TOOLS & TECHNIQUES

Brought to you by the publisher of Tax Facts

MW00345627

CHARITABLE PLANNING

LEIMBERG
ALLEN
HAYS
MACNAB
SHUMAKER
YANG
ZIPSE

Cover photograph: Jonathan J. Spille

ISBN 978-0-87218-936-2
Library of Congress Control Number: 2007931472

THE NATIONAL UNDERWRITER COMPANY
Copyright © 2001, 2007
The National Underwriter Company
P.O. Box 14367
Cincinnati, Ohio 45250-0367

Second Edition

Printed in the United States of America

DEDICATION

Stephan R. Leimberg

To
Max and Aaron, my grandsons, who are the future, my mother, Sylvia Leimberg,
for her sense of humor, my father, Edward Leimberg, who faithfully watered
the money tree and fed the three-legged brown cow that lived under the boardwalk and
gave chocolate milk, and to my Zeda, who, when asked at age 89 if he'd ever flown,
looked up from his rocker toward the sky and answered, "Not Yet!"

Jim Allen

To my wonderful wife and kids, Brenda, Brandon, and Lauren:
I love you very much!

Johnine Hays

To my husband Dave
for all his support and encouragement, and to my mother for her lifetime of love.

JJ MacNab

To my husband, Tim,
and all my online planned giving friends
for sharing their humor, stories, and legal acumen.

Roger Shumaker

With all my love to my wife, Cheri, my children,
Don, Bill and Cristy and my grandchildren,
Charlotte, Wesley and Madison and my parents
who taught me the importance of generosity.

Wesley Yang

To my wife, Mary Ann,
and my children, Margaret and Thomas,
for their continuing love and support.

Randy L. Zipse

To my loving wife, Teri, and our three fantastic sons,
who have been understanding and supportive
of my legal career.

ABOUT THE AUTHORS

Stephan R. Leimberg

Stephan R. Leimberg is CEO of Leimberg and LeClair, Inc., an estate and financial planning software company, CEO of LISI, Leimberg Information Services, Inc., an e-mail newsletter service, and President of Leimberg Associates, Inc., a publishing and software company. He is an Adjunct Professor in the Masters of Taxation Program of Villanova University School of Law and former adjunct at Temple University School of Law. He holds a B.A. from Temple University, and a J.D. from Temple University School of Law. Leimberg is the Editor of the American Society of Financial Service Professionals audio publication, *Keeping Current*.

Leimberg is the author or co-author of numerous books on estate, financial, and employee benefit and retirement planning and a nationally known speaker. Leimberg is the creator and principal author of the entire nine book *Tools and Techniques* series including *The Tools and Techniques of Estate Planning, The Tools and Techniques of Financial Planning, The Tools and Techniques of Employee Benefit and Retirement Planning, The Tools and Techniques of Life Insurance Planning, The Tools and Techniques of Charitable Planning, The Tools and Techniques of Investment Planning, The Tools and Techniques of Risk Management, The Tools and Techniques of Practice Management,* and *The Tools and Techniques of Retirement Income Planning*. Leimberg is co-author of *Tax Planning with Life Insurance* with noted attorney Howard Zaritsky, *The Book of Trusts* with attorneys Charles K. Plotnick and Daniel Evans, and *How to Settle an Estate* with Charles K. Plotnick. He was also a contributing author of the American Bar Association's *The Lawyer's Guide to Retirement*.

Leimberg is co-creator of many software packages for the financial services professional including Estate and Financial Planning *NumberCruncher* (estate planning), DeCoupleCruncher (estate planning), *Financial Analyzer II* (financial calculations), *Estate Planning Quickview* (Estate Planning Flow Charts), Life Settlement Number-Cruncher (life settlement buy-hold analysis), *Planning Ahead for a Secure Retirement* (PowerPoint Client Seminar) and *Toward a Zero Estate Tax* (PowerPoint Client Estate Planning Seminar).

A nationally known speaker, Professor Leimberg has addressed the Miami Tax Institute, the NYU Tax Institute, the Federal Tax Bar, the Notre Dame Law School and Duke University Law School's Estate Planning Conference, the National Association of Estate Planners and Councils, the AICPA's National Estate Planning Forum, the ABA Section on Taxation, and The Annual Meeting of the American Society of Financial Service Professionals. Leimberg has also spoken to the Federal Bureau of Investigation, and the National Aeronautics and Space Administration.

Leimberg was awarded the Excellence in Writing Award of the American Bar Association's Probate and Property Section. He has been honored as Estate Planner of the Year by the Montgomery County Estate Planning Council and as Distinguished Estate Planner by the Philadelphia Estate Planning Council. He is also recipient of the President's Cup of the Philadelphia Life Underwriters, a two time Boris Todorovitch Lecturer, and the First Ben Feldman Lecturer.

Leimberg was named Edward N. Polisher Lecturer of the Dickinson School of Law and 2004 recipient of the National Association of Estate Planners and Councils Distinguished Accredited Estate Planner award,

Leimberg's LISI e-mail newsletter/data base http://www.leimbergservices.com is used daily by thousands of estate, financial, employee benefit, charitable, and retirement planning practitioners.

James R. Allen, Jr.

James R. Allen, Jr. is Director of Advanced Markets for MetLife Independent Distribution. Prior to joining MetLife, he was Director of Business & Charitable Planning for Pacific Life. Mr. Allen has a broad range of experience in the financial services industry as an insurance agent, registered securities representative, "fee only" financial planner, and as Director of Advanced Marketing for a national life insurance marketing organization.

Mr. Allen received his BA in Business Communications from California State University Fullerton and his Masters Degree in Financial Services from the American College. Allen holds the Certified Financial Planner (CFP), Chartered Advisory in Philanthropy (CAP), Chartered Life Underwriter (CLU) and Chartered Financial Consultant (ChFC) designations.

Allen writes frequently and his articles have been published in a variety of publications, including *The Journal of Deferred Compensation, The Journal of Financial Service Professionals, National Underwriter, and California Broker*. Mr. Allen has twice been the recipient of the *SFSP Journal* author award and has been a featured speaker at national and regional broker/dealer and professional organization meetings throughout the country. He is a member of the Society of Financial Service Professionals (SFSP) and the Association for Advanced Life Underwriting (AALU).

Johnine (Johni) R. Hays

Johnine (Johni) R. Hays is the Senior Planned Giving Consultant for The Stelter Company, a national publisher of planned giving newsletters and Web products for charities. She has been quoted in the *Wall Street Journal* and has published charitable planning articles in *Estate Planning Magazine, Life Insurance Selling, Fundraising Success* and the *National Underwriter*. She is also the author of the book, *Essentials of Annuities*.

Ms. Hays has extensive experience in estate and charitable planning, life insurance, annuities, retirement planning, and federal income, estate, and gift taxation. Johni is a featured speaker at national and regional conferences such as the National Committee on Planned Giving and the Association of Fundraising Professionals. She also frequently lectures to groups of professional advisors, planned giving officers and donors on various topics including estate and charitable planning, probate, living wills, annuities, life insurance, retirement planning, IRAs, and taxes.

Ms. Hays previously served as the Executive Director of the Greater Des Moines Community Foundation Planned Giving Institute. She has also served as a member of the Advanced Markets team for several life insurance companies including ManuLife Financial in their U.S. headquarters in Boston. In addition, she practiced law as an estate planning attorney with Myers Krause & Stevens, Chartered law firm in Naples, Florida, where she specialized in life insurance as a part of the overall estate plan.

Ms. Hays graduated cum laude with a Juris Doctor degree from Drake University in Des Moines, Iowa in 1993. She also holds a Bachelor of Science degree in Business Administration from Drake University where she majored in insurance, and graduated magna cum laude in 1988.

Ms. Hays is a member of the National Committee on Planned Giving, the Mid-Iowa Planned Giving Council, and currently serves as the President of the Mid-Iowa Estate & Financial Planners Council. She is a Chartered Advisor in Philanthropy (CAP) and a Chartered Life Underwriter (CLU). She has been a member of both the Iowa Bar and the Florida Bar since 1993.

JJ MacNab

JJ MacNab is an independent planner, analyst, and author who has been working with high net worth individuals, corporations, and family offices for the past 20 years. She specializes in advanced tax, charitable, and insurance analysis and research.

Ms. MacNab has published numerous technical, consumer-oriented, and editorial articles on insurance analysis, tax planning trends, and charitable techniques for *Forbes, Planned Giving Today, CA Trusts & Estates Quarterly, Keeping Current, Journal of Planned Giving, Financial Planning, Chronicle of Philanthropy,* and other national publications.

In addition to being a writer, analyst, and researcher, Ms. MacNab is one of only a handful of fee-only insurance analysts in the US. As owner and analyst of Insurance Barometer LLC, she provides technical insurance research for high net worth individuals, family offices, trustees, corporations, and professional advisors across the country. She also prepares annual reports on key insurance companies for consumers who need a second opinion for potential acquisitions, or who would like to monitor the performance of their insurance portfolio on a regular basis.

Ms. MacNab is a frequent source of information and is quoted regularly in such respected publications as *Forbes, Fortune, Wall Street Journal, USA Today, Smart Money, Worth, Financial Times, Chronicle of Philanthropy, New York Times, San Francisco Chronicle, Baltimore Sun, Investment News, Journal of Financial Planning, Currents, Annuity Market News,* and *Dow Jones Investment Advisor.* She has been interviewed as an expert on NBC Nightly News, CBS Marketwatch, CNN, CNN Financial, and ABC World News Tonight, and has appeared as a featured guest on C-SPAN.

Ms. McNab's professional memberships include: California Association of Insurance Analysts (Past President); Co-Chair of the Exempt Organization Committee and the Consumer Education Committee of the American Bar Association; National Capital Gift Planning Council; National Association of Philanthropic Planners; and the Society of Financial Service Professionals.

Ms. MacNab is a graduate of the University of California at Berkeley. She lives and works in Bethesda, MD and is working on a book on the subject of tax protesters

Roger L. Shumaker

Roger L. Shumaker is a member in the law firm of McDonald Hopkins LLC with offices in Cleveland, Columbus, Chicago, Detroit and West Palm Beach. Mr. Shumaker focuses his practice on estate planning, probate and trust administration, charitable planning, succession planning for middle-market and closely held businesses, and individual and fiduciary income taxation. He is listed in *The Best Lawyers in America* for trusts and estates law and in Ohio *SuperLawyers* and is a frequent writer and speaker on the topic of using computers in the delivery of legal services and on a host of estate planning, charitable, tax, and probate issues. He has presented at the Heckerling Institute on Estate Planning, the Notre Dame Estate Planning Institute, at meetings of the American College of Trust and Estate Counsel, the American Bar Association, the AICPA and numerous local professional and lay groups.

Mr. Shumaker graduated with distinction from Manchester College and subsequently received his Juris Doctor degree from Case Western Reserve University School of Law. He is licensed to practice in Ohio, Michigan, and Indiana.

Mr. Shumaker's professional associations include the Cleveland Bar Association, the Ohio State Bar Association, the American Bar Association (Real Property, Probate & Trust Law Section Council, 1991-1997), the American College of Trust and Estate Counsel, the Estate Planning Council of Cleveland (President, 1990-1991 and Distinguised Estate Planner of 2005), the Northern Ohio Planned Giving Council (Board of Trustees, 1994-1997), and Kingdom Advisors (Charter and Certified Member).

Mr. Shumaker is actively involved in numerous community organizations, including the Cleveland Museum of Art Planned Giving Council (Chairman, 1998), University Hospitals Diamond Advisory Group, the Salvation Army of Cleveland (Secretary and Chair of Development Committee), The City Mission, the Ohio Presbyterian Retirement and Services Foundation, the Breckenridge Village Retirement Community, the Western Reserve Emmaus Community, Inc., the Northeast Ohio Chrysalis Community, and Garfield Memorial United Methodist Church.

Wesley Yang

Mr. Yang is a tax attorney and certified public accountant specializing in the areas of business and tax law and estate planning. Mr. Yang is a shareholder in the law firm of Leech Tishman Fuscaldo & Lampl, LLC, where he concentrates his practice in the areas of estate and asset protection planning for high net worth individuals, executives, and owners of closely held businesses, international taxes, executive compensation, and corporate reorganizations, including management succession issues. Mr. Yang specializes in protecting and preserving wealth for clients through the use of irrevocable insurance trusts, family partnerships and limited liability companies, asset protection trusts, multigenerational dynasty trusts, charitable trusts, captive insurance companies, and offshore trusts and entities as part of their overall financial and estate plans.

Mr. Yang is a nationally recognized author. He is the co-author of several books, including *Estate Planning and Administration in Pennsylvania* and *Representing Physicians*. In addition, Mr. Yang is the author of two chapters of the *CCH Federal Tax Service* ("The Section 179 Expensing Election" and "Special Rules of Depreciation"), and has published numerous articles in prestigious national tax publications such as *The Journal of Taxation*, *The Tax Advisor*, *TAXES – The Tax Magazine*, and *The Tax Executive*. He is also a frequent lecturer at local and national conferences on taxation and accounting.

Mr. Yang was recognized as one of the country's top 100 attorneys by *Worth Magazine* in 2005 and 2006. Mr. Yang is listed in *Who's Who in American Law* (7th Ed.) and was picked as one of Pennsylvania's "Super Lawyers" in 2004.

Mr. Yang was previously employed as a tax supervisor at Coopers & Lybrand, as Manager of International Taxes at Dravo Corporation, and as Assistant Professor of Taxation and Accounting at Duquesne University. Prior to joining Leech Tishman Fuscaldo & Lampl, Mr. Yang was affiliated with several other law firms in Pittsburgh, PA. Mr. Yang received his B.A. (cum laude) from the University of Pittsburgh in 1972, with a double major in East Asian Studies and Chinese language (Departmental Honors in both majors), and his J.D. from the University of Pittsburgh Law School in 1975. In addition, Mr. Yang holds a Graduate Chef's Certificate from the South China Institute of Catering in Hong Kong, BCC.

Randy L. Zipse

Randy L. Zipse is Vice President of Advanced Markets for John Hancock (USA). Mr. Zipse is responsible for the Advanced Markets group, which provides estate and business planning support to home office employees, field personnel, and producers. Mr. Zipse has written numerous articles on trust taxation, estate planning, and business succession planning that have appeared in the *Journal of Financial Service Professionals*, *Broker World*, *Estate Planning*, *Life Insurance Selling*, *LAN*, and the *National Underwriter*. Mr. Zipse is on The Board of Advisers of *Keeping Current*. He is also a frequent lecturer at industry meetings, including such major events as the AALU, Million Dollar Round Table, and New York University Tax Institute.

Prior to joining John Hancock, Mr. Zipse was Sr. Counsel and VP of the Manulife Financial Advanced Markets team. Before that he worked as an attorney in the private practice. Mr. Zipse has been associated with several large firms, including Jones Day Reavis & Pogue and Gardere & Wynne – both in Dallas, Texas. As a private practice attorney, Mr. Zipse concentrated on estate planning, deferred compensation, business succession planning, and charitable planning. Prior to becoming an attorney, Mr. Zipse worked as a CPA with Deloitte Haskins & Sells.

An honors graduate of the University of Northern Iowa (B.A. in accounting), Mr. Zipse subsequently received his JD from Drake University College of Law (Order of the Coif, class rank number one), and is a member of the Iowa, Texas, and Missouri Bars.

ACKNOWLEDGMENTS

We wish to thank a number of people who inspired, taught, or created, or otherwise made a difference – either educationally or ethically or inspirationally in helping others help others through charitable planning. These special people include Conrad Teitell, Jerry J. McCoy, Christopher Hoyt, Larry Stelter, Frank Minton, Scott Fithian, Sandra Kerr, Charles Schultz, Lee Hoffman, Marc Hoffman, Gary Pforzheimer, Paul Brooks, Elton Brooks, Emil Kallina, Marc Carmichael, Terry Simmons, Jon Heintzelman, Bill Sturtevant, Vaughn Henry, Dave Dunlop, Bob Sharpe, Jr., Gordon Caswell, Winton Smith, Debra Ashton, Doug White, Kathryn Miree, Paul Comstock, Eric Dryburgh, Lynda Moerschbaecher, and Doug Freeman.

Special thanks to the editorial staff of The National Underwriter Company's Professional Publishing Division who were responsible for technical accuracy and did more than merely "polish up" our work. Thank you Sonya E. King, J.D., LL.M.; John H. Fenton, J.D., M.S.B.A.; Deborah A. Miner, J.D., CLU, ChFC; Joseph F. Stenken, J.D., CLU, ChFC; and William J. Wagner, J.D., LL.M., CLU. They proofed voluminous copy, meticulously checked each point for accuracy, tackled the thankless and difficult job of updating the text for a just-passed tax law, and assured an up-to-the-last-minute update before second edition of THE TOOLS AND TECHNIQUES OF CHARITABLE PLANNING went to press.

Most importantly, the authors want to acknowledge you, our loyal and growing body of readers, for keeping the *Tools and Techniques* series alive and prospering.

SPECIAL ACKNOWLEDGMENTS

We wish to thank attorney, Robert E. Harley (of Martin, Browne, Hull & Harper in Springfield, Ohio), for providing the practical suggestions for handling conservation easements in Chapter 18.

Special thanks to Roger Shumaker's colleagues, Deviani Kuhar, who assisted in research, writing and rewriting the chapters on Charitable Gift Annuities, Charitable Remainder Annuity Trusts and Supporting Organizations (first edition) and D. W. Craig Dreyer who assisted with this Edition in researching and confirming websites and in updating and rewriting of several chapters.

PREFACE TO THE SECOND EDITION

In 1975, the concept of a series of *Tools and Techniques* books was born. Its objective was to provide practitioners with concise, accurate, objective, and ethically-based information, packaged in a manner that would significantly reduce the time it takes to learn or review complex and broad-based concepts. Our goal then – as it is now – was to provide information and insight for performance.

After successfully launching *The Tools and Techniques of Estate Planning, The Tools and Techniques of Financial Planning, The Tools and Techniques of Employee Benefit and Retirement Planning,* and *The Tools and Techniques of Life Insurance Planning,* I dreamed of a fifth book, one which would help professionals who help others through charitable planning. Although there were a number of scholarly texts and others that covered one segment or another of the charitable planning process, there was no one book that incorporated all the aspects of the process that was designed for a student, novice, or long-time professional who needed to quickly grasp or revisit the pros and cons of the various tools and techniques and understand which (or which combination) would best meet the objectives of the client, the client's family, and the intended charity(ies).

When we launched the first edition of THE TOOLS AND TECHNIQUES OF CHARITABLE PLANNING, we stated that this book would put great emphasis on ethics and objectivity. Our authors stressed the distinction between a strictly legalistic approach in which the mere avoidance of legal violations or appearance of a conflict of interest is sufficient and a strong pro-active awareness and practice of the highest standards, particularly where tax law is concerned. Here, as much, if not more than in any of our other *Tools and Techniques* texts, intellectual creativity must be combined with moral imagination, cost efficacy, and legitimacy in making suggestions to both clients and charities, many of whom are greatly dependent on the professional. Time has shown how important ethics and values are to the planner.

Stephan R. Leimberg

CONTENTS

SELLING THE DREAM

CHAPTER 1

THE GROWTH OF CHARITY

Since the days of the cave, people have banded to-gether for self-protection. Survival and self-interest have always been among humanity's strongest motivators and primal driving forces. Caring and doing for others, including the giving of time and money to help make a meaningful and positive difference in someone else's life, came much later and represented a quantum leap forward in our human progression.

The concept of organizations and formal entities whose sole or major purpose was the alleviation of pain and suffering, the enhancement of the quality of life, the furthering of noble and just causes, the enablement of intellectual and physical growth through education and sports, and the attainment of other social investments in ideas, ideals, and people, all came still later.

The growth of formal charities has been on a con-tinuum that has tracked roughly, but not precisely, with the economic change starting with mere survival and moving toward what many (but unfortunately not all) in our country are enjoying, the highest standard of living ever experienced in history.

SELLING THE DREAM OF "BETTER"

It is important for all of our readers to understand that the act of paying the price of the dream of "better," whether it is an investment in a better world, a better community, a better chance for a child to learn, or a better chance for someone with AIDS, cancer, or heart disease to live, generally must be "sold."

Yes. There are those who volunteer their time and give money without being asked. But most charitable gifts, whether those that sustain charitable organizations day to day, or those larger gifts that bulwark the future, are "sold," in the finest and broadest sense of the word.

WHO IS SELLING THE DREAM?

"Better" is sold from the pulpit, through direct mail, by phone, by fax, by e-mail, on web sites, or face-to-face. It is sold by professionals who raise funds for charities on a full-time basis, either as an employee of a charity or as a consultant. It is sold by professionals who are not full-time fund raisers but who see an opportunity to help both their clients and the charities that their clients wish to support.

And, unfortunately, "better" is sometimes sold by opportunists: those who use charities or charitable ideas merely as a means of selling a product or service, and have little concern about the financial fortune or future of the charity itself. (We'll have more to say about the category of opportunists who prey on unsuspecting individuals with unlawful or at-and over- the-edge schemes rather than legitimate dreams).

SELLING THE DREAM REQUIRES AN IN-DEPTH UNDERSTANDING OF WHY PEOPLE GIVE

There are a multiplicity of motivating forces that ex-plain charitable giving. It is likely that most individuals are moved to make gifts for more than one reason. The subject of giving in general and charitable giving in par-ticular is as complex and as difficult to understand and use as a prediction base as the human soul itself. But it cannot be ignored. To the professional whose mission it is to help finance a charity's mission, a working knowledge of the major gift-giving forces is essential.

Here are some of the factors the authors have found most important:

"I really care!"

People often make charitable gifts because they have a genuine concern about the day-to-day good things the charity is doing. They want to help the charity do more, or do it better! They are genuinely concerned. They want to help. For example, many of those reading this book, and several of the authors, have benefited from Scouting and want it to continue. They know their money can make a positive difference in the lives of the youngsters of today who will be the adults and community leaders of tomorrow.

Assure continuation of charity's mission

People give because they are motivated to support what they see as important causes. They want to turn dreams into reality. One donor said, "I give, not just for the emotional satisfaction of giving, but because the organization is accomplishing something." The donor wants to be sure that the mission or the work of a religious organization, local hospital, or school continues beyond today or this year. Philanthropist Carol Auerbach in Philadelphia said, "In our minds the reason we gave the money was to make certain these programs could exist in Philadelphia." So some donors who give do it with the express intention of helping assure the continuation of the charity they believe in by taking action now.

People they respect have given

People often give because people they care about and respect, those that have inspired and guided them, such as parents or close friends, support the charity's mission. In a true sense these donors are "pre-sold" on the charity's worth and credibility, and they are motivated by the example of these role models and mentors. They want to help the organizations their "teachers" and "mentors" want to help. Often, a part of the motivation for wanting to help an organization is not primarily due to the donor's own strong belief in the recipient charity, but is a way to say, "Thanks" and tell their "heroes," "I want you to know I learned something important from you about what *is* important."

To transmit values

People sometimes not only give because they really care but because they want their children and grandchildren, and their friends, to *see* that they care. They want to transmit and project a spirit of personal philanthropy to their children and others to help create a "multiplier effect." They understand that significant, continual, and publicly apparent giving is a way to transfer and promote important family values to children, grandchildren, and other family members. They are teaching others by example. The authors have found that more and more high net-worth families are searching for ways to teach and share both the mechanics and the spirit of philanthropy to their children and others. For instance, each year, one of the authors hands his grandson 12 envelopes, each with a $10 bill inside and a postcard addressed to the grandparents. The grandson is entrusted (in consultation with his parents) to make a gift to a different charity each month and to write on the postcard to tell his grandparents the name of the charity and why that particular charity was selected.

As a way to assure remembrance

If you've ever wondered why the soldiers guarding the temples in ancient Rome or the ancient castles throughout Europe carved their initials and the dates into the columns, or why, all across Europe in the Second World War, GIs wrote "Kilroy was here!" on walls and fences, perhaps remembrance is an answer. Each of us wants to be remembered; to have someone in the future see and acknowledge that we were here in the past.

Significant gifts to charity can provide some assurance that the donor (or others whose names the donor selects, such as a parent or spouse, a brother or sister) will be remembered (and have a measure of meaning and worth) beyond his death, and remembered in a positive manner. By this lasting mark, a donor obtains a measure of immortality. This is why you see so many plaques on walls of temples and churches and the names of benefactors on the doorways to rooms and buildings.

To honor or be honored

Many people give to honor other people or to be honored themselves. By being honored, they attain a measure of immortality for others or themselves.

To become a leader among peers

Calvin Coolidge said that "No one has ever been honored for what he *received*. Honor is our reward when we *give*." Some give large gifts because they know that making a significant gift to charity can help make the giver a leader among peers.

Competitiveness

Some give to show others how much they *can* give, and to *more* than match the gifts of their lifelong friends, business associates, and competitors. Charitable giving becomes a sport in which *everyone* wins.

Enhanced social image

Some give to enhance their own, or their children's, social, political, or business position in the community. Sometimes gifts enable them to be known by and reach people who are otherwise unreachable. Charitable giving, particularly significant planned giving, places family members in strategic social positions and helps them to meet people they might not otherwise meet on more favorable terms.

Sense of indebtedness

Some give because they have a sense that they have received and feel an obligation, and a need, to give back.

Share good fortune

Those fortunate enough to have "sufficient surplus wealth" (as they define the term) to share with others and wise enough to enjoy it often copiously do so.

Sense of purposeful stewardship

Some people feel they are merely "trustees of wealth," "stewards" of the money that goes through their hands. They feel that, although the money is not theirs permanently, that they want to take an active role in *where* it goes and *how* it is used. Or as one humorist said, "If you're giving while you're living, then you're knowing where it's going." (And, of course, these individuals have the pleasure and honor of enjoying the charity's use of their gift).

Sense of guilt

It is likely that a number of large and memorable gifts (such as those of Nobel and Carnegie) were motivated by the donor's sense of guilt or shame for some past act or lifestyle. These donors have a driving need for redemption, to make amends, and to "set things right."

Protect themselves or their children

Many individuals heed the ancient words of Horace, who said, "Riches either serve or govern the possessor." They are afraid that great wealth can spoil or corrupt themselves or their children. Warren Buffett said, "I want my children to inherit enough wealth so that they can afford to do *anything*, but not enough wealth for them to be able to afford to do *nothing*!" Many successful individuals are hesitant to leave their children more than a specified amount or percentage of their estates. Charity has long been a viable recipient of any perceived excess.

Have no one to leave it to

There are those who have no close relatives to leave their estates to and choose charities over an escheat to the state. Others have only relatives who never cared about them (or whom they never cared about) and would rather have their wealth pass to one or more charities. There are even situations where money is left to charity to spite and anger the logical heirs, and perhaps to remind them of who really won some ancient feud or slight.

Want an income tax deduction

In addition to personal satisfaction and accomplishment, an income tax deduction, which can translate into increased net spendable income, is an important motivational element for large charitable lifetime gifts. An income tax deduction means the donor will pay less in taxes, have more for retirement, have more to give to his children, and have even more to give to charity.

Of course, the authors are well aware that no large charitable gifts are, or should be, motivated *solely* by an income tax deduction. Because tax rates, and therefore deductions, are not 100%

and therefore do not reduce income taxes dollar for dollar, no one gives, nor *should* anyone give, merely to obtain a tax deduction.

Avoid capital gains

As we will note later in this book in much more detail, arranged properly, highly appreciated property can be donated to a charity and result in a large deduction, but avoid or defer any capital gain on that growth. For instance, suppose a client purchased property for $10,000 and it is now worth $60,000. Her gift directly to a charity will result in a $60,000 charitable deduction, and she is not subject to a current tax on the $50,000 in appreciation.

Tax benefits translate to more wealth–and more control over it

As noted above and throughout this book, arranged properly, charitable gifts can generate significant tax deductions. These deductions translate into savings which in turn translate into more spendable money left over to direct to where the donor wants it to go.

As long as federal and state death taxes in one form or another continue to exist or the threat of them continues, individuals have the choice of two beneficiaries with respect to a sizable portion of their income and estate. They can do nothing and by default choose a branch of the U.S. and state governments. Or they can hand-pick one or more charities. Put another way, a person can choose "directed philanthropy," and choose *who* receives a sizable portion of his or her income and wealth (and when and how), or do nothing and allow federal and state lawmakers to decide. That is what some planners call "Involuntary Philanthropy." The choice is the client's.

Remove financial uncertainty

A gift to charity can be a means of providing the donor, or someone else the donor chooses, with an annuity–a stream of dollars that can *never* be outlived. At the same time, by using one or more of the charitable tools described in this book, the donor can avoid or reduce the need to worry about the ups and downs of the stock market or the risks of other investments. Some of these tools or techniques will also help

shift the burden of management of investments, at least in part, away from the donor and to wealth-management professionals.

Benefit family members

Charitable gifts are made for one or more of these reasons, and these gifts can be structured to provide surprisingly generous, legislatively-sanctioned benefits for the donor, the donor's spouse, other family members, and even non-family friends.

WHY PEOPLE DON'T GIVE MORE?

It is not sufficient for professionals to understand the motivations for giving; they must understand why some individuals don't give anything or give very little.

Here are some of the reasons the authors have found that some of those who could make significant gifts to charity choose not to do so:

No one told them how

All too often, no one has told them how to make a meaningful gift. They just did not think they could, so they didn't.

Never took the time

Associated with the answer that no one told them how is that many people are so involved in their daily routines that they have never taken the time to think, or talk to their professional advisors, about what is important to them, or how they can accomplish those goals. Charitable planning gives a person the opportunity to see into the future, and more importantly, to help *determine* it!

Concern about impact on lifestyle

Some individuals do not give more because they are concerned that doing more financially for a charity, even one whose mission is very important to them, could adversely affect their own financial situation and lifestyle. They feel they cannot afford it.

Obviously, this fear is well founded in *some* situations. But in many cases, being charitable does *not* mean disinheriting children or suffering financially. Often, it is just that no one shared with those individuals the tools and techniques that would enable them and their family, as well as their charity, to *all* benefit. Although planners must know (and must be sure their clients know) that all charitable giving comes with a cost, it is a basic premise of this book that it *is* possible for *all* the parties to a charitable gift to benefit in one way or another.

Most people cling to wealth. One reason is a worry that they may not have enough to achieve and maintain sufficient financial independence for as long as they live. Before prospective donors make any significant gifts to charity, they should be assured that under *any* reasonable assumption enough wealth and income will remain to maintain a desired standard of living. It is the duty of the charitable planning team to make sure before the gift is made, that the donor will be financially secure after the gift.

Fear that a contribution will be misused

A woman once came up to one of this book's authors after he gave a talk on charitable giving. She mentioned that she had a daughter with Cerebral Palsy. She told him that although she knew how important the organization's role was with children and parents in her situation, she did not give a nickel to the local organization because she was told that it had very high administrative expenses. She was afraid that too little was getting to the children the organization was supposed to serve.

Ironically, the local United Cerebral Palsy Foundation (UCP) in her area has one of the lowest overheads and highest payout to the clients of the charity of any other charity in the country. And when, at the author's suggestion, she went to UCP's website and then confirmed its figures with the website of the state's attorney general, she confirmed that she had been very mistaken and that the UCP organization in her area was one of the most cost-efficient of all charities.

Donors such as this woman must be told where their money goes and how it is spent. They want assurance there *is* due diligence and oversight, a reasonable level of both self and outside monitoring. They are also concerned with how much of their donations each year actually are used for charitable purposes rather than bloated executive salaries or fund-raising costs.

Don't know how to find who can help them—or who they can trust for advice

Look in the phone book and see how many professionals you can find that advertise: "Charitable Consultant to the Public." Few attorneys, CPAs, life insurance agents, or financial planners have rigorously trained or taken more than one or two courses in this most complex and multi-disciplinary field. In many cases, charitable planning is an accidental and incidental offshoot of a legal, accounting, insurance, or financial practice where its difficult rules, complex practicalities, and ethical dilemmas are rarely encountered. So all too often the professional giving advice often is not a professional in the charitable field, and those that are well versed are difficult to find, identify, and confirm. (Think of how difficult it would be for a lay person to analyze the level of a professional's competency in this area).

In addition to wanting advice from someone who is technically competent in the tax implications and tools and techniques of charitable planning, potential donors want someone who is also client-centered rather than product-driven; someone on the same side of the table as them. Donors want someone looking to help them shape out their dreams for their families and themselves, and then help them find meaningful solutions to their multiple objectives. As you will note in our material on the ethics of charitable planning, this ethical objectivity is more easily (and often) said than realized.

Fear of loss of control

Potential donors worry about control. Some worry that they will lose control over both their money and over the use of their money by the charity. Of course, that is exactly what *will* happen if they do nothing–the IRS and state revenue agencies gain control. Lifetime planning, and interaction with the charity, can mean they control not only where their money goes, but how it is used.

Many individuals deliberately make gifts to smaller local charities rather than larger national organizations because they feel they have more influence as to how their money will be distributed and used. The larger the influence they perceive they will have, the more likely they are to make the gift. Charitable planners must therefore ask: " How important is it to you to foster the principals and values that you believe in? Doesn't it make sense to be proactive and plan gifts, rather than have your loved ones and your favorite charity take what's left over after the tax authorities?"

Don't think they can make a gift large enough to really matter

All too often, the reason that no gift is made is that the potential donor feels that he cannot make a gift that is large enough to make a meaningful difference. Planners that read through the chapters of this book will know that almost anyone can make a sizable and important gift.

No one asked!

The basic premise of this chapter is that a charity's dreams must be sold. Someone must ask a donor for a contribution. Ironically, the single biggest reason many individuals do not make meaningful gifts to charities is that no one asked them—or asked them again. Charities are sometimes so focused on the "here and now" that they have hesitated to think of the future, or they are afraid that asking for donations for the future will interfere with the cash demands they have now.

In some cases the charity simply has not taken the time or devoted the resources to create a planned giving program, one that concentrates on the charity's long-term large scale future needs. Of course, potential donors don't think of the importance of funding the future of their charities if the charities themselves don't. So it is essential that charities tell people about their dreams.

It is essential that charities dream big dreams. Charities should help prospective donors buy into the charity's dream or, better yet, help people work with the charity to create a dream that both parties share! And once a person really buys into the dream, the "sale" is made.

WHERE CAN I FIND OUT MORE ABOUT IT?

1. Prince, Russ Alan, et al., *The Charitable Giving Handbook*, 1st edition (Cincinnati, OH: The National Underwriter Company, 1997).

GENERAL RULES FOR CHARITABLE DEDUCTIONS

CHAPTER 2

OVERVIEW

Charitable giving has become a significant element in the financial and estate plans of many individuals, whether they are of modest means or in the wealthiest 2% of our population. The total dollar amount of charitable contributions made by individuals and corporations increases every year, proving that Americans feel supporting charities is important, if not essential. It is, therefore, a topic that a financial services professional cannot afford to ignore, and about which professional competence is critical.

WHAT IS IT?

A charitable gift is a donation of cash or other property—or an interest in property—to, or for the use of, a qualified organization.[1] It is a freely given and voluntary gift, a transfer made with the primary—if not sole—intention of benefiting a charity or its causes and beneficiaries. Furthermore, it is a gift from which any benefit to the donor generally (i.e., absent a specific Code provision to the contrary, such as in the case of a charitable remainder trust or charitable gift annuity) is insubstantial and insignificant. The gift is also made from what is essentially a detached and disinterested generosity, rather than a "let's make a deal" *quid pro quo*.

A charitable gift for income tax deduction purposes must generally be a gift of the donor's entire interest in the property, subject to several specific statutory exceptions for gifts of partial interests. Exceptions are made for a remainder interest in a personal residence or farm, transfers to charitable remainder trusts, pooled income funds, charitable lead trusts, conservation easements, or an undivided portion of the donor's entire interest. (The partial interest rules are explained in detail in Chapter 5 of this book.)

Under IRC Section 170, a taxpayer is allowed an income tax deduction for charitable gifts made during the taxable year. The gift must be made to a qualified charity.

Qualified Charities Defined

Contributions to the following types of organizations are eligible for an income tax charitable deduction:[2]

1. a community chest, corporation, trust, fund or foundation organized under United States law, that is operated and organized solely for religious, charitable, educational, scientific, literary purposes, or for the prevention of cruelty to children or animals;

2. a war veterans' organization such as a post or auxiliary;

3. a domestic fraternal society only if the donation is used for the purposes described in item (1), above;

4. certain nonprofit cemetery companies; or

5. the United States or any particular state, U.S. possession, political subdivisions, or Indian tribal government, if the gift is made for exclusively public purposes.

In general terms, qualified charities will include most churches, temples, synagogues, mosques, and other religious organizations, nonprofit hospitals, nonprofit educational organizations, colleges, museums, public parks, and recreations areas.[3]

Noncharitable groups include lobbying groups, social clubs, labor unions, chambers of commerce, civic leagues, for-profit groups, and individuals.

A complete listing of approved charitable organizations is available from the IRS in Publication 78, Cumulative List of Charitable Organizations. This information is available on the Internet at www.irs.gov under the heading "Charities & Non-Profits." The IRS updates this list every three months. If a particular charity is not listed, the donor should contact the charity directly and ask for documentation on its tax-exempt status.

Direct Gifts

Charitable contributions can be made in many ways. For example, a gift can be a direct lifetime gift, or can be made at death (testamentary). Also, a gift can be total, absolute, and outright or can take the form of a partial interest, such as a gift to a charitable remainder trust. This chapter will focus primarily on direct lifetime gifts. This type of charitable contribution is an outright gift of property or cash to a qualifying charity involving no retained interest, strings attached, or partial interest.

Cash Gifts

Gifts of cash are the easiest to give to charity in terms of substantiation (assuming the donor writes a check) and for ease of determining the value of the gift. Examples of direct gifts of cash include weekly contributions to a church or other religious organization, payroll deductions to a charity such as the United Way, or donations to the policemen's ball, and so on. The full value of a cash gift is deductible in the year the contribution is made within the income percentage limits (see Chapter 3 and Appendix D). Generally, the donor may take a current deduction of up to 50% of adjusted gross income (AGI) in the year a cash gift is made.

Ordinary Income Property

Gifts of ordinary income property include gifts that, if the property were sold, would produce ordinary income to the donor. Examples include works of art if the donor was the artist, capital assets held one year or less, and inventory.

Gifts of ordinary income property are generally deductible only up to the amount of the donor's cost basis. (The fair market value of ordinary income property must be reduced by the amount of the ordinary gain that would be realized if the property were sold; thus, the fair market value minus the gain is generally the donor's cost basis.)

Example: Nationally known fine art photographer, Douglas Mellor, donates a photograph he created to the United Cerebral Palsy of Philadelphia and Vicinity. Regardless of the appraisal value of the photo, his deduction would be limited to the cost he incurred for materials and photo chemistry.

Long-term Capital Gain Property

Gifts of long-term capital gain property include property that, if sold, would result in long-term capital gain to the donor. Capital assets held more than one year are long-term capital gain assets. Examples of capital assets include stocks, bonds, cars, furniture, real estate, and collectibles, such as art or coins.

Normally, no gain or loss is recognized by the donor when items of long-term capital gain property are donated to a qualified charity. This is one of the major tax advantages of a charitable gift of appreciated property. The accumulated capital gain escapes tax entirely when the gift is made directly and outright to the charity. Contributions of capital gain assets are generally deductible at the item's fair market value at the time the contribution is made; however, the deduction may be limited to the donor's cost basis in some cases, depending on the status of the charitable recipient, or the percentage limitation chosen. See Chapter 5 for details on the rules for gifts of property.

Life Insurance

A gift of life insurance is deductible only if the charitable organization is made (or names itself) the absolute owner of all the economic rights in the policy. This "lock, stock, and barrel" requirement means no one other than the charity can have any meaningful rights in the policy. Consequently, when a client merely names a charitable organization as the beneficiary of the life insurance policy, no current charitable deduction is allowed for income tax purposes. (However, see Chapter 23 for the estate tax effects of naming a qualified charity as beneficiary of a life insurance policy).

The donor may deduct the value of an existing life insurance policy as of the date of transfer of the ownership to the charity (provided an absolute assignment is made). The value for income tax deduction purposes is the cost basis in the life insurance policy, or the fair market value if it is lower than the cost basis. Note that no deduction is ever allowed if the policy is subject to a debt—no matter how small—at the time the policy is transferred to the charity.

Once the charity owns and is the beneficiary of a life insurance policy, the donor may then deduct all future premiums paid to the charity to cover the premium obligations. To allow for the highest deductible amount, avoid litigation, and minimize the potential for an IRS audit, it is suggested that the donor contribute the future premiums directly to the charity. This allows the donor to deduct the premiums up to 50% of adjusted gross income (AGI). If instead the donor pays the premium gifts directly to the insurance company, the gifts may be considered gifts "for the use of" the charity and, as such, limited to 30% of the taxpayer's AGI. (Although there is some question as to this point, prudence suggests the more conservative approach. In fact, it is suggested that the donor "round up" the check to the charity for two reasons. For example, if the premium is $4,856, the donor should round the check to an even $5,000. Cosmetically, this makes it easier to document the size and date of the gift without calling to the IRS's attention that it is other than an outright gift of cash. Consequently, an audit is less likely. Second, the charity will likely have other such policies and will inevitably incur some administrative costs, which the additional rounding will help to cover.)

Annuities

Annuities are not the most tax-favored assets to give to a charity or non-charitable beneficiary. The reason a gift of an annuity to charity is typically contra-indicated is that the full value of the deferred "gain" inside the annuity is taxed to the annuity owner in the year of the charitable gift. (Of course, a charitable deduction is allowed for the gift, which at least to some extent creates a "wash" and may even offset the entire reportable income). Once the charity has received the annuity, its full value is deductible by the former annuity owner.

Example: Assume that Jackie Miller purchased an annuity on March 21, 1994. The value of the

annuity is currently $100,000 with an original cost basis of $30,000. If Jackie contributes the annuity to the Red Cross during this taxable year, she must first realize and recognize $70,000 ($100,000 value minus $30,000 cost basis) of ordinary income. Jackie can then deduct $100,000 (to the extent it does not exceed 50% of her AGI) for the tax year.

These rules apply to annuities purchased after April 22, 1987. For annuities purchased prior to April 23, 1987, the amount of the deferred gain in the annuity is taxable as ordinary income to the annuity owner, not in the year of the gift, but during the year of the surrender of the annuity by the new owner. The taxpayer is limited to a deduction of only the cost basis in the annuity, not the current value.

Series E and EE Bonds

Savings bonds issued by the United States government, such as Series E or EE bonds, are also inefficient assets for lifetime giving. The major reason they are not favored assets is that the ownership of these assets cannot be transferred to a charity during the donor's lifetime. Instead, the donor would have to cash in the bonds, pay income tax on the deferred gain, and then contribute the net cash remaining to the charitable organization.

Gifts of Tangible Personal Property

Contributions of tangible personal property (generally items such as jewelry, art, stamps, collections, etc.) are deductible at the item's fair market value or cost basis, whichever is lower. This is especially evident with items that depreciate over time (e.g., automobiles). Normally, with depreciating items, the fair market value will be less than the cost basis and the taxpayer will be able to deduct only the current fair market value.

In contrast, the taxpayer may deduct the full fair market value of property that is donated to a charity and used in the charity's mission. This is referred to as a "related use" gift. A typical example of a related use gift would be the donation of a Monet painting to an art museum. If the museum displays the newly donated painting in its art collection, the taxpayer could deduct the painting's full fair market value, not merely the cost basis. However, if the museum does *not* use the donated property for the mission of the charity, the taxpayer may deduct only the property's cost basis.[4]

In other words, if the art museum immediately sold a donated painting and used the cash proceeds to build a new wing on its building, or if the painting were given to the United Cerebral Palsy Association (which, of course, could not use it in a use-related manner since its mission does not encompass the displaying of art to the public), only the donor's cost basis would be deductible. Even if the art museum sells the Monet painting to another art museum, the taxpayer would be allowed to deduct only the cost basis of the painting. Donors of tangible personal property who wish to deduct the full fair market value of a gift should, therefore, obtain documentation from the donee charity attesting to the fact that the gift will be used by the recipient in a use-related manner at the time it is received (e.g., IRS Form 8283).

Recapture of tax benefit if not used for exempt purpose. Effective for income tax returns filed after September 1, 2006, if a charity disposes of tangible personal property within three years of the gift and the donor had taken a fair market value deduction for the property based on the related use rule, the taxpayer must adjust his tax benefit by including as ordinary income the amount equal to the excess of the amount of the deduction taken over the taxpayer's cost basis. An exception applies if the charity certifies the property was actually used for a related use or the related use became impossible. This provision only applies to property for which a deduction of more than $5,000 was claimed. A penalty of $10,000 applies to a person who knowingly identifies that property as related use property when it is not intended to be used as related use property.[5]

Fractional interests. Charitable lifetime gifts or bequests of fractional interests in tangible personal property made after August 17, 2006, are subject to recapture. Donors who fail to follow up a previously made fractional gift with a contribution of all the remaining interest in the property before the earlier of 10 years from the initial gift or the donor's death must recapture as ordinary income all the previously taken charitable contribution deductions for this gift, plus interest. The provision also imposes an additional 10% penalty tax on the amount recaptured. The amounts of the additional charitable contribution deductions are based on the lesser of the fair market value of the property at the time of the initial fractional gift or the fair market value of the property at the time of the additional charitable contribution.[6]

Clothing/Household Items

For contributions made after August 17, 2006, no deduction is allowed for donations of clothing or household items unless the items are in good condition or better. Household items include furniture, furnishings, electronics, appliances, and linens. This provision does not apply to food, paintings, antiques, art objects, jewelry, gems and collections. Further, no deduction is allowed for items with minimal value such as used socks and used undergarments. A taxpayer can deduct an item of clothing or a household item that is not in good condition if its value is more than $500 and the taxpayer includes a qualified appraisal with the tax return.[7]

Vehicles, Boats and Airplanes

Deductions for charitable gifts of automobiles, other vehicles, boats or planes where the value exceeds $500 changed effective January 1, 2005. The deduction under these circumstances is limited to the gross sales price received by the charity for the subsequent sale of the donated vehicle, or the fair market value, if lower. If the charity makes a material improvement to the vehicle, has a significant intervening use for the vehicle, or will transfer it to a needy individual then the fair market value may be used to determine the charitable deduction. The charity must complete IRS Form 1098-C and provide the gross sales price or certify if one of the exceptions applies. In addition, the charity must provide the donor with IRS Form 8283, and if it sells the vehicle it must also provide IRS Form 8282.[8]

Nondeductible Gifts or Contributions

Raffle tickets. Contributions toward raffle tickets, lottery tickets, or bingo games are not qualified gifts to a charitable organization and, thus, cannot be deducted by the donor.

Gifts to a specific individual or person. Gifts to individuals are not deductible gifts. For example, a bank sets up a fund to receive donations to help a local family who lost their home in a house fire. Contributions to the family are not deductible charitable contributions even if the money is contributed to the bank for the specific and sole benefit of the needy family.

Gifts of contribution of services. No charitable deduction is allowed for contributions of time spent donating services to charitable organizations, or for lost wages for time spent donating services.[9] Neither is the value of time spent donating blood a deductible expense. However, reasonable expenditures for meals, lodging, and other minor out-of-pocket expenses incurred while donating services are deductible.

Gifts of a partial interest in property. Gifts of a partial interest in property generally are not deductible. For example, if stock were contributed to a qualified charity, but the donor reserved the right to vote the shares or receive the income they produced, the gift would be a contribution of only part of the interest the donor had in the stock, and no charitable deduction would be allowed for any part of the gift. Several very specific and carefully restricted statutory exceptions to this general rule are provided for gifts to charitable remainder trusts, charitable lead trusts, pooled income funds, charitable gift annuities, or a remainder interest in a farm or personal residence.[10]

Gifts to nonqualified organizations. No income tax deduction is permitted for a contribution to an organization that is not a qualified charity, such as a chamber of commerce, civic league, country club, labor union, political organization, or homeowner's association.

Gifts with a quid pro quo. Generally gifts donated to charity coupled to or conditioned on a *quid pro quo* ("this for that") are not deductible for income tax purposes. An example of a *quid pro quo* is a large donation to a particular school in exchange for the donor's child being accepted by the school when the student's grades otherwise would not qualify for admission. If a charitable organization receives any *quid pro quo* contribution in excess of $75, it must provide a donor with a written disclosure including an estimate of the value of the goods or services received by the donor.[11]

Earmarked gifts. A gift given to a charity but earmarked by the donor for the benefit of a particular individual is not a deductible gift. For example, if a particular donor or business makes a gift to a local family of cash, property, or tangible items such as clothing for having the first set of surviving sextuplets, the gift would not be deductible. Even if the donor instead made the gift to a local community foundation or other group, but earmarked the gift for the benefit of the family, the gift still would not be deductible.

Use of property. The rent-free use of the donor's facilities such as office space, storage space, vehicles, cars, or artwork provided to a charity is not deductible by the donor no matter how valuable the rental use might be.[12]

Gifts to foreign charities. Charitable contributions given to foreign charities are not eligible for an individual income tax deduction. The charity must be a United States organization. However, the charity can certainly provide work and assistance in a foreign country and still be a qualified charity for income tax purposes.

Gifts of future interests in tangible personal property. Gifts of a future interest in tangible personal property are not deductible until the qualified charity actually receives possession of the property and no further strings are attached. For example, if a donor gives an antique tractor to the state museum, but retains the right to keep the tractor on the donor's farm until his death, the gift is not currently deductible by the donor. Instead, the gift would be deductible by the donor's estate upon the death of the donor and the delivery of the tractor to the museum.

VALUE AND SUBSTANTIATION OF GIFTS

Fair Market Value

The value of property donated (if not cash), for purposes of the deduction, is its fair market value. For a detailed explanation of how fair market value is defined and ascertained, see Appendix J.

The manner in which fair market value is determined for gifts of property can vary widely depending on the type of property. For special rules applying to gifts of property, see Chapter 4, and for details on the valuation of property gifts, see Appendix J.

Substantiation

All charitable contributions are subject to some form of substantiation requirements, depending on the value and type of gift. In the event that an appraisal is required, it must provide specific information; for details, see Appendix J. The substantiation requirements are summarized in Figure 2.1.

Figure 2.1

TYPE OF GIFT REQUIRED	SUBSTANTIATION TO THE IRS	HOW TO REPORT
Cash gift of less than $250	A cancelled check, bank record or an acknowledgement from the charity	Schedule A on IRS Form 1040
Cash gift of $250 or more	Acknowledgement from the charity	Schedule A on IRS Form 1040
Non-cash gift of less than $250	Receipt from the charity unless impractical	Schedule A on IRS Form 1040
Non-cash gift of $250 but less than $500	Acknowledgement from the charity	Schedule A on IRS Form 1040
Non-cash gift of $500 but less than $5,000+	Acknowledgement from the charity and specific written records	Attach Section A of Form 8283 to IRS Form 1040
Automobile, planes, boats valued at more than $500, but less than $5,000	Acknowledgement from the charity	Attach Form 8283 to IRS Form 1040 and IRS Form 1098-C
Non-cash gift of $5,000 or more	Acknowledgement from the charity and specific written records plus a qualified appraisal. No appraisal is required for gifts of publicly held securities*	Attach Section B of IRS Form 8283 (attach Form 1098-C if gift was a vehicle, boat or plane)
Non-cash gift of more than $500,000	Acknowledgement from the charity and specific written records plus a qualified appraisal	Attach Section B of IRS Form 8283 and attach the qualified appraisal to IRS Form 1040

*If a gift is made of over $5,000, but $10,000 or less of non-publicly traded securities, no appraisal is required, just a partially completed appraisal summary form.

+Excluding automobiles, airplanes and boats.

Gifts of Less Than $250

For each charitable contribution of cash or currency, a taxpayer must maintain a receipt from the charity showing the name, date, and amount of the contribution.[13] Prior to the Pension Protection Act of 2006, donors were not required to obtain receipts from the charity for actual gifts of currency under $250, but instead they could have "reliable records" of their own. Now even small gifts such as $20 made in cash need to have a receipt from the charity in order to be deductible.

For gifts under $250 made via check, a taxpayer must maintain a cancelled check (i.e., bank record) or a receipt from the charity.

Non-cash gifts require a receipt from the charity showing the name of the charity, the date and location of the gift, and a description of the property (the fair market value does not have to be stated on the receipt). However, in the donor's tax records the fair market value must be evidenced as well as the donor's cost basis.[14] An exception exists if the taxpayer doesn't have a receipt from the charity and the reason is that obtaining the receipt is impractical (e.g., leaving a bag of clothing at a shelter's doorstep).

Gifts of $250 or More

No deduction is allowed to any taxpayer for any gift of $250 or more unless the taxpayer has substantiation by contemporaneous written acknowledgement of the donation from the charity.[15] The acknowledgement is considered contemporaneous if it is received by the donor before he files his income tax return. In other words, the acknowledgement must be received by the donor on or before the due date of the donor's income tax return, including any extra time for extensions filed.

The acknowledgement must include a description of the property donated, the amount of cash contributed, a statement of whether the charity provided any goods or services in consideration for any property gifted, and a description and good faith estimate of the value of any goods or services.[16]

Gifts of More Than $500

Taxpayers claiming a deduction for a gift of more than $500 must include IRS Form 8283 (Noncash Charitable Contributions) with the income tax return. The $500 amount is determined prior to the application of any deduction limits. In addition to the foregoing substantiation requirements, for property gifts of $500 or more the donor must also have records reflecting how the donor originally acquired the property, and the cost basis.[17]

Gifts of More Than $5,000

Gifts of property (other than cash or marketable securities) that are valued at more than $5,000 require a qualified appraisal of the donated property. The appraisal summary must be attached to the donor's tax return. If the property is nonpublicly traded stock, only a summary appraisal is necessary. A "qualified appraisal" is one is prepared by a qualified appraiser as defined by the Pension Protection Act of 2006 in accordance with generally accepted appraisal standards and any Treasury regulations. For details, see Appendix J.

If a donated life insurance policy has a value of $5,000 or more, it is necessary to obtain a formal appraisal from someone other than the insurer or the agent who sold the policy.

Gifts of More Than $500,000

For gifts valued at more than $500,000 which are not cash, inventory, publicly traded stock or intellectual property, the taxpayer must attach a qualified appraisal to the return.

Gifts of Artwork More Than $20,000

Gifts of artwork valued at $20,000 or more require that the full written appraisal (not the summary) be attached to the donor's income tax return. If one piece of artwork alone is valued at $20,000 or more, the IRS reserves the right to request an 8 x 10 inch color photograph of the artwork.

Gifts of Artwork Valued at More Than $50,000

For gifts of artwork valued at $50,000 or more, the donor can request a Statement of Value from the IRS. This statement must be requested by the donor prior to the filing of the income tax return. The donor must pay $2,500 to obtain the Statement of Value, and the request must be accompanied by the donor's qualified appraisal of the property.

Loss of Deduction

The donor may be denied an income tax deduction if he fails to comply with the substantiation requirements. To illustrate, in *Tokh v. Commissioner*,[18] the taxpayer had self-generated receipts for contributions to charitable organizations. The taxpayer, not the charitable recipient, had listed the items donated and the value of the donated items. The original costs, ages or conditions of the donated items were not included on the receipts. The taxpayer argued to the court that he was too busy to comply with record keeping requirements. The Tax Court found the receipts were unreliable and held the taxpayer failed to meet the substantiation requirements set forth in IRS regulations. The court denied the charitable deduction to the taxpayer and assessed penalties as well.

WHAT ARE THE TAX IMPLICATIONS?

Income Tax

Lifetime gifts to qualified charitable organizations are eligible for an income tax deduction, subject to certain limitations depending on several factors. Those factors include:

- the type of property that was contributed (e.g., long-term capital gain property, ordinary income property, cash, etc.);

- whether the gift was an outright gift or a partial interest gift;

- the amount of the taxpayer's adjusted gross income (AGI);

- whether the taxpayer itemizes income tax deductions;

- the type of charitable organization to which the gift is made (public charity or private family foundation); and

- whether the gift was "to" or "for the use of" the charity.

Depending on the type of property donated, the amount of the income tax charitable deduction may be limited. Gifts of cash are generally deductible up to 50% of AGI (30% for private family foundations). Gifts of long-term capital gain property are deductible up to 30% of AGI for public charities (20% for family private foundations). For details on the income percentage limits, see Chapter 3.

The general rule with respect to donations of long-term capital gain property is that no gain or loss is recognized by the donor upon the contribution of the appreciated property directly to a qualified charity. This rule does not apply to other types of property such as deferred annuities, savings bonds or debt-encumbered property. The rules affecting gifts of property are explained in detail in Chapter 4.

Gifts of partial interests are generally not deductible at all; however, there are several statutory exceptions for specific types of partial interest gifts. These exceptions are explained in Chapter 5, and separate chapters explain the special rules for charitable trusts, pooled income funds, and other specific types of gifts. Very generally, the donor

of these special types of partial interest gifts cannot take an income tax deduction equal to the fair market value of the property. Instead, these gifts are only partially deductible, based on the actuarial value of the interest actually received (or to be received) by the charity.[19]

The larger the amount of AGI the donor has, the greater the amount of his potential charitable deduction. For example, a donor with an AGI of $100,000 can potentially deduct up to $50,000 of cash gifts. A donor with an AGI of $40,000 can deduct up to only $20,000 of cash gifts.

If the donor does not itemize income tax deductions on his or her income tax return, the donor will not be eligible to claim the charitable deduction to reduce taxable income.

Itemized deductions are reduced dollar for dollar for certain upper-income taxpayers. If the donor's AGI is above a certain income level ($156,400 in 2007; $78,200 for married individuals filing separately; $159,950 and 79,975, respectively, in 2008), the amount of most itemized deductions (including charitable contributions) must be reduced by the lesser of (a) 3% of the taxpayer's AGI over the threshold level or (b) 80% of the itemized deductions otherwise allowable for that year. This preliminary reduction amount is itself then reduced by multiplying it by 2/3 in 2006 and 2007, 1/3 in 2008 and 2009, and 0 in 2010. Itemized deductions for this purpose do not include medical expenses, investment interest or casualty or theft losses.[20]

Example: Assume that a taxpayer has $200,000 of AGI and gives a cash gift of $45,000 to a public charity in 2007. The taxpayer's charitable deduction is limited to $44,128. This amount is calculated as follows:

(a) .03 x ($200,000 - $156,400) = $1,308

(b) .80 x $45,000 = $36,000

The lesser of (a) or (b) = $1,308

$1,308 x 2/3 = $872 reduction

$45,000 - $872 = $44,128

The donor's allowable deduction is also affected by the type of charity to which the property is donated. Most charities can be categorized as one of two types:

public charities (50%-type charities) and private family foundations (30%-type charities). For more information on the differences between the types of charities, see Chapter 3, and Appendix D.

Another potential determinant of the amount of the charitable deduction is whether the donor made the gift "to" the charity or "for the use of" the charity. This issue is also explained in Chapter 3.

Gift Tax

As a general rule, most (but not all) lifetime charitable gifts will qualify for the gift tax exemption. The difference between the gift tax exemption and the charitable income tax deduction is more visible with certain deferred gifts. The failure to qualify for the gift tax exemption means the donor's remaining unified credit must be used to offset the gift or, if the gift exceeds even that, the donor must pay out-of-pocket gift taxes.

Outright lifetime gifts to qualified charities can qualify for unlimited gift tax exemptions. Therefore, there is no limit to how much cash or property a donor can give without incurring a gift tax. However, the donor's income tax deduction in any given year may be limited as discussed earlier.

Under EGTRRA 2001, the gift tax rates are scheduled for incremental reduction through 2009, and further reduction in 2010.[21] In addition, the gift tax exemption increased to $1 million in 2002 and thereafter.[22]

Estate Tax

If a donor makes an outright lifetime charitable gift of an asset, the value of the asset is removed from his estate. Therefore, upon the donor's death, the asset will not be includable in the donor's estate for federal estate tax purposes.

Under EGTRRA 2001, the estate tax rates are scheduled for incremental reduction through 2009, and for repeal in 2010.[23] In addition, the exemption equivalent of the estate tax unified credit is scheduled to increase through 2009.[24] For most purposes, the repeal of the estate tax for only one year means that planning should be done as though there were no repeal.

Testamentary gifts made by a decedent to qualified charitable organizations are eligible for an unlimited estate tax charitable deduction. The donor is not limited upon death as to the amount of property he may donate. Furthermore, the amount of the charitable estate tax deduction is not dependent on the status of the charitable recipient as long as the charity qualifies as either a 30% or 50% charity. As a result, a decedent could contribute his or her entire estate to charitable organizations and the estate would escape any federal estate taxation that may otherwise apply. (For details regarding testamentary gifts, see Chapter 23.)

Partial interest gifts made at death, such as gifts to testamentary charitable remainder trusts or pooled income funds, and remainder interests in farms or personal residences, are not eligible for a full charitable estate tax deduction. Only the present value of the charity's remainder interest is eligible for the estate tax charitable deduction. The part of the gift given to a noncharitable beneficiary is generally included in the donor's estate.

PENALTY FOR OVERVALUATION

The IRS can impose a variety of penalties against taxpayers for certain offenses. The penalties that can apply with respect to a charitable deduction include penalties for negligence, substantial valuation misstatements, gross valuation misstatements, and fraud.

20% Negligence Penalty

The IRS may impose a negligence penalty against a taxpayer for acts of negligence with respect to completion of an income tax return. Negligence is defined as any failure to make a reasonable attempt to comply with the provisions of the Internal Revenue Code.[25]

Valuation Misstatement Penalties

20% Substantial Valuation Misstatement Penalty

A 20% penalty applies to certain valuation misstatements.[26] This penalty is applied to the amount by which the donor underpaid the tax, due to the overstatement of value of the item contributed to charity. The penalty applies only if the value of the property claimed in the tax return is more than 150% of the actual value of the property. Furthermore, the donor must also have underpaid the tax by more than $5,000 due to the overstatement; otherwise, the penalty will not apply.[27]

Example: Richard Shearson donates gem stones to the Smithsonian Institution in Washington, D.C. Richard values the amount of the gemstones at $32,000. The IRS, upon an audit, determines that the value of the gemstones is actually $15,000. The IRS may impose a 20% substantial valuation misstatement penalty against Richard, since the claimed value ($32,000) is more than 150% times the actual value ($15,000).

Richard is in a 35% income tax bracket For Richard's income tax bracket, the amount of the additional income tax owed is $5,950 (35% x $17,000), which exceeds the $5,000 threshold at which the penalty becomes applicable. Richard will be assessed an additional tax of $5,950 plus a penalty of $1,190 ($5,950 x 20%).

40% Gross Valuation Misstatement Penalty

The 20% penalty described above can increase to 40% if the value claimed on the taxpayer's return is 200% or more of the actual value. The amount of the tax underpaid must be more than $5,000 for the 40% gross misstatement penalty to be applicable.[28]

The negligence and valuation misstatement penalties are not stacked upon one another for multiple infractions of IRC Section 6662. For example, the maximum penalty would be 20% even if the donor's return showed both negligence and a substantial misstatement.[29]

A reasonable cause exception to the valuation overstatement penalties is available if the claimed value was based on a qualified appraisal made by a qualified appraiser and, in addition to obtaining the appraisal, the donor made a good faith investigation of the value of the contributed property. This exception, however, does not apply in the case of gross valuation misstatements.[30]

75% Fraud Penalty

If any part of the underpayment of tax required to be shown is due to fraud, the fraud penalty can be imposed in an amount equal to 75% of the underpayment.[31]

$1,000 Civil Penalty

In addition, a civil penalty can be imposed on any person who aids or assists in understatements of tax liability. The penalty is $1,000 and is in addition to any other penalties.[32] Providing a false substantiation statement to a donor may subject the charity to this penalty.

APPRAISER PENALTIES

The Pension Protection Act of 2006 imposes a civil penalty on any person who prepares an appraisal used to support a tax position if the appraisal results in a substantial or gross valuation misstatement. The penalty is $1,000 or 10% of the understatement of tax resulting from the misstatement (whichever is greater) up to a maximum of 125% of the gross income derived from the appraisal. An exception to the penalty applies if the appraiser establishes that it is "more likely than not" that the appraisal was correct.[33]

TIMING OF DEDUCTION

The charitable gift must be complete and, generally speaking, unconditional. If the gift would be complete but for the happening of a specific subsequent event preventing or reversing the gift, then the gift is considered a completed gift only if the possibility of the event happening is so remote as to be negligible.[34] For this purpose, "remote" generally means that the likelihood of the event happening has an actuarial value of 5% or less.[35]

A charitable contribution is deductible in the year the contribution was made by the donor.[36] In determining when the contribution is made, the delivery date of the gift to the charity is considered the date the gift is made.[37] The donor cannot retain the property in any way. The property (or a deed evidencing the transfer of the property) must be received by the charitable organization.

A pledge made to a charitable organization may be complete for gift tax purposes, but not for income tax purposes. A pledge is not considered a completed charitable gift. It is merely an agreement to make a future gift.

A promissory note given to a charity is not deductible for income tax purposes by the maker of the note. The amount of the note is deductible only when it is actually paid to the charity.

Checks. A contribution made by a check mailed to a charity is considered made on the date the check is mailed, not the date the check is actually received by the charity. For example, if the donor mails a check on December 29 and the check is received by the charitable organization on January 2 of the following year, the donor may take an income tax deduction for the amount of the check in the previous tax year. But, the gift is not deductible if the check is later dishonored by the bank.

Credit card. Credit card contributions are deductible when charged to the credit card company. The date of the gift is the date the charge is made by the donor, not the date the donor actually pays the bill from the credit card company.[38]

Tangible personal property. Gifts of tangible personal property are deductible in the year in which the property is delivered and received by the charitable organization. Specific rules for various types of personal property are explained in detail in Chapter 3 and Appendix J.

Stock/securities. With stock certificates, the date that the certificates are hand-delivered to the charity is the date of the gift. For delivery by mail and not in person, the contribution is considered made on the date of mailing. In the case of stock given to the donor's stockbroker to be transferred into the charity's name, the gift is made when the stock is transferred on the corporate books. Stocks registered in street name are not completed gifts until they are transferred to the charity's account on the books of the brokerage firm. For additional information on gifts of stock, see Chapter 3 (regarding the various types of securities) and Appendix J (valuation).

Real estate. Gifts of real estate are not completed gifts and, thus, not deductible for income tax purposes until the deed is actually given to the charity. The actual land or real estate itself cannot be "delivered," but the deed operates as the substitute for the property; therefore, the deed must be delivered. The recording or non-recording of the deed in the public record, in most states, has no effect on the timing or completeness of the gift.

CHAPTER ENDNOTES

1. "To" and "for the use of" are defined in the Code. The terms are explained in Chapter 3.

2. See IRC Secs. 170(b)(1)(A), 170(c), 7871(a)(1)(A). The extent to which a particular gift is deductible as between various charitable organizations may vary; see Chapter 3 for details.

3. While contributions to religious organizations are generally deductible, no part of the tuition and fees paid to private day schools providing religious and secular education is deductible. See *Sklar v. Commissioner*, 125 TC 14 2005; *Sklar v. Commissioner*, 282 F.3d 610 (9th Cir. 2002) *aff'g*. T.C. Memo. 2000-18.

4. Treas. Reg. §1.170A-4(b)(3)(i).

5. IRC Secs. 170(e)(1)(B), as amended by PPA 2006; 170(e)(7), as added by PPA 2006.

6. IRC Sec. 170(o), as added by PPA 2006.

7. IRC Sec. 170(f)(16), as added by PPA 2006.

8. IRC Sec. (f)(12), as added by AJCA 2004. See also Notice 2005-44, 2005-1 C.B. 1287.

9. Treas. Reg. §1.170A-1(g).

10. See IRC Sec. 170(f). The rules for gifts of partial interests are explained in detail in Chapter 5.

11. IRC Sec. 6115.

12. IRC Sec. 170(f)(3)(a); Treas. Reg. §1.170A-7(a).

13. Treas. Reg. §1.170A-13(a).

14. Treas. Reg. §1.170A-13(b)(2).

15. IRC Sec. 170(f)(8).

16. IRC Sec. 170(f)(8)(B).

17. Treas. Reg. §1.170A-13(b)(3).

18. TC Memo 2001-45.

19. Calculations of deductions for partial interest gifts can easily be done on software such as *NumberCruncher*, or *Charitable Gift Analyzer*.

20. IRC Sec. 68.

21. IRC Secs. 2001(c), 2502(a).

22. IRC Sec. 2502(a), as amended by EGTRRA 2001.

23. IRC Sec. 2210, as amended by EGTRRA 2001.

24. IRC Sec. 2010(c), as amended by EGTRRA 2001.

25. IRC Sec. 6662(c).

26. IRC Sec. 6662(b)(3).

27. IRC Secs. 6662(e), as amended by PPA 2006.

28. IRC Sec. 6662(h).

29. Treas. Reg. §1.6662-2(c). The maximum would be 40% if the donor's return showed both negligence and a gross valuation misstatement.

30. IRC Sec. 6664(c), as amended by PPA 2006.

31. IRC Sec. 6663(a).

32. IRC Sec. 6701.

33. See IRC Sec. 170(f)(11)(E), as amended by PPA 2006; IRC Sec. 6695A, as added by PPA 2006.

34. Treas. Reg. §1.170A-1(e).

35. Rev. Rul. 70-452, 1970-1 CB 199.

36. IRC Sec. 170(a)(1); Treas. Reg. §1.170A-1(a).

37. Treas. Reg. §1.170A-1(b).

38. Rev. Rul. 78-38, 1978-1 CB 67.

INCOME PERCENTAGE LIMITATIONS

CHAPTER 3

WHAT IS IT?

Lifetime gifts made to charities are not fully deductible by the taxpayer in every circumstance. Charitable gifts are deductible up to only a specific percentage of the donor's "contribution base." The donor's "contribution base" is defined as adjusted gross income (AGI) computed without net operating loss carryback.[1] For purposes of this chapter, the term "adjusted gross income" (AGI) will be used instead of "contribution base."

The percentage of AGI limitation varies depending on several factors, such as:

1. the type of charity;

2. the type of property donated;

3. whether the donor makes a specific election with respect to long-term capital gain property donated to public charities;

4. whether the donor is an individual or a corporation; and

5. whether the gift is made "to" the charity, or "for the use of" the charity.

The type of charity. In general terms, charities can be divided into two categories: "50% charities" or "public charities" (e.g., churches, schools, hospitals, and governmental entities); and "30% charities" (e.g., usually private family foundations). Gifts made to public charities are deductible at a higher percentage of the donor's AGI than are gifts made to private family foundations.

The type of property donated. The second factor involves the type of property the donor gives to charity. Types of property include cash, long-term capital gain property, short-term capital gain property, tangible personal property, and ordinary income property.

Long-term capital gain election. The third factor depends on whether the donor makes a special election with respect to long-term capital gain property. If the donor chooses the election, the property can be deducted up to 50% of AGI, but the donor can deduct only his cost basis. Without the election, the fair market value of the property is deductible up to 30% of AGI. This election does not apply to gifts to 30% charities.

Identity of the donor. The fourth factor is the identity of the donor. Individual donors have different rules than do corporate donors with respect to the amount of the income tax deduction.

Gifts "to" or "for the use of" the charity. The fifth and final factor is whether a cash gift is given "to" the charity or "for the use of the charity." Gifts "for the use of" the charity are limited to 30% of AGI, while gifts "to" public charities are deductible up to 50% of the donor's AGI.

In any event, the overall charitable deduction cannot be greater than 50% of the donor's AGI for the year. Any taxpayer who donates 20% or less of his AGI each year will not be affected by any limitations. Contributions in excess of these limits are subject to carryover rules for up to five years after the year of the gift. Each of these rules is discussed in detail below.

Public (50%) Charities

"Fifty percent charities" include: churches; schools; universities; hospitals; the United States government, and state and local governments; community chests, funds, community foundations, donor advised funds, or foundations organized and operated only for charitable, religious, scientific, literary, or educational purposes; private operating foundations; private non-operating foundations that distribute 100% of their contributions within two and one-half months of the year in which they receive those contributions (commonly known as "passthrough" foundations); pooled fund private foundations; and certain supporting organizations.[2]

According to the Internal Revenue Code, any charitable contribution of cash to the following types of charities is deductible up to 50% of the donor's AGI:

1. a church or a convention or association of churches;

2. an educational organization that normally maintains a regular faculty and curriculum and normally has a regularly enrolled body of pupils or students in attendance at the place where its educational activities are regularly carried on;

3. an organization the principal purpose or functions of which are the providing of medical or hospital care or medical education or medical research, if the organization is a hospital, or if the organization is a medical research organization directly engaged in the continuous active conduct of medical research in conjunction with a hospital, and during the calendar year in which the contribution is made such organization is committed to spend such contributions for such research before January 1 of the fifth calendar year that begins after the date such contribution is made;

4. an organization that normally receives a substantial part of its support (exclusive of income received in the exercise or performance by such organization of its charitable, educational, or other purpose or function constituting the basis for its exemption under Code Section 501(a)) from the United States or any state or political subdivision thereof or from direct or indirect contributions from the general public, and that is organized and operated exclusively to receive, hold, invest, and administer property and to make expenditures to or for the benefit of a college or university, and that is an agency or instrumentality of a state or political subdivision thereof, or that is owned or operated by a state or political subdivision thereof or by an agency or instrumentality of one or more states or political subdivisions;

5. a governmental unit;[3]

6. an organization that normally receives a substantial part of its support (exclusive of income received in the exercise or performance by such organization of its charitable, educational, or other purpose or function constituting the basis for its exemption under Code Section 501(a)) from a governmental unit or from direct or indirect contributions from the general public;

7. a private foundation that is an operating foundation, a passthrough private foundation or a pooled fund private foundation (none of these include a non-operating private foundation);[4] or

8. certain supporting organizations of public charities.[5]

HOW IS IT DONE?

Public (50%) Charities

The effect of the percentage limitation on public charities is that:

- Cash gifts "to" the charity (see discussion below) are deductible up to 50% of AGI.[6]

- Cash gifts "for the use of" the charity are deductible up to 30% of AGI.[7]

- Gifts of ordinary income property are deductible by the donor up to 50% of the donor's AGI. This type of property includes deferred annuities, business inventory, and property that if sold would result in ordinary income to the donor.[8]

- Gifts of short-term capital gain property are deductible up to 50% of the donor's AGI. Short-term capital gain property is property that, if sold by the donor, would result in short-term capital gain income. Generally, short-term capital gain property is a capital asset that has been held by the donor for *one year or less*.[9]

- Gifts of long-term capital gain property are deductible up to 30% of AGI. Long-term capital gain property is property that, if sold, would produce long-term capital gain.[10] Generally, long-term capital gain property is a capital asset that has been held for *more than one year*.[11] Examples of capital assets include stocks, bonds, real estate, jewelry, cars, boats, etc.

Special election. Under a special election for long-term capital gain property, the donor may take a deduction for up to 50% of AGI if the donor values the property at the lesser of fair market value or his *adjusted cost basis*. No carryover is allowed for the amount of the reduced long-term capital gain. This election applies to all long-term capital gain property in that tax year. The election is made on the donor's income tax return.[12]

Example: A donor gives $100,000 of highly appreciated stock to the American Lung Association. The cost basis of the property is $45,000. The donor can deduct $100,000 up to 30% of his AGI or, if elected, the donor could deduct $45,000 up to 50% of his AGI. If the election is made to use the cost basis of $45,000, the reduced amount ($100,000 - $45,000 = $55,000) is not eligible to be carried forward into future years.

- Gifts of tangible personal property that are "related" to the charity's use are deductible at fair market value up to 30% of AGI, or the donor may deduct the cost basis in the property up to 50% of AGI.[13]

    Tangible personal property "unrelated" to the charity's use is deductible up to 50% of AGI, but the value is based on the lesser of its fair market value or cost basis.[14] "Unrelated" to the use generally means a use that is unrelated to the exempt purpose or function of the charity.[15]

    The charitable organization is responsible for determining whether the charity puts the property to a "related" use or an "unrelated" use. The charity will make this determination on IRS Form 8283 for non-cash gifts valued at more than $500. For details on "related" and "unrelated" use property, see Chapter 4.

    Gifts of future interests in tangible personal property are not deductible until all the intervening interests in, and rights to, the possession or use of the property have expired.[16]

Private Family Foundations
(30% Charities)

Thirty percent charities include veterans' associations, fraternal groups, and private non-operating founda-

tions, which are commonly referred to as private family foundations.

"Private foundation" means a domestic or foreign organization described in Code Section 501(c)(3) (i.e., a community chest, fund, or foundation organized and operated exclusively for religious, charitable, scientific, literary, or educational purposes) *other than*:

1. an organization described in Code Section 170(b)(1)(A) (i.e., other than a private operating foundation, a "passthrough" foundation, or a pooled fund foundation)—in other words, 50% charities;

2. an organization that normally receives more than one-third of its support from grants, gifts, contributions, etc., from persons other than disqualified persons (i.e., from the general public), *and* that normally receives not more than one-third of its support from gross investment income and unrelated business taxable income;

3. an organization that is organized and at all times is operated exclusively for the benefit of one or more specified organizations described in paragraphs 1 or 2, above; or

4. an organization that is organized and operated exclusively for testing for public safety.[17]

The effect of the percentage limitations on private foundations is that:

- Cash gifts donated "to" or "for the use of" the private foundation are deductible up to 30% of AGI.

- Ordinary income and short-term capital gain property gifts are deductible up to 30% of the donor's AGI.[18]

- Gifts of long-term capital gain property are deductible up to 20% of AGI.[19]

- Qualified stock gifts (long-term capital gain stock for which market quotations are readily available on an established securities market) made to private family foundations are deductible at fair market value up to 20% of AGI.[20] This provision for qualified stock applies only if the gift is 10% or less of the total outstanding shares of the corporation. When determining

the 10% limitation, gifts made by the donor's siblings, spouse, ancestors and descendants are also counted.[21]

- Gifts of tangible personal property (whether related or unrelated to the use of the 30% charity) are deductible only to the extent of *the lesser of* fair market value *or* cost basis up to 20% of AGI.[22]

Order of Charitable Deductions Allowed

The percentage limitations are not "stacked"; in other words, each level is reduced by contributions deducted (or carried over) at the next higher level. In general, a donor's charitable deductions must be accounted for in the following order for income tax purposes:

1. Gifts subject to the 50% limitation, only, up to 50% of the donor's AGI.

2. Gifts subject to the 30% limitation, up to the *lesser of*:

   - 30% of the donor's AGI, *or*

   - the *excess* of:

     (a) 50% of the donor's AGI *over*

     (b) the amount of the allowable contributions made to 50% organizations.

   Caution: Contributions of long-term capital gain property to 50% organizations, which ordinarily would be subject to the 30% limitation, must nevertheless be included in the latter amount.

3. Gifts of long-term capital gain property subject to the 30% limitation, up to 30% of the donor's AGI.

4. Contributions subject to the 20% limitation, up to the *lesser* of:

   - 20% of the donor's AGI, *or*

   - the excess of:

     (a) 30% of the donor's AGI *over*

     (b) the amount of contributions of long-term capital gain property to 50% organizations to which the 30% limitation applies.

Gifts exceeding these limitations may be subject to carryover for up to five years (see "Carryover Rules" below). Table 4 from IRS Publication 526, Charitable Contributions helps to determine the amount and order of charitable contributions that are deductible as well as the carryover amount, if any (see Figure 3.1 at the end of this chapter).

The following examples illustrate the order of deduction rules:

Example: Norma Greenfield had $50,000 of AGI last year. She donated $2,000 in cash to St. Jude's Children's Research Hospital. She also gave $5,000 in cash to a private family foundation (i.e., a 30% charity). Her third charitable contribution for the year was a piece of real estate purchased in 1998 with a cost basis of $22,000 and a fair market value of $28,000, which she gave to the American Heart Association. Norma did not choose the special election for long-term capital gain property. Therefore, she may deduct the fair market value of the property up to 30% of her AGI.

First, the $2,000 cash donation to St. Jude's is fully deductible up to 50% of her AGI (50% x $50,000 = $25,000). Since $2,000 is less than $25,000, $2,000 of the cash gift is fully deductible to Norma.

In the pecking order of deductions, the gift to the private foundation is considered before the gift of long-term capital gain property to the 50% organization. Norma's total contributions to the 50% charities equal $30,000 ($28,000 + $2,000). But 50% of her AGI is equal to $25,000, so her total contributions exceed the amount she can deduct for the year. Therefore, the $5,000 gift to the 30% charity is not deductible for the year. However, it can be carried forward to future years.

The gift of land is considered next and is deductible up to 30% of her AGI, or $15,000 (30% x $50,000 = $15,000). Norma's carryover for the year is determined by subtracting the deductible amount from the fair market value of the land ($28,000 - $15,000 = $13,000).

Norma's total charitable deductions for the tax year are $17,000 ($2,000 + $15,000). Her carryover generated from this tax year is equal to $18,000 ($5,000 + $13,000).

Effect of the special election. If Norma had chosen the special election for long-term capital gain property, she could have deducted the cost basis of the real property, which was $22,000. Recall that Norma's AGI was $50,000. Because she had a cash gift of $2,000 to St. Jude's, her total contributions of the real property and the cash gift totalled $24,000 ($2,000 + $22,000). Since 50% of her AGI is $25,000, she could have deducted both contributions in full. So far she has deducted only $24,000. Consequently, $1,000 of the $5,000 cash gift to the private family foundation would be deductible in the current tax year.

Her total charitable deductions for the tax year would be $25,000 ($2,000 + $22,000 + $1,000), and her carryover generated from this tax year would be $4,000 ($5,000 - $1,000).

Reduction from Fair Market Value to Cost Basis

Long-term capital gain property. The "reduction to cost basis rule" requires that the fair market value of the property *not* be used to determine the donor's charitable deduction for the donation of such property to a private family foundation. Instead the fair market value must be *reduced* by the amount of the long-term capital gain in the property. The general rule is that long-term capital gain is equal to the amount that would have been taxed as long-term capital gain if the property had been sold as of the date of the gift. A capital asset is generally an asset that the donor has held for more than one year. The net effect is that the property's cost basis is deducted, not the fair market value.[23]

Short-term capital gain property. For any capital asset held for one year or less, the property is generally considered short-term capital gain property. The amount of the charitable deduction for short-term capital gain property is determined by using the property's fair market value *minus* the short-term capital gain included in the property as if the property had been sold. The deductible amount is generally the property's cost basis.[24]

Inventory. Similarly, inventory property, accounts and notes receivable, and copyrights are valued for

charitable contribution purposes at the property's fair market value *minus* the amount that would have been ordinary income if the property had been sold.[25]

Patents and Intellectual Property. The donor's deduction for patents, copyrights, software, or intellectual property donated after June 3, 2004 is limited to the donor's cost basis or fair market value, whichever is less. The donor can also claim subsequent charitable deductions (if the gift is not made to a private foundation) based on a percentage of the income the charity receives as a result of the contributed asset. The deductions can be taken for a period of years. For more information on these types of assets, see Chapter 4.[26]

Qualified stock to private foundations. Ordinarily, if long-term capital gain property is contributed to a private family foundation, the fair market value of the property must be reduced by the amount of the long-term capital gain. An exception to this rule applies to "qualified appreciated stock." With qualified appreciated stock, no reduction from the property's fair market value to cost basis is required. "Qualified appreciated stock" is defined as long-term capital gain stock for which market quotations are readily available on an established securities market.[27]

Tangible personal property. Gifts of tangible personal property that are "unrelated" to the use of the charity (see Chapter 4) are deductible using, as a general rule, the donor's cost basis. As with gifts of long-term capital gain property, the fair market value of the tangible personal property must be *reduced* by the amount of the capital gain in the property.[28]

Property subject to depreciation recapture. If a donor gives property that has been previously depreciated on the taxpayer's income tax return, the donor must reduce the value of the property by the amount of depreciation subject to recapture (if the property had been sold).[29] If the property has long-term capital gain *and* has been depreciated, the taxpayer must reduce the property's value by both (1) the amount of the long-term capital gain, *and* (2) the depreciable amount subject to recapture.

Example: Kathy Foll owns a commercial office building that she uses to rent office space to several businesses. The building is worth $1,000,000 today. Kathy has depreciated part of the building's cost basis since purchasing

the building three years ago. Her cost basis is $800,000 and the total depreciation to date that is subject to recapture is $120,000. Kathy donates the commercial building to Goodwill. If she decides to elect the cost basis deduction (see "Special Election," above), she can deduct $800,000 (cost basis) minus $120,000 (depreciation recapture), or $680,000, up to 50% of her AGI. Otherwise, if she decides *not* to elect the cost basis deduction, she can deduct $1,000,000 (fair market value) minus $120,000 (depreciation recapture) or $880,000, up to 30% of her AGI.

Fair Market Value Less Than Cost Basis

If a taxpayer donates property that has a current fair market value *lower* than the taxpayer's cost basis, the donor is limited to a deduction of the lower fair market value rather than the cost basis.[30]

Example: John Smith purchased a building for $140,000 three years ago. John donates the building to the local elementary school this year. The building currently appraises for only $125,000 due to the building's new neighbor, a landfill operation. John can deduct only $125,000, not $140,000, up to 30% of AGI.

Property Subject to a Debt

Taxpayers who contribute property subject to a debt must reduce the fair market value of the property by the amount of the debt regardless of whether the recipient or another individual assumes the debt. This rule does not apply to gifts of life insurance (see Chapter 13).[31]

Example: Jay Carson owns a building in Fargo, North Dakota worth $750,000. Jay has a mortgage on the building worth $200,000. If he donates the building to the Smithsonian Institution, the value of his charitable contribution ($750,000) is reduced by the amount of the debt ($200,000). Therefore, Jay can deduct $550,000 ($750,000 - $200,000) up to 30% of his AGI.

Gifts Made by a Corporation

Generally, a C corporation may deduct gifts to qualified charities up to 10% of the corporation's taxable income. C corporations also have a 5-year carryforward provision.[32]

An S corporation can make gifts of corporate assets. The S corporation, as a passthrough entity, will pass the charitable deductions on to its individual shareholders each year through the annual K-1 Form.[33]

"TO" VERSUS "FOR THE USE OF"

Charitable gifts are classified into two groups: (1) those that are considered gifts made "to" the charity; and (2) those that are considered gifts given "for the use of" the charity.

In general terms, a gift "to" a charity involves an outright gift with no strings attached. A gift "for the use of" the charity is viewed as something less than a direct outright gift.[34] The IRS regulations poorly describe what is meant by "for the use of." (The term does *not* refer to gifts such as the rent-free use of property owned by the donor; such gifts are nondeductible. See Chapter 5.) The following are examples of gifts "for the use of" a charity:

- a contribution of a *remainder* interest to a charity that is *held in trust for the benefit of the charity* (however, a contribution of a remainder interest is a contribution "to" the charity);

- a contribution of an *income* interest in property (e.g., a charitable lead trust).[35]

The distinction between gifts "to" a charity and gifts "for the use of" a charity is important because the rules for most charitable gift deductions imply that the gift is being given "to" a charity. However, gifts "for the use of the charity" have *lower* percentage limitations than gifts "to" charities:

- Cash gifts "to" a public charity are deductible up to 50% of the donor's AGI.[36]

- Cash gifts "for the use of" a public charity are deductible up to 30% of AGI.[37]

- Cash gifts "to" a private non-operating family foundation are deductible up to 30% of the donor's AGI.[38]

- Cash gifts "for the use of" a private non-operating family foundation are deductible up to 30% of the donor's AGI.[39]

This limitation is especially critical with gifts of life insurance policies to charitable entities. When a charity purchases a life insurance policy on the life of its donor, and the donor makes annual contributions to the charity to cover future premium obligations, those contributions are considered to be made "to" the charity.

But, if, in the alternative, the donor pays the premiums directly to the insurance company instead of "to" the charity owning the policy, the IRS considers those contributions a gift "for the use of" the charity.[40] The consequence of this distinction is that the deduction for the cash contributions is limited to 30% of the donor's AGI instead of 50%.[41]

Example: Nathan Adams buys a $100,000 life insurance policy for the local Methodist church. The annual premiums are $1,950. Nathan makes an annual donation of $2,000 directly to the church to cover the cost of the premium. Nathan can deduct $2,000 as a charitable contribution of cash up to 50% of his AGI. If, however, Nathan pays the premium directly to the life insurance company, instead of the church, Nathan can only deduct $2,000 up to 30% of his AGI.

CARRYOVER RULES

To the extent the donor has charitable contributions in any tax year in excess of the percentage limitations, he may carry over the excess unused portion to the extent deductible, in each of the five succeeding tax years until it is used up. Carried-over deductions retain the same character (e.g., 50%-type or 30%-type) in the carryover years as in the year of the initial contribution.[42]

If a taxpayer has carryover allowances from several prior years, the taxpayer must use the carryover from the earliest year first, rather than the most recent year. The carryover provision is available only for the 5-year period immediately following the year the excess was created. A donor cannot pick and choose which five years to use.

Example: Jayne King has the following excess charitable contributions of cash gifts:

2004	$10,000
2005	$ 5,000
2006	$12,000

In 2007, Jayne did not make any charitable contributions and her AGI in 2007 is $40,000. Jayne must use all the excess contribution from 2004 before she can use up the contributions from 2005 or 2006. Jayne can use the $10,000 carryover from 2004, $5,000 from 2005, and $5,000 of the $12,000 from 2006, for a total of $20,000. The remaining $7,000 from 2006 can be carried forward to 2008.

Contributions in carryforward years are subject to the same percentage limitation they were subject to in the year the excess was created.[43] For instance, if the donor has $20,000 of capital gain property carryover (30% property), then in the next five years, that contribution is only deductible up to 30% of AGI.

The excess charitable contribution cannot be used in a tax year earlier than the year of the gift. In other words, no carryback is allowed for the excess contribution, only a carryforward is allowed.

Example: If the donor has an excess charitable contribution for 2007, the donor cannot use the excess to reduce his taxable income in a tax year before 2007 (e.g., 2005 or 2006). The excess charitable contribution can be used only in the years 2008 through 2010.

The following are examples of the carryover rules:

Example 1: Cindy Ray has $24,000 of AGI this year. Cindy made a gift of $6,000 cash to her local synagogue. She also made a gift of $3,000 of long-term capital gain property to the synagogue. She did not choose the special election so she will deduct this property up to 30% of her AGI at its fair market value. Cindy also has a carryover from last year of $5,000 for long-term capital gain property donated to the same synagogue.

Cindy's income tax charitable deduction for this year cannot be more than her AGI multiplied by the percentage limitation ($24,000 x 50%), or $12,000. Since her gift of $6,000 cash falls within the $12,000 limitation, Cindy can deduct the $6,000 cash gift in full.

Next, to determine her deduction for the long-term capital gain property for this year, she determines her AGI multiplied by the percentage limitation ($24,000 x 30% = $7,200). She compares that number ($7,200) to her total limitation of $12,000 *reduced* by the current cash gift of $6,000 *plus* the carryover amount of $5,000, or $12,000 *minus* ($5,000 + $6,000) = $1,000. The lesser of these two amounts ($7,200 or $1,000) is $1,000. Therefore, her deduction for the $3,000 long-term capital gain property is $1,000.

Her deduction for the $5,000 carryover amount is limited to the smaller of $7,200 or $6,000 ($12,000 - $6,000). Since the $5,000 carryover is less than $7,200 or $6,000, it can be deducted in full.

Cindy's total deduction for this year is $12,000 ($6,000 cash + $1,000 of long-term capital gain + $5,000 of carryover from last year). Cindy can carry over $2,000 of long-term capital gain property until next year ($3,000 capital gain property - $1,000 allowable deduction this year = $2,000 carryover for next year).

Example 2: Assume that Bernie and Barb Milligan (who file jointly as a married couple) have an AGI as follows:

AGI for year 1: $50,000

AGI for year 2: $40,000

In year 1 they gave:

• $26,500 cash contribution to Georgetown University

• $1,000 cash contribution to a private non-operating foundation

In year 2 they gave:

• $19,000 cash contribution to Georgetown University

• $600 cash contribution to the same private non-operating foundation

Since Bernie and Barb's AGI in year 1 was $50,000, their maximum charitable income tax deduction is:

$50,000	AGI for Year 1	
x 50%	Percentage Limitation	
$25,000	Maximum Allowable Deduction for Year 1	

Therefore, they can claim $25,000 of the $26,500 donated to Georgetown University as a charitable income tax deduction.

The excess amount eligible for the 5-year carryforward provision is:

$26,500	Total Contributions for Year 1
- 25,000	Allowable Contributions
$ 1,500	Carryover from Year 1

No deduction is allowed for the contribution of $1,000 to the private non-operating foundation. The donors may carry it forward as well.

The total carryover for year 1 is:

$1,500	
+1,000	
$2,500	Total Carryover for Year 1

In year 2, the maximum deductible amount is:

$40,000	AGI for Year 2
x 50%	Percentage Limitation
$20,000	Maximum Allowable Deduction for Year 2

$20,000	Maximum Allowable Deduction
- 19,000	Total Cash Gifts Made in Year 2
$ 1,000	Excess from Year 2

In year 2, $1,000 of the $2,500 carryover from year 1 is eligible for a charitable deduction. Therefore, $1,500 is still leftover as a carryover for year 3.

No current year deduction is available for the $600 donated to the private non-operating foundation in year 2.[44] It can be carried over, however.

The total carryover for year 2 equals:

$1,500
+ 600
$2,100 Total Carryover for Year 2

The following is an example of the carryover rules when capital gain property is involved:

Example: Assume that Steve and Tanya Rucker (who file jointly as a married couple) have an AGI as follows:

AGI in year 1: $50,000

AGI in year 2: $40,000

In year 1 they gave:

• $20,000 in cash to the Mayo Clinic in Rochester, Minnesota; *plus*

• $13,000 of long-term capital gain property to the Boy Scouts of America;

• for a total of $33,000.

In year 2 they gave:

• $5,000 in cash to the Mayo Clinic; *plus*

• $10,000 in long-term capital gain property to the Boy Scouts;

• for a total of $15,000.

Since their AGI was $50,000 in Year 1, the maximum charitable income tax deduction is:

$50,000 AGI for Year 1
x   50% Percentage Limitation
$25,000 Maximum Allowable Deduction

In year 1, they can claim as a charitable income tax deduction $25,000 of the $33,000.

The excess amount eligible for the 5-year carryforward provision is:

$33,000 Total Contributions for Year 1
- 25,000
$ 8,000 Carryover from Year 1

The $8,000 carryover is treated as a contribution of 30% long-term capital gain property in each of the five carryforward years.

In year 2, the maximum deductible amount is:

$40,000 AGI for Year 2
x   50% Percentage Limitation
$20,000 Maximum Allowable Deduction
$20,000 Maximum Allowable Deduction
- 5,000 Cash Gift
$15,000

$40,000 AGI for Year 2
x   30% Long-Term Capital Gain Property
$12,000 Maximum Allowable Deduction
         for Year 2
$12,000 Maximum Allowable Deduction
- 10,000 Capital Gain Property
$ 2,000

Of the $8,000 carryover from year 1, $2,000 is eligible for a charitable deduction. Therefore $6,000 is still left over as a carryover for year 3.

$8,000 Carryover
- 2,000 Used in Year 2
$6,000 Unused Charitable Deduction
        Carryforward of 30% property[49]

Effect of Subsequent Events on Carryover Provisions

Death. The carryover provisions are not available to a taxpayer after the year of the taxpayer's death. Therefore, any unused carryover is lost after the decedent's final income tax return is filed. A surviving spouse cannot use the deceased spouse's carryover amount.[46]

Example: Larry and Avis Bjork filed a joint return in year 1 with excess charitable contributions such that the carryover was $10,000. Larry dies in year 1. In year 2, Avis files a separate return. Of the $10,000 carryover, $6,000 was due to Larry's contributions and $4,000 was due to Avis' contributions. The $6,000 allocated to Larry cannot be used on Avis' year 2 return. Avis can claim only the $4,000 allocated to her.

The $6,000 representing Larry's portion can be used only on the decedent's final income tax return in year 1.

Changing status from separate to married filing jointly. If a couple has filed separately in a year in which one spouse made an excess charitable contribution, the excess contribution is aggregated and available for use on the joint return. The same theory applies if two single individuals have charitable carryforwards and then get married in a later tax year—the carryforward amount is eligible for use on the joint return.[47]

Changing status from married filing jointly to separate. If a married couple files a joint tax return that creates a charitable deduction carryforward, and during one of the five carryforward years the couple files separate returns, the carryforward amount is allocated to each spouse. The allocation is made as if each spouse filed a separate return in the year of the charitable contribution creating the carryforward. The result is that each spouse will have his or her own share of the charitable deductions based on the amount of the total charitable contribution made by each spouse.[48]

Remarriage during the carryover years. In the case of a taxpayer who has previously filed a joint return with a spouse where a carryover of charitable income tax deductions was created, if the couple gets divorced and either spouse subsequently remarries within the 5-year carryover period, the carryover remains available. Each taxpayer can use his or her allocation of the excess carryover from the prior marriage on his or her subsequent joint return with a new spouse.[49]

Taking the standard deduction in a carryover year. A donor can choose to use the standard deduction in one of the years for which the 5-year carryover provision applies, but if he does so, part of the carryover is treated as used for that year, even though no charitable deduction is actually taken.[50]

Information to Support a Carryover Deduction

A donor who claims a carryover deduction must attach to his income tax return a statement showing:

- the excess contributions made in each year;

- the years in which those contributions were made;

- the amount of excess contribution that is 30% capital gain property; and

- the amount of the carryover that has been used in each year since the original excess contribution was made.[51]

CHAPTER ENDNOTES

1. IRC Sec. 170(b)(1)(F).
2. IRC Sec. 170(b)(1)(A).
3. See IRC Sec. 170(c)(1).
4. IRC Sec. 170(b)(1)(E).
5. IRC Sec. 170(b)(1)(A). The rules for eligible supporting organizations are set forth in IRC Secs. 509(a)(2) and 509(a)(3).
6. IRC Sec. 170(b)(1)(A); Treas. Reg. §1.170A-8(b).
7. IRC Sec. 170(b)(1)(B).
8. IRC Sec. 170(b)(1)(A); Treas. Reg. §1.170A-4(b)(1).
9. IRC Secs. 170(b)(1)(A), 1222(1).
10. IRC Secs. 170(b)(1)(C)(i), 170(b)(1)(C)(iv); Treas. Reg. §1.170A-8(d)(1).
11. IRC Sec. 1222(3).
12. IRC Secs. 170(b)(1)(C)(iii), 170(e)(1); Treas. Reg. §1.170A-8(d)(2).
13. IRC Sec. 170(b)(1)(C)(i).
14. IRC Secs. 170(b)(1)(A), 170(e)(1)(B)(i).
15. Treas. Reg. §1.170A-4(b)(3).
16. IRC Sec. 170(a)(3).
17. IRC Sec. 509(a).
18. IRC Sec. 170(b)(1)(B).
19. IRC Sec. 170(b)(1)(D)(i).
20. IRC Secs. 170(e)(5)(A), 170(e)(5)(B), 170(b)(1)(D)(i).
21. IRC Secs. 170(e)(5)(C), 267(c)(4).
22. IRC Sec. 170(e)(1)(B)(ii).
23. IRC Secs. 170(e)(1)(B)(ii), 1222(3).
24. IRC Secs. 170(e)(1)(A), 1222(1); Treas. Reg. §1.170A-4(a)(1).
25. IRC Sec. 170(e)(1)(A).
26. IRC Sec. 170(m), as added by AJCA 2004. See also Notice 2005-41, 2005-23 IRB 1203.
27. IRC Secs. 170(e)(1)(B)(ii), 170(e)(5).
28. IRC Sec. 170(e)(1)(B)(i).
29. IRC Sec. 170(e)(1)(A).
30. Treas. Reg. §1.170A-1(c)(1).
31. *Tidler v. Comm.*, TC Memo 1987-268; *Scott v. Comm.*, 61 TC 654 (1974). See also *Douglas v. Comm.*, 58 TC Memo 563 (1989).
32. IRC Secs. 170(b)(2), 170(d)(2); Treas. Reg. §1.170A-11(c).
33. IRC Secs. 1366(a), 1366(b).
34. IRC Sec. 170(b)(1)(B); Treas. Reg. §1.170A-8(a)(2).
35. Treas. Reg. §1.170A-8(a)(2).
36. IRC Sec. 170(b)(1)(A); Treas. Reg. §1.170A-8(b).

37. IRC Sec. 170(b)(1)(B).

38. IRC Sec. 170(b)(1)(B).

39. IRC Sec. 170(b)(1)(B).

40. Some national commentators make the legal argument that cash gifts paid directly to insurance companies for life insurance policies owned by public charities are deductible up to 50% of AGI. In any event, there is no case law directly on point or IRS authority to substantiate this view.

41. IRC Sec. 170(b)(1)(B)(i); Treas. Reg. §1.170A-8(b).

42. IRC Secs. 170(b)(1)(D)(ii), 170(d)(1); Treas. Regs. §§1.170A-10(b), 1.170A-10(c).

43. IRC Secs. 170(b)(1)(D)(ii), 170(d)(1); Treas. Regs. §§1.170A-10(b), 1.170A-10(c).

44. Treas. Reg. §1.170A-10(b)(1), Example 1.

45. Treas. Reg. §1.170A-10(c)(1), Example 1.

46. Treas. Reg. §1.170A-10(d)(4)(iii).

47. Treas. Reg. §1.170A-10(d)(4)(ii).

48. Treas. Reg. §1.170A-10(d)(4)(i).

49. Treas. Reg. §1.170A-10(d)(4)(ii).

50. Treas. Reg. §1.170A-10(b)(2), Example 1.

51. Treas. Reg. §1.170A-10(e).

Figure 3.1

Worksheet 2. **Applying the Deduction Limits**   *Keep for your records*

If the result on any line is less than zero, enter zero. For other instructions, see page 15.

Step 1. Enter any qualified conservation contributions (QCCs).

1. If you are a qualified farmer or rancher, enter any QCCs eligible for the 100% limit **1**
2. Enter any QCCs not entered on line 1. Do not include this amount on line 3, 4, 5, 6, or 8 . . . . **2**

Step 2. List your other charitable contributions made during the year.

3. Enter your contributions to 50% limit organizations. (Include contributions of capital gain property if you reduced the property's fair market value. Do not include contributions of capital gain property deducted at fair market value.) **Do not** include any contributions you entered on line 1 or 2 . . . . **3**
4. Enter your contributions to 50% limit organizations of capital gain property deducted at fair market value **4**
5. Enter your contributions (other than of capital gain property) to qualified organizations that are not 50% limit organizations **5**
6. Enter your contributions "for the use of" any qualified organization. (But do not enter here any amount that must be entered on line 8.) **6**
7. Add lines 5 and 6 . . . . **7**
8. Enter your contributions of capital gain property to or for the use of any qualified organization. (But do not enter here any amount entered on line 3 or 4) **8**

Step 3. Figure your deduction for the year and your carryover to the next year.

9. Enter your adjusted gross income **9**
10. Multiply line 9 by 0.5. This is your 50% limit **10**

			Carryover
Contributions to 50% limit organizations			
11. Enter the smaller of line 3 or line 10	**11**		
12. Subtract line 11 from line 3	**12**		
13. Subtract line 11 from line 10	**13**		
Contributions not to 50% limit organizations			
14. Add lines 3 and 4	**14**		
15. Multiply line 9 by 0.3. This is your 30% limit	**15**		
16. Subtract line 14 from line 10	**16**		
17. Enter the smallest of line 7, 15, or 16	**17**		
18. Subtract line 17 from line 7	**18**		
19. Subtract line 17 from line 15	**19**		
Contributions of capital gain property to 50% limit organizations			
20. Enter the smallest of line 4, 13, or 15	**20**		
21. Subtract line 20 from line 4	**21**		
22. Subtract line 17 from line 16	**22**		
23. Subtract line 20 from line 15	**23**		
Other contributions of capital gain property			
24. Multiply line 9 by 0.2. This is your 20% limit	**24**		
25. Enter the smallest of line 8, 19, 22, 23, or 24	**25**		
26. Subtract line 25 from line 8	**26**		
27. Add lines 11, 17, 20, and 25	**27**		
28. Subtract line 27 from line 10	**28**		
29. Enter the smaller of line 2 or line 28	**29**		
30. Subtract line 29 from line 2	**30**		
31. Subtract line 27 from line 9	**31**		

32. Enter the smaller of line 1 or line 31 . . . . **32**
33. Add lines 27, 29, and 32. Enter the total here and on Schedule A (Form 1040), line 15 or line 16, whichever is appropriate **33**
34. Subtract line 32 from line 1 . . . . **34**
35. Add lines 12, 18, 21, 26, 30, and 34. Carry this amount forward to Schedule A (Form 1040) next year **35**

GIFTS OF PROPERTY

CHAPTER 4

WHAT IS IT?

While many charitable donations are made by personal check, larger donations tend to involve gifts of non-cash property. The rules that are applied to each charitable gift vary depending on the type of asset donated, the category to which the charitable donee is assigned, and the timing and structure of the gift vehicle used. The laws and regulations governing donations of property were relatively stable from the last major revisions of the charity tax laws in 1969 up until the late 1990s. As a result of Congressional hearings detailing abuses and numerous stories in the press about greedy donors and aggressive techniques, restrictive legislation and regulations have recently been passed. Most of the abuses that have been shut down involved inflated tax deductions, appraisals that provided unrealistic property values, and situations where donors benefited significantly while the charities involved received little or nothing of value. Since further scrutiny from lawmakers is likely, it is imperative that both advisers and charities not only keep current on the changes in the law, but also avoid situations which are likely to trigger more legislative restrictions.

WHEN IS THE USE OF SUCH A DEVICE INDICATED?

1. When a donor has non-cash assets that he or she no longer needs or wants and also is charitably inclined.

2. When a donor wants to combine tax planning with charitable donations.

3. When a donor wishes to give particular assets that the charity can use in its day-to-day operations.

TANGIBLE PERSONAL PROPERTY

Since the deduction rules differ between tangible and intangible gifts, it is important to properly characterize each gift accordingly.

There is an almost unlimited assortment of tangible property donated to charity. Such gifts might include automobiles, furniture, jewelry, art, books, coins, livestock, timber, and crops. IRS Publication 526 *Charitable Contributions* defines "tangible property" in a charitable context as "any property other than land or buildings that can be seen or touched." Although coins, such as cash money, are considered intangible, collectible coins that have a numismatic value are considered tangible assets.

The income tax deduction limits for tangible property gifts depend on a variety of factors.

Related Use

Will the donated property be used by the charity in a manner consistent with its charitable purpose? For example, a donation of a valuable book collection to a library which will display the collection in its archives and make the books available for reading by scholars and researchers clearly falls into this category. A donation of office furniture to a charity that uses the gift to furnish its offices again is a related use gift. In comparison, the gift of a rare medieval manuscript to a modern art museum is unrelated, since it is unrealistic that the museum will display the manuscript as part of its collection.

For "related use" gifts that do not fall within the rules for investments or future interests (see below), the donor may deduct the full fair market value up to 30% of his adjusted gross income (AGI). For "unrelated use" gifts, the donor may deduct the lesser of (a) fair market value or (b) adjusted basis, up to 50% of adjusted gross income.[1]

In situations where the donor takes a full fair market value income tax deduction but the charity fails to put the donated property to a related use, the Pension Protection Act of 2006 introduced a new recapture provision for gifts where the value is greater than $5,000. When a charity disposes of a related use item within three years of the gift, the excess of the deduction claimed over the donor's basis is included in the donor's income in the year that the charity disposes of the tangible property. If the disposition by the charity takes place in the same year that the gift is made, the donor's deduction is limited to his or her basis. This new recapture rule only applies to gifts made after September 1, 2006 where the fair market value exceeds $5,000. An exception to this new recapture rule is available when the charity certifies in writing under penalty of perjury detailing how the property was indeed related to the nonprofit's charitable purpose. Any fraudulent certification is subject to a $10,000 penalty.[2]

Investment or Inventory?

If a donor has held tangible personal property as an investment for more than one year, it is generally considered a capital asset and if the related use test, above, is also met, the deduction is equal to the fair market value as of the date of the gift. It is important to distinguish between an investment and inventory. A coin collection held by a hobbyist, for example, would be considered an investment. On the other hand, a similar collection held by a dealer would be considered inventory. If characterized as inventory, the deduction is limited to the lesser of adjusted basis or fair market value, and the deduction is subject to the 50% of AGI limitation.[3]

There are two exceptions to the rule allowing a deduction for gifts of inventory:

- *Gifts of inventory by C corporations used for the care of the ill, needy, or infants.*[4] The deduction is limited to the lesser of (1) adjusted basis plus 50% of the difference between basis and list price, and (2) 200% of adjusted basis.

- *Gifts of qualified research property made to an institution of higher education or scientific research.*[5] The deduction is limited to the lesser of (1) adjusted basis plus 50% of the difference between basis and list price, and (2) 200% of adjusted basis.

In 2005, Congress enacted temporary legislation that broadened the deduction limits for donations of food inventory and books to qualified victims of Hurricane Katrina. Anyone (not just C corporations) who donated

Figure 4.1

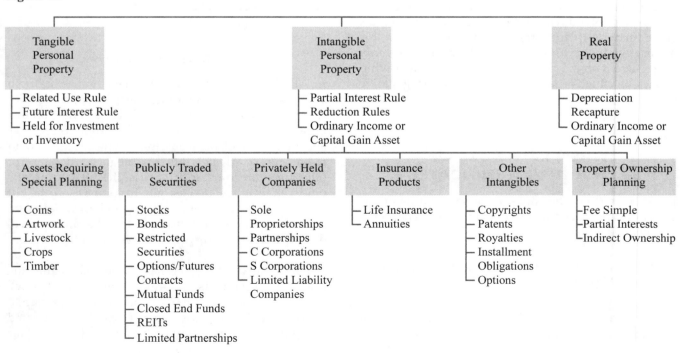

food inventory that met quality and labeling standards, could claim an enhanced deduction, and C corporations who donated book inventories to qualified schools were allowed the enhanced deduction if the school certified that the books were suitable for their teaching and education purposes. While this law affected only donations made between August 28, 2005 and January 1, 2006, it is possible that the Katrina Act may be used as a model for future natural disasters, and advisors should keep an eye on legislative relief at those times.

Future Interest in Tangible Personal Property

If a donor gives a charity a future interest in tangible property, the gift is not considered complete and there is no tax deduction allowed until the asset passes in its entirety to the charity.[6] Ordinarily, gifts to charity via a charitable remainder trust (CRT) or pooled income fund would be considered future interest gifts because the charity's actual receipt of the donated property is delayed; nevertheless, such gifts are deductible at the time of the gift *if* the trust meets strict statutory requirements. On the other hand, gifts made to charitable gift annuities, in which the transfer of the property to the charity occurs immediately, are considered to be part outright gift and part sale.

Fractional Interest in Tangible Personal Property

Prior to 2004, a donor could give a fractional interest in tangible personal property (a painting, for example) to a charity and receive a charitable tax deduction equal to the percentage of the asset donated—even if the asset remained in the possession of the donor. The deduction was allowed as long as the donor made the artwork available to the museum for a percentage of the year equal to the percentage donated. This was a popular technique because (1) it allowed a donor to spread a sizable tax deduction over decades when it would otherwise be limited by a percentage of adjusted gross income, (2) if the asset increased in value, each fractional interest donated would result in an larger deduction, and (3) the donor continued to enjoy the property in his home or business for at least part, if not all, of the year.

The Pension Protection Act of 2006 curtailed some of the more abusive arrangements for these fractional gifts. Under the new law, a donor's tax deduction is recaptured if the donor's entire interest in the asset isn't donated to the charity within 10 years of the original fractional interest gift. The deduction is also recaptured if the charity fails to take physical possession or use the property for its exempt purposes during that time. In either situation, the donor is also fined a 10% penalty in addition to the recaptured tax deduction. And finally, the new laws, in effect for all donations made after August 17, 2006, limit the value of the asset for future tax deduction calculations to the *lesser* of (1) fair market value as of the date of the original fractional interest donations, *or* (2) the fair market value when subsequent fractional interests are donated.[7]

Unusual and Special Asset Types

A few types of tangible property have special rules and requirements:

- *Used cars, boats, and planes:* For donations made after December 31, 2004, new rules apply.[8] The charitable donee must now provide a "contemporaneous" written acknowledgement within 30 days of the gift that discloses to the donor whether (1) the vehicle will be used for the direct purposes of the charity, or (2) the charity plans to sell the vehicle. If the vehicle is donated for the charity's related use, the donor is entitled to a deduction equal to the fair market value as of the date of the gift. If the charity sells a related use vehicle within three years of the donation, it must report the sale to the IRS if the proceeds exceed $500 (the prior threshold was $5,000). However, if the vehicle is donated to a charity which plans on selling it, then the donor's charitable income tax deduction is now limited to the gross proceeds of the sale.

These new rules substantially curbed the abuses where a donor would call up an accommodating nonprofit to tow away their unwanted and practically worthless car, the donor would deduct the Kelly Blue Book value (which is based on a working car in good condition), but the charity would only receive a few dollars for the vehicle in a used car auction. When Congress and the IRS found that numerous taxpayers had taken deductions of $2,000 to $5,000 and more for cars that the charity liquidated at auction netting only an average of $75, it was not surprising that this abuse was shut down.

- *Clothing and household items:* For donations made after August 17, 2006, the Pension Protection Act of 2006 eliminated the deduction for gifts of used clothing and household unless the items were in "good used condition or better." This disallowance would not apply for items valued at greater than $500 if the donor obtains and files a qualified appraisal with his or her tax return. Certain items such as paintings, coins, jewelry and collectibles, for example, are exempt from this new law and are addressed elsewhere in this section.

- *Coins.* As mentioned earlier, if coins have a numismatic value that differs from their currency value, they are considered tangible personal property for charitable gift purposes. An exception is made for coins such as Krugerrands, Canadian Maple Leaf coins, and newly issued United States Mint gold coins, where the IRS has concluded that such gifts are equivalent to cash.[9] The IRS has further ruled that such coins can be used to fund a charitable remainder trust since they are readily convertible to other income producing assets.[10]

- *Artwork.* If an artist donates his own painting to a museum—even if he kept it for more than one year, and the donation meets the related use test—the deduction is, nevertheless, limited to the cost of his canvas, brushes, and paint. (The value of his time, experience, talent, or reputation is irrelevant in measuring the value of the deduction.) If a non-artist donor gives the same painting to a museum, it is instead deductible at full market value *if* it was held for more than one year by the donor and *if* it meets the related use test. Furthermore, art can be divided into two components: (1) it is a tangible property in that is can be seen or touched; and (2) it may hold a copyright, which is intangible and can be transferred separately from the work of art itself. Because partial gifts of tangible property do not qualify for a tax deduction, if a donor gives a painting to the museum but retains the copyright, the gift is incomplete and no income tax deduction is allowed. However, this particular partial interest gift would qualify for gift and estate tax deduction purposes.

Example: Mr. Hanford owns an extensive collection of original cartoon art valued at $18,000 that he would like to donate to the San Francisco Cartoon Art Museum. Since Mr. Hanford is neither the artist who created the cartoon art nor a dealer who trades in such pieces, the gift is considered one of an investment rather than inventory. Since he has owned the pieces for more than one year prior to donation, the artwork is considered a long-term capital gain asset. Furthermore, since the cartoon art is being donated to a museum that regularly exhibits such pieces and the museum has promised to display the art to the public, Mr. Hanford's gift will meet the related use test. And finally, Mr. Hanford is making an outright gift of the art this year and is not retaining any use or enjoyment of the pieces, thus avoiding the future and partial interest rules.

To transfer the artwork to the museum, Mr. Hanford delivers the pieces to the museum's planned giving officer. The officer provides him with a receipt that describes the gift and states that he will receive nothing of value in return for making the donation. Mr. Hanford will need to obtain a qualified appraisal of the collection since it is worth more than $5,000 (see Chapter 2). But he will not have not to attach a copy of that appraisal to the IRS Form 8283 because the value of his art gift is not greater than $20,000.

- *Livestock.* A donor can claim a tax deduction at full fair market value for gifts of livestock donated to a charity that then places the livestock into a related use. In particular, the donor must have owned cattle and horses for more than two years. All other livestock (specifically, hogs, mules, donkeys, fur-bearing animals, goats, sheep and other mammals) must have been held for more than one year.[11]

- *Crops.* Unharvested crops are considered part of the land. Assuming that the land has been held for more than one year, land that includes crops is long-term capital gain property. In this case, the crops are considered intangible property and the related use test does not apply. Gifts of harvested crops, on the other hand, constitute a tangible property donation; thus, the related use test would apply. However, most crops are produced in a trade or business and are, therefore, inventory. As inventory, crops are considered ordinary income property. This limits the donor's deduction to the lesser of fair market value or basis, and makes the deduction subject to the 50% of adjusted gross income limitation. Finally, a gift of yet-to-be-harvested crops is characterized as a donation of a futures contract, which again limits the income tax deduction to the donor's adjusted basis.

- *Timber.* Similar to crops, the characterization of a gift of timber depends on whether the timber is still standing and being donated with the land, or whether it has been cut and is being donated separate from the land. Standing timber is considered intangible property and the related use test is irrelevant. If the donor were in the business of producing timber, a gift of cut timber would be considered a donation of inventory. However, if the donor was not in the business but was clearing land that had been held for investment purposes, such a gift would be characterized as tangible personal property.

- *Taxidermy:* According to stories in the press and a Congressional hearing in 2004, some aggressive promoters were selling hunting and safari packages as tax deductible vacations. The promoters claimed their clients could deduct all travel costs incurred in hunting *if* the client would simply donate the mounted animals to a charity. The accommodating charity would warehouse the mounted animals for two years, to avoid the IRS reporting requirements, and then sell the animals for far less than the thousands of dollars of deduction claimed by the donors. For donations of taxidermy property made after July 25, 2006, a new law requires the charity to report any sale within three years, not two, and the deduction is limited to the lesser of the donor's basis or fair market value. The basis in this case is limited to the cost of preparing, stuffing, and mounting the animal, not the travel and hunting expenses.[12]

INTANGIBLE PROPERTY

Intangible property has a value that is separate from any physical, intrinsic worth of the assets. Rather than specifically defining intangible assets, the IRS simply provides an outline of examples. In general, intangible gifts are not subject to the related use and future interest rules. Instead, the IRS subjects such gifts to other tests:

1. *Partial interest rule.* When a donor gives less than a complete interest in an asset to charity, the IRS generally allows no income, gift, or estate tax deduction—unless the gift falls within one of the statutorily specified forms (charitable remainder trust, charitable lead trust, and pooled income fund)[13] or it is one of few other exceptions specifically carved out in the Internal Revenue Code. These exceptions include: (1) a remainder interest in a farm or personal residence; (2) an undivided portion of a donor's interest in a property; (3) qualified conservation contributions; and (4) works of art separated from their copyright (deductible for gift and estate taxes only).[14]

2. *Section 170 reduction rules.* While most assets donated to charity are subject to long-term capital gains tax, some are characterized as ordinary income property. For such assets, the principal reduction rule states that the charitable income tax deduction is to be reduced by the amount of gain that would have been recognized if the asset were sold and the proceeds were donated to charity. The second reduction rule states that if long-term capital gain property is donated to a private foundation (other than an operating, pooled fund, or pass-through foundation), the deduction is reduced by the amount of gain that would have been recognized if sold. An exception is carved out for donations of "qualified appreciated stock" defined as publicly traded stock that would have been subject to long-term capital gains treatment if sold.

While these rules apply in general to all gifts of intangible property, special planning is required for certain type of gifts:

- *Copyrights.* The American Jobs Creation Act of 2004 completely changed the tax consequences of such donations.[15] For gifts made after June 3, 2004, the law now allows for a multi-year deduction for gifts of intellectual property. The donor's deduction is now equal to basis in the year the donation is made, but the deduction is reduced by any long-term capital gain.[16] Over the next twelve years, the donor can claim additional deductions that are calculated based on a sliding scale percentage of the royalties received by the charity. The donor qualifies for these additional deductions only after the income amounts exceed the initial basis. The donor must advise the charity at the time of contribution that he or she intends to claims the additional deductions, and the charitable donee

has a new burden of tracking the royalty income for that purpose. In order to complete the gift of a copyright to a charity, the transfer must be made in writing, signed by the copyright owner or owner's agent, and the original or certified copy mailed to the Register of Copyrights along with the appropriate fee.

- *Patents*. Under prior law, the gift of a patent by its creator was considered the gift of a capital asset and was, therefore, deductible at its full fair market value, reduced by any depreciation that had been taken. Under the American Jobs Creation Act of 2004, the tax treatment of patents and copyrights were brought into parity.[17]

- *Royalties*. Similar to a copyright, royalty income is separate from the item that produces that income. If one is donated without the other, the partial interest rules apply. In addition, most royalties are considered ordinary income assets. (However, royalties on oil and gas interests are usually treated as gifts of real property unless the donor is in the trade or business of producing oil or gas.) And finally, royalties are generally exempt from being characterized as unrelated business income (although this issue should be researched in detail prior to making a gift).

- *Installment obligations*. The charitable gift of a note or mortgage is considered a taxable disposition that triggers gain recognition at the time of the transfer. However, the donor is entitled to an offsetting charitable income tax deduction equal to the note or mortgage's fair market value.

- *Life insurance*. While this topic is covered in significant detail in Chapter 13, charitable donations of life insurance are subject to a complex set of rules. Since life insurance is an ordinary income asset, the income tax deduction is limited to the lesser of fair market value or adjusted basis. All interests in the policy must be transferred to charity or the gift will fail the partial interest test. The donor cannot receive any value from the contract, directly or indirectly, or the policy will be considered a personal benefit contract and the charity will face a 100% excise tax. And finally, donations of contracts subject to loans may be considered a forgiveness of debt and cause the transfer to be treated as a bargain sale.

- *Annuities*. Depending on the issue date of the annuity and the type of contract donated, the tax consequences of this gift can vary widely. For all annuity contracts issued on or after April 23, 1987, upon transfer to a charity, the donor must recognize all gain in the contract as ordinary income and can claim a tax deduction equal to the fair market value. For matured contracts issued after this date, that the donor can deduct the maturity value of the contract. Note, however, that the donor must recognize the gain in the annuity as ordinary income. For nonmatured contracts issued prior to April 23, 1987, the gain is recognized as ordinary income, but the donor's deduction is limited to adjusted basis.[18]

- *Options*. Listed options and futures contracts are covered under the section below entitled "*Publicly traded securities*." Charitable planning with employee stock options, however, is a particularly complex field. In general, the gift of an unexercised nonqualified stock option to a charity or charitable trust will result in the donor recognizing ordinary income on the spread between the fair market value and exercise price. Furthermore, since the donor has no basis in the option, there is no offsetting charitable income tax deduction, meaning that the donor pays income taxes to make a charitable donation.[19] Testamentary gifts of nonstatutory options are treated more favorably—any compensation income will be recognized by the charity rather than by the donor's estate.[20]

Example: Ms. Duckworth is an executive at a small, successful software company and has received substantial bonuses in the form of nonstatutory employee stock options. She would like to make a sizable donation of some of these options to the Literacy Volunteers of America and needs to know the best way to structure such a gift.

With nonstatutory options, the employee must generally recognize compensation income when the option is exercised, sold, or transferred in an arm's length transaction. Any offsetting charitable deduction depends on how and when the gift is made:

1. If the stock option plan permits transfers, Ms. Duckworth can simply donate her unexer-

cised options to charity. The transfer to charity will not immediately trigger income taxes.[21] But as soon as the charity exercises the options, she—not the charity—will be taxed on the income realized (the difference between the fair market value on the date of exercise and the option price). Since this is an ordinary income gift, her charitable deduction is limited to the lesser of Ms. Duckworth's adjusted basis or the fair market value. Depending on the timing of the charity exercising the options, Ms. Duckworth could face income tax with no offsetting charitable deduction.

2. If she exercises the options prior to donation, she will have to raise the funds to pay the exercise price, and pay taxes on the difference between the fair market value and the exercise price. Assuming that she donates the options in the same year she exercises the shares, she will qualify for a deduction equal only to the lesser of her adjusted basis and fair market value. If she holds the stock acquired by exercising the options for more than one year prior to donation, she will receive a larger charitable deduction, but it will not occur in the same year as the taxes were realized.

3. If Ms. Duckworth arranges for a testamentary transfer of the options, she will avoid the recognition of income while she is alive. But she has a long life expectancy, and would like to see her favorite charity benefit in the near future.

One potentially favorable planning option for this case is to have the corporation itself donate stock options to charity. With this approach, Ms. Duckworth will not pay taxes on any portion of the options, and the corporation will receive a tax deduction at the time the charity exercises the options.

PUBLICLY TRADED SECURITIES

Aside from cash gifts made by personal check, the asset most commonly given to charity is publicly traded securities. From a donor's point of view, such gifts are popular because they: (1) are often highly appreciated and, therefore, generate a large deduction; (2) are relatively simple to transfer; (3) do not usually require expensive appraisals or incur any significant transfer costs; and (4) are welcomed by the charitable donee since they are often readily liquidated.

While highly appreciated stocks are the most common property donated of this type, many advisors also recommend charitable donations of mutual fund shares, closed-end investment company shares, restricted securities, real estate investment trust shares, options and futures contracts, and debt instruments such as bonds.

Gifts of certain publicly traded securities, however, hold potential tax traps, and care should be taken to plan around, or in some cases, completely avoid, such gifts.

There are nine major types of publicly traded securities that are most often used to fund charitable donations:

1. *Common and preferred stock.* If traded on a public exchange, such investments are considered capital assets.[22] As a result, as long as the donor has held the stock for more than one year, the deduction for such gifts is equal to the fair market as of the date the gift is complete. Otherwise, stock is considered ordinary income property and the deduction is limited to the lesser of the donor's adjusted basis or the fair market value. Fair market value for such gifts is the mean between the highest and lowest quoted selling price on the date the gift is completed.[23]

Example: Mrs. Price wants to make a sizable donation to the San Luis Obispo Symphony. After consulting with her advisor, she has decided to donate highly appreciated stock rather than cash. The end of the tax year is only a few days away, and in order to complete the gift in the current year, special care must be taken to ensure that the delivery requirements are met in time.

Mrs. Price has two major stock holdings that she wishes to donate. She keeps her shares of IBM stock in a safe deposit box in town, but holds her AT&T stock in a brokerage account, which keeps the securities in the street name of the brokerage firm.

To transfer the IBM stock, Mrs. Price will first have to retrieve the certificates from her safe deposit box. She will then have to endorse the certificates over to charity, taking care to sign her name exactly as the shares reflect her as the owner. For example, if the shares show that the owner's name is Sandra J. Price, she will have to sign her name with the middle initial, even if her signature does not usually include such information. As an alternative, she can sign an endorsement form and attach the form to the original certificate. Prior to completing the paperwork, Mrs. Price contacts the charity to review their gift acceptance policy and to determine the exact legal wording of the charity's name to which the shares must be transferred.

If Mrs. Price, her agent, or her broker delivers the IBM shares personally to the charity, her delivery date (the date on which she qualifies for a tax deduction) will be the day she hands the endorsed certificates or the certificates plus the assignment form to the charity. If she chooses to mail the endorsed certificate and/or forms, her gift is complete as of the date of the mailing, assuming that all the forms are accurately endorsed. She should send the documents certified mail with a "return receipt requested." If she delivers the shares to her broker, bank, or IBM to be reissued in the name of the charity, the gift is not considered complete until the date the change is reflected in IBM's corporate books. Since timing is important to Mrs. Price, it is recommended that she meet with an officer of the charity and personally deliver the stocks.

The AT&T stock is held in the street name of the brokerage firm and Mrs. Price must contact her broker to transfer the stock to SLO Symphony. The gift of stock is not considered complete, however, until the brokerage firm actually transfers title to the charity and the change is reflected on AT&T's corporate books. Since this may take a little time, it is important that Mrs. Price begin this process as soon as possible to meet her year-end deadline.

Since these are publicly traded securities, the value of Mrs. Price's deduction will be determined by taking the mean of the highest and lowest quoted selling prices on the day her gift is complete. She will need to file an IRS Form 8283, since the value of each stock gift is greater than $5,000. No qualified appraisal will be required since the gift is of publicly traded securities.

2. *Debt instruments*. These gifts include corporate bonds, mortgage backed securities, municipal bonds, and United States Treasury obligations. If such assets, when sold, would result in capital gain tax treatment, then they would make favorable charitable donations—that is, the tax deduction would be equal to the fair market value as of the date of the gift. Some debt instruments, such as zero coupon bonds, often result in ordinary income on sale or redemption. A gift of these assets to charity receives less favorable tax treatment. The donor does not recognize the income when the gift is made, but the ordinary income portion of the bond is not deductible.[24]

3. *United States Savings Bonds*. For lifetime gifts, Series E, EE, H, and HH savings bonds result in a tax deduction equal to the fair market value of the bond (Series H and HH bonds are no longer sold). The donor, however, will also be taxed on all unrealized income as of the date of the contribution. This diminishes the attractiveness of such gifts from a tax planning viewpoint.

4. *Restricted securities*. Some stocks are subject to sales restrictions by the SEC, by corporate charter, or by trust agreement. As a result, charitable gifts of private placement holdings, controlled stock, and unregistered securities can be both difficult and fraught with problems. For example, when a donor places restricted stock into a charitable remainder or lead trust, since the donor retains an interest in the stock, the restrictions remain in place. For outright charitable donations, however, as long as the charitable organization does not own at least 10% of the company's outstanding shares and the charity is not considered an affiliate, outright donations of restricted stock will generally be deductible as long as two years have elapsed since the donor acquired the stock from the issuer. While donations of listed securities do not generally require a qualified appraisal, if the restrictions placed on a stock alter its value in any way, an appraisal may be required.[25]

5. *Options and futures contracts*. Since all gains and losses from listed options (also called Section 1256 contracts) are taxed according to the "60-40 Rule" (i.e., gains and losses and allocated 60% to long-term capital gain or loss and 40% to short-term capital gain or loss), charitable gifts

of such assets will trigger the reduction rules for the short-term capital gain or loss portion of the gift. Section 1256 contracts include all listed equity and nonequity options, including stock index futures and foreign currency contracts.

6. *Mutual funds.* Like stocks, these investments make popular charitable gifts since they are considered capital assets; therefore, the deduction is based on the fair market value as of the date of the gift, provided that the donor had held the mutual fund shares for more than one year. The fair market value is defined as the public redemption price for the date of the gift. However, if there is no public redemption price because the gift was made on a Saturday, Sunday, or holiday, then the market value is the public redemption price for the first day preceding the date of the gift for which a quote is available.[26] Furthermore, in some cases, where the mutual fund company has withheld taxes from the account, the donor is entitled to a refund for the amount withheld.

7. *Closed-end investment companies.* These investments trade in a manner similar to publicly traded stock, are valued in the same manner as listed stock and are, therefore, subject to the same favorable tax deduction.

8. *Real estate investment trusts (REITs).* Many REITs produce income that may result in unrelated business taxable income (UBTI) to the charitable organization. Other investment trusts specifically prohibit transfers to charitable entities. Great care should be taken in arranging such gifts.

9. *Publicly traded master limited partnerships (MLPs).* Since many MLPs may trigger unrelated business income tax (UBIT), it is imperative that such gifts be carefully reviewed prior to donation.

PRIVATELY HELD BUSINESSES

In terms of tax planning, charitable donations of privately held businesses are among the most complex and potentially troublesome. There are five primary types of business structures, each of which has a distinct combination of ownership, tax, liquidity, and transferability issues. Planners must navigate around numerous potential traps to successfully arrange such donations.

Sole Proprietorships

In general, this is a very simple business structure, with one person who owns and controls the entire business. The company's value may include tangible, intangible, or capital assets. All risk, income, and losses inure to the sole proprietor.

- *Outright gifts.* Charitable donations of sole proprietorships generally make poor gifts from the charity's perspective. This is because any income generated by the business will be considered unrelated business income and, therefore, taxable to the charitable donee. If the gift is substantial in relation to the charity's other assets, such high levels of unrelated business income may even jeopardize the tax-exempt status of the charity. A good alternative may be for the sole proprietor to donate individual assets of the company to charity instead.

- *Planned gifts.* A charitable remainder trust cannot own a sole proprietorship. This is because any income will generally be considered unrelated business income and cause the trust to be subject to a 100% excise tax. For grantor charitable lead trusts, this is not a problem—the income is taxable to the donor anyway. For nongrantor trusts, however, the trust receives a deduction for the amounts distributed to charity, but such a deduction is unavailable for unrelated business income.

Partnerships

This business structure can be either general (all partners share management, control, income and expenses) or limited (varying levels of control are assigned to different classes of ownership).

- *Outright gifts.* Charitable donations of partnership interests must, first of all, be specifically allowed under the terms of the business agreement. Furthermore, the planner must be aware that the intermediate sanction rules may apply in the case of outright gifts to public charities, and penalties for self-dealing, excess business holding, and jeopardy investments may apply when partnership interests are donated to private foundations. And, similar to gifts of sole proprietorships, unrelated business income taxes are a substantial concern when donating

partnership interests. To plan around this potential problem, gifts of underlying partnership assets may be more appropriate than gifts of partnership interests.

- *Planned gifts.* Under the Tax Relief and Health Care Act of 2006, a charitable remainder trust is subject to a 100% excise tax in any year in which the trust generates unrelated business income—no matter how little unrelated business income it receives. Furthermore, if the partnership has any debt whatsoever, the transfer of partnership interests to a charitable remainder trust would be considered relief of indebtedness to the donor. On the other hand, gifts of partnership interests to grantor charitable lead trusts can be quite advantageous.

C Corporations

Gifts of nonpublicly traded (i.e., closely held) C corporation shares can generate sizable charitable deductions as long as certain restrictions are met and the donor plans around the potential problems carefully.

- *Outright gifts.* Once again, unrelated business income taxes are a concern for the charitable donee and the gift must not violate private foundation self-dealing rules and public charity intermediate sanction rules. Furthermore, if the donor directly or indirectly receives any significant benefit from the charitable donation, the IRS may consider such benefit as an indirect taxable dividend to the donor and disallow the donor's deduction.

- *Planned gifts.* If closely held stock is transferred to a charitable trust and held for investment, unrelated business income, self-dealing, excess business holdings, and jeopardy investment rules may apply. The liquidation of nonpublic traded C corporation stock through a charitable remainder trust, however, can be quite advantageous to the donor if careful attention is paid to the details. If a donor transfers stock to a charitable remainder trust and then the trust sells it to an unrelated third party, the donor recognizes no capital gains tax (unless the sale is considered to have been prearranged).

For donations to charitable lead trusts, if the closely held stock is to be held as an investment, income planning to pay the charitable income

beneficiary is extremely important. Furthermore, if a nongrantor lead trust is established, the donor may be required to recognize income without receiving a corresponding deduction if the lead interest is characterized as unrelated business income.

S Corporations

For donations made on or after January 1, 1998, a charitable organization is eligible to own S corporation stock. The stockholder agreement, of course, must permit such transfers, and a gift to several different charities may cause the S corporation to lose its status if the resulting ownership is divided among too many shareholders.

- *Outright gifts to qualified charities.* The same three main issues apply to S corporation donations as to C corporation gifts. The donor must consider self-dealing rules if the donation is made to a private foundation, or intermediate sanction rules if donated to a public charity. Finally, if the holding of the underlying business triggers unrelated business taxable income (UBTI), the charitable donee will face taxes and potentially lose its tax-exempt status. One planning option to consider is having the S corporation donate assets to the charity rather than having the shareholders donate S corporation stock. The tax benefit will be claimed by the shareholder and UBTI risk will no longer be a problem. Furthermore, the valuation discounts such as the lack of marketability discount or minority interest discount will not reduce the amount of the tax deduction available if underlying assets are donated rather than the shares themselves.

- *Recent improvements in the laws effecting donations of S corporation shares:* The Pension Protection Act of 2006 provided temporary additional incentives for gifts made in 2006 and 2007. For gifts in those years, shareholders could reduce the basis in their stock only by the pro rata share of the entire contribution. This effectively made that tax treatment the same as a partnership. In other tax years, however, basis had to be reduced by the shareholder's pro rata share of the entire contribution.

- *Planned gifts.* While outright gifts of S corporation stock to a qualified charity are deductible, transfers of S stock to charitable remainder trusts are generally not deductible. If such a transfer occurs, the company will lose its S corporation status. Even if this consequence is acceptable to the remaining shareholders, self-dealing and unrelated business income issues still apply. S corporation stock can be transferred to a charitable lead trust as long as it is a grantor trust for income tax purposes or, if established at death, as long as the trustee is able to make a small business trust election. If transferred to a grantor trust, unrelated business income is not an issue because all income is taxable to the donor. Furthermore, when transferred to a lead trust, the donation must adhere to all self-dealing, excess business holding and jeopardy investment rules.

Example: Mr. Holm is a shareholder in a successful technology firm that is structured as an S corporation. In recent years, he has made a substantial profit in the business. He is considering donating some of his shares to a charitable remainder trust for the future benefit of the American Cancer Society.

Upon reviewing the situation with an advisor, Mr. Holms reconsiders his decision. First of all, there is a buy-sell agreement in place that limits Mr. Holm's ability to transfer shares to anyone other than an existing shareholder. Secondly, a charitable remainder is not considered to be a Qualified Subchapter S Corporation Trust (QSST). So, a transfer of the S corporation stock to a charitable remainder trust will cause a loss of the S corporation's special status and immediately convert the entity to a C corporation. This could trigger substantial income taxes for all of the shareholders. After discussing these disadvantages with his advisor, Mr. Holm decides to donate other highly appreciated, publicly traded stock instead.

Tax Shelter Notice involving S Corporation Donations

The IRS issued Notice 2004-30 to address an abusive tax shelter that closely resembled the Charitable Family Limited Partnership (CharFLP).[27] The scheme that had been promoted attempted to shift income taxes from the S corporation shareholder to the tax exempt entity, and was labeled as a "listed transaction" by the IRS for the purpose of tax shelter disclosure requirements.

According to the terms of the plan, the S corporation would issue both voting and non-voting stock plus warrants that were exercisable to non-voting stock. The non-voting stock would be donated to charity, the donors would take a charitable deduction for the gift, and all income from the company would be allocated to the non-voting stock. Later, the charity's stock would be redeemed or repurchased by the voting stockholders, but by claiming that the strike price of the warrants was equal to the value of all the non voting stock, the promoters artificially reduced the fair market value of the non-voting stock to zero.

Limited Liability Companies (LLCs)

While LLC rules and requirements vary by state law, in general, these companies are taxed either as a partnership or as a corporation. If an LLC is treated as a partnership, the partnership information discussed above applies. If treated as a corporation, any donation will be treated the same as the C corporation gifts outlined earlier.

REAL PROPERTY

Gifts of real estate generally fall into five main categories: (1) residential property; (2) investment property; (3) raw land; (4) agricultural land; and (5) commercial property. When helping clients plan charitable donations involving these assets, it is imperative that the advisor takes into account the various real property ownership structures.

Fee Simple

This is the most common and simplest form of real property ownership. The term "fee simple" means the owner holds all rights to the property, including the right to transfer the property during lifetime or at death. Donating fee simple property is a rather simple transaction from a legal viewpoint although the actual steps involved in transferring title may be quite complex and will be outlined in more detail in the later example entitled "Gift of Real Estate."

Example: Ms. Baldessari owns an apartment complex and is considering contributing it to a charitable remainder trust that will benefit the University of California upon her death. She knows that several other complexes in the area have recently sold for a very high price. Ms. Baldessari knows that her building could sell easily if it were listed in the near future. Since she is planning on leaving a sizable bequest to the University anyway, contributing it to a charitable remainder trust makes sense for Ms. Baldessari.

Ms. Baldessari owns the property outright and, therefore, does not need to plan around any transfer restrictions that might be associated with partial interest or indirect ownership structures. She has owned the property for more than one year as an investment. However, she does have an outstanding mortgage on the property, and has depreciated the asset on her past tax returns.

If Ms. Baldessari transfers her property subject to a mortgage to a charitable remainder trust, several problems arise. She may run afoul of the grantor trust rules, and the transfer may be considered an act of self-dealing. She may also face problems with prohibited payments, bargain sale treatment, and unrelated debt-financed income. Ms. Baldessari decides to repay the mortgage with other assets prior to transferring the real estate to the charitable remainder trust.

As a final step, the advisor calculates Ms. Baldessari's tax deduction, taking into account the depreciation amount that she has deducted on past tax returns. While she will not have to realize this amount upon transferring the property to the charitable remainder trust, the fair market value of the asset will have to be reduced by the amount that would have been recaptured as ordinary income had she sold the property instead of donating it to the charitable remainder trust.

Once all of the background planning is complete, Ms. Baldessari must complete many detailed steps to fund her charitable trust. First of all, the donor must be able to prove that she owns the property by producing a Full Covenant and Warranty Deed. To complete the transfer to the charitable remainder trust, she must transfer the title of property to the trust, generally through an escrow company or attorney. As part of their services, the escrow company

or attorney will usually perform a title search, arrange for title insurance, contract for a survey of the property, hire a specialist to perform an environmental hazard report, contract for an inspection report, outline all the necessary disclosures, and make arrangements to bring the property up to local code.

And finally, in order to qualify for an income tax deduction, Ms. Baldessari must obtain a qualified written appraisal from an independent appraiser no earlier than 60 days prior to the transfer to the trust, and no later than the date on which she files her income tax return. Once the property is transferred to the charitable remainder trust, the trustee is free to sell the complex and reinvest in other investments, from which Ms. Baldessari will receive income for her lifetime.

Partial Interests

Ownership of less than a fee simple in real property can take several forms, each of which requires specialized planning when transferring the donor's ownership to a charity. The following are examples of partial ownership of real estate:

- *Community property.* Currently, several states are community property states and while property ownership laws vary somewhat between these states, in general, real property purchased by spouses during marriage is considered to be owned equally by both spouses.[28] Community property can be donated to charity either during life or at death, with each spouse controlling the disposition of his half of the property.

- *Tenancy by the entirety.* In some non-community property states, when spouses co-own assets, it is assumed that each spouse owns the entire property. When one dies, the entire asset passes directly to the survivor; as a result, charitable bequests of such property cannot be arranged by will or trust. For partial donations during life, the transfer to charity severs the tenancy by the entirety and the remaining owner becomes a tenant in common with the charity (see below).

- *Joint tenancy with right of survivorship.* With this form of ownership, two or more people own equal but undivided shares of a property. At the death of a joint tenant, his ownership interest passes automatically to the remaining owners. Many clients have established this form of ownership under the misconception that it will remove the asset from their taxable estate. Although it is true that property transferred under a joint tenancy with rights of survivorship avoids probate, such a transfer does not avoid estate taxes. Instead, by entering into a joint tenancy with their children, many parents may have inadvertently triggered a taxable gift. A joint tenant (in a tenancy with right of survivorship) cannot leave a charity his interest at death since by contract it must pass to the surviving joint owner. It is possible to make a gift of such an interest during the joint tenants' lifetimes. If a gift of one tenant's interest is made during lifetime, the joint tenancy is severed and the charity becomes a tenant in common with the remaining owner.

- *Tenancy in common.* Commonly referred to as a "TIC," tenancy in common occurs when two people own undivided fractional interests in a property. They may own equal or unequal percentages of the property, and both income and expenses are divided proportionately depending on their ownership percentages. Before a TIC interest is contributed, it is imperative to ascertain that the donor has the right to dispose of his share to an outside party. If a tenant donates his interest to a charity, then the charity becomes a tenant in common.

- *Condominiums.* This is a form of co-ownership where two or more owners retain exclusive rights to inhabit or rent a specific unit on the property while sharing ownership and expenses of the common grounds. Each owner has the right to sell, transfer, or donate his interests during life or at death. Condominium ownership between two or more persons can also take the form of community property, tenants in common, tenants by the entirety, or joint tenancy (as explained above).

- *Life estates.* In addition to concurrent forms of ownership, property can be divided between current and future rights. For example, one person may have to right to use, control, and enjoy property for life (i.e., a life estate) or for a specified period of years, at which time, the same or different rights

pass to a second party. Naturally, any transfers to charity cannot violate the terms of the life estate. If the life tenant has a right to *use* the property for life, but is prohibited from *selling* the property, he can donate the use of the property to the charity only for the length of his life.

- *Leaseholds.* In some situations, property may be subject to a long or short-term lease of the land and/or structures on that land. If the donor is both the owner and lessor of the land, the gift is fairly straightforward, so long as the donor gives away his entire interest. However, if the donor gives the lease by itself to the charity, the transfer would most likely be considered a gift of a partial interest and would, therefore, be nondeductible.

(For rules governing "partial interest gifts," which are more commonly gifts of less than the donor's entire interest, see Chapter 5.)

Indirect Ownership

In some situations, the donor may own an interest in an entity, which in turn owns real property. When the donor wishes to transfer the real property to charity, special planning considerations should be taken into account depending on the type of indirect ownership structure:

- *Inter vivos trusts.* Many donors hold title to their real property through a revocable living trust. In this situation, it is often advisable to transfer the title to the donor first, who then makes a direct donation to the charity. This extra step will ensure the donor an unambiguous charitable deduction.

- *Partnerships.* When real estate is held by a partnership, it is important to remember that the partnership owns the real property and the partners (either general or limited) own interests in the partnership. The partnership agreement may place limitations on the transfer of partnership interests during life or at death and must be carefully reviewed prior to making any charitable donations. Charitable planning can then take on either of two forms depending on the goals of the donor: (1) the partnership can donate the real property to charity; or (2) the partners can donate partnership interests. If the

latter gift is chosen, it is imperative to review the partnership terms and income characterization to ensure that the charity will not realize unrelated business income.

- *Corporations.* Similar to a partnership, a donor may have established a corporation to own and manage his real property. Again, the donor will have a choice of donating corporate shares to charity or having the corporation make a donation of the underlying property to charity.

- *Cooperative housing corporations.* Often referred to as a "co-op," this property ownership is usually a multi-tenant residential property that finances the purchase by selling equity shares in the corporation. Some tenants/shareholders have arranged their co-op shares to be considered real property; others have characterized them as intangible personal property.

WHERE CAN I FIND OUT MORE ABOUT IT?

1. Internal Revenue Service, Publication 526 *Charitable Contributions,* (2006).

2. Toce, Joseph, Abbin, Byrle, Vorsatz, Mark, and Page, William, *Tax Economics of Charitable Giving 2006-2007* (Warren Gorham & Lamont, 2006).

3. Teitell, Conrad. *Guide to Tax Benefits for Charitable Gifts,* updated regularly (PG Calc, distributed by *Trusts and Estates* Magazine).

4. Lyon, James. "Reflections on Deductibility of Contribution of Items of Tangible Personal Property to Museums", February 16, 2007 at: www.pgdc.com.

5. Ashton, Debra. *The Complete Guide to Planned Giving, Revised Third Edition* (Ashton Associates, 2004).

6. Kestenbaum, Avi. "Know the Differences: Why All Charitable Contributions Are Not Equal," *Trusts & Estates Magazine* (May 2006).

7. Raby, Burgess and Raby, William, "Property Contributions: It's All About the Details," Tax Analysts *Tax Practice* (March 20, 2006).

8. Fox, Richard. "Practical Charitable Planning for Employee Stock Options," *Estate Planning Journal* (May 2005).

9. Internal Revenue Service Publication 561 *Determining the Value of Donated Property* (April 2007).

QUESTIONS AND ANSWERS

Question – Why is it often better to donate highly appreciated assets rather than cash?

Answer – With a cash donation to charity, the asset has a 100% adjusted basis. By choosing to donate an appreciated long-term capital gain asset instead, a donor can reduce future taxes significantly. For example, let us suppose a donor has two assets: $10,000 of cash in a checking account (adjusted tax basis of $10,000), and Microsoft shares that have been held for several years worth $10,000 (adjusted tax basis of $3,000.) If the donor writes a check for $10,000 to the American Lung Foundation, he is effectively giving away cash and keeping the Microsoft investment intact. If the donor instead gives $10,000 of Microsoft stock, the charity will still receive a gift worth $10,000, but the donor will now have $10,000 of cash that he can *reinvest* (after a 30-day waiting period) in Microsoft stock. With both options, the donor is left with $10,000 of Microsoft stock. But by donating the highly appreciated asset to charity instead of cash, the donor has increased the tax adjusted basis in his holdings by $7,000. Should the donor later choose to sell the stock, his future gain—and therefore his taxes—would be substantially reduced. Of course, the income percentage limitations (see Chapter 3) should also be considered.

Question – What is a Charitable Family Limited Partnership?

Answer – Sometimes referred to as a "Char-FLP," in this planning technique a donor establishes a family limited partnership with his heirs, then donates a substantial percentage of the partnership interests (anywhere between 30% and 98% is typical) to a public charity.[29] While the donor's charitable income tax deduction is reduced by a variety of valuation discounts (e.g., marketability and minority discounts), the immediate tax deduction can be significant. In addition to the upfront charitable deduction, the partnership is able to sell the highly appreciated asset and reinvest the proceeds with much of the resulting capital gains tax being absorbed by the charity's tax-exempt status. (Since the charity owns—say 98% of the limited partnership interests—98% of the capital gain is attributable to the charity, which of course is tax-exempt.)

While these plans vary substantially depending on the planner or promoter involved, there are some significant problems that are likely to be addressed either through future legislation or through Treasury regulations. In particular, the donor's children or other future heirs usually purchase the charity's interests a few years into the plan for an amount that is substantially less than either the fair market value of the interests or the deduction taken by the donor when the interests were donated. Secondly, this plan is more of a business arrangement than a charitable contribution, and as such, the donor's deduction may be at risk; furthermore, the charity is likely to be subjected to unrelated business income taxes.[30] For additional details, see Appendix A.

Question – Is there any advantage to donating tax shelter interests to charity?

Answer – Contributions of "burned-out" tax shelters offer little or no benefit to either a donor or a charity. The value of the gift must be reduced by the full amount of the debt associated with it. Furthermore, charities must be wary of such gifts since debt-financed shelters could potentially result in unrelated business income.

Question – Are there any circumstances in which a donor can donate S corporation stock to a charitable remainder trust without forfeiting the S corporation status of the company?

Answer – Under the Small Business Job Protection Act of 1996, Congress changed the S corporation laws to permit charities to own S corporation stock when the donation was made directly to the charity. Unfortunately, it did not extend the safe harbor rules to include charitable remainder trusts. Some planning options do exist for donors who desire to make such gift. These possibilities range from being relatively simple to quite complex. One of the more creative solutions is for the S corporation itself to establish the charitable remainder trust. The charitable contribution deduction will then pass through to the S corporation's shareholders.[31]

Question – Is there any way to fund a charitable remainder trust with real estate subject to a mortgage?

Answer – By using a specially designed Real Estate Investment Trust (REIT), donors may be able to convert appreciated, debt-encumbered real estate to a debt free security that can then be donated to a charitable remainder trust without triggering gain recognition or potential self-dealing problems.[32]

CHAPTER ENDNOTES

1. IRC Sec. 170(e)(1)(B).
2. IRC Sec. 170(e)(7).
3. Treas. Reg. §1.170A-4(b)(1).
4. IRC Sec. 170(e)(3)(A)(i).
5. IRC Sec. 170(e)(4).
6. IRC Sec. 170(a)(3).
7. IRC Sec. 170(o)(1)(A), Sec. 170(o)(3), and Sec. 2522(e)(3).
8. IRC Sec. 170(f)(12), Sec. 170(e)(3).
9. Rev. Rul. 69-63, 1969-1 CB 63.
10. Let. Rul. 9225036.
11. IRC Sec. 1231.
12. IRC Sec.170(f)(15).
13. IRC Secs. 170(f)(2)(A), 2055(e)(2)(A) and 2522(c)(2)(A).
14. IRC Secs. 170(f)(3)(B), 2055(e)(2) and 2522(c)(2).
15. IRC Sec. 170(m).
16. IRC Sec. 170(e)(1)(B)(iii).
17. IRC Sec. 170(e)(1)(B)(iii).
18. Treas. Reg. §1.170A-4(a).
19. Rev. Rul. 98-21, 1998-1 CB 975, Rev. Proc. 98-34, 1998-1 CB 983.
20. Treas. Reg. §1.421-6(d)(5).
21. Treas. Reg. §1.83-7; Let. Rul. 9713012.
22. IRC Sec. 1221.
23. Treas. Reg. §1.170A-13(c).
24. IRC Secs. 1271, 1272, 1273, 1274, 1275.
25. Rev. Rul. 77-287, 1977-2 CB 319.
26. Treas. Regs. §§20.2031-8(b)(1), 25.2512-6(b)(1).
27. 2004-1 CB 828.
28. Ten states are community property states: Alaska, Arizona, California, Idaho, Louisiana, Nevada, New Mexico, Texas, Washington, and Wisconsin.
29. See Stephan R. Leimberg, "Charitable Family Limited Partnerships: Prudent Planning or Evil Twin," at: http://www.pgdc.com/usa/item/?itemID=24424&g11n.enc=ISO-8859-1.
30. See, e.g., Field Service Advice 200122011, in which the IRS determined that a formula clause, which allocated additional value to a charity if the value of the transferred property was redetermined for transfer tax purposes, was ineffective.
31. Let. Rul. 9340043.
32. Let. Rul. 199952071.

PARTIAL INTEREST RULES

CHAPTER 5

WHAT IS IT?

A partial interest gift is a gift in which the donor retains a "substantial" right or interest in the donated property. The general rule for gifts of partial interests is that a donor who contributes less than his entire interest in property receives no income tax charitable deduction.[1] However, there are several very narrow exceptions to this rule for gifts of:

1. an "undivided portion" of the donor's entire interest in the property (explained below);[2]

2. an irrevocable remainder interest in a personal residence or farm (explained below);[3]

3. an interest transferred in the form of a charitable lead trust, charitable annuity trust, charitable remainder unitrust, or pooled income fund (see Chapters 14, 15, 16, and 20, respectively); or

4. a qualified conservation or facade easement (see Chapter 18).[4]

Aside from these exceptions, the law generally does not permit any income,[5] gift,[6] or estate tax[7] deduction for partial interest gifts.

WHEN IS THE USE OF SUCH A DEVICE INDICATED?

1. When the donor wishes to generate or retain income from the donated property.

2. When the donor wants to share partial ownership in a related use gift, such as sharing artwork with a museum that will display it for a portion of the year.[8]

3. When the donor wants to continue using a personal residence or farm during life, but receive a current deduction for an irrevocable contribution of a remainder interest in the property at his death.

4. When the donor wants to make a testamentary gift while providing an interest or control during life for a spouse, child, or other non-charitable beneficiary.

ADVANTAGES

- A partial interest gift that qualifies for a deduction permits a donor to retain some use of property while providing a current income and gift tax charitable deduction for the absolute gift of another portion of the same property.

- The partial interest rules permit a donor to divide substantial interests in the same property between two or more charitable organizations.[9] This allows a donor to benefit more than one charity at a time.

- A qualifying remainder interest in a personal residence does not have to be the taxpayer's principal residence. So long as the taxpayer uses the property as a personal residence, a current income tax deduction for the irrevocable gift of a remainder interest is available.

DISADVANTAGES

- A partial interest gift must either meet the stringent requirements of a gift in trust, or fall within a narrow group of exceptions; otherwise, the donor will generally not receive a tax deduction (income, gift, or estate tax). Such a donor would not only be denied the deduction but may also be making a taxable gift.

- Depending on the type of partial interest gift, the amount of the charitable deduction may be insufficient to justify the time and expense involved in establishing a partial interest gift. In the case of a right to use property, no deduction is available at all.

WHAT ARE THE REQUIREMENTS?

Undivided Portion of Donor's Entire Interest

A donor may receive an income tax charitable deduction for a gift of an "undivided portion" of the donor's entire interest in the property.[10] An undivided portion is a "fraction or percentage of each and every substantial interest or right owned by the donor in such property and must extend over the entire term of the donor's interest in such property and in other property into which such property is converted."[11]

In order to make a partial interest gift, immediately before the contribution, all of the interests in the contributed property must be owned by the donor or by the donor and the donee organization.[12] The donee organization must also receive all interests in the contributed property at the earlier of the donor's death or the expiration of 10 years from the date of the initial contribution.[13] If the donor fails to contribute all of the remaining interests in the property to the donee organization within 10 years of the initial donation, a recapture provision will be triggered. This recapture provision recovers all income and gift tax deductions plus interest from the date of the initial contribution.[14] These recapture provisions are also triggered if the donee organization fails to take substantial physical possession of the property such that it is used for the organization's charitable purpose or function within 10 years of the initial contribution.[15]

The exception for an undivided portion of a taxpayer's entire interest does not apply if the taxpayer transfers some specific rights in the property and retains other substantial rights.[16] For example, assume Ted contributes an interest in certain historic motion pictures to a charitable organization and retains exclusive rights to make reproductions of the films and to commercially sell the reproductions. Because Ted transfers some rights but retains other substantial rights, Ted's gift does not qualify as a contribution of an undivided interest in the films.[17]

A contribution of property will not be treated as a partial interest gift if the donor retains only an insubstantial interest in the property.

Example: Assume that Douglas W. Mellon transfers certain of his fine art photographs to a museum for display, subject to the terms of a loan and gift agreement. Under the agreement, Douglas and his successors in interest retain certain rights regarding the way the photographs are displayed and the publicity surrounding his gift. Furthermore, the terms of the loan and gift agreement specify any retained rights are to be consistently exercised with "good museum standard" practices.

In the event of a dispute, the terms of the loan and gift agreement further specify that the parties must submit such disagreements to arbitration. The retained rights would be considered largely fiduciary powers exercisable in furtherance of the donee's exempt purpose. In such circumstances, the gifts of the fine art photographs would qualify for a charitable deduction as an undivided interest since the retained rights represent an insubstantial interest in the property.[18]

Remainder Interest in Personal Residence

A second exception to the partial interest rules exists for a gift of a remainder interest in a personal residence.[19] The gift of a remainder interest in a personal residence usually follows the expiration of a life estate. (See Chapter 4 for an explanation of the various forms of partial ownership of real estate.) This exception allows a donor to retain the use of a personal residence, while obtaining a current income deduction for a gift of a future interest in the property. The gift must be in the form of an irrevocable contribution, and not made by a transfer in trust.[20] The gift must also consist of a remainder interest in the personal residence itself rather than in any sale proceeds of the property.[21]

For purposes of this exception, the term "residence" means any property the taxpayer uses as a personal residence. This remains the case even though the taxpayer does not use the property as his *principal* residence. Therefore, a vacation home that a taxpayer uses as a personal residence qualifies for a deduction. Furthermore, the term personal residence can also include stock owned by the taxpayer as a tenant-stockholder in a cooperative housing corporation, so long as the taxpayer uses the dwelling unit that the shares represent as a personal residence.[22]

The term personal residence can even include a yacht.[23] But a personal residence does not include household furnishings or other tangible personal property.[24] Therefore, the exception for a gift of a remainder interest in a personal residence does not apply to a remainder interest in home furnishings or other tangible property.

Remainder Interest in Farm

A third exception to the partial interest rule exists for a gift of a remainder interest in a farm.[25] For purposes of this exception, the term "farm" refers to land used by the taxpayer or a tenant for the production of crops, fruits, or other agricultural products, or the sustenance of livestock. The term also includes land improvements located on the farm. The regulations define livestock to include several different types of animals.[26] (See Chapter 4 for details regarding outright gifts of farm property, livestock or crops.)

The rules described above for gifts of a remainder interest in a personal residence apply equally to contributions of a remainder interest in a farm; the gift must be an irrevocable transfer, and not made in trust. In addition, the gift must be an interest in the farm itself, not in sales proceeds.

Finally, a gift of a remainder interest in a farm need not be the entire farm acreage. This means a gift of a remainder interest in a farm may be in any portion of the total acreage used as a farm.[27]

Example: Assume that a farmer owns a 10-acre farm that includes eight acres of pasture and two acres of non-pasture land. The two acres of non-pasture land contain a lake, the farmer's house, tenant houses, farm buildings, other farm structures, and fences. The farmer leases the property, except for the residence, tenant homes, and certain other structures, on an annual basis to an unrelated third party. The tenant uses the farm property to raise cattle and to produce other agricultural products. The farmer subsequently makes a gift of an irrevocable remainder interest, not in trust, of four acres of pasture land to a charitable organization. The farmer continues to lease the four acres of pasture land after the contribution. The lessee does not reside on any portion of the farm. Under these circumstances, the IRS has concluded that the farmer's gift of a remainder interest in the four acres of farm property qualified as a charitable contribution.[28]

Other Partial Interest Gifts

A gift of a future interest in tangible personal property does not generate an income tax deduction until all intervening interests in and all rights to the actual possession or enjoyment of the property expire or are held by a person other than the donor or a person standing in close relationship to the donor.[29]

A gift is not considered a partial interest gift if the result of a combination of gifts is that all the donor's interests in the property go to charitable organizations.[30] For example, suppose a taxpayer contributes a life estate with an income interest in real estate to his church, with a remainder interest in the property going to a local university. An income tax deduction would be allowed for each partial interest gift since the two gifts in combination result in all of the donor's interest going to charitable organizations. The taxpayer would be permitted to claim a current income (and gift) tax deduction for the entire value of the property. Note, the result would not be the same if the taxpayer owns a fee simple interest in the property and contributes a gift of just a life interest or remainder interest in the property to charity.[31] In that case, neither an income nor a gift tax deduction would be allowed.

Similarly, if the taxpayer gives away the only interest he owns (e.g., a life estate), a deduction will be permitted even though it is not the entire ownership interest of the property. But, this rule will not apply if partial interests were created to avoid the general rule disallowing the deduction for partial interest gifts.[32]

Right to Use Property

A contribution of the right to _use_ property is treated as a gift of a partial interest.[33] Consequently, a donor will not be allowed an income tax deduction for the rent-free use of either tangible personal or real property, no matter how valuable that right may be. For instance, even if the owners of the Empire State Building allowed a charitable organization to use the building rent free for 20 years, the owners would receive no income tax deduction. Furthermore, the rent-free use of real or personal property does not augment the gift portion of any transaction subject to the bargain sale rules (see Chapter 10).[34]

Similarly, a donor who contributes the rent-free use of a vacation home to a charity is not entitled to any income tax deduction for the gift, nor for any time or effort donated to assist in such a transaction.[35] Only the donor's out-of-pocket costs in making the property available to the charity would be allowed as a deduction.

HOW IS IT DONE?

Valuation of a Deduction for an Undivided Interest in Property

The valuation of a partial interest gift of an undivided portion of the donor's entire interest in property is not complex. Generally, the amount of the deduction will be the fair market value of the fractional interest. When the subsequent contribution of the remaining interests in the property is made, the available deduction is determined using the lesser of the fair market value at the time of the initial contribution or the fair market value of the property at the time of the subsequent contribution.[36]

Example: Glenn Evans owns an oil painting valued by experts at $200,000. Glenn acquired the painting 15 years ago at a cost of $100,000. While Glenn wishes to share the painting with the general public, he is reluctant to completely part with it. Glenn resolves this dilemma by making a donation of an undivided one-fourth interest in the painting to a publicly supported art institute. Glenn reserves possession of the painting for nine months of the year for the earlier of Glenn's death or ten years from the date of the initial contribution. The art institute obtains absolute and unquestioned possession of the painting for the other three months of the year when Glenn leaves the country to live at a tropical vacation spot.

Assuming the art institute puts the painting to a related use, Glenn should be able to claim a deduction for as much as $50,000 (one-fourth of $200,000).[37] This deduction is subject to the 30% limitation on gifts of appreciated long-term capital gain property (see Chapter 3). If Glenn were to grant the art institute a one-half interest (i.e., to use the painting for six months out of each year), he should receive a deduction of as much as $100,000. At the end of the ten

years, when the painting is worth $300,000, Glenn makes his subsequent gift of the remaining interests in the oil painting, he obtains an additional income tax deduction of $150,000 (which is three-fourths of the initial $200,000 fair market value of the oil painting), regardless of the additional $100,000 of appreciation in the oil painting.[38]

Valuation of a Deduction for a Contribution of a Remainder Interest in a Personal Residence

The valuation of a partial interest gift of a remainder interest in a personal residence often involves a slightly more complex set of computations. The process of determining the amount of the deduction involves the use of both an appropriate remainder interest factor and a depreciation adjustment factor derived from appropriate factors in *IRS Publication 1459*. An example of a gift of a remainder interest in a personal residence will help reveal the tax implications of such a transaction.

On October 1, 2007, a donor, age 65, contributes a remainder interest in a personal residence to Drake University, while reserving the use of the property for his life. The total value of the residence is $500,000. The value of the underlying land on which the residence sits is $50,000. An estimate of the remaining useful life of the house is 40 years with no estimate of any residual value at the end of such time. In calculating the deduction amount, the total value of the residence must be split into two parts. These two parts include the land and home portion of the property.

Nondepreciable portion (land)	$ 50,000
Depreciable portion (home)	450,000
Total Value	$500,000

The remainder interest factor for a life tenant, age 65, using the Section 7520 interest rate of 5.2% for October, 2007, equals .46062. This factor is used to value the land portion of the gift. To determine the value of the remainder interest in the depreciable portion, a series of computational steps (described in IRS Publication 1459) must occur. The result of these computations produces an appropriate depreciation adjustment remainder factor of .32360. Therefore, the total value of the remainder interest in the personal residence is as follows:

Nondepreciable property $50,000 x .46062	$ 23,031
Depreciable property $450,000 x .32360	$145,620
Amount of contribution	$168,651

Based on these computations, the taxpayer in this example should obtain an income tax deduction of $168,651 for the gift of a remainder interest in his personal residence.

WHAT ARE THE TAX IMPLICATIONS?

The partial interest rules in the Internal Revenue Code disallow most deductions for gifts of property of less than a taxpayer's entire interest. As described above, the law prohibits the deduction of a partial interest gift unless one of a narrow group of exceptions applies.

Assuming one of the exceptions applies, the taxpayer's deduction is generally calculated as some portion of the fair market value of the property contributed. However, some partial interest gifts may require special calculations or considerations to determine the amount of an allowable deduction. The calculation of the deduction amount for a gift of an undivided interest in property, or a gift of a remainder interest in a personal residence, are both explained above.

The tax implications of charitable remainder annuity trusts, charitable remainder unitrusts, and pooled income funds, are explained at Chapters 15, 16, and 20, respectively.

WHAT ARE THE ALTERNATIVES?

1. An outright gift of cash or property (see Chapters 2 and 4) is simpler to make and administer.

2. A bargain sale (see Chapter 10) can allow a donor to sell property to a charity at a reduced price, resulting in a transaction that is partly a taxable sale and partly a deductible gift.

WHERE CAN I FIND OUT MORE ABOUT IT?

1. Leimberg, Stephan R., et al., *The Tools & Techniques of Estate Planning*, 14th edition (Cincinnati, OH: The National Underwriter Company, 2006).

2. Toce, Joseph, Abbin, Byrle, Vorsatz, Mark, and Page, William, *Tax Economics of Charitable Giving 2007-2008* (Warren Gorham & Lamont, 2007).

3. Osteen, Carolyn M., et al., *The Harvard Manual on Tax Aspects of Charitable Giving*, 8th edition (Boston, MA: 1999).

QUESTIONS AND ANSWERS

Question – Do fractional interests (expressed in terms of a percentage of time, months, or a specific portion of a year) in art objects qualify for a deduction under the partial interest rules?

Answer – A fractional interest in an art object may qualify for a deduction as an undivided portion of the donor's entire interest in the property.[39] This method of giving can permit a deduction for a gift of a partial interest in related-use property. The circumstances may be such that a donor does not give up as much as it may appear. For example, a donor may contribute a one-fourth interest in a piece of artwork to a museum. The artwork may be kept at the principal residence of the donor for nine months. When a donor lives at a vacation home or travels for the other three months of the year, the artwork could be on display at the museum.

Question – Suppose a donor purchases shares of stock and later wishes to donate a remainder interest in the stock to a charitable organization. The donor's tax advisor tells him that if he donates only the remainder interest, a partial gift will occur and no deduction will be permitted. Subsequently, the donor transfers a life estate to his daughter, so that all he owns is the remainder interest. Can he take a deduction for a gift of his remainder interest?

Answer – No deduction will be permitted if the IRS determines that the ownership of the property was split solely for the purpose of circumventing the partial interest rules.[40] Among the circumstances the IRS would evaluate in making such a determination is whether a significant passage of time occurred between the donor's division of property interests and the contribution of the remainder interest to charity. A significant passage of time creates the impression that the donor's purpose in making the property division was not to circumvent the partial interest rules. In one private letter ruling, the Service determined that a seven-year passage of time was sufficient to permit a charitable deduction.[41]

Question – Does an individual receive a charitable deduction for a gift loan to a charitable organization?

Answer – Treasury regulations disallow an income tax charitable deduction for the value of a no-interest or a below-market loan to charity under the "partial interest" rules.[42] This rule would seem to apply to both principal and interest amounts. However, this rule may not apply to the deemed interest amount. The legislative history for the below market loan rules suggests that Congress intended such deemed payments to receive treatment as cash contributions and not as a contribution of a partial interest in property. Neither the IRS nor the courts have ruled on this issue. See Chapter 11 for details on the application of the below-market loan rules to no-interest or "partial interest" gift loans to a charitable organization.

Question – If a charitable organization delays taking possession of a piece of artwork (say for a year or two), will the donor still receive an immediate income tax deduction?

Answer – The IRS will trigger the deduction recapture rules if the donee organization has not had substantial possession of the property and used the property in a manner that is related to the charitable donee's tax-exempt purpose or function by the earlier of the donor's death or the expiration of ten years from the date of the initial contribution.[43]

Question – If a donor imposes a condition on a remainder interest in a personal residence, will the condition result in a disallowance of a deduction?

Answer – The answer depends on whether or not the possibility that the condition could defeat the charity's interest is so remote as to be negligible. Suppose the donor of a remainder interest in a personal residence imposes the following condition. "In the event I cannot continue to occupy my personal residence for good reason and decide to sell my life estate interest, the charitable organization must also sell its remainder interest. The sale proceeds are to be divided in accordance with the values of the life estate and remainder interest at the time of the sale." According to the IRS, this language creates the possibility the charitable organization will not receive the residence itself. Furthermore, the IRS considered such a gift not to be an irrevocable contribution of a remainder interest in the personal residence itself. Therefore, the IRS concluded that no current income tax deduction would be available.[44]

Question – A homeowner sometimes rents a part of his home to others. Assuming the home is a personal residence of the taxpayer, can the taxpayer still make a deductible gift of a remainder interest in the property?

Answer – The fact that a residence is partially rented does not affect the deduction under the partial interest rules for a remainder interest in a personal residence.[45]

Question – Will the making of a qualified conservation contribution result in unfavorable tax consequences to the donor?

Answer – Sometimes a qualified conservation contribution causes unfavorable tax consequences to the donor. For example, the IRS has made a determination that a contribution of a facade easement for an historic structure to a local historical society caused a partial recapture of the investment tax credit previously taken on the property.[46] In a second example, the IRS also has ruled that a contribution of a conservation easement on a farm with respect to which an estate had made a special use valuation election caused the election to be invalidated.[47] For additional details on conservation and facade easements, see Chapter 18.

CHAPTER ENDNOTES

1. IRC Sec. 170(f)(3).
2. IRC Sec. 170(f)(3)(B)(ii).
3. IRC Sec. 170(f)(3)(B)(i); Treas. Regs. §§1.170A-7(b)(3), 1.170A-7(b)(4).
4. IRC Sec. 170(f)(3)(B)(iii).
5. IRC Sec. 170(f)(3)(A); Treas. Reg. §1.170A-7(a)(1).
6. IRC Sec. 2522(c)(2); Treas. Reg. §25.2522(c)-3(c)(1)(i).
7. IRC Sec. 2055(e)(2); Treas. Reg. §20.2055-2(e)(1)(i).
8. See the Pension Protection Act of 2006, Sec. 1218; IRC Sec. 170(o), Sec. 2055(g) and Sec. 2522(e).
9. See IRC Sec. 170(f)(3)(A); Treas. Reg. §1.170A-7(a)(2)(ii).
10. IRC Sec. 170(f)(3)(B)(ii).
11. Treas. Reg. §1.170A-7(b)(1).
12. IRC Sec. 170(0(1)(A).
13. IRC Sec. 170(o)(3)(A).
14. IRC Sec. 170(o)(3)(B).
15. IRC Sec. 170(o)(3)(B).
16. See Treas. Reg. §1.170A-7(b)(1)(ii); Rev. Rul. 76-331, 1976-2 CB 52. In Revenue Ruling 76-331, the donor did not obtain a charitable deduction for a contribution of real property to a charitable organization when the donor retained mineral rights or rights to payments under a 60-year timber lease.
17. See Treas. Reg. §1.170A-7(b)(1); Rev. Rul. 88-37, 1988-1 CB 97.

18. See Let. Ruls. 9303007, 200223013 and 200223014.

19. IRC Sec. 170(3)(B)(i); Treas. Reg. §1.170A-7(b)(3).

20. Treas. Reg. §20.2055-2(e)(2)(ii) and (iii); Treas. Reg. §1.170A-7(b)(3) and (4); Treas. Reg. §25.2522(c)-(3)(c)(2)(ii) and (iii).

21. See Rev. Rul. 77-169, 1977-1 CB 286; Rev. Rul. 77-305, 1977-2 CB 72.

22. Treas. Reg. §1.170A-7(b)(3).

23. See Let. Rul. 8015017; Treas. Reg. §1.121-1(b)(1).

24. Rev. Rul. 76-165, 1976-1 CB 279.

25. IRC Sec. 170(f)(3)(B)(i); Treas. Reg. §1.170A-7(b)(3).

26. Treas. Reg. §1.170A-7(b)(4).

27. Rev. Rul. 78-303, 1978-2 CB 122.

28. See Rev. Rul. 78-303, 1978-2 CB 122.

29. IRC Sec. 170(a)(3); Treas. Reg. §1.170A-7(a)(2)(ii).

30. Treas. Reg. §1.170A-7(a)(2)(ii).

31. See Rev. Rul. 75-420, 1975-2 CB 79. The IRS commented that a gift of a tenancy in common for a taxpayer's life (where the taxpayer owns the entire fee simple interest) does not result in a deduction, because it is not a gift of an undivided portion of the taxpayer's entire interest in property. For an explanation of the various types of partial property interests, see Chapter 4.

32. Treas. Reg. §1.170A-7(a)(2)(i).

33. IRC Sec. 170(f)(3)(A); Treas. Reg. §1.170A-7(a)(1).

34. Treas. Reg. §1.170A-4(c)(2)(ii). Chapter 10 of this book discusses this issue in more detail.

35. See Rev. Rul. 89-51, 1989-1 CB 89.

36. See IRC Sec. 170(o)(2).

37. See Treas. Reg. §1.170A-7(c).

38. See IRC Sec. 170(o)(2).

39. Let. Rul. 9303007.

40. Treas. Reg. §1.170A-7(a)(2)(i).

41. Let. Rul. 9124031.

42. IRC Sec. 170(f)(3)(A); Treas. Reg. §1.170-7(A)(d), Ex. 3. No deduction is permitted when a donor gives less than his or her entire interest in property.

43. See IRC Sec. 170(o)(3(A)(ii).

44. See Rev. Rul. 77-305, 1977-2 CB 72.

45. Let. Rul. 8711038.

46. Rev. Rul. 89-90, 1989-2 CB 3.

47. Let. Rul. 8940011.

E-PHILANTHROPY AND TECHNOLOGY ISSUES

CHAPTER 6

WHAT IS E-PHILANTHROPY?

First there was E-tailing, and then E-commerce. Everything else seems to have an "e" existence, so why not philanthropy? For purposes of this chapter, E-philanthropy is defined as *any philanthropic activity that is enhanced by combination with electronic technology.* The technology component includes computer software and Internet facilities such as e-mail and the World Wide Web. For the planner involved in facilitating or learning about philanthropy, the effects of these tools are broadest with respect to (1) electronic communications, (2) Internet-based information sites and publications, and (3) Internet-facilitated giving.

E-mail seems to be a given when it comes to maintaining routine contact with donors, provided the donor is connected. Much of the information that has been traditionally available via brochures and other printed media can be easily "delivered" to interested donors via the charity's Web site. Credit card donations are becoming commonplace for most charities with an "E-presence."

The educational value of Internet resources has grown exponentially. There are numerous Web sites of charitable entities, affiliated organizations, software providers, consultants and professional fund raising associations, which deliver information electronically through the World Wide Web or e-mail distribution. All of the software providers listed in Appendix H maintain Web sites that generally offer free information, articles, the opportunity to purchase software, and more.

Many charities now communicate with potential donors via e-mail, with most messages containing links to the sending charity's Web site or to an affiliated Web site. These communications can include the same information that has been sent via U.S. mail in the past but is now more efficiently delivered electronically. The quick e-mail

reminder may be the motivating factor in facilitating the gift, especially if it is timed near year-end, when donors may wish to complete a contribution.

With the proliferation of E-philanthropy comes a wider potential for errors or even abuse, with respect to lists of donor information, financial and personal privacy, and the identity of charitable organizations making contact (or being contacted) online. Efforts by the Association of Fundraising Professionals are underway to create an "E-donor Bill of Rights," to address concerns and challenges arising from Internet charitable giving.[1] Their website offers excellent resources on electronic fundraising issues.

Among the most interesting sites is the Planned Giving Design Center licensed to a local or national charity that, in turn, makes the resources maintained at the site available to other professionals. Crescendo Interactive's Gift Law site offers similar services through its web-based assistance to charitable organizations. Many allied professionals also provide charitable planning information and links to many of the Web sites that can be helpful in planning for charitable gifts, both immediate and deferred.

"The Charitable Giving Newsletter" is an example of another e-philanthropy service provided via an electronically published newsletter. It is supported by the Council for Advancement and Support of Education (CASE). Many charities operating locally and nationally publish periodic newsletters and solicitations that are delivered to donors' via email.

At least one private ruling has been issued with respect to the specific impact of the Internet on philanthropic activities. The organization requesting the ruling provided a widely-used Web site with a database of information on over 700,000 charities that had "become a major source about nonprofit organizations on the internet." Further-

more, the charity wanted to establish a donor advised fund. Contributors would be able to make contributions to the fund electronically and make recommendations for disbursement of the funds using the database. The IRS determined that donations to the fund would qualify as "public support," so that donors could claim charitable deductions for contributions to a "public charity" not subject to private foundation limitations.[2]

"Cyberspace" and "E-commerce" not only embrace charity, but can also enclose it, creating a system in which donors are solicited, contributions are made, and recommendations for charitable beneficiaries are reviewed and evaluated, all without ever leaving the Internet.

There are also some interesting sites that promote philanthropic activities and facilitate donations. Two offer the incentive of designating a percentage of every purchase through affiliates of the site to favorite causes. The other was started by a student at Case Western Reserve University to promote charitable donations to selected organizations. Some charities partner with search engine providers—donors are encouraged to use the search engine by a promise to credit the charity with a small cash payment for each search.

The Fidelity Gift Fund and other charitable gift funds promote giving via their Web sites. Other sites, such as iGive.com and Charitymall.com provide shopping links to providers of goods that are purchased with regularity over the Internet. Each has an extensive listing of vendors with the commission percentages allocable to charities listed. For each purchase, the "commission" is allocated to the purchaser's designated beneficiary or beneficiaries.

Accountability of charitable organizations has been enhanced by internet access to information through Guidestar (www.guidestar.org), Charity Navigator (www.charitynavigator.org), MinistryWatch (www.ministrywatch.com) and similar web-based providers of information about and evaluations of the effectiveness of charitable organizations. Prospective donors can research potential recipient charities in advance of a contribution. Importantly, this broader scrutiny by the independent evaluators has influenced charities to change policies and practices in areas that ensure greater benefits from the charitable activities.

As the donor community becomes increasingly dependent on the Internet for information, shopping and related services, it is likely that the charitable community will find ways to facilitate donation and planning processes, making it ever more easy for the donor to accomplish his or her own charitable objectives.

ADVANTAGES

- Information on a charitable organization or its activities can be made available to donors 24 hours a day, seven days a week.

- "Blast" e-mailing to a charity's e-mail distribution list is cost effective and typically more immediate than a "snail mail" letter or brochure on a recent development. More detailed information can typically be linked from the e-mail message directly to the charity's Web site.

DISADVANTAGES

- Initial costs for establishing a Web presence can be relatively high.

- The content of Web sites needs to be kept current, which entails time commitment and additional costs.

WHERE CAN I FIND OUT MORE ABOUT IT?

1. www.pgcalc.com provides links to important and helpful online resources.

2. www.giftlaw.com provides weekly e-mail service and other useful information from Crescendo Software.

3. www.leimbergservices.com provides information and commentary on the latest charitable cases, rulings, and legislation.

CHAPTER ENDNOTES

1. Principles of the "E-donor Bill of Rights" promulgated by the Association of Fundraising Professionals can be found at www.afpnet.org.
2. See Let. Rul. 200037053.

ETHICAL ISSUES IN CHARITABLE PLANNING

CHAPTER 7

WHAT IS IT?

Charity must first and foremost be about giving–not taking. An ethical inquiry is indicated whenever a product seller or promoter markets, a "donor" seeks, or a charity encourages a "quid pro quo" designed to motivate and reward the donor by something other than detached and disinterested generosity. Scrutiny is also indicated if the "donor" is to receive from the charity something economically substantial and significant.

There are many laws and regulations designed to limit egregious charitable planning practices. For issues that are less obvious or that are simply not addressed under current law, ethics plays a very important role. In the context of charitable planning, ethics can be defined as a set of principles or values that, if followed, result in a charitable plan that meets a donor's objectives, yields a suitable charitable gift, and complies with the spirit of tax and other laws that provide privileged status to charities. Ethics is not simply the act of following current laws; it is the professional restraint that begins where existing laws end.

WHEN IS THE USE OF SUCH A DEVICE INDICATED?

1. *Legislative consequences*: There are many advisors, donors, and charities that choose to take an aggressive rather than a balanced approach to charitable planning. Without self-moderation, the entire charitable community will likely face substantial, expensive, cumbersome, and limiting legislation on par with the financial, insurance, accounting, and legal industries.

   One of the aspects that makes charitable planning as popular as it is with advisors is the favored tax status of charities. If abused, this preferential treatment will be taken away, resulting in not only less powerful tools for the advisors who work in this field, but also substantially reduced donations for many worthy charities. Charities themselves will be more expensive to administer and the cost of raising development dollars will increase.

   Unlike the insurance, accounting, financial, and legal professions, the charitable industry does not and legally cannot hire powerful lobbying firms on a full-time basis to fight proposed legislation.

   As a result of a recent surge in aggressive plans and tax shelters involving tax exempt organizations, several pieces of restrictive legislation have been passed into law in recent years, and more legislation is likely to be introduced in the near future. While charity laws have been fairly stable since the last major reforms in 1969, several key bills and IRS pronouncements have attacked everything from charitable split dollar life insurance plans to tax shelters involving S Corporations, donor advised funds, supporting organizations, and car donation programs. The Senate Finance Committee has also assembled a long laundry list of abuses and problems, and there are strong indications that the era of restrictive legislation is far from over.[1]

2. *Risk to the parties involved*: Ethics has a practical side. When donors become involved in unethical planning, they risk the loss of a deduction, plus interest and penalties. Advisors who put donors and charity at risk by recommending unethical techniques and products face potential licensing problems, regulatory fines, and civil suits. And of course, they face the largest loss of all, the loss of the respect of fellow professionals and the trust of the public. The charitable split dollar debacle and the loss of prestige suffered by its promoters is a good example. Charities that engage in unethical fund-

raising practices face potential penalties, fines, loss of exempt status, and civil suits, in addition to the loss of respect and support of potential donors.

3. *Using charity for non-charitable purposes*: There are many individuals, companies, advisors, and even charities that use the tax-exempt status of charities for non-charitable purposes. This abuse likely will result in lost deductions, severe sanctions, fines, and, in the case of charities, penalty taxes and the possible loss of exempt status. The IRS has also indicated that additional resources will be allocated and a new emphasis placed on the criminal investigation and prosecution of the more aggressive participants and promoters.

4. *Loss of goodwill*: Perhaps one of the less obvious but most damaging consequences of unethical business practices is the loss of the public's respect for the charitable community. Charitable gifts require the utmost trust. When advisors and charitable representatives abuse that trust, future donors are less likely to willingly give their cash and other assets.

HOW IS IT DONE?

Depending on the role of person involved, the ethical issues and pressures vary. As the following descriptions and examples will show, all sides of the charitable planning triangle–donor, charity, and advisor–must be sensitive to, and continually practice, a higher than ordinary standard of ethics.

Donors

Most of the ethical issues faced by donors involve receiving a benefit that is more than relatively insubstantial or insignificant or is made for reasons other than a detached, disinterested generosity.

Inflated valuation/inflated charitable deduction

Perhaps the most common abuse by a donor involves some form of "cheating" on the amount deducted on an income tax return. This usually involves inflating the value of an asset donated, such as a work of art, an automobile, or other tangible property.

―――――――

Example: A donor owns an old grandfather's clock which has not run in two decades and which has suffered from rust and damage while sitting in the donor's garage. The donor calls up a charity to pick the clock up and take it away, and then asks a good friend who runs an antique store to write up an appraisal which values the clock at ten times the real value. The donor uses this appraised value even though the true fair market value for the clock was negligible.

―――――――

Example: A donor gives a coin collection to charity valued at roughly $500. The charity issues the donor a rather vague receipt that simply describes the gift as "coin collection." The donor inflates the value of the gift to $4,800 for the purposes of calculating his charitable deduction, realizing that, as long as the value is less than $5,000, he does not need a qualified appraisal.

―――――――

Private benefit

In order to qualify for a charitable tax deduction, the donor's charitable gift must be complete and the donor must receive no benefit in return (or something relatively insignificant and insubstantial, such as a mug or letter-opener). The gift must essentially be, from an economic standpoint, one of detached, disinterested generosity.

The only exceptions to these general rules are certain statutorily sanctioned and highly restricted and circumscribed split interest gifts such as charitable remainder trusts, in which the deduction is reduced by the present value of what the donor receives or retains. Strict rules and penalties are in place to prevent abuse of these split interest instruments.

If the donor or his family benefits economically in any other relatively significant way from a charitable gift, problems will ensue. All too often, promoters or donors approach charities with new schemes attempting to yield a full charitable tax deduction but which actually results in a significant benefit back to the donor.

―――――――

Example: A donor makes a gift to the University Foundation for the purpose of setting up an academic scholarship fund. According to the charity's gift acceptance policy, the donor cannot choose the actual scholarship recipients, but can establish the general guidelines of who will receive the grants. The donor submits a list that states that a full scholarship shall be paid to any student of a particular religious faith, who has chosen a specific major, and who graduated from a certain high school in the past year. The charity representative realizes that it is quite likely that the donor's grandchildren will be the only ones to benefit from this gift.

Example: A donor establishes a charitable remainder trust and names his local university as the revocable charitable remainder beneficiary. He then approaches the charity and requests that they pay for the qualified appraisal and the legal fees for drafting the trust. He implies that he will change the remainder beneficiary of the trust to a different charity if it does not assist with the implementation costs.

Example: A donor sets up a donor advised fund at a national charity that will be used to fund his family's reunion, pay the expenses associated with his spouse's hobby, and fund a "mission" for his 20-year-old twin daughters to spend the next year in Paris.

Lack of charitable intent

Many donors implement charitable techniques even though they have little or no interest in benefiting charity. Some "play the numbers" using CRTs, others establish donor advised funds where the fund principal passes indirectly to non-charitable beneficiaries. Since "charitable intent" is a sine qua non for receiving a charitable tax deduction, such planning is inherently flawed.

Example: A politician who is facing corruption charges wishes to make a sizable donation to a number of national charities and asks the charities' representatives to make sure that the gifts are well-publicized prior to his scheduled court date.

Example: A donor wishes to fund a charitable trust to sell his highly appreciated real estate. He sets up the trust such that the charitable beneficiary will receive the minimum amount required

by law. He then names his donor advised fund as the charitable beneficiary and arranges for his children to be compensated for their "volunteer" activities from the donor advised fund. In the end, the way the arrangement operates, little, if any, money will ever pass to charity despite the donor's significant tax savings. (This is also a "private benefit" example.)

Aggressive risk

A few donors will implement a plan that is so aggressive that, if caught by the IRS, they will likely end up in Tax Court or in the most extreme cases, explaining their case to a jury in a criminal trial. These plans usually involve untested techniques (for example, the Accelerated CRT, the Death Bed CLAT, charitable split dollar, or abusive donor advised funds) and often result in: (1) a loss of tax deduction, (2) restrictive legislation, (3) the loss of exempt status for the charity involved, or (4) negative publicity for the charitable community.

Example: A donor has talked with his advisors about setting up a highly aggressive planning technique. In order for his plan to work, he needs to find a charity willing to participate in the plan. After two larger charities turn him down, he narrows his search to smaller non-profits that are desperate for donations and will not question his scheme, or that do not have the budget to hire legal counsel to review the scheme.

Tax fraud

A small number of donors try to persuade the charity involved to commit or help commit fraud as a condition for receiving a gift. This might include changing the date the gift is considered complete or falsifying receipts.

Example: A donor wants to make a sizable donation to a charity but would like to apply the charitable deduction to her prior year's tax returns. Even though the gift was legally considered complete in January, the donor asks the charity to date the receipt for December 30th of the previous year.

Charity Board Members & Executives

Misuse of funds

If a donor is promised that his gift will be used for a restricted purpose, some charities simply ignore these promises once the gift is complete.

———————

Example: The charity receives a sizable gift from a donor who asks that the donation be used for a specific purpose that falls within the charity's mission. The charity agrees to the terms of the gift. But as soon as the donation is made, the money is placed in the organization's general funds and the donor's wishes are ignored.

———————

Example: A community foundation works with a donor to establish a long-term endowment program. The donor puts $20,000 into the program, which will grow undisturbed for 50 years. At the end of the time period, the fund will have grown to $2,300,000 and the charity will use the lump sum to endow a program with a local university. A few years later, the donor calls the foundation to inquire about the status of the fund, but the community foundation has no record of this plan.

———————

Private inurement

When insiders or persons wielding significant economic power over a charity's decision-making process (e.g., board members or executives) attempt to benefit from its assets or take advantage of its special status to receive unrealistic compensation or benefits, the charity faces substantial excise taxes and the potential loss of exempt status. These abuses might include using the charity's assets for personal use, or channeling business to a for-profit company owned by a charitable insider.

———————

Example: Upon the death of an elderly donor, the charity receives a new Mercedes sedan. One of the charity's board members decides that the car should be kept by the charity for his personal use.

———————

Example: A charity's board member, who is also a lawyer, tells the development officer that he expects her to direct some of the charity's wealthier contributors to his law firm to draft

their charitable remainder trust documents and other legal documents.

———————

Public disclosure

As more and more donors and advisors hold charities accountable for their expenses and investment choices, many charities have felt compelled to manipulate their public disclosure information, such as IRS Form 990, to better meet increased donor expectations.

———————

Example: The charity's accounting staff has become increasingly aware that donors have begun to scrutinize the charity's Form 990 to determine whether the charity is run efficiently. In an attempt to improve the appearance of the charity's expenses, the accounting department decides to hide the cost of the lease for a private jet under the section entitled "Utilities."

———————

Example: A university has received several comments from donors who feel that the charity's overhead costs are too high as a percentage of donations raised. The university sets up a separate foundation to raise funds but almost all of the foundation's overhead costs are paid by the parent charity. When donors now review the foundation's Form 990, they see a leanly run non-profit.

———————

Privacy

It is increasingly common for a charity to sell or trade donor information, including addresses, telephone numbers, and, in some cases, even donation amounts. This is a violation of a donor's privacy.

———————

Example: In an effort to raise annual funds, the charity's administration department sells the charity's donor lists, including names, addresses, and phone numbers, to a list company. They neither inform the donors of the sale of the information, nor do they give the donors any choice as to whether the information will be sold.

———————

Example: At the request of a local insurance agent, a charity's board member gives the agent a copy of the donor list, mailing addresses, phone numbers, and the amount of cumulative donations. The insurance agent solicits sales from this list and implies to the charity that he will make an effort to have additional gifts made to the charity.

Example: An insurance marketing firm approaches a national charity about setting up life insurance policies covering the lives of the nonprofit's wealthiest donors. It will not cost the donors or the charity anything, and at the end of two years, the charity will receive a moderate lump sum payment by selling each insurance policy into the secondary life insurance market. All the donors need to do is complete the insurance application and take a physical examination. At no time during the transaction does anyone disclose to the donors the future resale of the policies, and the fact that the donors' financial and medical information will be disclosed to anyone who is interested in purchasing the two year old policies.

Conflict of interest

It is often difficult to balance a donor's objectives with the charity's need to raise funds. In some cases, charity administrators and executives place unrealistic quotas and pressure on the planned giving and development staff to bring gifts into the charity.

Example: A planned giving officer works with a donor to put together a charitable plan. In the course of the planning, the planned giving officer decides that the donor does not have sufficient assets to commit to the program and recommends that the donor consider a bequest instead. Upon hearing this recommendation, the planned giving officer's supervisor assigns a different charitable representative to work with the donor and the lifetime gift is completed even though it is inconsistent with the donor's needs and circumstances.

Misuse of charity

Some unscrupulous individuals try to twist the positive associations of philanthropy into their own personal gain. This might include a person seeking a favorable judgment or pardon making a substantial donation to enlist the charity's recommendation on the donor's behalf.

Planned Giving & Development Officers

Competence

Planned giving is a relatively new field. Many charities are courting these types of gifts for the first time. As a result, many planned giving and development professionals may not be experienced in working with complex cases. They are often asked questions regarding a wide variety of issues only somewhat related to the planned gift. These questions include topics such as estate taxes, insurance needs, or the drafting of legal documents. Rather than lose control over the implementation of the gift, some planned giving professionals attempt to address all these needs regardless of their competency or proficiency in the topic.

Example: A new planned giving officer has recommended that a donor establish a charitable gift annuity with the organization. When the donor's advisors, all of whom recommended a charitable lead trust, question this recommendation, the planned giving officer admits to being new and only familiar with charitable gift annuities.

Example: A planned giving officer has been informed by an elderly donor that he wishes to leave his entire estate to the charity at his death. He has no surviving family and is living off of his Social Security income, as well as the income from his investments. He would like to make a lifetime donation, but he is worried that he does not have sufficient savings to give any away because he is worried about outliving his money. He has been thinking about purchasing long-term care insurance but the premiums seem a little high. The planned giving officer talks the elderly man out of buying the insurance, saying that a long-term care policy is a bad deal, and the man would be better off leaving his money with the charity instead of the insurance company.

Compensation

This is perhaps the most complex ethical issue faced by planned giving professionals. Some smaller charities cannot afford to pay competitive salaries and want to structure compensation as a percentage

of funds raised. Others seek to increase fund raising by offering percentage-based incentives to their development staff. Still others are tempted by offers to share investment or insurance commissions.

Example: Over the years, an elderly couple has become quite attached to the planned giving officer at the local charity. In an effort to thank him for his time and patience over the years, the couple decides to give him $1,000.

Example: A charity feels that it cannot afford to pay a fair market wage to its fund raising staff. Instead, it offers to pay them a percentage of the money raised. Also, the charity offers the planned giving officer a percentage of the present value of planned gifts.

Disclosure

While planned giving and development staff ultimately report to their charitable employer, they work closely with donors to educate and close outright and planned gifts. As part of this education, they must fully disclose the details of the recommended plan, including both the benefits and disadvantages.

Example: A planned giving officer works closely with a donor to establish a charitable remainder trust that names the charity as the sole, irrevocable remainder beneficiary. When the donor agrees to implement the plan, the charity recommends a local lawyer who is closely affiliated with the charity to draft the trust documents. In the course of the planning, the donor is never advised that the charitable beneficiary could be revocable if the donor left such an option open in the trust document.

Example: A planned giving officer prepares a charitable remainder unitrust illustration showing an annual increase in the donor's income if the trust earns 10% per year. At no time does the charity's representative illustrate or discuss the effect on the donor's income if the trust earns less than the projected amount or suffers losses during a downturn in the market.

Example: An environmental charity spends a substantial percentage of its donations on mass mail and telemarketing companies. In an attempt to make its fund raising expenses appear more reasonable on Form 990, the charity classifies the mass mail and telemarketing costs as public education and environmental activism.

Private benefit

Most private benefit situations are instigated by a donor or an advisor. However, in some cases, these benefits are promised by the planned giving and development staff as an inducement to complete a gift.

Example: A planned giving officer convinces a donor to establish a substantial charitable trust. When the donor balks at the high legal costs of implementing the trust and obtaining the qualified appraisal, the charity offers to pay these fees for the donor. (This example also illustrates "conflict of interest.")

Conflict of interest

In planned giving, a charity's gift is balanced against the interests retained by the donor. This places the planned giving officer directly into a conflict of interest. Many do not discuss these conflicts with their donors. Others go so far to hide the conflicts that they will draft the donor's legal documents themselves rather than involve an attorney.

Example: An elderly woman has no heirs and wants the local humane society to receive her estate. The planned giving officer tells her to simply name him personally as the executor of her will.

Example: A planned giving officer goes to work for a large state university art museum. Four years later, she changes jobs to work for a national art museum and takes the university's list of donors with her. Once settled in her new job, she calls on the donors she worked with in the past fours years and sets up appointments to discuss how they can benefit her new employer instead. (This is also a "privacy" example.)

Undue influence

Because seniors are the most likely candidates for planned gifts, special issues involving the elderly must be considered. A representative of a favorite charity is often, or often becomes, a senior's most trusted advisor. This trust must not be violated.

Example: A planned giving officer meets with an elderly donor and, despite several indications that the donor's competency is in question, arranges for the donor to implement a sizable gift.

Advisors

Competence

Many advisors consider themselves to be experts in several fields and incorporate charitable planning into their portfolio of services with little of no understanding of the special laws, rules, and restrictions faced by charities. Charitable trusts are often viewed as products to be sold. New, untested techniques are often stressed even though the advisor does not understand the consequences of these plans to the charity involved.

Example: At a monthly continuing education lunch, a planner hears that several of the other attendees have incorporated charitable planning into their practices. The planner decides that he would like to do the same and purchases a charitable remainder trust (CRT) marketing kit. The idea is so successful that the next five clients with whom the planner meets all agree to establish CRTs in combination with wealth replacement insurance. The planner wonders if there are other charitable planning techniques that can be presented to his clients.

Example: An insurance agent has recommended that a client sell his closely held company stock through a CRT. The client will use the charitable tax deduction to purchase a sizable insurance policy through a wealth replacement trust. When the plan is ready to be implemented, the client changes his mind when he learns that he will need to pay approximately $15,000 to a professional appraiser to value the business as of the date it is transferred to the trust. Realizing his insurance sale is at risk, the agent signs the appraisal form as a qualified appraiser.

Compensation

No other ethical issue seems to be raised as often as appropriate compensation and fees when it comes to advisors working with donors. Some charitable gifts appropriately result in insurance sales, others in increased investment product or service fees. But others result in lost "money-under-management" compensation to advisors who, as a result, dissuade clients from implementing lifetime charitable gifts.

Example: A financial planner has convinced his client to set up a CRT. The client's objective is to diversify her investment portfolio, currently highly appreciated stock, without current income tax cost. She is unsure which charities she wishes to benefit and asks her planner for advice. The planner visits several charitable planned giving officers and tells each one that he will require a finder's fee before introducing the donor to the charity. Without disclosing the financial fee he is to receive, he then advises his client to name as the CRT's remainder beneficiary the charity willing to pay the highest fee.

Example: An insurance agent is working with a client who has expressed some charitable intent. The agent recommends that the client purchase a large insurance policy to benefit the charity. Once the policy is in place, the agent approaches the charity and says that his client would like to make a gift of the new policy and will make future annual gifts to pay the premiums. When the charity's planned giving officer says that he does not believe that the annual gifts are invested prudently if life insurance is used, the agent says he will take the gift elsewhere.

Example: A donor is considering making a sizable outright gift to charity. His investment advisor, however, talks him out of the gift, convincing his client that the money is better left in the donor's possession (and under the advisor's fee-based management) until the client's death.

Example: An insurance agent approaches a charity with a plan: for every insurance policy purchased by a donor, the agent will pay a percentage of her commission to the charity.

Example: A doctor wishes to make a sizable gift to the medical school that he attended. The advisor recommends that the doctor instead fund a donor advised fund with a national charity that pays a substantial finder's fee and which will allow the advisor to continue to manage the money. As a result, the doctor's charity will not receive any gifts for years or even decades, and the amount eventually paid to the medical school will be reduced as a result of multiple fees and expenses paid to the advisor over the years.

Example: At his investment advisor's recommendation, a donor who wanted to make an outright gift instead sets up a CRT. The advisor knew, or should have known, that the CRT was not appropriate for the client's goals and objectives. The advisor would lose management fees if the immediate outright gift were made, but as advisor to the CRT, his quarterly management fees will continue.

Example: An insurance agent "sells" charitable gift annuities for a commission paid by a national charity.

Example: A local charity has approached a successful attorney about sitting on its advisory board. The attorney agrees, on the condition that he receives the first choice of donor referrals looking for legal advice.

Disclosure

Just as charities must disclose both benefits and disadvantages of a particular plan, an advisor must also ensure that clients understand all the factors behind the implementation decision.

Example: A financial planner recommends that her client sell a highly appreciated asset worth $75,000 through a CRT. The advisor discusses the income, capital gain, and estate tax benefits,

and shows how the charitable tax deduction can help offset the cost of the insurance purchased in a wealth replacement trust. But no mention is ever made of the fact that this type of trust is irrevocable, or that the annual administration expenses of a trust this size will quickly erode any tax savings.

Example: In an attempt to compete for a new client, a financial planner illustrates a cutting edge technique involving a family limited partnership and an obliging charity. He tells the client that, by using this strategy, in a few years' time the client can save millions in taxes without having to pay the charity more than a small amount. The planner never discloses that the idea has neither been tested in court nor is specifically addressed in the Internal Revenue Code.

Conflict of interest

Some advisors have a duty to the client. Others have a duty to the insurance companies, mutual funds, or other companies they represent. Such conflicts are seldom disclosed to the client.

Undue influence

With elderly or incapacitated clients, a particular advisor is often singled out as the one person that client trusts. Such unquestioning dependence must not be abused.

WHERE CAN I FIND OUT MORE ABOUT IT?

1. Freeman, Douglas. "Balancing the Scales: The Gift Planner's Dilemma," *Planned Giving Design Center* (www.pgdc.net), August 11, 1999.

2. Minton, Frank. "Compensation of Gift Planning and Financial Services Professionals," *Planned Giving Design Center* (www.pgdc.net), March 14, 2001.

3. Blum, Debra. "Fees Paid to Donors' Financial Advisers Stir Debate in the Philanthropic World," *Chronicle of Philanthropy*, November 16, 2000.

4. "Position Paper: Percentage-Based Compensation," *Association of Fundraising Professionals* (www.nsfre.org), 1992.

5. Ryan, Ellen. "The Good, the Bad, and the Money," *CASE Currents* (www.case.org), October, 1989.

6. Maryland Bar Association Committee on Ethics, Docket 2003-09: Attorney Cannot Participate on Church's Legacy Committee and Provide Pro Bono Estate Planning Services to Donors.

7. IRS Congressional Testimony: "Charitable Giving Problems and Best Practices," www.irs.gov/pub/irs-news/ir-04-081.pdf.

8. Elliot, Deni. *The Ethics of Asking: Dilemmas in Higher Education Fundraising*, The Johns Hopkins University Press, 1995.

QUESTIONS AND ANSWERS

Question – If a donor wants to implement an aggressive technique, why would he care what the consequences would be to the charity if it entered into the plan willingly?

Answer – If a donor enters into an aggressive plan which places the charity at risk, it is a fairly good indication that the donor's gift lacks charitable intent, one of the requirements for obtaining a charitable tax deduction. If the donor is entering into the agreement because his advisor recommended it, then the advisor is committing an unethical act that makes everyone look bad: (1) charities have a favored place in our society and the tax code, and aggressive planning risks legislation, loss of exempt status, and bad publicity for the entire charitable industry; (2) the donor risks losing a deduction; and (3) the advisor feeds into the negative stereotype that charities and donors have about for-profit advisors. With the most aggressive techniques, advisors often must "shop" charities to find one that is less discriminating about the types of plans it will support. Advisors who use these tactics just to make a quick dollar may cause irreparable damage to an entire community. In extreme cases, they may also be considered promoters of abusive tax shelters, subject to civil penalties, and may be required to maintain client lists.

Question – Is there a problem with a charity accepting money from questionable sources?

Answer – Many charities grapple with this issue. If a Wall Street trader known for his unethical business practices wants to donate $500,000 to a business school, should the school accept the money? If a notorious mobster wants to give $250,000 to his church, should the church cash the check? Every charity that faces these gifts needs to question what the benefits and disadvantages are of receiving them. On the positive side, the money can be used to fund important projects. On the negative, the charity may receive bad publicity, and in extreme cases might be unintentionally involved in money laundering. Most charities take a practical approach. A charity cannot judge a donor's motivation. A criminal who has served time in jail may truly become philanthropic. The mobster who gives money to his church may honestly wish to assist the church with its mission. The charity, however, should make an effort to determine whether the donor expects anything in return that would compromise the charity. The charity should also make every effort to ensure that it is not aiding the donor in any illegal activity such as money laundering.

Question – Can a charity accept money from a source whose business purpose runs counter to the charity's mission?

Answer – Many companies facing substantial lawsuits will donate money to a variety of charities in an attempt to limit their damages in the lawsuit. For example, should a hospital foundation that researches lung cancer accept donations from the tobacco industry? What if the gift is sufficiently large that the new building will be named after the donor? Every charity that faces this dilemma struggles with the pros and cons unique to each gift.

Question – Does private benefit include naming a building after a donor?

Answer – No, as long as there are no other hidden benefits, the IRS does not consider naming opportunities problematic.

Question – A donor is setting up a substantial charitable remainder trust that names Charity A as the irrevocable remainder beneficiary. What is wrong with Charity A paying for the donor's legal fees to draft this trust?

Answer – There are two key issues raised by this situation. First of all, the donor is taking a deduction for a gift and then receiving something of value in return. This would fall into the private benefit trap. Secondly, if Charity A pays the attorney's fees, then

the attorney would appear to be working for the charity and not for the donor. As Charity A and the donor are in direct conflict in this trust (the more income the donor takes, the less the charity receives), the attorney must be absolutely clear from the beginning whose interests (charity or donor) are represented.

Question – What steps has the non-profit industry taken to self-regulate?

Answer – All of the major gift planning associations have adopted an ethics code addressing issues like compensation, conflict of interest, use of funds, and privacy. A copy of each of the major association's codes has been included in Appendix E. Furthermore, many of the association have worked together to establish a Donor's Bill of Rights, which is also located in Appendix E. Furthermore, as a result of recent Senate hearings and numerous negative articles in the press, the various leading non-profit associations have worked diligently with Senate staff, Treasury attorneys, and IRS executives to formulate a plan to help clean up some of the worst abuses. This will likely be a process that continues for several years and further legislation is likely.

Question – How should a planned giving officer handle personal gifts from donors?

Answer – Over the years, charitable representatives often become close with their donors. This sometimes results in donors making personal gifts to planned giving officers as a way of thanking them for their years of help. Charity representatives should decline these gifts and suggest that all gifts be made to the charity instead. One polite way of handling this situation is to ask that the donor make the gift to the charity in the representative's name. That way the donor feels like they are giving something of emotional value to the representative.

Question – Why should an advisor involve a planned giving officer in the charitable planning process?

Answer – Charities operate under a very complex set of rules and regulations, and unless an advisor specializes exclusively in this field, the tax and regulatory traps can be substantial. Bringing a planned giving officer into the process ensures that someone on the planning team is making sure that the charitable laws are followed. Furthermore, charitable organizations can operate under a variety of structures.

Simply naming the charity as the beneficiary of a trust may not ensure that the money goes to the correct part of the charity or that the money will be used for a specific purpose desired by the donor. Even if the donor requires anonymity, the advisor can work with the charity on behalf of John and Jane Doe.

Question – Why is it important for a charity representative to make sure that a donor's advisors are involved in the process?

Answer – Planned giving and development officers usually know a great deal about charitable planning but simply cannot be specialists in all fields. Insurance questions should be forwarded to the donor's insurance advisor, legal questions to the lawyer, and tax questions to the tax professional. This team approach ensures that the donor receives competent advice from specialized advisors. Furthermore, donors are not always completely forthright with charities about the extent of their wealth for fear that the charity may ask for more or consider them selfish if they do not give enough.

Question – I manage a client's assets for a quarterly fee based on a percentage of the account value. If the donor gives this money to charity, I lose the management fee. If I recommend that the donor fund a donor advised fund through one of the mutual fund companies, it will pay me the same percentage fee that the client was paying me, and then everybody wins, right?

Answer – If the donor wants a chosen charity to receive money in the near future, the introduction of a donor advised fund intermediary solely for the purpose of paying the advisor is clearly in conflict with the donor's objectives. Prior to the charitable gift, the advisor worked for and was paid by the client. Once the gift is made, the advisor is being paid by, and therefore works for, the charity. If the advisor is not providing investment advice to the charity, the advisor is not working for that fee, which makes it a finder's fee. If the advisor continues to provide services to the donor, such as helping him choose between investment funds offered by the donor advised fund sponsor or helping him choose charitable grantees, then the donor is receiving something of value from the charity (the advisor's services) which will be considered a private benefit.

Question – My employer wants to withhold a percentage of my paycheck to go to a private foundation. I feel pressured from my supervisor to make this donation. Is this practice ethical?

Answer – No. Charitable donations should be made freely without pressure from employers. Charitable intent is extremely important in making donations, and any practice that results in resentment of the charitable industry is bad. Perhaps you can suggest that your employer entice employees to participate by using a matching funds program rather than intimidating employees through harassment.

Question – Are there any ethical guidelines that advisors can follow when working with charities?

Answer – There are number of common sense guidelines that apply to those who work in charitable planning.

- *Competence.* Hold yourself out as an expert only when you are actually an expert. If your knowledge base is insufficient in a particular area, involve other advisors who specialize in that area until your own experience is adequate.

- *Continued education.* The laws are rapidly changing in this field. Make an effort to stay up to date.

- *Compensation.* The commissions or fees you might earn should not drive your charitable planning advice. Sometimes, you may even lose money in the form of management fees when you recommend gifts to charity.

- *Full disclosure.* Always provide your clients with full disclosure about the gift planning they are considering. Clients must completely understand the benefits and disadvantages of their charitable decisions.

- *Charity involvement.* When at all possible, involve the charity in your client's planning. The client will benefit from its specialized experience.

- *Remember the important role of charities.* The non-profit organization holds a favored place with both the government and donors. Advisors should likewise value the role of charities and avoid planning techniques that put charities at risk or trigger negative publicity that makes it harder for non-profits to raise funds.

CHAPTER ENDNOTES

1. Tax Exempt Governance Proposals: Senate Staff Discussion Draft: http://finance.senate.gov/hearings/testimony/2004test/062204stfdis.pdf.

THE PLANNED GIVING OFFICE

CHAPTER 8

WHAT IS IT?

Even within the planned giving community, the definition of the term, "planned giving" varies. Some see it as "dealing with any non-cash gift." Others define it as "dealing with any gift in which a partial interest passes to the charity." This may be shaped in part by the size and sophistication of the professional fund-raising staff of the charity.

In general, however, most subscribe to the definition of planned giving provided by planned giving pioneer Robert F. Sharpe:

Any gift given for any amount, given for any purpose–operations, capital expansion, or endowment–whether for current or deferred use, which requires the assistance of a professional staff person, a qualified volunteer, or the donor's advisors to complete. In addition, it includes any gift that is carefully considered by a donor in light of estate and financial plans.

To put it simply, any gift that requires planning falls under the definition of planned giving. It is therefore the role of the planned giving office at a charity, no matter what it calls itself or even if it is a one-person operation, to provide donors with the needed expertise to arrange these gifts or to assist donors in finding the needed expertise.

WHEN IS THE USE OF SUCH A DEVICE INDICATED?

1. When a donor wants to give a charity a highly appreciated asset rather than simply a check.

2. When a donor would like to leave the charity a gift at death, either by bequest or through a beneficiary designation.

3. When a donor wants to arrange a split interest gift such as a charitable remainder trust, remainder interest in a home or farm, charitable lead trust, charitable gift annuity, pooled income fund, life estate, or bargain sale.

4. When a donor would like to make a substantial lifetime gift, but needs to coordinate that gift with other financial, tax, or retirement income planning objectives.

WHAT ARE THE REQUIREMENTS?

The configuration of a planned giving office varies depending on the budget and donor demographics of the charity. For example, a planned giving office might follow any of the following organizational structures:

*   A small, local charity employs a staff of three to manage its fund-raising office. One person handles the mass mailing and telemarketing tasks. The second person handles the processing of all donations under $5,000. The third person wears several hats: handling larger outright gifts, planned gifts, and the public relations for the charity.

*   A mid-size charity does not distinguish between planned gifts and outright gifts. There are three major gift development officers, all of whom offer planned giving services to the donors of the charity.

*   A university foundation that traditionally solicits only small outright donations from its alumni is considering adding a planned giving department because several of its donors have asked recently about charitable trusts. Currently all donors with these questions are passed to a

local attorney, but the university is uncomfortable that the donors must pay for donation advice. The foundation believes adding in-house counsel will strengthen its existing fund-raising efforts.

- A large non-profit hospital has an active planned giving department which consists of a senior planned giving officer who handles the largest and most complex gifts, as well as two assistant planned giving associates who handle the less complicated donations.

- A large national medical research organization has a central planned giving staff of ten located in Washington D.C. A Director of Planned Giving manages the overall program, and Senior Planned Giving Officers work closely with Regional Planned Giving Officers located throughout the United States. These experienced officers travel as needed to assist regional counsel with larger gifts, and coordinate their work with major gift and annual giving development officers on a case-by-case basis.

Regardless of the size and structure, all of these planned giving offices share a number of key goals, concerns, and potential problems. First, these charity representatives answer first and foremost to the mission statement of their employers. Second, they must balance the needs of their employer with those of the donors they solicit. And finally, they must be well versed in both the laws that govern charities as well as the tax laws surrounding the gift vehicles they recommend to donors.

HOW IS IT DONE? AN EXAMPLE

Last month, a financial planner named Gwen made a decision. She had been working as a comprehensive fee-based planner for a large financial services company for the past eight years and over the course of her career had become increasingly active in recommending planned gifts to her clients. As her interest in charitable planning grew, Gwen's interest in joining a charity as a planned giving professional also grew. When the ABC University Foundation offered her a job, she decided to take it.

When Gwen started working for the foundation, she felt quite comfortable with the ins and outs of charitable remainder trusts, and was also competent discussing such things as tax deduction limits, estate planning,

and retirement planning with her donors. She figured that her past financial and estate planning experience would give her a running start in soliciting gifts for her new charitable employer. What Gwen did not expect, however, was the amount of state and federal charity laws, rules, and regulations that she needed to learn in order to successfully represent her charity.

What is a Public Charity?

While the answer appeared obvious to Gwen as a planner, she found that the legal definition of her employer's status was much more complex. In order for her donors to receive favorable tax treatment on their charitable gifts, the charity must qualify as a "tax-exempt organization." To do this, the charity must be "organized and operated exclusively for purposes that are charitable, religious, scientific, testing for public safety, literary, educational, fostering amateur sports competition or preventing cruelty to children and animals."[1] If the charity falls under one of these purposes and the exempt status has been applied for and confirmed by the IRS in a determination letter, then contributions are tax-deductible for both income and estate and gift tax purposes.[2]

Other Requirements for Tax-Exempt Status

Gwen also learned that, in addition to having a tax-exempt purpose, her employer must meet five requirements, and in her dealings with the donors, she must ensure that none of these requirements were ever compromised:

1. *The charity must be organized exclusively for exempt purposes.* The ABC University, for example, was organized exclusively to provide a quality college education to its students.

2. *The charity must be operated primarily for that exempt purpose.* Gwen now understood why the ABC University Press, a highly profitable textbook publishing company, had been formed as a separate entity.

3. *No one running the charity may use it to benefit personally.* Such "private inurement" is prohibited and also includes a prohibition against using a privileged position of trust to exert substantial influence over the charity. Gwen read in the donor files about how a past board member, an executive at a major software company, had tried to

impose a requirement that the ABC University's computer department purchase and teach only his company's computer language.

4. *The charity may neither support nor oppose any political candidate.* In her capacity as a financial planner, Gwen had often written letters of support on company letterhead, endorsing a favorite candidate. Now that she worked for a charity, Gwen had to make sure that she used only her personal stationary or home email account and that it was clear that her endorsement was her opinion and not that of her employer.

5. *The charity may provide neither substantial support nor opposition to any legislation.* Upon joining her new employer, Gwen subscribed to an Internet listserv where pending charitable legislation was discussed. When the associations opposing new legislation asked the listserv participants to quickly email or fax a letter of opposition to their elected politicians, Gwen almost complied without checking with her supervisor. As it turned out, such an email or letter would require the approval of the charity's board and would need to be coordinated with other legislative efforts to ensure that the total expenditure would not be considered substantial.

As she watched the charity operate during her first few months on the job, Gwen realized that each of these tests would require that she be very careful in how she represented her employer in the future.

The Charity's Mission Statement

When Gwen first started working for the charity, she was given a copy of her employer's one page mission statement. She filed the mission statement in her drawer along with the charity's annual report. Within a week, she pulled the mission statement back out and memorized its contents. By the time she met with her first donor, she had enlarged and framed the statement and hung it on the wall in her office.

She realized the importance of putting the mission of the charity foremost in her dealings with donors. Unlike the financial services firm she once worked in, where the clients invested with her because they liked her, trusted her, and were happy with her service, the donors with whom she was now meeting "invested" their time and money in her charity primarily because they believed in

the charity's mission statement. In other words, Gwen concluded that her role was not to provide her services in the charity's name; she was selling her donors on the charity's purpose and her services would enable them to support that purpose in the most tax- and nontax-advantaged way.

Balancing the Needs of the Charity with Those of the Donor

When Gwen worked as a financial planner, she worked diligently on behalf of her clients and made recommendations that were in her clients' best interests. When she faced ethical dilemmas, it was usually involving her compensation. If she recommended option A, she would be paid $X, while if she recommended Option B, she would be paid $Y. Or if she put more hours into the solution, as a fee-only planner, she would receive more income.

While working as a planned giving professional, her donors' needs often conflict with those of her charitable employer. For example, when setting up a charitable remainder trust, the lower the payout rate to the donor, the larger the gift to charity in the future. If the donor could not decide between an outright gift and a split interest gift, she might feel compelled to recommend an outright gift. Unlike the compensation pressures she experienced as a planner, Gwen now had few compensation-related issues when making one recommendation over another. She did, however, need to formulate solutions that optimized the charitable gift while meeting the donor's goals and objectives and keeping the overall transaction within the donor's psychological comfort zone. Sometimes, she advised donors that they should not make a charitable gift at all, despite the fact that they wished to benefit her charity.

Major Gift Acceptance Policy[3]

A few weeks after starting her new job, Gwen was assigned the task of reviewing and modifying the foundation's Major Gift Acceptance Policy. This document, while quite lengthy, was designed to both protect the charity from potentially problematic gifts and provide a detailed set of instructions for the acceptance and disposition of all non-cash donations. The document also provided Gwen with instructions and workable guidelines on how to handle conflicts of interest, set limits on the types and size of trusts for which the foundation would act as trustee, and provide appropriate receipts to donors. It also had guidelines to be followed when hiring independent contractors, appraisers, investment managers, and other professional advisors to work on behalf of the charity.

Gwen found this document to be an indispensable part of her job. It not only gave her guidelines, it also provided her with the means to decline inappropriate gifts without offending the donor personally.

Donor Contact

When Gwen worked as a planner, she felt close to her clients. They would share information with her regarding their children and grandchildren, and would often relate personal goals and objectives. As a planned giving officer, however, Gwen was surprised to find that her donors were often even more relaxed. They respected her work with the charity and often asked about Gwen's daughter. In fact, Gwen felt as if she had made many close friends with her foundation's donors.

While Gwen enjoyed this aspect of her work very much, there were potential disadvantages. A few of these donors would try to make personal gifts to Gwen or to her daughter, which she could not accept. In some extreme cases, donors would try to include Gwen in their estate plans, either as executor, or even as a beneficiary.

Unless Gwen learned to maintain some distance from these donors, she worried that they would develop a stronger loyalty to her than they would to her charity. Furthermore, Gwen's supervisors made it clear that she needed to meet certain meeting quotas as a part of her job. Each week, she would report how many first appointments, second appointments, and so on, that she had, and if these figures were low she would be expected to increase them.

Compensation

As a planner, Gwen made a good living. As she became more experienced and more successful, she increased the minimum net worth requirements for her clientele and automated her practice to become as efficient as possible. As a planned giving officer, Gwen now made considerably less than she did as a planner. At first, Gwen did not mind the loss of income. She had more free time to spend with her family, and she felt that the time spent working with generous donors made up for the lost income.

After a few months, however, Gwen occasionally felt some resentment when planners and insurance agents to whom she would refer business would make more in one case than she did in an entire year. Gwen realized that there was no such thing as a perfect job and figured that the reduced income was balanced not only by her increased involvement with her donors, but also by seeing the results of her work in the success of her charity, and by feeling less restricted by the compensation-related conflicts that had been ever-present when she worked for fees or commissions.

Public Disclosure & Accountability

Gwen found that there was a rapidly growing trend for donors and their advisors to perform due diligence on her charity to ensure that money and other assets donated were used efficiently. The annual return filed by the charity was an integral part of her employer's accountability to donors.

Public charities (other than churches and small nonprofits with annual gross receipts of less than $25,000) are required to file an information return each year on IRS Form 990. A charity is required to make its Form 990 available for public inspection at its principal office (and certain regional or district offices) during regular business hours for three years after the filing date.[4] No information may be withheld from the public except the names and addresses of contributors. A public inspection requirement also applies, without any time limit, to an organization's exemption application and supporting papers and to the resulting IRS determination letter.

A charity is also required to provide a copy of IRS Form 990 immediately to anyone who requests it in person and to provide a copy within 30 days to anyone who requests it in writing. This must be done without charge except for a reasonable fee for any reproduction and mailing costs.[5] Finally, several states require that charities in that state file a copy of the Form 990 with the Division of Charities or Division of Consumer Affairs of the state Attorney Generals' office, which then records this data and discloses information about the charity to the public, sometimes over the Internet.

State Laws

In addition to the Form 990 disclosure rules, Gwen found that many states have specialized rules and requirements not only for charities located in those states but also for outside charities seeking gifts from residents of those states. In many states, there are registration requirements for those who solicit charitable gifts as well as a requirement of registration, licenses, or permits for certain charitable products such as charitable gift annuities. The definition of the unauthorized practice of law varies from state to state, so Gwen also had to make sure that she did not inadvertently violate these laws when working with out-of-state donors.

Marketing to Donors

In her first few weeks on the job, Gwen handled the open files on her desk that her predecessor had left behind. She received some leads from the Major Gifts department, and a few others from the Annual Gifts department. She quickly realized, however, that she needed to start prospecting for new gifts.

For out-of-state alumni, she started sending a quarterly newsletter, emphasizing both the charity's mission and the benefits of particular planned giving vehicles. For older and more established potential donors, she set up a system to call them occasionally and schedule appointments for the next time she would be in their area.

For local potential donors, she set up educational seminars, hosted by the university and given by professional advisors with whom she had a good working relationship. These, too, were followed up with personalized letters, telephone calls, and appointments.

Even once a planned gift was completed, Gwen would meet regularly with the donor to answer questions and ensure a continued interest in the mission of the charity. Such stewardship worked to make sure that revocable gifts were not diverted elsewhere, and gave the donors the opportunity to donate (both their time and money) again. She realized that many individuals wanted not only to give in a meaningful and significant way–but they also wanted to be involved in how that gift was used. The constant contact helped assure that their gift was used wisely and confirmed their wisdom in furthering the cause of the charity.

Networking with Advisors and Peers

From her prior work experience, Gwen knew that professional advisors often had access to very wealthy clients. She therefore retained her membership in the local Estate Planning Council and increased her activity with the various financial, insurance, and accounting associations.

Gwen became active with the local councils for the National Committee on Planned Giving[6] and the Association of Fundraising Professionals[7] and joined an online discussion group made up of other planned giving professionals around the nation. In a planned giving council meeting, she became friends with an experienced planned giving officer from a local hospital foundation who offered to mentor her through her first years in the field.

The Professional Advisory Board

When Gwen took over her position, the planned giving office had a reasonably good working relationship with several local and regional advisors. Gwen decided to try to establish a more formal arrangement with these professionals. After combing through the list of attorneys, CPAs, investment advisors, trust officers, and insurance agents, she chose a core group of the area's 25 most successful professionals and asked then to join the ABC University Foundation Advisory Board. She was somewhat surprised when 20 refused her invitation.

After sitting down and talking with a couple of these advisors, she realized that she needed to adjust her marketing efforts for this group. She had placed names on her list because she thought they would bring in donors. They had declined because they thought she wanted free legal and financial counseling.

She compiled another list, and instead of placing relative strangers on the list, she instead chose those advisors who cared most about the mission of her charity, and this time most responded affirmatively. Her group would meet quarterly to hear a seminar on a timely topic, and she would ask their advice about marketing to donors, how to handle an unusual gift, or ways that the Major Gift Acceptance Policy could be adapted to fit whatever new regulations or legislation that had recently been passed.

Continuing Education

Gwen regularly attended conferences, both local and national, subscribed to publications such as *Planned Giving Today*[8] and *Chronicle of Philanthropy*,[9] and received periodic updates from such websites at *GiftLaw*,[10] and

the *Planned Giving Design Center* and leimbergservices. com.[11] Gwen did all this to make sure she provided quality advice to her donors. She also did not want to jeopardize her charitable employer by relying on outdated laws and regulations. Unfortunately, there were many websites on the internet that contained authoritative but out of date articles, and Gwen found that it was safer to trust current seminars and conferences and a few carefully chosen online resources.

Gift Counting & Accounting

One of the more confusing aspects of Gwen's job was how to value the planned gifts she helped arrange for her charity. When a charity wished to keep a list of the value of donations for internal and campaign purposes, such valuation is called gift "counting." When a charity needs to value gifts for annual filing and report purposes, such valuation is referred to as gift "accounting."

For "counting" purposes, the current value of a planned gift depends on several factors:

1. Is the gift a pledge, made outright, or donated through a split interest vehicle? If a pledge, is it enforceable? If outright, will it be made during lifetime or as a bequest? If a split interest gift, will it be funded during lifetime or as a testamentary gift?

2. Is the charity named as a beneficiary of a retirement account, annuity, or insurance policy?

3. Is the gift revocable or irrevocable?

4. If the gift is deferred, what interest rate and mortality assumptions are used to calculate the present value?

For guidance on these questions, Gwen relied on the standards published by the Council for Advancement and Support of Education (CASE) that are further clarified in her charity's Gift Acceptance Policy.

Gift "accounting" is far more detailed and restrictive. Detailed instructions are provided in three Statements issued by the Financial and Accounting Standards Board (FASB).[12]

1. *FASB Statement No. 116*: Accounting for Contributions Received and Contributions Made (June 1993).

2. *FASB Statement No. 117*: Financial Statements of Not-for-Profit Organizations (June 1993).

3. *FASB Statement No. 124*: Accounting for Certain Investments Held by Not-for-Profit (November 1995).

Capital Campaign

A few months after she started with the charity, Gwen's supervisor informed her that the charity had decided to enter into a five-year, $200 million capital campaign. She would be meeting with a consultant in the next few weeks to discuss her role in the campaign. The planned giving department for the university foundation was relatively new, so her predecessors had never been involved in such a fund-raising effort.

She was advised by the consultant that 25% to 40% of the funds raised during the campaign would come from planned gifts and that her contribution to the increased marketing efforts would be measured by the campaign counting rules established by CASE. Only irrevocable gifts would be counted, and the only bequests included would be those made irrevocably by donors who were older than 75.

Gwen was aware of renewed marketing efforts by those in the Major Gifts and Annual Gifts departments but was unsure why the presence of a campaign would change her marketing efforts. As the campaign continued, she became aware of increasing pressure from her supervisor to close more irrevocable gifts, and she worried that this might affect her objectivity in balancing the needs of the donor with those of the charity's campaign goals.

Quotas & Other Job Pressures

As Gwen gained experience, she found that her new career was accompanied by some unexpected worries. The university was facing across-the-board budget cuts, and while decreasing the fund-raising office made no sense in times of a budget crisis, she worried that the gifts she was bringing in were difficult to quantify in the short-term and therefore made her job vulnerable.

At the same time, she became uncomfortable with the fact that her pay was significantly less than what it had been as a financial planner. She also found that her charity was often in competition with other charities and foundations, and that advisors were often steering gifts to community foundations and donor advised fund charities rather than encouraging direct donations to her charity. And finally, Gwen watched as planned giving professionals moved from charity to charity at a rather high turnover rate.

While she loved working on behalf of her charity and she cherished the closeness of her relationships with the many generous donors, Gwen was not immune to the many pressures faced by people in her position.

WHERE CAN I FIND OUT MORE ABOUT IT?

1. Adler, Betsy. *The Rules of the Road*, published by the Council on Foundations (www.cof.org) 1999.

2. White, Douglas. *The Art of Planned Giving: Understanding Donors and the Culture of Giving*, (New York, NY: John Wiley & Sons, 1998).

3. Moerschbaecher, Lynda. *Start at Square One: Starting and Managing the Planned Gift Program*, (Chicago, IL: Precept Press, 1998).

4. Barrett, Richard and Molly Ware. *Planned Giving Essentials: A Step by Step Guide to Success, 2nd Edition.* (New York, NY: Aspen Publishers Inc., 2002).

5. Jordan, Ronald & Quynn, Katelyn. *Planned Giving for Small Nonprofits*, (New York, NY: John Wiley & Sons, 2002).

6. Ashton, Debra. *The Complete Guide to Planned Giving, Revised Third Edition*, (Ashton Associates, 2004).

QUESTIONS AND ANSWERS

Question – How is a 501(c)(3) charity formed?

Answer – The first step is to prepare a business plan for the charity to determine the mission statement, potential donor base, initial funding, name of the organization, board members who will govern the charity, and how future board members will be selected.

Once these details are ironed out, the next step is to incorporate. This involves signing articles of incorporation that include the charitable purposes of the organization. The articles of incorporation are submitted to the Secretary of State with appropriate fees.

The third and lengthiest step is to apply for tax-exempt status with the Internal Revenue Service (IRS) on Form 1023. This is a fairly detailed form, and the IRS is likely to follow up with numerous questions regarding the function, activities, and likely source of future funds.

Once Form 1023 and the filing fee are submitted and approved, the IRS will issue a determination letter that grants the non-profit its 501(c)(3) status. There are numerous hazards in completing these forms, so most new charities should involve qualified legal and tax counsel in the process.

Question – Why do some charities have trustees while others have a board of directors?

Answer – While a charity's exempt status is determined by federal tax law, the legal structure of the underlying charity is governed by laws of the state in which it is located. A charity is generally organized as a non-profit corporation, a charitable trust, or an unincorporated non-profit association.

Charitable trusts are governed by trustees, while non-profit corporations and associations are governed by boards of directors. Most charities are non-profit corporations. The specific rules that apply to these corporations differ from state to state. A charity's directors are legally responsible for the charity's actions and omissions.

Question – Who governs or regulates charities?

Answer – The Internal Revenue Service (IRS) regulates the tax benefits associated with non-profits (tax deductions for donors and tax exemptions for the charities.) The IRS requires that annual returns be filed and may perform audits at its discretion. It may impose fines or penalties, and even revoke the tax-exempt status of errant organizations.

In most states, the attorney general of the state where the charity is located regulates the business and solicitation practices of the charity. Depending on the state, the attorney general may require the filing of regular reports and may also inspect the charity's books and records.

Question – What are intermediate sanctions?

Answer – Charitable insiders are prohibited from benefiting excessively from the activities and transactions of the charity. If such an excess benefit occurs, the IRS may impose sizable penalty taxes on both the insider who received the benefit and the person who approved the improper transaction. These penalty taxes are called intermediate sanctions. The penalty taxes can range from 10% to 200% of an excess benefit.[13]

Excess benefits include excessive compensation, employee benefits, or inappropriate property transfers to a "disqualified person" (generally anyone in a position to exert substantial influence over the charity). Typical examples of disqualified persons include someone who founded the charity, who is a substantial contributor to it, or who holds a managerial position within it.

Question – What happens if a charity engages in substantial lobbying regarding legislation?

Answer – The penalty is the loss of tax-exempt status. Charities may choose whether or not to be governed by something called the "expenditure test." Under the expenditure test, the charity may spend a set percentage (depending on the charity's size, from 5% to 20%, but no more that $1.5 million) of its exempt purpose expenditures on lobbying with no more than 25% of its lobbying expenditures spent on grass-roots lobbying efforts.[14] For charities that do not elect expenditure test treatment, the IRS has unfortunately never provided a clear definition of the word "substantial," and many charities prefer to avoid lobbying entirely rather than inadvertently trigger the harsh penalty of losing their tax-exempt status.

CHAPTER ENDNOTES

1. IRC Sec. 501(c)(3).
2. IRC Sec. 170.
3. A good example of a Major Gift Acceptance Policy can be found on the Duke University website at www.giftrecords.duke.edu/policies/gap.htm.
4. IRC Sec. 6104(d).
5. Treas. Reg. § 301.6104(d)-1(d)(3).
6. See www.ncpg.org.
7. See www.nsfre.org.
8. See www.pgtoday.com.
9. See www.philanthropy.com.
10. See www.giftlaw.com.
11. See www.pgdc.net.
12. See www.fasb.org for information on ordering these statements.
13. IRC Sec. 4958.
14. IRC Secs. 501(h), 4911.

THE PLANNED GIVING TEAM

CHAPTER 9

WHAT IS IT?

Many planned giving techniques directly affect a donor's tax, estate, financial, retirement, and insurance plans. As each of these fields is highly specialized, a team approach is almost always in a donor's best interest when planning a major gift. The framework of the planned giving team varies, depending on the donor's specific needs and goals, but is generally comprised of up to five key advisors—a planned giving officer, attorney, accountant, insurance representative, and investment advisor. Several other advisors may be added to the team to address specific needs, including a professional trustee, appraiser, trust accounting firm and, in some cases, even a family mediator.

In theory, each of the advisors handles specific duties, and the donor's best interest is carefully balanced among the various financial planning disciplines. The overall plan is designed to benefit both the donor and the chosen charity, and the team works smoothly to implement the plan and review it periodically to ensure its continued success.

In practice, the planned giving team (perhaps better labeled as a co-operative) is seldom so efficient. The process may be plagued with problems of control, personality conflicts, uneven levels of competence, and deep-seated prejudices regarding the objectives and agendas of other team members.

For the team approach to work, each advisor must understand the roles, responsibilities, and conflicts of interest faced by the other advisors. Each member of the team must agree to put aside petty differences to best serve the objectives and needs of the donor and to aid in the accomplishment of the charity's goals.

WHEN IS THE USE OF SUCH A DEVICE INDICATED?

1. When a donor wants to plan for both financial needs (either personally or for the benefit of his heirs) and charitable objectives.

2. When a donor wants to make a relatively large planned gift. A donor worth $10,000,000 may not need to assemble a planning team to donate $100,000 of appreciated stock to charity. To a donor worth $600,000, the same $100,000 gift has a substantially larger effect on his financial situation, and a team approach may be advisable.

3. When a donor's charitable planning is sufficiently complex that legal documents, beneficiary designations, or specialized tax preparation is needed to implement the planned gift.

4. When a planned giving technique has been proposed by one advisor and the potential donor would like a second or third opinion. It is also appropriate if the donor merely wants to obtain the suggestions and additional ideas of others.

ADVANTAGES

1. When a planning team functions smoothly, the donor is presented with a cohesive plan that is implemented quickly and efficiently.

2. By allocating tasks to specialists, the implementation fees are kept to a minimum, and fewer mistakes are made.

3. Full disclosure of compensation and conflicts of interest proactively address some of the potential misunderstandings, and gives the donor a better insight of the pressures faced by each advisor.

DISADVANTAGES

1. A planning team rarely runs as smoothly as the example that is provided near the end of this chapter.

2. Many advisors have strong personalities and the leadership of the team frequently shifts throughout the process, with different advisors trying to assume the leadership position at any one time.

3. The team's advisors often have preconceived biases about the other professionals on the team and, in some cases, none of the team members have sufficient practical experience to lead the group successfully.

4. The "ball" may be dropped and an important task is left undone.

WHAT ARE THE REQUIREMENTS?

In order for a team approach to work, each member of the team must be aware of the goals, pressures, and potential conflicts of interest of the other team members. Each advisor must also recognize the perceived stereotypes that other advisors may attempt to apply and work to overcome such biases.

The following is a brief outline of the general goals, possible problems, and ideal objectives for the three main advisor types: the planned giving officer, the insurance or investment advisor, and the legal or tax advisor. This outline is not meant to be complete but rather offers a generalized portrait of each advisor type.

Planned Giving Officers

While generalizations can often result in misleading stereotypes, there are some basic characteristics of planned giving officers:

- *Charitable mission.* Many planned giving officers are primarily motivated to work in their particular career to obtain the personal satisfaction of raising money to support their charitable employer's good deeds.

- *Work with generous people.* Once they begin working for the charity, most gift planners enjoy assisting philanthropic people arrange their charitable contributions.

- *Meet employer expectations.* As in any job, planned giving officers must show success in their efforts to keep their bosses happy. Planned giving officers gain advancement, raises, and job security by completing charitable gifts.

- *Cooperation of other advisors.* When planned giving officers recommend a charitable gift, there is usually some anxiety about other advisors dissuading the donor from making the gift, or recommending the use of an intermediary charity, such as a donor advised fund or a community foundation.

- *Competence.* Many planned giving officers want to be competent in the technicalities and laws surrounding charitable planning, and strive to remain up-to-date with changing laws and issues. Other planned giving officers focus more on the social aspects of soliciting gifts and prefer to leave the technical aspects of planning to outside advisors.

- *Good public relations for the charity.* There is a tongue-in-cheek question called the "*60 Minutes* test," which many planned giving officers apply to each gift situation. If the donor implements the charitable recommendation, will the charity feel comfortable seeing a *60 Minutes* journalist walk up to its door? Most planned giving officers take the good name of their particular employer and the charitable industry in general quite seriously.

Truths and Misconceptions Regarding Planned Giving Officers

Some of the following complaints may indeed be based on the truth, but quite often the complaint may reflect other advisors' biases more than any inherent characteristic in a planned giving officer. To successfully work with a non-profit advisor, a commercial sector professional must learn to distinguish truth from stereotype, and in cases where the complaint is justified, learn to work around the planned giving officer's limitations.

- *High turnover rate.* Planned giving is a fairly new field for most charities. According to a poll taken in 2002 by the National Committee on Planned Giving, 40% of the planned giving professionals who responded had less than five years of experience. Furthermore, 51% of planned giving officers had changed charitable employers within the prior three years. For charitable advisors who have significant experience or who remain loyal to one employer, mobility concerns should not pose a problem for other advisors. In situations where mobility or inexperience are issues, the other advisors should focus more on the charity's mission and less on the individual fund-raiser.

- *Under pressure to produce.* Many planned giving officers feel pressured by their charitable employer to close gifts, especially during capital campaigns or in times when the charity faces a shortage of funds. Some charities compound the pressure to close gifts by paying performance bonuses. These pressures can often be alleviated if the donor and other advisors request full disclosure from the fund-raiser of all deadlines and compensation pressures at the beginning of the charitable planning process.

- *Perceived as less competent than commercial sector advisors.* Many non-profit advisors are paid less than their commercial sector counterparts, and it is often erroneously assumed that they are therefore less knowledgeable. However, a large number of planned giving officers hold advanced degrees, including law degrees, and designations such as CPA and CFP. While many planned giving officers earn less than their commercial sector counterparts, this is usually the result of a career choice rather than an indication of competence.

- *Resentful of "for-profit" advisors.* There is a tendency by many in the tax-exempt industry to refer to professionals who work for a charity as "non-profit" advisors while those who work in the commercial sector are "for-profit" advisors. Buried within these labels is an implicit assumption that planned giving officers are charitably minded while commercial sector advisors are driven by profit and greed. Unfortunately, this bias is supported by planners and advisors who sell charitable planning as a product rather than a tool, and who urge clients to enter into complex charitable plans when donative intent is marginal or, in some cases, completely

lacking. It can also be fueled by the compensation discrepancies between the non-profit and commercial sector. If a planned giving officer recommends a large life insurance purchase, for example, as part of charitable remainder trust recommendation, the planned giving officer is quite aware that the insurance agent will earn a sizable commission for the insurance sale. In some extreme cases, this commission for one sale to one donor may be more than the planned giving officer makes in six months or even a year.

- *Appear to be ungrateful.* Many commercial sector advisors complain that when they arrange a planned gift to benefit a particular charity, they often face scrutiny and suspicion from the planned giving officer. For example, when an insurance agent arranges for a donor to purchase life insurance which will be owned by the charity, instead of saying "thank you," the planned giving officer may respond with criticism about insurance as an investment and in some cases, may even decline the gift. While commercial sector advisors may interpret this type of reaction as ungracious, it is more often because they do not understand the responsibilities, pressures, and laws that must be faced by the charitable recipient. Charities must be wary of gifts with too many strings attached, and the donation of cash on the condition that it be used to purchase insurance or any other specific investment is too restrictive and probably inappropriate for most charities.

- *Do not provide full disclosure.* Some non-profit advisors recommend advanced techniques to their donors without fully disclosing the inherent risks. For example, if a planned giving officer illustrates a NIMCRUT assuming a 5% payout and 12% annual return, the donor may not understand that if the assets experience a loss instead of a gain, the annual income could actually decrease. (See Chapter 16 for a discussion of NIMCRUTs.)

- *Designation of beneficiary.* Another area where planned giving officers face criticism is the designation of a charitable remainder beneficiary. Some planned giving officers recommend that their charitable employer act as the trustee of the CRT, and fail to disclose that the remainder beneficiary could have been revocable and that

the donor could have named either himself or a trusted relative, friend, or professional as trustee. As the charity directly benefits from this lack of disclosure, a commercial sector advisor should assist donors with a more complete picture of the options and opportunities available.

- *Willing to produce legal documents.* Some planned giving officers either recommend documents that are drafted by in-house counsel or simply provide donors with sample documents. In the former situation, the attorney represents the charity and not the donor; the donor should always retain separate counsel prior to signing the documents. Furthermore, while providing a sample document to a donor may seem like a good technique to educate donors, it often puts the donor's legal counsel in an awkward position. In the donor's mind, the attorney simply needs to change a few lines or add a paragraph or two, and the donor may resent the fact that the attorney charges the normal fee for drafting the documents. Some donors do not even see the need to involve an attorney at all when the donor thinks the sample document can be easily adjusted.

- *Expect donations from advisors.* Some planned giving officers expect advisors to give up commissions and fees because their work is being done while arranging a charitable gift. While asking advisors for donations is perfectly acceptable, asking for a split or rebate of commissions, investment fees, and legal fees may violate certain state laws and ethical guidelines. Furthermore, unless a charitable representative takes the time and effort to educate an advisor on the mission of the charity, it is unreasonable to ask that the advisor become a donor to that charity.

- *Want and expect free advice.* Most charities are understaffed, especially when it comes to specialized financial counsel. All too often, a charity will not have the funds to hire full-time planned giving officers or even outside advisors. They therefore frequently call on local counsel to answer questions free of charge. Once again, unless a charity has promoted the charity's mission to an advisor and asked for a donation in the form of services, it is unreasonable for a charity to expect gifts of time and research.

The Ideal Planned Giving Officer as a Member of the Planning Team

Most of the problems outlined above can be solved with clear communication, improved disclosure, and reasonable expectations on the part of both the planned giving officer and commercial sector advisors. The ideal planned giving officer will engage in the following activities:

1. Educate and involve the donor in the charity's mission.

2. Place the charity's mission before the personal services of the planned giving officer so that, in the event the charitable representative changes employers, the donor will remain comfortable working with the charity.

3. Put together a brief conceptual report for the donor on the recommended planned gift, and supply all supporting calculations to the appropriate advisors.

4. Work proactively with both the donor and advisors to ensure full disclosure of all relevant risks and options.

5. Work closely with the donor's attorney in the drafting of all documents that will be needed.

6. Meet with the donor periodically following the implementation of the planned gift to review the charitable plan and remind the donor of the charity's mission.

7. Resolve in a professional manner all issues and problems within the planning team.

Financial Advisors

Over the past twenty years, the financial services industry has developed a number of specialized professions. These include insurance agents, insurance consultants, stockbrokers, investment advisors, financial planners, and philanthropic planners. While the specific duties, compensation structures, and marketing practices for each type of profession are different, there are some general goals and issues that apply to most financial advisors.

- *Customer Service.* Most financial advisors offer their services in more than one field. There are insurance agents that perform estate or retirement planning, and investment advisors that offer comprehensive financial planning. Due to many clients having charitable objectives, it is natural that advisors want to include charitable planning among their services.

- *Compensation.* Unlike most planned giving officers, very few financial advisors earn a salary. Many advisors earn commissions, others earn fees, but most earn some combination of commissions and fees. Assuming that the advisor is performing a service or selling a product, it is reasonable for that person to be compensated accordingly.

- *Charitable Motivation.* Many financial advisors have added charitable planning to their list of services because they enjoy helping clients arrange substantial gifts to charity. These advisors are often active with their local planned giving council and generously volunteer their time and services for their favorite causes.

- *Competition.* If other planners and financial professionals have added charitable planning to their list of services, then a planner who does not may lose clients to those who do.

- *Networking.* Planned giving generally requires three or four advisors to work together on a donor's behalf. Team planning gives a financial professional access to new legal, accounting, and charitable advisors.

Some Truths and Misconceptions Regarding Financial Advisors

Over the years, other advisors who work with financial professionals have formed generalized ideas and biases that must be understood and addressed in order to develop a productive working relationship.

- *Too much focus on compensation.* Planned giving officers, tax advisors, and legal counsel all complain that many financial professionals focus more on compensation levels that they do on what is right for the customer.

Example: An insurance agent sells a client on the use of a CRT to liquidate highly appreciated stock, even though the client has expressed no interest in making a charitable donation.

Example: A client wishes to invest in a charitable gift annuity offered by ABC University. His insurance agent recommends that the client purchase a charitable gift annuity through a national foundation instead, with ABC University as the ultimate beneficiary. The agent does not disclose that he will earn a 7% commission from the foundation, and that ABC University's gift from the foundation will be delayed by several years.

Example: A client wishes to make an annual donation to her local art museum. Her agent advises that life insurance is the most advantageous way of funding this gift, and she purchases a sizable policy. The museum, however, does not accept insurance gifts.

Example: An investment advisor has a client who wishes to set up a $1 million donor advised fund to benefit several charities. The advisor "shops" several donor advised fund charities and recommends that the client establish an account with a charity that pays 1% of the account balance each year to the advisor. The internal fees on this fund are significantly higher than with other funds, substantially reducing the amount available for charitable grants, and the advisor recommends that minimal annual grants be made so that her annual fee does not decrease.

- *Lacks competence in charitable laws.* Many financial planners and insurance agents have started to include charitable planning in their list of client services. Some of these advisors hold themselves out as experts but, in far too many cases, their education and practical experience is limited. A few advisors are state of the art in their own field and mistakenly assume that charitable laws are similar to the laws that govern their business clientele. The charitable split dollar debacle is a good example of this misunderstanding. Split dollar funding of life insurance is a sound, ethical, and relatively common technique in the estate, employee benefit, and business planning marketplace. But when applied to a charitable organization, the split dollar technique violated laws that could cause the loss of a non-profit's tax-exempt status.

The other advisors on the planning team can often mitigate the concern of inadequate education or experience by requesting a list of client referrals, charities, and other advisors with whom the financial advisor has worked on planned gifts. Although there is nothing inherently wrong with working with a financial advisor who has no prior charitable experience, it is vitally important to determine the level of each team member's competence when the overall program is designed. In addition to providing a list of references, financial advisors who do have significant experience in charitable planning can provide each team member with sample reports and a list of related continuing education that has been completed.

- *Wants to control the planning process.* Many planned gifts originate with a financial planner or insurance professional. While it is only natural that this advisor should assume the team leader position, that may or may not be advisable. Sometimes legal counsel may be a more appropriate choice as leader, because the attorney will be held accountable for the legal documents that are drafted during the process. Alternatively, the team leader should often be the planned giving officer, who can afford to spend more hours on the details of the process because the client is not paying for his services. Often, the planned giving officer will have more experience, and often specific legal expertise, than the client's attorney. Assuming that the agent or planner has properly disclosed any conflicts of interest, and has made sound recommendations, ceding the leadership of the plan should not pose significant risk to this advisor's involvement.

- *Often recommends techniques that are too aggressive.* Many financial advisors are adept at matching the risk level of a particular plan with the risk tolerance of their client. The more aggressive the client, the higher the risk of the underlying advice. With planned giving, however, there are two parties to every gift. In addition to assessing the donor's risk, the planner must take into account the risk tolerance of the charity. When a charity violates tax laws, the consequences to the charity may be significantly harsher than the

consequences to a client or business, because a violation could result in the loss of the charity's tax-exempt status with the accompanying catastrophic consequences to both those who work for, and benefit from, the charity.

- *Thinks of planning techniques as products.* Many insurance, brokerage, and mutual fund companies have "packaged" charitable trusts as a product to be sold. When presented to a client as a tax-savings tool, advisors have found that these "products" can be quite lucrative in terms of insurance commissions and investment fees. However, planned gifts should be considered as a planning technique, rather than as a product, and considerable research and planning should be done to ensure that the recommended technique is suitable for the client's individual objectives and needs.

- *In an effort to sell the plan, the advisor may hide the disadvantages.* Several lawsuits have recently emerged regarding (1) charitable trusts that did not perform as projected; (2) premiums that did not vanish in year six, the last year that the client carried forward a charitable tax deduction to cover the premium costs; (3) "pass through foundations" that did not distribute funds to charitable grantees as promised; and (4) clients who face considerable tax, interest, and penalties from being sold charitable split dollar plans that could not provide the benefit that was promised. Financial advisors have learned a valuable lesson in these cases: in order to give a client sufficient information to make an informed decision, the risks must be disclosed as well as the benefits. These disclosed risks should include whether newer and sophisticated concepts have been tested before the IRS or the courts.

The Ideal Financial Advisor as a Member of the Planning Team

An agent, financial planner, or investment advisor who wants to work successfully with charities and their donors should consider the following:

1. Take an interest in the mission of the charity.

2. Provide honest, clear, accurate, and constant communication to all team members as well as to the donor.

3. Provide full disclosure regarding compensation methods and conflicts of interest.

4. Yield to the charity on charitable law issues, and to the donor's attorney and tax advisor on legal and tax issues.

5. Take the lead in performing annual reviews of all insurance or investment parts of the plan.

6. Handle all service and information requests promptly.

7. Resolve in a professional manner all issues and problems within the planning team.

Tax Advisors or Estate Planning Attorneys

While the education, business practices, and state regulation may vary between tax advisors and legal counsel, in the context of the planned giving team, these two advisor groups share many of the same goals, biases, and conflicts of interest.

- *Compensation.* Advisors who work for larger firms often earn some form of base salary but their overall compensation is highly dependent on the number of billing hours they complete. For smaller firms, advisors' pay is even more dependent on the fees they bring in. Unlike a planned giving officer whose salary is fixed, or an insurance agent, who occasionally earns larger commissions on some cases to help offset other sales that are small, tax and legal advisors depend almost entirely on billable hours.

- *Competition.* In an effort to attract and maintain wealthy clients, tax and legal advisors must remain state-of-the-art and offer services that appeal to high-end clients. Philanthropic planning is one of these services.

- *Charitable involvement.* Many accountants and attorneys are active with their local planned giving council and will volunteer as much time as they have with their favorite charities.

- *Avoid conflicts of interest and liability.* Attorneys and accountants have a fiduciary duty to their clients and must put their clients' needs first (this may mean even ahead of the charity's interests).

They must fully disclose all conflicts of interest, and in the event that their recommendations and plans are found to be problematic, it is probable that they will be sued, and in a worst case scenario they may lose their professional licenses.

- *Networking.* Just like financial advisors and planned giving officers, attorneys and tax advisors must generate new business. By working with other advisors on a planned giving team, they can build new relationships that will in turn bring in new clients.

Some Truths and Misconceptions Regarding Tax Advisors and Estate Planning Attorneys

Most of the stereotypes surrounding these advisors stem from their unusually long work hours and stringent business and ethical restrictions. By understanding the pressures particular to these professions, the other members of the planning team can develop a much more satisfactory business relationship with the team attorney and accountant.

- *These advisors do not care for charitable giving.* Many planned giving officers believe that attorneys and accountants try to talk potential donors out of making gifts that are recommended by planned giving officers because of a dislike of charity. In reality, while some advisors may not be charitably inclined, most find that their clients come to them to validate whether the gift is feasible and can generate benefits beyond the joy and personal satisfaction of giving. Sometimes it is simply not in the client's best interests to structure a current gift and, in some cases, the client is uncomfortable turning the charity down and is simply using the advisor as an excuse for delaying or declining to make the gift.

- *Advisor fees for charitable giving are too high.* Many planned giving officers believe that attorneys and accountants should prepare their plans, documents, and tax forms at a discounted rate because the client is making a charitable gift. While planned giving officers may spend a considerable amount of time educating donors about the charity's mission, they often expect advisors to make a donation of time and services without giving these advisors a similar education. Furthermore, attorneys and tax advisors face the same liability and professional issues with charitable planning as they do with non-charitable work. While many advisors do perform work on a pro bono basis, such services are generally reserved for those who cannot otherwise afford legal counsel. Rather than foster resentment in a client's mind about the expense of the legal and tax work, planned giving officers might instead point out that the tax and legal advisors actions are protecting the donor's (rather than the charity's) rights and that legal and accounting expenses can usually be more than offset by the tax savings and the accomplishment of other personal objectives resulting from the plan.

- *These advisors are stingy with their time.* Most legal and accounting professionals work substantially more than 40 hours per week, with many working as many as 60 hours or more per week. Any hours spent helping charities will generally reduce what little time is available for family, friends, errands, and hobbies.

- *These advisors like to only set up private foundations.* There are indeed a number of advisors who recommend that their clients establish private foundations. This trend, however, is reversing as more and more advisors become aware of the alternatives such as donor advised funds and supporting organizations.

- *Will not talk about the charity with other donors.* Planned giving officers often approach commercial sector advisors looking for potential donors among the advisor's client lists. Most legal and tax advisors are not in a position to recommend new or specific charitable causes to their clients. Indeed, they would generally consider these recommendations as a solicitation on behalf of the charity.

- *Legal counsel is averse to using a charity's documents.* Attorneys and accountants resent being asked to rubber stamp plans they did not prepare and they rightfully worry that they will be charged with malpractice if anything is done incorrectly. Other advisors on the planning team should respect the professional constraints faced by these advisors.

The Ideal Tax Advisor or Estate Planning Attorney as a Member of the Planning Team

An attorney or accountant who wants to work successfully as a member of a planned giving team should attempt to follow several basic guidelines:

1. Take an interest in the mission of the charitable beneficiary.

2. Assume the role of team leader when it is suitable and respect the leadership of a different team leader if appropriate, particularly if the other person has a superior educational and experiential background or specializes in charitable planning.

3. Take steps to remain up-to-date and competent on charitable planning, and either decline a case or work with co-counsel if inexperienced with the charitable planning concepts that are recommended by other members of the team.

4. Yield to other team members on matters in which they are more qualified.

5. Handle all communications and requests promptly.

6. Provide full disclosure regarding fees and conflicts of interest.

7. Resolve in a professional manner all issues and problems within the planning team.

Technical Competence

In a 1997 study, Russ Alan Prince polled several wealthy donors regarding their planned giving experiences. Fifty-eight percent of those polled were unhappy with the charitable planning proposed by charity representatives and 62% were dissatisfied with plans proposed by their commercial sector advisors. The most common reason for their frustration with advisors was found to be lack of technical competence. Not surprisingly, when advisors were asked to rank which aspects of their professional practice were most important, they place technical competence last.[1] If the various professionals want to offer their clients quality service in charitable planning, they need to place more emphasis on learning the technical aspects of this field.

HOW IS IT DONE?

Mr. Thomas, a successful businessman, has been meeting with the planned giving officer for the Huntington Library. He has decided that he would like to fund a major planned gift and after reviewing several techniques with the charity's representative, the use of a deferred NIMCRUT (net income with makeup charitable remainder unitrust, see Chapter 16) seems to fit his planning objectives.

After reviewing the basic conceptual report provided by the charity, Mr. Thomas agrees to the plan and asks what the next step should be. The planned giving officer says that, in order to implement the plan, Mr. Thomas' other advisors should be brought together to discuss and iron out the details. Mr. Thomas provides the names and phone numbers of his various advisors and gives the planned giving officer permission to share the details of his case with the various people involved:

1. Mr. Thomas' estate planning attorney is needed to review the plan and draft the necessary documents.

2. His accountant will review the income tax consequences of the gift to ensure the optimization of the charitable deduction. The accountant will also provide trust accounting for the CRT on an annual basis.

3. The donor's financial planner will handle the transfer of highly appreciated stock to fund the trust and will then manage the liquidation and reinvestment of the assets within the CRT.

4. The insurance agent will handle the recommendations and implementation of the insurance policy that will be purchased through a Wealth Replacement Trust. Furthermore, the agent will perform an annual review of the policy and insurance.

After a brief meeting, the advisors agree that the attorney has significant practical experience in establishing CRTs, so she will lead the team. All correspondence from each advisor will pass through her office, and she will ensure that everything is done in a timely manner so that the donor's gift can be completed by the end of the current tax year.

In order to begin the work, the team leader asks that each advisor, including the planned giving officer, put together a package for the donor to review. This package should include (1) a professional biography, (2) a contract, if it is required by the professional, (3) a clear and detailed estimate of all fees or commissions that will be charged or earned throughout the CRT implementation, and (4) a letter outlining any potential conflicts of interest and promising Mr. Thomas a professional commitment to make sure that his plan will be implemented as quickly and as efficiently as possible.

Each team member complies, and the analysis begins. The planned giving officer provides his numerical analyses to the attorney and accountant, who each work to revise some of the details so that they better fit Mr. Thomas' actual financial situation. Meanwhile the insurance agent begins the medical and financial underwriting process, while the investment advisor prepares the necessary documents to transfer the stock and researches a recommended portfolio for the CRT once the stock has been liquidated.

While there are some disagreements among the advisors regarding the planning details or the allocation of different tasks, these are handled professionally. When disagreements cannot be readily resolved, the choices are presented clearly and openly to Mr. Thomas, who makes the final decision.

The CRT is drafted, funded, and completed by the end of the year, and the advisors prepare separate letters to Mr. Thomas outlining each of their responsibilities and estimated fees, if any, for managing and reviewing the plan on a periodic basis. Furthermore, the advisors have learned that they work fairly well together and plan to refer business to each other in the future.

WHERE CAN I FIND OUT MORE ABOUT IT?

1. Henry, Vaughn, "Team Building and Expanding Your Practice," *Journal of Practical Estate Planning* (April-May 2001, pp. 30-41).

2. Prince, Russ Alan and File, Karen Maru, *Cultivating the Affluent II: Leveraging High Net Worth Client and Advisor Relationships* (Institutional Investor: 1997).

3. Breitstein, Joel, "Donor/Client: The Two Faces of a Prospect," Planned Giving Design Center Website at www.pgdc.net, 1998.

4. Leave a Legacy™ Website at www.leavealegacy.org.

5. Mangone, Betsy. "Professional Advisors and Non-Profits: A Collaboration to Shape our Philanthropic Future,"www.pgdc.com, June 02, 2006.

6. Mangone, Betsy. "A Professional Advisors Guide to Working with Non-Profit Organizations,"www.pgdc.com, June 23, 2004.

7. Miree, Kathryn. "Nonprofit Marketing Strategies to Reach Donor-Advisors," *The Journal of Gift Planning*, Fall 2004.

QUESTIONS AND ANSWERS

Question – What is the donor's role in the planned giving team?

Answer – Because the donor generally chooses the team members, it is imperative that conflicting personalities be kept to a minimum. If one team member is not working well with the others, the donor should address this situation quickly by either speaking with the advisor about the problem or, in some cases, replacing the advisor with a new team member. Also, the donor must be willing to trust the various team members to make clear decisions when needed.

Question – Who should lead the planned giving team?

Answer – The attorney is the most likely leader as document drafting and review are usually involved, and because the attorney may have substantial liability if any aspects of the plan are found to be problematic. However, in cases where other team members are more experienced, the team leader could possibly fall on other shoulders. The planned giving officer, for example, might be a suitable leader if that professional has significant experience and in cases where fees are an issue. The planned giving professional's time is covered by the charitable employer rather than paid for directly by the donor.

Question – How can an insurance agent develop a long-term and profitable relationship with a charity?

Answer – There are numerous opportunities for a professional insurance agent to develop long-term, profitable, working relationships with local charities. Charities often receive unusual or confusing gifts of life insurance, annuities and, more recently, viatical settlements. An insurance agent can be available to the charity as a valuable resource for these questions. By offering quality and unbiased advice, and by avoiding some key pitfalls such as asking for donor lists, an insurance agent can quickly become a member of the charity's team. While free advice may appear to be a waste of an agent's time, charities are often in a position to recommend insurance products to their donors. Charities also prefer to work with an agent who is familiar with their organization and who understands the quirks and nuances of charitable gifts involving life insurance products. This passive marketing may seem foreign to the insurance industry, but the traditional methods such as asking for referrals, or even a charity's donor list, do not generally work with non-profit organizations.

Question – How can a tax or estate planning attorney develop a long-term and profitable relationship with a charity?

Answer – Unlike an insurance agent, who works on commission, most accountants and attorneys do not have the ability or freedom to spend hours cultivating referrals. In general, the best method for these advisors involves less free advice and more professional expertise. While many advisors hold themselves out as competent in the charitable field, very few are actually experts. Advisors who wish to work in this field should enroll in related continuing education courses, and make an effort to become a specialist.

Question – How does a professional advisory board work and what are its strengths and limitations?

Answer – Many charities assemble groups of local practitioners to participate on advisory boards. In theory, the goal of these boards is two-fold: (1) the charity has a periodic opportunity to educate these advisors on the mission of the charity, and (2) the charity can test new planning ideas and concepts on a panel of experts. In practice, the effectiveness of these boards varies dramatically. Most advisors are not in a position to recommend specific charities to their clients. Furthermore, many of the more successful local advisors tend to avoid commitments because they are time consuming and the possibility of obtaining referrals from a charity that has 20 other advisors on the board is less likely.

CHAPTER ENDNOTES

1. Prince, Russ Alan, et al., *The Charitable Giving Handbook*, 1st edition (Cincinnati, OH: The National Underwriter Company, 1997), pp. 26-28.

BARGAIN SALE TRANSACTIONS

CHAPTER 10

WHAT IS IT?

A bargain sale is the sale of an asset to a charitable organization at a price below the asset's fair market value (FMV).[1] A bargain sale is treated for income tax purposes as: (1) part sale (or exchange) of property to charity; and (2) part charitable contribution.[2] It's as if the donor sold a portion of the property to the charitable organization and donated the balance.[3]

Sometimes a taxpayer may not be aware that a transaction is a bargain sale transaction until after the transaction is complete. For example, this could occur when a taxpayer makes an outright gift of an asset at a time when the property is subject to a debt. If a charitable organization receives debt-encumbered property, the donor is treated as if the charitable organization paid him cash equal to the amount of the debt, even though no cash payment is actually made by the charitable organization or received by the donor.[4] As a result, the deemed property sale is treated as a bargain sale.

WHEN IS THE USE OF SUCH A DEVICE INDICATED?

1. When a donor wants to make a contribution of property, but wants or needs to receive some cash consideration for the asset.

2. When a donor seeks to lower income taxes with a current income tax deduction and to remove appreciated property from his or her estate.

3. When the donor and charity desire a significant degree of flexibility in making a property transfer. For instance, the donor may structure a bargain sale so that payments occur over a period of years, rather than all at once. The use of such a payment method permits a donor to receive income over an

extended period of time and also allows the donor to report the taxable gain (including any capital gain portion) over a period of years under the installment method. The use of the installment method also eases the cash flow burden to the charitable organization and may enable it to acquire property it otherwise could not afford.

ADVANTAGES

Advantages to the Donor

1. A donor can lower income and estate taxes through the income tax deduction that a bargain sale generates and also remove a highly appreciated asset from his or her estate.

2. A donor may structure a bargain sale so that payments occur over a period of years, rather than all at once. The use of such a payment method permits a donor to receive a steady income over an extended period of time and also allows the donor to report the taxable gain (including any capital gain portion) over a period of years under the installment method.

3. Bargain sales remain an easy way to make a large current gift to charity with no diminution of current cash flow.

Advantages to the Charitable Organization

1. The charitable organization obtains property at a fraction of its full fair market value.

2. The charitable organization receives an immediate gift of an asset from a donor, instead of waiting until the donor's death.

3. Bargain sale transactions are easy to arrange and require no ongoing administration.

4. The charitable organization may use the installment method of payment to reduce the current cash flow strain from the transaction.

DISADVANTAGES

Disadvantages to the Donor

1. A donor who uses the bargain sale technique makes an irrevocable gift. As a result, he loses dominion, use, and control over the asset upon completion of the bargain sale.

2. A donor who uses the bargain sale technique cannot avoid capital gains tax on highly appreciated assets.

3. Any realized gain from a bargain sale must be recognized in the year of the gift, even if a charitable deduction is allowed for the "bargain portion" of the gift. Depending on the circumstances, the tax incurred in a bargain sale may or may not be offset by the deductible gift portion of the transaction.

4. An "unintentional" bargain sale transaction may result from an outright gift of debt-encumbered property. In such a case, the donor is deemed to have made a sale, with the debt viewed as partial consideration.

Disadvantages to the Charitable Organization

1. The charitable organization needs cash to acquire an asset.

2. The charitable organization may become part of a bidding war with another charitable organization or other "qualified" organization for the purchase of the asset.

3. The charitable organization must be alert for any problems with the asset. For example, a donor may attempt to pass off damaged or problem property (such as an asset with an environmental issue) in a bargain sale transaction.

4. The donor may ask the charitable organization to assume or pay the debt on an encumbered piece of property. The debt assumption or payment does not relieve the donor from exposure to the bargain sale rules. The donor may later attempt to seek payment of an unforeseen capital gains tax from the charitable organization. This scenario may include an additional complication if the donor represents a major or consistent benefactor to the charitable organization, and there are either current ongoing donations in progress or plans for future donations.

WHAT ARE THE REQUIREMENTS?

1. The sale transaction must involve a "qualified" charitable organization under IRC Section 170(c). IRS Publication 78 contains a lengthy list of "qualified" charitable organizations.[5] Examples of "qualified" charitable organizations include nonprofit schools, hospitals, churches, and synagogues, The United Way, YMCA, YWCA, The American Red Cross, the Boy Scouts, the Girl Scouts, and the American Heart Association. For a detailed explanation of the requirements for qualified organizations, see Chapter 2.

2. The subject of the transaction must be "property,"[6] rather than any services the taxpayer may provide in connection with the subsequent use of the property by the organization. This requirement precludes any deduction for the "free use" of the property prior to or in connection with the bargain sale. Therefore, a rent-free use of real or personal property does not augment the bargain sales transaction any more than a contribution of personal services by the taxpayer.[7]

3. The sale price or debt encumbrance (if any) on the asset must be lower than the fair market value of the asset. This requirement reflects the "bargain" element in the transaction. The "sale price" may reflect either a cash purchase or an amount of debt encumbrance.[8] In fact, the transfer of property subject to debt will trigger the bargain sale rules even if the charitable organization does not specifically agree to or make an assumption of payment for the debt.

4. If the deduction portion of the transaction exceeds $5,000, a "qualified appraisal" must be performed in order to establish and document the fair market value of the bargain sale property.[9] "Qualified appraisal" means an appraisal of such property that

(1) is treated as a qualified appraisal under Treasury regulations or other IRS guidance, and (2) is conducted by a qualified appraiser in accordance with generally accepted appraisal standards and any regulations or other guidance.[10]

A qualified appraisal summary and IRS Form 8283 must accompany the taxpayer's return to substantiate the charitable deduction.[11]

5. For purposes of this valuation process, a "qualified appraiser" means an individual who: (1) has earned an appraisal designation from a recognized professional appraiser organization, or has otherwise met minimum education and experience requirements set forth in Treasury regulations; (2) regularly performs appraisals for which the individual receives compensation; and (3) meets such other requirements as may be prescribed in Treasury regulations or other guidance.[12] A qualified appraiser must be qualified to render an appraisal of the type of property in question.[13] Finally, a qualified appraiser must understand that an overstatement of property value may lead to the imposition of tax penalties.[14] The appraiser may not be: (a) the donor,[15] (b) any person from whom the property was acquired,[16] or (c) the organization that receives the property.[17]

6. There must be an irrevocable transfer of the ownership interest by the donor to the charitable organization in the year for which the deduction is claimed.

HOW IS IT DONE?

A bargain sale for cash consideration allows a donor to make a contribution of property while obtaining partial payment for it. This may be particularly attractive when a donor owns property that is desirable to a charity, but he does not wish to donate the entire amount.

Example: Luke Oliver purchased land 20 years ago that is valued at $2 million. The property is adjacent to land owned by his alma mater, Villanova Law School. Luke would like to transfer the land to Villanova, but he would also like to obtain cash for a portion of the fair market value (FMV) of the property. Luke and the university agree on a bargain sale price of $500,000, the amount of his adjusted basis.

Luke transfers his complete ownership of the land to the university and receives payment of $500,000 in the same year. But, the $500,000 price that Luke receives does not simply represent a return of his cost basis. Instead, Luke must allocate his adjusted basis in the property ($500,000) between the sale and gift portions of the transaction based upon their relative proportions to the property's fair market value.[18] Since the "bargain" element ($1,500,000/$2,000,000) is 75% of the FMV of the property, $375,000 (75% of the property's $500,000 adjusted basis) is allocated to the gift portion of the transaction.

The remaining 25% of the property's adjusted basis ($125,000) is allocated to the sales portion of the transaction. This means that with respect to the $500,000 sale portion, Luke has a return of basis of $125,000 and a taxable gain of $375,000. Assuming a 15% capital gains tax rate, Luke will be required to pay a capital gains tax of $56,250 (15% of $375,000).

Would Luke be better off selling the property to the university at the $500,000 bargain sales price, or selling the property outright for its FMV and then making a cash contribution to charity in the amount of the gain? Assuming an income tax bracket rounded up to 40%, sufficient income to deduct the full amount in one year, and no state tax considerations, the results would be as shown in Figure 10.1.

As the example shows, Luke saves $168,750 in capital gains taxes through the use of a bargain sale rather than an outright sale coupled with a gift. The bargain sale technique could be made more advantageous to Luke by structuring payments to be made to him over time. Installment payments would provide him with an annual income stream for a number of years, and would permit him to report the taxable capital gain as the receipt of payments occurs. A portion of each periodic payment would represent a long-term capital gain. Otherwise Luke must report the entire capital gain in the year of sale.[19]

A bargain sale is sometimes the unintended result of a gift of property subject to a debt encumbrance.[20] For a donor who expected to be able to deduct the full fair market value of the gift, the bargain sale results can be tantamount to a harsh penalty. The donor is

Figure 10.1

	Bargain Sale	Outright Sale
Sale Proceeds	$500,000	$2,000,000
Adjusted Basis	(125,000)	(500,000)
Recognized Gain	375,000	1,500,000
Capital Gains Tax Rate	15%	15%
Capital Gains Tax	$ 56,250	$ 225,000
Amount of Charitable Contribution	$1,500,000	$1,500,000
Tax Benefit of Charitable Deduction at 40%	$600,000	$600,000
Sale Proceeds Retained	500,000	500,000
Capital Gains Tax at 15%	(56,250)	(225,000)
Net Cash Flow Increase After Taxes	$1,043,750	$ 875,000

essentially treated as though he received partial consideration for the property, in the amount of the debt encumbrance.

Example: Assume the same facts as in the example above, except that Luke Oliver has an outstanding mortgage of $200,000 on a parcel of land, and he makes an outright gift of the land rather than entering into a bargain sale. Since the debt encumbrance represents 10% of the FMV of the property, 10% of the adjusted basis of the property ($50,000) is allocated to the deemed sales portion. Is Luke better off transferring the property subject to the mortgage, or paying the mortgage off first, then making the transfer? Assuming that in either event Luke will pay the $200,000 mortgage himself, the results of the two alternatives compare as shown in Figure 10.2.

As the example shows, Luke saves $102,500 in tax costs by paying the $200,000 mortgage off prior to giving the land away rather than making a gift that involves debt encumbered property. The additional tax cost in this example includes a $22,500 capital gains tax plus a reduction in the tax benefit of the taxpayer's charitable tax deduction in the amount of $80,000. Even if the charitable organization agrees to assume the debt and pays it off, the additional $102,500 tax cost still burdens and reduces the economic benefits of this transaction. Obviously, an "unin-

tentional" bargain sale transaction may produce significant tax ramifications and diminish the total effectiveness of a charitable contribution.

A donor should carefully consider the economic, social, and tax implications of any bargain sale transaction. As these examples indicate, a bargain sale transaction may produce unintended tax consequences.

WHAT ARE THE TAX IMPLICATIONS?

1. The donor in a bargain sale is required to recognize taxable income on the sales portion of the transaction. To calculate this taxable income, the donor must allocate his adjusted basis between the portion sold and the portion of the property contributed to charity. This basis allocation is determined by the relative proportions of the sale portion and the gift portion.[21]

2. In order to claim a deduction for the charitable gift portion of the transaction, the donor must determine that a deductible contribution was made and be able to document the value of it by meeting the appraisal requirements described above. Of course any ultimate deduction is also subject to the income percentage limits set forth in the Internal Revenue Code.[22]

3. The property that is the subject to the bargain sale is removed from the donor's estate once an irrevocable

Figure 10.2

	Bargain Sale	Mortgage Payoff
Deemed Sale Proceeds	$200,000	
Adjusted Basis	(50,000)	
Recognized Gain	150,000	
Capital Gains Tax Rate	15%	
Capital Gains Tax	$ 22,500	
Amount of Charitable Contribution	$1,800,000	$2,000,000
Tax Benefit of Charitable Deduction at 40%	$ 720,000	$ 800,000
Capital Gains Tax at 15%	(22,500)	0
Mortgage Payment	(200,000)	(200,000)
Net Cash Flow Increase After Taxes	$ 497,500	$ 600,000

transfer is made; however, any amounts remaining payable to the donor under the sale portion of the transaction will remain includable for federal estate tax purposes.

WHERE CAN I FIND OUT MORE ABOUT IT?

1. Toce, Joseph, Abbin, Byrle, Vorsatz, Mark, and Page, William, *Tax Economics of Charitable Giving 2006-2007* (Warren Gorham & Lamont, 2006).

2. Osteen, Carolyn M., et al., *The Harvard Manual on Tax Aspects of Charitable Giving*, 8th edition (Boston, MA: 1999).

QUESTIONS AND ANSWERS

Question – An attorney, O.J. Bailey, seeks to sell a piece of property with a FMV of $100,000 and an adjusted basis of $50,000 to Temple University for $75,000. In addition, Mr. Bailey agrees to perform all legal services in connection with the transfer of this property the university at no charge. Is Mr. Bailey permitted a charitable deduction for the value of his services in connection with transaction?

Answer – No deduction is allowable for a taxpayer's performance of services for, or on behalf of, a charitable organization.[23]

Question – What types of property should (or should not) be the subject of a bargain sale?

Answer – Charitable contributions of "ordinary income" property are reduced by the amount of ordinary income a sale of such property at its fair market value would generate.[24] Because of these negative tax ramifications, an intentionally structured bargain sale transaction does not usually include ordinary income property.

Ordinary income property generally includes the following types of property:

1. Property held by the donor primarily for sale to customers in the ordinary course of a trade or business (inventory);

2. A work of art created by the donor;

3. A manuscript prepared by the donor;

4. Letters and memoranda prepared by or for the donor; and

5. All capital assets held by the donor for one year or less.[25]

The best type of property to use in an intentional bargain sale is highly appreciated capital gain property, which the donor has held for more than one year.

Question – What are the tax consequences if a charitable organization agrees to assume or pay a debt when a bargain sale transaction includes a debt-encumbered piece of property?

Answer – Even if the charitable organization agrees to assume or pay a debt, the amount of the indebtedness is still treated as partial consideration payable to the donor. The donor is in the same tax position regardless of whether the charitable organization assumes the liability and pays off the debt. This treatment is the same whether the property is subject to recourse debt or nonrecourse debt, and whether the contribution is real property subject to a mortgage[26] or a pledge of personal property.[27]

Question – What are the tax ramifications of making a bargain sale transaction of debt-encumbered property to a charitable remainder trust (CRT)?

Answer – Donors should avoid transferring mortgaged property to a CRT. The IRS has determined that such transactions disqualify a charitable remainder unitrust (CRUT) because the trust income may be used to discharge an obligation of the owner.[28] Since the IRS considers the donor to be the owner of such a trust, it will not qualify under the CRT rules. (See Chapters 15 and 16 for details on CRTs.)

Question – Does the transfer of a debt-encumbered life insurance contract to a charitable organization result in a bargain sale transaction? What are the tax ramifications to the donor and charitable organization in such a transaction?

Answer – Donors should not transfer any insurance policy subject to an outstanding loan to a charitable organization. First, the transaction will be considered a bargain sale and trigger gain taxed at ordinary income rates. Second, even if a transfer of a life insurance policy subject to a loan were deductible (which it is not), the donor's deduction would be limited to his cost basis. But the issue is moot, because under the charitable split dollar rules (see the Questions and Answers in Chapter 11), such a transfer would cost the donor not only the present deduction, but a deduction for all future premiums as well.

CHAPTER ENDNOTES

1. See IRC Sec. 170(c).
2. Treas. Reg. §1.170A-4(c)(2)(ii).
3. See IRC Sec. 1011(b).
4. Treas. Reg. §1.1011-2(a)(3).
5. IRS Publication 78.
6. Treas. Reg. §1.170A-4(c)(2)(ii).
7. Treas. Reg. §1.170A-1(g).
8. Treas. Reg. §1.1011-2(a)(3).
9. IRC Secs. 170(f)(11)(C), 170(f)(11)(E); Treas. Reg. §1.170A-13(c).
10. IRC Sec. 170(f)(11)(E). See also Notice 2006-96, 2006-46 IRB 902.
11. Treas. Reg. §1.170A-13(c)(4)(i)(A).
12. IRC Sec. 170(f)(11)(E). See also Notice 2006-96, 2006-46 IRB 902.
13. Treas. Reg. §1.170A-13(c)(5)(i)(B).
14. IRC Sec. 6695A(a).
15. Treas. Reg. §1.170A-13(c)(5)(iv)(A).
16. Treas. Reg. §1.170A-13(c)(5)(iv)(B).
17. Treas. Reg. §1.170A-13(c)(5)(iv)(C).
18. IRC Sec. 1011(b) and Treas. Regs. §§1.1011-2(b), Ex. 1, and 1.1011-2(c).
19. Treas. Regs. §§1.1011-2(b), Ex. 2, 1.1011-2(c).
20. Treas. Reg. §1.1011-2(a)(3).
21. IRC Secs. 170(e)(2) and 1011(b), Treas. Reg. §1.170A-4(c)(2)(i).
22. See IRC Sec. 170(b)(1). These limitations are explained in Chapter 3.
23. Treas. Reg. §1.170A-1(g); *Grant v. Comm.*, 84 TC 809 (1985), *affirmed in unpublished opinion,* 800 F.2d 260 (4th Cir. 1986).
24. IRC Sec. 170(e)(1)(A).
25. Treas. Reg. §1.170A-4(b)(1).
26. See *Tidler v. Comm.*, TC Memo 1987-268 (taxpayer transferred mortgage property to charity, the mortgage liability was treated as an amount realized, even though the property had a special warranted deed whereby the taxpayer remained personally responsible for the debt).
27. Rev. Rul. 70-626, 1970-2 CB 158. Ruling involved a taxpayer who pledged stock as collateral for a loan. The taxpayer later donated the stock to charity, subject to the pledge. Although the taxpayer remained personally liable to repay the loan, the charity agreed to pay the debt. At the time of the contribution, the indebtedness was less than the FMV of the property and greater than its adjusted basis. Service ruled the pledge of stock to secure indebtedness should receive the same treatment as a mortgage on real property. The transfer created a bargain sale to the charity.
28. See Let. Rul. 9015049.

BELOW-MARKET INTEREST LOANS

CHAPTER 11

WHAT IS IT?

A below-market loan is the extension of credit either interest free, or with a stated interest rate less than the current market rates. Most below-market loans are between a corporation and one of its employees. Below-market loans may also include the lending of money between a parent and child or some other family member. Most importantly in the context of philanthropy, below-market loans may even occur between individuals and charitable organizations.

The Internal Revenue Code lists six types of below-market loans that are subject to its statutory rules. Most below-market loans fall into one of these categories, but if a loan does not, it will not be treated as a below-market loan. The categories are:

1. Gift loans,

2. Compensation-related loans,

3. Corporation-shareholder loans,

4. Tax avoidance loans,

5. Loans that have a "significant tax effect," and

6. Loans to continuing care facilities.[1]

Within all of these categories, a below-market loan is either a term loan or a demand loan. From a philanthropic standpoint, the most important of these techniques is the gift loan; however, the characteristics of each of the other types of loans are explained briefly below.

WHEN IS THE USE OF SUCH A DEVICE INDICATED?

1. When an individual wants to help a charitable organization overcome a temporary cash flow problem, benefit from the time value of money, or take advantage of a financial opportunity.

2. When a donor who has "maxed out" his deductible contributions for the year wishes to provide additional financial assistance to a charitable organization.

ADVANTAGES

1. A below-market loan can permit a donor to help a charitable organization with immediate or significant cash-flow needs, without the donor having to make a large outright gift.

2. A donor who has reached (or is near reaching) the income percentage limits on deductible contributions for a year (see Chapter 3) can make a much larger amount available to the charity with a below-market loan than could be deducted as an outright gift.

DISADVANTAGES

1. The tax implications of below-market loans may prove quite costly, since interest income is imputed to the lender and interest expense is imputed to the borrower. Even when a donor makes a below-market loan to a charitable organization, he may or may not receive a full offsetting charitable deduction. Therefore, these loans are typically motivated more by economic and personal objectives than by the tax implications.

2. Depending on the type of below-market loan (see below), favorable tax treatment may require the existence of a special relationship and might not apply to the more common arm's length transaction. Therefore, the availability of below-market loan techniques may be rather limited.

3. The IRS has attempted to apply the limitations on below-market loans in a variety of ways that were detrimental to taxpayers, as explained in the questions and answers at the end of this chapter. One notable example was the Service's treatment of certain split dollar insurance contracts as below-market loans.[2]

WHAT ARE THE REQUIREMENTS?

A below market loan is defined in the Internal Revenue Code as either a demand loan or a term loan, depending on the repayment terms. A loan under any of the six categories listed above (and described in more detail at "How is it Done") can be either a demand loan or a term loan.

1. *Demand loans.* A demand loan is a loan that is payable in full at any time upon the demand of the lender, or a loan with an indefinite maturity. Furthermore, a demand loan includes loans whereby the borrower cannot transfer the benefits of the interest arrangement and such benefits remain conditioned upon future performance of services by the individual.[3]

   The borrower in the case of a demand loan must compute and report an amount of forgone interest. (See "How is it done" for details.) The forgone interest represents the difference between the appropriate AFR and stated rate of interest on the below-market loan. A gift loan that is a term loan also receives treatment as a demand loan for income tax purposes.[4]

2. *Term loan.* A term loan is any loan that is not a demand loan.[5] In the case of term loans, taxpayers must compute the excess of the amount loaned over the present value of all payments due under the loan.[6]

HOW IT IS DONE?

Gift Loans

A gift loan is a loan for which failure to charge interest at the applicable federal rate is in the nature of a gift.[7] This can occur regardless of whether the lender or borrower is a natural person. Gift loans may be either direct or indirect; for instance, a direct gift loan occurs when a parent decides to lend a child a sum of money with no interest or a below-market rate of interest. An indirect gift loan can occur if a parent makes an interest-free or below-market loan to a corporation or a partnership in which the parent's child is a shareholder or partner.[8]

Example: Bobbie Whiteburn wants to enable the local YMCA to build a new gymnasium. Bobbie loans the local organization $2,500,000 and receives a promissory note with terms that include no interest and an indefinite time for repayment. This transaction occurs on July 1 of the current year. The entire loan remains outstanding on December 31 of Year 1. Assume that the annual AFR is 6%. Since the transaction amount exceeds the $250,000 limit, the below-market loan exception for gift loans to charitable organizations does not apply.

Furthermore, this gift loan receives treatment under the below-market loan rules as a demand loan. In such cases, the individual taxpayer will be deemed to have received interest income for the amount of forgone interest. Since the loan in this example is $2,500,000, the Mr. Whiteburn needs to use the exact method of interest calculation.[9] Because this example includes a full semiannual period, the below-market loan rules will deem the borrower as having made a $75,000 ($2,500,000 times .06/2) interest payment to the lender on the last day of the first year.

Consequently, Mr. Whiteburn will need to report this deemed interest income as an item on Schedule B of his personal tax return for each year. Mr. Whiteburn will also be able to report the deemed interest amount (subject to any income percentage limitations) as a charitable deduction on Schedule A of his personal tax return for each year. The lender will need to compute this forgone interest for each year and until the day when the balance of the gift loan drops below $250,000.

Interest Calculations for Gift Loans

The demand loan provisions require taxpayers to compute an amount of forgone interest on the gift loan each year the loan balance exceeds $250,000.[10] Computation of the forgone interest requires the use of either the exact method[11] or the approximate method[12] of interest calculation. The use of the exact method of interest computation assumes a daily compounding of interest.[13] The approximate method uses a computation of simple interest within any compounding period.[14] The below-market loan rules limit the use of the approximate method to interest computations on loans under $250,000.[15]

In the event of a short year, the computation of forgone interest for demand loans requires that the year be broken down into two semiannual compounding periods.[16] Assuming the short-term AFR at 6%, the semiannual compounding of interest for a full semiannual period is calculated by multiplying the loan balance at the beginning of the period by 3% (.06/2). In addition, the below-market loan rules will deem the lender to have made periodic gifts of the deemed interest to the charitable organization.[17] The net tax effect to the lender also depends on whether a charitable deduction arises from these deemed payments.[18]

The lender must compute and report each subsequent year's forgone interest annually based upon the appropriate (short-term, mid-term, or long-term) AFR for the year.

Compensation-Related Loans

A below-market loan is considered compensation-related if it is made in connection with the performance of one of the following types of services:

1. Between an employer and employee;[19]

2. Between an independent contractor and a person for whom such independent contractor provides services;[20] or

3. Between a partnership and a partner if the loan is made in consideration for services performed by the partner acting other than in his capacity as member of the partnership.[21]

In the case of a compensation-related loan, the Internal Revenue Code deems the forgone interest amount as having been transferred by the lender to the borrower as taxable compensation.

Corporation-Shareholder Loans

A corporation-shareholder loan is a below-market loan between a corporation and any shareholder of the corporation.[22] As in the case of compensation-related loans, a transfer of income is deemed made by the corporation (the lender) to the shareholder (the borrower), which is taxable as a dividend and a deemed retransfer of the same amount (the imputed interest) back to the corporation.

Tax Avoidance Loans

A loan will be treated as a below-market loan if one of the principal purposes of the interest arrangement is to avoid federal tax.[23] The tax avoidance may be with respect to either party to the transaction. The proposed regulations view a loan as having tax avoidance as a principal purpose where a principal factor of the structure of the transaction is to reduce the tax liability of either or both parties (rather than to make a below-market interest rate loan and a payment by the lender to the borrower).[24]

Significant Tax Effect Loans

Significant tax effect loans include any loan in which the interest arrangement has a significant effect on the federal tax liability of the lender or borrower.[25] The proposed regulations contain a reserved section for future provisions on significant tax effect loans.[26] The temporary regulations list four factors that might receive consideration as to whether a below-market loan has a significant tax effect. These four factors include:

1. Whether items of income and deduction that are generated by the loan offset each other;[27]

2. The amount of such items;[28]

3. The cost to the taxpayer of complying with IRC Section 7872 if it applies;[29] and

4. The non-tax reasons to structure the loan as a below-market loan rather than a market interest rate loan and payment by the lender to the borrower.[30]

Loans to Qualified Continuing Care Facilities

Below-market loans may also include any loan (including refundable and partially refundable deposits characterized as loans) to any qualified continuing care facility pursuant to a continuing care contract.[31] The below-market loan rules exempt certain loans under some circumstances.[32] For calendar years before 2006, an exemption is provided for any below-market loan made by a lender to a qualified continuing care facility if the lender (or the lender's spouse) attains age 65 before the close of the calendar year.[33] This exemption applies only if the outstanding balance of the loans is less than $90,000, as adjusted for inflation. In 2005, this amount was $158,100.[34]

An additional exemption exists for loans under a written continuing care contract to a qualified continuing care facility entered into after 2005. Those loans are exempt from the below-market rules if the lender (or the lender's spouse) has reached age 62 by the close of the calendar year. The dollar limitation imposed by the pre-2006 rules does not apply for calendar years after 2005; instead, the exception for below-market loans to qualified continuing care facilities applies without regard to the aggregate amount of the outstanding loan.[35]

Exceptions to the Below-Market Loan Rules

There are several exceptions to the rules for below-market loans. For philanthropic purposes, the most important exception is the exemption from the below-market loan rules for gift loans of $250,000 or less. Regulations provide that gift loans of $250,000 or less made to a charitable organization are exempt from the below-market loan rules.[36] This exemption applies on a *per charitable organization* basis; thus, a wealthy donor can make no-interest or below-market interest loans up to $250,000 to as many charitable organizations as he or she may like. The Service treats effectively controlled charitable organizations as one organization for purposes of this exemption.[37] A single loan with a balance in excess of $250,000 will completely lose its exemption.

A de minimis exception for loans of $10,000 or less applies to gift loans between individuals, compensation-related loans, and corporation-shareholder loans.[38] Furthermore, for gift loans between individuals, the Internal Revenue Code limits the lender's imputed interest income to the borrower's net investment income.[39] (This exception is not available for any day in which the aggregate balance of such loans exceeds $100,000.[40] The exception also is not available if one of the purposes of the loan is tax avoidance.[41])

WHAT ARE THE TAX IMPLICATIONS?

1. The Internal Revenue Code treats a below-market loan as, in effect, two transactions: (1) an arm's-length loan requiring payment of interest ("imputed interest") at the applicable federal rate; and (2) a transfer of funds by the lender to the borrower ("imputed transfer").[42] The treatment of the imputed interest in the hands of the lender and the deduction (if any) to the borrower depends on the nature of the loan and the parties to it, as described above. (See the Questions and Answers, at the end of this chapter, regarding whether a charitable deduction is available to the lender.)

2. In the case of a compensation-related loan, the amount of forgone interest is treated as compensation to the borrower.[43] The regulations specify that a loan from a qualified pension, a profit sharing plan, or a stock bonus plan, to a participant of the plan will not be treated, either directly or indirectly, as a compensation-related loan.[44]

3. Regardless of whether a term has been specified, all gift loans are treated as demand loans for income tax purposes.[45] This means that the lender is treated as having transferred to the borrower and the borrower is deemed to have transferred to the lender an amount equal to the forgone interest.[46] This forgone interest amount is included in the gross income of the lender. However, gift loans of $250,000 or less made to a charitable organization are exempt from the below-market loan rules.[47]

WHAT ARE THE ALTERNATIVES?

1. A bargain sale (see Chapter 10) may provide the opportunity for a donor to make funds or property available to a charitable organization without making an outright gift of the entire amount.

2. A charitable lead trust (see Chapter 14), while somewhat more complex, provides a means for donors to give a partial interest to a charitable organization while retaining a future interest in the property.

WHERE CAN I FIND OUT MORE ABOUT IT?

1. Leimberg, Stephan R., et al., *The Tools & Techniques of Estate Planning*, 14th edition (Cincinnati, OH: The National Underwriter Company, 2006).

2. Toce, Abbin, Pace, & Vorsatz, *Tax Economics of Charitable Giving*, 2006-2007 edition (Warren, Gorham & Lamont, 2006).

QUESTIONS AND ANSWERS

Question - Does an individual receive a charitable deduction for a gift loan to a charitable organization?

Answer – Treasury regulations disallow an income tax charitable deduction for the value of a no-interest or below-market loan to a charitable organization under the "partial interest" rules.[48] (See Chapter 5 for details.) This rule would seem to apply to both principal and interest amounts. However, this rule may not apply to the deemed interest amount. The explanation in the "Blue Book" on the Joint Committee on Taxation indicates Congress intended such payments to receive treatment as a cash contribution and not as a contribution of a partial interest in property. Neither the IRS nor the courts have ruled on this issue.

Question – How does the cumulative amount of forgone interest affect the compounding of interest on a below-market loan that spans a term of years?

Answer – At the beginning of each successive calendar year, the principal balance returns to the original amount, since the rules also deem the accrued interest to be paid on December 31. This process repeats until the borrower repays the loan.

Question – The proposed regulations state that the applicable federal rate is the federal statutory rate in effect for semiannual periods and the alternate federal rates published by the IRS on a monthly basis. What exactly are these rates and are loans still subject to these rules?

Answer – When the proposed regulations were drafted, the IRS determined and announced the applicable federal rate (AFR) twice a year. The AFR became effective for the 6-month period following the announcement. For example, the AFR determined from the data for the 6-month period ending September 30 was the rate effective for the following January 1 to June 30 period, and the rate based from the data for the period ending March 31 was the rate effective for the following July 1 to December 31 period. The proposed regulations refer to this rate as the "federal statutory rate"[49] and the two periods as the first

and second semiannual periods.[50] Subsequently, it became apparent that market rate volatility many times rendered these rates obsolete. Therefore, the IRS no longer determines this 6-month rate. Instead, the IRS determines and announces the AFRs on a monthly basis.

While the former 6-month statutory rate is no longer determined, this rate still remains an integral part of the regulations with respect to the computation of forgone interest. The regulations treat a loan made on January 1 as having sufficient interest for the period ending June 30 if the stated interest is at least equal to the statutory AFR in effect for the semiannual period. Therefore, the alternate rate (now statutory rate) for January and July of each year should replace the former 6-month rate and provide the same safe harbor effect for the below-market loans. It should not be necessary to adjust this rate each month when the alternate rate increases.

Question – May a charitable organization enter into a split dollar arrangement with an employee? If so, may the parties characterize the arrangement as a below-market loan transaction under the final split dollar regulations?

Answer – While no legal authority approves split dollar in the charitable context, a charitable organization may provide reasonable compensation to its employees.[51] So long as employee benefits under a split dollar arrangement constitute (together with all other income and benefits) reasonable compensation, the IRS should not contest the arrangement.[52] In the final split dollar regulations,[53] the IRS permitted parties to a split dollar arrangement to treat the arrangement as a below-market loan under IRC Section 7872 if certain requirements are met. In some cases, particularly with older employees, the parties may prefer to apply below-market loan treatment to a collateral assignment non-equity type split dollar arrangement.[54] This preference may exist because the imputed interest will be lower than the new Table 2001 rates and taxation of the inside build up of cash value under IRC Section 83 can be avoided. Such treatment is not available in the private foundation context, because such a loan, even though compensation-related, constitutes self-dealing between the foundation and the employee.[55] On the other hand, a public charity may make a compensation-related loan to one of its employees. Furthermore, a public charity organization and its employee should be able to choose below-market loan treatment.[56] However,

it may be advisable for the public charity to seek a private letter ruling prior to the inception of such an arrangement.

The Service has issued two favorable private letter rulings dealing with a split dollar arrangement between a charitable organization and an employee.[57] Both of these rulings involved private foundations. The IRS stated in both rulings that such split dollar arrangements would not (1) adversely affect the private foundation's exempt status (i.e., violate the rules against private inurement and private benefit); (2) constitute prohibited self-dealing between the employee and the foundation; or (3) amount to a prohibited taxable expenditure of the foundation's funds. In reaching its conclusion, the IRS noted the general rule that charitable organizations may pay compensation to employees (even if they are insiders or disqualified persons) so long as the total compensation package is reasonable in amount and furthers the charitable organization's exempt purposes.[58] The IRS also viewed compensation in the form of a split dollar arrangement as an acceptable method of employee compensation.

However, each of these two private letter rulings involved endorsement split dollar insurance. The foundation maintained control over both the policy and cash value. The rulings were unclear as to whether the foundation's control over the policy may have been a significant factor for the IRS's favorable position. Therefore, it may be advisable to structure any such arrangement through endorsement split dollar insurance.

CHAPTER ENDNOTES

1.   See IRC Sec. 7872(c)(1).

2.   See Notice 2001-10, 2001-5 CB 459; Notice 2002-8, 2002-4 CB 398; and Treas. Reg. §1.7872-15.

3.   IRC Sec. 7872(f)(5).

4.   IRC Secs. 7872(d)(2), 7872(f)(3).

5.   IRC Sec. 7872(f)(6).

6.   IRC Sec. 7872(b). The taxpayer obtains the present value of the loan by discounting all payments due at the applicable federal rate appropriate to the loan.

7.   For term loans, the AFR is the rate in effect under the original issue discount rules, on the day the loan is made, compounded semiannually. See IRC Sec. 7872(f)(2)(A). For demand loans, the AFR is the short-term AFR in effect for the period for which forgone interest is being calculated, compounded semiannually. See IRC Sec. 7872(f)(2)(B).

8.   See Prop. Treas. Reg. §1.7872-4(g)(1)(ii).

9.   See Prop. Treas. Reg. §1.7872-13(b)(1).

10.   Temp. Treas. Reg. §1.7872-5T(b)(9).

11.   Prop. Treas. Reg. §1.7872-12(c)(1).

12.   Prop. Treas. Reg. §1.7872-12(c)(2).

13.   Prop. Treas. Reg. §1.7872-12(c)(1).

14.   Prop. Treas. Reg. §1.7872-12(c)(2).

15.   Prop. Treas. Reg. §1.7872-13(b)(1)(ii).

16.   See Prop. Treas. Reg. §1.7872-3(b)(3). The periods for semiannual compounding include January 1 to June 30 and July 1 to December 31.

17.   Prop. Treas. Reg. §1.7872-1(a). Although the deemed receipt of interest income and subsequent deemed gift of the interest to the charitable organization use the same amount, it is possible the lender will not have exactly corresponding offsetting amounts for income tax purposes. The charitable deduction is subject to the income percentage limitations explained in Chapter 3.

18.   The explanation by the Joint Committee on Taxation states that Congress intends the deemed payment from the lender to the borrower to receive treatment as a cash distribution and not as a contribution of a partial interest under IRC Section 170(f)(3)(A). See *General Explanation of the Revenue Provisions of the Deficit Reduction Act of 1984 (H.R. 4170, 98th Congress P.L. 98-369)* (JCS-41-84), p. 530 (the DEFRA Blue Book).

19.   Prop. Treas. Reg. §1.7872-4(c)(1)(i).

20.   Prop. Treas. Reg. §1.7872-4(c)(1)(ii).

21.   Prop. Treas. Reg. §1.7872-4(c)(1)(iii). See also IRC Sec. 707(a)(1), which governs transactions between a partnership and a partner. IRC Sec. 707(a)(1) treats certain transactions between a partnership and a partner as though those transactions occur between the partnership and one who is not a partner. Examples of such transactions include loans between a partner and the partnership, sales of property between a partner and the partnership, *performance of services* by the partner for the partnership, and leases between a partner and the partnership.

22.   Prop. Treas. Reg. §1.7872-4(d)(1).

23.   IRC Sec. 7872(c)(1)(D).

24.   Prop. Treas. Reg. §1.7872-4(e).

25.   IRC Sec. 7872(c)(1)(E).

26.   Prop. Treas. Reg. §1.7872-4(f).

27.   Temp. Treas. Reg. §1.7872-5T(c)(3)(i).

28.   Temp. Treas. Reg. §1.7872-5T(c)(3)(ii).

29.   Temp. Treas. Reg. §1.7872-5T(c)(3)(iii).

30.   Temp. Treas. Reg. §1.7872-5T(c)(3)(iv). The Service wants to limit situations in which below-market loans have the potential to convert otherwise nondeductible personal expenses into the equivalent of deductible expenses. Examples of such situations include: (1) loans to a membership organization in lieu of part or the entire fee; (2) loans to colleges and secondary schools in lieu of part or full payment of tuition, room and board, and books that would otherwise be charged; (3) loans to institutions providing meals, lodging, and medical services (i.e., to a continuing care facility); and (4) loans to an employee or independent contractor by an employer in lieu of payment for services. Many of these transactions have a significant potential for distortion of tax liability.

31.   IRC Sec. 7872(c)(1)(F).

32.   IRC Sec. 7872(g).

33. IRC Sec. 7872(g)(1).

34. Rev. Rul. 2004-108, 2004-2 CB 853.

35. IRC Sec. 7872(h)(1), Conf. Rept. No. 109-455 (PL 109-222) p. 209.

36. See Temp. Treas. Reg. §1.7872-5T(b)(9).

37. See Treas. Reg. §1.482-1(a)(1) for the Service's meaning of effectively controlled organizations that shall be seen as one organization for purposes of this limitation.

38. IRC Secs. 7872(c)(2), 7872(c)(3).

39. IRC Sec. 7872(d)(1)(A).

40. IRC Sec. 7872(d)(1)(D).

41. IRC Sec. 7872(d)(1)(B).

42. Prop. Treas. Reg. §1.7872-1(a).

43. Prop. Treas. Reg. §1.7872-4(c)(1).

44. Prop. Treas. Reg. §1.7872-4(c)(1).

45. IRC Secs. 7872(d)(2), 7872(f)(3). For gift tax purposes, the term loan provisions of IRC Sec. 7872 continue to apply.

46. IRC Sec. 7872(a)(1).

47. See Temp. Treas. Reg. §1.7872-5T(b)(9).

48. IRC Sec. 170(f)(3)(A) and Treas. Reg. §1.170A-7(a). No deduction is permitted when a donor gives less than his or her entire interest in property.

49. Prop. Treas. Reg. §1.7872-3(b)(2)(ii).

50. Prop. Treas. Reg. §1.7872-3(b)(3)(i).

51. See, generally, Rev. Rul. 73-126, 1973-1 CB 220.

52. The anti-charitable split dollar legislation, which was passed in 1999 and codified at IRC Sec. 170(f)(10), raises the concern of whether compensation-related split dollar is still viable in the charitable context. In Let. Rul. 200020060, the IRS indirectly addressed the issue in light of Notice 99-36, 1999-1 CB 1284, which warned against abusive charitable split dollar transactions. The IRS held that based upon the taxpayer's representations, Notice 99-36 was inapplicable. Specifically, the IRS noted that the split dollar arrangement was a true contributory plan, with the employee paying his share of the premium directly to the insurance company. Under no circumstances would the employee's share ever be paid to or through the charitable organization. In light of the IRS's analysis, IRC Sec. 170(f)(10) should be inapplicable to a compensation-related split dollar arrangement so long as the employee is required to pay his or her share of the premium directly to the insurance company.

53. Treas. Reg. §§1.61-22; 1.7872-15.

54. There are no published rulings in which the IRS approves the use of a collateral assignment split dollar arrangement between a charitable organization and an employee. If a charitable organization and an employee desire to use collateral assignment split dollar, parties should likely seek a private letter ruling.

55. See Let. Rul. 9530032. This assumes the employee is a disqualified person. This likely will be the case because split dollar arrangements typically involve key people, such as officers and directors who are disqualified persons for purposes of the self-dealing rules of the Code. See IRC Sec. 4946.

56. Let. Rul. 9530032. The IRS ruled the loan arrangement would not "jeopardize" the exempt status of the organization. The IRS based this ruling on circumstances such as (1) the foundation became a public charity (a public charity is not subject to the self-dealing rules of the Internal Revenue Code), and (2) the taxpayer represented the below-market loan was part of a reasonable compensation package for its key employees.

57. See Let. Ruls. 200020060, 9539016.

58. Reasonable compensation issues are governed by the provisions of IRC Sec. 162(a).

CHARITABLE GIFT ANNUITIES

CHAPTER 12

WHAT IS IT?

A charitable gift annuity is a contract between a donor and a qualified charity. The donor transfers cash or appreciated property to the charity, and in return the charity makes an unsecured promise to pay an annuity to the donor or another designated annuitant. The annuity can be for one life or for two lives as a joint and survivor annuity. A gift annuity can also be thought of as the purchase of an annuity contract from a charity in combination with an immediate gift of a future interest to that charity.

The most common approach is for the donor to be the annuitant for life and for the first payment from the charity to be made within a year after the annuity agreement is signed. Payments under the annuity can be monthly, quarterly, semi-annually, or annually. There are variations of a charitable gift annuity available, including the following:

- The donor is the first joint-life annuitant and the donor's spouse is the second.

- The source of funds can be from the donor alone or jointly from a husband and wife as joint donors.

- The annuitant can be a person other than the donor or the donor's spouse.

- The annuity payments can begin immediately (within one year of the transfer establishing the annuity), or the payments can be deferred for a number of years. Some charities allow the donor to choose when payments will begin (the decision on when payments begin may itself be deferred until the annuitant wants payments to begin).

Each of these variations presents slightly different tax consequences which will be reviewed below.

Deferring the start of the annuity payments will impact directly on the actuarial determination of the donor's tax deduction. Likewise, naming more than one annuitant, such as a spouse, another family member, or a friend, will also have an effect on the value of the donor's income tax deduction.

WHEN IS THE USE OF SUCH A DEVICE INDICATED?

1. The charitable gift annuity typically works best with smaller contributions, or where the donor is interested in increasing the cash flow from the donated property. For example, while a donor might give appreciated property to purchase a charitable gift annuity to benefit the charity, he may also want to receive an income stream that the appreciated property is not currently providing.

2. A charitable gift annuity can also be an effective way to provide a benefit to another individual. However, when a person other than the donor's spouse is named as annuitant, the donor is making a gift to that person of the present value of the annuitant's interest in the charitable gift annuity. The IRS ruled favorably on the use of a deferred charitable gift annuity as a means of funding the education of a child/grandchild (the annuitant) that included an option for the annuitant to sell or assign the interest in the annuity to the university in exchange for a lump sum payment or installment payments over several years.[1] It is important to remember that the annuitant in a situation like this is not required to use the annuity payments for college expenses.

ADVANTAGES

1. The charitable gift annuity is convenient, simple, easy to understand and explain, and a highly cost-

effective charitable planning device. Many charitable organizations have reduced the process to a one or two page annuity contract with a few pages of supporting information, including an illustration of the benefit to the donor and the computation of the anticipated tax consequences.

2. In most cases little or no legal or accounting work is involved at the time of implementation. The payments from the charity to the donor (or the designated annuitant, if not the donor), will be reported for tax purposes on a Form 1099R.

3. For a number of reasons, the donor-annuitant's after-tax cash flow typically increases (in some cases significantly). First, in most cases the donated asset produced a small amount of (or no) income prior to the transfer to charity. Second, unlike dividends, which are entirely ordinary income, part of each annuity payment is considered a return of capital and, if appreciated property is given to the charity, part of each payment receives favorable capital gain treatment. Finally, in most cases the annuity rate far exceeds the dividends, interest, or rent that is otherwise payable due to the risk factor that is built into the size of the annuity payment because the charity takes the principal at the annuitant's death.

DISADVANTAGES

1. The donor is "at risk" economically to some extent because the promise of the charity to pay the annuity is a general claim against the charity's assets and cannot be collateralized. This is to be distinguished from the charitable remainder trust, where the assets are held in a separate trust, outside the reach of the creditors of the charitable remainder beneficiaries or the charity itself.

2. Typically, it is not possible to establish a single charitable gift annuity for the benefit of more than one charity. The reason is that the charity issuing the annuity will not generally agree to distribute part of the remainder to another charity. This is sometimes a characteristic that weighs in favor of a charitable remainder trust.

HOW IS IT DONE?

A donor wishes to give money or property to a charity, but may also be interested in receiving a stream of income. The donor may want the stream of income for a number of reasons. One reason may be so that the gift will not cause a financial hardship if the donor lives longer than expected. The donor may also want to receive income from a highly appreciated, but non-income producing, asset and is willing to donate a portion of the value of the asset (such as publicly-traded stock) to a charity.

In some ways, a charitable gift annuity is like a commercial annuity. The donor gives money or property to a charity, and the charity agrees to provide an income stream to the donor for the donor's lifetime. The payout to the donor will be less than would be paid out of a commercial annuity, because part of the amount paid to the charity is designed to be retained by the charity as a charitable donation.

To determine the amount to pay out to the donor, most charities use the rates suggested by the American Council on Gift Annuities (ACGA). Periodically, the ACGA publishes a table of annuity rates for single-life and two-life charitable gift annuity contracts. (See Appendix B for the ACGA's current recommended charitable gift annuity rates.) These tables assume that approximately 50% of the value of the donor's initial gift will be left at the end of the annuitant's life expectancy. Utilization of the uniform rates is intended to ensure that there will be a benefit to the charity at the end of the annuitant's life (except for the extremely long-lived annuitant) and to limit competition among charities based on offered rates.

The donor will receive an income tax deduction equal to the difference between the fair market value of the donated property and the present value of the annuity. If the donor donates cash, a portion of each annuity payment will represent a return of principal, and a portion will represent ordinary income to the annuitant. If the donor gives the charity appreciated property, a portion of the payment representing a return of principal will be treated as a capital gain, so that the capital gain is spread over the life expectancy of the annuitant.

Example: Donald, age 70, wants to provide a delayed contribution to his alma mater, ABC University. He owns 1,000 shares of publicly-traded common stock valued at $50 per share, paying an annual dividend of 75 cents per share (1.5% of the current value). His basis in the stock is $10 per share. He transfers the stock to ABC in return for an annuity of 6.5% per year, which is the suggested rate from the ACGA for his age. This results in an annual payment from ABC to Donald of $3,250 ($50,000 x .065).

Assuming a Section 7520 interest rate of 6.0%, the present value of the annuity is $27,621 (see Appendix K for valuation tables and examples of single life annuity calculations), so the gift to charity is $22,379 ($50,000 - $27,621). Donald's life expectancy is another 15.5 years (see Appendix B), so he can expect to receive a total of $50,375 from the annuity ($3,250 x 15.5).

Each payment will be broken down into three different parts for income tax purposes. Part will be taxed as a capital gain, part as ordinary income, and the rest will be a non-taxable return of principal.

Of the $3,250 that Donald receives each year, $1,469 will be ordinary income. Of the remaining $1,781, $1,426 will be treated as a capital gain each year, and the remaining $355 will be a return of principal, which will not be taxed. After basis ($5,524) and gain ($22,097) allocated to the annuity are recovered in approximately the 16th payment, all amounts are treated as ordinary income.

Age: 70	Annual Payments
Gift Annuity Rate: 6.5%	Sec. 7520 Rate: 6.0%
Fair Market Value: $50,000	Adjusted Basis: $10,000
Annuity Payment:	$50,000 x 6.5% = $3,250
Annuity Factor:	8.4988
Annuity Adj. Factor:	1.0000
Present Value of	
Annuity:	$3,250 x 8.4988 x 1.0000 = $27,621
Charitable Gift:	$50,000 - $27,621 = $22,379
Table V Expected Return Multiple	
w/ Frequency Adjustment:	15.5
Allocated Basis:	$10,000 x ($27,621 ÷ $50,000) = $5,524
Allocated Gain:	$27,621 - $5,524 = $22,097
Expected Return:	$3,250 x (15.5 x 1) = $50,375
Exclusion Ratio:	$27,621 ÷ $50,375 = 54.8%
Exclusion (Basis and Gain):	$3,250 x 54.8% = $1,781
Ordinary Income Portion:	$3,250 - $1,781 = $1,469
Gain Portion:	22,097 ÷ (15.5 x 1) = $1,426
Basis Portion:	$3,250 - ($1,469 + $1,426) = $355

WHAT ARE THE TAX IMPLICATIONS?

Income Tax Treatment to the Donor and Annuitant

Generally, for income tax purposes each payment will be divided into an ordinary income portion, a capital gain portion (if appreciated property is donated), and a portion that is not taxed, as it represents a return of capital.[2] The donor is allowed to receive–income tax free–his investment in the contract over the expected term of the annuity. After the annuitant has recovered the investment in the contract (which will generally occur if the annuitant lives past his life expectancy), succeeding payments are treated entirely as ordinary income.[3] If the donor is the annuitant or the joint donors are spouses and the annuitants, this general rule applies. However, if the annuitant and donor are different persons, the general rule does not apply and the donor must report any capital gain immediately.[4] In either case, the annuitant's investment in the contract will generally be the present value of the annuity.[5]

If the annuity payments are deferred beyond one year, the general rules also apply, but the present value will be different because of the deferred starting date. While the calculation of the charitable deduction is essentially the same – based on the difference between the fair market value of the property transferred to the charity and the present value of the annuity – the present value of the deferred annuity would be less and, thus, the charitable deduction would be greater.

If there is no certain annuity starting date (e.g., the annuity allows the annuitant to elect that payments will begin at any time after reaching a specified age (such as 65)), the donor's deduction will probably be based on the maximum possible present value of the annuity (and therefore the minimum charitable deduction). In a private letter ruling, the charity promised the donor a fixed annuity for as long as he lived. The donor, 50 at the time the contract was signed, retained the right to have payments start at any time after he reached age 55. At that point, the actual annual payment was based on his age at the annuity starting date as applied to tables in effect when the annuity contract was signed. The charity provided the donor with an estimated value of the charitable contribution at an amount reflecting the maximum possible present value of the annuity, even though the donor could decide to defer the starting date of the annuity, which could reduce the non-charitable value of the contract.[6]

If the donor dies prior to reaching his life expectancy, the donor's estate is permitted an income tax deduction on the decedent's final income tax return in the amount of the unrecovered investment in the contract. If a donor other than an annuitant dies, the deduction is reportable by the annuitant on the final income tax return.[7]

Gift Tax Issues

When the donor and the annuitant are the same, there is only a gift of the remainder to charity. Although this is a gift and should be reported on a gift tax return showing the amount of the gift, the donor is allowed a corresponding gift tax charitable deduction.[8] This rule will also apply when a husband and wife establish a joint life annuity from jointly owned assets.

When the donor and spouse are the annuitants, there is a gift attributable to the transfer to the spouse of the joint-life annuity interest. Again, a gift tax return is technically required. But there would be a corresponding and offsetting gift tax marital deduction available.[9]

When the donor is not the annuitant, the donor has made a gift of the actuarial value of the annuitant's interest. If the annuitant begins receiving annuity payments under an immediate annuity, the interest of the annuitant will qualify for the $12,000 (as indexed for 2007) annual exclusion for gift tax purposes.

When the donor is a joint annuitant with someone other than a spouse, the donor has made a gift of the actuarial value of the other annuitant's interest. If the donor and the other joint annuitant share immediately in the annuity payments, the interest of the other annuitant will qualify for the $12,000 (as indexed for 2007) annual exclusion for gift tax purposes. If the interests are in succession, the non-donor's annuity interest would be a completed gift not qualifying for the annual exclusion. However, if the donor retained the right to revoke the interest of the other annuitant, the gift would not be complete and therefore not reportable until complete.

When the annuity payments are deferred to a later time and someone other than the donor is an annuitant, the gift to the annuitant will not be eligible for the gift tax annual exclusion. A currently taxable gift can be avoided by having the donor retain the right to revoke the annuitant's interest.

Estate Tax Issues

When the donor-annuitant dies, there is nothing reportable because the interest has terminated. When the donor-annuitant dies and is survived by a non-contributing joint annuitant, the value of the annuity will be includable in the donor's estate. If the non-contributing joint annuitant is a spouse, the value of the spouse's interest will qualify for the estate tax marital deduction.

Obviously, the actuarial determination of the surviving joint annuitant can be complicated. See Appendix K for valuation tables and examples of calculating a single life annuity. Most of the software listed in Appendix H can assist in the calculation of these values.

WHERE CAN I FIND OUT MORE ABOUT IT?

Most charities offer charitable gift annuities as one of their planned giving opportunities. A pre-printed brochure will likely be available for the asking. Many of the web sites listed in Appendix L offer calculators to help a donor in the planning process. For the professional charitable planner, CPA, or attorney, most of the software listed in Appendix H will perform the pertinent calculations. The National Committee on Planned Giving web site (www.ncpg.org) also contains a significant amount of information.

The American Council on Gift Annuities, 233 McCrea Street, Suite 400, Indianapolis, IN 46225, Phone: (317) 269-6271, www.acga-web.org. The information on this web site includes the current rate tables and other related information.

QUESTIONS AND ANSWERS

Question – Can I get a better annuity rate by "shopping" with different charities?

Answer – Perhaps. The purpose of the uniform rates is to avoid competition among charities, based on an assumption that most donors want to benefit a particular charity and are not necessarily looking for the "best" rate of return. However, not all charities limit themselves to the uniform rates and many offer rates that are higher (and a few offer rates that are lower). Remember that a higher annuity rate means a lower charitable income tax deduction, and if the annuitant is not the donor or the donor's spouse, the value of the taxable gift to the annuitant will be larger.

Question – What happens if the charity goes out of business or bankrupt?

Answer – Because the annuitant's claim is unsecured (there is no specific property guaranteeing the obligation of the charity to pay the annuity), the annuitant will be among the general creditors of the charity. This means that after all of the preferred and secured creditors are paid, the annuitant will share with other creditors in seeking satisfaction of his claim. In a typical bankruptcy situation, unsecured creditors may receive only 10% of the amounts they are owed.

Question – What happens if the annuitant dies before his normal life expectancy has elapsed?

Answer – There is an additional income tax deduction available to the donor-annuitant or the non-donor annuitant (if the annuity is for the life of someone other than the donor) for the unrecovered investment in the contract that will pass to the charity.[10] Most charities are familiar with this calculation.

Question – How does the annuitant know how much income to report each year?

Answer – The charity or its designated administrator will send the annuitant a Form 1099R reflecting the allocation of the payments among taxable income, capital gains, and nontaxable return of principal.

Question – How does the donor know how much to report as a charitable income tax deduction?

Answer – The charity will typically provide the donor with a letter summarizing the amount of the charitable deduction and the income tax treatment of the payments. Most tax professionals will be familiar with the tax consequences and can determine the amount of the charitable income tax deduction.

Question – Can I transfer encumbered property to the charity in return for a charitable gift annuity?

Answer – Yes. Unlike the rules applicable to the transfer of debt-encumbered property to a charitable remainder trust, it is permissible to transfer such property to a charity in return for a charitable gift annuity. Of course, the net value of the property, after a reduction for the amount of the debt, will be used to determine the amount of the annuity and

the donor's deduction. However, it should be noted that any capital gain attributable to the debt would be reported immediately.[11]

Question – When a charity purchases a commercial annuity to insure its obligation, are there any charitable split dollar insurance implications?

Answer – No. Under the Tax Relief Extension Act of 1999, which imposed severe restrictions on what were considered abusive charitable split dollar arrangements, there is a specific exemption to the restrictions for charitable gift annuities.[12]

Question – Will a transfer of appreciated property to a charity in return for a charitable gift annuity result in the recognition of capital gain?

Answer – Yes, but not immediately. Under the bargain sale rules, the capital gain is reported as the annuity payments are received, based on the number of years over which the annuity is expected to be paid (the life of the annuitant or lives of the annuitants).[13] However, if the annuity is assignable to someone other than the charity or if the donor is not one of the annuitants, then the gain is immediately recognized.[14]

Question – Can the creation of a charitable gift annuity be subject to the generation-skipping transfer tax?

Answer – Yes. If there is a completed gift to a non-donor annuitant who is a skip-person (generally, a person more than one generation younger than the donor), the value of the interest transferred to that person may be subject to the generation-skipping transfer tax. To the extent that the $12,000 (as indexed for 2007) annual exclusion is not available for a generation-skipping transfer, the donor may need to allocate the generation-skipping transfer exemption.

Question – Can a life income beneficiary under a charitable remainder unitrust exchange his unitrust interest for a charitable gift annuity?

Answer – Yes. The IRS ruled favorably on this type of exchange taking into account the differences in the value of the interests to determine the income and gift tax charitable deductions, the treatment of undistributed capital gains, and the donor's adjusted basis in the annuity.[15]

Question – Can an IRA be left at the owner's death to a charity in exchange for a charitable gift annuity?

Answer – Yes. The IRS approved this arrangement, indicating that a charitable estate tax deduction would be allowed for the charitable portion, that the receipt would not be unrelated business taxable income and that the character of the IRA proceeds as income in respect of a decedent would continue in the hands of the charity.[16] While not specifically addressed, one would conclude that the annuitant would not have any portion of the payments excludable as capital gain—see above for a discussion of the income tax implications to an annuitant.

CHAPTER ENDNOTES

1. PLR 200233023.

2. See Treas. Reg. §1.1011-2(c), Ex. 8.

3. IRC Sec. 72(b)(2).

4. IRC Sec. 72(e)(4)(C); Treas. Reg. §1.1011-2(a)(4).

5. Treas. Reg. §1.72-10(a).

6. Let. Rul. 9743054; but see Let. Rul. 9017071.

7. IRC Sec. 72(b)(3).

8. IRC Sec. 2522.

9. IRC Sec. 2523.

10. IRC Sec. 72(b)(3).

11. Treas. Reg. §1.1011-2(a)(3).

12. IRC Sec. 170(f)(10)(D).

13. Treas. Reg. §1.1011-2(c), Ex. 8.

14. Treas. Reg. §1.1011-2(a)(4).

15. Let. Rul. 200152018.

16. Let. Rul. 200230018.

CHARITABLE GIVING USING LIFE INSURANCE

CHAPTER 13

WHAT IS IT?

Life insurance often plays a crucial and highly useful role in the charitable planning process. Insurance and annuity contracts can provide needed liquidity to fund major gifts and endowment funds, replace value otherwise lost to heirs, or act as a tax-advantaged investment for donors, charities, and planned giving vehicles.

This field, however, is quite complex, and any advisor who recommends insurance products and techniques in a charitable context must take extra steps to learn the intricacies of state and federal laws as they apply to both insurance products and charities. From a charity's point of view, unless a planned giving professional has an extensive insurance background and has remained proficient in this field, care should be taken when advising donors on specific products.

The insurance advisor should realize that the rules are complex, strictly construed, and often encompass state as well as federal laws–often extending beyond mere tax considerations. The consequences to both the charity and the donor can be quite severe if planning and implementation are flawed. It is also essential that all parties are exceptionally sensitive to ethical considerations and that potential conflicts of interest are constantly considered and monitored (see Chapter 7).

As a result of a Senate Finance Committee hearing in 2004,[1] several negative stories in the national press involving charities engaging in speculative investor owned life insurance (IOLI) programs, and a two year report prepared by the Treasury Department, restrictive legislation is likely to be passed in the near future. It is imperative that both advisors and charities keep up to date on all legal and regulatory changes prior to making any recommendations regarding charities and life insurance.

WHEN IS THE USE OF SUCH A DEVICE INDICATED?

1. When a donor wishes to give an existing insurance or annuity contract to charity. Such a gift might be a life insurance contract that was purchased in the past, but that is no longer needed or is now relatively insignificant to the donor.

2. When the donor wants to replace all or some of the value of an asset donated to charity. One of the most common objections to charitable donations, either outright or through a split interest vehicle, is that the donor's heirs will receive a smaller inheritance. Insurance can often replace some or all of that lost value.

3. When the trustee of a split interest trust wants to control the timing and distribution of the income.

4. When a charity wishes to ensure that a lump sum endowment is fully funded at a donor's death, even if there is a premature death.

5. When a charity wishes to "reinsure" a charitable gift annuity program.

6. When the charity wishes to invest in a pool of policies in a manner similar to corporate-owned life insurance.

OUTRIGHT GIFTS AT DEATH

Life Insurance Policies

Unfortunately, very few policy owners review their beneficiary designations regularly after the policy is originally delivered. The lack of a regular review, which ideally should be performed at least every two to three

years (and more frequently if the client's circumstances change), often results in an undesired disposition. It is quite common for an ex-spouse or deceased family member to have inadvertently been left as the policy beneficiary.

Both advisors and charities therefore should recommend that donors: (1) review all beneficiary designations to make sure the designations are current; and (2) consider naming a charity as either a primary, secondary, or ultimate contingent beneficiary. If a donor has only one heir, a spouse or child for example, naming a favorite charity as a secondary beneficiary may be appropriate in the event the heir predeceases the donor. Because the beneficiary designation is usually revocable, the donor can be assured that the beneficiary designation can later be changed to reflect the donor's changing needs. This might occur, for example, if the donor later remarries or has children. In most cases, naming a charity as the ultimate contingent beneficiary in the remote possibility that all named primary and secondary beneficiaries predecease the insured costs nothing and avoids the possibility that the insurance proceeds will escheat to the state.

In addition, many donors do not consider their group term life insurance benefits to be particularly important in their overall financial plan. In planning an estate or in calculating income replacement needs, these relatively small policies (the average size is roughly $50,000) are often disregarded because the donor often loses them when changing jobs or upon retirement. These policies, however, often result in income taxation to the employee. Anyone who has a group term policy in excess of $50,000 must include the Table I cost for the excess amount in their income tax return each year.[2] Should a donor, however, name a charitable organization the sole beneficiary for amounts in excess of $50,000, no income taxes are due.[3] The designation of the charity can be revocable and there is no "recapture" in later years should the donor change his mind and name someone else as beneficiary. In other words, group term insurance is an excellent tool for a donor to make a sizable gift at death without any current outlay. If death occurs while a charity is named as beneficiary, the insurance will be includable in the insured's estate, but will then be allowed as a charitable deduction for the estate.

Outright gifts of life insurance contracts at death are relatively simple and the planning is easy to implement. The seeds for these gifts can be planted in a brief postscript on a donor letter, in a paragraph in a quarterly newsletter, or as part of a larger checklist when helping donors and clients plan their charitable gifts and bequests. Of course, because no gift is made to charity

during the donor's lifetime, there are no income tax benefits to naming a charity as beneficiary, even if the designation is made irrevocably (which is rarely, if ever, appropriate). The estate of the donor, however, will receive a charitable deduction equal to the death benefit paid to the charity, so the donation will, in most cases, be effectively tax-neutral.

Example: Last summer, the XYZ University Foundation sent out an educational newsletter to all of its donors discussing the reasons for having a coordinated estate plan. In a brief sidebar to the article, they included a paragraph that reminded donors to review all beneficiary designations regularly and to consider charity as either a primary or successor beneficiary for their life and annuity contracts. A few weeks later, the university received a call from one of its retired professors who said that he had changed his beneficiary designation on his life insurance policy to include XYZ University for $50,000 of the death benefit. He laughed rather sheepishly and admitted that, even though he had been paying the premiums for many years, he forgot to remove his ex-wife as beneficiary after his divorce eight years ago.

Naming the charity as the successor owner of a policy. There are many planning situations in which a donor may own a life insurance contract on someone else's life. This might occur when policies are cross-purchased between spouses or business owners. For example, A and B are business partners with each partner owning a $200,000 policy on the other's life. When the first partner dies, the surviving partner will receive the $200,000 death benefit which will be paid to the deceased partner's estate in return for the interest in the business. The insurance the decedent's estate owns on the surviving shareholder's life, however, will no longer be needed. Worse yet, the fair market value of that policy will be includable in the deceased partner's estate. By naming a favorite charity as the successor owner of the policy, the charity will take over ownership of the policy at the deceased's death and the deceased's estate will receive a charitable deduction to offset any estate taxes.

Annuity Contracts

There are many investors who currently own either fixed or variable annuities that were purchased primarily as retirement savings vehicles. At death, however, these investments have unfavorable tax consequences because they do not receive a stepped up basis and are considered income in respect of a decedent. (EGTRRA 2001 replaces stepped-up basis with a modified carryover basis for one year for property received from decedents dying in 2010.) In other words, any gain in the contract will be subject to ordinary income tax rates at the annuity owner's death. By naming a tax-exempt charity as the beneficiary of the contract, no income taxes will be paid, and the donor can effectively leverage a charitable bequest. For example, suppose a person owns an annuity that is worth $100,000 and has a $20,000 income tax basis. He wants to make significant gifts at his death both to his children and to his favorite charity. Assuming a 40% income tax rate, family members receiving that annuity would receive after-tax income of only $68,000 ($100,000 - $32,000, i.e., 40% of the $80,000 gain). On the other hand, if the donor left the full $100,000 to charity by simply naming it as the beneficiary of the annuity, the charity, as a tax-exempt entity, will pay no income tax and receive the entire $100,000. So by leaving his intended beneficiaries only $68,000 of other assets and leaving the charity the annuity, he will maximize the potential of both of his objectives. If he wanted his children to have $100,000 at his death, he could give them sufficient cash each year to purchase $32,000 of life insurance on his life. The children would net $68,000 from the annuity and receive an additional $32,000 of income-tax-free and estate-tax-free life insurance, for a total of $100,000. (EGTRRA 2001 repeals the estate tax for one year for decedents dying in 2010.)

OUTRIGHT GIFTS DURING LIFE

Life Insurance Policies

It is not unusual to find that donors who purchased life insurance several years ago now find that the insurance is no longer needed. For example, children may have become financially independent or even become alienated from the family or, in a few cases, may have predeceased their parents. In other situations, the donor may simply have purchased more life insurance than was really needed. In the business life insurance market, donors may own insurance for a buy sell agreement that is no longer applicable because the underlying business has gone public or merged with a competitor. Regardless of the reason, these older policies make up the core of many insurance donation programs.

In order to qualify as a completed gift, the ownership of the contract and the beneficiary designation must be transferred completely to the charity.[4] In order to make the value of the policy and future premiums tax deductible, the donor may retain no incidents of ownership or any interests in the contract, no matter how small or seemingly unimportant. Such rights include, but are not limited to, the ability to change beneficiaries, surrender the policy, use the policy as collateral for a loan, or borrow from the contract. As seen in the 1999 charitable split dollar legislation and IRS Notice 99-36,[5] even an indirect benefit to the donor or family, as in the case of charitable split dollar, is sufficient to disqualify a deduction for the gift.

For practical purposes, the gift of a life insurance contract is considered complete when the charity is listed as the policy owner on the insurance company's records. The amount of the tax deduction is based on the policy values and the donor's cost basis as of that date. Figure 13.1 provides a brief summary of how the tax deduction is calculated for a life insurance policy. The amount of the deduction is based on the lesser of (a) cost basis, or (b) fair market value, with the latter number defined by the age and premium payment status of the underlying contract.[6]

Once the gift is complete, the charity should issue an appropriate receipt for the donor's tax records. The receipt should contain the donor's name, the date of the gift, and a general description of the policy including the insurance company, policy number, face amount, and insurance type. The charity should also include a statement that the donor received no goods or services in return for the gift.

And finally, the charity should complete IRS Form 8283 (Noncash Charitable Contributions) with the appropriate information, most of which will need to be obtained from the insurance company on a signed IRS Form 712 (Life Insurance Statement). The donor must also obtain a qualified appraisal if the fair market value of the policy is $5,000 or more. This qualified appraisal can be performed only by someone who does not have a financial interest in the contract (in other words, neither the agent nor the insurance company may do the valuation), who offers appraisals on a regular basis, and who is qualified by education or experience to appraise insurance policies. The appraisal must be signed no earlier than 60 days prior to the date of contribution and no later than April 15th of the following year.[7]

Figure 13.1

CHARITABLE INCOME TAX DEDUCTION LIMITS FOR GIFTS OF LIFE INSURANCE

- **Recently Issued Policy:** The deduction is equal to the lesser of

  o the cost basis, or
  o the fair market value of the contract. This is defined as the first premium paid.

- **Existing Life Policy in Premium Paying Mode:** The deduction is equal to the lesser of

  o the cost basis, or
  o the fair market value of the contract. This is defined as the interpolated terminal reserve plus unearned premium. This latter number is roughly equal to the cash surrender value but that is an approximation only.

- **Paid Up Life Insurance Policy:** The deduction is equal to the lesser of

  o the cost basis, or
  o the fair market value of the contract. This is defined as the replacement value of the contract. This latter number is equal to what the donor would have to pay for a new single premium policy with the same death benefit at his or her current age.

Definition of Cost Basis: In general, the cost basis is the sum of all premiums paid to date less (1) amounts surrendered or (2) dividends received in cash.

Policy Valuation: If requested, the insurance company will provide free of charge either (1) the interpolated terminal reserve plus unearned premium, or (2) the replacement cost for the policy on Form 712.

Before any insurance or financial professional agrees to prepare a qualified appraisal and sign the IRS Form 8283, it is imperative that he or she review the new appraisal rules passed into law on August 17, 2006 as part of the Pension Protection Act of 2006. This new law requires that an appraiser include a copy of his or her qualifications as part of the appraisal, outlining all education and experience in valuing this type of asset. The appraiser must also state that he or she has never been banned from practice before the IRS. The appraiser must have earned an appraisal designation from a recognized organization or have otherwise met education and experience requirements, and he or she must regularly perform such appraisals.[8] There are new penalties imposed if the IRS determines that the value differs substantially from that determined by the appraiser.[9]

Example: One of ABC Medical Foundation's long-term donors has decided to give ABC a $1 million whole life policy. She originally purchased the insurance several years ago to benefit her son. The policy is now paid up and no further premiums are required. Her son is now grown, has become a successful physician, and the donor feels that she no longer needs to keep the insurance. She now has questions regarding her deduction and the steps she needs to take to complete the donation.

Prior to processing this gift, two steps should occur: (1) the charity must determine whether it should and will accept the gift; and (2) the donor must review her overall financial situation to decide whether the insurance policy is the most appropriate asset to donate.

When presented with a copy of the policy and a current in-force illustration, the charity compares the contract to the minimum standards set out in their gift acceptance policy (discussed in more detail in the "Questions and

Figure 13.2

CHARITABLE INCOME TAX DEDUCTION LIMITS FOR GIFTS OF COMMERCIAL ANNUITIES			
	Annuity contracts issued on or after April 23, 1987	**Annuity contracts issued April 22, 1987 or earlier that have matured**	**Annuity contracts issued April 22, 1987 or earlier that have not matured**
Charitable Deduction	Value of the contract	Value of the contract	Limited to the donor's cost basis in the contract
Income Tax Due	Upon gift to charity, donor recognizes all gain in the contract as ordinary income	Upon gift to charity, donor recognizes all gain in the contract as ordinary income	Upon gift to charity, donor recognizes all gain in the contract as ordinary income
Net Result	Donor's net deduction is limited to the cost basis in the contract	Donor's net deduction is limited to the cost basis in the contract	Donor can only deduct difference between basis and gain. If donor's gain is larger than the basis, the donor may actually have to pay income taxes upon gifting the contract to charity
Example Tax Basis = $10,000 FMV = $50,000	Donor recognizes $40,000 in ordinary income and receives a $50,000 charitable deduction. Net deduction is $10,000	Donor recognizes $40,000 in ordinary income and receives a $50,000 charitable deduction. Net deduction is $10,000	Donor recognizes $40,000 in ordinary income and receives a $10,000 charitable deduction. Net income recognized by donor is $30,000

Answers," below) and determines that the gift is acceptable. At the same time, the donor reviews the deduction limits with her tax counsel and, even though the charitable tax deduction for life insurance is not as favorable as it is with other highly appreciated assets, she decides to donate the policy.

Annuity Contracts

For a variety of reasons, there are many donors who currently own variable and fixed annuities and would like to give them to charity. However, as outlined in Figure 13.2, the tax code does not favor lifetime gifts of commercial annuities. Donors are usually best advised to either keep the annuity and donate other highly appreciated property, or to hold on to the annuity and simply name the charity as the beneficiary of the contract at death. In rare cases where the donor wishes to donate a highly appreciated annuity despite the deduction limitations, the steps to complete the gift are similar to those outlined regarding life insurance gifts.

Once the gift is complete, a receipt should be issued by the charity. The receipt should name the donor, state the date of the gift, and describe the policy in detail (type of contract, insurance company, issue date, death benefit if applicable, and contract number.) The charity should prepare an IRS Form 8283 (Noncash Charitable Contributions) for the donor and, if the value of the contract exceeds $5,000, the donor must obtain a qualified appraisal.

Example: A new donor has indicated that he would like to participate in PDQ Community Foundation's capital campaign. Upon reviewing his portfolio, he decides to donate a highly appreciated variable annuity. He purchased the contract in 1990. It has grown from $50,000 to $250,000 during this time.

Once again, there are two steps to be completed before processing this gift. First, the charity should determine whether the gift falls within the limitations defined by its gift acceptance policy. Second, PDQ should recommend that the donor discuss the tax ramifications of such a gift with tax counsel to determine whether this asset is the most appropriate choice to give.

As outlined in Figure 13.2 above, the tax system does not favor lifetime gifts of commercial annuities. Because the donor's contract was purchased after April 22, 1987, he will receive a charitable income tax deduction of $250,000. However, he will also include the entire gain in the annuity ($200,000) on his income tax return in the year that he gives it to the charity.[10] In the end, the donor will receive a net tax deduction of only $50,000 even though he is donating an asset worth $250,000. Upon reviewing this tax information, the donor agrees that he might be better off keeping the annuity in place and instead giving the charity some of his highly appreciated stock.

NEW LIFE INSURANCE PURCHASES

The preceding section addressed the special planning techniques involving gifts of existing contracts (life insurance or annuity contracts that were purchased by donors in prior years that no longer suit their original purpose.) There are also two main planning scenarios which involve gifts of new life insurance policies.

Insuring Against the Loss of a Major Donor

Many charities have loyal donors without whose annual gifts the charity would face financial hardship. If a donor's primary focus is lifetime gifts rather than bequests, it might make sense for the charity to purchase life insurance equal to the present value of the donor's anticipated future gifts to the charity. In many instances, if the charity explains to the donor that the purpose of this insurance purchase is to ensure that the good deeds currently funded by that donor will continue even if the donor dies prematurely, the donor may either offer to donate an extra amount each year to cover the cost of the premiums or may decide to arrange a bequest to cover this same risk.

Gifts of Premiums Earmarked for New Insurance

There are a rapidly growing number of donors who wish to donate new insurance to charity. In its simplest form, the charity purchases a policy on the life of a donor, who funds the premium payments by making an ongoing annual contribution. In its more common form, the donor buys the policy and then, immediately after issue, donates the contract to the charity.

While quite conventional, this latter technique has several potential problems and great care should be taken in arranging such gifts.

State Insurable Interest Rules

To prevent people from speculating on the lives of strangers and random acquaintances, only someone with an insurable interest in the life of the insured may purchase a policy on that person. In order for an insurance policy to be considered valid, it must meet the insurable interest rules in the state in which it is issued.

If the policy is found to have violated these rules when it was issued, the insurance company can later argue that the policy was void from the beginning, and may refuse to pay the death benefit at the insured's death. While a charity is assumed to have an insurable interest in the life of a donor in most states, there may be unusual quirks in a particular state's laws that must be followed to the letter in order to avoid having the contract nullified later. For example, if a charity located in New York purchases a policy on the life of a donor residing in California, the insurable interest rules for New York (the location of the policy owner) must be met.

If one party purchases a policy but the ownership is immediately transferred to another party, the insurance company may later attempt to void the contract if the insurable interest rules for either owner are in any way not met. In the case above, if the California donor purchases the policy on his own life and then immediately transfers the policy to the New York charity, the policy could be found void if New York's insurable interest laws are not closely followed. Technically, California's laws should apply because the policy was issued in California, but the insurance company can assert that New York's laws should apply because the policy was only temporarily owned by a California resident in anticipation of transferring it to the New York charity.

Finally, in cases where the insurance purchase did not meet state insurable interest laws, the IRS has denied income, gift, and estate tax charitable deductions. For example, if the California donor purchases the policy and immediately transfers it to the New York charity without meeting the specific terms of the New York insurable interest laws, the income tax deduction for the gift could be lost. Also, because the donor originally owned the contract, the death benefit will be in his taxable estate for three years following the date of the donation. If he should die within this time frame, the charity would receive the death benefit but absent an insurable interest, the donor's estate would have no offsetting charitable deduction. Furthermore, the decedent's personal representative could arguably have the right to be reimbursed by the charity for the estate taxes due on the death benefit.

As a result of intense lobbying by groups selling Investor Owned Life Insurance programs to charities, several states have recently amended their insurable interest laws. It is imperative that insurance professionals, professional advisors, and charities all verify the applicable law prior to setting up a one of these programs to ensure that the plan is in compliance in the state (or states) where it is implemented.

State Laws Governing the Contract

The laws regarding the rights of the policy owner, the beneficiary, and the insured vary from state to state. These rights might involve everything from policy disclosure requirements to suicide contestability periods. These rights will also define the fiduciary relationship, if any, between the agent, the insurance company, and the charity.

The state laws where the policy was originally purchased govern that policy for its duration, even if the policy is then donated to an out-of-state charity. As described above, if a California donor purchases a contract in California and later transfers it to a New York charity,

the California state insurance laws will still apply for the life of the contract.

Risk Assessment and Insurance Illustrations

If a donor and agent put together a new insurance plan without including the charity in the decision-making process, significant fiduciary responsibility problems may arise for the charity. In most cases, the agent and the donor have already decided on the amount, company, funding level, and product type. They usually present the charity with only a sales illustration, a copy of the policy, and a Change of Ownership Form for the charity's signature. Prior to signing such a form, the agent should prepare an in-depth explanation for the charity of the following contract features:

- *Policy guarantees.* What specifically is guaranteed under worst-case scenario assumptions?

- *Current assumptions.* What does the illustration look like at 1% below the current rate? At 2% below? Does the illustration have any non-guaranteed bonus rate assumptions? Does the company assume that mortality rates will improve in the future? Do they assume a higher than normal or current lapse rate?

- *Term mixes.* Does the policy include any term mixes or riders? How do these affect the volatility of the contract?

- *Bells and whistles.* What riders and extra policy features have been added to the policy? What is the cost for these riders?

- *Insurance company due diligence.* What research has been done into the financial strength and stability of the company beyond a brief review of third party ratings?

A Gift with Strings Attached

When insurance giving plans are presented to a charity, there is often an implied or even outright condition to the gift. The donor is giving annual gifts to the charity to pay for a new insurance policy, but if the charity does not purchase the policy or later decides to surrender it, the annual gifts will likely cease.

Some charities address this situation by stating in their gift acceptance policy that they will accept no gifts of insurance policies where premiums are still required. Other charities simply shrug, and figure a gift of life insurance premiums is better than no gift at all. From a pragmatic point of view, this may be true, but unfortunately this logic masks an underlying weakness. It must be the charity's (informed) choice whether or not to invest in and maintain life insurance; not the donor's, not the agent's. If a potential donor were to approach a charity and say, "I want to give you $5,000 per year on the condition that you invest it all in XYZ stock," clearly, the investment restrictions attached to this gift would be unacceptable. And yet, when a donor approaches a charity with a similar proposal, "I'll give you $5,000 per year to buy life insurance on my life through XYZ Insurance Company," few charities recognize that this arrangement may be just as problematic as the stock example.

Duty to Invest Prudently

Charities have a fiduciary responsibility to invest their assets wisely. If a donor makes an unrestricted gift to charity, it is highly unlikely that the charity would independently invest in life insurance without some guarantee from the donor that annual donations would be made to pay the premiums. Furthermore, when a donor puts together an insurance giving program with an agent, it is usually assumed that the agent will continue servicing and managing that contract after it is donated to the charity. For variable life contracts, this can be problematic. Even if the charity chooses to delegate investment management responsibilities to the insurance agent involved, the charity must first verify that the agent is qualified, ethical, and knowledgeable. Then, the charity has a fiduciary duty to continually review and monitor the agent's recommendations.

Percentage-Based Fund Raising Fees

The National Committee on Planned Giving's Model Standards of Practice clearly prohibit the "payment of finders fees, commissions or other fees by a donee organization to an independent gift planner as a condition for the delivery of a gift." Assume an insurance agent and a potential donor approach a charity with a plan which provides that the donor will make annual contributions to the charity, which in turn will use those contributions to purchase life insurance on the life of the donor through the insurance agent. By agreeing to this pre-arranged plan, this charity is effectively, if indirectly, ensuring that the insurance agent is paid a commission from the

insurance company as a condition for arranging this gift. If this is truly an unrestricted gift, the charity has a choice. They can, instead, purchase no load insurance using the same premium money. Or, they can purchase the insurance (or different insurance) using a different insurance agent.

But if "the deal is" that the agent will take the donor (and his contributions) elsewhere if the charity does not purchase the insurance through him, then clearly the gift is conditioned on receiving the commission and the ethics rule is applicable.

Future Premiums

Finally, budgeting for future premiums is one of the largest inherent problems in soliciting or receiving gifts of new life insurance. If the donor loses interest in making annual gifts to pay the premiums, the policy may lapse. The charity could effectively end up with a valueless gift.

Of course, if the policy has sufficient cash value, the policy could provide term insurance for an extended period of time (called "extended term"). The death benefit can be reduced and the policy could be made paid up for the insured's life (called "reduced paid-up coverage), or the charity could pay the premiums out of other assets or income. The charity could also surrender the contract, or sell it to a high-net-worth settlement or viatical company.

How to Proceed

The problems inherent in gifts of new life insurance are not insurmountable, but they are numerous and should be addressed thoroughly and openly between the donor, agent, and charity. While the insurance agent may decide that it is more expedient to have the donor apply for the insurance and transfer ownership immediately following policy issue, the potential risks involving taxes and insurable interest make such planning precarious. To minimize these risks: (1) the charity should be the original applicant, owner, and beneficiary of the policy; (2) the charity should investigate the insurance agent's background, experience, and licenses; (3) the charity should be given a choice of companies and products; and (4) all potential conflicts of interest should be discussed and resolved prior to implementation. The agent or financial advisor who understands these issues and who works with the charity to resolve them professionally will likely develop a long and profitable relationship with that charity.

———————

Example: Dr. Schoen wants to give $5,000 of appreciated stock each year to his favorite charity so the charity can purchase a $250,000 life insurance policy on his life. After meeting with Dr. Schoen and his agent, the charity decides that there are no conditions on this gift, and that the agent, the insurance company, and the product recommended are all suitable. Upon reviewing the program in more detail, however, the charity decides instead to purchase $240,000 of insurance with an annual premium of $4,800 and uses the remaining $200 gift to cover the annual expenses of managing the policy. The charity will be billed each year by the insurance company, and the charity will contact the donor at that time to request the next donation. Furthermore, the charity will: (1) review the policy annually to ensure that it is performing as expected; (2) verify that the insurance company is still financially strong; and (3) issue a receipt to the donor for each premium payment.

———————

In cases where insurance gifts are found to be appropriate, it is imperative that implementation be handled correctly. Once a product is chosen, medical and financial underwriting are complete, the policy is issued, and it is time to pay the premium, the donor and charity have two choices in arranging for the first and future payments.

1. *Donor writes a check to charity each year.* In this scenario, the donor writes a check (or in the best case scenario, gives highly appreciated property) to the charity each year for an amount sufficient to cover the annual premium payment. Many charities ask that the donor pay somewhat more than the annual premium each year to cover the expenses of administering the policy or, in some cases, the charity will purchase slightly less insurance. Rounding up the check is often preferable because it makes it easier to explain and document the charitable gift with tax authorities. For instance, for a premium of $1,845, the check might be rounded up to $2,000. If the client is audited or must otherwise prove the charitable contribution, a photostat of both sides of the check is less likely to cause needlessly bothersome questions.

2. *Donor pays the premium directly to the insurance company.* It is often simpler for the donor to write the check directly to the insurance company each year. This scenario is less advantageous for a number of reasons: (1) the donor will need to fund the policy with cash rather than highly appreciated property; (2) issuing a charitable receipt for this situation is problematic; and (3) it is difficult for the charity to determine on what date the gift was considered complete. Despite its problems, if the charity and donor decide to use this payment method, the donor should send a copy of the check to the charity when it is mailed to the insurance company, and the charity should verify that the insurer received the check.

In the past, conventional wisdom said that the tax deduction percentage limits applied to these two different payment situations would differ. A 50% deduction limit was applied to donations made to the charity to pay premiums, while a 30% limit was assumed for premiums paid directly to the insurer. According to some authorities' interpretation of case law, however, both situations above would qualify for the 50% deduction limit.

Prior to choosing one method or another, it is imperative that the charity verify the state's insurable interest laws. One jurisdiction, for example, allows a charity to purchase life insurance on the life of a donor only if the donor makes the first three premium payments. [11]

LIFE INSURANCE AS A WEALTH REPLACEMENT TOOL

Many donors would like to make significant charitable gifts or bequests, but decide against them because they worry about disinheriting or upsetting their heirs. Will their children have sufficient funds for emergencies and lifestyle needs? Will there be enough for the grandchildren's college education? Will the heirs feel slighted if money is left to charity instead of to them?

Life insurance can alleviate many of these concerns, effectively replacing some or all of a charitable donation in the form of a cash benefit for the heirs. This concept is often referred to as "wealth replacement" and if, as a result of combining charitable planning and life insurance, the heirs end up with more than they would have had no planning been done, the phrase "wealth enhancement" is sometimes used.

Example: Mr. Jones has a 200 acre parcel valued at $210,000 which sits adjacent to a university's land. Upon his death, he wishes to leave this land to the university, but he does not want to disinherit his daughter. The simplicity of life insurance appeals to Mr. Jones and he simply gives his daughter sufficient funds each year to pay the premiums on a $210,000 insurance policy on his life. Upon his death, the charity receives the land, his daughter collects the insurance death benefit, and the rest of his estate is distributed according to his estate plan.

Many planned giving officers and advisors think that a wealth replacement trust is a specialized charitable insurance trust. However, it is simply another name for an irrevocable life insurance trust (also called an ILIT or a Crummey Trust) which is used in combination with charitable planning. In the most common arrangement, the donor makes an annual gift to the trust on the heirs' behalf, which is then used to purchase life insurance on the donor's life. At the donor's death, the trust collects the death benefit to distribute to the children.

Example: Professor Bernstein is quite wealthy. He wants to donate $500,000 of stock to his favorite charity, but he is somewhat concerned that his son will be upset at not receiving this money. On the advice of the planned giving officer, Professor Bernstein uses some of the savings from his charitable tax deduction to fund an ILIT which purchases a $250,000 life insurance policy for his son's benefit. As he explains to his son, this is the amount that the son would have received from that stock portfolio after estate taxes, if applicable, were paid.

There are a variety of factors that must be considered in designing an appropriate wealth replacement insurance portfolio. A planner must keep in mind: (1) the overall estate planning goals of the donor; (2) from what source the donor will pay the annual premiums; (3) the appropriate size and structure of the life insurance policy; and (4) what type of charitable planning will be implemented. If providing for heirs is a key concern for a donor, the life insurance death benefit, which often can be paid for out of a charitable tax deduction, can provide the donor with both planning flexibility and peace of mind.

But even as the insurance community has picked up the pace on marketing this idea, the planned giving community has been far more cautious in recent years about promoting these plans. In the mid to late 1980s, the charitable remainder trust (CRT) and wealth replacement life insurance combination was quite popular, and the structure of choice with many planners and agents was to match the tax deduction (spread out over six years) with a "six-pay" insurance policy.

Unfortunately for consumers, interest and dividend rates have dropped considerably since then. The intent was for the policyowner to be able to finance the policy after the sixth year with anticipated ever-increasing dividends. However, these optimistic projections did not materialize. "Six-pay" policies are now not likely to be self-sustaining and the required payments are not likely to "vanish" until well beyond the originally projected period. Planned giving officers who recommended the original planning now feel responsible for the donor discontent resulting from the need to continue to pay premiums.

Example: Using life insurance to replace a charitable donation works especially well in the case of a charitable remainder trust. For example, Mr. and Mrs. Donor (ages 70 and 65, respectively) have recently retired from a publicly traded company, LMN, Inc., that they helped found many years ago. They wish to sell approximately $1 million of their LMN stock (with a $10,000 basis) in order to diversify their investment portfolio. They have been discussing the use of a charitable remainder unitrust to avoid current capital gains tax, but have hesitated to implement this plan because they want their children to receive some benefit from this business. (Please refer to Figures 13.3 and 13.4 for details of this plan.)

Their goals include: (1) reinvest the proceeds from the sale of the stock to increase their current income; (2) provide a sizable benefit for their favorite charity; (3) minimize income and estate taxes; and (4) make sure that their children have a reasonable financial safety net.

After careful consideration, Mr. and Mrs. Donor decide to set up a net income with make-up charitable remainder unitrust (NIMCRUT) with a 7% payout and a targeted rate of return of 10%. This will provide them with an annual

Figure 13.3

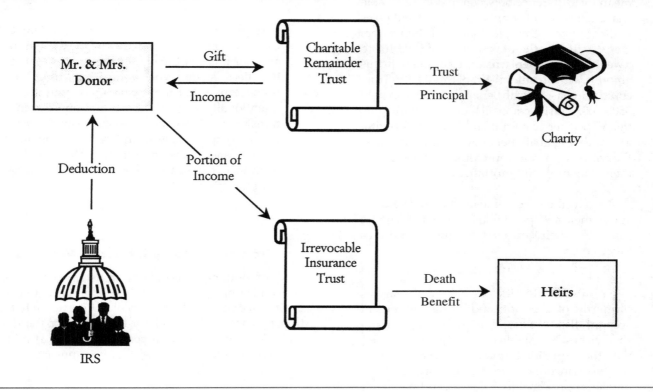

CHARITABLE REMAINDER TRUST WITH WEALTH REPLACEMENT

Figure 13.4

CRT WITH WEALTH REPLACEMENT TRUST BENEFITS

	Sale Without CRT	Sale With CRT	Sale With CRT + WRT
Annual Income (inc at 3%/yr)	$50,596	$70,000	$63,000
Tax Savings (40% tax bracket)	$0	$103,168	$0
Net to Heirs (55% estate tax bracket)	$325,260	$0	$500,000
Charity (Present value at 3%)	$0	$1,000,000	$1,000,000

income of $70,000 that will increase at a rate of roughly 3% per year to keep up with inflation. Assuming a 7.2% Section 7520 rate, this structure will give them a total income tax deduction of approximately $257,920, the unused portion of which they can carry forward for an additional five years as needed.

By selling and reinvesting the stock through the CRT, Mr. and Mrs. Donor will significantly increase their spendable annual income, their charity will receive a sizable benefit upon the second spouse's death, and the charitable deduction will result in an income tax savings of approximately $17,195 per year for six years. They understand that the gift to the CRT is irrevocable, that there will be some increased annual administration expenses to maintain this planning, and that eventually, the charity will receive the principal in the trust. The only remaining problem that prevents them from moving forward is their children's inheritance.

In this situation, the role of life insurance can mean the difference between making a sizable charitable gift and simply paying current taxes while giving nothing to charity. If the Donors were to transfer their tax savings of $103,168 to a wealth replacement trust, and supplement this amount with an annual gift of $7,000, the Trust could purchase a death benefit of approximately $500,000.[12] Furthermore, if they continue to give that $7,000 per year for their lifetimes, applying an increasing death benefit option could cause the policy to grow to approximately $800,000 by their statistical joint mortality of 20 years.

By using their tax savings and a small percentage of their net spendable income, the Donors can solve their concerns for their children's inheritance.

Example: Ms. Maddock's net worth consists primarily of a sizable individual retirement account (IRA). At the advice of her accountant, she wishes to establish a testamentary CRT with these qualified funds. Instead of paying a combined income and estate tax that could be as high as approximately 75% (depending on her date of death), her heirs will receive a substantial annual income from the trust. In order for this planning to work, however, there must be sufficient liquidity from non-IRA assets to pay the estate taxes due on the testamentary CRT at Ms. Maddock's death. Life insurance owned by an insurance trust is the natural solution for her planning dilemma, and she withdraws sufficient extra income from the IRA each year which, after taxes, will cover the premiums for this policy.

Example: As part of an overall estate plan, Mr. Carsten sets up a testamentary $1 million charitable lead annuity trust (CLAT) from which his favorite school will receive 9% per year for 23 years. After that, the trust principal will pass to his children. Because it is likely that his heirs will not receive any benefit from this trust until many years after his death, Mr. Carsten's advisor recommends that he set up an insurance trust for his children's benefit to supplement their inheri-

tance. With this planning, the children receive a lump sum from the insurance at his death, with an additional amount passing to them from the CLAT at the end of the trust term.

Example: Miss Pine wants to set up a sizable CLT to benefit her church during the trust term and her niece at the end of the term. Because her niece is somewhat unhealthy, Miss. Pine is concerned that the use of a CLT might unintentionally trigger the generation-skipping transfer tax if her niece passes away prior to the end of the trust term and the trust principal passes instead to her grandnieces. The use of life insurance in this case would allow Miss Pine to plan for this possibility.

Transfers into Split Interest Vehicles

Many donors would like to transfer existing insurance and annuity contracts into split interest gifts in the most tax-advantaged way possible. Unfortunately, these transfers are not particularly beneficial for the donor and in some cases are quite costly. Split interest vehicles should be funded with other, highly-appreciated assets whenever possible.

Charitable Remainder Trust

Because many donors own older insurance policies, transferring cash-heavy contracts into a charitable remainder trust (CRT) would seem beneficial. Under current law, however, the tax deduction for the donation of an insurance policy to charity is limited to the lesser of the cost basis or the fair market value. For highly appreciated insurance policies, this means the donor's gross tax deduction is the cost basis, which is then further reduced by the present value of the CRT's future income stream to the donor. For highly appreciated policies, the net tax deduction to the donor is often a small percentage of the policy's actual value. Unfortunately, this transfer cannot qualify for 1035 exchange treatment because the original owner of the policy (the donor) is not the same as the new owner (the CRT).

Example: Mr. Partridge owns a $1 million life insurance policy with a $400,000 cash surrender value and a $100,000 cost basis. He has read somewhere that a CRT can invest in life insurance, so now he wants to transfer this existing policy into a CRT or "1035 exchange" his current policy into a new policy inside the CRT. As mentioned earlier, the deduction for insurance gifts is the lesser of the cost basis ($100,000) or the fair market value ($400,000). The gross deduction ($100,000) will further be reduced by the applicable present value of the future income stream based on the Section 7520 rate. Assuming that the charitable remainder interest for the CRT is 30%, this means that the donor's deduction is limited to only $30,000, even though the policy is worth $400,000. Furthermore, this transfer cannot qualify for a "1035 exchange" because the owner of the old policy must be the same as the owner of the new policy.

Charitable Gift Annuity

Another technique that is often considered by donors is the transfer of an existing commercial annuity to fund a charitable gift annuity (CGA). Again, this transfer does not qualify for the 1035 exchange exemption and the resulting tax consequences are mediocre at best.

A charitable gift annuity is technically considered to be part sale, part gift, and if a commercial annuity is used to fund a CGA, the tax consequences will be prorated accordingly between sale and gift. For example, Donor A paid $5,000 for an annuity which now has a value of $20,000. If Donor A transfers the contract to a CGA with a 50% deduction percentage, 50% of the annuity will be considered a gift, and 50% a sale. Because the donor's deduction is limited to his basis, the net tax deduction for setting up this CGA would be only $2,500. Furthermore, when the donor begins receiving income from the CGA, rather than having each income payment be part return of basis, part capital gain, and part ordinary income, under current law it would appear that this income would be part return of principal, with the remainder taxed as ordinary income.[13] See Chapter 12 for a more detailed discussion of charitable gift annuities.

Example: Mrs. Barnett owns a $500,000 variable annuity with a $100,000 cost basis. She wishes to exchange this commercial annuity for a 50% charitable gift annuity issued by the VP Educational Foundation. Because a CGA is part gift, part sale, the donor would receive a tax deduction equal to approximately $50,000 (50% of the cost basis). She cannot qualify for a 1035 exchange from commercial annuity to charitable gift annuity for two reasons: (1) the exchange must be between like contracts; and (2) the owner must be the same for both old and new contracts.

INSURANCE AS AN INVESTMENT

In general, the economics of life insurance are relatively simple. An individual purchases coverage to provide a lump sum benefit in event of death prior to statistical mortality. On the other side of the coin, an insurance company issues and prices a large number of policies based on the assumption that it will need to pay a certain number of claims each year. Some insureds will die early and others will live long lives; as long as the overall death rate of a large pool of insureds is fairly predictable, the insurance company will make a profit.

In addition to this, life insurance is a highly tax-favored product. Realizing that insurance death benefits serve an important social purpose, Congress has given life insurance special tax incentives: the cash values grow tax-deferred and the death benefit is paid to the beneficiary free of federal income tax.

A charity can benefit from the statistical play (if the insured dies early, the charity as policy owner will financially benefit), but the tax advantages are usually irrelevant because the charity is already exempt from taxes. As a result of the fairly large cost for having a tax-deferred wrapper on the underlying investment, a well-diversified and carefully managed stock or mutual fund portfolio will almost always outperform an insurance policy if the insured lives beyond statistical mortality. On the other hand, if the insured dies earlier than the average person, the charity will have a difficult time using traditional investments to exceed the return from the policy's death benefit.

Individual Insurance

Many donors would like to make a sizable donation but either do not have the available funds, or do not want to commit to a substantial amount during their lifetime. Many have found that helping the charity purchase an insurance policy on their lives is a good compromise.

Figure 13.5

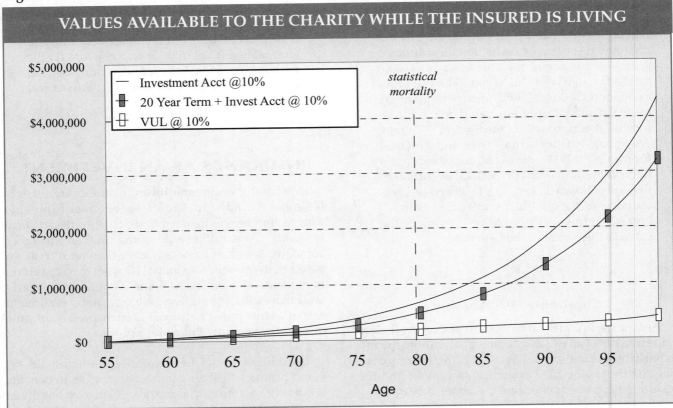

VALUES AVAILABLE TO THE CHARITY WHILE THE INSURED IS LIVING

— Investment Acct @10%
▬ 20 Year Term + Invest Acct @ 10%
▢ VUL @ 10%

statistical mortality

Age

It fills a psychological desire to make a substantial gift (the death benefit) while only requiring a relatively small annual outlay (the premium.)

As seen earlier in this chapter, however, there are some inherent problems in having a charity begin an insurance program on a donor's life. If the charity is truly free to invest the annual donations freely, it may find that more traditional investments yield a higher return. Because, without insurance, the charity would lose money if a regular and substantial donor died prematurely, mixing traditional investments with term insurance may prove to be the optimal solution. There is no "one size fits all" answer. An advisor must analyze each gift on a case-by-case basis.

Example: Mr. MacDonald has been talking with his financial planner about his desire to benefit the ABC Medical Foundation. He would really like to make a significant gift and his planner has shown him that if he donates $5,500 per year, he can fund a $400,000 low load variable universal life insurance policy (VUL) where the Foundation will be the sole owner and

beneficiary. When Mr. MacDonald sees that ABC will receive a substantial lump sum at his death, he approaches the Foundation to announce his gift. The planned giving officer explains to Mr. MacDonald that one of the key aspects that make life insurance attractive–the tax benefits–is irrelevant when working with a tax-exempt organization. Instead, the charity representative recommends a different approach.

Using the same $5,500 per year, the planned giving officer prepares two charts in which she compares the insurance as proposed by the planner to: (1) the charity simply investing in mutual funds; and (2) the charity purchasing term insurance on the donor's life with the remaining amount invested in mutual funds. Figure 13.5 shows the values available to the charity in each year assuming the donor lives to age 100. As Mr. MacDonald can see, simply investing the annual donation in the general investment fund yields the best return to the charity. Purchasing term insurance has a slightly lower yield and the permanent insurance model offers a fairly low return.

Figure 13.6

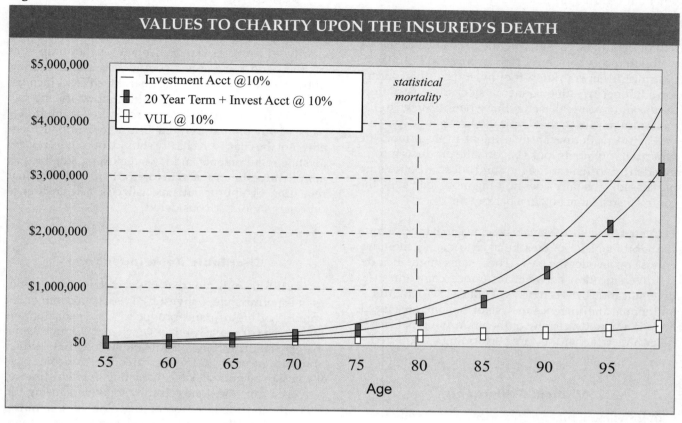

The planned giving officer then turns to Figure 13.6 which shows the same three scenarios but illustrates the value to charity if Mr. MacDonald should pass away in any given year prior to age 100. In the earlier years, the option which does not include insurance has the lowest return to the charity while VUL insurance option is not as appealing in the long term. After reviewing these charts, Mr. MacDonald decides the VUL insurance may not make as much sense as he previously thought but that the term insurance plus mutual fund investments looks appealing.

Group Policies

Another popular insurance program involves a charity investing in a large pool of policies. For example, a university might take a portion of its invested assets and purchase insurance policies on the lives of 5,000 alumni, beginning on the twentieth anniversary of their graduation. All that each insured needs to do is complete a simple one-page form giving the university permission to purchase the insurance. The charity pays the annual premiums out of its current cash flow and in many cases, within a few years, starts collecting the death benefits of those who pass away.

Such a program can offer substantial returns to the charity. But it will also require a significant commitment of time and resources for it to work. From the charity's point of view, it needs to track the lives of all 5,000 alumni in order to collect the death benefits in a timely manner. Furthermore, the charity has the daunting task of monitoring this large pool of policies to ensure that the contracts are performing as expected. Many charities who implemented this type of plan in the 1970s and 1980s unfortunately found that their investment in group insurance had more problems than benefits when the policies did not "vanish" as illustrated.

A charity has a fiduciary duty under state laws to manage the charity's funds in a prudent manner. While the details of this duty may vary from state to state, the majority of the states impose some sort of "prudent investor" duty on a charity's directors. Prior to investing in a sizable group, or even a modest individual insurance program, a charity must assess the inherent risk and

potential return as it would any other investment. In California, for example, a charity's board must "[a]void speculation, looking instead to the permanent disposition of the funds, considering the probable income, as well as the probable safety of the corporation's capital."[14] Charities, in general, know they must apply this concept to traditional investments such as stocks, bonds, mutual funds, and even real estate. But when it comes to life insurance products, they typically take a more passive view. In considering an investment in insurance, the typical charity rarely looks beyond the products recommended by an insurance agent, and once the policies are purchased, it usually does nothing more than store the contracts in a large box in a back room.

Even if the charity's analysis shows that the program can be profitable, steps must be taken to manage the inherent risk on an ongoing basis. These steps might include: (1) diversification between insurance companies; (2) diversification between types of policies; (3) a thorough and annual due diligence analysis of the companies used; and (4) a periodic review of the underlying policies to determine whether they are performing as expected.

Viatical Settlements

A growing number of charities are currently being approached by viatical and senior settlement advisors to either sell the charity's existing contracts or invest in viatical pools. Because the only policies that the promoters are willing to purchase are those that have the highest short- to mid-term potential, charities should not viaticate any policies in their insurance portfolio unless keeping the insurance in force is otherwise impossible. In terms of investing in viatical settlement pools, these assets have little or no regulation and should be considered extremely speculative investments.

Annuities

Annuities have some benefit for certain individual investors because they offer a tax-deferred means of investing in both mutual funds and fixed-interest accounts. Because a charity is already tax-exempt, there is no benefit from a tax standpoint in investing in commercial annuity products. There are a number of relatively new annuity products that offer contractual guarantees even if the underlying account values are exposed to stock market risk. They may sound appealing, but the internal fees for such guarantees can be quite high.

Reinsuring Charitable Gift Annuities

In this planning situation, a donor funds a charitable gift annuity (CGA) with various appreciated assets. The charity, in turn, takes a percentage of the lump sum invested and purchases a commercial immediate annuity that pays the donor the guaranteed CGA income. If the donor lives beyond statistical mortality, the risk is transferred to the insurance company. If the donor passes away prematurely, the insurance company benefits, not the charity. A charity should, of course, review all state requirements and laws regarding suitable gift annuity investments, and in cases where it decides that reinsurance is appropriate, specialized CGA reinsurance products should be considered.

Charitable Remainder Trust

The IRS has indicated that, under certain circumstances, it is permissible to invest CRT assets in commercial annuity and life insurance products.[15] Commercial annuities can be particularly effective when the donor wants to delay taking income for a relatively long time. When annuities are used, the timing and control of income payments can be quite flexible. Investing in life insurance, however, must be done carefully to avoid causing the CRT to be considered a grantor trust. With life insurance, the donor's goal should realistically be to delay income payments until after the insured's death.

WHERE CAN I FIND OUT MORE ABOUT IT?

1. Charitable Life Insurance Evaluation Guidelines: A Tool for Charitable Gift Planners," *National Committee on Planned Giving*, June 2005.

2. Newton, Mark A. and Clontz, Bryan K. "An Analysis of Commercial Insurance as an Alternative Gift Annuity Financing Option," *Journal of Gift Planning* (October, 1998).

3. Stucker, Hal. "Agents Advised to Avoid CGA Commissions," *National Underwriter, Life & Health/Financial Services Edition*, March 6, 2000.

4. Leimberg, Stephan & Zipse, Randy. "Life Insurance and Charitable Planning: How to Stay on the Right Side of the Comfort Line in the (Quick) Sand," *The Journal of Gift Planning*, Fall 2006.

5. Leimberg, Stephan. "Stranger Owned Life Insurance (SOLI): Killing the Goose that Lays Golden Eggs," *Estate Planning*, January 2005.

6. Abramson, Eric. "Evaluating Creative Planned Giving Scenarios Involving Life Insurance," *The Journal of Gift Planning*, Fall 2004.

QUESTIONS AND ANSWERS

Question—What are IOLI, CHOLI, FOLI, and SOLI?

Answer—In the context of charitable planning, these are all variations of the same plan. In Investor Owned Life Insurance (IOLI), a group of policies are established on the lives of the charity's wealthier donors. The charity (or a trust controlled by the charity) purchases the policies and pays the premiums, sometimes using a financing or bond program arranged for by the plan promoter, for a minimum of two years. At the end of that period, the charity sells the policies to an investor or investor group. Since the investors could not otherwise purchase these policies directly, the charity effectively is renting out their insurable interest to benefit this investor group. CHOLI stands for Charity Owned Life Insurance, FOLI is Foundation Owned Life Insurance, and SOLI is Stranger Owned Life Insurance.

Many of these plans vary in how they are established – the source of the premiums, the arrangement for the charity to keep or sell the policies at the end of the contestability period, and so on – but in the long run, the result will be the same. The Senate Finance Committee has proposed a 100% excise tax on all costs involved in these transactions, and while this legislation has not yet passed into law, restrictive legislation in some form is almost certainly to be passed in the near future.

To gather information to better form this future legislation, the Pension Protection Act of 2006 imposed a two-year reporting requirement on all charities that have entered into arrangements where life insurance interests are in anyway split between the charity and private investors. Furthermore, the Treasury Department has been charged with assembling a report to Congress detailing whether these plans are suitable for a charity's tax exempt purpose.[16]

Question – What is charitable split dollar (and charitable reverse split dollar)?

Answer – In both of these arrangements, donors use a charity as a conduit to purchase large amounts of life insurance on a tax-deductible basis. The plans mimicked a similar corporate split dollar technique and while the strategy may or may not have worked under insurance law, it violated several aspects of charity law, in particular private benefit rules.

The IRS effectively shut down this technique with IRS Notice 99-36,[17] and Congress imposed harsh penalties for becoming involved in such plans by enacting legislation in December, 1999 that makes it clear that no deduction is (or was) allowed for the donation of a personal benefit contract.[18] Current law defines a "personal benefit contract" as "any life insurance, annuity, or endowment contract if any direct or indirect beneficiary under such contract is the transferor, any member of the transferor's family, or any other person (other than [certain charitable organizations]) designated by the transferor." Charities that continue to pay premiums on personal benefit contracts must report all payments made after February 8, 1999 to the IRS on Form 8870 and must pay a 100% excise tax on all premiums paid after December 17, 1999.

Because the legislation that was passed in December 1999 made it clear that charitable split dollar and charitable reverse split dollar never did give rise to an income tax deduction, it is possible that some of the charities involved will face legal suits and may even lose their tax-exempt status as a result of their participation in promoting or agreeing to implement these programs.[19]

Question – Can charitable gift annuities pay agents commissions just like annuities issued by insurance companies?

Answer – Several charities are offering substantial commissions to insurance agents who "sell" gift annuities for those charities. But this practice violates the National Council on Planned Giving (NCPG) Model Practice Standards and may also violate state and federal charity laws.

Question – What is "financed charitable life insurance"?

Answer – This is a technique that is also growing in popularity in the non-charitable marketplace. To summarize, the charity takes out a loan from a bank to pay premiums on a pool of insurance contracts.

The death benefits, or in some cases other assets of the charity, are used as collateral for the cumulative loan. This planning is problematic in several ways. Depending on the circumstances, it may trigger unrelated business taxable income, and if the policy does not perform as well as projected, the underlying contract could lapse and the charity would be forced to repay a substantial cumulative loan plus interest with nothing to show in return. Such planning should be considered highly speculative and be scrutinized carefully by legal counsel.[20]

The authors caution practitioners to carefully evaluate the actual performance of the policies and the economic viability of the overall strategies. The more money borrowed, the greater the risk the client is taking and the higher the cost–because the ultimate loan balance must be paid either out-of-pocket during the insured's lifetime or from death proceeds. If the intent is to pay the loan off at death, then sufficient additional death proceeds must be purchased to satisfy the obligation and still have enough proceeds to accomplish the objective of the insurance. The authors suggest that if premium financing is used to support a large life insurance contract, that advisors borrow as little as possible, keep the duration of the loan relatively short, consider worst case scenarios, and develop an "exit strategy" before implementing the plan. Constant monitoring of policy performance and disclosure of the cost and risk to the client are essential.

Question – What are the consequences if a policyowner donates a life insurance contract that has sizable policy loans?

Answer – In the 1980s, a substantial number of life insurance policies were sold as retirement plans or as informal funding for executive deferred compensation plans. A doctor, for example, might invest $30,000 per year into a universal life contract for twelve years. Starting in year 20, he would withdraw $40,000 per year in tax-free loans over the next fifteen years. When interest and dividend rates rapidly declined in the 1980s and 1990s, these insurance policies could no longer support the promised income stream, and contracts which were projected to last until age 100 are now lapsing. As a result, these investors are faced with enormous, unanticipated tax bills in the years the policies lapse and advisors are looking for ways to quickly dispose of these contracts without triggering that tax.

At first glance, a donation of the policy to charity seems to offer that solution. In reality, the transfer will likely be considered a bargain sale, and the donor will recognize the gain as ordinary income. Furthermore, the transaction may violate prohibited self-dealing rules and possibly any deduction will be barred under the new charitable split dollar laws. The legislative history of the charitable split dollar rules says the following:

> If a transferor contributes a life insurance contract to a section 170(c) organization and designates one or more section 170(c) organizations as the sole beneficiaries under the contract, generally, it is not intended that the deduction denial rule under the provision apply. If, however, there is an outstanding loan under the contract upon the transfer of the contract, then the transferor is considered as a beneficiary.

Thus, it appears that any loan against the policy at the time it is donated to a charity, no matter how small that loan is, will result in a disallowance of any deduction for either the contribution of the policy itself or for future premiums. There is no de minimis amount and no way to revive the deduction by paying off the loan after the policy is transferred to the charity.

Question – Can a donor give viatical settlement interests to charity?

Answer – In the past ten years, a secondary market for life insurance has emerged. When policies are purchased from terminally ill insureds, the transaction is called a viatical settlement, and when investors purchase the contracts from elderly or from someone only somewhat unhealthy, it is called a senior, or lifetime, settlement. A large number of investors purchased these investments in anticipation of receiving high, often triple-digit returns. As it turned out, few of these investments have paid what was promised. In many cases, in order to keep their investment from collapsing, investors have been forced into adding more money to pay additional premiums. When investors need to choose between adding more money or losing their investment entirely, it is not surprising that they are looking for ways out of the deal in the most advantageous way possible. In theory, by donating viatical investments to charity, they can receive a substantial deduction for what will shortly be a worthless asset. However, charities should generally not accept these gifts unless the underlying policies have been thoroughly checked to ensure they meet the charity's written gift acceptance policy.

Question – What is an Insurance Product Gift Acceptance Policy?

Answer – Just as a charity's major gift acceptance policy has been designed to screen out toxic real estate assets or illiquid, speculative stock, both of which would be considered inappropriate investments, a charity should also establish written guidelines for which insurance gifts to accept, what should be done regularly to monitor insurance gifts, and under what circumstances existing insurance gifts should be surrendered or sold. In order to ensure that all investments are and remain appropriate, a non-profit organization should establish a minimum set of acceptance standards with the provision that if those standards are not met at the time of the gift or at some later date, that it would only be prudent for the organization to surrender or sell the policy and reinvest the proceeds in more suitable assets. The following is a brief description of the basic criteria used in determining the efficacy of an insurance gift.

- *Required information.* A charity should consider an insurance gift only if the complete contract and a current vanishing in-force illustration are provided for review. For policies that are not contractually "paid-up," a second vanishing in-force illustration should be obtained which assumes a 1-2% reduction in the interest or dividend rate.

- *Complete gift.* The acceptance policy should clearly state that the organization will accept a contract (by absolute assignment or change-of-ownership) only if all incidents of ownership are transferred to the charity, with no ownership interest, benefit, assignment, or endorsement held by or inuring to any party other than the charity.

- *Company quality.* The charity should establish minimum quality standards including: (1) third party ratings; (2) key financial ratios; (3) operating performance; and (4) market profile measures. All of these factors should be reviewed annually as they could expose some serious problems about the insurance company's long-term viability.

- *Paid-up status.* As many charities have come to realize in recent years, "paid-up" and "vanished" mean very different things. A paid-up contract means that the policy owner is guaranteed that no additional premiums are required beyond a specified date. A vanished policy means that, at current rates, the projected interest and dividends will be sufficient to keep the policy in force. If interest rates or dividends decrease, substantial additional payments may be required. A written gift acceptance policy should outline ongoing supervision for vanished policies.

- *Policy loans.* If interest is not paid annually on outstanding loans, an insurance policy can quickly collapse from the compounding debt. If a charity is unwilling to service loans, the gift acceptance policy should prohibit it from accepting such contracts unless it plans to immediately surrender the policy. Furthermore, the gift policy should caution the charity from taking new policy loans and reinvesting this cash in yet another income-producing investment, because income produced by the investment purchased with the loan proceeds would be "debt-related income" and would be considered unrelated business income and therefore taxable. And finally, if the organization is a private foundation, all gifts of life insurance with an outstanding loan balance should be refused, because acceptance of such contracts is a prohibited transaction.

- *Term blends.* Most planned giving professionals realize that a $100,000 whole life policy has different charges and guarantees than a $100,000 term policy. Few development officers understand the consequences and risks when a policy is made up of both term and permanent elements. In some cases, a high percentage of term insurance adds a tremendous amount of volatility to a contract. In other cases, the use of term insurance can substantially reduce the outlay without greatly increasing risk. A well written policy statement should place limits on the percentage of term insurance that is acceptable if volatility is anticipated.

Question – How does a charity "count" insurance gifts?

Answer – For a variety of reasons, charities must take a written inventory of the completed gifts in their planned giving portfolio on a regular basis. Because planned gifts can be valued in a variety of ways (nominal value or present value, fair market value or discounted value), in order to establish some consistency, most charities follow the guidelines established by the Council for Advancement and Support of Education (CASE).

To make things even more confusing, charities often count planned gifts using different methods for different purposes: annual counting (similar to an annual inventory) often differs from campaign counting (when the charity is in the middle of a special fund raising drive which often lasts for two or more years.) While the question of counting insurance contracts arises regularly, there is unfortunately no authoritative work that completely or accurately reflects the value of insurance contracts to a charity.

The following is a brief outline of the CASE guidelines, but these are neither comprehensive nor, in some cases, appropriate.

- *Annual counting.* For contracts where the donor transfers all ownership interests to the charity, the gift is reported as an outright gift at the cash surrender value. Premium payments made by a donor are reported as outright gifts. If the charity is named the beneficiary, but not owner, of a contract, the value of the gift is the death benefit and is only credited on the date the death benefit is paid to the charity as a result of the donor's death.

- *Capital campaigns.* Some charities do not include insurance gifts in their capital campaign totals, while others have a choice of counting methods. Under the simpler method, the annual counting rules above are used. In a more complex approach, a discount factor is applied to the policy's death benefit. This amount would also be adjusted to reflect policy loans, automatic premium loans, and decreasing future death benefits.

Neither of the above counting guidelines reflects the true value of an insurance contract. For example, assume a donor has been diagnosed with a terminal illness and has a life expectancy of only one year. He is currently taking care of his final affairs and gives his favorite charity a $1 million renewable term policy. Because there is no cash value for this type of contract, the CASE guidelines suggest that the policy has no value. But if the charity can expect to receive $1 million within the next year, clearly the real value of this contract is significantly higher.

And finally, the question often arises of how to value gifts of life insurance for donor recognition purposes. Several charities give credit for the present value of the death benefit, while others actually credit the nominal face value of the policy. At this time, there appears to be no set standards regarding these gifts.

Question – What is involved in monitoring a charity's insurance portfolio?

Answer – In an environment of declining interest rates and dividends and rapidly changing company structures, the age of simply storing life insurance contracts in a box in the back room until it is time to collect a death benefit is gone. Contracts require regular monitoring and review just like any other significant investment.

When managing a portfolio on a case-by-case basis, the following approach should be considered:

- When a charity first receives or purchases a policy, it should be sure to obtain the illustration that was valid as of the date of the gift or gift. The charity based its original decision to invest in this policy (or accept it as a gift) on these figures, and by comparing future values to the original illustration, the charity can determine whether the contract is performing on track.

- Each year, on or around the policy anniversary date, a charity should request a copy of an in-force illustration from the insurance company at both current interest or dividend rates and at 1% below current rates. Many charities faced financial problems with their portfolios when dividend rates started declining in the mid to late 1980s. Had these charities been reviewing these in-force illustrations each year, they would have had ample warning that the contracts would require additional outlay in the future.

- As part of the annual review, a charity should check the insurance company's financial health through third party rating services, news services, and other insurance trade publications.

If charities and their advisors had put the same time and effort into managing their insurance portfolio that they put into managing their other investment holdings, many of the problems and losses experienced over the past ten years could have been avoided. If they cannot dedicate the necessary time and staff to maintaining these investments in a prudent manner, then they should consider accepting only larger, established, paid-up policies or, in the extreme, avoiding insurance gifts completely.

Question – What should a charity consider if an insurance policy is no longer sustainable?

Answer – Should a charity decide that it is no longer feasible to keep an insurance contract, it should consider all of its options rather than simply canceling the policy.

- *Discuss additional premium payments with the donor.* If, for whatever reason, a charity cannot, or feels it should not, pay the premiums, the donor who originally gave the contract should be contacted to determine whether he is willing to assist with this outlay.

- *Reduce the death benefit.* If a charity no longer wants to pay the premiums, one favorable option is to reduce the death benefit to a level where current cash values are sufficient to pay up the policy. This is called placing the policy on "reduced paid-up" status.

- *Sell the policy.* In the event that the insured is unhealthy, or the policy is particularly valuable in the secondary market (high face amount with an insured over age 70), a viatical or senior settlement should be considered.

- *Surrender the contract.* Should the charity decide that surrendering the contract is the most appropriate option, care should be taken to time the surrender for the best value. For example, if the policy is a whole life contract that pays dividends annually on the policy anniversary date, surrendering the contract two weeks before that date could net the charity significantly less.

CHAPTER ENDNOTES

1. "Charity Oversight and Reform: Keeping Bad Things from Happening to Good Charities", Senate Finance Committee, http://finance.senate.gov/hearings/testimony/2004test/062204jmtest.pdf.

2. IRC Sec. 79(a); Treas. Reg. §1.79-3(d)(2).

3. IRC Sec. 79(b)(2)(B); Treas. Reg. §1.79-2(c)(3).

4. IRC Sec. 170(f)(3)(A); Rev. Rul. 76-143, 1976-1 CB 63.

5. IRC Sec. 170(f)(10); Notice 99-36, 1999-1 CB 1284.

6. IRC Sec. 170(e)(1)(A); see Treas. Reg. §25.2512-6(a), Exs. 3 & 4.

7. Treas. Reg. §1.170A-13(c).

8. IRC Sec.170(f)(11).

9. IRCSec. 6695A.

10. Treas. Reg. §1.170A-4(a).

11. D.C. Code Ann. §31-4716.

12. Assumes a rate of return that is 1% below the current credited interest rate.

13. The taxation of charitable gift annuities funded with ordinary income property such as insurance or annuities is untested at this time.

14. Cal. Corp. Code Sec. 5240.

15. See Let. Rul. 8745013, Let. Rul. 9227017, TAM 9825001, Let. Rul. 199915045.

16. IRC Sec. 6050V.

17. Notice 99-36, 1999-1 CB 1284.

18. IRC Sec. 170(f)(10).

19. See commentary on charitable split dollar at www.leimbergservices.com.

20. See Stephan Leimberg and Albert Gibbons, "Premium Financing: The Last Choice - Not the First Choice," *Estate Planning* (January, 2001), p. 35.

CHARITABLE LEAD TRUSTS

CHAPTER 14

WHAT IS IT?

A charitable lead trust (CLT) is a form of split-interest charitable trust. Conceptually, the charitable lead trust is the opposite of the charitable remainder trust (CRT) because the charity receives the annuity stream, and the grantor (or his heirs) receives the remainder value. Conversely, in a CRT the grantor (or his heirs) receives the annuity stream, and the charity receives the remainder value (see Chapter 16). Technically, CLTs resemble CRTs in some respects, but differ from CRTs in other respects. The differences between CLTs and CRTs will be explained below in "Questions and Answers."

Each year's annuity stream can be set up to be paid *either* as a sum certain (i.e., an annuity trust), *or* as a fixed percentage of the trust (i.e., a unitrust). When the charity's income interest ends, the assets in the trust are

Figure 14.1

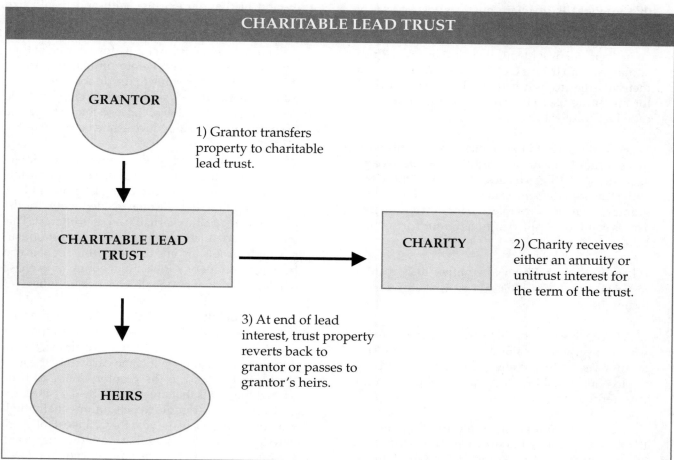

CHARITABLE LEAD TRUST

GRANTOR

1) Grantor transfers property to charitable lead trust.

CHARITABLE LEAD TRUST

CHARITY

2) Charity receives either an annuity or unitrust interest for the term of the trust.

3) At end of lead interest, trust property reverts back to grantor or passes to grantor's heirs.

HEIRS

passed to a noncharity beneficiary (e.g., the grantor's children), or the assets are paid back to the grantor.

Charitable lead trusts can be set up during lifetime or created at a client's death. CLTs may provide income, gift, or estate tax benefits while also meeting a client's charitable giving aspirations. Figure 14.1 graphically depicts a CLT.

There are two types of charitable lead trusts: one that does not provide an income tax deduction, and one that does. The type that does *not* provide an income tax deduction is *not* taxable to the grantor/donor, while the type that does provide an income tax deduction up front is taxable to the grantor/donor in all of the following years. These two types of lead trusts are explained in more detail below.

WHEN IS THE USE OF SUCH A DEVICE INDICATED?

- When a client is charitably inclined and has property that he would like to retain, but does not necessarily need the current income from the property.

    A client can provide his favorite charity with an annuity stream from a CLT for a period of time and then have the property in the CLT revert back to him for his future use. This type of CLT is commonly called a "grantor lead trust."

- When a client would like to pass assets to his heirs in the future, but with reduced gift or estate tax consequences. A CLT can be designed so that the assets in the trust pass to heirs instead of going back to the grantor when the charitable lead interest terminates. This is commonly called a "nongrantor" or "family lead trust."

- When a client seeks an alternative to a grantor retained annuity trust (GRAT) as an estate freezing technique.

    A GRAT is a noncharitable split-interest trust in which the grantor retains an annuity interest for a term of years, with the remainder typically passing to noncharitable beneficiaries at the end of the trust term.

    A CLT can be a viable estate freezing alternative to a GRAT in situations where: (1) the client is concerned about inclusion of the GRAT in his

estate due to age or poor health; or (2) where the client does not need the income stream that would be paid from the GRAT.

The gift tax value of the property transferred to a GRAT (and therefore to the GRAT's beneficiaries) is reduced by the value of the income interest retained by the grantor. Gifts to a CLT have a similar impact—the gift tax value of the property transferred to a CLT is reduced by the present value of the charity's right to receive the annuity stream for a specified period of time.

However, because the grantor retains an annuity interest in the GRAT, the date of death value of the income stream from the trust is included in the grantor's estate if death occurs before the trust terminates.[1] Alternatively, in a family lead trust, the assets do not revert back to the grantor. Consequently, the value of the CLT is not brought back into the grantor's estate when the grantor dies.

- When the client would like to benefit both charity and his heirs upon his death and would like to accomplish this with reduced estate taxation. A "testamentary" CLT can be established that would provide for payments to charity for a period of time after the donor's death before ultimately passing the trust remainder value to the donor's heirs. The estate is entitled to a sizable estate tax charitable deduction for the value of the lead interest payable to charity, which will reduce estate taxes.

- When a client would like to create an immediate income tax deduction to offset unusually high taxable income in a particular year. Using a "grantor" CLT creates an immediate income tax deduction for the present value of the charitable income interest. This income tax deduction can be used to offset unusually high taxable income received from the sale of a business, receipt of a substantial bonus, or exercise of a large block of nonqualified stock options.

    The trade-off or cost of obtaining a large, immediate deduction is that beginning with the year following the year the deduction is claimed, and in all future tax years, the income earned by the lead trust will be taxed to the grantor/donor as if he owned the assets that are actually held by the CLT. Of course, if the donor expects an unusually high amount of income in the year the CLT is established, and significantly lower taxable income in later years, the trade-off might be very advantageous.

ADVANTAGES

1. Charitable lead trusts can provide a benefit to charity without having to permanently "give away" the asset. The CLT is one of only a few forms of split-interest charitable gifts that qualify for the income, gift, or estate tax charitable deduction.

2. If designed as a "grantor lead trust," an income tax charitable deduction is allowed at the date the trust is funded for the actuarial value of the annuity stream payable to the specified charity (or charities).

3. Unlike some other wealth transfer techniques (e.g., GRATs or qualified personal residence trusts, "QPRTs"), lead trusts can be created either while the donor is alive (i.e., an inter vivos trust) or upon death (i.e., a testamentary trust).

4. It may be possible to create a lead trust that is both a "grantor trust" for income tax purposes and an irrevocable trust for gift and estate tax purposes (i.e., a "defective grantor trust"). This would provide an income tax deduction for the grantor, while also ultimately passing the lead trust assets to the grantor's heirs with reduced gift taxation.

5. Unlike charitable remainder trusts (CRTs), which are restricted on the term length that can be used, charitable lead trusts can be for virtually any term length desired by the grantor/donor.

DISADVANTAGES

1. Unlike charitable remainder trusts, lead trusts are *not* tax-exempt entities. If the lead trust is a "grantor trust," all of the income earned by the trust (including the lead interest paid to charity) will be taxed to the grantor rather than to the trust. On the other hand, a family lead trust will have to pay income tax on any trust income it receives in excess of the lead interest it pays to charity.[2]

2. Contributions to a charitable lead trust do not always generate an income tax deduction. An income tax deduction is allowed only if the lead trust is a "grantor trust" for income tax purposes.

3. Lead trusts must comply with many of the private foundation rules.[3]

WHAT ARE THE REQUIREMENTS?

1. Payments to the charity (i.e., the "lead" interest) must be paid in the form of:

   - a *guaranteed annuity interest*, which is an irrevocable right to receive payment of a sum certain at least annually (i.e., charitable lead annuity trust or CLAT); or

   - a *unitrust interest*, which is an irrevocable right to receive at least annually a fixed percentage of trust assets, as revalued each year (i.e., charitable lead unitrust or CLUT).[4]

2. The term of the lead interest can be *either* for a specified term of years (e.g., 5, 10, 15, 20, or 25 years) selected by the donor, *or* for the life of an individual (or the lives of individuals). If the lead interest is based on the life of an individual (or the lives of individuals), the individual or individuals must be alive at the time the property is transferred to the trust. (Only one or more of the following individuals may be used as the measuring life or lives: (1) the donor; (2) the donor's spouse; (3) a lineal ancestor of all the remainder beneficiaries; or (4) the spouse of a lineal ancestor of all the remainder beneficiaries.)[5]

   The lead interest (annuity or unitrust) can also be paid for the life of an individual *plus* a term of years.[6] Unlike a charitable remainder trust, which has a "term of years" limit of 20 years, there is no limitation on the term length for a "term of years" CLT. Furthermore, a guaranteed annuity interest may be made to continue for the shorter of (1) a term of years, or (2) lives in being *plus* a term of years.[7]

3. In order to receive an income tax deduction, the grantor of the CLT must be treated as the owner of the trust for income tax purposes (i.e., a "grantor trust"). In a "grantor trust," the trust is ignored for income tax purposes and the grantor pays the income tax on all trust taxable income. The result of this requirement is that the grantor will receive an immediate income tax deduction for the value of the lead interest, but will pay income tax each year on all taxable income generated by the trust (including the income used to pay the lead interest to the specified charity).[8]

4. Charitable lead trusts must comply with many of the private foundation rules (see Chapter 21). Therefore, the trust document should prohibit certain activities such as engaging in self-dealing, excess busi-

ness holdings, jeopardy investments, and taxable expenditures.[9]

5. The Internal Revenue Service has published sample declarations of trust which can be used a guide when creating an inter vivos or testamentary CLAT.[10]

HOW IS IT DONE – EXAMPLES

Example 1: Reversionary grantor lead trust. Brenda Lang owns Decorating Unlimited, a floral and wedding consulting business. Brenda's interest in Decorating Unlimited has a fair market value of $1,000,000 with a cost basis of $250,000. Besides her business interest, she also owns a sizable portfolio of tax-exempt bonds.

Brenda has received an offer to sell her interest in the business. But she is concerned about the large capital gains tax she would incur if she were to sell. One way for Brenda to reduce the potential tax burden on the sale of the business would be to transfer her tax-exempt bond portfolio to a "grantor charitable lead annuity trust" for a specified term of years. Brenda would be entitled to an immediate charitable income tax deduction for the calculated value of the charitable lead interest, which could then be used to offset the taxable income incurred from the sale of the business. At the end of the trust term, the bond portfolio would revert back to Brenda.

If Brenda contributes $500,000 of tax-exempt bonds to a 12-year CLAT paying 6.5%, the value of the charitable lead interest for income tax deduction purposes will be $269,513 (assuming that payments would be made at the end and not the beginning of the year, and also assuming a Section 7520 rate of 6.2%).[11] In a 40% income tax bracket, this will save $107,805. Because the maximum income tax deduction allowed in any one year for a contribution to a charitable lead trust is 30% of adjusted gross income (AGI), Brenda's AGI would need to exceed $898,377 in order to take full advantage of the tax savings in the current year.[12] Assuming a 15% capital gains rate, if Brenda sells the business for $1,000,000 and has a cost basis of $250,000, the capital gains tax on the sale will be $112,500 ($750,000 gain x 15%). Therefore, the tax savings of $107,805 generated by creating the lead trust would effectively reduce the taxes due on the sale of the business from $112,500 to $4,695 ($112,500 tax - $107,805 tax savings = $4,695 net tax). Figure 14.2 details the calculation of the income tax deduction allowed for the lead interest.[13]

In addition to the income tax savings provided by creating the lead trust, Brenda's favorite charity (or charities) would receive an annuity payment of $32,500 (6.5% x $500,000) every year for the next 12 years. This is attractive to Brenda because she is actively involved in several charitable organizations.

Because the lead trust is a "grantor" type trust, Brenda would have to pay income tax on *all* of

Figure 14.2

Trust Type:	Term
§7520 Rate:	6.2%
FMV of Trust:	$500,000
Percentage of Payout:	6.500%
Payment Period:	Annual
Payment Timing:	End
Term:	12

Annual Payout:	$32,500
Term Certain Annuity Factor:	8.2927
Payout Frequency Factor:	1.0000
Present Value of Annuity:	$269,513
Remainder Interest = FMV of Trust less PV of Annuity:	$230,487
Charitable Deduction for Income Interest:	$269,513
Donor's Deduction as Percentage of Amount Transferred:	53.903%

the income generated by the trust. This would include any income used to make the annuity payment to charity as part of the lead interest. However, since the trust would be funded with tax-exempt bonds, there may be little, if any taxes actually due on the trust income.

Thus, by using a "grantor lead trust," Brenda can reduce the taxes incurred from the sale of the business, provide an immediate benefit to her favorite charities through the lead interest, and enjoy the benefits of the bond portfolio at the end of the trust term.

Example 2: Family CLAT as an estate freeze tool. Brandon and Lauren Lang have a net estate of $6,000,000, with a significant portion of the estate consisting of rental real estate. Brandon and Lauren have two children, Brandon Jr. and Chelsea, to whom they are currently making annual gifts equal to the available gift tax exclusion ($12,000 in 2007). They have not yet used any of their available gift tax unified credit applicable exclusion amount ($1,000,000). They are, however, making sizable charitable gifts each year, and have considered establishing a private foundation.

Because they are charitably inclined and wish to reduce the estate tax bill that will be incurred at the survivor's death, the Langs have decided to create a CLAT and a private foundation. They will fund the CLAT with $2,000,000 of real estate,

with the CLAT paying a 6% annuity for a term of 20 years. The annuity stream from the CLAT will be paid to their newly established foundation. At the end of the lead interest, the real estate will pass to Brandon Jr. and Chelsea.

Since the assets in the CLAT will not revert back to Brandon and Lauren, but instead will ultimately pass to their heirs (Brandon, Jr. and Chelsea), the transfer to the CLAT will be a completed gift to the children for gift tax purposes. However, the value of that transfer for gift tax purposes will be reduced by the value of the annuity interest paid to the foundation. Assuming a Section 7520 rate of 6.2%, the lead interest for a 20-year annuity of 6% will be $1,354,320. Therefore, the value of the taxable gift for gift tax purposes is $645,680 ($2,000,000 - $1,354,320), against which the Lang's gift tax unified credit applicable exclusion amount ($1,000,000) can be applied, resulting in no gift tax.

Assuming the real estate grows 3% per year (after reduction for annuity payments to foundation), it will be worth $3,612,222 at the end of the trust term. Consequently, the Langs will have transferred over $3.6 million of wealth to their children without having incurred any gift or estate taxes. In addition, they will have funded their private foundation with $2,400,000 ($120,000 per year x 20 years) over the term of the CLAT. Figure 14.3 details the calculation of the lead interest for this example.[14]

Figure 14.3

Trust Type:	Term
§7520 Rate:	6.2%
FMV of Trust:	$2,000,000
Percentage of Payout:	6.000%
Payment Period:	Annual
Payment Timing:	End
Term:	20
Annual Payout:	$120,000
Term Certain Annuity Factor:	11.2860
Payout Frequency Factor:	1.0000
Present Value of Annuity:	$1,354,320
Remainder Interest = FMV of Trust less PV of Annuity:	$645,680
Charitable Deduction for Income Interest:	$1,354,320
Donor's Deduction as Percentage of Amount Transferred:	67.716%

WHAT ARE THE TAX IMPLICATIONS?

In order to qualify for the income, gift, or estate tax charitable deduction, the lead trust must be structured as either a *guaranteed annuity interest* or a *unitrust interest*. If payments are not made in this manner, charitable income, gift, or estate tax deductions will not be allowed.[15] The present value of the charitable lead interest (i.e., the charity's right to the annuity stream) is deductible for income, gift, or estate tax purposes. In a grantor lead trust, a charitable income tax deduction is allowed. In an inter vivos family lead trust, a charitable gift tax (but no income tax) deduction is allowed. Finally, in a testamentary lead trust, an estate tax charitable deduction is allowed.

Charitable Lead Annuity Trust (CLAT). In a CLAT, the charitable income beneficiary is granted an irrevocable right to a guaranteed sum certain, paid at least annually, for the term of the trust. Unlike the charitable remainder trust however, there are no minimum or maximum percentages that are required to be used to determine the annuity payment.[16] Once the annuity amount is determined, it is guaranteed. Consequently, if the income earned by the trust is insufficient to make the annuity payment, the trustee must invade trust principal to satisfy the annuity interest that has been promised to charity.

Charitable Lead Unitrust (CLUT). In a CLUT, the charitable beneficiary must be paid a fixed percentage of the trust assets each year for the term of the trust. Unlike the charitable remainder trust, there are no specific minimum or maximum unitrust percentages that must be used in a CLUT. So it is possible (at least theoretically) to select any percentage as the payout rate.

Valuing the Charitable Deduction

In general, the value of an income, gift, or estate tax charitable deduction is the present value of the lead (annuity or unitrust) interest payable to charity. The primary factors used in the computation of the present value of the lead interest are: (1) the length of the trust term; (2) the annuity or unitrust rate to be paid to charity; (3) the frequency of payment, and (4) the Section 7520 rate in effect at the time the trust is funded. The Section 7520 rate is 120% of the federal applicable midterm rate (rounded to the nearest two-tenths of 1%), and is published by the IRS on a monthly basis.

Generally, a larger deduction can be obtained by stretching out the trust term. Likewise, the charitable deduction can be increased by increasing the payout rate. In contrast, for annuity trusts in particular, using a higher Section 7520 rate yields a smaller charitable deduction. The grantor has the choice of using the Section 7520 rate in effect the month the trust is funded, or the rate in effect for either of the two previous months.[17]

Grantor Lead Trust

Income tax consequences. In order to qualify for the income tax charitable deduction, the grantor must be treated as the owner of the trust for income tax purposes ("a grantor trust").[18] The deductible amount is the present value of the annuity or unitrust lead interest payable to the charitable beneficiary. However, the charitable lead interest is considered a gift "for the use of" charity rather than a gift "to" charity (see Chapter 3). Therefore, the donor's current charitable deduction will be limited to 30% of AGI (20% for gifts of appreciated property).[19] Note that the excess is not lost. Any portion of the lead interest that cannot be deducted in the current year due to the deduction limitations can be carried over for an additional five years.[20]

If the trust ceases to be a grantor trust because the grantor dies, or relinquishes grantor trust powers, the charitable income tax deduction is recaptured. The amount recaptured is equal to the initial charitable deduction less the discounted amounts that were actually paid to the charitable beneficiary up to the time the trust ceased to be a grantor trust.[21]

As explained above, in a grantor trust the grantor is taxed personally on all trust income including the lead interest payable to charity. In essence, a grantor trust is treated as if the trust was nonexistent for income tax purposes. Because of this tax consequence, grantor lead trusts are typically funded with tax-exempt assets, such as municipal bonds.

Gift and estate tax consequences. If the trust proceeds will revert back to the grantor at the end of the lead interest, the value of the assets in the CLT will be included in the grantor's estate at death.[22] In addition, where the CLT remainder reverts back to the grantor, the transfer of assets to the CLT is not a completed gift subject to gift taxes.

Family Lead Trust

Income tax consequences. The grantor of a family lead trust is *not* entitled to an income tax deduction and is *not* taxed on trust income. Instead, the trust is taxed as a complex trust and the trust receives an income tax deduction for trust income paid to charity as part of the lead interest.[23] All trust income above the annuity or unitrust lead interest paid to charity is taxed to the trust.

Gift and estate tax consequences. The transfer of assets to a family lead trust is a completed gift for gift tax purposes. In essence, there are two gifts being made—a gift of the lead interest to charity, and a gift of the remainder interest to the grantor's heirs. When properly structured, a charitable gift tax deduction is allowed for the present value of the lead interest passing to charity. However, the present value of the remainder interest passing to the donor's heirs is a gift subject to gift taxation. Because the remainder interest in the trust is a completed gift while the donor is living, the value of the trust is *not* included in the estate of the grantor at death.

Under EGTRRA 2001, the *gift* tax rates are scheduled for incremental reduction through 2009, and further reduction in 2010.[24] The *estate* tax rates are also scheduled for incremental reduction through 2009, and for *repeal* in 2010 and restoration in 2011.[25]

Generation-skipping tax consequences. If the remainder interest in a family CLT passes to heirs two generations or lower than the grantor (for example, grandchildren or great-grandchildren), the generation skipping tax (GST) will also apply. Due to the way the GST tax is calculated and the GST exemption is applied with a CLT, use of a CLAT can potentially cause GST tax problems.[26] In general, a CLUT should be considered if a CLT is to be designed as a generation-skipping trust.

Under EGTRRA 2001, the generation-skipping tax is scheduled for incremental reduction through 2009, and for *repeal* in 2010 and restoration in 2011.[27]

WHERE CAN I FIND OUT MORE ABOUT IT?

1. Toce, Joseph, Abbin, Byrle, Vorsatz, Mark, and Page, William, *Tax Economics of Charitable Giving 2007-2008* (Warren Gorham & Lamont, 2007).

2. Colliton, James W., *Charitable Gifts,* 3rd edition (Warren Gorham & Lamont, 1998).

3. Leimberg, Stephan R., et al., *The Tools & Techniques of Estate Planning,* 14th edition (Cincinnati, OH: The National Underwriter Company, 2007).

4. Osteen, Carolyn M., et. al., *The Harvard Manual on Tax Aspects of Charitable Giving,* 8th edition (Boston, MA: 1999).

QUESTIONS AND ANSWERS

Question – How is a charitable lead trust different from a charitable remainder trust?

Answer – While both are split-interest charitable trusts, there are significant differences between charitable lead trusts and charitable remainder trusts. The most obvious difference is that the income and remainder beneficiary roles are reversed. In a lead trust, a charity is entitled to the annuity or unitrust interest and a noncharitable beneficiary is entitled to the remainder. Conversely, in a charitable remainder trust, the noncharitable beneficiary is entitled to the annuity or unitrust interest with a charitable beneficiary receiving the remainder interest.

Aside from the reversed trust interest roles, there are other differences. For example, charitable remainder trusts are tax-exempt entities whereas charitable lead trusts are not. Additionally, charitable remainder trusts have minimum and maximum payout rates, as well as maximum term limits. Charitable lead trusts do not have these same requirements.

Question – What types of assets are typically used to fund a CLT?

Answer – Almost any type of asset can be transferred to a CLT. However, assets that are both income producing (to pay the lead income interest) and rapidly appreciating (to pass increased wealth to heirs with reduced gift and estate taxes) are preferred. Assets that often work well in a CLT include rental real estate, dividend-paying stock, or a balanced portfolio of securities.

Since the grantor is taxed on all trust income in a grantor lead trust, tax-exempt securities such as municipal bonds are commonly used to fund a grantor lead trust in order to reduce the taxable income the grantor must pay.

Question – Are there "problem assets" that should *not* be used to fund a CLT?

Answer – Caution must be used when transferring mortgaged property or closely held business interests to a CLT.

Transferring mortgaged property to a CLT can cause problems for the grantor. If the debt on the property exceeds the grantor's basis in the property, the transfer will be treated as part gift/part sale and the grantor may have gain recognition on the transfer. Also, depending on when the debt was placed on the property, the transfer of encumbered property to a CLT may cause unrelated business taxable income (UBTI). If the trust has UBTI, a portion of the trust's deduction for payment of the lead interest to charity may be disallowed.[28]

The transfer of closely-held stock or partnership interests to a CLT may cause problems with the prohibition against "excess business holdings." Charitable lead trusts must comply with the private foundation restriction against excess business holdings. In general, the CLT cannot hold more than 20% of the voting interests in a business without running afoul of the excess business holdings restriction. An excise tax is imposed on the value of any excess business holdings that exceed the 20% threshold.[29]

There are exceptions to the excess business holdings restriction that may apply to transfers of closely-held business interests to a CLT and allow for a transfer of more than 20% of the voting interests:

1. If the CLT receives property through a gift or bequest that may cause an excess business holdings problem, the trust has five years from the date it acquires the holdings to dispose of that property.

2. As long as the value of the charitable lead interest does not exceed 60% of the value of the total fair market value of the trust, *and* the entire income interest (but none of the remainder interest) is payable to charity, an exception to the excess business holdings restriction will apply.[30]

Question – What is a charitable lead "super trust"?

Answer – A "super trust" is a CLT that is considered a grantor lead trust for income tax purposes, but a family lead trust for gift and estate tax purposes. This type of trust design is commonly called a "defective grantor trust." By structuring the trust in this manner, the grantor can benefit in the following ways:

- receive an immediate income tax deduction allowed for a grantor lead trust;

- reduce gift taxation on the assets that will ultimately pass to his heirs; and

- remove the assets, including future appreciation, from the taxable estate at death.

Designing a "super lead trust" requires careful drafting of the trust document so that provisions are included that will make the trust a grantor trust for income tax purposes, but will not cause the trust proceeds to be included for estate tax purposes. *Caution*: This is an unproven technique, and it is not certain that the desired results will be achieved.

CHAPTER ENDNOTES

1. IRC Sec. 2036(a)(1); Prop. Treas. Reg. §20-2036-1; REG-119097-05, 72 Fed. Reg. 31487 (6-7-2007).
2. IRC Secs. 671, 642(c)(1).
3. IRC Secs. 4947(a)(2), 4941, 4943, 4944, 4945.
4. IRC Secs. 170(f)(2)(B), 2055(e)(2)(B), 2522(c)(2)(B).
5. Treas. Regs. §§ 1.170A-6(c)(2), 20.2055-2(e)(2), 25.2522(c)-3(c)(2).
6. Treas. Regs. §§ 1.170A-6(c)(2), 20.2055-2(e)(2), 25.2522(c)-3(c)(2).
7. Rev. Rul. 85-49, 1985-1 CB 330; Rev. Proc. 2007-45, 2007-29 IRB 89; Rev. Proc. 2007-46, 2007-29 IRB 102.
8. IRC Sec. 170(f)(2)(B); Treas. Reg. §1.170A-6(c)(1).
9. IRC Secs. 4947(a)(2), 4941, 4943, 4944, 4945.
10. Rev. Proc. 2007-45, 2007-29 IRB 89; Rev. Proc. 2007-46, 2007-29 IRB 102.
11. This example assumes a Section 7520 rate of 6.2%. Section 7520 rates are issued monthly by the IRS. Donors may use the rate for the month the trust is funded or may "look back" in either of the two prior months and choose the best rate of the three. In fact, by waiting until the IRS releases the next month's rates—typically between the 18th and the 22nd of each month—it is possible to select the best of four month's rates. Section 7520 rates are available at Leimberg.com and taxfactsonline.com.
12. Contributions to a charitable lead trust are considered to be gifts "for the use of" charity rather than as gifts "to" charity. Thus, the donor's contribution is subject to a limitation of 30% of adjusted gross income as the maximum deduction that can be taken in one year. IRC Sec. 170(b)(1)(B); Treas. Regs. §§1.170A-8(a)(2), 1.170A-8(c).
13. Computation courtesy of NumberCruncher software (Leimberg.com).
14. Computation courtesy of NumberCruncher software (Leimberg.com).
15. IRC Secs. 170(f)(2)(b), 2055(e)(2)(B), 2522(c)(2)(B).
16. A charitable remainder trust is required to pay an annuity or unitrust amount of not less than 5% and not more than 50% of the net fair market value of the trust assets. IRC Secs. 664(d)(1), 664(d)(2).

17. IRC Secs. 7520(a)(1), 7520(a)(2).

18. IRC Sec. 170(f)(2)(B); Treas. Reg. §1.170A-6(c)(1).

19. IRC Sec. 170(b)(1)(B); Treas. Regs. §§1.170A-8(a)(2), 1.170A-8(c).

20. IRC Secs. 170(b)(1)(B), 170(b)(1)(D)(ii).

21. See Treas. Reg. §1.170A-6(c)(4).

22. IRC Secs. 2036, 2038.

23. IRC Secs. 641(a), 642(c)(1).

24. IRC Secs. 2001(c), 2502(a).

25. IRC Sec. 2210, as amended by EGTRRA 2001.

26. Under IRC Section 2642(e), the final determination of the amount of trust exempt from GST is not made until the end of the lead interest. Consequently, there is the possibility that a portion of a CLAT could be subject to GST, or that some of the GST exemption applied could be wasted because the trust remainder value ends up being less than the exemption amount allocated.

27. IRC Secs. 2001(c), 2010(c), 2631(c), 2641, 2664.

28. Treas. Reg. §1.681(a)-2(b).

29. IRC Sec. 4943.

30. IRC Sec. 4943(c)(6); Treas. Reg. §1.170A-(6)(c)(2)(i)(d).

CHARITABLE REMAINDER ANNUITY TRUSTS

CHAPTER 15

WHAT IS IT?

A charitable remainder annuity trust (CRAT) is a form of split-interest trust established between one or more donors and a trustee. (A split-interest trust is a trust that has both charitable and noncharitable beneficiaries.) Typically the donor transfers cash or other property into the trust. The trust then pays a fixed annuity for a term of years or the life (or lives) of one or more individuals. At the end of that specified term (or when the noncharitable annuitants have all died), the trust is continued for, or its assets are distributed to, one or more qualified charities.

Ordinarily, a taxpayer receives a charitable deduction only for a gift of a complete interest in property. A gift of a partial interest does not qualify for a charitable deduction unless a specific provision in the Internal Revenue Code allows for such a partial interest deduction. (See Chapters 5, 14, and 16 for explanations of partial interest gifts.) One such statutory exception to the partial interest rule is the CRAT.

The donor can claim an income and gift tax charitable deduction for the actuarially determined present value of the charity's remainder interest; an estate tax deduction can be taken if the trust is funded by a transfer at death.

WHEN IS THE USE OF SUCH A DEVICE INDICATED?

1. When the donor wishes to make a large charitable gift while retaining an annuity interest in the donated property.

2. When the donor does not anticipate making additions to the trust (see "What are the Requirements," below).

3. When the donor is risk-averse and would like to "fix" the payments and, thus, avoid a potential decrease in payments should the market value of the charitable remainder unitrust's (CRUT's) assets decline at some point in the future.

4. When the donor wants to make a gift at death while providing an annuity benefit for one or more individuals, with the remainder passing to one or more charities. However, it is not the preferred giving technique if the property being transferred is debt-encumbered.[1]

ADVANTAGES

1. There is no risk of the reduced cash flow that might result with a CRUT due to a decline in the value of the trust assets.

2. There is no risk of loss of principal as with a charitable gift annuity. The property is in the hands of the CRAT's trustee until the expiration of the annuity interest.

3. The CRAT can also be an effective way to provide a benefit (i.e., an income stream) to another individual. Of course, if the donor names someone other than the donor or the donor's spouse as an annuitant, a portion of the transfer to the trust is a gift. Depending on the actuarial value of the annuity to be paid to that person other than the donor or the donor's spouse, the gift may be taxable to the donor.

4. The administrative burdens are generally less than with a CRUT because no annual revaluation is required with a CRAT as compared to the CRUT.

DISADVANTAGES

1. Once it is established, no additional contributions may be made to a CRAT. One solution to this problem may be to establish one or more additional CRATs.

2. The set-up costs in a CRAT are higher, and the administrative tasks more burdensome than with a charitable gift annuity.

3. Annuity payments are not guaranteed. So, if the value of the CRAT assets falls to zero, the annuity payments cease.

4. Charitable remainder trusts are treated as private foundations for various purposes, including the application of the prohibition on self-dealing. As a result, a CRAT may not enter into sales, leases, loans, or certain other transactions with the donor or related parties.[2]

WHAT ARE THE REQUIREMENTS?

Like the other split-interest gifts (i.e., CRUT, pooled income fund), the CRAT must meet stringent requirements.[3] Foremost among them are:

1. There must be a written trust instrument that is valid under state law. The Internal Revenue Service has promulgated sample forms for CRATs.[4]

2. The trust must provide for: (a) a specific amount; (b) at least annually; (c) to one or more beneficiaries; at least one of which is not a charity; (d) for life *or* for a term of years (not to exceed 20 years); (e) with an irrevocable remainder interest to be held for the benefit of, or paid over to, charity.[5]

3. The trust must be a CRAT from its inception to its termination—it cannot alternate between different types of payments. In other words, a CRAT cannot provide a fixed annuity payment in one year (i.e., as is required with a CRAT), and then provide a percentage of the value of the trust assets in the next year (i.e., as would be the case with a CRUT).[6]

4. The trust must have at least one noncharitable beneficiary and the recipient must be an individual other than a charitable organization.[7]

5. The trust must require that the trustee pay the noncharitable beneficiary a fixed dollar amount for life, *or* for a term of not more than 20 years. This amount may be expressed as either a stated sum *or* as a percentage of the initial value of the trust assets. For example, the annuity amount could be stated as $20,000 or 5% of the trust's initial value ($400,000).[8]

6. The annuity amount must not be less than 5% nor more than 50% of the initial net fair market value of all property placed into the trust.[9]

7. The present value of the charitable remainder interest must be at least 10% of the initial fair market value of the contributed property. This computation is affected by the age of the annuitant, the term of the trust, and the annuity rate.[10]

8. The trust must be protected from the payment of any estate tax due in the donor's estate (i.e., the CRAT's value will be included in the donor's estate if the donor is the life income beneficiary). If someone other than the donor's spouse is a beneficiary, the value of that interest will be a taxable disposition; consequently, some of the deceased donor's applicable unified credit amount may have to be used, or estate tax may be due (after taking into account the charitable deduction for the remainder value). (Under EGTRRA 2001, the estate tax unified credit is scheduled to increase through 2009.)

9. No additions may be made to a charitable remainder annuity trust after its creation.[11]

10. In a ruling predating the "10% remainder interest requirement," described above, the IRS ruled that a gift of a remainder interest through a CRAT must meet the "5% probability test." The revenue ruling states that no deduction will be allowed "unless the possibility that the charitable transfer will not become effective is so remote as to be negligible." Essentially, this means that if the actuarial possibility of a charity receiving a remainder interest is less than 5%, it is "so remote as to be negligible" and the deduction will be denied. This could happen, for example, where the annuity payout is for the joint life expectancy of a young couple and the trust was drafted before the 10% remainder interest requirement went into effect.[12]

HOW IS IT DONE?

First, a charitable remainder trust document must be drafted, which defines the term of the annuity interest based on a fixed number of years *or* the life of the beneficiary. (The lives of the beneficiaries may be used if more than one annuitant is designated.) The trust document must also specify the annuity rate and the identity of the remainder beneficiary (or that the remainder beneficiary must be a "qualified charity" (see Chapter 4). The statutory requirements discussed in the previous paragraphs must also be met.

The drafter may use one of the model forms promulgated by the IRS (see the reference about and "Questions and Answers," below). However, drafters should be aware that these model forms are incomplete and require insertion of administrative provisions to create a complete document. Furthermore, it may not be enough to have a properly prepared trust document if the trust is not administered properly. In *Atkinson v. Commissioner*, the failure of the trustee to follow the terms of the trust resulted in the loss of the charitable estate tax deduction.[13]

> *Example*: William, age 70, desires to provide a benefit to his alma mater. He would also like to receive favorable tax treatment and a fixed level of income for as long as he lives. William transfers appreciated securities to a CRAT, with an annuity payout of 7.5% of the initial value of the trust assets to be distributed to him for his lifetime, and the remainder to go to his alma mater.
>
> The stock William places in the trust has a low cost basis and pays dividends annually. Trust distributions to William will be taxed under the 4-tier income tax system described below.

WHAT ARE THE TAX IMPLICATIONS?

Income Tax

Trust. CRATs are not subject to income tax on their general investment income (i.e., dividends, royalties, interest, and gains from the sale or exchange of property) because the trust itself is tax-exempt.[14] However, if the trust has "unrelated business taxable income" (UBTI) during a year, the trust will be taxed on the UBTI *plus* all of its other income as well. UBTI in these cases generally falls into one of two distinct classes of income: (1) income from the regular conduct of an unrelated trade or business; or (2) "unrelated debt financed income."[15] An in-depth explanation of UBTI is beyond the scope of this discussion, but planners should be aware of its application to charitable remainder trusts.

Annuity recipients. The recipients of the annuity amounts are subject to income tax on the distributions made to them. The distributions received by the annuitants are taxed under a 4-tier income tax reporting rule. Under this 4-tier approach, payouts will be taxed in the following order: (1) ordinary income; (2) capital gain; (3) other income (generally tax-exempt income); and (4) return of capital.[16]

Donor. The donor receives an immediate income tax charitable deduction for the present value of the remainder interest. The remainder interest is generally the initial fair market value of the trust assets *minus* the present value of the recipient's annuity interest determined using IRS tables issued under Section 7520. For details on this calculation, see Appendix K.

Gift Tax

When the donor and the recipient of the annuity amount are the same, there is a gift of the remainder to charity. This should be reported on a gift tax return (Form 709) by showing the amount of the gift and by taking a corresponding gift tax charitable deduction. Likewise, when the sole recipient of the annuity amount is the donor's spouse, the gift tax marital deduction will be available.

If the recipient of the annuity amount is someone other than the donor (or the donor's spouse), the annuity interest is a separate taxable gift. If there is only one recipient to whom a taxable gift is made, the gift will qualify for the $12,000 (in 2007) annual exclusion. If there are successive recipients, only the gift to the first recipient qualifies for the annual exclusion.[17] If there are co-recipients and their percentage interests are not fixed and certain (i.e., as when the trustee can allocate the annuity amount among recipients), no part of the gift will qualify for the annual exclusion.[18]

When payment of the annuity amounts are deferred until a later time (as in a testamentary trust), the gift to the recipient will not qualify for the annual exclusion. However, the necessity of reporting a taxable transfer

can be avoided altogether if the donor retains the right to revoke the recipient's annuity interest.

Estate Tax

If the donor dies prematurely and is the sole recipient (or one of the recipients) of the annuity amount, the donor's estate will include a portion of the value of the CRAT under IRC Section 2036—specifically, the amount necessary at the specified payout rate to yield the guaranteed annual payment. However, the full value of the CRAT should be includable under IRC Section 2039. This does not cause a problem if the donor is the only recipient of the annuity amount because a corresponding amount can be deducted from his gross estate. However, if there is a successive noncharitable income recipient, the amount included in the donor's estate for that successive interest is not deductible.[19]

A testamentary bequest or devise of a charitable remainder interest in the form of a CRAT qualifies for the estate tax charitable deduction. An interest left to the donor's spouse qualifies for the marital deduction. Interests left to any recipients other than the donor's spouse are not deductible and will be includable in the donor's estate.

WHERE CAN I FIND OUT
MORE ABOUT IT?

1. Toce, Joseph, Abbin, Byrle, Vorsatz, Mark, and Page, William, *Tax Economics of Charitable Giving 2006-2007* (Warren Gorham & Lamont, 2006).

2. Hopkins, Bruce R., *The Law of Tax Exempt Organizations*, 9th edition (New York, NY: John Wiley & Sons, Inc., 2007, periodic updates).

3. Phelan, Marilyn E., *Nonprofit Enterprises: Corporations, Trust and Associations* (West Group-Clark, Boardman, Callaghan, Inc., 1997-2000).

4. The Planned Giving Design Center (www.pgdc.net). The information on this web site is available through a subscribing local charitable organization. The site contains numerous articles on various charitable remainder planning strategies.

5. Most charities offer CRATs as one of their planned giving opportunities. A preprinted brochure will likely be available for the asking. Many of the web sites listed in Appendix L offer calculators to help the donor in the planning process. For the professional charitable planner, CPA, or attorney, most of the computer programs listed in Appendix H can perform the pertinent calculations. The National Committee on Planned Giving web site (www.pgdc. com; see Appendix L) contains a significant amount of information and provides links to several web sites of interest to the charitable gift planner.

QUESTIONS AND ANSWERS

Question – How does the CRAT differ from the CRUT?

Answer – The major distinction between a CRAT and a CRUT is that payments from a CRAT are set as a fixed amount or as a fixed percentage of the initial fair market value of the trust's assets at its inception. In comparison, the unitrust payment amount from a CRUT varies from year to year since unitrust payments are a fixed percentage of the annually re-determined fair market value of the trust's assets.

Another important distinction is that with a CRAT, no subsequent additions are permitted after the initial contribution, whereas with a CRUT additions are permitted by the donor (and certain others). This difference alone frequently serves as a compelling reason for donors to choose a CRUT over a CRAT. Because the amount payable under a CRAT becomes fixed on the date that the trust is created, it is the charity rather than the annuitant(s) that benefits from any increases in value of the trust fund. On the other hand, if the trust does not produce income or does not grow sufficiently, the charity will suffer due to the loss of principal in paying the annuity amount.[20]

Question – How does the CRAT differ from the charitable gift annuity?

Answer – The CRAT is distinguishable from the charitable gift annuity in its being a separate trust that is not commingled with the charitable remainder beneficiary's assets. Instead, the property in a CRAT is held by the trustee in a fiduciary capacity. The CRAT is also distinguishable from the charitable gift annuity because of its ability to have the annuity paid for a term of years *and* over multiple lives rather than being limited to the single (or joint) life annuity available with a charitable gift annuity.

The trustee of a CRAT is required to make the annuity payments during the term of the trust, which can be (1) for a number of years *or* (2) for the life or lives of the annuitant(s). At the end of the term of years, or at the death of the last surviving annuitant, the trustee will continue to hold the trust property for, or distribute the trust property to, the remainder beneficiary (or beneficiaries), which must be qualified charities.

The annuity rate of the CRAT can be selected by the donor as compared to the uniform rates used with most charitable gift annuities. (Charitable gift annuity rates vary with age and are calculated to assure that, on average, at least 50% of the value of the fund will go to the charity at the expiration of the annuitant's normal life expectancy. See Chapter 12.) With a CRAT, a higher annuity rate will decrease the amount of the charitable income tax deduction available to the donor, and will increase the amount of the taxable gift to the annuitant (if the annuitant is not the donor). Furthermore, the value of the remainder interest must be at least 10% of the trust's initial fair market value for it to qualify as a CRAT.

Question – Is there any limit to how many annuity beneficiaries may be named by the donor?

Answer – No. Both CRATs and CRUTs are required to have at least one noncharitable beneficiary of the annuity amount or the unitrust amount, respectively, who is a person other than a charitable organization described in Code Section 170(c). There may be multiple noncharitable recipients of the annuity amount to be paid each year. However, the greater the number of income beneficiaries, the smaller the value of the remainder interest, which must be at least 10% of the trust's initial fair market value in order for the trust to qualify as a CRUT or a CRAT. Thus, practically speaking, multiple lives may result in the trust failing to qualify under the 10% minimum charitable deduction requirement.[21]

An independent trustee can be given the right to allocate the annuity amount among a class of named noncharitable beneficiaries; however, if he has "sprinkle power" to vary the amount and frequency of payouts to noncharitable beneficiaries, the trust will not qualify.[22] If the annuity amount is to be paid for the joint lives of a group of individuals, all of the individuals must be alive and ascertainable when the trust is created. Therefore, after-born or after-adopted children may not be added to the trust, nor may after-acquired spouses be substituted. This makes practical sense because the addition of such beneficiaries would change the actuarial assumptions upon which the donor's tax deduction is based. For this reason, if the trust is to continue for a fixed number of years (rather than for the beneficiaries' lives), the trust may provide for after-born, after-adopted, and after-acquired spouses.

Question – Is there any minimum annuity amount that must be paid to the individual beneficiary?

Answer – Yes. Generally, the annuity amount payable to the noncharitable beneficiary must not be less than 5% of the initial trust value. However, there are two safe harbor exceptions to the 5% minimum payout rule. The first exception under the Treasury regulations provides that the 5% test will not be violated if the reduction in the annuity amount occurs under the following circumstances: (1) the reduction in the annuity amount must occur as a result of the death of the income recipient *or* the expiration of the term of years; (2) the distribution must be made to a "qualified charity" (within the meaning of IRC Section 170(c)) *either* at the time of the income recipient's death *or* on the termination of a term of years; *and* (3) the total amounts payable each year as the annuity payments "after such distribution are not less than a stated dollar amount which bears the same ratio to 5% of the initial net fair market value of the trust immediately after such distribution bears to the net fair market value of the trust assets immediately before such distribution."[23]

Under the second exception to the 5% rule, the Treasury regulations also provide relief when the 5% minimum payout is violated because of a good faith error in the valuation of the trust assets.[24] If the grantor of an inter vivos CRAT establishes a fixed dollar amount in good faith, and later learns that the trust assets are worth a much greater amount, the grantor may enter into an agreement with the IRS District Director consenting to fix the value of the trust, for charitable deduction purposes, at 20 times the value of the annuity.

Question – Is there any maximum payout limit for the annuity of the noncharitable beneficiary?

Answer – Yes. The annuity amount may not be greater than 50% of the value of the property, valued at the time of the initial contribution to the trust.[25]

Question – Can the donor name a trust or other entity as the annuity beneficiary?

Answer – Yes. The Code provides that a CRAT must have at least one annuity recipient other than a charity described in IRC Section 170(c), meaning the grantor (or another individual). However, the additional annuity beneficiary can be another trust, an estate, a partnership, or a corporation.[26]

Question – Can amounts be paid to the charitable beneficiaries early?

Answer – Yes. Treasury regulations permit the transfer of trust principal or excess income to the charitable remainderperson prior to the conclusion of the measuring term of the trust. However, a CRAT may distribute the annuity amount, only, to a noncharitable income recipient. Furthermore, no increased or additional deduction is allowed for an early payout.

Question – Can highly appreciated property be used to fund the trust?

Answer – Yes. Charitable remainder trusts are often funded with appreciated property. Typically, the contributed property is sold by the trust at a later date. In fact, the property may have to be sold, in the case of a CRUT to provide liquidity for payment of the annuity. However, it is important to make sure that any gain on the sale of appreciated property by the trust will not be attributed to the donor. Thus, the donor should not retain control (either directly or indirectly) over the asset. Nor should there be a prearranged plan for the trustee to sell the property. The IRS has taken the position in some transactions that a charity (or trustee of a charitable trust) may be viewed as the donor's agent in disposing of appreciated assets. These transactions can generally be classified as involving either: (1) the redemption of stock pursuant to a prior binding agreement; (2) the resale of assets by the trust to the grantor pursuant to an understanding; or (3) the sale by the trust of appreciated property, and subsequent reinvestment in tax-exempt bonds.[27]

Question – Can the donor use retirement benefits to fund the CRAT?

Answer – Yes, but planners should be particularly sensitive to the possible tax consequences (see Chapter 22). If a lifetime gift to charity consists of an individual's qualified plan benefit, the donor will have to include the entire amount of the benefit in his gross income. The same gift using an IRA, however, will expose only the amount of the benefits that were not previously included in his gross income (i.e., the nondeductible portion of the IRA) to income tax. Under both circumstances, the amounts transferred to the trust that represent the remainder interest that will eventually pass to charity should be eligible for the income and gift tax deduction.

If the transfer is made at the donor's death, however, the adverse income tax consequences do not arise. A donor may designate a charitable remainder trust as the beneficiary of the donor's retirement plan or IRA benefits. Although the IRA or retirement plan payout will be accelerated at death (because the charitable remainder trust is not a "designated beneficiary"), the tax-exempt status of the CRAT (or CRUT) should shield the retirement benefits from income tax. If the surviving spouse is named as the annuity beneficiary, the use of the marital and charitable deductions should shield the retirement benefits from estate tax at the death of the first spouse.[28]

Question – Can the donor use debt-encumbered property to establish the trust?

Answer – Technically such funding is possible, but planners must be particularly sensitive to potential tax traps. The contribution of debt-encumbered property to a charitable remainder trust is treated as part charitable gift, part taxable sale. The transfer is treated as a gift to the extent that the value of the property exceeds the underlying debt. But the same transaction is also treated for tax purposes as a sale to the extent the debt to which the property is subject exceeds the transferor's basis in the sale portion of the gift.[29] Note that the donor's basis in the property must be apportioned; consequently, a certain amount of basis is carried away by the gift portion. This results in increasing the donor's gain on the sale portion.

Example: Lynn Schneider owns real estate that has a fair market value of $500,000, an adjusted basis of $100,000, and is subject to a mortgage of $250,000. Lynn creates a CRAT and funds it with the property as a charitable gift, which the trust takes subject to the mortgage. Lynn realizes a gain of $200,000 and is deemed to have made a $250,000 gift to the trust as follows:

Sale Portion

Amount realized	$250,000
Basis allocable to the sale	
($250,000/$500,000) x 100,000	- 50,000
Recognized gain	$200,000

Gift Portion

Value of transferred property	$500,000
Amount realized	- 250,000
Gift Element	$250,000

In addition, donors should be aware that several other issues may arise including the creation of "debt financed income"[30] and treatment of the property as a constructive sale to the trust, which in turn may be considered an act of "self-dealing" (which is forbidden under IRC Section 4911). This problem can be avoided by using a charitable gift annuity (see Chapter 12).

Question – Can the donor use operating business assets to fund the CRAT?

Answer – While this is possible (although the deduction would be limited to basis), it may cause the CRAT to earn Unrelated Business Taxable Income (UBIT or UBTI as defined in IRC Section 515). Prior to the enactment of the Tax Relief and Health Care Act of 2006, a CRT would lose its tax exempt status for any year in which UBIT/UBTI was received. This change lessens this burden by providing a 100% tax on net UBIT/UBTI, allowing other taxable income to avoid tax under the general exemption available to CRTs.[31]

Question – Can the donor add property to the CRAT after it is established?

Answer – The donor may not add additional property to the trust once it is established.[32]

Question – Can the donor establish the charitable remainder trust at the time of his death?

Answer – Yes, a CRAT created under a will or revocable trust is deemed created at the date of the donor's death even if it is not funded until the end of a reasonable period of estate administration. The payment of the annuity amount may be deferred until the end of the taxable year of the trust in which the trust is fully funded. However, the trust must be obligated to pay the annuity amount from the date of death, and a makeup distribution must be made to adjust

for the failure to pay the full amount during the estate administration.[33]

Question – Can the donor reserve the right to change the remainder beneficiary?

Answer – Yes. The donor may reserve the right to change the remainder beneficiary. But that right must be restricted to only "qualified charities" (described in IRC Section 170(c)).

Question – What types of charities can be named as the remainder beneficiaries of a charitable remainder annuity trust?

Answer – According to the Internal Revenue Code, charities described in Section 170(c) may be named as charitable remainder beneficiaries. Trust drafters may also want to include charities described in IRC Section 170(b)(1)(A), due to the fact that IRC Section 170(c) applies to public charities and private foundations. Use of the public charity category under IRC Section 170(b)(1)(A) would increase the income percentage limitation applicable for the donor's charitable deduction.[34]

Question – When must the annuity amount be paid to the beneficiary named in the trust document?

Answer – The annuity amount must be paid at least annually (or more often). It must also be paid during the taxable year *or* within a reasonable time after the close of the year. The IRS will treat any payment made before the filing date of the trust tax return (including extensions) as a timely payment for this purpose.[35] The recipient must include the trust distribution in income for the recipient's taxable year in which the trust taxable year ends.[36]

Question – Can the trustee make distributions *other than* the annuity amount to the trust income beneficiaries?

Answer – No, the trustee cannot distribute amounts in excess of the annuity amount to the *income* beneficiaries. However, the trustee may make additional distributions of trust principal to the *charitable* beneficiary (or another qualified charity). Although such payments will not jeopardize the charitable deduction for the donation of the remainder interest, the donor will not receive any additional deduction for contributions to the trust.[37]

Question – May a CRAT make a distribution "in-kind?"

Answer – A CRAT may satisfy the annuity amount by making a distribution "in-kind" instead of a cash payment. However, the trust will be deemed to have sold the asset and, thus, will have to recognize a gain (or loss) on the sale. Furthermore, the resulting capital gain may eventually be taxable to the donor as part of a later annuity payment.

Question – Are there IRS model forms for CRATs?

Answer – Yes. From time to time the IRS has published model forms for creating charitable remainder annuity trusts.[38] In fact, there is a 4-part test that ensures IRS recognition of the trust as being qualified under IRC Section 664. However, the model forms do *not* cover all situations. Many commentators advise great care in using model documents in their original form. Additional drafting is generally required to contour the trust clauses to fit the particular needs of the client(s).

Question – Can a transfer to a CRAT be subject to the generation-skipping tax?

Answer – Yes. If there is a completed gift to a non-donor annuity beneficiary who is a skip person (i.e., a person who is more than one generation younger than the donor), the value of the interest transferred to that person would be subject to the generation-skipping transfer tax. The donor would need to allocate generation-skipping exemption to exempt the interest from this tax.

CHAPTER ENDNOTES

1. IRC Sec. 1011; Treas. Reg. §1.1011-2(a)(3).
2. IRC Sec. 4947(a)(2); Treas. Reg. §1.664-1(b).
3. See IRC Sec. 664(d)(1)(B); Treas. Reg. §1.664-1(a)(2).
4. See Rev. Proc. 2003-54, 2003-31 IRB 236.
5. IRC Sec. 664(d)(1).
6. See Treas. Reg. §1.664-1(a)(2).
7. IRC Sec. 664(d)(1)(A); Treas. Reg. §1.664-2(a)(3)(i).
8. IRC Sec. 664(d)(1)(A); Treas. Reg. §1.664-2(a)(1)(iii).
9. Treas. Regs. §§1.664-2(a)(1)(i), 1.664-2(a)(2)(i). 1.664-2(a)(5)(i).
10. IRC Sec. 664(d)(1)(D).
11. Treas. Reg. §1.664-2(b).
12. Rev. Rul. 77-374, 1977-2 CB 329; *Tax Economics of Charitable Giving* 2006-2007, p. 17-3 (Warren, Gorham, & Lamont, 2006).
13. *Atkinson v. Comm.*, 115 TC 26 (2000).
14. IRC Sec. 664(c); *Newhall Unitrust v. Comm.*, 104 TC 236 (1995), *aff'd*, 105 F.3d 482 (9th Cir. 1997).
15. Treas. Reg. §1.664-1(c).
16. Treas. Reg. 1.664-1(d)(1).
17. Treas. Reg. §25.2503-3(c), Example 5.
18. Treas. Reg. §25.2503-2.
19. Rev. Rul. 82-105, 1982-1 CB 133. See also REG-119097-05, 72 Fed. Reg. 31487 (June 7, 2007).
20. IRC Sec. 664(b).
21. See IRC Sec. 664(d).
22. Rev. Rul. 77-73, 1977-1 CB 175.
23. Treas. Reg. §1.664-2(a)(ii).
24. Treas. Reg. §1.664-2(a)(iii).
25. IRC Sec. 664(d)(1)(A).
26. IRC Secs. 664(d)(1)(A), 7701(a).
27. See, Treas. Reg. §1.664-1(e)(2); Rev. Rul. 78-197, 1978-1 CB 83; *Blake v. Commissioner*, 697 F.2d 473 (2d Cir. 1982); Rev. Rul. 60-370, 1960-2 CB 203.
28. IRC Sec. 2056(b)(8). See also Let. Rul. 9634019.
29. IRC Sec. 1011.
30. IRC Sec. 514.
31. IRC Sec. 664(c) as revised by Section 424 of the Tax Relief and Health Care Act of 2006.
32. IRC Sec. 664(d)(1)(A); Treas. Reg. §1.664-2(b).
33. Treasury regulations §§1.664-1(a)(5)(i) and 1.664-1(a)(5)(ii) provide guidance on calculating the make-up distribution.
34. The IRS has ruled in favor of such a description of the description of the charitable remaindermen in Letter Ruling 903702.
35. Treas. Reg. §1.664-2(a)(1)(i).
36. Treas. Regs. §§1.652(c)-1, 1.662(c)-1.
37. Treas. Reg. §1.664-2(a)(4); Rev. Rul. 82-128, 1982-2 CB 71.
38. The latest iteration of sample forms for CRATs is set forth in Rev. Proc. 2003-54, 2003-31 IRB 236, and Rev. Proc. 2003-54, 2003-31 IRB 236. For an excellent discussion of these forms, see Pusey, J. Michael, *Gift Planner's Digest*, "Exploring the New Model Charitable Remainder Trust Forms" (September 17, 2003), The Planned Giving Design Center, at: www.pdgc.com.

CHARITABLE REMAINDER UNITRUSTS

CHAPTER 16

WHAT IS IT?

A charitable remainder unitrust (CRUT) is an irrevocable, split-interest trust in which the donor reserves a unitrust interest for himself or at least one other noncharitable beneficiary, and through which the remainder interest in the property is donated to a qualified charity. The noncharitable unitrust interest can be measured by (1) the beneficiary's lifetime (or beneficiaries' lifetimes), (2) a term of years not to exceed 20, or (3) some combination thereof.

A CRUT resembles a charitable remainder annuity trust (CRAT—see Chapter 15), but provides a great deal more flexibility. The primary difference between a CRUT and a CRAT is that the noncharitable interest in a CRAT is a *fixed* annual annuity (i.e., a fixed dollar amount), whereas the noncharitable interest in a CRUT is a *variable* annuity (i.e., measured as a fixed percentage of the trust value each year). For a detailed explanation of the differences between CRUTs and CRATS, see "Questions and Answers," below.

WHEN IS THE USE OF SUCH A DEVICE INDICATED?

1. When the client has appreciated or non-income producing property from which he wishes to increase his return.

2. When the donor wants to make a testamentary gift of qualified retirement plan or IRA assets without giving up the lifetime payout from them.

Testamentary gifts of retirement plan dollars are a popular tool for charitable giving because such gifts allow donors to avoid the negative tax results imposed on such gifts after death. It is not uncommon for a donor to name a testamentary charitable remainder trust as the beneficiary of a retirement plan. A detailed explanation of charitable gifts of retirement assets is contained in Chapter 22.

ADVANTAGES

1. A charitable remainder trust (CRT) allows the donor to make a currently deductible gift without giving up future income on the asset. Furthermore, the income stream from the CRT can be greater than the income the asset was providing prior to establishing the CRT.

2. A CRUT can offer the donor maximum flexibility with respect to the trust payout.

DISADVANTAGES

1. A gift to a CRT is irrevocable. If the donor expects to employ wealth replacement (see "Joint Life CRUT with Life Replacement Trust," below), it is important that his insurability be ascertained prior to the transfer.

2. The use of a CRT involves setup and administrative expenses that may not be justified for smaller gifts.

WHAT ARE THE REQUIREMENTS?

Basic Requirements

The requirements for a CRUT resemble the requirements imposed on a CRAT.[1] In order to qualify for income, estate, and gift tax charitable deductions, the CRUT's structure must meet certain guidelines set forth in the

Code, applicable Treasury regulations, and IRS interpretations of the Code.[2] The requirements include:

1. A fixed percentage of the net fair market value of the trust principal, as revalued annually, must be payable to one or more noncharitable beneficiaries each year. At least one of the noncharitable beneficiaries must be an individual other than a charitable organization.[3] This interest is sometimes referred to as the "unitrust" interest. The donor may retain this unitrust interest for himself.[4]

2. The fixed percentage payable annually must not be less than 5% nor more than 50% of the trust value.[5] The actual frequency of the payments may vary from once a year to semi-annual, quarterly, or monthly.[6] There is a slight adjustment to the size of the income tax deduction depending upon which payment schedule is selected, and whether the payment is made at the beginning or the end of the time period.[7]

3. The unitrust interest, which is payable to one or more noncharitable beneficiaries, must be made *either* for a term of years (not to exceed 20) *or*, in the case of individual beneficiaries, for the life or lives of those noncharitable individuals.[8] Unitrust beneficiaries must be alive at the creation of the trust if they are to receive an interest for life. Thus, if a donor wishes to provide for a class of beneficiaries that might be expanded by future births (such as grandchildren), the unitrust interest must be limited to a term of years (not to exceed 20).[9]

4. The present value of the charitable remainder interest, as determined at the time that the CRUT is first created, must be equal to at least 10% of the initial trust value.[10] A donor can make multiple contributions to a CRUT since it is valued annually (this differs from a CRAT, to which only one contribution can be made). The 10% minimum remainder rule applies to the initial contribution *and* to any additional contributions that are made to the unitrust.[11] There is no requirement that a certain amount actually pass to the qualified charity at the termination of the trust. Depending upon actual trust performance and duration, the charitable remainder interest may be more or less than the value of the charitable remainder

interest determined at the time of the CRUT's inception.

5. No amount other than the specified unitrust interest can be paid to or for the benefit of any person other than a qualified charitable organization. This requires that the *entire* remainder interest must go to a qualified charitable organization (see Chapter 2).[12]

Net Income Exception CRUT (NICRUT)

The preceding requirements apply to a "standard" CRUT—sometimes known as a "SCRUT." With a standard CRUT, the annual unitrust payment is paid regardless of trust income—even if the CRUT does not have sufficient income to make the payment. In other words, the trustee could be forced to sell or otherwise invade the trust principal. However, some assets do not have an established market and, thus, may be difficult to sell promptly to generate the required income. But there are two other types of CRUTs, each of which provides an alternative to the required unitrust payment in the event the CRUT does not have sufficient income to make such payments. These are collectively known as "income exception" CRUTs, meaning that both methods provide that the unitrust beneficiary will receive the lesser of the fixed percentage of the trust's value or the net income earned by the trust.

The first alternative form of CRUT is the "net income CRUT" or "NICRUT." A NICRUT provides that the unitrust beneficiary will receive each year the *lesser of*:

- the unitrust amount specified in the trust instrument (i.e., a fixed percentage of the value of the trust assets), *or*

- the net income earned by the trust during the year.

Example: Assume that a CRUT is established with assets worth $10,000,000, and that it provides an annual payout equal to the lesser of (1) 5% of the trust's value (as redetermined annually), or (2) the trust's actual earned income for that year. The trust earns $300,000 in a year in which the trust has a value of $10,000,000. A standard CRUT would require that the unitrust beneficiary receive $500,000—even though that amount exceeds the trust income. However, if the trust instrument is a NICRUT, it would require the unitrust beneficiary to receive only $300,000. If the amount of any year's payout to the unitrust beneficiary is less than the stated percentage payout amount, any excess is forfeited for that year and the process repeats for each successive year.

Net Income with Make-up Provision CRUT (NIMCRUT)

The second alternative form of CRUT is the "net income with make-up CRUT," or "NIMCRUT." A NIMCRUT resembles a NICRUT in that the unitrust beneficiary will receive the *lesser of* the fixed percentage of the trust's value *or* the net income earned by the trust However, a NIMCRUT differs from a NICRUT in that a "make-up" account accrues in those years when net income is less than the fixed percentage of the trust's value. A make-up account is simply an accounting record of the cumulative net shortfall in the unitrust amounts actually paid out to the unitrust beneficiary each year. In a subsequent year, if trust net income is greater than the fixed unitrust percentage, net income will be paid out up to the total of the current year's unitrust percentage, *plus* any balance in the make-up account.

Example: Assume that the NIMCRUT is funded with $10,000,000 on January 1, 2007. The unitrust percentage is 5% of the trust's value (measured at the beginning of the year). During 2007, the trust earns income of $300,000. Because $300,000 of income is less than 5% of the trust value (5% x $10,000,000 = $500,000), the unitrust beneficiary receives only $300,000. The $200,000 difference between the fixed percentage amount and the actual income earned (and distributed) is recorded in the "make-up" account.

Further assume that the trust has a value of $11,000,000 on January 1, 2008. Based upon this revaluation, the unitrust percentage amount is $550,000 for 2008 (i.e., 5% x $11,000,000). If the trust earns $700,000 in 2008, the unitrust beneficiary will receive the entire $700,000. The distribution will represent $550,000 for the 2008 unitrust percentage and $150,000 from the make-up account (i.e., earned in 2007). At the end of 2008, the make-up account will have a

balance of $50,000 (i.e., the $200,000 that was not distributed in 2007, *minus* the $150,000 in "excess" earnings distributed in 2008). The make-up account is not adjusted for the time value of money.

Caution: Although the use of a NIMCRUT provides numerous planning opportunities, especially for appreciated property, it is important that the donor fully understand that no unitrust payment will be made *until* and *unless* the NIMCRUT earns "income" (as defined in a trust accounting sense).[13] In one case, a state appeals court judge remanded a case to the trial court for a determination of fraud and negligent misrepresentation when the donor alleged that he did not realize that distributions from a NIMCRUT would not be made until after the contributed real estate has been sold and the NIMCRUT earned income. In this case, nonproductive real estate was contributed to the NIMCRUT and the trustee was unable to immediately find a buyer for the property, causing a delay in distributions to the unitrust beneficiary.[14]

"FLIP" Unitrust

From the discussion above, it is clear that by using a NIMCRUT when contributing highly appreciated property, the trustee need not make distributions-in-kind or undergo a forced sale of contributed property to make the annual unitrust payments to the trust's unitrust beneficiary. Instead, the trustee can sell the trust property at the most opportune time and "make up" payments to the unitrust beneficiary later when the trust receives income. In some instances, NIMCRUT investments are intentionally selected to allow the trustee to postpone the unitrust distributions until income is needed by the beneficiary—in effect making the NIMCRUT a tool for supplemental income at a later time, such as retirement. However, at some point, the unitrust beneficiary may prefer the more predictable distributions that can be obtained with a standard CRUT.

The advantages of a NIMCRUT (income deferral) and a standard CRUT (reliable distributions) are sometimes combined into another type of trust, known as a "FLIP Unitrust" or a "FLIP-CRUT." A FLIP Unitrust ordinarily begins as a NIMCRUT, and at some future time changes or "flips" to a standard CRUT. The "flip" is permitted to occur only upon the happening of a *triggering event* that is not, and must not, be within the control of the donor, unitrust beneficiary, trustee, or any other person.[15] Commonly, the trust will provide for the "flip" to occur upon the sale of unmarketable funding assets, such as real estate. Other triggering events could include the removal of restrictions on Rule 144 stock (i.e., restricted stock), a beneficiary's 65th birthday, or the death of a beneficiary's spouse.[16] While there is no specific authority, it seems that tying the "flip" to a beneficiary's retirement could violate the rule that the event not be within the control of the beneficiary.

A CRUT is allowed to "flip" only once. The "flip" must be from a NIMCRUT or NICRUT to a standard CRUT – a "reverse flip" from a standard CRUT to a NIMCRUT or NICRUT is *not* allowed.[17] Once the triggering event occurs, the change in payout method will occur on January 1 of the year *following* the year in which the triggering event occurred.[18]

HOW IS IT DONE?

Joint Life CRUT with Wealth Replacement Trust

First, the charitable advisor gathers information from the prospective donors pertaining to their financial situation, goals, and whether they have a desire to donate money to a particular charitable organization. The advisor determines that the clients want to meet the following goals: defer capital gains taxes on the appreciated assets; secure a lifetime annuity stream; create an endowment for the charity of their choice; and provide for their children. A CRUT provides a grantor with a current income tax deduction and an ongoing income stream. Additionally, the grantor can use a CRUT to "avoid" paying capital gains taxes on appreciated assets immediately. However, once assets are transferred to a CRUT, and out of the grantor's estate, those assets are not available to the grantor's heirs after the grantor's death. A "wealth replacement trust" funded by life insurance can complement a CRUT and restore assets to the grantor's heirs.

The charitable advisor, working with other professional advisors, prepares a plan that includes using a wealth replacement trust in conjunction with a CRUT. After the clients have reviewed the plan and agreed to it, the determination is made whether they qualify for the life insurance that will be used as the wealth replacement portion of the plan. When the donors'

insurability is verified, the CRUT document is drafted by an attorney experienced in drafting CRUTS and life insurance trusts. After the CRT document is drafted, the donors can execute (i.e., sign) and fund the wealth replacement trust with life insurance; then, the donors transfer their highly appreciated stock to the CRUT. Once the life insurance is in force, the donors execute the CRUT document, and their attorney re-registers their stock in the name of the CRUT. The CRUT trustee then sells the stock and reinvests the proceeds in a diversified portfolio of securities.[19]

Example: Bob and Mary Smith are ages 64 and 62, respectively. They own $1,000,000 of appreciated stock with a very low basis ($100,000). Although this stock has appreciated greatly, it is not producing much income for Bob and Mary. The Smiths are charitably inclined and have made substantial cash gifts to charities in the past. They are interested in three things: (1) deferring capital gains taxes on the appreciated assets; (2) securing an income stream for life; and (3) providing for their heirs. A CRUT could be the solution for them.

Bob and Mary decide to donate the stock to a CRUT where the remainder beneficiary will be Bob's alma mater, Drake University. The Smiths will receive 7% of the trust assets (valued annually each year) as income for as long as either of them is alive. After they both die, Drake University will receive whatever money is left in the trust.

Bob and Mary will receive an immediate income tax deduction based on the remainder value as calculated under IRS guidelines. These guidelines take into account Bob's and Mary's ages, the unitrust percentage they will receive each year, the current Section 7520 rate, and their life expectancies. Based upon a Section 7520 rate of 6.8%, Bob and Mary would receive a total income tax deduction of $224,700 (see Figure 16.1). Assuming they are in a 40% tax bracket, this would result in total income tax savings of $89,880. Should their family income not be high enough for them to take the full income tax deduction in the year of donation, they may carry over the remainder of the deduction for up to five years, or until the deduction is completely used.[20]

Figure 16.1

CHARITABLE REMAINDER UNITRUST INCOME TAX DEDUCTION CALCULATION*	
Table Rate	6.8%
Fair Market Value of Trust	$1,000,000
Rate of Annuity	7%
Payment Periods in Year	1
Number of Months Valuation Date Precedes First Payout	12
Ages	64, 62
Payout Sequence Factor	0.936330
Adjusted Payout Rate	6.554%
Interpolation: Factor at 6.4%	0.23217
Factor at 6.6%	0.22247
Difference: 0.00970	
(6.554% - 6.4%)/0.2% = X/0.00970; Therefore X = 0.00747	
Life Remainder Factor = Factor at 6.4% Minus X:	0.22470
Present Value of Remainder Interest = $1,000,000 x 0.22470:	$224,700
Donors' Deduction:	$224,700
Donors' Deduction as a Percentage of Amount Transferred	22.470%
* Courtesy NumberCruncher Software (http://www.leimberg.com)	

Bob and Mary will also receive income from the CRUT. Every year, the trust assets will be valued at the beginning of the year, and 7% of that value will be paid at the end of the year. For instance, in year one Bob and Mary will receive $70,000 from the unitrust (see Figure 16.2). Assuming that the trust assets grow at 6% each year, Bob and Mary will receive a gross income of $1,500,253 over their joint life expectancy of 24 years. If the trust grows at more than 6% per year, the annual payout to Bob and Mary will increase as the value of the CRUT increases.

Bob and Mary decide to use some of this income to create an irrevocable life insurance trust (ILIT) that will buy a survivorship universal life insurance contract with long-term policy guarantees. At their ages and using standard

Figure 16.2

Yr.	Age 1	Age 2	Contribution to Unitrust	Gross Income from Unitrust	Unitrust Value at End of Year
1	64	62	$ 1,000,000	70,000	990,000
5	68	66	0	67,242	950,990
10	73	71	0	63,946	904,382
15	78	76	0	60,812	860,058
20	83	81	0	57,832	817,907
24	87	85	0	55,553	785,678
		Totals:	$1,000,000	$1,500,253	

Figure 16.3

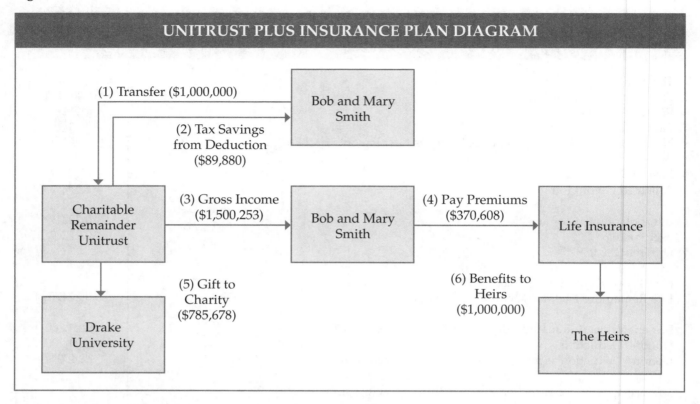

UNITRUST PLUS INSURANCE PLAN DIAGRAM

underwriting, assume the premium that would guarantee coverage for their joint lives would be $15,442.[21] Over their joint life expectancy of 24 years, this would represent total premiums of $370,608.[22] Every year, Bob and Mary will give $15,442 cash to the trust, and the trust will pay the insurance premium. Upon the death of the surviving spouse, the proceeds of the ILIT will go to their heirs (see Figure 16.3).

In this way, Bob and Mary have satisfied the following goals: secured a current income tax deduction; secured a lifetime annuity stream; created an endowment for the charity of their choice; and provided for their children.

WHAT ARE THE TAX IMPLICATIONS?

Ordinarily, a taxpayer receives a charitable deduction only for a gift of a complete interest in property. Gifts of partial interests do not qualify for charitable deductions unless a specific provision in the Internal Revenue Code allows for such deductions.[23] One such statutory exception to the partial interest rule is the CRUT.[24]

All charitable remainder trusts, including CRUTs, have two distinct tax characteristics. First, the donor is entitled to a deduction for income, gift, and estate tax purposes. The donor's charitable deduction is equal to the present value of the remainder interest to be given to the qualified charity when the income stream terminates. Second, the CRUT itself is exempt from federal income taxes, provided that the CRUT continues to qualify as a charitable remainder trust, and does not engage in certain prohibited activities that give rise to a special type of earnings (i.e., "unrelated business taxable income" (UBTI)). The two tax characteristics of a CRUT are discussed in more detail below.

At the time that a donor contributes highly appreciated property to a charitable remainder trust—frequently a CRUT—he can claim a current income tax charitable deduction for the present value of the remainder interest, which will eventually pass to a qualified charity. Because the assets in the CRUT will ultimately pass to a qualified charity, the CRUT is exempt from federal income taxation. Since the CRUT is exempt from federal income taxation, the trustee can sell the appreciated property without incurring an immediate capital gain tax. Because there is no capital gain tax imposed on the charitable trust, the trustee can reinvest 100% of the sale proceeds in income-generating assets. However, it is important to note that income tax cannot be completely avoided when using a CRUT—in actuality, the tax is deferred. When the unitrust beneficiary of the CRUT receives the income stream from the trust, he must recognize income (i.e., ordinary income, capital gains, or other (tax-exempt) income). See "Taxation of CRUT Income and Payouts" below.

Value of the Charitable Deduction

Income tax charitable deduction. A CRUT may be created during the donor's lifetime (i.e., inter vivos) or at the donor's death (i.e., testamentary). The donor of an inter vivos CRUT receives an immediate income tax deduction equal to the present value of the remainder interest that will eventually pass to a qualified charitable remainder beneficiary. In general, the present value of the charitable remainder interest (i.e., the amount of the deduction) is determined by *multiplying* the fair market value of the property transferred to the CRUT by the appropriate unitrust remainder factor.[25] (See Appendix K for a detailed explanation of the calculation.) The value of the unitrust remainder interest can be determined from comprehensive tables provided by the IRS.[26] The factors considered in determining the value of the charitable remainder interest are as follows:

1. the fair market value of the property being donated to the CRUT;

2. the term of the trust;[27]

3. the form of trust payout to the unitrust beneficiaries (i.e., standard payout, net income, or net income with make-up);

4. the stated unitrust payout rate;

5. the frequency of the payments (annually, semiannually, quarterly, or monthly);

6. the timing of the payments; *and*

7. the IRS discount rate (i.e., the Section 7520 rate) in effect for the month of the gift, *or* either of the two months immediately preceding the gift.[28]

Although in practice the noncharitable distribution under a NICRUT or NIMCRUT may be smaller than under a standard CRUT, the calculation of the value of the charitable remainder interest (and, thus, the income tax deduction) is the same for all three types of CRUTs.

The remainder value is identical because the IRS tables assume that the full unitrust payment will be made at the earliest date under both the NICRUT and NIMCRUT.

The donor's income tax charitable deduction is subject to the same percentage limitations and carryforward rules that apply to outright charitable gifts made during life (see Chapter 3).[29] Unlike outright charitable gifts, CRT gifts do not require that the donor obtain a contemporaneous written acknowledgement of the contribution by the donee organization.[30]

Gift tax charitable deduction. If the retained unitrust interest is given to anyone other than the donor, the donor has made a gift that must be reported for federal gift tax purposes.[31] The full value of the donated property must be reported on a federal gift tax return (Form 709); however, the donor will be entitled to a gift tax charitable deduction for the value of the remainder interest passing to the qualified charitable organization. Even if no taxable gift is made in connection with the establishment of the CRUT, a federal gift tax return must still be filed for the year of the gift to the CRUT.[32]

Estate tax charitable deduction. If the donor creates an inter vivos CRUT and retains for himself a lifetime unitrust interest in the trust, the full fair market value of the CRUT will be includable in the donor's gross estate. However, an estate tax charitable deduction can be claimed for the amount of the remainder interest donated to charity.[33]

Taxation of CRUT Income and Payouts

Taxation of CRUT income. The CRUT itself is exempt from all federal income taxes unless it has unrelated business taxable income (UBTI). Care must be taken to avoid UBTI because *any* UBTI will cause *all* trust income to be subject to federal income taxation.[34]

Taxation of amounts received by noncharitable beneficiaries. At times, some promoters make it appear that ordinary income or capital gains tax can be completely avoided by contributing appreciated property to a CRUT. In reality, it is more appropriate to say that these taxes can be *deferred* (and, at times, reduced) by contributing appreciated property to a CRUT. This deferral is accomplished through what is called a "4-tier system." The 4-tier system characterizes distributions from a CRUT and ensures that any income that escapes taxation at the trust level (due to the tax-exempt status of the trust) will be taxed when received by the noncharitable unitrust beneficiary.[35]

Amounts distributed from a CRUT are taxed under the 4-tier system in the following order:

1. *Ordinary income.* Distributions to the noncharitable beneficiary are taxable as ordinary income to the extent that the CRUT earned ordinary income in that tax year. If distributions exceed current year ordinary income, the distributions will nevertheless be taxable as ordinary income if the CRUT earned ordinary income in a previous year that was not previously distributed.

2. *Capital gains.* Distributions will be treated as *short-term* capital gain to the extent that the CRUT had short-term capital gains in that year (or had such gains in a previous year that have not yet been distributed). If the distribution exceeds ordinary income and short-term capital gains (both current year and undistributed gains from previous years), the distribution will be characterized as *long-term* capital gain to the extent that there is current year long-term capital gain (and previously undistributed long-term capital gains).

3. *Other income (e.g., tax-exempt income).* If the distribution exceeds ordinary income (current and past year), short-term capital gains (current and past year), and long-term capital gains (current and past years), the distribution will represent other income to the extent that there is such other income for current and past years. Other income includes income that is tax-exempt for federal income tax purposes.

4. *Return of principal.* Finally, and only after all current year income and all previously undistributed prior year income is deemed to be distributed, a distribution from a CRUT will be characterized as a nontaxable return of principal.[36]

Clearly, the 4-tier system makes it impossible for a donor to avoid taxes indefinitely when appreciated property is contributed to a CRUT and later sold by the trustee. Even if the trustee were to invest the proceeds from the sale of the appreciated property entirely in tax-exempt municipal bonds, the distributions to the noncharitable unitrust beneficiary would represent income (either in the form of short-term or long-term capital gain) until the cumulative distributions equaled the total amount of capital gain incurred on the sale of appreciated property. However, while the tax on the gain cannot be avoided, the ability to *defer* the taxation can provide a significant benefit to the grantor.

Determination of Trust Income

For a NICRUT or a NIMCRUT, a distribution can only be made only from trust income. Despite the obvious importance of income determination, the Code provides surprisingly little guidance on what constitutes trust income. Specifically, the Code provides only that trust income is determined by terms of the governing trust instrument or under local (i.e., state) law.[37] In response to adoption of some version of the Uniform Principal and Income Act by most states, the Service has stated that it will respect allocations of amounts between income and principal pursuant to local law.[38] Conversely, definitions of income within a trust document that depart fundamentally from local law will not be respected by the Service.[39] Treasury regulations and IRS rulings provide the following limited guidance about the appropriate classification of capital gain income:

- *Post-contribution capital gains.* Ordinarily, a post-contribution capital gain is considered a return of trust principal, and not trust income. However, the IRS has ruled that a CRUT instrument can specifically classify post-contribution capital gain as income if it does not "represent a fundamental departure from state law." The characterization of post-contribution capital gains as trust income appears to be a commonly accepted practice among practitioners—especially when creating a NIMCRUT.[40]

- *Pre-contribution capital gains.* At one time, some practitioners believed that pre-contribution capital gains could be classified as trust income by specifying such treatment in the trust instrument.[41] The benefits of this are obvious when funding a NIMCRUT with highly-appreciated property. However, Treasury regulations make it clear that built in appreciation at the time of contribution is properly treated as principal—regardless of what the trust instrument provides.[42]

WHERE CAN I FIND OUT MORE ABOUT IT?

1. Toce, Joseph, Abbin, Byrle, Vorsatz, Mark, and Page, William, *Tax Economics of Charitable Giving 2006-2007* (Warren Gorham & Lamont, 2006).

2. Leimberg, Stephan R., et al., *The Tools & Techniques of Estate Planning*, 14th edition (Cincinnati, OH: The National Underwriter Company, 2006).

3. Osteen, Carolyn M., et. al., *The Harvard Manual on Tax Aspects of Charitable Giving*, 8th edition (Boston, MA: 1999).

QUESTIONS AND ANSWERS

Question – What factors should be considered when deciding between a charitable remainder annuity trust (CRAT) and a CRUT?

Answer – A CRAT offers the primary benefits of simplicity and certainty. With a CRAT, the retained interest is a fixed dollar amount. Therefore, since the amount is fixed, there is no need for an annual revaluation as with a CRUT. For that reason (i.e., no annual revaluation requirement), a CRAT will be considerably easier, and less expensive to administer than a CRUT, especially when there are hard-to-value assets being contributed to the trust.

A second consideration is the need (or desire) for a fixed return. With a CRAT, the annual payout is fixed. The unitrust interest will not be reduced if the value of the trust decreases, unless the trust is completely liquidated by distributions.

A third consideration is the need for a hedge against inflation. While a CRAT offers the promise of a fixed annual return, this fixed annual payout can be a significant detriment in the event of inflation. For this reason, younger donors often prefer the flexible unitrust payment that is available with a CRUT, as opposed to the fixed payment guaranteed by a CRAT.

With a CRAT or a CRUT, in many instances the cash flow created from the trustee's investment of 100% of the sales proceeds on a tax-free basis will be significantly more than the cash flow that would have been earned by the donor from the contributed asset. Furthermore, the donor's source of income can be diversified by selling the contributed asset inside the CRAT or the CRUT and allowing the trustee to invest the proceeds in a diversified portfolio.

A fourth consideration is whether additional contributions to the trust are contemplated. A donor can make multiple contributions to a single CRUT, but the *initial* contribution is the *only* contribution that can be made to a CRAT.

Question – Many closely-held businesses are incorporated as S corporations. Can S corporation stock be contributed to a CRUT?

Answer – Yes, S corporation stock may be contributed to a CRUT. However, if this happens, the corporation's status as an S corporation will be *automatically terminated*.[43] In some situations, termination of S corporation status may be an acceptable consequence. However, any decision to transfer S corporation stock to a CRUT should be made only after careful consideration. Termination of the S corporation status will affect all shareholders, not just the shareholder contemplating the transfer.

In some instances (especially when the prospective donor owns all or most of the outstanding S corporation stock), it may be beneficial for the S corporation to create a CRUT. Any corporate contribution of property is treated as having been made *pro rata* by the shareholders of the S corporation.[44] Note, however, that contributions made by an S corporation will reduce a shareholder's basis in his or her corporate stock by the fair market value of the property contributed.[45] The result of this rule is a shifting of unrealized appreciation in the property to the S corporation stock—meaning larger gains if the stock is eventually sold.[46] This rule has no impact for cash and property that is not appreciated; in other words, the corporation's contribution of the property to the CRUT will have essentially the same impact as if the shareholder had created the trust.

Question – Why is it common for a NIMCRUT to invest in a deferred annuity contract?

Answer – In many instances, the grantor of a NIMCRUT does not want, or need, an immediate distribution from the CRUT. For instance, a donor with an irregular income pattern may want to time distributions from the NIMCRUT to occur in years when his other income is lower. In fact, this is a primary reason for selecting a NIMCRUT instead of a standard CRUT. (With a standard CRUT, payments must be made from trust principal if income is insufficient.) For a donor who wants to "time" distributions of income from the NIMCRUT to meet his or her needs, a deferred annuity can provide the desired investment vehicle. By specifying in the trust agreement that distributions from a deferred annuity contract should be treated as trust income, the trustee of a NIMCRUT can virtually "turn on and off" a NIMCRUT's income stream to suit the need of the unitrust beneficiary. This ability to control the recognition of income by the NIMCRUT provides yet another planning opportunity: the trustee can allow the assets in the NIMCRUT to accumulate on a tax-deferred basis for many years, and then control distributions in later years for supplemental retirement benefits. Few, if any, investment choices offer the trustee such flexibility.

Question – Has the IRS approved the use of a deferred annuity to control the timing of distributions from a NIMCRUT?

Answer – Although the IRS has addressed this issue on several instances, there is no final, formal guidance on this point.[47] The IRS first addressed this issue in the proposed charitable remainder trust regulations in 1997. At that time, the IRS stated that it was "studying" whether NIMCRUTs that were invested in assets that are used to control the timing of the receipt and taxation of the beneficiary's income could qualify as a valid charitable remainder trust. Furthermore, the IRS said that it would not issue letter rulings on such trusts.[48] However, in 1998 the IRS issued a Technical Advice Memorandum (TAM)[49] in which it said that a NIMCRUT's purchase of two deferred annuities was not an act of self-dealing and did not disqualify the trust. Furthermore, the IRS training manual for its agents states that the "vast majority" of NIMCRUTs will not engage in self-dealing if they invest in deferred annuities.[50] While a TAM constitutes guidance from the IRS' National Office to another IRS official in the field, it cannot be relied upon as authority by a taxpayer other than the taxpayer involved in the specific transaction at issue.[51]

Question – Can the grantor serve as trustee of a CRUT?

Answer – Subject to certain restrictions, the grantor of a CRUT can serve as trustee. However, neither the grantor nor any other person can be given a power that would cause the grantor to be treated as the owner of the trust under the grantor trust rules.[52] Otherwise, the CRUT will fail to satisfy the requirements of a valid charitable remainder trust.[53] In situations where the grantor is not the unitrust beneficiary, the grantor/trustee should *not* be given the sole power to (1) identify the eventual charitable remainder beneficiary, or (2) make discretionary distributions among a class of permissible unitrust beneficiaries. These powers can cause estate tax inclusion where it could otherwise be avoided.[54]

If the CRUT holds assets that do not have a readily determinable fair market value, the value of those assets should be determined by an independent trustee or by a qualified appraiser.[55]

Question – Can the donor contribute his home to a CRUT?

Answer – Yes, but the donor must vacate the property prior to making the contribution, to avoid self-dealing. The donor's use of the property after the transfer would constitute self-dealing even if the donor entered into an arm's-length lease with the CRUT.[56]

Question – If debt-encumbered appreciated real estate is to be contributed to a charitable remainder trust, does that create any special considerations?

Answer – Yes, several issues must be considered before contributing debt encumbered real estate to a charitable remainder trust, including a CRUT. In fact, it is generally recommended that the transfer of debt encumbered real estate be *avoided*. The following are some of the issues that should be considered before undertaking this risky transaction:

First, if the property is subject to a mortgage and the donor is relieved of the mortgage, the transfer should be treated as a bargain sale (see Chapter 10). If there is a bargain sale, the donor will be required to pay a capital gains tax.[57]

Second, a transfer of debt-encumbered property could disqualify the charitable remainder trust if the trustee pays the mortgage. The reason is that if the trustee makes the mortgage payment, it appears that the charitable remainder trust is a grantor trust for income tax purposes and, as a result, cannot qualify as a charitable remainder trust.[58]

Third, a transfer of debt-encumbered property may constitute self-dealing for the donor and the trustee.[59] This appears to be the case even if the debt is not assumed by the trust.[60]

Fourth, if the debt was placed on the property within five years of the date of transfer, the charitable remainder trust could be treated as receiving debt-financed income. If a charitable remainder trust realizes any debt-financed income, *all* trust income may be taxable.[61]

At one time, it was thought that these issues could be avoided by transferring an option to purchase debt encumbered property to the charitable remainder trust. However, the IRS has since ruled that a charitable remainder trust funded with such an option would not qualify as a valid charitable remainder trust.[62] One possible solution to this problem is to contribute the appreciated property to a partnership, and then contribute the partnership interest to the charitable remainder trust. The IRS has not specifically ruled on this use of a partnership.

Question – Can a charity be a unitrust beneficiary of a CRUT?

Answer – The answer is unclear. A CRUT must have one or more noncharitable unitrust beneficiaries. However, in addition to the noncharitable unitrust beneficiary, the CRUT can also have a charitable unitrust beneficiary. It is not clear whether the existence of a charitable unitrust beneficiary would reduce the value of the unitrust interest for gift tax purposes. There seems to be a conflict of authority on this point. In a private letter ruling, the IRS approved an estate tax deduction for the value of the current interest payable to the charity. While this ruling involved a charitable remainder annuity trust (CRAT) and not a CRUT, this distinction should not be of importance. But, in a revenue ruling, the IRS denied an estate tax deduction for the value of the current annuity interest payable to the charitable beneficiary.[63] This charitable annuity interest would not have been payable until the death of the noncharitable annuitants. This ruling also involved a CRAT, and not a CRUT.

Question – Does the charitable remainder beneficiary have to be determined at the time that the CRUT is created?

Answer – No. The selection of the ultimate qualified charitable beneficiary may be left to the trustee, the unitrust beneficiary, the donor, or a third person.[64] However, unless the CRUT instrument mandates that the ultimate charitable beneficiary qualify as a public charity, the grantor's income tax deduction will be treated as a remainder gift to a private foundation. Gifts to a private foundation receive less favorable income tax treatment than gifts to a public charity (see Chapter 3). Gifts of cash to

a private foundation are subject to the 30% of adjusted gross income (AGI) limitation rather than the more favorable 50% limitation. Gifts of appreciated property (other than certain marketable securities) are subject to the 20% limitation, and the value of the contributed property is limited to the grantor's adjusted basis.[65] Thus, unless the ultimate charitable beneficiary of a CRUT is intended to be a private foundation, the CRUT instrument should be drafted to explicitly limit the beneficiary of the remainder interest in the CRUT to public charities. Moreover, if a private foundation is intended to be the ultimate remainder beneficiary of a CRUT, the CRUT should be funded with cash or qualified marketable securities, to maximize the donor's charitable income tax deduction.

Question – Since a CRUT must have one or more noncharitable beneficiaries, must the noncharitable unitrust beneficiary be an individual?

Answer – No, the noncharitable beneficiary is not required to be an individual. The noncharitable beneficiary of a CRUT can be an individual, trust, estate, partnership, association, company or corporation. However, the payment to a *non*individual beneficiary must be limited to a term of years not to exceed 20. The IRS has made limited exceptions to this rule for trusts created for the benefit of incompetent individuals. In a revenue ruling, the IRS approved a charitable remainder trust that provided distributions for the benefit of an incompetent individual for that person's life.[66] At one time it also appeared that a trust for the benefit of a competent person could be a permissible unitrust beneficiary. In a private letter ruling, the IRS determined that a separate trust for a competent beneficiary was a permissible unitrust beneficiary of a CRUT because the competent beneficiary had the absolute and unqualified right to withdraw all property from the trust and, thus would be treated as the owner of the trust property for federal income tax purposes (under IRC Section 678). However, in another private letter ruling, the IRS reversed its position and stated that only a trust for the benefit of an incompetent beneficiary qualifies as a permissible unitrust beneficiary. The IRS' position in the latest letter ruling has been criticized as unwarranted under both the explicit language and spirit of the Code.[67]

Question – What are the estate planning opportunities for using ESOPs and CRTs?

Answer – An individual may have a large portion of his wealth tied up in the stock of a single corporation and may seek to diversify such holdings. If those shares are highly appreciated, a sale will generally result in the recognition of significant capital gain for federal income tax purposes. However, if such a sale is instead made to the corporation's employee stock ownership plan (ESOP), diversification can be achieved with a concomitant deferral of any capital gain so long as the sale proceeds are reinvested in "qualified replacement property" (generally, securities traded on an established secondary market).[68] If a sale to an ESOP is made, capital gain is recognized only if the qualified replacement property is later sold, and the gain recognized is measured by the difference between the sale price of the qualified replacement property and the owner's original cost basis in his corporate stock. If the individual dies owning qualified replacement property, the individual's capital gain will never be recognized because such property receives a stepped-up basis as a result of the individual's death.[69] Thus, after the individual's death his heirs can sell the qualified replacement property and invest in other property with little or no gain realized on such later sale.

A sale of stock to an ESOP, and reinvestment of the proceeds in qualified replacement property, can be a useful income and estate tax planning strategy. However, once an individual elects to defer capital gain through the purchase of qualified replacement property, he is "locked in" to that portfolio. In other words, the individual cannot reinvest any portion of the qualified replacement property without accelerating the deferred gain. This is a significant drawback of this strategy, as illustrated by the example below:

Example: Assume that Robert Boyd (age 50) wishes to diversify his holdings in his corporation. He elects to sell his stock to the corporation's ESOP. Because Robert is relatively young, he elects to reinvest the sale proceeds in growth stock that constitutes qualified replacement property. Under IRC Section 1042, Robert will be able to defer the capital gain on the sale of his stock to the ESOP, but only for so long as he holds onto the original stock portfolio. When he reaches retirement age, it may be desirable for Robert to shift his emphasis from growth to current income for supplemental retirement planning needs. However, he will not be able to do so without accelerating the deferred capital gain.

However, it appears that this problem can be solved with a gift of the qualified replacement property to a charitable remainder trust. Generally, the transfer of highly appreciated, long-term capital gain property to a charitable remainder trust allows the donor to avoid immediate recognition of the gain in such property. This is so because the trust's later sale of the property is not attributed to the donor and, as a tax-exempt entity, the trust does not have to pay tax on the gain. Thus, by transferring the qualified replacement property to a charitable remainder trust, the donor is able to (1) achieve diversification on an ongoing basis through the trust's investment strategy, and (2) receive supplemental retirement income through a retained annuity or unitrust interest. Moreover, if the transfer of the replacement property is made to a NIMCRUT, the donor can achieve maximum planning flexibility.

Example: Assume that Robert transfers the replacement property to a NIMCRUT sometime after the sale to the ESOP. The individual does not need supplemental retirement income until retirement at age 65, which is approximately 15 years later. Therefore, the NIMCRUT can reinvest the qualified replacement properties in a growth portfolio until Robert reaches age 65. This will allow for significant growth in the principal of the trust without any diminution of the principal due to current unitrust payments. Later, when Robert retires, the trust's portfolio can be shifted from a growth emphasis to stress the production of current income instead. Because there will be a larger value from which to determine the individual's unitrust payments in retirement, and because additional distributions can be recouped from the NIMCRUT's make-up account, supplemental income from the NIMCRUT can be maximized without an adverse impact on the amount ultimately passing to the charitable remainderperson.

While the IRS has approved of this approach in several private letter rulings, it has done so with little legal analysis.[70] In those letter rulings, the IRS concluded that the transfer of qualified replacement property to a charitable remainder trust constituted a disposition within the meaning of IRC Section 1042(e). Code Section 1042(e) and its legislative history seem to provide for taxation upon disposition of qualified replacement property.[71] Nevertheless, the IRS has consistently determined that recognition of capital gain is avoided on the transfer of qualified replacement property to the trust. Apparently, the IRS views the transfer of qualified replacement property to a charitable remainder trust as a gift that is eligible for the gift exception of IRC Section 1042(e). However, in each of the rulings, the IRS noted that the trustee of the charitable remainder trust in question was under no obligation (express or implied) to sell the qualified replacement property, "nor [could] the trustee be legally bound to sell" such property. In summary, the planner would be well-advised to include similar language in any charitable remainder trust that will hold qualified replacement property.

Question – How are CRUTS used in closely-held businesses transfer planning?

Answer – The use of a CRUT to effectuate the transfer of a business from the current owner to the new ownership can benefit the business owner in several ways. By contributing stock to a CRUT, the business owner can take a current income tax charitable deduction for the present value of the charitable remainder interest. In addition, the business owner may also be able to benefit from an increased income stream in the future, as illustrated by the following example:

Example: Alexander owns 100% of the stock of Imperial Importers, Inc. At age 60, Alexander is anxious to implement a plan that will allow him to pass the business to his three sons, Nicholas, George, and Michael. Alexander will complete the transfer through the use of a CRUT. He will take the following steps to complete the transfer of the business:

First, Alexander will make gifts of Imperial Importers, Inc. stock to his three children. To accomplish this, Alexander will make annual exclusion gifts of stock to Nicholas, George, and Michael.[72]

Second, Alexander will transfer his remaining shares to a CRUT. Alexander will be permitted a current income tax deduction for the value of the remainder interest passing to charity.

If Alexander structures the CRUT to pay the unitrust interest to him for his lifetime, there will be no current taxable gift.

Third, at some future time, Imperial Importers will offer to redeem all outstanding shares of the company's stock. Assuming that the CRUT tenders its shares for redemption, but the children do not, the three children will then own all of the remaining outstanding shares of stock.[73] If there are sufficient assets in the corporation, the shares can be redeemed for cash, and the unitrust distribution amount can be used as supplemental retirement income for Alexander. In some instances, the corporation will redeem the stock for a note. The corporation will then purchase key-person insurance policy on the life of Alexander. Upon the death of Alexander, the corporation can use the life insurance proceeds to satisfy the obligation under the note.

Caution: While this strategy appears appropriate under the language of the Code, it should be noted that the Treasury regulations contain an example that appears to explicitly prohibit redemption via a note transaction because it constitutes self-dealing. Other commentators have also suggested that this example is invalid in light of the broad language of the redemption exception in IRC Section 4941.[74] State redemption laws should also be considered. Some state laws prevent a corporation from redeeming stock if that redemption can cause the corporation to become insolvent; other states prevent redemption of stock for debt.

Fourth, once Imperial Importers has redeemed all of the stock from Alexander, Nicholas, George, and Michael will own 100% of the remaining outstanding shares, regardless of the number of shares each owns individually, and regardless of the percentage they collectively owned before the redemption.

The only significant downside to this transaction (assuming that the redemption is allowable under state law in the applicable jurisdiction) is that Nicholas, George, and Michael will have a cost basis in their corporate stock equal to the cost basis in the shares they received from Alexander. In effect, their cost basis will be nominal in most instances. But, in situations where the stock in the

family business cannot be transferred to children without considerable estate and gift tax cost, the fact that the children will have little cost basis in their interests is not a high price to pay for transferring the business to the next generation.

As discussed earlier in this chapter, a grantor can establish several different types of CRUTs. In this instance, Nicholas is likely to choose a NIMCRUT because he realizes the closely-held stock owned by the CRUT is unlikely to generate sufficient income to cover the annual unitrust payment. Stated another way, if Alexander does not use a NIMCRUT (or NICRUT), the trustee may be forced to sell some of the CRUT assets (i.e., stock) or make in-kind (i.e., stock) distributions to Alexander in satisfaction of his annual unitrust interest.

CHAPTER ENDNOTES

1. See Chapter 15.
2. IRC Secs. 664(d)(2), 664(d)(3); Treas. Regs. §§1.664-1, 1.664-3.
3. IRC Sec. 664(d)(2)(A); Treas. Reg. §1.664-3(a)(1).
4. According to a 1995 private letter ruling, an inter vivos charitable remainder trust cannot have more than one donor. Let. Rul. 9547004. However, commentators have noted that this ruling seems to lack authority in the Code and regulations. Moreover, it appears inconsistent with other rulings in which the IRS approved of charitable remainder trusts in which both the husband and the wife were donors of a single trust. Rev. Proc. 2005-52. The IRS has also ruled that trusts or limited liability companies (that are taxed as a partnership) are permissible CRUT donors. Let. Ruls. 9821029, 199952071.
5. IRC Sec. 664(d)(2)(A); Treas. Reg. §1.664-3(a)(2).
6. Treas. Reg. §1.664-3(a)(1)(i)
7. Treas. Regs. §§1.664-3(c) and 1.665-4.
8. Treas. Reg. §1.664-2(a)(5)(i). IRC. Sec. 7701(a)(1) defines person as "an individual, trust, estate, association, company corporation or partnership." Therefore, while it is uncommon, the unitrust interest can be payable to a corporation or partnership if limited to a term of years not to exceed 20. Let. Rul. 9419021 (limited partnership as beneficiary), Let. Rul. 9205031 (corporation).
9. Rev. Rul. 2002-20, 2002-17 IRB 794 provides an exception to the 20-year term limitation for a CRUT beneficiary that meets the definition of "financially disabled."
10. See IRC Sec. 664(d)(2)(D); Treas. Reg. §1.664-3(b).
11. Treas. Reg. §1.664-3(b).
12. IRC Sec. 664(d)(2)(C). A qualified organization is an organization described in IRC Secs. 170(c), 2055(a), or 2522(a).
13. For the rules revising the definition of "income" under IRC Section 643(b) to take into account changes in the definition of trust accounting income under state laws, see Treas. Reg. §1.643(b)(3).
14. *Martin v. Ohio State University Foundation*, 139 Ohio App.3d 89, 742 N.E.2d 1198 (10th Dist. 2000). See Let. Rul. 200219012 rescinding CRUT where there was no trust income.

15. Treas. Reg. §1.664-3(a)(1)(i)(c)(1).
16. Treas. Reg. §1.664-3(a)(1)(i)(d).
17. Treas. Reg. §1.664-3(a)(1)(i)(c)(3).
18. Treas. Reg. §1.664-3(a)(1)(i)(c)(2).
19. The steps for implementing a CRUT-wealth replacement trust approach were adopted from *The Charitable Remainder Trust Case Illustration Series: The Santiagos* (Carmel, IN: Renaissance, Inc. 1997).
20. IRC Sec. 170(d)(1).
21. Manulife Survivorship UL 2000, Male NS Standard Age 64, Female NS Standard Age 62, Maximum Policy Protection Rider.
22. Should Bob and Mary live past the anticipated life expectancy, they would have to continue making premium payments of $15,442 until the younger insured reaches age 100.
23. IRC Sec. 170(f)(3)(A); see Chapter 5.
24. IRC Secs. 664(d)(2), 664(d)(3).
25. In some instances, the value of the property contributed to the CRUT may be limited to the donor's cost basis in that property. See IRC Sec. 170(e).
26. Comprehensive tables for valuing the remainder interest in a CRUT are contained in IRS Publication 1458, Actuarial Values (Beta Volume). See Appendix K.
27. The value of a noncharitable beneficiary's life payout (or a payout over the lives of multiple noncharitable unitrust beneficiaries) is ordinarily determined in accordance with the life expectancies provided by the IRS tables. However, an individual who is terminally ill may not use the IRS life expectancy tables. Treas. Regs. §§1.7520-3(b)(3), 20.7520-3(b)(3), and 25.7520-3(b)(3).
28. The IRS discount rate is determined under IRC Section 7520 and is equal to 120% of the applicable federal mid-term rate.
29. See Chapter 3.
30. Treas. Reg. §1.170A-13(f)(13).
31. IRC Sec. 6019(3).
32. Treas. Reg. §25.6019-1(f).
33. IRC Secs. 2036(a)(1), 2039, 2055(e)(2)(A). However, the IRS has also ruled that if the income interest rate equivalent to the adjusted payout rate of the CRUT is less than the rate used to value the unitrust interest in the donor's life estate, then only a proportion of the trust property will be includable in the gross estate under IRC Section 2036. However, the full value would be includable under IRC Section 2039. Rev. Rul. 76-273, 1976-2 CB 268.
34. IRC Sec. 664(c); *Leila G. Newhall Unitrust v. Comm.*, 104 TC 236 (1995), *aff'd*, 105 F.3d 482 (9th Cir. 1997).
35. IRC Sec. 664(b); Treas Reg. §1.664-1(d)(1).
36. IRC Sec. 664(b); Treas. Reg. §1.664-1(d)(1).
37. IRC Sec. 643(b).
38. Treas. Reg. §1.643(b)-1.
39. Treas. Reg. §1.643(b)-1; see also Let. Rul. 9018015.
40. Treasury Regulations state that with respect to NICRUTs and NIMCRUTs, post-contribution capital gain may be allocated to income pursuant to applicable local law and the terms of the governing instrument, only, but not pursuant to a discretionary power granted to the trustee. See Treas. Reg. §1.664-3(b)(3).
41. See Let. Rul. 9442017.
42. Treas. Reg. §1.664-3(a)(1)(i)(b)(4).
43. Rev. Rul. 92-48, 1992-1 CB 301.

44. See, generally, IRC Sec. 1366(a)(1)(A).

45. See, generally, IRC Sec. 1367(a)(2)(b).

46. The possible impact of the Treasury regulations promulgated under IRC Section 337(d) should be considered when substantially all the assets of the S corporation will be contributed to the CRUT.

47. See H.R. Rep. No. 91-413, 60 (TRA '69), *reprinted in* 1969-3 CB 239. In the legislative history to the charitable remainder trust rules, Congress expressed its concern that charitable remainder trusts not be used as a means to manipulate the size of trust distributions for the donor's benefit.

48. Rev. Proc. 97-23, 1997-1 CB 654; Rev. Proc. 99-3, 1999-1, I.R.B. 103.

49. TAM 9825001.

50. See Teitel, "Charitable Remainder Trusts – Final Regulations," *Trusts and Estates*, August, 1999, p. 44. See *Internal Revenue Service Exempt Organizations Continuing Professional Education (CPE) Text for Fiscal Year 1999*, Topic P: Thirty Years after the 1969 TRA–Recent Developments Under Chapter 42.

51. IRC Sec. 6110(k)(3).

52. IRC Secs. 671, 672, 673, 674, 675, 676, 677, 678.

53. Treas. Reg. §1.664-1(a)(4).

54. See IRC Sec. 2036(a)(2).

55. Treas. Reg. §1.664-1(a)(7). The definitions of "qualified appraisal" and "qualified appraiser" are contained at IRC Sec. 170 (f) (11) (E).

56. Treas. Reg. §53.4941(d)-(2)(b).

57. IRC Sec. 1011(b).

58. Let. Rul. 9015049, citing Treas. Regs. §§1.664-1(a)(4), 1.677(a)-1(d).

59. But see Treas. Reg. §53.4941(d)-1(a).

60. IRC Sec. 4941(d)(2)(A).

61. IRC Secs. 664(c), 514(c)(2)(B).

62. Let. Rul. 9501004.

63. Let. Rul. 8845012; Rev. Rul. 76-225, 1976-1 CB 281.

64. Treas. Reg. §1.664-3(a)(4). See also, *e.g.*, Rev. Proc. 2005-52 through Rev. Proc. 2005-58; Rev. Rul. 76-371, 1976-2 CB 305, (trustee); Rev. Rul. 76-8, 1976-1 CB 179 (grantor); Rev. Rul. 76-7, 1976-1 CB 179 (beneficiaries); Let. Rul. 9504012 (grantors); Let. Rul. 9326049 (grantor); Let. Rul. 9014033 (beneficiaries); Let. Rul. 9022014 (beneficiary).

65. IRC Sec. 170(e).

66. IRC Sec. 7701(a)(1); Rev. Rul. 76-270, 1976-2 CB 194. See Rev. Rul. 2002-20, 2002-17 IRB 794 extending the 20-year term limitation for a CRUT beneficiary that meets the definition of "financially disabled."

67. Let. Ruls. 9619044, 9710008. See, e.g., Teitel at 245-46, note 4, above.

68. See IRC Sec. 1042.

69. See IRC Secs. 1042(e), 1014.

70. See Let. Ruls. 9547023, 9547022, 9438021, 9438012, and 9234023.

71. IRC section 1042(e) provides that: "If a taxpayer disposes of any qualified replacement property, then, notwithstanding any other provision of this title, gain (if any) shall be recognized….." The legislative history provides: "the Act (Section 1042(e)) overrides all other provisions permitting nonrecognition and requires that gain realized upon the disposition of qualified replacement property be recognized at that time." Sen. Rep. 99-313, 1032 (1986), *reprinted in* 1986-3 CB 1032.

72. IRC section 2503(b) allows each individual to make a present interest gift of up to $10,000 (adjusted for inflation in $1,000 increments) to each recipient without current gift tax, or without use of the grantor's estate and gift tax exemption.

73. See IRC Sec. 4941(d)(2)(F).

74. Treas. Reg. §53.4941(d)-3(d)(2), Example 2. See Muller, *Private Foundations – Self-Dealing (Section 4941)*, 89 T.M. A-33 (1994).

COMMUNITY FOUNDATIONS

CHAPTER 17

WHAT IS IT?

A community foundation is essentially a charitable grant-making organization that is formed to benefit a particular community or area. Traditionally, donors have made contributions to a community foundation as an endowment to support community needs, leaving the exact determination of the expenditures to a grant-making committee of the foundation. Over the years, community foundations have developed extensive procedures for determining how to maximize benefits to the community through such grants. These include prudent management and investment of the contributions that are received, investigation of the needs of the community, and monitoring the grant expenditures by recipient organizations.

The first community foundation was established in 1914 by a prominent Cleveland attorney and banker, Frederick H. Goff, out of a desire to support the community and to aggregate trusts for common charitable purposes. Other civic and industrial leaders lent support to the cause of establishing and building up the size of the foundation.[1] Numerous other communities have since formed community foundations for similar broad public purposes. There are now over 700 community foundations operating in the United States. In most cases, a single individual will not be able to establish a community foundation, but many individual donors will choose to support their community through contributions to their local community foundation in the form of current and deferred gifts—that is, gifts taking effect at the death of the donor or following the termination of a charitable split-interest arrangement.

WHEN IS THE USE OF SUCH A DEVICE INDICATED?

1. Whenever the donor wants to provide funding for the general community supported by the community foundation.

2. When the donor has an interest in continuing involvement in a donor advised fund.

ADVANTAGES

1. Amounts that are donated to a community foundation are eligible for the higher deduction limits of public charities rather than the lower limits on donations to private foundations (see Chapter 3).

2. A community foundation offers a donor a degree of control over donations without an obligation to be involved in the day-to-day administration of the fund. The donor and family members can take an active role in working with the community foundation to accomplish the charitable purposes of the donor and the donor's family. However, they can also leave it to the foundation to make the decisions on how to use the funds in the context of the stated purpose of a particular fund.

3. A community foundation is not subject to excise taxes and other restrictions that apply to a private foundation.

4. Many donors prefer community foundations because the reporting requirements and restrictions on certain activities that apply to private foundations make them appear unattractive, especially for contributions of less than $500,000.

DISADVANTAGES

1. The community foundation may have a policy that eventually adds the assets of a particular fund to the general funds of the community foundation, thereby eliminating the donor's involvement in distribution decisions.

2. Many community foundations allow only two or three younger generations of the donor's family to continue to be involved in grant making. After these generations have passed away, the community foundation takes over the grant-making authority.

3. Some community foundations have geographic restrictions, preferring to keep grants within a particular community. Donors who intend to benefit national or regional causes may not be able to accomplish these objectives through a named fund established with their local community foundation.

WHAT ARE THE REQUIREMENTS?

1. In order for a community foundation to be treated as a public charity, the foundation must be treated as a "publicly supported" organization. To be considered a publicly supported organization, the foundation must fulfill one of two public support tests.

    a. *One-third support test.* The community foundation generally must derive at least one-third of its annual support from contributions from the general public and certain governmental units. If a community foundation is not able to meet the first test, it may qualify as a public charity under the "facts and circumstances" test.[2]

    b. *Facts and circumstances test.* The community foundation must receive at least 10% of its annual support from contributions from the general public and certain governmental units. Also, the foundation must be organized and operated to attract new and additional public or government support on a continuous basis. In addition to these two requirements, there must be taken into account other factors to determine whether the community foundation is publicly supported. These factors include: (1) the amount of support actually received from the general public and governments; (2) the sources of the foundation's support; and (3) whether the governing body of the foundation represents the broad views of the public or the interests of a limited number of donors.[3]

In determining whether support comes from the general public for either the one-third test or the 10% test, contributions by individuals, corporations, or trusts will be counted as support from the general public only if the amount contributed by each person or entity does not exceed 2% of the foundation's total support.[4]

2. The requirements that a community foundation places on donors to be able to give to a named fund within the foundation or a donor advised fund varies with each community foundation. For example, the Cleveland Foundation will accept a donor advised fund as small as $10,000.[5] Typical minimums for giving to a named fund range from $100,000 and higher. In many cases, the funding may occur over several years and may be completed with a gift at death.

HOW IS IT DONE?

Community foundations often maintain separate trusts or funds within the foundation. These separate funds are subject to varying degrees of control by the foundation's governing body. However, these different funds will be treated as one entity for tax purposes if certain requirements are met.[6] The different funds in a community foundation fall into two general categories: restricted and unrestricted. As the name indicates, funds in an unrestricted fund may be used for community needs as determined by the foundation itself. Restricted funds allow donors to make recommendations for the use of the funds. There can also be different types of restricted funds (e.g., scholarship funds and field of interest funds, which support a specific cause that the donor is interested in). A restricted fund can also be used by a donor to support several charities without the need to make a number of different gifts. Restricted funds are also sometimes called "named funds" or "donor advised funds." The Pension Protection Act of 2006 (PPA 2006) has extended several of the regulatory requirements applicable to private foundations to donor advised funds. For more information, see Chapter 19.

The donor can establish a named fund or donor advised fund with a community foundation by: (1) a single lifetime gift; (2) a series of lifetime gifts; or (3) a transfer at the donor's death. The latter can be accomplished by a gift, a bequest under a trust or a will, or a distribution from a charitable remainder trust. In some situations, other family members or friends of the donor will make additional contributions to the fund during the life or after the death of the original donor.

Example 1: Donald wishes to establish a fund bearing his family's name with a local community foundation. He transfers $100,000 cash, and publicly traded securities with a fair market value of $900,000 and a cost basis of $200,000. He is entitled to a $1 million deduction, subject to the 50% adjusted gross income (AGI) limitation on the donation of cash and the 30% AGI limitation on the donation of capital gain property. The foundation agrees to make distributions from the fund based on Donald's stated general purpose to support the development of educational programs and training for blues musicians. Donald agrees that if students of the blues cannot be found to take advantage of the educational support, the funds may be distributed to promote the training of jazz musicians. He also requests that at least half of the distributions each year be made in the form of scholarships.

Example 2: Charlotte wants to establish a donor advised fund into which she will periodically deposit cash or securities. She will consult with the community foundation staff about how to expend the funds, with an expectation that she will direct the distribution of at least 5% of the fund balance each year. She makes her initial contribution in the amount of $10,000 and directs the foundation to distribute one-half of that contribution to her alma mater. In the second year, Charlotte adds $10,000 and directs a distribution of $6,000, $3,000 to her alma mater and $3,000 to several other charitable organizations. She also writes a letter to the foundation requesting that her daughter be permitted to direct distributions from the fund after Charlotte's death, provided the fund meets the community foundation's size requirement to allow for continued family involvement in directing distributions. The community foundation imposes a .5% management fee on the funds in the donor advised fund to cover investment and administrative expenses.

WHAT ARE THE TAX IMPLICATIONS?

If the community foundation meets the requirements to be treated as a public charity, gifts to the community foundation receive the most favored tax treatment: a charitable deduction may be taken up to 50% of adjusted gross income (AGI) for donations of cash, and 30% of AGI for donations of capital gain property.[7] If the amount that is donated to a community foundation exceeds these limits, the deduction may be carried forward up to five additional years (if the percentage limit is not used up in those years).[8]

If long-term capital gain property is donated to a community foundation, the donor will generally be able to deduct the full fair market value of the property, but with the lower 30% AGI limitation.[9] The donor may elect to deduct the basis of capital gain property to take advantage of the higher 50% AGI limitation. However, if this election is taken it applies to all capital gain property donated during the tax year.[10]

A community foundation is tax exempt under IRC Section 501(c)(3) as a grant-making organization.

WHAT ARE THE ALTERNATIVES?

In the last several years, many community foundations have developed donor advised funds as an alternative to private foundations, thereby affording donors the opportunity to be involved on a continuing basis in the grant-making process with the full availability of the foundation's resources to assure accomplishment of the donor's objectives. Under these arrangements, a donor makes a gift to the community foundation but reserves the right to be involved in determining how the income and principal of the fund will be expended. At some point in the future, the fund will become subject to exclusive control of the community foundation, but it is not unusual for at least one younger generation of the donor's family to continue to be involved in advising the community foundation on the distributions from the fund.

The donor advised fund is a suitable alternative to a private foundation or supporting organization whenever the resources to be contributed are relatively small (perhaps less than $500,000) or where the donor is not interested in incurring the set-up costs and ongoing participation and expenses involved in a private foundation or supporting organization. See Chapter 19 for more detailed information about donor advised funds.

WHERE CAN I FIND OUT MORE ABOUT IT?

1. Council on Foundations, 2121 Crystal Drive, Suite 700, Arlington, VA 22202, www.cof.org. Its Web site includes information on all types of charitable foundations and includes a "foundation locator" search function to help donors find community and other foundations to which they may want to make contributions.

2. Each year the Internal Revenue Service publishes, *Exempt Organizations Continuing Professional Educa-*

tion Technical Instruction Program (Internal Revenue Service, Freedom of Information Reading Room, Room 1621, 1111 Constitution Ave., N.W., Washington, DC 20224).

3. Toce, Joseph, Abbin, Byrle, Vorsatz, Mark, and Page, William, *Tax Economics of Charitable Giving 2006-2007* (Warren Gorham & Lamont, 2006).

QUESTIONS AND ANSWERS

Question – Why would someone choose to contribute to a community foundation rather than to a private foundation?

Answer – The reporting requirements and restrictions on certain prohibited activities that apply to private foundations often make a private foundation appear somewhat cumbersome, especially with contributions of less than $500,000. In addition, there are costs associated with establishing and operating a private foundation that may be perceived as prohibitive. The community foundation avoids these problems and also makes available to the donor the grant-making capacity and monitoring of expenditures that many private foundations cannot cost-effectively duplicate.

Contributions of cash to a community foundation are deductible up to 50% of the taxpayer's adjusted gross income (AGI), while contributions of cash to a private foundation are deductible only up to 30% of the taxpayer's AGI. If capital gain property is given to a community foundation, the fair market value of the property is deductible up to 30% of the taxpayer's AGI, while donations of capital gain property are deductible only for the basis of the property, and may be deductible only up to 20% of the taxpayer's AGI.

Question – Why would someone choose to make a contribution to a community foundation rather than an outright gift to a charity?

Answer – As with a private foundation, a primary benefit of donating to a community foundation is the ability to monitor the ultimate distribution each year to various charities. In many cases, donors are concerned about the application of the funds contrary to their wishes. With the administrative support offered by a community foundation, the handling of the funds by the recipient charity can be evaluated, and if found unsatisfactory the donor can advise the community foundation on the redirection of future

grants to organizations that more nearly meet the donor's objectives. In other cases, there may be a concern about the ability of the recipient to invest and manage the funds over a long period of time. A community foundation should be able to more effectively manage the investments on a pooled basis for all of the contributions received and for longer term endowment funds.

Question – Can a scholarship fund be established through a community foundation?

Answer – Yes. The IRS closely scrutinizes private foundations that have as their primary activity the granting of scholarships due to a concern about abusive practices, such as granting scholarships to relatives of the donor or carrying out discriminatory practices. A community foundation does not receive the same type of scrutiny because it has in place policies and procedures to prevent abusive practices. Further, the burden of the selection of scholarship recipients can be more cost-effectively managed by the personnel and resources of the community foundation.

Question – Why would someone choose a donor advised fund at a community foundation rather than a charitable gift fund sponsored by a mutual fund?

Answer – A donor may be more confident of local investment management and be averse to the relatively limited investment options available through a mutual fund operated charitable gift fund. Additionally, a local community foundation often can provide assistance in selecting worthy charities and in monitoring the expenditure of the funds that were distributed to a particular charity.

CHAPTER ENDNOTES

1. Cynthia Jones Eisenman, "Value Added: Donor Advised Funds at Community Foundations," *Trusts & Estates*, March 1997, p. 16.
2. Treas. Reg. §1.170A-9(e)(10).
3. Treas. Reg. §1.170A-9(e)(3).
4. Treas. Reg. §1.170A-9(e)(6).
5. The Cleveland Foundation, 1422 Euclid Avenue, Suite 1400, Cleveland, OH 44115; (216) 861-3810, at: www.clevelandfoundation.org.
6. Treas. Reg. §1.170A-9(e)(11).
7. IRC Sec. 170(b).
8. IRC Secs. 170(b)(1)(B), 170(d)(1).
9. IRC Sec. 170(b)(1)(B).
10. IRC Sec. 170(b)(1)(C)(iii).

QUALIFIED CONSERVATION CONTRIBUTIONS

CHAPTER 18

WHAT IS IT?

A *qualified conservation contribution* is a contribution of a qualified real property interest to a qualified organization exclusively for conservation purposes.

Qualified real property interests include:

1. the donor's entire interest in property (except that the donor may retain a "qualified mineral interest" without jeopardizing his income tax charitable deduction);

2. a remainder interest; or

3. a restriction granted in perpetuity on the use that may be made of the real property (i.e., an easement).

Details as to these requirements are explained below.

Over the past several years, conservation easements have become very popular. According to the Land Trust Alliance, "landowners have found that conservation easements can be flexible planning tools, and yet provide a permanent guarantee that the land won't be developed."[1] The National Land Trust Census Report, which provides land protection statistics through the end of 2005, reflects remarkable growth, stating that: "Total acres covered by local, state and national land trusts increased 54% to 37 million acres in just the past five years. This is an area 16.5 times the size of Yellowstone National Park. The pace of conservation by local and state land trusts more than tripled between successive five-year periods. The number of land trusts grew to 1,667, a 32% increase over five years."[2]

WHEN IS THE USE OF SUCH A DEVICE INDICATED?

1. When the donor wants to protect land from commercial or residential development.

2. When the donor wants to protect a historic building from development or alteration.

3. When the donor wants to preserve land for environmental reasons.

4. When the donor wants to permanently set aside land for use by the general public.

5. When the donor has a need to reduce his overall taxable estate for federal estate tax purposes.

6. When the executor wants to exclude a percentage of the property subject to a previously donated easement, and the ownership and other requirements have been met.

WHAT ARE THE REQUIREMENTS?

Qualified Conservation Contribution Requirements

Qualified Real Property Interest

The first requirement of a gift of qualified conservation property is that the contribution be a "qualified real property interest." There are three types of interests that will meet this requirement:

1. The donor can make a gift of his *entire interest* in real estate (although he may retain a "qualified mineral interest" as defined below). A contribution of the donor's entire interest in real property means a gift of 100% of his ownership stake in the real property. For instance, if a landowner who owns a parcel of land that adjoins a public park donates use of the lake to the public park during the summer months of each year, the donation would not constitute a contribution of a qualified real property interest because the donor did not contribute 100% of his ownership stake in the land.

   Note, however, that even though the donor must give his entire interest in the property to properly claim the deduction that does not mean that the donor cannot perform certain activities on the property after the donation has occurred. For example, the donor can continue to conduct certain agricultural activities or engage in certain recreational activities on the land. (But for purposes of the estate tax exclusion, the ability to use the land for certain activities after the donation has occurred is severely limited. See "Estate Tax Exclusion Requirements," below.)

   Qualified mineral interest. A "qualified mineral interest" is the donor's interest in subsurface oil, gas, or other minerals, and the right to access such minerals. Generally, a contribution will not be treated as having been made "exclusively for a conservation purpose" unless the conservation purpose is protected in perpetuity. However, where a donor contributes any interest in property and retains a qualified mineral interest, the above requirement will deemed to be satisfied *if*:

   - the ownership of the surface estate and mineral interests were separated prior to the contribution of the property (and have remained separated), *and*

   - the probability of surface mining occurring on the property is so remote as to be negligible.[3]

2. The gift may be a *remainder interest* in real property, following a life estate or a term of years (see Chapter 5). Note that the remainder interest under a qualified conservation gift must be to a "qualified organization" (see below).

(This requirement contrasts with the gift of a remainder interest in a personal residence or farm, which can be made whether or not the donee is a qualified organization, and whether or not the gift is exclusively for conservation purposes.)[4]

3. The donor can contribute a *perpetual conservation restriction*.[5] A "perpetual conservation restriction" limits the use that can be made of the real property in perpetuity. Three examples of interests that qualify as "perpetual conservation restrictions" include:

   (a) an easement;

   (b) a restrictive covenant (i.e., a provision in a deed requiring the property owner to limit the use of his property); and

   (c) an equitable servitude (i.e., a building restriction, or a restriction on the use of the land, where the restriction itself constitutes an interest in the land).[6]

Treasury regulations provide that the terms "easement," "conservation restriction," and "perpetual conservation restriction" have the same meaning. Effective for gifts after 1986, a gift of an easement represents a safe harbor partial interest gift for gift and estate tax purposes.[7]

   As stated above, a conservation easement is a restriction on the owner's use of the property. A popular form of conservation easement is the *open space or scenic easement*, where the landowner agrees to set the land aside to preserve natural, scenic, historic, scientific and recreational areas for public enjoyment.[8] A variation on the conservation easement is the use of a *facade easement*, where the landowner agrees *not* to alter the facade or modify the architectural characteristics of a particular building.[9] For new restrictions on façade easements, see Questions & Answers, below.

Example: In 1982, Fred Farmer purchased 23 acres of unimproved farmland located on a river. Fred donates to a qualified organization a conservation easement that restricts in perpetuity any improvement on the property to one single-family residence and some minor outbuildings to be built on a contiguous 3-acre home site. This easement qualifies as a perpetual conservation restriction.[10]

_____

Qualified Organization

To be deductible, a gift of a qualified conservation contribution must be made to a *qualified organization*. Treasury regulations provide that an eligible organization must have a commitment to protect the conservation purposes of the donated property. The needed commitment level will be deemed to be present if the recipient organization operates solely, or primarily, for a conservation purpose. The regulations also require the recipient organization to possess the resources necessary to enforce the restrictions on the contribution in perpetuity.[11] Nonprofit land trusts that have qualified as public charities (under Section 501 (c)) are frequently used as recipient organizations for donations of conservation contributions. For additional details as to the organizations that are qualified, see Chapter 2.

Exclusively for Conservation Purposes

In order to generate a deduction for income tax purposes, a qualified conservation contribution must be made for one or more of the following conservation purposes:

1. the preservation of land areas for outdoor recreation by, or for the education of, the general public;

2. the protection of a relatively natural habitat of fish, wildlife, or plants, or similar ecosystems;

3. the preservation of open space (including farmland and forest land) where such preservation will yield significant public benefit *and* is for the scenic enjoyment of the general public, *or* pursuant to a clearly delineated federal, state, or local governmental conservation policy; and

4. the preservation of an historically important land area or a certified historic structure.[12]

For gift and estate tax purposes, a gift of an easement in real property that otherwise qualifies as a qualified conservation contribution can result in a deduction regardless of the fact that it does not meet the conservation purpose requirement.[13]

Note that the conservation purpose must be protected in perpetuity to be treated as exclusive.[14] The Tax Court has held that in order to be protected in perpetuity, the deed of gift used to transfer the easement (once properly recorded as required under state law), must not be subordinate to a mortgage holder's security interest.[15]

Estate Tax Exclusion Requirements

In general, the requirements listed above that apply to conservation easements also apply to conservation easement exclusions for estate tax purposes. Therefore, except as explained below, the qualified conservation easement must be made to a qualified organization, used exclusively for conservation purposes, and the restriction must be protected in perpetuity.[16]

A qualified conservation easement for purposes of the estate tax exclusion is one that meets the following additional requirements:

1. The land has been continuously owned by the decedent, or a member of the decedent's family, during the three years immediately preceding the decedent's death.[17]

2. A *qualified conservation contribution* (defined above) was granted by the decedent, a member of his family, the executor of the decedent's estate, or the trustee of a trust holding the land, no later than the date of the election, which must be made by the due date for filing the estate tax return.[18]

3. The easement has been granted for a *conservation purpose*. The term "conservation purpose" generally has the same meaning for purposes of the estate tax exclusion as it does for the income tax charitable deduction (see above). Note, however, that the preservation of historically important land area or certified historic property does *not* qualify as a conservation purpose with respect to the estate tax exclusion.[19]

4. The donor may *not* retain a *development right*. A "development right" is generally any right to use the land for a commercial purpose other than farming, or the support of farming. It is important to note that the prohibition on development under the estate tax exclusion is stricter than under the income tax provision.[20]

5. For decedents dying after December 31, 2000, any land in the United States or its possessions otherwise meeting the requirements above may be the subject of a qualified conservation contribution. Prior to EGTRRA 2001, a proximity requirement limited the exclusion to land located (a) in or within 25 miles of a metropolitan area, National Wilderness Preservation system, or (b) in or within 10 miles of an Urban National Forest.[21]

EGTRRA 2001 also clarified that for purposes of calculating the applicable percentage of the value of the land subject to a qualified conservation easement, the value of the land and the value of the easement are determined as of the *date of the contribution of the easement*, instead of the date of the donor's death.

6. The election to take the exclusion must be made on the estate tax return and, once made, is irrevocable.[22]

HOW IS IT DONE?

A conservation easement represents an agreement between a landowner and a qualified charitable organization (or governmental agency). A basic scheme for implementing a conservation easement may run as follows: (1) gathering of information from the prospective donors; (2) preparation of a plan for the client's review; (3) approval of the plan by clients; (4) appraisal of the land to be donated; (5) drafting of the documents outlining the contribution purposes, and defining the retained and donated rights; (6) execution of the documents by the donors and the land trust trustees; (7) transfer of the legal title to the land trust; and (8) maintenance and protection of the land by the land trust trustees.

Before an attorney experienced in drafting conservation easements prepares the necessary documents, certain information must be gathered. Obviously, basic facts must be obtained (e.g., the current financial situation of the donors, the amount of land being considered for the easement, the manner in which the land is titled). However, among the other information and issues (both objective and subjective) that must also be considered, are:

Family control. Conservation easements should be entered into carefully, because once the donation has been made, the restriction on the use of the land must last "in perpetuity." A perpetual conservation restriction affects not only the donor, but also his heirs, because a conservation easement restricts the family's control over the property. It is important to remember that the development rights in the land are being given up. Thus, serious consideration should be given to the family situation, specifically, is there harmony among the donor and his heirs? Conflicts may arise after the restriction is placed on the land if some family members later decide to do something different with the property. For example, some family members may want to divide the property into lots, but cannot do so because of the perpetual restriction. These types of issues should be taken into account *before* the property interest is donated to the land trust.

Conservation purpose. The past use of the land and the various purposes for which the land can be used are important issues to be considered when defining the conservation purpose. Charitable planners should also be aware that there are varying degrees of strictness among the jurisdictions with respect to environmental issues that must also be taken into account in (e.g., grazing and fishing rights in many western states, wetlands in Ohio, etc.).

Retained landowner rights and land trust rights. When contributing the donor's interest in property to a land trust, the rights of the land trust and the rights of the property owners must be clearly defined so that a change in trustees at the land trust does not affect the ongoing oversight of the easement.

Appraisals. Specialized appraisers who are familiar with conservation easement issues should be used to value property because they will be familiar with the important valuation issues that are endemic to conservation easement contributions.

The laws and regulations on conservation easements are quite lengthy and complex. The regulations have been drafted to prevent tax abuse and describe the general intent of the law. Because these rules are complex, careful planning and document drafting are required. Several private letter rulings contain various issues that are scrutinized by the IRS in this area.[23]

WHAT ARE THE TAX IMPLICATIONS?

The "partial interest rule" generally bars deductions for charitable contributions of partial interests in property (see Chapter 5). However, an exception to the "partial interest rule" permits a deduction for a contribution of certain real property interests even though the gift is less than the donor's entire interest in the property. If the gift is for one of the proscribed "conservation purposes" (described below), and certain other requirements are met, a donor may be able to claim an income tax charitable deduction for the value of the qualified conservation contribution. If additional requirements are met, an executor may be able to exclude from the decedent's estate, a certain percentage of the value of the land that is subject to a qualified conservation easement.

Income Tax

In general, the donor can claim a deduction for the fair market value of a qualified conservation contribution at the time of the gift, provided the requirements described above are met.[24] However, certain additional rules must also be satisfied depending on the specific type of property interest being donated, as explained below.

Entire interest of the donor (other than a mineral interest). The value of a contribution of a donor's entire interest in property is the fair market value of the *surface* rights in the contributed property. The value of the contribution must be computed without regard to the *mineral* rights.[25]

Remainder interest in real property. For a contribution of a remainder interest for conservation purposes, the current fair market of the property (which must be reduced as outlined in the regulations), must take into account any pre-existing or contemporaneously recorded rights limiting, for conservation purposes, the use of the donated property.[26]

Perpetual conservation restriction (e.g., an easement). The value of a perpetual conservation restriction is the fair market value of the perpetual conservation restriction at the time of the contribution.[27] There are two methods for valuing perpetual conservation restrictions: (1) the comparable sales method; and (2) the "before-and-after" method.[28]

- If there is a substantial record of sales of easements that are comparable to the one donated, the fair market value of the donated easement is based on the sales prices of the comparable easements. As a practical matter, however, records of comparable sales of easements frequently are not available.

- If no substantial record of market place sales is available to use as a meaningful or valid com-

parison then, as a general rule, the fair market value of an easement is equal to the difference between the fair market value of the property it encumbers *before* and *after* the granting of the restriction. In other words, the value of the total property owned by the donor (including adjacent property that is not encumbered by the easement) *before* granting the easement is determined, and then the value of the property *after* granting the easement is subtracted to determine the value of the easement.[29] Practically speaking, the "before and after" approach is the method most commonly used for valuing conservation easements. For purposes of determining the value of the property before granting of the easement, the Tax Court ruled that the highest and best use of the property had to be taken into account.[30]

Miscellaneous rules. It is important to note that increases in the value of any property owned by the donor (or a related person) that result from the donation, whether or not the other property is contiguous to the donated property, reduce the amount of the donor's income tax charitable deduction. The reduction is equal to the amount of the increase in the value of the other property, as illustrated below:

Example: Edward Jones owns 10 one-acre lots that are currently woods and park land. The fair market value of Edward's lots is $15,000 and the basis of each lot is $3,000. Edward grants to the county a perpetual conservation easement to use and maintain eight of the acres as a public park and to restrict any future development on those eight acres. As a result of the restrictions, the value of the eight acres is reduced to $1,000 an acre. However, by restricting development on this portion of the land in perpetuity, Edward has ensured that the remaining two acres will always be bordered by park land, thus increasing their fair market value to $22,500 each. If the eight acres represented all of Edward's land the fair market value of the easement would be $112,000, an amount equal to the fair market value of the land before granting the easement (8 acres x $15,000 = $120,000) *minus* the fair market value of the encumbered land after the granting of the easement (8 x $1,000 = $8,000). However, because the easement only covered a portion of the taxpayer's contiguous land, the amount of the deduction is reduced to $97,000 ($150,000 - $53,000), that is, the difference between the fair market value of the entire tract of land before ($150,000) and after [(8 x $1,000) + (2 x $22,500)] the granting of the easement.[31]

In general, the value of an easement and, therefore, the amount of the charitable deduction are much smaller than the fair market value of the property itself.

Example: Gene Payton owns 100 acres of land adjacent to a city park. The land is undeveloped and completely natural. Gene has always loved nature and has turned down many offers by developers to purchase his property. By preserving the land as part of the city's park system, Gene can assure that new riding and hiking trails will be built and a larger area will exist for wildlife to thrive. In 2007, Gene agreed to grant a perpetual conservation easement on his land to the city park system so that the land can never be developed or used for anything other than the enjoyment of nature by the community. Gene's land is worth $5 million, and the value of the easement is worth approximately $1 million. Because Gene is in the highest tax bracket in 2007 (35%), his contribution can generate approximately $350,000 in income tax savings.

For tax years other than 2006 and 2007, qualified conservation contributions of capital gain property are generally subject to the same income percentage limitations and carryforward rules as are other charitable contributions of capital gain property (see Chapter 3). However for qualified conservation contributions made in 2006 and 2007, under PPA 2006 increased percentage limitations apply to such contributions and a longer carryover period is available. See Questions & Answers, below.

Property taxes. By donating a conservation easement, the donor decreases the value of his land and, correspondingly, reduces his property taxes.

Estate Tax

Estate Tax Exclusion for Land Subject to Permanent Conservation Easement

For estate tax purposes, an executor may elect to exclude the lesser of (1) the applicable percentage of the value of land subject to the qualified conservation easement, or (2) the maximum exclusion amount ($500,000). The applicable percentage of the value of the land subject to a qualified conservation easement that may be excluded from the decedent's gross estate is equal to 40% of such value, reduced by 2% for each 1% (or fraction thereof) by which the value of the easement is less than 30% of the value of the land.[32]

The exclusion can function like a "saving provision" by reducing the decedent's estate (and thus the estate taxes) by the exclusion amount. The consequences of claiming an estate tax exclusion for land subject to a permanent conservation easement are as follows:

1. The decedent's gross estate is reduced by the value of the qualified conservation easement exclusion.

2. To the extent that the value of the land is excluded from the gross estate, the property is *not* stepped-up to its fair market value on the date of the decedent's death. Instead, the basis of such land acquired from a decedent's estate is the same as in the hands of the decedent before death (i.e., carryover basis).[33]

Example: Martha Parsons inherited a ranch in an area located next to a national park. The ranch had been in her family for over 50 years. In her will, Martha conveyed a qualifying easement worth $250,000, which represented 25% of the value of the property ($1,000,000, without taking into account the easement). Martha donated the easement to the Friends of the Earth, a Section 501(c) publicly supported charitable organization. She retained the right to operate the property for ranching and farming, only, and retained no rights to develop the property. Martha died in 2007.

Because only 25% of the property's value was conveyed, the 40% exclusion percentage must be reduced by 2% for each 1% by which the value of the easement is below 30% of the entire property value. The reduction equals 10% [(30% - 25%) x 2%]. This results in a 30% exclusion (i.e., 40% *minus* the 10% reduction). Martha's estate benefits from an estate tax exclusion in the amount of $225,000 (i.e., 30% x $750,000). Because this calculated amount is less than the maximum exclusion amount ($500,000), Martha's estate will be able to exclude the entire $225,000.

WHERE CAN I FIND OUT MORE ABOUT IT?

1. Englebrecht, T. and Robins, D., "Conservation Easements: Tax and Valuation Attributes of Contributions of Partial Interest in Property," 17 *Journal of Taxation of Investments* 195 (Delta Hedge Publications (formerly RIA Group), Spring 2000).

2. Leimberg, Stephan R., et al., *The Tools & Techniques of Estate Planning*, 14th edition (Cincinnati, OH: The National Underwriter Company, 2006).

3. Small, S., *The Federal Tax Law of Conservation Easements*, Third Supplement (Boston, MA: Landowner Plann g Center, 1995).

QUESTIONS AND ANSWERS

Question – Is there any advantage to making a qualified conservation contribution during the landowner's lifetime over making a testamentary gift?

Answer – According to Russell Shay, Director of Public Policy for The Land Trust Alliance, "the existence of the post-mortem option is not a substitute for good estate planning by a landowner. The power of an executor to make a post-mortem donation of an easement may be limited by state probate law … and a disagreement among heirs could easily frustrate the use of these provisions to preserve family lands from development. In addition, good estate planning by a landowner can yield substantial additional benefits, including income tax deductions under Code section 170(h), which are not allowed in cases where estate tax benefits are taken for easement donations made post-mortem."[34]

Question – What other method can a donor use to convey land to a land trust and receive a tax benefit, other than with a qualified conservation contribution?

Answer – A *bargain sale* is a sale of land by a landowner to a land trust for less than its fair market value. A bargain sale is treated as a part gift, part sale for income tax purposes (see Chapter 10). By making a bargain sale, a donor can not only receive immediate income but also avoid at least some of the capital gain that would otherwise be recognized if the property were sold at fair market value.[35]

Question – What are the positive and negative changes affecting qualified conservation contributions under the Pension Protection Act of 2006 (PPA 2006)?

Answer – On the positive side, PPA 2006 provides more flexibility in charitable planning with respect to (1) income percentage limitations, and (2) carryovers of unused deductions. In tax years 2006 and 2007, the income percentage limit for qualified conservation contributions is increased from 30% of adjusted gross income (AGI) to 50%.[36] Qualifying individual farmers and ranchers may deduct up to 100% of AGI in 2006 and 2007 so long as the qualified real property interest includes a restriction that the property remain generally available for agriculture or livestock production.[37]

In addition, qualified conservation contributions exceeding the 50% limitation may be carried forward for up to 15 years (instead of five years, as under current law).[38]

However, PPA 2006 negatively impacts façade easements by instituting stricter rules. Under the new law, a charitable deduction is still permitted with respect to buildings (as is currently the case), but the "qualified real property interest" (see above) relating to the exterior of the building must now preserve the *entire exterior* of the building—that means the front, sides, and rear of the building, as well as the space above the building. The qualified real property interest must also prohibit any change in the exterior of the building that is inconsistent with the historical character of such exterior. Furthermore, the building or land must either be listed in the National Register, or located in a registered historic district and certified as being or historic significance to the district. In addition, requirements concerning the donee organization's status must also be satisfied, a $500 fee must be paid for claimed deductions in excess of $10,000, and certain documents (e.g., a qualified appraisal) must be attached to the donor's tax return.[39]

PPA 2006 also requires a reduction of the qualified conservation contribution deduction in order to take into account the rehabilitation credit.[40]

CHAPTER ENDNOTE

1. Land Trust Alliance, Frequently Asked Questions, at: http://www.lta.org/faq/.

2. Land Trust Alliance, *National Land Trust Census*, at: http://www.lta.org/census/2005_report.pdf.

3. IRC Secs. 170(h)(5)(B), 170(h)(6).

4. IRC Sec. 170(h)(2)(B).

5. IRC Sec. 170(h)(2).

6. IRC Sec. 170(h)(2)(C); Treas. Reg. §1.170A-14(b)(2). See *Nicoladis v. Comm*, TC Memo 1988-163.

7. IRC Secs. 2055(f), 2522(d); Treas. Reg. §1.170A-14(b)(2). A gift of an easement for estate and gift tax purposes does not need to have a conservation purpose to satisfy the requirements of a deductible partial interest gift.

8. IRC Sec. 170(h)(4), as amended by PPA 2006; Treas. Reg. §1.170A-14(d)(4). See, e.g., Rev. Rul. 75-373, 1975-2 CB 77; Rev. Rul. 74-583, 1974-2 CB 80; Let. Ruls. 200002020, 199952037.

9. IRC Sec. 170(h)(4), as amended by PPA 2006. See, e.g., Let. Rul. 199933029.

10. *Higgins v. Comm.*, TC Memo 1990-103.

11. Treas. Reg. §1.170A-14(c)(1). However, the donee does not have to set aside funds to see that the restrictions remain in force.

12. IRC Sec. 170(h)(4)(A); Treas. Reg. §1.170A-14(d)(1).

13. IRC Secs. 2055(f), 2522(d).

14. IRC Sec. 170(h)(5); Treas. Reg. §1.170A-14(b)(2).

15. *Satullo v. Comm.*, TC Memo 1993-614, *aff'd without opinion*, 67 F.3d 314 (11th Cir. 1995).

16. EGTRRA 2001 repeals the estate tax for one year for decedents dying in 2010.

17. IRC Sec. 2031(c)(8)(A)(ii).

18. IRC Secs. 2031(c)(6), 2031(c)(8)(A)(iii).

19. IRC Secs. 170(h)(4), 2031(c).

20. IRC Sec. 2031(c)(5)(A). For the treatment of *terminated* retained development rights, see IRC Sec. 2031(c)(5)(B).

21. IRC Sec. 2031(c)(8)(A)(i).

22. IRC Sec. 2031(c)(6).

23. See, e.g., Let. Ruls. 200002020, 199952037, 9632003, 9603018, 9420008, 9318017, 921871, 9052058, 8713018, 8641017, 8623037, 8544036, 8518024, 8313123, 8248069.

24. IRC Sec. 170(f)(3)(B)(iii); Treas. Reg. §1.170A-14(h)(3).

25. Treas. Regs. §§1.170A-14(h)(1), 1.170A-14(h)(4), Example 1.

26. Treas. Reg. §1.170A-14(h)(2).

27. Treas. Reg. §1.170A-14(h)(3).

28. Treas. Reg. §1.170A-14(h)(3).

29. Treas. Reg. §1.170A-14(h)(3). See also Rev. Rul. 76-376, 1976-2 CB 53; Rev. Rul. 73-339, 1973-2 CB 892; *Symington v. Comm.*, 87 TC 892 (1986); *Fannon v. Comm.*, TC Memo 1986-572.

30. *Schapiro v. Comm.*, TC Memo 1991-128.

31. Treas. Reg. §1.170A-14(h)(3).

32. IRC Sec. 2031(c).

33. IRC Sec. 1014(a)(4).

34. R. Shay, *New Conservation Options for Heirs to Land*, p. 3 (Land Trust Alliance, September 15, 2001). IRC Sec. 2031(c)(9) provides that the exclusion is *not* available if the easement is granted after the death of the decedent *and* anyone receives an income tax deduction.

35. See *Conservation Options for Landowners* published by the Land Trust Alliance (http://www.lta.org/conserve/options.htm).

36. IRC Sec. 170(b)(1)(E)(i), as added by PPA 2006. For guidance regarding deductions by individuals with respect to the percentage limitation, see Notice 2007-50, 2007-25 IRB 1430.

37. IRC Sec. 170(b)(1)(E)(iv), as added by PPA 2006.

38. IRC Sec. 170(b)(1)(E)(ii), as added by PPA 2006 For guidance regarding deductions by individuals with respect to amounts carried over, see Notice 2007-50, 2007-25 IRB 1430.

39. See IRC Sec. 170(h)(4)(B), as added by PPA 2006; IRC Sec. 170(h)(4)(C), as amended by PPA 2006.

40. See IRC Sec. 170(f)(14), as added by PPA 2006.

DONOR ADVISED FUNDS

CHAPTER 19

WHAT IS IT?

Although the donor advised fund has been around since 1931 as a planning tool, neither the Internal Revenue Code nor the tax regulations contained any definition of it until the Pension Protection Act of 2006 was passed into law on August 17, 2006. Under this new law, a donor advised fund is now defined as a fund or account: (1) that is separately identified by reference to contributions of a donor or donors; (2) that is owned and controlled by a sponsoring organization; and (3) with respect to which a donor (or any person appointed or designated by such donor) has, or reasonably expects to have, advisory privileges with respect to the distribution or investment of amounts held in such fund or account by reason of the donor's status as a donor.[1]

A fund will be considered as "separately identified" when the money donated by a donor is kept separate (either in a unique account or tracked by bookkeeping entries) from the donations made by other donors.[2] The sponsoring charity's general fund would, therefore, not be considered a donor advised fund, nor would a special purpose fund where donations are taken in from several donors. A sponsoring organization is a public charity other than a supporting organization.

The second prong of the new definition concerns whether the sponsoring charity owns and controls the fund. In order to qualify for a charitable income tax deduction, a donor must make a completed gift to a qualified charity. For a gift to be complete, the donor must relinquish both the ownership of and control over the money given. If a donor attempts to retain control over the fund (or delegate control to a chosen third party) in an attempt to avoid the donor advised fund categorization, the donor may lose the ability to deduct the value of the gift.[3]

Finally, the third prong of the new definition addresses the donor's role in advising the separately identified fund in regards to distributions and investment management. This advisory privilege is not a legally enforceable right, the presence of which would cause the fund to be considered a private foundation instead of a donor advised fund.[4]

There are two exceptions to the above rules. If the fund makes distribution to only a single identified charity, it would not be considered a donor advised fund.[5] For example an account funded by a single donor for the sole purpose of endowing a particular chair at a university would not be a donor advised fund, even if the fund is named after the donor, and even if the donor exercises some advisory capacity over the timing of the distributions and investment management. Furthermore, a fund established to make grants for travel and study expenses of certain individuals would not be considered a donor advised if a committee not controlled by the donor advises the fund and all grants are made using a written objective policy approved by the charity's governing board.[6]

There are numerous advantages to using donor advised funds. A wide variety of nonprofit organizations, including community foundations, universities, and foundations set up by mutual fund companies, have established or are considering establishing such programs.

Unfortunately, as the popularity of these plans grew over the years, so did the abuses and potential abuses. Some less scrupulous advisors and charities were taking advantage of perceived ambiguities and weaknesses in the Internal Revenue Code to provide benefits to donors which would be impossible without using such funds as intermediaries. While the new legislation provides some clarity to the rules, and many of the abuses have successfully been curbed, additional legislation and Treasury regulations are likely to be introduced in the near future. Congress has requested that the Treasury (1) prepare a study of the donor advised fund marketplace, and (2) make specific recommendations that would effectively shut down any remaining abusive planning situations.

WHEN IS THE USE OF SUCH A DEVICE INDICATED?

1. When a donor wants to make a substantial donation quickly (by year-end, for example) but needs more time to decide which charities should ultimately benefit from the gift.

2. When a donor would like to maintain more control over multi-year donations to his or her chosen charities. If a chosen charity does not continue to meet the donor's criteria or expectations, the donor can recommend that future annual grants be distributed to other charities.

3. When a donor wishes to fund a program but appoint others (such as children or grandchildren) to choose the charitable grantees.

4. When the donor would like to obtain advantages similar to those of a private foundation without the regulatory hassles, expense, lower deduction limits, and increased compliance rules.

5. When a donor would like to build a significant endowment fund over the next few years, allowing assets to grow tax-free until distributed.

ADVANTAGES

The benefits of setting up a donor advised fund are numerous:

- The donor receives an immediate charitable deduction, even if grants are spread out for years.

- Compared to private foundations, donations made to a donor advised fund receive favorable tax treatment. If cash is donated, the donor's deduction can be applied to as much as 50% of his adjusted gross income. If highly appreciated assets are donated, the deduction is limited to 30% of adjusted gross income.

- The donor gets a choice of name recognition or anonymity. Since the donor is allowed to choose the name of the fund, he can use the family name, thus ensuring a lasting family legacy. Alternatively, the donor(s) can choose a name that does not reveal who is making the gift. When grants are distributed from the fund, the charitable grantee will see only the name of the fund, and not the donor.

- The donor has the ability to recommend a number of charitable grantees. As long as the sponsoring charity approves the distribution and ensures that no private benefit is inuring to the donor, the fund can benefit numerous charitable causes. This comes in particularly handy when a donor wants to give a highly appreciated asset to several charities.

- A donor can change his or her mind about which charities will receive grants from year to year.

- A donor advised fund is generally very simple to understand and easy to use. Once it is funded, the donor can make several grants per year to a variety of charities.

- Compared to many other charitable planning techniques, a donor can establish a donor advised fund relatively quickly. And many sponsoring organizations now offer the donor the ability to set up and manage his or her account online. This can be very useful in year-end tax planning.

- The cost of setting up a donor advised fund is signifcantly less than setting up a private foundation. The donor does not need to hire an attorney to draft documents or provide legal advice.

- The minimum donation requirements are considerably less with a donor advised fund than with a private foundation. Many sponsoring organizations have limits as low as $5,000 with minimum grants of only $100. In comparison, just the legal and administrative fees for setting up a private foundation often run more than $15,000.

DISADVANTAGES

- The gift is irrevocable. Many donors who established donor advised funds have mistakenly thought that the money could be returned to them at a later date.

- There are usually annual fees and charges imposed by the sponsoring charity. Depending on the sponsoring charity, these fees can be substantial.

- Some charities put restrictions on grants made immediately after the fund is established. Others disallow grants that exceed a fixed percentage of the assets in the fund. And still others require that a high minimum amount be paid out.

- The donor's rights to control the management and distribution of the fund assets are limited.

- No grants can be made to individuals for any purpose without triggering a substantial excise tax.

- Further restrictive legislation is likely to be passed in the future, and lack of certainty about future laws makes long-term planning difficult.

WHAT ARE THE REQUIREMENTS?

Over the past few years, donor advised funds have become extremely popular. Often referred to as the "poor man's private foundation," these funds have emerged as one of the fastest growing tools in charitable planning today. Since the benefits can be substantial if the fund is established correctly, it is imperative that donors and advisors choose the sponsoring charity carefully and that all applicable regulations and laws are followed both literally and in keeping with the spirit of the law. Although the Internal Revenue Code and regulations are not yet complete in how they address donor advised funds, donors and advisors should practice common sense and appropriate ethics, keeping the spirit of the existing charitable law in mind when designing these programs. In areas where the new laws are not yet fleshed out by applicable Treasury regulations, the Joint Committee on Taxation's Technical Explanation of the Pension Protection Act may be consulted.[7]

The following is a brief outline of the types of donor funds currently being used, the rules that apply to each type of fund, and a summary of the rules and requirements that must be followed for these funds to qualify for tax-exempt status. Since additional legislation is likely to be passed in the foreseeable future, it is imperative that donors, charities, and advisors remain up to date on relevant changes.

TYPES OF DONOR FUNDS

Component fund: With this type of fund, a community trust, commonly called a "community foundation," establishes separate funds or trusts to receive and manage donors' contributions. If a donor's fund can qualify as a component fund, there are significant advantages. Even though the community foundation does not generally hold title to these component funds or trusts, a completed gift by a donor to such a trust is considered a donation to the community foundation; therefore, it is subject to the 50% deduction limits for cash gifts. (See Chapter 3 for additional details.) Furthermore, each trust does not file a separate tax return since all the component trusts are included on the consolidated return of the community foundation.

To qualify as a component fund, certain tests must be met:

- the community foundation's organizational documents must meet the single entity regulations;[8]

- the component fund must be subject to the governing instrument of the community foundation; and

- the gift to the community foundation must be complete without the donor imposing any material restrictions or retaining any substantive rights.

If the rules applicable to component funds are not followed closely, the donor's account will be characterized as a separate non-profit, and must file for its own tax-exempt status. Alternatively, it will be considered a private foundation and, thus, be subjected to additional strict—and harsh—rules.

Donor directed fund: Often referred to as a "pooled common fund," a donor directed fund is a type of private foundation that is treated as if it is a public charity for tax deduction purposes. A donor directed fund is defined in the Internal Revenue Code as a "private foundation all of the contributions to which are pooled in a common fund."[9]

To achieve the preferential tax treatment of a public charity, the following rules must be met:

- all the contributions must be pooled in a common fund, except that the donor, or donor's

spouse, may designate annual distributions to public charities; and

- the fund must be paid out entirely within a year of (1) the donor's death, or (2) the death of the donor's spouse if he or she has the right to designate charitable recipients.

Donor advised fund: In this popular arrangement, a donor enters into a written agreement with a sponsoring charity to establish an account to benefit the donor's causes. He then transfers cash or other assets to the account, receives an immediate charitable deduction, and over the next days, months, or years, requests that the sponsoring charity make grants to the donor's chosen charities. The donor receives regular statements from the sponsoring charity and, in some cases, may nominate an investment advisor or choose between a small number of investment funds.

The sponsoring charity usually receives a small annual fee for managing the account and may provide services, ranging from performing due diligence on the donor's selected grants to providing a list of worthy grant recipients that match the donor's goals and criteria.

APPLICABLE RULES AND RESTRICTIONS

Contrary to promises made by a few charities, a donor advised fund is not simply a charitable checking account for donors. Several rules and restrictions apply to these funds, as follows.

Deduction rules: A donor will qualify for a charitable tax deduction for income, estate, and gift tax purposes for contributions made to a donor advised fund as long as the charity provides a written receipt and acknowledgment to the donor that explains that the charity assumes all legal control over the monies in the fund. The charity must provide this receipt no later than the due date for the donor's filing of his or her tax returns. The deduction limits for gifts to a donor advised fund are the same as for gifts made directly to a public charity (see Chapter 2).[10]

Charity reporting requirements: A sponsoring charity must report the number of donor advised funds that they have, the total value of the funds, and the total contribution(s) made to and distribution(s) made from the funds. For new charities that plan on offering donor

advised funds, a detailed plan must be disclosed on the organization's tax exempt application.

Permitted distributions: A donor advised fund may make grants and distributions to: (1) the sponsoring organization's general fund; (2) a public charity other than a supporting organization; (3) a private operating foundation; (4) another donor advised fund; (5) a foreign charity; or (6) a non charitable organization. In the last two cases, special care must be taken by the sponsoring charity to ensure that the grants are made to meet a charitable purpose and to ensure than distributions are appropriate.

Taxable distributions: Any grant or distribution to (1) any individual for any purpose, or to (2) an organization that does not have a charitable, education, religious, or other exempt purpose[11] is considered a taxable distribution. The sponsoring charity must exercise the same "expenditure responsibility" found under the private foundation rules[12] prior to approving all distributions. Distributions to (a) Type III supporting organizations that are not "functionally integrated" and to (b) any supporting organization that is directly or indirectly controlled by the donor, his or her advisor, or his or her family members would also be taxable distributions.

Excise tax on taxable distributions: When the sponsoring charity makes a taxable distribution, the charity will be penalized with a new 20% excise tax on the amount of the distribution. In addition to this hefty penalty, any charity manager[13] who knowingly approves a taxable distribution will be subject to a 5% excise tax on the entire distribution, up to a maximum of $10,000 per distribution.[14]

Excise tax on prohibited benefits: If a donor, his or her advisor, a family member, or an entity that is more than 35% controlled by the donor or advisor recommends a distribution where "more than an incidental benefit" inures to the donor or one of these related parties, a 125% excise tax is applied on the amount of the benefit.[15] Any charity manager who approves such a distribution will pay a 10% excise tax on the benefit amount, with a maximum of $10,000 per distribution. An example of a benefit that would not violate this incidental benefit rule would be a logo coffee mug given to the donor as a thank you gift.[16]

Excess benefit transactions: If a donor advised fund makes any grant, loan, compensation, or other payments to a donor, his or her advisor, or someone related to the donor or that advisor, it is automatically characterized as an excess benefit transaction.[17] One hundred percent of the distribution will be considered excess benefit subject to the 125% excise tax and 10% charitable manager excise tax penalties, even if the recipient provides something of value back to the fund in exchange for the distribution. This new rule for donor advised funds is even tougher than the laws that regulate private foundations because private foundations are allowed to pay reasonable compensation to donors, advisors, and their family. Since advisors are included in the list of disqualified persons, compensation paid to an investment advisor who manages the fund's assets would be considered an excess benefit. Such compensation must, therefore, be paid by the sponsoring charity and not the donor advised fund itself.[18]

Excess business holdings: The new law extends the private foundation rules concerning excess business holdings to donor advised funds.[19] Under these rules, a donor advised fund can own no more than 20% of the voting stock of a corporation or similar ownership interests of any business enterprise,[20] reduced further by any voting stock controlled by the donor, his or her advisor, or their families. An exception is made for business entities where more than 95% of the entity's income is passive (e.g., from dividends and capital gains). When a donor contributes a business to a donor advised fund, the fund will have up to five years to liquidate the asset before the penalties are triggered,[21] and for donor advised funds that were funded prior to August 17, 2006, there is a 20-year transitional period for the fund to liquidate the business holdings.[22] Under very limited circumstances, the five-year liquidation period can be extended to 10 years.[23]

Effective date: The rules and restrictions apply to tax years that start after the date of the Pension Protection Act's enactment (i.e., August 17, 2006). In other words, the following rules apply for 2007 and beyond to all new and existing donor advised funds, not just those put in place after 2006.

HOW IS IT DONE? EXAMPLES

Example: Gift of appreciated property. Mr. Zerbe has made significant donations to several of his favorite charities over the years. He has approached his advisors about coordinating the sale of his business with his many annual gifts. The company has a fair market value of approximately $1 million and there are several

competing companies that would be quite eager to purchase Mr. Zerbe's interest.

After talking to his advisors, Mr. Zerbe feels that his planning goals are as follows: (1) to make annual gifts to several charities over the next 10 or 20 years; (2) to maintain flexibility in choosing which charities will benefit from his generosity; (3) to add to the fund later as he liquidates other highly appreciated assets; (4) to involve his niece and nephew in the charitable process; (5) to liquidate the stock and future gifts without paying capital gains taxes; (6) to arrange the gift of the stock quickly in order to complete the gift by the end of the year, selling the stock while the market for his company is hot; and (7) to maximize his current charitable tax deduction.

Mr. Zerbe decides to set up a donor advised fund with a charity established by his brokerage company. He establishes the account, transferred the ownership of the stock to the charity by year-end, and hires an appraiser to perform a qualified appraisal of the company. He calls the account The Zerbe Family Foundation, and names his niece and nephew as co-advisors. Every few months, they all get together and decide which charities should receive grants from the account. Since all of the grantees are public charities, and because none of the advisors on the account are in any way personally benefiting from the grants paid, the charity disburses the funds as requested.

Mr. Zerbe receives a sizable charitable tax deduction that will offset up to 30% of his adjusted gross income this year. He can then carry forward unused deduction amounts for up to five additional years. While he has funded the account with the shares from his closely held business, the immediate liquidation of the shares fell well with the five-year requirement. Whenever he wishes to donate additional highly appreciated assets, he simply calls the charity to arrange for the transfer.

Example: Building an endowment. Mr. and Mrs. Thomas would like to endow a chair at the university they both attended. The amount needed to fund this endowment is $1 million; however, the Thomases have not yet amassed

that amount of discretionary savings. After talking with their advisors, they decide to set up a program with their local community foundation that will provide current income tax benefits and enable them to fund their endowment in a more efficient manner.

In the course of their planning, Mr. and Mrs. Thomas earmark certain assets that can be used for this purpose. These include some appreciated real estate, older mutual funds, and some low yielding government bonds roughly valued at $500,000. Based on realistic growth, income, and tax assumptions, the Thomas's financial planner determines that it will take 10.5 years for this amount to reach the $1 million. If the Thomases liquidate some of the investments and reinvest in a manner that better reflects their time frame and goal, they will have to pay income or capital gains taxes on any appreciation in those assets. The financial advisor calculates that the time frame needed to reach $1 million would be roughly 12 years because of the lower after-tax capital they would have available to invest.

By transferring the earmarked assets to a donor advised fund at their local community foundation, the Thomases can achieve their goal in just 7.2 years. The charity can liquidate the assets, reinvest as needed, and the assets will grow tax-free. In addition to accelerating the timing of their endowment, the Thomases will receive an immediate tax deduction of $500,000, which can offset 30% of their adjusted gross income in the current year with any unused deduction carried forward for up to five additional years.

Example: Testamentary gift. Mr. Floyd has a dilemma. He has three grandchildren and worries that they are spoiled and selfish. Rather than leaving them money when he passes away, he would like to leave them with a sense of civic responsibility. His lawyer recommends that Mr. Floyd use his IRA account to meet that goal.

The lawyer explains that, upon death, Mr. Floyd's $1 million IRA will be subject to income and possibly estate taxes, leaving his heirs with a net inheritance of about $250,000. If Mr. Floyd establishes a donor advised fund with a small donation now and names this fund as the beneficiary of his IRA, the full $1 million will

be available for future charitable grants. Mr. Floyd's grandchildren can be the co-advisors for this testamentary fund, and each year they will be able to research and choose which charities will receive sizable grants.

Mr. Floyd loves the idea. His grandchildren cannot benefit financially from the plan. But they can have both a first-hand experience of philanthropy and the opportunity to grow emotionally. Their influence over the charitable recipients may also be socially advantageous.

WHERE CAN I FIND OUT MORE ABOUT IT?

1. Bjorklund, Victoria. "Provisions of Interest to Charitable Organizations and their Donors in H.R. 4, the Pension Protection Act of 2006," August 24, 2006, at: http://www.stblaw.com/content/Publications/pub569.pdf.

2. Joint Committee on Taxation, *Technical Explanation of H.R. 4, the "Pension Protection Act of 2006,"* as Passed by the House on July 28, 2006, and as Considered by the Senate on August 3, 2006 (JCX-38-06), August 3, 2006, p. 344, at: http://www.house.gov/jct/x-38-06.pdf.

3. Council on Foundations at: www.cof.org.

4. Fidelity Charitable Gift Fund at: www.charitablegift.org.

5. Fox, Richard. "Planning for Donor Control and Other Strings Attached to Charitable Contributions," *Charitable Giving and Solicitation, Bulletin No. 63* (Warren, Gorham & Lamont, March 18, 2003).

6. IRS Notice 2007-21, Study on Donor Advised Funds and Supporting Organizations, at: http://www.irs.gov/pub/irs-drop/n-07-21.pdf.

QUESTIONS AND ANSWERS

Question – What's the difference between a donor advised fund and a private foundation?

Answer – On the surface, the donor advised fund and a private foundation appear to be quite similar. A donor gives cash or appreciated assets to a charitable account that periodically distributes funds to chosen charitable causes. But in reality, the two planning tools face very different rules, restrictions, deduction limits, taxes, and costs. The chart in Figure 19.1 compares and contrasts the key features of both.

Question – When would a donor want to use a community foundation and when would a mutual fund established by a charity be more appropriate?

Answer – Community foundations (see Chapter 17) have been offering donor advised funds for many years and have developed an excellent system for educating donors and helping them implement their charitable objectives. For a donor who would like assistance or recommendations in research-

ing charitable donees, or who would like a fairly high percentage of the account assets to go to local charities, a community foundation is highly recommended. In comparison, mutual fund and brokerage house gift funds are relatively new and have literally exploded in popularity among donors and advisors. Such gift funds are recommended for donors who already know to which charities they would like to issue grants and whose interests are more national than local. In addition to these two groups, there are specialized national foundations, such as religious foundations or universities, which have started donor advised fund programs for their members.

Question – What factors should be considered in choosing between mutual fund company donor advised funds?

Figure 19.1

	PRIVATE FOUNDATION	DONOR ADVISED FUND
Structure	Either corporate or trust structure established as a private foundation	A written agreement between the donor and the sponsoring charity
Cost to Establish	Significant legal and accounting fees	Between $0 and $250, depending on the charity
Cost to Run	Annual legal, accounting, administration and operation expenses	Usually a flat fee ranging from .25% to 2% of asset value
Minimum Donation to Fund	Minimum recommended is $1 - $2 million	Usually $10,000 but depends on charity's policy
Donor's Deduction Limits (as a percentage of adjusted gross income in one year)	Gifts of Cash: 30% Appreciated Assets: 20%	Gifts of Cash: 50% Appreciated Assets: 30%
Tax-exempt Status	Must file its own application for tax-exempt status	Falls under the tax-exempt umbrella of the public charity offering the fund
Minimum annual grants required	Must pay out at least 5% of asset value	Depends on the charity's policy. Is as low as 0%.
Annual Taxes	2% of net gain, including capital gains	None
Annual Tax Filings	Tax and information returns with required schedules and attachments	Included in the charity's filings

Answer – There are several mutual funds and brokerage houses that have established separate charitable entities offering donor advised funds. Although they have only been around for a few years, three of these have already grown to be among the largest charities in the nation.[24]

When helping a donor decide between these funds, an advisor should keep two main factors in mind: service and cost. Some of the funds specialize in assisting donors with transferring unusual or difficult assets (e.g., restricted stock, privately held company stock, or real estate). Other funds offer only basic assistance. Furthermore, the annual fees between funds range from .65% to 2.95%. The higher the fees, the less the donor has available to designate to his or her chosen charities. So advisors should be performing due diligence on such programs just as they would mutual funds or investment managers.

Question – Can an investment advisor be paid a finder's fee or commission for helping a client set up a donor advised fund?

Answer – Under current law, a charity is prohibited from providing a private benefit to any individual. Furthermore, the ethics rules of all the major gift planning associations prohibit the payment of finder's fees and commissions. Unless the advisor performs work on an ongoing basis to the charity, the charity may not compensate the advisor without running afoul of the private benefit rules. Simply introducing the donor to the charity cannot justify the payment of a fee or commission. Many advisors argue that they are providing continued service to the donor (e.g., helping the donor choose grantees, or assisting with other estate planning needs), but that also violates the private benefit rule since the charity is paying the fee but the donor is receiving the benefit. And finally, the new donor advised fund laws that were passed in 2006 prohibit any payment from the fund itself to an advisor, family of the advisor or entity controlled by the advisor.

Question – Can a donor advised fund be used as a qualified plan alternative? How does this work?

Answer – There are a small number of national charities that were promoting this plan and national news stories of its abusive nature are what triggered the recent restrictive legislation. To summarize briefly, a donor would set up a donor advised fund with one of these charities and allow the money to grow tax

free for a number of years. Later, when the donor was ready to retire, the fund would compensate the donor for volunteering his or her time to charitable causes. Considering that a donor cannot take a current deduction for volunteering, it was unrealistic to assume that the donor could take a current deduction for assets which were accumulated to compensate the donor for volunteering at a later date. Such "charitable compensation" was found to be abusive and the new law prohibits any grants or distributions made to any individual, with very heavy penalties and fines if monies are ever paid out to the donor.

Question – Can the donor name his or her own investment advisor to manage the donor advised fund investments?

Answer – The donor can recommend an advisor to the sponsoring charity, but cannot pay the advisor out of the assets in the donor advised fund. The decision as to whether or not to use the advisor's services must be up to the charity and any compensation to the advisor must be made by the sponsoring charity. Since the charity has a fiduciary duty to invest the fund's assets prudently and retain and maintain control of investment decisions, the charity must choose the investment managers carefully. If the donor's advisor does not meet the charity's requirements at all times, the charity can and should terminate the investment advisor's contract. And finally, the investment advisor should prepare a statement to the charity which shows that his or her fees are at or below the market rates for such advisory work.

Question – A donor who has established a sizable donor advised fund at a community foundation and wishes to make distributions to a wide variety of causes. Is this acceptable under the new rules?

Answer – In general, yes, subject to the approval and review of the charitable managers of the donor advised fund. In this case, the community foundation reviewed the donor's list and approved the following grant distributions: (1) the American Cancer Society (a large 501(c)(3) charity); (2) the donor's local SPCA, a very small but efficiently run non profit; and (3) the community foundation's general fund to provide much needed funds for local issues of the sponsoring organization's choosing.

Question – A major charity offers a variety of gifts and benefits for long-term donors. Is it acceptable under the new rules for a donor who sets up a donor advised fund to receive such gifts?

Answer – In general, no. The new laws strictly limit any benefit received by a donor to something of minimal value (e.g., a coffee mug with the charity's logo). All charities that offer donor advised funds should immediately establish a policy or plan that established a separate membership category for donor advised fund donors to avoid this potential inadvertent trap.

Question – A donor's son uses his credit card to pay for the internet fees to set up a website for the family's donor advised fund. Can he be reimbursed by the donor advised fund for this expense?

Answer – No. Any payment to the donor, his family, or his advisors for any purpose—even if it is to reimburse that person for a charity related expense—would be considered a taxable distribution subject to a 20% excise tax. Furthermore the manager at the sponsoring charity who allowed such a reimbursement would be subject to an additional 5% excise penalty.

CHAPTER ENDNOTES

1. IRC Secs. 4966(d)(1), 4966(d)(2); Joint Committee on Taxation, *Technical Explanation of H.R. 4, the "Pension Protection Act of 2006,"* as Passed by the House on July 28, 2006, and as Considered by the Senate on August 3, 2006 (JCX-38-06), August 3, 2006, p. 344, at: http://www.house.gov/jct/x-38-06.pdf.

2. Id. at pp. 342-343.

3. Id. at p. 343.

4. Id.

5. IRC Sec.4966(d)(2)(B)(i).

6. IRC Sec.4945(g).

7. Joint Committee on Taxation, *Technical Explanation of H.R. 4, the "Pension Protection Act of 2006,"* as Passed by the House on July 28, 2006, and as Considered by the Senate on August 3, 2006 (JCX-38-06), August 3, 2006, p. 344, at: http://www.house.gov/jct/x-38-06.pdf.

8. Treas. Reg. §1.170A-9(e)(11).

9. IRC Sec. 170(b)(1)(E)(iii).

10. IRC Secs. 170(f)(18), 2055(e)(5), 2522(c)(5).

11. IRC Sec 170(c)(2)(B).

12. IRC Secs. 4945(h), 4945(g).

13. IRC Sec. 4966(d)(3).

14. IRC Secs. 4966(a), 4966(d)(3).

15. IRC Sec. 4948(f).

16. Rev. Proc. 90-12, 1990-1 C.B. 471.

17. IRC Sec. 4958(c)(2).

18. IRC Sec. 4967.

19. IRC Sec. 4943(e)(1).

20. IRC Sec. 4943(d)(3).

21. IRC Sec. 4943(c)(6).

22. IRC Sec. 4942(e)(3).

23. IRC Sec. 4943(d)(7).

24. See *The Chronicle of Philanthropy's* Annual Philanthropy 400 Survey at: http://philanthropy.com/free/articles/v19/i02/02000601.htm.

POOLED INCOME FUNDS

CHAPTER 20

WHAT IS IT?

A pooled income fund is a type of trust created and managed by a charity, into which a donor transfers property. This charitable contribution provides an irrevocable remainder interest in the property to or for the use of a particular charity. At the same time an income interest is provided to the income beneficiary, typically the donor and/or the donor's spouse.

In exchange for the donation, the income beneficiary receives a lifetime income paid from the earnings of the pooled income fund.[1] The donor does not necessarily have to be the income beneficiary, but this arrangement is the most common. The donor can name his spouse as the income beneficiary or as a joint income beneficiary with the donor. Or, the donor could name other family members or non-family members as the income beneficiaries. (Naming anyone other than the donor and/or the donor's spouse as the income beneficiary can result in gift tax consequences. For additional details, see "Tax Implications" later in this chapter.)

The assets within the pooled income fund are managed by the particular charity that established the fund. The donated property must be commingled with the other assets in the pooled income fund.

The donor is given a certain number of pooled income fund "units of participation" in exchange for the gift of property. The income earned by these commingled assets is then distributed proportionately according to the number of units of participation held among all the beneficiaries of the fund. In this sense, it is similar to a mutual fund.

Upon the death of the income beneficiary, or if more than one income beneficiary is named, then upon the death of the last surviving income beneficiary, the value of the remainder interest in the property is re-moved from the pooled income fund and transferred to the charity.[2]

WHEN IS THE USE OF SUCH A DEVICE INDICATED?

1. When the potential donor is looking for lifelong income for the donor and/or the donor's spouse. In the alternative, the donor could be looking to provide income to another family member or third party.

2. When the potential donor has assets with sizable built-in capital gains and may be reluctant to sell the property due to the capital gains taxation.

3. When the potential donor has a need to reduce his or her overall taxable estate for federal estate tax purposes (see "Tax Implications," below).

4. When the donor is looking for an immediate income tax deduction.

5. When the donor has charitable intent toward a specific charity.

6. When the donor does not wish to incur the costs and legal fees of establishing a charitable remainder trust or private foundation.

7. When the donor does not have a large enough asset to warrant the expense associated with a charitable remainder trust or private foundation.

8. When the donor wishes to receive variable income rather than a level income generated by a charitable gift annuity (see Figure 20.1 for a comparison of pooled income funds with charitable gift annuities).

9. When the donor does not have the investment experience to manage a charitable remainder trust, making the professional investment management of the pooled income fund more attractive.

ADVANTAGES

1. The donor or the donor's named income beneficiary receives income for life.

2. The donor receives a charitable income tax deduction.

3. Capital gains taxes on highly appreciated assets can be avoided.

4. Estate taxes can be saved on the present value of the charity's remainder interest.

5. No gift administration is necessary by the donor.

6. No trust must be created or maintained by the donor.

7. The donor can use wealth replacement with income from the pooled income fund to make the heirs "whole" in their inheritance.

DISADVANTAGES

1. A gift to a pooled income fund is irrevocable.

2. The amount of the income earned is variable and is out of the donor's control.

3. The donor's favorite charity might not offer a pooled income fund.

4. The charity may not receive the gift or the use of its income until sometime in the distant future.

5. If the donor does not use a "wealth replacement" technique, the donor's heirs may lose their perceived inheritance of the asset.

WHAT ARE THE REQUIREMENTS?

Treasury regulations set forth the following eight requirements[3] that a fund must meet to be qualified as a pooled income fund:

1. *Contribution of remainder interest to charity.* Each donor must transfer property to the fund and contribute an irrevocable remainder interest in such property to or for the use of a public charity, retaining for himself, or creating for another beneficiary or beneficiaries, a life income interest in the transferred property.

2. *Creation of life income interest.* Each donor must retain for himself for life an income interest in the property transferred to such fund, or create an income interest in such property for the life of one or more beneficiaries, each of whom must be living at the time of the transfer of the property to the fund by the donor.

3. *Commingling of property.* The property transferred to the fund by each donor must be commingled with, and invested or reinvested with, other property transferred to the fund by other donors.

4. *Prohibition against tax-exempt securities.* The property transferred to the fund by any donor must not include any tax-exempt securities and the fund must not invest in such securities. The governing instrument of the fund must contain specific prohibitions against accepting or investing in tax-exempt securities.

5. *Maintenance by charitable organization required.* The fund must be maintained by the same public charity to or for the use of which the irrevocable remainder interest is contributed.

6. *Prohibition against donor or beneficiary serving as trustee.* Neither the donor nor an income beneficiary may serve as a trustee of the pooled income fund. Furthermore, the governing instrument must prohibit the fund from having a donor or income beneficiary as a trustee. An exception to this rule exists where the public charity to (or for the use of) whom the remainder interest is contributed is the income beneficiary.

7. *Income of beneficiary to be based on rate of return of fund.* Each beneficiary entitled to income for any taxable year of the fund must receive the income in an amount determined by the rate of return earned by the fund for the taxable year with respect to his income interest. (Regulations specify the method for calculating each beneficiary's income interest.[4])

8. *Termination of life income interest.* Upon the termination of the income interest, the trustee must sever from the fund an amount equal to the value of the remainder interest in the property upon which the income interest is based.

HOW IS IT DONE?

Irrevocable Gift

When the donor transfers assets into a pooled income fund, it is an irrevocable gift. Therefore, the property cannot be accessed by the donor or reacquired by the donor in the future.

Property Suitable to Donate

The most beneficial property to donate into a pooled income fund is property with significant built-in, long-term capital gain. This would include property such as highly appreciated stock or other securities.

Cash is always an appropriate asset to donate. However, with cash, the donor does not have the ability to avoid taxation on long-term capital gain. So, between highly appreciated securities and cash, a donation of highly appreciated stock has better tax leveraging advantages for the donor.

Types of property that are not appropriate to give to a pooled income fund include any property with a mortgage or encumbrance on the property, real estate, tax-exempt securities, certain government bonds, deferred annuities, qualified plan accounts and IRAs, closely held stock, restricted stock, and life insurance policies.

What Can the Pooled Income Fund Do With the Assets?

The pooled income fund is not bound to keep the asset in the form it was donated. In other words, the fund is free to sell the specific donated asset and reinvest the proceeds. Generally, depending on the type of pooled fund and its investment objectives, the fund will invest the proceeds in bonds and dividend paying stocks. The trustee is not allowed, however, to invest in tax-exempt securities. The trustees of the pooled income fund are bound by prudent investor standards as they buy and sell assets within the fund.

The assets within the pooled income fund must be commingled with all other donated gifts. However, these assets within the pooled income fund are held in trust. They are separate and distinct from the assets of the charity itself. The pooled income fund assets cannot be commingled with other charitable remainder trusts or endowment funds of the charity. The pooled income fund assets cannot be used by the charity until the final income beneficiary named by the donor dies. At that time, an amount equal to the value of the remainder interest in the property is removed from the fund and transferred to the charity.

Units of Participation

The donor is given units of participation in the fund in exchange for the donated asset.[5] The number of units of participation awarded to the donor is determined by dividing the value of the property donated by the current value of one unit of participation.

Example: A donor donates appreciated securities with a value of $100,000 to a pooled income fund. Before the gift, the pooled income had a total value of $1,000,000, and 10,000 units of participation. By dividing the total fund value ($1,000,000) by the number of units of participation (10,000 units), the value of one unit of participation can be determined ($100).

In exchange for the $100,000 gift, the donor receives 1,000 units of participation in the fund valued at $100 per unit ($100,000 / $100 = 1,000 units). The respective value of each unit of participation may change with additional contributions to the fund and with changes to the fair market value of the fund's assets. The pooled fund's value has now risen from $1,000,000 in value to $1,100,000.

At the end of the year, the total income earned by the fund is divided by the total number of units of participation. Then, for each beneficiary, the amount of income earned by each unit of participation is multiplied by the number of his units to determine the total amount of income per beneficiary. Adjustments are made for income beneficiaries who hold units for less than a full tax year.[6]

Example: Jerry Novak, age 60, contacts his State University. Jerry would like to make a donation of $200,000 of highly appreciated stock to the university. Jerry originally purchased these stocks in the early 1980's for $30,000. Jerry does not want to incur capital gains tax on $170,000 of income ($200,000 fair market value minus $30,000 cost basis).

One of Jerry's objectives is also to divest his portfolio of the stock because it produces a low dividend income of approximately 1% each year. He would like to receive a higher amount of income from this investment. State University has four different pooled income funds from which to choose.

Jerry signs a contractual agreement with the university agreeing to transfer $200,000 of stock to one of the pooled income funds in exchange for quarterly income payable to Jerry for his lifetime. Then he transfers the stock ownership to the State University pooled income fund. The newly donated assets are pooled together with other assets in the fund.

Following the transfer, Jerry is assigned a specific number of units of participation in the fund. The number of units assigned is the portion his gift of $200,000 bears to the total value of the pooled fund.

Jerry's income tax deduction is based on the pool's prior highest rate of return of 4.8% over the last three years. In this case, the amount of the income tax deduction equals $83,792, based on the present value of the university's remainder interest. This amount is deductible by Jerry up to 30% of his adjusted gross income (AGI; see Chapter 3). He also files a gift tax return.

Summary of Benefits to the Donor

Based on the example above, the donor receives the following benefits:

- income for life;

- an income tax deduction of $83,792 which is deductible up to 30% of his adjusted gross income (AGI);

- avoidance of long-term capital gains tax on $170,000 gain on the asset ($170,000 x 15% capital gains tax rate = $25,500 in capital gains tax savings);

- removal of $200,000 from his estate for estate tax purposes (see "Tax Implications" below); and

- the ability to make a substantial, yet deferred gift to his favorite charity.

Note that as the donor's age increases (all else being equal), the amount of the income tax deduction also increases. For example, in the above scenario using the same $200,000 gift, a 70-year-old donor would be entitled to a deduction of $110,990 versus the 60-year-old's deduction of $83,792. The increase in the deduction with age is due to the increased actuarial probability that the charity will receive the money more quickly. The income beneficiary receives income based on the pool's income, and the funds are taxed to him as ordinary income.

Upon the donor's death, the value of his units of participation is includable in his federal taxable estate. However, an offsetting charitable deduction equal to the value of his units of participation is allowed and, thus, the donor has effectively removed the entire contribution amount from his estate. In the example above, if Jerry's federal estate were in a 45% marginal estate tax bracket, Jerry's estate would have saved $90,000 in federal estate taxes by using the pooled income fund technique. Following Jerry's death, the pooled income fund will remove $200,000 from the fund and transfer this amount to the University for its use. (See "Tax Implications," below, regarding the reduction and eventual repeal of the estate tax under EGTRRA 2001.)

Wealth Replacement Technique

When a donor has a family or other beneficiaries who would otherwise be entitled to the assets a donor contemplates giving to charity, wealth replacement may be a necessary component of the overall charitable plan. Wealth replacement is the process of providing the heirs with an equal inheritance from other assets not donated to charity, without reducing the heirs' overall inheritance. Life insurance is often used as the funding tool for wealth replacement.

Normally this technique involves the donor using part or all of the income generated by the pooled income fund, together with income tax savings, to make a gift to his children or to a trust on their behalf. The responsible adult child (or children), or a trust on their behalf, purchases a life insurance policy on the donor's life (or possibly on the lives of the donor and his or her spouse under a survivorship contract to reduce the outlay or increase the death benefit). The face amount of the policy normally equals the fair market value of the donated asset. This policy is purchased either directly by the donor's intended beneficiaries or inside an irrevocable life insurance trust using annual exclusion gifts into the trust to fund the premium payments. Upon the donor/insured's death, the death proceeds are distributed directly to the beneficiaries of the policy owner or to the trust (and then from the trust to the heirs), free of estate taxes and free of income taxes.

This technique benefits the heirs in that their inheritance is now free of both income and estate taxes and the proceeds are equal to the value of the donated asset. Had the donor instead bequeathed the asset directly to the beneficiary and not the pooled income fund at death, the heirs would have inherited the asset with a stepped-up cost basis and avoided capital gains, but the asset would have been exposed to estate taxes, thus eroding the value of the beneficiary's inheritance. (Under EGTRRA 2001, the results would be different for a death occurring in 2010; see below.)

WHAT ARE THE TAX IMPLICATIONS?

Income Tax

The donor of cash or property who gives an asset to a pooled income fund is eligible for an income tax charitable deduction. The amount of the deduction is an amount equal to the present value of the charity's remainder interest.[7] The factors that determine the amount of the income tax deduction include: the ages of the income beneficiaries; the fair market value of the donated asset; and the highest rate of return of the pooled income fund over the last three taxable years.[8]

The income beneficiary is taxed on the income received from the pooled income fund. The taxation of the income is determined under the rules for complex trusts. The pooled income fund does not have the 4-tiered income taxation attributes that a charitable remainder trust has (see Chapters 15 and 16) or the exclusion ratio attributes of a charitable gift annuity (see Chapter 12). Instead, the distributions to the income beneficiary will be taxed each year as ordinary income. The income interest will end with the last payment paid before the death of the beneficiary or paid on a pro rata basis up to the date of death.

Determining rate of return. For purposes of calculating the amount of the charitable deduction, the present value of the income interest is determined on the basis of the highest rate of return earned by the fund for any of the three taxable years immediately preceding the taxable year in which the transfer is made.[9] Even if the first year is not a full taxable year of the fund, the rate from that short year may still be used in the calculation. Accordingly, the charity should provide the last three year's rates of return on the pooled income fund in order to assist the taxpayer in determining the amount of the income tax deduction.

In the case of funds in existence less than three taxable years preceding the taxable year of the fund in which a transfer is made, the rate of return is determined by: (1) averaging the monthly Section 7520 rates for each of the previous three years; (2) taking the highest of the three rates determined in (1); and (3) subtracting 1% from this number.[10] The rate of return to use for 2007 is 4.8%.

The income tax deduction is available to the donor in the year the property is transferred to the pooled income fund, and may be carried over for up to five years thereafter (see Chapter 2). Generally, cash gifts and gifts of ordinary income property are deductible up to 50% of AGI; long-term capital gain property gifts are deductible up to 30% of AGI.[11]

Nonrecognition of gain. When a donor transfers appreciated property into a pooled income fund, the transfer of that property will not trigger taxation of long-term capital gain to the donor.[12] This nonrecognition of capital gain is one of the many benefits of donating appreciated assets to charity. For example, assume a donor transfers 1,000 shares of stock held for more than one year, with a fair market value of $500 per share. Assume also that the donor's cost basis is $30 per share. The donor will not incur a capital gain tax upon donation of the shares; therefore, $470,000 (($500 - $30 = $470) x 1,000 shares = $470,000) of capital gain income avoids taxation.

Furthermore, the pooled income fund will not realize or recognize capital gain income upon sale of the donated asset and reinvestment of the proceeds in another asset. Therefore, the gift of an appreciated long-term capital gain asset to a pooled income fund will, in effect, bypass taxation of long-term capital gain on the gift.

Gift Tax

Donors who transfer property or cash to a pooled income fund are not subject to a gift tax on the present value of the income interest as long as the donor is the sole income beneficiary. The rationale is that the donor cannot make a gift of the income interest the donor has retained for himself.

But what if the donor had named his spouse as income beneficiary? If the income beneficiary is the donor's spouse, the spouse's income interest will be a taxable (present interest) gift because in this instance the gift tax marital deduction is not available. To the extent it exceeds the donor's available annual exclusion, it will generate tax. Under EGTRRA 2001, the gift tax rates are scheduled for incremental reduction through 2009, and further reduction in 2010.[13]

However, the gift of the income interest to a donor's spouse can be kept incomplete—and, therefore, not taxable—by including in the donor's will a right to revoke the surviving spouse's interest. That provision makes the gift to the surviving spouse revocable and, thus, makes the gift incomplete and therefore nontaxable. If the donor does not include the power to revoke the spouse's interest in the will, there is another technique that may avoid gift tax: the donor may be able to qualify the gift under the qualified terminable interest property (QTIP) rules.[14]

When the donor names someone other than the donor or the spouse as the income recipient, then the donor has effectively made a present interest gift to the income beneficiary. Of course, to the extent the present value of the income beneficiary's interest is less than the annual exclusion amount (as indexed, $12,000 in 2007), the gift will not be taxable. Another alternative is for the donor to retain the right in his or her will to revoke the gift. As noted above, such a clause would make the gift to the third party income beneficiary incomplete and prevent any gift tax until the gift is completed.

Regardless of whom the donor names as the income beneficiary, the donor must file a gift tax return for the calendar year in which the gift to the pooled income fund was made.[15]

Estate Tax

Under EGTRRA 2001, estate tax rates are scheduled for incremental reduction through 2009, and for repeal in 2010.[16] In addition, the exemption equivalent of the estate tax unified credit is scheduled to increase through 2009.[17] For most purposes, the repeal of the estate tax for only one year means that planning should be done as though there were no repeal.

If the donor names himself as the income beneficiary, upon the donor's death, the value of the units of participation in the pooled income fund are includable in his estate for federal estate tax purposes.[18] However, the estate will receive an estate tax charitable deduction in an equal amount. Hence, this technique is, in essence, a way of removing the donated asset from the donor's taxable estate.

If the donor names his or her surviving spouse as an income beneficiary along with the donor, the property may qualify for the QTIP election and, thus, not be exposed to estate taxes. Upon the surviving spouse's death, the property may be subject to an estate tax charitable deduction. Consequently, in both estates the property could escape estate taxation.

If the donor names a third party as an income beneficiary and retains the power to revoke the gift in his will, then the donor's estate is entitled to a charitable deduction equal to the present value of the charity's interest as of the date of the donor's death. However, the income beneficiary's interest is includable in the donor's estate.[19] Hence the asset is only partially removed from the donor's estate when the donor names someone other than the donor or the donor's spouse as the income beneficiary.

Since the value of a non-spouse income beneficiary's interest is subject to estate tax, but the asset itself has been irrevocably donated to a pooled income fund, the estate will not have the asset to liquidate to pay the estate taxes. Therefore, careful planning by the estate planner is necessary to insure that adequate liquidity exists within the estate to pay any associated estate taxes under these circumstances.

Taxation of the Pooled Income Fund

The pooled income fund is not a tax-exempt fund. Instead, the pooled fund is taxed as a complex trust. Since the object of the pooled fund is to distribute its income each year to the income beneficiaries, the fund itself will not normally have taxable income at the fund level. Additionally, short-term capital gains, if allocated to income, will also avoid taxation at the fund level.

WHERE CAN I FIND OUT MORE ABOUT IT?

1. Toce, Joseph, Abbin, Byrle, Vorsatz, Mark, and Page, William, *Tax Economics of Charitable Giving 2006-2007* (Warren Gorham & Lamont, 2006).

2. Osteen, Carolyn, Donaldson, David, *The Harvard Manual on Tax Aspects of Charitable Giving*, 8th edition (Boston, MA: 1999).

3. Aston, Debra, *The Complete Guide to Planned Giving*, 3rd Edition (Ashton Associates) Quincy, MA: 2004).

4. Miree, Kathryn, *Professional Advisors Guide to Planned Giving*, 2006 edition (Aspen Publishers, Inc: 2005).

QUESTIONS AND ANSWERS

Question – Can a donor donate tax-exempt securities to a pooled income fund?

Answer – No. Treasury regulations prohibit pooled income funds from accepting gifts of tax-exempt securities. Therefore, a donor will not be able to contribute these types of securities to a pooled income fund, nor will the fund be able to accept them.

Question – Can a gift to a pooled income fund be made at death under the provisions of the donor's will or a trust?

Answer – Yes. The donor may direct in his will or a trust instrument that a gift of a fixed dollar amount or a specific asset be donated to a pooled income fund. The donor should also designate who the income beneficiaries will be.

As explained above, the donor's estate will be entitled to a federal estate tax charitable deduction in an amount equal to the present value of the pooled income fund's remainder interest.

The income interest will be includable in the donor's estate. If the income interest is given to the donor's spouse, the interest can qualify for the QTIP election.

Question – Can the charity itself be an income beneficiary in addition to being the pooled income fund's remainder beneficiary?

Answer – The charity can be a co-income beneficiary. However, the donor is not allowed an income tax deduction for the value of the income interest going to the charity.[20] Therefore, it is more practical for the donor to retain the income interest himself and then, upon receipt of the income, make an outright gift of that amount directly to the charity each year. This will enable the donor to receive a recurring income tax charitable deduction for the amount of the income, although the donor would have to pay income taxes on the income first.

A second alternative is for the donor to divide the initial gift into two amounts: one for a direct current gift to the public charity qualifying for an immediate income tax deduction, and a second gift directly to the pooled income fund.

Question – Do most pooled income funds generally have a minimum amount required in order to become a donor?

Answer – Yes, generally the minimum gift amount for a pooled income fund is $10,000. A few pooled income funds accept gifts of as little as $2,500.

Question – Can any person of any age make a gift to a pooled income fund?

Answer – The Internal Revenue Code does not prohibit a person from contributing to a pooled income fund based on age; however, the individual charities themselves may have minimum age restrictions (e.g., 50 or 55) to be an income beneficiary of their pooled income fund. For example, Harvard University has three pooled income funds with restrictions on beneficiary ages from age 25, 40 and 50 years old.

Question – Can the donor designate how the funds are used?

Answer – Some pooled income funds allow the donor to designate the particular use of the funds. For example with educational pooled income funds, the donor can generally designate which college department within the university is to receive the remainder.

Question – Can the donor name multiple income beneficiaries?

Answer – Typically yes. But again, the individual pooled fund may restrict the number of income beneficiaries to two or less. Additionally, the amount of the donor's income tax deduction will be determined in part by the relevant ages of the income beneficiaries.

Example: A donor who names two income beneficiaries (age 60 and age 40) donates a $100,000 gift using a 4.8% highest return payout. The donor is eligible for a charitable income tax deduction of $18,087. If the donor only chooses one income beneficiary (age 60), the income tax deduction rises to $41,896. In contrast, had the donor only chosen the single income beneficiary to be the 40 year-old, the income tax deduction would be $20,620.

Question – Can the pooled income fund charge a fee or other administrative costs against the pooled income fund's earnings?

Answer – Yes. For example, one pooled income fund charges 120 basis points as a management fee. The fee is based on the pool's net fair market value and is charged against both income and principal.

Question – How are the pooled income funds invested? What if the client wants growth over income?

Answer – The donor must check with the specific fund for the types of investments within each fund and the objectives of the fund. For example, one charity offers several funds from which donors may choose (e.g., a balanced fund, a growth fund, an international bond fund, an international equity fund, etc).

Question – Will most funds accept additional gifts at a future date?

Answer – Yes. Nearly all pooled income funds will accept additional contributions at a future date. Normally, a minimum amount limit will apply to the additional

contribution. However, the minimum amount for additional contributions is almost always much less than the requirement for the initial contribution to the pooled income fund.

Question – Can the donor receive a contribution back if the donor experiences a financial hardship?

Answer – No. The donation of cash or property to a pooled income fund is an irrevocable gift and cannot be returned to the donor at any time. Prior to making such a charitable gift, the donor should be in a solid financial situation, such that removal of these assets from his or her balance sheet is not reasonably likely to lead to a financial hardship at any time in the foreseeable future. Accordingly, these gifts should be made only after serious thought and consideration has been given to the donor's financial circumstances and standard of living.

Question – Can a donor choose a class of beneficiaries, such as all his or her grandchildren living and those yet unborn?

Answer – No. The named income beneficiaries must be alive and identifiable at the time of the gift into the pooled income fund. However, a gift to members of a class may be named if all are identifiable at the time of the gift.[21]

Question – Can the donor ever revoke the income payable to the income beneficiary?

Answer – Yes, the donor may retain the power to revoke the interest of an income beneficiary, but this power is exercisable only via the donor's will. Keeping this power in the donor's will prevents the gift from being a completed gift for gift tax purposes. Gifts of this nature are not subject to current gift tax.[22]

Question – Can the donor change the charity at any time?

Answer – No. The instant the gift is made, it is irrevocable. The donor cannot revoke the charity's interest under any circumstances. However, the pooled income fund itself may have a provision that in the event the particular charity is no longer a viable public charity, the assets will alternatively go to another public charity.

Question – Can the donor name himself as the sole income beneficiary for his life and then upon his

Figure 20.1

	COMPARISON OF A CHARITABLE GIFT ANNUITY TO A POOLED INCOME FUND	
	Charitable Gift Annuity	**Pooled Income Fund**
Description	Donor gives an asset to a charity and donor (or donor's chosen beneficiary) receives an income stream for life	Donor gives asset into a pooled income fund and donor (or donor's chosen beneficiary) receives an income stream for life, then assets pass to charity
Income tax deduction available to donor	Yes, for present value of the remainder interest to charity	Yes, for present value of the remainder interest to charity
Income paid to the beneficiary	Yes, level income. Income amount is commonly determined using rates from the American Council on Gift Annuities. Donor doesn't choose the amount of income paid	Yes, variable income. Income beneficiary receives the pro-rata income earned from the pooled assets; amount depends on the earnings within the fund. Donor doesn't choose the amount of income paid
Remainder assets to charity	Immediately upon gift by donor	Upon last of income beneficiaries to die
Length of time income is paid	Life only	Life only
Life expectancy used	Single or two life only	Single or joint life or multiple life
Taxation of income payments	Each payment is part ordinary income/capital gains/and return of principal	Taxable income to recipient as a distribution of income from a complex trust
Administration of asset required by donor	None	No, the pooled income fund does the administration of the fund/assets
Donor retains control over asset	No	No
Can the donor give tax-exempt securities?	Yes	No
Can life insurance become a part of the overall gift plan?	The income from the gift annuity can be used by the donor to purchase life insurance to replace the value of the donated assets for the donor's heirs	The income from the pooled income fund can be used by the donor to purchase life insurance to replace the value of the donated assets for the donor's heirs

death have his daughter receive income for her life, and then upon her death direct that the assets are to be distributed to the public charity?

Answer – Yes. The income interests can be named concurrently, consecutively, or both concurrently and consecutively.[23]

Question – Must the income beneficiary's interest last for the life of the beneficiary, or in the alternative, can the income period extend for a fixed number of years (an option available for charitable remainder trusts)?

Answer – No. The income period must be for the life of the income beneficiary and cannot last for a fixed number of years (as is available for charitable remainder trusts).

Question – Do the private foundation rules against self-dealing and the associated excise taxes apply to any aspects of pooled income funds?

Answer – Yes. These restrictions also apply to pooled income funds. The self-dealing excise taxes under IRC Section 4940, taxes on excess business holdings under Section 4941, jeopardy investments under Section 4944, and taxes on taxable expenditures under Section 4945 all apply to pooled income funds.

Question – Can any organization, other than a public charity under IRC Section 501(c)(3), have pooled income funds (e.g., a family foundation)?

Answer – No. The charity underlying the pooled income fund must be a 50% public charity under IRC section 170(b)(1)(A) (other than described in clauses (vii) and (viii)).[24] Therefore, pooled income funds do not have the broader choices for remainder charities as those available for charitable remainder trusts.

Question – Does the IRS provide any sample provisions for pooled income fund governing documents?

Answer – Yes. See Revenue Procedure 88-53, 1988-2 CB 712, for sample pooled income fund documents.

Question – Can a donor terminate his or her interest in a pooled income fund prior to death?

Answer – At first blush the answer is "no." Gifts to pooled income funds are irrevocable and, hence, the donor cannot unwind the gift. However, many pooled

income funds have not been able to produce the income payments at a level consistent with other giving opportunities. This has caused some organizations to terminate their pooled income funds prematurely and offer the donors one of three options: (1) an outright distribution back to the donor of the donor's income interest based on the then current life expectancy of the income beneficiary; (2) instead of receiving the income interest based on (1) above, the donor can choose to donate the income interest as a direct gift back to the charity and receive an income tax charitable contribution deduction for the then current value of the gift; and (3) the donor can take his or her income interest based on (1) above and give it back to the charitable organization in exchange for a charitable gift annuity. The donor's income interest is a capital asset with a tax basis of zero.

CHAPTER ENDNOTES

1. For final rules revising the definition of "income" under IRC section 643(b), to take into account changes in the definition of trust accounting income under state laws, see TD 9102, 69 Fed. Reg. 12, 13 (1-2-2004).

2. Treas. Reg. §1.642(c)-5(b)(8).

3. Treas. Reg. §1.642(c)-5(b).

4. See Treas. Reg. §1.642(c)-5(c).

5. Treas. Reg. §1.642(c)-5(c)(2).

6. Treas. Reg. §1.642(c)-5(c)(2)(i)(c).

7. Treas. Reg. §1.642(c)-5(a)(4). Pooled income computations can easily be performed on software programs, such as the Charitable Gift Planner.

8. IRC Sec. 642(c)(5). These numbers are available at www.leimbergservices.com.

9. IRC Sec. 642(c)(5).

10. Treas. Reg. §1.642(c)-6(e)(4).

11. IRC Sec. 170(b)(1). For additional details on gifts of property, see Chapter 4.

12. Treas. Reg. §1.642(c)-5(a)(3).

13. IRC Secs. 2001(c), 2502(a), as amended by EGTRRA 2001.

14. IRC Secs. 2523(f), 2056(b)(7)(A).

15. IRC Secs. 6019, 6075(b).

16. IRC Sec. 2210, as amended by EGTRRA 2001.

17. IRC Sec. 2010(c), as amended by EGTRRA 2001.

18. IRC Sec. 2036.

19. IRC Sec. 2038.

20. Treas. Reg. §1.642(c)-5(b)(2).

21. Treas. Reg. §1.642(c)-5(b)(2).

22. Treas. Reg. §1.642(c)-5(b)(2).

23. Treas. Reg. §1.642(c)-5(b)(2).

24. IRC Sec. 642(c)(5)(a).

PRIVATE FOUNDATIONS

CHAPTER 21

WHAT IS IT?

A private foundation (also sometimes called a "family foundation") is a charitable organization created, funded, and usually controlled by a single donor or by members of the donor's family.

Provisions regulating private foundations were originally inserted into the tax code as part of the Tax Reform Act of 1969. These rules were in reaction to what was perceived by some members of Congress as abuses of the tax-exempt, charitable status conferred on certain charities, particularly ones that were not subject to public oversight or scrutiny. As a result, Congress chose to place into the tax code rules that generally classify charities into two groups: public charities and private foundations. Private foundations are subject to a very restrictive set of rules and potential excise taxes, which were designed to prohibit the sort of behavior by foundations and their managers that Congress was concerned about when it enacted the private foundation rules. There are also punitive excise taxes that may be levied on both the foundation and individuals if these rules are violated. The Pension Protection Act of 2006 (PPA 2006) increased these restrictions and penalties on foundations making grants to supporting organizations.

Of all the possible tools and techniques of charitable planning, private foundations provide the greatest degree of long-term control and flexibility to a donor in terms of how a substantial charitable gift will be applied to charitable purposes. Many charitably inclined donors who have substantial wealth prefer utilizing a private foundation despite the presence of the restrictive tax rules because of the degree of control and involvement that the donor's family may have with a private foundation. This control often would be diluted or even nonexistent if the donor's contribution was made directly to a public charity.

Most private foundations do not engage directly in charitable activities themselves (e.g., operating a food bank), but instead distribute funds to other charities that perform charitable activities. There is a separate category of private foundations, called private operating foundations, that is subject to less restrictive rules than private foundations. However, private operating foundations have specific expenditure requirements, and must directly participate in charitable activities rather than simply make contributions to other charitable organizations. Under a change made by the PPA of 2006, grants made by private foundations to supporting organizations of public charities that are not "functionally integrated" (explained further below) with their public charities will not count toward the foundation's 5% distribution requirement.

WHEN IS THE USE OF SUCH A DEVICE INDICATED?

1. When the donor is charitably inclined and intends to make substantial gifts to charity (at least $1 million) either during his lifetime or at death.

2. When the donor has substantial wealth (generally at least $5 million) and cannot reduce the taxable estate in any other acceptable fashion. Typically a private foundation grantor prefers the scenario where 100% of the amount going into the private foundation will be devoted to charitable purposes and causes favored by the donor rather than losing a significant amount to death taxes, with only the remainder after taxes going to the donor's heirs. Typically, the donor's heirs have received or will receive substantial gifts or future inheritances apart from the amount going into the private foundation.

3. When the donor desires a high degree of control over the manner in which the funds inside the

private foundation will be expended for charitable purposes.

4. When the donor likes the idea of utilizing a private foundation as a vehicle for his family to come together on a regular basis to discuss the expenditure of a portion of the family's wealth on charitable causes. The donor also likes the fact that these meetings and discussions will teach the family the need for social responsibility.

5. When the donor likes the idea of having his name or family's name associated with a foundation that can raise the social profile of the donor and family in local charitable giving circles and in the community in general. Similarly, a corporate donor can raise its public profile by forming its own private foundation.

ADVANTAGES

1. A private foundation provides the donor and family significant control over the timing and manner (subject to the private foundation rules discussed below) in which charitable expenditures are made by the foundation, and substantial year by year flexibility in the choice of recipients.

2. Capital gains taxes can be avoided on highly appreciated assets transferred to the private foundation.

3. A full fair market value deduction can be taken for appreciated publicly traded securities donated to the foundation.

4. A private foundation can provide the donor and the donor's family with significant visibility in a local community for the charitable work.

5. A private foundation can act as the focal point for a family's charitable activities, and instill in the original donor's children and descendants a lasting sense of social responsibility and awareness that might not be achievable through other means.

6. If the donor regularly makes charitable contributions that cause the donor (either individual or corporate) to consistently exceed the donor's percentage limitation on charitable deductions, use of a private foundation can assist, since the foundation can make charitable contributions from its income that otherwise would be made by the donor.

DISADVANTAGES

1. Administrative costs can be high. These include costs to create the foundation, obtain tax-exempt status, annually ensure the foundation complies with the private foundation rules, and file the necessary annual reports.[1]

2. Application of the private foundation rules creates constant exposure to excise taxes for failure to stay within the rules, not only for the foundation, but for its managers as well. This requires constant monitoring and vigilance by both the foundation's board and its tax advisors.

3. The private foundation tax rules restrict a foundation's ability to expend funds for charitable purposes to a greater extent than a public charity is restricted.

4. Lower annual charitable contribution percentage limits apply to donations made to a private foundation (generally, 30% vs. 50% of AGI for contributions of cash, and 20% vs. 30% for contributions of capital gain property) compared with donations made to a public charity.

5. Holders of interests in closely-held businesses are denied a deduction for the fair market value of interests contributed to a private foundation.

6. The excess business holdings rule means that typically owners of closely held businesses cannot contribute their interests to a private foundation unless the foundation disposes of the interest within certain time limits (generally, five years).

WHAT ARE THE REQUIREMENTS?

A charity must request classification as either a public charity or a private foundation at the same time that it applies to the Service for recognition of its tax exempt status.

The tax code classifies a charity as a "private foundation" in the negative; that is, a charity is automatically classified as, and therefore is considered and taxed as, a private foundation unless it fits into one of the following categories:[2]

1. *activity-based public charity* – a charity that is deemed to be a public charity by virtue of the

inherently public nature of its activities (e.g., a hospital, church, or school);

2. *publicly-supported organization* – a charity that receives most of its donations and support from a broad spectrum of the general public (e.g., a museum), as opposed to from a single individual, a single family, or a limited number of persons or organizations; or

3. *supporting organization* – an organization that is operated, supervised, or controlled by or in connection with a public charity. There are three types of supporting organizations. See Chapter 24 for details on supporting organizations.

Private Foundation Excise Taxes

A charity classified as a private foundation (and any individual deemed to be a "disqualified person" related to that foundation) is subject to the following excise taxes.

1. *Tax on investment income.* A 2% excise tax is levied on the net investment income[3] of a domestic private foundation. This rate is reduced to 1% if the foundation's qualifying charitable distributions equal or exceeds the sum of: (1) an amount equal to the assets of the foundation multiplied by the average percentage payout of the foundation's assets for the previous five years; and (2) 1% of the net investment income for that year. The foundation must also not have been subject to the tax on failure to distribute income (discussed below) for the previous five years, in order to qualify for the 1% rate. Certain private operating foundations are exempt from this tax.[4] Foreign private foundations are subject to an annual 4% tax on gross investment income from United States sources.[5]

2. *Taxes on self-dealing.* A private foundation is subject to an excise tax if it participates in a "prohibited transaction" with a "disqualified person."[6] The term "disqualified person" includes: a substantial contributor to the foundation; a foundation manager; an owner of 20% or more of a substantial contributor to the foundation; and any family member of the preceding. Also included in the definition of a disqualified person is a corporation, partnership, estate or trust *if* more than 35% of the organization is

owned by individuals who satisfy the first four (4) conditions. Finally, government officials are disqualified persons.[7]

"Prohibited transactions" include: (1) any direct or indirect sale, exchange, or leasing of property between a private foundation and a disqualified person; (2) any direct or indirect lending of money or other extension of credit between a private foundation and a disqualified person; (3) any direct or indirect furnishing of goods, services, or facilities between a private foundation and a disqualified person; (4) any direct or indirect payment of compensation, or payment of reimbursed expenses, by a private foundation to a disqualified person; (5) any direct or indirect transfer to, or use by or for the benefit of, a disqualified person of the income or assets of a private foundation; and (6) any direct or indirect agreement by a private foundation to make any payment of money or other property to a government official, other than an agreement to employ the official for any period after termination of government service if the official is terminating that service within 90 days. There is an exception in the latter case for reasonable compensation paid to a disqualified person (other than certain government officials) for personal services performed to carry out the foundation's exempt purposes.

Self-dealing can result in two types of excise taxes, each with two levels of tax, as explained below. The taxes are imposed on disqualified persons and private foundation managers.[8] The tax will apply even if the transaction was on an arms-length basis, and even if the result of the transaction was not overly favorable to the disqualified person.

One self-dealing excise tax is imposed on each act of self-dealing between a private foundation and a disqualified person.[9] The second self-dealing excise tax is imposed on a foundation manager who knowingly participates in an act of self-dealing between a private foundation and a disqualified person—that individual is personally subject to a tax of 5% of the amount involved.

A first level tax of 10% of the amount involved is imposed on a disqualified person who engages in an act of self-dealing (as defined above) with a private foundation. The maximum amount of tax on self dealing that may be imposed on a foundation manager is $10,000 for each level of tax.[10]

A second level tax of 200% of the amount involved is imposed on a disqualified person if the self dealing is not corrected. If a foundation manager refused to agree to part or all of the correction, another self-dealing excise tax of 50% of the self-dealing amount is imposed on the foundation manager. Again, the maximum amount of tax on self dealing that may be imposed on a foundation manager is $20,000 for each act of self-dealing.[11]

3. *Tax on failure to distribute income.* An excise tax is generally levied on a private foundation (other than certain private operating foundations) that fails to distribute at least 5% of its investment assets annually for charitable purposes. (See the Q&A section of this chapter for which distributions qualify under this rule.)

An initial tax of 30% of the undistributed amount is levied if the foundation has failed to make the required distribution by the first day of the year succeeding the year the distribution was required to have been made. An additional tax of 100% of the amount that remains undistributed is imposed if the foundation does not correct the failure to distribute the funds by the time the IRS mails a notice of deficiency or the tax is assessed.[12]

4. *Tax on excess business holdings.* Private foundations are not allowed to own more than 20% of the voting stock in a corporation (35% where it can be established that an independent third party has effective control over the corporation). Stock owned by disqualified persons is included in calculating the permissible limits for stock owned by a foundation. A 2% de minimis exception is available. A comparable rule applies to the holdings of non-corporate enterprises, such as partnerships.

Excess business holdings are the amount of stock in a corporation (or interests in an unincorporated business enterprise) that a private foundation is not permitted to hold. These non-permissible holdings include and must count the stock or interests held by disqualified persons.

The initial tax is 10% of the excess business holdings amount; however, this 10% tax can be avoided in certain situations if the foundation disposes of the excess business holdings within 90 days of learning of the excess business holdings. Failure to dispose of the excess business holdings by the time the first tier tax is assessed or a deficiency notice is mailed exposes the foundation to a 200% tax.

Special rules permit private foundations to dispose of a business interest that was received by a gift or bequest over a five-year period without triggering the excise tax. In certain circumstances, this five-year period may be extended to 10 years.[13]

5. *Tax on investments that jeopardize charitable purposes.* A private foundation (and a foundation manager) is subject to an excise tax if it makes investments that are deemed to jeopardize its charitable purposes.[14] While there are no specific investments that are defined under the tax law to be *per se* violations of this rule, the regulations direct special attention to be paid to the following practices and investments: (a) trading securities on margin; (b) trading in commodities futures; (c) working interests in oil and gas; (d) puts, calls, straddles, and warrants; and (e) selling securities short.

A 10% tax is separately imposed on both a foundation and its managers for making an investment that jeopardizes the charitable purposes (limited to $10,000 per investment on a foundation manager). A foundation manager must have participated in the investment knowingly and that participation must have been willful and not due to reasonable cause to be held liable for this excise tax.[15] An additional tax of 25% is levied for failure to correct these investments (limited to $20,000 per investment on a foundation manager).

6. *Tax on taxable expenditures.* A private foundation is subject to an initial tax of 20%, and its foundation managers who knowingly made a taxable expenditure are subject to an initial tax of 5% on any "taxable expenditures" (limited to $10,000 on foundation managers).

"Taxable expenditures" include: (a) amounts spent to influence legislation; (b) amounts spent to participate in a political campaign; (c) grants made to individuals or noncharitable organizations that fail to meet certain objective criteria that ensure the funds are used for certain approved purposes or goals (such as a scholarship award to an individual to permit the grantee to achieve a specific objective or enhance a particular talent); and (d) expenditures for noncharitable purposes, among others.

Under a change made by PPA 2006, distributions to non-functionally integrated Type III supporting organizations and to Type I and Type II supporting organizations that are controlled (directly or indirectly) by foundation insiders or disqualified persons relative to the distributing foundation may also be considered taxable expenditures unless the foundation exercises "expenditure responsibility" (explained further in the Q&A section of this chapter).

An additional tax of 100% on the foundation and 50% on the foundation manager (limited to $20,000 on foundation managers) can be levied for failure to correct the taxable expenditure.[16]

HOW IS IT DONE?

1. The donor creates a nonprofit corporation or a charitable trust under the applicable state law.

2. The corporation or trust applies to the Internal Revenue Service for recognition of its tax-exempt charitable status, and for classification as a private foundation using IRS Form 1023, "Application for Recognition of Exemption Under Section 501(c)(3) of the Internal Revenue Code" (revised June 2006).

3. The donor transfers cash or title of the property to be given to the private foundation to the corporation or trust.

4. The donor receives an income tax deduction for the contribution. The income tax deduction is limited to 30% of the donor's adjusted gross income in the year of the contribution (20% for contributions of capital gain property). The donor is also allowed to carry over any excess for up to five future years, subject to the same limitations.

5. The donor files a federal gift tax return (IRS Form 709, "United States Gift (and Generation-Skipping Transfer) Tax Return") to report the gift.

6. The private foundation files information returns IRS Form 990-PF, "Return of Private Foundation") annually.

Example: Even after implementing an estate plan that has already substantially reduced her taxable estate, Mary Ann McDunn has a net worth of $10 million, mostly in publicly traded securities. Mary Ann has already transferred significant portions of her wealth to her heirs through estate planning devices such as family partnerships, GRATs, sales to defective grantor trusts, and other methods. She regularly donates substantial amounts to charity, and finds the idea of The Mary Ann McDunn Foundation very appealing. She has an annual income of approximately $1 million.

Mary Ann has in her portfolio of securities a block of shares in a publicly traded corporation worth approximately $1 million. She has a very low basis, as these shares were received as a gift from her father many years ago. Her broker has advised Mary Ann that she should sell the stock because (1) he feels the stock is presently overvalued in the market, and (2) that Mary Ann's portfolio is not sufficiently diversified because of the presence of this large block of stock. Mary Ann is unwilling to sell because of the substantial capital gains tax she will pay if she sold the shares; however, she is willing to part with these shares to start The Mary Ann McDunn Foundation.

Mary Ann's attorney creates a nonprofit corporation under local state law and applies to the IRS for charitable tax-exempt status. The board of directors of the new corporation consists of Mary Ann and some of her family members. Mary Ann is the president and sole officer of the corporation. The IRS approves the application for charitable tax-exempt status and classifies the new corporation as a private foundation.

Mary Ann transfers the $1 million of low basis, publicly traded securities to the private foundation. Mary Ann will receive an income tax deduction of $1 million for the full fair market value of the shares donated to the foundation. She will not report the gain (or be able to recognize any loss) on the difference between her tax basis and the fair market value of the stock.

Because her adjusted gross income (AGI) is $1 million for the year of contribution, her deduction will be limited to $200,000 for that year (20% of her AGI). But the excess of $800,000 may be carried over and deducted over up to five subsequent years, subject to the same 20% AGI limitation for those years.

During Mary Ann's lifetime, the foundation board meets regularly and decides to contribute to those charitable causes that Mary Ann traditionally supports with her direct annual contributions. As the foundation is making these gifts, Mary Ann can reduce or eliminate her direct personal contributions to these same charitable organizations, except when she desires to make unusually large donations (e.g., for a capital campaign). Mary Ann can also continue to add to the foundation's endowment as her investment decisions and the percentage limitations on the deductions for her charitable contributions permit.

Mary Ann also changes her will so that everything above the statutorily protected amount ($2,000,000 in 2007) will pass to The Mary Ann McDunn Foundation at her death. Her heirs have essentially received their inheritances during Mary Ann's lifetime as a result of careful estate planning (or perhaps from life insurance on her life purchased with lifetime gifts that she made to them), so the net effect of creating the foundation and passing everything to it at Mary Ann's death effectively results in no federal estate taxes imposed on Mary Ann's estate.

Private Operating Foundations

A private foundation that engages primarily in the active conduct of charitable, religious, educational, or similar activities, and meets certain income and asset tests may be classified as a private operating foundation. Private operating foundations are not subject to the income distribution requirements and the tax on investment income that otherwise apply to private foundations.

A private operating foundation must spend the lesser of: (1) its annual adjusted net income, or (2) 5% of its investment assets directly in the active conduct of charitable, religious, educational or similar purposes for which it was organized, and also meet certain asset, endowment or support tests.[17] For purposes of the annual percentage limitation on charitable contributions, a private operating foundation is treated as a public charity (in other words, contributions of cash are deductible up to 50% of the taxpayer's adjusted gross income, as opposed to the lower 30% limit for contributions of cash to private foundations).

WHAT ARE THE TAX IMPLICATIONS?

1. The donor of cash or property to a private foundation is eligible for an income tax deduction. The amount of the deduction in the case of long-term capital gain property is the fair market value of the property, so long as the property consists of publicly traded securities. Otherwise, the deduction is limited to the tax basis in the property. For contributions of property that would give rise to short term capital gains or ordinary income if sold by the donor, the donor must reduce the deduction by the amount of short term capital gain or ordinary income that would have been recognized if the property had been sold. In other words, the deduction is limited to his adjusted basis.

   An individual donor's annual percentage limitation is limited to 30% of adjusted gross income (AGI) for cash donations made to private foundations and to 20% of AGI for donations of capital gain property to private foundations. Private operating foundations are treated as public charities for these purposes. A corporation may deduct up to 10% of its taxable income (with certain adjustments) in any one taxable year.[18]

   No gain (or loss) is recognized on the contribution of property to a private foundation. Generally, a later sale of the property by the foundation will not cause recognition of gain or loss to the donor. But there is an important exception: if the circumstances indicate that the sale of the property had in fact already been consummated by the donor prior to the contribution to the foundation, and the contribution was a mere assignment of income, the donor will be taxed on any gain on the sale.[19]

2. Donors of cash or property to a private foundation are not subject to gift tax on the value of the amount transferred due to an unlimited gift

tax charitable deduction. Likewise, the value of the property donated to a private foundation is excluded from an individual donor's estate. If the transfer to a private foundation occurs at a person's death, the donor's estate receives an estate tax deduction for the value of the amount bequeathed to the private foundation.

WHAT ARE THE ALTERNATIVES?

Community foundations are charitable organizations that typically make grants to benefit local communities and local community organizations. They are classified as public charities[20] and, hence, are free of most of the restrictions applicable to private foundations. These organizations usually permit donors contributing a minimum amount set by the foundation to create a separate account (also known as a "donor advised fund"— see Chapter 19).

The donor advised fund makes it possible for the donor or members of the donor's family to recommend (but not dictate) how distributions from the separate account will be made. Although these foundations are usually community based, donor advised funds are not geographically limited, with a number of national financial institutions having established separate organizations that are classified as public charities. Donor advised funds relieve the donor of most of the administrative burdens associated with private foundations. Community foundations are discussed in more detail in Chapter 17. See Figure 21.1 for a comparison of the advantages and disadvantages of a community foundation account as compared to a private foundation (and supporting organizations). Supporting organizations are discussed in Chapter 24.

WHERE CAN I FIND OUT MORE ABOUT IT?

1. Toce, Joseph, Abbin, Byrle, Vorsatz, Mark, and Page, William, *Tax Economics of Charitable Giving 2006-2007* (Warren Gorham & Lamont, 2006).

QUESTIONS AND ANSWERS

Question – Can a foundation manager, who is also a donor or a member of the donor's family, accept a salary and benefits (e.g., group term life, split dollar life insurance, death benefit only, or a pension plan) from the foundation?

Figure 21.1

COMPARISON OF A PRIVATE FOUNDATION TO A SUPPORTING ORGANIZATION AND A COMMUNITY FOUNDATION ACCOUNT			
	Supporting Organization to an Operating 501(c)(3) Charity	**Community Foundation Account**	**Private Foundation**
What other names might it be called?	"Supporting organization," "Foundation," or "Auxiliary"	"Donor Advised Account"	"Family Foundation"
Is it considered a 501(c)(3) organization?	Yes	Yes	Yes
Individual AGI deduction limit on cash gifts?	50%	50%	30%
Individual AGI deduction limit on gifts of appreciated property?	30%	30%	20%
Corporate deduction limit on cash gifts or gifts of appreciated property?	10% of taxable income (with certain adjustments)	10% of taxable income (with certain adjustments)	10% of taxable income (with certain adjustments)

Figure 21.1 (cont'd)

	Supporting Organization to an Operating 501(c)(3) Charity	Community Foundation Account	Private Foundation
Carry forward of deductions that exceed AGI or taxable income limits available?	Yes, 5 Years	Yes, 5 Years	Yes, 5 Years
Values of appreciated property for deduction purposes?	Fair Market Value	Fair Market Value	Fair Market Value for publicly traded stock only; cost basis for other property
Engaged directly in charitable activities?	Often	Often	Not Usually
Sources of funding?	Public gifts, grants, single source individual family or endowment	Public gifts	Single source such as an individual family; or a limited number of donors
Objective with money raised?	Currently spent or Endowment	Currently spent or Endowment	Endowment
Minimum payout requirements?	No	No	Yes, generally 5% of investment assets
Tax for failure to meet minimum payout requirement?	No	No	Yes, 15% tax on undistributed amounts
Subject to investment tax?	No	No	Yes, 2% of investment income; can be reduced to 1% if amounts in excess of minimum required payout are distributed
Subject to self-dealing tax?	No	No	Yes
Subject to excess business holdings tax?	No	No	Yes
Tax on jeopardy type investment?	No	No	Yes
Tax on restricted activities?	No	No	Yes

COMPARISON OF A PRIVATE FOUNDATION TO A SUPPORTING ORGANIZATION AND A COMMUNITY FOUNDATION ACCOUNT

Figure 21.1 (cont'd)

COMPARISON OF A PRIVATE FOUNDATION TO A SUPPORTING ORGANIZATION AND A COMMUNITY FOUNDATION ACCOUNT			
	Supporting Organization to an Operating 501(c)(3) Charity	**Community Foundation Account**	**Private Foundation**
Informational return required for IRS	Form 990	Form 990	Form 990PF
When is Form 990 or 990-PF required?	Gross receipts over $25,000	Always filed at CF level	Always
Cost to set up and maintain?	Expensive to start, and costs are incurred to continue operations	Typically no up front cost, but investment management fee/year is charged as a percentage of the account (usually .5%-1%)	Expensive to start, and costs are incurred to continue operations
Eligible receivers of grants?	Supported organizations that are also 501(c)(3) organizations	501(c)(3) organizations	What the donor desires, but most often grants to other 501(c)(3) organizations
When is it used?	When a donor is willing to give up some control and flexibility in exchange for escaping classification as a private foundation	As either a donating or endowment alternative which allows some family involvement without private foundation rules and at a very reasonable cost	When donors wish to pursue their own charitable endeavors and create flexibility to change the foundation's purpose; usually want to create a permanent endowment and are not concerned about overhead costs

Answer – Yes. But the salary and benefits must be reasonable relative to the value of services that are actually performed by the manager.

Question – If a foundation wishes to avoid private foundation status by demonstrating that it receives support from the general public, how much support is required?

Answer – There are two categories of private foundations that can qualify as "publicly supported organizations:"

1. An organization that: (a) receives at least one-third of its support from certain government sources or the general public, or (b) receives at least 10% of its support from government sources or the general public and in addition meets a facts and

circumstances test demonstrating that it is organized and operated to attract additional government or public support.[21]

2. An entity that normally receives more than one-third of its support from members of the general public (exclusive of disqualified persons) and receives no more than one-third of its revenue from gross investment income.[22]

Question – What sort of transactions can give rise to a prohibited act of self-dealing?

Answer – Acts of self-dealing include: any direct or indirect sale, exchange, or leasing of property between a private foundation and a disqualified person; any direct or indirect lending of money or other extension of credit between a private foundation and a disqualified person; any direct or indirect furnishing of goods, services, or facilities between a private foundation and a disqualified person; any direct or indirect payment of compensation, or payment of reimbursed expenses, by a private foundation to a disqualified person; any direct or indirect transfer to, or use by or for the benefit of, a disqualified person of the income or assets of a private foundation; and any direct or indirect agreement by a private foundation to make any payment of money or other property to a government official, other than an agreement to employ the official for any period after termination of government service if the official is terminating that service within 90 days.

It is important to bear in mind that the above transactions constitute acts of self-dealing even if a particular transaction is done at arms-length and the foundation suffered no economic loss or detriment and the recipient received no special benefit or advantage as a result of the transaction.

Question – What distributions qualify for purposes of satisfying the requirements that a private foundation distribute at least 5% of its investment assets each year?

Answer – Grants to public charities or governmental agencies. Most commonly, private foundations satisfy their distribution requirements by making grants to other organizations. Grants to public charities (excepting certain 509(a)(3) supporting organizations detailed below) or governmental agencies will qualify so long as the public charity is not controlled by the

foundation, or the terms of the grant do not cause the grant to be treated as earmarked for, or used by, the foundation itself. Grants to a "functionally integrated" Type III supporting organization also satisfy the distribution requirement. A Type III supporting organization is "functionally integrated" (according to interim IRS guidance) if the activities engaged in by the Type III supporting organization carried out for and on behalf of the supported public charities are activities that perform the functions of, or to carry out the purposes of the supported organizations and, *but for* the involvement of the supporting organization, such activities would normally be engaged in by the supported organizations themselves. An example of this would be a blood bank operating as a supporting organization to a hospital.

Grants to 509(a)(3) supporting organizations that are (i) non-functionally integrated type III supporting organizations, and (ii) any other supporting organization if a disqualified person of the distributing private foundation directly or indirectly controls the supporting organization or one of its supported organizations, are *not* qualifying distributions (even if the foundation exercises "expenditure responsibility" with respect to the grant, as "expenditure responsibility" relates only to whether the grant may be a taxable expenditure, not a qualifying distribution). See Chapter 24 on Supporting Organizations for a more detailed discussion of Type I, II, and III supporting organizations.

Grants to a private operating foundation. Grants to private operating foundations may qualify so long as the donor private foundation exercises Section 4945 expenditure responsibility, as described below.

Grants to a foreign charity. Distributions made to a foreign charity may qualify so long as the private foundation has made a good faith determination that the foreign charity would qualify as a public charity or a private operating foundation if it were located in the United States. The foreign organization must provide sufficient documentation to the foundation to permit the IRS to confirm such a determination.[23]

Grants to noncharitable organizations. Grants made to a noncharitable exempt organization (e.g., a trade association) or to a for-profit entity may qualify for the distribution requirement so long as the foundation has assured itself that the grant will be applied for charitable purposes by exercising Section 4945 expenditure responsibility.

Set-asides. Amounts set aside for a charitable purpose (but not currently distributed) may be counted towards the distribution requirement if the set-aside meets either a suitability test or a cash distribution test. Approval for the set-aside must be obtained from the Service.[24]

Question – May a private foundation ever make a grant to a private individual?

Answer – Yes. But the foundation must be very careful in making that grant. It must be: (1) made for study, travel, or similar purposes, (2) a scholarship, fellowship, prize, or award, (3) awarded on an objective and nondiscriminatory basis under a procedure approved in advance, or (4) intended to achieve a specific objective, produce a report or other similar product, or improve or enhance a literary, artistic, musical, scientific, teaching, or other similar capacity, skill or talent of the grantee.

Question – What constitutes Section 4945 expenditure responsibility?

Answer – A grantor may rely on information in the IRS Business Master File ("BMF") or the grantee's current letter from the IRS granting exempt status (to ensure the donee organization is not a 509(a)(3) Type III, non-functionally integrated; see Chapter 24). The preferred method is to use the grantee organization's letter from the IRS granting exempt status because the BMF is relatively inaccessible. To determine whether a 509(a)(3) grantee organization is a Type I, Type II, or functionally-integrated Type III supporting organization , a private foundation may:

(1) Rely on a written representation signed by an officer, director, or trustee of the grantee that the organization is a Type I or II supporting organization. The grantor must also review and retain copies of the governing documents of the grantee organization and the written representation must describe the selection of the grantee organization's officers, directors, and trustees, and reference specific provisions within the governing documents creating a Type I or Type II supporting organization.

(2) Rely on a written representation signed by an officer, director or trustee of the grantee

that the organization is a Type III functionally-integrated supporting organization, as long as:

- one or more supported organization(s) is identified;

- the governing documents and/or any other documents are collected and reference such a relationship; and

- an officer, director, or trustee of each supported organization provides a written representation confirming that it is functionally-integrated and describing the activities of the supporting organization.

A grantor may always rely on written opinion of counsel of either the grantor or grantee in the alternative.

Question – Are there significant non-tax benefits to creating a private foundation?

Answer – Although there are as many non-tax reasons for creating and funding a private foundation as there are potential donors, many donors and their families find that a private foundation can provide a focal point for family members to work together as they implement the mission of the foundation. Thus, a private foundation can serve as a way to both insure the passing on of the family's values, and to encourage the cooperation of family members with each other. Younger family members can often acquire valuable business and management skills through their involvement in the foundation's activities, and can also gain access and exposure to important local business and political leaders in their communities through the foundation. Family members can receive compensation for services rendered to the foundation, so long as the compensation is reasonable relative to the actual value of the services rendered to the foundation, and the work performed is actually needed by the foundation.

Question – What are a private foundation's annual reporting requirements?

Answer – Private foundations must file an annual information return with the IRS on Form 990-PF, "Return of Private Foundation."[25] This return is a public document and the foundation must make it available to any citizen who requests inspection of it. Any foundation that is subject to any of the excise taxes discussed above (except the tax on investment income, which is reported on and paid with the Form 990-PF) must file Form 4720, "Return of Certain Excise Taxes," and pay the excise tax imposed on it with the return. In addition, there may be state or local filing requirements that vary by jurisdiction.

Question – Who is a "substantial contributor" to a private foundation?

Answer – Anyone who makes a donation or bequest of more than $5,000, if the amount donated exceeds 2% of the foundation's total contributions and bequests received by the end of the year the donation is received.[26] Donations by a spouse or a trust are treated as made by the individual or the creator of the trust, respectively. Once a person has become a substantial contributor with respect to a private foundation, he retains that status until: (1) he makes no contributions to the foundation for 10 years, (2) he (and any related person) is not a foundation manager during the same 10-year period, and (3) the IRS deems the contributions to be insignificant relative to the contributions of one other person. If someone is a substantial contributor, that person is also considered a disqualified person for purposes of the excise taxes that are imposed on transactions involving self-dealing.

Example: If Mr. Wong makes a donation of $10,000 to a private foundation, and in the year of the donation the foundation's total contributions and bequests received were $100,000, Mr. Wong would be a substantial contributor relative to that private foundation. However, if the foundation received $1,000,000 in total contributions and bequests in the year of Mr. Wong's donation, he would not be considered a substantial contributor, as his contribution does not exceed 2% of $1,000,000 (i.e., $20,000).

CHAPTER ENDNOTES

1. The fees for establishing and maintaining private foundations can vary depending on the location of the foundation, the size of the legal and accounting firms involved, and their experience, and the volume of work they do in this highly specialized area. There is, therefore, a considerable difference in opinion as to the size of the overall charitable gift that will make the creation of a private foundation economically cost-effective and viable. Some commentators feel a private foundation can be justified from a cost/benefit standpoint even in cases where much lower amounts than $1 million are involved. Others suggest alternative techniques should be considered for more modest overall gifts.

2. IRC Sec. 509(a).

3. Net investment income = Gross Investment Income (includes income from interest, dividends, rents, and royalties as well as similar sources) + Capital Gain Net Income (gain/loss on all property, except for gains from exempt use property held for at least one year).

4. IRC Sec. 4940.

5. IRC Sec. 4948(a).

6. IRC Sec. 4941.

7. IRC Sec. 4946(a).

8. IRC Sec. 4941(a).

9. IRC Sec. 4941(a)(1).

10. IRC Sec. 4941.

11. IRC Sec. 4941.

12. IRC Sec. 4942.

13. IRC Sec. 4943.

14. IRC Sec. 4944.

15. Treas. Reg §53.4944-1.

16. IRC Sec. 4945.

17. IRC Sec. 4942(j)(3).

18. IRC Sec. 170(b)(2).

19. *Blake v. Comm.*, 83-1 USTC 86,081 (2nd Cir. 1982).

20. Treas. Regs. §§1.170A-9(e)(10), 1.170A-9(e)(11), 1.170A-9(e)(12), 1.170A-9(e)(13), -1.170A-9(e)(14).

21. IRC Sec. 170(b)(1)(A)(vi).

22. IRC Sec. 509(a)(2).

23. Treas. Reg. §53.4942(a)-3(a)(6).

24. IRC Sec. 4942(g)(2).

25. IRC Sec. 6033.

26. IRC Secs. 4946(a)(2), 507(d)(2).

RETIREMENT PLAN GIFTS

CHAPTER 22

WHAT IS IT?

A charitable retirement plan gift is a contribution from a qualified plan or IRA[1] to a charity, typically upon the donor's death. Retirement plan gifts to charitable organizations have become very popular gift planning techniques. One reason for the growing popularity of these gifts is that more people are building larger qualified retirement plan balances, mostly through the increasing use of employer-sponsored 401(k) plans. Growth during bull markets also has led to substantial retirement plan balances; in some cases, more than participants can use during their lifetimes.

But perhaps the most important factor leading toward the use of retirement assets as charitable gifts is the awakening of professionals, the press, and the public to the fact that after death, retirement accounts are "junk assets." That is, even though IRAs, pension plans, 401(k) plans, and simplified employee pensions (SEPs) may be excellent vehicles for building and distributing money for lifetime retirement needs, as a wealth transfer mechanism, these plans provide little after-tax security for their intended noncharitable beneficiaries. They are seen as "tax heavy" and "utility light."

"Tax heavy" means that upon the participant's death, bequests of qualified plan or IRA assets to anyone other than the surviving spouse will, in many cases, be subject to both income and estate taxes. So, after state and federal taxes, they become in the hands of their recipients, "utility light." When IRA owners or qualified plan participants realize how little their intended beneficiaries will actually benefit from these plans, they will often decide to bequeath these assets to a charitable organization and leave other, more tax-favorable assets to their noncharitable heirs. This chapter will concentrate on these types of charitable planning techniques.

WHEN IS THE USE OF SUCH A DEVICE INDICATED?

1. When the potential donor has IRA, HR-10, SEP, 401(k) or other retirement assets and his estate's value is likely to exceed the exemption equivalent amount of the estate tax unified credit (see "Tax Implications," below).

2. When the potential donor has a need to reduce his or her overall taxable estate for federal estate tax purposes.

3. When the donor has charitable intent toward a specific charity or several charities.

4. When the plan participant understands the tax-heavy nature of qualified plan and IRA assets.

ADVANTAGES

1. The use of retirement plan assets for charitable giving at death provides excellent tax planning opportunities. Since retirement plan assets are subject to both income and estate taxes at the participant's death, these assets should be the first selected to fund testamentary charitable gifts. Clients with large qualified plan balances who leave those assets to charity upon their death can avoid both estate and income taxes otherwise due on these assets.

2. When a participant makes a retirement plan gift, the charity receives its inheritance directly from the qualified plan or IRA trustee without going through the probate process. This alleviates much of the time delay, red tape, and cost associated with probate. Hence the charity receives the inheritance more quickly and cost-efficiently than if the gift had been made from the probate estate.

3. The charity receives a cash gift upon the donor's death. This means that instead of inheriting a complex and administratively cumbersome asset such as real estate, the charity receives a liquid asset. Most charities prefer gifts of cash above all other types of gifts.

4. The gift allows the donor to prevent the undesirable result of the heirs receiving only a fraction of the retirement plan assets after taxes.

5. With the use of wealth replacement (the purchase of life insurance on the life of one or both donors to make up for the amount of the plan benefit contributed to the charity), the donor's heirs can receive a much larger tax-free inheritance than would otherwise be possible.

DISADVANTAGES

1. For a donor desiring to make a lifetime gift, the tax treatment of retirement plan assets is generally very unfavorable (see "Tax Implications," below).

2. A direct gift of retirement plan or IRA assets upon the participant's death may result in the surviving spouse lacking necessary retirement funds.

3. Since retirement plan gifts are typically revocable testamentary gifts, the charity has no guarantee as to the amount of the gift, nor whether the gift will in fact be made.

4. Unless the donor employs a "wealth replacement" technique as described below, the donor's heirs may lose part of their perceived inheritance as a result of the gift.

WHAT ARE THE REQUIREMENTS?

1. The plan participant must obtain a change of beneficiary form from the pension plan administrator or IRA custodian. The donor names a charity or multiple charities as the direct beneficiary of the retirement plan or IRA assets upon death.

2. In the case of a qualified retirement plan (not an IRA), the plan participant's spouse must sign a waiver allowing the participant to designate a nonspouse beneficiary.

3. The beneficiary designation is revocable. The plan participant (or IRA owner) may change the charitable beneficiary at any time in the future, and maintains total control over the retirement plan values during his lifetime.

4. Regardless of who is named as beneficiary of the account, the participant or IRA owner generally must begin taking required minimum distributions shortly after age 70½ .[2] Under regulations finalized in 2002, the designation of the charity as beneficiary has no effect on the amount required to be distributed to the participant during life.[3]

5. For purposes of the minimum distribution requirements after the participant's death, a charitable organization will not qualify as a "designated beneficiary." However, any estate tax resulting from naming the charity as beneficiary will be offset by the charitable deduction.

6. The donor is not required to file any type of gift tax return, because the mere naming of a charity as a retirement plan beneficiary is not a completed gift.

HOW IS IT DONE? AN EXAMPLE

There are several types of planning options a donor may choose when he decides to use IRA or qualified plan dollars for a charitable gift. Lifetime or testamentary gifts are possible; however, as explained at "Tax Implications" below, the tax treatment of lifetime gifts of retirement plans assets generally makes them unfeasible. For that reason, this section will focus on testamentary gifts.

Testamentary gifts of retirement plan dollars are a very effective planning tool. The donor may choose to name a charity as the primary or contingent beneficiary of the account. Another option is to establish a testamentary charitable remainder trust (CRT), and name it as the beneficiary of the account. A third alternative builds on the CRT technique by naming the participant's family foundation as the charity underlying the testamentary CRT.

Example: Eric and Christy Williams , both age 67, have four adult children and the following assets:

$1,000,000	Appreciated stocks
300,000	Personal residence
200,000	Florida vacation home
500,000	Certificates of deposit
1,000,000	Dan's IRA
$3,000,000	total assets

Christy is the primary beneficiary of Eric's estate under his will, as well as the beneficiary of his IRA. Upon discussing their situation with their financial planner, Christy learns that if Eric dies before her, she will inherit all the assets without any estate taxes imposed, due to the unlimited marital deduction. Further, Christy as the IRA beneficiary, can roll over the IRA into her name following Eric's death. Christy will not pay any income taxes on the IRA when she rolls it into her own name.

Eric and Christy also learn the following could occur at Christy's later death when the assets pass to their four children:

- The federal estate taxes due on just the IRA would be $450,000 [$1,000,000 x 45%][4]

- The income tax due on just the IRA would be $192,500 [($1,000,000 - $450,000) x 35%][5]

- When both income and estate taxes are paid, only $357,500 [$1,000,000 – ($450,000 + $192,500)] is left of the $1,000,000 IRA for their children.[6]

Estate tax	$450,000
Income tax	+ 192,500
Total taxes on the IRA	$642,500
Value of IRA	$1,000,000
Total IRA taxes	- 642,500
Net left for the children after parents' deaths:	$ 357,500

Eric and Christy are stunned to learn that even though they have spent many years building a retirement fund, their hard-earned nest egg is consumed at their deaths by estate and income taxes so that only approximately 36% of the $1,000,000 IRA would actually reach their children. Two potential charitable planning alternatives for the IRA proceeds are discussed below.

Testamentary Gift Directly to Charity

Eric can name his favorite charity or several charities as the primary beneficiary of his IRA. This technique would provide a direct gift to the charity upon his death, without the retirement plan assets being subjected to income tax or going through the probate process. However, this may leave Christy, the surviving spouse, without needed retirement income.

In the alternative, Eric could name Christy as the primary beneficiary of the IRA and the charity as the contingent beneficiary. Christy will then have the opportunity to roll the IRA over into her own name upon his death, or she can leave the account in her husband's name. In either event, she can continue to name the charity as the primary beneficiary of the inherited IRA, so that upon her later death, the retirement values would pass directly to charity.

This technique will minimize the taxes on the IRA proceeds. No income or estate taxes will be due at the first death due to the unlimited marital deduction and the spousal rollover. At the second death the estate taxes are offset by the charitable deduction. No income taxes would be payable on the IRA proceeds since the charitable recipient is a tax-exempt entity.

Naming the spouse as the primary beneficiary with the charity as a contingent beneficiary provides a gift to charity at presumably a significantly later time than if the charity were the direct beneficiary of the IRA, since the distribution to the charity would not occur until both the husband and the wife are deceased. This timing issue is generally not of great importance to the clients, but, nonetheless, should be discussed. The use of a spousal rollover gives Christy more control over the IRA proceeds than the CRT alternatives which follow.

Testamentary Gift Using a Charitable Remainder Trust

Several options are available for using a charitable remainder trust (CRT) as beneficiary of a retirement plan account. Of course, since a CRT is required to pay income to a noncharitable beneficiary for a term or life, the ultimate charitable gift (and the resulting deduction) will be much smaller than if the account were payable directly to the charity. (For details on the requirements and planning techniques using CRTs, see Chapters 15 and 16.)

The CRT may be named as the primary or the contingent beneficiary of the account. If the participant wishes to maximize the surviving spouse's flexibility, he or she could name the surviving spouse as primary beneficiary and name the CRT as contingent beneficiary.

CRT as contingent beneficiary. Assume that in the example above, instead of naming the charity as a direct beneficiary of the IRA, Eric names Christy as primary beneficiary and a testamentary CRT as the contingent beneficiary. If Eric predeceases his wife, she, as the surviving spouse, can roll the IRA over into her own name, or she may leave it in her husband's name. (The minimum distributions required under each or these scenarios will vary, as explained later in this chapter.) In either event, assuming she keeps the CRT as beneficiary, the funds will be distributed into the CRT upon her death. At that point, their children can be life income beneficiaries of the CRT. Following the death of the last child to die, the remaining assets in the CRT will pass to the charity.

CRT as primary beneficiary. As a third alternative, Eric could establish a testamentary CRT and name it as the primary beneficiary of the IRA. The CRT could then provide Christy with lifetime income. Upon her later assumed death, the funds would then be distributed to the charity. This technique provides the surviving spouse with the least amount of flexibility with respect to the retirement plan funds. Christy would not be able to roll the IRA over into her own name, nor would she be able to take distributions of principal. (However, some CRUTs can be designed to provide a measure of flexibility to the unitrust beneficiary; see Chapter 16.)

When the CRT is the primary beneficiary of a retirement plan and the decedent names the surviving spouse as the income (annuity or unitrust) beneficiary, it is possible to avoid estate taxes on the account proceeds. At the husband's death, the present value of the charity's interest is includable in his estate, but will be offset by the estate tax charitable deduction. The present

value of the wife's income (annuity or unitrust) interest would be eligible for the federal estate tax marital deduction, and would cease at her death. Hence, both the marital and the charitable interests combined can avoid estate taxes at the first and second deaths.

Caution: If a nonspouse is named as a co-income beneficiary of a testamentary CRT with the spouse, a marital deduction will *not* be allowed for the spouse's interest; consequently, not all estate taxes would be avoided.

Distributions as IRD

When a retirement plan or IRA makes a distribution to a CRT at the death of the participant or second spouse, the distribution is treated as income in respect of a decedent (IRD–see "Tax Implications" below). However, since the CRT is a tax-exempt entity, no income tax is owed by the trust on the distribution. However, the IRD income taxation becomes apparent when the CRT makes income distributions to the individual (non-charitable) beneficiaries. Distributions to these beneficiaries are taxable under the 4-tiered accounting system for CRTs (for details, see Chapters 15 and 16). Since the retirement plan assets are an IRD item, they are considered tier one ordinary income.

The income beneficiaries of the CRT are not eligible to take an income tax deduction against the estate taxes paid on the present value of their income interest, as discussed below. Instead, the IRD deduction is given to the trust as a tier four distribution of principal.

Example: Assume a $300,000 contribution was made into a testamentary CRT from the decedent's retirement plan, and that the present value of the charity's remainder interest is $90,000. Thus, the taxable portion is roughly $210,000. At a 45% marginal estate tax bracket, the estate taxes are $94,500 ($210,000 x 45% = $94,500). The trust will show $205,500 ($300,000 - $94,500 = $205,500) as tier one income and $94,500 becomes tier four principal.[7]

Wealth Replacement

"Wealth replacement" refers to a technique designed to provide replacement assets to a participant's estate when a significant charitable gift has been made. When a wealth replacement technique is employed, the participant can assure that his children or other heirs are provided with what they perceive to be a fair inheritance when the parent has given the retirement funds (or another large gift) to a charity.

This technique requires that life insurance be purchased on the plan participant's life by his intended beneficiaries or by a trust on their behalf. Generally, life insurance is received income tax free by the beneficiary, provided that state insurable interest laws are satisfied and that there has been no transfer for value of the policy. If the participant is counting on life insurance to satisfy the needs of heirs, it is very important to determine that he is insurable, before the charitable gift is made.

If the value of the donor's estate exceeds the exemption equivalent amount,[8] the life insurance should typically be owned by an irrevocable life insurance trust. Generally, this should remove the ownership of the life insurance policy from the estate, so that it is not subjected to federal estate tax. To accomplish this, a policy insuring the donor's life (or perhaps a survivorship contract on the lives of the donor and the donor's spouse to lower the annual premiums) should be purchased by the trustee of the trust. The beneficiaries of the trust should be those individuals who would have been the beneficiaries of the retirement plan. In many cases this will be the donor's children. (The trust is the owner and beneficiary of the life insurance policy.)

The amount of the life insurance purchased by the trustee should be coordinated with the expected value of the retirement account as of the assumed date of the plan participant's death. To illustrate, assume Gary Franklin is age 65 and that his retirement plan account has a value of $700,000. He assumes his plan will grow by 5.5% per year and that he will live until the age of 80. By age 80, his account could be worth over $1,000,000 (even after taking distributions). If Gary makes a charitable gift of the retirement plan account, he should consider purchasing a $1,000,000 policy because this amount is truly wealth replacement to his children. However, the donor could choose to replace only the value of the current plan at $700,000 without accounting for any future growth.

The irrevocable life insurance trust can fund the premiums using after-tax distributions from the retirement plan. To accomplish this, Gary should take withdrawals from the retirement plan since this is the most tax heavy asset. It is most tax efficient to deplete this asset first. Therefore, by withdrawing from the most tax heavy

asset and turning those withdrawals into tax-free life insurance, Gary is making the best use of his assets and reducing the taxes at the same time.

The retirement plan withdrawals should be large enough to cover the annual life insurance premiums, plus enough to cover the income taxes due on the withdrawal. For example, if Gary is in a 40% state and federal income tax bracket and will pay $20,000 in annual life insurance premiums, he should withdraw $33,333 [$20,000 ÷ (1 - 0.40)]. In most situations, these premium contributions made by the donor to the trustee should be arranged to qualify as annual exclusion gifts using "Crummey" withdrawal rights.

WHAT ARE THE TAX IMPLICATIONS?

Income Tax

It is possible for a donor to choose to donate part or all of his retirement plan benefit outright to a charity during his lifetime. Alternatively, the donor may choose to create a lifetime charitable remainder trust (CRT) and transfer the retirement plan dollars to the CRT. However, lifetime gifts of retirement plan assets are seldom contemplated due to the adverse income tax treatment.

First, to make a lifetime gift of retirement plan or IRA assets, the participant must receive a distribution of the funds, which results in income taxation, generally of the entire distribution, in the year it is received. Further, if the participant is under age 59½ at the time of the gift, a penalty will generally be imposed on the participant equal to 10% of the taxable amount.[9]

Of course, because the donor is in fact making a gift to charity, he will receive a charitable deduction for the value of that gift. The resulting income tax charitable deduction (up to 50% of the participant's adjusted gross income (AGI), assuming a cash gift to a public charity) may offset the income tax due on the distribution.

Example: Don Burr has $20,000 in his 401(k) account from a previous employer. If Don decides to contribute this amount today to his alma mater, Drake University, he will have to first take a distribution of it, resulting in $20,000 of additional taxable income. Assuming he contributes the entire amount, his income tax deduction is $20,000 (limited to 50% of his AGI).

Assuming a marginal income tax rate of 35.0%, both the income tax on the distribution and the dollar value of the deduction would be $7,000, resulting in a near "wash" from a tax standpoint. But, if Don was under 59½ at the time of the distribution, he would probably be subject to a 10% penalty tax on the taxable amount of the distribution, in addition to the income tax. This additional $2,000 expense would not be offset.

Pension Protection Act of 2006

To avoid some of the inherent problems with making lifetime charitable gifts from IRAs, Congress included in the Pension Protection Act of 2006 a provision that allows IRA owners age 70½ or older to use their IRAs to make a lifetime gift to a qualified charitable organization—called a qualified charitable distribution or QCD—without claiming the amount taken from the IRA as taxable income. The IRA owner, however, may not also use the amount given to charity as a charitable contribution deduction on the federal income tax return. The ceiling on the amount allowed under this provision is $100,000 in 2007 and in 2006. A spouse with his or her own IRA who is also age 70½ or older at the time of the gift may also contribute up to $100,000 in 2007 as well as 2006.

This provision is especially helpful for taxpayers who do not need their required minimum distributions. They can transfer those payments directly to an eligible organization and will not have to pay income tax on the required distributions as long as their IRA gifts total $100,000 or less for the year.

The distribution should be sent electronically or by a check made payable to the charitable organization. If the IRA administrator makes the check payable to the donor and the donor deposits it into his or her bank account and writes a personal check for the charitable gift, the transaction will not be an eligible QCD.

The QCD funds must come from an IRA. Other types of retirement accounts including SEPs, SIMPLEs, TSAs or 403(b)s, 401(k)s, and pension or profit sharing accounts are not eligible. If clients who are age 70½ or older have funds in these other retirement accounts, they may be able to move a portion of that money into a Rollover IRA (which excludes any required distributions form the other retirement account); and then perform a QCD from the Rollover IRA. For the best results, taxpayers should make sure these transactions occur on separate days.

Supporting organizations, private foundations, charitable gift annuities, donor advised funds and charitable trusts are not eligible recipients of these funds. Without further legislative action, this provision of the Pension Protection Act expires December 31, 2007.

Distributions of Employer Securities

One exception to the adverse treatment of lifetime charitable gifts of retirement benefits exists for gifts of employer securities. Special rules apply to participants who have employer securities in their qualified retirement plans.

Ordinarily, a distribution during life from an IRA or qualified plan results in taxable income to the participant in the year of receipt. However, a participant who receives a lump sum distribution of employer securities may defer any current income taxation on the securities until a sale or other disposition occurs. The amount of the tax deferral is equal to the net unrealized appreciation (NUA).[10] The net unrealized appreciation is the excess of the fair market value of the employer securities on the date of distribution over the cost basis. The cost basis to the participant is equal to the cost basis the qualified plan had in the stock.[11]

Later, if the participant decides to sell the employer securities, the amount of the NUA is treated as long-term capital gain, not ordinary income.[12] The actual holding period that an employer security was held by a qualified plan need not be calculated in order to determine whether the NUA qualifies for long-term capital gain treatment. However, the participant's holding period after the date of distribution must be calculated for purposes of determining whether appreciation in the employer securities after the date of distribution is long-term or short-term capital gain.[13]

From a planning standpoint, this is one of the few instances where a lifetime distribution of a qualified plan asset may be advantageous, since the plan participant does not have to currently recognize gain on the NUA.

Example: Assume that prior to her retirement, Julia Jones was a participant in a qualified retirement plan that invested in employer securities. As a result of her retirement, Ms. Jones received a lump sum distribution that included employer securities with a fair market value of $1,000,000.

The cost basis of the stock in the plan was $150,000; therefore Ms. Jones has $850,000 in NUA. The amount currently includable in the year of distribution is only the $150,000 difference between the fair market value and the NUA. The NUA will not be includable until Ms. Jones sells or otherwise disposes of the stock.

Income in Respect of a Decedent

"Income in respect of a decedent" (IRD) is the term given to gross income to which the decedent was entitled prior to death, but which was neither taxed during the decedent's lifetime nor included on the decedent's final income tax return.[14] Common examples of IRD items include final wages, vacation pay, bonuses, proceeds from qualified retirement plans, IRAs and deferred compensation plans, life insurance commissions, and attorney and accountant fees for work in progress. IRD is taxable income to the beneficiary receiving it.

Example: Susan Berch had an IRA worth $50,000 of which her daughter, Samantha, was the beneficiary. At Susan's death, Samantha received the IRA proceeds of $50,000 and will have to include the $50,000 as income in the year she received it.[15] Samantha is entitled to a deduction on her income tax return for the amount of any estate taxes paid on these IRA proceeds, regardless of whether she was directly responsible for paying the associated estate taxes.[16] The deduction is taken as an itemized deduction on Schedule A. It is not subject to the 2% floor.[17]

Computation of income tax on IRD. It may seem that a double tax is imposed on retirement plan proceeds, when both income and estate taxes are imposed. However, since the income beneficiary is entitled to an income tax deduction for the estate taxes paid, it is not truly a double tax.

But how is the value of the IRD deduction calculated? In simple terms, the first step is to determine the estate taxes on the estate both with – and without – the value of the IRD asset. The increase in the federal taxes owed by reason of the asset is the amount available as an income tax deduction on the beneficiary's income tax return. (If more than one individual receives a portion of the IRD, the deduction is prorated among the individuals who receive it. Similarly, if the IRD is received over several years, the deduction is prorated over the years it is received.)

Example: The Williams have a taxable estate valued at $3,000,000, including an IRA valued at $1,000,000, which has no cost basis. Assume that the estate taxes on the $2,000,000 estate without the IRA would be $0, and that the $3 million estate is subject to estate taxes of $450,000. The amount of estate tax attributable to the IRA is therefore $450,000.

Next, the income tax is computed based on the value of the IRA ($1,000,000) less the amount of federal estate tax ($450,000) attributable to the IRA:

$$\begin{array}{r} \$1,000,000 \\ -450,000 \\ \hline \$550,000 \end{array}$$

Assuming an income tax rate of 35%,[18] the income tax would be:

$$\begin{array}{r} \$550,000 \\ \times.35 \\ \hline \$192,500 \end{array}$$

$1,000,000	IRA balance at death
- 450,000	federal estate taxes
- 192,500	federal income tax after IRD deduction
$ 357,500	net amount left for heirs after both taxes

This excessive taxation makes retirement assets ideal for charitable giving at death. The charity receives them on a much more tax-efficient basis, effectively free of both income and estate taxes. For children or other heirs, a bequest of assets that receive a stepped-up cost basis at death is a better, more tax-efficient plan.

Example: Assume that Eric and Christy want to leave $1,000,000 to their children, and they have both a choice of assets and strong charitable inclinations. It would be much more tax efficient to leave the children the $1,000,000 of appreciated stock instead of the $1,000,000 of IRA proceeds. The children will receive a stepped-up cost basis for the stock to the date of death value of $1,000,000. When the children sell the stock, their cost basis will be $1,000,000; thus, they will realize minimal or no capital gains. In contrast, if the children inherit the IRA, they will end up with only $357,500.

It is important to note that under EGTRRA 2001, a carryover basis system is scheduled to replace the stepped-up basis system for property acquired from a decedent dying in 2010 (the year for which the federal estate tax is repealed). However, since all provisions of EGTRRA 2001 are scheduled to sunset for years beginning after December 31, 2010, long-term planning for these changes is speculative.

Required Minimum Distributions

In order to obtain the tax-favored treatment that allows account balances to grow tax deferred during the participant's working life, qualified retirement plans, IRAs and tax sheltered annuities must meet certain distribution requirements set forth in the Internal Revenue Code. Generally, minimum annual distributions must be made beginning no later than April 1 of the year after the participant reaches age 70½.[19]

Proposed regulations were originally issued in 1987 setting forth lengthy and complex procedures for meeting these requirements. New proposed regulations were issued in January 2001 governing qualified retirement plans, IRAs, and tax sheltered annuities. Finalized regulations were issued in 2002. Although the 2002 regulations make the required distribution amounts lower and easier to calculate than under earlier regulations, the requirements remain complex and the regulations should be reviewed with respect to any specific case. Generally, the minimum distribution requirements include the following:

1. Minimum annual distributions generally must begin no later than April 1 of the year after the participant reaches age 70½.[20] This is referred to as the individual's required beginning date.

2. The distribution required each year is determined by dividing the participant's account balance as of December 31 of the preceding year by the participant's life expectancy, taken from the Uniform Lifetime Table shown in Figure 22.1.[21] The participant's age is his attained age as of his birthday in the year the distribution is made.

3. If a participant has a spouse beneficiary who is more than 10 years younger than the participant, a joint and survivor life expectancy may be used, which results in lower distribution amounts than those derived from the table in Figure 22.1.[22]

4. Except for the rule for a younger spouse, the age and status of the beneficiary do not affect the amount of a participant's lifetime distributions in any way, nor do lifetime changes to the beneficiary designation.[23]

5. The determination of the existence and identity of the designated beneficiary will generally be made as of September 30 of the year after the participant's death. Consequently, if an individual or entity was named as beneficiary at the time of death but is no longer named as of September 30 of the following year (e.g., he receives a benefit before that date, or disclaims his entitlement), he will not be considered in determining the requirements for after-death distributions.[24]

6. Distributions after the death of the participant depend on whether he dies before or after his required beginning date. If the participant dies before his required beginning date one of two methods must be used: the life expectancy rule, or the five year rule.

   a) The life expectancy rule applies if any portion of the account is payable to or for the benefit of an individual beneficiary. If the individual is a nonspouse beneficiary, distributions generally must begin by December 31 of the year after the participant's death, and be made over the individual's single life expectancy.[25]

   b) The life expectancy rule is more lenient if the sole beneficiary is the participant's surviving spouse. Distributions are not required to begin until the later of (i) December 31 of the year after the participant's death, or (ii) the end of the calendar year in which the participant would have reached age 70½.[26]

   c) Under the five year rule, the entire account balance must be distributed by December 31 of the year that contains the fifth anniversary of the participant's death.[27]

If the participant dies after distributions have begun (i.e., after his required beginning date), the remaining balance must be distributed at least as rapidly as under the method in effect at the date of death.[28] If the participant has a designated beneficiary (determined as of September 30 of the year after death), the beneficiary's interest is distributed over the beneficiary's life expectancy.[29] If the participant does not have a designated beneficiary, the remaining balance is distributed over the participant's remaining life expectancy, using his age in the calendar year of his death, reduced by one for each calendar year that elapses thereafter.[30]

7. The regulations state that an entity other than an individual or a trust meeting special requirements may not be a designated beneficiary for purposes of meeting the minimum distribution requirements.[31]

The penalty for failure to make minimum distributions is 50% of the amount involved, and it is imposed against the participant, not the plan.[32]

Planning Opportunities

The 2002 final regulations governing minimum distributions offer a number of charitable planning opportunities:

1. A charity can be named as beneficiary or co-beneficiary of a qualified plan or IRA during the participant's lifetime without adverse tax consequences, since the designation of a charity as a beneficiary will not affect the calculation of lifetime required distributions. (Under the pre-2001 regulations, such a designation could result in some acceleration of income tax.)

2. Since the identity of the "designated beneficiaries" is not determined until September 30 following the year of the decedent's death, charitable beneficiaries can be paid their share of a retirement plan benefit prior to the September 30 cutoff date. In this way, designated beneficiaries who want to "stretch-out" their distributions can remain beneficiaries for purposes of the post-death minimum distribution rules.

Example: David Wine is an IRA owner who has an account balance of $1,000,000 as of December 31, 2005. David's date of birth was March 3, 1936; thus, he reached age 70½ on September 3, 2006 and has a required beginning date of April 1, 2007. David's required minimum distribution is not affected by the identity or existence of a designated beneficiary, unless

Figure 22.1

Age of the Employee	Distribution Period	Age of the Employee	Distribution Period	Age of the Employee	Distribution Period
70	26.2	86	13.1	101	5.3
71	25.3	87	12.4	102	5.0
72	24.4	88	11.8	103	4.7
73	23.5	89	11.1	104	4.4
74	22.7	90	10.5	105	4.1
75	21.8	91	9.9	106	3.8
76	20.9	92	9.4	107	3.6
77	20.1	93	8.8	108	3.3
78	19.2	94	8.3	109	3.1
79	18.4	95	7.8	110	2.8
80	17.6	96	7.3	111	2.6
81	16.8	97	6.9	112	2.4
82	16.0	98	6.5	113	2.2
83	15.3	99	6.1	114	2.0
84	14.5	100	5.7	115 and older	1.8
85	13.8				

he has a spouse more than 10 years younger who is named as the beneficiary of the account. Using the table set forth in Figure 22.1, David's distribution is calculated as follows:

$1,000,000 /27.4 years = $36,496

This means that if David names his favorite charity as the beneficiary of his retirement plan, his lifetime minimum distributions will not be affected. Furthermore, distributions after David's death will not be affected by the designation of the charity as a beneficiary as long as the charity is paid its share of the retirement plan prior to September 30 of the year following David's death.

Suppose David names the American Cancer Society and his daughter, Claire, each as 50% beneficiaries of his IRA, and then he dies in 2007. If the American Cancer Society takes receipt of the 50% distribution before September 30, 2008, Claire will be the only "designated beneficiary" for distribution purposes. Claire may stretch the IRA distributions out over her remaining life expectancy.

Estate Tax

Under EGTRRA 2001, the federal estate tax rates are scheduled for incremental reduction through 2009, and for repeal in 2010.[33] For most purposes, the repeal of the estate tax for only one year means that planning should be done as though there were no repeal.

Upon the death of the plan participant, the account proceeds generally may pass to the surviving spouse free of income and estate taxes due to the unlimited marital deduction and the spousal rollover option.

If a charitable contribution of the plan proceeds is made at the second spouse's death, the account proceeds will escape income taxation because the charity is a tax-exempt entity. In addition, the account values will effectively escape estate taxation at the second spouse's death. While the estate will technically include the values of the account in the decedent's gross estate, the estate will also receive an estate tax charitable deduction for the same amount – thus equating to a "wash," and no estate taxes will be assessed. See "How is it Done" above for an example of the effect of a charitable gift on the treatment of an IRA.

WHERE CAN I FIND OUT MORE ABOUT IT?

1. Leimberg, Stephan R., et al., *The Tools & Techniques of Estate Planning*, 11th edition (Cincinnati, OH: The National Underwriter Company, 1998).

2. Prince, Russ Alan, et al., *The Charitable Giving Handbook*, 1st edition (Cincinnati, OH: The National Underwriter Company, 1997).

3. Toce, Joseph P., *Tax Economics of Charitable Giving*, 2005-2006 edition (Warren Gorham & Lamont of RIA, 2005).

4. Osteen, Carolyn M., et al., *The Harvard Manual On Tax Aspects of Charitable Giving*, 8th edition (Boston, MA: 1999).

5. Aston, Debra, *The Complete Guide to Planned Giving*, 3rd edition (Quincy, MA: Ashton Associates, 2004).

6. Miree, Kathryn, *Professional Advisors Guide to Planned Giving*, 2006 edition (Aspen Publishers, Inc: 2005).

QUESTIONS AND ANSWERS

Question – What types of retirement plans can be used for charitable planning?

Answer – The rules explained in this chapter apply to any plan qualified under IRC Section 401, which includes pensions, profit sharing plans, 401(k) plans, ESOPs, and money purchase plans. In addition, these rules apply (with some minor exceptions as noted) to Keogh plans, tax sheltered annuities, traditional IRAs, SEPs, and SIMPLE IRAs.

Question – Can the planning techniques described in this chapter be used for Roth IRAs?

Answer – The lifetime planning techniques and minimum distribution rules described in this chapter are not applicable to Roth IRAs. However, Roth IRAs are subject to the same after-death minimum distribution requirements as traditional IRAs.[34]

Question – Is an estate tax charitable deduction available where a private non-operating "family" foundation is named as beneficiary of an IRA or plan benefit?

Answer – Probably. The IRS addressed this issue in a 1999 private ruling,[35] where a taxpayer owned an IRA of which he named a private foundation as the beneficiary. The Service determined that his estate would be entitled to a federal estate tax charitable deduction for the amount paid from the IRA to the foundation. The Service also determined that the proceeds would be taxed to the foundation, not his estate.

The IRS also determined in a 1998 ruling that distributions of retirement plan assets to a private family foundation upon the death of the plan participant did not trigger excise taxes under IRC Section 4940, because the proceeds retained their character as deferred compensation, not investment income.[36]

Question – Are there any restrictions on participants who name a charity as the beneficiary of a qualified plan benefit instead of the surviving spouse?

Answer – In order to be qualified, a retirement plan must meet certain requirements set forth in the Internal Revenue Code designed to protect the interests of married individuals in their spouses' qualified plan benefits. Consequently, a married participant in a qualified retirement plan must obtain written consent to any designation of a nonspouse (e.g., a charity) as beneficiary of the account.[37] This requirement does not extend to IRAs.

Question – Should the donor designate a charity as the retirement plan beneficiary in his will or revocable living trust document?

Answer – No. The retirement plan administrator will have its own documentation to name the beneficiary of the account. If the plan participant does not name a beneficiary, most plans name the estate of the participant as the default beneficiary.

Question – Is an estate entitled to a charitable deduction if the beneficiary designation form names the "estate of the participant" as the primary beneficiary, and the participant's will directs which charity is to receive the account balance?

Answer – An estate tax charitable deduction is available for the value of a plan benefit that is paid by the estate to charity. However, this course of action is bound to cause trouble. Since the plan beneficiary is the estate, the estate will receive the distribution and must pay income tax on it as income in respect of a decedent (IRD). This exposes the distribution to potential claims of creditors against the estate, and results in unnecessary income taxes. To avoid this situation, the charity should be named as beneficiary of the account. The participant should never name his estate as beneficiary if his intention is to make a charitable gift of the retirement funds.

CHAPTER ENDNOTES

1. The rules explained in this chapter apply to traditional IRAs. For SEPs and SIMPLE IRAs, the rules described in this chapter are generally the same as for traditional IRAs unless otherwise noted. Different rules apply to Roth IRAs, which are funded with after-tax dollars.

2. See IRC Sec. 401(a)(9).

3. See Treas. Reg. §1.401(a)(9)-5, A-4(a).

4. This example assumes a federal estate tax rate of 45%, and that the unified credit has been used for other assets. For details on the tax implications of this example and the effect of EGTRRA 2001 on the federal estate tax, see "What are the Tax Implications?"

5. The top marginal income tax bracket of 35% in 2007 is assumed for this example. The IRA is income in respect of a decedent (IRD) and the estate tax attributable to the IRA is deductible for income tax purposes.

6. This does not take into account the value of the heirs' income tax deduction for income in respect of a decedent, which is explained later in this chapter.

7. Let. Rul. 199901023.

8. Under EGTRRA, the exemption equivalent amount is scheduled to increase through 2009. IRC Sec. 2010(c), as amended by EGTRRA 2001.

9. See IRC Sec. 72(t). In the case of a SIMPLE IRA, the penalty is 25% during the first two years of participation.

10. IRC Sec. 402(e)(4).

11. Treas. Reg. §1.402(a)-1(b)(2)(I).

12. Notice 98-24, 1998-1 CB 929.

13. IRS Notice 98-24, above. See also Let. Rul. 199919039.

14. Treas. Reg. §1.691(a)-1(b).

15. See IRC Secs. 691(a)(1), 102.

16. See IRC Sec. 691(c)(1)(a); Treas. Reg. §1.691(c)-1a).

17. See IRC Sec. 67(b)(7).

18. This example assumes a marginal rate of 35%, which is the top income tax rate in effect for 2007.

19. IRC Secs. 408(a)(6), 408(b)(3), 401(a)(9), 403(b)(10).

20. This required beginning date applies to all IRA owners. For qualified plan participants, the required beginning date is April 1 of the calendar year following the *later* of (a) the year in which the employee attains age 70«, or (b) the year in which the employee (other than a 5% owner) retires from the employer maintaining the plan. IRC Sec. 401(a)(9)(C).

21. Treas. Reg. §1.401(a)(9)-5, A-4(a).

22. See Treas. Reg. §1.401(a)(9)-5, A-4(b). (The life expectancy table for this purpose is determined under Table VI of Treas. Reg. §1.72-9.)

23. See Treas. Reg. §1.401(a)(9)-5, A-4.

24. Treas. Reg. §1.401(a)(9)-4, A-4(a).

25. IRC Sec. 401(a)(9)(B)(iii); Treas. Reg. §1.401(a)(9)-3, A-1(a). Generally, Tables V and VI of Treas. Reg. §1.72-9 are to be used to determine life expectancies. Treas. Reg. §1.401(a)(9)-5, A-6.

26. See IRC Sec. 401(a)(9)(B)(iv); Treas. Reg. §1.401(a)(9)-3, A-3.

27. IRC Sec. 401(a)(9)(B)(ii), Treas. Regs. §§1.401(a)(9)-3, A-1(a); 1.401(a)(9)-3, A-2.

28. See IRC Sec. 401(a)(9)(B)(i).

29. Treas. Reg. §1.401(a)(9)-5, A-5(a)(1).

30. See Treas. Reg. §1.401(a)(9)-5, A-5(c)(3).

31. Treas. Reg. §1.401(a)(9)-4, A-3.

32. See IRC Sec. 4974. However, the penalty will be waived if it can be shown the shortfall was due to reasonable error, and that reasonable steps are being taken to remedy the shortfall. Treas. Reg. §54.4974-2, A-7(a).

33. IRC Sec. 2210, as amended by EGTRRA 2001.

34. See IRC Sec. 408A(c)(5).

35. See Let. Rul. 199939039.

36. See Let. Rul. 9838028.

37. See IRC Sec. 417(a)(2); Treas. Reg. §1.401(a)-20, A-31.

TESTAMENTARY GIFTS

CHAPTER 23

WHAT IS IT?

Testamentary gifts are gifts made at the death of the donor. Such gifts may arise from one of several different legal documents, such as from the donor's last will and testament or revocable living trust. Also, gifts can be made directly to the charity at the donor's death through contractual methods such as beneficiary designations of life insurance, retirement plans, annuities, IRAs, 401(k) plans, and other vehicles.

These types of testamentary gifts are popular charitable gifts. One of the reasons for their popularity is that donors don't have to deprive themselves of ownership, control, or use of the asset during their lifetimes. Instead they retain control over the asset during their lifetime and don't have to part with it until death. Many donors want to retain control and ownership of their assets for as long as possible. The security of knowing the asset is always available if needed is important to many donors. Hence, testamentary gifts are far more common, and in many cases significantly larger, than lifetime gifts.

The type of testamentary gift arising from the decedent's last will and testament or revocable living trust can be made in one of several ways:

- Pecuniary Amount

- Percentage/Fractional Bequests

- Specific/General Bequests

- Contingent Bequests

- Testamentary Split Interest Gifts

Pecuniary Amount

This technique is the simplest type of testamentary gift. It is a flat dollar amount directed to a particular charity (e.g., "I direct $800,000 to be paid from my estate to the Greater Des Moines Community Foundation").

Percentage/Fractional Bequests

The decedent may state in the last will and testament or trust that either a percentage of the estate or a fractional share be transferred to a charitable organization. A gift of a percentage of the residuary estate can be exemplified by, "I direct 30% of my estate assets to the American Lung Association." These types of gifts can easily track with increases or decreases in the donor's estate values from the date of execution of the will or trust until the date of death.

There are both potential advantages – and disadvantages – to each of these two types of testamentary techniques: pecuniary amounts and percentage/fractional bequests. For example, assume the decedent has a total estate of $4,000,000. He leaves a pecuniary amount of $1,000,000 of his estate (not a fractional bequest of 1/4) to a charitable organization. If the estate loses value and is only worth $3,000,000 as of the date of death, the charity receives $1,000,000, 1/3 of the estate. On the other hand, if the decedent's will (or trust) provided for a 25% interest to be paid to the charity, the charity would receive $750,000 and not $1,000,000. Obviously, the difference can be quite significant – both to the charity and to the decedent's other beneficiaries. So it is important that the client understand the implications of the two different types of wording.

Specific/General Bequests

A specific charitable bequest is a gift of a very specific or particular asset. For example, "I bequeath my 2005 Oldsmobile LSS to the Miami Women's Shelter." If, as of the date of death, the decedent no longer owned the

specific asset (in this case, the car) but had instead traded that car in for a 2007 model, the charity will not receive the 2007 car. They will receive nothing. To avoid any problems or confusion, gifts of specific assets should generally use the phrase, "if I own it upon my death" as part of the bequest.

A general charitable bequest can be described in the following manner: "I give any car I may own upon my death to the Miami Women's Shelter." In the above example, had the decedent made a general bequest, the charity would receive the 2007 car and would not have been disinherited. (Often, the bequest will also specify that it includes any insurance on the asset – so if the car is in an accident and totaled – the bequest would still be completed and the beneficiary would receive the casualty insurance proceeds.)

Contingent Bequests

A contingent bequest can be stated in the following format, "I bequeath my Renoir painting to the Public Art Museum of Washington DC for as long as the Renoir is displayed in the Washington Museum."

If, as of the date of the decedent's death, a transfer to a charity is dependent upon the performance of an act or happening of an event, no charitable deduction is allowed unless the possibility that the charity might not receive the property is so remote as to be considered negligible.[1] "Remote" is defined as where the probability of the charity not receiving the property is 5% or less.[2]

Therefore, a bequest of unimproved land to the local Methodist church, for as long as the church uses the land for a playground, must show the contingency to "be so remote as to be negligible" or else the charitable deduction will be disallowed by the IRS. In this example, the church will receive the land upon the donor's death, but only as long as it holds the land for the children's playground. If the possibility that the land will not be used for a playground is not that remote as to be negligible, the charitable deduction will be disallowed.

TESTAMENTARY
SPLIT INTEREST GIFTS

The following types of gifts can be made while the grantor of the gift is living or upon the death of the decedent. These gifts are called "split-interest" gifts. The interest is split between the charity and a noncharitable beneficiary. Accordingly, the full value of the asset is not eligible for a charitable deduction. In fact, no portion of a charitable gift of less than the donor's entire interest is deductible for either estate, gift, or income tax purposes – unless the gift falls within one of the four following statutorily excepted categories:[3]

- Charitable Remainder Trusts (CRTs)

- Charitable Lead Trusts (CLTs)

- Pooled Income Funds

- Remainder Interests in a Farm or Personal Residence

Even if the gift does meet the strict IRC definition and requirements of one of these four exceptions from the general rule (that a partial interest gift is not deductible), only the value of the charity's interest will be deductible. No deduction will be allowed for that portion of the value of the gift that will remain with – or pass to – any noncharitable beneficiary.

Charitable Remainder Trusts

A charitable remainder trust (CRT) is the most common form of split interest gifts. A CRT will provide a stream of payments to a noncharitable beneficiary for either (a) one or more specified lifetime(s), or (b) a term of up to 20 years. At the end of the noncharitable beneficiary's interest, the remainder of the assets in the trust is transferred to the charity as specified in the trust document. Two major types of charitable remainder trusts are available, a charitable remainder unitrust (CRUT) or a charitable remainder annuity trust (CRAT).

A testamentary charitable remainder trust may be created from the decedent's last will and testament or as a "pour over" from a previously existing living trust. The donor will name the noncharitable beneficiary to receive the annuity or unitrust payments in the document, as well as the percentage or amount to be paid. The will/trust will also designate the remainder charitable beneficiary.

Upon the funding of the CRT at the donor's death, the decedent's estate will be eligible for an estate tax charitable deduction. That deduction will be based on the present value of the charity's remainder interest.[4] The value of the noncharitable beneficiary's interest is subject to estate taxes. However, if the noncharitable beneficiary is solely the decedent's surviving spouse, that spouse's interest will typically qualify for the unlimited marital deduction and eliminate any federal estate tax. But the present value (measured as of the date of the donor's death) of the interest of a noncharitable beneficiary other than the spouse will remain in the decedent's taxable estate.

Example: Donna Smith establishes a testamentary CRAT upon her death. The trust is funded with $1,000,000. The trust provides a fixed annual annuity of 5.5% of the initial trust corpus, i.e., $55,000 a year. The annuity beneficiary is her niece and the annuity is payable for the niece's lifetime. The estate tax deduction is equal to the excess of the value of the property transferred to trust over the present value of a stream of $55,000 a year for the lifetime of a person the niece's age. So if the niece were age 55, and the appropriate federal discount (IRC Section 7520) rate[5] was 6.0%, assuming annual payments made at the end of each year, the deduction would be $348,475.[6] If the annuity beneficiary were older, the income tax deduction would be larger (e.g., $602,081 at age 75).

If Donna had created a testamentary CRUT at her death, again funding it with $1,000,000, and the trust provided a variable annual annuity equal to 5.5% of the annually re-valued trust principal (i.e., a unitrust), the estate's deduction would have been $316,520 assuming payments were to be made for the life of a 55 year old, the same 6.0% Section 7520 rate, and assuming payout at the end of each year (i.e., 12 months after annual valuation of trust assets). (Note: In a CRUT, the deduction is essentially "payout" driven rather than determined on the Section 7520 rate. This means even relatively large changes in the Section 7520 rate will not significantly – or in most cases – visibly – change the size of the deduction). What does have a significant and obvious impact on the size of the deduction is an upward or downward change in the payout percentage.)

Charitable Lead Trusts

A decedent may create a charitable lead trust (CLT) from his last will and testament or revocable living trust.

A charitable lead trust will provide a stream of payments to a charity for a specified period of time or for one or more lives. At the end of the period, the trust assets are transferred to noncharitable beneficiaries, commonly family members.

A charitable lead trust can be categorized as either a charitable lead annuity trust (CLAT) or a charitable lead unitrust (CLUT). The estate receives an estate tax deduction for the present value of the charity's annuity or unitrust interest.[7] In other words, the estate will receive a deduction equal to the present value of the right to receive an annuity or unitrust for the specified number of years.

The testamentary document will name the specific charitable beneficiary, the percentage or amount of the trust's principal to pay to the charity in the form of an annuity or unitrust, and the length of time (generally in whole years) that payments will be made. The noncharitable remainder beneficiary is also named in the document.

The benefit of a testamentary CLT is that the donor is allowed to transfer an asset to his heirs at a deferred date with a reduced estate tax cost. In the meantime, the asset will generate income that will benefit the donor's favorite charity.

Example: Assume Jack Ryan donates 500 acres of land in Arizona worth $1,000,000 to a charitable lead annuity trust. The trust will pay to one or more specified charity(ies) a fixed 7% annuity for a 10-year period. At the end of the 10-year period, the trust will transfer the land to Jack's daughter, Nina (or hold it for her benefit). The charity will receive $700,000 ($70,000 a year for 10 years, at the end of each year). Assuming a 6.0% Section 7520 rate, Jack's estate would receive a charitable estate tax deduction of $515,207. Nina receives the 500 acres of land in 10 years. Assuming no growth in the value of the land, Nina receives property worth $1,000,000 but Jack's estate only paid taxes based on a value of $484,793 ($1,000,000 - $515,207). Any further appreciation in the land's value after the date of death will escape taxation. So the CLT is particularly useful where it is highly likely that the property placed into it will generate income and appreciation equal to or greater than the payout rate promised to the charity.

All else being equal, the longer the term of years the charity will receive the annuity or unitrust, or the higher percentage of the trust's value paid to the charity as an annuity or unitrust, the larger the charitable estate tax deduction from a CLT.

Pooled Income Funds

The decedent may establish in his last will and testament a bequest to a pooled income fund (PIF). A pooled income fund is a trust to which a donor gives property while retaining an income stream for one or more noncharitable beneficiary(ies). The testamentary document may name the specific pooled income fund as the remainder beneficiary or the document may leave that discretion to the decedent-donor's executor or trustee. The donor will also name the individuals who will be the income beneficiaries. The income paid to the beneficiaries is a function of the total income earned by the fund, which pools all the donated assets together. The total income is divided by the number of units of participation each beneficiary owns and is distributed accordingly.

The donor's estate will be entitled to a federal estate tax charitable deduction for the amount of the gift equal to the present value of the pooled income fund's remainder interest. The present value of the income beneficiary's interest will be subject to estate tax. The only exception is if the spouse of the donor is the income beneficiary. In that case, the election can be made to qualify the property for the marital deduction as QTIP property. With a spouse as the income beneficiary, the full value of the asset given to the pooled income fund should escape all federal estate taxes.

Example: Assume Joe Brown donates $1,000,000 to a pooled income fund at his death. The pooled income fund will pay to his niece, age 55, a share of the income of the pooled income fund each year for her life. At her death, the charity receives the niece's share of the pooled income fund (essentially, whatever remains of the original $1,000,000 after investment and payments). Assuming the highest rate of return for the pooled income fund for the preceding three years was 4.8%, Joe's estate would receive a charitable estate tax deduction of $356,830.[8]

Remainder Interest in a Farm or Personal Residence

This type of charitable gift is evidenced by a devise of a life estate in the decedent's farm or personal residence to a noncharitable beneficiary. Upon the death of the holder of the life estate, the remainder interest in either the farm or personal residence is transferred to the specified charity.

Example: Dennis and Karen Johnson wish to leave their farmland to the local Make-A-Wish Foundation. When Dennis dies, in his will, he leaves Karen a life estate in the farm. He provides that the remainder interest passes at Karen's death to the charity.

The present value of the remainder interest in the farm or personal residence is the value eligible for an estate tax charitable deduction.[9] The value of the life estate is includable in the decedent's gross estate, unless the spouse is the holder of the life estate. In that situation, the value of the life estate can qualify for the unlimited marital deduction and will eliminate any federal estate tax it would otherwise have generated.

WHEN IS THE USE OF SUCH A DEVICE INDICATED?

Testamentary gifts made upon the death of the donor are particularly suitable for donors who would rather not make lifetime gifts but instead would like to keep the assets available for their lifetime use.

This technique is also valuable for donors who may not need a current income tax deduction, but may have an estate tax problem upon death. Testamentary gifts offer charitable estate tax deductions, not lifetime charitable deductions.

The revocable nature of testamentary gifts is also a key advantage for those donors who don't wish to, or aren't ready to, make a permanent lifetime gift. Testamentary gifts made via the donor's will or revocable living trust are amendable or revocable at any time prior to death just as any other will or trust provision is amendable or revocable prior to death. This enables the donor to retain complete and total control and flexibility over the asset for life.

ADVANTAGES

1. The donor retains lifetime control over the asset.

2. The gift is revocable at anytime until the date of death.

3. Testamentary gifts provide the donor with a full charitable estate tax deduction.

4. The donor can make a gift to a 30% charity without affecting the amount of the charitable deduction.

5. Using the wealth replacement trust concept (see Chapter 13), the donor's heirs can still receive their full inheritance.

DISADVANTAGES

1. Unless the donor employs the wealth replacement technique, the donor's heirs may feel disinherited with respect to the asset given to charity.

2. The donor doesn't have the ability to see the charity put the gift to immediate use.

WHAT ARE THE REQUIREMENTS?

The donor must generally use a will valid under state law or a trust document valid in the state of situs to provide a testamentary gift. To repeat: The state requirements for a valid will or trust must be followed in order for the document to be valid under state law.

At first blush, this type of gift may appear simple to construct in the will or trust. However, the technical requirements for a charitable deduction can be more difficult to qualify for than one may think.

The amount of the charitable estate tax deduction is equal to the fair market value of the gift. The deduction is reduced by the amount of any debt or encumbrance on the property.

Example: Jim Ray has property worth $1,000,000 with a mortgage of $200,000. If that property is bequeathed outright to charity upon Jim's death, the fair market value of the asset is $1,000,000 minus the debt of $200,000. Hence, Jim's estate tax charitable deduction is equal to $800,000.

The amount of the charitable bequest must be ascertainable and definite. This means that the document must be clear in stating the specific amount transferred to charity.

The key to a qualifying testamentary bequest is that the personal representative or executor must not have any discretion with respect to the amount of the charitable gift or the estate tax deduction will be disallowed. Words that have proven fatal for an estate tax charitable deduction are "empowering" a trustee or executor with the ability to determine the amount of the charitable bequest, or giving the trustee/executor the "discretion," the "option," or the "ability" to decide as they deem best.

The requirement for definiteness does not apply to the identity of the charitable beneficiary as long as the bequest is to a "qualified" charity. (The "rule of thumb" test of a qualified charity is that a person would receive an income tax deduction for a lifetime gift to that charity. See below for more on this.) For example, the executor or trustee generally can be given the authority to choose the charitable organizations that will be the recipients of the stated bequest (or even vary the percentage of gifts) as long as the amount of the overall bequest is certain. The person holding the authority does so in a fiduciary capacity.

Cy Pres Doctrine

Cy pres is a legal term that literally means "as near as possible." Cy pres has become a doctrine that courts can use when the charitable beneficiary is not definite, or, at the time of the actual gift, is no longer a viable charity, or the charitable purpose of the donor is impossible. The court, by using this doctrine, attempts to make the charitable bequest in the form and manner "as nearly as possible" to what the court believes the decedent intended. If the cy pres doctrine is not followed by the court in a given situation (not all states recognize the cy pres doctrine), the charitable estate tax deduction will not be allowed.

WHICH CHARITIES QUALIFY FOR AN ESTATE TAX CHARITABLE DEDUCTION?

The decedent has more flexibility in the types of charitable organizations to name as recipients of testamentary

gifts than he does in naming lifetime charitable recipients for income tax purposes. More specifically, the types of charities that can receive a decedent's charitable bequest at death are not divided into 50% and 30% charities. Gifts to both types of organizations are eligible for a full and unlimited estate tax charitable deduction. However, the charitable recipient must be a qualified charity under IRC Section 2055(a).

Section 2055(a) charitable organizations are as follows:

(1) The United States, any State, any political subdivision thereof, or the District of Columbia, for exclusively public purposes;

(2) Any corporation organized and operated exclusively for religious, charitable, scientific, literary, or educational purposes, including the encouragement of art, or to foster national or international amateur sports competition (but only if no part of its activities involve the provision of athletic facilities or equipment), and the prevention of cruelty to children or animals, no part of the net earnings of which inures to the benefit of any private stockholder or individual, which is not disqualified for tax exemption under IRC Section 501(c)(3) by reason of attempting to influence legislation, and which does not participant in, or intervene in (including the publishing or distributing of statements), any political campaign on behalf of (or in opposition to) any candidate for public office;

(3) A trustee or trustees, or a fraternal society, order, or association operating under the lodge system, but only if such contributions or gifts are to be used by such trustee or trustees, or by such fraternal society, order or association, exclusively for religious, charitable, scientific, literary, or educational purposes, or for the prevention of cruelty to children or animals, such trust, fraternal society, order or association would not be disqualified for tax exemption under IRC Section 501(c)(3) by reason of attempting to influence legislation, and such trustee or trustees, or such fraternal society, order, or association does not participate in, or intervene in, (including the publishing or distributing of statements), any political campaign on behalf of (or in opposition to) any candidate for public office;

(4) Any veteran's organization incorporated by Act of Congress, or of its departments or local chapters or posts, no part of the net earnings of which inures to the benefit of any private shareholder or individual; or

(5) An employee stock ownership plan if such transfer qualifies as a qualified gratuitous transfer of qualified employer securities within the meaning of IRC Section 664(g).

Although in most cases, there will be no practical distinction, planners should be aware that slight – and at times and under special circumstances – significant – and meaningful differences will exist between the charities that qualify for an income tax deduction (IRC Section 170) and the charities that qualify for an estate tax deduction (IRC Section 2055) or a gift tax deduction (IRC Section 2522). Section 2055(a) does not require that a charitable trust be organized and operated exclusively for charitable purposes, only that a contribution to a trust be used exclusively for charitable purposes. Further, there is no limit on the dollar amount an estate can deduct at death; limitations exist on the dollar amount available for lifetime charitable income tax deductions. Further, in testamentary gifts to charity, no distinction is made between gifts of long term capital gain property and ordinary income property.

HOW IS IT DONE?

Example: Patty Edwards has a will drafted by a local estate planning attorney. She stipulates in her will that she would like 25% of her residuary estate to go to the local chapter of the American Lung Association. Her estate consists of $4,000,000 of stock. Her only other beneficiary is her husband and he is to receive 75% of the residuary estate.

The probate estate will then distribute $3,000,000 to the spouse and $1,000,000 to the American Lung Association.

The federal taxable estate is:

$4,000,000	gross estate
- $1,000,000	charitable estate tax deduction
- $3,000,000	unlimited marital deduction
$ 0	taxable estate

Figure 23.1

Lifetime Gifts vs. Testamentary Gift		
	Lifetime Charitable Gifts	**Testamentary Charitable Gifts**
What IRC Section generally applies?	IRC Sec. 170	IRC Sec. 2055
Tax base against which charitable deduction is allowed.	Income tax base	Estate tax base
Is the amount of the charitable deduction limited?	Yes, the amount of the charitable income tax deduction is limited to a percentage of the donor's Adjusted Gross Income.	No. The decedent can give any amount of his/her estate to a qualified charity without limitation.
Do differences exist in the amount of the eligible tax deduction depending on the type of charity receiving the gift?	Yes. Gifts to public charities, supporting foundations, and private operating foundations (50% charities) are eligible for a larger potential deduction than gifts to private family foundations (30% charities).	No. The decedent's estate is entitled to a charitable deduction of the same amount regardless of whether the recipient is a 50% or a 30% charity.
Do different tax deductible amounts exist for gifts of tangible personal property?	Yes, depending on whether the gift is of an object that is related to the charity's use and operation.	No.
Does a difference exist in the amount of the charitable deduction if the property donated is long-term capital gain property versus ordinary income property?	Yes. Gifts of long-term gain property are generally given a lower overall percentage of AGI (30/20%) over ordinary income property (50%).	No.
Is the charitable deduction based on the property's fair market value at the time of the gift?	Not always. Certain gifts are limited to the lesser of fair market value or cost basis. See the Appendix for full details.	Yes.

Therefore, no estate taxes are due at Patty's death.

ISSUES WITH SPECIFIC PROPERTY

Tangible Personal Property

The decedent who transfers tangible personal property (e.g., a valuable work of art) outright at death is entitled to an estate tax deduction equal to the fair market value of the property. Donating tangible personal property to a public charity at the death of the donor may be preferable to lifetime gifts. The advantage is due to the fact that the income tax charitable deduction lifetime gift restrictions (e.g., property put to an unrelated use) on tangible personal property do not apply for testamentary gifts. This may be especially important with respect to gifts to charity by an artist or creator of other intellectual property. Such a gift, if made during lifetime, generates an income tax deduction limited to the creator's out-of-pocket costs – rather than the value of the assets. But if made at death, the entire fair market value is deductible for estate tax purposes – without limit.

Income in Respect of a Decedent

Income in respect of a decedent (IRD) is income still owed to the decedent as of the date of death – but untaxed by that time. A common example of IRD includes wages, bonuses, commissions, and fees earned but not yet paid or taxed. Other assets which contain income and gains that have never been taxed (such as pensions, IRAs, deferred compensation, and stock options[10]) are also considered items of IRD. The tax treatment of items of IRD follows the asset to the beneficiary. To illustrate, if the beneficiary of an IRA is a named beneficiary (and not the decedent's "estate"), the tax on the IRD is assessed to the IRA beneficiary, not the decedent's estate. The tax is imposed at the time of receipt.

Items of IRD are treated differently than other estate assets. IRD assets do not receive a stepped-up cost basis as of the date of death. However, the beneficiary is allowed an income tax deduction for the recipient's portion of any estate taxes paid on the IRD asset.

Due to the "double tax" against IRD items (estate and income taxes), these assets are generally the most tax-inefficient assets one can inherit. Some planners even call these "junk assets." Accordingly, IRD assets are prime targets for charitable gifts. By donating IRD assets to charity, both the income taxes and the estate taxes can be entirely eliminated, since the charity is a tax-exempt entity.

Testamentary Gifts of Life Insurance

Charitable gifts of life insurance are one of the most effective and efficient ways to make charitable bequests.

If the decedent is the policy owner and the insured, the value of the proceeds are in the decedent's gross estate for federal estate tax purposes. When the policy owner names a charity as the specific beneficiary of the policy proceeds, the estate is allowed an estate tax charitable deduction for the full amount of the death benefit paid.

A testamentary gift of life insurance to a charity is a gift free of both estate and income taxes. Because of the contractual nature of life insurance, death proceeds will also bypass the probate process when the policy owner names a specific beneficiary, other than the insured's estate.

The donor is not entitled to an income tax deduction for the amount of premiums paid on the policy when the donor has merely named a charity as the beneficiary of the death proceeds. The donor would need to make a lifetime gift of the policy's ownership and the charity would have to own absolute and complete rights over the policy in order to be entitled to an income tax deduction for paying the insurance policy premiums.

If the insured makes a lifetime gift of the policy to a charity, the charity normally also names itself as the policy beneficiary. In this situation, when the insured dies, the policy is not taxed in the insured's gross estate if the insured has lived at least three years from the date of the gift.

If, on the other hand, the insured dies within three years of transferring the policy to a charity, the policy is included in the insured's gross estate, but the estate is entitled to a charitable estate tax deduction for the amount of the proceeds. This amounts to a complete "wash," and hence no estate taxes are assessed on the value of the life insurance policy

Commercial Annuities

Commercial annuities are excellent assets to give at death to charity. When annuities are bequeathed to a noncharitable beneficiary, the beneficiary generally must pay income tax on the gain in the annuity. But, if a qualified charity is the beneficiary of a deferred annuity, the charity, as a tax-exempt entity, will receive the annuity free of any income tax liability. Therefore, it is more tax efficient for a decedent to give a commercial deferred annuity to charity than to a noncharitable beneficiary.

WHAT ARE THE TAX IMPLICATIONS?

Charitable Estate Tax Deduction

The assets donated outright to charity at death are included in the gross estate of the decedent as property owned by the decedent. (EGTRRA 2001 repeals the estate tax for one year in 2010.) The estate tax charitable deduction is then subtracted from the gross estate. The charitable estate tax deduction is generally equal to the fair market value of the property, reduced by any mortgage or other debt. This is true whether the property is long-term capital gain type property or ordinary income property.

Property Included in Decedent's Gross Estate

Two requirements are necessary for a testamentary bequest to qualify for the estate tax charitable deduction:

1. The property must be included in the donor/decedent's gross estate for estate tax purposes, and

2. The property must be transferred by the decedent.[11]

A person's gross estate is not the same as a decedent's probate estate. Therefore, even nonprobate property, i.e., assets passing outside probate by contract or by law (e.g., life insurance, deferred annuities, qualified plans, and IRAs) can be eligible for an estate tax charitable deduction.

The requirement that the property must be included in the gross estate can be illustrated by the following example: Larry Hogan has life insurance owned in his own name and also has life insurance inside an irrevocable life insurance trust for which he is the grantor. If both policies name his synagogue as the beneficiary, the personally owned policy will receive a charitable estate tax deduction. The policy payable from the life insurance trust will not. The policy owned by the life insurance trust was not included in Larry's gross estate. Incidentally, neither policy was part of Larry's probate estate.

Payment of Estate Taxes

Depending on the will or trust document, the payment of estate taxes may be payable from the assets donated to charity or may be payable from the decedent's residuary estate.

The decedent always has the right to direct in his will or trust the source from which property the estate taxes will be paid. For example, the will could state, "I direct all taxes to be paid from the residuary estate." Or, "I direct all taxes to be paid proportionately from each beneficiary."

Absent a specific provision in the will, the general rule (state law controls) is, under the Uniform Apportionment of Estate Tax Act, that each beneficiary of the estate bears his proportionate share of the estate taxes. Hence, the charitable beneficiary would not normally have a share of the estate tax to pay since the charitable gifts incurred or generated no estate tax liability. The implication is that the noncharitable beneficiaries would therefore have to share the estate tax burden, a result the client may – or may not – have anticipated or desired.

The decedent's estate tax return is required to disclose the amount of the charitable estate tax deduction.[12] The executor must declare the charitable gifts on Schedule O of the U.S. Estate Tax Return (Form 706).

Note, however, for testamentary charitable remainder trusts, the estate taxes cannot be paid from the CRT assets. To do (or even permit) so would disqualify the charitable remainder trust. Therefore, other estate assets must be used to pay for any estate taxes incurred on the annuity or unitrust beneficiary's interest.

QTIP Property

The donor may wish to make a charitable contribution with property, but at the same time, make a lifetime income interest available to the surviving spouse.

This technique can be implemented by setting up a QTIP trust which will provide lifetime income interest to the surviving spouse and, then, upon the death of the surviving spouse, the remainder interest would be transferred to the charity named in the donor's trust documents.

The donor's estate is not given a full estate tax deduction in this instance. Instead, the entire value is given an unlimited marital deduction.

In the surviving spouse's estate, the remainder value of the property is then given a charitable deduction. Hence, the bottom line is the entire QTIP trust bypasses all estate taxes, but the process occurs over two estates.

Example: Bill and Renee Baldwin have $500,000 of land in Florida. Bill sets up in his last will and testament that his land becomes part of a QTIP trust. The trust will pay all the income to Renee for her remaining lifetime. In Bill's estate, the $500,000 of QTIP property qualifies for the unlimited marital deduction.

Upon Renee's later death, the land is transferred directly to the University of Miami. The $500,000 of land is in her gross estate for federal estate tax purposes, but is then given a $500,000 estate tax charitable deduction. The land, therefore, escapes all federal estate taxation.

Powers of Appointment

General Power of Appointment

If a decedent exercises a general power of appointment upon death in favor of a charity, the transfer is eligible for an estate tax charitable deduction. General power of appointment property is included in the decedent's gross estate. Hence, the property is considered transferred by the decedent and thus meets the two-pronged test to qualify for the estate tax charitable deduction.

Special Power of Appointment

The exercise of a special (or limited) power of appointment (where one person directs the disposition of another person's assets, but the assets can't be paid to the powerholder, the powerholder's estate, creditors, or creditors of his estate) is a transfer that doesn't qualify for an estate tax deduction. Property transferred under a special power of appointment is not included in the powerholder's estate. Therefore, the charitable estate tax deduction is not allowed for the transfer.

Disclaimers

If a person makes a qualified disclaimer of property from the decedent's estate and the property then passes to a charitable organization, the estate will be eligible for an estate tax charitable deduction. The transfer is considered made by the decedent to the charity, and not from the person who made the disclaimer.[13]

Income Earned During Estate Administration

Generally, income earned on an asset that is the subject of a bequest follows to the beneficiary that receives the asset. Therefore, the income earned on the charitable asset during the administration of the estate is also donated to the charitable organization.[14]

QUESTIONS AND ANSWERS

Question – If the decedent's last will and testament names the beneficiary of the decedent's commercial annuity as a qualified public charity, and the beneficiary on the insurance company's beneficiary form is the "estate" of the decedent, will a charitable estate tax deduction be allowed?

Answer – Yes. But the annuity will be IRD to the estate. The correct way to set up this gift is to name the charity as the beneficiary of the annuity. The will should have no reference to this gift. The charity will then receive the annuity payments by contract. Neither the estate nor the charity will pay income tax on the annuity, and the estate will receive a charitable estate tax deduction for the amount of the annuity.

Question – What if the charity loses its tax-exempt status between the time the will was executed and the date of the decedent's death?

Answer – The status of the charity is determined as of the date of death. Therefore, if the charity is no longer a viable 501(c)(3) organization as of the decedent's date of death, the bequest will not qualify for an estate tax charitable deduction. Of course, if this situation was anticipated by the naming of a back-up charity, the problem would be avoided. It is always a wise move to consider contingent beneficiaries.

Question – Can a charitable testamentary gift be made to the decedent's family foundation (non-operating private family foundation)? Will the estate still receive a full estate tax charitable deduction?

Answer – Yes. Testamentary gifts to private family foundations are eligible for a full charitable estate tax deduction. This is in contrast to lifetime gifts to private foundations which have limitations on the percentage of AGI which can be deducted for income tax purposes.

Question – Would a client normally name a charitable beneficiary in an irrevocable life insurance trust?

Answer – No. A traditional irrevocable life insurance trust is outside of the decedent's estate for federal estate tax purposes. From a purely estate tax perspective, it would be a waste of the utility of the irrevocable trust and, presumably, "Crummey" gifts to name a charity as a beneficiary of the assets within an irrevocable life insurance trust; the assets in such a trust are already outside the ambit of the federal estate tax. Hence, assets within the life insurance trust are generally directed to family members, while assets otherwise subject to federal estate taxes are earmarked for testamentary charitable gifts.

Question – Can a donor's estate receive an estate tax deduction if the donor establishes a scholarship fund in his last will and testament?

Answer – Scholarship bequests can be tricky. A testator may wish to create a scholarship fund. But in order to receive an estate tax charitable deduction, the scholarship must benefit members of the general public, not just a private group of family members. The testator may have some restrictions and limitations as to who can qualify, but cannot have limitations such that the only people who can qualify are relatives of the decedent.

CHAPTER ENDNOTES

1.   Treas. Reg. §20.2055-2(b).
2.   Rev. Rul. 70-452, 1970-2 CB 199.
3.   IRC Sec. 2055(e)(2); Treas. Regs. §§20.2055-2(e)(1), 20.2055-2(e)(2).
4.   Treas. Regs. §§20.2055-2(f)(2)(i), 20.2055-2(f)(2)(ii).
5.   Section 7520 rates for each month are available at www.leimberg.com and www.taxfactsonline.com. The Section 7520 rate is based on the monthly federal midterm rate – which is then multiplied by 120% and rounded to the nearest 2/10ths of 1 percent. Note that in charitable planning, it is permissible to use the Section 7520 rate for the month the trust is funded – or to look back to either of the prior two months' Section 7520 rates – and to choose the rate that produces the highest deduction.
6.   See Appendix K for valuation tables and example calculations.
7.   IRC Sec. 2055(e)(2)(B); Treas. Regs. §§20.2055-2(e)(2)(vi), 20.2055-2(e)(2)(vii).
8.   See Appendix K for valuation tables and example calculations.
9.   Treas. Regs. §§20.2055-2(e)(2)(ii), 20.2055-2(e)(2)(iii), 20.2031-7-(d).
10. Let. Rul. 200002011.
11. Treas. Reg. §20.2055-1(a).
12. Treas. Reg. §20.2055-1(c).
13. IRC Sec. 2518(a).
14. IRC Sec. 642(c)(2).

SUPPORTING ORGANIZATIONS

CHAPTER 24

WHAT IS IT?

A supporting organization is an entity formed under state law as a trust or corporation that meets the various tax qualification rules under IRC Section 509(a)(3). As the name suggests, a supporting organization's primary purpose is to support another qualified charitable organization. It enjoys the benefits of a public charity (and is spared some of the restrictions of a private foundation), including the availability to the donor of the more expansive contribution deduction limits applicable to public charities.

Generally speaking, there are three types of supporting organizations (Type I, Type II and Type III), which were previously defined by Treasury regulations, but the definitions of which have now become a part of the Internal Revenue Code under the Pension Protection Act of 2006 (PPA 2006).[1] The distinctions between these three types of supporting organizations are based on the amount of control the supported charities are able to exercise over the supporting organizations.

In addition to the basic definitions, Congress authorized the Treasury Department in PPA 2006 to issue regulatory guidance, especially as to Type III supporting organizations. The initial guidance came in an advance notice of proposed rulemaking, which establishes a new framework designed to address perceived abuses.[2] The proposed rules, when released, will of course be subject to finalization. Readers are encouraged to review the most recent Treasury regulations applicable to supporting organizations.

WHEN IS THE USE OF SUCH A DEVICE INDICATED?

1. When the donor wants continued influence and "indirect control" over the distributions to one charity or a group of related charities.

2. When the donor is willing to share control with one charity or a group of related charities.

3. When the donor desires to make a significant gift now for deferred distribution without the disadvantages normally associated with a private foundation. (However, some of the more restrictive requirements associated with private foundations have been extended to supporting organizations under PPA 2006; see "Disadvantages" below.)

ADVANTAGES

1. A supporting organization is generally entitled to more favored tax treatment than a private foundation (but see the discussion below as to Type III supporting organizations).

2. Organizational operations and expenses of the supporting organization can be shared with the supported charity.

3. Much like a private foundation, a supporting organization can provide the donor and the donor's family with significant visibility in the local community for their charitable work.

4. The income distribution requirement (generally at least 85% of income) of certain types of supporting organizations will usually require smaller distributions than does the requirement for private foundations (generally at least 5% of the annual value of the foundation's assets). Some commentators have proposed imposing the same private foundation required distribution of 5% of annual value of the organization's assets on certain types of supporting organizations.[3] These proposals are included in the advance notice of proposed rulemaking, which provides that a Type III supporting organization that is "not functionally integrated" will

be required to distribute annually to or for the use of its supported organizations an amount equal to at least 5% of the aggregate fair market value of all its assets (other than assets that are used, or held for use, directly in supporting the charitable programs of its supported organizations). Further, the advance notice of proposed rulemaking indicates that as to Type III supporting organizations that are "not functionally integrated" and created on or after Aug. 17, 2006, the number of supported charities will be limited to five. Existing Type III organizations may still qualify if existing tests are met, subject to transitional rules to be issued.[4]

DISADVANTAGES

1. Some donors believe that they will have less control over a supporting organization than they would over a private foundation.

2. The various qualification tests for a supporting organization may be perceived as too restrictive and complex compared to the requirements of a donor advised fund.

3. The costs of compliance may be as high (or higher) than the compliance costs of a private foundation, and are certainly higher than the costs of using a donor advised fund. Compliance costs of Type I and Type II supporting organizations will likely be lower than with a Type III organization.

4. The increased scrutiny and requirements imposed by PPA 2006 will likely limit the prior flexibility of certain supporting organizations, especially Type III supporting organizations. In response to these concerns, the IRS has issued two administrative pronouncements: (1) Announcement 2006-93, providing guidance to supporting organizations changing to public charity status to qualify for tax-free distributions from IRAs (the so-called "Charitable IRA Rollover"), and to avoid new restrictions on distributions from donor advised funds and private foundations; and (2) Notice 2006-109, directed to supporting organizations, donor advised funds, and private foundations that make grants to supporting organizations.[5]

WHAT ARE THE REQUIREMENTS?

1. As noted above, there are three types of supporting organizations with the classification based on the relationship between the *supporting* organization and the *supported* public charity or charities. The discussion in the advance notice of proposed rulemaking summarizes this basic principle:

"To be classified as a supporting organization, an organization must satisfy an organizational test, an operational test, a relationship test, and a disqualified person control test. The organizational and operational tests require that the organization be organized and at all times thereafter operated exclusively for the benefit of, to perform the functions of, or to conduct the purposes of one or more publicly supported organizations [described in IRC Sections 509(a)(1) or 509(a)(2)]. The relationship test requires that the organization be operated, supervised, or controlled by or in connection with one or more publicly supported organizations. Finally, the disqualified person control test requires that the organization not be controlled directly or indirectly by certain disqualified persons."[6]

The following more fully describes the three types of relationships that a supporting organization may have with supported charities:[7]

*   Type I – *Operated, supervised, or controlled by.* This relationship requires a substantial degree of direction over the policies, programs, and activities of a supporting organization by one or more publicly supported charities. Such a relationship is similar to that of a parent and subsidiary, where the subsidiary is under the direction of, and accountable or responsible to, the parent.[8] PPA 2006 adds a provision that will convert a Type I supporting organization to a private foundation if it accepts a gift from a direct or indirect control person and charitable contributions will not be deductible if the donor or advisor controls a Type I supporting organization.[9]

*   Type II – *Supervised or controlled in connection with.* This relationship can be described as one that involves a brother-sister relationship. There must be common supervision or control by the persons supervising or controlling both the supporting organization and the supported charities. This control is to ensure that the supporting organization will be responsive to the needs and requirements of the publicly supported charity.[10]

- Type III – *Operated in connection with or functionally integrated*. The advance notice of proposed rulemaking creates two sub-types of Type III organizations: (1) "functionally integrated" and (2) "not functionally integrated." An announcement issued by the Service states "it is expected that Type III supporting organizations that are 'functionally integrated' will be required to meet: (A) the 'but for' test…; (B) an expenditure test that will resemble the qualifying distributions test for private operating foundations; and (C) an assets test that will resemble the alternative assets test for private operating foundations. Finally, it is expected that a Type III supporting organization that is 'not functionally integrated' will be required to meet a payout requirement equal to the qualified distribution requirement of a private non-operating foundation. In addition, there will be a limit on the number of publicly supported organizations a non-functionally integrated Type III supporting organization may support" (i.e., no more than five). The "operated in connection with" test requires that the supporting organization be responsive to, and significantly involved in, the operations of the publicly supported charity.[11]

The "functionally integrated" supporting organization is described as an organization that is not required under Treasury regulations to make payments to supported organizations due to activities of the organization related to performing the functions of, or carrying out the purposes of, such supported organizations. In other words, it is more like a private operating foundation in carrying out the charitable functions of the supported organization as opposed to a "not functionally integrated" supporting organization, which makes distributions to the supported charity similar to a grant-making private foundation. Further, a supporting organization fails the "functionally integrated" test if it is operated in connection with any supported organization not organized in the United States.[12] PPA 2006 provided the Treasury Department with the authority to require all Type III organizations to meet the functionally integrated test in future regulations, very likely along the lines of the current proposed regulations. Generally, supported charities have less control over a Type III organization, but Type III organizations are subject to more restrictions than Type I or Type II organizations.

2. Supporting organizations must also meet a control test—that is, they cannot be controlled by a disqualified person.[13] With Type I and Type II supporting organizations, control is essentially vested in the supported charities, so the possibility of control by a disqualified person is usually not an issue. However, the control of a Type III supporting organization is less direct than with a private foundation, so the rules are intended to limit control by the donor, his family, and any indirect control through entities (corporations, partnerships, etc.) controlled directly by the donor or members of his family. The concerns of the IRS are reflected in the new provisions enacted by Congress in PPA 2006 as discussed throughout this chapter, as amplified by the proposed Treasury regulations (as set forth in the advance notice).

3. All supporting organizations must meet both the "organizational" test and the "operational" test:

   a. The organizational test focuses primarily on the restricted purposes set forth in the organization's articles of organization (corporate charter and by-laws or the trust document creating the organization), which must relate to qualified charitable purposes for public charities, and which must avoid restricted non-charitable activities. Nevertheless, the Treasury regulations permit very broad charitable purposes in support of a qualified charity and provide numerous examples of permissible and impermissible purposes. For example, the Treasury regulations state that a Type I or Type II supporting organization "will be considered as meeting the requirements of this paragraph if the purposes set forth in its articles are similar to, but no broader than, the purposes set forth in the articles of its controlling [IRC Section 509(a)(1) or Section 509(a)(2)] organizations."[14] A Type III supporting organization's articles of organization must specifically name the supported charity. In most cases, experienced counsel can guide donors through meeting this test.

   b. The operational test relates to the activities of the supporting organization, which must be "exclusively to support one or more specified publicly supported organizations." To meet this test the supporting organization must engage "solely in activities which support or benefit the specified publicly supported organizations." This can include making payments to, or for

the use of, or providing services or facilities for, individual members of the charitable class benefited by the specified publicly supported organization. A supporting organization may also, for example, make a payment indirectly through another unrelated organization to a member of a charitable class benefited by the specified publicly supported organization, but only if such a payment constitutes a grant to an individual rather than a grant to an organization. However, an organization will not be regarded as operated exclusively if any part of its activities is in furtherance of a purpose other than supporting or benefiting one or more specified publicly supported organizations.[15]

4. The Treasury regulations also provide specific guidance on the relationships between the supported charity or charities and the supporting organization, depending on the type of supporting organization:

    a. A Type I relationship "presupposes a substantial degree of direction over the policies, programs, and activities of a supporting organization by one or more publicly supported organizations. ... This relationship is established by the fact that a majority of the officers, directors, or trustees of the supporting organization are appointed or elected by the governing body, members of the governing body, officers acting in their official capacity, or the membership of one or more publicly supported organizations."[16]

    b. A Type II relationship requires that "there must be common supervision or control by the persons supervising or controlling both the supporting organization and the publicly supported organizations to insure that the supporting organization will be responsive to the needs and requirements of the publicly supported organizations. Therefore, in order to meet such a requirement, the control or management of the supporting organization must be vested in the same persons that control or manage the publicly supported organizations."[17]

    c. Because Type III organizations are not as tightly controlled by the supported charity or charities, they must also meet other tests to maintain their qualification. These tests are referred to as the "responsiveness test" and the "integral part" test. The Treasury regulations explain in detail the procedures for complying with these complex tests and contain helpful examples.[18]

For more details on the enhancement of these tests, review the final version of the regulations resulting from the advance notice of proposed rulemaking.[19]

(i) Under the "responsiveness test," a supporting organization will be considered as operated in connection with one or more publicly supported organizations only if it "is responsive to the needs or demands of the publicly supported organizations." The Treasury regulations set forth the ways in which the "responsiveness test" may be met by the supporting organization. The advance notice of proposed rulemaking offers the following guidance: "Accordingly, a Type III supporting organization will be expected to demonstrate the necessary relationship between its officers, directors or trustees and those of its supported organization(s), and further show that this relationship results in the officers, directors or trustees of its supported organization(s) having a significant voice in the operations of the supporting organization" (the same as in current Treasury regulations).[20]

Under PPA 2006, the use of a charitable trust to meet the "responsiveness test" has been eliminated, so a charitable trust must prove that it is responsive. Consequently, as to charitable trusts post-PPA 2006, the advance notice of proposed rulemaking states the following:

"Consistent with Section 1241(c) of the PPA, . . . the proposed regulations will provide that charitable trusts must satisfy the responsiveness test under Treasury Regulation Section 1.509(a)-4(i)(2)(ii). Thus, for instance, a trust would be expected to show that its trustees have a close, continuous working relationship with the officers, directors, or trustees of the publicly supported organization(s) it supports and that through such relationship the officers, directors or trustees of its publicly supported organization(s) have a significant voice in the operations of the supporting organization."[21]

As set forth above, the functionally integrated Type III supporting organization is one that is not required under the Treasury regulations to make payments to supported organizations due to activities of the organization related to performing the functions of, or carrying out the purposes of, such supported organizations (i.e., by the nature of its activities, it *is* functionally integrated).[22] As a result of meeting this test, the Type III organization is not subject to the excise taxes and other requirements imposed on non-functionally integrated Type III supporting organizations.

(ii) Under the "integral part test," a supporting organization must "maintain a significant involvement in the operations of one or more publicly supported organizations and such publicly supported organizations are, in turn, dependent upon the supporting organization for the type of support that it provides."[23] One way a supporting organization can meet this test is if the supporting organization performs activities for a public charity that the charity itself would perform if it were not for the supporting organization performing those particular activities (commonly referred to as the "but for" test). Another way a supporting organization can meet the integral part test is if it makes payments of substantially all of its income to or for the use of one or more publicly supported charities, and the support received by the publicly supported charities is sufficient to insure the attentiveness of the public charity to the operations of the supporting organization (commonly referred to as the "attentiveness" test). The Service has determined that this requirement will be met if the supporting organization distributes at least 85% of its income to the supported organization.[24] The consequence of failing the integral part test is treatment as a private foundation.[25]

The advance notice of proposed rulemaking proposes to amplify these rules as follows.

- The "but for" test is satisfied if "the activities engaged in [by the supporting organization] for or on behalf of the publicly supported organizations are activities to perform the functions of, or to carry out the purposes of, such organizations, and, but for the involvement of the supporting organization, would normally be engaged in by the publicly supported organizations themselves."

AND

- "The "attentiveness" test is satisfied if it "requires a supporting organization to (1) make payments of substantially all of its income to or for the use of one or more publicly supported organiza-

tions, (2) provide enough support to one or more publicly supported organizations to insure the attentiveness of such organizations to the operations of the supporting organization, and (3) pay a substantial amount of the total support of the supporting organization to those publicly supported organizations that meet the attentiveness requirement." (Revenue Ruling 76-208 states that "substantially all of its income" means at least 85% of its adjusted net income.)[26]

5. Obviously, the ongoing operational issues for supporting organizations are very complex. Different rules apply to each of the three types of supporting organizations with ever-increasing complexity applying to Type III supporting organizations, where the nature and extent of the "control and supervision" by supported charities is the lowest. These operational issues should be addressed with the donor during the planning phase. Once a supporting organization is established, reliance upon competent legal and accounting advisors is essential.

HOW IS IT DONE?

A supporting organization can be formed by a charity, a donor, or both. Typically a supported charity will initiate the creation of a Type I or Type II supporting organization with the assistance of key donors.

In some circumstances, an existing charitable organization may find it beneficial to isolate certain activities in a supporting organization (likely a Type I or Type II organization). For example, if real estate operations must be segregated from other operations without losing control of those operations, the existing charity could establish a supporting organization to be used to promote donor support of the real estate operations.

Individual donors are more likely to form and contribute to a Type III supporting organization so that they can have more control over the organization than would be permissible with a Type I or Type II organization. However in light of PPA 2006 and the advance notice of proposed Treasury regulations, many commentators fear that once regulations are finalized, the Type III organizations that are "not functionally integrated" will be so difficult to work with, that they will be seldom used (see Treacy article, below). Like most other charitable gifts, a contribution to a supporting organization can be augmented or established by a transfer at the time of the donor's death. However, if the donor expects to have his or her family involved in the operation of the supporting organization after death, some pre-planning will likely be required to arrange for this family involvement, within the limits and restrictions imposed by IRC Section 509(f)(2)(B).

Example: Cristy is a successful alumnus of High Tech University and has been very successful in her "dot.com" career. She wants to establish a program to fund scholarships for women students to encourage them to pursue technical careers. She would also like to have ongoing involvement with the program and receive the maximum tax benefits for her contribution. Her advisors review with her the use of a private foundation, a named endowment fund, and a supporting organization. Due to the close scrutiny by the IRS of private foundations granting scholarships, and the reduced tax deduction limits, the private foundation is considered less attractive. The named endowment fund is attractive from the contribution limitation standpoint, but does not assure Cristy of the active role she desires. Cristy chooses to establish a supporting organization with $1,000,000 of appreciated stock of her employer. Her advisors form the "Cristy Scholarship Foundation for High Tech University." Two of her former professors, two university administrators, Cristy, and her attorney act as trustees of the foundation. The university has authority to name two-thirds of the foundation's trustees and Cristy reserves the right to designate the remaining trustees.

Cristy's initial and all subsequent contributions will enjoy the most favored tax treatment: the 50% of AGI limitation for donations of cash, and the 30% of AGI limitation for contributions of long-term capital gain property (see Chapter 3).

WHAT ARE THE TAX IMPLICATIONS?

1. The donor to a supporting organization is permitted a deduction of up to 50% of AGI for donations of cash, and 30% of AGI for donations of long-term capital gain property. This is in contrast to the lower deduction limits (generally 30%) that are afforded contributions to a private foundation.

2. Supporting organizations that are Types I, Type II, and functionally integrated Type III organizations are tax-exempt under IRC Section 501(c)(3).

3. A supporting organization is not subject to the 2% excise tax that applies to a private foundation in Type I and Type II supporting organizations because it is accorded public charity status, but may become taxable in a Type III supporting organization if it does not meet the functionally integrated Test.[27] However, if a Type I supporting organization accepts a gift from a direct or indirect control person. it will convert to a private foundation and charitable contributions will not be deductible if the donor or advisor controls a Type I supporting organization (see note 9).

4. A supporting organization must file an annual tax return (Form 990) with the Internal Revenue Service, and will likely be subject to state tax filing requirements as well.

5. Excise taxes on certain prohibited activities applicable to private foundations that make grants to controlled organizations also apply to supporting organizations.[28]

WHAT ARE THE ALTERNATIVES?

If the donor does not want to play an active role in the operations of a charitable organization, the donor should consider: a restricted endowment gift to the charity; a named fund or donor advised fund within a public charity; or a community foundation or a charitable gift fund sponsored by a mutual fund manager. If the donor would like to have more control over the charitable organization, a private foundation may be used. (See Chapter 17 for more information on community foundations; see Chapter 19 for more information on donor advised funds; see Chapter 21 for more information on private foundations; see Figure 21.1 in Chapter 21 for a comparison of supporting organizations, community foundations, and private foundations).

WHERE CAN I FIND OUT MORE ABOUT IT?

1. Toce, Joseph, Abbin, Byrle, Vorsatz, Mark, and Page, William, *Tax Economics of Charitable Giving 2006-2007* (Warren Gorham & Lamont, 2006).

2. Davine, Jeffrey D., "Everything You Ever Wanted to Know about Type III Supporting Organizations," *Gift Planner's Digest* (June 28, 2000), at: www.pgdc.net.

3 Fox, Richard L., Steve Leimberg's Charitable Planning Email Newsletter #120, April 9, 2007, reviewing IRS Notice 2006-109.

4. Hopkins, Bruce R., *The Law of Tax Exempt Organizations*, 9th edition (New York, NY: John Wiley & Sons, Inc., 2007, periodic updates).

5. Martin, Patrick D., "Supporting Organizations: Creation, Operation and Use," *Gift Planner's Digest*, April 28, 1999, at: www.pgdc.net.

6. Phelan, Marilyn E., *Nonprofit Enterprises: Corporations, Trusts and Associations* (West Group-Clark, Boardman, Callaghan, Inc., 1997-2000).

7. Treacy, Gerald B., "What's Left of SO's" (Committee Report: Philanthropy), *Trusts and Estates*, Oct. 2006.

8. Webel, Merrie Jeanne, "The Supporting Organization: A Beneficial (but Tangled) Alternative for the Directed Donor," *Probate and Property*, (March-April 2001), American Bar Association Real Property, Probate, and Trust Law Section.

9. Wruck, Craig and Helen Monroe, "Family Foundations: Donor Advised Funds and Supporting Organizations as Alternatives to Private Foundations," *Gift Planner's Digest*, February 1, 1999, at: www.pgdc.net.

QUESTIONS AND ANSWERS

Question – How much control must be exercised over the supporting organization by the supported charity?

Answer – With the Type I and Type II supporting organizations, the control is extensive. Practically speaking, a cooperative arrangement will likely exist; that is, the goodwill of the donor is essential to keeping the flow of contributions coming into the supporting organization. With the Type III supporting organization, the control is limited, but the other qualification requirements will ensure a continuing close connection with the supported charity or charities.

Question – Is there a preference for the type of entity for the different types of supporting organizations?

Answer – While most commentators have preferred the corporate form, a trust entity can also be an attractive form for any supporting organization. However, under PPA 2006, Type III supporting organizations must meet more stringent requirements in meeting the "responsiveness test" under IRC Section 1241(c).

Question – Is it possible to operate a supporting organization in connection with a community foundation?

Answer – Yes. Many community foundations encourage larger gifts to be made in the form of a supporting organization, with the community foundation as the supported charity. This approach also allows a family to leave open its charitable purposes by naming the community foundation as the supported charity under the governing instrument for a Type III supporting organization. Great flexibility is retained should the charitable focus of the family's philanthropic objectives change, and these changes can be carried out through the community foundation. These arrangements are similar to the donor advised fund, but can accommodate longer-term family involvement in the supported organization. It is likely this arrangement will fall within the definition of a "not functionally integrated" Type III supporting organization, which may limit the effectiveness of this arrangement.

Question – Why would a donor prefer a supporting organization over a private foundation?

Answer – A donor who uses a supporting organization often does so because he wants to obtain the more expansive contribution deduction limits that are available to public charities, which is true as to Type I, Type II and functionally integrated Type III supporting organizations. A supporting organization is also exempt from the private foundation excise taxes and administrative requirements, subject, however, to the new requirements that will likely result from the proposed rules.[29]

Question – Why would a charity prefer to have the donor establish a supporting organization rather than make an outright gift to the charity?

Answer – Direct control remains with the charity in the Type I and Type II supporting organizations. For a charity with a donor who is willing to cede control, this is obviously more attractive and is nearly the same as receiving an outright gift or one with some restrictions. With a Type III supporting organization, the charity will also likely view the gift favorably, because only limited, indirect control is permitted and the charity must receive the support. Primarily, it is a matter of "donor meddling" in the process, but in most cases the practicalities of the arrangement should ensure a harmonious result. However, if this arrangement falls within the definition of a "not functionally integrated" Type III supporting organization, its effectiveness will be less than under prior law.

Question – Can a supporting organization establish a donor advised fund?

Answer – Yes. In Letter Ruling 200149045, the IRS approved donor advised funds to be established by a supporting organization, which was a member organization organized as a supporting organization. The plan was to permit members to designate contributions to the supporting organization as donor advised funds for deferred distribution to the supported charitable organizations. This strategy might also be used to engage other donors who wish to assist with the activities of the supporting organization, but are unwilling to allow the supporting organization to use the funds on a current basis and/or without consultation with the donor as the advisor. It is likely this arrangement will fall within the definition of a "not functionally integrated" Type III supporting organization, which may limit the perceived effectiveness of this arrangement.

CHAPTER ENDNOTES

1. Pension Protection Act of 2006 (P.L. 109-208).

2. REG-155929-06, 72 Fed. Reg. 42335 (8-2-2007) (Payout Requirements for Type III Supporting Organizations That Are Not Functionally Integrated). See, also, Announcement 2007-87, 2007-40 IRB 753 (10-1-2007). For a detailed discussion of the regulations as currently proposed, see Fox, Richard L., Steve Leimberg's Charitable Planning Email Newsletter – Archive Message #125, dated Aug. 13, 2007. The effective date for the proposed regulations will be the date the proposed rules are published in the Federal Register as final or temporary regulations.

3. See the New York State Bar Association Tax Section's comments on supporting organizations in response to IRS Notice 2007-21, 2007-9 IRB 611, at: http://www.pgdc.com/usa/print_item/?itemID=416593. See similar comments from Ruth M. Madrigal,

Esq., to Susan Brown, Department of the Treasury, regarding Type III supporting organizations (May 17, 2007), at: http://www.pgdc.com/usa/print_item/?itemID=413131.

4. REG-155929-06, 72 Fed. Reg. 42335 (8-2-2007).

5. Announcement 2006-93, 2006-48 IRB 1017, Notice 2006-109, 2006-51 IRB. 1121.

6. REG-155929-06, 72 Fed. Reg. 42335 (8-2-2007).

7. These relationships are set forth in IRC Sec. 509(a)(3)(A). See also Treas. Reg. §1.509(a)-4.

8. Treas. Reg. §1.509(a)-4(g).

9. IRC Sec. 509(f)(2), as defined in IRC Sec 509(f)(2)(B)(i)-(iii).

10. Treas. Reg. §1.509(a)-4(h).

11. Announcement 2007-87, 2007-40 IRB 753; Treas. Reg. §1.509(a)-4(i).

12. IRC Sec. 509(f)(1)(B)(i).

13. IRC Sec. 509(a)(3)(C). "Disqualified persons" include: (1) a substantial contributor to the foundation, (2) a foundation manager, (3) an owner of more than 20% of a business or trust that is a substantial contributor to the foundation, and (4) a member of the family of any of the these individuals. IRC Sec. 4946(a). The term "substantial contributor" means a person who has given an organization more than $5,000, if the amount given is more than 2% of the total amount that has been given to the organization by all contributors. IRC Sec. 507(d)(2).

14. Treas. Reg. §1.509(a)-4(c).

15. Treas. Reg. §1.509(a)-4(e).

16. Treas. Reg. §1.509(a)-4(g).

17. Treas. Reg. §1.509(a)-4(h).

18. Treas. Reg. §1.509(a)-4(i).

19. REG-155929-06, 72 Fed. Reg. 42335 (8-2-2007).

20. Treas. Reg. §1.509(a)-4(i)(2); REG–155929–06, 72 Fed. Reg. 42335, 42339 (8-2-2007).

21. REG–155929–06, 72 Fed. Reg. 42335, 42339 (8-2-2007).

22. IRC 4943(f)(5)(B).

23. Treas. Reg. §1.509(a)-4(i)(3).

24. Rev. Rul. 76-208, 1976-1 CB 161.

25. See *Lapham Foundation Inc. v. Comm.*, TC Memo 2002-93 (a supporting organization that failed the integral part test is reclassified as a private foundation; affirmed on appeal in *Lapham Foundation, Inc. v. Comm.*, 94 AFTR 2d 2004-6880 (389 F.3d 606) 11-18-2004.

26. REG–155929–06, 72 Fed. Reg. 42335, 42336 (8-2-2007); Rev. Rul. 76-208, 1976-1 CB 161.

27. IRC Secs. 509(a)(3), 4942(g).

28. See IRC Secs. 4941, 4942, 4943, 4944, 4945. The provisions as to excess business holdings now apply to Supporting Organizations by the addition of sub-paragraph (f) to Sec. 4943 and as to excess benefits transactions for Type III Supporting Organizations under IRC Section 4958. The latter extends the private foundation concepts of disqualified persons/insiders and more than incidental benefits to persons involved with supporting organizations under IRC Section 4967.

29. See REG–155929–06, 72 Fed. Reg. 42335 (8-2-2007).

PLANNED GIVING TRENDS

In the past two decades, charitable planning has grown from a small, isolated industry into a full-fledged branch of financial planning. Traditionally, most advisors had included charitable recommendations only if a client insisted. Even then, generally such planning was limited to a sentence or two in a client's financial plan, usually in the form of a bequest or a lifetime cash gift.

In the mid-1980s, many advisors realized that the charitable remainder trust was a powerful planning tool (see Chapters 15 and 16). More and more professionals began incorporating CRTs into their client recommendations. In an effort to remain competitive and because of increased sophistication, these advisors are now recommending other advanced tools such as charitable lead trusts, donor advised funds, charitable gift annuities, supporting organizations, and private foundations.

As planned giving becomes more widespread, the charitable planning community is facing some substantial growing pains. Current trends include both positive and negative aspects:

1. *Resurgence of big name philanthropists.* In the past few years, several prominent business owners have made substantial charitable donations either outright or through private foundations. Such names include Bill Gates of Microsoft, Inc., Ted Turner, the founder of CNN Inc., and Berkshire Hathaway Chairman Warren Buffett. While each has made donations with a value of at least $1 billion, equally important is the fact they have all heavily and deliberately publicized these gifts in an attempt to persuade others to follow in their path. Other business owners and wealthy individuals have risen to the challenge, and have caused many observers to compare these modern philanthropists to John D. Rockefeller and Andrew Carnegie.

2. *The promotion of charitable giving techniques to less wealthy individuals.* As interest in charitable planning grows among advisors, sophisticated techniques that were once presented only to high net worth individuals are now being recommended to less affluent clients. While this may be appropriate in some cases, in many situations, large irrevocable transfers to charitable trusts, funds, and other planned giving vehicles, may not be suitable for those who do not have sufficient discretionary funds to make such gifts.

3. *The introduction of online donations.* As many development officers will verify, courting small annual donations is a time intensive and financially expensive effort. Many use mass mailings and telephone solicitations. Charities who are more cutting edge or who have a younger, more technical donor base, are turning to the Internet. The use of e-mail and Web sites to solicit gifts is growing steadily, though the efficacy of online solicitation has yet to be proven. Other charities have started using the Internet to court larger planned gifts, making interactive split interest calculators available on their Web sites as well as offering more planning information for donors to read online at their leisure.

4. *The increasing role of planned giving officers.* Twenty years ago, only the larger and more established charities had staff positions dedicated to planned giving. Most charities had development and annual giving staff in place. When planned giving cases and questions came up, they simply turned such queries over to these fundraisers. Today, larger charities often have entire departments set up to raise and administer planned gifts, mid-sized charities usually have at least one planned giving professional on staff, and even small and new charities are considering

planned giving staff as part of their initial start up requirements.

5. *Specialized consultants.* As planned giving grows in popularity, an entire community of commercial providers has arisen to service this market. These include planned giving consultants who offer their services to charities who do not have their own dedicated departments, trust accounting firms who specialize in charitable trust management, professional charitable trustees and fiduciaries, insurance appraisers who value donations of insurance, investment firms who provide services and funds only to non-profits, bequest tracking firms, and software companies who design products for the nonprofit marketplace.

6. *Financial firms now offer charitable planning.* Within the financial planning community, there has been a rapid shift from comprehensive planning to investment planning. Many of these asset management firms are now starting to include charitable planning in their portfolio of services, in addition to asset protection and more traditional investment management.

7. *Mutual fund and brokerage companies who establish foundations.* Several large mutual fund companies and brokerage firms have started separate charitable foundations, usually to administer donor advised funds and pooled income funds. Despite the assertions made by many critics that these funds lack independence from their founding corporations (all of the underlying investments are usually managed by the fund or company that established the charity), these vehicles have proven extremely popular. While such funds have only existed for the past ten years or so, four of these charities are now ranked in the 100 largest nonprofits in the United States.

8. *Increase in donor advised fund subsidiaries run by traditional charities.* In an effort to compete with the new donor advised fund programs established by the investment companies, several larger charities are establishing similar entities. In particular, universities are currently researching or running such funds, usually through a subsidiary or sister foundation.

9. *Negative Press.* While there has always been a fair amount of press covering charity scandals

in the past, in the years following the 9-11 tragedy and the Katrina disaster, the press took a particularly harsh view of the practices of fairly well established disaster assistance charities. Following 9-11, for example, a handful of major charity were heavily criticized by the press for not distributing aid money quickly enough to the families of those who had been killed. Following Hurricane Katrina, the same charities were again heavily criticized for cutting too many checks to confidence artists and scammers and for not reacting quickly enough to assist the many thousands who were suddenly homeless and in need. Furthermore, as a result of a Senate Finance Committee hearing in 2004,[1] the press has focused considerable attention on a number of problems found in otherwise respectable charities. Issues such as property valuation, board governance, executive compensation, misuse of donor advised funds, and lax enforcement by the IRS have all come under attack in recent years.

10. *A changing tax environment.* For the first time since 1969, Congress has passed some major charitable legislation into law and more changes are anticipated in the near future. The American Jobs Creation Act of 2004 put an end to abusive car donation programs, and the Pension Protection Act of 2006[2] contained a wide array of both charitable benefits (the IRA to Charity Rollover and improved rules for donating property to conservation easement charities) and restrictions (new rules affecting donor advised funds, supporting organizations, and a host of smaller provisions.)

11. *More changes on the way.* The Senate Finance Committee published a checklist in 2004 of charitable projects and problems that the Committee planned to address in future legislation.[3] This laundry list includes the following provision, all of which have the potential to become future charitable legislation:

- Investor Owned Life Insurance programs involving charities,

- Additional donor advised fund legislation,

- Additional supporting organization reform,

- Charitable governance issues and weaknesses,

- Excessive executive compensation received by non-profit leaders,

- Increased supervision responsibilities over charities by the IRS,

- Revocation of tax exempt status for organizations involved in tax shelters,

- Increased penalties for self dealing,

- Enhanced disclosure requirements, and

- Renewed focus on the prudent investor rules.

12. *Undoing Overly Complicated Charitable Plans.* There was a heavy emphasis on establishing complex plans involving split interest charitable trusts in the 1980s and 1990s. Unfortunately, many donors went into these plans without a complete understanding of the costs and limitations of keeping such trusts in place. Many of these donors have taken the steps needed to unravel their charitable trusts and more are likely to do the same in the next few years.

13. *Politicking by charities.* Non profits and politics are not supposed to mix. As a result of a growing number of churches preaching which candidate their flock should back, the IRS has started to crack down on the worst offenders.

14. *The IRS is starting to focus on charitable abuses.* As a result of almost non-existent audit rates of charities, the IRS has developed a reputation as a dog with no teeth. As a result of the renewed interest by Congress and the press, this is changing. Charity audits are going up, state attorneys general have taken a renewed interest in shutting down the worst offenders, and the IRS has indicated that they will be increasing not only civil actions against abusive charities and scheme, but will be working on building criminal cases as well. One such recent case involved an insurance agent in California who used his donor advised fund to pay the grade school tuition at his children's private school. He pleaded guilty, and was sentenced to five months in prison, five months of home detention,

and two years of supervised release. There are indications that other charity-related criminal cases are in the works.

AGGRESSIVE CHARITABLE PLANNING TECHNIQUES

As more and more advisors become active in planned giving, the desire to stay competitive and cutting edge has driven several to offer risky and untested techniques. In order to attract and maintain the wealthier clientele, such advisors usually attempt to maximize the benefits of the charitable tax deduction while minimizing any actual gifts to charity. The following is a brief list of some of the more notorious aggressive techniques that have recently been attempted:

1. *IOLI, CHOLI, SOLI, FOLI.* Nothing has been more aggressively marketed to charitable organizations in recent years than Investor Owned Life Insurance. Since these investors can not purchase life insurance on random wealthy people without violating state laws, they have come up with increasingly aggressive ways to convince charities to act as a middle man in arranging the purchase in exchange for a comparatively small payment to the charity. While the details of these plans vary from promoter to promoter, the scheme is generally the same. The charity arranges for their richest donors to take an insurance physical and complete an application. The investors arrange for moneys for the charities to purchase the policies for a brief period, at the end of which the investors take ownership of the policies and pay the charities a token amount for the plan. Congress has commissioned a study on the use of the plans and restrictive legislation is expected in the next few years.

1. *Tax deductible life insurance.* Finding a way to use pre-tax or tax deductible money to purchase large amounts of life insurance has long been the Holy Grail of the insurance and estate planning industries. While planners have attempted to use retirement accounts and business funds to achieve this goal, many considered the charitable tax deduction to hold the secret.

2. *Charitable split dollar and charitable reverse split dollar.* Several non-profits and literally hundreds of insurance agents marketed the charitable

split dollar plan and in the 5-year period prior to its demise in 1999, an estimated 5,000 plans were implemented. The donor would make a substantial "tax deductible gift" to an accommodating charity which would then purchase a life insurance policy on the donor's life on a split-dollar or reverse split dollar basis. The donor's heirs, either directly or through an irrevocable life insurance trust, would claim to pay the cash value portion of the policy and receive all of the policy's cash values and the bulk of the death benefit while the charity would net a small (if any) benefit from "investing" in this policy.

In 1999, the IRS issued guidance[4] stating that under existing law, such plans had never produced the tax results claimed by their promoters. Late in 1999, legislation was passed that increased the penalties for any charity that participated in such plans.[5] And finally, this technique has faced decisive losses in Federal court. In the case of Addis v. Commissioner, in 2004 the Ninth Circuit Appeals Court ruled that the taxpayers could not deduct the premiums in a charitable split dollar plan. The case was appealed to the Supreme Court which, in 2005, allowed the appellate decision to stand.

3. *Vulture trusts.* Also known as a "Ghoul Trust" or "Sickbed CLAT" by its critics and a "CLT per autre vie" by its promoters, this short-lived program took advantage of a relatively simple loophole in the Internal Revenue Code. In brief, a donor would establish a substantial charitable lead annuity trust (see details at Chapter 14) which would provide income to charity for the life of the annuitant, with the principal passing to the donor's heirs at the termination of the trust. There was nothing specifically in the Code, however, that stated that the measuring life used for the CLAT had to be the donor's. A handful of aggressive planners were therefore purchasing medical records of and permission from young, terminally ill people with a predictable life expectancy of two to five years. They would then use these unhealthy individuals as their measuring lives. For example, if a CLAT is established for a 35-year-old annuitant with a statistical life expectancy of 45 years, the present value of the income paid to charity is very high while the present value of the future gift (and therefore the gift tax) to the heirs is very

low. When the 35-year-old annuitant dies two or three years later, the money passes to the intended heirs with almost no estate or gift taxes. Of course, since the trust was a lead trust paying only an annuity for the duration of the measuring life, very little (by design) was paid to charity. Regulations amended early in 2001 closed this loophole.[6]

4. *Accelerated CRT and "son of accelerated" CRT.* By combining a short term CRT (typically two years) with a very high payout rate (e.g., 80%) and creative trust accounting, the promoters of this program offered their clients the ability to convert highly appreciated assets to cash while avoiding almost all capital gains. In 1997, Congress shut this plan down with legislation that limited the maximum payout rate to non-charitable beneficiaries and imposed a minimum 10% remainder interest to the charity. Only a few months later, the promoters were back, marketing a revised program (later called the "Son of Accelerated CRT") which supposedly would meet the new laws and still provide enormous tax benefits by incorporating a loan strategy into the original plan. The IRS followed with regulations, finalized in early 2001, shutting this plan down.[7]

5. *Charitable family limited partnerships.* Yet another plan (which, as of the publication of this book, is still being marketed) is the Charitable Family Limited Partnership or CHAR-FLP. While the details of this program vary widely, in general, a donor

- places a substantial and highly appreciated asset into a family limited partnership,

- retains a small percentage (almost always a general partnership interest which carries absolute control of the newly formed entity),

- gives or sells some or all of that interest to his intended heirs, and

- donates the balance of the partnership interests to a charity.

The donor takes a sizable deduction for the charitable gift, and causes the highly appreciated asset inside the partnership to be sold. Eventually, the charity's interest is bought back from the charity by the donor's heirs.

Promoters of CHAR-FLPs claim that little capital gains tax is due since most of the tax liability belongs to the partner that owns the largest interest (i.e., the charity). Unfortunately for the charity, there is a catch. The partnership is restrictive, and, by design, partners (the charity) cannot control, sell, or otherwise liquidate its partnership interest for a significant period of time, such as 50 years; therefore, the charity often has a strong incentive to sell its partnership interests to the donor's children at a very deep discount, rather than wait many years for a payout.

In the end, the donor receives a charitable deduction that may be, in reality, significantly higher than the value of the interest that passes to charity. The charity has been used to "launder" the built-in capital gains in the partnership's highly appreciated asset(s). So the asset is liquidated with little, if any, capital gains tax consequences to the donor or the donor's family. And partnership interests pass to the donor's heirs with almost no estate or gift tax consequences. While the IRS has not yet acted on these too-good-to-be-true arrangements, the Exempt Organizations Continuing Professional Education Text for Fiscal Year 2001 specifically addresses the inherent problems with such planning and indicates that the IRS will likely act on such programs in the future.

6. *Fraud.* In general, consumers trust charities. Specifically, individuals particularly trust those who wrap their charitable vehicles in religious garb. It is not surprising, therefore, that a number of con artists use charitable or religious organizations as a cover for their scams. In the past few years, there has been an incredible increase in stories about pseudo-religious entities that turn out to be nothing more than promoters of a Ponzi scheme, or phony charity telemarketers and solicitors who end up being nothing more than thieves.

ENDNOTES

1. http://finance.senate.gov/sitepages/hearing062204.htm.
2. http://www.dol.gov/ebsa/pdf/ppa2006.pdf.
3. http://finance.senate.gov/hearings/testimony/2004test/062204stfdis.pdf.
4. Notice 99-36, 1999-1 CB 1284.
5. See www.leimbergservices.com for extensive commentary on charitable split dollar and Char-FLPs.
6. Reg. §1.170A-6, as amended by T.D. 8923, 2001-6 IRB 485.
7. See Regs. §§1.663, 1.643(a)-8, as amended by T.D. 8926, 2001-6 IRB 492.

CHARITABLE GIFT ANNUITY RATES AND IRS EXPECTED RETURN MULTIPLES

SUGGESTED CHARITABLE GIFT ANNUITY RATES

Approved by the American Council on Gift Annuities on April 2, 2007
Effective July 1, 2007 through June 30, 2008

Age	Rate	Age	Rate	Age	Rate
0-1	3.70%	41	4.8	66	6.1
2-5	3.8	42	4.8	67	6.2
6-12	3.9	43	4.9	68	6.3
13-19	4.0	44	5.0	69	6.4
20	4.0	45	5.0	70	6.5
21	4.1	46	5.1	71	6.6
22	4.1	47	5.2	72	6.7
23	4.1	48	5.2	73	6.8
24	4.1	49	5.3	74	6.9
25	4.1	50	5.3	75	7.1
26	4.2	51	5.4	76	7.2
27	4.2	52	5.4	77	7.4
28	4.2	53	5.5	78	7.6
29	4.3	54	5.5%	79	7.8
30	4.3	55	5.5	80	8.0
31	4.3	56	5.6	81	8.3
32	4.4	57	5.6	82	8.5
33	4.4	58	5.7	83	8.8
34	4.4	59	5.7	84	9.2
35	4.5	60	5.7	85	9.5
36	4.5	61	5.8	86	9.9
37	4.6	62	5.9	87	10.2
38	4.6	63	5.9	88	10.6
39	4.7	64	6.0	89	11.0
40	4.7	65	6.0	90+	11.3

WARNING: These annuity rates, for both immediate and deferred annuities and for both single life and two lives, should not be used if the gift portion, based on IRS tables and the applicable discount rate, is not more than 10% of the amount paid for the annuity.

NOTES:
1. The rates are for ages at the nearest birthday.
2. For immediate gift annuities, these rates will result in a charitable deduction of more than 10% if the CMFR [IRC Sec. 7520 interest rate] is 4.0% or higher, whatever the payment frequency. If the CMFR is less than 4.0%, the deduction will be less than 10% when annuitants are below certain ages.
3. For deferred gift annuities with longer deferral periods, the rates may not pass the 10% test when the CMFR is low.
4. To avoid adverse tax consequences, the charity should reduce the gift annuity rate to whatever level is necessary to generate a charitable deduction in excess of 10%.

[See Chapter 12 regarding charitable gift annuities.]

Source: American Council on Gift Annuities

SUGGESTED CHARITABLE GIFT ANNUITY RATES

	Two Lives – Joint and Survivor					
Younger Age	**Older Age**	**Rate**	**Younger Age**	**Older Age**	**Rate**	
0-1	All	3.5	58	64+	5.4	
2-5	2+	3.6	59	59-61	5.4	
6-12	6+	3.7	59	62+	5.5	
13-19	13+	3.8	60	60	5.4	
20	20+	3.8	60	61+	5.5	
21	21+	3.8	61	61-65	5.5	
22	22+	3.8	61	66+	5.6	
23	23+	3.9	62	62-64	5.5	
24	24+	3.9	62	65-70	5.6	
25	25+	3.9	62	71+	5.7	
26	26+	3.9	63	63	5.5	
27	27+	3.9	63	64-68	5.6	
28	28+	3.9	63	69+	5.7	
29	29+	4.0	64	64-66	5.6	
30	30+	4.0	64	67-72	5.7	
31	31+	4.0	64	73+	5.8	
32	32+	4.0	65	65	5.6	
33	33+	4.1	65	66-70	5.7	
34	34+	4.1	65	71+	5.8	
35	35+	4.1	66	66-68	5.7	
36	36+	4.1	66	69-73	5.8	
37	37+	4.2	66	74+	5.9	
38	38+	4.2	67	67	5.7	
39	39+	4.2	67	68-71	5.8	
40	40+	4.3	67	72-76	5.9	
41	41+	4.3	67	77+	6.0	
42	42+	4.3	68	68-70	5.8	
43	43+	4.4	68	71-74	5.9	
44	44+	4.4	68	75-78	6.0	
45	45+	4.5	68	79+	6.1	
46	46+	4.5	69	69	5.8	
47	47+	4.6	69	70-72	5.9	
48	48+	4.6	69	73-76	6.0	
49	49+	4.7	69	77-80	6.1	
50	50+	4.7	69	81+	6.2	
51	51+	4.8	70	70-71	5.9	
52	52+	4.9	70	72-74	6.0	
53	53+	4.9	70	75-77	6.1	
54	54+	5.0	70	78-82	6.2	
55	55+	5.0	70	83+	6.3	
56	56-57	5.1	71	71-73	6.0	
56	58+	5.2	71	74-76	6.1	
57	57-58	5.2	71	77-79	6.2	
57	59+	5.3	71	80-83	6.3	
58	58-63	5.3	71	84+	6.4	

SUGGESTED CHARITABLE GIFT ANNUITY RATES

Two Lives — Joint and Survivor

Younger Age	Older Age	Rate	Younger Age	Older Age	Rate
72	72	6.0	78	87-89	7.2
72	73-74	6.1	78	90-92	7.3
72	75-77	6.2	78	93+	7.4
72	78-80	6.3	79	79	6.8
72	81-84	6.4	79	80-81	6.9
72	85+	6.5	79	82	7.0
73	73	6.1	79	83-84	7.1
73	74-75	6.2	79	85-86	7.2
73	76-78	6.3	79	87-88	7.3
73	79-81	6.4	79	89-90	7.4
73	82-84	6.5	79	91-93	7.5
73	85+	6.6	79	94+	7.6
74	74	6.2	80	80	6.9
74	75-76	6.3	80	81	7.0
74	77-79	6.4	80	82	7.1
74	80-81	6.5	80	83-84	7.2
74	82-84	6.6	80	85	7.3
74	85+	6.7	80	86-87	7.4
75	75	6.3	80	88-89	7.5
75	76-77	6.4	80	90-91	7.6
75	78-79	6.5	80	92-94	7.7
75	80-82	6.6	80	95+	7.8
75	83-85	6.7	81	81	7.1
75	86-88	6.8	81	82-83	7.2
75	89+	6.9	81	84	7.3
76	76	6.4	81	85	7.4
76	77-78	6.5	81	86-87	7.5
76	79-80	6.6	81	88	7.6
76	81-82	6.7	81	89-90	7.7
76	83-84	6.8	81	91-92	7.8
76	85-87	6.9	81	93-94	7.9
76	88+	7.0	81	95+	8.0
77	77	6.5	82	82-83	7.3
77	78-79	6.6	82	84	7.4
77	80	6.7	82	85	7.5
77	81-82	6.8	82	86	7.6
77	83-84	6.9	82	87	7.7
77	85-87	7.0	82	88-89	7.8
77	88-90	7.1	82	90	7.9
77	91+	7.2	82	91-92	8.0
78	78-79	6.7	82	93-94	8.1
78	80-81	6.8	82	95+	8.2
78	82	6.9	83	83	7.4
78	83-84	7.0	83	84	7.5
78	85-86	7.1	83	85	7.6

SUGGESTED CHARITABLE GIFT ANNUITY RATES

Two Lives — Joint and Survivor					
Younger Age	**Older Age**	**Rate**	**Younger Age**	**Older Age**	**Rate**
83	86	7.7	87	91	8.9
83	87	7.8	87	92	9.0
83	88	7.9	87	93	9.1
83	89	8.0	87	94	9.2
83	90-91	8.1	87	95+	9.3
83	92	8.2	88	88	8.7
83	93-94	8.3	88	89	8.8
83	95+	8.4	88	90	8.9
84	84	7.6	88	91	9.1
84	85	7.8	88	92	9.2
84	86	7.9	88	93	9.3
84	87	8.0	88	94	9.4
84	88-89	8.1	88	95+	9.5
84	90	8.2	89	89	9.0
84	91	8.3	89	90	9.1
84	92	8.4	89	91	9.3
84	93-94	8.5	89	92	9.4
84	95+	8.6	89	93	9.5
85	85	7.9	89	94	9.7
85	86	8.0	89	95+	9.8
85	87	8.1	90	90	9.3
85	88	8.2	90	91	9.5
85	89	8.3	90	92	9.6
85	90	8.4	90	93	9.8
85	91	8.5	90	94	9.9
85	92	8.6	90	95+	10.1
85	93-94	8.7	91	91	9.6
85	95+	8.8	91	92	9.8
86	86	8.1	91	93	10.0
86	87	8.2	91	94	10.1
86	88	8.4	91	95+	10.3
86	89	8.5	92	92	10.0
86	90	8.6	92	93	10.2
86	91	8.7	92	94	10.4
86	92	8.8	92	95+	10.6
86	93	8.9	93	93	10.4
86	94	9.0	93	94	10.6
86	95+	9.1	93	95+	10.8
87	87	8.4	94	94	10.8
87	88	8.5	94	95+	11.0
87	89	8.6	95 & over	95+	11.1
87	90	8.8			

TOOLS & TECHNIQUES

Brought to you by the publisher of Tax Facts

EXPECTED RETURN MULTIPLES

In determining the treatment of portions of payments from a charitable gift annuity (see Chapter 12) as ordinary income, gain, or recovery of basis, it is necessary to calculate the expected return. The expected return is equal to: one annuity payment x the number of payments per year x the expected return multiple.

The expected return multiple is obtained from Table V or Table VI, with an adjustment for frequency of payment (use the Frequency of Payment Adjustment Table). Table V is used for a single life and Table VI is used for two lives (joint and survivor). Additional Table VI factors are available at taxfactsonline.com.

For example, assume semiannual payments, payable at the end of each period, of $10,000 for an individual age 70. The Table V factor for age 70 is 16.0. The factor from the Frequency of Payment Adjustment Table for semiannual payments at the end of each period is -.2. The frequency adjusted expected return multiple equals 15.8 (16.0 - .2). The expected return equals $316,000 ($10,000 x 2 x 15.8).

Frequency of Payment Adjustment Table

If the number of whole months from the annuity starting date to the first payment date is	0-1	2	3	4	5	6	7	8	9	10	11	12
And payments under the contract are to be made:												
Annually	+0.5	+0.4	+0.3	+0.2	+0.1	0	0	-0.1	-0.2	-0.3	-0.4	-0.5
Semiannually	+ .2	+ .1	0	0	- .1	- .2	....	....	....	....	....	....
Quarterly	+ .1	0	- .1	....	....	....	....	....	....	....	....	....

TABLE V — ORDINARY LIFE ANNUITIES —

ONE LIFE — EXPECTED RETURN MULTIPLES

Age	Multiple	Age	Multiple	Age	Multiple
5	76.6	42	40.6	79	10.0
6	75.6	43	39.6	80	9.5
7	74.7	44	38.7	81	8.9
8	73.7	45	37.7	82	8.4
9	72.7	46	36.8	63	7.9
10	71.7	47	35.9	84	7.4
11	70.7	48	34.9	85	6.9
12	69.7	49	34.0	86	6.5
13	68.8	50	33.1	87	6.1
14	67.8	51	32.2	88	5.7
15	66.8	52	31.3	89	5.3
16	65.8	53	30.4	90	5.0
17	64.8	54	29.5	91	4.7
18	63.9	55	28.6	92	4.4
19	62.9	56	27.7	93	4.1
20	61.9	57	26.8	94	3.9
21	60.9	58	25.9	95	3.7
22	59.9	59	25.0	96	3.4
23	59.0	60	24.2	97	3.2
24	58.0	61	23.3	98	3.0
25	57.0	62	22.5	99	2.8
26	56.0	63	21.6	100	2.7
27	55.1	64	20.8	101	2.5
28	54.1	65	20.0	102	2.3
29	53.1	66	19.2	103	2.1
30	52.2	67	18.4	104	1.9
31	51.2	68	17.6	105	1.8
32	50.2	69	16.8	106	1.6
33	49.3	70	16.0	107	1.4
34	48.3	71	15.3	108	1.3
35	47.3	72	14.6	109	1.1
36	46.4	73	13.9	110	1.0
37	45.4	74	13.2	111	.9
38	44.4	75	12.5	112	.8
39	43.5	76	11.9	113	.7
40	42.5	77	11.2	114	.6
41	41.5	78	10.6	115	.5

TABLE VI – ORDINARY JOINT LIFE AND LAST SURVIVOR ANNUITIES –

TWO LIVES – EXPECTED RETURN MULTIPLES

AGES	35	36	37	38	39	40	41	42	43	44	45	46	47	48	49	50
35	54.0	...	...	...	...	...	...	...	...	...	...	...	...	...	...	...
36	53.5	53.0	...	...	...	...	...	...	...	...	...	...	...	...	...	...
37	53.0	52.5	52.0	...	...	...	...	...	...	...	...	...	...	...	...	...
38	52.6	52.0	51.5	51.0	...	...	...	...	...	...	...	...	...	...	...	...
39	52.2	51.6	51.0	50.5	50.0	...	...	...	...	...	...	...	...	...	...	...
40	51.8	51.2	50.6	50.0	49.5	49.0	...	...	...	...	...	...	...	...	...	...
41	51.4	50.8	50.2	49.6	49.1	48.5	48.0	...	...	...	...	...	...	...	...	...
42	51.1	50.4	49.8	49.2	48.6	48.1	47.5	47.0	...	...	...	...	...	...	...	...
43	50.8	50.1	49.5	48.8	48.2	47.6	47.1	46.6	46.0	...	...	...	...	...	...	...
44	50.5	49.8	49.1	48.5	47.8	47.2	46.7	46.1	45.6	45.1	...	...	...	...	...	...
45	50.2	49.5	48.8	48.1	47.5	46.9	46.3	45.7	45.1	44.6	44.1	...	...	...	...	...
46	50.0	49.2	48.5	47.8	47.2	46.5	45.9	45.3	44.7	44.1	43.6	43.1	...	...	...	...
47	49.7	49.0	48.3	47.5	46.8	46.2	45.5	44.9	44.3	43.7	43.2	42.6	42.1	...	...	...
48	49.5	48.8	48.0	47.3	46.6	45.9	45.2	44.5	43.9	43.3	42.7	42.2	41.7	41.2	...	...
49	49.3	48.5	47.8	47.0	46.3	45.6	44.9	44.2	43.6	42.9	42.3	41.8	41.2	40.7	40.2	...
50	49.2	48.4	47.6	46.8	46.0	45.3	44.6	43.9	43.2	42.6	42.0	41.4	40.8	40.2	39.7	39.2
51	49.0	48.2	47.4	46.6	45.8	45.1	44.3	43.6	42.9	42.2	41.6	41.0	40.4	39.8	39.3	38.7
52	48.8	48.0	47.2	46.4	45.6	44.8	44.1	43.3	42.6	41.9	41.3	40.6	40.0	39.4	38.8	38.3
53	48.7	47.9	47.0	46.2	45.4	44.6	43.9	43.1	42.4	41.7	41.0	40.3	39.7	39.0	38.4	37.9
54	48.6	47.7	46.9	46.0	45.2	44.4	43.6	42.9	42.1	41.4	40.7	40.0	39.3	38.7	38.1	37.5
55	48.5	47.6	46.7	45.9	45.1	44.2	43.4	42.7	41.9	41.2	40.4	39.7	39.0	38.4	37.7	37.1
56	48.3	47.5	46.6	45.8	44.9	44.1	43.3	42.5	41.7	40.9	40.2	39.5	38.7	38.1	37.4	36.8
57	48.3	47.4	46.5	45.6	44.8	43.9	43.1	42.3	41.5	40.7	40.0	39.2	38.5	37.8	37.1	36.4
58	48.2	47.3	46.4	45.5	44.7	43.8	43.0	42.1	41.3	40.5	39.7	39.0	38.2	37.5	36.8	36.1
59	48.1	47.2	46.3	45.4	44.5	43.7	42.8	42.0	41.2	40.4	39.6	38.8	38.0	37.3	36.6	35.9
60	48.0	47.1	46.2	45.3	44.4	43.6	42.7	41.9	41.0	40.2	39.4	38.6	37.8	37.1	36.3	35.6
61	47.9	47.0	46.1	45.2	44.3	43.5	42.6	41.7	40.9	40.0	39.2	38.4	37.6	36.9	36.1	35.4
62	47.9	47.0	46.0	45.1	44.2	43.4	42.5	41.6	40.8	39.9	39.1	38.3	37.5	36.7	35.9	35.1
63	47.8	46.9	46.0	45.1	44.2	43.3	42.4	41.5	40.6	39.8	38.9	38.1	37.3	36.5	35.7	34.9
64	47.8	46.8	45.9	45.0	44.1	43.2	42.3	41.4	40.5	39.7	38.8	38.0	37.2	36.3	35.5	34.8
65	47.7	46.8	45.9	44.9	44.0	43.1	42.2	41.3	40.4	39.6	38.7	37.9	37.0	36.2	35.4	34.6
66	47.7	46.7	45.8	44.9	44.0	43.1	42.2	41.3	40.4	39.5	38.6	37.8	36.9	36.1	35.2	34.4
67	47.6	46.7	45.8	44.8	43.9	43.0	42.1	41.2	40.3	39.4	38.5	37.7	36.8	36.0	35.1	34.3
68	47.6	46.7	45.7	44.8	43.9	42.9	42.0	41.1	40.2	39.3	38.4	37.6	36.7	35.8	35.0	34.2
69	47.6	46.6	45.7	44.8	43.8	42.9	42.0	41.1	40.2	39.3	38.4	37.5	36.6	35.7	34.9	34.1
70	47.5	46.6	45.7	44.7	43.8	42.9	41.9	41.0	40.1	39.2	38.3	37.4	36.5	35.7	34.8	34.0
71	47.5	46.6	45.6	44.7	43.8	42.8	41.9	41.0	40.1	39.1	38.2	37.3	36.5	35.6	34.7	33.9
72	47.5	46.6	45.6	44.7	43.7	42.8	41.9	40.9	40.0	39.1	38.2	37.3	36.4	35.5	34.6	33.8
73	47.5	46.5	45.6	44.7	43.7	42.8	41.8	40.9	40.0	39.0	38.1	37.2	36.3	35.4	34.6	33.7
74	47.5	46.5	45.6	44.7	43.7	42.7	41.8	40.9	39.9	39.0	38.1	37.2	36.3	35.4	34.5	33.6
75	47.4	46.5	45.5	44.7	43.6	42.7	41.8	40.8	39.9	39.0	38.1	37.1	36.2	35.3	34.5	33.6
76	47.4	46.5	45.5	44.7	43.6	42.7	41.7	40.8	39.9	38.9	38.0	37.1	36.2	35.3	34.4	33.5
77	47.4	46.5	45.5	44.7	43.6	42.7	41.7	40.8	39.8	38.9	38.0	37.1	36.2	35.3	34.4	33.5
78	47.4	46.4	45.5	44.5	43.6	42.6	41.7	40.7	39.8	38.9	38.0	37.0	36.1	35.2	34.3	33.4
79	47.4	46.4	45.5	44.5	43.6	42.6	41.7	40.7	39.8	38.9	37.9	37.0	36.1	35.2	34.3	33.4
80	47.4	46.4	45.5	44.5	43.6	42.6	41.7	40.7	39.8	38.8	37.9	37.0	36.1	35.2	34.2	33.4
81	47.4	46.4	45.5	44.5	43.5	42.6	41.6	40.7	39.8	38.8	37.9	37.0	36.0	35.1	34.2	33.3
82	47.4	46.4	45.4	44.5	43.5	42.6	41.6	40.7	39.7	38.8	37.9	36.9	36.0	35.1	34.2	33.3
83	47.4	46.4	45.4	44.5	43.5	42.6	41.6	40.7	39.7	38.8	37.9	36.9	36.0	35.1	34.2	33.3
84	47.4	46.4	45.4	44.5	43.5	42.6	41.6	40.7	39.7	38.8	37.8	36.9	36.0	35.0	34.1	33.2
85	47.4	46.4	45.4	44.5	43.5	42.6	41.6	40.7	39.7	38.8	37.8	36.9	36.0	35.0	34.1	33.2
86	47.3	46.4	45.4	44.5	43.5	42.5	41.6	40.6	39.7	38.8	37.8	36.9	36.0	35.0	34.1	33.2
87	47.3	46.4	45.4	44.5	43.5	42.5	41.6	40.6	39.7	38.7	37.8	36.9	35.9	35.0	34.1	33.2
88	47.3	46.4	45.4	44.5	43.5	42.5	41.6	40.6	39.7	38.7	37.8	36.9	35.9	35.0	34.1	33.2
89	47.3	46.4	45.4	44.4	43.5	42.5	41.6	40.6	39.7	38.7	37.8	36.9	35.9	35.0	34.1	33.2
90	47.3	46.4	45.4	44.4	43.5	42.5	41.6	40.6	39.7	38.7	37.8	36.9	35.9	35.0	34.1	33.2

TABLE VI — ORDINARY JOINT LIFE AND LAST SURVIVOR ANNUITIES —

	TWO LIVES — EXPECTED RETURN MULTIPLES															
AGES	**51**	**52**	**53**	**54**	**55**	**56**	**57**	**58**	**59**	**60**	**61**	**62**	**63**	**64**	**65**	**66**
51	38.2	…	…	…	…	…	…	…	…	…	…	…	…	…	…	…
52	37.8	37.3	…	…	…	…	…	…	…	…	…	…	…	…	…	…
53	37.3	36.8	36.3	…	…	…	…	…	…	…	…	…	…	…	…	…
54	36.9	36.4	35.8	35.3	…	…	…	…	…	…	…	…	…	…	…	…
55	36.5	55.9	35.4	34.9	34.4	…	…	…	…	…	…	…	…	…	…	…
56	36.1	35.6	35.0	34.4	33.9	33.4	…	…	…	…	…	…	…	…	…	…
57	35.8	35.2	34.6	34.0	33.5	33.0	32.5	…	…	…	…	…	…	…	…	…
58	35.5	34.8	34.2	33.6	33.1	32.5	32.0	31.5	…	…	…	…	…	…	…	…
59	35.2	34.5	33.9	33.3	32.7	32.1	31.6	31.1	30.6	…	…	…	…	…	…	…
60	34.9	34.2	33.6	32.9	32.3	31.7	31.2	30.6	30.1	29.7	…	…	…	…	…	…
61	34.6	33.9	33.3	32.6	32.0	31.4	30.8	30.2	29.7	29.2	28.7	…	…	…	…	…
62	34.4	33.7	33.0	32.3	31.7	31.0	30.4	29.9	29.3	28.8	28.3	27.8	…	…	…	…
63	34.2	33.5	32.7	32.0	31.4	30.7	30.1	29.5	28.9	28.4	27.8	27.3	26.9	…	…	…
64	34.0	33.2	32.5	31.8	31.1	30.4	29.8	29.2	28.6	28.0	27.4	26.9	26.4	25.9	…	…
65	33.8	33.0	32.3	31.6	30.9	30.2	29.5	28.9	28.2	27.6	27.1	26.5	26.0	25.5	25.0	…
66	33.6	32.9	32.1	31.4	30.6	29.9	29.2	28.6	27.9	27.3	26.7	26.1	25.6	25.1	24.6	24.1
67	33.5	32.7	31.9	31.2	30.4	29.7	29.0	28.3	27.6	27.0	26.4	25.8	25.2	24.7	24.2	23.7
68	33.4	32.5	31.8	31.0	30.2	29.5	28.8	28.1	27.4	26.7	26.1	25.5	24.9	24.3	23.8	23.3
69	33.2	32.4	31.6	30.8	30.1	29.3	28.6	27.8	27.1	26.5	25.8	25.2	24.6	24.0	23.4	22.9
70	33.1	32.3	31.5	30.7	29.9	29.1	28.4	27.6	26.9	26.2	25.6	24.9	24.3	23.7	23.1	22.5
71	33.0	32.2	31.4	30.5	29.7	29.0	28.2	27.5	26.7	26.0	25.3	24.7	24.0	23.4	22.8	22.2
72	32.9	32.1	31.2	30.4	29.6	28.8	28.1	27.3	26.5	25.8	25.1	24.4	23.8	23.1	22.5	21.9
73	32.8	32.0	31.1	30.3	29.5	28.7	27.9	27.1	26.4	25.6	24.9	24.2	23.5	22.9	22.2	21.6
74	32.8	31.9	31.1	30.2	29.4	28.6	27.8	27.0	26.2	25.5	24.7	24.0	23.3	22.7	22.0	21.4
75	32.7	31.8	31.0	30.1	29.3	28.5	27.7	26.9	26.1	25.3	24.6	23.8	23.1	22.4	21.8	21.1
76	32.6	31.8	30.9	30.1	29.2	28.4	27.6	26.8	26.0	25.2	24.4	23.7	23.0	22.3	21.6	20.9
77	32.6	31.7	30.8	30.0	29.1	28.3	27.5	26.7	25.9	25.1	24.3	23.6	22.8	22.1	21.4	20.7
78	32.5	31.7	30.8	29.9	29.1	28.2	27.4	26.6	25.8	25.0	24.2	23.4	22.7	21.9	21.2	20.5
79	32.5	31.6	30.7	29.9	29.0	28.2	27.3	26.5	25.7	24.9	24.1	23.3	22.6	21.8	21.1	20.4
80	32.5	31.6	30.7	29.8	29.0	28.1	27.3	26.4	25.6	24.8	24.0	23.2	22.4	21.7	21.0	20.2
81	32.4	31.5	30.7	29.8	28.9	28.1	27.2	26.4	25.5	24.7	23.9	23.1	22.3	21.6	20.8	20.1
82	32.4	31.5	30.6	29.7	28.9	28.0	27.2	26.3	25.5	24.6	23.8	23.0	22.3	21.5	20.7	20.0
83	32.4	31.5	30.6	29.7	28.8	28.0	27.1	26.3	25.4	24.6	23.8	23.0	22.2	21.4	20.6	19.9
84	32.3	31.4	30.6	29.7	28.8	27.9	27.1	26.2	25.4	24.5	23.7	22.9	22.1	21.3	20.5	19.8
85	32.3	31.4	30.5	29.6	28.8	27.9	27.0	26.2	25.3	24.5	23.7	22.8	22.0	21.3	20.5	19.7
86	32.3	31.4	30.5	29.6	28.7	27.9	27.0	26.1	25.3	24.5	23.6	22.8	22.0	21.2	20.4	19.6
87	32.3	31.4	30.5	29.6	28.7	27.8	27.0	26.1	25.3	24.4	23.6	22.8	21.9	21.1	20.4	19.6
88	32.3	31.4	30.5	29.6	28.7	27.8	27.0	26.1	25.2	24.4	23.5	22.7	21.9	21.1	20.3	19.5
89	32.3	31.4	30.5	29.6	28.7	27.8	26.9	26.1	25.2	24.4	23.5	22.7	21.9	21.1	20.3	19.5
90	32.3	31.3	30.5	29.5	28.7	27.8	26.9	26.1	25.2	24.3	23.5	22.7	21.8	21.0	20.2	19.4

TABLE VI – ORDINARY JOINT LIFE AND LAST SURVIVOR ANNUITIES –

TWO LIVES – EXPECTED RETURN MULTIPLES

AGES	67	68	69	70	71	72	73	74	75	76	77	78	79	80	81	82
67	23.2	...	...	...	...	...	...	...	...	...	...	...	...	...	...	...
68	22.8	22.3	...	...	...	...	...	...	...	...	...	...	...	...	...	...
69	22.4	21.9	21.5	...	...	...	...	...	...	...	...	...	...	...	...	...
70	22.0	21.5	21.1	20.6	...	...	...	...	...	...	...	...	...	...	...	...
71	21.7	21.2	20.7	20.2	19.8	...	...	...	...	...	...	...	...	...	...	...
72	21.3	20.8	20.3	19.8	19.4	18.9	...	...	...	...	...	...	...	...	...	...
73	21.0	20.5	20.0	19.4	19.0	18.5	18.1	...	...	...	...	...	...	...	...	...
74	20.8	20.2	19.6	19.1	18.6	18.2	17.7	17.3	...	...	...	...	...	...	...	...
75	20.5	19.9	19.3	18.8	18.3	17.8	17.3	16.9	16.5	...	...	...	...	...	...	...
76	20.3	19.7	19.1	18.5	18.0	17.5	17.0	16.5	16.1	15.7	...	...	...	...	...	...
77	20.1	19.4	18.8	18.3	17.7	17.2	16.7	16.2	15.8	15.4	15.0	...	...	...	...	...
78	19.9	19.2	18.6	18.0	17.5	16.9	16.4	15.9	15.4	15.0	14.6	14.2	...	...	...	...
79	19.7	19.0	18.4	17.8	17.2	16.7	16.1	15.6	15.1	14.7	14.3	13.9	13.5	...	...	...
80	19.5	18.9	18.2	17.6	17.0	16.4	15.9	15.4	14.9	14.4	14.0	13.5	13.2	12.8	...	...
81	19.4	18.7	18.1	17.4	16.8	16.2	15.7	15.1	14.6	14.1	13.7	13.2	12.8	12.5	12.1	...
82	19.3	18.6	17.9	17.3	16.6	16.0	15.5	14.9	14.4	13.9	13.4	13.0	12.5	12.2	11.8	11.5
83	19.2	18.5	17.8	17.1	16.5	15.9	15.3	14.7	14.2	13.7	13.2	12.7	12.3	11.9	11.5	11.1
84	19.1	18.4	17.7	17.0	16.3	15.7	15.1	14.5	14.0	13.5	13.0	12.5	12.0	11.6	11.2	10.9
85	19.0	18.3	17.6	16.9	16.2	15.6	15.0	14.4	13.8	13.3	12.8	12.3	11.8	11.4	11.0	10.6
86	18.9	18.2	17.5	16.8	16.1	15.5	14.8	14.2	13.7	13.1	12.6	12.1	11.6	11.2	10.8	10.4
87	18.8	18.1	17.4	16.7	16.0	15.4	14.7	14.1	13.5	13.0	12.4	11.9	11.4	11.0	10.6	10.1
88	18.8	18.0	17.3	16.6	15.9	15.3	14.6	14.0	13.4	12.8	12.3	11.8	11.3	10.8	10.4	10.0
89	18.7	18.0	17.2	16.5	15.8	15.2	14.5	13.9	13.3	12.7	12.2	11.6	11.1	10.7	10.2	9.8
90	18.7	17.9	17.2	16.5	15.8	15.1	14.5	13.8	13.2	12.6	12.1	11.5	11.0	10.5	10.1	9.6

TABLE VI – ORDINARY JOINT LIFE AND LAST SURVIVOR ANNUITIES –

TWO LIVES – EXPECTED RETURN MULTIPLES

AGES	83	84	85	86	87	88	89	90
83	10.8	...	...	...	...	...	...	...
84	10.5	10.2	...	...	...	...	...	...
85	10.2	9.9	9.6	...	...	...	...	...
86	10.0	9.7	9.3	9.1	...	...	...	...
87	9.8	9.4	9.1	8.8	8.5	...	...	...
88	9.6	9.2	8.9	8.6	8.3	8.0	...	...
89	9.4	9.0	8.7	8.3	8.1	7.8	7.5	...
90	9.2	8.8	8.5	8.2	7.9	7.6	7.3	7.1

CHARITABLE REMAINDER TRUST (CRT) ADMINISTRATION

Administration of a charitable remainder trust (CRT) can be a complex task. There are numerous tax and private foundation rules to be concerned with (even though CRTs are not technically private foundations), as well as a number of recordkeeping, accounting, valuation, and tax reporting responsibilities.

The consequences of improperly administering a CRT can be severe and may even include disqualification of the trust as a CRT. It is also possible to cause the CRT to incur excise tax by creating unrelated business taxable income (UBTI). Consequently, it is crucial to appoint a trustee who is sensitive to these issues and who is willing and able to perform the myriad administrative responsibilities associated with a CRT.

The duties of a CRT trustee include:

- investing trust assets;

- maintaining trust records and filing the appropriate tax and informational returns;

- determining and paying the required annuity or unitrust payment to the income beneficiary;

- following the 4-tier ordering system for payments to the income beneficiary;

- valuing trust assets; and

- complying with the private foundation rules and maintaining the tax-exempt status of the trust.

CHOOSING A CHARITABLE TRUSTEE

There are no specific limitations regarding who can serve as trustee of a CRT. However, the trustee of a CRT assumes a substantial amount of responsibility and must be able to perform all of the duties described above.

In general, the trustee will be chosen from one of the following three categories:

1. an institutional trustee, such as a bank or trust company;

2. the charitable remainderman; or

3. the grantor.

Institutional Trustee

Using an institutional trustee may be the appropriate choice in most cases because banks and trust companies are highly experienced in managing trusts. Institutional trustees familiar with managing CRTs should be able to avoid many potential CRT administration pitfalls, such as violating the private foundation rules or creating unrelated business taxable income. In addition, institutional trustees may have access to investment opportunities (such as common trust funds) that might not be available to a charity or grantor trustee. Institutional trustees can invest in common trust funds without jeopardizing the tax-exempt status of the CRT or the grantor's charitable deduction.[1]

On the other hand, using an institutional trustee will require paying an annual fee for the institution's services, which could run as high as 1.5% to 2% of the principal of the trust. Many of the operational costs of a CRT that are associated with using an institutional trustee may be reduced—perhaps significantly—if the grantor or the charitable remainderman serves as trustee.

Another drawback to using an institutional trustee is the loss of control over how CRT assets will be invested. Because an institutional trustee has a fiduciary obligation to invest CRT assets prudently, the institution may invest CRT assets more conservatively than desired by the grantor. Investing trust assets conservatively could reduce the annual amount paid to the trust income beneficiary (usually the grantor), particularly in a CRUT where the payout is a percentage of the trust assets.

Charity as Trustee

Charitable organizations are sometimes willing to serve as trustee of a CRT if they are designated as the sole or majority charitable remainderman. This can be convenient for the grantor, and may lower the cost to the donor of administering the CRT if the charity is willing to serve as trustee at no charge.

Like the institutional trustee, though, the charity trustee may invest trust assets more conservatively than desired by the grantor because the board of directors or trustees of the charity also have a fiduciary obligation to invest prudently. An additional drawback may be that, unlike the institutional trustee, many smaller or medium sized charities may not have staff skilled in managing CRTs, or may not posses the investment experience or the administrative capabilities of a large institutional trustee.

A charity trustee can invest CRT assets in its general endowment fund or with the assets of other CRTs.[2] However, a charity that manages and commingles donor funds (including CRTs) must provide a disclosure statement to a donor. This statement must disclose, in writing and at the time of donation, the material terms of the operation of the fund.[3]

Grantor as Trustee

There are no specific legal prohibitions against a grantor serving as trustee of his own CRT. But that is far from a green light indicating that such a course of action is either safe or appropriate. For instance, if the grantor serves as trustee, and retains any powers that would cause the trust to be treated as a grantor trust, the trust will be disqualified as a CRT.[4] Consequently, where the grantor will serve as trustee of the CRT, the trust document should be carefully drafted so as to avoid inadvertently causing grantor trust status. For example, giving the grantor the power to "sprinkle" trust income between the trust income beneficiaries would cause the trust to be treated as grantor trust, which would then disqualify the trust as a CRT.[5] The tax consequences of disqualification of the CRT would include taxation of the trust's income *and* a denial of the donor's charitable contribution deduction.

Hard-to-value assets. In the past, an independent trustee was needed where a CRT was funded with unmarketable assets that did not have an objective, ascertainable value (i.e., "hard-to-value" assets). However a grantor may serve as trustee in this situation as long as a current qualified appraisal from a qualified independent appraiser is used to value the hard-to-value assets.[6] If the grantor intends to serve as a trustee of a CRT funded with hard-to-value assets (such as annuities, closely-held business interests, or limited partnership units), a qualified independent appraiser must be used to value those assets.

Use of a third party administrator. When the grantor is serving as trustee, it is common for the grantor/trustee to hire an experienced administrative service to handle the day-to-day operation of the trust. There are many such administrative services that specialize solely in administering CRTs for a fee.

Typically, the administrative service will handle trust compliance, maintain appropriate records, file tax returns, and make trust distributions. In addition to hiring an administrative service, a grantor/trustee may hire a professional money manager to invest trust proceeds. Alternatively, the grantor/trustee could retain investment responsibility while hiring out the administrative responsibilities.

Trustee's fees. A grantor can be paid for his services as trustee provided that the fees are reasonable *and* do not exceed the amount customarily paid to independent trustees under applicable state law.[7] Regardless of who serves as trustee, trustee fees cannot be paid from the income beneficiary's annuity or unitrust payment.[8]

INVESTING TRUST ASSETS

A trust will not qualify as a CRT if the trust document places unreasonable restrictions on the trustee's ability to invest trust assets.[9] For example, requiring the trustee to invest solely in tax-exempt bonds, or requiring the trustee to receive approval from the income beneficiary prior to making an investment change will potentially disqualify the trust as a CRT.

However, there can be *reasonable* restrictions placed on the trustee's investment selection. For instance, the grantor may restrict the trustee's ability to invest in hard-to-value assets, such as closely-held stock.

Unrelated Business Taxable Income (UBTI)

A charitable remainder trust is ordinarily tax-exempt for income tax purposes. However, if the trust has what is considered "unrelated business taxable income " or "debt-financed income" (collectively UBTI), the trust must pay an excise tax equal to the amount of the UBTI. For example if a trust has $10,000 of income and $1,000 is considered UBTI, the trust will pay a $1,000 excise tax.[10] This excise tax is effective for taxable years beginning after December 31, 2006. While this is a harsh result, prior to the enactment of The Tax Relief and Health Care Act of 2006, if the trust had even $1 of UBTI, the trust lost tax exempt status for that year.[11]

Because of this potential negative consequence, the trustee of a CRT should avoid investing trust property in a manner that may create UBTI.

There are certain "problem investments" that may cause UBTI for a CRT:

1. mortgaged real estate or other debt-financed property;

2. closely-held stock where the CRT owns more than 49% of the combined voting power of all classes of stock; or

3. certain partnership interests (depending on the underlying partnership investments).

The trustee must evaluate closely whether these (or other) assets will create UBTI for the trust before investing trust assets.

TAX REPORTING REQUIREMENTS

Unless the trust has UBTI, a CRT is an entity that is exempt from income tax. However, whether or not there is UBTI, and even though the CRT may have no income tax liability, there are still tax reporting requirements that must be met.

Because CRTs are required to adopt a calendar year, all tax forms must be filed by April 15th of the following year.[12] In general, the following forms must be filed annually with IRS:

- Form 5227 (Split-Interest Trust Information Return);

- Form 1041-A (U.S. Information Return, Trust Accumulation of Charitable Amounts); and

- Schedule K-1 of Form 1041 (Beneficiary's Share of Income, Deductions, Credits, etc.).

In addition to federal tax reporting, there may be state tax returns that must be filed with the trust's state of domicile. Any state income tax reporting requirements will depend on state law and will vary from state to state.

Form 5227 (Split-Interest Trust Information Return)

With few exceptions, all charitable remainder trusts, pooled income funds, and charitable lead trusts must file Form 5227 each year. The purpose of this form is to report all trust income, deductions, accumulations, distributions, and the annuity or unitrust amounts that were paid to the income beneficiary. In addition, a completed trust balance sheet is required on this form. A sample of Form 5227 is included in Appendix F.

Form 1041-A (U.S. Information Return, Trust Accumulation of Charitable Amounts)

This form is an informational return that has much of the same information as Form 5227. It is used to report trust income and deductions, and also includes a balance sheet showing beginning-of-year and end-of-year asset values.

In general, CRTs are required to file this form annually, with the exception of "net income only" trusts (see Chapter 16), in which all of the trust income is distributed for that calendar year.

A sample of Form 1041-A is included in Appendix F.

Schedule K-1 of Form 1041 (Beneficiary's Share of Income, Deductions, Credits, etc.)

This form is used to report the tax character of the annuity or unitrust payment made to the income beneficiary. All payments to the income beneficiary must be accounted for under the 4-tier ordering system required of CRTs. A sample of Schedule K-1 is included in Appendix F.

Form 8282 (Donee Information Return)

Form 8282 must be filed when any property, which required an appraisal when it was contributed to the CRT, is subsequently sold within two years of the contribution. Charitable contributions of property (other than cash and publicly traded securities) exceeding $5,000 ($10,000 for closely-held stock) require a qualified appraisal at the time of contribution.[13]

The purpose of Form 8282 is to allow the IRS to compare the value of the property claimed as a deduction by the donor to the value the trustee actually received upon disposition of the property. The form requires disclosure of the following information:

- a description of the property received;

- the date the property was received by the trust;

- the value received by the trust upon disposition;

- the date of the disposition; and

- the name and address of the donor.

A copy of this form must also be sent to the donor.

Other Tax Reporting Requirements

In certain circumstances, additional tax reporting may be required. For instance, if a charitable remainder trust has UBTI, the trustee must file Form 1041. Also, if the trustee violates any of the private foundation rules, Form 4720 (Excise Tax Return) must be filed.

Short tax year exception to the calendar year requirement. As previously mentioned, all CRTs must use a calendar tax year. However, during the initial and final tax years of the trust, it is likely that the trust will not be in effect for the entire calendar year. For instance, a donor can establish a CRT at any time during the year, and it is unlikely that the income beneficiary receiving a lifetime payout will die exactly on December 31st. Consequently, the initial and final years of the trust will most likely be short tax years.

For the initial short calendar tax year, the trust document must provide for a prorated payment of the annuity or unitrust amount based on the actual number of days the trust was in effect for that year.[14] For example, if an annuity trust was established on June 30th (the 181st day of most years), the trust would be in effect for 184 of the 365 calendar days of the year. Therefore, the annual annuity payment would be multiplied by .504 (184/365) to determine the initial payment.

For the final tax year of a lifetime payment, the prorated payment would be based on the number of days the income beneficiary lived during the year. For instance if the income beneficiary of an annuity trust died on June 30th (the 181st day of most years), the annual annuity payment would be multiplied by .496 (181/365) to determine the final payment.

ACCOUNTING FOR ANNUITY OR UNITRUST PAYMENTS TO THE INCOME BENEFICIARY

The 4-Tier Ordering System

The tax character of the annuity or unitrust amount paid to the income beneficiary is determined using the 4-tier ordering system. The general policy of the 4-tier system is to treat the income beneficiary as receiving income taxable at the highest tax rate before receiving any distributions of income that are taxable at lower rates (e.g., long-term capital gains).

Under the 4-tier system, distributions are treated as from:

Tier One: Ordinary income (taxable at ordinary income rates);

Tier Two: Capital gains (taxable at capital gains rates);

Tier Three: Other income (such as tax-exempt income); and

Tier Four: Trust principal or corpus (tax-free return of capital).[15]

Current and prior undistributed income from each tier must be exhausted before any income earned in the next tier will be treated as distributed to the income beneficiary. If the trust has unrelated business taxable income, the excise tax paid is allocated to principal, and therefore does not reduce taxable income under the four tier system.[16]

Example: Assume Mr. Dawson owns stock (which he purchased 10 years ago) with a fair market value of $1,000,000 and a cost basis of $100,000. He contributes this stock to a standard charitable remainder unitrust (see Chapter 16) with an 8% payout valued as of the beginning of the year. The trustee of the CRUT sells the stock and reinvests the proceeds in a bond fund earning 5% per year. The first payment from the CRUT would be $80,000 (8% x $1,000,000).

Using the 4-tier ordering system, Mr. Dawson's unitrust payment would be taxed as follows: $50,000 as ordinary income (which represents the total amount of the bond fund income earned by the trust), and $30,000 of capital gains from the sale of the stock, leaving $870,000 of undistributed capital gains in the trust (i.e., $900,000 long-term gain *minus* $30,000 distributed capital gain).

It is the responsibility of the trustee to account for annuity or unitrust payments to the income beneficiary using the 4-tier system. The tax character of all unitrust or annuity payments to the income beneficiary during the year is determined as of the end of the calendar year for which the payment is required. If there are two or more income beneficiaries, each is treated as receiving a pro rata portion of the distribution.

Paying the Annuity or Unitrust Amount

Caution: A CRT that does not pay the required annuity or unitrust payment to the beneficiary within the calendar year will lose its tax-exempt status for that year. However, as long as the payment consists of only income or property (i.e., no principal and no tax-exempt income), the trustee can pay the annuity or unitrust amount within

a reasonable time after the close of the calendar year (but generally no later than the filing date of IRS Form 5227.[17] In most cases, this would be April 15th following the close of the calendar year.)

If the unitrust or annuity payment includes tax-exempt income or trust principal, all payments must be made during the calendar year. For trusts created prior to December 10, 1998, payments can be made up to the filing date of Form 5227 as long as the annuity or unitrust amount is 15% or less.[18]

Occasionally, the income beneficiary may not be using a calendar tax year, in which case the tax years of the CRT and the income beneficiary would be different. In this situation, the trust will be treated as having made the annuity or unitrust payment in the trust's calendar tax year, not the beneficiary's fiscal tax year.

If property is distributed as part of the annuity or unitrust amount, the distribution is essentially treated as if the trust had sold the property and paid the sale proceeds to the income beneficiary. Consequently, the trust will recognize either a gain or loss on the transfer of the property, which must be taken into account when determining the tax character of the annuity or unitrust amount under the 4-tier system.

The tax character of distributions to the income beneficiary using the 4-tier system is reported on Schedule K-1 of Form 1041.

RECORDKEEPING REQUIREMENTS

The trustee of a CRT must keep detailed records of all transactions involving the trust. Examples of the recordkeeping that must be done include:

- tracking the cost basis of all trust assets for purposes of determining the income tax treatment of dispositions under the 4-tier ordering system;

- determining the value of any tax preference items for purposes of calculating the alternative minimum tax. Any tax preference items need to be allocated to the income beneficiary in each year the income is distributed;

- calculating all gains, losses, and deductions associated with trust investment activities;

- determining the character of trust receipts as either principal or income;

- determining the annual value of trust assets in the case of charitable remainder unitrusts (CRUTs); and

- accounting for the amount owed to the income beneficiary as "make-up" in a net income with make-up provisions unitrust (NIMCRUT).

VALUATION OF CRT ASSETS

Determining the proper value of trust assets is important for a variety of reasons. For instance, valuation is needed:

1. to determine the donor's tax deduction for income, gift, or estate tax purposes;

2. to fix the sum certain of the annual annuity amount for a charitable remainder annuity trust (CRAT);

3. to make the annual recomputation of the unitrust payment for a charitable remainder unitrust (CRUT); and

4. to determine the selling price of assets held in the trust.

Charitable Remainder Annuity Trust (CRAT)

With a CRAT, the annuity payment is determined based on the initial contribution and subsequent annual valuations are not necessary (see Chapter 15). However, if an annuity payment is made and it is later determined that an incorrect valuation was used, the payment must be corrected.[19] If the trust was undervalued, the trustee must pay the additional amount due the income beneficiary. Similarly, if the trust was overvalued, the income beneficiary must repay the trust for the overpayment.

Charitable Remainder Unitrust (CRUT)

Because the annual payment to the income beneficiary is a fixed percentage of the trust assets, an annual valuation is required for a CRUT (see Chapter 16). The timing and method of valuation must be determined when the CRUT is established.

There are no requirements that valuation must occur on a specific date or in a specific manner. The trustee has the choice of valuing trust assets on a specific date, or using an average valuation based on more than one date. However, once the valuation date (or dates) is selected by the trustee, that date must also be used in each subsequent year, and must be disclosed on the trust's initial Form 5227 filed with the IRS.[20]

Valuation of additional contributions. If the CRUT document allows for additional contributions, the trust document must provide for valuation of the contributions for calculating the unitrust payment to the income beneficiary. The method used for valuing the unitrust payment will depend on whether the additional contribution is made before or after the valuation date used by the trustee.

If the additional contribution is made before the valuation date, the value of the additional contribution and its earnings are included on the valuation date. But these are prorated based on the number of days in the calendar year that the contribution is included in the trust.

This prorated amount is then multiplied by the unitrust percentage to determine the unitrust payment attributable to the additional contribution.[21]

Example: If an additional contribution is made on June 30th, the additional contribution would be in the trust for 184 days of the year. Consequently, the value of the additional contribution and its earnings would be multiplied by .504 (184/365) to determine the amount that would be multiplied by the unitrust percentage.

If the additional contribution is made after the valuation date, the value of the additional contribution (but not its earnings) is prorated based on the number of days in the calendar year the contribution is included in the trust. This prorated value is then multiplied by the unitrust percentage to determine the unitrust payment attributable to the additional contribution.[22]

TERMINATION OF A CHARITABLE REMAINDER TRUST

A charitable remainder trust is required to make an annuity or unitrust payment to the income beneficiary for a specified period of time, typically for life *or* for a term of years (not greater than 20). Once that period of time has expired, the trust will either (1) terminate and pay the trust corpus to the selected charitable remainderman, or (2) continue as a non-tax-exempt Section 4947 charitable trust. If the trust continues as a Section 4947 charitable trust, it must comply with all of the private foundation rules, and the trust will not be tax-exempt unless it can qualify as a tax-exempt entity (such as a supporting organization).

When the trust terminates, the trustee has a reasonable period of time to settle the affairs of the trust (e.g., pay the final annuity or unitrust amount to the income beneficiary's estate).

COMPLYING WITH THE PRIVATE FOUNDATION RULES

A trustee of a charitable remainder trust must comply with many of the complex, and sometimes harsh, private foundation rules.

These rules include prohibitions against:

1. self-dealing;[23]

2. excess business holdings;[24]

3. jeopardy investments;[25] and

4. taxable expenditures.[26]

A properly drafted trust document will contain provisions prohibiting the trustee from engaging in any activities that may be considered a prohibited transaction. Penalties may be imposed on the trust if a prohibited transaction occurs. So the trustee must act carefully to avoid engaging in a prohibited transaction.

Example: If the trustee engages in an act of self-dealing, a tax equal to 10% of the amount involved could be imposed on the trust. If the act of self-dealing is not corrected, a second excise tax of 200% of the amount involved could also be imposed.[27]

ENDNOTES

1. Rev. Rul. 73-571, 1973-2 CB 213, amplified by Rev. Rul. 83-19, 1983-1 CB 115.
2. Rev. Rul. 83-19, 1983-1 CB 115; Let. Ruls. 8121067, 8220120, 8903019.
3. Philanthropy Protection Act of 1995 (P.L. 104-62).
4. See IRC Secs. 671, 672, 673, 674, 675, 676, 677; Treas. Reg. §1.664-1(a)(4).
5. IRC Sec. 674.
6. Treas. Reg. §1.664-1(a)(7). See also IRC Sec. 170(f)(11)(E).
7. Let. Ruls. 8033026, 8035078, 9104035.
8. Rev. Rul. 74-19, 1974-1 CB 155; Let. Ruls. 7807096, 7828006.
9. Treas. Reg. §1.664-1(a)(3).
10. IRC §664(c)(2).
11. *Leila G Newhall Unitrust v. Comm*, 105 F.3rd 482 (9th Cir. 1997).
12. IRC Sec. 644.
13. See also IRC Sec. 170(f)(11)(E).
14. Treas. Regs. §§1.664-2(a)(1), 1.664-3(a)(1).
15. IRC Sec. 664(b).
16. Treas. Reg. §1.664-1(d)(2).
17. Treas. Regs. §§1.664-2(a)(1), 1.664-3(a)(1).
18. Treas. Reg. §1.664-3(h).
19. This rule also applies to unitrusts.
20. Treas. Reg. §1.664-3(a)(1)(iv).
21. Treas. Reg. §1.664-3(b), Example 2.
22. Treas. Reg. §1.664-3(b), Example 1.
23. IRC Sec. 4941(d).
24. IRC Sec. 4943(c).
25. IRC Sec. 4144.
26. IRC Sec. 4945(d).
27. IRC Sec. 4941.

INCOME PERCENTAGE LIMITS FOR LIFETIME CHARITABLE GIFTS*

TYPE OF GIFT:	"50% CHARITIES"	"30% CHARITIES"
	Public Charities, Private Operating Foundations, Pass-through Private Foundations, Pooled Fund Private Foundations, Certain Supporting Organizations	Private Non-Operating Foundations ("Family Foundations"), Other Qualified Non-50% type Charities (veteran's associations, fraternal groups)
Cash or cash equivalents	Up to 50% of AGI	Up to 30% of AGI
Ordinary income property or short-term capital gain property	Generally, cost basis up to 50% of AGI	Generally, cost basis up to 30% of AGI
Long-term capital gain property	FMV up to 30% of AGI. (Under a special election, the taxpayer may choose to deduct the cost basis up to 50% of AGI.)	Generally, cost basis up to 20% of AGI
"Qualified Stock" (long-term capital gain stock with readily ascertainable market quotes)	Not Applicable	FMV up to 20% of AGI (The stock cannot be more than 10% of the value of the corporation's shares.)
Tangible personal property (held long-term)	Related to the charity's use: FMV up to 30% of AGI (or, the cost basis is deductible up to 50% of AGI) Unrelated to use: Generally, cost basis up to 50% of AGI	Related or unrelated to the charity's use: Generally, cost basis up to 20% AGI
Gifts "for the use of" the charity instead of "to" the charity (e.g., contribution of remainder interest held in trust for benefit of charity)	Up to 30% of AGI	Up to 30% of AGI
• Life insurance premiums paid directly "to" the charity on policies owned by the charity	Up to 50% of AGI	Up to 30% of AGI

| • Life insurance premiums paid to the life insurance company, or "for the use of" the charity on a policy owned by the charity | Up to 30% of AGI ** | Up to 30% of AGI | |

See Chapter 3 for details

** Some national commentators have made a legal argument that this limitation should not apply, and that gifts of premiums paid to the life insurance company for payments on policies owned by a public charity should be deductible up to 50% of AGI.

CODE
OF ETHICS

PROFESSIONAL CODES

Giving Institute

Giving Institute Membership Standards

Preamble

Member Firms of Giving Institute are organized to provide professional services as described in the Standards of Membership, Standards of Practice and the Professional Code of Ethics to not-for-profit organizations. Member Firms share a deep commitment to philanthropy and respect for the men and women who voluntarily commit their time and resources in the service of the philanthropic organizations operating today throughout society.

These tenets are a result of decades of service and experience by Member Firms, and have been carefully formulated to address the best interests of not-for-profit client organizations and their extraordinarily generous donor constituencies.

The philanthropic community recognizes the high ideals, competence, and integrity of the individuals who comprise the Member Firms. Through years of experience, these professionals have honed their skills and achieved acknowledged leadership in strengthening and expanding the philanthropic potential of their clients.

Standards of Practice

Member Firms of Giving Institute shall strive to:

- Provide service to not-for-profit organizations that serve the public's best interest.

- Engage clients that represent the broadest interest of society such as: religious, educational, health care, human service, arts, cultural, humanitarian, environmental, international, and other organizations benefiting humankind.

- Offer services that advance the goals of a client that directly relate to philanthropy such as: studies, campaign management, annual development programs, planned giving, strategic planning, direct mail, telemarketing, management services, executive search, public relations, marketing and communications, software developers, organization development/management, prospect research, and training.

Professional Code of Ethics

Member Firms believe it is in the best interest of the client that:

- Initial meetings with prospective clients should not be construed as services for which payment is expected.

- No payments or special consideration should be made to an officer, director, trustee, employee, or advisor of a not-for-profit organization as compensation for influencing the selection of fundraising counsel.

- Fees should be mutually agreed upon in advance of services.

- A flat, fixed fee is charged based on the level and extent of professional services provided. Fees are not based on the amount of charitable income raised or expected to be raised.

- Contracts providing for a contingent fee, a commission, or a fee based on percentage of funds raised are prohibited. Such contracts are harmful to the relationship between the donor and the institution and detrimental to the financial health of the client organization.

- Fundraising expenditures are within the authority and control of the not-for-profit organization.

- Member Firms feel it is in the best interest of clients that solicitation of gifts is undertaken by Board members, staff and other volunteers.

- Subsequent to analysis or study, a Member Firm should engage a client only when the best interest of the client is served.

- Member Firms should not profit directly or indirectly from materials provided by others, but billed to the Member Firm, without disclosure to the client.

- Member Firms do not engage in methods that are misleading to the public or harmful to their clients; do not make exaggerated claims of past achievement; and do not guarantee results of promise to help clients achieve goals.

- Any potential conflict of interest should be disclosed by the firm to clients and prospective clients.

- Member Firms will not acquire or maintain custody of funds and/or gifts directed to the client organization.

Reprinted with permission Giving Institute: Leading Consultants to Nonprofits (www.givinginstitute.org).

Association of Fundraising Professionals (AFP)

AFP Code of Ethical Principles and Standards of Professional Practice

Code of Ethical Principles

Adopted 1964; amended October 2004.

The Association of Fundraising Professionals (AFP) exists to foster the development and growth of fundrais-

ing professionals and the profession, to promote high ethical standards in the fundraising profession and to preserve and enhance philanthropy and volunteerism.

Members of AFP are motivated by an inner drive to improve the quality of life through the causes they serve. They serve the ideal of philanthropy; are committed to the preservation and enhancement of volunteerism; and hold stewardship of these concepts as the overriding principle of their professional life. They recognize their responsibility to ensure that needed resources are vigorously and ethically sought and that the intent of the donor is honestly fulfilled. To these ends, AFP members embrace certain values that they strive to uphold in performing their responsibilities for generating philanthropic support.

AFP members aspire to:

- practice their profession with integrity, honesty, truthfulness and adherence to the absolute obligation to safeguard the public trust;

- act according to the highest standards and visions of their organization, profession and conscience;

- put philanthropic mission above personal gain;

- inspire others through their own sense of dedication and high purpose;

- improve their professional knowledge and skills, so that their performance will better serve others;

- demonstrate concern for the interests and well being of individuals affected by their actions.

- value the privacy, freedom of choice and interests of all those affected by their actions;

- foster cultural diversity and pluralistic values, and treat all people with dignity and respect;

- affirm, through personal giving, a commitment to philanthropy and its role in society;

- adhere to the spirit as well as the letter of all applicable laws and regulations;

- advocate within their organizations, adherence to all applicable laws and regulations;

- avoid even the appearance of any criminal offense or professional misconduct;

- bring credit to the fundraising profession by their public demeanor;

- encourage colleagues to embrace and practice these ethical principles and standards of professional practice; and

- be aware of the codes of ethics promulgated by other professional organizations that serve philanthropy.

Standards of Professional Practice

Furthermore, while striving to act according to the above values, AFP members agree to abide by the AFP Standards of Professional Practice, which are adopted and incorporated into the AFP Code of Ethical Principles. Violation of the Standards may subject the member to disciplinary sanctions, including expulsion, as provided in the AFP Ethics Enforcement Procedures.

Professional obligations

1. Members shall not engage in activities that harm the members' organization, clients, or profession.

2. Members shall not engage in activities that conflict with their fiduciary, ethical and legal obligations to their organizations and their clients.

3. Members shall effectively disclose all potential and actual conflicts of interest; such disclosure does not preclude or imply ethical impropriety.

4. Members shall not exploit any relationship with a donor, prospect, volunteer or employee to the benefit of the members or the members' organizations.

5. Members shall comply with all applicable local, state, provincial, federal, civil and criminal laws.

6. Members recognize their individual boundaries of competence and are forthcoming and truthful about their professional experience and qualifications.

Solicitation and use of philanthropic funds

7. Members shall take care to ensure that all solicitation materials are accurate and correctly reflect their organization's mission and use of solicited funds.

8. Members shall take care to ensure that donors receive informed, accurate and ethical advice about the value and tax implications of potential gifts.

9. Members shall take care to ensure that contributions are used in accordance with donors' intentions.

10. Members shall take care to ensure proper stewardship of philanthropic contributions, including timely reports on the use and management of funds.

11. Members shall obtain explicit consent by the donor before altering the conditions of contributions.

Presentation of information

12. Members shall not disclose privileged or confidential information to unauthorized parties.

13. Members shall adhere to the principle that all donor and prospect information created by, or on behalf of, an organization is the property of that organization and shall not be transferred or utilized except on behalf of that organization.

14. Members shall give donors the opportunity to have their names removed from lists that are sold to, rented to, or exchanged with other organizations.

15. Members shall, when stating fundraising results, use accurate and consistent accounting methods that conform to the appropriate guidelines adopted by the American Institute of Certified Public Accountants (AICPA)* for the type of organization involved. (* In countries outside of the United States, comparable authority should be utilized.)

Compensation

16. Members shall not accept compensation that is based on a percentage of contributions; nor shall they accept finder's fees.

17. Members may accept performance-based compensation, such as bonuses, provided such bonuses are in accord with prevailing practices within the members' own organizations, and are not based on a percentage of charitable contributions.

18. Members shall not pay finder's fees, commissions or percentage compensation based on contributions and shall take care to discourage their organizations from making such payments.

Amended October 2004

Association for Healthcare Philanthropy

Statement of Professional Standards and Conduct

All members shall comply with the Association's Statement of Professional Standards and Conduct:

Association for Healthcare Philanthropy members represent to the public, by personal example and conduct, both their employer and their profession. They have, therefore, a duty to faithfully adhere to the highest standards and conduct in:

I. Their promotion of the merits of their institutions and of excellence in health care generally, providing community leadership in cooperation with health, educational, cultural, and other organizations;

II. Their words and actions, embodying respect for truth, honesty, fairness, free inquiry, and the opinions of others, treating all with equality and dignity;

III. Their respect for all individuals without regard to race, color, sex, religion, national origin, disability, age or any other characteristic protected by applicable law;

IV. Their commitment to strive to increase professional and personal skills for improved service to their donors and institutions, to encourage and actively participate in career development for themselves and others whose roles include support for resource development functions, and to share freely their knowledge and experience with others as appropriate;

V. Their continuing effort and energy to pursue new ideas and modifications to improve conditions for, and benefits to, donors and their institution;

VI. Their avoidance of activities that might damage the reputation of any donor, their institution, any other resource development professional or the profession as a whole, or themselves, and to give full credit for the ideas, words, or images originated by others;

VII. Their respect for the rights of privacy of others and the confidentiality of information gained in the pursuit of their professional duties;

VIII. Their acceptance of a compensation method freely agreed upon and based on their institution's usual and customary compensation guidelines which have been established and approved for general institutional use while always remembering that:

1. any compensation agreement should fully reflect the standards of professional conduct; and,

2. antitrust laws in the United States prohibit limitation on compensation methods.

IX. Their respect for the law and professional ethics as a standard of personal conduct, with full adherence to the policies and procedures of their institution;

X. Their pledge to adhere to this Statement of Professional Standards and Conduct, and to encourage others to join them in observance of its guidelines.

Reprinted with permission by the Association for Healthcare Philanthropy (AHP), 313 Park Avenue, Suite 400, Falls Church, VA 22046, www.ahp.org.

Council for Advancement and Support of Education (CASE)

CASE Statement of Ethics

Institutional advancement professionals, by virtue of their responsibilities within the academic community, represent their colleges, universities, and schools to the larger society. They have, therefore, a special duty to exemplify the best qualities of their institutions and to observe the highest standards of personal and professional conduct.

In so doing, they promote the merits of their institutions, and of education generally, without disparaging other colleges and schools.

Their words and actions embody respect for truth, fairness, free inquiry, and the opinions of others.

They respect all individuals without regard to race, color, sex, sexual orientation, marital status, creed, ethnic or national identity, handicap, or age.

They uphold the professional reputation of other advancement officers and give credit for ideas, words, or images originated by others.

They safeguard privacy rights and confidential information.

They do not grant or accept favors for personal gain, nor do they solicit or accept favors for their institutions where a higher public interest would be violated.

They avoid actual or apparent conflicts of interest and, if in doubt, seek guidance from appropriate authorities.

They follow the letter and spirit of laws and regulations affecting institutional advancement.

They observe these standards and others that apply to their professions and actively encourage colleagues to join them in supporting the highest standards of conduct.

The CASE Board of Trustees adopted this Statement of Ethics to guide and reinforce our professional conduct in all areas of institutional advancement. The statement is also intended to stimulate awareness and discussion of ethical issues that may arise in our professional activities. The Board adopted the final text in Toronto on July 11, 1982, after a year of deliberation by national and district leaders and by countless volunteers throughout the membership.

Reprinted with permission by the Council for Advancement and Support of Education (CASE), 1307 New York Avenue NW, Suite 1000, Washington, DC 20005-4701, www.case.org.

Council on Foundations

Statement of Ethical Principles

The Council on Foundations and its members promote the highest standards of ethical behavior. In recognition of the importance of philanthropy toward the public good and those we serve, we adopt these ethical principles.

- Mission: Our members are committed to the public benefit and to their philanthropic purposes and act accordingly.

- Stewardship: Our members manage their resources to maximize philanthropic purposes, not private gain; and actively avoid excessive compensation and unreasonable or unnecessary expenses. They pursue maximum benefit through their work, how they work, and by supporting the work of partners, colleagues and grantees.

- Accountability and Transparency: In carrying out their philanthropic activities, our members embrace both the letter and the spirit of the law. They welcome public interest, take responsibility for their actions and communicate truthfully.

- Diversity and Inclusiveness: Our members seek diversity and inclusiveness in order to reflect the communities they serve and to ensure that a range of perspectives contribute to the common good and the development of their mission in a changing society.

- Governance: Our members' governing bodies understand and embrace their responsibility to oversee the mission, strategic direction, finances and operations of their respective organizations, and do so honestly and with integrity. They establish clear and understandable policies and ensure that they are followed.

- Respect: Members interact respectfully with grantees, colleagues, donors and peers.

Approved: June 28, 2005

Reprinted courtesy of the Council of Foundations, 2121 Crystal Drive, Suite 700, Arlington, VA 22202, www.cof.org.

National Committee on Planned Giving (NCPG)

Model Standards of Practice for the Charitable Gift Planner

PREAMBLE

The purpose of this statement is to encourage responsible gift planning by urging the adoption of the following Standards of Practice by all individuals who work in the charitable gift planning process, gift planning officers, fund raising consultants, attorneys, accountants, financial planners, life insurance agents and other financial services professionals (collectively referred to hereafter as "Gift Planners"), and by the institutions that these persons represent.

This statement recognizes that the solicitation, planning and administration of a charitable gift is a complex process involving philanthropic, personal, financial, and tax considerations, and as such often involves professionals from various disciplines whose goals should include working together to structure a gift that achieves a fair and proper balance between the interests of the donor and the purposes of the charitable institution.

I. PRIMACY OF PHILANTHROPIC MOTIVATION

The principal basis for making a charitable gift should be a desire on the part of the donor to support the work of charitable institutions.

II. EXPLANATION OF TAX IMPLICATIONS

Congress has provided tax incentives for charitable giving, and the emphasis in this statement on philanthropic motivation in no way minimizes the necessity and appropriateness of a full and accurate explanation by the Gift Planner of those incentives and their implications.

III. FULL DISCLOSURE

It is essential to the gift planning process that the role and relationships of all parties involved, including how and by whom each is compensated, be fully disclosed to the donor. A Gift Planner shall not act or purport to act as a representative of any charity without the express knowledge and approval of the charity, and shall not, while employed by the charity, act or purport to act as a representative of the donor, without the express consent of both the charity and the donor.

IV. COMPENSATION

Compensation paid to Gift Planners shall be reasonable and proportionate to the services provided. Payment of finders fees, commissions or other fees by a donee organization to an independent Gift Planner as a condition for the delivery of a gift are never appropriate. Such payments lead to abusive practices and may violate certain state and federal regulations. Likewise, commission-based compen-

sation for Gift Planners who are employed by a charitable institution is never appropriate.

V. COMPETENCE AND PROFESSIONALISM

The Gift Planner should strive to achieve and maintain a high degree of competence in his or her chosen area, and shall advise donors only in areas in which he or she is professionally qualified. It is a hallmark of professionalism for Gift Planners that they realize when they have reached the limits of their knowledge and expertise, and as a result, should include other professionals in the process. Such relationships should be characterized by courtesy, tact and mutual respect.

VI. CONSULTATION WITH INDEPENDENT ADVISORS

A Gift Planner acting on behalf of a charity shall in all cases strongly encourage the donor to discuss the proposed gift with competent independent legal and tax advisers of the donor's choice.

VII. CONSULTATION WITH CHARITIES

Although Gift Planners frequently and properly counsel donors concerning specific charitable gifts without the prior knowledge or approval of the donee organization, the Gift Planners, in order to insure that the gift will accomplish the donor's objectives, should encourage the donor, early in the gift planning process, to discuss the proposed gift with the charity to whom the gift is to be made. In cases where the donor desires anonymity, the Gift Planners shall endeavor, on behalf of the undisclosed donor, to obtain the charity's input in the gift planning process.

VIII. DESCRIPTION AND REPRESENTATION OF GIFT

The Gift Planner shall make every effort to assure that the donor receives a full description and an accurate representation of all aspects of any proposed charitable gift plan. The consequences for the charity, the donor and, where applicable, the donor's family, should be apparent, and the assumptions underlying any financial illustrations should be realistic.

IX. FULL COMPLIANCE

A Gift Planner shall fully comply with and shall encourage other parties in the gift planning process to fully comply with both the letter and spirit of all applicable federal and state laws and regulations.

X. PUBLIC TRUST

Gift Planners shall, in all dealings with donors, institutions and other professionals, act with fairness, honesty, integrity and openness. Except for compensation received for services, the terms of which have been disclosed to the donor, they shall have no vested interest that could result in personal gain.

Adopted and subscribed to by the National Committee on Planned Giving and the American Council on Gift Annuities, May 7, 1991. Revised April 1999.

Reprinted with permission by the National Committee on Planned Giving (NCPG), 2333 McCrea Street, Suite 400, Indianapolis, IN 46225, www.ncpg.org.

DONOR BILL OF RIGHTS

Donor Bill of Rights

To assure that philanthropy merits the respect and trust of the general public, AFP and other fundraising organizations declare that all donors have the following rights.

Philanthropy is based on voluntary action for the common good. It is a tradition of giving and sharing that is primary to the quality of life. To ensure that philanthropy merits the respect and trust of the general public, and that donors and prospective donors can have full confidence in the nonprofit organizations and causes they are asked to support, we declare that all donors have these rights:

I.   To be informed of the organization's mission, of the way the organization intends to use donated resources, and of its capacity to use donations effectively for their intended purposes.

II.   To be informed of the identity of those serving on the organization's governing board, and to expect the board to exercise prudent judgment in its stewardship responsibilities.

III. To have access to the organization's most recent financial statements.

IV.   To be assured their gifts will be used for the purposes for which they were given.

V.   To receive appropriate acknowledgement and recognition.

VI.   To be assured that information about their donation is handled with respect and with confidentiality to the extent provided by law.

VII. To expect that all relationships with individuals representing organizations of interest to the donor will be professional in nature.

VIII. To be informed whether those seeking donations are volunteers, employees of the organization or hired solicitors.

IX.   To have the opportunity for their names to be deleted from mailing lists that an organization may intend to share.

X.   To feel free to ask questions when making a donation and to receive prompt, truthful and forthright answers.

Copyright 2007, Association of Fundraising Professionals (AFP), all rights reserved. Reprinted with permission.

Principles of the E-Donor Bill of Rights

An "E-Donor Bill of Rights" is being created to address concerns and challenges arising from Internet charitable giving.

AFP is working with other philanthropic organizations as well as online service providers to ensure that online donors have greater confidence in the nonprofit organizations and causes they are asked to support.

The E-Donor Bill of Rights is intended to relate to AFP's long-standing Donor Bill of Rights, created in 1993 by AFP in conjunction with other fundraising and nonprofit groups. The document was developed to ensure donor awareness of the responsibilities that a charity has to its donors, and the expectations that donors should have of charities when making a charitable gift. The AFP Donor Bill of Rights lists ten rights that a donor has–ten best practices that all charities and donors should be always aware of.

Since the creation of the Donor Bill of Rights, the philanthropic landscape has changed dramatically. One critical change has been the growing use of technology to

facilitate charitable giving, primarily through the Internet. While the Internet holds great potential as a charitable giving tool, it also creates new challenges – both for the donor and the charity. Because the Internet is such a new medium for giving, best practices are just beginning to be identified, and many donors and charities are unsure as to their online rights and responsibilities.

Principles of the E-Donor Bill of Rights

The E-Donor Bill of Rights is intended to complement the original document and provide further and more detailed guidance for the new world of online giving. In addition to the rights outlined in the Donor Bill of Rights, online donors should demand the following of their online solicitors:

- To be clearly and immediately informed of the organization's name, identity, nonprofit or for-profit status, its mission, and purpose when first accessing the organization's website.

- To have easy and clear access to alternative contact information other than through the website or email.

- To be assured that all third-party logos, trademarks, trustmarks and other identifying, sponsoring, and/or endorsing symbols displayed on the website are accurate, justified, up-to-date, and clearly explained.

- To be informed of whether or not a contribution entitles the donor to a tax deduction, and of all limits on such deduction based on applicable laws.

- To be assured that all online transactions and contributions occur through a safe, private, and secure system that protects the donor's personal information.

- To be clearly informed if a contribution goes directly to the intended charity, or is held by or transferred through a third party.

- To have easy and clear access to an organization's privacy policy posted on its website and be clearly and unambiguously informed about what information an organization is gathering about the donor and how that information will be used.

- To be clearly informed of opportunities to opt out of data lists that are sold, shared, rented, or transferred to other organizations.

- To not receive unsolicited communications or solicitations unless the donor has "opted in" to receive such materials.

IRS FILING AND REPORTING REQUIREMENTS

REVENUE PROCEDURE 83-32, 1983-1 CB 723

Section 1. Purpose

.01 The purpose of this revenue procedure is to update Rev. Proc. 73-29, 1973-2 C.B. 483, which sets forth the return filing requirements for charitable and split-interest trusts.

.02 This revenue procedure sets forth the following changes in filing requirements, effective for taxable years beginning after December 31, 1980:

(1) Trusts described in section 4947(a)(1) of the Internal Revenue Code that are treated as private foundations file form 990-PF. Other section 4947(a)(1) trusts file Form 990 (and Schedule A Form 990). Section 4947(a)(1) trusts do not file Form 5227 or Form 1041-A.

(2) Section 664 trusts do not file Form 1041-B, which is discontinued.

(3) Foundation managers do not file Form 990-AR, which is discontinued.

.03 Subsequent to the publication of Rev. Proc. 73-29, section 664 trusts, pooled income funds under section 642(c)(5), and all other split-interest trusts described in section 4947(a)(2) were required to file Form 5227. For taxable years ending on or after December 31, 1975, Form 5227 replaced Schedule PF (Form 1041). This revenue procedure incorporates this change.

Sec. 2. Background

.01 The charitable trust returns, forms, and schedules (hereinafter referred to as returns) to which this revenue procedure is applicable are the following:

(1) Form 990, Return of Organization Exempt from Income Tax.

(2) Schedule A (Form 990), Organization Exempt Under 501(c)(3).

(3) Form 990-PF, Return of Private Foundation.

(4) Form 999-T, Exempt Organization Business Income Tax Return.

(5) Form 1041, U.S. Fiduciary Income Tax Return.

(6) Form 5227, Split-interest Trust Information Return.

(7) Form 1041-A, Trust Accumulation of Charitable Amounts.

(8) Form 4720, Return of Certain Excise Taxes on Charities and Other Persons Under Chapters 41 and 42 of the Internal Revenue Code.

.02 The charitable and split-interest trusts that file one or more of these returns are:

(1) Trusts exempt from income tax under section 501(a) of the Code as organizations described in section 501(c)(3) (hereinafter referred to as exempt charitable trusts).

(2) Non-exempt charitable trusts described in section 4947(a)(1) of the Code, including charitable trusts created prior to October 10, 1969, that have not applied to the Internal Revenue Service for recognition as organizations described in section 501(c)(3) (hereinafter referred to as section 4947(a)(1) trusts); and

(3) Charitable remainder trusts described in section 664 of the Code, pooled income funds described in section 642(c)(5), and all other section 4947(a)(2) trusts treated as if they were private foundations.

Sec. 3. Table of Filing Requirements

The following table shows the filing requirements for these charitable trusts:

KIND OF RETURN

KIND OF TRUST	990	Sch A (990)	990-PF	990-T	1041	1041-A	5227	4720
Exempt charitable trusts that are not private foundations	yes[A]	yes[A]	no	yes[B]	no	no	no	no
Exempt charitable trusts that are private foundations	no	no	yes	yes[B]	no	no	no	yes[F]
Charitable trusts (described in section 642(c)(6)) that are treated as taxable private foundations	no	no	yes	no	yes	no	no	yes[F]
4947(a)(1) trusts that are not treated as private foundations	yes[A]	yes[A]	no	no	yes[G]	no	no	no
4947(a)(1) trusts that are treated as private foundations	no	no	yes	no	yes[G]	no	no	yes[F]
Charitable remainder trusts under section 664	no	no	no	no	yes[C]	yes[D]	yes	yes[F]
Pooled income funds under section 642(c)	no	no	no	no	yes	yes[D]	yes[E]	yes[F]
All other section 4947(a)(2) trusts treated as if they were private foundations	no	no	no	no	yes	yes[D]	yes	yes[F]

[A] Excluding trusts whose gross receipts normally do not exceed $25,000 during the taxable year.

[B] But only if the trust has $1,000 or more of gross income from an unrelated trade or business.

[C] But only if there is unrelated business taxable income (as defined in section 512).

[D] But not if all net income is required to be distributed currently to beneficiaries.

[E] Only with respect to amount transferred in trust after May 26, 1969.

[F] If there is liability for a Chapter 42 excise tax (excluding section 4940).

[G] If the trust has zero taxable income under Subtitle A of the Code, Form 990 or Form 990-PF may be used to satisfy the requirements of filing Form 1041.

Sec. 4. Effect on Other Revenue Procedures

This revenue procedure supersedes Rev. Proc. 73-29.

Sec. 5. Effective Date

.01 Changes in filing requirement set forth in section 1.02 of this revenue procedure are effective for taxable years beginning after December 31, 1980.

.02 Changes in filing requirements discussed in section 1.03 of this revenue procedure are effective for taxable years ending on or after December 31, 1975.

To print or view IRS forms, please go to the IRS Internet Web site: http://www.irs.ustreas.gov/forms_pubs/index.html.

IRS FILING REQUIREMENTS

CHARITABLE SPLIT-INTEREST TRUSTS & PRIVATE FOUNDATIONS

FORM	DESCRIPTION	WHEN TO FILE	WHERE TO FILE
1023	Application for Recognition of Exemption	Generally, within 27 months after the end of the month the organization was formed	Internal Revenue Service P.O. Box 192 Covington, KY 41012-0192
990	Return of Organization Exempt from Income Tax	By the 15th day of the 5th month after the organization's accounting period ends	Internal Revenue Service Center Ogden, Utah 84201-0027
990-EZ	Short Form Return of Organization Exempt from Income Tax	By the 15th day of the 5th month after the organization's accounting period ends	Same as Form 990
990-N	Electronic Notice (e-Postcard) for Tax-Exempt Organizations Not Required to File Form 990 or Form 990-EZ	Beginning in 2008, by the 15th day of the 5th month after the organization's accounting period ends	To be Announced www.irs.gov/eo
990-PF	Return of Private Foundation	By the 15th day of the 5th month following the close of the foundation's accounting period	Same as Form 990
990-T	Exempt Organization Business Income Tax Return	By the 15th day of the 5th month after the end of the tax year	Same as Form 990
Form 1041-A	U.S. Information Return - Trust Accumulation of Charitable Amounts	On or before April 15 following the close of the calendar year	Same as Form 990
Form 4720	Return of Certain Excise Taxes on Charities and Other Persons Under Chapters 41 and 42 of the Internal Revenue Code	By the due date (not including extensions) for filing the organization's Form 990, Form 990-PF or Form 5227	Same as Form 990
Form 5227	Split-Interest Trust Information Return	On or before April 15 following the close of the calendar year	Same as Form 990

INDIVIDUALS, TRUSTS & ESTATES

FORM	DESCRIPTION	WHEN TO FILE	WHERE TO FILE
Form 1040	U.S. Individual Income Tax Return	Generally, by the 15th day of April following the close of the calendar year	Depends on where the taxpayer's "residence" is located
Schedule A	Itemized Deductions	Attachment to Form 1040	Same as Form 1040
Schedule K-1	Beneficiary's Share of Income, Deductions, Credits, etc.	Attachment to Form 1040	Same as Form 1040
Form 8283	Noncash Charitable Contributions	Attachment to Form 1040	Same as Form 1040
Form 1041	U.S. Income Tax Return for Estates and Trusts	*Calendar Year Trusts & Estates:* By the 15th day of April following the close of the calendar year *Fiscal Year Trusts & Estates:* By the 15th day of the 4th month following the close of the tax year	Depends on the where the trust or estate is "domiciled"
Form 706	U.S. Estate Tax Return	Within 9 months after the date of the decedent's death	Internal Revenue Service Center Cincinnati, OH 45999
Schedule O	Charitable, Public and Similar Gifts and Bequests	Attachment to Form 706	Same as Form 706
Form 709	U.S. Gift Tax Return	On or before the 15th day of April following the close of the calendar year	Internal Revenue Service Center Cincinnati, OH 45999

IRS FORMS

661106

☐ Final K-1	☐ Amended K-1	OMB No. 1545-0092

**Schedule K-1
(Form 1041)**

20**06**

Department of the Treasury
Internal Revenue Service

For calendar year 2006,

or tax year beginning _____ , 2006

and ending _____ , 20 _____

Beneficiary's Share of Income, Deductions, Credits, etc.

▶ See back of form and instructions.

Part I	Information About the Estate or Trust

A Estate's or trust's employer identification number

B Estate's or trust's name

C Fiduciary's name, address, city, state, and ZIP code

D ☐ Check if Form 1041-T was filed and enter the date it was filed

_____ / _____ / _____

E ☐ Check if this is the final Form 1041 for the estate or trust

F ☐ Tax shelter registration number, if any _____

G ☐ Check if Form 8271 is attached

Part II	Information About the Beneficiary

H Beneficiary's identifying number

I Beneficiary's name, address, city, state, and ZIP code

J ☐ Domestic beneficiary ☐ Foreign beneficiary

Part III	Beneficiary's Share of Current Year Income, Deductions, Credits, and Other Items

1	Interest income
2a	Ordinary dividends
2b	Qualified dividends
3	Net short-term capital gain
4a	Net long-term capital gain
4b	28% rate gain
4c	Unrecaptured section 1250 gain
5	Other portfolio and nonbusiness income
6	Ordinary business income
7	Net rental real estate income
8	Other rental income
9	Directly apportioned deductions
10	Estate tax deduction

11	Final year deductions
12	Alternative minimum tax adjustment
13	Credits and credit recapture
14	Other information

*See attached statement for additional information.

Note: A statement must be attached showing the beneficiary's share of income and directly apportioned deductions from each business, rental real estate, and other rental activity.

For IRS Use Only

For Paperwork Reduction Act Notice, see the Instructions for Form 1041.

Cat. No. 11380D

Schedule K-1 (Form 1041) 2006

Form **1041-A**

(Rev. December 2000)

Department of the Treasury
Internal Revenue Service

U.S. Information Return
Trust Accumulation of Charitable Amounts

For calendar year 20......

OMB No. 1545-0094

Name of trust	Employer identification number

Name of trustee

Number, street, and room or suite no. (or P.O. box)

City or town, state, and ZIP code

Part I Income and Deductions (See the instructions for Form 1041 or Form 5227.) If total income is $25,000 or less, skip lines 1–8 and enter total income on line 9.

Income

1	Interest income	1
2	Dividends	2
3	Business income or (loss) (attach Schedule C or C-EZ (Form 1040))	3
4	Capital gain or (loss) (attach Schedule D (Form 1041))	4
5	Rents, royalties, partnerships, other estates and trusts, etc. (attach Schedule E (Form 1040))	5
6	Farm income or (loss) (attach Schedule F (Form 1040))	6
7	Ordinary gain or (loss) (attach Form 4797)	7
8	Other income (state type of income) _____	8
9	**Total** income (combine lines 1 through 8)	9

Deductions

10	Interest	10
11	Taxes	11
12	Charitable deduction (itemize by charitable purpose; include payee's name and address)	12
13	Trustee fees	13
14	Attorney, accountant, and return preparer fees	14
15	Other deductions (attach schedule)	15

Part II Distributions of Income Set Aside for Charitable Purposes (see instructions)

16	Accumulated income set aside in prior tax years for which a deduction was claimed under section 642(c)	16
17	Income set aside in prior tax years for which a deduction was claimed under section 642(c) and which was distributed during the current tax year (itemize by charitable purpose; include payee's name and address)	
a	_____	17a
b	_____	17b
c	_____	17c
d	_____	17d
e	_____	17e
18	Total (add lines 17a through 17e)	18
19	Balance (subtract line 18 from line 16)	19
20	Income set aside during the current tax year for which a deduction was claimed under section 642(c) (included in Part I, line 12)	20
21	Carryover (add lines 19 and 20)	21

Part III Distributions of Principal for Charitable Purposes (see instructions)

22	Principal distributed in prior tax years for charitable purposes	22
23	Principal distributed during the current tax year for charitable purposes (itemize by charitable purpose; include payee's name and address)	
a	_____	23a
b	_____	23b
c	_____	23c
d	_____	23d
e	_____	23e
24	**Total** (add lines 23a through 23e)	24

For Paperwork Reduction Act Notice, see instructions.   Cat. No. 10615B   Form **1041-A** (Rev. 12-2000)

Form 1041-A (Rev. 12-2000)

Page **2**

| **Part IV** | **Balance Sheets** (see instructions). If line 9, page 1, is $25,000 or less, complete only lines 38, 42, and 45 (see instructions). | | |

Assets		(a) Beginning-of-Year Book Value	(b) End-of-Year Book Value
25 Cash—non-interest bearing	25		
26 Savings and temporary cash investments	26		
27a Accounts receivable. 27a			
b Less: allowance for doubtful accounts. 27b			
28a Notes and loans receivable 28a			
b Less: allowance for doubtful accounts. 28b			
29 Inventories for sale or use	29		
30 Prepaid expenses and deferred charges	30		
31 Investments—U.S. and state government obligations (attach schedule) . .	31		
32 Investments—corporate stock (attach schedule)	32		
33 Investments—corporate bonds (attach schedule)	33		
34a Investments—land, buildings, and equipment: basis 34a			
b Less: accumulated depreciation 34b			
35 Investments—other (attach schedule)	35		
36a Land, buildings, and equipment: basis 36a			
b Less: accumulated depreciation 36b			
37 Other assets (describe ▶ _____)	37		
38 **Total assets** (add lines 25 through 37)	38		
Liabilities			
39 Accounts payable and accrued expenses	39		
40 Mortgages and other notes payable (attach schedule)	40		
41 Other liabilities (describe ▶ _____)	41		
42 **Total liabilities** (add lines 39 through 41)	42		
Net Assets			
43 Trust principal or corpus	43		
44 Undistributed income and profits	44		
45 Total net assets (add lines 43 and 44)	45		
46 **Total liabilities and net assets** (add lines 42 and 45)	46		

Sign Here	Under penalties of perjury, I declare that I have examined this return, including accompanying schedules and statements, and to the best of my knowledge and belief, it is true, correct, and complete. Declaration of preparer (other than trustee) is based on all information of which preparer has any knowledge.		
	▶ _____ Signature of trustee or officer representing trustee	▶ _____ Date	

Paid Preparer's Use Only	Preparer's signature ▶	Date	Check if self-employed ▶ ☐
	Firm's name (or yours, if self-employed), address, and ZIP code ▶		
			Phone no. ( )

Form **5227**

Department of the Treasury
Internal Revenue Service

Split-Interest Trust Information Return

▶ See separate instructions.

OMB No. 1545-0196

20**06**

Full name of trust

Name of trustee

Number, street, and room or suite no. (If a P.O. box, see page 3 of the instructions.)

City, state, and ZIP code

C Fair market value (FMV) of assets at end of tax year

D Date the trust was created

E Check applicable boxes (see instructions)
☐ Initial return   ☐ Final return   ☐ Amended return
Change in trustee's ▶   ☐ Name   ☐ Address

A Employer identification number

B Type of Entity
(1) ☐ Charitable lead trust
(2) ☐ Charitable remainder annuity trust described in section 664(d)(1)
(3) ☐ Charitable remainder unitrust described in section 664(d)(2)
(4) ☐ Pooled income fund described in section 642(c)(5)
(5) ☐ Other

F Did the split-interest trust have any unrelated business taxable income (section 664 trusts only)? If "Yes," file Form 1041 . . . . ☐ Yes   ☐ No

Part I	Ordinary Income (Section 664 trust only)		
1	Interest income	1	
2a	Qualified dividends (see instructions) . . . . . . [2a]		
b	Ordinary dividends (including qualified dividends)	2b	
3	Business income or (loss). Attach Schedule C or C-EZ (Form 1040) .	3	
4	Rents, royalties, partnerships, other estates and trusts, etc. Attach Schedule E (Form 1040)	4	
5	Farm income or (loss). Attach Schedule F (Form 1040)	5	
6	Ordinary gain or (loss). Attach Form 4797	6	
7	Other income. State nature of income ▶	7	
8	**Total** ordinary income. Combine lines 1, 2b, and 3 through 7	8	

Deductions Allocable to Ordinary Income

9	Interest	9	
10	Taxes	10	
11	Other deductions. Attach a separate sheet listing deductions . . .	11	
12	**Total** deductions. Add lines 9 through 11	12	
13	Ordinary income less deductions. Subtract line 12 from line 8. Enter here and on line 21, column (a)	13	

Capital Gains (Losses) and Allocable Deductions

14	Total short-term capital gain or (loss) for tax year. Attach Schedule D (Form 1041) . . . . [14]		
15	Deductions allocable to short-term capital gains . . . . [15]		
16	**Balance.** Subtract line 15 from line 14. Enter here and on line 21, column (b)	16	
17a	Total long-term capital gain or (loss) for tax year. Attach Schedule D (Form 1041) . . . . [17a]		
b	28% rate gain or (loss) . . . . . . [17b]		
c	Unrecaptured section 1250 gain . . . [17c]		
18	Deductions allocable to long-term capital gains [18]		
19	**Balance.** Subtract line 18 from line 17a. Enter here and on line 21, column (c)	19	

Part II	Accumulation Schedule (Section 664 trust only)			
Accumulations	(a) Ordinary income	Capital gains and (losses)		(d) Nontaxable income
		(b) Net short-term	(c) Net long-term	
20 Undistributed from prior tax years				
21 Current tax year (before distributions)				
22 **Total.** Add lines 20 and 21				
23 Undistributed at end of tax year				

Part III	Current Distributions Schedule (Section 664 trust only)					
Name of recipient	Identifying number	(a) Ordinary income	Capital gains		(d) Nontaxable income	(e) Corpus
			(b) Short-term	(c) Long-term		
24a						
b						
c						

For Privacy Act and Paperwork Reduction Act Notice, see page 10 of the instructions.   Cat. No. 13227T   Form **5227** (2006)

Form 5227 (2006)

Page **2**

Part IV   Balance Sheet (see page 6 of the instructions)

			(a) Beginning-of-Year Book Value	(b) End-of-Year Book Value	(c) FMV (see instructions)
Assets					
25	Cash—non-interest-bearing	25			
26	Savings and temporary cash investments	26			
27a	Accounts receivable	27a			
b	Less: allowance for doubtful accounts	27b			
28	Receivables due from officers, directors, trustees, and other disqualified persons (attach schedule)	28			
29a	Other notes and loans receivable	29a			
b	Less: allowance for doubtful accounts	29b			
30	Inventories for sale or use	30			
31	Prepaid expenses and deferred charges	31			
32a	Investments—U.S. and state government obligations (attach schedule)	32a			
b	Investments—corporate stock. Attach schedule.	32b			
c	Investments—corporate bonds. Attach schedule	32c			
33a	Investments—land, buildings, and equipment: basis (attach schedule)	33a			
b	Less: accumulated depreciation	33b			
34	Investments—other (attach schedule)	34			
35a	Land, buildings, and equipment: basis	35a			
b	Less: accumulated depreciation	35b			
36	Other assets. Describe ▶	36			
37	**Total assets.** Add lines 25 through 36 (must equal line 47)	37			
Liabilities					
38	Accounts payable and accrued expenses	38			
39	Deferred revenue	39			
40	Loans from officers, directors, trustees, and other disqualified persons	40			
41	Mortgages and other notes payable. Attach schedule	41			
42	Other liabilities. Describe ▶	42			
43	**Total liabilities.** Add lines 38 through 42	43			
Net Assets					
44	Trust principal or corpus	44			
45a	Undistributed income	45a			
b	Undistributed capital gains	45b			
c	Undistributed nontaxable income	45c			
46	**Total net assets.** Add lines 44 through 45c	46			
47	**Total liabilities and net assets.** Add lines 43 and 46	47			

Part V-A   Charitable Remainder Annuity Trust Information (to be completed **only** by a section 664 charitable remainder annuity trust)

48a	Enter the initial fair market value (FMV) of the property placed in the trust	48a
b	Enter the total annual annuity amounts for all recipients. Attach schedule showing the amount for each recipient if more than one	48b

Part V-B   Charitable Remainder Unitrust Information (to be completed **only** by a section 664 charitable remainder unitrust)

49a	Enter the unitrust fixed percentage to be paid to the recipients	49a %
	If there is more than one recipient, attach a schedule showing the percentage of the total unitrust dollar amount payable to each recipient.	
b	**Unitrust amount.** Subtract line 43, column (c), from line 37, column (c), and multiply the result by the percentage on line 49a. Do not enter less than -0-	49b
	Note. *Complete lines 50a through 51b **only** for those unitrusts whose governing instruments provide for determining required distributions with reference to the unitrust's income. Otherwise, enter the amount from line 49b on line 52.*	
50a	Trust's accounting income for 2006	50a
b	Enter the smaller of line 49b or line 50a here, and on line 52 on page 3, unless the **Caution** below applies	50b
	Caution: *Lines 51a and b need to be completed by those unitrusts whose governing instruments provide for current distributions to make up for any distribution deficiencies in previous years due to the trust income limit. See Regulations section 1.664-3(a)(1)(i)(b)(2). For these trusts, when completing line 52, enter the smaller of line 50a or line 51b.*	

Form **5227** (2006)

Form 5227 (2006)   Page **3**

51a	Total accrued distribution deficiencies from previous years (see page 8 of the instructions) . . .	**51a**	
b	Add lines 49b and 51a	**51b**	
52	Unitrust distributions for 2006.	**52**	
53	Carryover of distribution deficiency. Subtract line 52 from line 51b	**53**	

54 Did the trustee change the method of determining the fair market value of the assets? . . . . . . ☐ **Yes** ☐ **No**
    If "Yes," attach an explanation.

55 Were any additional contributions received by the trust during 2006? . . . . ☐ **Yes** ☐ **No**
    If "Yes," attach a schedule that lists the assets and the date(s) received.

Part VI-A   **Statements Regarding Activities** (see page 8 of the instructions)

			Yes	No
1	Are the requirements of section 508(e) satisfied either:			
	• By the language in the governing instrument; or			
	• By state legislation that effectively amends the governing instrument so that no mandatory directions that conflict with the state law remain in the governing instrument?	**1**		
2	Are you using this return only to report the income and assets of a segregated amount under section 4947(a)(2)(B)?	**2**		

Part VI-B   **Statements Regarding Activities for Which Form 4720 May Be Required**

File Form 4720 if any item is checked in the "Yes" column (to the right), unless an exception applies.

			Yes	No
1	Self-dealing (section 4941):			
a	During 2006, did the trust (either directly or indirectly):			
	(1) Engage in the sale or exchange, or leasing of property with a disqualified person?. ☐ **Yes** ☐ **No**			
	(2) Borrow money from, lend money to, or otherwise extend credit to (or accept it from) a disqualified person? . . . . ☐ **Yes** ☐ **No**			
	(3) Furnish goods, services, or facilities to (or accept them from) a disqualified person? ☐ **Yes** ☐ **No**			
	(4) Pay compensation to, or pay or reimburse the expenses of, a disqualified person? ☐ **Yes** ☐ **No**			
	(5) Transfer any income or assets to a disqualified person (or make any of either available for the benefit or use of a disqualified person)? . . . . ☐ **Yes** ☐ **No**			
	(6) Agree to pay money or property to a government official? (**Exception.** Check "No" if the trust agreed to make a grant to or to employ the official for a period after termination of government service, if terminating within 90 days.) . . . . ☐ **Yes** ☐ **No**			
b	If any answer is "Yes" to 1a(1) through (6), did **any** of the acts fail to qualify under the exceptions described in Regulations sections 53.4941(d)-3 and 4, or in a current Notice regarding disaster assistance (see page 9 of the instructions)?	**1b**		
	Organizations relying on a current Notice regarding disaster assistance, check here . . . . ▶ ☐			
c	Did the trust engage in a prior year in any of the acts described in 1a, other than excepted acts, that were not corrected before January 1, 2006?.	**1c**		
2	Does section 4947(b)(3)(A) or (B) apply? (See page 9 of the instructions.) (If "Yes," check the "N/A" box in questions 3 and 4.) . . . . ☐ **Yes** ☐ **No**			
3	Taxes on excess business holdings (section 4943): ☐ **N/A**			
a	Did the trust hold more than a 2% direct or indirect interest in any business enterprise at any time during 2006? . . . . ☐ **Yes** ☐ **No**			
b	If "Yes," did the trust have excess business holdings in 2006 as a result of (1) any purchase by the trust or disqualified persons after May 26, 1969; (2) the lapse of the 5-year period (or longer period approved by the Commissioner under section 4943(c)(7)) to dispose of holdings acquired by gift or bequest; or (3) the lapse of the 10-, 15-, or 20-year first phase holding period? . . . . Use Schedule C, Form 4720, to determine if the trust had excess business holdings in 2006.	**3b**		
4	Taxes on investments that jeopardize charitable purposes (section 4944): ☐ **N/A**			
a	Did the trust invest during 2006 any amount in a manner that would jeopardize its charitable purpose?.	**4a**		
b	Did the trust make any investment in a prior year (but after December 31, 1969) that could jeopardize its charitable purpose that had not been removed from jeopardy before January 1, 2006?	**4b**		
5	Taxes on taxable expenditures (section 4945) and political expenditures (section 4955):			
a	During 2006, did the trust pay or incur any amount to:			
	(1) Carry on propaganda, or otherwise attempt to influence legislation (section 4945(e))? ☐ **Yes** ☐ **No**			
	(2) Influence the outcome of any specific public election (see section 4955); or to carry on, directly or indirectly, any voter registration drive?. . . . . ☐ **Yes** ☐ **No**			
	(3) Provide a grant to an individual for travel, study, or other similar purposes? . . . ☐ **Yes** ☐ **No**			
	(4) Provide a grant to an organization other than a charitable, etc., organization described in section 509(a)(1), (2), or (3), or section 4940(d)(2)?. . . . . ☐ **Yes** ☐ **No**			
	(5) Provide for any purpose other than religious, charitable, scientific, literary, or educational, or for the prevention of cruelty to children or animals?. . . . . . ☐ **Yes** ☐ **No**			

Form **5227** (2006)

Form 5227 (2006)

Page **4**

5b If any answer is "Yes" to 5a(1) through (5), did **any** of the transactions fail to qualify under the exceptions described in Regulations section 53.4945, or in a current Notice regarding disaster assistance (see page 9 of the instructions)? . . . .

Organizations relying on a current Notice regarding disaster assistance, check here . . . . ▶ ☐

c If the answer is "Yes" to question 5a(4), does the trust claim exemption from the tax because it maintained expenditure responsibility for the grant? (See page 9 of the instructions.) . . . . ☐ Yes ☐ No

If "Yes," attach the statement required by Regulations section 53.4945-5(d).

6 Personal benefit contracts (section 170(f)(10)):

a Did the trust, during the year, receive any funds, directly or indirectly, to pay premiums on a personal benefit contract? . . . . ☐ Yes ☐ No

b Did the trust, during the year, pay premiums, directly or indirectly, on a personal benefit contract? . .

If "Yes" to 6b, file Form 8870 (see instructions).

	Yes	No
5b		
6b		

Part VII **Questionnaire for Charitable Lead Trusts, Pooled Income Funds, and Charitable Remainder Trusts**

Section A—Charitable Lead Trusts

1 Does the governing instrument require income in excess of the required annuity or unitrust payments to be paid for charitable purposes? . . . . ☐ Yes ☐ No

2 Enter the amount of any excess income required to be paid for charitable purposes for 2006 . . .	**2**	
3 Enter the amount of annuity or unitrust payments required to be paid to charitable beneficiaries for 2006	**3**	
4 Enter the amount of annuity or unitrust payments required to be paid to private beneficiaries for 2006	**4**	

Section B—Pooled Income Funds

1 Enter the amount of contributions received during 2006	**1**	
2 Enter the amount required to be distributed for 2006 to satisfy the remainder interest	**2**	
3 Enter any amounts that were required to be distributed to the remainder beneficiary that remain undistributed	**3**	
4 Enter the amount of income required to be paid to private beneficiaries for 2006	**4**	
5 Enter the amount of income required to be paid to the charitable remainder beneficiary for 2006	**5**	

Section C—Charitable Remainder Trusts and Other Information
(All split-interest trusts, check applicable boxes.)

1 Check this box if you are filing for a charitable remainder annuity trust or a charitable remainder unitrust whose charitable interests involve only cemeteries or war veterans' posts . . . . ▶ ☐

2 Check this box if you are making an election under Regulations section 1.664-2(a)(1)(i)(a)(2) or 1.664-3(a)(1)(i)(g)(2) to treat income generated from certain property distributions (other than cash) by the trust as occurring on the last day of the tax year. (See page 10 of the instructions.) . . . . ▶ ☐

3 Check this box if any of the split-interest trust's income interests expired during 2006 . . . . ▶ ☐

Sign Here	Under penalties of perjury, I declare that I have examined this return, including accompanying schedules and statements, and to the best of my knowledge and belief, it is true, correct, and complete. Declaration of preparer (other than trustee) is based on all information of which preparer has any knowledge.	
	▶ _____ Signature of trustee or officer representing trustee	▶ _____ Date

Paid Preparer's Use Only	Preparer's signature ▶	Date	Check if self-employed ☐	Preparer's SSN or PTIN
	Firm's name (or yours if self-employed), address, and ZIP code ▶		EIN	
			Phone no. ( )	

Form **5227** (2006)

MODEL FORMS FOR CHARITABLE REMAINDER TRUSTS

In 2003 and 2005 the IRS published a total of 16 model forms for different types of charitable remainder trusts. One form for each type of trust covered in those documents is reproduced in the pages that follow. The IRS has stated that taxpayers who make transfers to a trust that substantially follows one of these sample forms may be assured that the Service will recognize the trust as meeting all of the requirements of a charitable remainder unitrust or charitable remainder annuity trust (as the case may be), provided that the trust operates in a manner consistent with the terms of the instrument creating the trust and provided it is a valid trust under applicable local law.

The text of the model forms is set forth below in the following order:

- Inter Vivos Charitable Remainder Unitrust: One Life[1]

- Inter Vivos Charitable Remainder Unitrust: Term of Years[2]

- Inter Vivos Charitable Remainder Unitrust: Two lives, Consecutive Interests[3]

- Inter Vivos Charitable Remainder Unitrust: Two Lives, Concurrent and Consecutive Interests[4]

- Testamentary Charitable Remainder Unitrust: One Life[5]

- Testamentary Charitable Remainder Unitrust: Term of Years[6]

- Testamentary Charitable Remainder Unitrust: Two Lives, Consecutive Interests[7]

- Testamentary Charitable Remainder Unitrust: Two Lives, Concurrent and Consecutive Interests[8]

- Inter Vivos Charitable Remainder Annuity Trust: One Life[9]

- Inter Vivos Charitable Remainder Annuity Trust: Term of Years[10]

- Inter Vivos Charitable Remainder Annuity Trust: Two Lives, Consecutive Interests[11]

- Inter Vivos Charitable Remainder Annuity Trust: Two Lives, Concurrent and Consecutive Interests[12]

- Testamentary Charitable Remainder Annuity Trust: One Life[13]

- Testamentary Charitable Remainder Annuity Trust: Term of Years[14]

- Testamentary Charitable Remainder Annuity Trust: Two Lives, Consecutive Interests[15]

- Testamentary Charitable Remainder Annuity Trust: Two Lives, Concurrent and Consecutive Interests[16]

In all cases, the termination of the life interests must be followed by distribution of the trust assets to the

charitable remainder beneficiary, and the trust must be a valid trust under applicable local law.

The Service has stated that if the trust provisions are substantially similar to those in one of the model forms, the Service will recognize the trust as satisfying all of the applicable requirements of Sections 664(d)(2) and 664(d)(3) of the Code (in the case of a CRUT) or Section 664(d)(1) (in the case of a CRAT) and the corresponding regulations.

According to the IRS, a document will be considered to be substantially similar to one of the samples even though, for example, the wording is varied to comport with local law and practice as necessary to create trusts, define legal relationships, pass property by bequest, provide for the appointment of alternative and successor trustees, or designate alternative charitable remaindermen. Moreover, for transfers to a qualifying charitable remainder unitrust or charitable remainder annuity trust, the remainder interest will be deductible under sections 170(f)(2)(A), 2055(e)(2)(A), and 2522(c)(2)(A) for income, estate, and gift tax purposes, respectively, if the charitable remainder beneficiary otherwise meets all of the requirements of those provisions. Therefore, it will not be necessary for a taxpayer to request a ruling on the qualification of a substantially similar trust.

A trust that contains substantive provisions in addition to those provided by these model forms (other than provisions necessary to establish a valid trust under applicable local law) or that omits any of those provisions will not necessarily be disqualified but neither will it be assured of qualification under the provisions of these revenue procedures.

ENDNOTES

1. See Rev. Proc. 2005-52, 2005-34 IRB 326.
2. See Rev. Proc. 2005-53, 2005-34 IRB 339.
3. See Rev. Proc. 2005-54, 2005-34 IRB 353.
4. See Rev. Proc. 2005-55, 2005-34 IRB 367.
5. See Rev. Proc. 2005-56, 2005-34 IRB 383.
6   See Rev. Proc. 2005-57, 2005-34 IRB 392.
7. See Rev. Proc. 2005-58, 2005-34 IRB 402.
8. See Rev. Proc. 2005-59, 2005-34 IRB 412.
9. See Rev. Proc. 2003-53, 2003-31 IRB 230.
10. See Rev. Proc. 2003-54, 2003-31 IRB 236.
11. See Rev. Proc. 2003-55, 2003-31 IRB 242.
12. See Rev. Proc. 2003-56, 2003-31 IRB 249.
13. See Rev. Proc. 2003-57, 2003-31 IRB 257.
14. See Rev. Proc. 2003-58, 2003-31 IRB 262.
15. See Rev. Proc. 2003-59, 2003-31 IRB 268.
16. See Rev. Proc. 2003-60, 2003-31 IRB 274.

I. INTER VIVOS CHARITABLE REMAINDER UNITRUST — ONE LIFE

On this _____ day of _____, 20__, I, _____ (hereinafter "the Donor"), desiring to establish a charitable remainder unitrust within the meaning of Rev. Proc. 2005–52 and § 664(d)(2) of the Internal Revenue Code (hereinafter "the Code"), hereby enter into this trust agreement with _____ as the initial trustee (hereinafter "the Trustee"). This trust shall be known as the _____ Charitable Remainder Unitrust.

1. *Funding of Trust.* The Donor hereby transfers and irrevocably assigns, on the above date, to the Trustee the property described in Schedule A, and the Trustee accepts the property and agrees to hold, manage, and distribute the property, and any property subsequently transferred, under the terms set forth in this trust instrument.

2. *Payment of Unitrust Amount.* In each taxable year of the trust during the unitrust period, the Trustee shall pay to [*permissible recipient*] (hereinafter "the Recipient") a unitrust amount equal to [*a number no less than 5 and no more than 50*] percent of the net fair market value of the assets of the trust valued as of the first day of each taxable year of the trust (hereinafter "the valuation date"). The first day of the unitrust period shall be the date property is first transferred to the trust and the last day of the unitrust period shall be the date of the Recipient's death. The unitrust amount shall be paid in equal quarterly installments at the end of each calendar quarter from income and, to the extent income is not sufficient, from principal. Any income of the trust for a taxable year in excess of the unitrust amount shall be added to principal. If, for any year, the net fair market value of the trust assets is incorrectly determined, then within a reasonable period after the correct value is finally determined, the Trustee shall pay to the Recipient (in the case of an undervaluation) or receive from the Recipient (in the case of an overvaluation) an amount equal to the difference between the unitrust amount(s) properly payable and the unitrust amount(s) actually paid.

3. *Proration of Unitrust Amount.* For a short taxable year and for the taxable year during which the unitrust period ends, the Trustee shall prorate on a daily basis the unitrust amount described in paragraph 2, or, if an additional contribution is made to the trust, the unitrust amount described in paragraph 5.

4. *Distribution to Charity.* At the termination of the unitrust period, the Trustee shall distribute all of the then principal and income of the trust (other than any amount due the Recipient under the terms of this trust) to [*designated remainderman*] (hereinafter "the Charitable Organization"). If the Charitable Organization is not an organization described in §§ 170(c), 2055(a), and 2522(a) of the Code at the time when any principal or income of the trust is to be distributed to it, then the Trustee shall distribute the then principal and income to one or more organizations described in §§ 170(c), 2055(a), and 2522(a) of the Code as the Trustee shall select, and in the proportions as the Trustee shall decide, in the Trustee's sole discretion.

5. *Additional Contributions.* If any additional contributions are made to the trust after the initial contribution, the unitrust amount for the year in which any additional contribution is made shall be [*same percentage used in paragraph 2*] percent of the sum of (a) the net fair market value of the trust assets as of the valuation date (excluding the assets so added and any post-contribution income from, and appreciation on, such assets during that year) and (b) for each additional contribution during the year, the fair market value of the assets so added as of the valuation date (including any post-contribution income from, and appreciation on, such assets through the valuation date) multiplied by a fraction the numerator of which is the number of days in the period that begins with the date of contribution and ends with the earlier of the last day of the taxable year or the last day of the unitrust period and the denominator of which is the number of days in the period that begins with the first day of such taxable year and ends with the earlier of the last day in such taxable year or the last day of the unitrust period. In a taxable year in which an additional contribution is made on or after the valuation date, the assets so added shall be valued as of the date of contribution, without regard to any post-contribution income or appreciation, rather than as of the valuation date.

6. *Deferral of the Unitrust Payment Allocable to Testamentary Transfer.* All property passing to the trust by reason of the death of the Donor (hereinafter "the testamentary transfer") shall be considered to be a single contribution that is made on the date of the Donor's death. Notwithstanding the provisions of paragraphs 2 and 5 above, the

obligation to pay the unitrust amount with respect to the testamentary transfer shall commence with the date of the Donor's death. Nevertheless, payment of the unitrust amount with respect to the testamentary transfer may be deferred from the date of the Donor's death until the end of the taxable year in which the funding of the testamentary transfer is completed. Within a reasonable time after the end of the taxable year in which the testamentary transfer is completed, the Trustee must pay to the Recipient (in the case of an underpayment) or receive from the Recipient (in the case of an overpayment) the difference between any unitrust amounts allocable to the testamentary transfer that were actually paid, plus interest, and the unitrust amounts allocable to the testamentary transfer that were payable, plus interest. The interest shall be computed for any period at the rate of interest, compounded annually, that the federal income tax regulations under § 664 of the Code prescribe for this computation.

7. *Unmarketable Assets*. Whenever the value of a trust asset must be determined, the Trustee shall determine the value of any assets that are not cash, cash equivalents, or other assets that can be readily sold or exchanged for cash or cash equivalents (hereinafter "unmarketable assets"), by either (a) obtaining a current "qualified appraisal" from a "qualified appraiser," as defined in § 1.170A–13(c)(3) and § 1.170A–13(c)(5) of the Income Tax Regulations, respectively, or (b) ensuring the valuation of these unmarketable assets is performed exclusively by an "independent trustee," within the meaning of § 1.664–1(a)(7)(iii) of the Income Tax Regulations.

8. *Prohibited Transactions*. The Trustee shall not engage in any act of self-dealing within the meaning of § 4941(d) of the Code, as modified by § 4947(a)(2)(A) of the Code, and shall not make any taxable expenditures within the meaning of § 4945(d) of the Code, as modified by § 4947(a)(2)(A) of the Code.

9. *Taxable Year*. The taxable year of the trust shall be the calendar year.

10. *Governing Law*. The operation of the trust shall be governed by the laws of the State of _____. However, the Trustee is prohibited from exercising any power or discretion granted under said laws that would be inconsistent with the qualification of the trust as a charitable remainder unitrust under § 664(d)(2) of the Code and the corresponding regulations.

11. *Limited Power of Amendment*. This trust is irrevocable. However, the Trustee shall have the power, acting alone, to amend the trust from time to time in any manner required for the sole purpose of ensuring that the trust qualifies and continues to qualify as a charitable remainder unitrust within the meaning of § 664(d)(2) of the Code.

12. *Investment of Trust Assets*. Nothing in this trust instrument shall be construed to restrict the Trustee from investing the trust assets in a manner that could result in the annual realization of a reasonable amount of income or gain from the sale or disposition of trust assets.

13. *Definition of Recipient*. References to the Recipient in this trust instrument shall be deemed to include the estate of the Recipient with regard to all provisions in this trust instrument that describe amounts payable to and/or due from the Recipient. The prior sentence shall not apply to the determination of the last day of the unitrust period.

II. INTER VIVOS CHARITABLE REMAINDER UNITRUST — TERM OF YEARS

On this _____ day of _____, 20__, I, _____ (hereinafter "the Donor"), desiring to establish a charitable remainder unitrust within the meaning of Rev. Proc. 2005–53 and § 664(d)(2) of the Internal Revenue Code (hereinafter "the Code"), hereby enter into this trust agreement with _____ as the initial trustee (hereinafter "the Trustee"). This trust shall be known as the _____ Charitable Remainder Unitrust.

1. *Funding of Trust.* The Donor hereby transfers and irrevocably assigns, on the above date, to the Trustee the property described in Schedule A, and the Trustee accepts the property and agrees to hold, manage, and distribute the property, and any property subsequently transferred, under the terms set forth in this trust instrument.

2. *Payment of Unitrust Amount.* In each taxable year of the trust during the unitrust period, the Trustee shall pay to [*permissible recipient*] (hereinafter "the Recipient") a unitrust amount equal to [*a number no less than 5 and no more than 50*] percent of the net fair market value of the assets of the trust valued as of the first day of each taxable year of the trust (hereinafter "the valuation date"). The unitrust period shall be a period of [*a number not more than 20*] years. The first day of the unitrust period shall be the date property is first transferred to the trust and the last day of the unitrust period shall be the day preceding the [*ordinal number corresponding to the length of the unitrust period*] anniversary of that date. The unitrust amount shall be paid in equal quarterly installments at the end of each calendar quarter from income and, to the extent income is not sufficient, from principal. Any income of the trust for a taxable year in excess of the unitrust amount shall be added to principal. If, for any year, the net fair market value of the trust assets is incorrectly determined, then within a reasonable period after the correct value is finally determined, the Trustee shall pay to the Recipient (in the case of an undervaluation) or receive from the Recipient (in the case of an overvaluation) an amount equal to the difference between the unitrust amount(s) properly payable and the unitrust amount(s) actually paid.

3. *Proration of Unitrust Amount.* For a short taxable year and for the taxable year during which the unitrust period ends, the Trustee shall prorate on a daily basis the unitrust amount described in paragraph 2, or, if an additional contribution is made to the trust, the unitrust amount described in paragraph 5.

4. *Distribution to Charity.* At the termination of the unitrust period, the Trustee shall distribute all of the then principal and income of the trust (other than any amount due the Recipient under the terms of this trust) to [*designated remainderman*] (hereinafter "the Charitable Organization"). If the Charitable Organization is not an organization described in §§ 170(c), 2055(a), and 2522(a) of the Code at the time when any principal or income of the trust is to be distributed to it, then the Trustee shall distribute the then principal and income to one or more organizations described in §§ 170(c), 2055(a), and 2522(a) of the Code as the Trustee shall select, and in the proportions as the Trustee shall decide, in the Trustee's sole discretion.

5. *Additional Contributions.* If any additional contributions are made to the trust after the initial contribution, the unitrust amount for the year in which any additional contribution is made shall be [*same percentage used in paragraph 2*] percent of the sum of (a) the net fair market value of the trust assets as of the valuation date (excluding the assets so added and any post-contribution income from, and appreciation on, such assets during that year) and (b) for each additional contribution during the year, the fair market value of the assets so added as of the valuation date (including any post-contribution income from, and appreciation on, such assets through the valuation date) multiplied by a fraction the numerator of which is the number of days in the period that begins with the date of contribution and ends with the earlier of the last day of the taxable year or the last day of the unitrust period and the denominator of which is the number of days in the period that begins with the first day of such taxable year and ends with the earlier of the last day in such taxable year or the last day of the unitrust period. In a taxable year in which an additional contribution is made on or after the valuation date, the assets so added shall be valued as of the date of contribution, without regard to any post-contribution income or appreciation, rather than as of the valuation date.

6. *Deferral of the Unitrust Payment Allocable to Testamentary Transfer.* All property passing to the trust by reason of the death of the Donor (hereinafter "the testamentary transfer") shall be considered to be a single contribution

that is made on the date of the Donor's death. Notwithstanding the provisions of paragraphs 2 and 5 above, the obligation to pay the unitrust amount with respect to the testamentary transfer shall commence with the date of the Donor's death. Nevertheless, payment of the unitrust amount with respect to the testamentary transfer may be deferred from the date of the Donor's death until the end of the taxable year in which the funding of the testamentary transfer is completed. Within a reasonable time after the end of the taxable year in which the testamentary transfer is completed, the Trustee must pay to the Recipient (in the case of an underpayment) or receive from the Recipient (in the case of an overpayment) the difference between any unitrust amounts allocable to the testamentary transfer that were actually paid, plus interest, and the unitrust amounts allocable to the testamentary transfer that were payable, plus interest. The interest shall be computed for any period at the rate of interest, compounded annually, that the federal income tax regulations under § 664 of the Code prescribe for this computation.

7. *Unmarketable Assets*. Whenever the value of a trust asset must be determined, the Trustee shall determine the value of any assets that are not cash, cash equivalents, or other assets that can be readily sold or exchanged for cash or cash equivalents (hereinafter "unmarketable assets"), by either (a) obtaining a current "qualified appraisal" from a "qualified appraiser," as defined in § 1.170A–13(c)(3) and § 1.170A–13(c)(5) of the Income Tax Regulations, respectively, or (b) ensuring the valuation of these unmarketable assets is performed exclusively by an "independent trustee," within the meaning of § 1.664–1(a)(7)(iii) of the Income Tax Regulations.

8. *Prohibited Transactions*. The Trustee shall not engage in any act of self-dealing within the meaning of § 4941(d) of the Code, as modified by § 4947(a)(2)(A) of the Code, and shall not make any taxable expenditures within the meaning of § 4945(d) of the Code, as modified by § 4947(a)(2)(A) of the Code.

9. *Taxable Year*. The taxable year of the trust shall be the calendar year.

10. *Governing Law*. The operation of the trust shall be governed by the laws of the State of _____. However, the Trustee is prohibited from exercising any power or discretion granted under said laws that would be inconsistent with the qualification of the trust as a charitable remainder unitrust under § 664(d)(2) of the Code and the corresponding regulations.

11. *Limited Power of Amendment*. This trust is irrevocable. However, the Trustee shall have the power, acting alone, to amend the trust from time to time in any manner required for the sole purpose of ensuring that the trust qualifies and continues to qualify as a charitable remainder unitrust within the meaning of § 664(d)(2) of the Code.

12. *Investment of Trust Assets*. Nothing in this trust instrument shall be construed to restrict the Trustee from investing the trust assets in a manner that could result in the annual realization of a reasonable amount of income or gain from the sale or disposition of trust assets.

13. *Definition of Recipient*. References to the Recipient in this trust instrument shall be deemed to include the estate of the Recipient with regard to all provisions in this trust instrument that describe amounts payable to and/or due from the Recipient. The prior sentence shall not apply to the determination of the last day of the unitrust period.

III. INTER VIVOS CHARITABLE REMAINDER UNITRUST — TWO LIVES, CONSECUTIVE INTERESTS

On this _____ day of _____, 20__, I, _____ (hereinafter "the Donor"), desiring to establish a charitable remainder unitrust, within the meaning of Rev. Proc. 2005–54 and § 664(d)(2) of the Internal Revenue Code (hereinafter "the Code"), hereby enter into this trust agreement with _____ as the initial trustee (hereinafter "the Trustee"). This trust shall be known as the _____ Charitable Remainder Unitrust.

1. *Funding of Trust.* The Donor hereby transfers and irrevocably assigns, on the above date, to the Trustee the property described in Schedule A, and the Trustee accepts the property and agrees to hold, manage, and distribute the property, and any property subsequently transferred, under the terms set forth in this trust instrument.

2. *Payment of Unitrust Amount.* In each taxable year of the trust during the unitrust period, the Trustee shall pay to [*permissible recipient*] (hereinafter "the Initial Recipient") until the Initial Recipient's death, and thereafter to [*permissible recipient*] (hereinafter "the Successor Recipient"), a unitrust amount equal to [*a number no less than 5 and no more than 50*] percent of the net fair market value of the assets of the trust valued as of the first day of each taxable year of the trust (hereinafter "the valuation date"). The first day of the unitrust period shall be the date property is first transferred to the trust and the last day of the unitrust period shall be the date of the death of the survivor of the Initial Recipient and the Successor Recipient. The unitrust amount shall be paid in equal quarterly installments at the end of each calendar quarter from income and, to the extent income is not sufficient, from principal. Any income of the trust for a taxable year in excess of the unitrust amount shall be added to principal. If, for any year, the net fair market value of the trust assets is incorrectly determined, then within a reasonable period after the correct value is finally determined, the Trustee shall pay to the Initial Recipient and/or the Successor Recipient (in the case of an undervaluation) or receive from the Initial Recipient and/or the Successor Recipient (in the case of an overvaluation) an amount equal to the difference between the unitrust amount(s) properly payable and the unitrust amount(s) actually paid.

3. *Payment of Federal Estate Taxes and State Death Taxes.* The lifetime unitrust interest of the Successor Recipient will take effect upon the death of the Initial Recipient only if the Successor Recipient furnishes the funds for payment of any federal estate taxes and state death taxes for which the Trustee may be liable upon the death of the Initial Recipient. If the funds are not furnished by the Successor Recipient, the unitrust period shall terminate on the death of the Initial Recipient, notwithstanding any other provision in this instrument to the contrary.

4. *Proration of Unitrust Amount.* For a short taxable year and for the taxable year during which the unitrust period ends, the Trustee shall prorate on a daily basis the unitrust amount described in paragraph 2, or, if an additional contribution is made to the trust, the unitrust amount described in paragraph 6. If the Successor Recipient survives the Initial Recipient, the Trustee shall prorate on a daily basis the next regular unitrust payment due after the death of the Initial Recipient between the estate of the Initial Recipient and the Successor Recipient.

5. *Distribution to Charity.* At the termination of the unitrust period, the Trustee shall distribute all of the then principal and income of the trust (other than any amount due the Initial Recipient and/or the Successor Recipient under the terms of this trust) to [*designated remainderman*] (hereinafter "the Charitable Organization"). If the Charitable Organization is not an organization described in §§ 170(c), 2055(a), and 2522(a) of the Code at the time when any principal or income of the trust is to be distributed to it, then the Trustee shall distribute the then principal and income to one or more organizations described in §§ 170(c), 2055(a), and 2522(a) of the Code as the Trustee shall select, and in the proportions as the Trustee shall decide, in the Trustee's sole discretion.

6. *Additional Contributions.* If any additional contributions are made to the trust after the initial contribution, the unitrust amount for the year in which any additional contribution is made shall be [*same percentage used in paragraph 2*] percent of the sum of (a) the net fair market value of the trust assets as of the valuation date (excluding the assets so added and any post-contribution income from, and appreciation on, such assets during that year) and (b) for each additional contribution during the year, the fair market value of the assets so added as of the valuation date (including any post-contribution income from, and appreciation on, such assets through the valuation

date) multiplied by a fraction the numerator of which is the number of days in the period that begins with the date of contribution and ends with the earlier of the last day of the taxable year or the last day of the unitrust period and the denominator of which is the number of days in the period that begins with the first day of such taxable year and ends with the earlier of the last day in such taxable year or the last day of the unitrust period. In a taxable year in which an additional contribution is made on or after the valuation date, the assets so added shall be valued as of the date of contribution, without regard to any post-contribution income or appreciation, rather than as of the valuation date.

7. *Deferral of the Unitrust Payment Allocable to Testamentary Transfer.* All property passing to the trust by reason of the death of the Donor (hereinafter "the testamentary transfer") shall be considered to be a single contribution that is made on the date of the Donor's death. Notwithstanding the provisions of paragraphs 2 and 6 above, the obligation to pay the unitrust amount with respect to the testamentary transfer shall commence with the date of the Donor's death. Nevertheless, payment of the unitrust amount with respect to the testamentary transfer may be deferred from the date of the Donor's death until the end of the taxable year in which the funding of the testamentary transfer is completed. Within a reasonable time after the end of the taxable year in which the testamentary transfer is completed, the Trustee must pay to the Initial Recipient and/or the Successor Recipient (in the case of an underpayment) or receive from the Initial Recipient and/or the Successor Recipient (in the case of an overpayment) the difference between any unitrust amounts allocable to the testamentary transfer that were actually paid, plus interest, and the unitrust amounts allocable to the testamentary transfer that were payable, plus interest. The interest shall be computed for any period at the rate of interest, compounded annually, that the federal income tax regulations under § 664 of the Code prescribe for this computation.

8. *Unmarketable Assets.* Whenever the value of a trust asset must be determined, the Trustee shall determine the value of any assets that are not cash, cash equivalents, or other assets that can be readily sold or exchanged for cash or cash equivalents (hereinafter "unmarketable assets"), by either (a) obtaining a current "qualified appraisal" from a "qualified appraiser," as defined in § 1.170A–13(c)(3) and § 1.170A–13(c)(5) of the Income Tax Regulations, respectively, or (b) ensuring the valuation of these unmarketable assets is performed exclusively by an "independent trustee," within the meaning of § 1.664–1(a)(7)(iii) of the Income Tax Regulations.

9. *Prohibited Transactions.* The Trustee shall not engage in any act of self-dealing within the meaning of § 4941(d) of the Code, as modified by § 4947(a)(2)(A) of the Code, and shall not make any taxable expenditures within the meaning of § 4945(d) of the Code, as modified by § 4947(a)(2)(A) of the Code.

10. *Taxable Year.* The taxable year of the trust shall be the calendar year.

11. *Governing Law.* The operation of the trust shall be governed by the laws of the State of _____. However, the Trustee is prohibited from exercising any power or discretion granted under said laws that would be inconsistent with the qualification of the trust as a charitable remainder unitrust under § 664(d)(2) of the Code and the corresponding regulations.

12. *Limited Power of Amendment.* This trust is irrevocable. However, the Trustee shall have the power, acting alone, to amend the trust from time to time in any manner required for the sole purpose of ensuring that the trust qualifies and continues to qualify as a charitable remainder unitrust within the meaning of § 664(d)(2) of the Code.

13. *Investment of Trust Assets.* Nothing in this trust instrument shall be construed to restrict the Trustee from investing the trust assets in a manner that could result in the annual realization of a reasonable amount of income or gain from the sale or disposition of trust assets.

14. *Definition of Initial Recipient and Successor Recipient.* References to the Initial Recipient and/or the Successor Recipient in this trust instrument shall be deemed to include the estate of the Initial Recipient and/or the Successor Recipient with regard to all provisions in this trust instrument that describe amounts payable to and/or due from the Initial Recipient and/or the Successor Recipient. The prior sentence shall not apply to the determination of the last day of the unitrust period.

IV. INTER VIVOS CHARITABLE REMAINDER UNITRUST — TWO LIVES, CONCURRENT AND CONSECUTIVE INTERESTS

On this _____ day of _____, 20__, I, _____ (hereinafter "the Donor"), desiring to establish a charitable remainder unitrust within the meaning of Rev. Proc. 2005–55 and § 664(d)(2) of the Internal Revenue Code (hereinafter "the Code"), hereby enter into this trust agreement with _____ as the initial trustee (hereinafter "the Trustee"). This trust shall be known as the _____ Charitable Remainder Unitrust.

1. *Funding of Trust.* The Donor hereby transfers and irrevocably assigns, on the above date, to the Trustee the property described in Schedule A, and the Trustee accepts the property and agrees to hold, manage, and distribute the property, and any property subsequently transferred, under the terms set forth in this trust instrument.

2. *Payment of Unitrust Amount.* In each taxable year of the trust during the unitrust period, the Trustee shall pay to [*permissible recipient*] and to [*permissible recipient*] (hereinafter "the Recipients") in equal shares during their joint lives, a unitrust amount equal to [*a number no less than 5 and no more than 50*] percent of the net fair market value of the assets of the trust valued as of the first day of each taxable year of the trust (hereinafter "the valuation date") and, upon the death of one (hereinafter "the Predeceasing Recipient"), the Trustee shall pay the entire unitrust amount to the survivor (hereinafter "the Survivor Recipient"). The first day of the unitrust period shall be the date property is first transferred to the trust and the last day of the unitrust period shall be the date of the Survivor Recipient's death. The unitrust amount shall be paid in equal quarterly installments at the end of each calendar quarter from income and, to the extent income is not sufficient, from principal. Any income of the trust for a taxable year in excess of the unitrust amount shall be added to principal. If, for any year, the net fair market value of the trust assets is incorrectly determined, then within a reasonable period after the correct value is finally determined, the Trustee shall pay to the Predeceasing Recipient and/or the Survivor Recipient (in the case of an undervaluation) or receive from the Predeceasing Recipient and/or the Survivor Recipient (in the case of an overvaluation) an amount equal to the difference between the unitrust amount(s) properly payable and the unitrust amount(s) actually paid.

3. *Payment of Federal Estate Taxes and State Death Taxes.* The lifetime unitrust interest of the Survivor Recipient will take effect upon the death of the Predeceasing Recipient only if the Survivor Recipient furnishes the funds for payment of any federal estate taxes and state death taxes for which the Trustee may be liable upon the death of the Predeceasing Recipient. If the funds are not furnished by the Survivor Recipient, the unitrust period shall terminate on the death of the Predeceasing Recipient, notwithstanding any other provision in this instrument to the contrary.

4. *Proration of Unitrust Amount.* For a short taxable year and for the taxable year during which the unitrust period ends, the Trustee shall prorate on a daily basis the unitrust amount described in paragraph 2, or, if an additional contribution is made to the trust, the unitrust amount described in paragraph 6. Upon the death of the Predeceasing Recipient, the Trustee shall prorate on a daily basis the next regular unitrust payment due after the death of the Predeceasing Recipient between the estate of the Predeceasing Recipient and the Survivor Recipient.

5. *Distribution to Charity.* At the termination of the unitrust period, the Trustee shall distribute all of the then principal and income of the trust (other than any amount due the Predeceasing Recipient and/or the Survivor Recipient under the terms of this trust) to [*designated remainderman*] (hereinafter "the Charitable Organization"). If the Charitable Organization is not an organization described in §§ 170(c), 2055(a), and 2522(a) of the Code at the time when any principal or income of the trust is to be distributed to it, then the Trustee shall distribute the then principal and income to one or more organizations described in §§ 170(c), 2055(a), and 2522(a) of the Code as the Trustee shall select, and in the proportions as the Trustee shall decide, in the Trustee's sole discretion.

6. *Additional Contributions.* If any additional contributions are made to the trust after the initial contribution, the unitrust amount for the year in which any additional contribution is made shall be [*same percentage used in paragraph 2*] percent of the sum of (a) the net fair market value of the trust assets as of the valuation date (excluding the assets so added and any post-contribution income from, and appreciation on, such assets during that year) and (b) for each additional contribution during the year, the fair market value of the assets so added as of the valuation date (including any post-contribution income from, and appreciation on, such assets through the valuation

date) multiplied by a fraction the numerator of which is the number of days in the period that begins with the date of contribution and ends with the earlier of the last day of the taxable year or the last day of the unitrust period and the denominator of which is the number of days in the period that begins with the first day of such taxable year and ends with the earlier of the last day in such taxable year or the last day of the unitrust period. In a taxable year in which an additional contribution is made on or after the valuation date, the assets so added shall be valued as of the date of contribution, without regard to any post-contribution income or appreciation, rather than as of the valuation date.

7. *Deferral of the Unitrust Payment Allocable to Testamentary Transfer.* All property passing to the trust by reason of the death of the Donor (hereinafter "the testamentary transfer") shall be considered to be a single contribution that is made on the date of the Donor's death. Notwithstanding the provisions of paragraphs 2 and 6 above, the obligation to pay the unitrust amount with respect to the testamentary transfer shall commence with the date of the Donor's death. Nevertheless, payment of the unitrust amount with respect to the testamentary transfer may be deferred from the date of the Donor's death until the end of the taxable year in which the funding of the testamentary transfer is completed. Within a reasonable time after the end of the taxable year in which the testamentary transfer is completed, the Trustee must pay to the Predeceasing Recipient and/or the Survivor Recipient (in the case of an underpayment) or receive from the Predeceasing Recipient and/or the Survivor Recipient (in the case of an overpayment) the difference between any unitrust amounts allocable to the testamentary transfer that were actually paid, plus interest, and the unitrust amounts allocable to the testamentary transfer that were payable, plus interest. The interest shall be computed for any period at the rate of interest, compounded annually, that the federal income tax regulations under § 664 of the Code prescribe for this computation.

8. *Unmarketable Assets.* Whenever the value of a trust asset must be determined, the Trustee shall determine the value of any assets that are not cash, cash equivalents, or other assets that can be readily sold or exchanged for cash or cash equivalents (hereinafter "unmarketable assets"), by either (a) obtaining a current "qualified appraisal" from a "qualified appraiser," as defined in § 1.170A–13(c)(3) and § 1.170A–13(c)(5) of the Income Tax Regulations, respectively, or (b) ensuring the valuation of these unmarketable assets is performed exclusively by an "independent trustee," within the meaning of § 1.664–1(a)(7)(iii) of the Income Tax Regulations.

9. *Prohibited Transactions.* The Trustee shall not engage in any act of self-dealing within the meaning of § 4941(d) of the Code, as modified by § 4947(a)(2)(A) of the Code, and shall not make any taxable expenditures within the meaning of § 4945(d) of the Code, as modified by § 4947(a)(2)(A) of the Code.

10. *Taxable Year.* The taxable year of the trust shall be the calendar year.

11. *Governing Law.* The operation of the trust shall be governed by the laws of the State of _____. However, the Trustee is prohibited from exercising any power or discretion granted under said laws that would be inconsistent with the qualification of the trust as a charitable remainder unitrust under § 664(d)(2) of the Code and the corresponding regulations.

12. *Limited Power of Amendment.* This trust is irrevocable. However, the Trustee shall have the power, acting alone, to amend the trust from time to time in any manner required for the sole purpose of ensuring that the trust qualifies and continues to qualify as a charitable remainder unitrust within the meaning of § 664(d)(2) of the Code.

13. *Investment of Trust Assets.* Nothing in this trust instrument shall be construed to restrict the Trustee from investing the trust assets in a manner that could result in the annual realization of a reasonable amount of income or gain from the sale or disposition of trust assets.

14. *Definition of Predeceasing Recipient and Survivor Recipient.* References to the Predeceasing Recipient and/or the Survivor Recipient in this trust instrument shall be deemed to include the estate of the Predeceasing Recipient and/or the Survivor Recipient with regard to all provisions in this trust instrument that describe amounts payable to and/or due from the Predeceasing Recipient and/or the Survivor Recipient. The prior sentence shall not apply to the determination of the last day of the unitrust period.

V. TESTAMENTARY CHARITABLE REMAINDER UNITRUST — ONE LIFE

I give, devise, and bequeath [*property bequeathed*] to my Trustee in trust to be administered under this provision. I intend this bequest to establish a charitable remainder unitrust, within the meaning of Rev. Proc. 2005–56 and § 664(d)(2) of the Internal Revenue Code (hereinafter "the Code"). The trust shall be known as the _____ Charitable Remainder Unitrust and I hereby designate _____ as the initial trustee (hereinafter "the Trustee").

1. *Payment of Unitrust Amount.* In each taxable year of the trust during the unitrust period, the Trustee shall pay to [*permissible recipient*] (hereinafter "the Recipient") a unitrust amount equal to [*a number no less than 5 and no more than 50*] percent of the net fair market value of the assets of the trust valued as of the first day of each taxable year of the trust (hereinafter "the valuation date"). The first day of the unitrust period shall be the date of my death and the last day of the unitrust period shall be the date of the Recipient's death. The unitrust amount shall be paid in equal quarterly installments at the end of each calendar quarter from income and, to the extent income is not sufficient, from principal. Any income of the trust for a taxable year in excess of the unitrust amount shall be added to principal. If, for any year, the net fair market value of the trust assets is incorrectly determined, then within a reasonable period after the correct value is finally determined, the Trustee shall pay to the Recipient (in the case of an undervaluation) or receive from the Recipient (in the case of an overvaluation) an amount equal to the difference between the unitrust amount(s) properly payable and the unitrust amount(s) actually paid.

2. *Deferral Provision.* The obligation to pay the unitrust amount shall commence with the date of my death, but payment of the unitrust amount may be deferred from this date until the end of the taxable year in which the trust is completely funded. Within a reasonable time after the end of the taxable year in which the trust is completely funded, the Trustee must pay to the Recipient (in the case of an underpayment) or receive from the Recipient (in the case of an overpayment) the difference between any unitrust amounts actually paid, plus interest, and the unitrust amounts payable, plus interest. The interest shall be computed for any period at the rate of interest, compounded annually, that the federal income tax regulations under § 664 of the Code prescribe for this computation.

3. *Proration of Unitrust Amount.* For a short taxable year and for the taxable year during which the unitrust period ends, the Trustee shall prorate on a daily basis the unitrust amount described in paragraph 1.

4. *Distribution to Charity.* At the termination of the unitrust period, the Trustee shall distribute all of the then principal and income of the trust (other than any amount due the Recipient under the terms of this trust) to [*designated remainderman*] (hereinafter "the Charitable Organization"). If the Charitable Organization is not an organization described in §§ 170(c) and 2055(a) of the Code at the time when any principal or income of the trust is to be distributed to it, then the Trustee shall distribute the then principal and income to one or more organizations described in §§ 170(c) and 2055(a) of the Code as the Trustee shall select, and in the proportions as the Trustee shall decide, in the Trustee's sole discretion.

5. *Additional Contributions.* No additional contributions shall be made to the trust after the initial contribution. The initial contribution, however, shall be deemed to consist of all property passing to the trust by reason of my death.

6. *Unmarketable Assets.* Whenever the value of a trust asset must be determined, the Trustee shall determine the value of any assets that are not cash, cash equivalents, or other assets that can be readily sold or exchanged for cash or cash equivalents (hereinafter "unmarketable assets"), by either (a) obtaining a current "qualified appraisal" from a "qualified appraiser," as defined in § 1.170A–13(c)(3) and § 1.170A–13(c)(5) of the Income Tax Regulations, respectively, or (b) ensuring the valuation of these unmarketable assets is performed exclusively by an "independent trustee," within the meaning of § 1.664–1(a)(7)(iii) of the Income Tax Regulations.

7. *Prohibited Transactions.* The Trustee shall not engage in any act of self-dealing within the meaning of § 4941(d) of the Code, as modified by § 4947(a)(2)(A) of the Code, and shall not make any taxable expenditures within the meaning of § 4945(d) of the Code, as modified by § 4947(a)(2)(A) of the Code.

8. *Taxable Year*. The taxable year of the trust shall be the calendar year.

9. *Governing Law*. The operation of the trust shall be governed by the laws of the State of _____. However, the Trustee is prohibited from exercising any power or discretion granted under said laws that would be inconsistent with the qualification of the trust as a charitable remainder unitrust under § 664(d)(2) of the Code and the corresponding regulations.

10. *Limited Power of Amendment*. This trust is irrevocable. However, the Trustee shall have the power, acting alone, to amend the trust from time to time in any manner required for the sole purpose of ensuring that the trust qualifies and continues to qualify as a charitable remainder unitrust within the meaning of § 664(d)(2) of the Code.

11. *Investment of Trust Assets*. Nothing in this trust instrument shall be construed to restrict the Trustee from investing the trust assets in a manner that could result in the annual realization of a reasonable amount of income or gain from the sale or disposition of trust assets.

12. *Definition of Recipient*.

VI. TESTAMENTARY CHARITABLE REMAINDER UNITRUST — TERM OF YEARS

I give, devise, and bequeath [*property bequeathed*] to my Trustee in trust to be administered under this provision. I intend this bequest to establish a charitable remainder unitrust, within the meaning of Rev. Proc. 2005–57 and § 664(d)(2) of the Internal Revenue Code (hereinafter "the Code"). The trust shall be known as the _____ Charitable Remainder Unitrust and I hereby designate _____ as the initial trustee (hereinafter "the Trustee").

1. *Payment of Unitrust Amount.* In each taxable year of the trust during the unitrust period, the Trustee shall pay to [*permissible recipient*] (hereinafter "the Recipient") a unitrust amount equal to [*a number no less than 5 and no more than 50*] percent of the net fair market value of the assets of the trust valued as of the first day of each taxable year of the trust (hereinafter "the valuation date"). The unitrust period shall be a period of [*a number not more than 20*] years. The first day of the unitrust period shall be the date of my death and the last day of the unitrust period shall be the day preceding the [*ordinal number corresponding to the length of the unitrust period*] anniversary of that date. The unitrust amount shall be paid in equal quarterly installments at the end of each calendar quarter from income and, to the extent income is not sufficient, from principal. Any income of the trust for a taxable year in excess of the unitrust amount shall be added to principal. If, for any year, the net fair market value of the trust assets is incorrectly determined, then within a reasonable period after the correct value is finally determined, the Trustee shall pay to the Recipient (in the case of an undervaluation) or receive from the Recipient (in the case of an overvaluation) an amount equal to the difference between the unitrust amount(s) properly payable and the unitrust amount(s) actually paid.

2. *Deferral Provision.* The obligation to pay the unitrust amount shall commence with the date of my death, but payment of the unitrust amount may be deferred from this date until the end of the taxable year in which the trust is completely funded. Within a reasonable time after the end of the taxable year in which the trust is completely funded, the Trustee must pay to the Recipient (in the case of an underpayment) or receive from the Recipient (in the case of an overpayment) the difference between any unitrust amounts actually paid, plus interest, and the unitrust amounts payable, plus interest. The interest shall be computed for any period at the rate of interest, compounded annually, that the federal income tax regulations under § 664 of the Code prescribe for this computation.

3. *Proration of Unitrust Amount.* For a short taxable year and for the taxable year during which the unitrust period ends, the Trustee shall prorate on a daily basis the unitrust amount described in paragraph 1.

4. *Distribution to Charity.* At the termination of the unitrust period, the Trustee shall distribute all of the then principal and income of the trust (other than any amount due the Recipient under the terms of this trust) to [*designated remainderman*] (hereinafter "the Charitable Organization"). If the Charitable Organization is not an organization described in §§ 170(c) and 2055(a) of the Code at the time when any principal or income of the trust is to be distributed to it, then the Trustee shall distribute the then principal and income to one or more organizations described in §§ 170(c) and 2055(a) of the Code as the Trustee shall select, and in the proportions as the Trustee shall decide, in the Trustee's sole discretion.

5. *Additional Contributions.* No additional contributions shall be made to the trust after the initial contribution. The initial contribution, however, shall be deemed to consist of all property passing to the trust by reason of my death.

6. *Unmarketable Assets.* Whenever the value of a trust asset must be determined, the Trustee shall determine the value of any assets that are not cash, cash equivalents, or other assets that can be readily sold or exchanged for cash or cash equivalents (hereinafter "unmarketable assets"), by either (a) obtaining a current "qualified appraisal" from a "qualified appraiser," as defined in § 1.170A–13(c)(3) and § 1.170A–13(c)(5) of the Income Tax Regulations, respectively, or (b) ensuring the valuation of these unmarketable assets is performed exclusively by an "independent trustee," within the meaning of § 1.664–1(a)(7)(iii) of the Income Tax Regulations.

7. *Prohibited Transactions.* The Trustee shall not engage in any act of self-dealing within the meaning of § 4941(d) of the Code, as modified by § 4947(a)(2)(A) of the Code, and shall not make any taxable expenditures within the meaning of § 4945(d) of the Code, as modified by § 4947(a)(2)(A) of the Code.

8. *Taxable Year.* The taxable year of the trust shall be the calendar year.

9. *Governing Law.* The operation of the trust shall be governed by the laws of the State of _____. However, the Trustee is prohibited from exercising any power or discretion granted under said laws that would be inconsistent with the qualification of the trust as a charitable remainder unitrust under § 664(d)(2) of the Code and the corresponding regulations.

10. *Limited Power of Amendment.* This trust is irrevocable. However, the Trustee shall have the power, acting alone, to amend the trust from time to time in any manner required for the sole purpose of ensuring that the trust qualifies and continues to qualify as a charitable remainder unitrust within the meaning of § 664(d)(2) of the Code.

11. *Investment of Trust Assets.* Nothing in this trust instrument shall be construed to restrict the Trustee from investing the trust assets in a manner that could result in the annual realization of a reasonable amount of income or gain from the sale or disposition of trust assets.

12. *Definition of Recipient.* References to the Recipient in this trust instrument shall be deemed to include the estate of the Recipient with regard to all provisions in this trust instrument that describe amounts payable to and/or due from the Recipient. The prior sentence shall not apply to the determination of the last day of the unitrust period.

VII. TESTAMENTARY CHARITABLE REMAINDER UNITRUST — TWO LIVES, CONSECUTIVE INTERESTS

I give, devise, and bequeath [*property bequeathed*] to my Trustee in trust to be administered under this provision. I intend this bequest to establish a charitable remainder unitrust, within the meaning of Rev. Proc. 2005–58 and § 664(d)(2) of the Internal Revenue Code (hereinafter "the Code"). The trust shall be known as the _____ Charitable Remainder Unitrust and I hereby designate _____ as the initial trustee (hereinafter "the Trustee").

1. *Payment of Unitrust Amount.* In each taxable year of the trust during the unitrust period, the Trustee shall pay to [*permissible recipient*] (hereinafter "the Initial Recipient") until the Initial Recipient's death, and thereafter to [*permissible recipient*] (hereinafter "the Successor Recipient"), a unitrust amount equal to [*a number no less than 5 and no more than 50*] percent of the net fair market value of the assets of the trust valued as of the first day of each taxable year of the trust (hereinafter "the valuation date"). The first day of the unitrust period shall be the date of my death and the last day of the unitrust period shall be the date of the death of the survivor of the Initial Recipient and the Successor Recipient. The unitrust amount shall be paid in equal quarterly installments at the end of each calendar quarter from income and, to the extent income is not sufficient, from principal. Any income of the trust for a taxable year in excess of the unitrust amount shall be added to principal. If, for any year, the net fair market value of the trust assets is incorrectly determined, then within a reasonable period after the correct value is finally determined, the Trustee shall pay to the Initial Recipient and/or the Successor Recipient (in the case of an undervaluation) or receive from the Initial Recipient and/or the Successor Recipient (in the case of an overvaluation) an amount equal to the difference between the unitrust amount(s) properly payable and the unitrust amount(s) actually paid.

2. *Deferral Provision.* The obligation to pay the unitrust amount shall commence with the date of my death, but payment of the unitrust amount may be deferred from this date until the end of the taxable year in which the trust is completely funded. Within a reasonable time after the end of the taxable year in which the trust is completely funded, the Trustee must pay to the Initial Recipient and/or the Successor Recipient (in the case of an underpayment) or receive from the Initial Recipient and/or the Successor Recipient (in the case of an overpayment) the difference between any unitrust amounts actually paid, plus interest, and the unitrust amounts payable, plus interest. The interest shall be computed for any period at the rate of interest, compounded annually, that the federal income tax regulations under § 664 of the Code prescribe for this computation.

3. *Proration of Unitrust Amount.* For a short taxable year and for the taxable year during which the unitrust period ends, the Trustee shall prorate on a daily basis the unitrust amount described in paragraph 1. If the Successor Recipient survives the Initial Recipient, the Trustee shall prorate on a daily basis the next regular unitrust payment due after the death of the Initial Recipient between the estate of the Initial Recipient and the Successor Recipient.

4. *Distribution to Charity.* At the termination of the unitrust period, the Trustee shall distribute all of the then principal and income of the trust (other than any amount due the Initial Recipient and/or the Successor Recipient under the terms of this trust) to [*designated remainderman*] (hereinafter "the Charitable Organization"). If the Charitable Organization is not an organization described in §§ 170(c) and 2055(a) of the Code at the time when any principal or income of the trust is to be distributed to it, then the Trustee shall distribute the then principal and income to one or more organizations described in §§ 170(c) and 2055(a) of the Code as the Trustee shall select, and in the proportions as the Trustee shall decide, in the Trustee's sole discretion.

5. *Additional Contributions.* No additional contributions shall be made to the trust after the initial contribution. The initial contribution, however, shall be deemed to consist of all property passing to the trust by reason of my death.

6. *Unmarketable Assets.* Whenever the value of a trust asset must be determined, the Trustee shall determine the value of any assets that are not cash, cash equivalents, or other assets that can be readily sold or exchanged for cash or cash equivalents (hereinafter "unmarketable assets"), by either (a) obtaining a current "qualified ap-

praisal" from a "qualified appraiser," as defined in § 1.170A–13(c)(3) and § 1.170A–13(c)(5) of the Income Tax Regulations, respectively, or (b) ensuring the valuation of these unmarketable assets is performed exclusively by an "independent trustee," within the meaning of § 1.664–1(a)(7)(iii) of the Income Tax Regulations.

7. *Prohibited Transactions*. The Trustee shall not engage in any act of self-dealing within the meaning of § 4941(d) of the Code, as modified by § 4947(a)(2)(A) of the Code, and shall not make any taxable expenditures within the meaning of § 4945(d) of the Code, as modified by § 4947(a)(2)(A) of the Code.

8. *Taxable Year*. The taxable year of the trust shall be the calendar year.

9. *Governing Law*. The operation of the trust shall be governed by the laws of the State of _____. However, the Trustee is prohibited from exercising any power or discretion granted under said laws that would be inconsistent with the qualification of the trust as a charitable remainder unitrust under § 664(d)(2) of the Code and the corresponding regulations.

10. *Limited Power of Amendment*. This trust is irrevocable. However, the Trustee shall have the power, acting alone, to amend the trust from time to time in any manner required for the sole purpose of ensuring that the trust qualifies and continues to qualify as a charitable remainder unitrust within the meaning of § 664(d)(2) of the Code.

11. *Investment of Trust Assets*. Nothing in this trust instrument shall be construed to restrict the Trustee from investing the trust assets in a manner that could result in the annual realization of a reasonable amount of income or gain from the sale or disposition of trust assets.

12. *Definition of Initial Recipient and Successor Recipient*. References to the Initial Recipient and/or the Successor Recipient in this trust instrument shall be deemed to include the estate of the Initial Recipient and/or the Successor Recipient with regard to all provisions in this trust instrument that describe amounts payable to and/or due from the Initial Recipient and/or the Successor Recipient. The prior sentence shall not apply to the determination of the last day of the unitrust period.

VIII. TESTAMENTARY CHARITABLE REMAINDER UNITRUST — TWO LIVES, CONCURRENT AND CONSECUTIVE INTERESTS

I give, devise, and bequeath [*property bequeathed*] to my Trustee in trust to be administered under this provision. I intend this bequest to establish a charitable remainder unitrust, within the meaning of Rev. Proc. 2005–59 and § 664(d)(2) of the Internal Revenue Code (hereinafter "the Code"). The trust shall be known as the _____ Charitable Remainder Unitrust and I hereby designate _____ as the initial trustee (hereinafter "the Trustee").

1. *Payment of Unitrust Amount.* In each taxable year of the trust during the unitrust period, the Trustee shall pay to [*permissible recipient*] and to [*permissible recipient*] (hereinafter "the Recipients") in equal shares during their joint lives, a unitrust amount equal to [*a number no less than 5 and no more than 50*] percent of the net fair market value of the assets of the trust valued as of the first day of each taxable year of the trust (hereinafter "the valuation date") and, upon the death of one (hereinafter "the Predeceasing Recipient"), the Trustee shall pay the entire unitrust amount to the survivor (hereinafter "the Survivor Recipient"). The first day of the unitrust period shall be the date of my death and the last day of the unitrust period shall be the date of the Survivor Recipient's death. The unitrust amount shall be paid in equal quarterly installments at the end of each calendar quarter from income and, to the extent income is not sufficient, from principal. Any income of the trust for a taxable year in excess of the unitrust amount shall be added to principal. If, for any year, the net fair market value of the trust assets is incorrectly determined, then within a reasonable period after the correct value is finally determined, the Trustee shall pay to the Predeceasing Recipient and/or the Survivor Recipient (in the case of an undervaluation) or receive from the Predeceasing Recipient and/or the Survivor Recipient (in the case of an overvaluation) an amount equal to the difference between the unitrust amount(s) properly payable and the unitrust amount(s) actually paid.

2. *Deferral Provision.* The obligation to pay the unitrust amount shall commence with the date of my death, but payment of the unitrust amount may be deferred from this date until the end of the taxable year in which the trust is completely funded. Within a reasonable time after the end of the taxable year in which the trust is completely funded, the Trustee must pay to the Predeceasing Recipient and/or the Survivor Recipient (in the case of an underpayment) or receive from the Predeceasing Recipient and/or the Survivor Recipient (in the case of an overpayment) the difference between any unitrust amounts actually paid, plus interest, and the unitrust amounts payable, plus interest. The interest shall be computed for any period at the rate of interest, compounded annually, that the federal income tax regulations under § 664 of the Code prescribe for this computation.

3. *Proration of Unitrust Amount.* For a short taxable year and for the taxable year during which the unitrust period ends, the Trustee shall prorate on a daily basis the unitrust amount described in paragraph 1. Upon the death of the Predeceasing Recipient, the Trustee shall prorate on a daily basis the next regular unitrust payment due after the death of the Predeceasing Recipient between the estate of the Predeceasing Recipient and the Survivor Recipient.

4. *Distribution to Charity.* At the termination of the unitrust period, the Trustee shall distribute all of the then principal and income of the trust (other than any amount due the Predeceasing Recipient and/or the Survivor Recipient under the terms of this trust) to [*designated remainderman*] (hereinafter "the Charitable Organization"). If the Charitable Organization is not an organization described in §§ 170(c) and 2055(a) of the Code at the time when any principal or income of the trust is to be distributed to it, then the Trustee shall distribute the then principal and income to one or more organizations described in §§ 170(c) and 2055(a) of the Code as the Trustee shall select, and in the proportions as the Trustee shall decide, in the Trustee's sole discretion.

5. *Additional Contributions.* No additional contributions shall be made to the trust after the initial contribution. The initial contribution, however, shall be deemed to consist of all property passing to the trust by reason of my death.

6. *Unmarketable Assets.* Whenever the value of a trust asset must be determined, the Trustee shall determine the value of any assets that are not cash, cash equivalents, or other assets that can be readily sold or exchanged for

cash or cash equivalents (hereinafter "unmarketable assets"), by either (a) obtaining a current "qualified appraisal" from a "qualified appraiser," as defined in § 1.170A–13(c)(3) and § 1.170A–13(c)(5) of the Income Tax Regulations, respectively, or (b) ensuring the valuation of these unmarketable assets is performed exclusively by an "independent trustee," within the meaning of § 1.664–1(a)(7)(iii) of the Income Tax Regulations.

7. *Prohibited Transactions.* The Trustee shall not engage in any act of self-dealing within the meaning of § 4941(d) of the Code, as modified by § 4947(a)(2)(A) of the Code, and shall not make any taxable expenditures within the meaning of § 4945(d) of the Code, as modified by § 4947(a)(2)(A) of the Code.

8. *Taxable Year.* The taxable year of the trust shall be the calendar year.

9. *Governing Law.* The operation of the trust shall be governed by the laws of the State of _____. However, the Trustee is prohibited from exercising any power or discretion granted under said laws that would be inconsistent with the qualification of the trust as a charitable remainder unitrust under § 664(d)(2) of the Code and the corresponding regulations.

10. *Limited Power of Amendment.* This trust is irrevocable. However, the Trustee shall have the power, acting alone, to amend the trust from time to time in any manner required for the sole purpose of ensuring that the trust qualifies and continues to qualify as a charitable remainder unitrust within the meaning of § 664(d)(2) of the Code.

11. *Investment of Trust Assets.* Nothing in this trust instrument shall be construed to restrict the Trustee from investing the trust assets in a manner that could result in the annual realization of a reasonable amount of income or gain from the sale or disposition of trust assets.

12. *Definition of Predeceasing Recipient and Survivor Recipient.* References to the Predeceasing Recipient and/or the Survivor Recipient in this trust instrument shall be deemed to include the estate of the Predeceasing Recipient and/or the Survivor Recipient with regard to all provisions in this trust instrument that describe amounts payable to and/or due from the Predeceasing Recipient and/or the Survivor Recipient. The prior sentence shall not apply to the determination of the last day of the unitrust period.

IX. INTER VIVOS CHARITABLE REMAINDER ANNUITY TRUST — ONE LIFE

On this _____ day of _____, 20__, I, _____ (hereinafter "the Donor"), desiring to establish a charitable remainder annuity trust, within the meaning of Rev. Proc. 2003–53 and § 664(d)(1) of the Internal Revenue Code (hereinafter "the Code"), hereby enter into this trust agreement with _____ as the initial trustee (hereinafter "the Trustee"). This trust shall be known as the _____ Charitable Remainder Annuity Trust.

1. *Funding of Trust.* The Donor hereby transfers and irrevocably assigns, on the above date, to the Trustee the property described in Schedule A, and the Trustee accepts the property and agrees to hold, manage, and distribute the property under the terms set forth in this trust instrument.

2. *Payment of Annuity Amount.* In each taxable year of the trust during the annuity period, the Trustee shall pay to [*permissible recipient*] (hereinafter "the Recipient") an annuity amount equal to [*a number no less than 5 and no more than 50*] percent of the initial net fair market value of all property transferred to the trust, valued as of the above date (that is, the date of the transfer). The first day of the annuity period shall be the date the property is transferred to the trust and the last day of the annuity period shall be the date of the Recipient's death. The annuity amount shall be paid in equal quarterly installments at the end of each calendar quarter from income, and to the extent income is not sufficient, from principal. Any income of the trust for a taxable year in excess of the annuity amount shall be added to principal. If the initial net fair market value of the trust assets is incorrectly determined, then within a reasonable period after the value is finally determined for federal tax purposes, the Trustee shall pay to the Recipient (in the case of an undervaluation) or receive from the Recipient (in the case of an overvaluation) an amount equal to the difference between the annuity amount(s) properly payable and the annuity amount(s) actually paid.

3. *Proration of Annuity Amount.* The Trustee shall prorate the annuity amount on a daily basis for any short taxable year. In the taxable year of the trust during which the annuity period ends, the Trustee shall prorate the annuity amount on a daily basis for the number of days of the annuity period in that taxable year.

4. *Distribution to Charity.* At the termination of the annuity period, the Trustee shall distribute all of the then principal and income of the trust (other than any amount due the Recipient or the Recipient's estate under the provisions above) to [*designated remainderman*] (hereinafter "the Charitable Organization"). If the Charitable Organization is not an organization described in §§ 170(c), 2055(a), and 2522(a) of the Code at the time when any principal or income of the trust is to be distributed to it, then the Trustee shall distribute the then principal and income to one or more organizations described in §§ 170(c), 2055(a), and 2522(a) of the Code as the Trustee shall select, and in the proportions as the Trustee shall decide, in the Trustee's sole discretion.

5. *Additional Contributions.* No additional contributions shall be made to the trust after the initial contribution.

6. *Prohibited Transactions.* The Trustee shall not engage in any act of self-dealing within the meaning of § 4941(d) of the Code, as modified by § 4947(a)(2)(A) of the Code, and shall not make any taxable expenditures within the meaning of § 4945(d) of the Code, as modified by § 4947(a)(2)(A) of the Code.

7. *Taxable Year.* The taxable year of the trust shall be the calendar year.

8. *Governing Law.* The operation of the trust shall be governed by the laws of the State of _____. However, the Trustee is prohibited from exercising any power or discretion granted under said laws that would be inconsistent with the qualification of the trust as a charitable remainder annuity trust under § 664(d)(1) of the Code and the corresponding regulations.

9. *Limited Power of Amendment.* This trust is irrevocable. However, the Trustee shall have the power, acting alone, to amend the trust from time to time in any manner required for the sole purpose of ensuring that the trust qualifies and continues to qualify as a charitable remainder annuity trust within the meaning of § 664(d)(1) of the Code.

10. *Investment of Trust Assets.* Nothing in this trust instrument shall be construed to restrict the Trustee from investing the trust assets in a manner that could result in the annual realization of a reasonable amount of income or gain from the sale or disposition of trust assets.

X. INTER VIVOS CHARITABLE REMAINDER ANNUITY TRUST — TERM OF YEARS

On this _____ day of _____, 20__, I, _____ (hereinafter "the Donor"), desiring to establish a charitable remainder annuity trust, within the meaning of Rev. Proc. 2003–54 and § 664(d)(1) of the Internal Revenue Code (hereinafter "the Code"), hereby enter into this trust agreement with _____ as the initial trustee (hereinafter "the Trustee"). This trust shall be known as the _____ Charitable Remainder Annuity Trust.

1. *Funding of Trust*. The Donor hereby transfers and irrevocably assigns, on the above date, to the Trustee the property described in Schedule A, and the Trustee accepts the property and agrees to hold, manage, and distribute the property under the terms set forth in this trust instrument.

2. *Payment of Annuity Amount*. In each taxable year of the trust during the annuity period, the Trustee shall pay to [*permissible recipient*] (hereinafter "the Recipient") an annuity amount equal to [*a number no less than 5 and no more than 50*] percent of the initial net fair market value of all property transferred to the trust, valued as of the above date (that is, the date of the transfer). The annuity period is a term of [*a number not more than 20*] years. The first day of the annuity period shall be the date the property is transferred to the trust and the last day of the annuity period shall be the day preceding the [*ordinal number corresponding to the length of the annuity period*] anniversary of that date. The annuity amount shall be paid in equal quarterly installments at the end of each calendar quarter from income, and to the extent income is not sufficient, from principal. Any income of the trust for a taxable year in excess of the annuity amount shall be added to principal. If the initial net fair market value of the trust assets is incorrectly determined, then within a reasonable period after the value is finally determined for federal tax purposes, the Trustee shall pay to the Recipient (in the case of an undervaluation) or receive from the Recipient (in the case of an overvaluation) an amount equal to the difference between the annuity amount(s) properly payable and the annuity amount(s) actually paid.

3. *Proration of Annuity Amount*. The Trustee shall prorate the annuity amount on a daily basis for any short taxable year. In the taxable year of the trust during which the annuity period ends, the Trustee shall prorate the annuity amount on a daily basis for the number of days of the annuity period in that taxable year.

4. *Distribution to Charity*. At the termination of the annuity period, the Trustee shall distribute all of the then principal and income of the trust (other than any amount due the Recipient under the provisions above) to [*designated remainderman*] (hereinafter "the Charitable Organization"). If the Charitable Organization is not an organization described in §§ 170(c), 2055(a), and 2522(a) of the Code at the time when any principal or income of the trust is to be distributed to it, then the Trustee shall distribute the then principal and income to one or more organizations described in §§ 170(c), 2055(a), and 2522(a) of the Code as the Trustee shall select, and in the proportions as the Trustee shall decide, in the Trustee's sole discretion.

5. *Additional Contributions*. No additional contributions shall be made to the trust after the initial contribution.

6. *Prohibited Transactions*. The Trustee shall not engage in any act of self-dealing within the meaning of § 4941(d) of the Code, as modified by § 4947(a)(2)(A) of the Code, and shall not make any taxable expenditures within the meaning of § 4945(d) of the Code, as modified by § 4947(a)(2)(A) of the Code.

7. *Taxable Year*. The taxable year of the trust shall be the calendar year.

8. *Governing Law*. The operation of the trust shall be governed by the laws of the State of _____. However, the Trustee is prohibited from exercising any power or discretion granted under said laws that would be inconsistent with the qualification of the trust as a charitable remainder annuity trust under § 664(d)(1) of the Code and the corresponding regulations.

9. *Limited Power of Amendment*. This trust is irrevocable. However, the Trustee shall have the power, acting alone, to amend the trust from time to time in any manner required for the sole purpose of ensuring that the trust

qualifies and continues to qualify as a charitable remainder annuity trust within the meaning of § 664(d)(1) of the Code.

10. *Investment of Trust Assets.* Nothing in this trust instrument shall be construed to restrict the Trustee from investing the trust assets in a manner that could result in the annual realization of a reasonable amount of income or gain from the sale or disposition of trust assets.

XI. INTER VIVOS CHARITABLE REMAINDER ANNUITY TRUST — TWO LIVES, CONSECUTIVE INTERESTS

On this ____ day of _____, 20__, I, _____ (hereinafter "the Donor"), desiring to establish a charitable remainder annuity trust, within the meaning of Rev. Proc. 2003–55 and § 664(d)(1) of the Internal Revenue Code (hereinafter "the Code"), hereby enter into this trust agreement with _____ as the initial trustee (hereinafter "the Trustee"). This trust shall be known as the _____ Charitable Remainder Annuity Trust.

1. *Funding of Trust.* The Donor hereby transfers and irrevocably assigns, on the above date, to the Trustee the property described in Schedule A, and the Trustee accepts the property and agrees to hold, manage, and distribute the property under the terms set forth in this trust instrument.

2. *Payment of Annuity Amount.* In each taxable year of the trust during the annuity period, the Trustee shall pay to [*permissible recipient*] (hereinafter "the Initial Recipient") until the Initial Recipient's death, and thereafter to [*permissible recipient*] (hereinafter "the Successor Recipient") (subject to any proration in paragraph 4), an annuity amount equal to [*a number no less than 5 and no more than 50*] percent of the initial net fair market value of all property transferred to the trust, valued as of the above date (that is, the date of the transfer). The first day of the annuity period shall be the date the property is transferred to the trust and the last day of the annuity period shall be the date of the death of the survivor of the Initial Recipient and the Successor Recipient. The annuity amount shall be paid in equal quarterly installments at the end of each calendar quarter from income, and to the extent income is not sufficient, from principal. Any income of the trust for a taxable year in excess of the annuity amount shall be added to principal. If the initial net fair market value of the trust assets is incorrectly determined, then within a reasonable period after the value is finally determined for federal tax purposes, the Trustee shall pay to the Initial Recipient and/or Successor Recipient (in the case of an undervaluation) or receive from the Initial Recipient and/or Successor Recipient (in the case of an overvaluation) an amount equal to the difference between the annuity amount(s) properly payable and the annuity amount(s) actually paid.

3. *Payment of Federal Estate Taxes and State Death Taxes.* The lifetime annuity interest of the Successor Recipient will take effect upon the death of the Initial Recipient only if the Successor Recipient furnishes the funds for payment of any federal estate taxes and state death taxes for which the Trustee may be liable upon the death of the Initial Recipient. If the funds are not furnished by the Successor Recipient, the annuity period shall terminate on the death of the Initial Recipient, notwithstanding any other provision in this instrument to the contrary.

4. *Proration of Annuity Amount.* The Trustee shall prorate the annuity amount on a daily basis for any short taxable year. If the Successor Recipient survives the Initial Recipient, the Trustee shall prorate on a daily basis the next regular annuity payment due after the death of the Initial Recipient between the estate of the Initial Recipient and the Successor Recipient. In the taxable year of the trust during which the annuity period ends, the Trustee shall prorate the annuity amount on a daily basis for the number of days of the annuity period in that taxable year.

5. *Distribution to Charity.* At the termination of the annuity period, the Trustee shall distribute all of the then principal and income of the trust (other than any amount due the Recipients or their estates under the provisions above) to [*designated remainderman*] (hereinafter "the Charitable Organization"). If the Charitable Organization is not an organization described in §§ 170(c), 2055(a), and 2522(a) of the Code at the time when any principal or income of the trust is to be distributed to it, then the Trustee shall distribute the then principal and income to one or more organizations described in §§ 170(c), 2055(a), and 2522(a) of the Code as the Trustee shall select, and in the proportions as the Trustee shall decide, in the Trustee's sole discretion.

6. *Additional Contributions.* No additional contributions shall be made to the trust after the initial contribution.

7. *Prohibited Transactions.* The Trustee shall not engage in any act of self-dealing within the meaning of § 4941(d) of the Code, as modified by § 4947(a)(2)(A) of the Code, and shall not make any taxable expenditures within the meaning of § 4945(d) of the Code, as modified by § 4947(a)(2)(A) of the Code.

8. *Taxable Year.* The taxable year of the trust shall be the calendar year.

9. *Governing Law.* The operation of the trust shall be governed by the laws of the State of _____. However, the Trustee is prohibited from exercising any power or discretion granted under said laws that would be inconsistent with the qualification of the trust as a charitable remainder annuity trust under § 664(d)(1) of the Code and the corresponding regulations.

10. *Limited Power of Amendment.* This trust is irrevocable. However, the Trustee shall have the power, acting alone, to amend the trust from time to time in any manner required for the sole purpose of ensuring that the trust qualifies and continues to qualify as a charitable remainder annuity trust within the meaning of § 664(d)(1) of the Code.

11. *Investment of Trust Assets.* Nothing in this trust instrument shall be construed to restrict the Trustee from investing the trust assets in a manner that could result in the annual realization of a reasonable amount of income or gain from the sale or disposition of trust assets.

XII. INTER VIVOS CHARITABLE REMAINDER ANNUITY TRUST — TWO LIVES, CONCURRENT AND CONSECUTIVE INTERESTS

On this ____ day of _____, 20__, I, _____ (hereinafter "the Donor"), desiring to establish a charitable remainder annuity trust, within the meaning of Rev. Proc. 2003–56 and § 664(d)(1) of the Internal Revenue Code (hereinafter "the Code"), hereby enter into this trust agreement with _____ as the initial trustee (hereinafter "the Trustee"). This trust shall be known as the _____ Charitable Remainder Annuity Trust.

1. *Funding of Trust.* The Donor hereby transfers and irrevocably assigns, on the above date, to the Trustee the property described in Schedule A, and the Trustee accepts the property and agrees to hold, manage, and distribute the property under the terms set forth in this trust instrument.

2. *Payment of Annuity Amount.* In each taxable year of the trust during the annuity period, the Trustee shall pay to [*permissible recipient*] and to [*permissible recipient*] (hereinafter "the Recipients") in equal shares during their lifetimes, an annuity amount equal to [*a number no less than 5 and no more than 50*] percent of the initial net fair market value of all property transferred to the trust, valued as of the above date (that is, the date of the transfer), and upon the death of one (hereinafter "the Predeceasing Recipient"), the Trustee shall pay the entire annuity amount (subject to any proration in paragraph 4) to the survivor (hereinafter "the Survivor Recipient"). The first day of the annuity period shall be the date the property is transferred to the trust and the last day of the annuity period shall be the date of the Survivor Recipient's death. The annuity amount shall be paid in equal quarterly installments at the end of each calendar quarter from income, and to the extent income is not sufficient, from principal. Any income of the trust for a taxable year in excess of the annuity amount shall be added to principal. If the initial net fair market value of the trust assets is incorrectly determined, then within a reasonable period after the value is finally determined for federal tax purposes, the Trustee shall pay to the Recipients (in the case of an undervaluation) or receive from the Recipients (in the case of an overvaluation) an amount equal to the difference between the annuity amount(s) properly payable and the annuity amount(s) actually paid.

3. *Payment of Federal Estate Taxes and State Death Taxes.* The lifetime annuity interest of the Survivor Recipient will continue in effect upon the death of the Predeceasing Recipient only if the Survivor Recipient furnishes the funds for payment of any federal estate taxes and state death taxes for which the Trustee may be liable upon the death of the Predeceasing Recipient. If the funds are not furnished by the Survivor Recipient, the annuity period shall terminate on the death of the Predeceasing Recipient, notwithstanding any other provision in this instrument to the contrary.

4. *Proration of Annuity Amount.* The Trustee shall prorate the annuity amount on a daily basis for any short taxable year. Upon the death of the Predeceasing Recipient, the Trustee shall prorate on a daily basis the Predeceasing Recipient's share of the next regular annuity payment between the estate of the Predeceasing Recipient and the Survivor Recipient. In the taxable year of the trust during which the annuity period ends, the Trustee shall prorate the annuity amount on a daily basis for the number of days of the annuity period in that taxable year.

5. *Distribution to Charity.* At the termination of the annuity period, the Trustee shall distribute all of the then principal and income of the trust (other than any amount due the Recipients or their estates under the provisions above) to [*designated remainderman*] (hereinafter "the Charitable Organization"). If the Charitable Organization is not an organization described in §§ 170(c), 2055(a), and 2522(a) of the Code at the time when any principal or income of the trust is to be distributed to it, then the Trustee shall distribute the then principal and income to one or more organizations described in §§ 170(c), 2055(a), and 2522(a) of the Code as the Trustee shall select, and in the proportions as the Trustee shall decide, in the Trustee's sole discretion.

6. *Additional Contributions.* No additional contributions shall be made to the trust after the initial contribution.

7. *Prohibited Transactions.* The Trustee shall not engage in any act of self-dealing within the meaning of § 4941(d) of the Code, as modified by § 4947(a)(2)(A) of the Code, and shall not make any taxable expenditures within the meaning of § 4945(d) of the Code, as modified by § 4947(a)(2)(A) of the Code.

N

8. *Taxable Year.* The taxable year of the trust shall be the calendar year.

9. *Governing Law.* The operation of the trust shall be governed by the laws of the State of _____. However, the Trustee is prohibited from exercising any power or discretion granted under said laws that would be inconsistent with the qualification of the trust as a charitable remainder annuity trust under § 664(d)(1) of the Code and the corresponding regulations.

10. *Limited Power of Amendment.* This trust is irrevocable. However, the Trustee shall have the power, acting alone, to amend the trust from time to time in any manner required for the sole purpose of ensuring that the trust qualifies and continues to qualify as a charitable remainder annuity trust within the meaning of § 664(d)(1) of the Code.

11. *Investment of Trust Assets.* Nothing in this trust instrument shall be construed to restrict the Trustee from investing the trust assets in a manner that could result in the annual realization of a reasonable amount of income or gain from the sale or disposition of trust assets.

XIII. TESTAMENTARY CHARITABLE REMAINDER ANNUITY TRUST — ONE LIFE

I give, devise, and bequeath [*property bequeathed*] to my Trustee in trust to be administered under this provision. I intend this bequest to establish a charitable remainder annuity trust, within the meaning of Rev. Proc. 2003–57 and § 664(d)(1) of the Internal Revenue Code (hereinafter "the Code"). The trust shall be known as the _____ Charitable Remainder Annuity Trust and I hereby designate _____ as the initial trustee (hereinafter "the Trustee").

1. *Payment of Annuity Amount.* In each taxable year of the trust during the annuity period, the Trustee shall pay to [*permissible recipient*] (hereinafter "the Recipient") an annuity amount equal to [*a number no less than 5 and no more than 50*] percent of the initial net fair market value of all property passing to this trust as finally determined for federal estate tax purposes. The first day of the annuity period shall be the date of my death and the last day of the annuity period shall be the date of the Recipient's death. The annuity amount shall be paid in equal quarterly installments at the end of each calendar quarter from income, and to the extent income is not sufficient, from principal. Any income of the trust for a taxable year in excess of the annuity amount shall be added to principal. If the initial net fair market value of the trust assets is incorrectly determined, then within a reasonable period after the value is finally determined for federal estate tax purposes, the Trustee shall pay to the Recipient (in the case of an undervaluation) or receive from the Recipient (in the case of an overvaluation) an amount equal to the difference between the annuity amount(s) properly payable and the annuity amount(s) actually paid.

2. *Deferral Provision.* The obligation to pay the annuity amount shall commence with the date of my death, but payment of the annuity amount may be deferred from this date until the end of the taxable year in which the trust is completely funded. Within a reasonable time after the end of the taxable year in which the trust is completely funded, the Trustee must pay to the Recipient (in the case of an underpayment) or receive from the Recipient (in the case of an overpayment) the difference between any annuity amounts actually paid, plus interest, and the annuity amounts payable, plus interest. The interest shall be computed for any period at the rate of interest, compounded annually, that the federal income tax regulations under § 664 of the Code prescribe for this computation.

3. *Proration of Annuity Amount.* The Trustee shall prorate the annuity amount on a daily basis for any short taxable year. In the taxable year of the trust during which the annuity period ends, the Trustee shall prorate the annuity amount on a daily basis for the number of days of the annuity period in that taxable year.

4. *Distribution to Charity.* At the termination of the annuity period, the Trustee shall distribute all of the then principal and income of the trust (other than any amount due the Recipient or the Recipient's estate under the provisions above) to [*designated remainderman*] (hereinafter "the Charitable Organization"). If the Charitable Organization is not an organization described in §§ 170(c) and 2055(a) of the Code at the time when any principal or income of the trust is to be distributed to it, then the Trustee shall distribute the then principal and income to one or more organizations described in §§ 170(c) and 2055(a) of the Code as the Trustee shall select, and in the proportions as the Trustee shall decide, in the Trustee's sole discretion.

5. *Additional Contributions.* No additional contributions shall be made to the trust after the initial contribution. The initial contribution, however, shall be deemed to consist of all property passing to the trust by reason of my death.

6. *Prohibited Transactions.* The Trustee shall not engage in any act of self-dealing within the meaning of § 4941(d) of the Code, as modified by § 4947(a)(2)(A) of the Code, and shall not make any taxable expenditures within the meaning of § 4945(d) of the Code, as modified by § 4947(a)(2)(A) of the Code.

7. *Taxable Year.* The taxable year of the trust shall be the calendar year.

8. *Governing Law.* The operation of the trust shall be governed by the laws of the State of _____. How-

ever, the Trustee is prohibited from exercising any power or discretion granted under said laws that would be inconsistent with the qualification of the trust as a charitable remainder annuity trust under § 664(d)(1) of the Code and the corresponding regulations.

9. *Limited Power of Amendment.* This trust is irrevocable. However, the Trustee shall have the power, acting alone, to amend the trust from time to time in any manner required for the sole purpose of ensuring that the trust qualifies and continues to qualify as a charitable remainder annuity trust within the meaning of § 664(d)(1) of the Code.

10. *Investment of Trust Assets.* Nothing in this trust instrument shall be construed to restrict the Trustee from investing the trust assets in a manner that could result in the annual realization of a reasonable amount of income or gain from the sale or disposition of trust assets.

XIV. TESTAMENTARY CHARITABLE REMAINDER ANNUITY TRUST — TERM OF YEARS

I give, devise, and bequeath [*property bequeathed*] to my Trustee in trust to be administered under this provision. I intend this bequest to establish a charitable remainder annuity trust, within the meaning of Rev. Proc. 2003–58 and § 664(d)(1) of the Internal Revenue Code (hereinafter "the Code"). The trust shall be known as the _____ Charitable Remainder Annuity Trust and I hereby designate _____ as the initial trustee (hereinafter "the Trustee").

1. *Payment of Annuity Amount.* In each taxable year of the trust during the annuity period, the Trustee shall pay to [*permissible recipient*] (hereinafter "the Recipient") an annuity amount equal to [*a number no less than 5 and no more than 50*] percent of the initial net fair market value of all property passing to this trust as finally determined for federal estate tax purposes. The annuity period is a term of [*a number not more than 20*] years. The first day of the annuity period shall be the date of my death and the last day of the annuity period shall be the day preceding the [*ordinal number corresponding to the length of the annuity period*] anniversary of that date. The annuity amount shall be paid in equal quarterly installments at the end of each calendar quarter from income, and to the extent income is not sufficient, from principal. Any income of the trust for a taxable year in excess of the annuity amount shall be added to principal. If the initial net fair market value of the trust assets is incorrectly determined, then within a reasonable period after the value is finally determined for federal estate tax purposes, the Trustee shall pay to the Recipient (in the case of an undervaluation) or receive from the Recipient (in the case of an overvaluation) an amount equal to the difference between the annuity amount(s) properly payable and the annuity amount(s) actually paid.

2. *Deferral Provision.* The obligation to pay the annuity amount shall commence with the date of my death, but payment of the annuity amount may be deferred from this date until the end of the taxable year in which the trust is completely funded. Within a reasonable time after the end of the taxable year in which the trust is completely funded, the Trustee must pay to the Recipient (in the case of an underpayment) or receive from the Recipient (in the case of an overpayment) the difference between any annuity amounts actually paid, plus interest, and the annuity amounts payable, plus interest. The interest shall be computed for any period at the rate of interest, compounded annually, that the federal income tax regulations under § 664 of the Code prescribe for this computation.

3. *Proration of Annuity Amount.* The Trustee shall prorate the annuity amount on a daily basis for any short taxable year. In the taxable year of the trust during which the annuity period ends, the Trustee shall prorate the annuity amount on a daily basis for the number of days of the annuity period in that taxable year.

4. *Distribution to Charity.* At the termination of the annuity period, the Trustee shall distribute all of the then principal and income of the trust (other than any amount due the Recipient under the provisions above) to [*designated remainderman*] (hereinafter "the Charitable Organization"). If the Charitable Organization is not an organization described in §§ 170(c) and 2055(a) of the Code at the time when any principal or income of the trust is to be distributed to it, then the Trustee shall distribute the then principal and income to one or more organizations described in §§ 170(c) and 2055(a) of the Code as the Trustee shall select, and in the proportions as the Trustee shall decide, in the Trustee's sole discretion.

5. *Additional Contributions.* No additional contributions shall be made to the trust after the initial contribution. The initial contribution, however, shall be deemed to consist of all property passing to the trust by reason of my death.

6. *Prohibited Transactions.* The Trustee shall not engage in any act of self-dealing within the meaning of § 4941(d) of the Code, as modified by § 4947(a)(2)(A) of the Code, and shall not make any taxable expenditures within the meaning of § 4945(d) of the Code, as modified by § 4947(a)(2)(A) of the Code.

7. *Taxable Year.* The taxable year of the trust shall be the calendar year.

8. *Governing Law.* The operation of the trust shall be governed by the laws of the State of _____. However, the Trustee is prohibited from exercising any power or discretion granted under said laws that would be inconsistent with the qualification of the trust as a charitable remainder annuity trust under § 664(d)(1) of the Code and the corresponding regulations.

9. *Limited Power of Amendment.* This trust is irrevocable. However, the Trustee shall have the power, acting alone, to amend the trust from time to time in any manner required for the sole purpose of ensuring that the trust qualifies and continues to qualify as a charitable remainder annuity trust within the meaning of § 664(d)(1) of the Code.

10. *Investment of Trust Assets.* Nothing in this trust instrument shall be construed to restrict the Trustee from investing the trust assets in a manner that could result in the annual realization of a reasonable amount of income or gain from the sale or disposition of trust assets.

XV. TESTAMENTARY CHARITABLE REMAINDER ANNUITY TRUST — TWO LIVES, CONSECUTIVE INTERESTS

I give, devise, and bequeath [*property bequeathed*] to my Trustee in trust to be administered under this provision. I intend this bequest to establish a charitable remainder annuity trust, within the meaning of Rev. Proc. 2003–59 and § 664(d)(1) of the Internal Revenue Code (hereinafter "the Code"). The trust shall be known as the _____ Charitable Remainder Annuity Trust and I hereby designate _____ as the initial trustee (hereinafter "the Trustee").

1. *Payment of Annuity Amount.* In each taxable year of the trust during the annuity period, the Trustee shall pay to [*permissible recipient*] (hereinafter "the Initial Recipient") until the Initial Recipient's death, and thereafter to [*permissible recipient*] (hereinafter "the Successor Recipient") (subject to any proration in paragraph 3), an annuity amount equal to [*a number no less than 5 and no more than 50*] percent of the initial net fair market value of all property passing to this trust as finally determined for federal estate tax purposes. The first day of the annuity period shall be the date of my death and the last day of the annuity period shall be the date of the death of the survivor of the Initial Recipient and the Successor Recipient. The annuity amount shall be paid in equal quarterly installments at the end of each calendar quarter from income, and to the extent income is not sufficient, from principal. Any income of the trust for a taxable year in excess of the annuity amount shall be added to principal. If the initial net fair market value of the trust assets is incorrectly determined, then within a reasonable period after the value is finally determined for federal estate tax purposes, the Trustee shall pay to the Initial Recipient and/or Successor Recipient (in the case of an undervaluation) or receive from the Initial Recipient and/or Successor Recipient (in the case of an overvaluation) an amount equal to the difference between the annuity amount(s) properly payable and the annuity amount(s) actually paid.

2. *Deferral Provision.* The obligation to pay the annuity amount shall commence with the date of my death, but payment of the annuity amount may be deferred from this date until the end of the taxable year in which the trust is completely funded. Within a reasonable time after the end of the taxable year in which the trust is completely funded, the Trustee must pay to the Initial Recipient and/or the Successor Recipient (in the case of an underpayment) or receive from the Initial Recipient and/or the Successor Recipient (in the case of an overpayment) the difference between any annuity amounts actually paid, plus interest, and the annuity amounts payable, plus interest. The interest shall be computed for any period at the rate of interest, compounded annually, that the federal income tax regulations under § 664 of the Code prescribe for this computation.

3. *Proration of Annuity Amount.* The Trustee shall prorate the annuity amount on a daily basis for any short taxable year. If the Successor Recipient survives the Initial Recipient, the Trustee shall prorate on a daily basis the next regular annuity payment due after the death of the Initial Recipient between the estate of the Initial Recipient and the Successor Recipient. In the taxable year of the trust during which the annuity period ends, the Trustee shall prorate the annuity amount on a daily basis for the number of days of the annuity period in that taxable year.

4. *Distribution to Charity.* At the termination of the annuity period, the Trustee shall distribute all of the then principal and income of the trust (other than any amount due the Recipients or their estates under the provisions above) to [*designated remainderman*] (hereinafter "the Charitable Organization"). If the Charitable Organization is not an organization described in §§ 170(c) and 2055(a) of the Code at the time when any principal or income of the trust is to be distributed to it, then the Trustee shall distribute the then principal and income to one or more organizations described in §§ 170(c) and 2055(a) of the Code as the Trustee shall select, and in the proportions as the Trustee shall decide, in the Trustee's sole discretion.

5. *Additional Contributions.* No additional contributions shall be made to the trust after the initial contribution. The initial contribution, however, shall be deemed to consist of all property passing to the trust by reason of my death.

6. *Prohibited Transactions.* The Trustee shall not engage in any act of self-dealing within the meaning of § 4941(d) of the Code, as modified by § 4947(a)(2)(A) of the Code, and shall not make any taxable expenditures within the meaning of § 4945(d) of the Code, as modified by § 4947(a)(2)(A) of the Code.

7. *Taxable Year*. The taxable year of the trust shall be the calendar year.

8. *Governing Law*. The operation of the trust shall be governed by the laws of the State of _____. However, the Trustee is prohibited from exercising any power or discretion granted under said laws that would be inconsistent with the qualification of the trust as a charitable remainder annuity trust under § 664(d)(1) of the Code and the corresponding regulations.

9. *Limited Power of Amendment*. This trust is irrevocable. However, the Trustee shall have the power, acting alone, to amend the trust from time to time in any manner required for the sole purpose of ensuring that the trust qualifies and continues to qualify as a charitable remainder annuity trust within the meaning of § 664(d)(1) of the Code.

10. *Investment of Trust Assets*. Nothing in this trust instrument shall be construed to restrict the Trustee from investing the trust assets in a manner that could result in the annual realization of a reasonable amount of income or gain from the sale or disposition of trust assets.

XVI. TESTAMENTARY CHARITABLE REMAINDER ANNUITY TRUST — TWO LIVES, CONCURRENT AND CONSECUTIVE INTERESTS

I give, devise, and bequeath [*property bequeathed*] to my Trustee in trust to be administered under this provision. I intend this bequest to establish a charitable remainder annuity trust, within the meaning of Rev. Proc. 2003–60 and § 664(d)(1) of the Internal Revenue Code (hereinafter "the Code"). The trust shall be known as the _____ Charitable Remainder Annuity Trust and I hereby designate _____ as the initial trustee (hereinafter "the Trustee").

1. *Payment of Annuity Amount.* In each taxable year of the trust during the annuity period, the Trustee shall pay to [*permissible recipient*] and to [*permissible recipient*] (hereinafter "the Recipients") in equal shares during their lifetimes, an annuity amount equal to [*a number no less than 5 and no more than 50*] percent of the initial net fair market value of all property passing to this trust as finally determined for federal estate tax purposes, and upon the death of one (hereinafter "the Predeceasing Recipient"), the Trustee shall pay the entire annuity amount (subject to any proration in paragraph 3) to the survivor (hereinafter "the Survivor Recipient"). The first day of the annuity period shall be the date of my death and the last day of the annuity period shall be the date of the Survivor Recipient's death. The annuity amount shall be paid in equal quarterly installments at the end of each calendar quarter from income, and to the extent income is not sufficient, from principal. Any income of the trust for a taxable year in excess of the annuity amount shall be added to principal. If the initial net fair market value of the trust assets is incorrectly determined, then within a reasonable period after the value is finally determined for federal estate tax purposes, the Trustee shall pay to the Recipients (in the case of an undervaluation) or receive from the Recipients (in the case of an overvaluation) an amount equal to the difference between the annuity amount(s) properly payable and the annuity amount(s) actually paid.

2. *Deferral Provision.* The obligation to pay the annuity amount shall commence with the date of my death, but payment of the annuity amount may be deferred from this date until the end of the taxable year in which the trust is completely funded. Within a reasonable time after the end of the taxable year in which the trust is completely funded, the Trustee must pay to the Recipients (in the case of an underpayment) or receive from the Recipients (in the case of an overpayment) the difference between any annuity amounts actually paid, plus interest, and the annuity amounts payable, plus interest. The interest shall be computed for any period at the rate of interest, compounded annually, that the federal income tax regulations under § 664 of the Code prescribe for this computation.

3. *Proration of Annuity Amount.* The Trustee shall prorate the annuity amount on a daily basis for any short taxable year. Upon the death of the Predeceasing Recipient, the Trustee shall prorate on a daily basis the Predeceasing Recipient's share of the next regular annuity payment between the estate of the Predeceasing Recipient and the Survivor Recipient. In the taxable year of the trust during which the annuity period ends, the Trustee shall prorate the annuity amount on a daily basis for the number of days of the annuity period in that taxable year.

4. *Distribution to Charity.* At the termination of the annuity period, the Trustee shall distribute all of the then principal and income of the trust (other than any amount due the Recipients or their estates under the provisions above) to [*designated remainderman*] (hereinafter "the Charitable Organization"). If the Charitable Organization is not an organization described in §§ 170(c) and 2055(a) of the Code at the time when any principal or income of the trust is to be distributed to it, then the Trustee shall distribute the then principal and income to one or more organizations described in §§ 170(c) and 2055(a) of the Code as the Trustee shall select, and in the proportions as the Trustee shall decide, in the Trustee's sole discretion.

5. *Additional Contributions.* No additional contributions shall be made to the trust after the initial contribution. The initial contribution, however, shall be deemed to consist of all property passing to the trust by reason of my death.

6. *Prohibited Transactions.* The Trustee shall not engage in any act of self-dealing within the meaning of § 4941(d) of the Code, as modified by § 4947(a)(2)(A) of the Code, and shall not make any taxable expenditures within the meaning of § 4945(d) of the Code, as modified by § 4947(a)(2)(A) of the Code.

7. *Taxable Year.* The taxable year of the trust shall be the calendar year.

8. *Governing Law.* The operation of the trust shall be governed by the laws of the State of _____. However, the Trustee is prohibited from exercising any power or discretion granted under said laws that would be inconsistent with the qualification of the trust as a charitable remainder annuity trust under § 664(d)(1) of the Code and the corresponding regulations.

9. *Limited Power of Amendment.* This trust is irrevocable. However, the Trustee shall have the power, acting alone, to amend the trust from time to time in any manner required for the sole purpose of ensuring that the trust qualifies and continues to qualify as a charitable remainder annuity trust within the meaning of § 664(d)(1) of the Code.

10. *Investment of Trust Assets.* Nothing in this trust instrument shall be construed to restrict the Trustee from investing the trust assets in a manner that could result in the annual realization of a reasonable amount of income or gain from the sale or disposition of trust assets.

CHARITABLE PLANNING SOFTWARE

With the advent of the personal computer over 25 years ago, professional and amateur programmers sought to make complex calculations an achievable objective for those who were either mathematically challenged or wanted a more time and cost-effective means of performing "what-if" analysis.

Depending on the programmer's view of the market, more (or less) sophisticated applications became available to professionals in the financial and estate planning service industries, which for this purpose includes accountants, financial planners, attorneys, trust officers and charitable gift planners. With great progress having been achieved in software programming, the ease with which complex charitable planning calculations can be performed today is truly amazing.

There are several vendors in the charitable planning and planned giving areas that offer comprehensive computer software designed to assist charitable planners, planned giving professionals, and members of the allied professions. Other vendors offer programs that are less comprehensive, but that are often quite sufficient to assist planned giving professionals, such as CPAs, financial planners, attorneys and others in planning with their clients. The discussion of the latter type of software is addressed in this Appendix based on this distinction.

WHAT TO LOOK FOR— SELECTION CRITERIA

Choosing software suitable to a specific practice is often a difficult process. Over the years, it has become somewhat easier as tax and financial professionals have become more technologically proficient and software has become easier to use. The following issues will help focus thinking prior to making a software purchase.

Software that works the way the charitable planner does. Sophisticated software frequently forces the user to adapt to its operational viewpoint. In many situations, the charitable planner simply needs a factor to help the client or donor generally understand the magnitude of the benefit to the donor by adopting a particular planning technique. In other situations, the planner needs to present a polished and full-blown presentation to the donor that will help "sell" the donor on the merits of the specific plan. In yet other situations, the planner needs to provide precise and specific information to the donor for income tax reporting purposes.

The planner needs to decide the typical purposes for which the software will be applied. For someone who needs an occasional factor for determining the tax deduction for a charitable remainder trust, the purchase of a comprehensive reporting, presentation and administration system would be a misapplication of resources. The alternative is to design and program software that will meet specific needs, or to pay a professional programmer to do that. This will likely be a more expensive alternative than finding software that is "close enough" to the way the professional works.

Software that is relatively efficient. Most computer users want results fast. Depending on particular purposes and circumstances, a planner may need only the charitable deduction, and not a full-blown illustration. For example, some programs require the entry of the client's/donor's name and the value of the estate (if not the value of specific assets) before it will calculate the charitable deduction factors for a particular planning approach. That can be very frustrating. At the same time, a comprehensive administration system will need the donor's name, address, age, social security number and other vital statistics in order for it to fully perform its functions. So long as the program does not request needless information, it will meet most users' requirements for appropriate efficiency.

Software with a proven reputation. In most professions, there tends to be a reasonably free interchange of substantive and procedural information. That is the focus of professional continuing education programs. This type of information is frequently exchanged on an informal basis, over lunch, at professional meetings, or in casual conversation. Most satisfied users of computer programs are eager to share their experiences and overall satisfaction with a particular software program.

Likewise, if the software has not worked, most users will happily provide the negatives of their experience with a particular program. Prior to purchasing a computer program to assist you in charitable planning, be sure to talk to another user, more than one if possible. Frequently, the vendor can provide you names of other users, but be cautious because the vendor will not likely give out the name of an extremely dissatisfied user.

A vendor that can support the software over a long period of time. The financial commitment involved in implementing any computer program is significant. The initial cost to purchase adequate licenses may be small in comparison to related hardware costs and the time spent in learning the program or, with more sophisticated software, the cost of being trained in the use of the software. In most cases, there will be periodic maintenance fees and annual (or more frequent) upgrade costs. When selecting software, one need to look for a vendor that has a strong user base to sustain continued support – particularly because tax law, actuarial information, and other essential information change constantly.

TYPES OF SOFTWARE

There are several types of software that can be helpful to the charitable planning professional. The following list is arranged from least comprehensive (and typically least expensive to purchase, and least difficult to learn) to most comprehensive. For the reader's convenience, the vendor addresses, phone numbers and other contact information are provided at the end of this chapter.

Quick calculations. The following programs provide "quick and dirty" computations that show the basic tax consequences of many, if not most, charitable planning techniques. A visit to the vendor's web page to confirm exactly what the program will – or will not – do is suggested.

Data entry time for each of the following software programs is minimal. The results can be used to es-timate the potential tax consequences of a proposed charitable planning technique. Each of these programs would be an appropriate choice for advisors who do not routinely make detailed proposals to potential donors, and for many would be the only charitable planning software needed.

- *NumberCruncher*: provides fast and accurate essential numbers useful in evaluating various charitable planning techniques.

- *PhilanthroCalc on the Web* available from PhilanthroTec, which provides basic charitable planning calculations that can be performed online at its website: http://www.ptec.com.

- *Tiger Tables*: provides fast and accurate essential numbers useful in evaluating various charitable planning techniques.

- *zCalc*: provides fast and accurate essential numbers useful in evaluating various charitable planning techniques via Microsoft Excel spreadsheet "add-in." Also includes more comprehensive illustrations, as shown below.

Comprehensive Calculations and Illustrations

The following programs provide comprehensive calculations for various charitable planning techniques. Some integrate with estate planning illustrations so that the donor is informed of the overall implication to him and his family. They also include illustrations that are useful in discussions with donors. In this sense, they are an aid to the professional in "selling" the donor on a particular type of charitable gift:

- *Crescendo*: a comprehensive charitable planning program intended for use by charitable gift planning professionals (e.g., development and planned giving personnel).

- *PG Calc*: a comprehensive charitable planning program intended for use by charitable gift planning professionals (e.g., development and planned giving personnel); they also offer a new program "GiftStory", which can be used online, interactively by prospective donors or by professionals, to develop a presentation to meet specific donor objectives.

- *Philanthro Calc for Windows*: a program that includes comprehensive calculations, illustrations and explanatory reports.

- *zCalc*: provides illustrations through a series of tools that are integrated with Microsoft Excel spreadsheet "add-in." Also provides the factors for doing quick calculations, as shown above.

- *CharitableFinancialPlanner*: see below.

Administrative Software

The programs listed below include most of the features indicated above, and they also offer marketing and donor relations management:

- *Blackbaud Raiser's Edge*: manages the donor database and integrates the reporting of various types of information to donors.

- *PG Wrap (GiftWrap)*: administrative software that generates annual reports to donors, including tax reporting information.

These programs are intended for the professional fund raiser, especially those in the large, institutional setting.

WHERE CAN I FIND OUT MORE ABOUT IT?

The following is an alphabetical listing of the names and addresses of the software vendors whose software is discussed above:

The Raiser's Edge
Blackbaud, Inc.
2000 Daniel Island Drive
Charleston, SC 29492-7541
800-443-9441, Fax 843-216-6111
www.blackbaud.com

Charitable Financial Planner
Brentmark Software
3505 Lake Lynda Drive, Suite 212
Orlando, FL 32817-8327
800-879-6665, 407-306-6160
www.brentmark.com

Crescendo Interactive
Crescendo Interactive (Comdel, Inc.)
110 Camino Ruiz
Camarillo, CA 93012
800-858-9154, Fax 805-388-2483
www.crescendosoft.com

Tiger Tables
Larry Katzenstein, Esq.
Thompson Coburn LLP
Tiger Tables Software
4529 Pershing Place
St. Louis, MO 63108
www.tigertables.com

Charitable Financial Planner
NumberCruncher
Steve Leimberg
144 West Eagle Road
Havertown, PA 19083
610-924-0515
www.leimberg.com

PGCalc
GiftWrap
PG Calc, Inc.
129 Mount Auburn St.
Cambridge, MA 02138
617-497-4970
www.pgcalc.com

PhilanthroCalc
PhilanthroTec., Inc.
10820-E Independence Pointe Parkway
Matthews, NC 28105
800-332-7832, Fax 704-845-5528
www.ptec.com

ViewPlan
CCH Incorporated
4025 West Peterson Ave.,
Chicago, IL 60646-6085
888-879-5515, Fax 800-221-4240
www.cch.com

Intuitive Estate Planner
Thomson West
610 Upperman Drive
Eagan, MN 55123
800-344-5008
www.west.thomson.com

zCalc
Fast Tax
2395 Middway Road
Bldg. 1
Carrolton, TX 7506
888-706-1041, Ext 18778
www.fasttax.thomson.com

QUESTIONS AND ANSWERS

Question – What hardware is needed to use charitable planning software?

Answer – A computer is needed on which the specific software can be installed. Likely, a printer will also be needed to prepare the reports generated by the program.

Question – Is it possible to do computer calculations via the Internet?

Answer – Yes. Many of the web sites listed in this appendix (and in Appendix L) provide limited calculation services that can be helpful for occasional use. The results will be less useful than the printed reports from software that a user could run on the user's own computer. Nevertheless, these sites are helpful for "quick and dirty" computations. The printed reports will typically bear the logo of the vendor or charity making the calculations available, so they may be less useful when making a presentation to a specific client.

TAX TABLES

Income Tax

	Taxable Years Beginning in 2007	Taxable Years Beginning in 2008
STANDARD DEDUCTION:		
Married, filing jointly	$7,850	$10,900
Married, filing separately	5,350	5,450
Head of Household	7,850	8,000
Single	5,350	5,450
PERSONAL EXEMPTION*:	$3,400	$3,500

*Subject to phase out at higher levels of taxable income.

TAXABLE YEARS BEGINNING IN 2008

SCHEDULE X
SINGLE INDIVIDUALS

Taxable Income			Tax on Lower Amount	Tax Rate on Excess
$ -0-	to	$ 8,025	$ -0-	10.0%
8,025	to	32,550	803	15.0%
32,550	to	78,850	4,481	25.0%
78,850	to	164,550	16,056	28.0%
164,550	to	357,700	40,052	33.0%
357,700	to	......	103,792	35.0%

SCHEDULE Y-1 – JOINT RETURNS
AND SURVIVNG SPOUSES

Taxable Income			Tax on Lower Amount	Tax Rate on Excess
$ -0-	to	$ 16,050	$ -0-	10.0%
16,050	to	65,100	1,605	15.0%
65,100	to	131,450	8,963	25.0%
131,450	to	200,300	25,550	28.0%
200,300	to	357,700	44,828	33.0%
357,700	to	......	96,770	35.0%

SCHEDULE Y-2
MARRIED FILING SEPARATELY

Taxable Income			Tax on Lower Amount	Tax Rate on Excess
$ -0-	to	$ 8,025	$ -0-	10.0%
8,025	to	32,550	803	15.0%
32,550	to	65,725	4,481	25.0%
65,725	to	100,150	12,775	28.0%
100,150	to	178,850	22,414	33.0%
178,850	to	......	48,385	35.0%

SCHEDULE Z
HEAD OF HOUSEHOLD

Taxable Income			Tax on Lower Amount	Tax Rate on Excess
$ -0-	to	$ 11,450	$ -0-	10.0%
11,450	to	43,650	1,145	15.0%
43,650	to	112,650	5,975	25.0%
112,650	to	182,400	23,225	28.0%
182,400	to	357,700	42,755	33.0%
357,700	to	......	100,604	35.0%

ESTATES AND TRUSTS

Taxable Income			Tax on Lower Amount	Tax Rate on Excess
$ -0-	to	$ 2,200	$ -0-	15.0%
2,200	to	5,150	330	25.0%
5,150	to	7,850	1,067	28.0%
7,850	to	10,700	1,823	33.0%
10,700	to	......	2,764	35.0%

TAXABLE YEARS BEGINNING IN 2007

SCHEDULE X – SINGLE INDIVIDUALS

Taxable Income			Tax on Lower Amount	Tax Rate on Excess
$ -0-	to	$ 7,825	$ -0-	10.0%
7,825	to	31,850	783	15.0%
31,850	to	77,100	4,386	25.0%
77,100	to	160,850	15,699	28.0%
160,850	to	349,700	39,149	33.0%
349,700	to	......	101,469	35.0%

SCHEDULE Y-1 – JOINT RETURNS AND SURVIVNG SPOUSES

Taxable Income			Tax on Lower Amount	Tax Rate on Excess
$ -0-	to	$16,650	$ -0-	10.0%
16,650	to	63,700	1,565	15.0%
63,700	to	128,500	8,773	25.0%
128,500	to	195,850	24,973	28.0%
195,850	to	349,700	43,831	33.0%
349,700	to	......	94,601	35.0%

SCHEDULE Y-2 – MARRIED FILING SEPARATELY

Taxable Income			Tax on Lower Amount	Tax Rate on Excess
$ -0-	to	$7,825	$ -0-	10.0%
7,825	to	31,850	783	15.0%
31,850	to	64,250	4,386	25.0%
64,250	to	97,925	12,486	28.0%
97,925	to	174,850	21,915	33.0%
174,850	to	......	47,301	35.0%

SCHEDULE Z – HEAD OF HOUSEHOLD

Taxable Income			Tax on Lower Amount	Tax Rate on Excess
$ -0-	to	$11,200	$ -0-	10.0%
11,200	to	42,650	1,120	15.0%
42,650	to	110,100	5,838	25.0%
110,100	to	178,350	22,700	28.0%
178,350	to	349,700	41,810	33.0%
349,700	to	......	98,356	35.0%

TAX RATE SCHEDULE FOR ESTATES AND TRUSTS

Taxable Income			Tax on Lower Amount	Tax Rate on Excess
$ -0-	to	$2,150	$ -0-	15.0%
2,150	to	5,000	323	25.0%
5,000	to	7,650	1,035	28.0%
7,650	to	10,450	1,777	33.0%
10,450	to	......	2,701	35.0%

TAX RATE SCHEDULE FOR CORPORATIONS†

Taxable Income			Tax on Lower Amount	Tax Rate on Excess
$ -0-	to	$ 50,000	$ -0-	15%
50,000	to	75,000	7,500	25%
75,000	to	100,000	13,750	34%
100,000	to	335,000	22,250	39%*
335,000	to	10,000,000	113,900	34%
10,000,000	to	15,000,000	3,400,000	35%
15,000,000	to	18,333,333	5,150,000	38%**
18,333,333	to	......	6,416,667	35%

REDUCTION IN INCOME TAX RATES

2006-2010	25.0%	28.0%	33.0%	35.0%
2011	28.0%	31.0%	36.0%	39.6%

† Personal Service Corporations are taxed at a flat rate of 35%.

* A 5% surtax is imposed on income above $100,000 until the benefit of the 15 and 25% tax rates has been canceled. Thus, taxable income from $100,000 to $335,000 is taxed at the rate of 39%.

** Corporations with taxable income over $15,000,000 are subject to an additional tax of the lesser of 3% of the excess over $15,000,000 or $100,000. Thus, taxable income exceeding $18,333,333 is taxed at 35%. See Ann. 93-133, 1993-32 IRB 12.

GIFT AND ESTATE TAX

2007 – 2009 GIFT AND ESTATE TAX TABLE

Taxable Gift/Estate		Tax on Col. 1	Rate on Excess
From	To		
$0	$10,000	$0	18%
10,000	20,000	1,800	20%
20,000	40,000	3,800	22%
40,000	60,000	8,200	24%
60,000	80,000	13,000	26%
80,000	100,000	18,200	28%
100,000	150,000	23,800	30%
150,000	250,000	38,800	32%
250,000	500,000	70,800	34%
500,000	750,000	155,800	37%
750,000	1,000,000	248,300	39%
1,000,000	1,250,000	345,800	41%
1,250,000	1,500,000	448,300	43%
1,500,000	....	555,800	45%

2010 GIFT TAX ONLY TABLE

Taxable Gift		Tax on Col. 1	Rate on Excess
From	To		
$0	$10,000	$0	18%
10,000	20,000	1,800	20%
20,000	40,000	3,800	22%
40,000	60,000	8,200	24%
60,000	80,000	13,000	26%
80,000	100,000	18,200	28%
100,000	150,000	23,800	30%
150,000	250,000	38,800	32%
250,000	500,000	70,800	34%
500,000	....	155,800	35%

2011- GIFT AND ESTATE TAX TABLE

Taxable Gift/Estate From	To	Tax on Col. 1	Rate on Excess
$ 0	$ 10,000	$ 0	18%
10,000	20,000	1,800	20%
20,000	40,000	3,800	22%
40,000	60,000	8,200	24%
60,000	80,000	13,000	26%
80,000	100,000	18,200	28%
100,000	150,000	23,800	30%
150,000	250,000	38,800	32%
250,000	500,000	70,800	34%
500,000	750,000	155,800	37%
750,000	1,000,000	248,300	39%
1,000,000	1,250,000	345,800	41%
1,250,000	1,500,000	448,300	43%
1,500,000	2,000,000	555,800	45%
2,000,000	2,500,000	780,800	49%
2,500,000	3,000,000	1,025,800	53%
3,000,000	10,000,000	1,290,800	55%
10,000,000	17,184,000	5,140,800	60%
17,184,000	....	9,451,200	55%

IRC Sec. 2001(c), as amended by EGTRRA 2001.

2006 GIFT AND ESTATE TAX TABLE

Taxable Gift/Estate From	To	Tax on Col. 1	Rate on Excess
$ 0	$ 10,000	$ 0	18%
10,000	20,000	1,800	20%
20,000	40,000	3,800	22%
40,000	60,000	8,200	24%
60,000	80,000	13,000	26%
80,000	100,000	18,200	28%
100,000	150,000	23,800	30%
150,000	250,000	38,800	32%
250,000	500,000	70,800	34%
500,000	750,000	155,800	37%
750,000	1,000,000	248,300	39%
1,000,000	1,250,000	345,800	41%
1,250,000	1,500,000	448,300	43%
1,500,000	2,000,000	555,800	45%
2,000,000	....	780,800	46%

UNIFIED CREDIT

GIFT TAX UNIFIED CREDIT

Year	Exemption Equivalent	Unified Credit
2002-2009	$1,000,000	$345,800
2010	$1,000,000	$330,800
2011	$1,000,000	$345,800

ESTATE TAX UNIFIED CREDIT

Year	Exemption Equivalent	Unified Credit
2006-2008	$2,000,000	$780,800
2009	$3,500,000	$1,455,800
2010	NA	NA
2011	$1,000,000	$345,800

MAXIMUM CREDIT TABLE FOR STATE DEATH TAXES

The amount of any state death taxes paid may be subtracted from the federal estate tax as determined under the preceding tables, provided, however, that the maximum to be subtracted may not exceed the maximum determined under the following table:

MAXIMUM STATE DEATH TAX CREDIT*			
Taxable Estate		Credit on	Rate on
From	To	Column 1	Excess
$0	$100,000	$0	0%
$100,000	$150,000	$0	0.8%
$150,000	$200,000	$400	1.6%
$200,000	$300,000	$1,200	2.4%
$300,000	$500,000	$3,600	3.2%
$500,000	$700,000	$10,000	4.0%
$700,000	$900,000	$18,000	4.8%
$900,000	$1,100,000	$27,600	5.6%
$1,100,000	$1,600,000	$38,800	6.4%
$1,600,000	$2,100,000	$70,800	7.2%
$2,100,000	$2,600,000	$106,800	8.0%
$2,600,000	$3,100,000	$146,800	8.8%
$3,100,000	$3,600,000	$190,800	9.6%
$3,600,000	$4,100,000	$238,800	10.4%
$4,100,000	$5,100,000	$290,800	11.2%
$5,100,000	$6,100,000	$402,800	12.0%
$6,100,000	$7,100,000	$522,800	12.8%
$7,100,000	$8,100,000	$650,800	13.6%
$8,100,000	$9,100,000	$786,800	14.4%
$9,100,000	$10,100,000	$930,800	15.2%
$10,100,000	....	$1,082,800	16.0%

* This table resembles the table contained in IRC Section 2011(b), but it is not the same The table in the Code is based on the *adjusted taxable estate*, defined as the taxable estate reduced by $60,000 This table is a modification of that table and can be used directly from the *taxable estate*

The maximum state death credit calculated from the table is reduced by 25% for decedents dying in 2002, 50% for decedents dying in 2003, and 75% for decedents dying in 2004. Multiply the amount calculated above by 75% in 2002, 50% in 2003, and 25% in 2004. The state death tax credit is replaced by a deduction for state death taxes for 2005 to 2009. The federal estate tax is repealed for one year in 2010. The federal estate tax returns, along with the full state death tax credit, in 2011.

VALUATION ISSUES RELATING TO SPECIFIC ASSETS

GENERAL VALUATION RULES

Determining the value of a charitable contribution can be simple or complex, depending on the type of property being donated. Although valuing contributions of certain types of property (such as cash or marketable securities) is relatively easy, valuing others (such as artwork, real estate, or closely held stock) can be much more difficult.

In general, it is up to the donor to be able to prove the value of the property for deduction purposes. This will typically require substantiation of the value of the gift through a qualified independent written appraisal. It is best to have that valuation done and documented contemporaneously with the gift itself.

Fair Market Value

The value of the property for charitable deduction purposes is the fair market value of the property given.[1] Fair market value is defined as "the price at which the property would change hands between a willing buyer and a willing seller, neither being under any compulsion to buy or sell and both having reasonable knowledge of relevant facts."[2]

Once fair market value has been determined for income tax purposes, there are deduction limitations, as well as several "reduction rules," that come into play, depending on the type of property that is being contributed. These may reduce the fair market value of the property for deduction purposes, or limit the amount of deduction that can be taken in any one year.

Deduction Limitations

The limitations on charitable deductions are measured by a percentage of the taxpayer's "contribution base," which, with some relatively minor exceptions, is essentially the same as the taxpayer's adjusted gross income (AGI). For purposes of this appendix and throughout most of this book, the contribution base will be referred to as AGI.

The maximum charitable deduction allowed in one year is either 50% of AGI for gifts to public charities or 30% of AGI for gifts to private charities.[3] Because of this, charities are commonly referred to as either 50% or 30% organizations. This 50% - 30% limitation is a general limitation; deduction limits may be reduced further depending on the type of property donated.

In general, the 50% - 30% rule would apply to gifts of cash, ordinary income property, or long-term gain property where the deduction is limited to cost basis. As will be discussed below, if the subject of a charitable gift is appreciated property, the donor's current deduction is further limited. Gifts of appreciated property to a 50% (i.e., public) charity result in a current deduction limited to 30% of the donor's AGI, while gifts to a 30% (private) organization are deductible only up to 20%. Gifts that are made "for the use of" charity rather than to charity are also subject to the 30% limitations.

Deductions for contributions in excess of the limits discussed above are not lost. The excess, that part of the contribution over the currently deductible limit, can be carried over for an additional five years and applied in those years against otherwise taxable income.[4] However, if the donor dies or, for any other reason, is unable to deduct the remaining donation during the carryover period, the unused deduction is wasted. For example, if Mr. Donor has an AGI of $100,000 and donates a $500,000 piece of property to charity, he can deduct $50,000 in year 1 (based on a 50% of AGI deduction limit) and carryover the remaining $450,000. Assuming he can continue to deduct $50,000 per year for the five carryover years, his total deduction used is $300,000. The remaining deduction of $200,000 will expire unused after the sixth year. Obviously, this example illustrates the importance of careful planning to guarantee that the tax benefits of charitable gifts are not squandered.

Reduction Rule: Ordinary Income Property

One of the principal reduction rules is for "ordinary income property." This is defined as property which would not have created long-term gain had the property been sold by the donor for its fair market value rather than given to charity.[5]

Ordinary income property includes:

1. short term capital gain property (capital assets held one year or less)

2. inventory

3. depreciation recapture property

4. life insurance and annuities

5. accounts and notes receivable

In the case of ordinary income property, the deduction must be reduced by the value of the ordinary income the donor would have realized upon the sale of the asset. In other words, the deduction will be limited to the lesser of (a) adjusted cost basis or (b) market value at the time of the gift. The bottom line is, in many – but not all – cases, the donor's deduction for contributions of ordinary income property will be the donor's basis.

Example: Mr. Donor owns a life insurance policy that has a fair market value of $5,000. He has paid $2,000 in premiums (his cost basis). If Mr. Donor were to surrender or sell the policy, he would be taxed on the $3,000 gain as ordinary income. Therefore, for the purpose of valuing his donation of the policy to charity, he can deduct only his cost basis of $2,000. If instead, the cash value of Mr. Donor's policy is only $1,000, his deduction would

be limited to only the $1,000 fair market value of the policy rather than the $2,000 cost basis.

Reduction Rule: Long-Term Capital Gain Property

Contributions of long-term capital gain property made directly to charity are entitled to an unusual double tax benefit. First, in most instances, the donor is allowed a deduction based on the full fair market value of the gift. Second, the donor does not have to pay tax on the appreciation in the property given to charity, regardless of how much gain is built-in.[6] There is, however, a reduction in the deduction limitations for long-term capital gain property.

As noted above, the general limitation on charitable deductions is 50% of AGI for gifts to public charities, or 30% of AGI for gifts to private charities. When making a gift of appreciated property, the deduction limitations are reduced to 30% of AGI for public charities and 20% for private charities.[7]

Reduction Rule: Tangible Personal Property

Gifts of tangible personal property, such as works of art, musical instruments, or other collections made to public charities, are normally deducted at full fair market value. An important exception, however, is when a gift of tangible personal property is made to charity where the charity's use of the property is unrelated to its charitable purpose. In this situation, the deduction is reduced by the amount of built in capital gain in the value of the property.[8] For example, if a donor gives a painting to a public charitable organization to be displayed in their art museum, the use is related to the charitable function and the value of the property would be full fair market value. However, if the painting is given to a cancer research organization that intends to sell the painting to fund future research, the use is not related to the organization's charitable purpose. Consequently, the value of the property for income tax deduction purposes would be reduced to the donor's cost basis in the painting. So it is important to distinguish between and plan based on whether the client's property is "use related" or "use unrelated" to the tax-exempt functions of the charity. Obviously, it often is advantageous to obtain a letter from the recipient charity assuring the donor that use related property will in fact be use related (e.g., that art donated to an art museum will be displayed rather than sold to raise money).

Tangible personal property is subject to the same deduction limitations as other property. If the property is capital gain property, the limitations on capital gain property apply. Ordinary income property would be limited to the lesser of fair market value or cost basis.

Reduction Rule: Gifts of Appreciated Property to a Private Charity

Gifts of appreciated property (long-term capital gain property) are normally deducted at full fair market value, subject to the deduction limitations discussed above. However, if a gift of appreciated property is made to a private foundation, the value of the property for determining the income tax deduction is reduced by the long-term capital gain in the property. Consequently, the value for deduction purposes will be limited to the donor's cost basis.[9] For example, if a donor contributes real estate that has a fair market value of $500,000 and a cost basis of $250,000, the value of property for income tax deduction purposes is $250,000 (the donor's cost basis).

An exception to this limitation is where "qualified appreciated stock" is contributed to a private charity. Qualified appreciated stock is stock (or a mutual fund) that is publicly traded, provided the donor doesn't contribute (in the aggregate) more than 10% of the outstanding shares.[10] If the gift to a private charity is qualified appreciated stock, than the deduction value will based on fair market value rather than cost basis.

Summary

The following table details the income tax deduction limitations and reduction rules as applied to various types of charitable gifts.

Gift	% Public	Valuation	% Private	Valuation
Cash	50	FMV	30	FMV
Appreciated Property	30	FMV	20	Basis*
Ordinary Income Property	50	Basis	30	Basis
"For Use Of" Property	30	FMV	30	FMV
Tangible Personal Property (Related Use)	50	FMV	30	FMV
Tangible Personal Property (Unrelated Use)	50	Basis	30	Basis

* FMV for qualified appreciated stock

Appraisal Requirements

Generally, gifts of property that exceed $5,000 must have a qualified appraisal from a qualified appraiser.[11] In addition, a fully completed appraisal summary must be sent with the tax return and the donor must maintain certain records pertaining to the appraisal of the property.

Gifts of publicly traded securities or closely held stock fall within specific exceptions to this general rule.

- Gifts of publicly traded securities (securities for which market quotations are readily available on an established securities market) do not require a qualified appraisal.

- Gifts of closely held stock do not require a full appraisal unless the value of the stock exceeds $10,000.

A qualified appraisal must include the following information:

1. A description of the property in sufficient detail to determine that the property appraised is in fact the property transferred to charity.

2. The date of the contribution.

3. The valuation date.

4. Information about the qualified appraiser, including qualifications and relationship to the donor.

5. The appraised fair market value of the property.

6. The methodologies used in determining the valuation.

VALUATION ISSUES FOR SPECIFIC ASSETS

Clothing and Household Items

For gifts made after August 17, 2006, in order to deduct contributions of clothing and household items, the items must be in good used condition or better. Household items include furniture, electronics, appliances, and other similar items.[12] Deductions will not be allowed for contributions of clothing or other items that have a minimal monetary

value, e.g., used socks or undergarments. A deduction may be allowed for clothing and household items, regardless of condition, for single items over $500 that include a qualified appraisal of the item with the tax return.

Used Cars, Boats, and Airplanes

1. The value of used vehicles (cars, boats, and airplanes) that exceed $500 and that are contributed to a charity must be contemporaneous substantiated with a written acknowledgement from the charitable organization.[13] An acknowledgement is considered contemporaneous if made within 30 days of the contribution or, if the property is sold by the charity without any significant intervening use or material improvement, within 30 days of the sale of the vehicle. The acknowledgement must state the donor's tax ID and the vehicle ID, and that the donor did not receive any goods or services in connection with the donation of the vehicle.

   If the vehicle is sold by the charity without any significant intervening use or material improvement, the acknowledgement must certify that the vehicle was sold in an arm's length transaction between unrelated persons and state the amount of the gross proceeds from the sale. If the vehicle is not to be sold by the charity without any significant intervening use or material improvement, the charity must certify the intended use or material improvement and the intended duration of such use.

2. If the vehicle is to be sold by the charity without any significant intervening use or material improvement, the charitable deduction cannot exceed the gross proceeds received from the sale. In most cases, the value of the used vehicle is limited to the gross proceeds received by the charity upon the sale of the vehicle. However, if the charity uses the vehicle rather than selling or disposing of it, normal methods for determining fair market value (for example "blue book" values) may be used to the fair market value of the vehicle.

Real Estate

1. Gifts of appreciated real estate are generally valued at fair market value if transferred to a public charity, or cost basis if transferred to a private charity.

2. A qualified appraisal will be required if the value of the property exceeds $5,000.

3. Real estate is typically valued at its "highest and best" use, regardless of how the real estate is currently being used.

4. The value of the property for deduction purposes must be reduced by any debt. *Caution:* Transfers of mortgaged real estate may result in application of the bargain sale rules, which could trigger partial gain recognition.[14]

5. There are three general approaches to valuing real estate for charitable deduction purposes: comparable sales, capitalization of income, and new replacement cost. An appraisal may require the combined use of one or more of these approaches.

6. Valuation discounts may be applied if the use of the property is restricted, or if the gift is a fractional or undivided interest in the real estate. This will reduce the donor's charitable deduction.

Publicly Traded Stocks, Bonds, and Mutual Funds

1. Charitable gifts of publicly traded securities will generally be subject to the deduction limitations for gifts of appreciated property.

2. A qualified appraisal is not required for contributions of publicly traded securities.

3. The value of publicly traded stocks and bonds is determined by using the average between the highest and lowest quoted selling prices on the valuation date.[15] For example, if the highest selling price of a stock was $10 and the lowest $6, the valuation price would be $8 (($10 + $6) / 2).

4. If no sales occurred on the valuation date, a weighted average based on the closest trading dates before and after the valuation date is used.

5. The fair market value of a share of a mutual fund is the public redemption price in effect at the time of the gift.[16]

Closely Held Stock

1. Contributions of closely held stock will generally be subject to the deduction limitations for gifts of appreciated property.

2. Contributions of closely held stock that exceed $10,000 require a qualified appraisal.

3. Relevant factors to consider when valuing closely held stock include: the earning power of the company, the economic outlook of the industry, the value of securities issued by similar businesses, and the goodwill of the business.

4. Valuation discounts for lack of marketability and control may be applied when determining the fair market value of the donated property. This will reduce the donor's charitable deduction.

5. Transfers of S corporation stock to a charitable remainder trust will cause loss of S corporation status. Consequently, the transfer of S corporation stock to a CRT is not advisable.

Life Insurance

1. Charitable gifts of life insurance will generally be subject to the deduction limitations for gifts of ordinary income property.

2. For gifts of life insurance that exceed $5,000 in value, a qualified appraisal will be required. Obtaining a qualified appraisal for a life insurance policy can be difficult since neither the issuing insurance company nor the donor's agent would be allowed to perform the appraisal. It is likely that the IRS would accept an appraisal by another insurance agent, CLU, ChFC, or insurance analyst.

3. The value of a life insurance policy for charitable deduction purposes is its replacement cost. The manner in which replacement cost is determined depends on the nature of the policy. If the policy is a single premium or paid up policy, then the value of the policy is the amount the company would charge for a single premium contract of the same amount on the life of the insured as of the date of the gift.[17]

   If the policy requires additional premiums, the value is the interpolated terminal reserve, increased by unused premiums and accumulated dividends, less outstanding loans against the policy.[18]

   If the policy is newly issued, the value of the policy is the premium paid to bring the policy into force.[19]

4. In no event should a donor transfer a life insurance policy subject to a loan. Such a transfer may result in application of the bargain sale rules. This could trigger immediate partial taxation upon the transfer of the policy. Note also, that donors contributing life insurance policies with any loan – no matter how small – will be barred from ever deducting either the value of the policy itself or subsequent premiums.

Tangible Personal Property

1. The fair market value of contributions of tangible personal property that is unrelated to the purpose or function of the charity must be reduced by the long-term capital gain in the asset. Consequently, cost basis will be the value of the property for determining the charitable deduction. If the property is for a related use, then the fair market value of the property is used to determine the charitable deduction.

   For gifts of tangible personal property over $5,000 where fair market value is deducted, if the charity sells or disposes of the property within 3 years of the contribution, there are additional requirements in order to avoid a reduction in the value of the original contribution. The charity must certify that the property was intended to be used for a related purpose, how it was used, and that the continued use of the property by the charity is no longer feasible. Without this certification, the donor's deduction is limited to: (a) cost basis if the property is disposed of in the year of contribution, or (b) the donor must include back in his/her income the difference between the claimed deduction and cost basis if the property is disposed of after the year of contribution but before 3 years of the date of contribution.[20]

2. The value of certain artwork may be determined by the IRS Art Advisory Panel. This is a member group of art dealers, museum directors, and curators who assist the IRS in valuing artwork worth more than $20,000. The panel is used when the IRS and the donor disagree as to the value of the artwork.

3. For artwork valued at $50,000 or more, the donor can request a *Statement of Value* from the IRS. The cost for this statement is $2,500.

ENDNOTES

1. Treas. Reg. §1.170A-1(c)(1).
2. Treas. Reg. §1.170A-1(c)(2).
3. IRC Secs. 170(b)(1)(A), 170(b)(1)(B).
4. IRC Secs. 170(b)(1)(B), 170(b)(1)(C)(ii), 170(b)(1)(D)(ii), 170(d).
5. Treas. Reg. §1.170A-4(b)(1).
6. Important exceptions to this rule are charitable bargain sales, or where there is a "pre-arranged" sale by the donor.
7. IRC Secs. 170(b)(1)(C), 170(b)(1)(D).
8. IRC Sec. 170(e)(1)(B)(i).
9. IRC Sec. 170(e)(1)(B)(ii).
10. IRC Sec. 170(e)(5).
11. Treas. Reg. §1.170A-13(c)(2).
12. IRC Sec. 170(f)(16).
13. IRC Sec. 170(f)(12)(A).
14. Treas. Reg. §1.1011-2(a).
15. Treas. Reg. §25.2512-2(b).
16. Treas. Reg. §25.2512-6(b).
17. *U.S. v. Ryerson*, 312 U.S. 260 (1941); Treas. Reg. §25.2512-6(a), Ex. (3).
18. Treas. Reg. §25.2512-6(a); Rev. Rul. 59-195, 1959-1 CB 18.
19. *Powers v. Comm.*, 312 U.S. 259 (1941).
20. IRC Sec. 170(e)(7).

VALUATION TABLES

Valuation tables using up-to-date interest rates and mortality factors must be used in valuing interests in a charitable trust (or a charitable gift annuity) for income, gift, estate, and generation-skipping tax purposes. The value of such interests is generally determined under the following tables using an interest rate (rounded to the nearest 2/10ths of 1 percent) equal to 120% of the federal midterm rate in effect for the month in which the valuation date occurs. For additional valuation tables, see IRS Publications 1457, 1458, and 1459.

The Section 7520 valuation table interest rate for each month is published in a revenue ruling and is available at taxfactsonline.com as the rate becomes available. When a charitable deduction is involved, the taxpayer can use the interest rate for either of the two preceding months or the current month. However, if a transfer of more than one interest in the same property is made with respect to which the taxpayer could use the same interest rate, the taxpayer must be consistent and use such interest rate with respect to each such interest.

For purposes of these tables, round the age of any person whose life is used to measure an interest to the age of such person on his birthday nearest the valuation date.

CLATs, CRATs

In general, the value of the annuity interest in a charitable lead annuity trust (CLAT, see Chapter 14) or charitable remainder annuity trust (CRAT, see Chapter 15) equals the present value of the annuity interest. The value of the remainder interest in a CLAT or CRAT is equal to the excess of the value of the property transferred to the CLAT or CRAT over the value of the annuity interest. [Note: The examples below are for CRATs. If the transfers were to a CLAT rather than to a CRAT, the values received by the charitable and noncharitable beneficiaries would be switched.]

The value of an *annuity payable annually at the end of the year* is equal to the annual payment multiplied by the appropriate annuity factor. For an annuity payable for a term certain, use a Term Certain Annuity Factor. For an annuity payable for a person's life, use a Single Life Annuity Factor.

If the *annuity is payable semiannually, quarterly, monthly, or weekly at the end of such period*, an additional step is required. First, calculate the value of the annuity payable annually at the end of the year (see above). (Use the aggregate payments for the year as the annual payment for this purpose.) Second, multiply the value of the annuity payable annually at the end of the year by the appropriate factor from the Annuity Adjustment Factors Table A. The result is the value of an annuity payable less than annually at the end of each period.

If an *annuity is payable at the beginning of each period during a term certain*, the following steps are required. First, calculate the value of an annuity payable at the end of each year (see above). (Use the aggregate payments for the year as the annual payment for this purpose.) Second, multiply the value of the annuity payable annually at the end of the year by the appropriate factor from the Annuity Adjustment Factors Table B. The result is the value of an annuity payable at the beginning of each period during a term certain.

If an *annuity is payable at the beginning of each period during the life of one individual*, an additional step is required. First, calculate the value of an annuity payable at the end of each year or lesser period (see above). Second, to this value add the amount of one additional payment.

Example (single life): Ann transfers property worth $100,000 to a CRAT. Ann's daughter, Tina (age 45), receives a right to payments of $5,000 for life payable annually at the end of each year.

Charity receives the remainder. Assume a Section 7520 interest rate of 6.0% is used.

The value of the annuity received by Tina equals $67,618 [$5,000 x 13.5237 (Single Life Annuity Factor for 6.0% and age 45)]. The value of the charitable contribution equals $32,382 [$100,000 - $67,618].

Example: Assume, instead, that Tina receives a right to payments of $2,500 for life payable semiannually at the end of each period ($5,000 aggregate payment for the year). The value of the annuity received by Tina equals $68,619 [$67,618 x 1.0148 (Annuity Adjustment Factor Table A for semiannually and 6.0%)]. The value of the charitable contribution equals $31,381 [$100,000 - $68,619].

Example: Assume that Tina receives the right to payments at the beginning of each period. The value of an annual annuity received by Tina equals $72,618 [$67,618 + $5,000 (one payment)]. The value of the charitable contribution equals $27,382 [$100,000 - $72,618].

The value of a semiannual annuity received by Tina equals $71,119 [$68,619 + $2,500 (one payment)]. The value of the charitable contribution equals $28,881 [$100,000 - $71,119].

Example (term certain): Bob transfers property worth $100,000 to a CRAT. Bob retains the right to payments of $10,000 for 10 years payable annually at the end of each year. Charity receives the remainder. Assume a Section 7520 interest rate of 6.0% is used.

The value of the annuity retained by Bob equals $73,601 [$10,000 x 7.3601 (Term Certain Annuity Factor for 6.0% and 10 years)]. The value of the charitable contribution equals $26,399 [$100,000 - $73,601].

Example: Assume, instead, that Bob retains the right to payments of $5,000 for 10 years payable semiannually at the end of each period ($10,000 aggregate payment for the year). The value of the annuity received by Bob equals $74,690 [$73,601 x 1.0148 (Annuity Adjustment Factor Table A for semiannually and 6.0%)]. The value of the charitable contribution equals $25,310 [$100,000 - $74,690].

Example: Assume that Bob receives the right to payments at the beginning of each period. The value of an annual annuity received by Bob equals $78,017 [$73,601 x 1.0600 (Annuity Adjustment Factor Table B for annually and 6.0%)]. The value of the charitable contribution equals $21,983 [$100,000 - $78,017].

The value of a semiannual annuity received by Bob equals $76,898 [$73,601 x 1.0448 (Annuity Adjustment Factor Table B for semiannually and 6.0%)]. The value of the charitable contribution equals $23,102 [$100,000 - $76,898].

CLUTs, CRUTs

In general, the value of the unitrust remainder interest in a charitable lead unitrust (CLUT, see Chapter 14) or charitable remainder unitrust (CRUT, see Chapter 16) equals the present value of the unitrust remainder interest. The value of the unitrust interest in a CLUT or CRUT is equal to the excess of the value of the property transferred to the CLUT or CRUT over the value of the unitrust remainder interest. [Note: The examples below are for CRUTs. If the transfers were to a CLUT rather than to a CRUT, the values received by the charitable and noncharitable beneficiaries would be switched.]

If the unitrust payments are made annually at the beginning of each year and the annual payout rate is equal to an adjusted payout rate for which factors are given, the present value of the unitrust remainder interest can be calculated simply by multiplying the value of the property transferred to the unitrust by the appropriate unitrust remainder factor. For a unitrust payable for a term certain, use a Term Certain Unitrust Remainder Factor. For a unitrust payable for a person's life, use a Single Life Unitrust Remainder Factor. If the unitrust payments are made other than annually at the beginning of each year or the annual payout rate falls between adjusted payout rates for which factors are given, the calculation of the value of the unitrust remainder interest is more complex.

Example: Cathy transfers property worth $100,000 to a CRUT. Cathy (age 70) retains the right to payments of 10% of the trust corpus (valued annually) for life payable annually at the beginning of each year. Charity receives the remainder. The value of the unitrust remainder interest received by the charity equals $31,362 [$100,000 x .31362 (Single Life Unitrust Remainder Factor for 10.0% and age 70)]. The retained unitrust interest equals $68,638 [$100,000 - $31,362].

Example: Assume, instead, that payments to Cathy will be made at the end of each year. Also, assume a Section 7520 interest rate of 6.0% is used. The value of the unitrust remainder interest payable to charity is calculated as follows.

1. The Unitrust Payout Adjustment Factor for 6.0% and annual payments payable at the end of the year equals .943396.

2. The adjusted payout rate equals 9.434% [10% x .943396].

3. The Single Life Unitrust Remainder Factor for age 70 at a 9.4% adjusted payout rate equals .33197.

4. The Single Life Unitrust Remainder Factor for age 70 at a 9.6% adjusted payout rate equals .32568.

5. The difference between (3) and (4) equals .00629 [.33197 - .32568].

6. $\frac{9.434\% - 9.400\%}{9.600\% - 9.400\%} = \frac{X}{.00629}$

    X = .00107

7. The interpolated unitrust remainder factor equals .33090 [.33197 - .00107].

8. The value of the unitrust remainder equals $33,090 [$100,000 x .33090].

9. The retained unitrust interest equals $66,910 [$100,000 - $33,090].

PIFs

In general, the value of the remainder interest in a pooled income fund (PIF, see Chapter 20) equals the present value of the remainder interest. The value of the income interest in a PIF is equal to the excess of the value of the property transferred to the PIF over the value of the remainder interest.

The monthly Section 7520 valuation table interest rate does not apply to a PIF. Instead, the highest rate of return earned by the fund for any of the three years immediately preceding the taxable year of the fund during which the contribution is made is used. However, the IRS prescribes an annual rate for new funds which have not been in existence for three years.

A remainder factor is obtained by converting an annuity factor (use Single Life Annuity Factors) into a remainder factor. This is done in two steps. First, the annuity factor is converted into an income factor by multiplying the annuity factor by the appropriate rate of return (round to 5 places, e.g., .54322). Second, the income factor is converted into a remainder factor by subtracting the income factor from 1.

The value of the remainder interest in the PIF is then determined by multiplying the value of the property transferred to the PIF by the remainder factor. Interpolation is required when the rate of return is between interest rates for which factors are given.

Example: Dave transferred property worth $100,000 to a PIF. Income is to be paid to Dave (age 60) for life. The highest rate of return earned by the fund for any of the three immediately preceding years was 8.8%.

The value of the remainder interest payable to charity is calculated as follows.

1. The Single Life Annuity Factor for 8.8% and age 60 is equal to 8.6018.

2. The factor in (1) is converted to a remainder factor equal to .24304 [1 - (8.6018 x 8.8%)].

3. The remainder interest is equal to $24,304 [$100,000 x .24304].

4. The retained income interest equals $75,696 [$100,000 - $24,304].

Example: Assume, instead, that the highest rate of return earned by the fund for any of the three immediately preceding years was 8.75%. The value of the remainder interest payable to charity is calculated as follows.

1. The Single Life Annuity Factor for 8.6% and age 60 is equal to 8.7335.

2. The factor in (1) is converted to a remainder factor equal to .24892 [1 - (8.7335 x 8.6%)].

3. The Single Life Annuity Factor for 8.8% and age 60 is equal to 8.6018.

4. The factor in (3) is converted to a remainder factor equal to .24304 [1 - (8.6018 x 8.8%)].

5. The difference between (2) and (4) equals .00588 [.24892 - .24304].

6. $\dfrac{8.750\% - 8.600\%}{8.800\% - 8.600\%} = \dfrac{X}{.00588}$

   X = .00441

7. The interpolated remainder factor equals .24451 [.24892 - .00441].

8. The value of the remainder equals $24,451 [$100,000 x .24451].

9. The retained income interest equals $75,549 [$100,000 - $24,451].

CHARITABLE GIFT ANNUITIES

In general, the value of the annuity interest received in a charitable gift annuity (see Chapter 12) is equal to the present value of the annuity interest (for calculation of the value of such an annuity, see the discussion of single life CRATs above). The value of the charitable contribution with respect to a charitable gift annuity is equal to the excess of the value of the property transferred in exchange for the annuity over the value of the annuity.

ANNUITY ADJUSTMENT FACTORS TABLE A*

FREQUENCY OF PAYMENTS

INTEREST RATE	ANNUALLY	SEMI ANNUALLY	QUARTERLY	MONTHLY	WEEKLY
4.0%	1.0000	1.0099	1.0149	1.0182	1.0195
4.2%	1.0000	1.0104	1.0156	1.0191	1.0205
4.4%	1.0000	1.0109	1.0164	1.0200	1.0214
4.6%	1.0000	1.0114	1.0171	1.0209	1.0224
4.8%	1.0000	1.0119	1.0178	1.0218	1.0234
5.0%	1.0000	1.0123	1.0186	1.0227	1.0243
5.2%	1.0000	1.0128	1.0193	1.0236	1.0253
5.4%	1.0000	1.0133	1.0200	1.0245	1.0262
5.6%	1.0000	1.0138	1.0208	1.0254	1.0272
5.8%	1.0000	1.0143	1.0215	1.0263	1.0282
6.0%	1.0000	1.0148	1.0222	1.0272	1.0291
6.2%	1.0000	1.0153	1.0230	1.0281	1.0301
6.4%	1.0000	1.0158	1.0237	1.0290	1.0311
6.6%	1.0000	1.0162	1.0244	1.0299	1.0320
6.8%	1.0000	1.0167	1.0252	1.0308	1.0330
7.0%	1.0000	1.0172	1.0259	1.0317	1.0339
7.2%	1.0000	1.0177	1.0266	1.0326	1.0349
7.4%	1.0000	1.0182	1.0273	1.0335	1.0358
7.6%	1.0000	1.0187	1.0281	1.0344	1.0368
7.8%	1.0000	1.0191	1.0288	1.0353	1.0378
8.0%	1.0000	1.0196	1.0295	1.0362	1.0387
8.2%	1.0000	1.0201	1.0302	1.0370	1.0397
8.4%	1.0000	1.0206	1.0310	1.0379	1.0406
8.6%	1.0000	1.0211	1.0317	1.0388	1.0416
8.8%	1.0000	1.0215	1.0324	1.0397	1.0425
9.0%	1.0000	1.0220	1.0331	1.0406	1.0435
9.2%	1.0000	1.0225	1.0339	1.0415	1.0444
9.4%	1.0000	1.0230	1.0346	1.0424	1.0454
9.6%	1.0000	1.0235	1.0353	1.0433	1.0463
9.8%	1.0000	1.0239	1.0360	1.0442	1.0473
10.0%	1.0000	1.0244	1.0368	1.0450	1.0482
10.2%	1.0000	1.0249	1.0375	1.0459	1.0492
10.4%	1.0000	1.0254	1.0382	1.0468	1.0501
10.6%	1.0000	1.0258	1.0389	1.0477	1.0511
10.8%	1.0000	1.0263	1.0396	1.0486	1.0520
11.0%	1.0000	1.0268	1.0404	1.0495	1.0530
11.2%	1.0000	1.0273	1.0411	1.0503	1.0539
11.4%	1.0000	1.0277	1.0418	1.0512	1.0549
11.6%	1.0000	1.0282	1.0425	1.0521	1.0558
11.8%	1.0000	1.0287	1.0432	1.0530	1.0568

*For use in calculating the value of an annuity payable at the end of each period or, if the term of the annuity is determined with respect to one or more lives, an annuity payable at the beginning of each period.

ANNUITY ADJUSTMENT FACTORS TABLE B*

FREQUENCY OF PAYMENTS

INTEREST RATE	ANNUALLY	SEMI ANNUALLY	QUARTERLY	MONTHLY	WEEKLY
4.0%	1.0400	1.0299	1.0249	1.0215	1.0203
4.2%	1.0420	1.0314	1.0261	1.0226	1.0213
4.4%	1.0440	1.0329	1.0274	1.0237	1.0223
4.6%	1.0460	1.0344	1.0286	1.0247	1.0233
4.8%	1.0480	1.0359	1.0298	1.0258	1.0243
5.0%	1.0500	1.0373	1.0311	1.0269	1.0253
5.2%	1.0520	1.0388	1.0323	1.0279	1.0263
5.4%	1.0540	1.0403	1.0335	1.0290	1.0273
5.6%	1.0560	1.0418	1.0348	1.0301	1.0283
5.8%	1.0580	1.0433	1.0360	1.0311	1.0293
6.0%	1.0600	1.0448	1.0372	1.0322	1.0303
6.2%	1.0620	1.0463	1.0385	1.0333	1.0313
6.4%	1.0640	1.0478	1.0397	1.0343	1.0323
6.6%	1.0660	1.0492	1.0409	1.0354	1.0333
6.8%	1.0680	1.0507	1.0422	1.0365	1.0343
7.0%	1.0700	1.0522	1.0434	1.0375	1.0353
7.2%	1.0720	1.0537	1.0446	1.0386	1.0363
7.4%	1.0740	1.0552	1.0458	1.0396	1.0373
7.6%	1.0760	1.0567	1.0471	1.0407	1.0383
7.8%	1.0780	1.0581	1.0483	1.0418	1.0393
8.0%	1.0800	1.0596	1.0495	1.0428	1.0403
8.2%	1.0820	1.0611	1.0507	1.0439	1.0413
8.4%	1.0840	1.0626	1.0520	1.0449	1.0422
8.6%	1.0860	1.0641	1.0532	1.0460	1.0432
8.8%	1.0880	1.0655	1.0544	1.0471	1.0442
9.0%	1.0900	1.0670	1.0556	1.0481	1.0452
9.2%	1.0920	1.0685	1.0569	1.0492	1.0462
9.4%	1.0940	1.0700	1.0581	1.0502	1.0472
9.6%	1.0960	1.0715	1.0593	1.0513	1.0482
9.8%	1.0980	1.0729	1.0605	1.0523	1.0492
10.0%	1.1000	1.0744	1.0618	1.0534	1.0502
10.2%	1.1020	1.0759	1.0630	1.0544	1.0512
10.4%	1.1040	1.0774	1.0642	1.0555	1.0521
10.6%	1.1060	1.0788	1.0654	1.0565	1.0531
10.8%	1.1080	1.0803	1.0666	1.0576	1.0541
11.0%	1.1100	1.0818	1.0679	1.0586	1.0551
11.2%	1.1120	1.0833	1.0691	1.0597	1.0561
11.4%	1.1140	1.0847	1.0703	1.0607	1.0571
11.6%	1.1160	1.0862	1.0715	1.0618	1.0581
11.8%	1.1180	1.0877	1.0727	1.0628	1.0590

*For use in calculating the value of a term certain annuity payable at the beginning of each period.

TERM CERTAIN ANNUITY FACTORS

INTEREST RATE

YEARS	4.0%	4.2%	4.4%	4.6%	4.8%	5.0%	5.2%	5.4%	5.6%	5.8%
1	0.9615	0.9597	0.9579	0.9560	0.9542	0.9524	0.9506	0.9488	0.9470	0.9452
2	1.8861	1.8807	1.8753	1.8700	1.8647	1.8594	1.8542	1.8489	1.8437	1.8385
3	2.7751	2.7646	2.7542	2.7438	2.7335	2.7232	2.7131	2.7030	2.6929	2.6829
4	3.6299	3.6129	3.5959	3.5791	3.5625	3.5460	3.5295	3.5132	3.4971	3.4810
5	4.4518	4.4269	4.4022	4.3778	4.3535	4.3295	4.3056	4.2820	4.2586	4.2354
6	5.2421	5.2082	5.1746	5.1413	5.1083	5.0757	5.0434	5.0114	4.9797	4.9484
7	6.0021	5.9579	5.9143	5.8712	5.8285	5.7864	5.7447	5.7034	5.6626	5.6223
8	6.7327	6.6775	6.6229	6.5690	6.5158	6.4632	6.4113	6.3600	6.3093	6.2592
9	7.4353	7.3680	7.3016	7.2362	7.1716	7.1078	7.0449	6.9829	6.9217	6.8613
10	8.1109	8.0307	7.9518	7.8740	7.7973	7.7217	7.6473	7.5739	7.5016	7.4303
11	8.7605	8.6667	8.5745	8.4837	8.3944	8.3064	8.2199	8.1346	8.0508	7.9682
12	9.3851	9.2771	9.1710	9.0666	8.9641	8.8633	8.7641	8.6666	8.5708	8.4765
13	9.9856	9.8629	9.7423	9.6239	9.5077	9.3936	9.2815	9.1714	9.0633	8.9570
14	10.5631	10.4250	10.2896	10.1567	10.0264	9.8986	9.7733	9.6503	9.5296	9.4112
15	11.1184	10.9645	10.8138	10.6661	10.5214	10.3797	10.2408	10.1046	9.9712	9.8404
16	11.6523	11.4822	11.3159	11.1530	10.9937	10.8378	10.6851	10.5357	10.3894	10.2462
17	12.1657	11.9791	11.7968	11.6186	11.4444	11.2741	11.1075	10.9447	10.7854	10.6296
18	12.6593	12.4560	12.2575	12.0637	11.8744	11.6896	11.5091	11.3327	11.1604	10.9921
19	13.1339	12.9136	12.6987	12.4892	12.2847	12.0853	11.8907	11.7009	11.5156	11.3347
20	13.5903	13.3528	13.1214	12.8960	12.6763	12.4622	12.2536	12.0502	11.8519	11.6585

INTEREST RATE

YEARS	6.0%	6.2%	6.4%	6.6%	6.8%	7.0%	7.2%	7.4%	7.6%	7.8%
1	0.9434	0.9416	0.9398	0.9381	0.9363	0.9346	0.9328	0.9311	0.9294	0.9276
2	1.8334	1.8283	1.8232	1.8181	1.8130	1.8080	1.8030	1.7980	1.7931	1.7882
3	2.6730	2.6632	2.6534	2.6436	2.6339	2.6243	2.6148	2.6053	2.5958	2.5864
4	3.4651	3.4493	3.4336	3.4180	3.4026	3.3872	3.3720	3.3568	3.3418	3.3269
5	4.2124	4.1895	4.1669	4.1445	4.1222	4.1002	4.0783	4.0567	4.0352	4.0138
6	4.9173	4.8866	4.8561	4.8260	4.7961	4.7665	4.7373	4.7082	4.6795	4.6511
7	5.5824	5.5429	5.5039	5.4653	5.4271	5.3893	5.3519	5.3149	5.2784	5.2422
8	6.2098	6.1609	6.1127	6.0650	6.0179	5.9713	5.9253	5.8798	5.8349	5.7905
9	6.8017	6.7429	6.6848	6.6276	6.5710	6.5152	6.4602	6.4058	6.3521	6.2992
10	7.3601	7.2908	7.2226	7.1553	7.0890	7.0236	6.9591	6.8955	6.8328	6.7710
11	7.8869	7.8068	7.7280	7.6504	7.5739	7.4987	7.4245	7.3515	7.2796	7.2088
12	8.3838	8.2927	8.2030	8.1148	8.0280	7.9427	7.8587	7.7761	7.6948	7.6148
13	8.8527	8.7502	8.6494	8.5505	8.4532	8.3577	8.2637	8.1714	8.0807	7.9915
14	9.2950	9.1809	9.0690	8.9592	8.8513	8.7455	8.6415	8.5395	8.4393	8.3409
15	9.7122	9.5866	9.4634	9.3426	9.2241	9.1079	8.9940	8.8822	8.7726	8.6650
16	10.1059	9.9685	9.8340	9.7022	9.5731	9.4466	9.3227	9.2013	9.0823	8.9657
17	10.4773	10.3282	10.1823	10.0396	9.8999	9.7632	9.6294	9.4984	9.3702	9.2446
18	10.8276	10.6668	10.5097	10.3561	10.2059	10.0591	9.9155	9.7751	9.6377	9.5033
19	11.1581	10.9857	10.8174	10.6530	10.4924	10.3356	10.1824	10.0327	9.8863	9.7434
20	11.4699	11.2860	11.1066	10.9315	10.7607	10.5940	10.4313	10.2725	10.1174	9.9660

TERM CERTAIN ANNUITY FACTORS

INTEREST RATE

YEARS	8.0%	8.2%	8.4%	8.6%	8.8%	9.0%	9.2%	9.4%	9.6%	9.8%
1	0.9259	0.9242	0.9225	0.9208	0.9191	0.9174	0.9158	0.9141	0.9124	0.9107
2	1.7833	1.7784	1.7735	1.7687	1.7639	1.7591	1.7544	1.7496	1.7449	1.7402
3	2.5771	2.5678	2.5586	2.5494	2.5403	2.5313	2.5223	2.5134	2.5045	2.4956
4	3.3121	3.2974	3.2829	3.2684	3.2540	3.2397	3.2255	3.2115	3.1975	3.1836
5	3.9927	3.9718	3.9510	3.9304	3.9099	3.8897	3.8696	3.8496	3.8298	3.8102
6	4.6229	4.5950	4.5673	4.5399	4.5128	4.4859	4.4593	4.4329	4.4068	4.3809
7	5.2064	5.1709	5.1359	5.1012	5.0669	5.0330	4.9994	4.9661	4.9332	4.9006
8	5.7466	5.7033	5.6604	5.6181	5.5762	5.5348	5.4939	5.4535	5.4135	5.3740
9	6.2469	6.1953	6.1443	6.0940	6.0443	5.9952	5.9468	5.8990	5.8517	5.8051
10	6.7101	6.6500	6.5907	6.5322	6.4745	6.4177	6.3615	6.3062	6.2516	6.1977
11	7.1390	7.0702	7.0025	6.9357	6.8700	6.8052	6.7413	6.6784	6.6164	6.5553
12	7.5361	7.4586	7.3824	7.3073	7.2334	7.1607	7.0891	7.0187	6.9493	6.8810
13	7.9038	7.8176	7.7328	7.6495	7.5675	7.4869	7.4076	7.3297	7.2530	7.1776
14	8.2442	8.1493	8.0561	7.9645	7.8745	7.7862	7.6993	7.6140	7.5301	7.4477
15	8.5595	8.4559	8.3543	8.2546	8.1567	8.0607	7.9664	7.8738	7.7829	7.6937
16	8.8514	8.7393	8.6295	8.5217	8.4161	8.3126	8.2110	8.1114	8.0136	7.9178
17	9.1216	9.0012	8.8833	8.7677	8.6545	8.5436	8.4350	8.3285	8.2241	8.1218
18	9.3719	9.2433	9.1174	8.9942	8.8736	8.7556	8.6401	8.5269	8.4162	8.3077
19	9.6036	9.4670	9.3334	9.2028	9.0750	8.9501	8.8279	8.7084	8.5914	8.4769
20	9.8181	9.6737	9.5327	9.3948	9.2602	9.1285	8.9999	8.8742	8.7513	8.6311

INTEREST RATE

YEARS	10.0%	10.2%	10.4%	10.6%	10.8%	11.0%	11.2%	11.4%	11.6%	11.8%
1	0.9091	0.9074	0.9058	0.9042	0.9025	0.9009	0.8993	0.8977	0.8961	0.8945
2	1.7355	1.7309	1.7263	1.7217	1.7171	1.7125	1.7080	1.7035	1.6990	1.6945
3	2.4869	2.4781	2.4694	2.4608	2.4522	2.4437	2.4352	2.4268	2.4184	2.4101
4	3.1699	3.1562	3.1426	3.1291	3.1157	3.1024	3.0892	3.0761	3.0631	3.0502
5	3.7908	3.7715	3.7524	3.7334	3.7146	3.6959	3.6774	3.6590	3.6408	3.6227
6	4.3553	4.3299	4.3047	4.2797	4.2550	4.2305	4.2063	4.1822	4.1584	4.1348
7	4.8684	4.8365	4.8050	4.7737	4.7428	4.7122	4.6819	4.6519	4.6222	4.5928
8	5.3349	5.2963	5.2581	5.2204	5.1830	5.1461	5.1096	5.0735	5.0378	5.0025
9	5.7590	5.7135	5.6686	5.6242	5.5804	5.5370	5.4943	5.4520	5.4103	5.3690
10	6.1446	6.0921	6.0404	5.9893	5.9389	5.8892	5.8402	5.7917	5.7440	5.6968
11	6.4951	6.4357	6.3772	6.3195	6.2626	6.2065	6.1512	6.0967	6.0430	5.9900
12	6.8137	6.7474	6.6822	6.6180	6.5547	6.4924	6.4310	6.3705	6.3109	6.2522
13	7.1034	7.0304	6.9585	6.8879	6.8183	6.7499	6.6825	6.6162	6.5510	6.4868
14	7.3667	7.2871	7.2088	7.1319	7.0562	6.9819	6.9087	6.8368	6.7661	6.6966
15	7.6061	7.5200	7.4355	7.3525	7.2710	7.1909	7.1122	7.0349	6.9589	6.8842
16	7.8237	7.7314	7.6409	7.5520	7.4648	7.3792	7.2951	7.2126	7.1316	7.0521
17	8.0216	7.9233	7.8269	7.7324	7.6397	7.5488	7.4596	7.3722	7.2864	7.2022
18	8.2014	8.0973	7.9954	7.8954	7.7976	7.7016	7.6076	7.5154	7.4251	7.3365
19	8.3649	8.2553	8.1480	8.0429	7.9400	7.8393	7.7406	7.6440	7.5494	7.4566
20	8.5136	8.3986	8.2862	8.1762	8.0686	7.9633	7.8603	7.7594	7.6607	7.5641

SINGLE LIFE ANNUITY FACTORS

INTEREST RATE

AGE	4.0%	4.2%	4.4%	4.6%	4.8%	5.0%	5.2%	5.4%	5.6%	5.8%
0	23.1342	22.2019	21.3340	20.5247	19.7689	19.0619	18.3996	17.7782	17.1944	16.6452
1	23.2822	22.3483	21.4784	20.6670	19.9088	19.1994	18.5345	17.9106	17.3242	16.7723
2	23.2307	22.3035	21.4394	20.6330	19.8792	19.1736	18.5121	17.8911	17.3073	16.7576
3	23.1714	22.2512	21.3934	20.5923	19.8433	19.1418	18.4840	17.8661	17.2851	16.7379
4	23.1071	22.1943	21.3428	20.5475	19.8034	19.1063	18.4522	17.8378	17.2597	16.7152
5	23.0386	22.1333	21.2885	20.4990	19.7601	19.0675	18.4175	17.8066	17.2316	16.6899
6	22.9665	22.0691	21.2312	20.4477	19.7141	19.0262	18.3803	17.7731	17.2014	16.6626
7	22.8908	22.0014	21.1706	20.3934	19.6653	18.9823	18.3407	17.7373	17.1690	16.6331
8	22.8119	21.9307	21.1071	20.3363	19.6139	18.9359	18.2988	17.6993	17.1346	16.6019
9	22.7291	21.8563	21.0402	20.2760	19.5594	18.8866	18.2541	17.6588	17.0977	16.5682
10	22.6422	21.7781	20.9697	20.2122	19.5017	18.8343	18.2066	17.6155	17.0582	16.5321
11	22.5517	21.6964	20.8958	20.1453	19.4410	18.7791	18.1563	17.5696	17.0162	16.4937
12	22.4574	21.6112	20.8187	20.0754	19.3774	18.7212	18.1035	17.5213	16.9720	16.4531
13	22.3606	21.5236	20.7392	20.0032	19.3117	18.6613	18.0488	17.4713	16.9261	16.4110
14	22.2624	21.4347	20.6586	19.9300	19.2451	18.6006	17.9933	17.4205	16.8796	16.3683
15	22.1635	21.3451	20.5774	19.8562	19.1780	18.5395	17.9376	17.3696	16.8330	16.3255
16	22.0642	21.2553	20.4960	19.7824	19.1109	18.4784	17.8819	17.3187	16.7865	16.2829
17	21.9641	21.1647	20.4139	19.7079	19.0433	18.4169	17.8259	17.2676	16.7398	16.2402
18	21.8626	21.0729	20.3308	19.6325	18.9748	18.3546	17.7691	17.2159	16.6926	16.1971
19	21.7586	20.9787	20.2453	19.5549	18.9043	18.2904	17.7107	17.1626	16.6439	16.1526
20	21.6513	20.8813	20.1569	19.4746	18.8312	18.2238	17.6499	17.1071	16.5932	16.1062
21	21.5402	20.7805	20.0652	19.3911	18.7550	18.1544	17.5865	17.0491	16.5401	16.0575
22	21.4257	20.6763	19.9704	19.3046	18.6762	18.0824	17.5207	16.9889	16.4849	16.0068
23	21.3072	20.5684	19.8719	19.2148	18.5941	18.0072	17.4519	16.9258	16.4270	15.9537
24	21.1843	20.4562	19.7695	19.1211	18.5083	17.9287	17.3798	16.8597	16.3663	15.8978
25	21.0566	20.3395	19.6627	19.0232	18.4186	17.8463	17.3042	16.7901	16.3022	15.8387
26	20.9241	20.2181	19.5514	18.9212	18.3249	17.7601	17.2249	16.7170	16.2348	15.7765
27	20.7861	20.0916	19.4352	18.8143	18.2265	17.6696	17.1413	16.6399	16.1636	15.7107
28	20.6434	19.9604	19.3145	18.7032	18.1242	17.5751	17.0541	16.5593	16.0890	15.6416
29	20.4957	19.8244	19.1893	18.5877	18.0175	17.4766	16.9630	16.4750	16.0109	15.5692
30	20.3432	19.6838	19.0595	18.4679	17.9068	17.3741	16.8681	16.3870	15.9293	15.4934
31	20.1859	19.5386	18.9254	18.3438	17.7919	17.2678	16.7695	16.2955	15.8442	15.4143
32	20.0236	19.3886	18.7865	18.2153	17.6728	17.1572	16.6668	16.2001	15.7555	15.3317
33	19.8559	19.2333	18.6426	18.0818	17.5488	17.0420	16.5598	16.1004	15.6627	15.2452
34	19.6829	19.0729	18.4938	17.9435	17.4203	16.9225	16.4484	15.9967	15.5659	15.1548
35	19.5040	18.9067	18.3393	17.7998	17.2865	16.7978	16.3321	15.8882	15.4645	15.0601
36	19.3196	18.7352	18.1796	17.6510	17.1478	16.6683	16.2113	15.7752	15.3589	14.9612
37	19.1293	18.5579	18.0143	17.4968	17.0038	16.5338	16.0855	15.6575	15.2486	14.8578
38	18.9327	18.3745	17.8431	17.3368	16.8542	16.3938	15.9543	15.5345	15.1333	14.7496
39	18.7300	18.1851	17.6659	17.1710	16.6989	16.2483	15.8178	15.4065	15.0130	14.6365
40	18.5206	17.9891	17.4824	16.9990	16.5376	16.0968	15.6756	15.2727	14.8872	14.5182
41	18.3042	17.7862	17.2921	16.8204	16.3697	15.9391	15.5272	15.1330	14.7556	14.3941
42	18.0809	17.5766	17.0951	16.6351	16.1955	15.7750	15.3726	14.9873	14.6182	14.2643
43	17.8507	17.3601	16.8914	16.4434	16.0148	15.6046	15.2119	14.8356	14.4748	14.1288
44	17.6137	17.1369	16.6811	16.2450	15.8277	15.4279	15.0449	14.6777	14.3255	13.9874
45	17.3707	16.9078	16.4648	16.0408	15.6347	15.2455	14.8723	14.5144	14.1707	13.8408
46	17.1215	16.6724	16.2425	15.8306	15.4358	15.0572	14.6940	14.3453	14.0104	13.6886
47	16.8668	16.4316	16.0147	15.6149	15.2315	14.8636	14.5103	14.1710	13.8449	13.5314
48	16.6064	16.1851	15.7811	15.3935	15.0215	14.6643	14.3211	13.9913	13.6741	13.3689
49	16.3405	15.9330	15.5419	15.1665	14.8060	14.4595	14.1264	13.8061	13.4978	13.2010
50	16.0685	15.6748	15.2968	14.9336	14.5845	14.2488	13.9258	13.6150	13.3158	13.0275
51	15.7910	15.4110	15.0459	14.6949	14.3572	14.0323	13.7196	13.4184	13.1281	12.8484
52	15.5087	15.1424	14.7901	14.4512	14.1250	13.8109	13.5083	13.2167	12.9355	12.6644
53	15.2217	14.8690	14.5295	14.2026	13.8878	13.5844	13.2920	13.0100	12.7380	12.4754
54	14.9304	14.5911	14.2643	13.9494	13.6459	13.3533	13.0710	12.7986	12.5356	12.2817

SINGLE LIFE ANNUITY FACTORS

INTEREST RATE

AGE	4.0%	4.2%	4.4%	4.6%	4.8%	5.0%	5.2%	5.4%	5.6%	5.8%
55	14.6347	14.3087	13.9945	13.6915	13.3993	13.1173	12.8451	12.5823	12.3284	12.0830
56	14.3348	14.0219	13.7202	13.4290	13.1480	12.8766	12.6144	12.3611	12.1163	11.8796
57	14.0308	13.7310	13.4415	13.1621	12.8921	12.6313	12.3791	12.1353	11.8995	11.6713
58	13.7238	13.4368	13.1595	12.8915	12.6325	12.3821	12.1399	11.9055	11.6787	11.4590
59	13.4146	13.1402	12.8748	12.6183	12.3701	12.1300	11.8976	11.6725	11.4545	11.2433
60	13.1036	12.8415	12.5879	12.3426	12.1051	11.8751	11.6524	11.4365	11.2273	11.0246
61	12.7904	12.5404	12.2985	12.0641	11.8371	11.6172	11.4040	11.1973	10.9968	10.8023
62	12.4743	12.2363	12.0057	11.7822	11.5655	11.3555	11.1517	10.9540	10.7622	10.5759
63	12.1553	11.9290	11.7095	11.4967	11.2903	11.0899	10.8955	10.7067	10.5234	10.3453
64	11.8339	11.6191	11.4106	11.2082	11.0118	10.8211	10.6358	10.4558	10.2809	10.1109
65	11.5104	11.3067	11.1090	10.9169	10.7303	10.5490	10.3728	10.2014	10.0348	9.8728
66	11.1843	10.9916	10.8043	10.6223	10.4454	10.2733	10.1059	9.9431	9.7847	9.6305
67	10.8550	10.6729	10.4959	10.3238	10.1563	9.9933	9.8347	9.6802	9.5299	9.3834
68	10.5231	10.3515	10.1845	10.0219	9.8637	9.7096	9.5595	9.4133	9.2709	9.1320
69	10.1896	10.0281	9.8709	9.7177	9.5685	9.4231	9.2813	9.1432	9.0085	8.8771
70	9.8560	9.7043	9.5565	9.4124	9.2720	9.1350	9.0014	8.8711	8.7440	8.6199
71	9.5236	9.3814	9.2427	9.1074	8.9754	8.8466	8.7210	8.5983	8.4785	8.3615
72	9.1932	9.0601	8.9302	8.8034	8.6796	8.5587	8.4407	8.3254	8.2128	8.1027
73	8.8655	8.7411	8.6197	8.5011	8.3852	8.2719	8.1613	8.0531	7.9474	7.8440
74	8.5395	8.4235	8.3102	8.1995	8.0912	7.9853	7.8818	7.7806	7.6815	7.5846
75	8.2142	8.1064	8.0009	7.8977	7.7968	7.6980	7.6014	7.5068	7.4142	7.3236
76	7.8889	7.7888	7.6909	7.5950	7.5011	7.4093	7.3193	7.2312	7.1449	7.0603
77	7.5637	7.4711	7.3803	7.2915	7.2044	7.1192	7.0356	6.9537	6.8735	6.7948
78	7.2393	7.1538	7.0700	6.9878	6.9073	6.8283	6.7510	6.6751	6.6006	6.5276
79	6.9175	6.8387	6.7614	6.6857	6.6114	6.5385	6.4670	6.3968	6.3280	6.2604
80	6.6006	6.5282	6.4572	6.3875	6.3191	6.2519	6.1860	6.1213	6.0577	5.9953
81	6.2908	6.2245	6.1593	6.0952	6.0324	5.9706	5.9100	5.8504	5.7918	5.7343
82	5.9892	5.9284	5.8687	5.8100	5.7524	5.6957	5.6400	5.5852	5.5314	5.4785
83	5.6958	5.6402	5.5856	5.5319	5.4791	5.4272	5.3762	5.3259	5.2765	5.2280
84	5.4085	5.3578	5.3080	5.2590	5.2108	5.1633	5.1166	5.0707	5.0255	4.9810
85	5.1258	5.0798	5.0344	4.9898	4.9459	4.9026	4.8601	4.8181	4.7769	4.7362
86	4.8500	4.8082	4.7671	4.7265	4.6866	4.6473	4.6085	4.5704	4.5327	4.4957
87	4.5845	4.5466	4.5092	4.4725	4.4362	4.4005	4.3653	4.3306	4.2964	4.2626
88	4.3291	4.2949	4.2611	4.2277	4.1949	4.1625	4.1305	4.0990	4.0679	4.0372
89	4.0839	4.0529	4.0224	3.9922	3.9624	3.9331	3.9041	3.8755	3.8473	3.8195
90	3.8490	3.8210	3.7933	3.7660	3.7391	3.7125	3.6863	3.6604	3.6348	3.6096
91	3.6277	3.6024	3.5774	3.5527	3.5283	3.5042	3.4805	3.4570	3.4338	3.4109
92	3.4238	3.4009	3.3782	3.3558	3.3337	3.3119	3.2903	3.2689	3.2479	3.2270
93	3.2364	3.2156	3.1950	3.1747	3.1546	3.1347	3.1151	3.0957	3.0765	3.0576
94	3.0626	3.0437	3.0250	3.0065	2.9882	2.9701	2.9523	2.9346	2.9171	2.8998
95	2.8985	2.8813	2.8643	2.8475	2.8308	2.8144	2.7981	2.7820	2.7660	2.7502
96	2.7448	2.7292	2.7137	2.6984	2.6832	2.6682	2.6533	2.6386	2.6241	2.6097
97	2.6030	2.5887	2.5746	2.5606	2.5468	2.5331	2.5195	2.5061	2.4928	2.4797
98	2.4701	2.4571	2.4443	2.4315	2.4189	2.4064	2.3940	2.3818	2.3696	2.3576
99	2.3410	2.3292	2.3175	2.3059	2.2945	2.2831	2.2718	2.2606	2.2496	2.2386
100	2.2159	2.2052	2.1946	2.1841	2.1736	2.1633	2.1531	2.1429	2.1329	2.1229
101	2.0930	2.0833	2.0737	2.0642	2.0548	2.0455	2.0362	2.0271	2.0180	2.0090
102	1.9726	1.9639	1.9554	1.9468	1.9384	1.9300	1.9217	1.9134	1.9052	1.8971
103	1.8535	1.8458	1.8382	1.8306	1.8230	1.8156	1.8081	1.8008	1.7935	1.7862
104	1.7270	1.7202	1.7135	1.7069	1.7003	1.6937	1.6872	1.6807	1.6743	1.6679
105	1.6034	1.5975	1.5917	1.5860	1.5803	1.5746	1.5690	1.5634	1.5578	1.5523
106	1.4458	1.4410	1.4363	1.4316	1.4269	1.4223	1.4176	1.4130	1.4085	1.4039
107	1.2564	1.2527	1.2491	1.2455	1.2420	1.2384	1.2349	1.2313	1.2279	1.2244
108	0.9666	0.9643	0.9620	0.9597	0.9574	0.9551	0.9529	0.9506	0.9484	0.9462
109	0.4808	0.4798	0.4789	0.4780	0.4771	0.4762	0.4753	0.4744	0.4735	0.4726

SINGLE LIFE ANNUITY FACTORS

INTEREST RATE

AGE	6.0%	6.2%	6.4%	6.6%	6.8%	7.0%	7.2%	7.4%	7.6%	7.8%
0	16.1278	15.6396	15.1785	14.7424	14.3295	13.9381	13.5666	13.2136	12.8778	12.5581
1	16.2522	15.7615	15.2978	14.8592	14.4438	14.0499	13.6760	13.3207	12.9827	12.6608
2	16.2395	15.7505	15.2884	14.8511	14.4368	14.0440	13.6710	13.3165	12.9792	12.6579
3	16.2220	15.7349	15.2745	14.8387	14.4258	14.0341	13.6622	13.3086	12.9721	12.6516
4	16.2016	15.7165	15.2579	14.8238	14.4123	14.0219	13.6512	13.2986	12.9631	12.6434
5	16.1787	15.6959	15.2392	14.8068	14.3969	14.0079	13.6383	13.2869	12.9523	12.6335
6	16.1540	15.6734	15.2188	14.7882	14.3799	13.9924	13.6241	13.2739	12.9404	12.6225
7	16.1273	15.6491	15.1966	14.7679	14.3614	13.9754	13.6085	13.2595	12.9271	12.6103
8	16.0988	15.6231	15.1728	14.7462	14.3414	13.9570	13.5916	13.2439	12.9127	12.5969
9	16.0680	15.5950	15.1471	14.7225	14.3196	13.9369	13.5730	13.2267	12.8968	12.5821
10	16.0350	15.5646	15.1192	14.6968	14.2959	13.9150	13.5527	13.2078	12.8792	12.5658
11	15.9997	15.5322	15.0893	14.6692	14.2704	13.8914	13.5308	13.1874	12.8602	12.5480
12	15.9624	15.4978	15.0576	14.6399	14.2432	13.8661	13.5073	13.1655	12.8397	12.5289
13	15.9236	15.4621	15.0245	14.6093	14.2148	13.8398	13.4828	13.1427	12.8184	12.5089
14	15.8844	15.4259	14.9911	14.5784	14.1862	13.8132	13.4581	13.1197	12.7969	12.4888
15	15.8450	15.3897	14.9578	14.5476	14.1577	13.7868	13.4335	13.0968	12.7757	12.4690
16	15.8060	15.3538	14.9248	14.5172	14.1296	13.7608	13.4095	13.0745	12.7549	12.4497
17	15.7669	15.3180	14.8918	14.4869	14.1017	13.7350	13.3857	13.0525	12.7345	12.4307
18	15.7274	15.2818	14.8586	14.4564	14.0736	13.7092	13.3618	13.0305	12.7141	12.4119
19	15.6867	15.2445	14.8244	14.4249	14.0447	13.6825	13.3372	13.0078	12.6932	12.3925
20	15.6441	15.2054	14.7885	14.3919	14.0143	13.6546	13.3114	12.9839	12.6711	12.3720
21	15.5995	15.1644	14.7508	14.3572	13.9824	13.6250	13.2842	12.9587	12.6478	12.3504
22	15.5530	15.1217	14.7115	14.3210	13.9489	13.5942	13.2556	12.9323	12.6233	12.3277
23	15.5041	15.0767	14.6700	14.2827	13.9136	13.5615	13.2254	12.9044	12.5974	12.3036
24	15.4526	15.0292	14.6262	14.2423	13.8762	13.5269	13.1933	12.8746	12.5697	12.2779
25	15.3981	14.9789	14.5797	14.1992	13.8363	13.4899	13.1590	12.8427	12.5401	12.2504
26	15.3407	14.9258	14.5305	14.1536	13.7940	13.4507	13.1225	12.8087	12.5084	12.2209
27	15.2797	14.8693	14.4781	14.1050	13.7488	13.4086	13.0834	12.7722	12.4744	12.1890
28	15.2157	14.8099	14.4229	14.0537	13.7011	13.3641	13.0419	12.7335	12.4382	12.1552
29	15.1484	14.7474	14.3648	13.9996	13.6507	13.3171	12.9980	12.6925	12.3998	12.1193
30	15.0780	14.6819	14.3038	13.9427	13.5976	13.2676	12.9517	12.6492	12.3593	12.0813
31	15.0044	14.6133	14.2399	13.8831	13.5419	13.2155	12.9030	12.6036	12.3166	12.0412
32	14.9274	14.5415	14.1729	13.8205	13.4834	13.1608	12.8517	12.5555	12.2715	11.9989
33	14.8467	14.4661	14.1024	13.7546	13.4217	13.1030	12.7975	12.5047	12.2237	11.9540
34	14.7623	14.3872	14.0286	13.6854	13.3569	13.0422	12.7404	12.4510	12.1733	11.9065
35	14.6737	14.3042	13.9508	13.6125	13.2885	12.9779	12.6800	12.3942	12.1198	11.8561
36	14.5810	14.2174	13.8693	13.5360	13.2166	12.9103	12.6164	12.3343	12.0633	11.8029
37	14.4841	14.1264	13.7839	13.4556	13.1410	12.8391	12.5493	12.2711	12.0036	11.7465
38	14.3824	14.0308	13.6940	13.3710	13.0613	12.7640	12.4785	12.2041	11.9404	11.6868
39	14.2761	13.9307	13.5997	13.2822	12.9774	12.6848	12.4037	12.1335	11.8736	11.6235
40	14.1646	13.8256	13.5005	13.1886	12.8890	12.6013	12.3247	12.0587	11.8028	11.5564
41	14.0475	13.7151	13.3962	13.0899	12.7957	12.5130	12.2411	11.9794	11.7276	11.4851
42	13.9249	13.5993	13.2866	12.9862	12.6975	12.4198	12.1527	11.8956	11.6480	11.4094
43	13.7967	13.4779	13.1716	12.8772	12.5942	12.3218	12.0596	11.8071	11.5639	11.3294
44	13.6628	13.3510	13.0512	12.7630	12.4857	12.2187	11.9616	11.7139	11.4751	11.2448
45	13.5237	13.2190	12.9259	12.6439	12.3724	12.1110	11.8591	11.6163	11.3821	11.1561
46	13.3792	13.0817	12.7954	12.5198	12.2543	11.9985	11.7519	11.5140	11.2845	11.0630
47	13.2298	12.9396	12.6601	12.3910	12.1316	11.8815	11.6403	11.4075	11.1829	10.9659
48	13.0751	12.7923	12.5198	12.2572	12.0040	11.7597	11.5240	11.2965	11.0767	10.8644
49	12.9152	12.6399	12.3744	12.1184	11.8715	11.6332	11.4031	11.1808	10.9660	10.7584
50	12.7497	12.4819	12.2236	11.9743	11.7338	11.5014	11.2770	11.0601	10.8505	10.6477
51	12.5787	12.3185	12.0674	11.8249	11.5908	11.3646	11.1460	10.9345	10.7301	10.5322
52	12.4027	12.1502	11.9064	11.6708	11.4432	11.2231	11.0103	10.8045	10.6052	10.4123
53	12.2219	11.9771	11.7405	11.5119	11.2908	11.0770	10.8701	10.6698	10.4759	10.2881
54	12.0363	11.7992	11.5700	11.3483	11.1339	10.9263	10.7254	10.5308	10.3422	10.1595

SINGLE LIFE ANNUITY FACTORS

INTEREST RATE

AGE	6.0%	6.2%	6.4%	6.6%	6.8%	7.0%	7.2%	7.4%	7.6%	7.8%
55	11.8459	11.6165	11.3947	11.1800	10.9722	10.7709	10.5760	10.3871	10.2040	10.0265
56	11.6505	11.4290	11.2145	11.0068	10.8056	10.6108	10.4219	10.2387	10.0611	9.8889
57	11.4505	11.2366	11.0295	10.8289	10.6344	10.4459	10.2631	10.0858	9.9137	9.7467
58	11.2463	11.0402	10.8404	10.6468	10.4591	10.2769	10.1002	9.9287	9.7622	9.6005
59	11.0387	10.8403	10.6479	10.4613	10.2802	10.1044	9.9338	9.7681	9.6071	9.4507
60	10.8279	10.6371	10.4520	10.2724	10.0979	9.9286	9.7640	9.6041	9.4487	9.2977
61	10.6136	10.4304	10.2526	10.0798	9.9120	9.7490	9.5905	9.4365	9.2866	9.1409
62	10.3951	10.2195	10.0488	9.8830	9.7218	9.5651	9.4127	9.2644	9.1202	8.9798
63	10.1723	10.0041	9.8407	9.6817	9.5271	9.3767	9.2303	9.0879	8.9492	8.8141
64	9.9456	9.7849	9.6285	9.4764	9.3283	9.1842	9.0438	8.9072	8.7740	8.6443
65	9.7151	9.5617	9.4124	9.2670	9.1254	8.9875	8.8532	8.7223	8.5947	8.4703
66	9.4804	9.3342	9.1918	9.0532	8.9180	8.7863	8.6579	8.5327	8.4107	8.2916
67	9.2407	9.1017	8.9663	8.8342	8.7054	8.5799	8.4574	8.3380	8.2214	8.1076
68	8.9967	8.8648	8.7361	8.6106	8.4881	8.3687	8.2521	8.1383	8.0271	7.9186
69	8.7490	8.6240	8.5020	8.3830	8.2668	8.1533	8.0425	7.9343	7.8286	7.7253
70	8.4988	8.3806	8.2652	8.1525	8.0424	7.9348	7.8297	7.7270	7.6266	7.5285
71	8.2473	8.1357	8.0267	7.9202	7.8161	7.7143	7.6148	7.5175	7.4223	7.3292
72	7.9951	7.8900	7.7872	7.6867	7.5884	7.4923	7.3982	7.3062	7.2162	7.1280
73	7.7429	7.6440	7.5473	7.4526	7.3600	7.2694	7.1807	7.0938	7.0088	6.9255
74	7.4898	7.3970	7.3061	7.2172	7.1301	7.0448	6.9613	6.8795	6.7993	6.7208
75	7.2349	7.1480	7.0628	6.9795	6.8978	6.8177	6.7393	6.6624	6.5871	6.5132
76	6.9775	6.8963	6.8167	6.7388	6.6623	6.5874	6.5139	6.4418	6.3712	6.3018
77	6.7177	6.6421	6.5679	6.4952	6.4238	6.3539	6.2852	6.2178	6.1517	6.0868
78	6.4560	6.3858	6.3168	6.2492	6.1828	6.1176	6.0536	5.9908	5.9291	5.8686
79	6.1941	6.1290	6.0650	6.0023	5.9406	5.8801	5.8206	5.7622	5.7048	5.6484
80	5.9340	5.8738	5.8147	5.7566	5.6995	5.6433	5.5882	5.5340	5.4807	5.4283
81	5.6778	5.6222	5.5676	5.5139	5.4611	5.4092	5.3582	5.3080	5.2587	5.2101
82	5.4265	5.3753	5.3250	5.2754	5.2268	5.1788	5.1317	5.0853	5.0397	4.9948
83	5.1801	5.1331	5.0868	5.0413	4.9964	4.9523	4.9089	4.8661	4.8240	4.7825
84	4.9372	4.8940	4.8516	4.8097	4.7686	4.7280	4.6881	4.6487	4.6100	4.5718
85	4.6961	4.6567	4.6178	4.5796	4.5418	4.5047	4.4680	4.4320	4.3964	4.3613
86	4.4592	4.4232	4.3877	4.3527	4.3183	4.2843	4.2508	4.2177	4.1852	4.1530
87	4.2294	4.1966	4.1642	4.1324	4.1009	4.0699	4.0393	4.0091	3.9793	3.9499
88	4.0070	3.9772	3.9477	3.9187	3.8900	3.8618	3.8338	3.8063	3.7791	3.7523
89	3.7920	3.7649	3.7382	3.7117	3.6857	3.6599	3.6345	3.6094	3.5846	3.5602
90	3.5847	3.5600	3.5357	3.5117	3.4880	3.4646	3.4415	3.4186	3.3961	3.3738
91	3.3882	3.3659	3.3438	3.3220	3.3004	3.2791	3.2581	3.2373	3.2167	3.1964
92	3.2065	3.1861	3.1660	3.1462	3.1265	3.1071	3.0879	3.0690	3.0502	3.0317
93	3.0388	3.0203	3.0019	2.9838	2.9659	2.9482	2.9307	2.9133	2.8962	2.8792
94	2.8827	2.8658	2.8490	2.8325	2.8161	2.7999	2.7839	2.7680	2.7523	2.7368
95	2.7346	2.7192	2.7039	2.6888	2.6738	2.6590	2.6444	2.6299	2.6155	2.6013
96	2.5955	2.5813	2.5674	2.5536	2.5399	2.5263	2.5129	2.4996	2.4865	2.4735
97	2.4666	2.4537	2.4410	2.4283	2.4158	2.4034	2.3911	2.3789	2.3669	2.3549
98	2.3457	2.3339	2.3222	2.3106	2.2992	2.2878	2.2765	2.2654	2.2543	2.2434
99	2.2278	2.2170	2.2063	2.1958	2.1853	2.1749	2.1646	2.1544	2.1443	2.1343
100	2.1130	2.1032	2.0935	2.0839	2.0744	2.0649	2.0555	2.0462	2.0370	2.0279
101	2.0000	1.9911	1.9823	1.9736	1.9650	1.9564	1.9479	1.9394	1.9311	1.9228
102	1.8890	1.8810	1.8731	1.8652	1.8574	1.8497	1.8420	1.8344	1.8268	1.8193
103	1.7790	1.7719	1.7648	1.7577	1.7507	1.7438	1.7369	1.7301	1.7233	1.7166
104	1.6616	1.6553	1.6490	1.6428	1.6367	1.6305	1.6245	1.6184	1.6125	1.6065
105	1.5468	1.5414	1.5360	1.5306	1.5253	1.5199	1.5147	1.5094	1.5042	1.4990
106	1.3994	1.3949	1.3905	1.3860	1.3816	1.3772	1.3729	1.3685	1.3642	1.3600
107	1.2209	1.2175	1.2140	1.2106	1.2072	1.2039	1.2005	1.1972	1.1939	1.1906
108	0.9439	0.9417	0.9395	0.9373	0.9352	0.9330	0.9308	0.9287	0.9265	0.9244
109	0.4717	0.4708	0.4699	0.4690	0.4682	0.4673	0.4664	0.4656	0.4647	0.4638

SINGLE LIFE ANNUITY FACTORS

INTEREST RATE

AGE	8.0%	8.2%	8.4%	8.6%	8.8%	9.0%	9.2%	9.4%	9.6%	9.8%
0	12.2534	11.9627	11.6851	11.4198	11.1660	10.9229	10.6900	10.4667	10.2523	10.0464
1	12.3540	12.0612	11.7816	11.5143	11.2586	11.0137	10.7791	10.5540	10.3379	10.1304
2	12.3516	12.0594	11.7802	11.5133	11.2579	11.0134	10.7789	10.5541	10.3383	10.1309
3	12.3460	12.0543	11.7757	11.5093	11.2543	11.0101	10.7761	10.5515	10.3360	10.1289
4	12.3385	12.0475	11.7694	11.5036	11.2491	11.0053	10.7717	10.5475	10.3323	10.1255
5	12.3295	12.0392	11.7618	11.4965	11.2426	10.9993	10.7661	10.5423	10.3275	10.1210
6	12.3193	12.0298	11.7531	11.4885	11.2351	10.9924	10.7597	10.5363	10.3219	10.1158
7	12.3080	12.0193	11.7434	11.4794	11.2267	10.9845	10.7523	10.5294	10.3154	10.1097
8	12.2956	12.0078	11.7326	11.4694	11.2173	10.9758	10.7441	10.5218	10.3082	10.1029
9	12.2818	11.9949	11.7207	11.4582	11.2068	10.9659	10.7348	10.5130	10.3000	10.0951
10	12.2666	11.9807	11.7073	11.4457	11.1950	10.9548	10.7244	10.5031	10.2906	10.0863
11	12.2500	11.9651	11.6927	11.4319	11.1821	10.9426	10.7128	10.4922	10.2803	10.0765
12	12.2320	11.9483	11.6768	11.4170	11.1680	10.9293	10.7002	10.4803	10.2689	10.0657
13	12.2133	11.9307	11.6603	11.4014	11.1533	10.9154	10.6870	10.4677	10.2570	10.0543
14	12.1945	11.9130	11.6437	11.3858	11.1385	10.9014	10.6739	10.4553	10.2452	10.0431
15	12.1759	11.8957	11.6274	11.3705	11.1242	10.8879	10.6611	10.4432	10.2337	10.0322
16	12.1580	11.8789	11.6117	11.3558	11.1104	10.8749	10.6489	10.4317	10.2229	10.0220
17	12.1403	11.8625	11.5964	11.3415	11.0970	10.8624	10.6372	10.4207	10.2125	10.0122
18	12.1228	11.8462	11.5813	11.3274	11.0839	10.8502	10.6257	10.4100	10.2025	10.0028
19	12.1048	11.8295	11.5658	11.3130	11.0705	10.8377	10.6140	10.3990	10.1923	9.9932
20	12.0859	11.8119	11.5495	11.2978	11.0563	10.8245	10.6017	10.3875	10.1815	9.9831
21	12.0658	11.7933	11.5321	11.2816	11.0413	10.8104	10.5886	10.3752	10.1700	9.9724
22	12.0448	11.7737	11.5139	11.2647	11.0255	10.7957	10.5748	10.3623	10.1579	9.9611
23	12.0224	11.7529	11.4945	11.2466	11.0086	10.7799	10.5601	10.3486	10.1450	9.9490
24	11.9985	11.7307	11.4738	11.2273	10.9905	10.7630	10.5442	10.3337	10.1311	9.9359
25	11.9728	11.7067	11.4514	11.2063	10.9709	10.7447	10.5270	10.3176	10.1160	9.9217
26	11.9453	11.6810	11.4274	11.1838	10.9499	10.7249	10.5085	10.3002	10.0996	9.9062
27	11.9155	11.6531	11.4013	11.1594	10.9269	10.7034	10.4882	10.2811	10.0816	9.8893
28	11.8839	11.6235	11.3735	11.1333	10.9024	10.6803	10.4665	10.2607	10.0623	9.8711
29	11.8502	11.5919	11.3438	11.1054	10.8762	10.6556	10.4433	10.2388	10.0416	9.8516
30	11.8146	11.5585	11.3124	11.0759	10.8484	10.6294	10.4186	10.2154	10.0196	9.8307
31	11.7769	11.5231	11.2791	11.0446	10.8189	10.6016	10.3923	10.1907	9.9962	9.8086
32	11.7371	11.4857	11.2439	11.0114	10.7876	10.5721	10.3645	10.1643	9.9713	9.7850
33	11.6949	11.4459	11.2064	10.9760	10.7542	10.5406	10.3347	10.1361	9.9446	9.7597
34	11.6502	11.4038	11.1667	10.9386	10.7188	10.5071	10.3030	10.1062	9.9162	9.7328
35	11.6027	11.3589	11.1244	10.8985	10.6810	10.4713	10.2691	10.0740	9.8857	9.7038
36	11.5524	11.3114	11.0795	10.8561	10.6408	10.4332	10.2330	10.0398	9.8532	9.6730
37	11.4992	11.2611	11.0319	10.8110	10.5981	10.3927	10.1946	10.0033	9.8185	9.6400
38	11.4426	11.2076	10.9812	10.7629	10.5525	10.3494	10.1535	9.9642	9.7814	9.6047
39	11.3827	11.1508	10.9273	10.7118	10.5039	10.3033	10.1096	9.9225	9.7417	9.5668
40	11.3191	11.0904	10.8700	10.6573	10.4521	10.2540	10.0627	9.8778	9.6991	9.5262
41	11.2514	11.0261	10.8088	10.5991	10.3967	10.2012	10.0124	9.8298	9.6533	9.4825
42	11.1794	10.9576	10.7436	10.5371	10.3376	10.1448	9.9586	9.7784	9.6042	9.4356
43	11.1033	10.8851	10.6745	10.4711	10.2746	10.0848	9.9012	9.7236	9.5517	9.3853
44	11.0227	10.8082	10.6012	10.4011	10.2078	10.0208	9.8400	9.6651	9.4957	9.3317
45	10.9380	10.7274	10.5240	10.3274	10.1372	9.9534	9.7754	9.6032	9.4364	9.2749
46	10.8491	10.6425	10.4427	10.2496	10.0629	9.8821	9.7072	9.5378	9.3737	9.2147
47	10.7563	10.5537	10.3578	10.1683	9.9849	9.8074	9.6356	9.4691	9.3077	9.1513
48	10.6591	10.4607	10.2687	10.0829	9.9031	9.7289	9.5602	9.3967	9.2382	9.0845
49	10.5577	10.3634	10.1755	9.9935	9.8173	9.6466	9.4811	9.3207	9.1651	9.0142
50	10.4515	10.2616	10.0778	9.8997	9.7272	9.5600	9.3979	9.2406	9.0881	8.9400
51	10.3407	10.1552	9.9756	9.8015	9.6328	9.4692	9.3105	9.1565	9.0071	8.8620
52	10.2256	10.0446	9.8692	9.6992	9.5344	9.3745	9.2193	9.0687	8.9224	8.7803
53	10.1061	9.9298	9.7587	9.5929	9.4320	9.2758	9.1242	8.9770	8.8340	8.6950
54	9.9824	9.8107	9.6441	9.4825	9.3255	9.1732	9.0252	8.8815	8.7418	8.6060

SINGLE LIFE ANNUITY FACTORS

INTEREST RATE

AGE	8.0%	8.2%	8.4%	8.6%	8.8%	9.0%	9.2%	9.4%	9.6%	9.8%
55	9.8543	9.6873	9.5252	9.3678	9.2149	9.0665	8.9223	8.7821	8.6458	8.5132
56	9.7217	9.5594	9.4018	9.2488	9.1001	8.9556	8.8151	8.6785	8.5457	8.4164
57	9.5845	9.4270	9.2741	9.1254	8.9809	8.8404	8.7038	8.5709	8.4415	8.3157
58	9.4434	9.2907	9.1424	8.9982	8.8579	8.7215	8.5887	8.4595	8.3337	8.2113
59	9.2987	9.1510	9.0073	8.8675	8.7315	8.5992	8.4703	8.3449	8.2227	8.1037
60	9.1507	9.0079	8.8688	8.7335	8.6018	8.4736	8.3487	8.2270	8.1085	7.9930
61	8.9991	8.8611	8.7267	8.5960	8.4686	8.3445	8.2236	8.1057	7.9909	7.8789
62	8.8431	8.7100	8.5804	8.4541	8.3311	8.2112	8.0943	7.9803	7.8691	7.7607
63	8.6826	8.5544	8.4296	8.3078	8.1892	8.0735	7.9606	7.8505	7.7431	7.6383
64	8.5179	8.3947	8.2745	8.1574	8.0431	7.9316	7.8228	7.7167	7.6130	7.5118
65	8.3490	8.2307	8.1153	8.0027	7.8929	7.7856	7.6809	7.5787	7.4788	7.3813
66	8.1754	8.0621	7.9514	7.8434	7.7379	7.6350	7.5344	7.4361	7.3400	7.2462
67	7.9965	7.8881	7.7822	7.6788	7.5777	7.4790	7.3825	7.2882	7.1960	7.1059
68	7.8126	7.7091	7.6079	7.5091	7.4125	7.3180	7.2256	7.1353	7.0470	6.9605
69	7.6243	7.5256	7.4292	7.3349	7.2426	7.1524	7.0642	6.9778	6.8933	6.8106
70	7.4325	7.3386	7.2468	7.1570	7.0692	6.9832	6.8990	6.8166	6.7359	6.6569
71	7.2381	7.1490	7.0618	6.9764	6.8929	6.8110	6.7309	6.6524	6.5756	6.5002
72	7.0418	6.9573	6.8746	6.7936	6.7143	6.6365	6.5604	6.4858	6.4127	6.3410
73	6.8439	6.7640	6.6857	6.6090	6.5339	6.4602	6.3880	6.3171	6.2477	6.1796
74	6.6438	6.5684	6.4945	6.4220	6.3509	6.2812	6.2128	6.1458	6.0800	6.0154
75	6.4407	6.3697	6.3000	6.2316	6.1646	6.0988	6.0342	5.9709	5.9087	5.8476
76	6.2338	6.1670	6.1015	6.0373	5.9742	5.9122	5.8514	5.7917	5.7331	5.6755
77	6.0231	5.9606	5.8992	5.8389	5.7797	5.7215	5.6644	5.6083	5.5531	5.4989
78	5.8091	5.7506	5.6932	5.6368	5.5814	5.5269	5.4734	5.4208	5.3691	5.3183
79	5.5930	5.5385	5.4850	5.4324	5.3806	5.3298	5.2798	5.2306	5.1822	5.1346
80	5.3768	5.3262	5.2764	5.2274	5.1792	5.1318	5.0852	5.0394	4.9942	4.9498
81	5.1624	5.1154	5.0691	5.0236	4.9789	4.9348	4.8914	4.8487	4.8067	4.7653
82	4.9506	4.9071	4.8642	4.8221	4.7805	4.7397	4.6994	4.6597	4.6207	4.5822
83	4.7417	4.7015	4.6619	4.6229	4.5844	4.5466	4.5093	4.4725	4.4363	4.4006
84	4.5342	4.4971	4.4606	4.4246	4.3891	4.3541	4.3197	4.2857	4.2522	4.2192
85	4.3268	4.2927	4.2591	4.2260	4.1933	4.1611	4.1294	4.0980	4.0671	4.0367
86	4.1214	4.0901	4.0593	4.0289	3.9989	3.9693	3.9401	3.9113	3.8829	3.8549
87	3.9210	3.8923	3.8641	3.8363	3.8088	3.7816	3.7549	3.7284	3.7023	3.6765
88	3.7258	3.6997	3.6739	3.6484	3.6232	3.5984	3.5738	3.5496	3.5257	3.5020
89	3.5360	3.5121	3.4885	3.4653	3.4423	3.4195	3.3971	3.3749	3.3530	3.3314
90	3.3518	3.3300	3.3085	3.2872	3.2662	3.2455	3.2250	3.2047	3.1847	3.1649
91	3.1763	3.1565	3.1369	3.1175	3.0983	3.0793	3.0606	3.0421	3.0238	3.0056
92	3.0133	2.9952	2.9773	2.9595	2.9420	2.9247	2.9075	2.8905	2.8738	2.8572
93	2.8624	2.8459	2.8294	2.8132	2.7971	2.7813	2.7655	2.7500	2.7346	2.7193
94	2.7215	2.7063	2.6912	2.6763	2.6616	2.6470	2.6326	2.6183	2.6042	2.5902
95	2.5872	2.5733	2.5595	2.5459	2.5324	2.5190	2.5057	2.4926	2.4796	2.4668
96	2.4606	2.4478	2.4352	2.4227	2.4103	2.3980	2.3858	2.3738	2.3618	2.3500
97	2.3431	2.3314	2.3198	2.3083	2.2969	2.2856	2.2744	2.2633	2.2524	2.2415
98	2.2325	2.2218	2.2111	2.2006	2.1901	2.1797	2.1695	2.1593	2.1492	2.1392
99	2.1243	2.1145	2.1047	2.0951	2.0855	2.0760	2.0666	2.0572	2.0479	2.0388
100	2.0188	2.0098	2.0009	1.9921	1.9833	1.9746	1.9660	1.9575	1.9490	1.9406
101	1.9145	1.9063	1.8982	1.8902	1.8822	1.8743	1.8665	1.8587	1.8509	1.8433
102	1.8119	1.8045	1.7971	1.7898	1.7826	1.7754	1.7683	1.7613	1.7543	1.7473
103	1.7099	1.7032	1.6966	1.6901	1.6836	1.6772	1.6708	1.6644	1.6581	1.6518
104	1.6006	1.5947	1.5889	1.5831	1.5774	1.5717	1.5660	1.5603	1.5548	1.5492
105	1.4939	1.4888	1.4837	1.4787	1.4737	1.4687	1.4637	1.4588	1.4539	1.4491
106	1.3557	1.3515	1.3473	1.3431	1.3389	1.3348	1.3307	1.3266	1.3225	1.3185
107	1.1873	1.1840	1.1808	1.1775	1.1743	1.1711	1.1679	1.1647	1.1616	1.1585
108	0.9223	0.9202	0.9181	0.9160	0.9139	0.9118	0.9098	0.9077	0.9056	0.9036
109	0.4630	0.4621	0.4613	0.4604	0.4596	0.4587	0.4579	0.4570	0.4562	0.4554

SINGLE LIFE ANNUITY FACTORS

INTEREST RATE

AGE	10.0%	10.2%	10.4%	10.6%	10.8%	11.0%	11.2%	11.4%	11.6%	11.8%
0	9.8484	9.6580	9.4748	9.2982	9.1281	8.9640	8.8056	8.6527	8.5049	8.3621
1	9.9309	9.7390	9.5542	9.3763	9.2047	9.0393	8.8796	8.7254	8.5765	8.4325
2	9.9316	9.7398	9.5552	9.3773	9.2059	9.0405	8.8810	8.7268	8.5779	8.4340
3	9.9298	9.7382	9.5538	9.3761	9.2048	9.0396	8.8802	8.7262	8.5774	8.4335
4	9.9267	9.7353	9.5511	9.3737	9.2026	9.0376	8.8783	8.7244	8.5758	8.4320
5	9.9225	9.7315	9.5475	9.3703	9.1994	9.0346	8.8755	8.7218	8.5733	8.4297
6	9.9176	9.7269	9.5432	9.3662	9.1956	9.0310	8.8721	8.7186	8.5703	8.4268
7	9.9119	9.7215	9.5381	9.3614	9.1911	9.0267	8.8680	8.7148	8.5666	8.4234
8	9.9055	9.7154	9.5324	9.3561	9.1860	9.0219	8.8634	8.7104	8.5625	8.4194
9	9.8981	9.7085	9.5258	9.3498	9.1800	9.0162	8.8580	8.7052	8.5575	8.4147
10	9.8897	9.7005	9.5182	9.3426	9.1731	9.0096	8.8517	8.6992	8.5518	8.4092
11	9.8804	9.6916	9.5098	9.3345	9.1654	9.0022	8.8446	8.6924	8.5452	8.4029
12	9.8701	9.6818	9.5004	9.3255	9.1568	8.9940	8.8368	8.6848	8.5380	8.3959
13	9.8593	9.6715	9.4906	9.3161	9.1478	8.9854	8.8285	8.6769	8.5303	8.3885
14	9.8486	9.6613	9.4808	9.3068	9.1389	8.9768	8.8203	8.6690	8.5227	8.3812
15	9.8383	9.6515	9.4715	9.2979	9.1304	8.9687	8.8125	8.6615	8.5156	8.3743
16	9.8286	9.6423	9.4628	9.2896	9.1225	8.9612	8.8053	8.6547	8.5090	8.3681
17	9.8194	9.6336	9.4546	9.2818	9.1152	8.9542	8.7987	8.6484	8.5030	8.3624
18	9.8106	9.6253	9.4467	9.2744	9.1082	8.9476	8.7925	8.6425	8.4974	8.3570
19	9.8016	9.6169	9.4388	9.2670	9.1011	8.9410	8.7862	8.6365	8.4918	8.3517
20	9.7921	9.6080	9.4304	9.2591	9.0937	8.9340	8.7796	8.6303	8.4859	8.3461
21	9.7820	9.5985	9.4215	9.2507	9.0858	8.9265	8.7725	8.6236	8.4796	8.3401
22	9.7714	9.5885	9.4121	9.2419	9.0775	8.9187	8.7651	8.6167	8.4730	8.3339
23	9.7600	9.5779	9.4021	9.2324	9.0686	8.9103	8.7572	8.6092	8.4659	8.3272
24	9.7478	9.5663	9.3912	9.2222	9.0589	8.9012	8.7486	8.6010	8.4582	8.3199
25	9.7344	9.5537	9.3793	9.2110	9.0483	8.8911	8.7391	8.5921	8.4497	8.3118
26	9.7198	9.5400	9.3664	9.1988	9.0368	8.8802	8.7288	8.5822	8.4404	8.3030
27	9.7038	9.5249	9.3521	9.1853	9.0240	8.8681	8.7173	8.5713	8.4300	8.2931
28	9.6867	9.5086	9.3368	9.1707	9.0102	8.8550	8.7048	8.5595	8.4188	8.2824
29	9.6682	9.4912	9.3202	9.1550	8.9953	8.8409	8.6914	8.5467	8.4066	8.2708
30	9.6485	9.4725	9.3025	9.1382	8.9794	8.8257	8.6770	8.5330	8.3936	8.2584
31	9.6275	9.4526	9.2837	9.1204	8.9624	8.8096	8.6617	8.5184	8.3797	8.2452
32	9.6052	9.4314	9.2636	9.1013	8.9443	8.7924	8.6453	8.5028	8.3648	8.2310
33	9.5812	9.4087	9.2420	9.0808	8.9248	8.7738	8.6276	8.4860	8.3487	8.2157
34	9.5556	9.3845	9.2189	9.0588	8.9039	8.7539	8.6087	8.4680	8.3315	8.1992
35	9.5282	9.3583	9.1941	9.0352	8.8814	8.7325	8.5882	8.4484	8.3129	8.1814
36	9.4988	9.3304	9.1675	9.0099	8.8573	8.7095	8.5663	8.4275	8.2929	8.1623
37	9.4675	9.3006	9.1391	8.9828	8.8315	8.6848	8.5427	8.4050	8.2714	8.1417
38	9.4338	9.2685	9.1085	8.9536	8.8036	8.6582	8.5173	8.3806	8.2481	8.1194
39	9.3977	9.2341	9.0757	8.9223	8.7736	8.6296	8.4899	8.3544	8.2230	8.0954
40	9.3589	9.1971	9.0403	8.8884	8.7413	8.5986	8.4603	8.3260	8.1957	8.0693
41	9.3172	9.1571	9.0021	8.8519	8.7063	8.5651	8.4281	8.2952	8.1662	8.0409
42	9.2723	9.1142	8.9610	8.8125	8.6685	8.5289	8.3934	8.2619	8.1341	8.0101
43	9.2242	9.0681	8.9169	8.7702	8.6279	8.4899	8.3559	8.2259	8.0995	7.9768
44	9.1728	9.0188	8.8695	8.7248	8.5843	8.4480	8.3156	8.1871	8.0622	7.9409
45	9.1183	8.9665	8.8193	8.6765	8.5379	8.4034	8.2727	8.1458	8.0224	7.9025
46	9.0605	8.9110	8.7659	8.6252	8.4886	8.3559	8.2270	8.1017	7.9800	7.8616
47	8.9996	8.8525	8.7097	8.5711	8.4365	8.3057	8.1786	8.0551	7.9350	7.8182
48	8.9354	8.7907	8.6502	8.5138	8.3813	8.2525	8.1274	8.0057	7.8873	7.7722
49	8.8678	8.7256	8.5875	8.4534	8.3230	8.1963	8.0732	7.9534	7.8368	7.7234
50	8.7963	8.6567	8.5211	8.3894	8.2613	8.1368	8.0156	7.8978	7.7831	7.6715
51	8.7211	8.5842	8.4511	8.3218	8.1961	8.0738	7.9548	7.8389	7.7262	7.6164
52	8.6423	8.5082	8.3778	8.2510	8.1276	8.0076	7.8908	7.7771	7.6663	7.5585
53	8.5600	8.4286	8.3009	8.1767	8.0558	7.9382	7.8236	7.7121	7.6034	7.4975
54	8.4740	8.3456	8.2207	8.0991	7.9807	7.8655	7.7533	7.6439	7.5374	7.4336

SINGLE LIFE ANNUITY FACTORS

INTEREST RATE

AGE	10.0%	10.2%	10.4%	10.6%	10.8%	11.0%	11.2%	11.4%	11.6%	11.8%
55	8.3843	8.2588	8.1367	8.0179	7.9021	7.7894	7.6795	7.5725	7.4681	7.3664
56	8.2907	8.1682	8.0490	7.9329	7.8198	7.7096	7.6022	7.4975	7.3954	7.2959
57	8.1931	8.0738	7.9575	7.8443	7.7339	7.6263	7.5214	7.4191	7.3193	7.2220
58	8.0920	7.9758	7.8626	7.7522	7.6446	7.5397	7.4373	7.3375	7.2401	7.1450
59	7.9877	7.8747	7.7645	7.6571	7.5523	7.4501	7.3503	7.2530	7.1580	7.0652
60	7.8804	7.7706	7.6635	7.5590	7.4571	7.3576	7.2605	7.1657	7.0731	6.9827
61	7.7696	7.6631	7.5591	7.4577	7.3586	7.2619	7.1675	7.0753	6.9852	6.8972
62	7.6549	7.5516	7.4508	7.3524	7.2564	7.1625	7.0708	6.9812	6.8937	6.8081
63	7.5359	7.4360	7.3385	7.2432	7.1501	7.0591	6.9702	6.8833	6.7983	6.7153
64	7.4130	7.3165	7.2221	7.1300	7.0399	6.9519	6.8658	6.7816	6.6993	6.6187
65	7.2860	7.1928	7.1018	7.0128	6.9258	6.8407	6.7575	6.6761	6.5964	6.5184
66	7.1544	7.0647	6.9770	6.8912	6.8073	6.7252	6.6449	6.5663	6.4893	6.4139
67	7.0177	6.9315	6.8471	6.7646	6.6838	6.6047	6.5273	6.4515	6.3773	6.3046
68	6.8760	6.7932	6.7122	6.6330	6.5553	6.4793	6.4049	6.3319	6.2605	6.1905
69	6.7297	6.6504	6.5728	6.4968	6.4223	6.3494	6.2779	6.2079	6.1393	6.0720
70	6.5796	6.5038	6.4296	6.3568	6.2855	6.2157	6.1472	6.0800	6.0142	5.9496
71	6.4264	6.3541	6.2832	6.2137	6.1456	6.0788	6.0133	5.9490	5.8860	5.8242
72	6.2707	6.2018	6.1342	6.0680	6.0030	5.9392	5.8767	5.8153	5.7551	5.6959
73	6.1128	6.0473	5.9830	5.9200	5.8581	5.7973	5.7377	5.6792	5.6217	5.5653
74	5.9521	5.8899	5.8289	5.7690	5.7102	5.6524	5.5957	5.5400	5.4853	5.4316
75	5.7877	5.7288	5.6710	5.6143	5.5585	5.5037	5.4499	5.3970	5.3451	5.2940
76	5.6189	5.5633	5.5087	5.4551	5.4023	5.3505	5.2996	5.2495	5.2003	5.1519
77	5.4457	5.3933	5.3419	5.2913	5.2416	5.1927	5.1446	5.0973	5.0508	5.0051
78	5.2683	5.2191	5.1708	5.1232	5.0765	5.0305	4.9852	4.9407	4.8968	4.8537
79	5.0878	5.0418	4.9965	4.9519	4.9080	4.8649	4.8224	4.7805	4.7393	4.6988
80	4.9061	4.8630	4.8207	4.7790	4.7379	4.6975	4.6577	4.6185	4.5799	4.5419
81	4.7246	4.6845	4.6449	4.6060	4.5677	4.5299	4.4927	4.4561	4.4200	4.3844
82	4.5443	4.5070	4.4702	4.4339	4.3982	4.3630	4.3283	4.2941	4.2604	4.2271
83	4.3654	4.3308	4.2966	4.2629	4.2297	4.1969	4.1646	4.1328	4.1014	4.0704
84	4.1866	4.1545	4.1228	4.0916	4.0608	4.0304	4.0004	3.9708	3.9417	3.9129
85	4.0066	3.9770	3.9477	3.9188	3.8903	3.8622	3.8345	3.8071	3.7801	3.7534
86	3.8272	3.7999	3.7729	3.7463	3.7200	3.6941	3.6685	3.6432	3.6182	3.5935
87	3.6511	3.6260	3.6012	3.5767	3.5525	3.5286	3.5050	3.4817	3.4587	3.4359
88	3.4787	3.4556	3.4328	3.4103	3.3881	3.3661	3.3444	3.3230	3.3018	3.2808
89	3.3100	3.2888	3.2679	3.2473	3.2269	3.2067	3.1868	3.1671	3.1476	3.1283
90	3.1453	3.1259	3.1068	3.0879	3.0692	3.0507	3.0324	3.0143	2.9964	2.9788
91	2.9877	2.9700	2.9525	2.9351	2.9180	2.9010	2.8843	2.8677	2.8513	2.8350
92	2.8407	2.8245	2.8084	2.7925	2.7768	2.7612	2.7458	2.7306	2.7155	2.7005
93	2.7043	2.6893	2.6746	2.6600	2.6455	2.6312	2.6170	2.6030	2.5891	2.5753
94	2.5763	2.5626	2.5490	2.5356	2.5223	2.5091	2.4960	2.4831	2.4703	2.4577
95	2.4540	2.4414	2.4290	2.4166	2.4043	2.3922	2.3802	2.3683	2.3565	2.3448
96	2.3383	2.3267	2.3152	2.3039	2.2926	2.2814	2.2703	2.2594	2.2485	2.2377
97	2.2307	2.2200	2.2095	2.1990	2.1886	2.1783	2.1681	2.1579	2.1479	2.1380
98	2.1292	2.1194	2.1097	2.1000	2.0904	2.0809	2.0715	2.0622	2.0529	2.0437
99	2.0296	2.0206	2.0117	2.0028	1.9940	1.9852	1.9766	1.9680	1.9595	1.9510
100	1.9322	1.9240	1.9157	1.9076	1.8995	1.8915	1.8836	1.8757	1.8679	1.8601
101	1.8357	1.8281	1.8206	1.8132	1.8058	1.7985	1.7912	1.7840	1.7769	1.7698
102	1.7404	1.7335	1.7267	1.7200	1.7133	1.7066	1.7000	1.6935	1.6870	1.6805
103	1.6456	1.6394	1.6333	1.6272	1.6212	1.6152	1.6092	1.6033	1.5974	1.5915
104	1.5437	1.5382	1.5327	1.5273	1.5220	1.5166	1.5113	1.5060	1.5008	1.4956
105	1.4443	1.4395	1.4347	1.4299	1.4252	1.4206	1.4159	1.4113	1.4067	1.4021
106	1.3145	1.3105	1.3065	1.3025	1.2986	1.2947	1.2908	1.2870	1.2831	1.2793
107	1.1553	1.1522	1.1491	1.1461	1.1430	1.1400	1.1369	1.1339	1.1309	1.1279
108	0.9016	0.8996	0.8975	0.8955	0.8935	0.8916	0.8896	0.8876	0.8856	0.8837
109	0.4545	0.4537	0.4529	0.4521	0.4513	0.4505	0.4496	0.4488	0.4480	0.4472

UNITRUST PAYOUT ADJUSTMENT FACTORS

Interest Rate	Number of Months That Valuation Date Precedes First Payout		Factors For Payout At The End Of Each			
	At Least	But Less Than	Annual Period	Semiannual Period	Quarterly Period	Monthly Period
4.4	..	1	1.000000	.989350	.984054	.980533
	1	2	.996418	.985806	.980529	.977021
	2	3	.992849	.982275	.977017	
	3	4	.989293	.978757	.973517	
	4	5	.985749	.975251		
	5	6	.982219	.971758		
	6	7	.978700	.968277		
	7	8	.975195			
	8	9	.971702			
	9	10	.968221			
	10	11	.964753			
	11	12	.961298			
	12	.	.957854			

Interest Rate	At Least	But Less Than	Annual Period	Semiannual Period	Quarterly Period	Monthly Period
4.6	..	1	1.000000	.988882	.983354	.979680
	1	2	.996259	.985183	.979676	.976015
	2	3	.992532	.981498	.976011	
	3	4	.988820	.977826	.972360	
	4	5	.985121	.974168		
	5	6	.981436	.970524		
	6	7	.977764	.966894		
	7	8	.974107			
	8	9	.970463			
	9	10	.966832			
	10	11	.963216			
	11	12	.959613			
	12	.	.956023			

Interest Rate	At Least	But Less Than	Annual Period	Semiannual Period	Quarterly Period	Monthly Period
4.8	..	1	1.000000	.988415	.982657	.978830
	1	2	.996101	.984561	.978825	.975013
	2	3	.992217	.980722	.975008	
	3	4	.988348	.976898	.971206	
	4	5	.984494	.973089		
	5	6	.980655	.969294		
	6	7	.976831	.965515		
	7	8	.973022			
	8	9	.969228			
	9	10	.965448			
	10	11	.961684			
	11	12	.957934			
	12	.	.954199			

UNITRUST PAYOUT ADJUSTMENT FACTORS

	Number of Months That Valuation Date Precedes First Payout		Factors For Payout At The End Of Each			
Interest Rate	At Least	But Less Than	Annual Period	Semiannual Period	Quarterly Period	Monthly Period
5.0	..	1	1.000000	.987950	.981961	.977982
	1	2	.995942	.983941	.977977	.974014
	2	3	.991901	.979949	.974009	
	3	4	.987877	.975973	.970057	
	4	5	.983868	.972013		
	5	6	.979876	.968069		
	6	7	.975900	.964141		
	7	8	.971940			
	8	9	.967997			
	9	10	.964069			
	10	11	.960157			
	11	12	.956261			
	12	.	.952381			

Interest Rate	At Least	But Less Than	Annual Period	Semiannual Period	Quarterly Period	Monthly Period
5.2	..	1	1.000000	.987486	.981268	.977137
	1	2	.995784	.983323	.977132	.973018
	2	3	.991587	.979178	.973012	
	3	4	.987407	.975050	.968911	
	4	5	.983244	.970940		
	5	6	.979099	.966847		
	6	7	.974972	.962771		
	7	8	.970862			
	8	9	.966769			
	9	10	.962694			
	10	11	.958636			
	11	12	.954594			
	12	.	.950570			

Interest Rate	At Least	But Less Than	Annual Period	Semiannual Period	Quarterly Period	Monthly Period
5.4	..	1	1.000000	.987023	.980577	.976295
	1	2	.995627	.982707	.976289	.972026
	2	3	.991273	.978409	.972019	
	3	4	.986938	.974131	.967769	
	4	5	.982622	.969871		
	5	6	.978325	.965629		
	6	7	.974047	.961407		
	7	8	.969787			
	8	9	.965546			
	9	10	.961323			
	10	11	.957119			
	11	12	.952934			
	12	.	.948767			

UNITRUST PAYOUT ADJUSTMENT FACTORS

Interest Rate	Number of Months That Valuation Date Precedes First Payout		Factors For Payout At The End Of Each			
	At Least	But Less Than	Annual Period	Semiannual Period	Quarterly Period	Monthly Period
5.6	..	1	1.000000	.986562	.979888	.975455
	1	2	.995470	.982092	.975449	.971036
	2	3	.990960	.977643	.971029	
	3	4	.986470	.973214	.966630	
	4	5	.982001	.968805		
	5	6	.977552	.964416		
	6	7	.973124	.960047		
	7	8	.968715			
	8	9	.964326			
	9	10	.959958			
	10	11	.955609			
	11	12	.951279			
	12	.	.946970			

Interest Rate	At Least	But Less Than	Annual Period	Semiannual Period	Quarterly Period	Monthly Period
5.8	..	1	1.000000	.986102	.979201	.974618
	1	2	.995313	.981480	.974611	.970050
	2	3	.990647	.976879	.970043	
	3	4	.986004	.972300	.965496	
	4	5	.981382	.967743		
	5	6	.976782	.963206		
	6	7	.972204	.958692		
	7	8	.967646			
	8	9	.963111			
	9	10	.958596			
	10	11	.954103			
	11	12	.949631			
	12	.	.945180			

Interest Rate	At Least	But Less Than	Annual Period	Semiannual Period	Quarterly Period	Monthly Period
6.0	..	1	1.000000	.985643	.978516	.973784
	1	2	.995156	.980869	.973776	.969067
	2	3	.990336	.976117	.969059	
	3	4	.985538	.971389	.964365	
	4	5	.980764	.966684		
	5	6	.976014	.962001		
	6	7	.971286	.957341		
	7	8	.966581			
	8	9	.961899			
	9	10	.957239			
	10	11	.952603			
	11	12	.947988			
	12	.	.943396			

UNITRUST PAYOUT ADJUSTMENT FACTORS

Interest Rate	At Least	But Less Than	Annual Period	Semiannual Period	Quarterly Period	Monthly Period
6.2	..	1	1.000000	.985185	.977833	.972952
	1	2	.995000	.980259	.972944	.968087
	2	3	.990024	.975358	.968079	
	3	4	.985074	.970481	.963238	
	4	5	.980148	.965628		
	5	6	.975247	.960799		
	6	7	.970371	.955995		
	7	8	.965519			
	8	9	.960691			
	9	10	.955887			
	10	11	.951107			
	11	12	.946352			
	12	.	.941620			

Interest Rate	At Least	But Less Than	Annual Period	Semiannual Period	Quarterly Period	Monthly Period
6.4	..	1	1.000000	.984729	.977152	.972122
	1	2	.994844	.979652	.972114	.967110
	2	3	.989714	.974600	.967101	
	3	4	.984611	.969575	.962115	
	4	5	.979534	.964576		
	5	6	.974483	.959602		
	6	7	.969458	.954654		
	7	8	.964460			
	8	9	.959487			
	9	10	.954539			
	10	11	.949617			
	11	12	.944721			
	12	.	.939850			

Interest Rate	At Least	But Less Than	Annual Period	Semiannual Period	Quarterly Period	Monthly Period
6.6	..	1	1.000000	.984274	.976473	.971295
	1	2	.994688	.979046	.971286	.966136
	2	3	.989404	.973845	.966127	
	3	4	.984149	.968672	.960995	
	4	5	.978921	.963527		
	5	6	.973721	.958408		
	6	7	.968549	.953317		
	7	8	.963404			
	8	9	.958286			
	9	10	.953196			
	10	11	.948132			
	11	12	.943096			
	12	.	.938086			

UNITRUST PAYOUT ADJUSTMENT FACTORS

Interest Rate	Number of Months That Valuation Date Precedes First Payout		Factors For Payout At The End Of Each			
	At Least	But Less Than	Annual Period	Semiannual Period	Quarterly Period	Monthly Period
6.8	..	1	1.000000	.983821	.975796	.970471
	1	2	.994533	.978442	.970461	.965165
	2	3	.989095	.973092	.965156	
	3	4	.983688	.967772	.959879	
	4	5	.978309	.962481		
	5	6	.972961	.957219		
	6	7	.967641	.951985		
	7	8	.962351			
	8	9	.957089			
	9	10	.951857			
	10	11	.946653			
	11	12	.941477			
	12	.	.936330			

Interest Rate	At Least	But Less Than	Annual Period	Semiannual Period	Quarterly Period	Monthly Period
7.0	..	1	1.000000	.983368	.975121	.969649
	1	2	.994378	.977839	.969639	.964198
	2	3	.988787	.972342	.964187	
	3	4	.983228	.966875	.958766	
	4	5	.977700	.961439		
	5	6	.972203	.956033		
	6	7	.966736	.950658		
	7	8	.961301			
	8	9	.955896			
	9	10	.950522			
	10	11	.945178			
	11	12	.939864			
	12	.	.934579			

Interest Rate	At Least	But Less Than	Annual Period	Semiannual Period	Quarterly Period	Monthly Period
7.2	..	1	1.000000	.982917	.974449	.968830
	1	2	.994223	.977239	.968819	.963233
	2	3	.988479	.971593	.963222	
	3	4	.982769	.965980	.957658	
	4	5	.977091	.960400		
	5	6	.971446	.954851		
	6	7	.965834	.949335		
	7	8	.960255			
	8	9	.954708			
	9	10	.949192			
	10	11	.943708			
	11	12	.938256			
	12	.	.932836			

UNITRUST PAYOUT ADJUSTMENT FACTORS

| Interest Rate | Number of Months That Valuation Date Precedes First Payout | | Factors For Payout At The End Of Each | | | |
	At Least	But Less Than	Annual Period	Semiannual Period	Quarterly Period	Monthly Period
7.4	..	1	1.000000	.982467	.973778	.968013
	1	2	.994069	.976640	.968002	.962271
	2	3	.988172	.970847	.962260	
	3	4	.982311	.965088	.956552	
	4	5	.976484	.959364		
	5	6	.970692	.953673		
	6	7	.964935	.948017		
	7	8	.959211			
	8	9	.953521			
	9	10	.947866			
	10	11	.942243			
	11	12	.936654			
	12	.	.931099			

Interest Rate	At Least	But Less Than	Annual Period	Semiannual Period	Quarterly Period	Monthly Period
7.6	..	1	1.000000	.982019	.973109	.967199
	1	2	.993914	.976042	.967187	.961313
	2	3	.987866	.970103	.961301	
	3	4	.981854	.964199	.955451	
	4	5	.975879	.958331		
	5	6	.969940	.952499		
	6	7	.964037	.946703		
	7	8	.958171			
	8	9	.952340			
	9	10	.946544			
	10	11	.940784			
	11	12	.935058			
	12	.	.929368			

Interest Rate	At Least	But Less Than	Annual Period	Semiannual Period	Quarterly Period	Monthly Period
7.8	..	1	1.000000	.981571	.972442	.966387
	1	2	.993761	.975447	.966374	.960357
	2	3	.987560	.969361	.960345	
	3	4	.981398	.963312	.954353	
	4	5	.975275	.957302		
	5	6	.969190	.951329		
	6	7	.963143	.945393		
	7	8	.957133			
	8	9	.951161			
	9	10	.945227			
	10	11	.939329			
	11	12	.933468			
	12	.	.927644			

UNITRUST PAYOUT ADJUSTMENT FACTORS

Interest Rate	Number of Months That Valuation Date Precedes First Payout		Factors For Payout At The End Of Each			
	At Least	But Less Than	Annual Period	Semiannual Period	Quarterly Period	Monthly Period
8.0	..	1	1.000000	.981125	.971777	.965578
	1	2	.993607	.974853	.965564	.959405
	2	3	.987255	.968621	.959392	
	3	4	.980944	.962429	.953258	
	4	5	.974673	.956276		
	5	6	.968442	.950162		
	6	7	.962250	.944088		
	7	8	.956099			
	8	9	.949987			
	9	10	.943913			
	10	11	.937879			
	11	12	.931883			
	12	.	.925926			

Interest Rate	At Least	But Less Than	Annual Period	Semiannual Period	Quarterly Period	Monthly Period
8.2	..	1	1.000000	.980680	.971114	.964771
	1	2	.993454	.974261	.964757	.958455
	2	3	.986951	.967883	.958441	
	3	4	.980490	.961547	.952167	
	4	5	.974072	.955253		
	5	6	.967695	.949000		
	6	7	.961361	.942788		
	7	8	.955068			
	8	9	.948816			
	9	10	.942605			
	10	11	.936434			
	11	12	.930304			
	12	.	.924214			

Interest Rate	At Least	But Less Than	Annual Period	Semiannual Period	Quarterly Period	Monthly Period
8.4	..	1	1.000000	.980237	.970453	.963966
	1	2	.993301	.973670	.963952	.957509
	2	3	.986647	.967148	.957494	
	3	4	.980037	.960669	.951080	
	4	5	.973472	.954233		
	5	6	.966951	.947841		
	6	7	.960473	.941491		
	7	8	.954039			
	8	9	.947648			
	9	10	.941300			
	10	11	.934994			
	11	12	.928731			
	12	.	.922509			

UNITRUST PAYOUT ADJUSTMENT FACTORS

Interest Rate	Number of Months That Valuation Date Precedes First Payout		Factors For Payout At The End Of Each			
	At Least	But Less Than	Annual Period	Semiannual Period	Quarterly Period	Monthly Period
8.6	..	1	1.000000	.979794	.969794	.963164
	1	2	.993149	.973081	.963149	.956565
	2	3	.986344	.966414	.956550	
	3	4	.979586	.959793	.949996	
	4	5	.972874	.953217		
	5	6	.966209	.946686		
	6	7	.959589	.940199		
	7	8	.953014			
	8	9	.946484			
	9	10	.940000			
	10	11	.933559			
	11	12	.927163			
	12	.	.920810			

Interest Rate	At Least	But Less Than	Annual Period	Semiannual Period	Quarterly Period	Monthly Period
8.8	..	1	1.000000	.979353	.969136	.962364
	1	2	.992996	.972494	.962349	.955624
	2	3	.986041	.965683	.955609	
	3	4	.979135	.958919	.948916	
	4	5	.972278	.952203		
	5	6	.965468	.945534		
	6	7	.958706	.938912		
	7	8	.951992			
	8	9	.945324			
	9	10	.938703			
	10	11	.932129			
	11	12	.925600			
	12	.	.919118			

Interest Rate	At Least	But Less Than	Annual Period	Semiannual Period	Quarterly Period	Monthly Period
9.0	..	1	1.000000	.978913	.968481	.961567
	1	2	.992844	.971908	.961551	.954686
	2	3	.985740	.964954	.954670	
	3	4	.978686	.958049	.947839	
	4	5	.971683	.951193		
	5	6	.964730	.944387		
	6	7	.957826	.937629		
	7	8	.950972			
	8	9	.944167			
	9	10	.937411			
	10	11	.930703			
	11	12	.924043			
	12	.	.917431			

UNITRUST PAYOUT ADJUSTMENT FACTORS

Interest Rate	Number of Months That Valuation Date Precedes First Payout		Factors For Payout At The End Of Each			
	At Least	But Less Than	Annual Period	Semiannual Period	Quarterly Period	Monthly Period
9.2	..	1	1.000000	.978474	.967827	.960772
	1	2	.992693	.971324	.960755	.953752
	2	3	.985439	.964226	.953734	
	3	4	.978238	.957180	.946765	
	4	5	.971089	.950186		
	5	6	.963993	.943242		
	6	7	.956949	.936350		
	7	8	.949956			
	8	9	.943014			
	9	10	.936123			
	10	11	.929283			
	11	12	.922492			
	12	.	.915751			

Interest Rate	At Least	But Less Than	Annual Period	Semiannual Period	Quarterly Period	Monthly Period
9.4	..	1	1.000000	.978037	.967176	.959980
	1	2	.992541	.970742	.959962	.952820
	2	3	.985138	.963501	.952802	
	3	4	.977790	.956315	.945695	
	4	5	.970497	.949182		
	5	6	.963258	.942102		
	6	7	.956074	.935075		
	7	8	.948942			
	8	9	.941865			
	9	10	.934839			
	10	11	.927867			
	11	12	.920946			
	12	.	.914077			

Interest Rate	At Least	But Less Than	Annual Period	Semiannual Period	Quarterly Period	Monthly Period
9.6	..	1	1.000000	.977600	.966526	.959190
	1	2	.992390	.970161	.959171	.951890
	2	3	.984838	.962778	.951872	
	3	4	.977344	.955452	.944628	
	4	5	.969906	.948181		
	5	6	.962526	.940965		
	6	7	.955201	.933805		
	7	8	.947932			
	8	9	.940718			
	9	10	.933560			
	10	11	.926455			
	11	12	.919405			
	12	.	.912409			

UNITRUST PAYOUT ADJUSTMENT FACTORS

Interest Rate	Number of Months That Valuation Date Precedes First Payout		Factors For Payout At The End Of Each			
	At Least	But Less Than	Annual Period	Semiannual Period	Quarterly Period	Monthly Period
9.8	..	1	1.000000	.977165	.965878	.958402
	1	2	.992239	.969582	.958382	.950964
	2	3	.984539	.962057	.950945	
	3	4	.976898	.954591	.943565	
	4	5	.969317	.947183		
	5	6	.961795	.939832		
	6	7	.954331	.932539		
	7	8	.946924			
	8	9	.939576			
	9	10	.932284			
	10	11	.925049			
	11	12	.917870			
	12	.	.910747			

Interest Rate	At Least	But Less Than	Annual Period	Semiannual Period	Quarterly Period	Monthly Period
10.0	..	1	1.000000	.976731	.965232	.957616
	1	2	.992089	.969004	.957596	.950041
	2	3	.984240	.961338	.950021	
	3	4	.976454	.953733	.942505	
	4	5	.968729	.946188		
	5	6	.961066	.938703		
	6	7	.953463	.931277		
	7	8	.945920			
	8	9	.938436			
	9	10	.931012			
	10	11	.923647			
	11	12	.916340			
	12	.	.909091			

Interest Rate	At Least	But Less Than	Annual Period	Semiannual Period	Quarterly Period	Monthly Period
10.2	..	1	1.000000	.976299	.964588	.956833
	1	2	.991939	.968428	.956812	.949120
	2	3	.983942	.960622	.949099	
	3	4	.976011	.952878	.941448	
	4	5	.968143	.945196		
	5	6	.960339	.937577		
	6	7	.952597	.930019		
	7	8	.944918			
	8	9	.937301			
	9	10	.929745			
	10	11	.922250			
	11	12	.914816			
	12	.	.907441			

TERM CERTAIN UNITRUST REMAINDER FACTORS

ADJUSTED PAYOUT RATE

YEARS	4.0%	4.2%	4.4%	4.6%	4.8%	5.0%	5.2%	5.4%	5.6%	5.8%
1	.960000	.958000	.956000	.954000	.952000	.950000	.948000	.946000	.944000	.942000
2	.921600	.917764	.913936	.910116	.906304	.902500	.898704	.894916	.891136	.887364
3	.884736	.879218	.873723	.868251	.862801	.857375	.851971	.846591	.841232	.835897
4	.849347	.842291	.835279	.828311	.821387	.814506	.807669	.800875	.794123	.787415
5	.815373	.806915	.798527	.790209	.781960	.773781	.765670	.757627	.749652	.741745
6	.782758	.773024	.763392	.753859	.744426	.735092	.725855	.716716	.707672	.698724
7	.751447	.740557	.729802	.719182	.708694	.698337	.688111	.678013	.668042	.658198
8	.721390	.709454	.697691	.686099	.674677	.663420	.652329	.641400	.630632	.620022
9	.692534	.679657	.666993	.654539	.642292	.630249	.618408	.606765	.595317	.584061
10	.664833	.651111	.637645	.624430	.611462	.598737	.586251	.573999	.561979	.550185
11	.638239	.623764	.609589	.595706	.582112	.568800	.555766	.543003	.530508	.518275
12	.612710	.597566	.582767	.568304	.554170	.540360	.526866	.513681	.500800	.488215
13	.588201	.572469	.557125	.542162	.527570	.513342	.499469	.485942	.472755	.459898
14	.564673	.548425	.532611	.517222	.502247	.487675	.473496	.459701	.446280	.433224
15	.542086	.525391	.509177	.493430	.478139	.463291	.448875	.434878	.421289	.408097
16	.520403	.503325	.486773	.470732	.455188	.440127	.425533	.411394	.397697	.384428
17	.499587	.482185	.465355	.449079	.433339	.418120	.403405	.389179	.375426	.362131
18	.479603	.461933	.444879	.428421	.412539	.397214	.382428	.368163	.354402	.341127
19	.460419	.442532	.425304	.408714	.392737	.377354	.362542	.348282	.334555	.321342
20	.442002	.423946	.406591	.389913	.373886	.358486	.343690	.329475	.315820	.302704

ADJUSTED PAYOUT RATE

YEARS	6.0%	6.2%	6.4%	6.6%	6.8%	7.0%	7.2%	7.4%	7.6%	7.8%
1	.940000	.938000	.936000	.934000	.932000	.930000	.928000	.926000	.924000	.922000
2	.883600	.879844	.876096	.872356	.868624	.864900	.861184	.857476	.853776	.850084
3	.830584	.825294	.820026	.814781	.809558	.804357	.799179	.794023	.788889	.783777
4	.780749	.774125	.767544	.761005	.754508	.748052	.741638	.735265	.728933	.722643
5	.733904	.726130	.718421	.710779	.703201	.695688	.688240	.680855	.673535	.666277
6	.689870	.681110	.672442	.663867	.655383	.646990	.638687	.630472	.622346	.614307
7	.648478	.638881	.629406	.620052	.610817	.601701	.592701	.583817	.575048	.566391
8	.609569	.599270	.589124	.579129	.569282	.559582	.550027	.540615	.531344	.522213
9	.572995	.562115	.551420	.540906	.530571	.520411	.510425	.500609	.490962	.481480
10	.538615	.527264	.516129	.505206	.494492	.483982	.473674	.463564	.453649	.443925
11	.506298	.494574	.483097	.471863	.460866	.450104	.439570	.429260	.419171	.409298
12	.475920	.463910	.452179	.440720	.429527	.418596	.407921	.397495	.387314	.377373
13	.447365	.435148	.423239	.411632	.400320	.389295	.378550	.368081	.357879	.347938
14	.420523	.408169	.396152	.384465	.373098	.362044	.351295	.340843	.330680	.320799
15	.395292	.382862	.370798	.359090	.347727	.336701	.326002	.315620	.305548	.295777
16	.371574	.359125	.347067	.335390	.324082	.313132	.302529	.292264	.282326	.272706
17	.349280	.336859	.324855	.313254	.302044	.291213	.280747	.270637	.260870	.251435
18	.328323	.315974	.304064	.292579	.281505	.270828	.260534	.250610	.241044	.231823
19	.308624	.296383	.284604	.273269	.262363	.251870	.241775	.232065	.222724	.213741
20	.290106	.278008	.266389	.255233	.244522	.234239	.224367	.214892	.205797	.197069

TERM CERTAIN UNITRUST REMAINDER FACTORS

ADJUSTED PAYOUT RATE

YEARS	8.0%	8.2%	8.4%	8.6%	8.8%	9.0%	9.2%	9.4%	9.6%	9.8%
1	.920000	.918000	.916000	.914000	.912000	.910000	.908000	.906000	.904000	.902000
2	.846400	.842724	.839056	.835396	.831744	.828100	.824464	.820836	.817216	.813604
3	.778688	.773621	.768575	.763552	.758551	.753571	.748613	.743677	.738763	.733871
4	.716393	.710184	.704015	.697886	.691798	.685750	.679741	.673772	.667842	.661951
5	.659082	.651949	.644878	.637868	.630920	.624032	.617205	.610437	.603729	.597080
6	.606355	.598489	.590708	.583012	.575399	.567869	.560422	.553056	.545771	.538566
7	.557847	.549413	.541089	.532873	.524764	.516761	.508863	.501069	.493377	.485787
8	.513219	.504361	.495637	.487046	.478585	.470253	.462048	.453968	.446013	.438180
9	.472161	.463003	.454004	.445160	.436469	.427930	.419539	.411295	.403196	.395238
10	.434388	.425037	.415867	.406876	.398060	.389416	.380942	.372634	.364489	.356505
11	.399637	.390184	.380934	.371885	.363031	.354369	.345895	.337606	.329498	.321567
12	.367666	.358189	.348936	.339902	.331084	.322475	.314073	.305871	.297866	.290054
13	.338253	.328817	.319625	.310671	.301949	.293453	.285178	.277119	.269271	.261628
14	.311193	.301854	.292777	.283953	.275377	.267042	.258942	.251070	.243421	.235989
15	.286297	.277102	.268184	.259533	.251144	.243008	.235119	.227469	.220053	.212862
16	.263394	.254380	.245656	.237213	.229043	.221137	.213488	.206087	.198928	.192001
17	.242322	.233521	.225021	.216813	.208887	.201235	.193847	.186715	.179830	.173185
18	.222936	.214372	.206119	.198167	.190505	.183124	.176013	.169164	.162567	.156213
19	.205101	.196794	.188805	.181125	.173741	.166643	.159820	.153262	.146960	.140904
20	.188693	.180657	.172946	.165548	.158452	.151645	.145117	.138856	.132852	.127096

ADJUSTED PAYOUT RATE

YEARS	10.0%	10.2%	10.4%	10.6%	10.8%	11.0%	11.2%	11.4%	11.6%	11.8%
1	.900000	.898000	.896000	.894000	.892000	.890000	.888000	.886000	.884000	.882000
2	.810000	.806404	.802816	.799236	.795664	.792100	.788544	.784996	.781456	.777924
3	.729000	.724151	.719323	.714517	.709732	.704969	.700227	.695506	.690807	.686129
4	.656100	.650287	.644514	.638778	.633081	.627422	.621802	.616219	.610673	.605166
5	.590490	.583958	.577484	.571068	.564708	.558406	.552160	.545970	.539835	.533756
6	.531441	.524394	.517426	.510535	.503720	.496981	.490318	.483729	.477214	.470773
7	.478297	.470906	.463613	.456418	.449318	.442313	.435402	.428584	.421858	.415222
8	.430467	.422874	.415398	.408038	.400792	.393659	.386637	.379726	.372922	.366226
9	.387420	.379741	.372196	.364786	.357506	.350356	.343334	.336437	.329663	.323011
10	.348678	.341007	.333488	.326118	.318896	.311817	.304880	.298083	.291422	.284896
11	.313811	.306224	.298805	.291550	.284455	.277517	.270734	.264102	.257617	.251278
12	.282430	.274989	.267729	.260646	.253734	.246990	.240412	.233994	.227734	.221627
13	.254187	.246941	.239886	.233017	.226331	.219821	.213486	.207319	.201317	.195475
14	.228768	.221753	.214937	.208317	.201887	.195641	.189575	.183684	.177964	.172409
15	.205891	.199134	.192584	.186236	.180083	.174121	.168343	.162744	.157320	.152065
16	.185302	.178822	.172555	.166495	.160634	.154967	.149488	.144191	.139071	.134121
17	.166772	.160582	.154609	.148846	.143286	.137921	.132746	.127754	.122939	.118295
18	.150095	.144203	.138530	.133069	.127811	.122750	.117878	.113190	.108678	.104336
19	.135085	.129494	.124123	.118963	.114007	.109247	.104676	.100286	.096071	.092024
20	.121577	.116286	.111214	.106353	.101694	.097230	.092952	.088853	.084927	.081166

TERM CERTAIN UNITRUST REMAINDER FACTORS

ADJUSTED PAYOUT RATE

YEARS	12.0%	12.2%	12.4%	12.6%	12.8%	13.0%	13.2%	13.4%	13.6%	13.8%
1	.880000	.878000	.876000	.874000	.872000	.870000	.868000	.866000	.864000	.862000
2	.774400	.770884	.767376	.763876	.760384	.756900	.753424	.749956	.746496	.743044
3	.681472	.676836	.672221	.667628	.663055	.658503	.653972	.649462	.644973	.640504
4	.599695	.594262	.588866	.583507	.578184	.572898	.567648	.562434	.557256	.552114
5	.527732	.521762	.515847	.509985	.504176	.498421	.492718	.487068	.481469	.475923
6	.464404	.458107	.451882	.445727	.439642	.433626	.427679	.421801	.415990	.410245
7	.408676	.402218	.395848	.389565	.383368	.377255	.371226	.365279	.359415	.353631
8	.359635	.353147	.346763	.340480	.334297	.328212	.322224	.316332	.310535	.304830
9	.316478	.310063	.303764	.297579	.291507	.285544	.279690	.273944	.268302	.262764
10	.278501	.272236	.266098	.260084	.254194	.248423	.242771	.237235	.231813	.226502
11	.245081	.239023	.233102	.227314	.221657	.216128	.210725	.205446	.200286	.195245
12	.215671	.209862	.204197	.198672	.193285	.188032	.182910	.177916	.173047	.168301
13	.189791	.184259	.178877	.173640	.168544	.163588	.158766	.154075	.149513	.145076
14	.167016	.161779	.156696	.151761	.146971	.142321	.137809	.133429	.129179	.125055
15	.146974	.142042	.137266	.132639	.128158	.123819	.119618	.115550	.111611	.107798
16	.129337	.124713	.120245	.115927	.111754	.107723	.103828	.100066	.096432	.092922
17	.113817	.109498	.105334	.101320	.097450	.093719	.090123	.086657	.083317	.080098
18	.100159	.096139	.092273	.088554	.084976	.081535	.078227	.075045	.071986	.069045
19	.088140	.084410	.080831	.077396	.074099	.070936	.067901	.064989	.062196	.059517
20	.077563	.074112	.070808	.067644	.064614	.061714	.058938	.056280	.053737	.051303

ADJUSTED PAYOUT RATE

YEARS	14.0%	14.2%	14.4%	14.6%	14.8%	15.0%	15.2%	15.4%	15.6%	15.8%
1	.860000	.858000	.856000	.854000	.852000	.850000	.848000	.846000	.844000	.842000
2	.739600	.736164	.732736	.729316	.725904	.722500	.719104	.715716	.712336	.708964
3	.636056	.631629	.627222	.622836	.618470	.614125	.609800	.605496	.601212	.596948
4	.547008	.541937	.536902	.531902	.526937	.522006	.517111	.512249	.507423	.502630
5	.470427	.464982	.459588	.454244	.448950	.443705	.438510	.433363	.428265	.423214
6	.404567	.398955	.393407	.387925	.382505	.377149	.371856	.366625	.361455	.356347
7	.347928	.342303	.336757	.331288	.325895	.320577	.315334	.310165	.305068	.300044
8	.299218	.293696	.288264	.282920	.277662	.272491	.267403	.262399	.257478	.252637
9	.257327	.251991	.246754	.241613	.236568	.231617	.226758	.221990	.217311	.212720
10	.221302	.216209	.211221	.206338	.201556	.196874	.192291	.187803	.183411	.179110
11	.190319	.185507	.180805	.176212	.171726	.167343	.163063	.158882	.154799	.150811
12	.163675	.159165	.154769	.150485	.146310	.142242	.138277	.134414	.130650	.126983
13	.140760	.136564	.132483	.128515	.124656	.120905	.117259	.113714	.110269	.106920
14	.121054	.117172	.113405	.109751	.106207	.102770	.099436	.096202	.093067	.090026
15	.104106	.100533	.097075	.093728	.090489	.087354	.084321	.081387	.078548	.075802
16	.089531	.086257	.083096	.080043	.077096	.074251	.071505	.068853	.066295	.063825
17	.076997	.074009	.071130	.068357	.065686	.063113	.060636	.058250	.055953	.053741
18	.066217	.063500	.060887	.058377	.055965	.053646	.051419	.049280	.047224	.045250
19	.056947	.054483	.052120	.049854	.047682	.045599	.043603	.041690	.039857	.038100
20	.048974	.046746	.044614	.042575	.040625	.038760	.036976	.035270	.033639	.032081

TERM CERTAIN UNITRUST REMAINDER FACTORS

ADJUSTED PAYOUT RATE

YEARS	16.0%	16.2%	16.4%	16.6%	16.8%	17.0%	17.2%	17.4%	17.6%	17.8%
1	.840000	.838000	.836000	.834000	.832000	.830000	.828000	.826000	.824000	.822000
2	.705600	.702244	.698896	.695556	.692224	.688900	.685584	.682276	.678976	.675684
3	.592704	.588480	.584277	.580094	.575930	.571787	.567664	.563560	.559476	.555412
4	.497871	.493147	.488456	.483798	.479174	.474583	.470025	.465501	.461008	.456549
5	.418212	.413257	.408349	.403488	.398673	.393904	.389181	.384503	.379871	.375283
6	.351298	.346309	.341380	.336509	.331696	.326940	.322242	.317600	.313014	.308483
7	.295090	.290207	.285393	.280648	.275971	.271361	.266816	.262337	.257923	.253573
8	.247876	.243194	.238589	.234061	.229608	.225229	.220924	.216691	.212529	.208437
9	.208216	.203796	.199460	.195207	.191034	.186940	.182925	.178987	.175124	.171335
10	.174901	.170781	.166749	.162802	.158940	.155160	.151462	.147843	.144302	.140837
11	.146917	.143115	.139402	.135777	.132238	.128783	.125410	.122118	.118905	.115768
12	.123410	.119930	.116540	.113238	.110022	.106890	.103840	.100870	.097978	.095162
13	.103665	.100501	.097428	.094441	.091538	.088719	.085979	.083318	.080733	.078223
14	.087078	.084220	.081449	.078763	.076160	.073637	.071191	.068821	.066524	.064299
15	.073146	.070577	.068092	.065689	.063365	.061118	.058946	.056846	.054816	.052854
16	.061442	.059143	.056925	.054784	.052720	.050728	.048807	.046955	.045168	.043446
17	.051612	.049562	.047589	.045690	.043863	.042104	.040412	.038785	.037219	.035713
18	.043354	.041533	.039784	.038106	.036494	.034947	.033462	.032036	.030668	.029356
19	.036417	.034805	.033260	.031780	.030363	.029006	.027706	.026462	.025271	.024130
20	.030590	.029166	.027805	.026505	.025262	.024075	.022941	.021858	.020823	.019835

ADJUSTED PAYOUT RATE

YEARS	18.0%	18.2%	18.4%	18.6%	18.8%	19.0%	19.2%	19.4%	19.6%	19.8%
1	.820000	.818000	.816000	.814000	.812000	.810000	.808000	.806000	.804000	.802000
2	.672400	.669124	.665856	.662596	.659344	.656100	.652864	.649636	.646416	.643204
3	.551368	.547343	.543338	.539353	.535387	.531441	.527514	.523607	.519718	.515850
4	.452122	.447727	.443364	.439033	.434735	.430467	.426231	.422027	.417854	.413711
5	.370740	.366241	.361785	.357373	.353004	.348678	.344395	.340154	.335954	.331797
6	.304007	.299585	.295217	.290902	.286640	.282430	.278271	.274164	.270107	.266101
7	.249285	.245060	.240897	.236794	.232751	.228768	.224843	.220976	.217166	.213413
8	.204414	.200459	.196572	.192750	.188994	.185302	.181673	.178107	.174602	.171157
9	.167620	.163976	.160403	.156899	.153463	.150095	.146792	.143554	.140380	.137268
10	.137448	.134132	.130889	.127716	.124612	.121577	.118608	.115705	.112865	.110089
11	.112707	.109720	.106805	.103961	.101185	.098477	.095835	.093258	.090744	.088291
12	.092420	.089751	.087153	.084624	.082162	.079766	.077435	.075166	.072958	.070810
13	.075784	.073416	.071117	.068884	.066716	.064611	.062567	.060584	.058658	.056789
14	.062143	.060055	.058031	.056071	.054173	.052335	.050554	.048830	.047161	.045545
15	.050957	.049125	.047354	.045642	.043989	.042391	.040848	.039357	.037918	.036527
16	.041785	.040184	.038640	.037153	.035719	.034337	.033005	.031722	.030486	.029295
17	.034264	.032870	.031531	.030242	.029004	.027813	.026668	.025568	.024511	.023494
18	.028096	.026888	.025729	.024617	.023551	.022528	.021548	.020608	.019706	.018843
19	.023039	.021994	.020995	.020038	.019123	.018248	.017411	.016610	.015844	.015112
20	.018892	.017991	.017132	.016311	.015528	.014781	.014068	.013388	.012739	.012120

SINGLE LIFE UNITRUST REMAINDER FACTORS

ADJUSTED PAYOUT RATE

AGE	4.0%	4.2%	4.4%	4.6%	4.8%	5.0%	5.2%	5.4%	5.6%	5.8%
0	.06864	.06177	.05580	.05061	.04609	.04215	.03871	.03570	.03307	.03075
1	.06253	.05543	.04925	.04388	.03919	.03509	.03151	.02838	.02563	.02321
2	.06444	.05716	.05081	.04528	.04045	.03622	.03252	.02927	.02642	.02391
3	.06666	.05920	.05268	.04699	.04201	.03765	.03382	.03046	.02750	.02490
4	.06908	.06143	.05475	.04889	.04376	.03926	.03530	.03182	.02876	.02605
5	.07167	.06384	.05697	.05095	.04567	.04103	.03694	.03334	.03016	.02735
6	.07440	.06637	.05933	.05315	.04771	.04292	.03870	.03497	.03168	.02876
7	.07727	.06905	.06183	.05547	.04987	.04494	.04058	.03673	.03332	.03029
8	.08027	.07186	.06445	.05792	.05216	.04708	.04258	.03859	.03506	.03192
9	.08343	.07482	.06722	.06052	.05460	.04936	.04471	.04060	.03694	.03369
10	.08674	.07793	.07015	.06327	.05718	.05179	.04700	.04274	.03896	.03559
11	.09021	.08120	.07323	.06617	.05991	.05435	.04942	.04502	.04111	.03762
12	.09382	.08461	.07645	.06920	.06277	.05706	.05197	.04744	.04339	.03978
13	.09753	.08812	.07976	.07234	.06574	.05985	.05461	.04993	.04576	.04202
14	.10129	.09168	.08313	.07552	.06874	.06269	.05729	.05247	.04815	.04428
15	.10509	.09527	.08652	.07872	.07176	.06554	.05999	.05501	.05055	.04655
16	.10889	.09886	.08991	.08192	.07478	.06839	.06267	.05754	.05294	.04880
17	.11273	.10249	.09334	.08515	.07782	.07126	.06537	.06008	.05533	.05105
18	.11662	.10616	.09680	.08842	.08090	.07415	.06809	.06264	.05774	.05332
19	.12061	.10994	.10037	.09178	.08407	.07714	.07091	.06529	.06023	.05566
20	.12473	.11384	.10406	.09527	.08737	.08025	.07383	.06805	.06283	.05811
21	.12900	.11790	.10790	.09891	.09080	.08349	.07690	.07094	.06555	.06068
22	.13341	.12208	.11188	.10267	.09436	.08686	.08008	.07395	.06839	.06336
23	.13798	.12643	.11601	.10659	.09808	.09038	.08342	.07710	.07138	.06618
24	.14272	.13095	.12031	.11069	.10197	.09408	.08692	.08042	.07452	.06915
25	.14766	.13567	.12481	.11497	.10605	.09795	.09060	.08392	.07784	.07230
26	.15279	.14058	.12950	.11945	.11032	.10202	.09447	.08760	.08134	.07563
27	.15814	.14571	.13442	.12415	.11481	.10631	.09856	.09149	.08505	.07916
28	.16368	.15104	.13953	.12904	.11949	.11078	.10284	.09558	.08895	.08288
29	.16943	.15656	.14484	.13414	.12438	.11546	.10731	.09986	.09304	.08679
30	.17537	.16229	.15034	.13943	.12946	.12034	.11198	.10433	.09732	.09089
31	.18150	.16821	.15605	.14493	.13474	.12541	.11685	.10900	.10179	.09517
32	.18783	.17433	.16196	.15063	.14023	.13069	.12193	.11387	.10647	.09966
33	.19438	.18068	.16810	.15655	.14595	.13620	.12723	.11897	.11137	.10437
34	.20115	.18724	.17446	.16270	.15189	.14193	.13275	.12430	.11650	.10930
35	.20816	.19405	.18107	.16910	.15808	.14791	.13853	.12987	.12187	.11448
36	.21540	.20109	.18791	.17574	.16451	.15414	.14455	.13569	.12749	.11990
37	.22287	.20838	.19500	.18263	.17120	.16062	.15083	.14177	.13337	.12558
38	.23060	.21593	.20236	.18979	.17816	.16739	.15739	.14813	.13953	.13154
39	.23858	.22374	.20998	.19723	.18540	.17442	.16423	.15477	.14597	.13779
40	.24684	.23183	.21789	.20496	.19294	.18177	.17138	.16172	.15272	.14434
41	.25538	.24021	.22611	.21299	.20079	.18943	.17885	.16899	.15980	.15123
42	.26421	.24889	.23463	.22134	.20896	.19741	.18665	.17660	.16721	.15845
43	.27332	.25786	.24344	.23000	.21744	.20572	.19477	.18453	.17496	.16601
44	.28271	.26712	.25257	.23896	.22625	.21435	.20322	.19281	.18305	.17391
45	.29235	.27665	.26196	.24821	.23534	.22328	.21198	.20139	.19145	.18213
46	.30225	.28644	.27163	.25774	.24472	.23251	.22105	.21028	.20018	.19068
47	.31238	.29647	.28155	.26754	.25438	.24201	.23040	.21947	.20919	.19952
48	.32275	.30676	.29173	.27760	.26431	.25181	.24004	.22896	.21852	.20868
49	.33335	.31729	.30217	.28794	.27453	.26190	.24999	.23876	.22817	.21817
50	.34419	.32808	.31289	.29856	.28505	.27229	.26026	.24889	.23814	.22799
51	.35528	.33912	.32387	.30946	.29585	.28299	.27083	.25933	.24845	.23815
52	.36657	.35038	.33507	.32060	.30691	.29395	.28168	.27005	.25904	.24861
53	.37805	.36185	.34651	.33198	.31821	.30517	.29280	.28106	.26993	.25937
54	.38972	.37352	.35815	.34358	.32976	.31664	.30418	.29234	.28110	.27042

SINGLE LIFE UNITRUST REMAINDER FACTORS

ADJUSTED PAYOUT RATE

AGE	4.0%	4.2%	4.4%	4.6%	4.8%	5.0%	5.2%	5.4%	5.6%	5.8%
55	.40157	.38539	.37002	.35542	.34155	.32836	.31583	.30390	.29256	.28177
56	.41361	.39746	.38209	.36748	.35358	.34034	.32774	.31574	.30431	.29342
57	.42582	.40971	.39437	.37976	.36584	.35257	.33992	.32785	.31634	.30536
58	.43817	.42212	.40682	.39222	.37829	.36500	.35231	.34019	.32862	.31756
59	.45061	.43464	.41939	.40482	.39090	.37759	.36488	.35272	.34109	.32996
60	.46314	.44726	.43207	.41754	.40364	.39034	.37761	.36542	.35375	.34257
61	.47577	.45999	.44488	.43041	.41655	.40326	.39053	.37833	.36662	.35540
62	.48852	.47286	.45785	.44345	.42964	.41639	.40367	.39146	.37974	.36848
63	.50141	.48589	.47098	.45667	.44293	.42972	.41703	.40484	.39311	.38184
64	.51440	.49903	.48426	.47005	.45638	.44324	.43060	.41843	.40671	.39544
65	.52749	.51229	.49766	.48357	.47001	.45694	.44435	.43223	.42054	.40927
66	.54069	.52568	.51121	.49726	.48381	.47084	.45833	.44626	.43461	.42337
67	.55404	.53924	.52495	.51115	.49784	.48498	.47256	.46056	.44898	.43778
68	.56751	.55293	.53883	.52521	.51205	.49932	.48701	.47511	.46360	.45246
69	.58105	.56671	.55283	.53940	.52640	.51382	.50165	.48985	.47844	.46738
70	.59461	.58052	.56687	.55365	.54084	.52843	.51639	.50473	.49342	.48245
71	.60813	.59431	.58091	.56791	.55529	.54306	.53118	.51966	.50847	.49761
72	.62158	.60804	.59490	.58213	.56973	.55768	.54598	.53461	.52357	.51283
73	.63493	.62168	.60881	.59629	.58411	.57227	.56076	.54955	.53866	.52806
74	.64822	.63528	.62268	.61042	.59848	.58686	.57555	.56453	.55380	.54335
75	.66149	.64887	.63657	.62458	.61290	.60151	.59041	.57959	.56904	.55875
76	.67478	.66249	.65049	.63880	.62739	.61625	.60538	.59478	.58443	.57432
77	.68807	.67612	.66446	.65307	.64194	.63108	.62046	.61009	.59995	.59005
78	.70134	.68975	.67843	.66736	.65654	.64596	.63561	.62548	.61558	.60590
79	.71451	.70330	.69233	.68160	.67109	.66081	.65074	.64088	.63123	.62178
80	.72749	.71666	.70605	.69566	.68548	.67550	.66573	.65615	.64676	.63755
81	.74019	.72975	.71950	.70946	.69961	.68994	.68047	.67117	.66205	.65310
82	.75256	.74250	.73263	.72293	.71342	.70407	.69490	.68589	.67705	.66837
83	.76461	.75493	.74542	.73608	.72690	.71788	.70902	.70031	.69175	.68333
84	.77641	.76712	.75798	.74900	.74016	.73147	.72292	.71451	.70624	.69810
85	.78802	.77913	.77037	.76175	.75326	.74491	.73668	.72859	.72061	.71276
86	.79937	.79086	.78248	.77423	.76610	.75808	.75019	.74241	.73474	.72719
87	.81030	.80218	.79418	.78628	.77850	.77083	.76326	.75580	.74844	.74118
88	.82081	.81307	.80544	.79790	.79047	.78313	.77589	.76874	.76169	.75473
89	.83091	.82355	.81628	.80909	.80200	.79500	.78808	.78125	.77450	.76783
90	.84060	.83360	.82668	.81985	.81309	.80642	.79982	.79330	.78685	.78048
91	.84973	.84308	.83650	.83000	.82357	.81721	.81092	.80470	.79855	.79246
92	.85814	.85182	.84556	.83937	.83325	.82718	.82119	.81525	.80937	.80356
93	.86587	.85985	.85390	.84800	.84215	.83637	.83064	.82497	.81936	.81379
94	.87305	.86732	.86164	.85601	.85044	.84491	.83944	.83402	.82865	.82333
95	.87983	.87437	.86895	.86359	.85827	.85300	.84778	.84260	.83746	.83237
96	.88618	.88097	.87582	.87070	.86563	.86060	.85561	.85066	.84575	.84088
97	.89204	.88708	.88216	.87727	.87243	.86762	.86285	.85811	.85341	.84875
98	.89753	.89280	.88810	.88343	.87880	.87420	.86964	.86511	.86061	.85614
99	.90287	.89836	.89388	.88943	.88501	.88062	.87626	.87193	.86763	.86336
100	.90804	.90375	.89948	.89525	.89103	.88685	.88269	.87856	.87445	.87037
101	.91313	.90905	.90500	.90097	.89696	.89298	.88902	.88509	.88118	.87729
102	.91811	.91425	.91040	.90658	.90278	.89900	.89524	.89150	.88778	.88408
103	.92304	.91939	.91575	.91214	.90854	.90496	.90139	.89785	.89432	.89081
104	.92828	.92485	.92144	.91805	.91467	.91131	.90796	.90463	.90131	.89800
105	.93340	.93020	.92701	.92383	.92067	.91751	.91437	.91125	.90813	.90502
106	.93992	.93701	.93411	.93122	.92834	.92546	.92260	.91974	.91689	.91405
107	.94778	.94522	.94268	.94013	.93760	.93507	.93254	.93002	.92750	.92499
108	.95981	.95782	.95583	.95385	.95187	.94989	.94791	.94593	.94396	.94199
109	.98000	.97900	.97800	.97700	.97600	.97500	.97400	.97300	.97200	.97100

SINGLE LIFE UNITRUST REMAINDER FACTORS

ADJUSTED PAYOUT RATE

AGE	6.0%	6.2%	6.4%	6.6%	6.8%	7.0%	7.2%	7.4%	7.6%	7.8%
0	.02872	.02693	.02534	.02395	.02271	.02161	.02063	.01976	.01898	.01828
1	.02109	.01922	.01756	.01610	.01480	.01365	.01263	.01171	.01090	.01017
2	.02170	.01975	.01802	.01650	.01514	.01393	.01286	.01190	.01104	.01028
3	.02260	.02056	.01876	.01717	.01575	.01449	.01336	.01235	.01145	.01064
4	.02366	.02155	.01967	.01800	.01652	.01520	.01401	.01296	.01201	.01116
5	.02487	.02266	.02071	.01896	.01741	.01603	.01479	.01368	.01269	.01179
6	.02618	.02389	.02184	.02003	.01841	.01696	.01566	.01450	.01345	.01251
7	.02761	.02522	.02309	.02120	.01950	.01799	.01663	.01540	.01431	.01332
8	.02914	.02665	.02444	.02246	.02069	.01910	.01768	.01640	.01524	.01420
9	.03079	.02821	.02590	.02384	.02199	.02033	.01884	.01750	.01629	.01520
10	.03259	.02990	.02750	.02535	.02342	.02169	.02013	.01872	.01745	.01631
11	.03450	.03172	.02922	.02698	.02497	.02316	.02153	.02006	.01872	.01752
12	.03655	.03365	.03106	.02872	.02663	.02474	.02303	.02149	.02010	.01884
13	.03867	.03566	.03297	.03054	.02835	.02638	.02460	.02299	.02154	.02021
14	.04081	.03770	.03490	.03237	.03010	.02804	.02619	.02450	.02298	.02159
15	.04296	.03973	.03682	.03419	.03182	.02968	.02775	.02599	.02439	.02294
16	.04508	.04173	.03871	.03598	.03352	.03129	.02926	.02743	.02576	.02424
17	.04720	.04372	.04059	.03775	.03519	.03287	.03076	.02884	.02710	.02551
18	.04933	.04573	.04248	.03953	.03686	.03444	.03224	.03024	.02842	.02676
19	.05153	.04780	.04443	.04137	.03859	.03607	.03378	.03169	.02978	.02804
20	.05384	.04997	.04647	.04329	.04040	.03778	.03539	.03321	.03122	.02940
21	.05626	.05226	.04862	.04532	.04232	.03958	.03709	.03481	.03274	.03083
22	.05879	.05465	.05088	.04745	.04432	.04148	.03888	.03650	.03433	.03234
23	.06146	.05716	.05325	.04969	.04645	.04348	.04077	.03830	.03603	.03394
24	.06427	.05983	.05578	.05208	.04871	.04562	.04280	.04021	.03784	.03566
25	.06726	.06266	.05846	.05463	.05112	.04791	.04497	.04227	.03980	.03752
26	.07042	.06566	.06131	.05734	.05369	.05035	.04729	.04448	.04189	.03951
27	.07379	.06887	.06436	.06024	.05646	.05298	.04979	.04686	.04416	.04168
28	.07733	.07225	.06758	.06331	.05938	.05577	.05245	.04940	.04658	.04398
29	.08106	.07581	.07099	.06656	.06248	.05873	.05528	.05210	.04916	.04645
30	.08498	.07956	.07457	.06998	.06575	.06186	.05827	.05495	.05189	.04906
31	.08909	.08348	.07833	.07358	.06920	.06515	.06142	.05797	.05478	.05182
32	.09339	.08761	.08228	.07736	.07282	.06863	.06475	.06116	.05783	.05475
33	.09791	.09195	.08645	.08136	.07666	.07231	.06828	.06454	.06108	.05786
34	.10265	.09651	.09082	.08557	.08070	.07619	.07200	.06812	.06452	.06117
35	.10764	.10131	.09545	.09002	.08498	.08030	.07596	.07193	.06818	.06469
36	.11287	.10635	.10031	.09470	.08949	.08465	.08015	.07596	.07206	.06842
37	.11835	.11165	.10542	.09963	.09424	.08923	.08457	.08022	.07617	.07238
38	.12412	.11722	.11081	.10484	.09927	.09409	.08926	.08475	.08054	.07661
39	.13017	.12308	.11648	.11032	.10458	.09922	.09422	.08955	.08518	.08109
40	.13653	.12925	.12246	.11612	.11020	.10466	.09949	.09465	.09011	.08587
41	.14322	.13575	.12877	.12225	.11614	.11043	.10508	.10007	.09537	.09097
42	.15025	.14259	.13542	.12871	.12243	.11654	.11101	.10583	.10097	.09640
43	.15762	.14977	.14242	.13552	.12905	.12298	.11729	.11193	.10690	.10217
44	.16534	.15731	.14976	.14269	.13604	.12979	.12391	.11838	.11318	.10828
45	.17338	.16516	.15743	.15017	.14334	.13691	.13086	.12516	.11979	.11472
46	.18174	.17334	.16544	.15800	.15099	.14438	.13816	.13228	.12674	.12150
47	.19041	.18184	.17375	.16613	.15895	.15217	.14576	.13972	.13400	.12860
48	.19941	.19066	.18240	.17461	.16724	.16029	.15371	.14749	.14161	.13604
49	.20873	.19981	.19138	.18342	.17588	.16875	.16201	.15562	.14956	.14383
50	.21839	.20931	.20072	.19259	.18489	.17759	.17067	.16412	.15790	.15199
51	.22840	.21917	.21042	.20212	.19426	.18679	.17971	.17299	.16660	.16054
52	.23872	.22933	.22043	.21198	.20395	.19633	.18909	.18220	.17566	.16943
53	.24934	.23981	.23076	.22216	.21399	.20621	.19881	.19176	.18506	.17867
54	.26026	.25060	.24141	.23267	.22434	.21642	.20886	.20166	.19480	.18826

SINGLE LIFE UNITRUST REMAINDER FACTORS

ADJUSTED PAYOUT RATE

AGE	6.0%	6.2%	6.4%	6.6%	6.8%	7.0%	7.2%	7.4%	7.6%	7.8%
55	.27149	.26171	.25239	.24351	.23504	.22697	.21927	.21192	.20491	.19821
56	.28303	.27313	.26369	.25468	.24608	.23787	.23003	.22254	.21538	.20854
57	.29488	.28487	.27531	.26618	.25746	.24912	.24114	.23351	.22622	.21923
58	.30699	.29688	.28722	.27798	.26914	.26067	.25257	.24481	.23738	.23025
59	.31932	.30913	.29937	.29002	.28107	.27249	.26427	.25639	.24882	.24157
60	.33186	.32159	.31175	.30231	.29325	.28457	.27623	.26823	.26055	.25317
61	.34463	.33429	.32437	.31485	.30571	.29692	.28848	.28037	.27257	.26507
62	.35767	.34728	.33730	.32770	.31847	.30960	.30106	.29285	.28495	.27734
63	.37100	.36057	.35053	.34087	.33157	.32262	.31400	.30569	.29769	.28998
64	.38458	.37412	.36404	.35433	.34498	.33596	.32726	.31887	.31078	.30298
65	.39841	.38794	.37783	.36809	.35868	.34961	.34085	.33239	.32422	.31633
66	.41252	.40205	.39193	.38216	.37272	.36361	.35479	.34628	.33804	.33008
67	.42696	.41650	.40639	.39661	.38715	.37800	.36915	.36059	.35230	.34428
68	.44169	.43126	.42117	.41139	.40193	.39277	.38390	.37530	.36697	.35890
69	.45666	.44628	.43622	.42648	.41703	.40787	.39898	.39037	.38201	.37391
70	.47181	.46150	.45149	.44178	.43236	.42321	.41433	.40571	.39735	.38922
71	.48707	.47683	.46689	.45723	.44785	.43873	.42987	.42126	.41290	.40476
72	.50239	.49225	.48238	.47279	.46346	.45439	.44556	.43697	.42862	.42048
73	.51774	.50770	.49793	.48841	.47915	.47013	.46135	.45280	.44447	.43635
74	.53316	.52324	.51358	.50416	.49498	.48603	.47731	.46880	.46051	.45243
75	.54872	.53894	.52939	.52008	.51100	.50214	.49349	.48505	.47681	.46877
76	.56446	.55483	.54543	.53624	.52728	.51852	.50996	.50160	.49344	.48546
77	.58037	.57091	.56167	.55263	.54380	.53516	.52671	.51845	.51038	.50247
78	.59643	.58716	.57809	.56922	.56053	.55203	.54372	.53557	.52760	.51980
79	.61253	.60346	.59459	.58590	.57738	.56904	.56086	.55286	.54501	.53732
80	.62853	.61969	.61102	.60252	.59419	.58601	.57800	.57014	.56243	.55487
81	.64433	.63571	.62726	.61897	.61082	.60283	.59499	.58729	.57974	.57232
82	.65984	.65146	.64324	.63515	.62722	.61942	.61176	.60423	.59683	.58957
83	.67506	.66693	.65893	.65108	.64335	.63575	.62828	.62093	.61371	.60660
84	.69010	.68222	.67447	.66684	.65934	.65195	.64468	.63753	.63049	.62356
85	.70503	.69742	.68993	.68255	.67528	.66812	.66106	.65411	.64727	.64053
86	.71974	.71241	.70517	.69805	.69102	.68410	.67727	.67054	.66390	.65736
87	.73402	.72696	.72000	.71313	.70635	.69967	.69307	.68656	.68014	.67381
88	.74786	.74108	.73438	.72777	.72125	.71480	.70845	.70217	.69597	.68985
89	.76125	.75475	.74832	.74198	.73571	.72951	.72339	.71734	.71137	.70547
90	.77418	.76796	.76180	.75572	.74971	.74376	.73788	.73207	.72633	.72065
91	.78645	.78049	.77460	.76878	.76302	.75732	.75168	.74610	.74058	.73512
92	.79780	.79211	.78647	.78089	.77537	.76990	.76449	.75913	.75383	.74858
93	.80829	.80283	.79743	.79208	.78679	.78154	.77634	.77119	.76610	.76105
94	.81806	.81283	.80765	.80253	.79744	.79240	.78741	.78247	.77756	.77270
95	.82733	.82233	.81737	.81245	.80757	.80274	.79795	.79320	.78849	.78382
96	.83605	.83126	.82651	.82180	.81712	.81248	.80788	.80332	.79880	.79431
97	.84413	.83953	.83498	.83046	.82597	.82152	.81710	.81271	.80836	.80404
98	.85171	.84731	.84294	.83860	.83429	.83002	.82577	.82155	.81737	.81321
99	.85911	.85490	.85071	.84656	.84243	.83832	.83425	.83020	.82618	.82219
100	.86632	.86229	.85828	.85431	.85035	.84642	.84252	.83864	.83478	.83095
101	.87342	.86958	.86575	.86195	.85818	.85442	.85069	.84698	.84329	.83962
102	.88040	.87674	.87310	.86947	.86587	.86229	.85873	.85518	.85166	.84815
103	.88732	.88384	.88038	.87694	.87351	.87010	.86671	.86334	.85998	.85663
104	.89471	.89143	.88817	.88492	.88169	.87847	.87526	.87207	.86889	.86573
105	.90193	.89885	.89578	.89272	.88967	.88664	.88361	.88060	.87760	.87461
106	.91122	.90840	.90559	.90278	.89999	.89720	.89442	.89165	.88888	.88613
107	.92249	.91999	.91750	.91501	.91253	.91005	.90758	.90511	.90265	.90019
108	.94002	.93805	.93609	.93412	.93216	.93020	.92824	.92629	.92434	.92239
109	.97000	.96900	.96800	.96700	.96600	.96500	.96400	.96300	.96200	.96100

SINGLE LIFE UNITRUST REMAINDER FACTORS

ADJUSTED PAYOUT RATE

AGE	8.0%	8.2%	8.4%	8.6%	8.8%	9.0%	9.2%	9.4%	9.6%	9.8%
0	.01765	.01709	.01658	.01612	.01570	.01532	.01497	.01466	.01437	.01410
1	.00951	.00892	.00839	.00791	.00747	.00708	.00672	.00639	.00609	.00582
2	.00959	.00896	.00840	.00790	.00744	.00702	.00664	.00629	.00598	.00569
3	.00992	.00926	.00867	.00814	.00765	.00721	.00681	.00644	.00611	.00580
4	.01039	.00970	.00908	.00851	.00800	.00753	.00711	.00672	.00636	.00604
5	.01098	.01026	.00960	.00900	.00846	.00796	.00751	.00710	.00672	.00637
6	.01166	.01089	.01019	.00956	.00899	.00846	.00799	.00755	.00715	.00678
7	.01242	.01161	.01088	.01021	.00960	.00905	.00854	.00808	.00765	.00726
8	.01326	.01241	.01163	.01093	.01029	.00970	.00917	.00867	.00822	.00781
9	.01421	.01331	.01249	.01175	.01107	.01045	.00988	.00936	.00889	.00845
10	.01526	.01432	.01346	.01268	.01196	.01131	.01071	.01016	.00965	.00918
11	.01643	.01543	.01453	.01370	.01295	.01226	.01162	.01104	.01051	.01001
12	.01769	.01664	.01569	.01482	.01403	.01330	.01263	.01202	.01145	.01093
13	.01901	.01791	.01691	.01600	.01516	.01440	.01369	.01304	.01245	.01190
14	.02033	.01918	.01813	.01717	.01629	.01548	.01474	.01406	.01343	.01285
15	.02162	.02041	.01931	.01831	.01738	.01653	.01576	.01504	.01437	.01376
16	.02286	.02160	.02044	.01938	.01841	.01752	.01670	.01595	.01525	.01460
17	.02406	.02274	.02152	.02041	.01940	.01846	.01760	.01680	.01607	.01539
18	.02524	.02386	.02258	.02142	.02035	.01936	.01846	.01762	.01685	.01613
19	.02646	.02500	.02367	.02245	.02132	.02029	.01933	.01845	.01764	.01689
20	.02773	.02621	.02481	.02353	.02235	.02126	.02025	.01933	.01847	.01768
21	.02909	.02749	.02603	.02468	.02344	.02229	.02124	.02026	.01936	.01852
22	.03052	.02884	.02730	.02589	.02458	.02338	.02227	.02124	.02029	.01940
23	.03203	.03028	.02867	.02718	.02581	.02454	.02337	.02229	.02128	.02035
24	.03367	.03183	.03013	.02857	.02713	.02580	.02456	.02342	.02236	.02138
25	.03543	.03350	.03172	.03008	.02857	.02717	.02587	.02467	.02355	.02251
26	.03732	.03530	.03344	.03172	.03013	.02865	.02729	.02602	.02484	.02375
27	.03939	.03727	.03532	.03351	.03183	.03028	.02885	.02751	.02627	.02511
28	.04159	.03937	.03732	.03543	.03367	.03204	.03052	.02911	.02780	.02658
29	.04394	.04162	.03947	.03748	.03564	.03392	.03233	.03084	.02946	.02818
30	.04644	.04401	.04176	.03967	.03773	.03593	.03425	.03269	.03124	.02988
31	.04908	.04654	.04419	.04200	.03996	.03807	.03630	.03466	.03312	.03169
32	.05189	.04923	.04676	.04447	.04233	.04034	.03849	.03676	.03514	.03363
33	.05488	.05210	.04952	.04711	.04487	.04278	.04083	.03901	.03731	.03571
34	.05805	.05515	.05245	.04993	.04758	.04538	.04333	.04142	.03962	.03794
35	.06144	.05841	.05558	.05295	.05048	.04818	.04603	.04401	.04212	.04035
36	.06503	.06187	.05892	.05616	.05358	.05116	.04890	.04678	.04480	.04293
37	.06885	.06555	.06247	.05958	.05688	.05435	.05198	.04975	.04766	.04570
38	.07293	.06949	.06627	.06325	.06043	.05777	.05528	.05295	.05075	.04868
39	.07726	.07368	.07032	.06717	.06421	.06143	.05882	.05637	.05406	.05189
40	.08189	.07816	.07465	.07137	.06827	.06537	.06263	.06006	.05764	.05535
41	.08683	.08295	.07930	.07587	.07264	.06960	.06674	.06405	.06150	.05910
42	.09210	.08807	.08427	.08069	.07733	.07415	.07116	.06833	.06567	.06315
43	.09771	.09352	.08957	.08585	.08233	.07902	.07589	.07294	.07014	.06750
44	.10367	.09932	.09521	.09134	.08768	.08423	.08096	.07787	.07495	.07218
45	.10994	.10543	.10117	.09715	.09334	.08974	.08634	.08311	.08005	.07716
46	.11656	.11189	.10747	.10329	.09933	.09559	.09204	.08867	.08548	.08245
47	.12349	.11866	.11408	.10974	.10564	.10174	.09805	.09454	.09121	.08805
48	.13077	.12577	.12103	.11654	.11228	.10823	.10439	.10074	.09727	.09397
49	.13839	.13323	.12833	.12368	.11926	.11506	.11107	.10728	.10366	.10022
50	.14639	.14107	.13601	.13120	.12663	.12228	.11813	.11419	.11043	.10685
51	.15477	.14928	.14407	.13910	.13437	.12987	.12558	.12149	.11758	.11386
52	.16350	.15785	.15248	.14735	.14247	.13781	.13337	.12913	.12508	.12122
53	.17258	.16678	.16124	.15597	.15093	.14612	.14153	.13714	.13294	.12893
54	.18201	.17606	.17037	.16493	.15974	.15478	.15004	.14550	.14116	.13700

SINGLE LIFE UNITRUST REMAINDER FACTORS

ADJUSTED PAYOUT RATE

AGE	8.0%	8.2%	8.4%	8.6%	8.8%	9.0%	9.2%	9.4%	9.6%	9.8%
55	.19182	.18570	.17986	.17428	.16893	.16382	.15893	.15424	.14976	.14546
56	.20199	.19573	.18974	.18400	.17851	.17325	.16821	.16338	.15875	.15430
57	.21254	.20613	.20000	.19412	.18848	.18307	.17789	.17291	.16814	.16355
58	.22343	.21688	.21060	.20458	.19880	.19325	.18792	.18280	.17788	.17316
59	.23461	.22793	.22151	.21535	.20943	.20374	.19827	.19301	.18795	.18309
60	.24608	.23927	.23272	.22642	.22036	.21454	.20893	.20354	.19834	.19334
61	.25786	.25092	.24425	.23782	.23163	.22567	.21993	.21440	.20907	.20393
62	.27001	.26295	.25616	.24961	.24329	.23721	.23134	.22568	.22021	.21494
63	.28255	.27538	.26847	.26180	.25537	.24916	.24316	.23738	.23179	.22639
64	.29545	.28817	.28116	.27438	.26783	.26150	.25539	.24949	.24377	.23825
65	.30871	.30134	.29423	.28735	.28069	.27426	.26803	.26201	.25618	.25054
66	.32238	.31493	.30772	.30075	.29399	.28746	.28113	.27500	.26906	.26331
67	.33651	.32899	.32170	.31464	.30780	.30118	.29475	.28852	.28248	.27663
68	.35108	.34349	.33614	.32901	.32209	.31538	.30887	.30256	.29643	.29047
69	.36604	.35841	.35100	.34381	.33683	.33005	.32346	.31707	.31085	.30481
70	.38132	.37366	.36620	.35896	.35193	.34509	.33844	.33197	.32568	.31957
71	.39685	.38916	.38167	.37440	.36732	.36043	.35372	.34720	.34084	.33466
72	.41257	.40486	.39736	.39006	.38295	.37602	.36927	.36270	.35629	.35005
73	.42844	.42074	.41323	.40591	.39878	.39182	.38504	.37843	.37198	.36568
74	.44454	.43685	.42934	.42202	.41488	.40791	.40110	.39446	.38798	.38165
75	.46092	.45326	.44577	.43846	.43132	.42435	.41754	.41088	.40438	.39802
76	.47766	.47004	.46259	.45530	.44818	.44122	.43442	.42776	.42125	.41488
77	.49475	.48718	.47979	.47255	.46547	.45853	.45175	.44511	.43861	.43225
78	.51216	.50467	.49735	.49017	.48314	.47626	.46951	.46290	.45643	.45008
79	.52978	.52239	.51515	.50806	.50110	.49427	.48759	.48102	.47459	.46828
80	.54745	.54018	.53304	.52603	.51916	.51242	.50580	.49930	.49292	.48666
81	.56503	.55788	.55085	.54396	.53718	.53053	.52399	.51757	.51126	.50507
82	.58242	.57540	.56851	.56173	.55506	.54851	.54207	.53574	.52951	.52339
83	.59962	.59274	.58598	.57933	.57279	.56635	.56001	.55378	.54765	.54161
84	.61674	.61002	.60341	.59690	.59049	.58418	.57796	.57184	.56582	.55988
85	.63389	.62734	.62090	.61454	.60828	.60211	.59603	.59004	.58414	.57832
86	.65091	.64455	.63828	.63210	.62600	.61999	.61406	.60821	.60244	.59675
87	.66756	.66139	.65531	.64930	.64337	.63752	.63175	.62605	.62043	.61488
88	.68380	.67783	.67194	.66612	.66037	.65469	.64908	.64354	.63807	.63267
89	.69963	.69387	.68817	.68254	.67698	.67148	.66605	.66068	.65537	.65012
90	.71503	.70947	.70398	.69855	.69318	.68786	.68261	.67742	.67228	.66719
91	.72972	.72437	.71908	.71385	.70867	.70354	.69847	.69345	.68848	.68357
92	.74338	.73823	.73314	.72810	.72310	.71816	.71326	.70841	.70361	.69886
93	.75604	.75109	.74618	.74132	.73650	.73173	.72700	.72232	.71768	.71308
94	.76789	.76312	.75839	.75370	.74905	.74445	.73988	.73536	.73087	.72643
95	.77918	.77459	.77004	.76552	.76104	.75660	.75220	.74783	.74350	.73920
96	.78985	.78543	.78105	.77670	.77238	.76810	.76386	.75964	.75546	.75131
97	.79976	.79550	.79128	.78709	.78293	.77880	.77470	.77063	.76659	.76258
98	.80908	.80498	.80091	.79687	.79286	.78888	.78492	.78099	.77709	.77322
99	.81822	.81428	.81036	.80647	.80261	.79877	.79496	.79117	.78741	.78367
100	.82714	.82336	.81959	.81586	.81214	.80845	.80478	.80113	.79751	.79390
101	.83597	.83234	.82873	.82515	.82158	.81804	.81451	.81101	.80753	.80406
102	.84466	.84119	.83774	.83431	.83089	.82750	.82412	.82076	.81742	.81409
103	.85331	.84999	.84670	.84342	.84016	.83691	.83368	.83046	.82726	.82408
104	.86258	.85944	.85632	.85321	.85011	.84703	.84396	.84090	.83786	.83483
105	.87163	.86866	.86570	.86276	.85982	.85690	.85399	.85109	.84820	.84532
106	.88338	.88065	.87792	.87520	.87248	.86978	.86708	.86440	.86172	.85905
107	.89774	.89530	.89286	.89042	.88799	.88557	.88315	.88073	.87833	.87592
108	.92044	.91849	.91654	.91460	.91266	.91072	.90879	.90685	.90492	.90299
109	.96000	.95900	.95800	.95700	.95600	.95500	.95400	.95300	.95200	.95100

SINGLE LIFE UNITRUST REMAINDER FACTORS

ADJUSTED PAYOUT RATE

AGE	10.0%	10.2%	10.4%	10.6%	10.8%	11.0%	11.2%	11.4%	11.6%	11.8%
0	.01386	.01363	.01342	.01323	.01305	.01288	.01272	.01258	.01244	.01231
1	.00557	.00534	.00512	.00493	.00474	.00458	.00442	.00427	.00414	.00401
2	.00542	.00518	.00495	.00474	.00455	.00437	.00421	.00405	.00391	.00377
3	.00552	.00526	.00502	.00480	.00459	.00440	.00422	.00406	.00391	.00376
4	.00574	.00546	.00521	.00497	.00475	.00455	.00436	.00419	.00402	.00387
5	.00606	.00576	.00549	.00524	.00501	.00479	.00459	.00440	.00423	.00406
6	.00644	.00613	.00584	.00557	.00532	.00509	.00488	.00468	.00449	.00432
7	.00690	.00657	.00626	.00598	.00571	.00547	.00524	.00502	.00482	.00464
8	.00743	.00707	.00675	.00644	.00616	.00590	.00565	.00542	.00521	.00501
9	.00804	.00766	.00732	.00699	.00669	.00641	.00615	.00591	.00568	.00547
10	.00875	.00835	.00798	.00764	.00732	.00702	.00675	.00649	.00624	.00602
11	.00956	.00913	.00874	.00838	.00804	.00772	.00743	.00715	.00689	.00665
12	.01045	.01000	.00959	.00920	.00884	.00851	.00819	.00790	.00762	.00737
13	.01139	.01091	.01048	.01007	.00969	.00933	.00900	.00869	.00840	.00813
14	.01231	.01181	.01135	.01092	.01052	.01014	.00979	.00947	.00916	.00887
15	.01320	.01267	.01218	.01173	.01130	.01091	.01054	.01019	.00987	.00956
16	.01401	.01345	.01294	.01246	.01201	.01160	.01121	.01084	.01050	.01018
17	.01476	.01418	.01364	.01313	.01266	.01222	.01181	.01143	.01107	.01073
18	.01547	.01486	.01429	.01375	.01326	.01279	.01236	.01196	.01158	.01122
19	.01619	.01554	.01494	.01438	.01385	.01336	.01291	.01248	.01208	.01170
20	.01694	.01626	.01562	.01503	.01448	.01396	.01348	.01303	.01260	.01220
21	.01774	.01702	.01635	.01573	.01514	.01460	.01409	.01361	.01316	.01274
22	.01859	.01782	.01711	.01645	.01584	.01526	.01472	.01422	.01374	.01330
23	.01949	.01868	.01793	.01724	.01658	.01597	.01540	.01487	.01437	.01390
24	.02047	.01962	.01883	.01809	.01740	.01675	.01615	.01558	.01505	.01455
25	.02155	.02065	.01981	.01903	.01830	.01762	.01698	.01638	.01581	.01528
26	.02273	.02178	.02089	.02006	.01929	.01856	.01789	.01725	.01665	.01609
27	.02404	.02303	.02209	.02122	.02040	.01963	.01891	.01824	.01760	.01700
28	.02545	.02439	.02339	.02247	.02160	.02079	.02002	.01931	.01863	.01800
29	.02698	.02585	.02480	.02382	.02290	.02204	.02123	.02047	.01976	.01908
30	.02861	.02742	.02631	.02527	.02430	.02339	.02253	.02172	.02096	.02025
31	.03035	.02910	.02793	.02683	.02579	.02482	.02391	.02306	.02225	.02149
32	.03221	.03089	.02965	.02849	.02739	.02636	.02540	.02449	.02363	.02282
33	.03422	.03282	.03151	.03028	.02912	.02803	.02701	.02604	.02513	.02427
34	.03637	.03489	.03350	.03220	.03097	.02982	.02873	.02771	.02674	.02583
35	.03869	.03713	.03567	.03429	.03299	.03177	.03061	.02953	.02850	.02753
36	.04118	.03953	.03798	.03653	.03515	.03386	.03263	.03148	.03039	.02936
37	.04385	.04211	.04048	.03894	.03748	.03611	.03481	.03359	.03243	.03134
38	.04674	.04490	.04318	.04155	.04001	.03856	.03719	.03589	.03466	.03350
39	.04984	.04791	.04609	.04437	.04274	.04120	.03975	.03837	.03707	.03583
40	.05320	.05116	.04924	.04742	.04571	.04408	.04254	.04108	.03970	.03839
41	.05683	.05469	.05267	.05075	.04894	.04722	.04559	.04405	.04258	.04119
42	.06077	.05851	.05638	.05436	.05245	.05063	.04891	.04728	.04573	.04425
43	.06500	.06263	.06039	.05827	.05625	.05433	.05252	.05079	.04915	.04759
44	.06956	.06707	.06472	.06248	.06035	.05834	.05642	.05459	.05286	.05121
45	.07441	.07180	.06933	.06698	.06474	.06262	.06059	.05867	.05684	.05509
46	.07958	.07685	.07425	.07178	.06943	.06720	.06507	.06304	.06110	.05926
47	.08504	.08218	.07946	.07687	.07440	.07205	.06981	.06768	.06564	.06369
48	.09083	.08784	.08499	.08228	.07969	.07722	.07487	.07262	.07047	.06842
49	.09695	.09382	.09085	.08801	.08530	.08271	.08024	.07788	.07562	.07346
50	.10344	.10018	.09707	.09410	.09127	.08856	.08597	.08349	.08112	.07885
51	.11031	.10691	.10367	.10057	.09761	.09477	.09206	.08946	.08697	.08459
52	.11752	.11399	.11061	.10738	.10429	.10132	.09849	.09577	.09316	.09066
53	.12509	.12142	.11791	.11454	.11132	.10823	.10526	.10242	.09969	.09707
54	.13302	.12921	.12556	.12206	.11870	.11548	.11239	.10942	.10657	.10383

SINGLE LIFE UNITRUST REMAINDER FACTORS

ADJUSTED PAYOUT RATE

AGE	10.0%	10.2%	10.4%	10.6%	10.8%	11.0%	11.2%	11.4%	11.6%	11.8%
55	.14134	.13738	.13359	.12995	.12646	.12311	.11989	.11679	.11382	.11096
56	.15004	.14595	.14202	.13824	.13462	.13113	.12778	.12456	.12146	.11847
57	.15914	.15491	.15084	.14693	.14317	.13955	.13607	.13272	.12949	.12638
58	.16861	.16424	.16004	.15599	.15209	.14834	.14473	.14125	.13789	.13465
59	.17840	.17390	.16955	.16537	.16134	.15746	.15371	.15010	.14662	.14325
60	.18851	.18387	.17939	.17507	.17091	.16689	.16302	.15927	.15566	.15217
61	.19898	.19420	.18958	.18513	.18084	.17669	.17268	.16881	.16506	.16145
62	.20985	.20494	.20020	.19561	.19119	.18691	.18277	.17877	.17490	.17115
63	.22117	.21613	.21126	.20654	.20199	.19758	.19331	.18918	.18518	.18131
64	.23291	.22774	.22274	.21791	.21322	.20869	.20429	.20004	.19592	.19192
65	.24508	.23979	.23467	.22971	.22490	.22025	.21573	.21135	.20710	.20299
66	.25774	.25233	.24709	.24202	.23709	.23231	.22767	.22318	.21881	.21457
67	.27095	.26543	.26009	.25489	.24985	.24496	.24021	.23560	.23111	.22676
68	.28469	.27908	.27363	.26833	.26319	.25819	.25332	.24860	.24400	.23954
69	.29894	.29324	.28769	.28230	.27705	.27195	.26699	.26216	.25746	.25288
70	.31362	.30783	.30219	.29671	.29137	.28618	.28112	.27619	.27139	.26672
71	.32864	.32277	.31706	.31150	.30608	.30079	.29565	.29063	.28573	.28096
72	.34396	.33803	.33225	.32661	.32112	.31575	.31052	.30542	.30044	.29559
73	.35955	.35356	.34772	.34201	.33645	.33101	.32571	.32053	.31547	.31053
74	.37547	.36943	.36354	.35778	.35215	.34666	.34129	.33604	.33091	.32590
75	.39181	.38574	.37980	.37400	.36833	.36278	.35735	.35205	.34686	.34178
76	.40865	.40256	.39660	.39076	.38505	.37947	.37400	.36864	.36340	.35827
77	.42601	.41991	.41394	.40808	.40235	.39674	.39124	.38585	.38056	.37539
78	.44386	.43777	.43180	.42594	.42020	.41457	.40906	.40365	.39834	.39314
79	.46209	.45602	.45007	.44422	.43849	.43287	.42735	.42193	.41661	.41139
80	.48052	.47449	.46856	.46275	.45704	.45143	.44592	.44051	.43519	.42997
81	.49898	.49300	.48712	.48134	.47566	.47008	.46460	.45921	.45391	.44870
82	.51737	.51145	.50563	.49990	.49427	.48873	.48328	.47792	.47265	.46746
83	.53567	.52983	.52407	.51841	.51284	.50735	.50195	.49663	.49139	.48624
84	.55403	.54828	.54261	.53702	.53151	.52609	.52075	.51549	.51030	.50519
85	.57258	.56693	.56135	.55586	.55044	.54510	.53983	.53464	.52952	.52447
86	.59113	.58560	.58013	.57474	.56943	.56418	.55901	.55390	.54886	.54389
87	.60939	.60398	.59864	.59337	.58817	.58303	.57795	.57294	.56799	.56310
88	.62733	.62206	.61685	.61170	.60662	.60159	.59663	.59173	.58688	.58209
89	.64493	.63980	.63474	.62972	.62477	.61987	.61503	.61024	.60551	.60083
90	.66217	.65719	.65227	.64741	.64259	.63783	.63312	.62846	.62385	.61928
91	.67870	.67388	.66912	.66440	.65973	.65511	.65053	.64600	.64152	.63708
92	.69415	.68949	.68487	.68030	.67577	.67129	.66685	.66245	.65809	.65378
93	.70852	.70401	.69954	.69511	.69072	.68637	.68205	.67778	.67355	.66935
94	.72202	.71765	.71332	.70902	.70477	.70055	.69636	.69222	.68810	.68403
95	.73494	.73072	.72653	.72237	.71825	.71416	.71010	.70608	.70209	.69813
96	.74720	.74311	.73906	.73504	.73105	.72709	.72316	.71926	.71539	.71155
97	.75860	.75465	.75073	.74684	.74297	.73914	.73533	.73155	.72780	.72407
98	.76937	.76555	.76175	.75798	.75424	.75052	.74683	.74317	.73953	.73591
99	.77995	.77626	.77260	.76895	.76534	.76174	.75817	.75462	.75109	.74759
100	.79032	.78676	.78323	.77971	.77622	.77274	.76929	.76586	.76245	.75906
101	.80062	.79719	.79379	.79040	.78703	.78368	.78035	.77704	.77375	.77048
102	.81078	.80749	.80422	.80096	.79772	.79450	.79130	.78811	.78494	.78178
103	.82091	.81775	.81461	.81149	.80838	.80529	.80221	.79914	.79609	.79306
104	.83182	.82881	.82582	.82284	.81988	.81693	.81399	.81106	.80815	.80525
105	.84245	.83959	.83674	.83391	.83108	.82826	.82546	.82267	.81988	.81711
106	.85638	.85373	.85108	.84844	.84581	.84319	.84058	.83797	.83537	.83278
107	.87352	.87113	.86875	.86636	.86399	.86161	.85925	.85689	.85453	.85218
108	.90106	.89913	.89721	.89529	.89337	.89145	.88953	.88762	.88571	.88380
109	.95000	.94900	.94800	.94700	.94600	.94500	.94400	.94300	.94200	.94100

SINGLE LIFE UNITRUST REMAINDER FACTORS

ADJUSTED PAYOUT RATE

AGE	12.0%	12.2%	12.4%	12.6%	12.8%	13.0%	13.2%	13.4%	13.6%	13.8%
0	.01219	.01208	.01197	.01187	.01177	.01168	.01159	.01151	.01143	.01135
1	.00389	.00378	.00367	.00358	.00348	.00340	.00331	.00323	.00316	.00309
2	.00365	.00353	.00342	.00331	.00322	.00312	.00304	.00295	.00288	.00280
3	.00363	.00350	.00339	.00327	.00317	.00307	.00298	.00289	.00281	.00273
4	.00373	.00359	.00347	.00335	.00324	.00313	.00303	.00294	.00285	.00276
5	.00391	.00377	.00363	.00351	.00339	.00327	.00317	.00306	.00297	.00288
6	.00415	.00400	.00386	.00372	.00359	.00347	.00335	.00325	.00314	.00305
7	.00446	.00430	.00414	.00400	.00386	.00373	.00360	.00349	.00338	.00327
8	.00482	.00465	.00448	.00432	.00417	.00403	.00390	.00378	.00366	.00354
9	.00527	.00508	.00490	.00473	.00457	.00442	.00428	.00414	.00402	.00389
10	.00580	.00560	.00541	.00523	.00506	.00490	.00475	.00460	.00446	.00433
11	.00642	.00620	.00600	.00581	.00563	.00546	.00529	.00514	.00499	.00485
12	.00712	.00689	.00668	.00647	.00628	.00610	.00593	.00576	.00560	.00545
13	.00787	.00763	.00740	.00718	.00698	.00678	.00660	.00642	.00626	.00610
14	.00860	.00834	.00810	.00787	.00766	.00745	.00726	.00707	.00689	.00673
15	.00928	.00901	.00875	.00851	.00828	.00807	.00786	.00767	.00748	.00730
16	.00988	.00959	.00932	.00907	.00883	.00860	.00839	.00818	.00799	.00780
17	.01041	.01011	.00983	.00956	.00930	.00907	.00884	.00862	.00842	.00822
18	.01088	.01057	.01027	.00999	.00972	.00947	.00923	.00900	.00879	.00858
19	.01135	.01101	.01070	.01040	.01012	.00985	.00960	.00936	.00914	.00892
20	.01183	.01148	.01115	.01083	.01054	.01026	.00999	.00974	.00950	.00927
21	.01235	.01197	.01162	.01129	.01098	.01068	.01040	.01014	.00988	.00964
22	.01288	.01249	.01211	.01176	.01143	.01112	.01082	.01054	.01027	.01002
23	.01345	.01304	.01264	.01227	.01192	.01159	.01127	.01098	.01069	.01042
24	.01408	.01364	.01322	.01283	.01246	.01210	.01177	.01145	.01115	.01087
25	.01478	.01431	.01387	.01345	.01306	.01268	.01233	.01199	.01168	.01137
26	.01556	.01506	.01459	.01415	.01373	.01333	.01295	.01260	.01226	.01194
27	.01644	.01591	.01541	.01494	.01449	.01407	.01367	.01329	.01293	.01259
28	.01740	.01684	.01631	.01580	.01533	.01488	.01445	.01405	.01367	.01330
29	.01845	.01785	.01728	.01675	.01624	.01577	.01531	.01488	.01447	.01408
30	.01957	.01893	.01833	.01776	.01723	.01672	.01623	.01578	.01534	.01493
31	.02077	.02010	.01946	.01885	.01828	.01773	.01722	.01673	.01627	.01582
32	.02206	.02134	.02066	.02002	.01940	.01883	.01828	.01776	.01726	.01679
33	.02346	.02270	.02197	.02128	.02063	.02002	.01943	.01887	.01835	.01784
34	.02497	.02415	.02338	.02265	.02195	.02130	.02067	.02008	.01951	.01897
35	.02661	.02574	.02492	.02414	.02340	.02270	.02203	.02140	.02080	.02022
36	.02838	.02746	.02658	.02575	.02496	.02422	.02350	.02283	.02218	.02157
37	.03030	.02932	.02838	.02750	.02666	.02586	.02510	.02438	.02369	.02303
38	.03239	.03135	.03035	.02941	.02851	.02766	.02685	.02608	.02534	.02464
39	.03466	.03355	.03249	.03149	.03053	.02962	.02876	.02793	.02715	.02640
40	.03714	.03596	.03484	.03377	.03275	.03178	.03086	.02998	.02914	.02833
41	.03987	.03861	.03742	.03628	.03520	.03416	.03318	.03224	.03134	.03048
42	.04285	.04152	.04025	.03903	.03788	.03678	.03573	.03473	.03377	.03285
43	.04610	.04468	.04333	.04205	.04082	.03965	.03853	.03746	.03644	.03546
44	.04963	.04813	.04670	.04533	.04403	.04278	.04159	.04045	.03936	.03832
45	.05342	.05183	.05032	.04887	.04748	.04616	.04489	.04368	.04252	.04141
46	.05750	.05582	.05421	.05267	.05121	.04980	.04846	.04717	.04593	.04475
47	.06183	.06006	.05836	.05673	.05518	.05369	.05226	.05089	.04958	.04832
48	.06646	.06459	.06279	.06107	.05943	.05785	.05634	.05488	.05349	.05216
49	.07140	.06942	.06752	.06571	.06397	.06230	.06070	.05916	.05768	.05626
50	.07667	.07459	.07259	.07068	.06884	.06708	.06538	.06376	.06219	.06069
51	.08231	.08012	.07801	.07599	.07406	.07220	.07041	.06869	.06703	.06544
52	.08826	.08596	.08375	.08163	.07959	.07763	.07574	.07392	.07218	.07049
53	.09456	.09214	.08982	.08759	.08544	.08338	.08139	.07948	.07763	.07586
54	.10120	.09867	.09623	.09389	.09164	.08946	.08737	.08536	.08342	.08154

SINGLE LIFE UNITRUST REMAINDER FACTORS

ADJUSTED PAYOUT RATE

AGE	12.0%	12.2%	12.4%	12.6%	12.8%	13.0%	13.2%	13.4%	13.6%	13.8%
55	.10820	.10556	.10301	.10055	.09819	.09591	.09371	.09159	.08955	.08757
56	.11560	.11283	.11016	.10759	.10511	.10272	.10042	.09819	.09605	.09397
57	.12338	.12050	.11771	.11502	.11243	.10993	.10751	.10518	.10293	.10075
58	.13153	.12852	.12562	.12281	.12011	.11749	.11496	.11252	.11016	.10787
59	.14001	.13687	.13385	.13092	.12810	.12537	.12273	.12017	.11770	.11531
60	.14880	.14554	.14240	.13935	.13641	.13356	.13080	.12813	.12555	.12305
61	.15795	.15457	.15130	.14813	.14507	.14210	.13923	.13644	.13375	.13113
62	.16753	.16402	.16063	.15734	.15415	.15107	.14808	.14518	.14237	.13964
63	.17757	.17393	.17042	.16700	.16370	.16049	.15738	.15437	.15144	.14860
64	.18805	.18429	.18065	.17712	.17369	.17036	.16714	.16400	.16096	.15800
65	.19899	.19511	.19135	.18769	.18415	.18070	.17735	.17410	.17094	.16787
66	.21045	.20645	.20257	.19880	.19513	.19157	.18810	.18473	.18146	.17827
67	.22252	.21841	.21441	.21052	.20673	.20305	.19947	.19599	.19259	.18929
68	.23519	.23096	.22685	.22284	.21895	.21515	.21146	.20786	.20436	.20094
69	.24843	.24409	.23987	.23575	.23175	.22784	.22404	.22033	.21672	.21320
70	.26216	.25772	.25339	.24918	.24507	.24106	.23715	.23333	.22961	.22598
71	.27631	.27178	.26735	.26304	.25882	.25471	.25070	.24679	.24296	.23923
72	.29084	.28622	.28170	.27729	.27298	.26877	.26467	.26065	.25673	.25290
73	.30571	.30100	.29639	.29189	.28749	.28320	.27899	.27489	.27087	.26694
74	.32100	.31621	.31152	.30694	.30246	.29807	.29378	.28959	.28548	.28146
75	.33681	.33195	.32719	.32253	.31797	.31351	.30914	.30486	.30067	.29657
76	.35324	.34832	.34350	.33877	.33415	.32961	.32517	.32082	.31656	.31238
77	.37032	.36535	.36047	.35570	.35101	.34642	.34192	.33750	.33317	.32892
78	.38803	.38302	.37811	.37329	.36856	.36392	.35937	.35490	.35051	.34621
79	.40627	.40124	.39630	.39145	.38669	.38201	.37742	.37291	.36848	.36413
80	.42484	.41980	.41485	.40998	.40520	.40050	.39588	.39134	.38688	.38249
81	.44357	.43854	.43358	.42871	.42392	.41921	.41457	.41001	.40553	.40112
82	.46235	.45733	.45238	.44752	.44273	.43802	.43338	.42881	.42431	.41989
83	.48116	.47616	.47123	.46638	.46161	.45690	.45227	.44770	.44320	.43877
84	.50015	.49519	.49030	.48548	.48073	.47604	.47143	.46688	.46239	.45797
85	.51949	.51458	.50974	.50496	.50025	.49560	.49102	.48650	.48204	.47763
86	.53898	.53413	.52935	.52463	.51998	.51538	.51084	.50636	.50194	.49758
87	.55828	.55351	.54881	.54416	.53957	.53503	.53055	.52613	.52176	.51744
88	.57736	.57268	.56806	.56349	.55898	.55451	.55010	.54574	.54144	.53718
89	.59620	.59162	.58710	.58262	.57819	.57382	.56949	.56520	.56097	.55678
90	.61477	.61030	.60588	.60151	.59718	.59290	.58866	.58447	.58032	.57621
91	.63269	.62834	.62403	.61977	.61554	.61136	.60722	.60312	.59907	.59505
92	.64950	.64527	.64107	.63692	.63280	.62872	.62468	.62068	.61672	.61279
93	.66519	.66107	.65699	.65294	.64893	.64495	.64101	.63711	.63323	.62940
94	.67998	.67597	.67200	.66806	.66415	.66027	.65643	.65262	.64884	.64509
95	.69421	.69031	.68645	.68262	.67881	.67504	.67130	.66759	.66390	.66025
96	.70774	.70396	.70021	.69648	.69279	.68912	.68548	.68186	.67828	.67471
97	.72037	.71670	.71305	.70943	.70584	.70227	.69872	.69520	.69171	.68824
98	.73232	.72875	.72521	.72169	.71819	.71472	.71127	.70784	.70444	.70106
99	.74411	.74065	.73721	.73379	.73040	.72703	.72368	.72035	.71704	.71375
100	.75569	.75234	.74901	.74570	.74241	.73914	.73589	.73265	.72944	.72625
101	.76722	.76399	.76077	.75757	.75438	.75122	.74807	.74494	.74183	.73873
102	.77864	.77552	.77241	.76932	.76625	.76319	.76015	.75712	.75411	.75111
103	.79003	.78703	.78403	.78106	.77809	.77514	.77221	.76929	.76638	.76348
104	.80236	.79948	.79662	.79377	.79093	.78810	.78528	.78248	.77969	.77691
105	.81435	.81159	.80885	.80612	.80340	.80069	.79799	.79530	.79262	.78995
106	.83020	.82763	.82506	.82250	.81995	.81741	.81488	.81235	.80983	.80732
107	.84984	.84749	.84516	.84283	.84051	.83819	.83587	.83356	.83126	.82896
108	.88189	.87999	.87808	.87618	.87428	.87238	.87049	.86859	.86670	.86481
109	.94000	.93900	.93800	.93700	.93600	.93500	.93400	.93300	.93200	.93100

SINGLE LIFE UNITRUST REMAINDER FACTORS

ADJUSTED PAYOUT RATE

AGE	14.0%	14.2%	14.4%	14.6%	14.8%	15.0%	15.2%	15.4%	15.6%	15.8%
0	.01128	.01121	.01115	.01108	.01102	.01096	.01091	.01085	.01080	.01075
1	.00302	.00296	.00290	.00284	.00279	.00274	.00269	.00264	.00259	.00255
2	.00273	.00267	.00260	.00254	.00248	.00243	.00238	.00233	.00228	.00223
3	.00265	.00258	.00252	.00245	.00239	.00233	.00228	.00222	.00217	.00212
4	.00268	.00261	.00253	.00247	.00240	.00234	.00228	.00222	.00217	.00211
5	.00279	.00271	.00263	.00256	.00249	.00242	.00236	.00229	.00224	.00218
6	.00295	.00286	.00278	.00270	.00262	.00255	.00248	.00242	.00235	.00229
7	.00317	.00308	.00299	.00290	.00282	.00274	.00266	.00259	.00252	.00246
8	.00344	.00333	.00324	.00314	.00305	.00297	.00289	.00281	.00273	.00266
9	.00378	.00367	.00356	.00346	.00336	.00327	.00318	.00310	.00302	.00294
10	.00421	.00409	.00398	.00387	.00376	.00366	.00357	.00348	.00339	.00330
11	.00472	.00459	.00447	.00435	.00424	.00413	.00403	.00393	.00384	.00375
12	.00531	.00518	.00505	.00492	.00480	.00469	.00458	.00447	.00437	.00428
13	.00595	.00580	.00567	.00553	.00541	.00529	.00517	.00506	.00495	.00485
14	.00657	.00641	.00627	.00613	.00600	.00587	.00574	.00563	.00551	.00540
15	.00714	.00697	.00682	.00667	.00653	.00640	.00627	.00614	.00602	.00591
16	.00762	.00745	.00729	.00714	.00699	.00685	.00671	.00658	.00646	.00633
17	.00804	.00786	.00769	.00753	.00737	.00722	.00708	.00694	.00681	.00668
18	.00839	.00820	.00802	.00785	.00769	.00753	.00738	.00724	.00710	.00697
19	.00871	.00852	.00833	.00815	.00798	.00782	.00766	.00751	.00737	.00723
20	.00905	.00885	.00865	.00846	.00828	.00811	.00794	.00779	.00763	.00749
21	.00941	.00920	.00899	.00879	.00860	.00842	.00825	.00808	.00792	.00777
22	.00978	.00955	.00933	.00912	.00892	.00873	.00854	.00837	.00820	.00804
23	.01017	.00992	.00969	.00947	.00926	.00906	.00886	.00868	.00850	.00833
24	.01060	.01034	.01009	.00986	.00963	.00942	.00922	.00902	.00883	.00865
25	.01109	.01081	.01055	.01030	.01006	.00984	.00962	.00941	.00921	.00902
26	.01163	.01134	.01106	.01080	.01055	.01030	.01007	.00985	.00964	.00944
27	.01226	.01195	.01166	.01138	.01111	.01085	.01061	.01037	.01015	.00993
28	.01296	.01263	.01231	.01201	.01173	.01145	.01119	.01094	.01070	.01047
29	.01372	.01336	.01303	.01271	.01240	.01211	.01183	.01157	.01131	.01107
30	.01453	.01416	.01380	.01346	.01313	.01282	.01253	.01224	.01197	.01171
31	.01540	.01500	.01462	.01426	.01391	.01358	.01326	.01296	.01267	.01239
32	.01634	.01591	.01551	.01512	.01475	.01439	.01405	.01373	.01342	.01312
33	.01736	.01691	.01647	.01606	.01566	.01528	.01492	.01457	.01424	.01392
34	.01846	.01798	.01751	.01707	.01664	.01624	.01585	.01548	.01512	.01478
35	.01967	.01915	.01866	.01818	.01773	.01729	.01688	.01648	.01610	.01573
36	.02098	.02043	.01989	.01938	.01890	.01843	.01799	.01756	.01715	.01676
37	.02241	.02181	.02124	.02069	.02017	.01967	.01920	.01874	.01830	.01788
38	.02397	.02333	.02272	.02214	.02158	.02105	.02053	.02004	.01957	.01912
39	.02568	.02500	.02434	.02372	.02312	.02254	.02200	.02147	.02096	.02048
40	.02757	.02684	.02614	.02546	.02482	.02421	.02362	.02305	.02251	.02199
41	.02966	.02888	.02813	.02741	.02672	.02606	.02543	.02482	.02424	.02368
42	.03198	.03114	.03034	.02957	.02883	.02812	.02744	.02679	.02617	.02557
43	.03453	.03363	.03277	.03195	.03116	.03040	.02967	.02897	.02830	.02766
44	.03732	.03637	.03545	.03457	.03372	.03291	.03213	.03138	.03066	.02997
45	.04034	.03932	.03834	.03740	.03650	.03563	.03480	.03399	.03322	.03248
46	.04362	.04253	.04148	.04048	.03951	.03859	.03769	.03684	.03601	.03521
47	.04711	.04595	.04484	.04377	.04274	.04175	.04080	.03988	.03899	.03814
48	.05087	.04964	.04845	.04731	.04621	.04516	.04414	.04316	.04222	.04130
49	.05490	.05359	.05233	.05111	.04995	.04882	.04774	.04669	.04568	.04471
50	.05924	.05785	.05651	.05522	.05398	.05278	.05163	.05051	.04944	.04840
51	.06391	.06244	.06101	.05964	.05832	.05705	.05582	.05464	.05349	.05239
52	.06887	.06731	.06581	.06435	.06295	.06160	.06030	.05904	.05782	.05664
53	.07415	.07249	.07090	.06936	.06788	.06645	.06506	.06373	.06243	.06118
54	.07974	.07799	.07631	.07468	.07311	.07160	.07013	.06871	.06734	.06601

SINGLE LIFE UNITRUST REMAINDER FACTORS

ADJUSTED PAYOUT RATE

AGE	14.0%	14.2%	14.4%	14.6%	14.8%	15.0%	15.2%	15.4%	15.6%	15.8%
55	.08567	.08383	.08206	.08034	.07868	.07708	.07552	.07402	.07257	.07116
56	.09197	.09003	.08816	.08635	.08460	.08291	.08127	.07968	.07814	.07665
57	.09864	.09661	.09464	.09273	.09089	.08910	.08737	.08570	.08408	.08250
58	.10567	.10353	.10146	.09945	.09751	.09563	.09381	.09205	.09033	.08867
59	.11299	.11075	.10858	.10648	.10444	.10246	.10055	.09869	.09688	.09513
60	.12063	.11828	.11600	.11380	.11166	.10958	.10757	.10561	.10371	.10187
61	.12860	.12614	.12376	.12145	.11921	.11703	.11492	.11286	.11087	.10893
62	.13699	.13443	.13194	.12952	.12717	.12489	.12267	.12052	.11843	.11639
63	.14584	.14316	.14056	.13804	.13558	.13319	.13087	.12862	.12643	.12429
64	.15513	.15234	.14963	.14699	.14443	.14193	.13951	.13715	.13485	.13262
65	.16488	.16198	.15916	.15641	.15374	.15113	.14860	.14614	.14373	.14140
66	.17517	.17215	.16921	.16635	.16357	.16086	.15822	.15565	.15314	.15070
67	.18608	.18295	.17990	.17693	.17403	.17121	.16847	.16579	.16317	.16062
68	.19762	.19437	.19121	.18813	.18513	.18220	.17935	.17656	.17384	.17119
69	.20976	.20641	.20314	.19995	.19684	.19381	.19084	.18795	.18513	.18237
70	.22244	.21898	.21561	.21232	.20910	.20596	.20289	.19989	.19696	.19410
71	.23559	.23203	.22855	.22515	.22183	.21859	.21542	.21232	.20929	.20632
72	.24915	.24549	.24192	.23842	.23500	.23165	.22838	.22518	.22205	.21899
73	.26310	.25935	.25567	.25208	.24856	.24511	.24174	.23845	.23522	.23206
74	.27753	.27368	.26991	.26622	.26261	.25907	.25561	.25222	.24889	.24563
75	.29255	.28862	.28476	.28098	.27728	.27365	.27009	.26661	.26319	.25984
76	.30828	.30426	.30032	.29646	.29268	.28896	.28532	.28175	.27825	.27481
77	.32475	.32067	.31666	.31272	.30886	.30507	.30135	.29769	.29411	.29059
78	.34198	.33783	.33376	.32976	.32583	.32197	.31818	.31445	.31080	.30720
79	.35985	.35565	.35153	.34747	.34348	.33957	.33571	.33193	.32821	.32455
80	.37818	.37394	.36977	.36567	.36163	.35767	.35377	.34993	.34615	.34244
81	.39678	.39250	.38830	.38417	.38010	.37609	.37215	.36827	.36445	.36068
82	.41553	.41124	.40701	.40285	.39875	.39471	.39074	.38682	.38297	.37917
83	.43441	.43011	.42587	.42169	.41757	.41352	.40952	.40558	.40169	.39786
84	.45361	.44930	.44506	.44088	.43676	.43269	.42868	.42473	.42082	.41698
85	.47329	.46901	.46478	.46061	.45649	.45243	.44842	.44446	.44055	.43670
86	.49327	.48901	.48481	.48066	.47656	.47252	.46852	.46457	.46068	.45683
87	.51317	.50896	.50479	.50068	.49661	.49259	.48862	.48470	.48082	.47699
88	.53296	.52880	.52469	.52062	.51659	.51262	.50868	.50479	.50095	.49714
89	.55263	.54853	.54448	.54047	.53650	.53257	.52869	.52484	.52104	.51728
90	.57214	.56812	.56413	.56019	.55629	.55242	.54860	.54481	.54106	.53735
91	.59107	.58712	.58322	.57935	.57553	.57173	.56798	.56426	.56057	.55692
92	.60890	.60504	.60122	.59743	.59368	.58996	.58628	.58263	.57901	.57542
93	.62559	.62182	.61808	.61437	.61070	.60706	.60345	.59986	.59632	.59280
94	.64138	.63769	.63404	.63041	.62681	.62325	.61971	.61620	.61272	.60927
95	.65662	.65303	.64946	.64592	.64240	.63891	.63546	.63202	.62862	.62524
96	.67118	.66767	.66419	.66074	.65731	.65390	.65052	.64717	.64384	.64053
97	.68480	.68138	.67798	.67461	.67126	.66793	.66463	.66135	.65809	.65486
98	.69770	.69437	.69106	.68776	.68450	.68125	.67802	.67482	.67163	.66847
99	.71048	.70724	.70401	.70080	.69762	.69445	.69130	.68818	.68507	.68198
100	.72307	.71992	.71678	.71366	.71056	.70748	.70441	.70136	.69834	.69532
101	.73565	.73259	.72954	.72652	.72350	.72051	.71753	.71457	.71162	.70869
102	.74813	.74517	.74222	.73928	.73636	.73346	.73057	.72769	.72483	.72198
103	.76060	.75773	.75488	.75204	.74921	.74640	.74360	.74081	.73804	.73528
104	.77414	.77139	.76864	.76591	.76319	.76048	.75779	.75510	.75243	.74976
105	.78729	.78464	.78200	.77936	.77674	.77413	.77153	.76894	.76636	.76379
106	.80482	.80232	.79983	.79735	.79488	.79242	.78996	.78751	.78507	.78264
107	.82666	.82438	.82209	.81981	.81754	.81527	.81301	.81075	.80850	.80625
108	.86293	.86104	.85916	.85728	.85540	.85352	.85165	.84978	.84790	.84604
109	.93000	.92900	.92800	.92700	.92600	.92500	.92400	.92300	.92200	.92100

SINGLE LIFE UNITRUST REMAINDER FACTORS

ADJUSTED PAYOUT RATE

AGE	16.0%	16.2%	16.4%	16.6%	16.8%	17.0%	17.2%	17.4%	17.6%	17.8%
0	.01070	.01065	.01060	.01056	.01051	.01047	.01043	.01039	.01035	.01031
1	.00251	.00247	.00243	.00239	.00236	.00232	.00229	.00226	.00223	.00220
2	.00219	.00215	.00211	.00207	.00203	.00200	.00196	.00193	.00190	.00187
3	.00208	.00203	.00199	.00195	.00191	.00187	.00184	.00180	.00177	.00173
4	.00206	.00202	.00197	.00193	.00188	.00184	.00180	.00177	.00173	.00170
5	.00213	.00207	.00202	.00198	.00193	.00189	.00185	.00180	.00177	.00173
6	.00223	.00218	.00212	.00207	.00202	.00197	.00193	.00188	.00184	.00180
7	.00239	.00233	.00227	.00222	.00216	.00211	.00206	.00201	.00197	.00192
8	.00259	.00253	.00246	.00240	.00234	.00229	.00223	.00218	.00213	.00208
9	.00287	.00279	.00272	.00266	.00259	.00253	.00247	.00242	.00236	.00231
10	.00322	.00315	.00307	.00300	.00293	.00286	.00280	.00273	.00267	.00261
11	.00366	.00358	.00350	.00342	.00334	.00327	.00320	.00313	.00307	.00300
12	.00418	.00409	.00400	.00392	.00384	.00376	.00369	.00361	.00354	.00347
13	.00475	.00465	.00456	.00447	.00438	.00430	.00422	.00414	.00406	.00399
14	.00530	.00520	.00510	.00500	.00491	.00482	.00474	.00465	.00457	.00450
15	.00580	.00569	.00559	.00549	.00539	.00530	.00521	.00512	.00504	.00496
16	.00622	.00611	.00600	.00589	.00579	.00570	.00560	.00551	.00542	.00534
17	.00656	.00645	.00633	.00622	.00612	.00602	.00592	.00582	.00573	.00564
18	.00684	.00672	.00660	.00649	.00638	.00627	.00617	.00607	.00597	.00588
19	.00709	.00696	.00684	.00672	.00661	.00650	.00639	.00628	.00618	.00609
20	.00735	.00721	.00708	.00696	.00684	.00672	.00661	.00650	.00640	.00630
21	.00762	.00748	.00734	.00721	.00708	.00696	.00684	.00673	.00662	.00651
22	.00788	.00774	.00759	.00745	.00732	.00719	.00707	.00695	.00684	.00672
23	.00817	.00801	.00786	.00771	.00757	.00744	.00731	.00718	.00706	.00694
24	.00848	.00831	.00815	.00800	.00785	.00771	.00757	.00744	.00731	.00719
25	.00884	.00866	.00849	.00833	.00817	.00802	.00788	.00774	.00760	.00747
26	.00924	.00906	.00888	.00870	.00854	.00838	.00822	.00808	.00793	.00779
27	.00972	.00953	.00933	.00915	.00898	.00881	.00864	.00848	.00833	.00818
28	.01025	.01004	.00984	.00964	.00945	.00927	.00910	.00893	.00877	.00861
29	.01083	.01061	.01039	.01018	.00998	.00979	.00961	.00943	.00926	.00909
30	.01146	.01122	.01099	.01077	.01055	.01035	.01015	.00996	.00978	.00960
31	.01212	.01187	.01162	.01139	.01116	.01094	.01073	.01053	.01033	.01014
32	.01284	.01256	.01230	.01205	.01180	.01157	.01135	.01113	.01092	.01072
33	.01362	.01332	.01304	.01277	.01251	.01226	.01202	.01179	.01157	.01135
34	.01445	.01414	.01384	.01355	.01327	.01300	.01275	.01250	.01226	.01203
35	.01538	.01505	.01472	.01441	.01412	.01383	.01355	.01329	.01303	.01278
36	.01639	.01603	.01568	.01535	.01503	.01472	.01442	.01414	.01386	.01359
37	.01748	.01709	.01672	.01636	.01602	.01569	.01537	.01506	.01476	.01448
38	.01869	.01827	.01787	.01749	.01712	.01676	.01642	.01609	.01577	.01546
39	.02001	.01957	.01914	.01872	.01832	.01794	.01757	.01722	.01687	.01654
40	.02149	.02101	.02055	.02010	.01967	.01926	.01886	.01848	.01811	.01775
41	.02314	.02263	.02213	.02165	.02119	.02074	.02031	.01990	.01950	.01912
42	.02499	.02443	.02390	.02338	.02288	.02240	.02194	.02150	.02107	.02065
43	.02703	.02644	.02586	.02531	.02477	.02426	.02376	.02328	.02281	.02237
44	.02930	.02866	.02804	.02744	.02687	.02631	.02578	.02526	.02476	.02428
45	.03176	.03107	.03041	.02977	.02915	.02855	.02798	.02742	.02688	.02636
46	.03445	.03371	.03299	.03230	.03164	.03100	.03038	.02978	.02920	.02864
47	.03732	.03653	.03576	.03503	.03431	.03362	.03296	.03232	.03169	.03109
48	.04043	.03958	.03876	.03797	.03720	.03647	.03575	.03506	.03439	.03375
49	.04377	.04286	.04199	.04114	.04032	.03953	.03877	.03802	.03731	.03661
50	.04740	.04643	.04549	.04459	.04371	.04287	.04205	.04125	.04048	.03974
51	.05132	.05028	.04928	.04832	.04738	.04648	.04560	.04475	.04393	.04313
52	.05550	.05440	.05334	.05231	.05131	.05034	.04941	.04850	.04762	.04677
53	.05997	.05880	.05767	.05657	.05551	.05448	.05348	.05251	.05157	.05066
54	.06473	.06348	.06228	.06111	.05998	.05888	.05782	.05679	.05579	.05481

SINGLE LIFE UNITRUST REMAINDER FACTORS

ADJUSTED PAYOUT RATE

AGE	16.0%	16.2%	16.4%	16.6%	16.8%	17.0%	17.2%	17.4%	17.6%	17.8%
55	.06980	.06848	.06720	.06596	.06476	.06359	.06246	.06136	.06030	.05926
56	.07521	.07381	.07246	.07114	.06987	.06863	.06742	.06626	.06512	.06402
57	.08098	.07950	.07806	.07667	.07531	.07400	.07273	.07149	.07028	.06911
58	.08706	.08550	.08398	.08251	.08108	.07969	.07834	.07702	.07574	.07450
59	.09343	.09178	.09018	.08862	.08711	.08564	.08421	.08282	.08147	.08015
60	.10008	.09834	.09665	.09501	.09342	.09186	.09035	.08888	.08745	.08606
61	.10705	.10522	.10344	.10171	.10003	.09839	.09680	.09524	.09373	.09226
62	.11442	.11249	.11062	.10880	.10703	.10530	.10362	.10198	.10039	.09883
63	.12222	.12020	.11823	.11631	.11445	.11263	.11086	.10914	.10746	.10582
64	.13044	.12832	.12626	.12425	.12229	.12038	.11852	.11670	.11493	.11321
65	.13912	.13690	.13473	.13263	.13057	.12857	.12661	.12470	.12284	.12103
66	.14831	.14599	.14373	.14152	.13937	.13726	.13521	.13321	.13126	.12935
67	.15814	.15571	.15335	.15104	.14878	.14658	.14443	.14234	.14029	.13828
68	.16860	.16607	.16360	.16119	.15883	.15653	.15429	.15209	.14995	.14785
69	.17967	.17704	.17447	.17196	.16951	.16711	.16476	.16247	.16023	.15803
70	.19131	.18857	.18590	.18329	.18074	.17824	.17579	.17340	.17106	.16878
71	.20343	.20059	.19782	.19511	.19245	.18986	.18732	.18483	.18239	.18001
72	.21599	.21306	.21019	.20738	.20462	.20193	.19929	.19671	.19417	.19169
73	.22896	.22593	.22296	.22005	.21720	.21441	.21167	.20899	.20637	.20379
74	.24244	.23931	.23625	.23324	.23030	.22741	.22458	.22180	.21908	.21641
75	.25656	.25334	.25018	.24708	.24404	.24106	.23813	.23526	.23245	.22968
76	.27144	.26813	.26488	.26169	.25856	.25549	.25247	.24951	.24660	.24375
77	.28714	.28374	.28041	.27714	.27392	.27077	.26766	.26462	.26162	.25868
78	.30367	.30020	.29680	.29345	.29015	.28692	.28374	.28061	.27753	.27451
79	.32095	.31742	.31394	.31052	.30716	.30385	.30059	.29739	.29424	.29115
80	.33878	.33519	.33165	.32817	.32474	.32137	.31805	.31479	.31157	.30840
81	.35698	.35334	.34975	.34621	.34273	.33930	.33593	.33260	.32932	.32610
82	.37542	.37174	.36810	.36452	.36099	.35752	.35409	.35071	.34738	.34410
83	.39409	.39037	.38670	.38308	.37951	.37599	.37252	.36910	.36573	.36240
84	.41318	.40943	.40574	.40209	.39850	.39495	.39144	.38799	.38458	.38121
85	.43289	.42914	.42543	.42177	.41815	.41458	.41106	.40758	.40414	.40075
86	.45303	.44927	.44556	.44190	.43828	.43470	.43117	.42768	.42423	.42082
87	.47320	.46946	.46576	.46211	.45849	.45492	.45139	.44789	.44444	.44103
88	.49338	.48966	.48598	.48235	.47875	.47519	.47167	.46819	.46474	.46133
89	.51355	.50987	.50622	.50261	.49904	.49551	.49201	.48855	.48513	.48173
90	.53368	.53004	.52644	.52287	.51934	.51585	.51239	.50896	.50556	.50220
91	.55331	.54973	.54618	.54266	.53918	.53573	.53232	.52893	.52558	.52225
92	.57187	.56835	.56486	.56140	.55797	.55457	.55121	.54787	.54456	.54128
93	.58931	.58585	.58242	.57901	.57564	.57230	.56898	.56569	.56243	.55919
94	.60584	.60245	.59908	.59574	.59242	.58913	.58587	.58263	.57942	.57623
95	.62188	.61855	.61525	.61197	.60872	.60549	.60228	.59910	.59595	.59281
96	.63725	.63399	.63075	.62754	.62435	.62119	.61804	.61492	.61182	.60875
97	.65165	.64846	.64529	.64214	.63902	.63591	.63283	.62977	.62673	.62371
98	.66532	.66220	.65910	.65602	.65296	.64991	.64689	.64389	.64090	.63794
99	.67891	.67586	.67283	.66981	.66682	.66384	.66088	.65794	.65502	.65211
100	.69233	.68935	.68639	.68345	.68053	.67762	.67473	.67185	.66899	.66615
101	.70578	.70288	.70000	.69713	.69428	.69144	.68862	.68582	.68303	.68025
102	.71915	.71633	.71353	.71074	.70797	.70520	.70246	.69972	.69700	.69430
103	.73253	.72980	.72707	.72436	.72167	.71898	.71631	.71365	.71100	.70837
104	.74711	.74447	.74184	.73923	.73662	.73402	.73144	.72887	.72630	.72375
105	.76123	.75867	.75613	.75360	.75107	.74856	.74605	.74356	.74107	.73859
106	.78021	.77779	.77538	.77297	.77058	.76819	.76581	.76343	.76107	.75871
107	.80401	.80177	.79954	.79731	.79509	.79287	.79065	.78845	.78624	.78405
108	.84417	.84231	.84044	.83858	.83672	.83487	.83301	.83116	.82931	.82746
109	.92000	.91900	.91800	.91700	.91600	.91500	.91400	.91300	.91200	.91100

SINGLE LIFE UNITRUST REMAINDER FACTORS

ADJUSTED PAYOUT RATE

AGE	18.0%	18.2%	18.4%	18.6%	18.8%	19.0%	19.2%	19.4%	19.6%	19.8%
0	.01028	.01024	.01021	.01017	.01014	.01011	.01007	.01004	.01001	.00998
1	.00217	.00214	.00211	.00209	.00206	.00204	.00201	.00199	.00197	.00195
2	.00184	.00181	.00178	.00175	.00173	.00170	.00168	.00166	.00163	.00161
3	.00170	.00167	.00164	.00162	.00159	.00156	.00154	.00151	.00149	.00147
4	.00166	.00163	.00160	.00157	.00154	.00151	.00149	.00146	.00143	.00141
5	.00169	.00166	.00162	.00159	.00156	.00153	.00150	.00147	.00144	.00142
6	.00176	.00172	.00169	.00165	.00162	.00158	.00155	.00152	.00149	.00146
7	.00188	.00184	.00180	.00176	.00172	.00168	.00165	.00161	.00158	.00155
8	.00203	.00199	.00194	.00190	.00186	.00182	.00178	.00174	.00171	.00167
9	.00225	.00220	.00216	.00211	.00206	.00202	.00198	.00193	.00189	.00186
10	.00256	.00250	.00245	.00240	.00235	.00230	.00225	.00221	.00216	.00212
11	.00294	.00288	.00282	.00277	.00271	.00266	.00261	.00256	.00251	.00246
12	.00341	.00334	.00328	.00322	.00316	.00310	.00305	.00299	.00294	.00289
13	.00392	.00385	.00378	.00372	.00366	.00359	.00353	.00348	.00342	.00336
14	.00442	.00435	.00428	.00421	.00414	.00408	.00401	.00395	.00389	.00383
15	.00488	.00480	.00473	.00465	.00458	.00451	.00445	.00438	.00432	.00426
16	.00525	.00517	.00509	.00502	.00494	.00487	.00480	.00474	.00467	.00461
17	.00555	.00547	.00539	.00531	.00523	.00516	.00509	.00502	.00495	.00488
18	.00579	.00570	.00562	.00553	.00545	.00538	.00530	.00523	.00515	.00509
19	.00599	.00590	.00581	.00573	.00564	.00556	.00548	.00541	.00533	.00526
20	.00620	.00610	.00601	.00592	.00583	.00575	.00567	.00559	.00551	.00543
21	.00641	.00631	.00622	.00612	.00603	.00594	.00586	.00577	.00569	.00561
22	.00662	.00651	.00641	.00631	.00622	.00613	.00604	.00595	.00586	.00578
23	.00683	.00672	.00661	.00651	.00641	.00631	.00622	.00613	.00604	.00596
24	.00707	.00695	.00684	.00673	.00663	.00653	.00643	.00633	.00624	.00615
25	.00735	.00722	.00711	.00699	.00688	.00677	.00667	.00657	.00647	.00637
26	.00766	.00753	.00741	.00728	.00717	.00705	.00694	.00684	.00673	.00663
27	.00804	.00791	.00777	.00764	.00752	.00740	.00728	.00717	.00706	.00695
28	.00846	.00832	.00818	.00804	.00791	.00778	.00766	.00754	.00742	.00731
29	.00893	.00878	.00863	.00848	.00834	.00820	.00807	.00795	.00782	.00770
30	.00943	.00927	.00911	.00895	.00880	.00866	.00852	.00838	.00825	.00812
31	.00996	.00978	.00961	.00945	.00929	.00914	.00899	.00884	.00870	.00857
32	.01052	.01034	.01015	.00998	.00981	.00965	.00949	.00933	.00918	.00904
33	.01114	.01094	.01075	.01056	.01038	.01020	.01003	.00987	.00971	.00956
34	.01180	.01159	.01138	.01118	.01099	.01080	.01062	.01044	.01027	.01011
35	.01254	.01231	.01209	.01187	.01167	.01147	.01127	.01108	.01090	.01072
36	.01334	.01309	.01285	.01262	.01240	.01218	.01197	.01177	.01157	.01138
37	.01420	.01394	.01368	.01343	.01319	.01296	.01274	.01252	.01231	.01210
38	.01517	.01488	.01460	.01434	.01408	.01383	.01358	.01335	.01312	.01290
39	.01622	.01591	.01562	.01533	.01505	.01478	.01452	.01427	.01402	.01378
40	.01741	.01707	.01675	.01644	.01614	.01585	.01557	.01529	.01503	.01477
41	.01875	.01839	.01804	.01770	.01738	.01706	.01676	.01646	.01618	.01590
42	.02025	.01986	.01949	.01912	.01877	.01843	.01810	.01779	.01748	.01718
43	.02193	.02151	.02111	.02072	.02034	.01997	.01962	.01927	.01894	.01861
44	.02381	.02336	.02292	.02250	.02209	.02169	.02131	.02094	.02058	.02023
45	.02586	.02537	.02490	.02444	.02400	.02357	.02316	.02276	.02237	.02199
46	.02810	.02758	.02707	.02658	.02610	.02564	.02519	.02476	.02433	.02392
47	.03051	.02994	.02940	.02887	.02835	.02786	.02737	.02690	.02645	.02601
48	.03312	.03251	.03192	.03135	.03080	.03026	.02974	.02924	.02875	.02827
49	.03594	.03529	.03466	.03404	.03345	.03287	.03231	.03177	.03124	.03072
50	.03902	.03832	.03764	.03698	.03634	.03572	.03512	.03453	.03396	.03341
51	.04236	.04161	.04088	.04017	.03949	.03882	.03817	.03755	.03693	.03634
52	.04594	.04514	.04436	.04360	.04286	.04215	.04146	.04078	.04012	.03949
53	.04977	.04892	.04808	.04727	.04648	.04572	.04498	.04425	.04355	.04286
54	.05387	.05295	.05206	.05120	.05035	.04954	.04874	.04796	.04721	.04648

SINGLE LIFE UNITRUST REMAINDER FACTORS

ADJUSTED PAYOUT RATE

AGE	18.0%	18.2%	18.4%	18.6%	18.8%	19.0%	19.2%	19.4%	19.6%	19.8%
55	.05825	.05728	.05632	.05540	.05450	.05363	.05278	.05195	.05114	.05036
56	.06295	.06191	.06090	.05991	.05895	.05802	.05711	.05623	.05537	.05453
57	.06797	.06687	.06579	.06474	.06372	.06273	.06176	.06082	.05990	.05900
58	.07329	.07212	.07098	.06986	.06878	.06772	.06669	.06569	.06471	.06376
59	.07887	.07763	.07641	.07523	.07408	.07296	.07186	.07080	.06976	.06875
60	.08471	.08339	.08210	.08085	.07963	.07844	.07727	.07614	.07504	.07396
61	.09083	.08943	.08807	.08674	.08545	.08419	.08296	.08176	.08059	.07944
62	.09732	.09584	.09441	.09300	.09163	.09030	.08900	.08772	.08648	.08527
63	.10422	.10266	.10114	.09966	.09821	.09680	.09542	.09408	.09276	.09148
64	.11153	.10988	.10828	.10672	.10519	.10370	.10224	.10082	.09942	.09807
65	.11926	.11752	.11584	.11419	.11257	.11100	.10946	.10796	.10649	.10505
66	.12748	.12566	.12389	.12215	.12045	.11879	.11717	.11559	.11403	.11252
67	.13633	.13442	.13255	.13072	.12894	.12719	.12548	.12381	.12218	.12058
68	.14580	.14379	.14183	.13992	.13804	.13621	.13441	.13265	.13093	.12925
69	.15589	.15379	.15174	.14973	.14776	.14584	.14395	.14211	.14030	.13853
70	.16654	.16434	.16220	.16010	.15804	.15602	.15405	.15211	.15022	.14836
71	.17767	.17539	.17315	.17095	.16880	.16670	.16463	.16261	.16062	.15868
72	.18926	.18688	.18455	.18226	.18002	.17782	.17567	.17355	.17148	.16944
73	.20127	.19879	.19636	.19398	.19165	.18936	.18711	.18490	.18274	.18062
74	.21379	.21122	.20870	.20622	.20380	.20141	.19907	.19678	.19452	.19231
75	.22697	.22430	.22169	.21912	.21660	.21413	.21170	.20931	.20696	.20466
76	.24095	.23819	.23549	.23283	.23022	.22765	.22513	.22265	.22022	.21782
77	.25579	.25295	.25016	.24741	.24471	.24206	.23945	.23688	.23436	.23188
78	.27154	.26861	.26574	.26291	.26013	.25739	.25470	.25205	.24944	.24688
79	.28810	.28510	.28215	.27924	.27638	.27357	.27080	.26807	.26538	.26274
80	.30529	.30222	.29919	.29622	.29329	.29040	.28756	.28476	.28200	.27928
81	.32292	.31979	.31670	.31366	.31066	.30771	.30480	.30193	.29910	.29632
82	.34087	.33768	.33454	.33144	.32838	.32537	.32240	.31947	.31658	.31373
83	.35912	.35588	.35269	.34954	.34643	.34336	.34034	.33735	.33440	.33150
84	.37789	.37461	.37137	.36818	.36503	.36191	.35884	.35581	.35281	.34985
85	.39740	.39409	.39082	.38760	.38441	.38126	.37815	.37507	.37204	.36904
86	.41745	.41412	.41084	.40759	.40437	.40120	.39806	.39496	.39190	.38887
87	.43765	.43432	.43102	.42776	.42453	.42134	.41819	.41507	.41198	.40893
88	.45796	.45463	.45133	.44807	.44484	.44164	.43848	.43535	.43225	.42919
89	.47838	.47506	.47177	.46851	.46529	.46210	.45894	.45582	.45272	.44966
90	.49887	.49558	.49231	.48908	.48587	.48270	.47956	.47644	.47336	.47031
91	.51896	.51570	.51246	.50926	.50609	.50294	.49982	.49673	.49367	.49064
92	.53803	.53480	.53161	.52844	.52530	.52218	.51910	.51604	.51300	.50999
93	.55599	.55280	.54965	.54652	.54342	.54034	.53728	.53426	.53125	.52827
94	.57307	.56994	.56682	.56374	.56067	.55763	.55462	.55162	.54865	.54571
95	.58970	.58662	.58355	.58051	.57750	.57450	.57153	.56857	.56564	.56274
96	.60569	.60266	.59965	.59666	.59369	.59074	.58781	.58491	.58202	.57915
97	.62071	.61773	.61477	.61183	.60891	.60601	.60313	.60026	.59742	.59459
98	.63499	.63207	.62916	.62627	.62340	.62054	.61771	.61489	.61209	.60931
99	.64922	.64635	.64350	.64067	.63785	.63504	.63226	.62949	.62674	.62400
100	.66332	.66051	.65772	.65494	.65218	.64943	.64670	.64398	.64128	.63860
101	.67749	.67474	.67201	.66930	.66659	.66391	.66123	.65857	.65593	.65330
102	.69161	.68893	.68626	.68361	.68097	.67834	.67573	.67313	.67054	.66797
103	.70575	.70314	.70054	.69795	.69538	.69281	.69026	.68772	.68520	.68268
104	.72121	.71868	.71616	.71365	.71115	.70867	.70619	.70372	.70127	.69882
105	.73613	.73367	.73122	.72878	.72635	.72393	.72151	.71911	.71671	.71433
106	.75635	.75401	.75167	.74934	.74702	.74470	.74240	.74009	.73780	.73551
107	.78185	.77967	.77748	.77531	.77313	.77096	.76880	.76664	.76449	.76234
108	.82562	.82377	.82193	.82009	.81826	.81642	.81459	.81275	.81093	.80910
109	.91000	.90900	.90800	.90700	.90600	.90500	.90400	.90300	.90200	.90100

CHARITABLE PLANNING WEBSITES

COMPREHENSIVE PROFESSIONAL RESOURCES	
Death and Taxes (Nonprofit information center; numerous charitable web site links; text of IRS releases and rulings; life insurance analysis)	www.deathandtaxes.com
Vaughn Henry's Charitable Trust & Estate Planning (Case studies and articles on charitable planning topics; IRS information, regulations and commentary on charitable legal issues; charitable web site links; planning articles and links)	www.gift-estate.com
Leimberg Associates, Inc. & Leimberg & LeClair, Inc. (Charitable planning software; books; tapes)	www.leimberg.com
Leimberg Information Services, Inc. (LISI) (Charitable newsletter provides, fast, frank, incisive analysis of recent charitable legislation, cases, and rulings; searchable database provides access to specific topics, references, and citations)	www.leimbergservices.com
Planned Giving Design Center (Provides technical information on charitable giving to professional advisors)	www.pgdc.net
Conrad Teitell's Taxwise Giving and Philanthropy Tax Institute	www.taxwisegiving.com
PROFESSIONAL EDUCATION	
American College (Offers the Chartered Advisor in Philanthropy (CAP) designation)	www.theamericancollege.edu
Gift College (Offers professional education and the Certified Gift Planning Associate certification)	www.giftcollege.com
American Institute for Philanthropic Studies (Offers Certified Specialist in Planned Giving (CSPG) designation)	www.plannedgivingedu.com
ASSOCIATIONS	
ABA - American Bar Association	www.abanet.org
ACTEC - American College of Trusts and Estate Counsel	www.actec.org

ASSOCIATIONS (cont'd)	
Advocis – The Financial Advisors Association of Canada	www.advocis.ca
AFP - Association of Fundraising Professionals	www.nsfre.org
AHP - Association for Healthcare Philanthropy	www.go-ahp.org
AICPA - American Institute of Certified Public Accountants	www.aicpa.org
ALDE - Association of Lutheran Development Executives	www.alde.org
American Grant Writers Association	www.agwa.us
ARNOVA - Association for Research on Nonprofit Organizations and Voluntary Action	www.arnova.org
ASA - American Society of Appraisers	www.appraisers.org
ATA - American Teleservices Association	www.ataconnect.org
BoardSource	www.boardsource.org
CAGP*ACPDP - Canadian Association of Gift Planners	www.cagp-acpdp.org
CAN - California Association of Nonprofits	www.canonprofits.org
CASE - Council for Advancement and Support of Education	www.case.org
CBA - Canadian Bar Association	www.cba.org/Gate.asp
CFP Board of Standards - Owners and Licensors of the CFP Certification Mark	www.cfp.net
The Center on Philanthropy at Indiana University	www.philanthropy.iupui.edu
CICA - Canadian Institute of Chartered Accountants	www.cica.ca
Civicus - World Alliance for Citizen Participation	www.civicus.org
Council on Foundations (A nonprofit association of grantmaking foundations)	www.cof.org
EFC - European Foundation Centre	www.efc.be
FPA - Financial Planning Association	www.fpanet.org
Forum of Regional Association of Grantmakers	www.givingforum.org
Foundation Center	foundationcenter.org
Giving Institute	www.aafrc.org
Institute for Charitable Giving (Training and Coaching for fundraisers)	www.instituteforgiving.org

ASSOCIATIONS (cont'd)	
Institute of Fundraising - UK	www.institute-of-fundraising.org.uk
ICFO - International Committee on Fundraising Organisations	www.icfo.de
Imagine Canada – (Organization of Canadian charities and non-profits)	www.imaginecanada.ca
Independent Sector	www.independentsector.org
International Association of Advisors in Philanthropy	www.advisorsinphilanthropy.org
NAELA - National Academy of Elder Law Attorneys	www.naela.org
NAEPC - National Association of Estate Planners and Councils	www.naepc.org
NAIFA – National Association of Insurance and Financial Advisors	www.naifa.org
NAPFA - National Association of Personal Financial Advisors	www.napfa.org
NCNA - National Council of Nonprofit Associations	www.ncna.org
NCPG - National Committee on Planned Giving	www.ncpg.org
Philanthropy Australia	www.philanthropy.org.au
Philanthropy News Digest	foundationcenter.org/pnd/
Philanthropy Roundtable	www.philanthropyroundtable.org
SAIF - Southern Africa Institute of Fundraising	www.saifundraising.org.za
SFSP - Society of Financial Service Professionals	www.financialpro.org
PUBLICATIONS	
Charitable Gift Planning News (Planned giving and related tax newsletter written by Lynda Moerschbaecher)	www.lmnopstuff.com
Chronicle of Philanthropy (Weekly newspaper covering the nonprofit world)	www.philanthropy.com
Contributions Magazine	www.contributionsmagazine.com
Financial Planning (Monthly magazine published by the IAFP)	www.fponline.com
501(c)(3) Monthly Letter (Monthly newsletter from the Great Oaks Communication Services)	www.501c3monthlyletter.com
Fund$Raiser Cyberzine (An online fundraising news magazine)	www.fundsraiser.com

PUBLICATIONS (cont'd)	
Gift Law (Weekly e-mail and other useful information from Crescendo Software)	www.giftlaw.com
Give & Take (A monthly planned giving newsletter from Robert F. Sharpe & Co.)	www.sharpenet.com/gt
Giving Magazine (Bi-monthly magazine written for donors)	www.givingmagazine.com
Grantsmanship Center Magazine htm (Quarterly newspaper covering nonprofit management)	www.tgci.com/publications/magazine.
Grassroots Fundraising Journal (Bi-monthly magazine published by Chardon Press)	www.grassrootsfundraising.org
GuideStar (Provides financial data and information on 650,000 charities)	www.guidestar.org
Internet Prospector (Free online newsletter covering prospect research)	www.internet-prospector.org
Investment News (A weekly newspaper published by Crain Communications)	www.investmentnews.com
Journal of Financial Planning (Monthly magazine published by the FPA)	www.journalfp.net
Journal of Gift Planning (Quarterly magazine published by NCPG)	www.ncpg.org
Don Kramer's Nonprofit Issues (Monthly newsletter covering nonprofit legal issues)	www.nonprofitissues.com
Nonprofit Nuts & Bolts (Monthly newsletter offering nonprofit management tips)	www.nutsbolts.com
Nonprofit Online News (News about online fundraising published by the Gilbert Center)	news.gilbert.org
Nonprofit Times (Monthly magazine on nonprofit management)	www.nptimes.com
Nonprofit World (Bi-monthly magazine from the Society for Nonprofit Organizations)	www.snpo.org/publications
News of the Week	www.leimbergservices.com
Philanthropy (Bi-monthly magazine from the Philanthropy Roundtable)	www.philanthropyroundtable.org

PUBLICATIONS (cont'd)	
Philanthropy News Digest (Weekly online news service from the Foundation Center)	fdncenter.org/newsletters
Philanthropy News Network	www.pnnonline.org
Planned Giving Today (Monthly newsletter for gift planning professionals)	www.liebertpub.com/pgtoday
Research Grant Guides (Free catalogue describing fundraising directories)	www.researchgrant.com
Responsive Philanthropy (Quarterly newsletter on social justice and philanthropy)	www.ncrp.org/publications/index.asp
The Stelter Company (Newsletters and collateral marketing materials for charities)	www.stelter.com
Taxwise Giving (Monthly newsletter published by Conrad Teitell)	www.taxwisegiving.com
Trusts & Estates (Weekly magazine offering estate, charitable, and tax planning analysis)	www.trustsandestates.com
RESEARCHING A NONPROFIT ORGANIZATION	
Action Without Borders (Global directory of 20,000 nonprofit websites)	www.idealist.org
American Institute of Philanthropy (Private watchdog group monitoring over 500 nonprofits)	www.charitywatch.org
Association of Small Foundations (Helps foundations with little or no staff)	www.smallfoundations.org
Better Business Bureau's Wise Giving Alliance (Reports on 200 charities)	www.give.org
Charities Review Council (Evaluates Minnesota charities)	www.smartgivers.org
Charities Today (Provides information and financial data)	www.charitiestoday.com
Evangelical Council for Financial Accountability (Evaluates 900 evangelical Christian charities)	www.ecfa.org
Forum of Regional Associations of Grantmakers	www.givingforum.org
GuideStar (Provides financial data and information on 650,000 charities)	www.guidestar.org

RESEARCHING A NONPROFIT ORGANIZATION (cont'd)

Internal Revenue Service (Publications, forms, and other information for tax-exempt organizations)	www.irs.gov/charities/index.html
IRS Exempt Organization Search (Online searchable database of 500,000 exempt organizations)	apps.irs.gov/app/pub78
Leave-A-Legacy (Encourages and educates the public and professional advisors about charitable giving techniques)	www.leavealegacy.org
MinistryWatch (Database of 400 Christian charities)	www.ministrywatch.com
Morethanmoney (An outreach program to encourage giving by wealthy young adults)	www.morethanmoney.org
National Center for Charitable Statistics	www.nccs.urban.org
National Center for Family Philanthropy (Encourages family giving)	ncfp.org
Women's Philanthropy Institute (Promotes giving and community activism among women)	women-philanthropy.org
VirtualGiving.com	www.virtualgiving.com

SOFTWARE

Access International (Integrated fundraising and trust accounting software)	www.accint.com
Advanced Solutions International (Exhibition management, fundraising, and fund accounting software)	www.advsol.com
Advantage Solutions (Fund accounting and fundraising database applications)	www.advantagesolutions.com
Batsch Systems (Estate and charitable planning, and information management database software)	www.batschgroup.com
Bipster International (Makers of BIPS - Bequest Income Processing Software)	www.bipster.com
Blackbaud (Fund accounting, matching gift, grant management, school administration and fundraising software packages)	www.blackbaud.com
Brentmark (Charitable Financial Planner software)	www.brentmark.com

SOFTWARE (Cont'd)	
Brick Marketing Services (Fundraising database management system)	www.brickmill.com
Bromelkamp Company (Integrated grant management and mailing list software)	www.bromelkamp.com
CCH - ViewPlan (Makers of BeneView and BeneQuick planned giving software	onlinestore.cch.com
Charitable Gift Planner (Charitable planning software from Steve Leimberg)	www.leimberg.com
Charity Auctions (Benefit auction software)	www.charityauctionhelp.com
Community TechKnowledge (Performance reporting software for foundations)	www.communitytech.net
Crescendo (Crescendo Pro) (Planned giving marketing proposals, graphics software)	www.crescendosoft.com
CTS (Software review and ratings)	www.ctsguides.com
Datatel (Higher education administration software)	www.datatel.com
Donation (Donor and donation tracking software)	www.software4nonprofits.com
Donor2 (Fundraising software system with modular add-ons)	www.donor2.com
Donor Ware (Web and data systems for ministries)	www.donorware.com
Donor Perfect (Campaign fundraising software)	www.donorperfect.com
Donorworks (Fundraising software)	www.donorworks.com
Ebase (Nonprofit offering a free interactive database)	www.ebase.org
Etapestry (Online donor tracking software)	www.etapestry.com
Executive Data Systems (Integrated fundraising and fund accounting software)	www.execdata.com

SOFTWARE (Cont'd)	
Firstgiving (Online fundraising program)	www.firstgiving.com
Fund EZ (Accounting and fundraising software)	www.fundez.com
FUNDimensions (Donations, pledges and membership database software)	www.fundimensions.com
Fundraisinginfo.com (Online fundraising support)	fundraisinginfo.com
FundTrack Software (Makers of PhilanthrAppeal 2000 + Donor Management Software)	www.fundtracksoftware.com
Gifted Memory (Prospect management system	www.giftedmemory.com
Insgift (Charitable planning software from Insmark)	www.insmark.com
Intrepid Systems (Campaign management and donation tracking software)	www.intrepidsystems.com
Kettley (Charitable Quick-Plan) (Analyzes benefits of planned gifts)	www.kettley.com
Kintera Fundware (Accounting system)	www.fundware.com
Linked Software (Membership management system)	www.linkedsoftware.com
LMNOP (Makers of Charitable Docs in a Box document drafting software)	www.lmnopstuff.com
Metafile Information Systems (Donor management, gift and pledge tracking software)	www.metafileweb.com
Microedge (Proposal tracking and grant management system software)	www.microedge.com/home
Northwest Software (Special event and auction tracking software)	www.nwsoftware.com
NumberCruncher (Estate planning and planned giving software from Steve Leimberg)	www.leimberg.com
Oaktree Systems (Database management software)	www.oaktreesys.com

SOFTWARE (Cont'd)	
PG Calc Inc. (Makers of Planned Giving Manager proposal software and GiftWrap gift administration software)	www.pgcalc.com
PhilanthroTec (Planned giving, data collection, trust marketing, and software training packages)	www.ptec.com
Plangiv (Canadian software for designing and planning gifts)	www.plangiv.com
PlannedGiving.com (Planned giving policy manual)	www.plannedgiving.com
Pledgemaker (Donor management software)	www.pledgemaker.com
Professional Support Software (Donor management software)	www.fundraiser-software.com
RDS (Inexpensive prospect management software for new and growing nonprofits	www.donorstrategies.com
Sage Software (Fundraising, accounting, and endowment management software)	www.sagenonprofit.com
Sherwood Systems funder (Fundraising and campaign software systems)	www.sherwoodsystems.ca/frequent-
Sungard Bi-Tech (Student information systems for higher education)	www.srn.com
SunGard (Trust accounting software)	www.sungard.com
Synergy Development Systems (Makers of Denari Fundraising Software)	www.denarisoft.com
Target Software (Fundraising system)	www.targetsite.com
Telosa Software (Fundraising and donor management software))	www.telosa.com
TRUST ADMINISTRATION	
Charitable Trust Administrators Inc. (CRT administration and accounting services)	www.ctai-ca.com
CRTPro.com (CRT administration and tax reporting services)	www.crtpro.com

TRUST ADMINISTRATION (Cont'd)	
Lifefund Services LLC (CRT administration services)	www.danbury.org/lfs/admin.htm
Premier Administration (Creates and administers tax-exempt trusts)	www.premieradministration.com
Renaissance, Inc. (Performs administration services for CRTs, CLTs, gift annuities, and pooled income funds)	www.charitabletrust.com
Yellowstone Trust Administration (Charitable trust administration services)	www.yellowstoneta.com

INDEX

GUIDE
TO THE
LEED® AP
Building Design and
Construction (BD+C) Exam

MICHELLE COTTRELL, LEED AP BD+C

WILEY

John Wiley & Sons, Inc.

Library of Congress Cataloging-in-Publication Data:

Cottrell, Michelle.

  Guide to the LEED AP building design and construction (BD + C) exam / Michelle Cottrell.

    p. cm.

  Includes index.

  ISBN 978-0-470-89042-4 (pbk.); ISBN 978-0-470-93397-8 (ebk); ISBN 978-0-470-93400-5 (ebk); ISBN 978-0-470-93401-2 (ebk); ISBN 978-0-470-95021-0 (ebk); ISBN 978-0-470-95045-6 (ebk)

  1. Leadership in Energy and Environmental Design Green Building Rating System–Examinations–Study guides. 2. Sustainable construction–Examinations–Study guides. I. Title.

  TH880.C678 2011

  690.028'6–dc22

                                        2010028362

Printed in the United States of America

10 9 8 7 6 5 4 3 2 1

Contents

Acknowledgments

I WOULD FIRST LIKE TO THANK MY MOM, as her continued enthusiasm is unprecedented! Mom, you have always been there for me, to listen or to laugh especially when I needed it most. Thank you for being you!

John Czarnecki, Assoc. AIA, senior editor at John Wiley & Sons, thank you for another opportunity and your support along the way. A special thanks to Sadie Abuhoff and Kerstin Nasdeo, as it has been a pleasure working with you both. I could not continue without your help along the way!

Next, I would like to thank each and every one of the image contributors, as this book and the rest of the LEED exam prep series would not be the same without your added visual integrity. Each of you helped to maintain my motivation with your interest, support, and excitement about the book with your great images and photos.

Zach Rose, Assoc. AIA, LEED AP, LEED Green Associate, thank you for your encouragement and support for not only this book and the others, but for your continued motivation. Thank you to the rest of my team at Green Education Services for your excitement and interest in the exam prep series!

Thank you to my family for granting me the time and space allowing me to focus on this book. I would like to thank all of my friends and colleagues for your understanding, as I "disappeared" for some months to accomplish yet another endeavor.

And finally my husband, Stefano, I could not have completed yet another book without your smiling face sitting across from me each day as I typed! Thank you for listening to me, making me laugh, and for giving me a life outside of writing. You have continued to be an incredible source of humor, amazing food, and a source of energy from the moment we met!

Introduction

Guide to the LEED® AP Building Design and Construction (BD+C) Exam is the resource to prepare for the Leadership in Energy and Environmental Design (LEED®) Accredited Professional (AP) Building Design + Construction (BD+C) exam. This exam prep guide provides a road map to studying for the LEED AP BD+C exam as administered by Green Building Certification Institute (GBCI). *Guide to the LEED® AP Building Design and Construction (BD+C) Exam* is aimed at those professionals seeking more information about the basic knowledge and understanding that is required in order to pass the exam and earn the LEED AP BD+C accreditation.

As a means to introduce myself, I am a LEED consultant and an education provider, focused on sustainable design and building operation concepts. I have traveled the country helping hundreds of students to prepare for the LEED Green Associate and LEED AP exams. The LEED AP BD+C classes typically are one-day seminars that review all of the information as presented in this book. During these classes, I share my LEED project experiences and study tips in order to help make sense of this challenging information and present it in a logical format to help streamline the studying efforts for my students. This book breaks down the difficult information to be retained into a coherent and straightforward approach, as compared to simply repeating what would be found in the study reference material outlined by GBCI.

 Keep an eye out for these STUDY TIPS! as they will point out the intricacies and nuances to remember.

EXAM PREP GUIDE STRUCTURE

Guide to the LEED® AP Building Design and Construction (BD+C) Exam is organized into three parts as a method to break down the information one can expect to see on the exam. First, an introduction is needed to review the concepts and process covered in the LEED Green Associate exam in order to then understand the next part, which covers the technologies and strategies to implement as detailed in each prerequisite and credit contained within each of the categories of the BD+C LEED rating systems. Finally, the appendices include charts and diagrams summarizing the critical information, as well as other resources to narrow down the amount of information to be studied as preparation to sit for and pass the LEED AP BD+C exam. The composition of the book is as follows:

Part I: *Ramping Up is composed of the following information:*

- Chapter 1: Understanding the Credentialing Process
- Chapter 2: Sustainability and LEED Basics Review
- Chapter 3: The LEED Rating Systems of the BD+C Reference Guide

 Be sure to review the eligibility requirements described in Chapter 1 to apply for the LEED AP BD+C exam.

Part II: Diving In: The Strategies and Technologies of LEED details the overlying concepts of the primary categories and the strategies to achieve each basic concept within. Part II is focused on organizing the information to remember and also to provide the concepts behind each prerequisite and credit. It is intended to work in tandem with the coordinating study worksheets included at the end of each chapter to help you remember the details, such as the intents, requirements, documentation requirements, and required calculations of each prerequisite and credit.

In Part II, the following LEED categories are reviewed:

- Chapter 4: Sustainable Sites
- Chapter 5: Water Efficiency
- Chapter 6: Energy and Atmosphere
- Chapter 7: Materials and Resources
- Chapter 8: Indoor Environmental Quality
- Chapter 9: Innovation in Design and Regional Priority

Part III: Study Tips and Appendices is dedicated to summarizing the critical information, details, and concepts to retain, as well as providing an overview of the testing center environment. The appendices include additional resources to help summarize the information presented in Parts I and II, such as scorecards and summary charts.

STUDY TIPS! are located throughout the book as tools to help stay focused on the pertinent information. They will include things to remember and point out side note type of information. While reading through this book, be sure to also keep an eye out for **FLASHCARD TIPS!**, as they will help to distinguish the important aspects for the exam and act as an indicator to create critical flashcards. All of the FLASHCARD TIPS! referenced throughout the book are collected at the end, following the index, although it is suggested to create your own to enhance your studying. It is recommended to purchase plain white note cards, as well as the color-coded note cards (i.e., pink, yellow, blue, green, and purple). Use the white ones for the information to be covered in Part I and the color-coded cards for Part II of this exam prep book. The FLASHCARD TIPS! suggest a starting point for flashcard creation, but feel free to make more as needed. If you decide to make your own with the help of the FLASHCARD TIPS!, be sure to refer to flashcards at the end for some additional flashcard suggestions. If you decide to use the flashcards from the book and not make your own, you can always use markers or highlighters to color-code them for streamlined studying.

Be sure to spot these **FLASHCARD** TIPS! to create flashcards along the way. Use the white cards for Part I and the color-coded ones for Part II.

One of the main concepts of sustainable design is the integrative fashion in which green buildings are designed and constructed. It is critical to understand how strategies and technologies have synergies and trade-offs. For example, green roofs can have an impact on a construction budget but can help save on operational energy costs, which may present a breakeven or surplus. Green roofs, as seen in Figure I.1, also have synergistic qualities because they can not only help reduce the heat burden on a building, but also help to manage stormwater. These types of concepts will be discussed in greater detail in Part II of this exam prep guide, but for now be sure to look for these **BAIT TIPS!** throughout Part II to help bring the concepts together.

Be sure to look out for these BAIT TIPS! as well. These tips will reinforce the important concepts and Bring All of It Together as synergies and trade-offs are pointed out for green building strategies and technologies.

Figure I.1 Holy Wisdom Monastery project in Madison, Wisconsin, by Hoffman, LLC, reduces the amount of stormwater runoff from the site, increases the amount of open space, promotes biodiversity, reduces cooling loads, and reduces the impacts of the urban heat island effect by implementing a vegetated roof. *Photo courtesy of Hoffman, LLC*

STUDY SCHEDULE

Week	Chapters	Pages
1	Part I: Ramping Up (Chapters 1– 3)	3-36
2	Part II: Sustainable Sites (Chapter 4)	37-104
3	Part II: Water Efficiency (Chapter 5)	105-128
4	Part II: Energy and Atmosphere (Chapter 6)	129-162
5	Part II: Materials and Resources (Chapter 7)	163-196
6	Part II: Indoor Environmental Quality (Chapter 8)	197-262
7	Part II: Innovation in Design and Regional Priority (Chapter 9) and Part III: Study Tips	263-282
8	Study flashcards, rewrite your cheat sheet a few times, and take online practice exams	
9	Register and take the LEED AP BD+C Exam!	

As the preceding table shows, it is recommended to read through Parts I and II of this exam prep book within seven weeks. Introductory terminology from Part I should be absorbed to get on the right path to understand the more critical exam-oriented information presented in Part II. The goal is to create a complete set of flashcards during the first seven weeks while reading through the material, thus allowing the following week (eighth week of studying) to focus on memorizing and studying the flashcards, followed by taking a few online practice exams, which are available at www.GreenEDU.com.

Although the exam format and structure will be reviewed in Part III of this book, there is one component that should be revealed up front. When at the testing center and about to take the exam, you will be prompted to take a tutorial on the

 After taking some practice exams, you may want to add to your cheat sheet and/or your flashcards.

computer. You will be allotted 10 minutes for the tutorial but will probably need only 4 to 5 minutes. It is highly advised to take advantage of those extra 5 to 6 minutes and jot down some thoughts and make a "cheat sheet" of sorts prior to starting the exam. Although you will not be allowed to bring any paper, books, or pencils into the exam area, you will be supplied with blank paper and a pencil (or a dry-erase board and a marker). So now that you know this opportunity is there, let's take advantage of it! Therefore, as a concept, strategy, referenced standard, or requirement is presented in this exam prep guide, make note of it on one single sheet of paper. At the end of Part II, this "cheat sheet" should be reviewed and then rewritten with the critical information you determine that you might forget during the exam. You are the only one who knows your weaknesses in terms of the information you need to learn—I can only make recommendations and suggestions. During Week Eight, you should rewrite your cheat sheet two to three more times. The more you write and rewrite your cheat sheet, the better chance you will have for actually retaining the information. It is also advised to monitor the time it takes to generate your cheat sheet, as time will be limited on exam day.

If you maintain the recommended study schedule, seven weeks from now a set of flashcards will be created and your cheat sheet started. Then you will have one week of consistent studying time to focus on the material in your flashcards. After studying your flashcards, it is recommended to take a few online practice exams to test your knowledge. The approach to these sample exams is described in Part III, Chapter 10, of this book, including the next steps for the cheat sheet. After a few practice exams, an assessment of your preparation should be completed to determine if you are ready for the exam. Your exam date should be scheduled at that time, as appointment times are readily available.

Before focusing on the exam material, be sure to read through Chapter 1 to understand the application requirements of the LEED AP BD+C exam to ensure your eligibility and to understand the exam application process.

PART I

RAMPING UP

CHAPTER 1

UNDERSTANDING THE CREDENTIALING PROCESS

BEFORE DIVING INTO THE EFFORT OF STUDYING and preparing for the LEED® AP BD+C exam, there are quite a few things to review to ensure your eligibility. Whenever I teach an exam prep course, this topic is not typically addressed until the end of the class, as it is easier to digest at that point; but it is important to present this information here in the first chapter, to make sure the test is applicable and appropriate for you. This chapter will provide the important concepts of the tiered credentialing system to ensure that the components, the exam application process, and the requirements for eligibility are understood.

This initial information begins with the new credentialing system for LEED accreditation, as it involves three tiers:

1. LEED Green Associate
2. LEED Accredited Professional (AP) with Specialty
3. LEED Fellow

THE TIERS OF THE CREDENTIALING PROCESS

The first step of comprehending the credentialing process begins with a brief understanding of the basics of LEED. LEED is the acronym for Leadership in Energy and Environmental Design, signifying a green building rating system designed to evaluate projects and award them certification based on their performance. The U.S. Green Building Council's® (USGBC's) website indicates that LEED has become the "nationally accepted benchmark for the design, construction, and operation of high performance green buildings." USGBC created the LEED Green Building Rating System back in the 1990s as a tool for the public and private commercial real estate markets to help evaluate the performance of the built environment.

 TIP Notice the LEED acronym does **not** contain an "S" at the end. Therefore, please note this first lesson: when referring to LEED, please do not say "LEEDS," as it is quite important to refer to the acronym correctly.

The First Tier of the Credentialing System: LEED Green Associate

The **LEED Green Associate** tier is applicable for professionals with a basic understanding of green building systems and technologies. Green Associate professionals have been tested on the key components of the LEED rating systems and the certification process. This level of credentialing is the first step to becoming a LEED Accredited Professional (AP).

The Green Associate exam is geared toward all professionals involved in the world of sustainable design, construction, and operations, beyond just the typical architecture and engineering design professionals. Therefore, the exam is available for lawyers, accountants, contractors, manufacturers, owners, and developers, as well. Any professional who works in the field of sustainable design and green building is eligible to sit for the exam, especially those with LEED project experience. For those who wish to sit without LEED project experience or are not employed in a sustainable field of work, participating in an educational course focused on sustainable design would qualify instead.

The Second Tier of the Credentialing System: LEED Accredited Professional with Specialty

The next tier, **LEED AP with Specialty**, is divided into five types (of specialties):

1. *LEED AP Building Design + Construction* (BD+C). This exam includes concepts related to new construction and major renovations, core and shell projects, and schools. This specialty will also cover retail and health care applications in the future.

2. *LEED AP Interior Design + Construction* (ID+C). This exam contains questions related to tenant improvement and fit-out project knowledge for commercial interior and retail professionals.

3. *LEED AP Operations + Maintenance* (O+M). This exam covers existing building project knowledge specific to operations and maintenance issues.

4. *LEED AP Homes.* This exam applies to professionals practicing in the residential market.

5. *LEED AP Neighborhood Development* (ND). This exam tests whole or partial neighborhood development project knowledge.

Because the LEED Green Associate credentialing tier is the first step to obtaining LEED AP status, the LEED AP exams are thought of in a two-part exam process beginning with the LEED Green Associate exam. You have the option to decide whether you wish to take both exams in one day or break the exam into two different testing appointments. The exams are quite challenging and mind intensive, and can be exhausting, so bear this in mind when deciding on which option to pursue.

LEED project experience is required in order to be able to sit for any of the LEED AP specialty exams. These exams cover more in-depth knowledge of each of the prerequisites and credits, the requirements to comply including documentation and calculations, and the technologies involved with the corresponding rating system. These exams are therefore applicable for those professionals working on LEED registered projects or those who have worked on a project within the last three years that has earned certification.

The Third Tier of the Credentialing System: LEED Fellow

Finally, the third tier of the credentialing system, **LEED Fellow**, is the highest level of credentialing, but not quite yet developed. It is meant to signify a demonstration of accomplishments, experience, and proficiency within the sustainable design and construction community. These individuals will have contributed to the continued development of the green building industry. The criteria for this credential is expected to be released at Greenbuild 2010, the international conference for those professionals seeking more information about green building strategies.

THE APPLICATION PROCESS

Now that there is an understanding about the three tiers of the credentialing system, whom each tier is geared for, and the eligibility requirements of each exam type, it is time to review the process for applying for the exam. The first step involves visiting the Green Building Certification Institute® (GBCI) website at www.gbci.org and downloading the *LEED AP BD+C Candidate Handbook* found in the Professional Credentials section of the website.

 TIP GBCI updates the candidate handbooks for each of the exam types at the beginning of each month, so make sure to have the most current version.

Each of the candidate handbooks details the following information:

- Study materials—including exam format, timing, references, and sample questions
- How to apply for the exam—including the application period, eligibility requirements, and exam fees
- How to schedule your exam once your eligibility is confirmed—including confirmation, canceling, and rescheduling your test date
- A pre-exam checklist
- What to expect on the day of your exam—including name requirements, scoring, and testing center regulations
- What to do after your exam—including the Credentialing Maintenance Program (CMP) (i.e., continuing education requirements) and certificates

Although the intention of this exam prep book is to consolidate all of the information needed to prepare for the LEED AP BD+C exam, some of the references are updated from time to time. Therefore, this book contains similar information as found in the handbooks to add efficiency, but it is best advised to refer to the latest version of the handbook appropriate to the LEED AP BD+C credential for the most up-to-date exam information, especially as related to the exam application process.

In order to understand why a different organization (other than USGBC) is the resource for information for LEED professional credentials and is the destination website to apply for the exam, the role of GBCI is presented next. As previously mentioned, LEED is an independent, third-party verified, voluntary rating system, and in order to be in compliance with ANSI/ISO/IEC 17024's accreditation requirements, USGBC created GBCI to separate the rating system development from the credentialing program. GBCI is now responsible for LEED project certification and professional credentialing, while USGBC is responsible for the development of the LEED rating systems and educating the industry for continuing efforts to help evolve the green building movement, and therefore transform the market. Case in point: the USGBC website should be visited to obtain information about each rating system or to purchase reference guides, while the GBCI website should be the resource for information about taking an exam or to register a project seeking certification and learn more about the certification process. Chapter 2 defines the roles of the two organizations in more detail.

 TIP It is important to refer not only to LEED correctly, but also to projects and professionals. Remember, buildings are **certified** and people are **accredited**. People will never be able to become LEED certified professionals—remember, there are LEED APs and not LEED CPs.

Additionally, LEED **certification** is meant for projects and buildings, not products. Not only will a LEED certified professional not be found, but also neither will a LEED certified chair, air-conditioning unit, appliance, paint, or glue.

Figure 1.1 The steps to register for the LEED AP BD+C exam.

TIP

It is *critical* to sign up and create the account with GBCI consistent with the account holder's name as it appears on the identification to be used to check in at the testing center. If they do not match on the day of the exam, exam fees may be lost, as the opportunity to take the exam may be forfeited. If your existing account with USGBC is not consistent with your identification, refer to the *LEED AP BD+C Candidate Handbook* for instructions on how to update your account information.

Once the handbook is downloaded and reviewed, the next step includes establishing an account with the GBCI website. If an account already exists with USGBC, the same one can be used for GBCI's website, as they are the same. Therefore, once an account is established with GBCI, the same login information will work on USGBC's website as well. Should a new account need to be established, navigate to the "Log In to My Credentials" section of the GBCI website to create an account.

APPLY!

Once an account is established with GBCI, the next step is to apply for eligibility. On the GBCI website, visit the "My Credentials" section to begin the process after logging in. Make sure the profile is correct and select the intended credentialing path. If you have already passed the LEED Green Associate exam, you will only need to have worked on a LEED project within the past three years to be eligible to sit for the LEED AP BD+C exam. Be sure to refer to the candidate handbook for more information about the requirements for project participation. Next, enter in the project information, such as name, location, and rating system in which it was registered or certified under and upload the documentation proving eligibility as described in the *LEED AP BD+C Candidate Handbook*. You will then need to pay the nonrefundable $100 application fee. Within seven days, you should receive an email indicating approval or denial, in order to move to the next step of the exam registration process. "Five to seven percent of all applications will be audited; you will be notified immediately if you are chosen for an audit and will be notified of your eligibility within seven days."[1] Should indication of ineligibility be received, it is required to wait 90 days to apply again.

REGISTER!

Your application is valid for up to one year, once approval notification is received. At this point, the next step of registering for the exam should be seen as an option within the "My Credentials" section of the website. Here, verification is required for the test to be registered for and confirmation of membership status. Remember, USGBC national company members can take advantage of reduced exam fees. This means the company that you work for must be a national member of USGBC. To receive the discount, you will need to ensure your USGBC/GBCI account profile contains the corporate ID associated with the company you work for.

SCHEDULE!

The next step is scheduling an appointment to take the exam at a Prometric testing center. As stated previously, it is advised to refrain from selecting an exam date until further along in the preparation for the exam. In the introduction of this exam prep book, a study and reading schedule is suggested. It is highly recommended to start studying and determine the level of knowledge of the test content before scheduling an exam date.

When ready to schedule an exam date, visit www.prometric.com/gbci, or if at the GBCI website, follow the links to the Prometric website to schedule a day to take the exam, from the "My Credentials" section. Remember, the eligibility code from GBCI is required to schedule an exam date. After an exam date is scheduled, a confirmation code is displayed on the screen. Keep this code! This code will be needed should the selected exam date need to be canceled, confirmed, or rescheduled with Prometric. A confirmation email containing your confirmation code will be sent from Prometric shortly after scheduling.

In addition, it is important to remember that candidates will have three allowed testing attempts per one-year application period. In the event that a retake is necessary (even though this is not the plan!), test takers will need only to pay an additional fee for the exam and not the application fee. Refer to the *LEED AP BD+C Candidate Handbook* for more information on this rule.

 TIP To reschedule or cancel an exam date, please consult the *LEED AP BD+C Candidate Handbook* for explicit instructions. They are quite meticulous about the procedure, so it is advised to be aware of the details to avoid risking a loss in fees paid.

WHY EARN LEED CREDENTIALS?

Just like green buildings are evaluated based on triple bottom criteria (social, economic, and environmental), deciding whether to earn LEED credentials can be approached in the same fashion, as there are individual, employer, and industry benefits to examine. From an individualistic standpoint, earning the LEED AP BD+C credential will grant a professional with a differentiator to market to a potential employer or client, provide them with exposure on the GBCI website database of LEED professionals, and earn them a certificate to display and recognition as a professional in the LEED certification process. An employer would also benefit by earning the eligibility to participate in LEED projects, as more projects are requiring LEED credentials for team members; building the firm's credentials when responding to requests for proposals (RFPs) and requests for qualifications (RFQs); and having the opportunity to encourage other staff members to aim for the same credential to help the firm to evolve. Finally, the market would also benefit as more professionals earn the LEED AP BD+C credential by helping the built environment to become more sustainable and the market to evolve, transform, and grow.

CHAPTER 2
SUSTAINABILITY AND LEED BASICS REVIEW

AS MENTIONED EARLIER, IT IS CRITICAL TO BE ON THE RIGHT PATH by remembering the basic concepts tested on the LEED® Green Associate exam before jumping into the details of the LEED categories as seen on the LEED AP BD+C exam. Therefore, sustainability and green building are described and detailed as a starting point. What is sustainability? The Wikipedia website refers to the concept as the "the capacity to endure."[1] For the purposes of LEED, it is important to take a step further beyond sustainability and think of **sustainable design** and development. Although the definition is not universally accepted, the Brundtland Commission of the United Nations' website is cited (for the purposes of the exam and LEED) for their definition: "development that meets the needs of the present without compromising the ability of future generations to meet their own needs."[2]

Within the design industry, sustainable design and sustainable building concepts are interchangeable with the term **green building**—the next vocabulary word to become familiar with. When referring to green buildings, it is understood that the buildings are sensitive to the environment, but one might wonder, how exactly? Green buildings are more efficient and use resources wisely, as they take energy, water, and materials into account (Figure 2.1). But one might ask, "How do they use resources more efficiently?" To answer this question, it is important to think of the different aspects of a building, for instance:

- *Site selection.* Is the project a redevelopment in an urban area, or does it support urban sprawl? How close is the project to public transportation to reduce the number of cars coming and going? How will the building need to be situated in order to take advantage of the natural breezes for ventilation and daylight to reduce the need for artificial lighting within the building?

- *Design of the building systems, such as mechanical equipment, building envelope, and lighting systems.* How do they work together? Were they designed independently of each other? Is the heat emitted from the lighting fixtures accounted for? Are there gaps in the envelope that allow conditioned air to escape?

- *Construction processes.* Think about the people on site during construction—are they being exposed to harmful fumes and gases? Are precautions being taken to reduce the chances for mold growth or other contaminants?

- *Operations of the building.* What kinds of items are purchased to support business? What about cleaning procedures?

- *Maintenance.* When was the last time equipment was tested to ensure that it is performing appropriately? Are there procedures in place to monitor for leaks?

9

Figure 2.1 Reasor's Supermarket in Owassa, Oklahoma, incorporates daylighting strategies and polished concrete floors together helping the project to earn multiple LEED credits within different categories, including Materials and Resources, Energy and Atmosphere, and Indoor Environmental Quality. *Photo courtesy of L&M Construction Chemicals, Inc.*

 TIP When thinking of green buildings, it is important to think of not only how the building is designed to function and how it is constructed, but also the environmental impacts from operations and maintenance.

■ *Waste management.* How is construction waste addressed? What about the garbage generated during operations? Is it going to the landfill? Who knows where those containers are going?!

THE BENEFITS OF GREEN BUILDINGS

Hopefully, the previous questions started to generate some thoughts of what is involved with green buildings. If not, maybe evaluating the benefits of green buildings might help; beginning with a review of the traditional buildings statistics and how they impact our planet. U.S. Green Building Council® (USGBC) has compiled information from the Energy Information Administration and the U.S. Geological Survey on the impacts of buildings on our natural resources in the United States. The USGBC website reports the following statistics for *conventionally* designed and built buildings:

39 percent primary energy use

72 percent electricity consumption

38 percent carbon dioxide (CO_2) emissions

14 percent potable water consumption[3]

It is important to digest the 38 percent CO_2 emissions statistic, as this percentage puts buildings at the top of the list, followed by transportation and industry. Buildings have a bigger impact on greenhouse gas emissions—the biggest, actually! These statistics have pushed the market to find better ways to design, construct, and operate buildings.

When looking at the statistics for green buildings, including LEED certified buildings, the General Services Administration (GSA) indicates that these projects have been able to achieve the following:

26 percent energy use reduction

40 percent water use reduction

70 percent solid waste reduction

13 percent reduction in maintenance costs[4]

These percentages reflect the benefits in the economic bottom line, but these green buildings have also reduced their impact on the environment, as well as demonstrated an improved indoor environment (such as air quality) and contribution to the community. Indoor air quality is extremely important when analyzing the benefits of green buildings, as the Environmental Protection Agency (EPA) reports Americans "spend, on average, 90 percent or more of their time indoors."[5] Green buildings have resulted in 27 percent higher levels of satisfaction[6] and allowed students the opportunity to perform better.[7]

TIP Write it, read it, say it, and hear it as many times as possible. The more senses you involve in your studying efforts, the more information you will be able to retain.

The Triple Bottom Line

The USGBC website summarizes the benefits of green buildings in three components: environmental, economic, and health and community benefits, as shown in Table 2.1. In the green building industry, these three concepts are defined as the *triple bottom line* (Figure 2.2). A conventional project usually assesses only the singular component of the economic prosperity for the project.

TABLE 2.1 The Benefits of Green Buildings[8]

Environmental Benefits	Enhance and protect ecosystems and biodiversity
	Improve air and water quality
	Reduce solid waste
	Conserve natural resources
Economic Benefits	Reduce operating costs
	Enhance asset value and profits
	Improve employee productivity and satisfaction
	Optimize life-cycle economic performance
Health and Community Benefits	Improve air, thermal, and acoustic environments
	Enhance occupant comfort and health
	Minimize strain on local infrastructure
	Contribute to overall quality of life

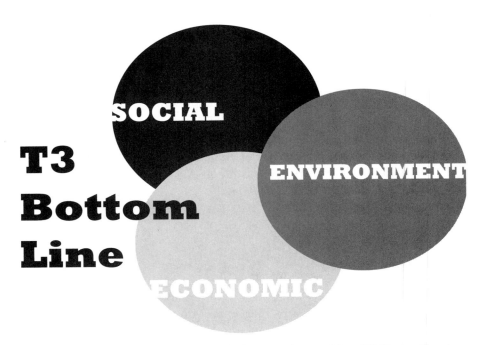

Figure 2.2 The triple bottom line.

However, when determining the goals for a project seeking LEED certification, the process typically begins with assessing the goals in comparison to the *triple bottom line* values. For example, should a client wish to install a green roof on their building, the team would assess the financial implications as compared to the environmental impacts versus the community benefits. These types of details will be discussed later, but understanding the three types of benefits is important at this time.

QUIZ TIME!

TIP These questions are formatted just as they would be on the exam. Notice the question indicates how many answers to select. The proper number of correct answers is required on the exam, as partial credit is **not** awarded.

TIP Answers to all of the quiz questions can be found in Appendix K.

Q2.1. Which of the following is an environmental benefit of green building strategies? (Choose one)

    A. Conserve natural resources

    B. Reduce solid waste

    C. Improve air and water quality

    D. Enhance and protect ecosystems and biodiversity

    E. All of the above

Q2.2. How much time, on average, do Americans spend indoors? (Choose one)

    A. 10 percent

    B. 90 percent

    C. 65 percent

    D. 35 percent

Q2.3. According to the Department of Energy's website, space heating is the largest energy use in the United States, followed by lighting. True or False?

    A. True

    B. False

Q2.4. Which of the following describes a high-performance green building? (Choose one)

  A. Conserves water and energy

  B. Uses spaces, materials, and resources efficiently

  C. Minimizes construction waste

  D. Creates a healthy indoor environment

  E. All of the above

TIP Don't worry if some of the questions presented are unfamiliar territory. The questions in this book are meant to present you with new information to learn from and to prepare you for the real exam, as there is bound to be information presented for which you will need to use the process of elimination to determine the best answers.

THE DESIGN AND CONSTRUCTION PROCESS

The Project Team Members

Understanding the processes of design and construction, from a traditional or conventional standpoint versus that of sustainable projects, begins with an understanding of the players involved in the process:

Architect. Responsible for the design of green building strategies, including overall site planning and interior spaces

MEP engineer. Responsible for the design of the energy and water systems of a building, more specifically, the mechanical, electrical, and plumbing components, including thermal impacts

Landscape architect. Responsible for the selection of trees and plants, the impacts of shading, and water efficiency for irrigation; also responsible for vegetated roof design

Civil engineer. Responsible for site design, including stormwater management, open space requirements, and site protection

Contractor. Typically referred to as the GC, short for general contractor; responsible for the demolition (if required) and construction of a facility, including site work

Facility manager. Also referred to as a building engineer; responsible for maintaining a building and its site during operations

Commissioning authority (CxA). Responsible for the commissioning process, including drawing review during design and equipment installation and performance review during construction

Owner. Defines the triple bottom line goals and selects the team members for a project; can be a developer and does not have to be the end user

End users/occupants. The inhabitants of a building and therefore should be the main priority when designing for comfort and productivity

For those not familiar with the professionals involved, create flashcards for each to remember their roles and importance.

Conventional Projects versus the Integrative Design Approach

The next step to understanding the process for design and construction involves comprehending the different types of projects, as well as the difference in the approach of conventionally designed buildings versus the integrative approach pursued by sustainably designed projects. Projects pursuing LEED certification are approached differently than conventional projects, as they use an integrative process that begins at the onset of the project, or as early as possible during design.

There are substantial differences between conventional and sustainably driven projects, specifically with the phases of the design and construction processes:

Phases of the Traditional Project Delivery:
- Predesign/Programming
- Schematic Design phase
- Design Development phase
- Construction Documents phase
- Agency Permit/Bidding
- Construction
- Substantial Completion
- Final Completion
- Certificate of Occupancy

Phases of the Integrative Project Delivery:
- Conceptualization
- Criteria Design
- Detailed Design
- Implementation Documents
- Agency Coordination/Final Buyout
- Construction
- Substantial Completion
- Final Completion
- Certificate of Occupancy

TIP Notice when all the players are introduced to the project and how they all work in a linear and independent fashion for a conventionally designed project.

The key difference of the phases depends on who is involved and when, when comparing a traditionally designed and constructed building to one that is designed with sustainable initiatives. For example, with a traditionally designed project, an owner may hire a civil engineering or environmental team once they select a piece of property. Once the environmental reports are completed and they have an idea of how their building can fit on the site, the site plan is handed off to an architect. The architect then works with the owner to detail the program requirements (known as the **Programming** phase) and then begins to design the building (known as the **Schematic Design** phase). The architect then works with an engineering team (typically composed of mechanical, electrical, and plumbing engineers and a structural engineer, if needed, depending on the project type). These professionals typically work independently of each other to complete their tasks (known as the **Design Development** phase). Remember, with a traditional design project, the architect has already designed the building and is now handing off the plans to the engineers to fit the building systems into the building that was designed without their input. Once the basic design elements are established, each professional works to complete a set of **construction documents** (CDs). Notice that the responsibilities are segmented just as the communication is fragmented.

What happens next with the CDs varies with different project types. Typically, these documents are first issued for permit review by the local municipality. It is quite common for most project types to send the CDs out for bid to a number of contractors about the same time as the drawings are issued for permit review (known as a Design-Bid-Build project type), while other project types have the contractor engaged as one entity with the architect from the beginning (known as a Design-Build project type).

At this point in a Design-Bid-Build project type, the contractor is given a short period of time in which to evaluate the drawings and provide the owner with a fee to provide demolition services (if required) and to construct the building, including site development work. They are given an opportunity to submit questions (known as requests for information, or RFIs) about the requirements or design elements during this bidding process, but then they are held to the quote they provide. Remember, the contractor was not engaged during the previous design phases, so they are not familiar with the project and have to dive in quickly, sometimes making assumptions about the construction requirements. Most of the time, projects are awarded based on the lowest bid, but think about the implications of doing so. If the lowest bidder wins the job, where are they cutting corners? Is quality being compromised? Was a critical element omitted? No one likes to lose money, as that is just bad business, but is this really the best way to select a contractor?

Once the permit is received, the contractor is selected and the construction cost is agreed upon, the phases of the design process are over and the construction process begins. Just as the design process has four phases, the construction process does as well. **Construction** commences the process, traditionally with little involvement from the design team. The next phase, **Substantial Completion**, includes the final inspection process and when the owner issues a "punch list." The owner compiles a punch list while walking the space with the contractor and notes any problems requiring the contractor's attention. **Final Completion** is next, followed by the **Certification of Occupancy**. Once the Certificate of Occupancy is received, the building is then permitted to be occupied.

When compared to the traditional project delivery method, the integrative design process for sustainable design projects involves different phases of design and construction as shown in the previous list, and remember the main differentiator is determined by the team members, particularly how and when they are involved. For a project seeking LEED certification, the owner may engage a number of consultants early in the process to assist in selecting the property or tenant space. They may retain an architect to evaluate the site for building orientation options to capitalize on natural ventilation or daylighting opportunities. They may hire a civil engineer to research the stormwater codes and to determine access to public transportation. A LEED consultant may be engaged to assist with evaluating the triple bottom line goals particular to a project site or tenant space. Think about the benefits of bringing the landscape architect and the civil engineer on board simultaneously so they could work together to reveal the opportunities to use stormwater collection for irrigation needs. If the site were already determined, the owner would bring all of the consultants (including the general contractor) together to review the economic, social, and environmental goals collaboratively. This goal-setting meeting, or *charette*, is a key component of the first step of a sustainable project and is therefore part of the first design phase of Programming or Predesign, as the integrative process should be started as early as possible. This early start concept is graphically represented in the Macleamy Curve on page 21 of the *Integrated Project Delivery: A Guide*. The Curve indicates

 Besides Design-Bid-Build and Design-Build, other project delivery types are Multiprime and Construction Manager at Risk.

 Remember, the integrative process needs to be implemented as early as possible in order for the true benefits to be achieved!

TIP Remember, an integrative project delivery (IPD) differs from a conventional project in terms of teams, process, risk, communications, agreement types, and phases.

the ability to impact functional capabilities during the early stages of the process as the cost of design changes increases as the project progresses.

Another key difference with a green building project is the use of energy modeling and Building Information Modeling (BIM). These tools allow the design team to find efficiencies and conflicts with their design intentions. They can model the proposed building systems to evaluate and predict the performance of the components specific to the elements and the project's location and site. These technologies allow the design team to specify systems and equipment sized appropriately for the specific building. Because the tools allow for the project to be evaluated from a three-dimensional perspective, design teams will also have the opportunity to find conflicts with building components and systems. The design teams can even use these tools to determine the estimated energy and water savings as compared to implementing traditional building systems. These tools are used throughout the design phases to bring more efficiency to the project for all team members.

Projects utilizing an integrative design approach bring the entire team together early in the design process, thus allowing the opportunity for everyone to work more collectively, which can actually save time and money. A project's schedule can be reduced because the project's goals are reinforced throughout every step of the process. An integrative project delivery (IPD) avoids the "value engineering" aspect that can happen on a conventionally designed project. Value engineering (VE) can take place when the bidding contractors respond with a construction cost much higher than anticipated by the owner and design professionals. In response to this high price, the design team begins to remove design elements from the original scope of work to try to get the construction cost better aligned with the project budget. IPD projects avoid this inefficiency because the contractor is evaluating the elements and drawings continuously throughout each of the design phases.

TIP Remember, with an IPD the risks may be shared across the team, but so are the rewards!

In summary, traditionally designed projects differ from IPDs in terms of teams, process, risk, communications, agreement types, and phases. Remember, conventional project teams are fragmented, whereas green building teams work more collectively. An IPD project's process is more holistically approached, while a traditional project is more linear. The risk is separated with a fragmented, traditional project as compared to an IPD. In terms of communicating ideas and concepts, traditional projects are presented in a two-dimensional format while sustainable projects work with BIM technologies to allow for the opportunity to find conflicts. Agreement types can vary, but with an IPD there is more collaboration to encourage a multilateral approach as compared to a unilateral approach of a conventional project. Finally, the phases change names from a traditional approach versus an IPD.

DO GREEN BUILDINGS COST MORE?

TIP Chapter 7 discusses the environmental components of LCAs.

When assessing the cost of any type of project, it is important to understand the different types of costs involved. Traditionally, only two types of costs are detailed in a project's pro forma: hard costs and soft costs. Hard costs are defined as construction costs including site work and demolition, while soft costs are related to the fees for professional services including legal and design. Soft costs also include pre- and postconstruction-related expenses, such as insurance. Green building projects take budgeting a step further by including a **life-cycle assessment** (LCA) cost. LCAs include the purchase price, installation, operation, maintenance, and replacement costs for each technology and strategy proposed to determine the appropriateness of the solution specific to the project.

USGBC has promoted many studies, including one from Davis Langdon (as found in the references listed in the *LEED AP BD+C Candidate Handbook*), indicating that green building does not have to cost more. This is especially true if the project starts the process early in the design phases. It is also important to bridge the gap between capital and operating budgets to understand the value of green building technologies and strategies. For example, the first or up-front cost of installing photovoltaic panels, high-efficiency mechanical systems, or an indoor water wall to improve indoor air quality may not fit in a typical budget, but if the utility cost savings were considered and evaluated, either one might make more sense. Another case in point, first costs may also be higher in a traditionally designed project because of the lack of integration. For example, a mechanical engineer may specify a larger mechanical system than what is actually needed because they may not realize that high-performance windows were specified by the architect, along with building insulation with a higher R-value. Remember, the economic bottom line is important, but a green building also evaluates the environmental and social impacts and benefits.

USGBC AND GBCI

Although Chapter 1 briefly introduced USGBC, it is important to remember the organization as "a 501(c)(3) nonprofit composed of leaders from every sector of the building industry working to promote buildings and communities that are environmentally responsible, profitable and healthy places to live and work," as posted on the USGBC website.[9] USGBC's mission statement is also listed on their website as "to transform the way buildings and communities are designed, built and operated, enabling an environmentally and socially responsible, healthy, and prosperous environment that improves the quality of life."[10] Remember also, USGBC created GBCI in January 2008 to "administer project certifications and professional credentials and certificates within the framework of the U.S. Green Building Council's Leadership in Energy and Environmental Design (LEED®) Green Building Rating Systems™," as indicated on the GBCI website.[11] GBCI's mission statement is stated as "to support a high level of competence in building methods for environmental efficiency through the development and administration of a formal program of certification and recertification."[12]

As indicated in Figure 2.3, USGBC is focused on developing the LEED Green Building Rating Systems, as well as providing education and research programs.

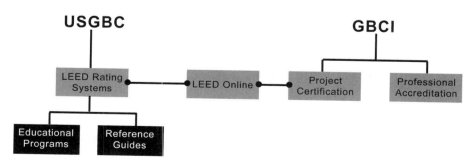

Figure 2.3 The roles of USGBC and GBCI.

Make a flashcard to remember what a TAG is.

In order to develop the rating systems, USGBC created a LEED Steering Committee composed of five technical advisory groups (TAGs) to help the main categories evolve. Eight regional councils are also a part of USGBC to help with the regional components of the rating systems.

GBCI was created in order to separate the rating system development from the certification and credentialing process. Therefore, GBCI is responsible for administering the process for projects seeking LEED certification and for professionals seeking accreditation credentials. GBCI administers the LEED certification process for projects with the help of certification bodies. These certification bodies are responsible for managing the review process, determining a building's compliance with LEED standards, and establishing the level of certification for which they qualify. Therefore, the certification bodies can be thought of as LEED customer service for teams working on a registered project. Ultimately, though, GBCI is responsible for the quality assurance during the certification and credentialing processes.

QUIZ TIME!

Q2.5. Risk is individually managed within an IPD. True or False?

    A. True

    B. False

Q2.6. When working on a green building project, when is the best time to incorporate an integrative design approach? (Choose one)

    A. Schematic design

    B. Construction documents

    C. Design development

    D. Beginning of construction

    E. Substantial completion

Q2.7. Life-cycle assessments (LCAs) are a beneficial tool to determine which of the following? (Choose one)

    A. Environmental benefits and potential impacts of a material, product, or technology

    B. Economics of building systems during the life of the building

    C. Environmental impacts of materials during construction

    D. Social impacts of policies during a fiscal year

    E. Maintenance implications, including cost, during the life of the building

Q2.8. The project team is looking to conduct a life-cycle cost analysis as a method of evaluating alternative flooring products. Which of the following should they take into consideration as input factors to that analysis? (Choose two)

    A. First costs, excluding the cost of installation

    B. First costs, including the cost of installation

C. Maintenance, life expectancy, and replacement cost

D. Maintenance and replacement cost, but not life expectancy

Q2.9. A LEED Accredited Professional is presented with a project that was started without sustainable design or LEED certification in mind. However, the owner and design team members involved thus far—none of which has significant experience with either LEED or sustainable design—have expressed interest in this path, in spite of the fact that the project is already well under way and moving rapidly toward the construction document phase. Given this situation, which of the following would tend to have the most influence on the effectiveness of the sustainable design process for a project aimed at LEED certification? (Choose three)

A. Starting the sustainable design process and consideration of LEED-related goals and getting objectives under way as soon as possible

B. Extensive research, evaluation, and life-cycle assessment for intended material and technology options

C. Aggressive value engineering of individual line items to ensure that the budget is not exceeded

D. Collectively delegating responsibility for specific target LEED credits and associated strategies to appropriate team members

E. Establishing means of collaborative, interdisciplinary communication among team members as a departure from a conventionally more segmented design process

Q2.10. Which of the following statements are true in reference to certification bodies? (Choose two)

A. Certification bodies are managed by USGBC.

B. Certification bodies are accredited to ISO standard 17021.

C. Certification bodies are assigned to a project once a project is registered.

D. Certification bodies are responsible for responding to appeals.

E. Certification bodies help individuals prepare for their accreditation exams.

CHAPTER 3

THE LEED RATING SYSTEMS OF THE *BD+C REFERENCE GUIDE*

THE LEED® AP BUILDING DESIGN AND CONSTRUCTION (BD+C) exam tests the knowledge of the rating systems contained within the *BD+C Reference Guide*. Not only is it important to know which three rating systems are included, it is also important to know when to use each one. The *BD+C Reference Guide* contains the LEED for New Construction and Major Renovations™ (LEED NC), LEED for Core & Shell™ (LEED CS), and LEED for Schools™ rating systems.

Use the white flashcards to remember each of the rating systems to remember which project types are best suited for each.

LEED FOR NEW CONSTRUCTION AND MAJOR RENOVATION (LEED NC)

LEED NC applies to most project types, although it was developed primarily for commercial office buildings. Other project types can include high-rise residential buildings (four or more stories), government buildings, institutional buildings (such as libraries and churches), and hotels. This rating system can also be applied to major renovation work, including heating, ventilation, and air conditioning (HVAC) or interior rehabilitations or significant envelope modifications. With LEED NC, the owner must occupy more than 50 percent of the leasable square footage. For projects at existing facilities with a smaller scope, the LEED for Existing Buildings: Operations & Maintenance™ rating system (EBOM) would be more appropriate. As with any LEED rating system, it is up to the project team to determine which system is best suited to their project.

TIP The majority of all LEED projects fall under the LEED NC rating system.

LEED FOR CORE & SHELL (LEED CS)

LEED CS was developed for the speculative development market where project teams are not responsible for all of the building's design and construction. For example, a developer may wish to build a new building but is not yet sure who will lease the interior space. Without knowing who the tenant will be, it is difficult to determine how the interior spaces will be finished and utilized. Similar to LEED NC, this rating system can be applied to commercial office buildings, medical

TIP The owner must occupy more than 50 percent of the leasable square footage for LEED NC projects and less than 50 percent for LEED CS projects.

Figure 3.1 Bill Stoller, the owner of Stoller Vineyards in Dayton, Ohio, holds the first LEED Gold plaque awarded to a winemaking facility. *Photo courtesy of Mike Haverkate, Stoller Vineyards*

office buildings, retail centers, warehouses, and lab facilities. The key difference between LEED NC and LEED CS relates specifically to occupancy. Remember, LEED NC requires the owner to occupy more than 50 percent of the leasable square footage, whereas the LEED CS rating system requires the owner to occupy less than 50 percent. Since the project team is left in the dark about the tenant(s), the rating system provides tools for guidance, such as default occupancy counts and energy modeling guidelines (specific for Core & Shell projects). The rating system appendix also includes tenant lease and sales agreement information specific to certification implications and LEED CS precertification guidelines.

PRECERTIFICATION

Precertification is available only within the LEED for Core & Shell rating system and is therefore unique. Remember, the rating system is aimed at the speculative development market where a marketing tool is desired and beneficial. Project teams are allowed to submit, for an additional flat rate fee, for precertification review based on declared environmental goals. Precertification is awarded based on the intentions of the project and not the actual achievement of the stated goals. The review process is intended to take less than one month but can be expedited for an additional fee. Note that the precertification fee is in addition to registration or regular certification review fees.

LEED FOR SCHOOLS

The LEED for Schools rating system applies best to the design and construction of new schools, as well as existing schools undergoing major renovations. This rating system is geared toward K–12 school types and can include any project situated on the grounds of such schools, such as administrative buildings, maintenance facilities, or dormitories. LEED for Schools uses the LEED NC rating system as a starting point and adds classroom acoustics, master planning, mold prevention, and environmental site assessment evaluation components. For post-secondary or prekindergarten projects, a project team can determine if LEED NC or LEED for Schools is more appropriate. Existing academic buildings can pursue the LEED for Existing Schools™ rating system.

THE CATEGORIES OF LEED

Each of the three LEED rating systems included in the *BD+C Reference Guide* has five main categories:

- Sustainable Sites (SS)
- Water Efficiency (WE)
- Energy & Atmosphere (EA)
- Materials & Resources (MR)
- Indoor Environmental Quality (EQ)

   The rating systems also include two other categories that provide bonus points: Innovation in Design (ID) and Regional Priority (RP).

PREREQUISITES AND CREDITS

As shown in Figure 3.2, within each category of each of the rating systems there are prerequisites and credits. For certification, it is critical to remember that

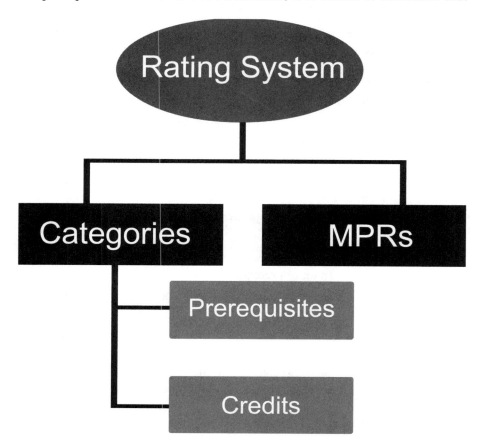

Figure 3.2 The components of a rating system.

prerequisites are absolutely required, while credits are optional. Not all categories contain prerequisites, but all of the categories have credits. All of the prerequisites of each primary category, required by the majority of the rating systems, are noted in the following list. These minimum performance features will be discussed in Part II, within each chapter broken out by category. It does not matter if a project intends to pursue credits in every category—*all* prerequisites are required and are mandatory within the rating system the project is working within.

Make a flashcard to remember the differences between credits and prerequisites. Be sure to include the following: credits are optional components that earn points, while prerequisites are mandatory, are not worth any points, and address minimum performance features.

The prerequisites covered in the **BD+C Reference Guide** *are sorted by category:*

Sustainable Sites
> Construction Activity Pollution Prevention
> Environmental Site Assessment (Schools Only)

Water Efficiency
> 20 Percent Water Use Reduction

Energy & Atmosphere
> Fundamental Commissioning of Building Energy Systems
> Minimum Energy Performance
> Fundamental Refrigerant Management

Materials & Resources
> Storage and Collection of Recyclables

Indoor Environmental Quality
> Minimum Indoor Air Quality Performance
> Environmental Tobacco Smoke (ETS) Control
> Minimum Acoustical Performance (Schools Only)

Each prerequisite and credit is structured the same, and both include the same components.

The components of prerequisites and credits:

- Credit name and point value

- Intent—describes the main goal or benefit for each credit or prerequisite

- Requirements—details the elements to fulfill the prerequisite or credit. Some credits have a selection of options to choose from to earn point(s)

- Benefits and issues to consider—discusses the triple bottom line values to the credit or prerequisite

- Related credits—indicates the trade-offs and synergies of credits and prerequisites

- Referenced standards—lists the standard referenced for establishing the requirements of the credit or prerequisite

- Implementation—suggests strategies and technologies to comply with the requirements of the credit or prerequisite

- Timeline and team—outlines which team member is typically responsible for the credit and when the effort should be addressed

- Calculations—although most calculations are completed online, this section describes the formulas to be used specific to the credit or prerequisite

- Documentation guidelines—describes the necessary documentation requirements to be submitted electronically for certification review

- Examples—demonstrates examples to satisfy requirements
- Exemplary performance—think of these as bonus points for achieving the next incremental level of performance
- Regional variation—speaks to issues as related to project's geographic location
- Operations and maintenance considerations—describes relevance of the credit or prerequisite after building is occupied, specific to the Existing Buildings: Operations & Maintenance rating system
- Resources—provides other tools or suggestions for more information on the topic
- Definitions—provides clarification for general and unique terms presented

Credit Weightings

Since prerequisites are required, they are not worth any points. All credits however, are worth a minimum of one point. Credits are always positive whole numbers, never fractions or negative values. All prerequisites and credits are tallied on scorecards (also referred to as checklists) specific to each rating system.

 TIP Remember, prerequisites are not worth any points but are mandatory in order for a project to receive certification.

Any project seeking certification must earn a minimum of 40 points, but this does not mean 40 credits must be earned as well; because different credits are weighted differently, they have varying point potentials. To determine each credit's weight, USGBC referred to the U.S. Environmental Protection Agency's (EPA's) 13 Tools for the Reduction and Assessment of Chemical and Other Environmental Impacts (TRACI) categories for environmental and health concerns including: climate change, resource depletion, human health criteria, and water intake. Once the categories of impact were determined and prioritized, USGBC referred to the National Institute of Standards and Technology (NIST) for their research to determine a value for each of the credits by comparing each of the strategies to mitigate each of the impacts.

 TIP Refer to the LEED scorecards in Appendices F, G, and H for a visual representation of how each category is composed of credits and prerequisites and the allocation of points.

As a result of the credit weighting and carbon overlay exercise, LEED values those strategies that reduce the impacts on climate change and those with the greatest benefit for indoor environmental quality, focusing on energy efficiency and carbon dioxide (CO_2) reduction strategies. For example, transportation is a very important element within LEED, and therefore any credits associated with getting to and from the project site are weighted more. Water is an invaluable natural resource, and therefore water efficiency and consumption reduction is weighted appropriately to encourage project teams to design accordingly to use less. Providing renewable energy on a project's site will lessen the burden on fossil fuels, and therefore is also suitably weighted.

 Remember, credit weightings are based on environmental impacts and human benefits, such as energy efficiency and CO_2 reduction for cleaner air.

In summary, USGBC created a simplified, 100-base-point scale for the four different certification levels.

- Certified: 40–49 points
- Silver: 50–59 points
- Gold: 60–79 points
- Platinum: 80 and higher

The 100 base points are totaled from the five main categories: SS, WE, EA, MR, and EQ. The last two categories make up 10 bonus points for a total of 110 available points. See Figure 3.3 for a breakdown of credits and point opportunities per category for each of the rating systems.

 Make a flashcard so you can quiz yourself on the certification levels and corresponding point ranges.

Credits				Possible Points		
NC	CS	Schools	Category	NC	CS	Schools
8	9	10	Sustainable Sites	26	28	24
3	3	4	Water Efficiency	10	10	11
6	6	6	Energy and Atmosphere	35	37	33
7	6	7	Materials and Resources	14	13	13
8	8	10	Indoor Environmental Quality	15	12	19
Subtotal				100	100	100
Innovation and/or Exemplary				6	6	6
Regional Priority				4	4	4
Total				110	110	110

Figure 3.3 The Point Distributions for BD+C Rating Systems

QUIZ TIME!

Q3.1. A developer in Phoenix is seeking LEED gold certification for a new lab facility to be built in the spring. They plan on occupying 32 percent of the facility. Which rating system should they register for? (Choose one)

A. LEED for New Construction

B. LEED for Commercial Interiors

C. LEED for Existing Buildings: Operations + Maintenance

D. LEED for Core & Shell

E. LEED for Schools

Q3.2. Which of the following statements are true in regard to credit weightings? (Choose two)

A. USGBC consulted with NIST and the U.S. EPA's TRACI tool to determine the credit weightings.

B. The LEED rating systems were reorganized, and new credits were introduced to recognize what matters most, such as transportation.

C. All of the BD+C LEED rating systems are based on a 100-point scale.

D. All credits are worth two points within LEED NC, but only one point within LEED CS.

Q3.3. If a university wishes to build a new administration building on their campus, they could look to LEED for New Construction or LEED for Schools rating systems and determine which one is more applicable. (Choose one)

A. True, but only if the mechanical systems are on one loop.

B. False, administration buildings cannot be certified under LEED NC.

C. True, the project team will need to determine which rating system is best suited to the project.

D. False, the university would need to look at the LEED for Universities rating system.

Q3.4. Which of the following is true about credit weightings and the carbon overlay? (Choose one)

A. Considers impact of direct energy use

B. Considers impact of transportation

C. Considers impact of embodied emissions of water, solid waste, and materials

D. All of the above

Q3.5. Incorporating green building strategies, such as high-efficiency mechanical systems, on-site photovoltaic systems, and an indoor water wall to help with the indoor air quality and air conditioning, plays a role in what type of cost implications? (Choose one)

A. Increased life-cycle costs

B. Increased first costs

C. Reduced construction costs

D. Increased soft costs

E. Reduced soft costs

Q3.6. If a project plans on earning silver certification under the LEED for Schools rating system, which point range would they aim for? (Choose one)

A. 50–59

B. 20–30

C. 40–49

D. 60–69

E. 30–39

THE LEED CERTIFICATION PROCESS

The typical project team members were previously outlined, but one member was not included: the LEED project administrator. The administrator is typically responsible for registering a project with Green Building Certification Institute (GBCI®) and for the coordination between all of the disciplines on the project team, by managing the documentation process until LEED certification is awarded. The LEED project administrator can be one of the team members previously mentioned in Chapter 2 and therefore would serve a dual-purpose role, or they can be an addition to the team. In either case, the administrator would grant access for each of the team members to LEED-Online, the online project management system.

TIP To learn more about LEED-Online, be sure to check out the demo video at www.youtube.com/ watch?v=fS3yzjZxcUA.

TIP Remember, only invited team members can see a project's LEED-Online page, after a project is registered.

TIP Remember, USGBC members pay a reduced fee for project registration and certification.

LEED-Online

LEED-Online is a web-based tool used to manage a project seeking LEED certification. It is the starting point to register a project with GBCI and communicate with the certification bodies, and is used to review the documentation submitted for both prerequisites and credits during design and construction. All projects seeking certification (except LEED for Homes™) are required to utilize LEED-Online to upload submittal templates and any required supporting documentation, such as drawings, contracts, and policies for review by the assigned certification body. Project teams receive reviewer feedback, can check the status of application reviews, and learn the certification level earned for their project through LEED-Online. Credit interpretation requests and appeals (both to be discussed later in the chapter) are also processed through LEED-Online.

When a team member is invited to a project on LEED-Online, they need to log in to the LEED-Online website to gain access. Once signed in, they would be greeted with the "My Projects" page to see a list of active projects they are assigned to. Upon selecting one of the projects, the "Project Dashboard" page would appear. This Dashboard serves as a project's home page and gives access to:

- The project's scorecard—shows which credits the team is pursuing and their status

- Credit interpretation requests (CIRs) and rulings

- LEED submittal templates—think of these as the "cover pages" for each credit and prerequisite. There is a submittal template for every prerequisite and credit, which must be submitted through LEED-Online. If a calculation is needed to show compliance, the template contains a spreadsheet with a built-in functionality that automatically completes the calculation after the required data is inputted according to the requirements described in the reference guides.

- Timeline—where a project administrator would submit for certification review

- Postcertification—to purchase plaques, certificates, and the like

Registration

The LEED certification process for projects begins with project registration. To register a project, the team administrator would sign in to LEED-Online and click on the "Register New Project" tab and follow the instructions provided. The registration process begins with a review of eligibility criteria including contact and USGBC membership verification. The next step involves selecting a rating system. LEED-Online provides assistance through a "Rating System Selector" to help the team to decipher which rating system is best suited to the specific project seeking certification. Before advancing to the "Rating System Results" step, the team administrator is prompted to confirm compliance with the seven minimum program requirements (MPRs) to be described in the next section. After confirming MPR compliance, the applicable LEED scorecard appears. The next step of registration includes entering specific project information, including owner contact information, project address and square footage, and the anticipated construction start and end dates. All of the information is then presented on screen for review, the payment is processed, and then the registration information is confirmed. The project administrator is then awarded access to the project's LEED-Online page through their "My Projects" tab and assigned a certification body for customer service.

Minimum Program Requirements

Just as there are prerequisites that must be achieved in each rating system, there are seven MPRs that must be met as well, in order for a project to receive certification. MPRs pertain to all the rating systems except LEED for Homes and LEED for Neighborhood Development. MPRs are critical components that are not listed on a project scorecard, but instead confirmed when registering a project on LEED-Online. Should noncompliance with any of the seven mandated MPRs be found at any time, a project could risk losing its certification, including any fees paid for registration and certification. The USGBC website details the following seven MPRs[1]:

MPR 1. Must comply with environmental laws

MPR 2. Must be a complete, permanent building or space

MPR 3. Must use a reasonable site boundary

The LEED project boundary must include and be consistent with all of the property as part of the scope of work of the new construction or major renovation, including any land that will be disturbed for the purpose of undertaking the LEED project during construction and operations.

The LEED project boundary may not include land that is owned by another party.

Campus projects seeking LEED certification must have project boundaries equal to 100 percent of the gross land area on the campus. If this causes a conflict with MPR 7, then MPR 7 takes precedence.

MPR 4. Must comply with minimum floor area requirements

A minimum of 1,000 square feet of gross floor area must be included in the scope of work.

MPR 5. Must comply with minimum occupancy rates

Full-time equivalent occupancy

The LEED project must be occupied by at least one full-time equivalent (FTE) occupant. If there is less than one annualized FTE, EQ credits will not be awarded, although compliance with EQ prerequisites is required.

MPR 6. Commitment to share whole-building energy and water usage data

Five years of actual whole-project utility data must be shared with U.S. Green Building Council (USGBC) and/or Green Building Certification Institute (GBCI).

MPR 7. Must comply with a minimum building area to site area ratio

The project's gross floor area must be no less than 2 percent of the gross land area within the LEED project boundary.

 TIP MPR 2 prohibits mobile homes, trailers, and boats from pursuing LEED certification.

 TIP Remember, all MPRs must be met in order to certify a project and to keep the certification once earned.

 TIP Be sure to make flashcards to remember the seven MPRs.

MPR 3 refers to the LEED project boundary. There are three types of boundaries to be aware of for the purposes of LEED: property boundary line, LEED project boundary line, and the building footprint (Figure 3.4). The property boundary line refers to the land owned according to a plot plan or legal property

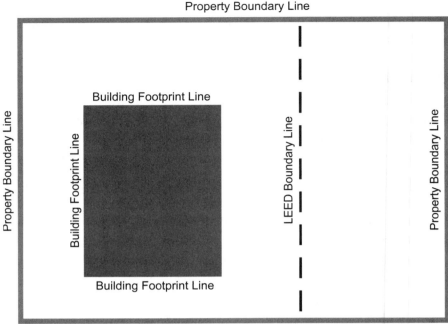

Property Boundary Line

Property Boundary Line

Building Footprint Line

Building Footprint Line

LEED Boundary Line

Property Boundary Line

Building Footprint Line

Property Boundary Line

Figure 3.4 The different types of boundaries for a LEED project.

 Make a flashcard to remember the three types of boundaries associated with LEED projects.

deed. The LEED project boundary line may or may not be the same as the property boundary. For example, a university may own acres of land but may wish to develop only a portion of it for one academic building. Therefore, the LEED project boundary line sets the limits for the scope of work to be included in the documents for certification. The building footprint is the amount of land on which the building resides.

Local municipalities are responsible for establishing sections of their towns for different uses and then characterize these areas into different zones, such as commercial, residential, and industrial. These sections of land are regulated based on:

■ Building type (commercial, residential, mixed-use, etc.)

■ Building height

■ Footprint, impervious versus pervious development (setbacks, parking, open space)

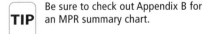 **TIP** Be sure to check out Appendix B for an MPR summary chart.

Project teams should be mindful of local regulations for land and the allowable uses. For the purposes of the exam, it is important to remember, although many credits may reference zoning, LEED will never override local, state, or federal requirements.

Credit Submittal Templates

TIP Remember, a submittal template acts as a cover page of sorts.

After a project is registered, the project administrator invites the other team members to the project's LEED-Online site and assigns each member their coordinating prerequisites and credits they will be responsible for. This means each prerequisite and credit has one responsible party assigned to it, and that person will generate and upload the required documentation specific to each prerequisite and credit.

When a team member is assigned a credit or prerequisite, they become the **declarant** to sign the credit submittal template. Each of these templates summarizes how the project team has satisfied the requirements for the specific credit or prerequisite. There is a submittal template for every prerequisite and credit, which must be submitted through LEED-Online. If a calculation is needed to show compliance, the template contains a spreadsheet and automatically completes the calculation after the required data is inputted according to the requirements described in the reference guides. It is suggested to visit the USGBC website to download the sample submittal templates (the link is available through the *Candidate Handbook* from GBCI).

Remember, all prerequisites and credits require a submittal template, and some may require additional documentation. The additional documentation may be exempt if the design team opts to use the licensed-professional exemption (LPE) path. This optional path is determined on the submittal template.

 TIP One team member can be assigned to more than one credit or prerequisite. Additional team members can be invited to LEED-Online and not be assigned any credit or prerequisite.

Make a flashcard to remember LPE!

Credit Interpretation Requests and Rulings

For those in the design and construction industry, it is helpful to think of **credit interpretation requests** (CIRs) like a request for information (RFI). Just as a contractor may issue an RFI to the design team for clarification about a detail to be constructed, a project team can issue a CIR to their assigned certification body in an effort to obtain clarification or more information. CIRs can be submitted any time after a project is registered via LEED-Online. Because the certification bodies are an integral part of the certification process, they are responsible for answering and responding to CIRs.

For a fee, team members of registered projects seeking LEED certification can submit CIRs for clarification about a credit or prerequisite within a LEED rating system. It is important to remember that CIRs are issued specific to *one* credit, prerequisite, or MPR. Note that CIR rulings are not considered final, nor are they definitive in determining if a particular strategy is satisfactory. Therefore, project teams are encouraged to upload their ruling with the coordinating credit, prerequisite, or MPR when submitting for a certification review through LEED-Online.

The USGBC website contains a database on previously issued CIRs for teams to query for more information before submitting a new one. Although these CIR postings serve as useful tools for a project team, they will no longer be used as supporting documentation for projects other than the one that submitted the CIR. For projects registered under the 2009, version 3 rating systems, CIRs are project specific and will not be posted to the database. With this change, teams are still encouraged to refer to the reference guides and the CIR database, as well as to contact their certification body before submitting a CIR, since there is a fee associated with issuing a new CIR.

 TIP When a CIR is responded to by a certification body, the reply is referred to as a **credit interpretation ruling**.

 TIP Be sure to check out the CIR guidelines on the GBCI website at www.gbci.org/Libraries/Credential_Exam_References/Guidelines-for-CIR-Customers.sflb.ashx.

Make a flashcard to remember the details of submitting a CIR.

Certification Review

Once the design team moves through the design phase and completes the construction documents, they are allowed to submit an application for a design review, although this is optional and not required. Optional split reviews provide the team with a preliminary status to see where the project stands with point-earning potential (at least from a design prerequisite and credit standpoint). If the team decides not to pursue this preliminary review at the end of design, they would wait to submit their documentation until after substantial completion. In

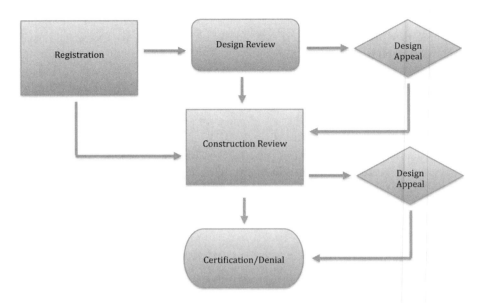

Figure 3.5 The certification review process.

Make a flashcard to remember the three components on which a project's certification fees are based.

summary, a project team can choose a split review for two certification reviews (one at the end of the design phase and another at the end of construction) or submit all documentation for a construction review after substantial completion.

At the time of a review submission, the LEED project administrator will need to pay a fee for certification review. This certification fee is based on the rating system the project is seeking certification with, the project's square footage, and whether the project was registered under a corporate membership account with USGBC. The project administrator will be required to submit a short project narrative to provide the certification body a background of the project, the intended use of the project, the location and surrounding areas, and any other details deemed appropriate for clarification purposes. Project photographs or renderings, elevations, floor plans, and any details should also be uploaded to LEED-Online.

The Time Frames of Certification Reviews

TIP Remember, USGBC members pay a reduced rate for registration and certification, including precertification for LEED CS projects.

Table 3.1 outlines the schedule associated with the submission and review times during the LEED certification review process. Bear in mind that the time frames listed apply to both design reviews and construction reviews. Once a project team submits for either type of review, they must then wait 25 business days to hear back from their assigned certification body. The certification body updates

Table 3.1 Certification Review Schedule

Process	Days
Preliminary design review or construction review	25 business days
Team reply	25 business days
Final review	15 business days
Team reply	15 business days
Appeal (if necessary)	25 business days
Appeal review (if necessary)	25 business days
Certification awarded	

LEED-Online to indicate whether a credit or prerequisite is "anticipated" or "denied," or will issue clarification requests to the team specific to any credits or prerequisites in question. The team then has 25 business days to respond with more information to explain how they satisfy the requirements of the credit or prerequisite requiring clarification. At that time, the team must wait 15 business days to receive indication whether the credit or prerequisite clarified is either "anticipated" or "denied." If the team submitted for a design review, they would repeat the steps listed earlier at the end of substantial completion in order to submit for a construction review. It is not until this review process that the final decision to award or deny credits and prerequisites takes place.

Should the team receive a "denied" status, they can issue an appeal to GBCI for a fee within 25 business days. GBCI would then have 25 business days to review the appeal and issue a ruling to the project team. Although GBCI leaves CIRs to the certification bodies to respond to and manage, they remain directly responsible for administering the appeals process. Once the appeal process ends, certification is awarded.

TIP Remember, GBCI is responsible for the appeals process!

QUIZ TIME!

Q3.7. Credit interpretation requests (CIRs) provide which of the following? (Choose two)

   A. Responses to written requests for interpretation of credit requirements

   B. Determination of whether a particular strategy can be used to satisfy two different credits at once

   C. Clarification of one existing LEED credit or prerequisite

   D. Definitive assurance that a particular method or strategy permitted on a previous project will be applicable to other projects in the future

Q3.8. Which of the following meets the MPR regarding minimum gross floor area for LEED for Schools rating system? (Choose one)

   A. 250 square feet

   B. 500 square feet

   C. 1,000 square feet

   D. 2,500 square feet

Q3.9. Which of the following statements are not true regarding MPRs? (Choose two)

   A. The LEED project boundary must include all contiguous land that is associated with normal building operations for the LEED project building, including all land that was or will be disturbed for the purpose of undertaking the LEED project.

   B. The owner must commit to sharing whole-building energy and water usage data for 10 years.

   C. LEED projects located on a campus must have project boundaries such that if all the buildings on campus become LEED certified, then 100 percent of the gross land area on the campus would be included within a LEED boundary.

    D. Any given parcel of real property may only be attributed to a single LEED project building unreasonable shapes for the sole purpose of complying with prerequisites.

    E. Gerrymandering of a LEED project boundary is allowed.

Q3.10. How many years must a project commit to sharing whole-building energy and water use? (Choose one)

    A. 7 years

    B. 10 years, unless the building changes ownership

    C. 6 months

    D. 1 year

    E. 5 years

Q3.11. Which of the following statements are true? (Choose two)

    A. Appeals are mailed to GBCI.

    B. Appeals can be submitted within 25 business days after final certification review.

    C. Appeals are free.

    D. Appeals can pertain only to credits, not prerequisites or MPRs.

    E. Appeals are submitted through LEED-Online.

Q3.12. Which of the following is new to all LEED rating systems under LEED 2009? (Choose one)

    A. Minimum program requirements

    B. Credit interpretation requests

    C. Regional Priority category

    D. Awareness and Education category

Q3.13. Design reviews can prove to be a beneficial option for a team to pursue since the project can be awarded points before construction begins. True or False?

    A. True

    B. False

Q3.14. LEED project registration provides which of the following? (Choose two)

    A. Three credit interpretation requests (CIRs)

    B. One preapplication USGBC review of project submittals and documentation

    C. One point toward LEED certification for registration prior to the development of construction documents

    D. Access to online LEED credit submittal templates for the project

E. Establishment of contact with GBCI and the assigned certification body

Q3.15. An application for LEED certification must contain which of the following? (Choose two)

A. Project summary information, including project contact, project type, project cost, project size, number of occupants, estimated date of occupancy, etc.

B. A list of all members of the design and construction team, including contact information, documented green building industry experience, and indication of all LEED Accredited Professionals

C. Completed LEED credit submittal templates for all prerequisites and attempted credits, plus any documentation specifically required to support those templates

D. Detailed documentation for all credits pursued, including full-sized plans and drawings, photocopies of invoices for all purchased materials, records of tipping fees, all energy modeling inputs and assumptions, and evidence of all calculations performed in support of LEED credits

Q3.16. When should the construction credits and prerequisites be submitted for certification review? (Choose one)

A. Beginning of construction

B. One year after occupancy

C. Substantial completion

D. Once permit is obtained

E. Six months after occupancy

Q3.17. Regarding the application process for LEED certification, which of the following is a correct statement? (Choose one)

A. LEED credit submittal templates and documentation may be submitted only after construction is complete.

B. All LEED credit submittal templates and documentation must be submitted prior to construction.

C. Prerequisites and credits marked as "Design" may be submitted and reviewed at the end of the design phase.

D. The optional design-phase submittal allows projects to secure points for specific LEED credits, for which a preliminary certification will be awarded if the project has earned a sufficient number of points.

Q3.18. How long does a project team have to submit an appeal after receiving certification review comments back from GBCI? (Choose one)

A. 15 business days

B. 25 business days

    C. 45 business days

    D. 1 week

    E. 1 month

Q3.19. Which of the following correctly characterize credit interpretation requests (CIRs)? (Choose three)

    A. Can be viewed only by the primary contact for a registered project

    B. Can be submitted any time after a project is registered

    C. Must be requested through LEED-Online

    D. Can be requested only in a written request mailed to GBCI

    E. Can address more than one credit or prerequisite

    F. Are relevant to one specific project and will not be referenced in the CIR database

Q3.20. Who is responsible for the appeals process? (Choose one)

    A. GBCI

    B. USGBC

    C. Certification bodies

    D. None of the above

PART II

DIVING IN: THE STRATEGIES AND TECHNOLOGIES OF LEED

CHAPTER **4**

SUSTAINABLE SITES

THIS CHAPTER BEGINS THE DETAILED STUDY OF THE INTENTIONS, requirements, and strategies described within the Sustainable Sites (SS) category's prerequisites and credits. The main topics include the factors applicable to site selection and location, design, construction, and maintenance of the site. As with making any other decision while working on a green building project, all components within the SS category are weighed on the triple bottom line values of environmental, economic, and community aspects.

Where a project is located and how it is developed can have multiple impacts on the ecosystem and water resources required during the life of a building. The site location can impact a building's energy performance with respect to orientation; it also could impact stormwater runoff strategies or the potential to pollute nearby waterways. How does the site fit into the existing infrastructure? Is it a contaminated site that can be remediated for redevelopment? Carbon emissions should be evaluated as well, as they may be impacted due to the transportation required to get to and from the site. Is there public transportation access available? How much parking is available for cars? Is the project site dependent on the use of cars? If so, are there incentives for carpools or vanpools? These concepts and questions should trigger some of the important factors to consider when deciding on a particular site and its true sustainable value. Once a site is selected, the project team needs to determine the most sustainable approach for development. They need to consider how much of the site will need to be developed and how much can be preserved or restored as open space. They need to work together to reduce the heat gain from the sun for the entire site, including rooftop areas. These types of site selection and site development strategies aid in the success of earning Leadership in Energy and Environmental Design (LEED®) certification, as proven by the project team for the Los Angeles Valley College Allied Health & Sciences Center (Figure 4.1).

Dedicate one color flashcard for all your flashcards within the SS category. This way anytime you see that color, you will associate that flashcard question with Sustainable Sites concepts and strategies.

Figure 4.1 The Los Angeles Valley College Allied Health & Sciences Center in California, by CO Architects, incorporates a stormwater retention system in the landscaping on the site and a PV system covered walkway, contributing to the achievement of earning LEED® Silver certification. *Photo courtesy of Robert Canfield, CO Architects*

Table 4.1 The Sustainable Sites (SS) Category

D/C	Prereq/ Credit	Title	Points NC	Points Schools	Points CS
C	Prereq 1	Construction Activity Pollution Prevention	R	R	R
C	Prereq 2	Environmental Site Assessment	N/A	R	N/A
D	Credit 1	Site Selection	1	1	1
D	Credit 2	Development Density and Community Connectivity	5	4	5
D	Credit 3	Brownfield Redevelopment	1	1	1
D	Credit 4.1	Alternative Transportation, Public Transportation Access	6	4	6
D	Credit 4.2	Alternative Transportation, Bicycle Storage and Changing Rooms	1	1	2
D	Credit 4.3	Alternative Transportation, Low-Emitting and Fuel-Efficient Vehicles	3	2	3
D	Credit 4.4	Alternative Transportation, Parking Capacity	2	2	2
C	Credit 5.1	Site Development, Protect or Restore Habitat	1	1	1
D	Credit 5.2	Site Development, Maximize Open Space	1	1	1
D	Credit 6.1	Stormwater Design, Quantity Control	1	1	1
D	Credit 6.2	Stormwater Design, Quality Control	1	1	1
C	Credit 7.1	Heat Island Effect, Nonroof	1	1	1
D	Credit 7.2	Heat Island Effect, Roof	1	1	1
D	Credit 8	Light Pollution Reduction	1	1	1
D	Credit 9	Tenant Design and Construction Guidelines	N/A	N/A	1
D	Credit 9	Site Master Plan	N/A	1	N/A
D	Credit 10	Joint Use of Facilities	N/A	1	N/A

TIP Remember to use the study worksheets at the end of the chapter to remember the details of each prerequisite and credit, such as the intent, requirements, and documentation and calculation requirements.

The SS category is compiled of the prerequisites and credits as shown in Table 4.1. Notice the points available to each credit and when the documentation is submitted for review: design (D) or construction (C). Use the table as a summary of the category, but for the purposes of the exam and an attempt to break down the information to remember, the category information is presented in this chapter by the overlying category strategies instead of a credit-by-credit approach as seen with the reference guide. Therefore, when preparing for the exam, it is helpful to remember that the SS category is broken down into the following four factors and the coordinating prerequisites or credits:

1. Site selection
2. Transportation
3. Site design and management
4. Stormwater management

SITE SELECTION

Make a flashcard to remember the definition of **floor-to-area ratio (FAR):** the proportion of the total floor area of a building to the total land area the building can occupy.

Determining the location of a green building project should be encouraged by previously developed locations to avoid sprawling development into the suburbs where undeveloped (**greenfield**) sites would then be disturbed. The idea is to build

Figure 4.2 Urban development in downtown Miami, Florida.

up and not out, to help increase density and reduce the negative environmental impacts of building on existing, cohesive natural habitats (Figure 4.2). Some municipalities offer an increased floor-to-area ratio (FAR) incentive to encourage the development of green buildings within certain communities. Zoning departments typically define building setback development lines based on the use and location of a neighborhood or town. Developers with an increased FAR allowance can build more within the setback lines and then in turn can sell or rent more space.

 An increased FAR increases the density and therefore preserves open space by building up and not out.

From an environmental perspective, the selection of a sustainable site would avoid the destruction of wildlife habitats to help lessen the threat of their ability to survive. The goal is to preserve land and therefore preserve plant and animal species. From an economic standpoint, avoiding sprawl development helps to lessen the burden of expanding infrastructure for both utilities and transportation. The social equity of the proper site selection could include the protection of the natural environment to be enjoyed and observed by future generations for ecological and recreational purposes.

 If less parking were provided due to urban redevelopment projects with access to public transportation, construction costs would be lower.

Site Location in Relation to LEED Compliance

Project teams are encouraged to address the following prerequisite and three credits when selecting a project site, as according to the BD+C LEED rating systems.

 Note that all of the following LEED strategies are addressed during the **Predesign phase.**

SS Prerequisite 2: Environmental Site Assessment (for Schools). Environmental reports required! Phase I is the starting point to determine if the site is contaminated. A Phase II Environmental Site Assessment is conducted if contamination is found. Remember, if the project site was once a landfill, it is not eligible for certification. School projects seeking certification for a **brownfield** site are also eligible for credit under SS Credit 3: Brownfield Redevelopment with proper remediation.

Make a flashcard to remember the six types of sensitive sites to avoid for SSc1: Site Selection.

Make a flashcard to remember that previously developed sites include not only properties with existing buildings and hardscape, but also those that were graded or somehow altered by human activity.

Related credits: Selecting an urban project location will help teams to achieve this credit along with SSc1: Site Selection and SSc4.1: Alternative Transportation, Public Transportation Access.

Make a flashcard to remember the definition of **building density**. It evaluates a building's total floor area as compared to the total area of the site and is measured in square feet per acre.

Be sure to review the study worksheet at the end of this chapter to remember the three equations associated with SS Credit 2 to determine the development density, density radius, and the average property density within density boundary for a project site.

SS Credit 1: Site Selection. Avoid the following six types of sensitive sites when selecting property in which to develop:

1. Prime farmland (defined by the U.S. Department of Agriculture): greenfield sites with soil appropriate for cultivation and agricultural growth and production

2. Floodplains/flood prone areas (predeveloped elevation is less than 5 feet above the 100-year floodplain level as defined by Federal Emergency Management Agency [FEMA])

3. Habitat for any **endangered or critical species:** where extinction is threatened due to human activities or environmental conditions

4. Land within 100 feet of wetlands (defined by the Code of Federal Regulations)

5. Previously undeveloped land within 50 feet of a body of water (Clean Water Act)

6. Public parkland (unless traded)

SS Credit 2: Development Density and Community Connectivity. Remember from the Green Associate exam the importance to increase density, maximize square footage, protect greenfields, and minimize impacts on land. When selecting a project site, developers should focus on **development density** or community connectivity concepts and to select a site with existing utility access. To comply, project teams can choose to document that the previously developed site is within an area with a density of **60,000 square feet per acre net** or is within a half mile of a residential neighborhood with an average density of 10 units per acre. The latter approach, referred to as community connectivity, also requires pedestrian access to at least 10 basic services from the new development. These basic services include local businesses and community services such as parks, grocery stores, banks, cleaners, pharmacies, and restaurants. Two of the basic services can be anticipated, but would only qualify if they intend to be operational within one year. Restaurants are the only type of basic service that can be counted twice. For example, if there were five restaurants, three banks, and two grocery stores within a half-mile of the project accessible by pedestrians, then two of the restaurants, one of the banks, and one of the grocery stores would count toward achieving this credit. The team would need to research the area to determine if there are at least six more basic services within the compliance area to achieve option 2 of this credit. For mixed-use projects, only one of the basic services located within the LEED project boundary may count toward the minimum 10 required for compliance. Physical education spaces, such as playing fields and playgrounds, are exempt from the development density calculations for projects pursuing certification under the LEED for Schools™ rating system.

Project teams have an opportunity to earn an Exemplary Performance credit if the project's density is double the average density of the calculated area or if the calculated area is doubled and the average density is at least 120,000 square feet per acre (double the credit requirement under option 1).

SS Credit 3: Brownfield Redevelopment. There are over 450,000 brownfield remediation and redevelopment opportunities in the United States available to help the reduction of sprawl developments and reuse land, thereby protecting the environment and undeveloped property.[1] These opportunities help to explain the long-term goals of USGBC to encourage regenerative projects. As a result

Figure 4.3 Villa Montgomery Apartments, a remediation project in Redwood City, California, by Fisher-Friedman Associates, earned LEED Gold certification under the LEED NC rating system, for compliance with multiple Sustainable Sites strategies including brownfield site selection and remediation. *Photo courtesy of FFA*

of this goal, USGBC teamed with the U.S. Environmental Protection Agency (EPA) to help encourage the **remediation** and redevelopment of brownfield sites by rewarding more points within the LEED rating systems (Figure 4.3), therefore weighting them more than other points.[2] Remediation methods applied to contaminated soil or groundwater may include physical, chemical, or biological means.

In 1980, the **Comprehensive Environmental Response, Compensation, and Liability Act (CERCLA),** also known as Superfund, was enacted by Congress to tax the chemical and petroleum industries on the release (or threatened release of) hazardous contaminants that may pose a public health risk. The tax is collected and dedicated to the remediation of brownfield sites, or Superfund sites. Another program, the **Resource Conservation and Recovery Act (RCRA),** was created to give the EPA authority to address projects involved with the disposal of hazardous wastes from cradle to grave.

In order to determine if a portion of land is a brownfield site, an examination is done via the ASTM E1903-97 Phase II Environmental Site Assessment, most commonly referred to as a Phase II report, where a "site's aboveground and subsurface characteristics, such as structure, geology and hydrology"[4] are evaluated for contamination. Should a site be contaminated, project teams could incorporate the following common remediation strategies to clean up their project site, depending on the type of contamination:

- Pump-and-treat methods
- Bioreactors, land farming
- **In situ (in place) remediation** to reduce site disturbance, such as "injection wells, reactive trenches, or other technologies that take advantage of the natural hydraulic gradient of groundwater."[5]

Make a flashcard to remember the definition of a **brownfield**: "real property, the expansion, redevelopment, or reuse of which may be complicated by the presence or potential presence of a hazardous substance, pollutant, or contaminant. Cleaning up and reinvesting in these properties protects the environment, reduces blight, and takes development pressures off green spaces and working lands."[3]

Make a flashcard to remember the ASTM referenced standard for brownfield sites: **E1903-97.**

QUIZ TIME!

Q4.1. What is the foundation for sustainable design for individual buildings? (Choose one)

 A. Carbon emissions

 B. Location

 C. Water use

 D. Orientation

 E. Energy use

Q4.2. What type of assessment is used to determine brownfield sites? (Choose one)

 A. ASTM C1540 Brownfield Testing

 B. ASTM E1903-97 Phase II Environmental Site Assessment

 C. ASTM E408 Standard Test Methods for Total Emittance of Surfaces, Using Inspection Meter Techniques

 D. ASTM E789 Standard Test Methods for Evaluation for Sites

Q4.3. Which of the following types of properties are best suited for a LEED project seeking SS Credit 1: Site Selection? (Choose two)

 A. Prime farmland

 B. Floodplains

 C. Habitat for any endangered species

 D. Within 500 feet of wetlands

 E. Within 250 feet of a body of water

 F. Public parkland

Q4.4. Which of the following represent in-situ remediation solutions for brownfield sites? (Choose two)

 A. Reactive trenches

 B. Pump and treat

 C. Injection wells

 D. Land farming

 E. Bioreactors

TRANSPORTATION

TIP Land use is the ultimate contributor to the demands of transportation.

Transportation is one of the key components addressed within the LEED rating systems as it accounts for 32 percent of the total U.S. greenhouse gas emissions in 2007, according to the U.S. Energy Information Administration.[6] As buildings traditionally have contributed to the need for transportation, green buildings have the opportunity to impact these statistics by reducing the "length and frequency of vehicle trips and encourage shifts to more sustainable modes of transportation."[7] The environmental benefits of sustainable strategies for transportation include a reduction in pollution including vehicle emissions, which have a dramatic impact on climate change, smog, and acid rain, among other air quality problems, according to Wikipedia.[8] The economic benefits include the reduction of the need to build and maintain roadways. The social component to reducing transportation impacts includes an improvement of human health by increasing the accessibility and therefore encouraging people to walk or bike from place to place.

Transportation is most impacted by four factors:

- Location—number and frequency of trips

- Vehicle technology—quantity and types of energy and support systems needed to move people and goods to and from the site

- Fuel—environmental impact of vehicle operation

- Human behavior—a daily transportation decision combining the listed impacts[9]

Transportation in Relation to LEED Compliance

The rating systems within the Building Design and Construction (BD+C) reference guide offer the following four alternative transportation credits to help reduce the environmental impacts of the use of cars. If more people carpooled, walked, or biked to work or school, there would be less pollution, as vehicles contribute to air pollution, **greenhouse gas** (GHG) emissions, and smog. GHGs "absorb and emit radiation at specific wavelengths within the spectrum of thermal infrared radiation emitted by the Earth's surface, the atmosphere itself, and by clouds."[10] The following alternative transportation strategies help to reduce the use of the automobile and therefore help to reduce these detrimental environmental impacts:

SS Credit 4.1: Public Transportation Access. Choose a site close to **mass transit** (Figure 4.4). Remember, one or more stops for two or more bus or streetcar lines is required to be within a quarter-mile walk of the building entrance. Projects could also comply if a rail station, ferry terminal, or tram terminal (existing or

Figure 4.4 Mass transit in New Jersey is designed to meet the commuting needs of large groups of people. *Photo courtesy of David Cardella*

TIP Remember, quarter-mile bus or half-mile rail.

Selecting a site within an urban context tends to allow project teams to achieve SS Credit 1, SS Credit 2, and SS Credit 4.1.

TIP For school projects to comply with Option 3: Pedestrian Access, the maximum walking radius must be less than three quarters of a mile for grades K–8 and less than a mile and a half for grades 9 and higher for 80 percent of the total student population.

planned and funded) is located within a half-mile walk of the building's entrance. Schools have a third option for compliance, if the team can prove 80 percent of the students within the **attendance boundary** live within less than a mile and a half radius from the school, then credit compliance is awarded. The attendance boundary includes the limits of the neighborhood that defines which households will attend which schools. With any of the three compliance path options, school projects must provide dedicated walking or biking lanes to the transit lines in two or more directions.

Project teams can pursue one Exemplary Performance point for any of the alternative transportation credits if a Comprehensive Transportation Management Plan is conducted to prove a measurable reduction in the use of a car to commute to the project site. In addition, NC and CS project teams can also pursue an Exemplary Performance credit under SS Credit 4.1 if the number of commuter rail, light rail, or subway lines is doubled or if the number of public or campus lines available increases from two to four.

SS Credit 4.2: Bicycle Storage and Changing Rooms. Projects seeking LEED certification are encouraged to incorporate bicycle storage (Figure 4.5) and changing rooms to help deter single-occupancy automobiles as a main source of transportation. Depending on the rating system being pursued and the type and size of the project, there are different requirements in which to comply with. Project teams will need to first determine the amount of bicycle racks to provide by calculating the amount of peak occupants, including **transient users.** Transient users can include higher education "students, volunteers, visitors, customers, etc."[11] Next, they will need to calculate the amount of **full-time equivalent (FTE)** occupants to then establish the number of showers and changing rooms to provide. Notice, FTE does not indicate full-time *employee,* but instead full-time *equivalent.* Therefore, to calculate an FTE, one would include regular building occupants (full-time and part-time) based on an occupancy period of 8 hours per day. For example, a full-time employee would have an FTE value of 1 because they spend 8 hours a day in the building and 8 divided by 8 is equal to 1. A part-time employee who works 4 hours per day would then have an FTE value of 0.5. Table 4.2 summarizes the requirements of this credit as project teams would need to know what percentage of the peak occupants and FTE to use in order to calculate the required number of bike racks and showers needed for compliance.

Figure 4.5 Bike racks at the Animal Care and Protective Services facility in Jacksonville, Florida provide the staff and visitors the opportunity to commute to the facility without a car. *Photo courtesy of Auld & White Constructors, LLC*

Table 4.2 The Requirements of SS Credit 4.2

Rating System	Project Type		Bike Racks	Showers/ Changing Rooms
NC	Commercial or Institutional		5% peak	0.5% FTE
CS	Commercial or Institutional	‹ 300,000 SF	3% yearly average	0.5% FTE
		› 300,000 SF	3% for 300,000 SF, then 0.5% for additional SF	0.5% FTE
Residential			15%	N/A
Schools			5% peak inc. staff and 3rd-grade+ students	0.5% FTE

NC and CS projects with a residential component will need to provide *covered* and secure bicycle storage. CS projects may need to utilize the default occupancy counts as depicted in the appendix of the *Reference Guide* to determine the number of showers and bike parking spaces to provide. School projects are required to include staff and students in the third grade and above in the bike rack calculations. Just like with SS Credit 4.1, school projects must provide dedicated walking or biking lanes to the transit lines in two or more directions in order to achieve this credit.

SS Credit 4.3: Low-Emitting and Fuel-Efficient Vehicles. Project teams have four options from which to choose in order to comply with this credit. All BD+C projects can pursue this credit if 5 percent of the total parking provided is reserved for **fuel-efficient vehicles** (FEVs). FEVs and low-emitting cars include some hybrid vehicles, but project teams should refer to the American Council for an Energy-Efficient Economy (ACEEE) to learn about compliant vehicles with a minimum green score of 40. If a school project pursues this first option by providing 5 percent for FEV **preferred parking** (Figure 4.6), it would also be required to provide a carpool drop-off area for FEVs. If a project is not capable of FEV reserved parking, project teams can opt to provide a 20 percent or more discounted parking rate instead. Option 2 can be pursued for NC and CS projects if the amount of alternative fuel, including electric recharging stations, is equivalent to 3 percent of the total vehicle parking. Schools can also pursue option 2 if 20 percent of the vehicle fleet (including buses and maintenance vehicles) is powered by an alternative fuel.

Options 3 and 4 are available only to NC projects. If 3 percent of the FTE occupants are provided with FEVs or **alternative-fuel vehicles**, such as those powered by natural gas, propane, hydrogen, ethanol, or biodiesel, along with preferred parking for the vehicles, compliance is awarded. Option 4 is applicable if at least 3 percent of the FTE occupants have access to a ride-share or carpool program.

SS Credit 4.4: Parking Capacity. In order to reduce the number of impervious surfaces and encourage the use of mass transit or bicycle commuting, sustainable projects should not have a surplus of parking. Reducing the amount of parking also minimizes the amount of land to be developed, therefore lowering construction costs. This alternative transportation credit limits the amount of parking based on nonresidential, residential, mixed-use, and school project types. Nonresidential project types have two compliance options. The first option is the same as the first option for school projects. For these two project types,

TIP Remember, showers and changing rooms are required to be located within 200 yards of the building entrance. This could indicate that the facilities can be located in another building.

TIP Preferred parking indicates designated and reserved parking closest to the building entrance other than handicapped spaces. A 20 percent discounted rate parking program could also comply if reserved parking is not an option, as long as the program is available to all of the occupants and available for at least two years.

TIP Zero- or low-emission vehicles (ZEVs) are standardized by California Air Resources Board (CARB), while FEVs are determined by ACEEE.

 Create a flashcard to remember the definition of an alternative-fuel vehicle: a vehicle that operates without the use of petroleum fuels, including gas-electric, or hybrid, vehicle types.

Figure 4.6 Providing preferred parking for car/vanpool vehicles could contribute to earning SS Credit 4.3.

 TIP Notice that option 1 for nonresidential and school projects is the same!

 Make a flashcard to remember the four alternative transportation credits.

local zoning requirements for parking capacity cannot be exceeded (not even by one space), and preferred parking for vanpools and/or carpools must be provided for at least 5 percent of the total parking capacity. Nonresidential projects could also pursue this credit if parking is provided for less than 5 percent of the FTE occupants in addition to a provision for carpool/vanpool reserved parking. Residential projects can pursue this credit if the local zoning parking capacity is not exceeded (preferred parking not required) while also encouraging carpooling. Mixed-use projects would need to determine the percentage of commercial use for the project in order to determine the compliance path that is appropriate for the project. If there is less than 10 percent commercial use, the project team is required to meet the residential compliance path mentioned previously. Otherwise, the project team would apply the nonresidential compliance path to the commercial area and the residential compliance path to the residential component in order to comply with this credit. School projects have a second compliance option in lieu of the aforementioned path. Teams would need to provide 25 percent fewer parking spaces than the standards detailed in the **Institute of Transportation Engineers (ITE) "Parking Generation"** study in order to comply. With any project type, project teams that avoid implementing any new parking would also comply with the intentions and requirements of this credit.

QUIZ TIME!

Q4.5. Which of the following alternative transportation credits is impacted by site selection? (Choose one)

A. SS Credit 4.1: Alternative Transportation, Public Transportation Access

B. SS Credit 4.2: Alternative Transportation, Bicycle Storage and Changing Rooms

    C. SS Credit 4.3: Alternative Transportation, Low-Emitting and Fuel-Efficient Vehicles

    D. SS Credit 4.4: Alternative Transportation, Parking Capacity

Q4.6. Which of the following represent the major factors that impact transportation effects on the environment? (Choose three)

    A. Vehicle technology

    B. Fuel

    C. Human behavior

    D. Quality of roads

    E. Suburban development

Q4.7. Which of the following are sustainable strategies that should be implemented on an auto-dependent green building? (Choose four)

    A. Provide priority parking for carpools/vanpools.

    B. Provide a mass transit discount program to employees.

    C. Supply alternative-fuel vehicles and accessibility to recharging stations.

    D. Offer discounted parking rates for multioccupant vehicles.

    E. Incorporate basic services (such as a bank, gym, cleaners, or pharmacy) for occupant usage in the new building.

Q4.8. Which of the following are effective and sustainable strategies to address transportation for a LEED project? (Choose three)

    A. Choose a site near a bus stop.

    B. Limit parking.

    C. Encourage carpooling.

    D. Provide sport-utility vehicles (SUVs) for all employees.

    E. Choose a greenfield site.

Q4.9. Which of the following BD+C rating systems has the opportunity to select from all four possible compliance path options for SSc4.3: Alternative Transportation, Low-Emitting and Fuel-Efficient Vehicles? (Choose one)

    A. LEED for Core & Shell

    B. LEED for Schools

    C. LEED for New Construction

    D. LEED for Commercial Interiors

    E. LEED for Existing Buildings: Operations & Maintenance

SITE DESIGN AND MANAGEMENT

Once a building's site is selected, site design and management become the next components to address when working on a green building project. The creation of natural, sustainable exterior environments that can be sustainably

Figure 4.7 The high-efficiency Duke Law Star Commons project in Durham, North Carolina, by Shepley Bulfinch, obtained its LEED certification by providing access to public transportation and reducing site disturbance and the heat island effect.
Photo courtesy of Kat Nania, Shepley Bulfinch

maintained add to the economic, environmental, and social equity of their green building projects and are therefore promoted within the LEED rating systems (Figure 4.7).

Site Design in Relation to LEED Compliance

Project teams are encouraged to utilize the concepts of sustainable landscaping techniques, including **native and/or adaptive plantings** with water-efficient irrigation systems, the preservation or restoration of open space, and the reduction of the heat island effect and light pollution. Core and shell projects are encouraged to develop guidelines for future tenants to follow to help continue the efforts in the future. Education facility projects are encouraged to develop site master plans and invite the community to share the facilities available at the school. The following credits address these sustainable strategies that project teams should be aware of when working on a project pursuing LEED certification.

SS Credit 5.1: Site Development, Protect or Restore Habitat. After a site is selected, project teams wishing to pursue this credit have two options depending on the site. For sites that have not been developed, or greenfield sites, project teams will need to limit the site disturbance with setbacks. These setbacks include 40 feet from the perimeter, 10 feet from hardscape, 15 feet from roads, and 25 feet from pervious surfaces. If the site was previously developed or graded, the project team will need to restore 50 percent of the site (not including the building footprint) or 20 percent of the total site including the building footprint, whichever is greater. The site is to be restored with native and/or adaptive plantings. If 75 percent of the site (minus the building footprint) or if 30 percent of the total site is restored with native and/or adaptive vegetation, the project may be eligible for an Exemplary Performance opportunity.

Native plantings refer to local vegetation that occurs naturally; while **adaptive plantings** once introduced, can adapt to their new surroundings. Both can survive with little to no human interaction or resources. Project teams should select plants that will not only require less water and maintenance, but also

TIP Green roof strategies comply with both SS Credits 2 and 5.1, but monoculture plantings (turf grass) do not, even if it is considered native or adaptive. To comply, teams are required to implement green roofs vegetated with native and adaptive plantings for a project in an urban area with zero setbacks and must ensure the roof promotes biodiversity and provides habitat.

TIP Create a flashcard to remember the setback requirements of this credit.

improve the nutrients in the soil and deter pests at the same time. Implementing these measures reduces the amount of chemicals introduced into the water infrastructure and therefore improves the quality of surface water and saves building owners from purchasing fertilizers and pesticides. Avoiding or reducing the amount of **potable water** (drinking water supplied by municipalities or wells) used for irrigation decreases the overall quantity of water required for building sites, and therefore reduces operation costs as well. Water-efficient irrigation and other water efficiency strategies will be discussed in the next chapter but for now it is important to connect site development decisions, such as vegetation selections, with environmental and economic operating and maintenance impacts.

SS Credit 5.2: Site Development, Maximize Open Space. Build small and reduce the size of a **building's footprint,** increase the FAR, and decrease the amount of land developed, therefore maximizing the amount of **open space.** If parking is required, use a tuck-under approach as another means to increase the ratio of open space to the **development footprint,** or the land impacted by a project, including all **hardscape** areas and the building footprint. Hardscape areas are paved, such as parking lots, roadways, walkways, and sidewalks.

Project teams pursuing this credit will need to refer to the local zoning ordinance for the applicable compliance path. If the area has a local open space requirement, the team will need to provide at least 25 percent more to comply. If the site does not have any zoning ordinances, the project team is required to provide open space equivalent to the size of the building footprint. If zoning requirements exist but do not include any open space requirements for the site, the project team will need to provide open space that is equal to 20 percent of the total site area for the project. A team can pick up an Exemplary Performance point if they provide double the amount of open space required by the applicable compliance path.

SS Prerequisite 1: Construction Activity Pollution Prevention. Project teams will need to comply with this prerequisite no matter which rating system they are working with or which credits they plan to pursue. The civil engineer will need to develop an erosion and sedimentation control (ESC) plan to provide the contractor with a strategy to avoid polluting the air and adjacent sites and erosion. The idea is to control erosion from stormwater runoff and/or wind, impacting neighboring waterways, such as storm sewers or streams, with **sedimentation** and particulates from entering the air. Allowing excess nutrients, such as nitrogen and phosphorus, to leave the site can lead to **eutrophication,** causing unwanted plant growth, such as weeds and algal blooms, that can alter the water quality and habitat environments in nearby streams. Project teams typically address these issues by stabilization methods, such as using vegetation to stabilize the soil or covering the soil with mulch, or by structural controls, such as silt fencing, earth dikes, or a constructed area to trap sediments.

All sites over one acre must conform to the EPA's construction general permit. This prerequisite applies the same provisions, including the National Pollutant Discharge Elimination System (NPDES) requirements, to all projects pursuing certification. The NPDES is a "permit program that controls water pollution by regulating point sources that discharge pollutants into waters of the United States."[12] Project teams need to determine the requirements pertaining to the specific site, as an ESC or stormwater pollution prevention plan could already exist.

 Xeriscaping can also be used as a sustainable landscaping strategy, as it uses drought-adaptable and minimal-water plant types along with soil covers, such as composts and mulches, to reduce evaporation.

 Create flashcards to remember each of the definitions for **native and adaptive plantings** and **potable water.**

 Create another flashcard to remember the definition of **building footprint:** the amount of land the building structure occupies, not including landscape and hardscape surfaces, such as parking lots, driveways, and walkways.

 Open space is considered pervious and vegetated land. Wetlands and natural ponds can count.

 Pedestrian and nonvehicular areas on urban sites can be considered as open space areas as well, including green roofs, therefore creating a synergy with SS Credit 2: Development Density and Community Connectivity.

 Create a flashcard to remember the definition for a **stormwater pollution prevention plan:** "describes all measures to prevent stormwater contamination, control sedimentation and erosion during construction, and comply with the requirements of the Clean Water Act."[13]

Besides low-albedo, nonreflective surface materials, car exhaust, air conditioners, and street equipment contribute to the heat island effect, while narrow streets and tall buildings make it worse.

It is the collective strategies that have the biggest reduction of building-associated environmental impacts, such as tuck-under parking with reserved spaces for low-emitting fuel types and carpools/vanpools.

Create two more flashcards to remember the definitions of **solar reflectance index (SRI)** and **albedo**. Also, remember the difference scales for each. Remember higher is better!

Create another flashcard to remember the definition of **heat island effect**: heat absorption by low-SRI hardscape materials that contribute to an overall increase in temperature by radiating heat.

Create a flashcard to remember the definition of **emissivity** as described in the BD+C reference guide: "the ratio of the radiation emitted by a surface to the radiation emitted by a black body at the same temperature."[14]

Heat Island Effect

Although energy use will be discussed in more detail in Chapter 6, materials used for site design and rooftops can efficiently impact the use of energy for two reasons. Think of summertime at the grocery store parking lot and how you can see heat emitting from the black asphalt surface. The sun is attracted to darker surfaces, where heat is then retained. Multiply this effect in a downtown, urban area to truly understand the impacts of the urban **heat island effect**. By specifying and implementing materials with a high **solar reflectance index (SRI)**, green building projects can reduce the heat island effect and the overall temperature of an area. A material's SRI value is based on the material's ability to reflect or reject solar heat gain measured on a scale from 0 (dark, most absorptive) to 100 (light, most reflective). Building materials are also evaluated based on their ability to reflect sunlight based on visible, infrared, and ultraviolet wavelengths on a scale from 0 to 1 (Figure 4.8). This solar reflectance is referred to as **albedo**; therefore, the terms *SRI* and *albedo* should be thought of synonymously for the purposes of the BD+C exam.

SS Credit 7.1: Heat Island Effect, Nonroof. Project teams have two options for complying with this credit and reducing the heat island effect. Option 1 addresses the hardscape, and option 2 impacts a parking provision strategy. Teams have the option to provide a combination of shading (within five years), high-SRI materials (minimum of 29), and/or open-grid paving (Figure 4.9) for 50 percent of the hardscape areas in order to comply with option 1. If high-SRI materials are used for surface paving, walkways, and rooftops, light can be distributed more efficiently at night to reduce the number of light fixtures required, which saves money during construction and later, during operations.

Option 2 requires 50 percent of the parking to be provided under cover. Keeping consistent with the other strategies, the roof of the parking structure must be covered with vegetation and/or solar panels, and/or the roofing material must have an SRI of at least 29. Not only does tuck-under parking help to reduce

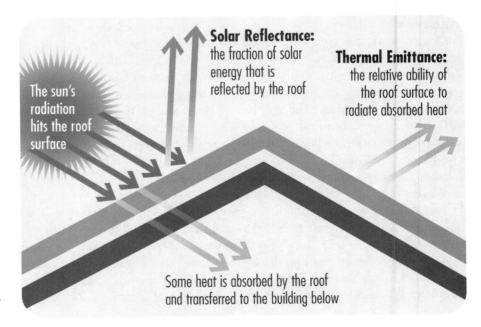

Figure 4.8 Diagram illustrating solar reflectance and thermal (or infrared) emittance. *Image courtesy of Cool Roof Rating Council*

Figure 4.9 Turfstone™ Open-Grid Pavers allow stormwater to pass through and encourage vegetation growth between each open cell, in order to recharge groundwater and reduce runoff. *Photo courtesy of Ideal*

the impacts of the urban heat island effect, but the strategy also helps to reduce impervious surfaces and to preserve open space for parking and nonparking uses. It is important for teams to determine ways to limit the number of impervious surfaces on the site, not only to reduce the heat island effect, but to reduce stormwater runoff as well. For the purposes of the exam, it is important to remember these types of synergies of strategies and credits.

If the team were seeking an Exemplary Performance credit, they would need to double either compliance option.

SS Credit 7.2: Heat Island Effect, Roof. Project teams have three options from which to choose in order to pursue this credit. The first addresses the roofing material. If a lighter roofing material is used, the mechanical systems do not have to compensate for the heat gain to cool a building, consequently reducing the use of energy. Therefore, if at least 75 percent of the roof surface (not including equipment, photovoltaic solar panels, and penetrations) is covered with a material with high SRI, then the project team could be awarded this credit and earn

 TIP Notice that a minimum of SRI 29 is used for both SSc7.1 and SSc7.2!

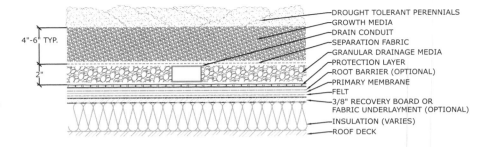

Figure 4.10 Assessing the different components of a green roof serves as a reminder of all of the different team members required to develop an appropriate solution. *Image courtesy of Roofscapes, Inc.*

one point. If the roof is low-sloped, the minimum required SRI is 78, while a steep-sloped roof can comply with a material with an SRI of at least 29. Option 2 requires at least 50 percent of the roof surface to be covered with vegetation (Figure 4.10). Option 3 allows the team to provide a combination of options 1 and 2 (Figure 4.11). If a project team doubles either compliance path option, they can pursue an Exemplary Performance credit.

SS Credit 8: Light Pollution Reduction. "Light pollution is waste light from building sites that produces glare, is directed upward to the sky, or is directed off the site."[15] To comply with LEED, project teams will not only need to address exterior lighting, but interior lighting as well for this design credit (Figure 4.12). In terms of site lighting, traditionally there has been little attention paid to the quality of the night sky and the effects on wildlife, or to the wasteful energy use approach for exterior lighting. It is inefficient to illuminate areas not used at night, light areas

Figure 4.11 The roof at Villa Montgomery Apartments in Redwood City, California, reduces the urban heat island effect with the installation of a combination of a high-SRI roof material with photovoltaic systems (generating a portion of the electricity needed for operations), along with a green roof, including a playground that offers residents the opportunity to enjoy the outdoor environment. *Photo courtesy of FFA*

Figure 4.12 The Utah Botanical Center's Wetland Discovery Point building at Utah State University in Kaysville was mindful of the nocturnal environment in which the center resides by providing very minimal exterior lighting and shielding any fixtures that would pollute the night sky. *Photo courtesy of Gary Neuenswander, Utah Agricultural Experiment Station*

beyond a property's boundary, or overcompensate light levels (**footcandle** levels). If vertical footcandle levels are minimized, light pollution is reduced, dark night skies are preserved, visibility at night is improved by the reduction of glare, and nocturnal animal habitats remain unaffected from sky glow. Project teams will need to follow the guidelines within ASHRAE 90.1-2007 for lighting power densities based on the lighting zones of IESNA RP-33 applicable to the site location (i.e., urban versus rural). Project teams will also look to IESNA RP-33 for the lighting distribution guidelines. The teams will need to determine if there is a stipulated curfew or lighting restriction times for the area; if not, a 10 P.M. default value can be used to determine the maximum distribution times. Typically, project teams will need to provide either full cutoff or semi-cutoff fixtures with minimal uplighting and **shielding** to direct and contain the light to appropriate areas in order to comply. Shielding a light fixture, or luminaire, involves a device or technique that helps to reduce glare, light trespass, and/or sky glow. Project teams will need to address egress areas, and light only for safety and comfort and not in excess. For example, in order to achieve this, the lighting designer could provide two low-light-output fixtures instead of one fixture with a higher light output.

Project teams have two options for complying with the interior light component of this credit. At any envelope openings, they can either provide a type of control to reduce the interior lighting power by 50 percent or they can shield all the nonemergency light fixtures with a controlled mechanism, such as automatic shades with a transmittance of less than 10 percent. Either option is to be provided following regular business hours, or between the hours of 11 P.M. and 5 A.M.

SS Credit 9: Tenant Design and Construction Guidelines (for CS). In an attempt to assist the future tenants of a CS project, this credit requires project teams to develop guidelines for the design and construction of leasable spaces within the building. The guidelines are to include the following topics along with examples of each, as indicated by the BD+C reference guide:

- Water use reduction

- Optimizing energy performance

    - Lighting power

Create a flashcard to remember the definition of a **footcandle**: a measurement of light measured in lumens per square foot.

TIP For CS projects, only lighting installed as part of the base building needs to comply. If no interior lighting is installed as part of the base building scope of work, compliance is met.

TIP School projects with outdoor sports fields are not required to follow the ASHRAE 90.1 guidelines for field locations, but are required to incorporate an automatic light shutoff at 11 P.M. with a manual override. The trespass calculations will also need to be conducted for two conditions: with the field lighting on and with the field lighting off.

TIP **Light trespass** is unwanted light shining on another's property.

Notice the majority of the strategies are derived from the EQ category (to be discussed in Chapter 8).

- Lighting controls
- Heating, ventilation, and air conditioning (HVAC)
- Energy use and metering
- Measurement and verification
- Ventilation and outdoor delivery
- Construction indoor air quality management
- Indoor chemical and pollutant source control
- Controllability of systems
- Thermal comfort
- Daylighting and views
- Commissioning
- Elimination or control of environmental tobacco smoke[16]

SS Credit 9: Site Master Plan (for Schools). School project teams that develop a master plan including the existing infrastructure, the current scope of work, and future construction are eligible to pursue this credit. In order to earn this credit, the team would also need to pursue and earn four out of the seven following Sustainable Site credits for the project and then recalculate those four SS credits for the entire campus:

- Credit 1: Site Selection
- Both of the site development credits (Credit 5)
- Both of the stormwater credits (Credit 6)
- Credit 7.1: Heat Island Effect, Nonroof
- Credit 8: Light Pollution Reduction

SS Credit 10: Joint Use of Facilities (for Schools). School project teams have three compliance path options from which to choose when pursuing this community-integrating credit. The first option is to provide a minimum of three shared spaces, such as a gym or auditorium, for the students and the general public to enjoy at the school. The second option includes collaboration with an outside company or organization to provide a minimum of two dedicated-use-type shared spaces, such as a library or a parking lot. The last option available to school project teams includes the provision of pedestrian access for students to shared spaces that are owned by others, such as a swimming pool or playing field. If a project team were to achieve at least two of the compliance path options, the project could earn an Exemplary Performance credit.

QUIZ TIME!

Q4.10. Which of the following is the best landscape design strategy to implement to reduce heat island effects? (Choose one)

  A. Absorption
  B. Xeriscaping
  C. Increased albedo
  D. Deciduous trees
  E. Increased imperviousness

Q4.11. The owner of a two-story office project has suggested that he is interested in the installation of a vegetated roof system and would like the design team to evaluate it as an option. Which set of team members best represents all of those who might offer meaningful input to this evaluation? (Choose one)

A. Architect, landscape architect, and civil engineer

B. Architect, contractor, and structural engineer

C. Landscape architect, contractor, civil engineer, and structural engineer

D. Architect, structural engineer, landscape architect, and civil engineer

E. Architect, structural engineer, landscape architect, civil engineer, and mechanical engineer

F. Architect, structural engineer, landscape architect, civil engineer, mechanical engineer, and contractor

Q4.12. Emissivity is an indication of which of the following material properties? (Choose one)

A. Ability to reflect light from light sources

B. Ability of a transparent or translucent material to admit solar gain

C. Ability of a material to absorb heat across the entire solar spectrum, including all nonvisible wavelengths

D. Ability of a material to give up heat in the form of long-wave radiation

Q4.13. The design team has attempted to address 50 percent of the hardscape surfaces on the project's site to meet the requirements to reduce the heat island effect for LEED compliance. Which of the following strategies should the LEED Accredited Professional discuss with the design team? (Choose three)

A. Effective tree-shaded area of hardscape features

B. Solar reflectance index for all nonstandard paving materials proposed

C. Percentage of perviousness for proposed open-grid paving materials

D. Emissivity of all low-albedo hardscape features in the design

E. Runoff coefficients for impervious paving materials selected

Q4.14. Which of the following statements is not true concerning infrared (or thermal) emittance? (Choose one)

A. Most building materials have an emittance of 0.9.

B. Emittance ranges from 0 to 1 (or 0% to 100%).

C. Glass is an exception to the rule and has an emittance of 0.1.

D. Untarnished galvanized steel has low emittance levels.

E. Aluminum roof coatings have intermediate emittance levels.

Q4.15. Which of the following are applicable only to LEED for Schools projects? (Choose two)

A. SS Credit 10: Joint Use of Facilities

B. SS Credit 1: Site Selection

C. SS Credit 7.1: Heat Island Effect, Nonroof

D. SS Credit 8: Light Pollution Reduction

E. SS Prerequisite 2: Environmental Site Assessment

Q4.16. How many credits does a school project need to earn in addition to developing a master plan for the site, in order to be in compliance with SS Credit 9: Site Master Plan? (Choose one)

A. Two of the seven eligible

B. Three of the five eligible

C. Four of the seven eligible

D. Four of the five eligible

E. Three of the seven eligible

Q4.17. What are the options from which project teams can select when pursuing SS Credit 8: Light Pollution Reduction for both interior and exterior lighting schemes? (Choose three)

A. Reduce 50 percent of the interior lighting power.

B. Shield all nonemergency light fixtures at all envelope openings.

C. Reduce interior lighting power by 25 percent from 11:00 p.m. to 5:00 a.m.

D. Follow the requirements of ASHRAE 90.1.

E. Follow the requirements of ANSI 33 for lighting power densities.

Q4.18. Which type of project has special lighting provisions as applicable to SS Credit 8: Light Pollution Reduction? (Choose one)

A. Schools

B. Office buildings

C. Hospitals

D. Core and shell

E. Dormitories

Q4.19. What percentage of the full-time equivalent (FTE) occupancy should teams determine in order to provide the minimum number of showers and changing rooms in order to comply with SS Credit 4.2, Alternative Transportation, Bicycle Storage and Changing Rooms? (Choose one)

A. 0.15 percent of FTE

B. 0.5 percent of FTE

C. 0.25 percent of FTE

D. 5 percent of FTE

E. 1 percent of FTE

STORMWATER MANAGEMENT

In the previous section, strategies were presented to address while designing a sustainable site, including the reduction of impervious surfaces to lower heat island effects. Another benefit of minimizing impervious surfaces is the reduction of **stormwater runoff,** which causes degradation of the surface water quality and reduces groundwater recharge to the local **aquifer,** an underground source of water for groundwater, wells, and springs. The reduction in surface water quality is caused by both a filtration decrease and the increase of hardscape areas containing contaminants. The increase of impervious surfaces and stormwater runoff has put water quality, aquatic life, and recreational areas at risk.

Nonpoint source pollutants, such as oil leaked from cars or fertilizers from plantings, are one of the biggest risks to the quality of surface water and aquatic life. These pollutants typically contaminate rainwater flowing along impervious surfaces on the journey to sewer systems or water bodies, especially after a heavy rainfall. Once this polluted rainwater is in the sewer system, it then contaminates the rest of the water and takes a toll on the process to purify it or it can contaminate the body of water into which it is discharged. These bodies of water also then suffer from soil erosion and sedimentation deteriorating aquatic life and recreational opportunities. Therefore, allowing rainwater to percolate through vegetation (Figure 4.13) or **pervious** surfaces, such as pervious concrete, porous pavement, or open-grid pavers that allows at least 50 percent of water to seep through, reduces

Create another flashcard to remember the definition of **stormwater runoff:** rainwater that leaves a project site flowing along parking lots and roadways, traveling to sewer systems and water bodies.

Nonpoint source pollutants are one of the biggest risks to the quality of surface water and aquatic life.

Create a flashcard to remember the definitions of **impervious surfaces:** surfaces that do not allow 50 percent of water to pass through them; and **pervious surfaces:** surfaces that allow at least 50 percent of water to percolate or penetrate through them.

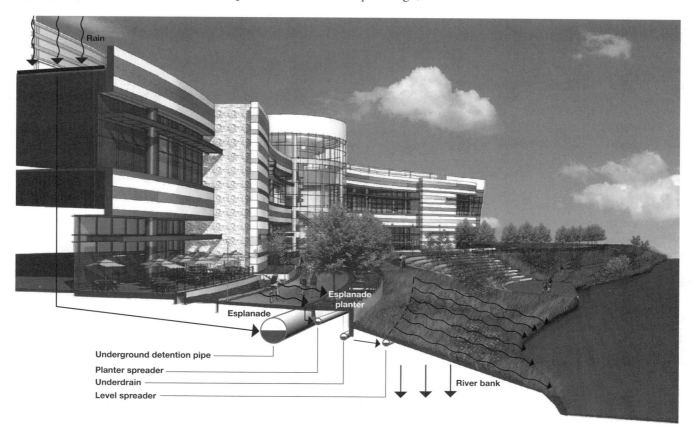

Figure 4.13 Rivers Casino Riverfront Park in Pittsburgh, Pennsylvania, addresses stormwater quantity and quality by incorporating filtration measures to capture and clean rainwater before releasing it into the nearby river. *Photo courtesy of Strada Architecture LLC*

the pollution of surface water, and is less of a burden on our ecosystem. For projects located in urban areas where space is limited, oil separators can be utilized to remove oil, sediment, and floatables. Within an oil separator, heavier solid materials settle to the bottom while floatable oil and grease rise to the top.

Stormwater Management in Relation to LEED Compliance

The triple bottom line benefits of managing stormwater include preserving the natural ecological systems that promote **biodiversity** that in turn help manage stormwater, such as wetlands (Figure 4.14). If the natural environment could manage stormwater, we could take advantage of the economic savings of creating manmade structures to do it for us, as well as the costs to maintain the structures. There is also social equity in managing runoff and maintaining clean surface water: the preservation of aquatic life and the ability to enjoy recreational activities. With the importance of these triple bottom line benefits, LEED addresses stormwater management within the following two credits:

SS Credit 6.1: Stormwater Design, Quantity Control. Project teams will need to determine the predevelopment imperviousness in order to determine which of the two compliance paths to pursue for this credit. If the existing imperviousness is less than 50 percent for the total site, then the team will be required to determine a strategy not to increase the imperviousness. If the existing imperviousness is more than 50 percent, they will need to decrease the runoff volume by 25 percent from the two-year, 24-hour design storm.

Project teams have a number of strategies from which to choose to reduce the amount of stormwater that leaves a project site, such as **wet** or **dry retention ponds.** Both of these approaches utilize excavated areas used to detain rainwater from leaving the site and, therefore, slow runoff. Three other options include on-site filtration methods. **Bioswales** (Figure 4.15), or engineered basins with vegetation, can be utilized to increase groundwater recharge and reduce peak stormwater runoff. The other options, vegetated filter strips and rain gardens, both function to collect and filter runoff while reducing peak discharge rates. Rooftops also contribute to the pollution of surface water, so implementing a

Figure 4.14 The Utah Botanical Center's Wetland Discovery Point project, at Utah State University in Kaysville, earned LEED Platinum certification for its efforts to create biodiversity. *Photo courtesy of Gary Neuenswander, Utah Agricultural Experiment Station*

Figure 4.15 Bioswales, an on-site filtration strategy, can help to recharge the groundwater and reduce stormwater runoff. *Photo courtesy of Thomas M. Robinson, EDR*

green, or vegetated, roof would also reduce stormwater runoff. Another option is to collect the water from the roof and use it for irrigation purposes (Figure 4.16) or toilet flushing. Be sure to review the six considerations of stormwater collection strategies in Chapter 5.

SS Credit 6.2: Stormwater Design, Quality Control. Project teams have two options from which to select when pursuing this credit. They can implement

 Reducing the amount of impervious surfaces, and increasing pervious surfaces, helps to reduce stormwater runoff and, therefore, also helps to save the quality of water.

Figure 4.16 Dick's Sporting Goods Corporate Headquarters in Pittsburgh, Pennsylvania, designed by Strada Architecture, LLC, incorporates roof water capture to reduce the stormwater runoff and reduce the need for potable water for irrigation. *Photo courtesy of Strada Architecture LLC*

Figure 4.17 This green roof at the Allegany County Human Resources Development Commission's community center in Cumberland, Maryland, minimizes impervious areas to reduce stormwater runoff.
Photo courtesy of Moshier Studio

 Green roofs have many synergies, including maximizing open space, creating a habitat for wildlife, and reducing stormwater runoff and the heat island effect, but they also help to insulate a building and therefore, reduce energy use. The trade-offs with green roofs include installation cost and maintenance.

 Create a flashcard to remember the two strategies to address stormwater management.

a "stormwater management plan that reduces impervious cover, promotes infiltration, and captures and treats the stormwater runoff from 90 percent of the average annual rainfall using acceptable best management practices (BMPs)."[17] In addition, the team must create a strategy that is able to remove 80 percent of the **total suspended solids** (TSS) load. Total suspended solids are particles that do not settle with gravity, but instead continue to move with the flow of stormwater and therefore need to be removed with filters instead to reduce contamination. Strategies to comply with this compliance option include vegetated swales, green roofs (Figure 4.17), and pervious paving.

The other compliance path requires the team to provide documentation for infield monitoring that complies with an accepted BMP monitoring practice, such as Technology Acceptance Reciprocity Partnership (TARP).

Project teams have an opportunity to earn one point for Exemplary Performance for the SS Credit 6 suite although there is not a defined compliance path. If a team develops a strategy that captures and treats stormwater above and beyond either of the two stormwater design credit requirements, they could earn one bonus point.

QUIZ TIME!

Q4.20. Which of the following are strategies to reduce stormwater runoff? (Choose three)

A. Green roofs

B. Impervious asphalt

C. Pervious pavers

D. Bioswales

Q4.21. Which of the following are LEED concepts that are *most* significantly influenced by site selection prior to design of the project? (Choose two)

  A. Heat island effect

  B. Alternative transportation: low-emitting and fuel-efficient vehicles

  C. Alternative transportation: public transportation access

  D. Stormwater management: quality control

  E. Brownfield redevelopment

Q4.22. How many basic services are required to comply with the BD+C LEED rating systems? (Choose one)

  A. 5

  B. 4

  C. 12

  D. 10

  E. 6

Q4.23. What is the minimum ACEEE score required for low-emitting and fuel-efficient vehicles by the BD+C LEED rating systems? (Choose one)

  A. 100

  B. 40

  C. 10

  D. 5

  E. 20

Q4.24. What roofing material would be best to comply with the BD+C LEED rating systems for heat island effect reductions? (Choose two)

  A. Gray asphalt with an SRI of 22

  B. Aluminum coating with an SRI of 50

  C. Red clay tile with an SRI of 36

  D. White EPDM with an SRI of 84

  E. White cement tile with an SRI of 90

  F. Light gravel on built-up roof with an SRI of 37

Q4.25. Using open-grid pavers would contribute to which LEED credit? (Choose two)

  A. Heat Island Effect

  B. Site Master Plan

  C. Stormwater Management: Quantity Control

  D. Site Selection

  E. Construction Activity Pollution Prevention

  F. Site Development

Q4.26. What is the default curfew time to be used if one does not exist? (Choose one)

A. 11:00 P.M.

B. 10:30 P.M.

C. 9:00 P.M.

D. 10:00 P.M.

E. 9:30 P.M.

Q4.27. Which of the following strategies does not align with erosion and sedimentation control measures? (Choose one)

A. Using vegetation to stabilize soil, also known as temporary and permanent seeding

B. Sediment traps and basins

C. Silt fencing

D. Earth dikes

E. Spraying the loose sand and dirt with water

Q4.28. Which of the following would qualify as public transportation for the purposes of LEED? (Choose three)

A. Campus bus

B. Light rail

C. Carpooling

D. Ferry service

E. Vanpooling

Q4.29. A project team is pursuing SS Credit 7.2: Heat Island Effect, Roof to reduce the heat gain and increase the efficiency of the building systems. The total flat roof surface is 50,000 square feet and they plan on installing 15,000 square feet of photovoltaic panels. The mechanical equipment occupies 5,000 square feet. How much of the roof surface has to be covered with a high-SRI material, and what is the minimum SRI of the material in order to comply with the credit? (Choose one)

A. 22,500 SF has to be covered with a roofing material with at least an SRI value of 78

B. 15,000 SF has to be covered with a roofing material with at least an SRI value of 78

C. 25,000 SF has to be covered with a roofing material with at least an SRI value of 78

D. 25,000 SF has to be covered with a roofing material with at least an SRI value of 29

E. 15,000 SF has to be covered with a roofing material with at least an SRI value of 29

Q4.30. A team pursuing LEED NC certification has to determine the FTE occupancy for a 312,000-square-foot facility. The new building will house 400 full-time employees and 600 part-time employees who work an average of four hours per day. In order to comply with SS Credit 4.2: Alternative Transportation, Bicycle Storage, and Changing Rooms, how many showers and bike racks need to be provided? (Choose one)

A. 4 showers and 35 bike racks

B. 3 showers and 21 bike racks

C. 3 showers and 35 bike racks

D. 4 showers and 21 bike racks

Q4.31. What is the maximum allowable distance showers can be located from the building's entrance for a project to comply with SS Credit 4.2: Alternative Transportation, Bicycle Storage, and Changing Rooms? (Choose one)

A. 200 feet

B. 300 feet

C. 200 yards

D. 100 feet

E. 100 yards

Q4.32. What strategy is defined in the reference guide that could earn a project a credit for Exemplary Performance within the SS Credit 6: Stormwater Design suite if implemented? (Choose one)

A. Double the quantity reductions for runoff.

B. Improve the runoff quality by removing 90 percent of the total suspended solids.

C. Increase the number of best management practices from 5 to 10.

D. A strategy is not defined in the reference guide.

E. Improve the runoff quality by removing 80 percent of the total suspended solids.

Q4.33. A project seeking LEED for Schools certification is looking for an Exemplary Performance strategy for SS Credit 10: Joint Use of Facilities. Which of the following could be implemented to help them comply? (Choose two)

A. Provide access to the parking lot, playing fields, and gymnasium for community events.

B. Provide access to the parking lot, playing fields, and toilets for community events.

C. Provide both a medical and a dental office on the school grounds.

D. Provide access to the library to the public.

E. Provide access to the swimming pool to the public.

CONSTRUCTION	SS Prerequisite 1:
	Construction Activity Pollution Prevention

PURPOSE

To minimize _____ _____ pollution by preventing the following:

- loss of soil from stormwater runoff and/or wind erosion, including protecting topsoil by stockpiling for reuse.
- sedimentation of storm sewer or receiving streams.
- contaminating the air with dust and particulate matter.

REQUIREMENTS

_____ Sedimentation Control Plan developed by _____ _____ and implemented by _____.

STRATEGIES

Stabilization Methods:

- Temporary & _____ seeding, mulching

Structural Control Methods:

- Earth dikes, silt fencing, _____ _____, & sediment basins

DOCUMENTATION

Erosion _____ Control Plan

REFERENCED STANDARD

2003 _____ Construction General Permit

Required	RESPONSIBLE PARTY:
	CONTRACTOR

SS Prerequisite 1:   **Construction Activity Pollution Prevention**

ANSWER KEY

PURPOSE

To minimize construction activity pollution by preventing the following:

- **loss of soil** from stormwater runoff and/or wind erosion, including protecting topsoil by stockpiling for reuse.
- **sedimentation** of storm sewer or receiving streams.
- **contaminating the air** with dust and particulate matter.

REQUIREMENTS

Erosion Sedimentation Control Plan developed by civil engineer and implemented by contractor

STRATEGIES

Stabilization Methods:

- Temporary & permanent seeding, mulching

Structural Control Methods:

- Earth dikes, silt fencing, sediment traps, & sediment basins

DOCUMENTATION

Erosion Sedimentation Control Plan

REFERENCED STANDARD

2003 EPA Construction General Permit

DESIGN	**SS Prerequisite 2:** **Environmental Site Assessment (SCHOOLS)**

PURPOSE

To protect the health of _____, perform the proper site _____ prior to school development

REQUIREMENTS

Conduct a _____ to determine existence of _____. Follow-up with a Phase II if contamination exists to determine proper _____.

STRATEGIES

Phase I assessment does not include soil samples but site research instead.

Phase II assessment includes soil sampling to determine appropriate remediation, such as:

- _____ & _____ methods

- bioreactors, land farming

- in situ (in place) remediation

DOCUMENTATION

Phase I and Phase II (if applicable) Environmental Site Assessments

REFERENCED STANDARD

ASTM E1527-05, Phase I Environmental Site Assessment

ASTM _____ Phase II Environmental Site Assessment

Required	**RESPONSIBLE PARTY:** **OWNER/DEVELOPER**

SS Prerequisite 2:

Environmental Site Assessment (SCHOOLS)

ANSWER KEY

PURPOSE

To protect the health of children, perform the proper site assessment prior to school development

REQUIREMENTS

Conduct a Phase I to determine existence of contamination. Follow-up with a Phase II if contamination exists to determine proper remediation.

STRATEGIES

Phase I assessment does not include soil samples but site research instead.

Phase II assessment includes soil sampling to determine appropriate remediation, such as:

- pump-and-treat methods

- bioreactors, land farming

- in situ (in place) remediation

DOCUMENTATION

Phase I and Phase II (if applicable) Environmental Site Assessments

REFERENCED STANDARD

ASTM E1527-05, Phase I Environmental Site Assessment

ASTM E1903-97 Phase II Environmental Site Assessment

DESIGN	**SS Credit 1:**
	Site Selection

PURPOSE

Avoid the _____ of inappropriate sites to mitigate harmful _____ impacts.

REQUIREMENTS

Avoid the following types of sites:

- Prime farmland (defined by the U.S. Department of Agriculture): greenfield sites with soil appropriate for cultivation and agricultural growth and production

- Floodplains/flood-prone areas (predeveloped elevation is less than ____ feet above the _____-year floodplain level as defined by Federal Emergency Management Agency [FEMA])

- Habitat for any_____ or _____ species: where extinction is threatened due to human activities or environmental conditions

- Land within 100 feet of wetlands (defined by the Code of Federal Regulations)

- Previously undeveloped land within _____ feet of a body of water (Clean _____ Act)

- Public _____

REFERENCED STANDARD

USDA Definition of Prime Agricultural Land (US CFR)

FEMA 100 Year Flood Definition

Endangered Species Lists (US Fish & Wildlife Service)

National Marine Fisheries Service, List of Endangered Marine Species

Definitions of Wetlands in the US CFR (40 CFR, Parts 230-233, 22)

1 pt.	**RESPONSIBLE PARTY:**
	OWNER/DEVELOPER

	SS Credit 1:
	Site Selection

ANSWER KEY

PURPOSE

Avoid the development of inappropriate sites to mitigate harmful environmental impacts.

REQUIREMENTS

Avoid the following types of sites:

- **Prime farmland** (defined by the U.S. Department of Agriculture): greenfield sites with soil appropriate for cultivation and agricultural growth and production

- **Floodplains/flood-prone areas** (predeveloped elevation is less than 5 feet above the 100-year floodplain level as defined by Federal Emergency Management Agency [FEMA])

- Habitat for any **endangered or critical species:** where extinction is threatened due to human activities or environmental conditions

- Land within **100 feet of wetlands** (defined by the Code of Federal Regulations)

- Previously undeveloped land within **50 feet of a body of water** (Clean Water Act)

- Public **parkland**

REFERENCED STANDARD

USDA Definition of Prime Agricultural Land (US CFR)

FEMA 100 Year Flood Definition

Endangered Species Lists (US Fish & Wildlife Service)

National Marine Fisheries Service, List of Endangered Marine Species

Definitions of Wetlands in the US CFR (40 CFR, Parts 230-233, 22)

DESIGN	SS Credit 2:
	Development Density and Community Connectivity

PURPOSE

To encourage the development or redevelopment of high density areas with _____ infrastructure, in order to preserve greenfield sites, _____, and natural resources.

REQUIREMENTS

Option 1: _____ Density

> Select a site within an existing neighborhood with a density of _____ square feet per acre including the project seeking certification

Option 2: Community _____

> • Develop a site within a half-mile of a residential area with an average density of _____ units per acre

> AND

> • Develop a site within a half-mile of _____ basic services with pedestrian access

EQUATIONS / DOCUMENTATION

Option 1: Development Density

> 1. Development _____ = Gross Building Area (sf) / Site Area (acres)

> 2. _____ Radius (lf) = 3 X √ [Site Area (acres) X 43,560 (sf/acres)]

> 3. Average Property Density within Density Boundary = Σ Square Footage/ Σ Site Area

Option 2: Community Connectivity

> Submit a vicinity plan with the neighborhood or residential area, the project, and a half-mile radius of _____ basic services.

EXEMPLARY PERFORMANCE

Option 1: Development Density

> Double the average density of the calculated area or if the calculated area is doubled, the average density is at least 120,000 square feet per acre (double the credit requirement).

	RESPONSIBLE PARTY:
4-5 pts.	**OWNER/DEVELOPER**

	SS Credit 2:
	Development Density and Community Connectivity

ANSWER KEY

PURPOSE

To encourage the development or redevelopment of high density areas with existing infrastructure, in order to preserve greenfield sites, habitats, and natural resources.

REQUIREMENTS

Option 1: **Development Density**

Select a site within an existing neighborhood with a density of **60,000 square feet per acre** including the project seeking certification

Option 2: **Community Connectivity**

- Develop a site within a half-mile of a residential area with an average density of 10 units per acre

AND

- Develop a site within a half-mile of **10 basic services** with pedestrian access

EQUATIONS / DOCUMENTATION

Option 1: Development Density

1. Development Density = Gross Building Area (sf) / Site Area (acres)

2. Density Radius (lf) = 3 X $\sqrt{}$ [Site Area (acres) X 43,560 (sf/acres)]

3. Average Property Density within Density Boundary = Σ Square Footage/ Σ Site Area

Option 2: Community Connectivity

Submit a vicinity plan with the neighborhood or residential area, the project, and a half-mile radius of 10 basic services.

EXEMPLARY PERFORMANCE

Option 1: Development Density

Double the average density of the calculated area or if the calculated area is doubled, the average density is at least 120,000 square feet per acre (double the credit requirement).

	SS Credit 3:
DESIGN	**Brownfield Redevelopment**

PURPOSE

To encourage the redevelopment of damaged and _____ sites in an effort to protect greenfield sites from development.

REQUIREMENTS

Option 1:

     Conduct an ASTM _____ Phase _____ Environmental Site Assessment to determine if a site is contaminated and is in need of remediation.

Option 2:

     Select a site that is classified as a brownfield by a local, _____, or federal government agency and perform appropriate remediation.

DOCUMENTATION

Phase II report or documentation from government agency along with remediation techniques implemented.

REFERENCED STANDARD

U.S. EPA, _____ of Brownfield

ASTM E1527-05, Phase _____ Environmental Site Assessment
ASTM _____ Phase II Environmental Site Assessment

	RESPONSIBLE PARTY:
1 pt.	**OWNER/DEVELOPER**

SS Credit 3:

Brownfield Redevelopment

ANSWER KEY

PURPOSE

To encourage the redevelopment of damaged and **contaminated** sites in an effort to protect greenfield sites from development.

REQUIREMENTS

Option 1:

Conduct an **ASTM E1903-97 Phase II Environmental Site Assessment** to determine if a site is contaminated and is in need of remediation.

Option 2:

Select a site that is classified as a brownfield by a local, state, or federal government agency and perform appropriate remediation.

DOCUMENTATION

Phase II report or documentation from government agency along with remediation techniques implemented.

REFERENCED STANDARD

U.S. EPA, Definition of Brownfield

ASTM E1527-05, Phase I Environmental Site Assessment

ASTM E1903-97 Phase II Environmental Site Assessment

DESIGN	**SS Credit 4.1:** **Alternative Transportation, Public Transportation Access**

PURPOSE

Reduce the negative environmental impacts from _____ use including _____ and _____ development.

REQUIREMENTS

Option 1: Rail

Site is within a _____ -mile of a commuter rail, light rail, rail, tram, or ferry station.

Option 2: Bus

Site is within a _____ mile of _____ or more bus (public or campus) lines.

Option 3: Pedestrian Access (SCHOOLS ONLY)

Site is within a three-quarter-mile radius of 80 percent of students attending grades K-8 and one-and-a- _____ -mile radius of _____ percent of the students attending grades 9 and above.

EQUATIONS / DOCUMENTATION

All Options:

Site _____ plan with walking distances labeled. Schools need to show pedestrian and bicycle paths from the building to the edge of the property are in at least _____ directions.

EXEMPLARY PERFORMANCE

Option 1: Rail

Site is within a half-mile of at least two existing commuter rail, light rail, rail, tram, or ferry stations.

Option 2: Bus

Site is within a quarter mile of _____ or more bus (public or campus) lines.

SCHOOLS: Include a school bus line and meet the requirements of Option 2.

All options:

Conduct a _____ Transportation _____ Plan in order to reduce a quantifiable amount of car use by implementing alternative options.

4-6 pts.	**RESPONSIBLE PARTY:** **OWNER/DEVELOPER**

	SS Credit 4.1:
	Alternative Transportation, Public Transportation Access

ANSWER KEY

PURPOSE

Reduce the negative environmental impacts from car use including pollution and land development.

REQUIREMENTS

Option 1: Rail

> Site is within a **half-mile** of a commuter rail, light rail, rail, tram, or ferry station.

Option 2: Bus

> Site is within a **quarter mile** of two or more bus (public or campus) lines.

Option 3: Pedestrian Access (SCHOOLS ONLY)

> Site is within a three-quarter-mile radius of 80 percent of students attending grades K-8 and one-and-a-half-mile radius of 80 percent of the students attending grades 9 and above.

EQUATIONS / DOCUMENTATION

All Options:

> Site vicinity plan with walking distances labeled. Schools need to show pedestrian and bicycle paths from the building to the edge of the property are in at **least two directions**.

EXEMPLARY PERFORMANCE

Option 1: Rail

> Site is within a half-mile of at least two existing commuter rail, light rail, rail, tram, or ferry stations.

Option 2: Bus

> Site is within a quarter mile of four or more bus (public or campus) lines.

> SCHOOLS: Include a school bus line and meet the requirements of Option 2.

All options:

> Conduct a Comprehensive Transportation Management Plan in order to reduce a quantifiable amount of car use by implementing alternative options.

DESIGN	SS Credit 4.2: Alternative Transportation, Bicycle Storage and Changing Rooms

PURPOSE

Reduce the negative environmental impacts from _____ use including _____ and _____ development.

REQUIREMENTS

NC Projects: Provide _____ percent of FTE occupants with bike storage and 0.5 percent of FTE with showers within 200 yards of building entrance.

CS Projects (<300,000 SF): Provide 3 percent of FTE occupants with bike storage and 0.5 percent of FTE with showers within _____ yards of building entrance.

CS Projects (>300,000 SF): Provide _____ percent of FTE occupants with bike storage up to 300,000 square feet and then 0.5 percent for additional square footage and 0.5 percent of FTE with showers within 200 yards of building entrance.

Residential Projects: Provide _____ percent of occupants with covered bike storage.

School Projects: Provide 5 percent of peak occupants (students from grade _____ and up) with bike storage and _____ percent of FTE with showers and changing rooms. Provide dedicated paths in at least _____ directions from edge of property.

EQUATIONS / DOCUMENTATION

All Options:

Create a plan with bike storage and shower and changing room locations in relationship to _____ entrance.

Calculate _____ and transient occupants. FTE = Total staff occupant hours / 8

EXEMPLARY PERFORMANCE

Conduct a _____ Transportation _____ Plan in order to reduce a quantifiable amount of car use by implementing alternative options.

1-2 pts.	RESPONSIBLE PARTY: ARCHITECT

SS Credit 4.2:

Alternative Transportation,

Bicycle Storage and Changing Rooms

ANSWER KEY

PURPOSE

Reduce the negative environmental impacts from car use including pollution and land development.

REQUIREMENTS

NC Projects: Provide 5 percent of FTE occupants with bike storage and 0.5 percent of FTE with showers within 200 yards of building entrance.

CS Projects (<300,000 SF): Provide 3 percent of FTE occupants with bike storage and 0.5 percent of FTE with showers within 200 yards of building entrance.

CS Projects (>300,000 SF): Provide 3 percent of FTE occupants with bike storage up to 300,000 square feet and then 0.5 percent for additional square footage and 0.5 percent of FTE with showers within 200 yards of building entrance.

Residential Projects: Provide 15 percent of occupants with covered bike storage.

School Projects: Provide 5 percent of peak occupants (students from grade 3 and up) with bike storage and 0.5 percent of FTE with showers and changing rooms. Provide dedicated paths in at least 2 directions from edge of property.

EQUATIONS / DOCUMENTATION

All Options:

Create a plan with bike storage and shower and changing room locations in relationship to building entrance.

Calculate FTE and transient occupants. **FTE = Total staff occupant hours / 8**

EXEMPLARY PERFORMANCE

Conduct a Comprehensive Transportation Management Plan in order to reduce a quantifiable amount of car use by implementing alternative options.

DESIGN	**SS Credit 4.3:**
	Alternative Transportation,
	Low-Emitting and Fuel-Efficient Vehicles

PURPOSE

Reduce the negative environmental impacts from _____ use including _____ and _____ development.

REQUIREMENTS

Option 1: Preferred Parking

> Of total parking, provide _____ percent preferred spaces for efficient vehicles. Schools to also provide at least 1 _____ drop-off area for efficient vehicles.

Option 2: Alternative Fueling Stations

> NC and CS Projects: Of total parking, provide _____ percent of the spaces with refueling stations for vehicles powered by alternative fuel.

> Schools: _____ percent of the fleet should be either fuel efficient or alternatively fuel powered.

Option 3: Provide FEVs to Occupants (NC ONLY)

> Provide _____ percent of the FTE with low-emitting or fuel-efficient vehicles.

Option 4: Vehicle Sharing Program (NC ONLY)

> Provide _____ percent of the FTE with access to a vehicle-share program with fuel-efficient cars.

EQUATIONS / DOCUMENTATION

Option 1: Preferred Parking

> Submit site plan with _____ parking spaces noted. If using discount parking program for compliance, submit program documentation.

Option 2: Alternative Fueling Stations

> Submit plan with location of refueling stations and information on fuel type and station capacity.

> Schools: Provide manufacturer and model numbers of vehicles and fuel consumption.

Option 3: Provide FEVs to Occupants (NC ONLY)

> Calculate FTE. FTE = Total staff occupant hours / 8.

> Provide vehicle information inlcuding make, model, and fuel type.

> Provide a site plan with preferred parking spaces noted.

Option 4: Vehicle Sharing Program (NC ONLY)

> Calculate FTE. FTE = Total staff occupant hours / 8.

> Provide contractual agreement for program indicating at least a _____-year commitment.

EXEMPLARY PERFORMANCE

Conduct a _____ Transportation _____ Plan in order to reduce a quantifiable amount of car use by implementing alternative options.

2-3 pts.	**RESPONSIBLE PARTY:**
	ARCHITECT

SS Credit 4.3:

Alternative Transportation,

Low-Emitting and Fuel-Efficient Vehicles

ANSWER KEY

PURPOSE

Reduce the negative environmental impacts from car use including pollution and land development.

REQUIREMENTS

Option 1: **Preferred Parking**

Of total parking, provide 5 percent preferred spaces for efficient vehicles. Schools to also provide at least 1 carpool drop-off area for efficient vehicles.

Option 2: **Alternative Fueling Stations**

NC and CS Projects: Of total parking, provide 3 percent of the spaces with refueling stations for vehicles powered by alternative fuel.

Schools: 20 percent of the fleet should be either fuel efficient or alternatively fuel powered.

Option 3: **Provide FEVs to Occupants (NC ONLY)**

Provide 3 percent of the FTE with low-emitting or fuel-efficient vehicles.

Option 4: **Vehicle Sharing Program (NC ONLY)**

Provide 3 percent of the FTE with access to a vehicle-share program with fuel-efficient cars.

EQUATIONS / DOCUMENTATION

Option 1: Preferred Parking

Submit site plan with preferred parking spaces noted. If using discount parking program for compliance, submit program documentation.

Option 2: Alternative Fueling Stations

Submit plan with location of refueling stations and information on fuel type and station capacity.

Schools: Provide manufacturer and model numbers of vehicles and fuel consumption.

Option 3: Provide FEVs to Occupants (NC ONLY)

Calculate FTE. FTE = Total staff occupant hours / 8.

Provide vehicle information inlcuding make, model, and fuel type.

Provide a site plan with preferred parking spaces noted.

Option 4: Vehicle Sharing Program (NC ONLY)

Calculate FTE. FTE = Total staff occupant hours / 8.

Provide contractual agreement for program indicating at least a **2-year commitment**.

EXEMPLARY PERFORMANCE

Conduct a Comprehensive Transportation Management Plan in order to reduce a quantifiable amount of car use by implementing alternative options.

DESIGN	SS Credit 4.4: Alternative Transportation, Parking Capacity

PURPOSE

Reduce the negative environmental impacts from _____ use including _____ and _____ development.

REQUIREMENTS

Case 1: Nonresidential Projects

Option 1: Parking capacity not to exceed _____ zoning ordinance. NC projects to also provide preferred parking for ride share vehicles for carpools/vanpools equal to _____ percent of total _____ capacity.

Option 2: Parking capacity is required to be less than 5 percent (____) or 3 percent (____) of _____ and preferred parking is required for carpools/vanpools (___ percent for NC and_____ percent for CS of ____ _____ _____).

Case 2: Residential Projects

Parking capacity not to exceed local zoning ordinance. Provide availability of shared vehicle program including _____ area, _____ _____ , and _____ boards.

Case 3: Mixed-Use Projects

Projects with a less than _____ percent commercial component shall follow Case _____.

Projects with a more than _____ percent commercial component, follow Case _____ for commercial area and Case _____ for residential area.

Case 4: Schools

Option 1: Parking capacity not to exceed local zoning ordinance and provide preferred parking for ride share vehicles for carpools/vanpools equal to _____ percent of total parking capacity.

Option 2: If no zoning ordinance exists, provide ____percent less parking capacity than the guidelines in the _____ referenced standard.

Case 5: All Project Types

Do not provide any new parking.

EQUATIONS / DOCUMENTATION

Case 1: Nonresidential Projects

Option 1: Plan showing the parking capacity for the site and minimum _____ percent preferred parking spaces.

Option 2: Calculate FTE. FTE = Total staff occupant hours / _____. Provide plan showing the parking capacity for the site and preferred parking spaces (5 percent for NC and 3 percent for CS)

Case 2: Residential Projects

Plan showing the parking capacity for the site, applicable preferred parking spaces for _____ and _____ drop-off areas.

Case 3: Mixed-Use Projects

Projects with less than 10 percent _____ component shall provide a plan showing the parking capacity for the site, applicable preferred parking spaces for vanpools, and carpool drop-off areas.

Projects with more than 10 percent commercial component, follow Case 1 for commercial area and Case 2 for residential area.

Case 4: Schools

Option 1: Plan showing the parking capacity for the site and minimum 5 percent preferred parking spaces for carpools and vanpools.

Option 2: Refer to the guidelines in the ITE referenced standard to determine how many spaces are recommended and then multiply by 75 percent to calculate number of maximum spaces to provide.

Case 5: All Project Types

Plan showing the parking capacity for the site.

REFERENCED STANDARD

Institute of Transportation Engineers (ITE), "_____ _____" study, 2003

EXEMPLARY PERFORMANCE

Conduct a _____ Transportation _____ Plan in order to reduce a quantifiable amount of car use by implementing alternative options.

2 pts.	RESPONSIBLE PARTY: ARCHITECT

	SS Credit 4.4:
	Alternative Transportation, Parking Capacity

ANSWER KEY

PURPOSE

Reduce the negative environmental impacts from car use including pollution and land development.

REQUIREMENTS

Case 1: Nonresidential Projects

Option 1: Parking capacity not to exceed local zoning ordinance. NC projects to also provide preferred parking for ride share vehicles for carpools/vanpools equal to 5 percent of total parking capacity.

Option 2: Parking capacity is required to be less than 5 percent (NC) or 3 percent (CS) of **FTE** and preferred parking is required for carpools/vanpools (5 percent for NC and 3 percent for CS of **total parking capacity**).

Case 2: Residential Projects

Parking capacity not to exceed local zoning ordinance. Provide availability of shared vehicle program including drop-off area, preferred parking, and ride boards.

Case 3: Mixed-Use Projects

Projects with a less than 10% commercial component shall follow Case 2.

Projects with a more than 10% commercial component, follow Case 1 for commercial area and Case 2 for residential area.

Case 4: Schools

Option 1: Parking capacity not to exceed local zoning ordinance and provide preferred parking for ride share vehicles for carpools/vanpools equal to 5 percent of total parking capacity.

Option 2: If no zoning ordinance exists, provide 25 percent less parking capacity than the guidelines in the ITE referenced standard.

Case 5: All Project Types

Do not provide any new parking.

EQUATIONS / DOCUMENTATION

Case 1: Nonresidential Projects

Option 1: Plan showing the parking capacity for the site and minimum 5 percent preferred parking spaces.

Option 2: Calculate FTE. FTE = Total staff occupant hours / 8. Provide plan showing the parking capacity for the site and preferred parking spaces (5 percent for NC and 3 percent for CS).

Case 2: Residential Projects

Plan showing the parking capacity for the site, applicable preferred parking spaces for vanpools and carpool drop-off areas.

Case 3: Mixed-Use Projects

Projects with less than 10 percent commercial component shall provide a plan showing the parking capacity for the site, applicable preferred parking spaces for vanpools, and carpool drop-off areas.

Projects with more than 10 percent commercial component, follow Case 1 for commercial area and Case 2 for residential area.

Case 4: Schools

Option 1: Plan showing the parking capacity for the site and minimum 5 percent preferred parking spaces for carpools and vanpools.

Option 2: Refer to the guidelines in the ITE referenced standard to determine how many spaces are recommended and then multiply by 75 percent to calculate number of maximum spaces to provide.

Case 5: All Project Types

Plan showing the parking capacity for the site.

REFERENCED STANDARD

Institute of Transportation Engineers (ITE), "Parking Generation" study, 2003

EXEMPLARY PERFORMANCE

Conduct a Comprehensive Transportation Management Plan in order to reduce a quantifiable amount of car use by implementing alternative options.

CONSTRUCTION	**SS Credit 5.1:** **Site Development, Protect or Restore Habitat**

PURPOSE

Promote _____ and provide _____ by conserving natural areas and restoring damaged areas.

REQUIREMENTS

Case 1: _____ Sites

Limit disturbance to:

- _____ feet from perimeter

- _____ feet from hardscape

- 15 feet from _____ _____ and utility trenches

- _____ feet from constructed permeable surfaces

Case 2: Previously _____ or Developed Sites

Restore at least _____ percent of the site (excluding the building footprint) or _____ percent with the building footprint - whichever is _____ - with native or _____ plantings.

EQUATIONS / DOCUMENTATION

Case 1: Greenfield Sites

Provide site plan depicting disturbance boundaries.

Case 2: Previously Graded or Developed Sites

Calculate 50 percent of site area (not including the building footprint) OR calculate 20 percent of total site area to determine minimum amount of area to be protected. Include _____ _____ square footage if also pursuing _____.

Provide site plan showing protected and/or restored areas with a list of _____.

EXEMPLARY PERFORMANCE

Restore at least _____ percent of the site (excluding the building footprint) or _____ percent with the building footprint - whichever is greater- with native or adaptive plantings.

1 pt.	**RESPONSIBLE PARTY:** **CIVIL ENGINEER or LANDSCAPE ARCHITECT**

SS Credit 5.1:

Site Development, Protect or Restore Habitat

ANSWER KEY

PURPOSE

Promote biodiversity and provide habitat by conserving natural areas and restoring damaged areas.

REQUIREMENTS

Case 1: Greenfield Sites

Limit disturbance to:

- **40** feet from perimeter

- **10** feet from hardscape

- **15** feet from roadway curbs and utility trenches

- **25** feet from constructed permeable surfaces

Case 2: Previously Graded or Developed Sites

Restore at least 50 percent of the site (excluding the building footprint) or 20 percent with the building footprint - whichever is greater- with native or adaptive plantings.

EQUATIONS / DOCUMENTATION

Case 1: Greenfield Sites

Provide site plan depicting disturbance boundaries.

Case 2: Previously Graded or Developed Sites

Calculate 50 percent of site area (not including the building footprint) OR calculate 20 percent of total site area to determine minimum amount of area to be protected. Include green roof square footage if also pursuing **SSc2**.

Provide site plan showing protected and/or restored areas with a list of vegetation.

EXEMPLARY PERFORMANCE

Restore at least 75 percent of the site (excluding the building footprint) or 30 percent with the building footprint - whichever is greater- with native or adaptive plantings.

	SS Credit 5.2:
DESIGN	**Site Development, Maximize Open Space**

PURPOSE

Promote _____ with a large proportion of _____ space as compared to the _____ footprint.

REQUIREMENTS

Case 1: Sites with Local Open Space Ordinances

Provide _____ percent more open space than that required.

Case 2: Sites with No Local Open Space Requirements

Provide an _____ amount of open space as compared to the building footprint.

Case 3: Sites with Local Zoning Ordinance but no Open Space Requirements

Provide open space equal to _____ percent of _____.

EQUATIONS/DOCUMENTATION

All Cases: Provide site plan with open space proportions noted.

Case 1: Sites with Local Open Space _____

Research local ordinance to determine required amount of open space and then multiply by 125 percent to determine amount required to comply with this credit.

Case 2: Sites with No _____ Open Space Requirements

Calculate proportions of building footprint to open space to ensure compliance.

Case 3: Sites with Local _____ Ordinance but no Open Space Requirements

Calculate square footage of site and the amount of open space provided to ensure a minimum of _____ percent is met.

EXEMPLARY PERFORMANCE

_____ the minimum amount of required _____ space provided for any of the compliance path options.

	RESPONSIBLE PARTY:
1 pt.	**CIVIL ENGINEER or LANDSCAPE ARCHITECT**

	SS Credit 5.2:
	Site Development, Maximize Open Space

ANSWER KEY

PURPOSE

Promote biodiversity with a large proportion of open space as compared to the development footprint.

REQUIREMENTS

Case 1: Sites with Local Open Space Ordinances

Provide 25 percent more open space than that required.

Case 2: Sites with No Local Open Space Requirements

Provide an equal amount of open space as compared to the building footprint.

Case 3: Sites with Local Zoning Ordinance but No Open Space Requirements

Provide open space equal to 20 percent of site.

EQUATIONS/DOCUMENTATION

All Cases: Provide site plan with open space proportions noted.

Case 1: Sites with Local Open Space Ordinances

Research local ordinance to determine required amount of open space and then multiply by 125 percent to determine amount required to comply with this credit.

Case 2: Sites with No Local Open Space Requirements

Calculate proportions of building footprint to open space to ensure compliance.

Case 3: Sites with Local Zoning Ordinance but No Open Space Requirements

Calculate square footage of site and the amount of open space provided to ensure that a minimum of 20 percent is met.

EXEMPLARY PERFORMANCE

Double the minimum amount of required open space provided for any of the compliance path options.

DESIGN	SS Credit 6.1:
	Stormwater Design, Quantity Control

PURPOSE

Increase _____ cover and on-site _____ to reduce _____ of runoff and the disruption of _____ hydrology.

REQUIREMENTS

Case 1: Sites with Existing Imperviousness of 50 Percent or Less

      Option 1: After development _____ discharge rate and quantity must not exceed the rate and quantity _____ to development.

      Option 2: Develop and implement a stormwater _____ plan that includes a stream _____ protection and quantity control strategies to prevent _____ erosion.

Case 2: Sites with Existing Imperviousness of More Than 50 Percent

      _____ the volume of stormwater runoff by _____ percent of the 2-year, _____-hour design storm

EQUATIONS / DOCUMENTATION

Case 1: Sites with Existing Imperviousness of 50 Percent or Less

      Option 1: Determine the predevelopment discharge quantity and rate for the site and compare to the _____ quantity and rate.

      Option 2: Provide measures and controls to be implemented to prevent excessive erosion along with calculations to demonstrate compliance

Case 2: Sites with Existing Imperviousness of More Than 50 Percent

      Determine the predevelopment and postdevelopment discharge _____ and _____ for the site and compare to the 2-year, 24-hour design storm to ensure a _____ percent decrease

1 pt.

RESPONSIBLE PARTY:

CIVIL ENGINEER or LANDSCAPE ARCHITECT

	SS Credit 6.1:
	Stormwater Design, Quantity Control

ANSWER KEY

PURPOSE

Increase pervious cover and on-site infiltration to reduce contamination of runoff and the disruption of natural hydrology.

REQUIREMENTS

Case 1: Sites with Existing Imperviousness of **50 Percent or Less**

Option 1: After development peak discharge rate and quantity must not exceed the rate and quantity prior to development.

Option 2: Develop and implement a stormwater management plan that includes a stream channel protection and quantity control strategies to prevent excessive erosion.

Case 2: Sites with Existing Imperviousness of **More Than 50 Percent**

Decrease the volume of stormwater runoff by 25 percent of the 2-year, 24-hour design storm

EQUATIONS / DOCUMENTATION

Case 1: Sites with Existing Imperviousness of 50 Percent or Less

Option 1: Determine the predevelopment discharge quantity and rate for the site and compare to the postdevelopment quantity and rate.

Option 2: Provide measures and controls to be implemented to prevent excessive erosion along with calculations to demonstrate compliance

Case 2: Sites with Existing Imperviousness of More Than 50 Percent

Determine the predevelopment and postdevelopment discharge quantities and rates for the site and compare to the 2-year, 24-hour design storm to ensure a 25 percent decrease

DESIGN	**SS Credit 6.2:** **Stormwater Design, Quality Control**

PURPOSE

Reduce _____ and _____ of runoff and the disruption of natural water flows.

REQUIREMENTS

Reduce _____ cover and promote infiltration to capture and treat runoff from _____ percent of the average annual rainfall using _____ _____ _____ (BMPs)

BMPs must remove at least _____ percent of the average annual postdevelopment _____ _____ _____ (TSS) load. BMPs must meet _____ of the following options:

Option 1:

      Are designed in accordance with _____ or _____ requirements

Option 2:

      _____ performance monitoring data exists proving compliance and conforms to accepted _____ for monitoring BMP strategies.

DOCUMENTATION

Stormwater management plan listing the BMPs including _____ and _____ measures to improve stormwater quality and the _____ of each measure.

1 pt.	**RESPONSIBLE PARTY:** **CIVIL ENGINEER or LANDSCAPE ARCHITECT**

SS Credit 6.2: **Stormwater Design, Quality Control**

ANSWER KEY

PURPOSE

Reduce contamination and pollution of runoff and the disruption of natural water flows.

REQUIREMENTS

Reduce impervious cover and promote infiltration to capture and treat runoff from 90 percent of the average annual rainfall using **best management practices** (BMPs)

BMPs must remove at least **80 percent** of the average annual postdevelopment **total suspended solids** (TSS) load. BMPs must meet one of the following options:

Option 1:

Are designed in accordance with local or state requirements

Option 2:

Infield performance monitoring data exists proving compliance and conforms to accepted protocol for monitoring BMP strategies.

DOCUMENTATION

Stormwater management plan listing the BMPs including structural and nonstructural measures to improve stormwater quality and the contribution of each measure.

CONSTRUCTION	SS Credit 7.1:
	Heat Island Effect, Nonroof

PURPOSE

Minimize impacts on _____ and habitats by reducing _____ islands.

REQUIREMENTS

Option 1: Combine any of the following strategies for _____ percent of the _____ areas on site:

- Shade within _____ years by the means of trees

- Shade from solar panel covered structures or architectural structures with an _____ of at least _____

- _____ surfaces with an _____ of at least _____

- Open-grid pavement system with at least _____ percent pervious

Option 2:

Place at least 50 percent of parking _____ or under cover by the means of either a green roof, roof surface with an _____ of at least _____, or solar panels.

DOCUMENTATION

Provide a _____ plan depicting nonroof hardscape area square footage and SRI values and/or pervious capabilities for compliant areas. If pursuing _____ strategies, calculate expected shade at 5 years at _____ a.m., 12 noon, and _____ p.m. on the _____ solstice to determine average and to prove compliance.

EXEMPLARY PERFORMANCE

Double the strategy for either compliance path option so that either _____ percent of the hardscape areas or _____ percent of all parking areas are addressed.

1 pt.	RESPONSIBLE PARTY:
	CIVIL ENGINEER or LANDSCAPE ARCHITECT

| | **SS Credit 7.1:** |
| | **Heat Island Effect, Nonroof** |

ANSWER KEY

PURPOSE

Minimize impacts on microclimates and habitats by reducing heat islands.

REQUIREMENTS

Option 1: Combine any of the following strategies for 50 percent of the hardscape areas on site:

- **Shade** within 5 years by the means of trees

- Shade from solar panel covered structures or architectural structures with an SRI of at least 29

- Hardscape surfaces with an **SRI** of at least 29

- **Open-grid pavement** system with at least 50 percent pervious

Option 2:

Place at least 50 percent of parking underground or under cover by the means of either a green roof, roof surface with an SRI of at least 29, or solar panels.

DOCUMENTATION

Provide a site plan depicting nonroof hardscape area square footage and SRI values and/or pervious capabilities for compliant areas. If pursuing shading strategies, calculate expected shade at 5 years at 10 a.m., 12 noon, and 3 p.m. on the summer solstice to determine average and to prove compliance.

EXEMPLARY PERFORMANCE

Double the strategy for either compliance path option so that either 100 percent of the hardscape areas or 100 percent of all parking areas are addressed.

| **DESIGN** | **SS Credit 7.2:**
Heat Island Effect, Roof |

PURPOSE

Minimize impacts on microclimates and _____ by reducing _____ islands.

REQUIREMENTS

Option 1: Cover _____ percent of the roof with roofing materials; must have a minimum _____ value of:

- _____ for low-sloped roofs

- _____ for steep-sloped roofs

Option 2: Implement a _____ roof for at least _____ percent of the roof surface

Option 3: Combination of Option 1 and Option 2

DOCUMENTATION

Calculate total roof area _____ any equipment and penetrations, such as skylights.

Provide roof plan with slopes and roofing materials with SRI values and/or vegetated roof areas.

EXEMPLARY PERFORMANCE

Cover _____ percent of the roof with a green roof.

REFERENCED STANDARD

ASTM International Standards for determining and measuring _____ and _____ reflectance.

| **1 pt.** | **RESPONSIBLE PARTY:**
ARCHITECT |

SS Credit 7.2:

Heat Island Effect, Roof

ANSWER KEY

PURPOSE

Minimize impacts on microclimates and habitats by reducing heat islands.

REQUIREMENTS

Option 1: Cover 75 percent of the roof with roofing materials; must have a minimum SRI value of:

- **78 for low-sloped roofs**

- **29 for steep-sloped roofs**

Option 2: Implement a vegetated roof for at least 50 percent of the roof surface

Option 3: Combination of Option 1 and Option 2

DOCUMENTATION

Calculate total roof area minus any equipment and penetrations, such as skylights.

Provide roof plan with slopes and roofing materials with SRI values and/or vegetated roof areas.

EXEMPLARY PERFORMANCE

Cover 100 percent of the roof with a green roof.

REFERENCED STANDARD

ASTM International Standards for determining and measuring emittance and solar reflectance.

	SS Credit 8:
DESIGN	**Light Pollution Reduction**

PURPOSE

Reduce light _____, sky glow, and the impacts from development while _____ night sky access and visibility through _____ reduction.

REQUIREMENTS

INTERIOR: At any and all _____ Openings:

Option 1: Reduce lighting _____ by at least _____ percent between 11:00 p.m. and 5:00 a.m.

Option 2: With a _____ device, shield all _____ light fixtures to allow a light transmittance of no more than _____ percent.

EXTERIOR:

Provide lighting power _____ in accordance with ANSI/ASHRAE/IESNA _____ - 2007 and follow light _____ requirements of IESNA RP-33 for applicable LZ1 to LZ4 zone.

ADDITIONAL REQUIREMENTS FOR SPORTS FIELDS FOR SCHOOLS:

_____ _____ are exempt from compliance with ASHRAE 90.1 but these areas must have an 11 p.m. automatic shut-off with _____ _____ capabilities AND comply with _____ requirements for when sports lighting is turned on and off. Depending on lighting zone footcandle levels vary at the site boundary line with a drop-off amount at either 10 feet for LZ1 and LZ2 and 15 feet for LZ3 and LZ4.

STRATEGIES

INTERIOR: At any and all Envelope Openings:

Option 1: Automatic sweep times, occupancy sensors, programmed master lighting controls panels

Option 2: Automatic shades with less than _____ percent _____

EXTERIOR: Provide site _____ plan depicting light levels

Low-intensity shielded fixtures and curfew controllers. Light only for safety and comfort utilizing down-lighting techniques instead of uplighting. Provide 2 fixtures with lower light outputs and better glare control as opposed to 1 fixture with a higher light output.

ADDITIONAL REQUIREMENTS FOR SPORTS FIELDS FOR SCHOOLS:

_____ _____ and controls

REFERENCED STANDARD

ANSI/_____/IESNA 90.1 - 2007

	RESPONSIBLE PARTY:
1 pt.	**LIGHTING DESIGNER**

DESIGN	**SS Credit 8:**
	Light Pollution Reduction

ANSWER KEY

PURPOSE

Reduce light trespass, sky glow, and the impacts from development while increasing night sky access and visibility through glare reduction.

REQUIREMENTS

INTERIOR: At any and all Envelope Openings:

Option 1: Reduce lighting power by at least 50 percent between 11:00 p.m. and 5:00 a.m.

Option 2: With a controlled device, shield all nonemergency light fixtures to allow a light transmittance of no more than 10 percent.

EXTERIOR:

Provide lighting power densities in accordance with ANSI/ASHRAE/IESNA 90.1 - 2007 and follow light distribution requirements of IESNA RP-33 for applicable LZ1 to LZ4 zone.

ADDITIONAL REQUIREMENTS FOR SPORTS FIELDS FOR SCHOOLS:

Playing fields are exempt from compliance with ASHRAE 90.1 but these areas must have an 11 p.m. automatic shut-off with manual override capabilities AND comply with trespass requirements for when sports lighting is turned on and off. Depending on lighting zone footcandle levels vary at the site boundary line with a drop-off amount at either 10 feet for LZ1 and LZ2 and 15 feet for LZ3 and LZ4.

STRATEGIES

INTERIOR: At any and all Envelope Openings:

Option 1: Automatic sweep times, occupancy sensors, programmed master lighting controls panels

Option 2: Automatic shades with less than 10 percent transmittance

EXTERIOR: Provide site photometric plan depicting light levels

Low-intensity shielded fixtures and curfew controllers. Light only for safety and comfort utilizing down-lighting techniques instead of uplighting. Provide 2 fixtures with lower light outputs and better glare control as opposed to 1 fixture with a higher light output.

ADDITIONAL REQUIREMENTS FOR SPORTS FIELDS FOR SCHOOLS:

Curfew timers and controls

REFERENCED STANDARD

ANSI/ASHRAE/IESNA 90.1 - 2007

DESIGN	**SS Credit 9:**
	Site Master Plans (SCHOOLS)

PURPOSE

To ensure the environmental site issues are continued for future improvements to the site caused by changes in programs or demography.

REQUIREMENTS

Project teams must also pursue and earn _____ of the _____ following credits and then apply them to the _____ campus:

- SS Credit 1: Site Selection

- SS Credit _____: Site Development, Protect or Restore Habitat

- SS Credit 5.2: Site Development, _____ _____ _____

- SS Credit 6.1: Stormwater Design, _____ Control

- SS Credit 6.2: Stormwater Design, _____ Control

- SS Credit 7.1: Heat Island Effect, _____

- SS Credit _____: Light Pollution Reduction

DOCUMENTATION

Submit master site plan, including _____ and current/future construction of buildings, parking, _____ and utilities.

Submit documentation showing compliance for campus for the _____ associated credits.

1 pt.	**RESPONSIBLE PARTY:**
	CIVIL ENGINEER

	SS Credit 9:
	Site Master Plans (SCHOOLS)

ANSWER KEY

PURPOSE

To ensure the environmental site issues are continued for future improvements to the site caused by changes in programs or demography.

REQUIREMENTS

Project teams must also pursue and earn **four of the seven** following credits and then apply them to the entire campus:

- SS Credit 1: Site Selection

- SS Credit 5.1: Site Development, Protect or Restore Habitat

- SS Credit 5.2: Site Development, Maximize Open Space

- SS Credit 6.1: Stormwater Design, Quantity Control

- SS Credit 6.2: Stormwater Design, Quality Control

- SS Credit 7.1: Heat Island Effect, Nonroof

- SS Credit 8: Light Pollution Reduction

DOCUMENTATION

Submit master site plan, including infrastructure and current/future construction of buildings, parking, paving, and utilities.

Submit documentation showing compliance for campus for the four associated credits.

DESIGN	SS Credit 9:
	Tenant Design and Construction Guidelines (CS)

PURPOSE

To reduce the impacts of tenant improvements by educating future tenants about sustainable design and construction strategies.

REQUIREMENTS

Create design and construction guidelines for the tenants to adopt within their leased areas. Guidelines to present LEED for Commercial Interiors rating system. The guidelines must provide examples and strategies for the following measures:

- Water Use Reduction

- Optimize energy performance for lighting power, lighting controls, and HVAC

- Energy use and metering

- Measurement and verification

- Ventilation and outdoor air delivery

- Construction indoor air quality management

- Indoor chemical and pollutant source control

- Controllability of systems

- Thermal comfort

- Daylighting and views

- Commissioning

- Elimination of control of environmental tobacco smoke

1 pt.

RESPONSIBLE PARTY:

OWNER

	SS Credit 9:
	Tenant Design and Construction Guidelines (CS)

ANSWER KEY

PURPOSE

To reduce the impacts of tenant improvements by educating future tenants about sustainable design and construction strategies.

REQUIREMENTS

Create design and construction guidelines for the tenants to adopt within their leased areas. Guidelines to present LEED for Commercial Interiors rating system. The guidelines must provide examples and strategies for the following measures:

- Water Use Reduction

- Optimize energy performance for lighting power, lighting controls, and HVAC

- Energy use and metering

- Measurement and verification

- Ventilation and outdoor air delivery

- Construction indoor air quality management

- Indoor chemical and pollutant source control

- Controllability of systems

- Thermal comfort

- Daylighting and views

- Commissioning

- Elimination of control of environmental tobacco smoke

DESIGN	**SS Credit 10:**
	Joint Use of Facilities

PURPOSE

To _____ the school into the community by sharing the _____ and _____ fields for _____ events and functions.

REQUIREMENTS

Option 1: Provide at least _____ of the following spaces (with a separate entry and access to toilets) to be shared with the general public:

- auditorium

- gymnasium

- cafeteria

- at least _____ classroom

- playing fields

- _____ parking

Option 2: Coordinate with the community to provide at least _____ of the following _____-use spaces in the building:

- _____ office

- _____ clinic

- Police offices

- _____ or media center

- Parking lot

- Community service center

- At least one commercial sector business

Option 3: Provide at least _____ of the following 6 spaces that are owned by other organizations or agencies with pedestrian access for students:

- auditorium

- _____

- cafeteria

- at least one classroom

- swimming pool

- playing fields

DOCUMENTATION

Provide plan showing shared spaces and documentation of _____ agreement or notice to public of available spaces along with _____ doors and gates and _____ restrooms

EXEMPLARY PERFORMANCE

Achieve _____ of the 3 compliance path options

1 pt.	**RESPONSIBLE PARTY:**
	ARCHITECT

	SS Credit 10:
	Joint Use of Facilities

ANSWER KEY

PURPOSE

To integrate the school into the community by sharing the building and playing fields for nonschool events and functions.

REQUIREMENTS

Option 1: Provide **at least 3** of the following spaces (with a separate entry and access to toilets) to be shared with the general public:

- auditorium

- gymnasium

- cafeteria

- at least one classroom

- playing fields

- shared parking

Option 2: Coordinate with the community to provide **at least 2** of the following dedicated-use spaces in the building:

- Commercial office

- Health clinic

- Police offices

- Library or media center

- Parking lot

- Community service center

- At least one commercial sector business

Option 3: Provide at least **2 of the following 6 spaces** that are owned by other organizations or agencies with pedestrian access for students:

- auditorium

- gymnasium

- cafeteria

- at least one classroom

- swimming pool

- playing fields

DOCUMENTATION

Provide plan showing shared spaces and documentation of joint-use agreement or notice to public of available spaces along with security doors and gates and accessible restrooms

EXEMPLARY PERFORMANCE

Achieve 2 of the 3 compliance path options

CHAPTER **5**

WATER EFFICIENCY

THIS CHAPTER FOCUSES ON THE STRATEGIES and technologies described within the Water Efficiency (WE) category of the BD+C Leadership in Energy and Environmental Design (LEED®) rating systems, including methods to reduce the consumption of water, our most precious resource that is often taken for granted. As the demand for water continues to increase and supplies are decreasing, it is challenging for municipalities to keep up. The U.S. Geological Survey estimates that buildings account for 12 percent of total water use in the United States. Potable water that is delivered to buildings and homes is first pulled from local bodies of water, treated, and then delivered. This water, commonly referred to as **potable water**, is typically used for toilets, urinals, sinks, showers, drinking, irrigation (Figure 5.1), and for equipment uses, such as mechanical systems, dishwashers, and washing machines. Once the wastewater leaves the building or home, it is treated and then delivered back to the body of water. When the influx supersedes the capacity of the wastewater treatment facilities, overflow will result. This overflow can pollute and contaminate nearby water bodies, the sources of potable water, consequently causing the need for more treatment facilities to be built. Therefore, it is critical to understand how to reduce the amount of potable water we consume, to reduce the burden on the entire cycle, especially as we are threatened with shortages in the near future.

Green building design teams have the opportunity to specify efficient fixtures, equipment, and appliances that require less water. They also have the ability to implement rainwater-harvesting technologies to capture nonpotable water to use for multiple applications indoors and out. In order to capture stormwater, runoff is collected from the roof or a permeable surface and stored in a cistern on site (Figure 5.1).

Not only is it important to reduce the amount of potable water that is required from the utility companies, but green buildings also have the opportunity to reduce the amount of wastewater that leaves a project site. Implementing biological wastewater treatment technologies can be cost prohibitive, so teams are encouraged to assess the return on investment (ROI) through the means of triple bottom line evaluation.

Building and site designs can help to reduce the amount of water that is required for operations and the amount of wastewater that leaves a site. Within the LEED BD+C rating systems, water efficiency for green buildings is addressed in the following three components:

1. Indoor water use

2. Outdoor water use (for irrigation)

3. Process water

Each of these strategies is referred to in the prerequisite and/or credits of the category, as seen in Table 5.1. Notice the prerequisite and all of the credits are submitted after construction documents are completed for a design side review. Do

Remember to pick a new color for flashcards created for the WE category topics.

Create a flashcard to remember the three types of water uses described in the WE category.

Water efficiency helps to reduce energy and therefore, costs, by reducing the amount of water that must be treated, heated, cooled, and distributed.

Figure 5.1 Capturing and storing rainwater to use for irrigation reduces the need for potable water. *Photo courtesy of Rainwater HOG, LLC*

Table 5.1 The Water-Efficiency (WE) Category

			Points		
D/C	Prereq/Credit	Title	NC	Schools	CS
D	Prereq 1	Water Use Reduction	R	R	R
D	Credit 1	Water-Efficient Landscaping	2–4	2–4	2–4
D	Credit 2	Innovative Wastewater Technologies	2	2	2
D	Credit 3	Water Use Reduction	2–4	2–4	2–4
D	Credit 4	Process Water Use Reduction	–	1	–

Figure 5.2 The Utah Botanical Center's Wetland Discovery Point project is located within a natural habitat requiring the team to address environmental impacts as a result of the new construction, such as water quality. In order to earn its Platinum certification, the team utilized a trombe wall as a thermal mass to capture the heat from the sun during the day and release it at night for heating. *Photo courtesy of Gary Neuenswander, Utah Agricultural Experiment Station*

not worry about remembering the exact credit name and number, as the exam will list them together, but it is important to know which are credits versus the prerequisite.

Similar to the strategies discussed within the Sustainable Sites category, there are triple bottom line values to water efficient strategies. From an environmental standpoint, the more we build with impervious surfaces, the harder it is for the groundwater to recharge naturally. From an economic viewpoint, the more we contribute to sprawl, the more we increase the demand for more facilities and additional distribution systems to be built at a cost to the public. In addition, the energy required to heat water is in direct comparison to the amount of water used; use less hot water, use less energy, save money. Although the social equity of water is drastically understated, as its economic value does not reflect its importance, maintaining clean sources of water is imperative to future generations. The Utah Botanical Center's Wetland Discovery Point project earned Platinum level LEED certification for addressing each of the triple bottom line components for the project (Figure 5.2).

INDOOR WATER USE

Indoor water use typically includes the water used for water closets, urinals, lavatories, and showers. Break room or kitchen sinks are also included in the calculations for indoor water use. For the purposes of the exam, it is important to understand and remember the differences between a flush fixture and a flow fixture and how the consumption of the fixture is measured. Flush fixtures, such as toilets and urinals (Figure 5.3), are measured in **gallons per flush** (gpf). Flow fixtures, such as sink faucets, showerheads, and aerators, are measured in **gallons per minute** (gpm).

 Create flashcards to remember flow and flush fixture types and how they are measured.

Indoor Water Use in Relation to LEED Compliance

When approaching the strategies to reduce water for a project seeking LEED certification, it is necessary for the project teams to calculate a **baseline** for water usage to compare to the amount the project is intended to require. The

Figure 5.3 Waterless urinals help to reduce the indoor water consumption. *Photo courtesy of SmithGroup, Inc.*

 Create a flashcard to remember the Energy Policy Act of 1992 (EPAct 1992) as the standard for the WE prerequisite and indoor water use credits.

WE prerequisite and some of the credits utilize the Energy Policy Act of 1992 (EPAct 1992) for flow and flush rates associated with conventional and efficient fixtures (see Table 5.2). Project teams should also reference the Energy Policy Act of 2005 (EPAct 2005), as it became U.S. law in August 2005.

Table 5.2 Water Consumption Assumptions According to EPAct 1992

Fixture Type	Gallons per Flush (gpf)
Conventional water closet (for baseline calculations)	1.6
Low-flow water closet	1.1
Ultra-low-flow water closet	0.8
Composting toilet	0.0
Conventional urinal (for baseline calculations)	1.0
Waterless urinal	0.0

TIP Notice that FTE is the acronym for **full-time equivalent** and not *full-time employee*. Make sure you account for part-time occupants as well!

Once the fixture water consumption is determined, project teams need to account for the occupant usage to calculate how much water is required for the building. Remember from the previous chapter, the full-time equivalent (FTE) occupancy is an estimation of actual building occupancy in terms of hours occupied per day and is used to determine the number of occupants for the building that will use the fixtures. As mentioned in the previous chapter, FTE is calculated by dividing the total number of occupant hours spent in the building per day by eight.

Create a flashcard to remember baseline versus design case: the amount of water a conventional project would use as compared to the design case.

Keeping within the lines of the basic concept to use less water, efficient indoor water strategies help to change the typically traditional, wasteful behavior of occupants. Project teams should conduct life-cycle cost assessments for determining the best solution for their projects. For example, waterless urinals might cost less to install as they do not require water, but their maintenance costs might be higher than a conventional fixture. Overall, most of the following strategies will not be noticeable, but will substantially reduce water consumption:

A low-flow water closet uses 30 percent less water than a conventional water closet.

WE Prerequisite 1: Water Use Reduction. The BD+C LEED rating systems define potable water use as an important component that green buildings should address and therefore, require a reduction in consumption as a minimal performance feature. This importance is characterized by the means of a prerequisite within the WE category. As a result, LEED certified projects must demand at least 20 percent or less indoor water as compared to conventionally designed buildings. The strategy to achieve this prerequisite involves implementing water-efficient flush and flow fixtures (Figure 5.4). As previously stated, project teams would need to calculate a baseline water consumption using the EPAct values based on the occupancy with a 1:1 male-to-female gender ratio. The declarant will then need to input the values

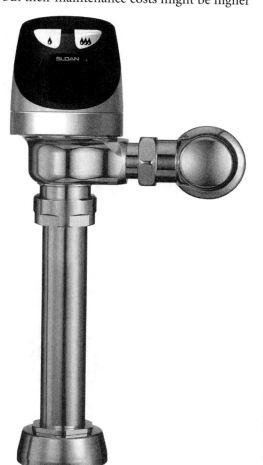

Figure 5.4 Using high-efficiency faucets and high-efficiency toilet (HET) fixtures and flushometers, which use 1.28 gpf or less, helps to achieve the water reduction prerequisite of 20 percent. *Photo courtesy of Sloan Valve Company*

specific to the fixtures specified for the specific project to then compare the different demanded consumptions to prove a 20 percent reduction. These calculations are completed on the submittal template on LEED-Online. Remember the built-in functionality of the submittal template determines compliance based on the data input. The template is configured to assume "the rule of three" to calculate consumption for both the baseline and design cases. The rule of three presupposes a female uses a water closet and a lavatory three times per day while a male only uses a water closet one time per day, a urinal two times per day, and a lavatory three times a day. Consumption is determined by multiplying water needs of each fixture type by sex based on FTE.

WE Credit 2: Innovative Wastewater Technologies. Project teams have two options from which to choose when pursuing this credit. Option 1 requires the project to reduce the potable water consumption used for urinals and toilets by 50 percent by using waterless fixtures or by using **graywater** or stormwater for flushing and to convey sewage.

Remember, stormwater collection was introduced in the previous chapter to reduce the runoff quantities for the site. Therefore, because there are multiple benefits of capturing stormwater, it is important to understand how a project team would design to collect and reuse the water. Project teams need to evaluate different options to determine the appropriate collection systems for their specific project. Systems can range from small barrels to large cisterns (Figures 5.5 and 5.6). Regardless of the system desired, project teams are encouraged to evaluate the following:

- *Water budget.* How much precipitation is expected versus how much water is needed for the purpose the water is intended?
- *Drawdown.* How much water is needed in between rainfalls?
- *Drainage area.* How will the water be collected on site to store? Will it be a permeable surface? If so, what is the size of the surface to determine how much water can be collected?

Create a flashcard to remember the definition of **graywater:** wastewater from showers, bathtubs, lavatories, and washing machines. This water has not come into contact with toilet waste according to the International Plumbing Code (IPC).

TIP Wastewater from toilets and urinals is considered **blackwater**. Kitchen sink, shower, and bathtub wastewater is also considered a source of blackwater. Remember, it's not the source that matters, but what could be in it! For example, washing machine wastewater could be considered blackwater, as it is used to wash cloth diapers.

Water-efficiency strategies incorporated into site design, such as collecting rainwater on site, can help to reduce the demand for indoor water for flush fixtures.

TIP Collected stormwater can be used for irrigation, fire suppression, flush fixtures, and custodial uses.

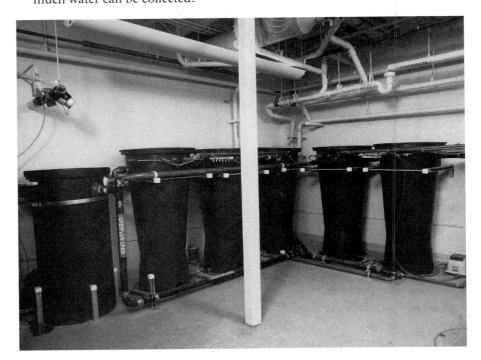
Figure 5.5 Stormwater is collected for reuse to reduce the need for potable water at the Natural Resources Defense Council's Robert Redford Building in Santa Monica, California. *Photo courtesy of Grey Crawford*

Figure 5.6 Stormwater is collected on site and stored in cisterns at the Utah Botanical Center's Wetland Discovery Point building and used to flush toilets, as well as irrigate the site, therefore reducing the need for potable water. *Photo courtesy of Gary Neuenswander, Utah Agricultural Experiment Station*

■ *Conveyance system.* Different pipes will be needed as stormwater and graywater pipes are not allowed to be connected to potable water lines.

■ *Pretreatment.* Screen and/or filters will be needed to remove debris from runoff.

■ *Pressurization.* A pump may be required depending on the system.

Option 2 of this credit requires the project and site to treat 50 percent of wastewater to tertiary standards. The treated water would then need to be used on site or infiltrated. This typically requires a large amount of property to do so and therefore lends itself to be an option for campus settings. The key is to avoid aquifer contamination as posed by current septic system technology. Teams should look to "constructed wetlands, mechanical recirculating sand filters, and anaerobic biological treatment reactors"[1] to comply with this compliance path option.

If 100 percent of the wastewater meets the requirements of the credit, a project team can pursue an Exemplary Performance credit under the Innovation in Design category.

WE Credit 3: Water Use Reduction. In order to comply with this credit, project teams will need to exceed the minimum threshold required by WE Prerequisite 1. Project teams can earn up to four additional points for achieving 30 percent, 35 percent, and 40 percent water reductions for indoor water use. They can pursue an exemplary performance opportunity to reducing water demand by 45 percent.

 TIP Remember, there are two compliance path options for this credit: one addresses the amount of wastewater coming to the site while the other refers to the amount of wastewater leaving the site.

 Create a flashcard to remember the different percentage thresholds to comply with this credit.

 Create a flashcard to remember the three opportunities that address indoor water use.

QUIZ TIME!

Q5.1. If an existing building undergoing a major renovation is seeking LEED NC certification but has a limited budget, which of the following water-efficiency strategies would be economically viable options? (Choose two)

A. Aerators

B. Low-flow toilets

    C. Waterless urinals

    D. Capturing rainwater for irrigation

    E. Flush valves

Q5.2. Which of the following products are not examples of a flow fixture? (Choose two)

    A. Lavatory faucets

    B. Toilets

    C. Sprinkler heads

    D. Aerators

    E. Showerheads

    F. Urinals

Q5.3. What is the minimum percentage of reduced water consumption required in order to comply with WE Prerequisite 1: Water Use Reduction? (Choose one)

    A. 10 percent

    B. 15 percent

    C. 20 percent

    D. 25 percent

    E. 30 percent

Q5.4. Which of the following are addressed for compliance with WE Credit 3: Water Use Reduction? (Choose three)

    A. Showerheads

    B. Sprinkler heads

    C. Hose bibs

    D. Janitor sinks

    E. Kitchen faucets

Q5.5. Which of the following are possible strategies to reach a 50 percent reduction in potable water use for sewage conveyance to earn WE Credit 2: Innovative Wastewater Technologies? (Choose three)

    A. Waterless urinals

    B. Composting toilets

    C. Treat wastewater on site

    D. Rainwater collection to flush toilets

    E. Using rainwater for custodial purposes

OUTDOOR WATER USE FOR IRRIGATION

> Remember, both composting and mulching optimize soil conditions to add to the efficiencies of native and adaptive plantings and high-efficiency irrigation systems.

Water used for irrigating landscaping accounts for the primary use of outdoor water usage, and is therefore a component to be addressed and reduced for projects seeking LEED certification. Remembering the concepts discussed in the previous chapter, site design including native and adaptive plants (Figure 5.7) can drastically reduce the amount of water required for irrigation, if not eliminate the need for irrigation all together. If irrigation is required, implementing a high-efficient system can also substantially reduce the amount of water required over conventional designs. Green building projects might also implement another sustainable option, including capturing rainwater to use for irrigation and indoor water flush functions.

Chapter 4 introduced the heat island effect and how it is responsible for an overall temperature increase of an area. Combining the impacts of greenhouse gas emissions, the heat island effect, and increased impervious surfaces from sprawling developments, water is thus evaporating at quicker rates and not getting delivered to plants and vegetation. Project teams need to be aware of these conditions and plan accordingly, efficiently, and sustainably.

 Create a flashcard to remember all of the uses of rainwater.

Figure 5.7 Native and noninvasive plantings do not require irrigation or fertilizers.

Outdoor Water Use in Relation to LEED Compliance

Pulling together the concepts and strategies from the Sustainable Sites category, such as native planting and xeriscaping (Figure 5.8), project teams could seek to achieve the following outdoor water use strategy:

WE Credit 1: Water-Efficient Landscaping. Project teams have two opportunities to earn points within this credit. If they design the site to use 50 percent less potable water for irrigation purposes, they can earn two points. Reducing the demand can be achieved by implementing a high-efficiency irrigation system with moisture sensors included. These irrigation system types include surface drip, underground, and bubbler systems. A team could also reduce the potable water demand by specifying native and adaptive plantings. A sustainable solution encompasses a decision of both vegetation and system types.

A number of calculations are required to document compliance for this credit. For the purposes of the exam, it is important to know the components of

> **TIP** Each of the calculations documenting compliance with this credit is based on irrigation needs during the month of July.

Figure 5.8 Xeriscaping helps to reduce the demand for potable water with the help of a high-efficient irrigation system and soil improvements for native plantings.

the calculations and not necessarily how to complete the calculations. The first step requires the landscape area to be determined, as it will be the same for both design and baseline cases. Next the **landscape coefficient** is calculated based on the vegetation type's **species factor** (water needs), **density factor** (spacing), and **microclimate factor** (environmental conditions such as humidity, temperature, and wind). The reference guide provides default values for each of these three components for different vegetation types such as trees, shrubs, and turfgrass for project teams to use. These default values do not need to be memorized for the purposes of the exam, just remember the three factors of the landscape coefficient calculation.

Next, the **evapotranspiration rate** is calculated for each landscape area followed by the amount of water actually delivered to vegetation by the proposed irrigation system and not blown away or evaporated. In order to do this, the declarant first determines the **irrigation efficiency** of the proposed type of system. The BD+C reference guide indicates a traditional irrigation system has a 0.625 efficiency default value while a drip system has a 0.90 irrigation efficiency default value. These values together with the controller efficiency value from the system's manufacturer will help to determine the total water usage for the design case. To create the baseline case, the conventional default values are used instead of project-specific efficient ones.

If a project team eliminates the need for potable water by the means of reusing water or by specifying native and adaptive plantings, they can earn another two points, for a total of four. This opportunity is available under WE Credit 1 and not as exemplary performance.

 TIP The amount of water delivered by sprinkler heads is measured in gallons per minute (gpm).

 TIP If a project team is required to use potable water for irrigation for public health reasons, the mandate does not hinder achieving this credit, as those areas can be excluded from the calculations. An example might include irrigating near a swimming pool.

 ! Remember the strategies discussed in the previous chapter. Proper site design will help to reduce water consumption for landscaping needs. Reducing water demands affects both the SS and WE categories.

QUIZ TIME!

Q5.6. Which of the following strategies might contribute to WE Credit 1: Water-Efficient Landscaping? (Choose three)

A. Planting of hardwood trees to provide shade

B. Planting native or adapted plant species

C. Installing turf grass

D. Reducing amount of pervious surface area

E. Combining vegetated swales and cisterns to capture rainwater to use for irrigation

Q5.7. A previously developed site is undergoing a major renovation. The plans include avoiding undeveloped areas and planting more than half of the site area with native and adapted vegetation. Retention ponds and bioswales will also be implemented with native vegetation. Which of the following LEED concepts might these design strategies contribute? (Choose four)

A. Heat island effect

B. Stormwater runoff reduction

C. Site disturbance

D. Water-efficient landscaping

E. Increase density

Q5.8. The major renovation of a four-story, 40,000-square-foot building in Florida includes repaving existing parking areas along the entire length of the south and west facades of the building. The building and parking areas compose the entire site to its boundaries, not leaving any green space. The common afternoon rain showers have led the design team to select open-grid paving with vegetated cells equivalent to 50 percent of its surface in lieu of a lower first cost solution, such as black asphalt. Based on the information provided, which of the following benefits and LEED strategies might the open-grid paving strategy contribute? (Choose three)

A. Reduced site disturbance

B. Water efficient landscaping

C. Heat island effect

D. Stormwater management

E. Optimize energy performance

F. Water use reduction

Q5.9. Which of the following would not reduce potable water used for irrigation? (Choose two)

A. Surface drip irrigation system

B. Sprinkler irrigation systems

C. Underground irrigation system

D. Bubbler irrigation systems

E. Installing native vegetation

F. Install invasive vegetation

PROCESS WATER

TIP   "A cooling tower uses water to absorb heat from air-conditioning systems and regulate air temperature in a facility."[2]

The types of water use reduction strategies previously described may be more obvious for green buildings to pursue as opposed to the third type: process water. Water used for building systems, such as heating and cooling air, is considered **process water**. Process water is used for industrial purposes, such as chillers, cooling towers, and boilers, and also includes water used for operations, such as washing machines, ice machines, and dishwashers. Typically, it is easier to remember the industrial purposes of process water than the operational aspects. To help remember these other types of process water think of restaurants, schools, or hotels and the need for water as part of business operations. For the purposes of the BD+C exam, it is critical to connect process water use reduction with projects seeking LEED for Schools certification, as it is the only rating system that addresses the strategy.

Facility managers and owners should be aware where process water is required and how much is consumed at those specific locations. Green building design teams know efficient building systems require less water. Taking advantage of closed-loop systems allows buildings to extend the use of water in a contaminant-free environment (Figure 5.9). Installing meters to understand the demands of water for building systems and how much is consumed could help economically, specifically in terms of cooling tower makeup water. This water is evaporated

Figure 5.9 Potable water can be reduced for a cooling tower by a closed-loop system. *Photo courtesy of SmithGroup, Inc.*

during the operation of a cooling tower and if metered, could be an opportunity for credit from the utility company, as it does not enter the sewer system, which would then need to be treated.

Process Water Use in Relation to LEED Compliance

Teams working on projects seeking LEED for Schools certification can pursue the following credit if process potable water is reduced:

WE Credit 4: Process Water Use Reduction. School project teams that implement at least four of the following water-efficient process items and can prove a 20 percent water reduction based on a benchmark or industry standard, are eligible to pursue this credit and earn one point:

■ Clothes washers

■ Dishwashers

■ Ice machines

■ Food steamers

■ Pre-rinse spray valves

Notice one-through cooling appliances and equipment, such as garbage disposals and refrigeration equipment, are not eligible. Also, notice the items listed are not addressed in any of the other WE credits or the prerequisite, nor are they addressed by EPAct 1992.

If the team can prove a 40 percent reduction in process water, they can also pursue an Exemplary Performance credit under the Innovation in Design category.

QUIZ TIME!

Q5.10. Which of the following are types of process water uses? (Choose three)

    A. Cooling towers

    B. Boilers

    C. Washing machines

    D. Cisterns

    E. Toilets

Q5.11. Which of the following are potential sources of nonpotable water? (Choose three)

    A. Blackwater

    B. Municipally supplied reclaimed water

    C. Captured rainwater

    D. Wastewater from a toilet

    E. Graywater

Q5.12. Which of the following uses are best described and suitable for nonpotable water? (Choose two)

    A. Drinking water

    B. Irrigation

    C. Clothes washing

    D. Process water

    E. Dishwashing

    F. Showers

Q5.13. Which of the following strategies can collected stormwater be used for? (Choose four)

    A. Landscape irrigation

    B. Fire suppression

C. Flush fixtures

D. Drinking water

E. Custodial uses

F. Shower water

Q5.14. Which of the following would not be impacted if a team were to install a stormwater collection system? (Choose one)

A. WE Credit 3: Water Use Reduction

B. SS Credit 6.1: Stormwater Design, Quantity Control

C. SS Credit 6.2: Stormwater Design, Quality Control

D. WE Credit 2: Innovative Wastewater Technologies

E. WE Credit 1: Water-Efficient Landscaping

DESIGN

PURPOSE

To ensure a reduction on the _____ of the municipal water supply and _____ systems by _____ water _____ within buildings.

REQUIREMENTS

Install low-flow and low-flush fixtures to _____ water consumption.

Calculate _____ consumption using occupancy uses for each fixture type based on _____ values.

Calculate _____ case consumption using occupancy uses for each fixture type based on _____ fixture values.

Assume a _____ gender ratio for calculations.

POINT DISTRIBUTION

20%		30%		35%		40%		45%
•Required		•2 points		•3 points		•4 points		•1 EP point

REFERENCED STANDARDS

The _____ Policy Act (EPAct) of 1992

The _____ Policy Act (EPAct) of 2005

The _____ Plumbing Code or International _____ Code

2–4 pts. for credit

	WE Prerequisite 1:
	Water Use Reduction
	20% Reduction

	WE Credit 3:
	Water Use Reduction
	30% to 40% Reduction

ANSWER KEY

PURPOSE

To ensure a reduction on the burden of the municipal water supply and wastewater systems by increasing water efficiency within buildings.

REQUIREMENTS

Install low-flow and low-flush fixtures to reduce water consumption.

Calculate baseline consumption using occupancy uses for each fixture type based on **EPAct values**.

Calculate design case consumption using occupancy uses for each fixture type based on actual fixture values.

Assume a 1:1 gender ratio for calculations.

POINT DISTRIBUTION

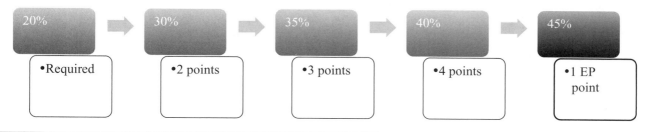

20%	30%	35%	40%	45%
•Required	•2 points	•3 points	•4 points	•1 EP point

REFERENCED STANDARDS

The Energy Policy Act (EPAct) of 1992

The Energy Policy Act (EPAct) of 2005

The Uniform Plumbing Code or International Plumbing Code

DESIGN	**WE Credit 1:**
	Water-Efficient Landscaping
	50% Reduction and No Potable Water Use

PURPOSE

To reduce the need for _____ water for landscape _____.

REQUIREMENTS

Option 1: (2 points)

Reduce the need for potable _____ for _____ by _____ percent.

Option 2: (4 points)

Use _____ or _____ to irrigate or plant _____-tolerant vegetation that does not require any watering. Temporary irrigation allowed for up to _____ year.

STRATEGIES

Use _____ and adaptive vegetation that can survive on natural rainfall

Use _____-efficiency irrigation systems

Use captured _____ for irrigation

CALCULATIONS

Calculate water demand based on the following factors:

Square footage of _____ area

Square footage for each type of _____

_____ factor, _____ factor, and _____ factor for each planting type

_____ rate for climate region

If irrigation system is to be used, type and controller _____

| **2–4 pts.** | **RESPONSIBLE PARTY:** |
| | **LANDSCAPE ARCHITECT** |

	WE Credit 1:
	Water-Efficient Landscaping
	50% Reduction and No Potable Water Use

ANSWER KEY

PURPOSE

To reduce the need for potable water for landscape irrigation.

REQUIREMENTS

Option 1: (2 points)

Reduce the need for potable water for irrigation by 50 percent.

Option 2: (4 points)

Use stormwater or graywater to irrigate or plant drought-tolerant vegetation that does not require any watering. Temporary irrigation allowed for up to one year.

STRATEGIES

Use native and adaptive vegetation that can survive on natural rainfall

Use high-efficiency irrigation systems

Use captured stormwater for irrigation

CALCULATIONS

Calculate water demand based on the following factors:

Square footage of landscaped area

Square footage for each type of vegetation

Species factor, density factor, and microclimate factor for each planting type

Evapotranspiration rate for climate region

If irrigation system is to be used, type and controller efficiency

DESIGN

PURPOSE

Reduce the amount of potable water used for _____ conveyance and the amount of _____ generated.

REQUIREMENTS

Option 1:

Reduce potable water used for sewage conveyance by _____ percent by implementing water-_____ fixtures or using _____ water sources, such as graywater and _____ stormwater.

Option 2:

Treat _____ percent of wastewater _____ site to _____ standards to be infiltrated or used on site to recharge the aquifer.

EXEMPLARY PERFORMANCE

Reduce the amount of wastewater generated by _____ percent or treat _____ percent of wastewater on site.

REFERENCED STANDARDS

The _____ Policy Act (EPAct) of 1992

The _____ Policy Act (EPAct) of 2005

The _____ Plumbing Code or International _____ Code

2 pts.

RESPONSIBLE PARTY:

PLUMBING ENGINEER

	WE Credit 2:
	Innovative Wastewater Technologies

ANSWER KEY

PURPOSE

Reduce the amount of potable water used for sewage conveyance and the amount of wastewater generated.

REQUIREMENTS

Option 1:

Reduce potable water used for sewage conveyance by **50 percent** by implementing water-conserving fixtures or using nonpotable water sources, such as graywater and captured stormwater.

Option 2:

Treat **50 percent** of wastewater on site to tertiary standards to be infiltrated or used on site to recharge the aquifer.

EXEMPLARY PERFORMANCE

Reduce the amount of wastewater generated by 100 percent or treat 100 percent of wastewater on site.

EXEMPLARY PERFORMANCE

For two years, purchase 70 percent of the building's electrical demand from a Green-e certified provider or purchase Green-e accredited renewable energy certificates (RECs).

REFERENCED STANDARDS

The Energy Policy Act (EPAct) of 1992

The Energy Policy Act (EPAct) of 2005

The Uniform Plumbing Code or International Plumbing Code

	WE Credit 4:
DESIGN	**Process Water Use Reduction (SCHOOLS)**

PURPOSE

To ensure a reduction on the burden of the municipal water supply and wastewater systems by _____ water efficiency within buildings.

REQUIREMENTS

Do not install garbage _____.

Do not use refrigeration equipment with _____-through cooling with _____ water.

Employ at least _____ of the following items and demonstrate a _____ percent water reduction:

    Clothes washers

    Dishwashers

    _____ machines

    _____ steamers

    _____ spray valves

EXEMPLARY PERFORMANCE

Reduce the amount of _____ water by _____ percent.

	RESPONSIBLE PARTY:
1 pt.	**MECHANICAL ENGINEER**

WE Credit 4:

Process Water Use Reduction (SCHOOLS)

ANSWER KEY

PURPOSE

To ensure a reduction on the burden of the municipal water supply and wastewater systems by maximizing water efficiency within buildings.

REQUIREMENTS

Do not install garbage disposals.

Do not use refrigeration equipment with once-through cooling with potable water.

Employ at least four of the following items and demonstrate a 20 percent water reduction:

Clothes washers

Dishwashers

Ice machines

Food steamers

Pre-rinse spray valves

EXEMPLARY PERFORMANCE

Reduce the amount of process water by 40 percent.

CHAPTER **6**

ENERGY AND ATMOSPHERE

THIS CHAPTER FOCUSES ON THE STRATEGIES and technologies to address energy use and consumption as described in the Energy & Atmosphere (EA) category of the Leadership in Energy and Environmental Design (LEED®) rating systems. By now, we all understand the environmental impacts of using fossil fuels to generate electricity. Each step of the electricity production process harms the environment and ecosystem in one way or another. For example, the burning of coal releases harmful pollutants and greenhouse gases that contribute to global warming and climate change, reducing air quality on a global scale.

Remember from Chapter 2, conventionally designed and built facilities account for 39 percent primary energy use, 72 percent electricity consumption, and 38 percent carbon dioxide (CO_2) emissions, according to the U.S. Green Building Council (USGBC®) website.[1] Therefore, the LEED rating systems put the most emphasis on the EA category by offering the largest opportunity to earn points, as an attempt to reduce the electrical consumption and corresponding CO_2 emissions of certified buildings. Project teams are encouraged to focus on the following four components in order to address the goals and intentions of the EA category to help reduce greenhouse gas emissions:

1. Energy efficiency
2. Tracking energy consumption
3. Managing refrigerants
4. Renewable energy

Each of these strategies is referred to in the prerequisites and credits of the category, as seen in Table 6.1. Remember from the previous chapters to note when the prerequisite or credit is eligible to be submitted for review, at the end of design or construction. Do not worry about remembering the exact credit name and number, but it is important to know which are credits versus prerequisites and therefore which ones are worth points and which ones are not.

 It's time to pick a different color for flashcards created for EA category topics.

 TIP Burning coal releases the following harmful pollutants into the atmosphere: carbon dioxide, sulfur dioxide, nitrogen oxide, and mercury.

 Create a flashcard to remember the four components of the EA category.

ENERGY EFFICIENCY

The integrative design process is critical within all the LEED categories, but is essential within the EA category, especially when determining the right components to deliver the correct holistic solution to reduce energy demand (Figure 6.1).

Table 6.1 The Energy & Atmosphere Category

D/C	Prereq/Credit	Title	Points		
			NC	Schools	CS
C	Prereq 1	Fundamental Commissioning of Building Energy Systems	R	R	R
D	Prereq 2	Minimum Energy Performance	R	R	R
D	Prereq 3	Fundamental Refrigerant Management	R	R	R
D	Credit 1	Optimize Energy Performance	1–19	1–19	3–21
D	Credit 2	On-Site Renewable Energy	1–7	1–7	4
C	Credit 3	Enhanced Commissioning	2	2	2
D	Credit 4	Enhanced Refrigerant Management	2	1	2
C	Credit 5	Measurement and Verification	3	2	—
C	Credit 5.1	Measurement and Verification, Base Building	—	—	3
C	Credit 5.2	Measurement and Verification, Tenant Submetering	—	—	3
C	Credit 6	Green Power	2	2	2

Energy performance, demands, and requirements are affected by multiple components, including:

- Site conditions, such as materials that contribute to heat island reduction, can reduce energy demand, as equipment will not need to compensate for heat gain from surrounding and adjacent areas.

- Building orientation can affect the amount of energy needed for artificial heating, cooling, and lighting needs by taking advantage of free energy by the means of passive design strategies, such as daylighting, natural ventilation, and implementing a trombe wall (Figure 6.2).

TIP Minimize solar gain in the summer and maximize it in the winter with the help of passive design strategies! Passive designs capitalize on the four natural thermal processes: radiation, conduction, absorption, and convection.

Figure 6.1 The Pennsylvania Department of Conservation and Natural Resources' Penn Nursery project incorporates radiant heat flooring to optimize its energy consumption. *Photo courtesy of Moshier Studio*

Figure 6.2 The Wetland Discovery Point building at Utah State University utilizes a trombe wall to capture heat from the sun, as well as radiant heat flooring to increase the energy efficiencies of the project. *Photo courtesy of Gary Neuenswander, Utah Agricultural Experiment Station*

- How much water needs to be heated or cooled? If building system equipment and fixtures require less water, less energy is therefore required. If all of the building equipment is sized appropriately and works efficiently, then less energy is demanded (Figures 6.3 and 6.4).

- Shifting loads to off-peak periods can help to reduce demand. Using thermal energy storage to take advantage of the temperature fluctuations associated with the daytime versus the night, allows project teams to refuse heat at night to provide cooling during the day in the summer and capture heat during the day to use at night in the winter (Figure 6.5).

- Roof design can impact how much energy is required for heating and cooling by implementing a green roof or a roof with a high solar reflectance index (SRI) value.

 Remember, SRI is the acronym for **solar reflectance index** and is synonymous with *albedo*. Do you remember the scale used for SRI? Is it better to have a higher or lower score?

- Building envelope thermal performance, including window selections, can reduce mechanical system sizing and energy demands by ensuring a thermal break between the interior and exterior environments (Figure 6.6). Insulating a building envelope can help to reduce the size of heating, ventilation, and air conditioning (HVAC) systems, and thus help to use less energy (Figure 6.7).

- Light fixture types and the lamps/bulbs they require can reduce energy use by providing more light per square foot, but require fewer kilowatts per hour and therefore optimize **lighting power density**, or the amount of lighting power installed per unit area.

The preceding bullet points describe the importance and need for project team members to work in a cohesive fashion to optimize the performance of a building and its site, ultimately reducing the amount of energy required for operations. Project teams are encouraged to take advantage of energy modeling and simulation software to study and evaluate how their specific project will function. Teams that utilize Building Information Modeling (BIM) software have an advantage to determine synergistic opportunities for their projects and to add

 The key to energy modeling and simulation is whole-building evaluation, not individual component assessments. How do all of the systems work together?

Figure 6.3 High-efficiency boilers can help to achieve energy performance and savings goals. *Photo courtesy of SmithGroup, Inc.*

efficiencies. Both of these design phase studies also contribute to whole-building life-cycle cost assessments to determine trade-offs between up-front costs and long-term savings.

Process Energy versus Regulated Energy

When a project team prepares and creates an energy simulation model (Figure 6.8), they should differentiate between **regulated** and **process energy**. LEED minimum energy performance criteria focuses on regulated energy, as

Figure 6.4 Installing high-efficiency chillers can help to achieve energy performance and savings goals. *Photo courtesy of SmithGroup, Inc.*

Figure 6.5 Ice ball thermal energy storage helps to provide cooling during the day from ice generated at night to reduce energy demands. *Photo courtesy of Cryogel*

Figure 6.6 Selecting insulated concrete forms (ICFs) as a building envelope material can increase the performance of a building. *Photo courtesy of Moshier Studio*

Figure 6.7 Spray foam insulation helps to seal any leaks of conditioned air to the exterior environment, therefore optimizing energy use. *Photo courtesy of BioBased Technologies*

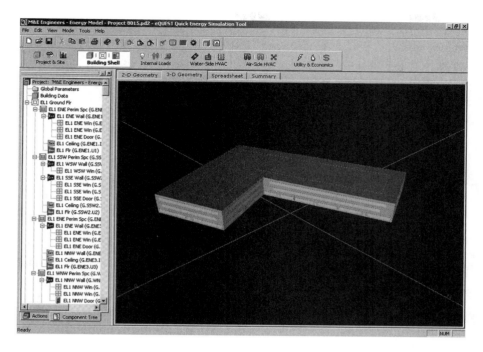

Figure 6.8 Modeling a proposed building can help project teams identify synergies to increase a building's performance and to calculate the energy saved based on those strategies. *Photo courtesy of M&E Engineers, Inc.*

process energy loads are calculated the same for both baseline and design case models. Regulated energy uses include the following:

- Lighting—interior and exterior applications (parking garages, facades, site lighting)
- HVAC—space heating, cooling, fans, pumps, toilet exhaust, ventilation for parking garages
- Domestic and space heating for service water

 Create a flashcard to remember the uses of regulated energy.

Process energy uses include computers, office equipment, kitchen refrigeration and cooking, washing and drying machines for laundry, and elevators and escalators. Miscellaneous items, such as waterfall pumps and lighting that is exempt from lighting power allowance calculations, such as lighting integrated into equipment, are also categorized as process energy uses. For the purposes of the LEED Accredited Professional (AP) Building Design and Construction (BD+C) exam, it is important to remember the different process energy uses to understand what is included in the energy modeling requirements to comply.

 Create a flashcard to remember the uses of process energy.

Energy Efficiency in Relation to LEED Compliance

Optimizing energy performance is presented as a prerequisite and a credit opportunity in order to require a minimum level of efficiency and to address the energy demand of green buildings, helping to save energy and therefore reducing greenhouse gas emissions and saving money.

EA Prerequisite 2: Minimum Energy Performance. Each of the BD+C LEED rating systems require buildings to perform to a minimum energy standard. Project teams have the opportunity to choose from a performance-based compliance path or a prescriptive approach, depending on the size of the project. The performance-based option requires an energy model to depict the assumed performance of the building and related energy consumption. Similar to the

 Create a flashcard to remember ASHRAE 90.1-2007, Appendix G, as the baseline standard for energy performance.

reference standard Energy Policy Act of 1992 (EPAct 1992; with the subsequent rulings of EPAct 2005), as discussed in the previous chapter, which is used to create a **baseline** for comparison to the **design case**, a baseline is needed for this performance-based compliance path to evaluate energy use reduction percentages of a project. Therefore, LEED references American Society of Heating, Refrigerating, and Air-Conditioning Engineers (ASHRAE) Standard 90.1-2007, Appendix G, to determine a baseline energy performance requirement for buildings seeking LEED for New Construction™ (LEED NC), LEED for Core & Shell™ (LEED CS), or LEED for Schools™ certification. Project energy models are required to demonstrate a minimum 10 percent energy savings as compared to the baseline modeled according to Appendix G of ASHRAE 90.1 in order to meet the requirements of this prerequisite. If the project is a major renovation, the project team will need to show only a 5 percent minimum energy savings as compared to the baseline in order to comply. School projects wishing to utilize a performance-based compliance path must also use the EPA's Target Finder Rating tool to determine an energy performance-rating goal.

TIP Any time you see ASHRAE 90.1, think ENERGY!

If a project team is looking for a prescriptive compliance path instead, they have two options from which to choose depending on the project type. The ASHRAE Advanced Energy Design Guide is used to define the prescriptive measures with which NC and CS projects are required to comply. For example, the maximum allowance for window areas is set for 40 percent of the gross wall area, and the skylight areas are required to be less than 5 percent of the gross roof area. The goal is to address minimum levels of performance for insulation and for fenestration assembly U-factor and solar heat gain coefficient with which teams must comply, depending on the applicable climate zone.

There are three paths within this option referencing the ASHRAE Advanced Energy Design Guide: one for office buildings under 20,000 square feet, another for retail spaces under 20,000 square feet, and a third for small warehouses less than 50,000 square feet. K–12 schools under 200,000 square feet are also required to comply with the Advanced Energy Design Guide if pursuing this prescriptive compliance path option. The second prescriptive option is available for projects seeking certification within each of the three BD+C rating systems if they are 100,000 square feet or less, although industrial warehouse, health care, or lab project types are not eligible for this compliance option. Eligible project types must follow the New Buildings Institute's Advanced Buildings™ Core Performance™ Guide prescriptive measures to comply with this other prescriptive compliance path option.

TIP Remember, only performance-based compliance paths require energy modeling; prescriptive compliance path options do not.

TIP Exemplary performance opportunities are available only to teams utilizing option 1 for EA Credit 1: Optimize Energy Performance.

EA Credit 1: Optimize Energy Performance. Whichever compliance path a project team pursues for EA Prerequisite 2, the same strategy is utilized to show compliance for this credit. For option 1, this performance-based option requires energy simulation, as points are awarded based on the percentage threshold achieved beyond the baseline model. Remember, to be in compliance with the prerequisite, the project must achieve 10 percent better performance than the baseline. To achieve at least the minimum number of points for this credit, a new construction project must achieve at least 12 percent better than the baseline, whereas an existing building undergoing a major renovation must achieve only 8 percent better than the baseline. For every two-percentage increment achieved, another point is awarded. Note, NC and School projects are awarded a different number of points when compared to a CS project. For example, an NC project that has achieved a 30 percent energy reduction would be awarded 10 points

(Figure 6.9), whereas a CS project that has achieved a 30 percent energy reduction would be awarded 12 points. Be sure to refer to the scorecards in Appendices F, G, and H for further clarification on point opportunities for each of the rating systems for this credit. Project teams are able to achieve these demand reductions by implementing the strategies presented earlier, such as installing high-performance mechanical systems including heat exchange systems (Figure 6.10).

Projects that are able to comply with the prescriptive compliance paths of options 2 and 3 can eliminate the need to develop an energy model, but are not eligible to earn as many points as compared to option 1. For example, option 2 awards only one point for complying with the requirements of the ASHRAE

 TIP For CS projects utilizing option 2 to pursue EA Credit 1, the requirements may involve the tenant's scope of work, therefore requiring language to be incorporated into the lease language to meet the requirements of this credit. This also implies that CS project teams can earn credit for the efficiencies within the tenant space and not within the base building.

 Remember, the majority of a building's energy use is consumed by space heating and lighting; therefore, both should be addressed to increase the efficiency and reduce the demand required.

Figure 6.9 The Wetland Discovery Point building at Utah State University in Kaysville utilized a ground-source heat pump to exchange heating and cooling loads between the building and the earth to reduce their energy consumption by 30 percent.
Photo courtesy of Gary Neuenswander, Utah Agricultural Experiment Station

Figure 6.10 Utilizing a heat exchange system can help to reduce energy demands and save an owner operating costs. *Photo courtesy of SmithGroup, Inc.*

Advanced Energy Design Guide. Option 3, however, awards up to three points for compliance with the New Building Institute's Advanced Buildings™ Core Performance™ Guide.

QUIZ TIME!

Q6.1. Which of the following strategies would help to reduce the energy demand of a new construction project? (Choose two)

A. Installing a high-performance envelope

B. Designing with BIM software

C. Using ENERGY STAR Portfolio Manager

D. Recovering waste heat

E. Recycling stormwater

Q6.2. How many percentage increments must a project seeking LEED certification improve the energy reduction to earn another point for EA Credit 1: Optimize Energy Performance? (Choose one)

A. 2 percent

B. 2 percent for NC and School projects, but 1 percent for CS projects

C. 1 percent

D. 5 percent

E. 1 percent for major renovation projects and 2 percent for all other project types

Q6.3. What is the minimum percentage reduction required in order to meet the EA energy performance prerequisite for new construction projects? (Choose one)

A. 2 percent

B. 4 percent

C. 5 percent

D. 10 percent

E. 12 percent

Q6.4. An 18,000-square-foot project seeking LEED for Core & Shell certification wishes to pursue a prescriptive compliance path for EA Prerequisite 2: Minimum Energy Performance. Which of the following compliance paths is appropriate to utilize? (Choose one)

A. Whole-building simulation

B. Advanced Buildings™ Core Performance™ Guide

C. ASHRAE Advanced Energy Design Guide

D. ENERGY STAR Portfolio Manager

E. ASHRAE 90.1-2007

Q6.5. Which of the following are true concerning energy for the purposes of LEED compliance? (Choose two)

A. Process energy is modeled the same for both the baseline case and design case.

B. Regulated energy is modeled the same for both the baseline case and design case.

C. Regulated energy uses include computers, office equipment, kitchen refrigeration and cooking, washing and drying machines for laundry, and elevators and escalators.

D. Process energy uses include computers, office equipment, kitchen refrigeration and cooking, washing and drying machines for laundry, and elevators and escalators.

E. Process energy includes lighting, HVAC, and domestic and space heating for service water.

Q6.6. Which of the following compliance paths are appropriate for a 55,000-square-foot warehouse project seeking LEED for New Construction certification? (Choose two)

A. Performance based

B. ASHRAE Advanced Energy Design Guide

C. Prescriptive based

D. Whole-building simulation

E. Advanced Buildings™ Core Performance™ Guide

TRACKING ENERGY CONSUMPTION

The BD+C Reference Guide details a number of means for project teams to address the monitoring and tracking of energy consumption. Projects seeking LEED certification are required not only to be designed and constructed to perform to a minimal energy performance, but must also implement procedures to ensure the performance, such as **commissioning** (Cx). Commissioning a building ensures that the equipment and systems are performing as they were intended, to maintain consistent and minimal energy demands. Just as with energy performance, the EA category addresses Cx in terms of a prerequisite and a credit opportunity.

The EA category also includes a number of other credits for the project teams to choose from to address the tracking of energy consumption. Depending on the rating system being utilized, project teams may have either one or two credits to pursue within the Measurement and Verification credit. By providing meters and other technology to track the consumption of energy, operations and maintenance staff members are able to detect inefficiencies, such as excessive demand, and therefore take corrective action. Metering utilities also ensures the ongoing accountability of energy usage (Figure 6.11).

Figure 6.11 Metering utilities to monitor consumption helps building owners and facility managers ensure that the building is functioning properly. *Photo courtesy of Gary Neuenswander, Utah Agricultural Experiment Station*

Tracking Energy Consumption in Relation to LEED Compliance

EA Prerequisite 1: Fundamental Commissioning. The first prerequisite of the EA category requires a new building to be commissioned by a commissioning agent (CxA). The CxA reports directly to the owner and represents the owner, responsible for coordinating with the design team and then the contractor during construction. Note, because of the role a CxA plays, he or she can be an employee of the developer/owner but may not be the engineer of record (see Study Tip). He or she must have experience commissioning at least two other projects to be qualified as the CxA on a project seeking LEED certification.

The commissioning process begins *early* in the design process in which the CxA works with the owner to establish the owner's project requirements (OPR). The OPR includes the environmental goals of the project and is issued to the design team to develop a basis of design (BOD) for the major building systems, such as lighting; domestic hot water; heating, ventilation, air conditioning, and refrigeration (HVAC&R); and any renewable energy generated on site. The BOD includes a description of these systems, the applicable indoor environmental quality measures, and any assumptions as related to the design. The report should also include any codes, ordinances, and regulations applicable to the project. The Cx process continues with the development of the Cx plan and incorporating the Cx requirements into the construction documents (CDs). The CxA works diligently during construction to ensure that the building system equipment is installed and calibrated correctly and performs appropriately and efficiently to avoid construction defects and equipment malfunctions by the means of **systems performance testing**. Finally, the CxA is responsible for completing a summary Cx report in order to comply with this prerequisite.

EA Credit 3: Enhanced Commissioning. Table 6.2 summarizes all of the Cx activities for both the prerequisite and the credit. As the table indicates, the

 TIP A commissioning agent (CxA) cannot be the engineer of record for the project. Think about it—who would double check the engineer's design if it were the same person? For projects smaller than 50,000 square feet, a qualified employee of one of the design team firms is eligible as long as they are not the same professional responsible for engineering services.

 TIP Remember, prerequisites are absolutely required, do not contribute to earning points, and ensure that certified buildings meet minimum performance criteria.

 TIP Commissioning of new buildings has an average payback of 4.8 years and typically costs about $1 per square foot, according to a study conducted by Lawrence Berkley National Laboratory.[2]

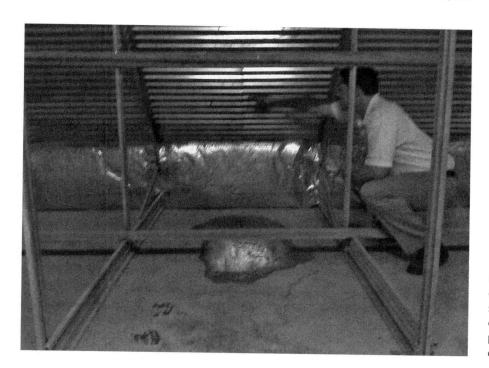

Figure 6.12 Inspecting building systems and educating the operations and maintenance staff on how the systems are intended to operate helps to ensure that a building performs the way it was designed. *Photo courtesy of ENERActive Solutions*

Table 6.2 Fundamental Commissioning versus Enhanced Commissioning

Phases	Task	Prerequisite 1: Fundamental Cx	Credit 3: Enhanced Cx
Predesign, Design	1. Designate CxA	Owner or project team	
	2. Document OPR and then develop BOD	Owner or CxA; design team	
	3. Review OPR and BOD	CxA	
	4. Develop and implement a Cx plan	Project team or CxA	
	5. Incorporate Cx requirements into CDs	Project team or CxA	
	6. Conduct Cx design review prior to midconstruction documents	—	CxA
Construction	7. Review contractor submittals applicable to systems being commissioned	—	CxA
	8. Verify installation and performance of commissioned systems	CxA	
	9. Develop systems manual for commissioned systems	—	Project team or CxA
	10. Verify that requirements for training are completed	—	Project team or CxA
	11. Complete a summary commissioning report	CxA	
Occupancy	12. Review building operation within 10 months after substantial completion	—	CxA

reference guide requires five extra tasks to be completed by the CxA in order to achieve this credit. These additional tasks begin prior to the completion of the CDs, as the CxA is required to review the design drawings and specifications to avoid design flaws and ensure that the environmental goals are included, such as water and energy use reductions, and they are in line with the OPR and BOD. The second task requires the CxA to review the construction submittals for the applicable systems to be commissioned. After functional testing of the systems is completed, but before the building is occupied, the CxA develops operation and maintenance manuals and helps to educate the facility management teams on the operation and maintenance strategies specific to the building (Figure 6.12). Finally, within 10 months after occupancy, the CxA returns to the site to ensure that the building systems are working accordingly and address any needed adjustments. Project teams can also seek an exemplary performance opportunity within the Innovation in Design (ID) category if comprehensive envelope commissioning is conducted.

EA Credit 5: Measurement and Verification (for NC and Schools); and EA Credit 5.1: Measurement and Verification, Base Building (for CS). Project

Create a flashcard to remember the benefits of utilizing a CxA:
1. Minimize or eliminate design flaws
2. Avoid construction defects
3. Avoid equipment malfunctions
4. Ensure that preventative maintenance is implemented during operations

teams seeking to achieve this credit will need to develop a measure and verification (M&V) plan in accordance with the International Performance Measure & Verification Protocol (IPMVP), Volume III. The plan should be implemented for at least one year after the project is completed, with corrective action details should the project not perform as anticipated.

Project teams have two options from which to choose in order to comply with this credit. They can follow option D of the reference standard for a calibrated simulation for a whole-building approach. In this case, actual energy data is calibrated with the energy model for the project and compared against a baseline, such as a local energy code. Or, if they are working with a smaller building, they can choose option B, as it is better suited to address individual **energy conservation measures** (ECMs). In either case, the teams will need to upload the M&V plan, along with a plan depicting metering locations for the electricity-using systems of the project. In either case, submetering equipment should be installed on all equipment that consumes large amounts of energy, such as HVAC, lighting, and plug loads.

EA Credit 5.2: Measurement and Verification, Tenant Submetering (for CS). CS project teams will need to plan for future tenant submetering along with an M&V plan to earn this credit. Therefore, a developer is not responsible for installing the submetering equipment, but instead should ensure future tenants will be able to submeter their usage, in order to comply with this credit.

 Create a flashcard to remember the prerequisite and four credits LEED utilizes to address the monitoring and tracking of energy consumption.

QUIZ TIME!

Q6.7. Which of the following is not required to be included in the BOD? (Choose one)

    A. Indoor environmental quality criteria

    B. Applicable codes

    C. Tenant design guidelines

    D. Energy-related system descriptions

    E. Design assumptions

Q6.8. When should the OPR be prepared? (Choose one)

    A. Schematic Design

    B. Construction Documents

    C. Design Development

    D. Beginning of Construction

    E. Substantial Completion

Q6.9. Which of the following are appropriate statements with regard to commissioning in the context of green building? (Choose two)

    A. The CxA should be a primary member of the design team who is directly responsible for the project design or construction management.

    B. The CxA should be separate and independent from those individuals who are directly responsible for project design or construction management (preferably from a separate firm).

C. The CxA is indirectly responsible for verifying the performance of building systems and equipment prior to installation, calibration, and operations.

D. The CxA is responsible for verifying the performance of building systems and equipment after installation.

Q6.10. Which of the following are required to be uploaded to LEED-Online for certification review to be in compliance with EA Credit 5: Measurement and Verification? (Choose two)

A. Tenant design guidelines

B. Plan with metering locations

C. Agreement with local utility provider

D. Meter type, manufacturer, and model number

E. Measurement and verification plan

F. Lease agreement with tenant(s)

Q6.11. What is the referenced standard for EA Credit 5: Measurement and Verification? (Choose one)

A. ASHRAE 90.1–2007

B. ASHRAE Advanced Energy Design Guide

C. IPMVP, Volume III

D. Advanced Buildings™ Core Performance™ Guide

MANAGING REFRIGERANTS

Besides commissioning and minimum energy performance prerequisites, the LEED rating systems also require buildings to manage refrigerants appropriately. Refrigerants enable the transfer of thermal energy and are therefore a critical component of air conditioning and refrigeration equipment for their ability to reject heat at high temperatures. Although they are cost effective, refrigerants have environmental trade-offs, as they contribute to ozone depletion and global warming. Therefore, project teams need to be mindful of the **ozone-depleting potential** (ODP) and **global warming potential** (GWP) of each refrigerant to determine the impact of the trade-offs, as an environmentally perfect refrigerant does not yet exist.

Managing Refrigerants in Relation to LEED Compliance

TIP Remember, chlorofluorocarbons (CFCs) are not allowed and hydrochlorofluorocarbons (HCFCs) are to be phased out, according to the Montreal Protocol.

 Create a flashcard to remember that refrigerants should be evaluated based on ODP and GWP impacts and what these acronyms stand for.

EA Prerequisite 3: Fundamental Refrigerant Management. To comply with this prerequisite, teams should refer to the Montreal Protocol when determining which refrigerants to use for their projects. The Montreal Protocol bans **chlorofluorocarbons** (CFCs) and requires **hydrochlorofluorocarbons** (HCFCs) to be phased out, as they have the biggest impact on ozone depletion. CFC-based refrigerants are highest in ODP, more than HCFCs. Hydrofluorocarbon (HFC)-based refrigerants have no ODP but have a high GWP. Although other options exist that are not as harmful to the ozone, they contribute more to the production of greenhouse gases. These alternative options are also not as efficient as CFCs

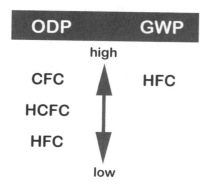

Figure 6.13 Comparing the ODP and GWP of refrigerants.

and HCFCs, and in turn cause cooling systems to be less efficient by using more energy per unit of cooling output. In summary, project teams are not allowed to use CFC-based refrigerants in new mechanical systems and fire suppression systems and are required to phase out CFC-based refrigerants for major renovation projects using the refrigerant in existing systems. The phase-out must be completed before the project is completed in order to comply, although exceptions are provided for existing chilled water systems.

EA Credit 4: Enhanced Refrigerant Management. This credit takes the requirements beyond the prerequisite to restrict the use of any refrigerants, as well as the use of **halons** and HCFCs for fire suppression systems. Halons, due to high ODP, have not been in production since they were banned in 1994 and are currently being phased out, as required by the Montreal Protocol. If refrigerants are used, project teams will need to document that they have minimal ODP and GWP by using the calculations provided within the reference guide. Equipment that uses less than a half–pound of refrigerants is exempt from compliance, as well as refrigerators and small water coolers.

 TIP For major renovation projects using CFC refrigerants where an economic analysis determines it unfeasible to phase out CFC-based refrigerants by the means of retrofitting or replacing the existing system, project teams are required to reduce the annual **leakage** to less than 5 percent, using EPA Clean Air Act, Title VI, Rule 608 procedures.

QUIZ TIME!

Q6.12. Which of the following refrigerants has the highest ODP? (Choose one)

   A. CFCs

   B. HCFCs

   C. HFCs

   D. NH_3

   E. Halons

Q6.13. Which of the following are not subject to LEED minimum energy requirements? (Choose three)

   A. Office equipment

   B. Elevators

   C. Chillers

   D. Process energy

   E. Regulated energy

Q6.14. When addressing refrigerants for a project and to comply with EA Prerequisite 3: Fundamental Refrigerant Management, which of the following should be considered? (Choose three)

A. Fan motors and variable-frequency drives for ventilation air handlers

B. Base building air conditioning systems

C. Boilers for heating systems

D. Reuse of existing HVAC&R systems

E. Elimination of substances with high ODP from use in air conditioning and refrigeration systems

Q6.15. Which of the following refrigerant is typically contained within fire suppression systems? (Choose one)

A. CFCs

B. HCFCs

C. HFCs

D. Hydrofluorocarbons

E. Halons

 Create a flashcard to remember the types of qualifying renewable energy sources. Ineligible systems include any architectural features, passive solar strategies, daylighting strategies, and geo-exchange systems using a ground-source heat pump. These heat pumps require electricity to operate and therefore are an ineligible renewable energy source. If it cannot be metered or uses electricity to operate, it cannot achieve this credit.

RENEWABLE ENERGY

Keeping with the same goals previously discussed, implementing renewable energy technologies into a green building project can reduce the need to produce and consume coal, nuclear power, and oil and natural gases for energy, therefore reducing pollutants and emissions, as well as increasing air quality. For the purposes of LEED compliance, eligible renewable energy sources include solar thermal, photovoltaic systems, wind, wave, some biomass systems, geothermal (heating and electric) power, and low-impact hydropower systems (Figure 6.14).

Figure 6.14 Sherman Hospital in Elgin, Illinois, utilizes geothermal energy to minimize energy demands from the grid. *Photo courtesy of Shepley Bulfinch*

Figure 6.15 Stoller Vineyards in Dayton, Oregon, generates electricity on site by the means of photovoltaic panels mounted on the roof. *Photo courtesy of Mike Haverkate, Stoller Vineyards*

The BD+C Reference Guide provides the following two strategies to incorporate renewable energy and reduce the use of fossil fuels for projects seeking LEED certification:

EA Credit 2: On-site Renewable Energy. Project teams are encouraged to evaluate the triple bottom line benefits of each of the eligible renewable energy sources to find the proper solution to install on site for the project (Figure 6.15). NC and School project teams will need to determine how much energy the system can provide (in terms of cost) in proportion to the total amount of energy required for the project (in terms of cost) to determine compliance and how many points can be earned, whereas CS project teams have only a single threshold to achieve. Project teams can use either the energy model generated for compliance with EA Prerequisite 2: Minimum Energy Performance or refer to the Commercial Buildings Energy Consumption Survey (CBECS) database compiled by the U.S. Department of Energy to estimate the electrical demand. All of the BD+C rating systems offer an exemplary performance opportunity for projects that surpass the applicable percentage threshold, depending on the rating system.

EA Credit 6: Green Power. In order to comply with this credit, project owners would need to purchase energy from a Green-e certified provider or **renewable energy certificates (RECs)** from a Green-e eligible source. The renewable energy associated with this credit is generated at a different location than the project site seeking LEED certification (Figure 6.16). Project teams would need to determine the energy demand of the project by the estimations of an energy model or by the CBECS database, just as with EA Credit 2. Project owners would need to then purchase 35 percent of the project's estimated energy demand for at least two years based on quantity, not the cost of energy (as with EA Credit 2), to comply. If they purchase 70 percent or more, the project could seek an Exemplary Performance point.

 TIP Project teams that implement an on-site renewable energy system that the project does not utilize can be eligible to pursue this credit if renewable energy certificates are sold for 200 percent of the system's output.

 TIP CS projects need to purchase only 35 percent of the core and shell square footage electrical demand (as opposed to the entire building's consumption), although there is a 15 percent square footage minimum.

 Create a flashcard to remember the meaning of the acronym REC.

 Create a flashcard to remember the two credits associated with renewable energy for LEED project teams to pursue.

Figure 6.16 Cedar Creek Wind Farm in Colorado helps to produce clean, renewable energy. *Photo courtesy of Brian Stanback, Renewable Choice Energy*

QUIZ TIME!

Q6.16. ASHRAE Standard 90.1-2007 is primarily concerned with which of the following? (Choose one)

A. Daylighting design

B. Ventilation effectiveness

C. Energy consumption

D. Ozone depletion

E. Indoor air quality

F. Thermal comfort

Q6.17. Which of the following are categorized as regulated energy? (Choose three)

A. Computers

B. HVAC

C. Refrigeration

D. Service hot water

E. Lighting

F. Drying machine

Q6.18. Which of the following could contribute to earning EA Credit 2: On-site Renewable Energy? (Choose three)

A. Passive solar design concept that captures winter heat from the sun

B. Photovoltaic panels that provide electricity to the building

C. A wind farm located within 500 miles of the project and operated by the local utility company

    D. A ground-source heat pump that takes heat from the ground

    E. Solar hot water system

    F. An on-site electric generator powered by geothermal energy

    G. A solar farm adjacent to the project site providing clean power to the grid

Q6.19. What is the primary intent of EA Credit 6: Green Power? (Choose one)

    A. To comply with the Montreal Protocol

    B. To encourage more solar farms in the United States and avoid carbon trading

    C. To encourage the development and use of renewable clean energy that is connected to the utility grid

    D. To minimize production of greenhouse gases by generating on-site renewable energy

Q6.20. The engineer working on a new corporate building project seeking LEED for Core & Shell certification has proposed a cogeneration system that provides electricity, cooling, heating, hot water, and dehumidification of outside air. The waste heat from the gas turbine–powered electric generator exhaust is designed and intended to drive an absorption chiller for cooling the building, therefore not using any CFCs or HCFCs. To which of the following LEED credits might these strategies contribute? (Choose two)

    A. Enhanced Commissioning

    B. On-Site Renewable Energy

    C. Enhanced Refrigerant Management

    D. Green Power

    E. Optimize Energy Performance

    F. Measure and Verification

Q6.21. What are the factors concerned with fenestration assemblies when pursuing a performance rating method for EA Credit 1: Optimize Energy Performance? (Choose two)

    A. Visible light transmittance

    B. U-factor

    C. Solar heat gain coefficient

    D. R-value

Q6.22. Which of the following tasks are not required to comply with EA Prerequisite 1: Fundamental Commissioning? (Choose two)

    A. Submittal review

    B. Operation and maintenance system manuals

    C. Commissioning plan

D. Basis of design

E. Functional testing procedures

F. Owner's program requirements

Q6.23. Which of the following credits are related to EA Credit 2: On-Site Renewable Energy? (Choose three)

A. SS Credit 7.1: Heat Island Effect, Nonroof

B. SS Credit 7.2: Heat Island Effect, Roof

C. SS Credit 8: Light Pollution Reduction

D. SS Credit 6: Green Power

E. EA Credit 1: Optimize Energy Performance

CONSTRUCTION	EA Prerequisite 1:
	Fundamental Commissioning of Building Energy Systems

	EA Credit 3:
	Enhanced Commissioning

PURPOSE

Prerequisite:

To ensure the _____-related systems of the building are _____, _____, and are performing accordingly and inline with the owner's _____ requirements, _____ of design, and construction documents.

Commissioning benefits include a reduction in _____ use, _____ costs, and contractor _____, an improvement in building documentation and occupant _____, and the verification of system _____.

Credit:

To start the commissioning process _____ in the design phases and complete additional tasks after the systems' performance has been _____.

REQUIREMENTS

Prerequisite - Complete the following _____ tasks:

1. Engage a commissioning agent (CxA)

    Must have commissioned at least _____ previous projects.

    CxA must report directly to the owner.

    Projects smaller than 50,000 gross square feet and not pursuing EA Credit 3, the CxA may be part of the design or construction teams but not the _____ of _____.

2. Record the owner's project _____ (OPR) and then the _____ of design (BOD) with the design team.

3. The commissioning activities must be included in the construction specifications.

4. A _____ plan must be created and implemented.

5. The installation and performance of the building's energy-related systems must be verified. These systems include:

    - HVAC & R systems and controls

    - Lighting and _____ controls

    - Domestic _____ water systems

    - On-site _____ energy systems

6. The _____ report must be completed.

Credit - In addition to the above listed tasks for prerequisite, complete the following _____ tasks:

1. CxA must review the design documents prior to mid-_____ document phase and ensure comments are addressed in _____ submission.

2. CxA must review the construction _____ for the _____-related systems to be commissioned to ensure alignment with _____ and _____.

3. Create a _____ manual.

4. Ensure building operations and maintenance staff have received required _____.

5. The CxA must return to the site within _____ months after substantial completion to review the building's performance and establish a plan to resolve any outstanding commissioning-related issues.

STRATEGIES

Credit:

    When selecting a CxA they must be an independent _____ party although they can be an employee of the _____.

        They cannot be an employee of the design firm but can be a consultant.

        The CxA must not be an employee or a consult to the _____ or _____ manager.

2 pts. for credit	**RESPONSIBLE PARTY:**
	COMMISSIONING AGENT

	EA Prerequisite 1:
	Fundamental Commissioning of Building Energy Systems

	EA Credit 3:
	Enhanced Commissioning

ANSWER KEY

PURPOSE

Prerequisite:

To ensure the energy-related systems of the building are installed, calibrated, and are performing accordingly and inline with the owner's project requirements, basis of design, and construction documents.

Commissioning benefits include a reduction in energy use, operating costs, and contractor callbacks, an improvement in building documentation and occupant productivity, and the verification of system performance.

Credit:

To start the commissioning process early in the design phases and complete additional tasks after the systems' performance has been verified.

REQUIREMENTS

Prerequisite - Complete the following six tasks:

1. Engage a commissioning agent (CxA)

    Must have commissioned at least two previous projects.

    CxA must report directly to the owner.

    Projects smaller than 50,000 gross square feet and not pursuing EA Credit 3, the CxA may be part of the design or construction teams but not the engineer of record.

2. Record the owner's project requirements (OPR) and then the basis of design (BOD) with the design team.

3. The commissioning activities must be included in the construction specifications.

4. A commissioning plan must be created and implemented.

5. The installation and performance of the building's energy-related systems must be verified. These systems include:

    - HVAC & R systems and controls
    - Lighting and daylighting controls
    - Domestic hot water systems
    - On-site renewable energy systems

6. The commissioning report must be completed.

Credit - In addition to the above listed tasks for prerequisite, complete the following five tasks:

1. CxA must review the design documents prior to mid-construction document phase and ensure comments are addressed in subsequent submission.

2. CxA must review the construction submittals for the energy-related systems to be commissioned to ensure alignment with OPR and BOD.

3. Create a systems manual.

4. Ensure building operations and maintenance staff have received required training.

5. The CxA must return to the site within 10 months after substantial completion to review the building's performance and establish a plan to resolve any outstanding commissioning-related issues.

STRATEGIES

Credit:

When selecting a CxA they must be an independent third party although they can be an employee of the owner.

They cannot be an employee of the design firm but can be a consultant.

The CxA must not be an employee or a consult to the contractor or construction manager.

DESIGN	**EA Prerequisite 2:**
	Minimum Energy Performance

	EA Credit 1:
	Optimize Energy Performance

PURPOSE

Prerequisite:

To ensure a _____ level of performance to increase efficiency and to reduce the environmental and _____ impacts from _____ energy demand.

Credit:

To achieve more efficiencies beyond the _____ to further reduce the environmental and economic impacts from excessive energy use.

REQUIREMENTS

Prerequisite Requirement for _____

 Use EPA's _____ Finder rating tool to establish an energy performance rating goal.

Option 1: Energy Simulation (1-19 POINTS for NC and SCHOOLS, 3-21 POINTS for CS)

 _____ the _____ and design case performance of the whole building in compliance with Appendix _____ of ASHRAE _____ to demonstrate at least a _____ percent energy savings.

 Project teams can earn an additional point for every _____ percentage points achieved for a reduction in energy demand.

Option 2: Prescriptive Compliance Path: ONE POINT for EA Credit 1

 Design the project to comply with the ASHRAE _____ Energy _____ Guide

Option 3: Prescriptive Compliance Path: Up to THREE POINTS for EA Credit 1

 Design the project to comply with New _____ Institute, Advanced Buildings™ _____ Performance™ Guide

REFERENCED STANDARDS

ANSI/ASHRAE/IESNA Standard _____

_____ Advanced Energy Design Guide for Small Warehouses and Self Storage Buildings 2008

ASHRAE Advanced Energy Design Guide for K-12 School Buildings

New Building Institute, _____ Buildings™ Core Performance™ Guide

_____ STAR Program, Target Finder Rating Tool

ASHRAE _____ Energy Design Guide for Small Office Buildings 2004

ASHRAE Advanced _____ Design Guide for Retail Buildings 2006

1–29 pts. for credit	**RESPONSIBLE PARTY:**
	MECHANICAL ENGINEER

	EA Prerequisite 2:
	Minimum Energy Performance

	EA Credit 1:
	Optimize Energy Performance

ANSWER KEY

PURPOSE

Prerequisite:

To ensure a minimum level of performance to increase efficiency and to reduce the environmental and economic impacts from excessive energy demand.

Credit:

To achieve more efficiencies beyond the prerequisite to further reduce the environmental and economic impacts from excessive energy use.

REQUIREMENTS

Prerequisite Requirement for SCHOOLS

Use EPA's Target Finder rating tool to establish an energy performance rating goal.

Option 1: Energy Simulation (1-19 POINTS for NC and SCHOOLS, 3-21 POINTS for CS)

Model the baseline and design case performance of the whole building in compliance with Appendix G of ASHRAE 90.1 to demonstrate at least a 10 percent energy savings.

Project teams can earn an additional point for every 2 percentage points achieved for a reduction in energy demand.

Option 2: Prescriptive Compliance Path: ONE POINT for EA Credit 1

Design the project to comply with the ASHRAE Advanced Energy Design Guide

Option 3: Prescriptive Compliance Path: Up to THREE POINTS for EA Credit 1

Design the project to comply with New Building Institute, Advanced Buildings™ Core Performance™ Guide

REFERENCED STANDARDS

ANSI/ASHRAE/IESNA Standard 90.1

ASHRAE Advanced Energy Design Guide for Small Warehouses and Self Storage Buildings 2008

ASHRAE Advanced Energy Design Guide for K-12 School Buildings

New Building Institute, Advanced Buildings™ Core Performance™ Guide

ENERGY STAR Program, Target Finder Rating Tool

ASHRAE Advanced Energy Design Guide for Small Office Buildings 2004

ASHRAE Advanced Energy Design Guide for Retail Buildings 2006

DESIGN	**EA Prerequisite 3:**
	Fundamental Refrigerant Management

	EA Credit 4:
	Enhanced Refrigerant Management

PURPOSE

Prerequisite:

To reduce the depletion of the _____.

Credit:

To encourage compliance with the _____ Protocol and reduce ozone depletion to minimize climate _____ contributions.

REQUIREMENTS

Prerequisite:

The use of _____-based refrigerants is prohibited in _____ HVAC&R systems.

A _____ out of existing CFC-based refrigerants is required for existing systems _____ to project completion.

Credit:

All projects must not use _____ depleting chemicals, such as CFCs, HCFCs, or _____, within the _____ suppression systems.

Option 1: Do not use _____ refrigerants in HVAC&R equipment.

Option 2: Evaluate the _____ _____ potential (ODP) and _____ _____ potential (GWP) of refrigerants to be used for HVAC&R equipment to ensure concentrations do not exceed maximum _____ allowed.

CALCULATIONS

Credit 1: Option 2:

Small equipment, such as HVAC units that use less than _____ pounds of refrigerant, refrigerators and small _____ coolers, are excluded from complying with this credit.

To determine ODP and GWP _____ and _____-of-_____ leakage rate concentrations, calculate the following factors:

- For HVAC&R equipment - Refrigerant _____, refrigerant _____, and equipment types

- Equipment life (provided default value)

- _____ rate (provided default value)

- End-of-life refrigerant loss (provided default value)

1–2 pts. for credit	**RESPONSIBLE PARTY:**
	MECHANICAL ENGINEER

	EA Prerequisite 3:
	Fundamental Refrigerant Management

	EA Credit 4:
	Enhanced Refrigerant Management

ANSWER KEY

PURPOSE

Prerequisite:

To reduce the depletion of the stratosphere.

Credit:

To encourage compliance with the Montreal Protocol and reduce ozone depletion to minimize climate change contributions.

REQUIREMENTS

Prerequisite:

The use of CFC-based refrigerants is prohibited in new HVAC&R systems.

A phase out of existing CFC-based refrigerants is required for existing systems prior to project completion.

Credit:

All projects must not use ozone depleting chemicals, such as CFCs, HCFCs, or halons, within the fire suppression systems.

Option 1: Do not use any refrigerants in HVAC&R equipment.

Option 2: Evaluate the ozone depleting potential (ODP) and global warming potential (GWP) of refrigerants to be used for HVAC&R equipment to ensure concentrations do not exceed maximum threshold allowed.

CALCULATIONS

Credit 1: Option 2:

Small equipment, such as HVAC units that use less than 0.5 pounds of refrigerant, refrigerators and small water coolers, are excluded from complying with this credit.

To determine ODP and GWP annual and end-of-life leakage rate concentrations, calculate the following factors:

- For HVAC&R equipment - Refrigerant charge, refrigerant types, and equipment types

- Equipment life (provided default value)

- Leakage rate (provided default value)

- End-of-life refrigerant loss (provided default value)

DESIGN	EA Credit 2:
	On-Site Renewable Energy

PURPOSE

To reduce the environmental and economic impacts of _____ fuel energy use by encouraging the generation of _____-site _____ energy for self-supply.

REQUIREMENTS

Install an _____ type of a renewable energy system on the project's site.

NC and School projects can earn _____ to _____ points for supplying a minimum of _____ percent of the building's energy (by cost).

CS projects can earn _____ points by supplying _____ percent of the base building's energy (by cost).

STRATEGIES

Eligible Systems include:

- solar thermal, _____ systems, wind, wave, some biomass systems, geothermal (heating and electric) power, and _____-impact hydropower systems

Ineligible systems include:

- _____ features, passive solar strategies, daylighting strategies, and geo-exchange systems using a _____-source heat pump

CALCULATIONS

Option 1:

Estimate energy demand of whole building by _____ to determine the value of the on-site generated power as a percentage of overall energy cost.

Option 2:

Use _____ database to estimate energy use of building to determine the value of the on-site generated power as a percentage of overall energy cost.

EXEMPLARY PERFORMANCE

NC and Schools: Generate more than _____ percent of building's energy use.

CS: Generate more than _____ percent of base building's energy use.

REFERENCED STANDARDS

ANSI/ASHRAE/IESNA Standard _____

U.S. Department of Energy's _____ Buildings Energy Consumption Survey (CBECS)

1–7 pts.

RESPONSIBLE PARTY:

ELECTRICAL ENGINEER

	EA Credit 2:
	On-Site Renewable Energy

ANSWER KEY

PURPOSE

To reduce the environmental and economic impacts of fossil fuel energy use by encouraging the generation of on-site renewable energy for self-supply.

REQUIREMENTS

Install an eligible type of a renewable energy system on the project's site.

NC and School projects can earn up to 7 points for supplying a minimum of 1 percent of the building's energy (by cost).

CS projects can earn 4 points by supplying 1 percent of the base building's energy (by cost).

STRATEGIES

Eligible Systems include:

- solar thermal, photovoltaic systems, wind, wave, some biomass systems, geothermal (heating and electric) power, and low-impact hydropower systems

Ineligible systems include:

- architectural features, passive solar strategies, daylighting strategies, and geo-exchange systems using a ground-source heat pump

CALCULATIONS

Option 1:

Estimate energy demand of whole building by simulation to determine the value of the on-site generated power as a percentage of overall energy cost.

Option 2:

Use CBECS database to estimate energy use of building to determine the value of the on-site generated power as a percentage of overall energy cost.

EXEMPLARY PERFORMANCE

NC and Schools: Generate more than 15 percent of building's energy use.

CS: Generate more than 5 percent of base building's energy use.

REFERENCED STANDARDS

ANSI/ASHRAE/IESNA Standard 90.1

U.S. Department of Energy's Commercial Buildings Energy Consumption Survey (CBECS)

CONSTRUCTION	**EA Credit 5 (CS Credit 5.1):** **Measurement and Verification** **Base Building (CS)**
	EA Credit 5.2: **Measurement and Verification** **Tenant Submetering (CS)**

PURPOSE

To provide the opportunity to _____ the building's _____ consumption over time.

REQUIREMENTS

Credit 5 and Credit 5.1: 2 points for Schools and 3 points for NC and CS

Option 1:

       Develop a _____ plan in compliance with IPMVP - Option _____: Calibrated _____

Option 2:

       Develop a _____ plan in compliance with IPMVP - Option _____: Energy Conservation _____ Isolation

Credit 5.2: 3 Points for CS

       Provide for an expandable metering network for _____ that is centrally monitored

REFERENCED STANDARD

International Performance _____ & _____ Protocol, Volume III (IPMVP)

2–3 pts. **RESPONSIBLE PARTY:**
ELECTRICAL ENGINEER

EA Credit 5 (CS Credit 5.1):
Measurement and Verification
Base Building (CS)

EA Credit 5.2:
Measurement and Verification
Tenant Submetering (CS)

ANSWER KEY

PURPOSE

To provide the opportunity to track the building's energy consumption over time.

REQUIREMENTS

Credit 5 and Credit 5.1: 2 points for Schools and 3 points for NC and CS

Option 1:

   Develop a M&V plan in compliance with IPMVP - Option D: Calibrated Simulation

Option 2:

   Develop a M&V plan in compliance with IPMVP - Option B: Energy Conservation Measure Isolation

Credit 5.2: 3 Points for CS

   Provide for an expandable metering network for tenants that is centrally monitored

REFERENCED STANDARD

International Performance Measure & Verification Protocol, Volume III (IPMVP)

CONSTRUCTION

EA Credit 6:

Green Power

PURPOSE

To reduce pollution generated by power plants by purchasing energy from _____-source, _____ energy systems.

REQUIREMENTS

For _____ years, purchase _____ percent of the building's electrical demand from a Green-e certified _____ or purchase Green-e accredited _____ energy _____ (RECs).

_____ projects: Energy use is determined by base building consumption based on a minimum of _____ percent of the total building square footage.

CALCULATIONS

Option 1:

Estimate energy demand of whole building by _____ to determine the value of the on-site generated power as a percentage of overall energy cost.

Option 2:

Use _____ database to estimate energy use of building to determine the value of the on-site generated power as a percentage of overall energy cost.

EXEMPLARY PERFORMANCE

For two years, purchase _____ percent of the building's electrical demand from a _____ certified provider or purchase _____ accredited renewable energy certificates (RECs).

REFERENCED STANDARD

Center for Resource Solutions, _____ Product Certification

2 pts.

RESPONSIBLE PARTY:

OWNER

	EA Credit 6:
	Green Power

ANSWER KEY

PURPOSE

To reduce pollution generated by power plants by purchasing energy from grid-source, renewable energy systems.

REQUIREMENTS

For two years, purchase 35 percent of the building's electrical demand from a Green-e certified provider or purchase Green-e accredited renewable energy certificates (RECs).

CS projects: Energy use is determined by base building consumption based on a minimum of 15 percent of the total building square footage.

CALCULATIONS

Option 1:

    Estimate energy demand of whole building by simulation to determine the value of the on-site generated power as a percentage of overall energy cost.

Option 2:

    Use CBECS database to estimate energy use of building to determine the value of the on-site generated power as a percentage of overall energy cost.

EXEMPLARY PERFORMANCE

For two years, purchase 70 percent of the building's electrical demand from a Green-e certified provider or purchase Green-e accredited renewable energy certificates (RECs).

REFERENCED STANDARD

Center for Resource Solutions, Green-e Product Certification

CHAPTER **7**
MATERIALS AND RESOURCES

Figure 7.1 Specifying green materials, such as these 3Form® panels with recycled content, is a strategy to reduce the detrimental impacts of construction and the need for virgin materials. *Photo courtesy of Skylar Nielson, 3Form*

AS THE PREVIOUS CHAPTERS POINTED OUT, the built environment can be quite tolling on the natural environment. This book has so far presented means of minimizing impacts from the project site and reducing water and energy demands, while this chapter details strategies to minimize the environmental impacts of building materials as depicted in the Materials & Resources (MR) category in the Leadership in Energy and Environmental Design (LEED®) rating systems

It's time to pick a different color for flashcards created for MR topics.

(Figure 7.1). This chapter details how to properly select materials and what to do with them after their useful life. These are two critical elements for the environment and the building industry, as buildings are a large consumer of natural resources and also contribute to the amount of solid waste generated, not only from an operational standpoint, but also in terms of construction. More specifically, a sustainability guide by San Mateo County suggests, "construction in the United States consumes 25% of all wood that is harvested, 40% of all raw stone, gravel and sand."[1] In terms of the quantity of waste generated, "according to the U.S. Environmental Protection Agency (EPA), an estimated 76 million tons of debris was generated in 1996 from commercial construction projects, including renovation and demolition activities.[2] As a result, green building project team members are advised to evaluate the environmental impact of their materials and product specifications and how to address waste during construction and operations.

Project teams may then find themselves asking, "Where does steel come from? What kinds of materials are used to make green building products? How far did the raw material for the windows have to travel to the manufacturing plant? How far is the manufacturing plant from the project site? What happens to the leftover gypsum wallboard scraps?" To help answer these types of questions, this chapter addresses three components for consideration as related to material and resource selection and disposal:

1. Salvaged materials and material reuse

2. Building material selection

3. Waste management

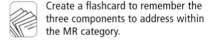

Create a flashcard to remember the three components to address within the MR category.

Each of these strategies is referred to in the prerequisites and credits of the category, as seen in Table 7.1. Remember from the previous chapters to note when the prerequisite or credit is eligible to be submitted for review: at the end of design or construction. Notice that only the prerequisite can be submitted after

Table 7.1 The Materials & Resources (MR) Category

D/C	Prereq/Credit	Title	NC	Schools	CS
			Points		
D	Prereq 1	Storage and Collection of Recyclables	R	R	R
C	Credit 1	Building Reuse; Maintain Existing Walls, Floors, and Roof	—	—	1–5
C	Credit 1.1	Building Reuse; Maintain Existing Walls, Floors, and Roof	1–3	1–2	—
C	Credit 1.2	Building Reuse, Maintain 50 percent of Interior Nonstructural Elements	1	1	—
C	Credit 2	Construction Waste Management	1–2	1–2	1–2
C	Credit 3	Materials Reuse	1–2	1–2	1
C	Credit 4	Recycled Content	1–2	1–2	1–2
C	Credit 5	Regional Materials	1–2	1–2	1–2
C	Credit 6	Rapidly Renewable Materials	1	1	—
C	Credit 7 (Credit 6 CS)	Certified Wood	1	1	1

construction documents (CDs) are completed, while all of the credits are submitted after substantial completion. Do not worry about remembering the exact credit name and number, but it is important to know which are credits versus prerequisites.

SALVAGED MATERIALS AND MATERIAL REUSE

Material selection should begin with the discovery of what is already existing that can be reused. From a large-scale perspective, reusing existing building stock can reduce the burden on the infrastructure, such as utility and road expansion. Reusing building components reduces the demand for virgin materials and the impacts from manufacturing, and can add to the character of a project (Figure 7.2). It also helps to reduce waste, as salvaged materials are reused as they are or **adaptively reused** (repurposed); in either case, they are diverted from landfills and incineration facilities and eliminate the need for packaging that is discarded. The BD+C rating systems address reuse in a number of ways to encourage pursuit by project teams.

Salvaged Materials and Material Reuse in Relation to LEED Compliance

MR Credit 1.1: Building Reuse: Maintain Existing Walls, Floors, and Roof (for NC and Schools); and MR Credit 1 (for CS). Project teams that look to reusing the existing building stock are eligible to pursue this credit if they are able to prove that a percentage of the **prior condition** of the project when it was selected, excluding exterior windows and doors, was maintained (Figure 7.3). Each of the

 Project teams need to be aware of maintaining compliance should the project include an expansion or addition. NC and School projects cannot double the existing square footage, while CS projects can build up to six times larger than the existing area to pursue these reuse credits.

Figure 7.2 The ebony oak wood for the reception desk at the One Haworth Center in Holland, Michigan, was recovered from the Great Lakes and other waterways to avoid depleting old-growth forests. *Photo courtesy of Haworth Inc.*

Figure 7.3 Finding new uses for existing buildings helps to extend the life of the existing building stock and avoids demolition and waste. *Photo courtesy of SmithGroup, Inc.*

 Materials are calculated by square footage for contribution. For interior doors and exterior walls, count one surface side, but for interior walls, include the square footage for both surfaces. Approach the calculations as if you were a painting contractor and bidding on the surface areas to be painted.

 MR Credit 1, Credit 1.1, and Credit 1.2 compliance is based on the square footage of the total preserved existing area in relation to the new square footage implemented applicable to the components of the credit (i.e., structural versus nonstructural).

TIP Reused materials are calculated as a percentage of total material cost of a project to prove compliance with MR Credit 3. Therefore, if a project team implements $50,000 worth of salvaged, reused, and/or **refurbished** materials on a project with a total material cost of $1 million, the project would earn one point.

rating systems presents different percentage thresholds to earn points within this credit. For example, in order to earn one point, LEED for Schools™ projects are required to achieve a 75 percent reuse of the **existing area,** while LEED for New Construction™ (LEED NC) projects need 55 percent and LEED for Core & Shell™ (LEED CS) projects need only 25 percent. To comply, project teams will need to attest that these components were preserved in their existing condition prior to the renovation and remain in the new completed project. Achieving an Exemplary Performance credit is available only to CS projects that are able to preserve 95 percent of the existing structure, envelope, and core components. Remember, reusing existing window assemblies and nonstructural-roofing materials cannot be included in the compliance calculations for this credit. However, these types of materials can be included in the calculations for construction waste management credit, as presented later in this chapter.

MR Credit 1.2: Building Reuse, Maintain 50 Percent of Interior Nonstructural Elements (for NC and Schools). NC and School project teams that preserve at least 5 percent (by area) of interior components, such as doors, ceilings, partitions, and walls, are eligible to pursue this credit. To be eligible for inclusion for this credit's calculations, these items must be used as they were originally intended. Just as with the previous credit, materials that do not meet the intentions of this credit can be used in the calculations for construction waste management credit. Also, projects cannot double the existing square footage for expansions and additions and pursue this credit.

MR Credit 3: Materials Reuse. This credit differs from the previous two, as it allows materials to be salvaged on site and also from off site. The qualifying attributes are determined by the intended use of the material to be reused. For example, if the material is found on site, it must be repurposed from its original intention, such as a door to be reused as a table, and cannot be used in the calculations for any other MR credit. Remember, those materials serving their intended function and found on site are to be used toward the previously described credits. If the material is salvaged from another location, it can serve the same purpose or have a new one to qualify with the intentions of this credit. Any off site, salvaged materials implemented on a project can also be applied toward MR Credit 5: Regional Materials, to be discussed later in the chapter. If the owner wishes to reuse the furniture from their existing location for the project seeking certification, documentation is required to show that the furniture was purchased at least two years prior to the relocation. The minimum threshold to earn this credit is 5 percent for each of the rating systems. NC and School projects have two point opportunities, while CS projects have only the one percentage threshold to achieve one point, although all of the BD+C rating systems offer the opportunity to earn an Exemplary Performance credit.

QUIZ TIME!

Q7.1. In order to comply with MR Credit 3: Materials Reuse, how many points could a project seeking LEED for Schools certification earn if they purchased $65,000 of salvaged lumber from a nearby facility and $55,000 of a refurbished raised access floor system? The team is planning on reusing the existing doors, with a value of $41,000, although they are relocating them to new locations throughout the project. The total material cost for the project has a value of $2 million. (Choose one)

   A. One

   B. Two

   C. This project does not meet the intentions of the credit

   D. Three, including one for exemplary performance

Q7.2. Which of the following credits could a project team pursue if the contractor purchased refurbished demountable partitions from a nearby supplier? (Choose two)

   A. MR Credit 4: Recycled Content

   B. MR Credit 5: Regional Materials

   C. MR Credit 1.1: Building Reuse; Maintain Existing Walls, Floors, and Roof

   D. MR Credit 3: Materials Reuse

   E. MR Credit 1.2: Building Reuse, Maintain 50 Percent of Interior Nonstructural Elements

Q7.3. Which of the following credits offer exemplary performance opportunities? (Choose three)

   A. SS Credit 2: Development Density and Community Connectivity

   B. MR Credit 3: Materials Reuse

   C. MR Credit 1: Building Reuse; Maintain Existing Walls, Floors, and Roof

   D. MR Credit 1.2: Building Reuse, Maintain 50 Percent of Interior Nonstructural Elements

   E. SS Prerequisite 1: Construction Activity Pollution Prevention

Q7.4. Which of the following are excluded from compliance with MR Credit 1: Building Reuse: Maintain Existing Walls, Floors, and Roof? (Choose three)

A. Window assemblies

B. Structural floor

C. Roof decking

D. Nonstructural roof material

E. Hazardous materials

Q7.5. Which of the following statements are true? (Choose two)

A. Compliance with MR Credit 3: Materials Reuse is based on purchasing salvaged materials with a value of at least 5 percent of the total material cost for the project.

B. Mechanical, electrical, and plumbing components cannot be salvaged and reused.

C. Existing structural building elements that are maintained can be included in all of the MR credits.

D. There is no limit on the square footage increase when calculating compliance for MR Credit 1.

E. Hazardous materials can be included in the MR credit calculations, as long as they are remediated to the ASHRAE 90.1 Standard.

BUILDING MATERIAL SELECTION

Implementing sustainable building materials impacts a project's triple bottom line, just as with site selection and energy and water demands. As introduced in Chapter 2, project teams should perform **life-cycle assessments (LCAs)** of building materials, prior to specification, to evaluate the "cradle-to-grave" cycle of each material, especially as related to the environmental components of pollution and the demand of natural resources. The cradle-to-grave cycle includes the **embodied energy,** such as the extraction location of raw materials, the manufacturing process and location, the impact on construction workers and building occupants, the expectancy term of use during operations, the disposal options available, and the energy contained within the product itself. With the evaluation of these components, the results of an LCA will help to determine the material selections to include in the construction purchasing policy to help guide the contractor.

Once the materials are selected, they should be evaluated for compliance with LEED. The credit opportunities will be presented in the next section, but first it is important to decipher how each is calculated and what should be included in the calculations. In the previous section, the MR Credits 1 and 2 calculations were based on area, whereas Credit 3: Materials Reuse was based on a percentage of the total material cost of the project. How does a team determine the total material cost of a project? There are two ways to comply: either by calculating the actual cost of materials (not including labor or equipment) or by assuming a

TIP Division 12: Furniture and Furnishings can also be included in the calculations, but if it is, then the furniture must be included consistently across all MR credits that are calculated based on the total material cost of the project.

45 percent default value. If calculating the actual cost, the number is determined by totaling Construction Specification Institute (CSI) MasterFormat™ Divisions 03–10, plus Foundations and Sections, Paving, Site Improvements, and Plantings. Mechanical, electrical, and plumbing equipment or any specialty items, such as elevators, are not included in any of the calculations.

Once the total material cost is determined for the project, the products are required to be tracked, measured, and calculated to prove compliance. Most of the MR credits are calculated in a similar way; for example, recycled content, regional materials, salvaged materials, and rapidly renewable animal or fiber products are calculated as a percentage of the total material cost for a project. Forest Steward-ship Council (FSC) wood products are calculated as a percentage of the total cost of new wood products purchased for a specific project. Remember, building reuse credits are based on area, not on cost. After construction, materials are then documented and tallied to show compliance to earn points. For example, should a project purchase 60 percent of their new wood products from a sustainably managed forest, they would earn one point, as the minimum threshold requires the team to purchase at least 50 percent FSC-certified wood of the total new wood purchased.

 Create a flashcard to remember how MR credits are calculated.

Project teams may be presented with a building component assembled with multiple materials. Each of the different materials could be manufactured with different environmental impacts, such as extraction and processing locations, and they can contain different amounts of postconsumer recycled content, pre-consumer recycled content, or none at all. In this case, the team would need to evaluate the **assembly recycled content** of the component. It does not matter if the assembly consists of multiple materials (think concrete) of multiple subcom-ponents (think furniture). To calculate compliance with MR Credit 4: Recycled Content, teams would need to divide "the weight of the recycled content by the overall weight of the assembly."[3] For example, if the window assemblies were assessed, the frame could have a different recycled content than the glass itself. The weight of the frame would need to be determined versus the weight of the glass, and then tallied with proportionate value of different types of recycled con-tents in order to determine the overall recycled content value of the assembled material. The same concept can be applied to MR Credit 5: Regional Materials.

Material Selection in Relation to LEED Compliance

Although it may not be feasible to conduct a full LCA for every product, project teams can refer to the BD+C Reference Guide for material selection assistance. The LEED rating systems suggest that project teams implement products with one or more of the following characteristics (see Table 7.2).

 Create a flashcard to remember that ISO 14021-1999: Environmental Label and Declarations is the referenced standard that declares a material having postconsumer/preconsumer recycled content.

MR Credit 4: Recycled Content. It is important to remember that this credit addresses the purchasing of materials with recycled content (Figure 7.4), not the actual recycling of materials, as that process will be addressed later. For project teams to comply with this credit, they will need to ensure that the contractor purchases materials with preconsumer and/or postconsumer recycled content equivalent to the cost of at least 10 percent of the total materials (based on cost) to be awarded one point. Table 7.2 defines the difference between the two types of recycled content and also provides examples of each. Project teams are eligible to earn two points if the amount reaches 20 percent and can earn a third for exem-plary performance for purchasing 30 percent.

 TIP Steel is the only material with a default recycled content value, as sometimes there is no documentation available to prove compliance. Project teams are then able to apply a 25 percent postconsumer value for any steel products implemented on the project when calculating their contribution toward earning MR Credit 4.

Figure 7.4 Permeable pavers made with recycled content not only help to recharge the groundwater, but also help to reduce the need for virgin materials. *Photo courtesy of Vast Enterprises, LLC*

 Create a flashcard to remember that regional materials must be extracted, processed, *and* manufactured within 500 miles of the project site to comply with MR Credit 5.

 Remember, salvaged materials recovered from within 500 miles of the project site can contribute toward earning both MR Credit 3 and MR Credit 5. The recovery location is the extraction point.

MR Credit 5: Regional Materials. Purchasing products from vendors nearby reduces transportation impacts, such as pollution, and also preserves the local economy (Figure 7.5). But what is considered local? This credit requires a project team to track not only the location from which a product was sold or distributed, but also the extraction points of the materials to make the product, where those materials were processed, and where the final product was manufactured and assembled. For the BD+C rating systems, each of these location points have to be determined for each of the materials contributing to earning this credit. Therefore, for the purposes of the exam, it is critical to remember that regional materials are extracted, processed, *and* manufactured within 500 miles of the project

Figure 7.5 Purchasing materials that are extracted, processed, and manufactured within 500 miles helps to reduce the transportation impacts associated with building materials. *Photo courtesy of Gary Neuenswander, Utah Agricultural Experiment Station*

site. Teams that purchase 10 percent of qualifying local materials can earn one point, and 20 percent earns two points. They can earn an Exemplary Performance credit for purchasing 30 percent of the total materials for the project (by cost) from within 500 miles.

As mentioned previously, for assembled materials with only a portion of the components that comply, that qualifying portion is calculated by weight for the purposes of documentation.

MR Credit 6: Rapidly Renewable Materials (for NC and Schools). Rapidly renewable materials are "agricultural products, both fiber and animal, that take 10 years or less to grow or raise and can be harvested in a sustainable fashion"[4] and therefore, preserve natural resource materials for future generations. NC and School project teams that purchase rapidly renewable materials worth 2.5 percent of the total material cost of the project are eligible to pursue this credit. If they purchase 5 percent or more, they can earn an Exemplary Performance credit. Be sure to refer to Table 7.2 for examples of rapidly renewable materials, and note that both animal and fiber types are included. CS projects are not eligible to pursue this credit.

MR Credit 7: Certified Wood (MR Credit 6 for CS). Wood certified by the **Forest Stewardship Council (FSC)** is addressed in this credit for each of the BD+C rating systems (although numbered differently). The certification proves compliance for responsible forest management, preserving materials for future generations and habitats, as well as maintaining biodiversity (Figure 7.6). Teams must purchase at least 50 percent of the new, permanently installed wood for the

Did you notice any commonalities between MR Credit 4 and MR Credit 5?

Create a flashcard to remember that rapidly renewable fiber or animal materials must be grown or raised in 10 years or less.

Which CSI Divisions are to be included in the MR calculations? Make a flashcard to remember them if you do not remember!

What types of green building materials are calculated the same for LEED documentation purposes? Which ones are calculated as a percentage of the total material volume or weight?

Fly ash can be a substitution for Portland cement for concrete products. It is the residual component that is left behind during the coal incineration or combustion process.

Create a flashcard to remember the difference between preconsumer and postconsumer recycled contents.

Do you remember what form the contractor would fill in to upload to LEED-Online to show compliance with the recycled content, local/regional materials, FSC wood, or rapidly renewable credits?

Table 7.2 Green Building Products

Characteristic		Description	Examples
Materials with recycled content		Products manufactured with material previously used	Masonry, concrete, carpet, acoustic ceiling tile, tile, rubber flooring, insulation, metal, and gypsum wallboard
	Preconsumer waste	Material left over from the manufacturing process and implemented into a new manufacturing process	Fly ash, sawdust, walnut shells, sunflower seed hulls, obsolete inventories, shavings, and trimmings
	Postconsumer waste	Manufactured products at the end of their useful life	Any products that were consumed (such as metals, plastics, paper, cardboard, glass), and demolition and construction debris
Local/regional materials		Products that are extracted, processed, and manufactured close to a project site	Materials obtained within 500 miles of the project site
Rapidly renewable materials		Animal or fiber materials that grow or can be raised in less than 10 years	Bamboo flooring and plywood, cotton batt insulation, linoleum flooring, sunflower seed board panels, wheatboard cabinetry, wool carpeting, cork flooring, bio-based paints, geotextile fabrics, soy-based insulation, and straw bales
FSC-certified wood materials		Sustainably managed forest resources	Contractors are required to show chain-of-custody (COC) documentation

Figure 7.6 Purchasing wood from sustainable and responsible forests helps to ensure resources for future generations. *Photo courtesy of Gary Neuenswander, Utah Agricultural Experiment Station*

Create a flashcard to remember that FSC wood requires chain-of-custody (COC) documentation.

project that is FSC certified and collect the vendor's or manufacturer's **chain-of-custody (COC)** certification documentation to prove compliance in order to earn this credit. Remember, this credit is calculated with only the new wood purchased for the project and not the total material cost, and it does not include temporarily installed wood, such as formwork or sidewalk protection. It can, however, include different types of FSC-certified products, such as FSC Pure, FSC Mixed Credit, and FSC Mixed (NN) percent. For the purposes of calculating compliance, FSC Pure and FSC Mixed Credit are valued at 100 percent of their cost, while FSC Mixed (NN) percent shall only have a value of its percentage of FSC product. For example, wood that is certified FSC Mixed (35) percent can contribute only 35 percent of its value toward compliance. FSC Recycled certified products do not meet the intentions of this credit, but can be included in the MR Credit 4: Recycled Content calculations.

QUIZ TIME!

Q7.6. Which of the following materials could contribute to earning an MR Credit 4: Recycled Content credit, as preconsumer recycled content? (Choose three)

A. Metal stud manufacturing scrap sent back into the same manufacturing process

B. Paper towels manufactured from cardboard used for packaging

C. Medium-density fiberboard panels manufactured with sawdust generated by the manufacturing of structural insulated panels

D. Concrete made with fly ash collected from coal-burning power plants

E. Carpet padding manufactured with waste fiber collected from textile manufacturing plants

Q7.7. The percentage calculation for MR Credit 6: Rapidly Renewable Materials accounts for which of the following? (Choose two)

    A. Cost of rapidly renewable materials

    B. Volume of rapidly renewable materials

    C. Combined weight for all rapidly renewable materials

    D. Total materials cost for the project

Q7.8. Which of the following is not an example of a rapidly renewable material? (Choose one)

    A. Strawboard

    B. Oak wood flooring

    C. Cotton insulation

    D. Cork flooring

    E. Wheatboard

Q7.9. A library is to be constructed with wood posts and beams salvaged from barns in the region and FSC-certified wood for doors and trim. The owner is interested in determining whether the project meets the requirements of MR Credit 7: Certified Wood for LEED compliance. The qualification of products and determination of their contribution to certified wood requires keeping track of which of the following? (Choose two)

    A. Cost of certified wood products as a percentage of the total material cost of the project

    B. Cost of certified wood products as a percentage of the total cost for wood products purchased for the project

    C. Weight of certified wood products as a percentage of all new wood products used on the project

    D. Chain-of-custody documentation for all FSC-certified wood products

    E. Chain-of-custody documentation for all new wood products purchased for the project

Q7.10. To help calculate compliance for MR credits, what is the default percentage value project teams can use to determine the total material cost for a project? (Choose one)

    A. 10 percent

    B. 20 percent

    C. 25 percent

    D. 45 percent

    E. 35 percent

Q7.11. Which of the following statements are not true? (Choose three)

    A. Furniture can be included in the calculations for MR credits.

    B. Specialty equipment cannot be included in the calculations for MR credits.

    C. Furniture cannot be included in the calculations for MR credits.

    D. Mechanical, electrical, and plumbing equipment and fixtures cannot be included in the calculations for MR credits.

    E. Mechanical, electrical, and plumbing equipment and fixtures can be included in the calculations for MR credits.

    F. Specialty equipment can be included in the calculations for MR credits.

7.12. Which of the following statements are true? (Choose two)

    A. FSC is the acronym for Forest Stewardship Council.

    B. FSC-certified wood and rapidly renewable materials can also count toward MR Credit 5: Regional Materials if they are extracted, processed, and manufactured within 500 miles of the project site.

    C. FSC-certified wood and rapidly renewable materials cannot count toward MR Credit 5: Regional Materials.

    D. FSC-certified wood and rapidly renewable materials can also count toward MR Credit 5: Regional Materials if they are extracted, processed, and manufactured within 100 miles of the project site.

    E. FSC is the acronym for Federal Society of Certified wood.

WASTE MANAGEMENT

 TIP Landfills require sunlight, moisture, and oxygen in order to decompose material—quite a challenging feat for a dark, enclosed environment, don't you think?

Construction processes and building operations should be addressed to minimize environmental impacts from disposal and waste. In the United States, building construction and demolition alone account for 40 percent of the total waste stream, while building operations account for 300 tons of waste per year for a building with 1,500 employees.[5]

When waste is collected and hauled from a construction site or an existing facility, it is typically brought to a landfill or an incineration facility, both of which contribute to greenhouse gas emissions. Landfills produce and then leak methane, and incineration facility processes produce carbon dioxide. As another environmental detriment, think about the potential for landfills to contaminate groundwater sources. As a result, green building project teams and facility managers are encouraged to address waste diversion strategies for projects under construction and operational buildings to avoid landfills and incineration facilities (Figure 7.7).

 Create a flashcard to remember the EPA statistic for current recycling rates of 32 percent.

 Create a flashcard to remember the 3Rs of waste management: Reduce, Reuse, and Recycle. Remember them in that order as a hierarchal approach for policies.

The EPA estimates a reduction of 5 million metric tons of carbon dioxide if recycling efforts were to increase just 3 percent above the current 32 percent rate.[6] To help reach this goal, the BD+C rating systems offer point opportunities for implementing waste management policies during construction, to divert waste by reuse and recycling strategies. Construction waste management plans should address whether waste will be separated on site into individually labeled waste containers or collected in a **commingled** fashion in one container and sorted off site (Figure 7.7). As with many of the components addressed within the LEED rating systems, there are trade-offs to address when deciding between the two

Figure 7.7 Separating waste on site is one method to comply with the construction waste management strategies to avoid landfills and incineration facilities. *Photo courtesy of Auld & White Constructors, LLC*

Figure 7.8 Dedicated waste container for masonry to be collected for recycling.

options. Commingled collection reduces the amount of space needed on site, while on-site collection may require additional labor to manage the sorting effort. In either case, land-clearing debris and soil should not be included in the calculations, but metals, concrete, and asphalt should all be collected for recycling and accounted for (Figure 7.8). Recycling options for paper, cardboard, plastics, and wood vary by region.

Figure 7.9 Recycling during operations is required of all projects seeking LEED certification. *Photo courtesy of Jason Hagopian, AIA, LEED AP*

 Create a flashcard to remember the minimum types of items to be recycled during operations to meet the requirements of the MR prerequisite: paper, corrugated cardboard, glass, plastics, and metals.

 TIP Waste is calculated in volume or weight (tons).

 Create a flashcard to remember the two strategies to reduce waste.

Waste Management in Relation to LEED Compliance

MR Prerequisite 1: Storage and Collection of Recyclables. Project teams are required to encourage recycling during operations by providing locations for collecting and storing materials to be recycled (Figure 7.9). At a minimum, the teams need to provide locations to collect paper, corrugated cardboard, glass, plastics, and metals. Calculations are not required to determine the size of the collection and storage locations, but the reference guide provides some guidance from the City of Seattle for the project teams to follow.

MR Credit 2: Construction Waste Management. This credit is addressed during construction, whereas the prerequisite prepares the building for the process to be conducted during operations. For this credit, project teams are required to develop a construction waste management plan to be implemented by the contractor during construction to divert nonhazardous demolition and construction debris from landfills and incineration facilities. The plan must describe the approach specific to each type of material and must instruct the contractor to collect the waste on site either in a commingled or separated fashion. The plan will also indicate the need for the contractor to collect the receipts from the waste hauler to document proof of diversion. A team will earn one point for diverting 50 percent and another for diverting 75 percent of demolition and construction waste. They can pursue an exemplary performance opportunity for recycling 95 percent. The percentage of waste diverted can be calculated based on weight or volume, as long as it is done consistently throughout the construction process.

QUIZ TIME!

Q7.13. Which of the following greenhouse gases is a by-product of landfills? (Choose one)

A. Carbon monoxide

B. Methane

C. Sulfur dioxide

D. Nitrous oxide

Q7.14. Which of the following statements are not true about green building materials? (Choose two)

A. Rapidly renewable materials are harvested within 10 years.

B. Cradle-to-grave materials can be recycled.

C. Products with postconsumer recycled content can contribute to earning MR Credit 4: Recycled Content, while products with preconsumer recycled content cannot.

D. Cotton insulation can be considered a type of rapidly renewable material.

Q7.15. Which of the following would the contractor upload to LEED-Online? (Choose two)

A. Stormwater management plan

B. Total amount of waste diverted from a landfill

C. The total material cost of the project and the percentage containing recycled content

D. Energy modeling calculations to show expected energy savings

Q7.16. When addressing materials and resources, a project team should incorporate which of the following to comply with the credits and prerequisites of the MR category within the BD+C LEED rating systems? (Choose three)

A. The purchasing policy of the manufacturer

B. Location of the manufacturing plant of steel

C. The type of car the CEO drives

D. Postconsumer recycled content of a chair

E. Extraction location of silica

Q7.17. How would a contractor show proof of compliance with MR Credit 7: Certified Wood? (Choose one)

A. Give the architect a spreadsheet summarizing all of the wood was purchased with 500 miles of the project site.

B. Upload receipts of FSC wood purchased to LEED-Online.

C. Upload chain-of-custody documentation to LEED-Online.

D. Complete a LEED credit template and upload it to LEED-Online, including the chain-of-custody numbers and invoice amounts.

E. Mail all documentation to USGBC.

Q7.18. How is waste hauled from a construction site calculated for the purposes of LEED? (Choose one)

A. As a percentage of total material cost of a project

B. As a percentage of the total material volume or weight

C. As a percentage of total cost of a project

D. In tons

Q7.19. Which of the following are not required for collection to comply with MR Prerequisite 1: Storage and Collection of Recyclables? (Choose two)

A. Glass

B. Plastics

C. Wood

D. Rubber

E. Corrugated cardboard

F. Metal

Q7.20. A contractor was provided with receipts from his waste hauler indicating that 20 tons of wood, plastic, and metal waste were sent to manufacturers for reuse. The hauler also indicated another 20 tons were landfilled, while 15 tons were sent to an incineration plant and 8 tons of soil and plant debris were sent to a site in need of mulching material. The hauler's receipts also show that 45 tons of concrete were sold to a concrete masonry unit manufacturing facility over 500 miles away from the project site. What percentage of waste was diverted in order to comply with MR Credit 2: Construction Waste Management? (Choose one)

A. 55 percent

B. 65 percent

C. 70 percent

D. 62.2 percent

DESIGN

MR Prerequisite 1:
Storage and Collection of Recyclables

PURPOSE

Reduce _____ generated by building occupants that is _____ to and _____ of in _____.

REQUIREMENTS

Design for the _____ and _____ of recyclable materials within the entire building.

At a minimum, plan to collect _____, corrugated cardboard, _____, _____, and _____.

DOCUMENTATION

Provide a _____ indicating storage and collection areas.

Required

RESPONSIBLE PARTY:
OWNER

	MR Prerequisite 1: **Storage and Collection of Recyclables**

ANSWER KEY

PURPOSE

Reduce waste generated by building occupants that is hauled to and disposed of in landfills.

REQUIREMENTS

Design for the collection and storage of recyclable materials within the entire building.

At a minimum, plan to collect **paper, corrugated cardboard, glass, plastics, and metals**.

DOCUMENTATION

Provide a plan indicating storage and collection areas.

CONSTRUCTION	MR Credit 1 (CS):
	MR Credit 1.1 (NC and Schools):
	Building Reuse,
	Maintain Existing Walls, Floors, and Roof (NC and SCHOOLS)

PURPOSE

To reduce the need for and the _____ and _____ impacts of new building materials by _____ the life cycle of the _____ building stock, _____ resources, retain _____ resources, reduce _____ and the environmental impacts of new buildings.

REQUIREMENTS

Preserve a percentage of the existing building _____ (including exterior skin and framing, not including window assemblies and nonstructural roofing material) and building _____ (including structural floor and roof decking).

_____ hazardous materials are not to be included in the calculations.

CS additions that are more than _____ times the original square footage are not eligible to pursue this credit.

NC additions that are more than _____ times the original square footage are not eligible to pursue this credit.

If reuse does not meet threshold minimums or if addition size disqualifies pursuit, salvaged materials can be included in calculation for MR Credit _____: _____ _____ Management.

POINT DISTRIBUTION

New Construction: Schools:

55%	→	75%	→	95%		75%	→	95%
•1 point		•2 points		•3 points		•1 point		•2 points

Core & Shell:

25%	→	33%	→	42%	→	50%	→	75%	→	95%
•1 point		•2 points		•3 points		•4 points		•5 points		•1 EP point

EXEMPLARY PERFORMANCE

CS: 95 percent of walls, floors, and roof must be preserved

1-5 pts.

RESPONSIBLE PARTY:

ARCHITECT

MR Credit 1 (CS):
MR Credit 1.1 (NC and Schools):

Building Reuse,

Maintain Existing Walls, Floors, and Roof (NC and SCHOOLS)

ANSWER KEY

PURPOSE

To reduce the need for and the manufacturing and transportation impacts of new building materials by extending the life cycle of the existing building stock, conserve resources, retain cultural resources, reduce waste and the environmental impacts of new buildings.

REQUIREMENTS

Preserve a percentage of the existing building envelope (including exterior skin and framing, not including window assemblies and nonstructural roofing material) and building structure (including structural floor and roof decking).

Remediated hazardous materials are not to be included in the calculations.

CS additions that are more than 6 times the original square footage are not eligible to pursue this credit.

NC additions that are more than 2 times the original square footage are not eligible to pursue this credit.

If reuse does not meet threshold minimums or if addition size disqualifies pursuit, salvaged materials can be included in calculation for MR Credit 2: Construction Waste Management.

POINT DISTRIBUTION

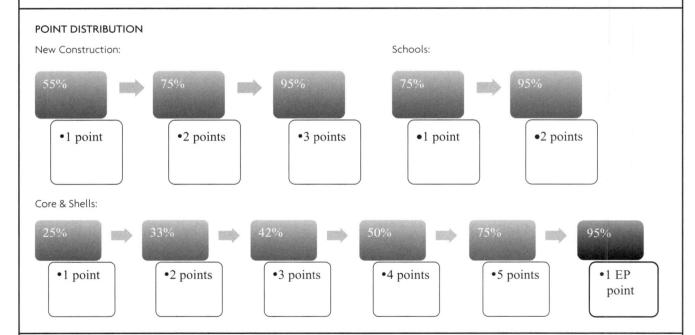

New Construction:

55%	75%	95%
•1 point	•2 points	•3 points

Schools:

75%	95%
•1 point	•2 points

Core & Shells:

25%	33%	42%	50%	75%	95%
•1 point	•2 points	•3 points	•4 points	•5 points	•1 EP point

EXEMPLARY PERFORMANCE

CS: 95 percent of walls, floors, and roof must be preserved

CONSTRUCTION

PURPOSE

To reduce the need for and the _____ and _____ impacts of new building materials by _____ the life cycle of the _____ building stock, _____ resources, retain _____ resources, reduce _____ and the environmental impacts of new buildings.

REQUIREMENTS

Preserve at least _____ percent of the existing _____ nonstructural elements (by area) of the total building square footage (including additions).

Interior nonstructural elements include walls, _____, floor coverings, and _____ systems.

Additions that are more than _____ times the original square footage are not eligible to pursue this credit.

1 pt.

RESPONSIBLE PARTY:

ARCHITECT

MR Credit 1.2:

Building Reuse,

Maintain 50 Percent of Interior Nonstructural Elements (NC and SCHOOLS)

ANSWER KEY

PURPOSE

To reduce the need for and the manufacturing and transportation impacts of new building materials by extending the life cycle of the existing building stock, conserve resources, retain cultural resources, reduce waste and the environmental impacts of new buildings.

REQUIREMENTS

Preserve at least **50 percent** of the existing interior nonstructural elements (by area) of the total building square footage (including additions).

Interior nonstructural elements include walls, doors, floor coverings, and ceiling systems.

Additions that are more than 2 times the original square footage are not eligible to pursue this credit.

CONSTRUCTION	MR Credit 2:
	Construction Waste Management

PURPOSE

_____ construction and _____ waste from _____ and _____ facilities and redirect the _____ material back into the manufacturing process or appropriate sites.

REQUIREMENTS

Create and implement a _____ _____ management plan.

Divert a percentage of construction and demolition debris by _____, _____, or _____.

POINT DISTRIBUTION

50% ➡ 75% ➡ 95%

- •1 point
- •2 points
- •1 EP point

DOCUMENTATION

Construction Waste Management Plan

Completed Submittal Form on LEED-Online with the following information:

- _____ description
- _____ of each type of waste (in terms of _____ or _____)
- _____ of disposal for each type of waste
- Percentage of total waste _____

EXEMPLARY PERFORMANCE

Divert more than _____ percent of construction waste from landfills and incineration facilities.

1-2 pts.

RESPONSIBLE PARTY:

CONTRACTOR

MR Credit 2:

Construction Waste Management

ANSWER KEY

PURPOSE

Divert construction and demolition waste from landfills and incineration facilities and redirect the reusable material back into the manufacturing process or appropriate sites.

REQUIREMENTS

Create and implement a **construction waste management plan**.

Divert a percentage of construction and demolition debris by recycling, donation, or salvaging.

POINT DISTRIBUTION

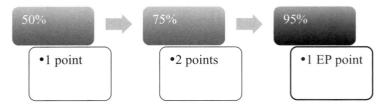

50%	75%	95%
•1 point	•2 points	•1 EP point

DOCUMENTATION

Construction Waste Management Plan

Completed Submittal Form on LEED-Online with the following information:

- Waste description

- Quantity of each type of waste (in terms of weight or volume)

- Destination of disposal for each type of waste

- Percentage of total waste diverted

EXEMPLARY PERFORMANCE

Divert more than 95 percent of construction waste from landfills and incineration facilities.

CONSTRUCTION

PURPOSE

Reduce the demand for _____ building materials and waste by _____ existing products, to reduce the impacts affiliated with the _____ and _____ of new materials.

REQUIREMENTS

Implement a percentage (based on cost) of _____, _____, or reused building materials and products.

CALCULATIONS

Materials from CSI _____ Divisions 03 to 10, _____ , and 32 are to be included in calculations.

Mechanical, _____, and plumbing elements and specialty items are not eligible to contribute to earning this credit.

Furniture can contribute to earning this credit, but must also be included in the calculations for MR credits _____ through _____ .

_____ can use actual material cost for project (excluding _____ and equipment) or they can use a _____ percent default value when completing calculations.

Items salvaged from on-site and off-site are eligible, but on-site items must serve a _____ purpose than originally intended.

POINT DISTRIBUTION

New Construction and Schools:

5%	→	10%	→	15%
•1 point		•2 points		•1 EP point

Core & Shell:

5%	→	10%
•1 point		•1 EP point

EXEMPLARY PERFORMANCE

For NC and SCHOOLS projects: Implement at least _____ percent of total material cost, salvaged, refurbished, or reused materials.

For CS projects: Implement at least _____ percent of total material cost, salvaged, refurbished, or reused materials.

1-2 pts.

RESPONSIBLE PARTY:

ARCHITECT

MR Credit 3:

Materials Reuse

ANSWER KEY

PURPOSE

Reduce the demand for virgin building materials and waste by reusing existing products, to reduce the impacts affiliated with the extraction and processing of new materials.

REQUIREMENTS

Implement a percentage (based on cost) of salvaged, refurbished, or reused building materials and products.

CALCULATIONS

Materials from CSI Masterformat Divisions 03 to 10, 31, and 32 are to be included in calculations.

Mechanical, electrical, and plumbing elements and specialty items are not eligible to contribute to earning this credit.

Furniture can contribute to earning this credit, but must also be included in the calculations for MR credits 3 through 7.

Contractors can use actual material cost for project (excluding labor and equipment) or they can use a **45 percent default value** when completing calculations.

Items salvaged from on-site and off-site are eligible but on-site items must serve a new purpose than originally intended.

POINT DISTRIBUTION

New Construction and Schools:

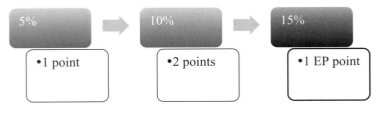

5%	10%	15%
•1 point	•2 points	•1 EP point

Core & Shell:

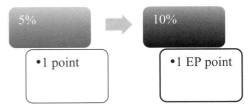

5%	10%
•1 point	•1 EP point

EXEMPLARY PERFORMANCE

For NC and SCHOOLS projects: Implement at least 15 percent of total material cost, salvaged, refurbished, or reused materials.

For CS projects: Implement at least 10 percent of total material cost, salvaged, refurbished, or reused materials.

CONSTRUCTION	MR Credit 4:
	Recycled Content

PURPOSE

To increase the demand for products with _____ content to reduce the impacts from extracting and processing _____ materials.

REQUIREMENTS

Implement a percentage (based on cost) of materials and products with recycled content such that the sum of the _____ amount plus _____ of the _____ amount of content reaches the minimum percentage threshold.

CALCULATIONS

Materials from CSI Masterformat Divisions 03 to _____, 31, and 32 are to be included in calculations.

Mechanical, electrical, and _____ elements and specialty items are not eligible to contribute to earning this credit.

_____ can contribute to earning this credit, but must also be included in the calculations for MR credits _____ through _____.

Contractors can use actual material cost for project (excluding labor and equipment) or they can use a _____ percent default value when completing calculations.

Recycled content of assembled materials is based on _____.

POINT DISTRIBUTION

10%	20%	30%
•1 point	•2 points	•1 EP point

EXEMPLARY PERFORMANCE

Implement at least _____ percent of total material cost, materials with recycled content.

REFERENCED STANDARD

International Standard _____ 14021-1999, Environmental Labels and Declarations, Self-_____ Environmental Claims (Type II Environmental Labeling)

1-2 pts.	RESPONSIBLE PARTY:
	CONTRACTOR

MR Credit 4:

Recycled Content

ANSWER KEY

PURPOSE

To increase the demand for products with recycled content to reduce the impacts from extracting and processing virgin materials.

REQUIREMENTS

Implement a percentage (based on cost) of materials and products with recycled content such that the sum of the postconsumer amount plus half of the preconsumer amount of content reaches the minimum percentage threshold.

CALCULATIONS

Materials from CSI Masterformat Divisions 03 to 10, 31, and 32 are to be included in calculations.

Mechanical, electrical, and plumbing elements and specialty items are not eligible to contribute to earning this credit.

Furniture can contribute to earning this credit, but must also be included in the calculations for MR credits 3 through 7.

Contractors can use actual material cost for project (excluding labor and equipment) or they can use a 45 percent default value when completing calculations.

Recycled content of assembled materials is based on **weight**.

POINT DISTRIBUTION

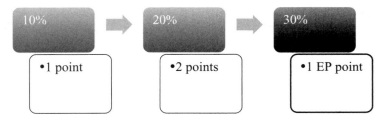

10% → 20% → 30%

- •1 point
- •2 points
- •1 EP point

EXEMPLARY PERFORMANCE

Implement at least 30 percent of total material cost, materials with recycled content.

REFERENCED STANDARD

International Standard **ISO 14021-1999,** Environmental Labels and Declarations, Self-Declared Environmental Claims (Type II Environmental Labeling)

CONSTRUCTION

PURPOSE

To increase the demand for products that are _____ extracted and manufactured to reduce the impacts from _____ and to support _____ resources.

REQUIREMENTS

Implement a percentage (based on cost) of materials and products that are _____, _____, and _____ within _____ miles of the project site.

CALCULATIONS

Materials from CSI Masterformat Divisions 03 to 10, 31, and _____ are to be included in calculations.

Mechanical, electrical, and _____ elements and _____ items are not eligible to contribute to earning this credit.

Furniture can contribute to earning this credit, but must also be included in the calculations for MR credits 3 through _____.

_____ can use actual material cost for project (excluding labor and equipment) or they can use a _____ percent _____ value when completing calculations.

If only a portion of an assembled material is _____, _____, and _____ within 500 miles of the project, the contributing value is based on _____.

POINT DISTRIBUTION

10%	20%	30%
•1 point	•2 points	•1 EP point

EXEMPLARY PERFORMANCE

Implement at least _____ percent of total material cost, materials that are extracted, processed, and manufactured within _____ miles of the project site.

1-2 pts.

MR Credit 5:

Regional Materials

ANSWER KEY

PURPOSE

To increase the demand for products that are locally extracted and manufactured to reduce the impacts from transportation and to support indigenous resources.

REQUIREMENTS

Implement a percentage (based on cost) of materials and products that are extracted, processed, and manufactured within **500 miles** of the project site.

CALCULATIONS

Materials from CSI Masterformat Divisions 03 to 10, 31 , and 32 are to be included in calculations.

Mechanical, electrical, and plumbing elements and specialty items are not eligible to contribute to earning this credit.

Furniture can contribute to earning this credit, but must also be included in the calculations for MR credits 3 through 7.

Contractors can use actual material cost for project (**excluding labor and equipment**) or they can use a 45 percent default value when completing calculations.

If only a portion of an assembled material is extracted, processed, and manufactured within 500 miles of the project, the contributing value is based on **weight**.

POINT DISTRIBUTION

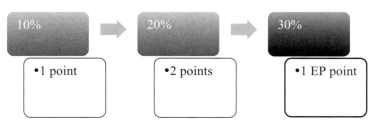

10%
- 1 point

20%
- 2 points

30%
- 1 EP point

EXEMPLARY PERFORMANCE

Implement at least 30 percent of total material cost, materials that are extracted, processed, and manufactured within 500 miles of the project site.

CONSTRUCTION	**MR Credit 6:**
	Rapidly Renewable Materials
	(NC and SCHOOLS)

PURPOSE

To increase the demand for _____ _____ materials to reduce the use and depletion of finite raw materials and materials with a _____ growth cycle.

REQUIREMENTS

Implement at least _____ percent (based on cost) of materials and products that are able to be regrown or harvested in less than _____ years.

CALCULATIONS

Materials from CSI Masterformat Divisions _____ to 10, 31 , and 32 are to be included in calculations.

Mechanical, electrical, and plumbing elements and _____ items are not eligible to contribute to earning this credit.

Furniture can contribute to earning this credit, but must also be _____ in the calculations for MR credits 3 through 7.

Contractors can use actual material cost for project (excluding labor and equipment) or they can use a _____ percent default value when completing calculations.

If only a portion of an assembled material is rapidly renewable, the contributing value is based on _____.

EXEMPLARY PERFORMANCE

Implement rapidly renewable materials with a cost of at least _____ percent of the total material cost for the project.

1 pt.	**RESPONSIBLE PARTY:**
	CONTRACTOR

	MR Credit 6: **Rapidly Renewable Materials** **(NC and SCHOOLS)**

ANSWER KEY

PURPOSE

To increase the demand for rapidly renewable materials to reduce the use and depletion of finite raw materials and materials with a long growth cycle.

REQUIREMENTS

Implement at least 2.5 percent (**based on cost**) of materials and products that are able to be regrown or harvested in less than **10 years**.

CALCULATIONS

Materials from CSI Masterformat Divisions 03 to 10, 31 , and 32 are to be included in calculations.

Mechanical, electrical, and plumbing elements and specialty items are not eligible to contribute to earning this credit.

Furniture can contribute to earning this credit, but must also be included in the calculations for MR credits 3 through 7.

Contractors can use actual material cost for project (excluding labor and equipment) or they can use a 45 percent default value when completing calculations.

If only a portion of an assembled material is rapidly renewable, the contributing value is based on weight.

EXEMPLARY PERFORMANCE

Implement rapidly renewable materials with a cost of at least 5 percent of the total material cost for the project.

CONSTRUCTION

MR Credit 7 (CS Credit 6):

Certified Wood

PURPOSE

To increase the demand for and encourage sustainably harvested renewable materials.

REQUIREMENTS

Implement at least _____ percent (based on cost) of new wood products certified by the Forest _____ Council (FSC).

CALCULATIONS

Only _____ installed _____ wood materials are to be included in calculations.

Furniture can contribute to earning this credit, but must also be _____ in the _____ for _____ credits 3–7.

Contractor will use the total _____ cost and not total _____ cost value when completing calculations.

Contractor will need to identify if wood products are FSC _____, FSC _____ Credit, or FSC Mixed (NN%).

DOCUMENTATION

_____-of-_____ documentation.

Invoices for _____ wood products purchased including percentage of certified wood.

EXEMPLARY PERFORMANCE

Implement rapidly renewable materials with a cost of at least _____ percent of the total material cost for the project.

REFERENCED STANDARD

_____ Stewardship _____'s Principles and Criteria

1 pt.

RESPONSIBLE PARTY:

CONTRACTOR

	MR Credit 7 (CS Credit 6):
	Certified Wood

ANSWER KEY

PURPOSE

To increase the demand for and encourage sustainably harvested renewable materials.

REQUIREMENTS

Implement at least 50 percent (based on cost) of new wood products certified by the Forest Stewardship Council (FSC).

CALCULATIONS

Only permanently installed **new wood** materials are to be included in calculations.

Furniture can contribute to earning this credit, but must also be included in the calculations for MR credits 3–7.

Contractor will use the total wood cost and not total material cost value when completing calculations.

Contractor will need to identify if wood products are FSC Pure, FSC Mixed Credit, or FSC Mixed (NN%).

DOCUMENTATION

Chain-of-custody documentation.

Invoices for new wood products purchased including percentage of certified wood.

EXEMPLARY PERFORMANCE

Implement rapidly renewable materials with a cost of at least 5 percent of the total material cost for the project.

REFERENCED STANDARD

Forest Stewardship Council's Principles and Criteria

CHAPTER 8

INDOOR ENVIRONMENTAL QUALITY

THIS CHAPTER FOCUSES ON THE ELEMENTS INVOLVED to improve the indoor environment as detailed in the Indoor Environmental Quality (EQ) category of the Leadership in Energy and Environmental Design (LEED™) rating systems. Remember that Chapter 2 introduced the importance of indoor environments, since Americans typically spend about 90 percent of their time indoors, according to the Environmental Protection Agency (EPA). The EPA also reports conventionally designed, constructed, and maintained indoor environments have significantly higher levels of pollutants than the outdoors.[1] However, studies have shown that green buildings with an improved interior environmental quality "have the potential to enhance the lives of building occupants, increase their resale value of the building, and reduce the liability for building owners."[2] Because employee salaries and benefits are typically the biggest cost for a business, larger than operating costs for facilities, such as utilities, the satisfaction and health of the occupants should be a high priority. Retaining employees in order to avoid the additional costs of training new hires can help to add efficiencies to the economic bottom line for businesses. Reducing absenteeism due to health impacts increases productivity and reduces liability of inadequate indoor environmental quality. Businesses, such as Haworth, will enjoy a return on their investment for increasing their employee satisfaction by providing a comfortable work environment (Figure 8.1). The BD+C LEED rating systems offer the following strategies to address to improve indoor environments:

It's time to pick a different color for flashcards created for EQ topics.

1. Indoor air quality
2. Thermal comfort
3. Lighting (natural and artificial)
4. Acoustics

Each of these strategies is referred to in the prerequisites and credits of the category, as seen in Table 8.1. Remember from the previous chapters to note when the prerequisite or credit is eligible to be submitted for review, at the end of design or construction. Notice only EQ Credits 3 and 4 can be submitted for review after substantial completion, while the prerequisites and all of the other credits can be submitted after construction documents are completed. Do not worry about remembering the exact credit name and number, but it is important to know which are credits versus prerequisites.

Create a flashcard to remember the four components of the EQ category.

Figure 8.1 Addressing such factors as daylighting, views, and low-emitting materials, helps to bring value to the indoor environmental quality. *Photo courtesy of Haworth Inc.*

Table 8.1 The Indoor Environmental Quality (EQ) Category

D/C	Prereq/Credit	Title	Points		
			NC	Schools	CS
D	Prereq 1	Minimum Indoor Air Quality Performance	R	R	R
D	Prereq 2	Environmental Tobacco Smoke (ETS) Control	R	R	R
D	Credit 1	Outdoor Air Delivery Monitoring	1	1	1
D	Credit 2	Increased Ventilation	1	1	1
C	Credit 3.1 (CS Credit 3)	Construction IAQ Management Plan—During Construction	1	1	1
C	Credit 3.2	Construction IAQ Management Plan—Before Occupancy	1	1	—
C	Credit 4.1	Low-Emitting Materials—Adhesives and Sealants	1	1	1
C	Credit 4.2	Low-Emitting Materials—Paints and Coatings	1	1	1
C	Credit 4.3	Low-Emitting Materials—Flooring Systems	1	1	1
C	Credit 4.4	Low-Emitting Materials—Composite Wood and Agrifiber Products	1	1	1
C	Credit 4.5	Low-Emitting Materials—Furniture and Furnishings	—	1	—
C	Credit 4.6	Low-Emitting Materials—Ceiling and Wall Systems	—	1	—
D	Credit 5	Indoor Chemical and Pollutant Source Control	1	1	1

D/C	Prereq/Credit	Title	Points		
			NC	Schools	CS
D	Credit 6.1	Controllability of Systems—Lighting	1	1	—
D	Credit 6.2 (CS Credit 6)	Controllability of Systems—Thermal Comfort	1	1	1
D	Credit 7.1 (CS Credit 7)	Thermal Comfort—Design	1	1	1
D	Credit 7.2	Thermal Comfort—Verification	1	1	—
D	Credit 8.1	Daylight and Views—Daylight	1	1	1
D	Credit 8.2	Daylight and Views—Views	1	1	1
D	Credit 9	Enhance Acoustical Performance	—	1	—
C	Credit 10	Mold Prevention	—	1	—

 Did you notice all of the credits within this category are only worth 1 point maximum?

INDOOR AIR QUALITY

The *LEED Reference Guide for Green Building Design and Construction* (BD+C) uses the American Society of Heating, Refrigerating, and Air-Conditioning Engineers' (ASHRAE's) definition for **indoor air quality** (IAQ) as it states it "is the nature of air inside the space that affects the health and well-being of building occupants."[3] Studies have shown that poor indoor air quality can lead to respiratory disease, allergies and asthma, and **sick building syndrome,** and can therefore impact the performance and productivity of employees. The LEED rating systems address components from a triple bottom line perspective, to improve air quality during construction and operations to avoid effects on human health and to improve the quality of life. In order to achieve this, the rating systems require project teams to address IAQ in terms of ventilation rates, construction practices, and minimizing exposure by prevention and segregation.

Ventilation Strategies in Relation to LEED Compliance

Project teams are encouraged to provide adequate ventilation for occupants without compromising energy use efficiencies, not to be a burden on the environment by contributing to the need for fossil fuels. Mechanical systems should work to thermally balance outdoor air with every air change; therefore, the key is to find the right balance. Too many air changes are wasteful and would impact economic and environmental bottom lines. However, too little ventilation can result in reduced quality of the indoor air, which would impact the health and satisfaction of occupants, thus also affecting the triple bottom line components. Therefore, project teams designing green buildings use the industry standard, **ASHRAE Standard 62.1, Ventilation for Acceptable Indoor Air Quality,** to adequately and appropriately size mechanical systems that will deliver the proper amounts of outside air while balancing energy demands. ASHRAE 62 describes proper **ventilation rates,** or the "amount of air circulated through a space, measured in air changes per hour."[4]

    EQ Prerequisite 1: Minimum Indoor Air Quality Performance. Just as with all the previous prerequisites described, this one sets a minimum level of performance required of all projects seeking LEED certification. The mechanical engineer should refer to ASHRAE 62.1-2007 or the local code (whichever is more

 Increasing ventilation may improve the overall IAQ, but it may increase the energy demand of heating, ventilation, and air conditioning (HVAC) systems at the same time. Therefore, it is important to recognize this category is about the occupants' well-being and not energy efficiency.

 TIP Any time you see ASHRAE 62, think IAQ! Say it out loud: IAQ 62, 62 IAQ!

stringent by requiring more outside air) to determine the outdoor air **ventilation rate** required to comply for a mechanically ventilated building. If the building has natural ventilation strategies, the mechanical engineer would consult paragraph 5.1 of ASHRAE 62.1. The standard addresses minimum requirements for ventilation rates in various building ventilation systems and types of occupied zones based on square footage, number of occupants and the associated activity, and the ventilation system itself. If the team is implementing a combination of natural and mechanical ventilation, or **mixed-mode ventilation,** these strategies are required to follow Chapter 6 of the referenced standard.

EQ Credit 1: Outdoor Air Delivery Monitoring. The mechanical engineer will need to develop a strategy to include carbon dioxide (CO_2) sensors to ensure that minimum requirements are maintained to help promote occupant comfort and well-being. The strategy must include provisions for an alarm (visual or audible) to be generated if the CO_2 levels vary by 10 percent or more in **densely occupied spaces** (25 people per 1,000 square feet). Compliance strategies could include using the building automation system (BAS) to monitor CO_2 levels. For mixed-mode and naturally ventilated buildings, the BAS could work with the windows to automatically open should the CO_2 levels reach unhealthy limits. For projects without a connection to a BAS, an audible or visual alarm could indicate that the windows should be opened to increase ventilation (Figure 8.2). Mechanically ventilated buildings could incorporate demand-controlled ventilation where airflow is increased if maximum setpoints are exceeded.

EQ Credit 2: Increased Ventilation. Building off of Prerequisite 1, project teams with mechanical or mixed-mode ventilation systems must increase the outdoor air supply to exceed the referenced standard or local code by at least 30 percent in order to meet the intentions of this credit. For naturally ventilated project types, the teams are directed to comply with the Carbon Trust's "Good Practice Guide 237." They will also need to complete the flow diagram process of Figure 1.18 as detailed in the Chartered Institution of Building Services Engineers (CIBSE) Applications Manual 10:2005, Natural Ventilation in Nondomestic Buildings. The mechanical engineer has two compliance paths from which to choose. Option 1 requires diagrams and calculations to prove the strategy's

> **TIP** Be sure to remember that CO_2 sensors must be located between 3 and 6 feet above the floor (the air we breathe). CO_2 concentrations greater than 530 parts per million (ppm) as compared to exterior environments are typically harmful to occupants.

Figure 8.2 Providing operable windows offers building occupants access to means of adequate ventilation. *Photo courtesy of Gary Neuenswander, Utah Agricultural Experiment Station*

effectiveness and compliance with the referenced standards, while option 2 requires an analytic model proving compliance with ASHRAE 62.1-2007, Chapter 6, for at least 90 percent of the occupied spaces. For the purposes of the exam, be sure to know how to comply, but not necessarily the details required to prove compliance, such as the details of the diagrams and calculations of CIBSE and the Good Practice Guide 237.

 Create a flashcard to remember the three ventilation strategies for improving indoor air quality.

QUIZ TIME!

Q8.1. Which of the following EQ credits are to be submitted after substantial completion and are not eligible for a design side review? (Choose two)

A. Credit 4: Low-Emitting Materials

B. Credit 2: Increased Ventilation

C. Credit 3: Construction IAQ Management Plan

D. Credit 1: Outdoor Air Delivery Monitoring

E. Credit 5: Indoor Chemical and Pollutant Source Control

Q8.2. Which of the following statements is not true? (Choose one)

A. All of the EQ credits are worth one point.

B. There are two prerequisites within the EQ category.

C. Although there are prerequisites within the EQ category, project teams only have to comply with at least one in order to pursue certification.

D. EQ prerequisites and credits intend to improve occupant well-being and comfort, and therefore productivity as well.

E. EQ credits may compensate energy efficiency of the project, but improve the indoor air quality.

Q8.3. What percentage above the referenced standard must the mechanical engineer increase the ventilation rate in order to comply with EQ Credit 2: Increased Ventilation? (Choose one)

A. 5 percent

B. 10 percent

C. 20 percent

D. 30 percent

E. 40 percent

Q8.4. What is considered a densely occupied area? (Choose one)

A. At least 10 people per 100 square feet

B. At least 25 people per 1,000 square feet

C. At least 25 people per 10,000 square feet

D. At least 25 people per 500 square feet

E. At least 15 people per 1,000 square feet

Q8.5. In order to comply with EQ Credit 1: Outdoor Air Delivery Monitoring, what should the alarm set points be set to? (Choose one)

A. +/– 1 percent

B. +/– 3 percent

C. +/– 5 percent

D. +/– 10 percent

E. +/– 15 percent

IAQ Practices during Construction in Relation to LEED Compliance

During construction, project teams should follow the practices recommended by the **Sheet Metal and Air Conditioning Contractors' National Association (SMACNA)** guidelines (Figure 8.3). Contractors need to be mindful of reducing or eliminating contaminants from entering the indoor environment, including mechanical systems, to deliver an environment with better air quality. Contaminants include **volatile organic compounds (VOCs),** carbon dioxide, particulates, and tobacco smoke. SMACNA guidelines recommend that VOCs from furniture, paints, adhesives, and carpets should be kept below defined maximum levels to avoid polluting the indoor environment (Figure 8.4). For the purposes of LEED, the indoor environment to be protected from high levels of VOCs includes any spaces where products and materials are applied on site and within the weather-proofing system.

Industry standards, such as Green Seal (for paints, coatings, adhesives, etc.), South Coast Air Quality Management District (SCAQMD) (for sealants), the Carpet and Rug Institute (CRI), and the FloorScore™ Program specify the

Figure 8.3 SMACNA-compliant practices include sealing off ductwork from dust and particulates.

Figure 8.4 Specifying materials with low to no VOCs helps to maintain good indoor air quality. *Photo courtesy of Sherwin-Williams*

maximum levels of VOCs, in grams per liter (g/L), not to be exceeded. Other standards, such as GREENGUARD and Scientific Certification Systems (SCS) Indoor Advantage, certify products, such as furniture, that do not off-gas harmful levels of pollutants.

The SMACNA guidelines also address ventilation as a means to maintain quality indoor air, as well as the requirements for filtration media at all air returns (Figure 8.5). The BD+C LEED rating systems follow suit with SMACNA practices and therefore, also recommend employing **Minimum Efficiency Reporting Value (MERV) filters** to ensure effectiveness. The rating of MERV filters ranges from 1 (lowest) to 16 (highest), where LEED requires a minimum of MERV 8 filters to be implemented at return air intake locations for compliance with one credit, while requiring MERV 13 filters in another.

The SMACNA guidelines also recommend good housekeeping practices during construction, to protect absorptive materials from moisture damage to later prevent the growth of toxic substances, such as mold. These materials, such as drywall, acoustic ceiling tiles, and carpet, should be stored in dry, elevated, and protected areas to avoid coming into contact with liquids (Figure 8.6).

 Create a flashcard to remember MERV and the 1–16 range of filters.

Figure 8.5 Installing MERV 8 filters or better will help to improve the indoor air quality by eliminating dust and particles. *Photo courtesy of Auld & White Constructors, LLC*

Figure 8.6 Elevating product storage protects against damage as suggested by SMACNA guidelines.

Create a flashcard to remember the 5 SMACNA standards: HVAC protection, source control, pathway interruption, housekeeping, and scheduling.

EQ Credit 3.1: Construction IAQ Management Plan—During Construction (CS Credit 3). Contractors will need to develop a Construction IAQ Management Plan to detail how the construction team will address the SMACNA guidelines during construction. The plan must include the strategies planned for the five SMACNA aspects: heating, ventilation, and air conditioning (HVAC) protection; source control; pathway interruption; housekeeping; and scheduling. The plan will also need to require any permanently installed air handlers that are used during the construction phase to have a minimum of a MERV 8 filter at each return air grille to protect the ductwork. The filtration media must be replaced prior to occupancy. LEED for Schools™ projects have the additional requirement to prohibit smoking within 25 feet of any entrances and inside the building once the building is enclosed. LEED for Core & Shell™ (LEED CS) projects that require tenants of the building to comply with an IAQ management plan are eligible to pursue an Exemplary Performance credit under the Innovation in Design (ID) category.

EQ Credit 3.2: Construction IAQ Management Plan—Before Occupancy (for NC and Schools). LEED for New Construction™ (LEED NC) and Schools project teams have the opportunity to decide which of the two compliance paths available to pursue for this credit. Typically, the decision is made because of limited time available in the schedule or the weather conditions at the time of year construction is completed. The first compliance path requires air quality testing in compliance with the EPA Compendium of Methods for the Determination of Air Pollutants in indoor air prior to occupancy to ensure nonharmful air levels for occupants. The reference guide lists the maximum concentration levels for contaminants, such as formaldehyde, particulates, total VOCs, 4-phenylcyclohexene (4-PCH), and carbon monoxide (CO) for the air quality testing to detect and determine compliance. If these contaminant levels are exceeded, the project has failed the test, the building must be flushed out, and then the air retested in order to prove compliance.

Remember, this credit is not available to LEED CS project teams, as base building construction typically does not include the finishing of the interiors in order for a flush-out or air quality testing to be implemented.

The other compliance path option requires conducting a building flush-out to eliminate any pollutants in the air caused by construction processes and activities. This compliance path requires the mechanical system to be flushed out with 14,000 cubic feet of outside air per square foot to remove residual contaminants prior to occupancy. The key to comply is to maintain an internal temperature of at least 60° F and for the relative humidity not to exceed 60 percent within the building. If the schedule does not permit project teams to complete the latter or if occupancy is desired, they could also comply if at least 3,500 cubic feet of outside air per square foot is delivered prior to occupancy and then once the space is occupied, ventilation is started three hours prior to occupancy each day and is continued during occupancy at a rate of 0.30 cubic feet per minute (cfm) per square foot until the 14,000 cubic feet of air have been delivered.

Low-Emitting Materials

The following credits have a few characteristics and commonalities to be remembered. First, in order to prove compliance, project teams are required to track and list all applicable products for each credit. The list would indicate that all products used are in compliance with the coordinating reference standard. Should a member of the construction team disregard the requirements and use a product out of compliance, the project team has the opportunity to pursue the credit with the VOC budget methodology. This option demonstrates that the overall VOC performance was ascertained.

The next two discussion points are specifically related to projects seeking LEED for school Schools certification. Although there are six-point opportunities available, school projects can be awarded only four points; therefore, project teams are required to choose the four with which they wish to comply. Finally, note that there is one reference standard listed for the majority of the credits

Make a flashcard to remember the referenced standard for School projects pursuing the EQ Credit 4 suite.

that school project types must comply with: California Department of Health Services Standard Practice for the Testing of Volatile Organic Emissions from Various Sources Using Small-Scale Environmental Chambers.

EQ Credit 4.1: Low-Emitting Materials—Adhesives and Sealants. For NC and CS projects, all adhesives, sealants, and sealant primers used within the building must comply with SCAQMD Rule 1168, while aerosol adhesives must comply with the Green Seal Standard for Commercial Adhesives, GS-36. School projects must comply with the California Department of Health Services Standard Practice for the Testing of Volatile Organic Emissions from Various Sources Using Small-Scale Environmental Chambers standard.

EQ Credit 4.2: Low-Emitting Materials—Paints and Coatings. For NC and CS projects, all paints and coatings must comply with the Green Seal Standard GS-11. Anticorrosive/antirust paints must comply with the Green Seal Standard GC-3, while wood finishes, floor coatings, stains, primers, and shellacs used inside the building must comply with SCAQMD Rule 1113. Just as with the previous credit, school projects must comply with the California Department of Health Services Standard Practice for the Testing of Volatile Organic Emissions from Various Sources Using Small-Scale Environmental Chambers standard.

EQ Credit 4.3: Low-Emitting Materials—Flooring Systems. For NC and CS projects, all carpet must comply with the Carpet and Rug Institute Green Label Plus program, and the carpet cushion must comply with the Carpet and Rug Institute Green Label program. Carpet adhesives must meet the requirements described in EQ Credit 4.1. The FloorScore™ Program standard is the compliance measure for all hard-surface flooring. Concrete, wood, bamboo, and cork floor finishes, such as stains and sealers, must be in compliance with EQ Credit 4.2 and meet SCAQMD Rule 1113. Tile-setting adhesives and grout must meet EQ Credit 4.1 and comply with SCAQMD Rule 1168. Just as with the previous two credits, school projects must comply with the California Department of Health Services Standard Practice for the Testing of Volatile Organic Emissions from Various Sources Using Small-Scale Environmental Chambers standard.

EQ Credit 4.4: Low-Emitting Materials—Composite Wood and Agrifiber Products. Composite wood and agrifiber products may also off-gas, and therefore must be evaluated for compliance with this credit. The BD+C reference guide defines composite wood and agrifiber products as "particleboard, medium-density fiberboard (MDF), plywood, wheatboard, strawboard, panel substrates and door cores."[5] These products, including oriented-strand board (OSB), are manufactured with resin products to bind the fibers to hold the products together and form the useful building material. To comply within the parameters of this credit, NC and CS projects with composite wood and agrifiber products cannot contain any added **urea-formaldehyde** resins, which off-gas at room temperature, to avoid contaminating the interior environment, and therefore avoid causing health problems. Although many exterior building products may contain **phenol-formaldehyde**, this resin off-gases only at high temperatures, and is therefore allowed within the confines of LEED compliance. Just as with the previous three credits, school projects must comply with the California Department of Health Services Standard Practice for the Testing of Volatile Organic Emissions from Various Sources Using Small-Scale Environmental Chambers standard.

EQ Credit 4.5: Low-Emitting Materials—Furniture and Furnishings (for Schools). Project teams have three compliance path options from which to choose when pursuing this credit addressing all desks, tables, and seats for students and

TIP The Green Seal standards contain either GS or GC prefixes.

TIP Hard-surface flooring included in the FloorScore Program addresses linoleum, ceramic flooring, laminate flooring, vinyl, wood flooring, rubber flooring, and wall base.

Notice the commonalities of SCAQMD Rules 1113 and 1168. On a similar note, which two credits share the requirements for carpet adhesive?

Create a flashcard to remember that urea-formaldehyde is not allowed, but phenol-formaldehyde is suitable.

Figure 8.7 Specifying GREENGUARD-certified furniture helps to maintain quality indoor air. *Photo courtesy of Steelcase, Inc.*

teachers. Furniture manufactured or refurbished within the year prior to occupancy are required to comply with one of the three compliance paths. The first option is to specify and install all GREENGUARD Children and Schools certified products (Figure 8.7). The second option is to specify and install furniture and seating that has passed the EPA Environmental Technology Verification (ETV) Large Chamber Test Protocol for Measuring Emissions of VOCs and Aldehydes test. The third and final option requires the furniture and seating to pass the ANSI/BIFMA M7.1 2007 and ANSI/BIFMA x7.1-2007 testing protocols.

EQ Credit 4.6: Low-Emitting Materials—Ceiling and Wall Systems (for Schools). When specifying gypsum board, insulation, wall coverings, and acoustic ceiling systems, project team members must ensure that the products comply with the California Department of Health Services Standard Practice for the Testing of Volatile Organic Emissions from Various Sources Using Small-Scale Environmental Chambers standard.

 Create a flashcard to remember what VOCs are, the different referenced standards, the types of VOCs, and that they are measured in grams per liter.

 Create a flashcard to remember the eight credits to pursue during construction to improve IAQ.

QUIZ TIME!

Q8.6. MERV filters range from which of the following? (Choose one)

    A. 1–30

    B. 0–50

    C. 1–110

    D. 1–16

    E. 1–100

Q8.7. Which of the following are the labeling standards applicable to carpets and carpet pads? (Choose two)

A. CRI Green Label+

B. Green-e

C. Green carpets

D. Green Seal

E. Green Seal 36

F. CRI Green Label

Q8.8. Which of the following are consistent with the requirements of EQ Credit 4.1: Low-Emitting Materials—Adhesives and Sealants? (Choose three)

A. All adhesives and sealants must not exceed the VOC limits set by ASHRAE 232-1998: Maximum VOC Emissions in Occupied Spaces with Recirculating Air.

B. Nonaerosol adhesives and sealants must be in compliance with VOC limits set by the SCAQMD Rule 1168.

C. Paints and coatings must contain no phenol-formaldehyde.

D. Adhesives and sealants must carry a Green Spec seal of approval.

E. Aerosol adhesives must meet VOC limits established by the Green Seal Standard (GS-36).

F. While projects are encouraged, but not required, to use low-VOC adhesives and sealants on exterior building elements, all adhesives and sealants inside of the building envelope weather seal must meet the requirements of the referenced standards.

Q8.9. SCAQMD Rule 1168 refers to which of the following? (Choose one)

A. Measures air-change effectiveness

B. Describes ventilation requirements for acceptable indoor air quality

C. Defines the use of urea- and phenol-formaldehyde in composite wood and agrifiber products

D. Sets the VOC maximum content for adhesives and sealants

E. Sets the VOC maximum content for paints and coatings

F. Defines the maximum VOC emissions from carpets and carpet cushions

Q8.10. Which of the following is not required by SMACNA standards? (Choose one)

A. Source control

B. Housekeeping

C. HVAC protection

D. Flush-out

E. Scheduling

Q8.11. How many maximum points can a school project seeking certification earn within the suite of EQ Credit 4? (Choose one)

A. 2 points maximum

B. 3 points maximum

C. 4 points maximum

D. 5 points maximum

E. 6 points maximum

Q8.12. How many credits within the EQ Credit 4 suite require compliance with California Department of Health Services Standard Practice for the Testing of Volatile Organic Emissions from Various Sources Using Small-Scale Environmental Chambers standard for projects seeking the LEED for Schools certification? (Choose one)

A. 4

B. 5

C. 6

D. 3

E. 2

Prevention and Segregation Methods in Relation to LEED Compliance

Assessing and managing indoor pollutants has become a major concern in the battle against sick building syndrome. If buildings can be designed with the ability of maintaining a safe and healthy environment, building occupants will be more productive and have a greater well-being. The following strategies address means to reduce contamination for a cleaner indoor environment.

EQ Prerequisite 2: Environmental Tobacco Smoke (ETS) Control. NC and CS project teams have a few options from which to choose in order to comply with this prerequisite, depending on the use of the project, whereas School projects have only one compliance path: option 1. Compliance with option 1 requires smoking to be prohibited in the building, and if smoking will be allowed on site, an area must be designated that is at least 25 feet away from any building entrances, outdoor air intakes, and operable windows. Option 2 allows NC and CS teams to permit smoking within the building, but only in designated areas. These areas must be separately exhausted to the outdoors, not to contaminate other areas in the building. This would require mechanical engineers to be mindful of those exhaust areas not to be located next to intake zones or building entrances. The rooms shall be enclosed with impermeable deck-to-deck partitions. Just as with option 1, if smoking will be allowed on site, an area must be designated that is at least 25 feet away from any building entrances, outdoor air intakes, and operable windows.

Residential and hospitality projects must prohibit smoking in all common areas within the building. All exterior doors and operable windows must be weather-stripped. All penetrations between units and vertical chases must be sealed to minimize contamination. Blower door tests must be conducted in accordance with ANSI/ASTM E779-03, Standard Test Method for Determining

Remember, EQ Credit 3.1: Construction IAQ Management Plan requires a minimum of a MERV 8 filter during construction, whereas this credit requires a MERV 13 filter to be installed after construction but prior to occupancy. If needed, make a flashcard to remember the minimum MERV filters required and for which credit.

Create a flashcard to remember the three strategies to improve IAQ by means of prevention and segregation.

Air Leakage Rate by Fan Pressurization for residential units to prove successful sealing. Continuing with the requirements mentioned for options 1 and 2, where smoking will be allowed outdoors, an area must be designated that is at least 25 feet away from any building entrances, outdoor air intakes, and operable windows.

EQ Credit 5: Indoor Chemical and Pollutant Source Control. Project teams will need to comply with four strategies in order to earn this credit. First, all regularly used entrances must employ an entryway system that is at least 10 feet long in the primary direction of travel to reduce the amount of dirt and contaminants from entering the building. Second, the team must ensure that any areas where hazardous gases or chemicals will be present are separately exhausted, are provided with self-closing doors, and are enclosed with deck-to-deck partitions or a hard-lid ceiling (not to contaminate adjacent spaces). These areas could include high-volume copy areas, laundry areas, laboratories, and art rooms. The mechanical engineer needs to ensure that the HVAC system will accommodate a MERV 13 filter or better. Finally, containment must be provided for any hazardous materials to be properly disposed of and separate drains at any locations where the mixing of hazardous materials occurs. It is important to remember this credit requires all four components to be adhered to, not just one or a combination of strategies in order to earn this credit.

EQ Credit 10: Mold Prevention (for Schools). In order to qualify for eligibility to pursue this credit, School project teams are also required to pursue three other EQ credits: EQ Credit 3.1: Construction IAQ Management Plan—During Occupancy, EQ Credit 7.1: Thermal Comfort—Design, and EQ Credit 7.2: Thermal Comfort—Verification. The mechanical engineer will need to design the HVAC system to achieve 60 percent or less humidity for all load conditions and occupancies. The team will need to also develop and implement an IAQ Management Plan for the operation and maintenance phases in accordance with the EPA document, *Building Air Quality: A Guide for Building Owners and Facility Managers.* The project should be designed to operate by eliminating the potential for condensation, especially for HVAC systems during dehumidification times, at pan and drain locations, and for humidification equipment that could potentially distribute mold. The project should properly address drainage during storms to avoid flooding, keep water away from the foundation, and maintain dry areas. Project teams should be mindful of climatic regions when specifying materials. For example, using carpet at entryways should be avoided in high-moisture areas. The plan should address the prevention of mold development during unoccupied periods and from leaking pipes or failed plumbing fixtures by inspection and commissioning activities.

QUIZ TIME!

Q8.13. Which of the following are standards for indoor air quality? (Choose three)

A. GREENGUARD

B. ASHRAE 90.1

C. CRI Green Label Plus

D. Green Seal

E. ENERGY STAR

Q8.14. What is the maximum level of humidity for which most project teams need to design, in order to comply with EQ Credit 10: Mold Prevention? (Choose one)

A. 45 percent

B. 50 percent

C. 60 percent

D. 65 percent

Q8.15. Which of the following are not required to comply with EQ Credit 5: Indoor Chemical and Pollutant Source Control? (Choose two)

A. MERV 18

B. MERV 13

C. Disposal containers and drains for hazardous waste

D. 10-foot-long entryway systems

E. 6-foot-long entryway systems

Q8.16. If smoking is going to be allowed on site, what is the minimum distance to designate smoking areas from building entrances, air intakes, and any operable windows in order to comply with EQ Prerequisite 2: ETS Control? (Choose one)

A. 10 feet

B. 15 feet

C. 20 feet

D. 25 feet

E. 50 feet

THERMAL COMFORT

Although temperature settings should vary with the seasons, buildings should allow for occupants to control their thermal conditions to optimize satisfaction and comfort. Remember, occupants who are satisfied and comfortable tend to be more productive! The *Green Building and LEED Core Concepts Guide* defines **thermal comfort** as "the temperature, humidity, and airflow ranges within which the majority of people are most comfortable, as determined by **ASHRAE Standard 55-2004.**"[6] ASHRAE 55 indicates that there are four environmental factors that impact thermal comfort determined by the building design: humidity, air speed, air temperature, and radiant temperature. For the purposes of LEED, occupants must be able to control one of the four components of thermal comfort in order to comply with the control strategy.

 TIP Anytime you see ASHRAE 55, think THERMAL COMFORT. What do you think of when you see ASHRAE 90.1? How about ASHRAE 62?

 Create a flashcard to remember the four environmental factors of thermal comfort defined by ASHRAE 55.

Thermal Comfort in Relation to LEED Compliance

EQ Credit 6.2: Controllability of Systems, Thermal Comfort (CS Credit 6). Project teams will need to provide access to control at least one of the four factors of thermal comfort for at least 50 percent of the building occupants in regularly

occupied areas to comply with this credit. Shared multioccupant areas, such as conference rooms, classrooms, or lecture halls, must have at least one method to control the thermal environment. Operable windows may be used for compliance instead of controls (Figure 8.8) if the occupants are located within 20 feet inside and no more than 10 feet side to side of the windows, and the windows comply with the requirements of ASHRAE 62.1-2007, paragraph 5.1, Natural Ventilation. Mechanically ventilated projects could implement a raised access floor for under-floor air distribution to comply with the intentions of this credit (Figure 8.9). CS projects may not have the opportunity to install a compliant system, but could be eligible if the base building is designed to accommodate a high level of occupant control for the tenant spaces.

EQ Credit 7.1: Thermal Comfort, Design (CS Credit 7). The mechanical engineer will need to ensure that the HVAC system is designed in accordance with ASHRAE 55-2004 in order to comply with the intentions of this credit. In

Figure 8.8 Wausau's LEED Silver facility in Wausau, Wisconsin, employs operable windows to give their employees access to fresh air. *Photo courtesy of Wausau Windows and Wall Systems*

Figure 8.9 Raised access floors provide the flexibility to grant occupants individual control of the amount of air supplied through diffusers for their thermal comfort. *Photo courtesy of Tate Access Floors, Inc.*

addition to the four building design factors of thermal comfort mentioned previously, the engineer will also need to address two other factors that are determined by occupancy: metabolic rate and clothing insulation. Natatoriums, or indoor swimming pool areas, for school projects must comply with the "typical Natatorium Design Conditions" as defined in Chapter 4 of the ASHRAE HVAC Applications Handbook. Just as mentioned in the previous credit, CS project teams need to ensure that tenant spaces will be able to meet the intentions of the credit in order to comply.

EQ Credit 7.2: Thermal Comfort, Verification (for NC and Schools). In addition to pursuing the previous credit, building owners will need to commit to conducting an anonymous occupant survey within 6 to 18 months after occupying the building to discover the overall satisfaction of the thermal comfort levels of the majority of the occupants to determine areas for improvement. A plan for corrective action must also be in place in order to comply with this credit. In order to ensure that building performance is in accordance with ASHRAE 55-2004, NC projects must also include a permanent monitoring system. Neither CS projects, nor residential projects are eligible to pursue this credit.

 Create a flashcard to remember the three credits that address thermal comfort.

QUIZ TIME!

Q8.17. When addressing thermal comfort, which two of the following are not addressed? (Choose two)

    A. Humidity

    B. Ventilation requirements

    C. Air movement

    D. Artificial light

    E. Average temperature

Q8.18. An Environmental Tobacco Smoke Control policy *best* addresses which of the following? (Choose one)

A. Providing ventilation requirements to effectively remove tobacco smoke

B. Providing dedicated smoking rooms 25 feet away from building entrances

C. Preventing tobacco smoke from contaminating indoor environments

D. Preventing tobacco smoke from entering the air occupied by nonsmokers

Q8.19. How long after occupancy should a thermal comfort survey be conducted in accordance with EQ Credit 7.2: Thermal Comfort, Verification? (Choose one)

A. Within 18 months

B. Within 12 months

C. Between 6 and 18 months

D. Between 6 and 12 months

E. Within 6 months

Q8.20. What is the minimum percentage of occupants that must have thermal control in order to comply with EQ Credit 7: Controllability of Systems, Thermal Comfort? (Choose one)

A. 10 percent

B. 25 percent

C. 90 percent

D. 50 percent

E. 75 percent

LIGHTING

TIP A study found students in daylit classrooms progressed 20 percent faster in math and 26 percent faster in reading as compared to students studying in artificially lit classrooms.[7]

The BD+C LEED rating systems address lighting in terms of naturally available daylight and artificially supplied light. When debating whether to incorporate daylighting strategies, project teams are advised to conduct a life-cycle cost analysis to determine the up-front costs and operational savings. For example, when using daylighting strategies, sensors could be installed to trigger alternative light sources when needed, which would impact up-front costs, although the costs can be offset by the energy saved during operations since less artificial light would be required. Daylighting can also result in improved occupant satisfaction and health due to access and connection to the exterior environment, also affecting the economic bottom line over time (Figure 8.10).

Besides daylighting, providing occupants with the ability to control their lighting needs can also benefit the triple bottom line. For example, occupant-controlled lighting contributes to employee satisfaction, as well as productivity, as light levels can be altered for specific tasks, needs, and preferences (Figure 8.11). Therefore, providing overall ambient light, as well as individual task lighting, is the best strategy to address lighting needs. Facilities can also see a reduction in energy usage for lighting needs by educating employees on the benefits of turning off fixtures after use.

Figure 8.10 A classroom at Northland Pines High School in Eagle River, Wisconsin, provides students and teachers accessibility to views of the outdoor environment, as well as daylighting to improve their satisfaction and productivity. *Photo courtesy of Hoffman, LLC*

Figure 8.11 Providing occupants with task lighting allows for more individual control of work environments to improve their satisfaction and productivity. *Photo courtesy of Skylar Nielson, 3Form*

Lighting in Relation to LEED Compliance

The BD+C rating systems offer the following three strategies to address lighting for projects seeking LEED certification:

EQ Credit 6.1: Controllability of Systems, Lighting (for NC and Schools). NC project teams will need to provide lighting controls for at least 90 percent of the building occupants and all shared multioccupant spaces. School project teams will also need to provide at least 90 percent of building occupants with individual lighting controls, but only in administrative offices or other (non-classroom) regularly occupied spaces. The classroom spaces must have controls to meet the needs of the group including general illumination and audio/visual needs.

EQ Credit 8.1: Daylight and Views, Daylight. Although each of the rating systems offer this credit, School projects are eligible for more points depending on the level of compliance. For NC and CS projects, teams must provide at least 75 percent of regularly occupied areas with daylight illumination to comply (Figure 8.12). School projects that provide classroom spaces with a minimum of 75 percent daylight will achieve one point and another point for providing 90 percent of the classroom spaces with daylight. If a School project delivers an additional 75 percent of daylight to all of the regularly occupied spaces they can pursue another point. All project types are eligible for an Exemplary Performance credit under the ID category. NC and CS projects that achieve 95 percent daylighting and School projects that provide 90 percent of their classrooms and 95 percent in all other regularly occupied areas are eligible to pursue an Exemplary Performance credit.

The most important factor for teams to address is consistent across all compliance path options for this credit: glare control. This strategy is important to address because avoiding it can hinder the productivity and comfort of the building occupants. Solar heat gain is another factor for teams to consider and address as it directly impacts energy efficiency. Different types of glass perform in different ways depending on how much light is reflected, absorbed, and transmitted. Transmitted light, or T_{vis}, and the amount of light absorbed impacts solar heat gain. For daylighting purposes, it is best to select glazing with a high T_{vis} to allow for the most amount of incident light to pass through the glazing. Therefore, project teams are challenged to find the balance between solar heat gain and T_{vis}.

All project teams can choose whether to pursue a performance-based or a prescriptive-based compliance path, similar to pursuing the energy performance prerequisite and credit within the EA category. The performance-based option includes a computer simulation demonstrating footcandle (fc) levels between 25 and 500 provided by daylight for the applicable spaces. The prescriptive path involves completing calculations to show compliance depending on top-lighting daylighting zones (using skylights) and side-lighting daylighting zones (using windows or glass doors). Top-lighting daylight strategies must include skylights with a minimum 0.5 visible light transmittance (VLT) for at least 3 to 6 percent of the roof area, and the distance between the skylights must not be more than 1.4 times the ceiling height. Only glazing areas 30 inches above the floor can be included in side-lighting daylight calculations. In this zone, the window-to-floor

 When one is designing, non–regularly occupied spaces should be placed at the core to allow offices, classrooms, and other regularly occupied areas to be placed along the window line.

 Remember, building orientation and passive design strategies impact the opportunity to utilize daylighting as an ambient light source. There is a direct relationship between the amount of vision glazing provided and the access to daylight and views.

TIP Project teams should design the overall illumination light level to be about 40 to 60 footcandles on an office work surface.

Figure 8.12 Providing interior environments with access to natural daylight not only improves the occupants' satisfaction and productivity levels, but also helps to reduce the need for artificial lighting to reduce operating costs. *Photo courtesy of Steelcase, Inc.*

ratio (WFR) multiplied by the VLT must be between 0.150 and 0.180 in order to comply with the requirements of this option. A third option is available for teams wishing to wait until the space is constructed in order to measure the actual light levels in the applicable spaces and a fourth option can be pursued to show compliance with this credit by combining any of the three other options.

EQ Credit 8.2: Daylight and Views, Views. Project teams will need to provide 90 percent of the regularly occupied areas with views to the exterior by the means of vision glazing in order to meet the requirements of this credit. Remember, vision glazing is the glass from 30 inches to 90 inches above the floor. Project teams will need to upload a plan view to show all of the perimeter glazing and a section view to depict the line of sight from the regularly occupied area to the perimeter glazing with the line of sight at 42 inches above the floor. CS project teams will need to prove tenant spaces have the opportunity to comply with the requirements in order to earn this credit.

 For private offices, all of the square footage may count toward credit compliance if 75 percent or more has a view to the exterior. This concept cannot be applied to multioccupant areas, as only the actual square footage compliant can be included in the calculations to achieve the minimum percentage threshold.

 Create a flashcard to remember the three EQ credits that address lighting.

Quiz Time!

Q8.21. What is the most common failure of daylighting strategies? (Choose one)

 A. Shallow floorplates

 B. Interior color schemes

 C. Shading devices

 D. Glare control

Q8.22. Which of the following are strategies to control glare? (Choose three)

 A. Blinds

 B. Louvers

 C. Light shelves

 D. Reflective glazing

 E. Building orientation

 F. Lower ceiling heights

Q8.23. In addition to addressing light levels, what are other strategies to be considered when designing for daylighting? (Choose three)

 A. Photovoltaic system energy contribution

 B. Direct beam penetration

 C. Integration with the electric lighting system

 D. Mechanical heat and cooling

 E. Interior color schemes

Q8.24. At what height is the line of sight drawn in section view in order to comply with EQ Credit 8.2: Daylight and Views, Views? (Choose one)

 A. 30 inches

 B. 32 inches

C. 34 inches

D. 36 inches

E. 42 inches

Q8.25. Which one of the following most closely represents an appropriate level of overall illumination on an office work surface, including daylighting, ambient artificial lighting, and task lighting? (Choose one)

A. 1–2 footcandles

B. 5–10 footcandles

C. 15–25 footcandles

D. 40–60 footcandles

E. 75–120 footcandles

F. 150–200 footcandles

ACOUSTICS

For those who have worked in an open plan office environment, there is an appreciation for attention to proper acoustic design components. The ability to communicate effectively, in person or via telecommunications, is impacted by the quality of acoustics. For educational environments, the LEED for Schools rating system addresses high-performance acoustic design for core learning spaces. Just as with thermal comfort and lighting controls, delivering high-performing interior acoustic environments adds to the satisfaction and well-being of building occupants and employees (Figure 8.13).

Acoustics in Relation to LEED Compliance

According to the BD+C Reference Guide, RT "is a measure of the amount of reverberation in a space and equal to the time required for the level of a study sound to decay by 60 dB after the sound has stopped. The decay rate depends on the amount of sound absorption in a room, the room geometry, and the frequency of the sound. RT is expressed in seconds."[8]

Remember, RT is calculated with the following four factors: volume of a room (in cubic feet), the square footage of interior surface area, sound absorption coefficients at 500-, 1,000-, and 2,000-Hertz frequencies for each fixed interior element, and the surface area for each fixed element.

Just as with commissioning and energy performance in the EA category and with IAQ performance for EQ Prerequisite 1 and Credit 2, acoustic strategies for LEED compliance are presented in a prerequisite and a credit opportunity for school projects to comply with. The only difference is the rating system, as the following two strategies are only included in the LEED for Schools rating system.

EQ Prerequisite 3: Minimum Acoustical Performance (for Schools). School project teams will need to consider the acoustic impacts of interior finishes, building geometry, and duct insulation that impact the ability for employees and staff to communicate and work effectively in order to comply with this third prerequisite. All core learning spaces will need to comply with the **reverberation time** (RT) requirements of ANSI Standard S12.60-2002, Acoustical Performance Criteria, Design Requirements and Guidelines for Schools. The background noise from HVAC systems must also be designed not to exceed 45 **dBA** (A-weighted decibel) in classrooms and other core learning areas. Depending on the size of the classrooms and core learning spaces, project teams will need to determine the compliance path to pursue. For these spaces of less than 20,000 cubic feet, the teams can either ensure 100 percent of the ceiling areas are finished with a materials with a **noise reduction coefficient** (NRC) of at least 0.70 or they can total the area of all acoustic absorbent surfaces exceeding the total ceiling area with materials with an NRC of at least 0.70. For core learning spaces larger than

Figure 8.13 Designing for proper acoustical performance also helps to improve the satisfaction and comfort levels of occupants by improving the ability to effectively communicate. *Photo courtesy of Steelcase, Inc.*

20,000 cubic feet, project teams are required to perform the calculations of ANSI Standard S12.60-2002 proving that all of the classrooms and core learning spaces have an RT of 1.5 seconds or less.

EQ Credit 9: Enhanced Acoustical Performance. Remember, the concept behind all of the prerequisites is to establish a baseline or minimum level of performance consistent for all LEED projects. Therefore, the two requirements of this credit build off of the requirements described for the prerequisite by specifically addressing sound transmission and background noise. For sound transmission compliance, the team must ensure that the building shell and the classroom and other core learning center partitions meet the **standard transmission class** (STC) requirements of ANSI Standard S12.60 and also ensure that windows within the core learning spaces have an STC rating of at least 35. For background noise compliance, project teams will need to exceed the requirements of the prerequisite and ensure that the background noise from HVAC systems is 40 dBA or less in all core learning spaces, whereas the prerequisite requires 45 dBA. Teams may pursue an Exemplary Performance credit under the ID category if the project's outdoor background noise level is 55 dBA for playground areas and 60 dBA for all

Although they have nothing to do with one another, both SRI and STC can be remembered as the higher the better in terms of performance! Do you remember what SRI refers to?

Create a flashcard to remember the two strategies to address acoustics in School projects.

other school grounds, including athletic fields. The project would also be eligible for an Exemplary Performance credit if the indoor noise level were 35 dBA.

QUIZ TIME!

Q8.26. A 60,000-square-foot existing timber frame building is undergoing a major renovation, including the addition of 140,000 square feet. This 200,000-square-foot renovation project reuses the existing structure, replaces single-pane windows with energy-efficient glazing manufactured in a nearby town, and installs salvaged wood floors donated from an adjacent property. Which of the following credits can the project team pursue? (Choose three)

A. MR Credit 7: Certified Wood

B. EQ Credit 4.4: Low-Emitting Materials, Composite Wood and Agrifiber Products

C. EA Credit 1: Optimize Energy Performance

D. MR Credit 5: Regional Materials

E. MR Credit 1: Building Reuse

Q8.27. Which of the following best describes the LEED strategy applicable to ASHRAE Standard 62.1-2007? (Choose one)

A. Exterior lighting levels

B. Thermal comfort by the means of controllability of systems

C. Environmental Tobacco Smoke (ETS) Control

D. Ventilation and indoor air quality

E. Building flush-out parameters and guidelines

Q8.28. A project team plans to use a raised access floor to include under-floor air distribution, allowing the use of floor-mounted operable diffusers at each workstation and therefore eliminating overhead ducts, thus maximizing the interior floor-to-ceiling height. The moderate supply air temperature required at the diffusers would reduce the amount of energy associated with cooling a consistently greater quantity of outside air needed to improve air quality. Which two LEED strategies are addressed? (Choose two)

A. Increased Ventilation

B. Construction IAQ Management

C. Regional Priority

D. Controllability of Systems: Thermal Comfort

E. Acoustical Performance

Q8.29. Which of the following design team deliverables and team members are most likely to play a significant role in achieving Construction IAQ Management Plan? (Choose two)

A. Project specifications

B. Civil engineer

C. Construction documents

D. Lighting designer

E. General contractor

F. Electrical engineer

Q8.30. To which standards should engineers design the ventilation systems for a LEED project? (Choose two)

A. ASHRAE 55

B. California Air Resources Board

C. ASHRAE 62.1

D. ASHRAE 90.1

E. ASTM 44

Q8.31. Which of the following strategies have proven to increase productivity and occupant satisfaction in green buildings? (Choose two)

A. Providing access to daylight

B. Selecting a site adjacent to a shopping center

C. Improving indoor air quality

D. Implementing a recycling program

E. Offering incentives for carpooling

Q8.32. A mid-sized hotel project plans on incorporating appropriate passive-solar orientation, geometry, and glazing to minimize summer cooling loads and to take advantage of the site's opportunities for winter solar gain. The building will be built from 8-inch-thick structural insulated panels (SIPs) with a pressed straw insulated core held together by the natural resins from the straw and using face sheets of exterior-grade oriented strand board (OSB) made from 100 percent preconsumer scrap wood and a phenol-formaldehyde-based resin. To which of the following LEED credits would these strategies contribute? (Choose three)

A. MR Credit 5: Regional Materials

B. EQ Credit 4.1: Low-Emitting Materials, Adhesives and Sealants

C. EA Credit 1: Optimized Energy Performance

D. EQ Credit 4.4: Low-Emitting Materials, Composite Wood

E. EA Credit 2: On-Site Renewable Energy

F. MR Credit 4: Recycled Content

Q8.33. Which of the following EQ credits are required to be submitted after substantial completion for certification review? (Choose two)

A. Credit 4: Low-Emitting Materials

B. Credit 2: Increased Ventilation

C. Credit 3: Construction IAQ Management Plan

D. Credit 8: Daylight and Views

E. Credit 1: Outdoor Air Delivery Monitoring

Q8.34. Which of the following is not used to calculate RT? (Choose one)

A. Surface area of fixed interior elements

B. Sound absorption coefficients for each interior fixed element

C. Volume of the room in cubic feet

D. NRC rating of each interior fixed element

E. Interior surface area (in square feet)

Q8.35. What are the following standard Hertz frequencies used to test reverberation times? (Choose three)

A. 500 Hz

B. 900 Hz

C. 1,000 Hz

D. 2,000 Hz

E. 1,500 Hz

Q8.36. What are some strategies schools can employ to reduce noise? (Choose three)

A. Use through-wall window units.

B. Locate computer equipment in separate rooms away from classrooms.

C. Specify and install low-NRC acoustic materials such as ceiling tiles.

D. Design HVAC systems with ductwork and diffusers away from teaching locations.

E. Use carpet tiles instead of a hard-surface flooring.

Q8.37. Which of the following is not related to EQ Credit 2: Increased Ventilation? (Choose one)

A. EA Prerequisite 1 and Credit 3: Fundamental and Enhanced Commissioning

B. EA Prerequisite 2 and Credit 1: Minimal and Enhanced Energy Performance

C. EQ Credit 7: Thermal Comfort

D. EA Credit 5: Measurement and Verification

E. EQ Credit 1: Outdoor Air Delivery Monitoring

Q8.38. How many components of EQ Credit 5: Indoor Chemical and Pollutant Source Control do project teams have to comply with in order to earn the point? (Choose one)

A. One

B. Two

C. Three

D. Four

E. Five

DESIGN	**EQ Prerequisite 1:** **Minimum Indoor Air Quality Performance**
	EQ Credit 2: **Increased Ventilation**

PURPOSE

Prerequisite:

To improve the indoor air quality in buildings to enhance the _____ and _____ - _____ of the occupants by establishing a _____ indoor air quality performance.

Credit:

To increase the_____ _____ _____ in buildings to enhance the comfort, well-being, and _____ of the occupants by providing _____ outdoor air ventilation.

REQUIREMENTS

Case 1: Mechanically Ventilated Buildings

Prerequisite:

> Comply with either the local code or _____ (whichever requires more outside air). For 62.1 - use the _____ _____ _____ which addresses both _____-related source contaminants and _____-related source contaminants. Ventilation rates are determined by the number of occupants and their activities for the former and background off-gassing for the latter.

> **CS Projects Additional Requirement** - Systems must be able to meet ventilation levels based on _____ requirements.

Credit:

> Provide at least _____ percent more outdoor air than that required by the Prerequisite.

Case 2: Naturally Ventilated Buildings

Prerequisite:

> Comply with either the _____ _____ or ASHRAE 62.1 - 2007 (whichever requires more outside air). For 62.1 - comply with the requirements for the location and _____ of ventilation openings.   Complying spaces must be within 25 feet of operable wall or roof openings and opening must be at least _____ percent of space's net occupied floor area. Other spaces without direct access comply if openings are not obstructed and at least _____ percent or 25 square feet of the area is free.

Credit: Meet recommendations of _____ Trust "Good Practice Guide _____" for occupied spaces and one of the following options:

> Option 1: Design building to meet recommendations described in _____ Applications Manual 10

> Option 2: Predict _____-by-_____ airflows with an analytic model to meet the minimum ventilation rates required by ASHRAE 62.1 - 2007 for at least _____ percent of the occupied spaces.

CALCULATIONS (for mechanically ventilated spaces)

_____ Zone Outdoor Airflow (vbz) = required design outdoor airflow in the breathing zone of an occupied space

> $$vbz = Rp \times Pz + Ra \times Az$$

> Rp = outdoor airflow rate required/person

> Pz = zone population

> Ra = outdoor airflow rate

> Az = zone floor area

Zone _____ Airflow (Voz) = the outdoor airflow required for the zone for the supply air distribution system

> $$Voz = \frac{Vbz}{Ez}$$

> Ez = zone air distribution effectiveness

REFERENCED STANDARDS

ASHRAE Standard 62.1 - 2007, _____ for Acceptable Indoor Air Quality

_____ Applications Manual 10 -2005, Natural Ventilation in Non-Domestic Buildings

1 pt. for credit	**RESPONSIBLE PARTY:** **MEP ENGINEER**

ANSWER KEY

PURPOSE

Prerequisite:

To improve the indoor air quality in buildings to enhance the comfort and well-being of the occupants by establishing a minimum indoor air quality performance.

Credit:

To increase the indoor air quality in buildings to enhance the comfort, well-being, and productivity of the occupants by providing additional outdoor air ventilation.

REQUIREMENTS

Case 1: Mechanically Ventilated Buildings

Prerequisite:

> Comply with either the local code or ASHRAE 62.1 - 2007 (whichever requires more outside air). For 62.1 - use the Ventilation Rate Procedure which addresses both people-related source contaminants and area-related source contaminants. Ventilation rates are determined by the number of occupants and their activities for the former and background off-gassing for the latter.

> **CS Projects Additional Requirement** - Systems must be able to meet ventilation levels based on tenant requirements.

Credit:

> Provide at least 30 percent more outdoor air than that required by the Prerequisite.

Case 2: Naturally Ventilated Buildings

Prerequisite:

> Comply with either the local code or ASHRAE 62.1 - 2007 (whichever requires more outside air). For 62.1 - comply with the requirements for the location and size of ventilation openings. Complying spaces must be within 25 feet of operable wall or roof openings and opening must be at least 4 percent of space's net occupied floor area. Other spaces without direct access comply if openings are not obstructed and at least 8 percent or 25 square feet of the area is free.

Credit: Meet recommendations of Carbon Trust "Good Practice Guide 237" for occupied spaces and one of the following options:

> Option 1: Design building to meet recommendations described in CIBSE Applications Manual 10

> Option 2: Predict room-by-room airflows with an analytic model to meet the minimum ventilation rates required by ASHRAE 62.1 - 2007 for at least 90 percent of the occupied spaces.

CALCULATIONS (for mechanically ventilated spaces)

Breathing Zone Outdoor Airflow (vbz) = required design outdoor airflow in the breathing zone of an occupied space

$$vbz = Rp \times Pz + Ra \times Az$$

Rp = outdoor airflow rate required/person

Pz = zone population

Ra = outdoor airflow rate

Az = zone floor area

Zone Outdoor Airflow (Voz) = the outdoor airflow required for the zone for the supply air distribution system

$$Voz = \frac{Vbz}{EZ}$$

Ez = zone air distribution effectiveness

REFERENCED STANDARDS

ASHRAE Standard 62.1 - 2007, Ventilation for Acceptable Indoor Air Quality

CIBSE Applications Manual 10 -2005, Natural Ventilation in Non-Domestic Buildings

DESIGN	**EQ Prerequisite 2:**
	Environmental Tobacco Smoke (ETS) Control

PURPOSE

NC and CS: To _____ or minimize environmental _____ smoke (ETS) from contaminating the indoor environment including occupants, _____, and ventilation systems.

SCHOOLS: To _____ environmental tobacco smoke (ETS) from contaminating the indoor environment including occupants, surfaces, and _____ systems.

REQUIREMENTS

Option 1: All project types

Do not allow smoking in the building.

Provide a _____ smoking area on site that is at least _____ feet away from any building entrances, outdoor air intakes, and operable windows.

Option 2: NC & CS

Do not allow smoking within the building except in dedicated areas with _____ and isolated ventilation and exhaust systems. Interior smoking areas also must have _____ deck-to-deck partitions.

Provide a dedicated smoking area on site that is at least _____ feet away from any building entrances, outdoor air _____, and _____ windows.

Option 3: Residential and Hospitality Projects Only

Do not allow smoking in the common areas of the building.

Provide a dedicated exterior smoking area on site that is at least 25 feet away from any building entrances, _____ air intakes, and operable windows (this includes balconies as well).

_____ all openings and seal all penetrations in each unit.

Conduct a _____ door test in accordance with reference standard to demonstrate acceptable sealing of units.

DOCUMENTATION

Smoking Policy and designated smoking areas shown on a plan

REFERENCED STANDARD

ANSI/ASTM _____, Standard Test Method for Determining Air Leakage Rate by Fan Pressurization

Residential Manual for Compliance with California's 2001 Energy Efficiency Standards (for Low-Rise Residential Buildings), Chapter 4

Required	**RESPONSIBLE PARTY:**
	OWNER/DEVELOPER

EQ Prerequisite 2: **Environmental Tobacco Smoke (ETS) Control**

ANSWER KEY

PURPOSE

NC and CS: To prevent or minimize environmental tobacco smoke (ETS) from contaminating the indoor environment including occupants, surfaces, and ventilation systems.

SCHOOLS: To eliminate environmental tobacco smoke (ETS) from contaminating the indoor environment including occupants, surfaces, and ventilation systems.

REQUIREMENTS

Option 1: All project types

Do not allow smoking in the building.

Provide a dedicated smoking area on site that is at least 25 feet away from any building entrances, outdoor air intakes, and operable windows.

Option 2: NC & CS

Do not allow smoking within the building except in dedicated areas with separate and isolated ventilation and exhaust systems. Interior smoking areas also must have impermeable deck-to-deck partitions.

Provide a dedicated smoking area on site that is at least 25 feet away from any building entrances, outdoor air intakes, and operable windows.

Option 3: Residential and Hospitality Projects Only

Do not allow smoking in the common areas of the building.

Provide a dedicated exterior smoking area on site that is at least 25 feet away from any building entrances, outdoor air intakes, and operable windows (this includes balconies as well).

Weatherstrip all openings and seal all penetrations in each unit.

Conduct a blower door test in accordance with reference standard to demonstrate acceptable sealing of units.

DOCUMENTATION

Smoking Policy and designated smoking areas shown on a plan

REFERENCED STANDARD

ANSI/ASTM E779-03, Standard Test Method for Determining Air Leakage Rate by Fan Pressurization

Residential Manual for Compliance with California's 2001 Energy Efficiency Standards (for Low-Rise Residential Buildings), Chapter 4

DESIGN	EQ Prerequisite 3:
	Minimum Acoustical Performance (SCHOOLS)

	EQ Credit 9:
	Enhanced Acoustical Performance (SCHOOLS)

PURPOSE

To improve _____ in the classroom for teachers and _____ by addressing classroom acoustic design.

REQUIREMENTS

Prerequisite:

Provide sufficient sound-absorptive finishes as detailed by _____ Standard S12.60-2002, for _____ learning spaces, such as classrooms.

HVAC systems must have a background noise level of _____ dBA maximum.

Case 1: Core Learning Areas Less Than _____ Cubic Feet:

Option 1: _____ percent of ceiling areas (not including return air grilles, lights, and diffusers) must be finished with a material with a noise reduction coefficient of _____ or higher.

Option 2: Calculate total area of acoustic wall panels, ceiling finishes, and other sound-absorbent finishes to confirm that the area meets or exceeds the total ceiling area of the room. Materials in calculation must have a noise reduction coefficient of 0.70 or higher.

Case 2: Core Learning Areas Greater Than or Equal to _____ Cubic Feet:

_____ time for core learning areas must be _____ seconds or less according to calculations per reference standard.

Credit:

_____ Transmission: Provide building envelope and core learning area partitions that meet the _____ transmission class (STC) requirements of ANSI Standard _____-2002. The minimum STC for windows is _____.

Background Noise: HVAC systems must have a background noise level of _____ dBA maximum (5 dBA better than the prereq).

CALCULATIONS

Reverberation time (RT) factors:

Volume (in cubic feet).

_____ surface area (in square feet).

Sound-absorbent coefficients at _____-Hz, 1,000-Hz, and _____-Hz frequencies for each interior _____ element.

_____ area of interior fixed element.

REFERENCED STANDARDS

ANSI Standard S12.60 - 2002, _____ Performance Criteria, Design Requirements, and Guidelines for Schools

_____ Handbook, Chapter 47, Sound and Vibration Control, 2003 HVAC Applications

1 pt. for credit	RESPONSIBLE PARTY:
	ACOUSTICAL ENGINEER

EQ Prerequisite 3:

Minimum Acoustical Performance (SCHOOLS)

EQ Credit 9:

Enhanced Acoustical Performance (SCHOOLS)

ANSWER KEY

PURPOSE

To improve communication in the classroom for teachers and students by addressing classroom acoustical design.

REQUIREMENTS

Prerequisite:

Provide sufficient sound-absorptive finishes as detailed by ANSI Standard S12.60-2002, for core learning spaces, such as classrooms.

HVAC systems must have a background noise level of **45 dBA maximum**.

Case 1: Core Learning Areas Less Than 20,000 Cubic Feet:

Option 1: 100 percent of ceiling areas (not including return air grilles, lights and diffusers) must be finished with a material with a noise reduction coefficient of 0.70 or higher.

Option 2: Calculate total area of acoustic wall panels, ceiling finishes, and other sound-absorbent finishes to confirm the area meets or exceeds the total ceiling area of the room. Materials in calculation must have a noise reduction coefficient of 0.70 or higher.

Case 2: Core Learning Areas Greater Than or Equal to 20,000 Cubic Feet:

Reverberation time for core learning areas must be 1.5 seconds or less according to calculations per reference standard.

Credit:

Sound Transmission: Provide building envelope and core learning area partitions that meet the sound transmission class (STC) requirements of ANSI Standard S12.60-2002. The minimum STC for windows is 35.

Background Noise: HVAC systems must have a background noise level of 40 dBA maximum (5 dBA better than the prereq).

CALCULATIONS

Reverberation time (RT) factors:

Volume (in cubic feet).

Interior surface area (in square feet).

Sound-absorbent coefficients at 500-Hz, 1,000-Hz, and 2,000-Hz frequencies for each interior fixed element.

Surface area of interior fixed element.

REFERENCED STANDARDS

ANSI Standard S12.60-2002, Acoustical Performance Criteria, Design Requirements, and Guidelines for Schools

ASHRAE Handbook, Chapter 47, Sound and Vibration Control, 2003 HVAC Applications

DESIGN	EQ Credit 1:
	Outdoor Air Delivery Monitoring

PURPOSE

Promote occupant comfort and well-being by providing ventilation system _____.

REQUIREMENTS

Provide _____ monitoring _____ sensors within the breathing zone (_____ to _____ feet above the floor) for all _____ occupied spaces for mechanically ventilated buildings and all spaces within a naturally ventilated building.

Sensors must provide an audible or visual alarm if CO_2 conditions vary by more than _____ percent.

Outdoor _____ rates must also be monitored to ensure ventilation effectiveness.

REFERENCED STANDARD

ASHRAE Standard _____ - 2007, Ventilation for _____ Indoor Air Quality

1 pt.	**RESPONSIBLE PARTY:**
	MECHANICAL ENGINEER

EQ Credit 1:
Outdoor Air Delivery Monitoring

ANSWER KEY

PURPOSE

Promote occupant comfort and well-being by providing ventilation system monitoring.

REQUIREMENTS

Provide permanent monitoring CO_2 sensors within the **breathing zone** (3 to 6 feet above the floor) for all densely occupied spaces for mechanically ventilated buildings and all spaces within a naturally ventilated building.

Sensors must provide an audible or visual alarm if CO_2 conditions vary by more than **10 percent**.

Outdoor airflow rates must also be monitored to ensure ventilation effectiveness.

REFERENCED STANDARD

ASHRAE Standard 62.1 - 2007, Ventilation for Acceptable Indoor Air Quality

CONSTRUCTION	**EQ Credit 3 (CS) and 3.1:**
	Construction IAQ Management Plan,
	During Construction

PURPOSE

Promote occupant _____ and well-being by reducing _____ air quality problems caused during _____.

REQUIREMENTS

Create and implement an _____ management plan during construction to comply with _____ IAQ Guidelines.

All _____ materials must be protected from _____ damage whether they are installed or stored on site.

Use a minimum of MERV _____ filters at all _____ air grilles for any permanently installed air handlers used during construction, per ASHRAE Standard _____. All filters to be replaced prior to occupancy.

_____ **Additional Requirement:** Once the building is enclosed, smoking must not be allowed within the facility and within _____ feet of any entrance.

STRATEGIES

_____ Guidelines:

Source Control

Pathway Interruption

_____

_____

HVAC Protection

EXEMPLARY PERFORMANCE

For _____ projects:

Require future tenants to implement a construction IAQ management plan during interior improvements for _____ percent of the tenant spaces.

REFERENCED STANDARDS

_____ Metal and Air Conditioning Contractors National Association (SMACNA) IAQ Guidelines for Occupied Buildings Under _____ 2nd Edition 2007, ANSI/SMACNA 008-2008 (Chapter 3)

ANSI/ASHRAE Standard 52.2 - 1999: Method of Testing General Ventilation Air-Cleaning Devices for Removal Efficiency by _____ Size

1 pt.

RESPONSIBLE PARTY:

CONTRACTOR

EQ Credit 3 (CS) and 3.1:

Construction IAQ Management Plan,

During Construction

ANSWER KEY

PURPOSE

Promote occupant comfort and well-being by reducing indoor air quality problems caused during construction.

REQUIREMENTS

Create and implement an IAQ management plan during construction to comply with SMACNA IAQ Guidelines.

All absorptive materials must be protected from moisture damage whether they are installed or stored on site.

Use a minimum of **MERV 8 filters** at all return air grilles for any permanantly installed air handlers used during construction, per ASHRAE Standard 52.2. All filters to be replaced prior to occupancy.

SCHOOLS Additional Requirement: Once the building is enclosed, smoking must not be allowed within the facility and within 25 feet of any entrance.

STRATEGIES

SMACNA Guidelines:

> Source Control
>
> Pathway Interruption
>
> Housekeeping
>
> Scheduling
>
> HVAC Protection

EXEMPLARY PERFORMANCE

For CS projects:

> Require future tenants to implement a construction IAQ management plan during interior improvements for 100 percent of the tenant spaces.

REFERENCED STANDARDS

Sheet Metal and Air Conditioning Contractors National Association (SMACNA) IAQ Guidelines for Occupied Buildings Under Construction, 2nd Edition 2007, ANSI/SMACNA 008-2008 (Chapter 3)

ANSI/ASHRAE Standard 52.2 - 1999: Method of Testing General Ventilation Air-Cleaning Devices for Removal Efficiency by Particle Size

CONSTRUCTION

EQ Credit 3.2:

Construction IAQ Management Plan,

Before Occupancy (NC and SCHOOLS)

PURPOSE

Promote occupant _____ and well-being by reducing _____ air quality problems caused during _____.

REQUIREMENTS

Option 1:
Flush-out

Provide _____ cubic feet of outside air per square foot of floor area maintaining an average of 60°F with a maximum of _____ percent relative humidity.

If occupancy is desired, provide at least _____ cubic feet of outside air per square foot of floor area. After occupancy, begin ventilation at least 3 hours prior to occupancy each day at a minimum rate of _____ cubic feet per minute per square foot of outside air (or the design minimum of EQ Prerequisite 1 - whichever is greater) until _____ cubic feet of outside air per square foot of floor area has been delivered.

Option 2: Air Testing

Complete testing after _____ but prior to _____ in accordance with the protocols of the reference standard.

Samples must be collected within _____ zone for at least _____ hours in areas with the _____ amount of ventilation.

If contaminant levels exceed threshold, the project may fail the test. If this is the case, the space will need to be _____ _____ and _____.

REFERENCED STANDARD

U.S. EPA _____ of Methods for the Determination of Air _____ in Indoor Air

1 pt.

RESPONSIBLE PARTY:

CONTRACTOR

EQ Credit 3.2:

Construction IAQ Management Plan,

Before Occupancy (NC and SCHOOLS)

ANSWER KEY

PURPOSE

Promote occupant comfort and well-being by reducing indoor air quality problems caused during construction.

REQUIREMENTS

Option 1: Flush-out

Provide **14,000 cubic feet** of outside air per square foot of floor area maintaining an average of **60°F** with a maximum of **60 percent** relative humidity.

If occupancy is desired, provide at least 3,500 cubic feet of outside air per square foot of floor area. After occupancy, begin ventilation at least 3 hours prior to occupancy each day at a minimum rate of 0.30 cubic feet per minute per square foot of outside air (or the design minimum of EQ Prerequisite 1 - whichever is greater) until 14,000 cubic feet of outside air per square foot of floor area has been delivered.

Option 2: Air Testing

Complete testing after construction but prior to occupancy in accordance with the protocols of the reference standard.

Samples must be collected within breathing zone for at least 4 hours in areas with the least amount of ventilation.

If contaminant levels exceed threshold, the project may fail the test. If this is the case, the space will need to be flushed out and retested.

REFERENCED STANDARD

U.S. EPA Compendium of Methods for the Determination of Air Pollutants in Indoor Air

CONSTRUCTION

EQ Credit 4.1:

Low-Emitting Materials,

Adhesives and Sealants

PURPOSE

To limit the amount of _____, irritating, and/or harmful contaminants used _____ to enhance the _____ and well-being of _____ and occupants.

REQUIREMENTS

NC and CS:

_____, sealants, and sealant _____ must not exceed the VOC limits of SMACNA _____.

Aerosol adhesives must not exceed the VOC limits of Green Seal Standard 36.

SCHOOLS:

Adhesives and _____' must comply with the _____ Department of Health Services Standard Practice for the Testing of Volatile Organic Emissions from Various Sources Using _____-Scale Environmental Chambers.

DOCUMENTATION

Contractor to submit a schedule of all adhesives, sealants, and sealant primers used on the interior of the space (inside of the _____ system and applied on site) with VOC level expressed in _____.

If not all products comply, contractor is to submit a _____ _____ to prove the _____ of all products comply.

REFERENCED STANDARDS

NC and CS:

South _____ Air Quality _____ District (SCAQMD) Rule #1168

Green Seal Standard 36

SCHOOLS:

California Department of _____ Services Standard Practice for the Testing of _____ Organic _____ from Various Sources Using Small-Scale Environmental Chambers

1 pt.

RESPONSIBLE PARTY:

CONTRACTOR

	EQ Credit 4.1:
	Low-Emitting Materials,
	Adhesives and Sealants

ANSWER KEY

PURPOSE

To limit the amount of odorous, irritating, and/or harmful contaminants used indoors to enhance the comfort and well-being of installers and occupants.

REQUIREMENTS

NC and CS:

Adhesives, sealants, and sealant primers must not exceed the VOC limits of **SMACNA 1168**.

Aerosol adhesives must not exceed the VOC limits of **Green Seal Standard 36**.

SCHOOLS:

Adhesives and sealants must comply with the California Department of Health Services Standard Practice for the Testing of Volatile Organic Emissions from Various Sources Using Small-Scale Environmental Chambers.

DOCUMENTATION

Contractor to submit a schedule of all adhesives, sealants, and sealant primers used on the interior of the space (inside of the weatherproofing system and applied on site) with VOC level expressed in **g/L**.

If not all products comply, contractor is to submit a VOC budget to prove the average of all products complies.

REFERENCED STANDARDS

NC and CS:

South Coast Air Quality Management District (SCAQMD) Rule #1168

Green Seal Standard 36

SCHOOLS:

California Department of Health Services Standard Practice for the Testing of Volatile Organic Emissions from Various Sources Using Small-Scale Environmental Chambers

CONSTRUCTION	**EQ Credit 4.2:**
	Low-Emitting Materials,
	Paints and Coatings

PURPOSE

To limit the amount of _____, irritating, and/or harmful contaminants used _____ to enhance the _____ and well-being of _____ and occupants.

REQUIREMENTS

NC and CS:

_____ and coatings must not exceed the VOC limits of Green _____ Standard _____.

Anticorrosive and _____ paints must not exceed the VOC limits of _____ Seal Standard _____.

Clear wood finishes, _____ _____, stains, primers, and shellacs applied to interior surfaces must not exceed the VOC limits of SMACNA #_____.

SCHOOLS:

Paints and _____ must comply with the _____ Department of Health Services Standard Practice for the Testing of Volatile Organic Emissions from Various Sources Using _____-Scale Environmental Chambers.

DOCUMENTATION

Contractor to submit a schedule of all _____ and _____ used on the interior of the space (inside of the weatherproofing system and applied _____ _____) with _____ level expressed in g/L.

If not all products comply, contractor is to submit a VOC budget to prove the average of all products complies.

REFERENCED STANDARDS

NC and CS:

South Coast Air Quality Management District (SCAQMD) Rule #1113

_____ _____ Standard 11 (GS-11)

Green Seal Standard _____ (_____-_____)

SCHOOLS:

California Department of _____ Services Standard Practice for the Testing of _____ Organic _____ from Various Sources Using Small-Scale Environmental Chambers.

1 pt.	**RESPONSIBLE PARTY:**
	CONTRACTOR

EQ Credit 4.2:

Low-Emitting Materials,

Paints and Coatings

ANSWER KEY

PURPOSE

To limit the amount of odorous, irritating, and/or harmful contaminants used indoors to enhance the comfort and well-being of installers and occupants.

REQUIREMENTS

NC and CS:

Paints and coatings must not exceed the VOC limits of Green Seal Standard **GS-11**.

Anticorrosive and antirust paints must not exceed the VOC limits of Green Seal Standard **GC-3**.

Clear wood finishes, floor coatings, stains, primers, and shellacs applied to interior surfaces must not exceed the VOC limits of **SMACNA #1113**.

SCHOOLS:

Paints and coatings must comply with the California Department of Health Services Standard Practice for the Testing of Volatile Organic Emissions from Various Sources Using Small-Scale Environmental Chambers.

DOCUMENTATION

Contractor to submit a schedule of all paints and coatings used on the interior of the space (inside of the weatherproofing system and applied on site) with VOC level expressed in g/L.

If not all products comply, contractor is to submit a VOC budget to prove the average of all products complies.

REFERENCED STANDARDS

NC and CS:

South Coast Air Quality Management District (SCAQMD) Rule #1113

Green Seal Standard 11 (GS-11)

Green Seal Standard 3 (GC-3)

SCHOOLS:

California Department of Health Services Standard Practice for the Testing of Volatile Organic Emissions from Various Sources Using Small-Scale Environmental Chambers

CONSTRUCTION	EQ Credit 4.3:
	Low-Emitting Materials,
	Flooring Systems

PURPOSE

To limit the amount of _____, irritating, and/or harmful contaminants used _____ to enhance the _____ and well-being of _____ and occupants.

REQUIREMENTS

NC and CS:

All _____ must comply with The Carpet and Rug Institute (CRI) Green Label _____ program.

All carpet _____ must comply with The Carpet and Rug Institute (CRI) _____ Label program.

All carpet adhesive must comply with the requirements of EQ Credit _____: Adhesives and Sealants.

All _____ surface flooring must comply with the requirements of the _____ standard and be certified by an independent third party. Hard surface flooring includes vinyl, _____, laminate, wood, ceramic, rubber, and _____ base.

Concrete, _____, bamboo, and cork floor finishes (sealer, _____, and finish) must not exceed the VOC limits of SMACNA #_____.

Tile setting adhesives and grout must not exceed the VOC limits of SMACNA #_____.

SCHOOLS:

All _____ products must comply with the _____ Department of Health Services Standard Practice for the Testing of _____ Organic Emissions from Various Sources Using Small-Scale Environmental Chambers.

DOCUMENTATION

Contractor to submit a schedule of all flooring products, _____, grout, and finishes used on the project and documentation proving compliance, including _____ levels.

REFERENCED STANDARDS

NC and CS:

The Carpet and Rug Institute (CRI) Green Label Plus Testing Program

South Coast Air Quality Management District (SCAQMD) Rule #1168

South Coast Air Quality Management District (SCAQMD) Rule #1113

FloorScore Program

SCHOOLS:

California Department of Health Services Standard Practice for the Testing of Volatile Organic Emissions from Various Sources Using Small-Scale Environmental Chambers

1 pt.

RESPONSIBLE PARTY:

CONTRACTOR

EQ Credit 4.3:

Low-Emitting Materials,

Flooring Systems

ANSWER KEY

PURPOSE

To limit the amount of odorous, irritating, and/or harmful contaminants used indoors to enhance the comfort and well-being of installers and occupants.

REQUIREMENTS

NC and CS:

All carpet must comply with **CRI Green Label Plus** program.

All carpet cushion must comply with **CRI Green Label** program.

All carpet adhesive must comply with the requirements of EQ Credit 4.1: Adhesives and Sealants.

All hard surface flooring must comply with the requirements of the **FloorScore** standard and be certified by an independent third party. Hard surface flooring includes vinyl, linoleum, laminate, wood, ceramic, rubber, and wall base.

Concrete, wood, bamboo, and cork floor finishes (sealer, stain, and finish) must not exceed the VOC limits of SMACNA #1113.

Tile setting adhesives and grout must not exceed the VOC limits of SMACNA #1168.

SCHOOLS:

All flooring products must comply with the California Department of Health Services Standard Practice for the Testing of Volatile Organic Emissions from Various Sources Using Small-Scale Environmental Chambers.

DOCUMENTATION

Contractor to submit a schedule of all flooring products, adhesives, grout, and finishes used on the project and documentation proving compliance, including VOC levels.

REFERENCED STANDARDS

NC and CS:

The Carpet and Rug Institute (CRI) Green Label Plus Testing Program

South Coast Air Quality Management District (SCAQMD) Rule #1168

South Coast Air Quality Management District (SCAQMD) Rule #1113

FloorScore Program

SCHOOLS:

California Department of Health Services Standard Practice for the Testing of Volatile Organic Emissions from Various Sources Using Small-Scale Environmental Chambers

CONSTRUCTION	**EQ Credit 4.4:**
	Low-Emitting Materials,
	Composite Wood and Agrifiber Products

PURPOSE

To limit the amount of _____, irritating, and/or harmful contaminants used _____ to enhance the _____ and well-being of _____ and occupants.

REQUIREMENTS

NC and CS:

_____ wood and agrifiber products must not contain any _____-formaldehyde resins.

Laminate _____ used to assemble on-site and shop-applied composite wood and agrifiber products must contain no added urea-_____ resins.

SCHOOLS:

All composite wood and _____ products must comply with the _____ Department of Health Services Standard Practice for the Testing of Volatile Organic Emissions from Various Sources Using Small-Scale Environmental Chambers.

DOCUMENTATION

Contractor to submit a schedule of all composite _____ and agrifiber products used on the project and documentation proving no urea-formaldehyde _____ were used.

Composite wood and agrifiber products include _____, medium-density fiberboard (MDF), _____, wheatboard, strawboard, panel substrates, and _____ cores.

REFERENCED STANDARDS

SCHOOLS:

California Department of Health Services _____ Practice for the Testing of Volatile Organic Emissions from Various Sources Using Small-Scale _____ Chambers

1 pt.	**RESPONSIBLE PARTY:**
	CONTRACTOR

EQ Credit 4.4:

Low-Emitting Materials,

Composite Wood and Agrifiber Products

ANSWER KEY

PURPOSE

To limit the amount of odorous, irritating, and/or harmful contaminants used indoors to enhance the comfort and well-being of installers and occupants.

REQUIREMENTS

NC and CS:

Composite wood and agrifiber products must not contain any **urea-formaldehyde** resins.

Laminate adhesives used to assemble on-site and shop-applied composite wood and agrifiber products must contain no added urea-formaldehyde resins.

SCHOOLS:

All composite wood and agrifiber products must comply with the California Department of Health Services Standard Practice for the Testing of Volatile Organic Emissions from Various Sources Using Small-Scale Environmental Chambers.

DOCUMENTATION

Contractor to submit a schedule of all composite wood and agrifiber products used on the project and documentation proving no urea-formaldehyde resins were used.

Composite wood and agrifiber products include particleboard, medium-density fiberboard (MDF), plywood, wheatboard, strawboard, panel substrates and door cores.

REFERENCED STANDARDS

SCHOOLS:

California Department of Health Services Standard Practice for the Testing of Volatile Organic Emissions from Various Sources Using Small-Scale Environmental Chambers

CONSTRUCTION

EQ Credit 4.5:

Low-Emitting Materials,

Furniture and Furnishings (SCHOOLS)

PURPOSE

To limit the amount of _____, irritating, and/or harmful contaminants used _____ to enhance the _____ and well-being of _____ and occupants.

REQUIREMENTS

All _____ furniture and seating that was manufactured, _____, or refinished within _____ year prior to _____ must:

Option 1:

be _____ Children and Schools certified.

Option 2:

not exceed the maximum indoor air concentrations for contaminants as determined by a procedure based on the EPA _____ Large Chamber Test Protocol for Measuring Emissions of VOCs and _____.

Option 3:

not exceed the maximum indoor air _____ for contaminants as determined by a procedure based on _____ / _____ M7.1 - 2007 testing protocol.

DOCUMENTATION

Contractor to submit a schedule of all furniture (_____ furniture and classroom furniture) and seating (_____ and guest chairs) used on the project and documentation proving compliance.

REFERENCED STANDARDS

ANSI/BIFMA x7.1 - 2007, Standard for _____ and TVOC Emissions of Low-Emitting Office Furniture _____ and Seating

Environmental Technology _____ (ETV) Large Chamber Test Protocol for Measuring Emissions of VOCs and Aldehydes

_____ Certification Program

1 pt.

RESPONSIBLE PARTY:

CONTRACTOR

EQ Credit 4.5:

Low-Emitting Materials,

Furniture and Furnishings (SCHOOLS)

ANSWER KEY

PURPOSE

To limit the amount of odorous, irritating, and/or harmful contaminants used indoors to enhance the comfort and well-being of installers and occupants.

REQUIREMENTS

All classroom furniture and seating that was manufactured, refurbished, or refinished within 1 year prior to occupancy must:

Option 1:

be **GREENGUARD** Children and Schools certified.

Option 2:

not exceed the maximum indoor air concentrations for contaminants as determined by a procedure based on the EPA ETV Large Chamber Test Protocol for Measuring Emissions of VOCs and Aldehydes.

Option 3:

not exceed the maximum indoor air concentrations for contaminants as determined by a procedure based on ANSI/BIFMA M7.1 - 2007 testing protocol.

DOCUMENTATION

Contractor to submit a schedule of all furniture (systems furniture and classroom furniture) and seating (task and guest chairs) used on the project and documentation proving compliance.

REFERENCED STANDARDS

ANSI/BIFMA x7.1 - 2007, Standard for Formaldehyde and TVOC Emissions of Low-Emitting Office Furniture Systems and Seating

Environmental Technology Verification (ETV) Large Chamber Test Protocol for Measuring Emissions of VOCs and Aldehydes

GREENGUARD Certification Program

CONSTRUCTION

EQ Credit 4.6:

Low-Emitting Materials,

Ceiling and Wall Systems (SCHOOLS)

PURPOSE

To limit the amount of _____, irritating, and/or harmful contaminants used _____ to enhance the _____ and well-being of _____ and occupants.

REQUIREMENTS

All _____ board, insulation, _____ ceiling systems, and _____ coverings must comply with the _____ Department of Health Services Standard Practice for the Testing of Volatile Organic _____ from Various Sources Using Small-Scale Environmental Chambers.

REFERENCED STANDARDS

California Department of _____ Services Standard Practice for the Testing of Volatile Organic _____ from Various Sources Using _____-Scale Environmental Chambers

1 pt.

RESPONSIBLE PARTY:

CONTRACTOR

EQ Credit 4.6:

Low-Emitting Materials,

Ceiling and Wall Systems (SCHOOLS)

ANSWER KEY

PURPOSE

To limit the amount of odorous, irritating, and/or harmful contaminants used indoors to enhance the comfort and well-being of installers and occupants.

REQUIREMENTS

All gypsum board, insulation, acoustical ceiling systems, and wall coverings must comply with the California Department of Health Services Standard Practice for the Testing of Volatile Organic Emissions from Various Sources Using Small-Scale Environmental Chambers.

REFERENCED STANDARDS

California Department of Health Services Standard Practice for the Testing of Volatile Organic Emissions from Various Sources Using Small-Scale Environmental Chambers

DESIGN	**EQ Credit 5**
	Indoor Chemical and Pollutant Source Control

PURPOSE

Reduce the _____ exposure to possible harmful _____ and chemical pollutants.

REQUIREMENTS

Install _____ entryway systems, such as _____, grates, and _____, at least _____ feet long in the direction of travel at building entrances.

Exhaust areas, such as high-volume copy areas, with _____ chemicals and gases. These areas should be located away from regularly occupied spaces.

Install MERV _____ or better filters at both _____ air and where outside air is supplied.

Provide for proper _____ and appropriate _____ of hazardous liquid wastes for housekeeping and laboratory spaces.

REFERENCED STANDARDS

ASHRAE Standard _____ - 1999: Method of Testing General Ventilation Air-_____ Devices for _____ Efficiency by _____ Size

1 pt.	**RESPONSIBLE PARTY:**
	ARCHITECT

EQ Credit 5

Indoor Chemical and Pollutant Source Control

ANSWER KEY

PURPOSE

Reduce the occupant's exposure to possible harmful particulates and chemical pollutants.

REQUIREMENTS

Install permanent entryway systems, such as grilles, grates, and mats, at least **10 feet long** in the direction of travel at building entrances.

Exhaust areas, such as high-volume copy areas, with hazardous chemicals and gases. These areas should be located away from regularly occupied spaces.

Install **MERV 13** or better filters at both return air and where outside air is supplied.

Provide for proper storage and appropriate disposal of hazardous liquid wastes for housekeeping and laboratory spaces.

REFERENCED STANDARDS

ASHRAE Standard 52.2 - 1999: Method of Testing General Ventilation Air-Cleaning Devices for Removal Efficiency by Particle Size

DESIGN	**EQ Credit 6.1:**
	Controllability of Systems,
	Lighting (NC and SCHOOLS)

PURPOSE

Increase the _____, comfort, and well-being for _____ by providing lighting system control to _____ occupants and groups in multi-occupant spaces.

REQUIREMENTS

NC Projects: Provide individual lighting _____ for at least _____ percent of occupants and all _____ multi-occupant spaces.

Schools Projects: Provide individual lighting _____ for at least _____ percent of occupants and all _____ spaces. Classrooms must have a lighting system that functions in at least _____ modes: general lighting and _____.

| **1 pt.** | **RESPONSIBLE PARTY:** |
| | **Electrical Engineer** |

	EQ Credit 6.1:
	Controllability of Systems,
	Lighting (NC and SCHOOLS)

ANSWER KEY

PURPOSE

Increase the productivity, comfort, and well-being for occupants by providing lighting system control to individual occupants and groups in multi-occupant spaces.

REQUIREMENTS

NC Projects: Provide individual lighting controls for at least 90 percent of occupants and all shared multi-occupant spaces.

Schools Projects: Provide individual lighting controls for at least 90 percent of occupants and all learning spaces. Classrooms must have a lighting system that functions in at least two modes: general lighting and A/V.

DESIGN	EQ Credit 6.2 (CS Credit 6)
	Controllability of Systems,
	Thermal Comfort

PURPOSE

Increase the _____, comfort, and well-being for _____ by providing _____ comfort system control to _____ occupants and groups in multi-occupant spaces.

REQUIREMENTS

Provide at least _____ percent of the building occupants and all of the shared _____-occupant spaces with thermal _____ controls.

Occupants must be able to control at least one of the _____ environmental factors of _____ comfort: air temperature, air _____, _____ temperature, and _____.

If _____ windows are used instead of controls, workstations must be located within _____ feet in front of and within _____ feet to either side. The window area must comply with ASHRAE _____ standards.

REFERENCED STANDARDS

_____ Standard _____ - 2007, _____ for Acceptable Indoor Air Quality

ASHRAE Standard _____ - 2004, _____ Environmental Conditions for Human _____

1 pt.

RESPONSIBLE PARTY:

Mechanical Engineer

EQ Credit 6.2 (CS Credit 6)

Controllability of Systems,

Thermal Comfort

ANSWER KEY

PURPOSE

Increase the productivity, comfort, and well-being for occupants by providing thermal comfort system control to individual occupants and groups in multi-occupant spaces.

REQUIREMENTS

Provide at least **50 percent** of the building occupants and all of the shared multi-occupant spaces with thermal comfort controls.

Occupants must be able to control at least one of the four environmental factors of thermal comfort: air temperature, air speed, radiant temperature, and humidity.

If operable windows are used instead of controls, workstations must be located within 20 feet in front of and within 10 feet to either side. The window area must comply with ASHRAE 62.1 standards.

REFERENCED STANDARDS

ASHRAE Standard 62.1 - 2007, Ventilation for Acceptable Indoor Air Quality

ASHRAE Standard 55 - 2004, Thermal Environmental Conditions for Human Occupancy

DESIGN

PURPOSE

Increase the _____ and _____-_____ for occupants by providing a comfortable _____ environment.

REQUIREMENTS

_____ systems must be designed to comply with ASHRAE _____ - 2004 and address the _____ occupancy factors (_____ rate and clothing _____) and the _____ building design factors (air _____, radiant temperature, air _____, and humidity).

    SCHOOLS: _____ must comply with Typical Natatorium Design Conditions of _____ Handbook.

    CS: Base building design must allow for _____ to be able to comply with this credit.

REFERENCED STANDARDS

ASHRAE Standard _____ - 2004, Thermal _____ Conditions for Human Occupancy

_____ Institute of Building _____ Engineers (CIBSE) _____ Manual 10-2005, Natural _____ in Non-Domestic Buildings

SCHOOLS: _____ HVAC Applications _____, 2003 Edition, Chapter 4 (Places of Assembly), Typical _____ Design Conditions

1 pt.

RESPONSIBLE PARTY:

Mechanical Engineer

EQ Credit 7.1 (CS Credit 7) **Thermal Comfort, Design**

ANSWER KEY

PURPOSE

Increase the productivity and well-being for occupants by providing a comfortable thermal environment.

REQUIREMENTS

HVAC systems must be designed to comply with **ASHRAE 55** - 2004 and address the two occupancy factors (metabolic rate and clothing insulation) and the four building design factors (air temperature, radiant temperature, air speed, and humidity).

> **SCHOOLS:** Natatoriums must comply with Typical Natatorium Design Conditions of ASHRAE Handbook.

> **CS:** Base building design must allow for tenants to be able to comply with this credit.

REFERENCED STANDARDS

ASHRAE Standard 55 - 2004, Thermal Environmental Conditions for Human Occupancy

Chartered Institute of Building Services Engineers (CIBSE) Applications Manual 10-2005, Natural Ventilation in Non-Domestic Buildings

SCHOOLS: ASHRAE HVAC Applications Handbook, 2003 Edition, Chapter 4 (Places of Assembly), Typical Natatorium Design Conditions

DESIGN	EQ Credit 7.2:
	Thermal Comfort, Verification (NC and SCHOOLS)

PURPOSE

Assess the _____ comfort of the occupants over time.

REQUIREMENTS

Pursue and _____ EQ Credit _____: Thermal Comfort, _____.

Confirm commitment to conducting an _____ thermal comfort survey _____ to _____ months after occupancy and have a _____ action plan developed.

    NC: Install a permanent _____ system to _____ and _____ the comfort criteria.

    _____ projects are not eligible to pursue this credit.

REFERENCED STANDARD

_____ Standard 55 - 2004, _____ Environmental Conditions for Human _____

1 pt.	RESPONSIBLE PARTY:
	Owner

EQ Credit 7.2: **Thermal Comfort, Verification (NC and SCHOOLS)**

ANSWER KEY

PURPOSE

Assess the thermal comfort of the occupants over time.

REQUIREMENTS

Pursue and earn EQ Credit 7.1: Thermal Comfort, Design.

Confirm commitment to conducting an anonymous thermal comfort survey **6 to 18 months** after occupancy and have a corrective action plan developed.

> **NC:** Install a permanent monitoring system to measure and record the comfort criteria.

> Residential projects are not eligible to pursue this credit.

REFERENCED STANDARD

ASHRAE Standard 55 - 2004, Thermal Environmental Conditions for Human Occupancy

DESIGN	**EQ Credit 8.1:** **Daylight and Views,** **Daylight**

PURPOSE

For _____ occupied areas, introduce _____ and views to provide the building occupants with a _____ to the outdoor environment.

REQUIREMENTS

NC and CS: Provide daylight to _____ percent of the regularly _____ spaces.

SCHOOLS: Provide daylight to _____ percent (1 point) or _____ percent (2 points) of the _____ spaces.

　　If at least _____ percent is achieved for the classroom areas, provide daylight to _____ percent of the _____ occupied spaces (additional 1 point).

COMPLIANCE PATH OPTIONS

OPTION 1: _____

　　Prove _____ percent of the spaces are daylit with between _____ and _____ footcandles.

OPTION 2: _____

　　Calculate the _____ zone for _____-lighting and/or _____-lighting strategies.

OPTION 3: _____

　　Record indoor light _____ levels to prove a minimum of _____ footcandles.

OPTION 4: _____

　　Choose from Options 1 through _____ to prove compliance.

STRATEGIES

All strategies must include _____ control.

OPTION 2: Prescriptive

　　_____-Lighting Daylight Zone:

　　　　Determine the _____ light _____ (VLT) for windows _____ inches above the floor. Multiply VLT by the _____-to-floor area ration (WFR) to prove a value between _____ and 0.180.

　　　　For ceiling-obstructed daylight, the related floor area must be _____ from the calculations.

　　_____-Lighting Daylight Zone:

　　　　Determine the daylight zone area under each _____ and add the _____ of the following three factors:

　　　　- _____ percent of the _____ height

　　　　- One-half the distance to the edge of the _____ skylight

　　　　- The distance to a fixed solid partition farther than _____ percent of the distance between the top of the wall and the ceiling

　　　　Skylight roof coverage must be between _____ and _____ percent of the roof area.

　　　　Skylights must have a minimum VLT of 0.5 and not be spaced apart more than _____ times the ceiling height.

　　　　If using a skylight _____ it is required to have a measured haze value of at least _____ percent and a _____ _____ of sight to the diffuser must be avoided.

EXEMPLARY PERFORMANCE

NC and CS: Provide daylight to _____ percent of the regularly occupied spaces.

SCHOOLS: Provide daylight to _____ percent for the _____ areas and provide daylight to 95 percent of the regularly occupied spaces.

REFERENCED STANDARD

_____ D1003-07E1, Standard Test for Method for _____ and Luminous Transmittance of Transparent _____

1-3 pts.	**RESPONSIBLE PARTY:** **ARCHITECT**

ANSWER KEY

PURPOSE

For regularly occupied areas, introduce daylight and views to provide the building occupants with a connection to the outdoor environment.

REQUIREMENTS

NC and CS: Provide daylight to 75 percent of the regularly occupied spaces.

SCHOOLS: Provide daylight to 75 percent (1 point) or 90 percent (2 points) of the classroom spaces.

> If at least 75 percent is achieved for the classroom areas, provide daylight to 75 percent of the regularly occupied spaces (additional 1 point).

COMPLIANCE PATH OPTIONS

OPTION 1: Simulation

> Prove 75 percent of the spaces are daylit with between 25 and 500 footcandles.

OPTION 2: Prescriptive

> Calculate the daylight zone for side-lighting and/or top-lighting strategies.

OPTION 3: Measurement

> Record indoor light footcandle levels to prove a minimum of 25 footcandles.

OPTION 4: Combination

> Choose from Options 1 through 3 to prove compliance.

STRATEGIES

All strategies must include glare control.

OPTION 2: Prescriptive

> Side-Lighting Daylight Zone:

>> Determine the visible light transmittance (VLT) for windows 30 inches above the floor. Multiply VLT by the window-to-floor area ration (WFR) to prove a value between 0.150 and 0.180.

>> For ceiling-obstructed daylight, the related floor area must be excluded from the calculations.

> Top-Lighting Daylight Zone:

>> Determine the daylight zone area under each skylight and add the *lesser* of the following three factors:

>> - 70 percent of the ceiling height

>> - One-half the distance to the edge of the closest skylight

>> - The distance to a fixed solid partition farther than 70 percent of the distance between the top of the wall and the ceiling

>> Skylight roof coverage must be between 3 and 6 percent of the roof area.

>> Skylights must have a minimum VLT of 0.5 and not be spaced apart more than 1.4 times the ceiling height.

>> If using a skylight diffuser, it is required to have a measured haze value of at least 90 percent and a direct line of sight to the diffuser must be avoided.

EXEMPLARY PERFORMANCE

NC and CS: Provide daylight to 95 percent of the regularly occupied spaces.

SCHOOLS: Provide daylight to 90 percent for the classroom areas and provide daylight to 95 percent of the regularly occupied spaces.

REFERENCED STANDARD

ASTM D1003-07E1, Standard Test for Method for Haze and Luminous Transmittance of Transparent Plastics

DESIGN	EQ Credit 8.2: Daylight and Views, Views

PURPOSE

For _____ occupied areas, introduce daylight and _____ to provide the building occupants with a _____ to the outdoor environment.

REQUIREMENTS

Provide direct _____ of sight to the _____ for at least _____ percent of regularly occupied areas.

Direct line of _____ is measured between _____ and _____ inches above the finish floor.

DOCUMENTATION

Provide a floor plan with _____ lines to _____ glazing.

Provide a section with direct line of sight to _____ glazing.

EXEMPLARY PERFORMANCE

Meet at least 2 out of the 4 measures:

- provide at least _____ percent of regularly occupied areas with numerous lines of sight in multiple directions and at least _____ degrees apart

- provide views for at least _____ percent of regularly occupied areas to at least two of the following: _____, human activity, or objects that are at least _____ feet from the glass

- provide unobstructed views for at least _____ percent of regularly occupied areas for a distance of _____ times the head height of the vision glazing

- provide views for at least _____ percent of regularly occupied areas that have a view factor of at least _____

1 pt.

RESPONSIBLE PARTY:

ARCHITECT

EQ Credit 8.2:

Daylight and Views,

Views

ANSWER KEY

PURPOSE

For regularly occupied areas, introduce daylight and views to provide the building occupants with a connection to the outdoor environment.

REQUIREMENTS

Provide direct line of sight to the exterior for at least 90 percent of regularly occupied areas.

Direct line of sight is measured between 30 and 90 inches above the finish floor.

DOCUMENTATION

Provide a floor plan with sight lines to perimeter glazing.

Provide a section with direct line of sight to perimeter glazing.

EXEMPLARY PERFORMANCE

Meet at least two out of the four measures:

- provide at least 90 percent of regularly occupied areas with numerous lines of sight in multiple directions and at least 90 degrees apart

- provide views for at least 90 percent of regularly occupied areas to at least two of the following: vegetation, human activity, or objects that are at least 70 feet from the glass

- provide unobstructed views for at least 90 percent of regularly occupied areas for a distance of three times the head height of the vision glazing

- provide views for at least 90 percent of regularly occupied areas that have a view factor of at least three

CONSTRUCTION

PURPOSE

To lessen the possibility of mold in schools by the means of _____ design and _____ strategies.

REQUIREMENTS

Pursue and earn the three following credits:

EQ Credit 3.1: Construction IAQ Management Plan, _____ _____

EQ Credit 7.1: Thermal Comfort, _____

EQ Credit 7.2: Thermal Comfort, _____

HVAC systems must be designed to achieve a _____ percent relative humidity at all times.

Create and implement an ongoing IAQ management plan in accordance with the EPA publication, _____ _____ _____: A Guide for Building Owners and Facility Managers.

STRATEGIES

Eliminate the _____ for condensation

Pay attention to known generators of _____

Prevent mold during _____ times

Address _____ and leaky/failed equipment

Design for mold _____

REFERENCED STANDARD

Building _____ Quality: A Guide for Building _____ and Facility Managers, U.S. Environmental _____ Agency, December 1991

1 pt.

RESPONSIBLE PARTY:

CIVIL ENGINEER or LANDSCAPE ARCHITECT

| | **EQ Credit 10:** |
| | **Mold Prevention (SCHOOLS)** |

ANSWER KEY

PURPOSE

To lessen the possibility of mold in schools by the means of preventative design and construction strategies.

REQUIREMENTS

Pursue and earn the three following credits:

> EQ Credit 3.1: Construction IAQ Management Plan, During Construction

> EQ Credit 7.1: Thermal Comfort, Design

> EQ Credit 7.2: Thermal Comfort, Verification

HVAC systems must be designed to achieve a 60 percent relative humidity at all times.

Create and implement an ongoing IAQ management plan in accordance with the EPA publication, Building Air Quality: A Guide for Building Owners and Facility Managers.

STRATEGIES

Eliminate the potential for condensation

Pay attention to known generators of condensation

Prevent mold during unoccupied times

Address floods and leaky/failed equipment

Design for mold prevention

REFERENCED STANDARD

Building Air Quality: A Guide for Building Owners and Facility Managers, U.S. Environmental Protection Agency, December 1991

CHAPTER 9

INNOVATION IN DESIGN AND REGIONAL PRIORITY

THE PREVIOUS FIVE CHAPTERS detailed the main categories of the Leadership in Energy and Environmental Design (LEED®) rating systems, while this chapter focuses on the two bonus categories of the Building Design and Construction (BD+C) rating systems: Innovation in Design (ID) and Regional Priority (RP). These categories are treated as bonus categories, as neither contains any prerequisites. The ID category encourages projects to explore new and innovative strategies and technologies, while the RP category offers additional point-earning opportunities focused on geographic environmental achievements.

 Remember to switch back to the white flashcards for ID and RP topics.

INNOVATION IN DESIGN

The ID category encourages the exploration and implementation of new green building technologies, as well as exceeding the thresholds defined in the existing LEED credits. As seen in Table 9.1, the BD+C rating systems offer up to six points for projects within the ID category by addressing four different strategies:

Create a flashcard to remember the strategies to earn ID points for the different rating systems.

1. Exemplary Performance
2. Innovation in Design
3. Including a LEED Accredited Professional on the project team
4. The School as a Teaching Tool credit

ID Credit 1: Innovation or Exemplary Performance

Three of the available six ID points can be used toward the achievement of exemplary performance. As mentioned in the previous chapters, Exemplary Performance credits are achieved once projects surpass the minimum performance-based thresholds defined in the existing LEED credits, typically the

Table 9.1 The Innovation in Design (ID) Category

D/C	Prereq/Credit	Title	Points		
			NC	Schools	CS
D/C	Credit 1	Innovation or Exemplary Performance	1–5	1–4	1–5
C	Credit 2	LEED Accredited Professional	1	1	1
C	Credit 3	The School as a Teaching Tool	—	1	—

next incremental percentage threshold. For example, projects can earn Exemplary Performance credits (within the ID category) for achieving the following:

- Diverting 95 percent of construction waste per the requirements of MR Credit 2: Construction Waste Management

- Reducing water consumption by more than 45 percent per the requirements of WE Credit 3: Water Use Reduction

- When 30 percent or more of the total material cost includes products with recycled content per the requirements of MR Credit 4: Recycled Content

If the team uses all three opportunities for exemplary performance achievements, they still have at least one more point opportunity for implementing an innovative strategy. If the team pursues less than three credits within the ID category for exemplary performance, then they can pursue more innovative strategies. The teams should research credit interpretation requests (CIRs) to see if their proposed strategy has been incorporated or presented in the past, or issue a new CIR to inquire about the award potential. Successful ID solutions include strategies that demonstrate quantitative performance with environmental benefits and can be replicated by other project teams. Some examples previously submitted and awarded include:

- Incorporating cradle-to-cradle (C2C) certified products (Figure 9.1)

- Implementing an educational program for occupants and visitors (Figure 9.2)

- Using large amounts of fly ash in concrete

- Achieving LEED credits from other rating systems, such as a LEED for New Construction and Major Renovations™ (LEED NC) project pursuing Acoustical Performance from the LEED for Schools™ rating system or Low-Emitting Materials, Systems Furniture and Seating from the LEED for Commercial Interiors™ (LEED CI) rating system

 TIP Remember the cradle-to-grave cycle from Chapter 7? C2C products are not only made of recycled products, but are recyclable after their useful life to avoid landfills and incineration facilities.

TIP Remember what fly ash is from Chapter 7?

Figure 9.1 C2C products help to extend the life of materials, although repurposed, reducing the need for virgin materials. *Photo courtesy of Steelcase, Inc.*

Figure 9.2 Providing opportunities to educate the end-users and community about the benefits and strategies of green building helps to further transform the market and therefore contribute to earning LEED certification. *Photo courtesy of Rainwater HOG, LLC*

When submitting for an Innovation in Design (ID) credit, each of the following four components need to be addressed for each credit being pursued:

1. Intent of strategy
2. Suggested requirements for compliance
3. Suggested documentation proving compliance with requirements
4. A narrative describing the strategy implemented

ID Credit 2: LEED Accredited Professional

The LEED rating systems also offer another point opportunity for including a LEED Accredited Professional (LEED AP) on the project team. Including a LEED AP on the project team can add efficiencies, as they are aware of the requirements of the LEED certification process. They are familiar with integrated design processes and understand how to evaluate the trade-offs and synergies of green building strategies and technologies. For the purposes of the exam, it is critical to remember that only **one point** can be awarded to projects for this credit; it does not matter how many LEED APs are on the project team, just as long as there is one. Note, LEED Green Associates do not qualify for the bonus point under this credit. The LEED AP credential certificate is required to prove compliance and earn the point.

ID Credit 3: The School as a Teaching Tool

This credit is available only for School projects to pursue. To comply, the owner will need to develop and then implement curriculum specific to the high-performance characteristics of the project within 10 months of earning LEED certification. Just as with any LEED rating system, the curriculum needs to be developed with a holistic, integrative approach encouraging an understanding of the human

Table 9.2 The Regional Priority (RP) Category

			Points		
D/C	Prereq/Credit	Title	NC	Schools	CS
D/C	Credit 1	Regional Priority	1–4	1–4	1–4

elements, ecological factors, and the school building and the impacts they have on one another. Besides meeting local or state standards, the school administrators must approve the curriculum. The curriculum should equate to at least 10 hours of classroom instruction per year, per full-time student. Some examples include:

- Implementing a sundial on site to reinforce astronomy and math
- Implementing agricultural areas to address food sources, growing practices, and nutrition or composting areas to address ecosystems and biology
- Implementing on-site renewable energy systems to address energy production to be estimated and analyzed by math students and economic students

REGIONAL PRIORITY

TIP Do you remember the point structure for LEED? How many points does a project need to achieve to earn Platinum status?

As seen in Table 9.2, the RP category offers the opportunity to earn up to four bonus points for achieving compliance of previously mentioned existing LEED credits. U.S. Green Building Council's (USGBC's) eight Regional Councils have consulted with the local chapters to determine which existing LEED credits are more challenging to achieve within certain zip codes. Based on the results of their findings, USGBC compiled a database of all the zip codes in the United States (available on the USGBC website) and chose six existing LEED credits to coordinate with each corresponding geographic region. For example, a project located in Dania Beach, Florida, could earn a bonus point within the RP category for purchasing 20 percent of their materials that are extracted, processed, and manufactured within 500 miles from the project site, as USGBC has recognized that South Florida has a few opportunities to obtain building materials to comply with MR Credit 5: Regional Materials. A project could earn up to four Regional Priority credits (RPCs) out of the six opportunities presented. For the purposes of the exam, it is critical to remember that RPCs are not *new* credits.

QUIZ TIME!

Q9.1. Exemplary performance generally requires which of the following? (Choose one)

    A. Develop an innovative strategy not presented in any existing LEED credit.

    B. Achieve either 20 percent or the next incremental percentage threshold established by the existing LEED credit that is being exceeded, whichever is greater.

    C. Meet or exceed the next percentage threshold as listed within the existing credit.

    D. Surpass the defined threshold of an innovative strategy being proposed by the team.

    E. Regardless of the LEED credit being pursued, achieve at least double the minimum effort described within the existing LEED credit, regardless of which credit is being exceeded.

Q9.2. Pursuing an Innovation in Design opportunity is appropriate when *at least one* of which of the following are true? (Choose two)

  A. The project is unable to meet the requirements established by an existing LEED credit.

  B. The compliance paths offered within an existing LEED credit are not possible to pursue.

  C. The project has exceeded or is projected to exceed the minimum performance established by an existing LEED credit.

  D. The project has achieved measurable performance in a LEED credit within another rating system.

Q9.3. Is it possible for the same building to earn multiple LEED certifications?

  A. Yes

  B. No

Q9.4. Which of the following statements are true regarding RPCs? (Choose three)

  A. Earning an RPC adds a bonus point to the project's total points.

  B. RPCs are new credits included in the LEED rating systems.

  C. Projects that are not registered with the 2009 versions of LEED are not awarded points within the Regional Priority category.

  D. Each zip code is assigned eight RPC opportunities.

  E. A project may earn up to four RPC bonus points.

Q9.5. How many points can be earned in the RP category? (Choose one)

  A. Six

  B. Three

  C. Two

  D. Four

  E. Ten

Q9.6. There are five LEED APs on the Botanical Center project, including three from the architectural firm, one from the mechanical engineering firm, and one from the electrical engineering firm. How many points can be achieved within the ID category for achieving this effort? (Choose one)

  A. One

  B. Two

  C. Three

  D. Four

Q9.7. What is the minimum number of hours required for curriculum per year, per full-time student in order to comply with ID Credit 3: The School as a Teaching Tool? (Choose one)

A. 6

B. 15

C. 8

D. 10

E. 20

Q9.8. How many additional prerequisites are projects required to comply if pursuing the LEED for Schools rating system as compared to the LEED NC rating system? (Choose one)

A. One

B. Two

C. Three

D. Four

Q9.9. How many additional credits are available in the LEED for Schools rating system as compared to the NC rating system? (Choose one)

A. One

B. Two

C. Three

D. Four

E. Five

Q9.10. A vegetated roof system using native and adapted plant species has the opportunity to contribute to earning which LEED credits? (Choose three)

A. MR Credit 6: Rapidly Renewable Materials

B. SS Credit 6.1: Stormwater Design: Quantity Control

C. SS Credit 7: Heat Island Effect

D. EQ Credit 4.4: Low-Emitting Materials: Composite Wood and Agrifiber Products

E. EA Credit 1: Optimize Energy Performance

Q9.11. A 100,000 square-foot existing building is undergoing a major renovation, including the addition of 240,000 more square feet. This 340,000 square-foot renovation project reuses the existing shell, diverts 97 percent of its construction waste, and purchases 22 percent of local regional material with recycled content. How many points can the team pursue by achieving these strategies? (Choose three)

A. 3 points for MR Credit 1.1: Building Reuse, Maintain Walls, Floors & Roof

B. 2 points for MR Credit 1.1: Building Reuse, Maintain Walls, Floors & Roof

C. 2 points for MR Credit 2: Construction Waste Management

D. 2 points for exemplary performance under ID Credit 1

E. 2 points for MR Credit 4: Recycled Content and 2 points for MR Credit 5: Regional Materials

F. 1 point for exemplary performance under ID Credit 1

DESIGN

PURPOSE

Allow for the opportunity to achieve _____ performance and/or _____ performance for green building strategies not addressed by the _____ Green Building _____ Systems.

STRATEGIES

PATH 1: Innovation in Design (Up to _____ points for NC and CS; up to ___ points for SCHOOLS)

    1. Propose a _____ and innovative performance achieved with an environmental benefit

    2. Proposed innovation must be applied comprehensively to the _____ project

    3. Must be _____ to other projects and considerably better than sustainable design strategies

PATH 2: Exemplary Performance (Up to 3 points)

    _____ the requirement of an existing LEED credit and/or achieve the stated _____ percentage _____

DOCUMENTATION

PATH 1:

    _____ of proposed strategy

    _____ of proposed strategy

    _____ proving compliance with proposed requirements

    _____ to achieve innovative performance

1-5 pts. for NC & CS
1-4 pts. for Schools

RESPONSIBLE PARTY:

PROJECT TEAM

	ID Credit 1:
	Innovation in Design

ANSWER KEY

PURPOSE

Allow for the opportunity to achieve exemplary performance and/or innovative performance for green building strategies not addressed by the LEED Green Building Rating Systems.

STRATEGIES

PATH 1: Innovation in Design **(Up to 5 points for NC and CS; up to 4 points for SCHOOLS)**

1. Propose a quantifiable and innovative performance achieved with an environmental benefit

2. Proposed innovation must be applied comprehensively to the entire project

3. Must be achievable to other projects and considerably better than sustainable design strategies

PATH 2: Exemplary Performance **(Up to 3 points)**

Double the requirement of an existing LEED credit and/or achieve the stated incremental percentage threshold

DOCUMENTATION

PATH 1:

Intent of proposed strategy

Requirements of proposed strategy

Submittals proving compliance with proposed requirements

Strategies/technologies to achieve innovative performance

CONSTRUCTION

PURPOSE

_____ the _____ and _____ process by encouraging the integration required by the LEED Green Building Rating Systems.

REQUIREMENTS

Engage at least _____ LEED AP as an integral project team member.

REFERENCED STANDARDS

LEED _____ Professional (AP)

Green Building _____ Institute (GBCI), www.gbci.org

1 pt.

RESPONSIBLE PARTY:

PROJECT TEAM

	ID Credit 2:
	LEED Accredited Professional (AP)

ANSWER KEY

PURPOSE

Streamline the application and certification process by encouraging the integration required by the LEED Green Building Rating Systems.

REQUIREMENTS

Engage **at least one** LEED AP as an integral project team member.

REFERENCED STANDARDS

LEED Accredited Professional (AP)

Green Building Certification Institute (GBCI), www.gbci.org

CONSTRUCTION

ID Credit 3:

The School as a Teaching Tool (SCHOOLS)

PURPOSE

Integrate with the school's _____ mission, a curriculum addressing the _____ features of the facility.

REQUIREMENTS

Develop a curriculum that addresses the sustainable and high-performance features of the school and implement it within _____ months of earning LEED certification.

The curriculum should address the features and how they relate to _____ and _____ ecology and the building itself.

The curriculum must be approved by school administrators and meet local and _____ standards.

The curriculum must provide at least _____ hours of classroom instruction per _____, per _____-time _____.

1 pt.

RESPONSIBLE PARTY:

OWNER

	ID Credit 3:
	The School as a Teaching Tool (SCHOOLS)

ANSWER KEY

PURPOSE

Integrate with the school's educational mission, a curriculum addressing the sustainable features of the facility.

REQUIREMENTS

Develop a curriculum that addresses the sustainable and high-performance features of the school and implement it within **10 months** of earning LEED certification.

The curriculum should address the features and how they relate to human and natural ecology and the building itself.

The curriculum must be approved by school administrators and meet local and state standards.

The curriculum must provide at least **10 hours** of classroom instruction per year, per full-time student.

PART III

STUDY
TIPS AND
APPENDICES

CHAPTER **10**

STUDY TIPS

AS MENTIONED EARLIER IN THE INTRODUCTION OF THIS BOOK, this chapter is dedicated to providing an approach for the rest of your study efforts. It includes tips for taking online practice exams and resources on where to find additional information while you continue to study, as well as providing an insight to the Prometric testing center environment and the exam format structure.

PREPARING FOR THE LEED AP BD+C EXAM: WEEK SEVEN

By the time you read this section, it should be Week Seven of your study efforts. You should have your white set of flashcards covering the basics of Leadership in Energy and Environmental Design (LEED®) (including Innovation in Design [ID] and Regional Priority [RP] bonus categories) and your color-coded cards separated into the five main categories of the LEED rating systems. This week will be a great opportunity to rewrite your cheat sheet at least three times. Note that your cheat sheet may evolve as you take a few online practice exams.

During Week Seven, you may need to refer to additional resources while studying. For example, if you want to learn more about the cost implications of LEED projects, refer to *Cost of Green Revisited* by Davis Langdon. Although a sample credit is provided in Appendix M of this book, I would recommend downloading one of the Building Design and Construction (BD+C) rating systems from the U.S. Green Building Council (USGBC) website and skim through it to see how the categories, prerequisites, and credits are organized and presented. I would also recommend reading through two more references: *Guidelines for CIR Customers* and *Guidance on Innovation & Design (ID) Credits*. All of these references are available to download from the *LEED AP Building Design + Construction Candidate Handbook* on the GBCI website for free. Again, it is highly recommended that you download the most current candidate handbook from the GBCI website, but as a point of reference, at the time of printing the references included:

 TIP Download and read through two of the references from the *LEED AP Building Design + Construction Candidate Handbook*:
- Guidelines for CIR Customers
- Guidance on Innovation in Design (ID) Credits

- *LEED for Building Design and Construction Reference Guide* (USGBC)

- *Cost of Green Revisited,* by Davis Langdon (2007)

- *Sustainable Building Technical Manual: Part II,* by Anthony Bernheim and William Reed (1996)

- *Guidance on Innovation & Design (ID) Credits* (USGBC, 2004)

- *Guidelines for CIR Customers* (USGBC, 2007)

- *Energy Performance of LEED® for New Construction Buildings: Final Report,* by Cathy Turner and Mark Frankel (2008)

- LEED-Online—sample credit templates (www.usgbc.org)

Some other resources include:

- ■ *www.usgbc.org*. You may want to check out some of the rating system scorecards or read about credit weightings of LEED v3. The USGBC website is also your primary source to learn about any updates to the LEED rating systems.

- ■ *www.gbci.org*. Make sure you download the current candidate handbook, and you may want to reference the disciplinary policy and the minimum program requirements and the project registration information.

- ■ *www.leedonline.com*. Even if you do not have any projects assigned to you, you will still be able to see what it looks like and watch a demo video.

Practice Exam Approach

TIP During the exam, you will have 2 hours, so time yourself during the practice exams.

Also during Week Seven, you should take some online practice exams. Although there are many sample exam questions provided in this book, it is helpful to practice for the real-life testing environment scenario. Search online, as you will find that there are a few options from which to choose for online practice exams, including www.GreenEDU.com. When you are taking a practice exam, pretend as if it is the real thing. For example, time yourself, have scratch paper and a pencil available, make a cheat sheet in about two to three minutes, do not use this book or your flashcards, and avoid any disruptions. Some of the online practice exams allow you to flag questions you are doubtful of to remind you to go back and answer later, so take advantage of this for practice as the real test is formatted in the same manner.

Most of the questions include multiple choices with multiple answers required. When approaching these types of questions, it is best advised to "hide" or "cover up" the provided answer options with your hand or a sheet of paper and formulate your own answers to help avoid getting sidetracked by the answer selection choices. Once you uncover or reveal the answer choices, make sure to read through all of the options before selecting your final answer(s). Be sure to read each question carefully and select the proper number of answers. After taking the practice exam, go through the answer key and evaluate your score. On the first practice exam, read through each question and answer one by one to understand how you decided on the correct answer and where you went wrong on the incorrect ones. Try to notice a pattern on your strengths and weaknesses to determine where your study efforts need to be devoted to improve your score. After taking the first practice exam, you may just want to focus on the questions you answered incorrectly.

THE TESTING CENTER ENVIRONMENT

The introduction of this book described the opportunity to make a cheat sheet after you completed the tutorial at the testing center, and Chapter 1 detailed how to schedule your exam date with a Prometric testing center. Hopefully, your exam date is still not scheduled at this point, as one more week of preparation time is suggested to review your flashcards, to refine your cheat sheet, and to give you the opportunity to take a few online practice exams. As stated earlier, it is best to assess your knowledge before scheduling your exam date.

During Week Nine, the week of your test date, there are a few things to remember before you sit for the exam:

■ Remember to visit the GBCI website and download the latest version of the *LEED AP Building Design + Construction Candidate Handbook*.

■ Confirm your exam date at least one day prior. When selecting an exam time, pick a time in which you will perform your best.

■ Find the Prometric testing center and map your path to make sure you know where you are going on your exam day. Be sure to take note of construction or traffic patterns that may impact the travel time to the testing center.

■ Keep rewriting your cheat sheet and studying your flashcards. Take your flashcards everywhere with you!

To be prepared on the day of your exam, please note the following:

■ Bring your picture ID with matching name, just as it is on your GBCI profile.

■ Dress comfortably and bring a sweater or a jacket, as the testing center may be cold.

■ Be sure to get plenty of rest and eat something, as you will not want to take any breaks during the exam to grab a bite or a drink (the clock can not be paused).

■ Be sure to **check in** at least 30 minutes prior to your testing time. If you miss your scheduled exam time, you will be considered absent and will have to forfeit your exam fees and the opportunity to take the exam.

■ Be sure to use the restroom after checking in and prior to being escorted to your workstation. Remember, no breaks!

■ You will be observed during your testing session and will be audio and video recorded as well.

■ You will not be allowed to bring any personal items to your workstation, such as calculators, paper, pencils, purses, wallets, food, or books.

> **TIP** A calculator will be provided should you be required to perform any calculations.

EXAM STRUCTURE

The exam is structured to test you on three components, as described in the candidate handbook provided by GBCI. You will be tested on recognition items, application items, and analysis items. The recognition items test your ability to remember factual data once presented in a similar environment to the exam references. For example, you may need to provide the definition for a term or recall a fact. The application items present a situation for you to solve using the principles and elements described in the exam format. These questions may require you to perform a calculation or provide the process or sequence of actions (i.e., CIRs, registration, certification). The analysis items are presented to determine your ability to evaluate a problem and create a solution. These question types are more challenging, as you must be able to decipher the different components of the problem and also assess the relationships of the components.

The exam questions are separated into categories of focus areas and then coordinate with an applicable rating system category. For example, project site factors coordinate with the Sustainable Sites (SS) category, and water management issues coordinate with the Water Efficiency (WE) category. Project systems and energy impacts coordinate with the Energy & Atmosphere (EA) category,

> **TIP** Remember, the exam is composed of multiple-choice questions. No written answers are required!

while acquisition, installation, and management of project materials coordinate with the Materials & Resources (MR) category. Improvements to the indoor environment coordinate with the Indoor Environmental Quality (EQ) category. Stakeholder involvement in innovation, project surroundings, and public outreach coordinate with the Innovation in Design (ID) and Regional Priority (RP) categories. Therefore, you should be familiar with each of the credit categories as presented earlier in Part II, Chapters 4 through 9.

When at the Testing Center

To give you an idea of what to expect, once you are at your workstation:

- You should dedicate 2 hours and 20 minutes to take the exam:
  - 10-minute tutorial
  - 2-hour exam
  - 10-minute exit survey

- The tutorial is computer based, so make sure your workstation's monitor, keyboard, and mouse are all functioning properly. After completing the tutorial, remember to then create your cheat sheet in the time left over prior to starting the exam.

- The 2-hour exam is composed of 100 multiple-choice questions. Just like with the practice exam questions, in order for the question to be counted as CORRECT, you must select **all** of the correct answers within each question, as there is no partial credit for choosing two out of the three correct answers.

- Although some of the practice exam questions in this book are formatted with a true or false statement or "All of the above" as an answer selection, you are less likely to find this on the real exam, as the questions tend to be straightforward and clear, to avoid any confusion.

- You will not see any credit numbers listed on their own, as all credit names will include the full name.

- Appendix L includes a list of commonly used acronyms. Although most of them are spelled out on the exam, it is still helpful to know what they are!

- During the exam, you will have the opportunity to mark or flag questions to come back to later. It is advised that you take advantage of this, as you may be short on time and want to revisit only the questions you were doubtful about. Note that any unanswered questions are marked INCORRECT, so it is best to at least try and then go back to the questions if you have time.

- The 10-minute exit survey is followed by your exam results—yes, instant and immediate results!

 TIP Remember to rely on your instincts. Typically, the first answer that comes to mind is often the right one!

Exam Scoring

The exams are scored on a scale from 125 to 200, where 170+ is considered passing. Do not worry about how the questions are weighted, just do your best! Should you need to retake the exam, your application is valid for one year, and therefore you will have three chances within the year to earn a score of 170 or more. Consult the candidate handbook for more information.

After the Exam

Once you have passed the LEED AP BD+C exam, remember to change your signature to reflect earning the credential! Although your certificate will not arrive immediately, remember, you must fulfill 30 hours of continuing education units over the next two years, including six LEED-specific continuing education units. The two-year reporting period begins the same day of your exam. Refer to the Credential Maintenance Program (CMP) handbook found on the GBCI website, for more information. There is also a code of conduct you must abide by, as stipulated in the disciplinary policy posted on the GBCI website at www.gbci.org/Files/Disc_ExamAppeals_Policy.pdf. It states that individuals with LEED credentials must:

A. Be truthful, forthcoming, and cooperative in their dealings with GBCI.
B. Be in continuous compliance with GBCI rules (as amended from time to time by GBCI).
C. Respect GBCI intellectual property rights.
D. Abide by laws related to the profession and to general public health and safety.
E. Carry out their professional work in a competent and objective manner.

 TIP The disciplinary policy found on the GBCI website also includes the exam appeals policy, if needed.

Appendix A

BD+C RATING SYSTEMS

Overview of the BD+C LEED Rating Systems

REFERENCE GUIDE	RATING SYSTEM	APPLICABLE PROJECT TYPES
BD+C	**LEED for New Construction & Major Renovations (NC)**	
		• New buildings
		• Major renovations: HVAC, envelope, and interior habilitation
		• Commercial occupancies: offices, institutional, hotels, residential with four or more stories
		• Shared tenant space: occupy more than 50% of leasable SF
	LEED for Core & Shell (CS)	
		• Developer controls core and shell but not tenant fit-out
		• Commercial and medical office buildings, retail centers, warehouses
		• Shared tenant space: occupy less than 50% of leasable SF
	LEED for Schools	
		• K–12 typically
		• New schools and renovations of existing
		• Following can be used for either LEED for Schools or NC:
		– Nonacademic buildings: admin offices, maintenance facilities, dorms
		– Postsecondary academic and prekindergarten buildings
	LEED for Healthcare	
	LEED for Retail: New Construction	

Appendix B

MINIMUM PROGRAM REQUIREMENTS (MPRs) FOR BD+C RATING SYSTEMS

Minimum Program Requirements

1	MUST COMPLY WITH ENVIRONMENTAL LAWS
NC, CS, SCHOOLS	Must comply with all applicable federal, state, and local building-related environmental laws and regulations in place where the project is located.
	This condition must be satisfied from the date of or the initiation of schematic design, whichever comes first, until the date that the building receives a certificate of occupancy or similar official indication that it is ready for use.

2	MUST BE A COMPLETE, PERMANENT BUILDING OR SPACE
NC, CS, SCHOOLS	All LEED projects must be designed for, constructed on, and operated on a permanent location on already existing land.
	No building or space that is designed to move at any point in its lifetime may pursue LEED certification.
	LEED projects must include the new, ground-up design and construction, or major renovation, of at least one building in its entirety.
	Construction prerequisites and credits may not be submitted for review until substantial completion of construction has occurred.

3	MUST USE A REASONABLE SITE BOUNDARY
NC, CS, SCHOOLS	1. The LEED project boundary must include all contiguous land that is associated with and supports normal building operations for the LEED project building, including all land that was or will be disturbed for the purpose of undertaking the LEED project.
	2. The LEED project boundary may not include land that is owned by a party other than that which owns the LEED project unless that land is associated with and supports normal building operations for the LEED project building.
	3. LEED projects located on a campus must have project boundaries such that if all the buildings on campus become LEED certified, then 100% of the gross land area on the campus would be included within a LEED boundary. If this requirement is in conflict with MPR 7, Must Comply with Minimum Building Area to Site Area Ratio, then MPR 7 will take precedence.
	4. Any given parcel of real property may be attributed to only a single LEED project building.
	5. Gerrymandering of a LEED project boundary is prohibited: the boundary may not unreasonably exclude sections of land to create boundaries in unreasonable shapes for the sole purpose of complying with prerequisites or credits.

4	MUST COMPLY WITH MINIMUM FLOOR AREA REQUIREMENTS
NC, CS, SCHOOLS	The LEED project must include a minimum of 1,000 square feet of gross floor area.

5	MUST COMPLY WITH MINIMUM OCCUPANCY RATES
NC, CS, SCHOOLS	Full-time equivalent occupancy
	The LEED project must serve one or more full-time equivalent (FTE) occupant(s), calculated as an annual average in order to use LEED in its entirety. If the project serves less than one annualized FTE, optional credits from the Indoor Environmental Quality category may not be earned (the prerequisites must still be earned).
6	COMMITMENT TO SHARE WHOLE-BUILDING ENERGY AND WATER USAGE DATA
NC, CS, SCHOOLS	All certified projects must commit to sharing with USGBC and/or GBCI all available actual whole-project energy and water usage data for a period of at least five years. This period starts on the date that the LEED project begins typical physical occupancy if certifying under NC, CS, Schools, or CI, or the date that the building is awarded certification if certifying under EBOM.
	This commitment must carry forward if the building or space changes ownership or lessee.
7	MUST COMPLY WITH A MINIMUM BUILDING AREA-TO-SITE AREA RATIO
NC, CS, SCHOOLS	The gross floor area of the LEED project building must be no less than 2% of the gross land area within the LEED project boundary.

Appendix C

LEED CERTIFICATION PROCESS

The Basic Steps in the LEED Certification Process

PROJECT REGISTRATION	
	Access to LEED Online
	– LEED Scorecard
	– LEED Credit Submittal Templates
	– Project team members can submit CIRs
	– Project team members receive access to CIR database
DESIGN APPLICATION PHASE (OPTIONAL)	
	Submit Credits and Prerequisites via LEED-Online
	– Comes back "Anticipated" or "Denied" (25 days)
	– No points awarded
	Clarification Request (25 days)
	Final Design Review (15 days)
	– Project team can:
	– ACCEPT: goes to Construction Application phase
	– APPEAL: goes to Design Appeal phase
DESIGN APPEAL PHASE	
	Changes made and submitted once again
	– Comes back "Anticipated" or "Denied" (25 days)
	No clarification requests
	Final Design Review (15 days)
CONSTRUCTION APPLICATION PHASE	
	Submit via LEED-Online (both design and construction)
	– Comes back "Anticipated" or "Denied" (25 days)
	– No points awarded yet
	Clarification Request (25 days)
	Final Construction Review (15 days)
	– Project team can:
	– ACCEPT: goes to Certification/Denial phase
	– APPEAL: goes to Construction Appeal phase

CONSTRUCTION APPEAL PHASE	
	Changes made and submitted once again
	– Comes back "Anticipated" or "Denied"
	No clarification requests
	Final Construction Review (15 days)
CERTIFIED / DENIAL PHASE	
	After Final Construction Review is ACCEPTED:
	– Certification Level Awards: Certified, Silver, Gold, or Platinum
	– Denied: project closed (appeals should be done in prior phases)

Appendix D

MAIN CATEGORY SUMMARIES

Sustainable Sites

Site Selection
- SS Prerequisite 2: Environmental Site Assessment (Schools)
- SS Credit 1: Site Selection
- SS Credit 2: Development Density and Community Connectivity
- SS Credit 3: Brownfield Redevelopment

Transportation
- SS Credit 4.1: Public Transportation Access
- SS Credit 4.2: Bicycle Storage and Changing Rooms
- SS Credit 4.3: Low-Emitting and Fuel-Efficient Vehicles
- SS Credit 4.4: Parking Capacity

Site Design and Management
- SS Prerequisite 1: Construction Activity Pollution Prevention
- SS Credit 5: Site Development
- SS Credit 7: Heat Island Effect
- SS Credit 8: Light Pollution Reduction
- SS Credit 9: Site Master Plan (Schools)
- SS Credit 10: Joint Use of Facilities (Schools)

Stormwater Management
- SS Credit 6.1: Quantity Control
- SS Credit 6.2: Quality Control

Water Efficiency

Indoor Water Use Reduction
- WE Prerequisite 1: Water Use Reduction—20 percent
- WE Credit 2: Innovative Wastewater Technologies
- WE Credit 3: Water Use Reduction

Outdoor Water Use Reduction
- WE Credit 1: Water-Efficient Landscaping

Process Water
- WE Credit 4: Process Water Use Reduction (Schools)

Energy & Atmosphere

Energy Efficiency
- EA Prerequisite 2: Minimum Energy Performance
- EA Credit 1: Optimize Energy Performance

Tracking Energy Consumption
- EA Prerequisite 1: Fundamental Commissioning
- EA Credit 3: Enhanced Commissioning
- EA Credit 5: Measurement and Verification
- EA Credit 5.1: Measurement and Verification, Base Building (for LEED CS)
- EA Credit 5.2: Measurement and Verification, Tenant Submetering (for LEED CS)

Managing Refrigerants
- EA Prerequisite 3: Fundamental Refrigerant Management
- EA Credit 3: Enhanced Refrigerant Management

Renewable Energy
- EA Credit 2: On-Site Renewable Energy
- EA Credit 6: Green Power

Materials & Resources

Salvaged Materials and Material Reuse
- MR Credit 1.1: Building Reuse, Maintain Existing Walls, Floors, and Roof (for NC and Schools)/ MR Credit 1 (for CS)
- MR Credit 1.2: Building Reuse, Maintain 50 Percent of Interior Nonstructural Elements (for NC and Schools)
- MR Credit 3: Materials Reuse

Building Material Selection
- MR Credit 4: Recycled Content
- MR Credit 5: Regional Materials
- MR Credit 6: Rapidly Renewable Materials (for NC and Schools)
- MR Credit 7: Certified Wood/MR Credit 6 (for CS)

Waste Management
- MR Prerequisite 1: Storage and Collection of Recyclables
- MR Credit 2: Construction Waste Management

Indoor Environmental Quality

Indoor Air Quality

Ventilation
- EQ Prerequisite 1: Minimum Indoor Air Quality Performance

- EQ Credit 1: Outdoor Air Delivery Monitoring
- EQ Credit 2: Increased Ventilation

IAQ Practices during Construction

- EQ Credit 3: Construction IAQ Management (for CS) / EQ Credit 3.1: Construction IAQ Management—During Construction /
- EQ Credit 3.2: Construction IAQ Management—Before Occupancy (for NC and Schools)
- EQ Credit 4.1: Low-Emitting Materials, Adhesives and Sealants
- EQ Credit 4.2: Low-Emitting Materials, Paints and Coatings
- EQ Credit 4.3: Low-Emitting Materials, Flooring Systems
- EQ Credit 4.4: Low-Emitting Materials, Composite Wood and Agrifiber Products
- EQ Credit 4.5: Low-Emitting Materials, Furniture and Furnishings (for Schools)
- EQ Credit 4.6: Low-Emitting Materials, Ceiling and Wall Systems (for Schools)

Prevention and Segregation Methods

- EQ Prerequisite 1: Environmental Tobacco Smoke (ETS) Control

- EQ Credit 5: Indoor Chemical and Pollutant Source Control
- EQ Credit 10: Mold Prevention (for Schools)

Thermal Comfort

- EQ Credit 6.2: Controllability of Systems, Thermal Comfort / EQ Credit 6 (for CS)
- EQ Credit 7.1: Thermal Comfort, Design / EQ Credit 7 (for CS)
- EQ Credit 7.2: Thermal Comfort, Verification (for NC and Schools)

Lighting

- EQ Credit 6.1: Controllability of Systems, Lighting (for NC and Schools)
- EQ Credit 8.1: Daylight and Views, Daylight
- EQ Credit 8.2: Daylight and Views, Views

Acoustics

- EQ Prerequisite 3: Minimum Acoustical Performance (for Schools)
- EQ Credit 9: Enhanced Acoustical Performance (for Schools)

Appendix E

RELATED PREREQUISITES AND CREDITS

			Sustainable Sites																	
			Prereq 1	Prereq 2 (Schools)	Credit 1	Credit 2	Credit 3	Credit 4.1	Credit 4.2	Credit 4.3	Credit 4.4	Credit 5.1	Credit 5.2	Credit 6.1	Credit 6.2	Credit 7.1	Credit 7.2	Credit 8	Credit 9 (CS)	Credit 9 (Schools)	Credit 10 (Schools)
Sustainable Sites	Prerequisite 1	Construction Activity Pollution Prevention										X	X	X	X						
	Prerequisite 2	Environmental Site Assessment (Schools)					X														
	Credit 1	Site Selection				X	X	X				X	X	X	X						
	Credit 2	Development Density & Community Connectivity			X		X														
	Credit 3	Brownfield Redevelopment	X	X																	
	Credit 4.1	Alternative Transportation, Public Transportation Access			X	X															
	Credit 4.2	Alternative Transportation, Bicycle Use											X	X	X						
	Credit 4.3	Alternative Transportation, Low-Emitting & Fuel-Efficient Vehicles									X										
	Credit 4.4	Alternative Transportation, Parking Capacity										X	X	X	X	X					
	Credit 5.1	Site Development, Protect or Restore Habitat											X	X	X	X	X				
	Credit 5.2	Site Development, Maximize Open Space												X	X	X	X				
	Credit 6.1	Stormwater Design, Quantity Control										X	X			X					
	Credit 6.2	Stormwater Design, Quality Control										X	X			X	X				
	Credit 7.1	Heat Island Effect, Non-Roof										X	X	X							
	Credit 7.2	Heat Island Effect, Roof										X	X	X	X						
	Credit 8	Light Pollution Reduction																			
	Credit 9	Tenant Guidelines (CS)																			
	Credit 9	Site Master Plan (Schools)			X							X	X	X	X			X			
	Credit 10	Joint Use of Facilities (Schools)				X															
Water Efficiency	Prerequisite 1	Water Use Reduction, 20% Reduction												X	X						
	Credit 1	Water Efficient Landscaping										X	X	X	X	X	X				
	Credit 2	Innovative Wastewater Technologies												X	X						
	Credit 3	Water Use Reduction												X	X						
	Credit 4	Process Water Use Reduction (Schools)																			
Energy & Atmosphere	Prerequisite 1	Fundamental Commissioning of the Building Energy Systems															X				
	Prerequisite 2	Minimum Energy Performance															X	X			
	Prerequisite 3	Fundamental Refrigerant Management																			
	Credit 1	Optimize Energy Performance															X	X			
	Credit 2	On-Site Renewable Energy																			
	Credit 3	Enhanced Commissioning																X			
	Credit 4	Enhanced Refrigerant Management																			
	Credit 5	Measurement & Verification																			
	Credit 6	Green Power															X				
Materials & Resources	Prerequisite 1	Storage & Collection of Recyclables																			
	Credit 1.1	Building Reuse, Maintain Existing Walls, Floors & Roof																			
	Credit 1.2	Building Reuse, Maintain 50% of Interior Non-Structural Elements																			
	Credit 2	Construction Waste Management					X														
	Credit 3	Materials Reuse																			
	Credit 4	Recycled Content																			
	Credit 5	Regional Materials																			
	Credit 6	Rapidly Renewable Materials (NC & Schools)																			
	Credit 7 (CSc6)	Certified Wood																			
Indoor Environmental Quality	Prerequisite 1	Minimum IAQ Performance					X	X	X	X	X										
	Prerequisite 2	Environmental Tobacco Smoke (ETS) Control																			
	Prerequisite 3	Minimum Acoustical Performance (Schools)																			
	Credit 1	Outdoor Air Delivery Monitoring						X	X	X	X										
	Credit 2	Increased Ventilation					X	X	X	X	X										
	Credit 3.1 (CSc3)	Construction IAQ Mgmt Plan: During Construction																			
	Credit 3.2	Construction IAQ Mgmt Plan: Before Occupancy (NC & Schools)																			
	Credit 4*	Low-Emitting Materials																			
	Credit 5	Indoor Chemical & Pollutant Source Control																			
	Credit 6.1	Controllability of Systems, Lighting (NC & Schools)																			
	Credit 6.2 (CSc6)	Thermal Comfort: Controllability																			
	Credit 7.1 (CSc7)	Thermal Comfort: Design																			
	Credit 7.2	Thermal Comfort: Verification (NC & Schools)																			
	Credit 8.1	Daylighting & Views: Daylight 75% of Spaces																			
	Credit 8.2	Daylighting & Views: Views for 90% of Spaces																			
	Credit 9	Enhanced Acoustical Performance (Schools)																			
	Credit 10	Mold Prevention (Schools)																			

*: Low-emitting material credits are all interrelated

	Water Efficiency					Energy & Atmosphere									Materials & Resources									Indoor Environmental Quality																	
	Prereq 1	Credit 1	Credit 2	Credit 3	Credit 4 (Schools)	Prereq 1	Prereq 2	Prereq 3	Credit 1	Credit 2	Credit 3	Credit 4	Credit 5	Credit 6	Prereq 1	Credit 1.1	Credit 1.2	Credit 2	Credit 3	Credit 4	Credit 5	Credit 6	Credit 7	Prereq 1	Prereq 2	Prereq 3 (Schools)	Credit 1	Credit 2	Credit 3.1	Credit 3.2 (NC & Schools)	Credit 4*	Credit 5	Credit 6.1	Credit 6.2	Credit 7.1	Credit 7.2 (NC & Schools)	Credit 8.1	Credit 8.2	Credit 9 (Schools)	Credit 10 (Schools)
		X																																						
		X																																						
				X				X																																
									X																										X					
				X				X		X		X													X		X	X	X		X	X	X	X	X	X	X	X	
	X	X	X	X	X	X			X		X																													
							X		X																															
X	X		X		X						X																													
X	X	X	X	X							X																													
					X								X																											
	X	X	X			X		X	X	X	X												X				X					X	X	X	X	X			
		X	X						X			X											X			X	X					X	X	X			X	X	
		X	X					X				X											X				X	X					X	X	X					
	X	X	X		X	X		X	X			X											X				X					X	X	X	X	X			
						X	X		X																											X				
					X	X		X	X	X																														
						X		X																																
														X	X																									
														X	X																									
														X	X	X		X	X	X																				
														X	X		X		X	X																				
														X	X	X	X																							
																	X												X											
			X					X		X															X			X	X											
			X				X		X		X												X			X	X													
			X					X		X																X														X
			X					X		X															X	X			X				X	X	X					
																							X				X	X		X	X	X	X						
																							X			X	X		X	X	X	X						X	
			X	X				X		X		X											X			X	X	X											
			X	X				X		X		X																X				X	X					X	X
			X	X				X		X			X																				X	X			X	X	
			X	X			X		X		X												X			X							X	X	X				
			X					X															X			X							X	X					
							X		X																									X	X			X	
							X		X																									X	X		X		
																								X															
																												X						X	X				

Appendix F

SAMPLE LEED NC SCORECARD[1]

Project Name

Date

LEED 2009 for New Construction and Major Renovation
Project Checklist

Sustainable Sites — 26 Possible Points

Yes ? No			
	Prereq 1	Construction Activity Pollution Prevention	Required
	Credit 1	Site Selection	1
	Credit 2	Development Density & Community Connectivity	5
	Credit 3	Brownfield Redevelopment	1
	Credit 4.1	Alternative Transportation, Public Transportation Access	6
	Credit 4.2	Alternative Transportation, Bicycle Storage & Changing Rooms	1
	Credit 4.3	Alternative Transportation, Low-Emitting & Fuel-Efficient Vehicles	3
	Credit 4.4	Alternative Transportation, Parking Capacity	2
	Credit 5.1	Site Development, Protection of Restore Habitat	1
	Credit 5.2	Site Development, Maximize Open Space	1
	Credit 6.1	Stormwater Design, Quantity Control	1
	Credit 6.2	Stormwater Design, Quality Control	1
	Credit 7.1	Heat Island Effect, Non-Roof	1
	Credit 7.2	Heat Island Effect, Roof	1
	Credit 8	Light Pollution Reduction	1

Water Efficiency — 10 Possible Points

Yes ? No			
	Prereq 1	Water Use Reduction – 20% Reduction	Required
	Credit 1	Water Efficient Landscaping	2 to 4
	Credit 2	Innovative Wastewater Technologies	2
	Credit 3	Water Use Reduction	2 to 4

Energy & Atmosphere — 35 Possible Points

Yes ? No			
	Prereq 1	Fundamental Commissioning of Building Energy Systems	Required
	Prereq 2	Minimum Energy Performance	Required
	Prereq 3	Fundamental Refrigerant Management	Required
	Credit 1	Optimize Energy Performance	1 to 19
	Credit 2	On-Site Renewable Energy	1 to 7
	Credit 3	Enhanced Commissioning	2
	Credit 4	Enhanced Refrigerant Management	2
	Credit 5	Measurement & Verification	3
	Credit 6	Green Power	2

Materials & Resources — 14 Possible Points

Yes ? No			
	Prereq 1	Storage & Collection of Recyclables	Required
	Credit 1.1	Building Reuse, Maintain Existing Walls, Floors & Roof	1 to 3
	Credit 1.2	Building Reuse, Maintain 50% of Interior Non-Structural Elements	1
	Credit 2	Construction Waste Management	1 to 2
	Credit 3	Materials Reuse	1 to 2

Materials & Resources, Continued — 14 Possible Points

Yes ? No			
	Credit 4	Recyled Content	1 to 2
	Credit 5	Regional Materials	1 to 2
	Credit 6	Rapidly Renewable Materials	1
	Credit 7	Certified Wood	1

Indoor Environmental Quality — 15 Possible Points

Yes ? No			
	Prereq 1	Minimum Indoor Air Quality Performance	Required
	Prereq 2	Environmental Tobacco Smoke (ETS) Control	Required
	Credit 1	Outdoor Air Delivery Monitoring	1
	Credit 2	Increased Ventilation	1
	Credit 3.1	Construction IAQ Management Plan – During Construction	1
	Credit 3.2	Construction IAQ Management Plan – Before Occupancy	1
	Credit 4.1	Low-Emitting Materials, Adhesives & Sealants	1
	Credit 4.2	Low-Emitting Materials, Paints & Coatings	1
	Credit 4.3	Low-Emitting Materials, Flooring Systems	1
	Credit 4.4	Low-Emitting Materials, Composite Wood & Agrifiber Products	1
	Credit 5	Indoor Chemical & Pollutant Source Control	1
	Credit 6.1	Controllability of Systems, Lighting	1
	Credit 6.2	Controllability of Systems, Thermal Comfort	1
	Credit 7.1	Thermal Comfort, Design	1
	Credit 7.2	Thermal Comfort, Verification	1
	Credit 8.1	Daylight & Views, Daylight	1
	Credit 8.2	Daylight & Views, Views	1

Innovation and Design Process — 6 Possible Points

Credit 1.1	Innovation or Exemplary Performance	1
Credit 1.2	Innovation or Exemplary Performance	1
Credit 1.3	Innovation or Exemplary Performance	1
Credit 1.4	Innovation	1
Credit 1.5	Innovation	1
Credit 2	LEED® Accredited Professional	1

Regional Priority Credits — 4 Possible Points

Credit 1.1	Regional Priority: Specific Credit	1
Credit 1.2	Regional Priority: Specific Credit	1
Credit 1.3	Regional Priority: Specific Credit	1
Credit 1.4	Regional Priority: Specific Credit	1

Total — 110 Possible Points

Certified: 40 to 49 points, **Silver:** 50 to 59 points, **Gold:** 60 to 79 points, **Platinum:** 80 to 110 points

Appendix G

SAMPLE LEED CS SCORECARD[1]

Project Name
Date

LEED 2009 for Core and Shell Development
Project Checklist

Yes ? No

Sustainable Sites — 28 Possible Points

		Points
Prereq 1	Construction Activity Pollution Prevention	Required
Credit 1	Site Selection	1
Credit 2	Development Density & Community Connectivity	5
Credit 3	Brownfield Redevelopment	1
Credit 4.1	Alternative Transportation, Public Transportation Access	6
Credit 4.2	Alternative Transportation, Bicycle Storage & Changing Rooms	2
Credit 4.3	Alternative Transportation, Low-Emitting & Fuel-Efficient Vehicles	3
Credit 4.4	Alternative Transportation, Parking Capacity	2
Credit 5.1	Site Development, Protection of Restore Habitat	1
Credit 5.2	Site Development, Maximize Open Space	1
Credit 6.1	Stormwater Design, Quantity Control	1
Credit 6.2	Stormwater Design, Quality Control	1
Credit 7.1	Heat Island Effect, Non-Roof	1
Credit 7.2	Heat Island Effect, Roof	1
Credit 8	Light Pollution Reduction	1
Credit 9	Tenant Design & Construction Guidelines	1

Water Efficiency — 10 Possible Points

		Points
Prereq 1	Water Use Reduction – 20% Reduction	Required
Credit 1	Water Efficient Landscaping	2 to 4
Credit 2	Innovative Wastewater Technologies	2
Credit 3	Water Use Reduction	2 to 4

Energy & Atmosphere — 37 Possible Points

		Points
Prereq 1	Fundamental Commissioning of Building Energy Systems	Required
Prereq 2	Minimum Energy Performance	Required
Prereq 3	Fundamental Refrigerant Management	Required
Credit 1	Optimize Energy Performance	3 to 21
Credit 2	On-Site Renewable Energy	4
Credit 3	Enhanced Commissioning	2
Credit 4	Enhanced Refrigerant Management	2
Credit 5.1	Measurement & Verification – Base Building	3
Credit 5.2	Measurement & Verification – Tenant Metering	3
Credit 6	Green Power	2

Materials & Resources — 13 Possible Points

		Points
Prereq 1	Storage & Collection of Recyclables	Required
Credit 1	Building Reuse, Maintain Existing Walls, Floors & Roof	1 to 5

Materials & Resources, Continued — 13 Possible Points

		Points
Credit 2	Construction Waste Management	1 to 2
Credit 3	Materials Reuse	1
Credit 4	Recyled Content	1 to 2
Credit 5	Regional Materials	1 to 2
Credit 6	Certified Wood	1

Indoor Environmental Quality — 12 Possible Points

		Points
Prereq 1	Minimum Indoor Air Quality Performance	Required
Prereq 2	Environmental Tobacco Smoke (ETS) Control	Required
Credit 1	Outdoor Air Delivery Monitoring	1
Credit 2	Increased Ventilation	1
Credit 3	Construction IAQ Management Plan – During Construction	1
Credit 4.1	Low-Emitting Materials, Adhesives & Sealants	1
Credit 4.2	Low-Emitting Materials, Paints & Coatings	1
Credit 4.3	Low-Emitting Materials, Flooring Systems	1
Credit 4.4	Low-Emitting Materials, Composite Wood & Agrifiber Products	1
Credit 5	Indoor Chemical & Pollutant Source Control	1
Credit 6	Controllability of Systems, Thermal Comfort	1
Credit 7	Thermal Comfort, Design	1
Credit 8.1	Daylight & Views, Daylight	1
Credit 8.2	Daylight & Views, Views	1

Innovation and Design Process — 6 Possible Points

		Points
Credit 1.1	Innovation or Exemplary Performance	1
Credit 1.2	Innovation or Exemplary Performance	1
Credit 1.3	Innovation or Exemplary Performance	1
Credit 1.4	Innovation	1
Credit 1.5	Innovation	1
Credit 2	LEED® Accredited Professional	1

Regional Priority Credits — 4 Possible Points

		Points
Credit 1.1	Regional Priority: Specific Credit	1
Credit 1.2	Regional Priority: Specific Credit	1
Credit 1.3	Regional Priority: Specific Credit	1
Credit 1.4	Regional Priority: Specific Credit	1

Total — 110 Possible Points

Certified: 40 to 49 points, **Silver:** 50 to 59 points, **Gold:** 60 to 79 points, **Platinum:** 80 to 110 points

Appendix H

SAMPLE LEED FOR SCHOOLS SCORECARD[1]

Project Name

Date

LEED 2009 for School New Construction and Major Renovation

Project Checklist

Sustainable Sites		Possible Points:	24
Prereq 1	Construction Activity Pollution Prevention		
Prereq 1	Environmental Site Assessment		
Credit 1	Site Selection	1	
Credit 2	Development Density & Community Connectivity	4	
Credit 3	Brownfield Redevelopment	1	
Credit 4.1	Alternative Transportation – Public Transportation Access	4	
Credit 4.2	Alternative Transportation – Bicycle Storage & Changing Rooms	1	
Credit 4.3	Alternative Transportation – Low-Emitting & Fuel-Efficient Vehicles	2	
Credit 4.4	Alternative Transportation – Parking Capacity	2	
Credit 5.1	Site Development – Protect or Restore Habitat	1	
Credit 5.2	Site Development – Maximize Open Space	1	
Credit 6.1	Stormwater Design – Quantity Control	1	
Credit 6.2	Stormwater Design – Quality Control	1	
Credit 7.1	Heat Island Effect – Non-Roof	1	
Credit 7.2	Heat Island Effect – Roof	1	
Credit 8	Light Pollution Reduction	1	
Credit 9	Site Master Plan	1	
Credit 10	Joint Use of Facilities	1	

Water Efficiency		Possible Points:	11
Prereq 1	Water Use Reduction – 20% Reduction		
Credit 1	Water Efficient Landscaping	2 to 4	
Credit 2	Innovative Wastewater Technologies	2	
Credit 3	Water Use Reduction	2 to 4	
Credit 3	Process Water Use Reduction	1	

Energy & Atmosphere		Possible Points:	33
Prereq 1	Fundamental Commissioning of Building Energy Systems		
Prereq 2	Minimum Energy Performance		
Prereq 3	Fundamental Refrigerant Management		
Credit 1	Optimize Energy Performance	1 to 19	
Credit 2	On-Site Renewable Energy	1 to 7	
Credit 3	Enhanced Commissioning	1	
Credit 4	Enhanced Refrigerant Management	2	
Credit 5	Measurement & Verification	2	
Credit 6	Green Power	2	

Materials & Resources		Possible Points:	13
Prereq 1	Storage & Collection of Recyclables		
Credit 1.1	Building Reuse – Maintain Existing Walls, Floors & Roof	1 to 2	
Credit 1.2	Building Reuse – Maintain 50% of Interior Non-Structural Elements	1	
Credit 2	Construction Waste Management	1 to 2	

Yes No ?

Materials & Resources, Continued		Possible Points:	13
Credit 3	Materials Reuse	1 to 2	
Credit 4	Recyled Content	1 to 2	
Credit 5	Regional Materials	1 to 2	
Credit 6	Rapidly Renewable Materials	1	
Credit 7	Certified Wood	1	

Indoor Environmental Quality		Possible Points:	19
Prereq 1	Minimum Indoor Air Quality Performance		
Prereq 2	Environmental Tobacco Smoke (ETS) Control		
Prereq 3	Minimum Acoustical Performance		
Credit 1	Outdoor Air Delivery Monitoring	1	
Credit 2	Increased Ventilation	1	
Credit 3.1	Construction IAQ Management Plan – During Construction	1	
Credit 3.2	Construction IAQ Management Plan – Before Occupancy	1	
Credit 4	Low-Emitting Materials	1 to 4	
Credit 5	Indoor Chemical and Pollutant Source Control	1	
Credit 6.1	Controllability of Systems – Lighting	1	
Credit 6.2	Controllability of Systems – Thermal Comfort	1	
Credit 7.1	Thermal Comfort – Design	1	
Credit 7.2	Thermal Comfort – Verification	1	
Credit 8.1	Daylight and Views – Daylight	1 to 3	
Credit 8.2	Daylight and Views – Views	1	
Credit 9	Enhanced Acoustical Performance	1	
Credit 10	Mold Prevention	1	

Innovation and Design Process		Possible Points:	6
Credit 1.1	Innovation in Design: Specific Tittle	1	
Credit 1.2	Innovation in Design: Specific Tittle	1	
Credit 1.3	Innovation in Design: Specific Tittle	1	
Credit 1.4	Innovation in Design: Specific Tittle	1	
Credit 2	LEED Accredited Professional	1	
Credit 3	The School as a Teaching Tool	1	

Regional Priority Credits		Possible Points:	4
Credit 1.1	Regional Priority: Specific Credit	1	
Credit 1.2	Regional Priority: Specific Credit	1	
Credit 1.3	Regional Priority: Specific Credit	1	
Credit 1.4	Regional Priority: Specific Credit	1	

Total		Possible Points:	110

Certified: 40 to 49 points, **Silver:** 50 to 59 points, **Gold:** 60 to 79 points, **Platinum:** 80 to 110 points

Appendix I

EXEMPLARY PERFORMANCE OPPORTUNITIES WITHIN THE BD+C LEED RATING SYSTEMS

Sustainable Sites

SSc2	Development Density and Community Connectivity	Project is double the density of the community average OR Community density of at least 120K square feet/acre in 2X the radius.
SSc4 (all credits)	Alternative Transportation	Comprehensive transportation management plan that shows quantifiable reduction in auto use.
SSc4.1	Alternative Transportation, Public Transportation	Within a 1/2 mile of at least two existing commuter rail, light rail, or subway lines OR within a 1/4 mile of at least four or more public or campus bus lines
SSc5.1	Site Development	Previously developed sites only: Protect/restore 75% of the site excluding building footprint, or 30% of the total site (including footprint), whichever is greater, with native/adapted vegetation.
SSc5.2	Maximize Open Space	Double the amount of open space required for credit achievement, regardless of option. Exceed zoning by 50% OR if a government project not subject to zoning open space should equal two times the building footprint OR if an urban project with no open space required open space should equal 40% of site area.
SSc6	Stormwater Management	Document comprehensive approach to capture and treat stormwater runoff demonstrating performance above and beyond credit requirements. SSc6.1 Quantity Control OR SSc6.2 Quality Control
SSc7.1	Heat Island Effect: Nonroof	100% nonroof hardscape is high-albedo, open grid, or shaded within five years OR 100% of parking spaces are under cover.
SSc7.2	Heat Island Effect: Roof	100% of the project's eligible roof area is vegetated.
SSc10	Joint Use of Facilities (Schools Only)	Meet 2 of the 3 options, rather than just 1

Water Efficiency

WEc2	Innovative Wastewater Technologies	100% reduction in potable water use for sewage conveyance OR on-site treatment of 100% of wastewater-treated water must be reused or infiltrated on-site.
WEc3	Water Use Reduction	45% reduction in projected potable water use, Exemplary performance calcs can include nonregulated fixtures (dishwashers and washing machines).
WEc4	Process Water Use Reduction (Schools Only)	Projected process water savings of 40%.

Energy & Atmosphere

EAc1	Optimize Energy Performance	Option 1 (simulation): 50% improvement over 90.1 for new construction and 46% for renovations.
EAc2	On-Site Renewable Energy	On-site renewable energy accounts for 15% (NC & Schools) or 5% (CS) of annual energy costs.
EAc3	Enhanced Commissioning	Comprehensive envelope commissioning. Demonstrate standards and protocol by which envelope was commissioned.
EAc6	Green Power	Purchase 70% of annual power needed from a renewable source for two years.

Materials & Resources

MRc1	Building Reuse (Core & Shell Only)	Maintain 95% or more of the existing walls, floors, and roof.
MRc2	Construction Waste Management	Divert 95% or more of total construction waste.
MRc3	Materials Reuse	NC and Schools: 15% of materials cost; CS: 10% of materials cost.
MRc4	Recycled Content	Total recycled content value is 30% or more of materials costs.
MRc5	Regional Materials	Regional materials value is 30% or more of materials costs.
MRc6	Rapidly Renewable Materials (NC and Schools Only)	5% or more of materials costs are attributed to rapidly renewable materials.
MRc7 (MRc6 for CS)	Certified Wood	FSC-certified wood value is 95% of total new wood value.

Indoor Environmental Quality

IEQc3	Construction Indoor Air Quality Management Plan (CS Only)	Enforce Construction IAQ Management plan for 100% of tenant spaces.
IEQc8.1	Daylight	95% (NC & CS) or 90% (Schools) daylight in regularly occupied spaces.
IEQc8.2	Views	Comply with two of the four additional measures for 90% of regularly occupied spaces: (1) Multiple lines of sight from directions at least 90 degrees apart; (2) Views of at least two of the three options: vegetation, humans, or objects at least 70 feet from the glazing; (3) Unobstructed views located within three times the head height of the vision glazing. (4) Views with a view factor of 3 or greater.
IEQc9	Enhanced Acoustical Performance (Schools Only)	Outdoor background noise level of either: (1) 55 dBA for playgrounds, 60 dBA for athletic fields and all other school grounds, OR (2) 35 dBA indoor noise level.
IEQc10	Mold Prevention (Schools Only)	No prescribed threshold; case-by-case basis.

Appendix J

REFERENCED STANDARDS OF BD+C

Sustainable Sites

SSp1	Construction Activity Pollution Prevention	2003 EPA Construction General Permit
SSp2	Environmental Site Assessment	ASTM E1527-05, Phase I Environmental Site Assessment
		ASTM E1903-97 Phase II Environmental Site Assessment
SSc1	Site Selection	USDA Definition of Prime Agricultural Land (US CFR)
		FEMA 100-Year Flood Definition
		Endangered Species Lists (US Fish & Wildlife Service)
		National Marine Fisheries Service, List of Endangered Marine Species
		Definitions of Wetlands in the US CFR (40 CFR, Parts 230-233, 22)
SSc3	Brownfield Redevelopment	ASTM E1903-97 Phase II Environmental Site Analysis
		ASTM E1527-05, Phase I Environmental Site Assessment
		EPA Brownfields Definition
SSc4	Alternative Transportation, Parking Capacity	Institute of Transportation Engineers, Parking Generation Study, 2003
SSc6.2	Stormwater Management, Quality Control	Guidance Specifying Mgmt Measures for Sources of Non-Point Pollution in Coastal Waters (US EPA 840B92002)
SSc7.1	Heat Island Effect, Nonroof	ASTM E408-71(1996)e1, Standard Test Methods for Total Normal Emittance of Surfaces Using Inspection-Meter Techniques
		ASTM C1371-04a Standard Test Method for Determination of Emittance of Materials Near Room Temperature Using Portable Emissometers
		ASTM C1549-04 - Determination of Solar Reflectance Near Ambient Temperature
		ASTM E1918-97 - Solar Reflectance of Horizontal and Low-Sloped Surfaces in Field
		ASTM E903-96 - Solar Absorbance, Reflectance, and Transmittance Integrating Sphere
SSc7.2	Heat Island Effect, Roof	ASTM E1980-01 - SRI of Horizontal and Low-Sloped Opaque Surfaces
		ASTM E408-71 - Total Normal Emittance of Surfaces Using Inspection Meter
		ASTM E903-96 - Solar Absorbance, Reflectance, and Transmittance Integrating Sphere
		ASTM E1918-97 - Solar Reflectance of Horizontal and Low-Sloped Surfaces in Field

		ASTM C1371-04 - Determination of Emittance of Materials Near Room Temp
		ASTM C1549-04 - Determination of Solar Reflectance Near Ambient Temperature
SSc8	Light Pollution Reduction	ASHRAE/IESNA 90.1-2004 (Lighting, Section 9 without amendments)

Water Efficiency

WEp1	Water Use Reduction	Energy Policy Act (EPAct 1992)
		Energy Policy Act (EPAct 2005)
		International Association of Plumbing and Mechanical Officials Publication IAPMO/ ANSI UPC 1-2006 section 402.0, Water-Conservation Fixtures and Fittings
		International Code Council, IPC 2006, section 604, Design of Building Water Distribution System
WEc2	Innovative Wastewater Technologies	Refer to WEp1 Standards
WEc3	Water Use Reduction	Refer to WEp1 Standards

Energy & Atmosphere

EAp2	Minimum Energy Performance	ASHRAE/IESNA 90.1-2007
		ASHRAE Advanced Design Guide for Small Office Buildings 2004
		ASHRAE Advanced Design Guide for Small Warehouses and Self-Storage Buildings 2008
		ASHRAE Advanced Design Guide for Retail Buildings 2006
		ASHRAE Advanced Energy Design Guide for K–12 School Buildings
		New Building Institute, Advanced Buildings Core Performance Guide
		ENERGY STAR Program, Target Finder Rating Tool
EAp3	Fundamental Refrigerant Management	U.S. EPA Clean Air Act, Title VI, Section 608, Refrigerant Recycling Rule
EAc1	Optimize Energy Performance	Refer to EAp2
EAc2	On-Site Renewable Energy	ASHRAE/IESNA 90.1-2007
EAc5	Measurement & Verification	IPMVP Volume III
EAc6	Green Power	Center for Resource Solutions' Green-e Product Certification Requirements

Materials & Resources

MRc4	Recycled Content	International Standard ISO14021-1999 - Environmental Labels and Declarations
MRc7	Certified Wood	Forest Stewardship Council's Principles and Criteria

Indoor Environmental Quality

EQp1	Minimum IAQ Performance	ASHRAE 62.1-2007 - Ventilation for Acceptable Indoor Air Quality
EQp2	Environmental Tobacco Smoke Control	ANSI/ASTM E779-03, Standard Test Method for Determining Air Leakage
		Residential Manual for Compliance w/ CA's 2001 Energy Efficiency Standards, Ch. 4
EQp3	Minimum Acoustical Performance	ANSI/ASHRAE S12.60-2002, Acoustical Performance Criteria, Design Requirements, and Guidelines for Schools
		ASHRAE Handbook, Chapter 47, Sound and Vibration Control, 2003 HVAC Applications
EQc1	Outdoor Delivery Monitoring	ASHRAE 62.1-2007 - Ventilation for Acceptable Indoor Air Quality
EQc2	Increased Ventilation	ASHRAE 62.1-2007 - Ventilation for Acceptable Indoor Air Quality
		The Carbon Trust Good Practice Guide 237 - Natural Ventilation in Nondomestic Buildings: A Guide for Developers, Architects, and Owners
		CIBSE Applications Manual 10: 2005, Natural Ventilation in Nondomestic Buildings
EQc3.1	Construction IAQ Management Plan: During Construction	ANSI/ASHRAE 52.2-1999 - Method of Testing General Ventilation Air-Cleaning Devices for Removal Efficiency by Particle Size
		IAQ Guidelines for Occupied Buildings Under Construction, SMACNA
EQc3.2	Construction IAQ Management Plan: Before Occupancy	US EPA "Compendium of Methods for the Determination of Air Pollutants in Indoor Air"
EQc4.1	Low-Emitting Materials: Adhesives and Sealants	South Coast Rule #1168, South Coast Air Quality Management District
		Green Seal Standard GS-36 (Commercial Adhesives)
EQc4.2	Low-Emitting Materials: Paints and Coatings	South Coast Air Quality Management District (SCAQMD) Rule #1113, Coatings
		Green Seal Standard GC-03 (anticorrosive and antirust paints)
		Green Seal Standard GS-11 (commercial flat and nonflat paints)
EQc4.3	Low-Emitting Materials: Carpet Systems	Carpet and Rug Institute Green Label Plus Testing Program
		South Coast Rule #1168, South Coast Air Quality Management District, VOC Limits
		South Coast Rule #1113, South Coast Air Quality Management District, Architectural Coatings
		Floor Score Program
		California Department of Health Services Standard Practice for Testing of Volatile Organic Emissions from Various Sources Using Small-Scale Environmental Chambers

		State of California Standard 1350, Section 9, Standard Practice for Testing of Volatile Organic Emissions from Various Sources Using Small-Scale Environmental Chambers, Testing Criteria
EQc4.4	Low-Emitting Materials: Composite Wood and Agrifiber Products	(Schools): California Department of Health Services Standard Practice for Testing of Volatile Organic Emissions from Various Sources Using Small-Scale Environmental Chambers
EQc4.5	Low-Emitting Materials: Furniture and Furnishings	(Schools): ANSI/Business and Institutional Furniture Makers' Association (BIFMA) x7.1-2007 Standard for Formalehyde and TVOC Emissions of Low-Emitting Office Furniture Systems and Seating
		Environmental Technology Verification (ETV) Large Chamber Test Protocol for Measuring Emissions of VOCs and Aldehydes, effective September 1999
		Greenguard Certification Program
EQc4.6	Low-Emitting Materials: Ceiling and Wall Systems	California Department of Health Services Standard Practice for Testing of Volatile Organic Emissions from Various Sources Using Small-Scale Environmental Chambers
EQc5	Indoor Chemical and Pollutant Source Control	ANSI/ASHRAE 52.2-1999 - Method of Testing General Ventilation Air-Cleaning Devices for Removal Efficiency by Particle Size
EQc6.2	Controllability of Systems: Thermal Comfort	ASHRAE 62.1-2007 - Ventilation for Acceptable Indoor Air Quality
		ASHRAE 55-2004 - Thermal Comfort Conditions for Human Occupancy
EQc7	Thermal Comfort	ASHRAE 55-2004 - Thermal Comfort Conditions for Human Occupancy
		CIBSE Applications Manual 10: 2005, Natural Ventilation in Non-Domestic Buildings
		(Schools): ASHRAE HVAC Applications Handbook, 2003 edition, Chapter 4 (Places of Assembly), Typical Natatorium Design Conditions
EQc7.2	Thermal Comfort: Verification	ASHRAE 55-2004 - Thermal Comfort Conditions for Human Occupancy
EQc8.1	Daylight and Views: Daylight	ASTM D1003-07e1, Standard Test Method for Haze and Luminous Transmittance of Transparent Plastics
EQc9	Enhanced Acoustical Performance	ANSI/ASHRAE S12.60-2002, Acoustical Performance Criteria, Design Requirements, and Guidelines for Schools
		ASHRAE Handbook, Chapter 47, Sound and Vibration Control, 2003 HVAC Applications
EQc10	Mold Prevention	Building Air Quality: A guide for Building Owners and Facility Managers, EPA Reference Number 402-F-91-102, effective December 1991

Innovation in Design

IDc2	LEED Accredited Professional	LEED Accredited Professional - (GBCI) Green Building Certification Institute

Appendix K

ANSWERS TO QUIZ QUESTIONS

CHAPTER 2: SUSTAINABILITY AND LEED BASICS REVIEW

Q2.1. **E.** All of the four options listed are environmental benefits of green building design, construction, and operational efforts.

Q2.2. **B.** According to the EPA website, Americans typically spend about 90 percent of their time indoors.

Q2.3. **A.** Thirty-eight percent of energy in the United States is used for space heating, followed by lighting with 20 percent of energy usage.

Q2.4. **E.** All of the four options listed describe high-performance green building strategies.

Q2.5. **B.** Risk is collectively managed in an IPD. The risks and rewards are both shared in an IPD project.

Q2.6. **A.** Incorporating green building strategies and technologies is best started from the very beginning of the design process. Schematic design is the earliest phase of the design process, and therefore the correct answer.

Q2.7. **A.** It is important to remember that LCAs look at not only the present impacts and benefits during each phase of the process, but future and potential impacts as well.

Q2.8. **B and C.** LCAs include the purchase price, installation, operation, maintenance, and upgrade costs for each technology and strategy proposed.

Q2.9. **A, D, and E.** Although it is strongly encouraged to begin the integrative design process and to incorporate green building technologies and strategies as early as possible in the design process, it is not intended to be an elaborate process. Value engineering should not be needed if the triple bottom line principles are applied.

Q2.10. **B and C.** Certification bodies are managed by GBCI and are assigned to a project team after registration, to assist with the process for a project seeking LEED certification, including the review of and response to credit interpretation requests (CIRs). GBCI is responsible for the appeals process.

CHAPTER 3: THE LEED RATING SYSTEMS OF THE *BD+C REFERENCE GUIDE*

Q3.1. **D.** The LEED Core & Shell rating system requires the developer/owner to occupy less than 50 percent of the building and therefore is the most appropriate rating system for this project.

Q3.2. **A and C.** Although the credits within the LEED rating systems are now weighted differently in the new version, the rating systems were not reorganized. The five main categories still exist, but now the rating systems are based on a 100-point scale. Each credit is now weighted in correlation to its impact on energy efficiency and CO_2 reductions.

Q3.3. **C.** Ultimately, it is up to the project team to decide which rating system is best suited to their project. A LEED for Universities rating system does not exist.

Q3.4. **D.** USGBC consulted with NIST and the EPA's TRACI tool to determine the credit weightings by assessing carbon overlay.

Q3.5. **B.** Although the strategies listed will increase the first costs for a project, it is important to remember the life-cycle costs, including purchase price, installation, operation, maintenance, and upgrade costs.

Q3.6. **A.** Make sure to remember the point range scales of the LEED certification levels for the purposes of the exam.

Q3.7. **A and C.** CIRs are submitted to the project's assigned GBCI certification body for review, electronically through LEED-Online. CIRs are limited to 600 words and should not be formatted as a letter. Since the CIR is submitted electronically through LEED-Online, the project and credit or prerequisite information is tracked; therefore, the CIR does not need to include this type of information. It is critical to remember that CIRs are submitted specific to one credit or prerequisite.

Q3.8. **C.** All projects seeking certification in any of the BD+C rating systems must include a minimum of 1,000 square feet of gross floor area per the MPRs listed on the USGBC website.

Q3.9. **B and E.** Be sure to remember each of the MPRs and how they pertain to each rating system, as posted on the GBCI website.

Q3.10. **E.** All projects seeking LEED certification must commit to sharing 5 years' worth of actual whole-project energy and water usage data with USGBC and/or GBCI.

Q3.11. **B and E.** Appeals are electronically submitted to GBCI through LEED-Online for a fee, within 25 business days after the final results from a design or construction certification review are posted to LEED-Online.

Q3.12. **C.** It is also important to remember, although the Regional Priority category is a new addition to the rating systems, no new prerequisites or credits were created to include within the new category. The Regional Priority category offers bonus points for achieving existing LEED credits detailed in the other categories.

Q3.13. **B.** Although design reviews can be beneficial, points are not awarded until final review after construction.

Q3.14. **D and E.** Registering with GBCI indicates a project is seeking LEED certification. GBCI assigns a certification body to help a project team through the process and to answer any CIRs. Project registration can be completed at any time, although it is strongly encouraged to do so as early as possible. GBCI does not grant the award of any points regardless when registration occurs. Registration will, however, grant the project team access to a LEED-Online site specific for the project, but does not include any free submissions of CIRs.

Q3.15. **A and C.** Although registering a project requires some information, including contact information, project location, and indication of compliance with MPRs, a team must submit all credit submittal templates for all prerequisites and attempted credits during the certification application. Required supplemental documentation, such as plans and calculations, must be uploaded as well.

Q3.16. **C.** The earliest construction prerequisites and credits can be submitted, along with design prerequisites and credits, for certification review is after substantial completion.

Q3.17. **C.** It is important to remember that points are awarded only once the project team submits for construction review, not at the design phase certification review. Design-side review is optional and therefore not required.

Q3.18. **B.** Project teams have 25 business days to issue an appeal to GBCI after receiving the final review comments.

Q3.19. **B, C, and F.** CIRs can be submitted through LEED-Online, to the GBCI certification body assigned to the project, any time after registration. CIRs specifically address one MPR, prerequisite, or credit. Although the project administrator submits the CIR, the certification body response is viewable by all team members invited to the LEED-Online site for the project. CIRs are project specific, and therefore CIR responses will no longer be published to a database as they once were.

Q3.20. **A.** GBCI is responsible for the appeals process as well as managing the certification bodies. It is best to remember USGBC as an education provider for the LEED rating systems they create, and GBCI as being responsible for the professional accreditation and project certification processes.

CHAPTER 4: SUSTAINABLE SITES

Q4.1. **B.** Where a project is located and how it is developed can have multiple impacts on the ecosystem and water resources required during the life of a building.

Q4.2. **B.** In order to determine if a portion of land is a brownfield site, an examination is done via the ASTM E1903-97 Phase II Environmental Site Assessment.

Q4.3. **D and E.** Although sites near wetlands and bodies of water should be avoided, to comply with the Sustainable Sites credit, LEED projects should not be within 100 feet of wetlands or 50 feet of a body of water.

Q4.4. **A and C.** Be sure to remember the difference between the three types of remediation strategies.

Q4.5. **A.** The process of elimination might be helpful to use to deduce the most appropriate answer.

Q4.6. **A, B, and C.** According to the *Green Building and LEED Core Concepts Guide*, transportation is most impacted by location, vehicle technology, fuel, and human behavior.

Q4.7. **A, C, D, and E.** If a LEED project's site does not offer mass transit accessibility, and is therefore dependent on car commuting, it is best to encourage the occupants to carpool, offer alternative fuel-efficient vehicles, or incorporate conveniences within the building or on site.

Q4.8. **A, B, and C.** Selecting a site near public transportation, limiting parking, and encouraging carpooling are all strategies to consider when working on a project seeking LEED certification. It is always best to redevelop a previously developed site, avoiding greenfield sites.

Q4.9. **C.** Do your best to remember all the nuances for each of the three rating systems.

Q4.10. **C.** The key to reducing heat island effects is to avoid implementing materials that will absorb and retain heat. Deciduous trees lose their leaves and therefore are not the best decision. Xeriscaping to reduce evaporation and increasing impervious surfaces to recharge groundwater are great strategies for sustainable site design, but do not help to reduce heat island effects. They, in turn, reap the benefits of reduced heat island effects. Implementing paving and roofing products with a higher albedo, or SRI, is therefore the best answer to reduce heat island effects.

Q4.11. **F.** It is best to involve all the players related to designing and installing a green roof in a collaborative setting. Understanding the requirements of a green roof will indicate the team members required, especially what type of vegetation will be utilized. Remember, a green roof impacts the thermal elements of a building, structural integrity, stormwater management, and the coordination of construction trades.

Q4.12. **D.** Emissivity is the ability of a material surface to give up heat in the form of radiation. It may be helpful to remember emittance is the opposite of reflectivity. Infrared reflectivity applies to low-emissivity materials. Therefore, these materials reflect the majority of long-wave radiation and emit very little, such as metals or special metallic coatings. High-emissivity surfaces, such as painted building materials, absorb a majority of long-wave radiation as opposed to reflecting it, and emit infrared or long-wave radiation more willingly.

Q4.13. **A, B, and C.** The LEED rating systems recommend to combine the following three strategies to reduce heat island effects: provide shade (within five years of occupancy), install paving materials with an SRI of at least 29, and implement an open-grid pavement system (less than 50 percent impervious).

Q4.14. **C.** Remember, some material in this book can be presented for the first time in the format of a question. Use these opportunities to test your knowledge, and if you are not familiar with the content, be sure to make a flashcard or make a note on your cheat sheet in order to remember the information.

Q4.15. **A and E.** Do your best to remember all the nuances for each of the three rating systems.

Q4.16. **C.** Dedicate a section of your cheat sheet to LEED for Schools to remember all the details of the rating system.

Q4.17. **A, B, and D.** Be sure to use the study worksheets at the end of each chapter to help remember the details of each prerequisite and credit.

Q4.18. **A.** Dedicate a section of your cheat sheet to LEED for Schools to remember all the details of the rating system.

Q4.19. **B.** Be sure to use the study worksheets at the end of each chapter to help remember the details of each prerequisite and credit.

Q4.20. **A, C, and D.** Impervious asphalt does not allow rainwater to percolate through and therefore allows stormwater to leave the site, carrying pollutants and debris, heading to storm sewers and nearby bodies of water.

Q4.21. **C and E.** Project teams can evaluate location and site-specific information prior to the beginning of designing a structure and the site, to determine the efficiencies of strategies and technologies for a green building project. These issues include the availability of mass transit and public transportation, and brownfield redevelopment. Strategies to reduce heat island effects, provisions for preferred parking, and technologies to reduce water use can all be addressed during the design process.

Q4.22. **D.** Access to 10 basic services, such as banks, post offices, grocery stores, schools, restaurants, fire stations, hardware stores, pharmacies, libraries, theaters, museums, and fitness centers, is required to comply with LEED.

Q4.23. **B.** LEED requires a minimum score of 40 for low-emitting and fuel-efficient cars. Refer to www.aceee.org/ for more information.

Q4.24. **D and E.** Selecting products with the highest SRI values is best suited for compliance with LEED.

Q4.25. **A and C.** Learning the strategies to comply with each of the credits and prerequisites is key for the exam. Try to remember the intent behind each to help decipher the appropriate strategy or technology.

Q4.26. **D.** Remember to use your cheat sheet for details that are difficult to remember!

Q4.27. **E.** Trust your memory and your logical senses! Using the precious resource of water is not a sustainable solution.

Q4.28. A, B, and D. Unfortunately, for the purposes of LEED, carpooling and vanpooling do not count as public transportation strategies. For a citywide approach to ride sharing, try doing a web search for "DC slug lines."

Q4.29. B. In order to qualify for this credit, 50 percent of the roof surface must comply by the means of a high-SRI roofing material and/or a green roof. Photovoltaic panels and mechanical equipment square footage is subtracted from the compliant roof surface calculations. Therefore, 50,000 – 15,000 – 5,000 = 30,000 SF eligible roof surface, where 50 percent would need to comply with the minimum SRI level.

Q4.30. A. First, determine the FTE where full-time employees have a value of 1 and part-time employees working an average of four hours per day have half value, therefore the FTE = 700. For bike parking, 5 percent of 700 = 35 and for showers, 0.5 percent of 700 = 3.5. For the purposes of LEED, it is appropriate to round up values for compliance.

Q4.31. C. Remember to use your cheat sheet for details that are difficult to remember!

Q4.32. D. A strategy is not defined in the reference guide as it is up to the team to prove exemplary performance specific to their project strategies.

Q4.33. A and C. Exemplary performance is met when two out of the three compliance path options are provided. Option B is not correct, as toilets are not eligible to comply. Options D and E are not correct, as two dedicated use spaces are required for both options 2 and 3.

CHAPTER 5: WATER EFFICIENCY

Q5.1. A and E. Aerators and flush valves are the two most economically feasible options if fixtures cannot be replaced.

Q5.2. B and F. Remember flow fixture and flush fixture types for the exam.

Q5.3. C. Use your flashcards to remember these types of details.

Q5.4. A, D, and E. Remember the components addressed by EPAct.

Q5.5. A, B, and D. The question asks for strategies to reduce the amount of water needed to flush fixtures, not how to meet the requirements of the credit where C would have been correct. E would reduce the indoor water use consumptions but would not help to reduce the water needed for sewage conveyance.

Q5.6. A, B, and E. Turf grass poses a maintenance, economic, and environmental concern by the amount of watering it requires. Reducing pervious surfaces does not address saving water for landscaping, and from an environmental aspect, project teams are encouraged to *increase* pervious surfaces to recharge groundwater.

Q5.7. A, B, C, and D. The site design strategies do not address increasing the density factor. Density can be increased by development design strategies, such as increasing floor-to-area ratio (FAR).

Q5.8. C, D, and E. Installing open-grid pavers in lieu of asphalt minimizes the contributions to the urban heat island effect, as pavers do not absorb the heat from the sun as opposed to asphalt. By reducing heat gain, energy use is optimized, as the building has less of a demand for cooling loads. The pavers also allow stormwater to penetrate through to reduce runoff.

Q5.9. B and F. Remember the types of high-efficiency irrigation systems, as traditional sprinkler or spray-type systems do not comply.

Q5.10. **A, B, and C.** Process water is the water needed for building systems and business operations.

Q5.11. **B, C, and E.** Blackwater is wastewater from a toilet. Remembering the different types of nonpotable water can help answer other questions about specific design strategies as related to water efficiency.

Q5.12. **B and D.** Sometimes the process of elimination helps to determine the correct answers. Although captured rainwater is used for custodial uses, cleaning dishes and clothes is best with potable water sources.

Q5.13. **A, B, C, and E.** Make a flashcard to remember this information if necessary.

Q5.14. **C.** Stormwater quality would not be impacted as collecting rainwater for reuse does not improve the quality of the water prior to leaving the site for the purposes of complying with SS Credit 6.2.

CHAPTER 6: ENERGY AND ATMOSPHERE

Q6.1. **A and D.** Learning the concepts to comply with each of the credits and prerequisites is key for the exam. Try to remember the intent behind each to help decipher the appropriate strategy or technology. Refer to Appendix D for a summary of concepts and related credits/prerequisites.

Q6.2. **A.** Remember to use your cheat sheet for details difficult to remember!

Q6.3. **D.** Use your flashcards to quiz yourself on these types of details.

Q6.4. **C.** Be sure to remember when to use which compliance path, especially for this credit as it has project size thresholds.

Q6.5. **A and D.** Refer to your flashcards to remember the difference between regulated energy and process energy.

Q6.6. **A and D.** Be sure to remember when to use which compliance path, especially for this credit, as it has project size thresholds.

Q6.7. **C.** Use your flashcards to quiz yourself on these types of details or make a note on your cheat sheet.

Q6.8. **A.** Remember, it is advised to incorporate integrative design strategies as early as possible in the design process.

Q6.9. **B and D.** Remember, commissioning agents should be independent third parties to perform their responsibilities for the owner. A CxA is responsible for minimizing design flaws and assessing the installation, calibration, and performance for the main building systems.

Q6.10. **B and E.** Be sure to use the study worksheets at the end of each chapter to help remember the details of each prerequisite and credit.

Q6.11. **C.** Consult Appendix J for a list of all of the referenced standards and use the study worksheets at the end of each chapter to help remember the details of each prerequisite and credit.

Q6.12. **A.** Make your own Figure 6.13 to remember the ranking of refrigerants in terms of ODP.

Q6.13. **A, B, and D.** Process energy is not included in minimum LEED requirements for the EA Minimum Energy Performance prerequisite. Process energy uses include computers, office equipment, kitchen refrigeration and cooking, washing and drying machines, and elevators and escalators. Miscellaneous items, such as a waterfall pumps and lighting that is exempt from lighting power allowance calculations, such as lighting integrated into equipment, are also categorized as process energy uses.

Q6.14. **B, D, and E.** Refrigerants do not apply to boilers, fan motors, or variable-frequency drives, which eliminates answer options A and C.

Q6.15. **E.** It is critical to remember the details about refrigerants for the purposes of the exam.

Q6.16. **C.** Remember each of the referenced standards and what each applies to. Remember to think "energy" every time you read "ASHRAE 90.1"!

Q6.17. **B, D, and E.** Regulated energy uses include lighting, HVAC, and domestic and space heating for service water.

Q6.18. **B, E, and F.** Passive solar design features and off-site strategies do not contribute to earning the On-Site Renewable Energy credit. Ground-source heat pumps do not qualify either, as they require power to function the pump.

Q6.19. **C.** Green power should be remembered with off-site renewable energy, as green power is purchased and not installed for the purposes of the exam.

Q6.20. **C and E.** Although a CxA will be responsible for verifying the installation, calibration, and performance of the cogeneration system, the strategy described in the question does not indicate any information involving a CxA. The question does not indicate any renewable energy to be generated on site, nor does it refer to any offsetting green power procurement.

Q6.21. **B and C.** Use your flashcards to quiz yourself on these types of details or make a note on your cheat sheet.

Q6.22. **A and B.** Remember Table 6.2! There are 12 tasks to comply with the Enhanced Commissioning credit, which is 5 more tasks than what is required by the prerequisite.

Q6.23. **A, B, and E.** Nonroof strategies can include the provision of solar panel–covered structures, and roof strategies can also include a photovoltaic system as both synergistic credits contribute to on-site renewable energy generation. EA Credit 2 is related, as the on-site power that is generated will reduce demand from grid and therefore optimize performance.

CHAPTER 7: MATERIALS AND RESOURCES

Q7.1. **D.** First, determine the eligible items based on the requirements of the credit. The doors are not eligible, as they are not repurposed; therefore, the total amount reused is $120,000 of the total $2 million, for 17 percent compliance. The percentage threshold for School projects is 15 percent.

Q7.2. **B and D.** Remember the differences of the intentions and requirements of MR Credit 4: Recycled Content and MR Credit 3: Material Reuse. Whenever you see "nearby," try to remember the possible connection to MR Credit 5: Regional Materials.

Q7.3. **A, B, and C.** Be sure to refer to Appendix I for a list of the exemplary performance opportunities.

Q7.4. **A, D, and E.** Window assemblies are excluded, as it is assumed the window should be upgraded for a more efficient system. Hazardous materials are excluded for obvious reasons, and nonstructural materials are not addressed in this credit but MR Credit 1.2 instead.

Q7.5. **A and B.** Use your flashcards to quiz yourself on these types of details or make a note on your cheat sheet.

Q7.6. **C, D, and E.** Remember, preconsumer recycled content refers to scrap and trim material generated from the manufacturing process, but does not enter into the consumer cycle of goods. Preconsumer recycled materials are used to manufacture a different product than what it was originally intended for.

Q7.7. **A and D.** Regional materials, salvaged materials, and rapidly renewable materials are calculated as a percentage of the total material cost for a project for the purposes of LEED.

Q7.8. **B.** Rapidly renewable products can be grown or raised in 10 years or less.

Q7.9. **B and D.** For the purposes of LEED, FSC wood products are calculated as a percentage of the total cost of wood products purchased for a specific project. Chain-of-custody documentation should be tracked and the certification number entered into the credit submittal templates for proof of compliance.

Q7.10. **D.** If you have not worked on a project seeking LEED certification during construction, this would not have as much value to you, but consider if this default number were not available and if the real number had to be determined and the amount of work that would entail.

Q7.11. **C, E, and F.** Use your flashcards to quiz yourself on these types of details or make a note on your cheat sheet.

Q7.12. **A and B.** Be sure to refer to Appendix L for a list of all acronyms and abbreviations.

Q7.13. **B.** Landfills produce methane, a powerful greenhouse gas. Although methane can be captured and burned to generate energy, if it is emitted, it is harmful to the environment.

Q7.14. **B and C.** Cradle-to-cradle products can be recycled, while cradle-to-grave materials are landfilled. Products with either or both preconsumer and postconsumer recycled content can contribute to earning the LEED credit.

Q7.15. **B and C.** Stormwater management plans are typically the responsibility of the civil engineer, while the energy modeling calculations are typically provided by the mechanical engineer.

Q7.16. **B, D, and E.** Although evaluating all of the vendor's procurement policies to ensure that sustainable purchasing procedures are in place could possibly contribute to earning an Innovation in Design credit, it is not required for compliance with any of the MR credits. The CEO's automobile choice is also not evaluated or assessed for LEED compliance.

Q7.17. **D.** FSC credit compliance requires the completion of a credit submittal template including invoice amounts and chain-of-custody certification numbers. Remember, all documentation is submitted for review via LEED-Online for all projects.

Q7.18. **D.** Waste is calculated in tonnage for the purposes of LEED documentation.

Q7.19. **C and D.** Use your flashcards to quiz yourself on these types of details or make a note on your cheat sheet.

Q7.20. **B.** It is critical to know what factors are appropriate to be included in the calculation. The 20 tons of wood, plastic, and metal and 45 tons of concrete = 65 tons diverted. The 20 tons landfilled plus the 15 tons sent to an incineration plant = 35 tons not diverted. 65 + 35 = 100 total tons, as the 8 tons are not eligible to be included in the calculations.

CHAPTER 8: INDOOR ENVIRONMENTAL QUALITY

Q8.1.   **A and C.** Be sure to remember which credits are eligible for a design side review. Knowing what the documentation requirements are can help with the process of elimination for answer selections.

Q8.2.   **C.** Use your flashcards to quiz yourself on these types of details or make a note on your cheat sheet.

Q8.3.   **D.** Be sure to use the study worksheets at the end of each chapter to help remember the details of each prerequisite and credit.

Q8.4.   **B.** Use your flashcards to quiz yourself on these types of details or make a note on your cheat sheet.

Q8.5.   **D.** Use your flashcards to quiz yourself on these types of details or make a note on your cheat sheet.

Q8.6.   **D.** LEED requires a minimum of MERV 8 filters to be installed for compliance.

Q8.7.   **A and F.** Be sure to review Appendix J for the referenced standards.

Q8.8.   **B, E, and F.** Remember, the specifics of the referenced standards and what they apply to. Phenol-formaldehyde and urea-formaldehyde relate to resin-manufactured building materials. Knowing the requirements of each of the materials would have helped to eliminate answer option C. Option D is eliminated, as Green Spec is not currently included in the referenced standards addressed in the LEED rating systems.

Q8.9.   **D.** Remember the specifics of the referenced standards and what they apply to.

Q8.10. **D.** Be sure to make a flashcard and make a note on your cheat sheet to remember the SMACNA standards.

Q8.11. **C.** Dedicate a section of your cheat sheet to LEED for Schools to remember all the details of the rating system.

Q8.12. **B.** Try to make a connection between credits or rating systems to find unique ways to remember important facts.

Q8.13. **A, C, and D.** ASHRAE 90.1 = Energy! ENERGY STAR applies to energy-efficient appliances, products, and buildings.

Q8.14. **C.** Dedicate a section of your cheat sheet to LEED for Schools to remember all the details of the rating system. Do you remember another credit with the same humidity level requirement?

Q8.15. **A and E.** Use your flashcards to quiz yourself on these types of details or make a note on your cheat sheet.

Q8.16. **D.** Use your flashcards to quiz yourself on these types of details or make a note on your cheat sheet.

Q8.17. **B and D.** ASHRAE 55 defines the three environmental components that impact thermal comfort, including humidity, air speed, and temperature.

Q8.18. **D.** Remember to read questions and answer options carefully to eliminate the incorrect answers and to depict the correct answer.

Q8.19. **C.** Use your flashcards to quiz yourself on these types of details or make a note on your cheat sheet.

Q8.20. **D.** Think about the logic behind this requirement. Is it really feasible to provide any higher of a percentage?

Q8.21. **D.** Glare control is required for each of the compliance paths as it is the most commonly forgotten element of most daylight strategies.

Q8.22. **A, B, and C.** Learning the strategies to comply with each of the credits and prerequisites is key for the exam. Try to remember the intent behind each to help decipher the appropriate strategy or technology.

Q8.23. **B, C, and E.** Remember, some material in this book can be presented for the first time in the format of a question. Use these opportunities to test your knowledge, and if you are not familiar with the content, be sure to make a flashcard or make a note on your cheat sheet in order to remember the information.

Q8.24. **E.** Use your flashcards to quiz yourself on these types of details or make a note on your cheat sheet.

Q8.25. **D.** Create a flashcard to remember this technical detail.

Q8.26. **C, D, and E.** The square footage indications are irrelevant. If any part of the envelope is being enhanced, typically EA Credit 1 is relevant. Remember to look for terms such as *nearby* and *adjacent* if MR Credit 5 is proposed as an answer choice. The Building Reuse credit comes into play as the existing structure is to remain. There was no mention of incorporating certified wood or low-emitting materials, therefore eliminating answer options A and B.

Q8.27. **D.** 62 IAQ, IAQ 62!

Q8.28. **A and D.** Remember the BAIT Tip to point out the trade-offs and synergies of increased ventilation strategies: better IAQ but reduced energy efficiency for mechanical systems to condition outside air.

Q8.29. **A and E.** Project specifications will give the contractor direction on how to comply with the IAQ credit requirements such as MERV filters, flush-out, and low-emitting materials.

Q8.30. **A and C.** Remember ASHRAE 55 = thermal comfort and 62 = IAQ, as both relate to ventilation system design.

Q8.31. **A and C.** Proximity to a shopping mall may increase satisfaction due to convenience, but not necessarily increase production as related to work. Carpooling and recycling are benefits to the environment and operations, not necessarily related to productivity or satisfaction.

Q8.32. **C, D, and F.** Remembering the strategies described in the EA and MR categories will help determine the correct answers. Review those flashcards!

Q8.33. **A and C.** Be sure to remember which credits are eligible for a design side review. Knowing what the documentation requirements are can help with the process of elimination for answer selections.

Q8.34. **D.** Use your flashcards to quiz yourself on these types of details or make a note on your cheat sheet.

Q8.35. **A, C, and D.** Use your flashcards to quiz yourself on these types of details or make a note on your cheat sheet.

Q8.36. **B, D, and E.** Learning the strategies to comply with each of the credits and prerequisites is key for the exam. Try to remember the intent behind each to help decipher the appropriate strategy or technology.

Q8.37. **C.** Thermal comfort is not related to this credit. Although it will improve air quality, the occupants' ability to control their thermal comfort is not addressed.

Q8.38. **D.** EQ Credit 5 differs from most credits, as it requires all of the strategies to be met in order to earn the point. Create a flashcard to help you remember the four components associated with this credit.

CHAPTER 9: INNOVATION IN DESIGN AND REGIONAL PRIORITY

Q9.1. **C.** Earning exemplary performance is credit-specific, so be aware of statements such as "regardless of which credit is being exceeded."

Q9.2. **C and D.** If unclear about ID credits, be sure to read through the Guidance on Innovation and Design (ID) credits on the GBCI website at www.gbci.org/ShowFile.aspx?DocumentID=3594.

Q9.3. **A.** A new green building project can earn the LEED NC certification and then earn the LEED EBOM certification during operations or a LEED Core & Shell building can be built and then earn multiple LEED CI certifications.

Q9.4. **A, C, and E.** Remember, the Regional Priority category is new but does not include any new credits. RPCs are earned by achieving existing LEED credits from other categories. Although earning a maximum of four RPCs is allowed, there are six opportunities available from which to choose.

Q9.5. **D.** Although earning a maximum of four RPCs is allowed, there are six opportunities available from which to choose for each zip code.

Q9.6. **A.** Regardless of how many LEED APs are on a project, only one point can be earned.

Q9.7. **D.** Dedicate a section of your cheat sheet to LEED for Schools to remember all the details of the rating system.

Q9.8. **B.** It might be helpful to compare one rating system against the other two in order to find differentiating characteristics to remember.

Q9.9. **E.** Narrowing down the specific credits and prerequisites to each of the rating systems will be helpful for the exam.

Q9.10. **B, C, and E.** Remember all of the BAIT Tips to remember all of the benefits of a green roof!

Q9.11. **C, E, and F.** It is important to remember the point opportunities for each credit and the percentage thresholds, especially for exemplary performance.

Appendix L

ABBREVIATIONS AND ACRONYMS

4-PCH	4-phenylcyclohexene
AFV	alternative-fuel vehicle
AIA	American Institute of Architects
ANSI	American National Standards Institute
AP	LEED Accredited Professional
ASHRAE	American Society of Heating, Refrigerating, and Air-Conditioning Engineers
ASTM	American Society for Testing and Materials
BAS	building automation system
BD+C	Building Design and Construction (LEED AP credential and also a reference guide)
BEES	Building for Environmental and Economic Sustainability software by NIST
BIFMA	Business and Institutional Furniture Manufacturer's Association
BIPV	building integrated photovoltaics
BIM	building information modeling
BMP	best management practice
BOD	basis of design
BOMA	Building Owners and Managers Association
CAE	combined annual efficiency
CBECS	Commercial Building Energy Consumption Survey (by DOE)
CDs	construction documents
CDL	construction, demolition, and land clearing
CE	controller efficiency
CFA	conditioned floor area
CFC	chlorofluorocarbon
CFL	compact fluorescent light
CFM	cubic feet per minute
CFR	U.S. Code of Federal Regulations
CI	Commercial Interiors (LEED CI rating system)
CIBSE	Chartered Institution of Building Services Engineers
CIR	credit interpretation request
CMP	Credentialing Maintenance Program
CO	carbon monoxide
CO_2	carbon dioxide
COC	chain of custody
COP	coefficient of performance
CRI	Carpet and Rug Institute
CS	Core & Shell (LEED CS rating system)
CSI	Construction Specifications Institute
CWMP	construction waste management plan
Cx	commissioning
CxA	commissioning agent or authority
dBA	A-weighted decibel
DHW	domestic hot water
DOE	U.S. Department of Energy

EA	Energy & Atmosphere category
EBOM	Existing Buildings: Operations & Maintenance (LEED EBOM rating system)
ECB	energy cost budget
ECM	energy conservation measure
EER	energy efficiency rating
EERE	U.S. Office of Energy Efficiency and Renewable Energy
EF	energy factor
EPA	U.S. Environmental Protection Agency
EPAct	U.S. Energy Policy Act of 1992 or 2005
EPEAT	electronic product environmental assessment tools
EPP	environmentally preferable purchasing
ESA	environmental site assessment
ESC	erosion and sedimentation control
ET	evapotranspiration
ETS	environmental tobacco smoke
ETV	Environmental Technology Verification
EQ	Indoor Environmental Quality category
fc	footcandle
FEMA	U.S. Federal Emergency Management Agency
FF&E	fixtures, furnishings, and equipment
FSC	Forest Stewardship Council
FTE	full-time equivalent
GBCI	Green Buildings Certification Institute
GBOM	Green Buildings Operations + Maintenance reference guide
GF	glazing factor
GHG	greenhouse gas
GPF	gallons per flush
g/L	grams per Liter
GPM	gallons per minute
GWP	global warming potential
HCFC	hydrochlorofluorocarbon
HEPA	high-efficiency particle absorbing
HERS	Home Energy Rating Standards
HET	high-efficiency toilet
HFC	hydrofluorocarbon
HVAC	heating, ventilation, and air conditioning
HVAC&R	heating, ventilation, air conditioning, and refrigeration
IAQ	indoor air quality
ICF	insulated concrete form
ID	Innovation & Design category
ID+C	Interior Design + Construction (LEED AP credential and also a reference guide)
IE	irrigation efficiency
IEQ	Indoor Environmental Quality category
IESNA	Illuminating Engineering Society of North America
IPD	integrated project delivery
IPM	integrated pest management
IPMVP	International Performance Measurement and Verification Protocol
ISO	International Organization for Standardization
KW	kilowatt
KWH	kilowatt per hour

LCA	life-cycle assessment/analysis
LCC	life-cycle cost
LCGWP	life-cycle global warming potential
LCODP	life-cycle ozone depletion potential
LED	light-emitting diode
LEED	Leadership in Energy and Environmental Design
LPD	lighting power density
MDF	medium density fiberboard
MERV	minimum efficiency reporting value
MPR	Minimum Program Requirement
MR	Materials & Resources category
MSDS	material safety data sheet
M&V	measurement and verification
NBI	New Building Institute
NC	New Construction (LEED NC rating system)
ND	Neighborhood Development (LEED ND rating system)
NH3	ammonia
NIST	National Institute of Standards and Technology
NRC	noise reduction coefficient
ODP	ozone-depleting potential
O&M	operations and maintenance
O+M	Operations + Maintenance (LEED AP credential)
OPR	owner's program requirements
OSB	oriented strand board
PV	photovoltaic
PVC	polyvinyl chloride
REC	renewable energy certification
RESNET	Residential Energy Services Network
RFC	request for clarification
RFI	request for information
RFP	request for proposal
RP	Regional Priority category
RT	reverberation time
SCAQMD	South Coast Air Quality Management District
SCS	Scientific Certification Systems
SEER	seasonal energy efficiency rating
SHGC	solar heat gain coefficient
SIP	structural insulated panels
SMACNA	Sheet Metal and Air-Conditioning Contractor's Association
SS	Sustainable Sites category
SRI	solar reflective index
STC	standard transmission class
TAG	Technical Advisory Group
TASC	Technical Advisory Subcommittee
TP	total phosphorus
TRACI	Tool for the Reduction and Assessment of Chemical and Other Environmental Impacts
TSS	total suspended solids
Tvis	visible transmittance
UL	Underwriter's Laboratory
USGBC	U.S. Green Building Council

VLT	visible light transmittance
VOC	volatile organic compound
WE	Water Efficiency category
WF	water factor
WFR	window-to-floor ratio
WWR	window-to-wall ratio
ZEV	zero emission vehicle

Appendix M

SAMPLE CREDIT

MR CREDIT 5: REGIONAL MATERIALS

1–2 Points

Intent

To increase demand for building materials and products that are extracted and manufactured within the region, thereby supporting the use of indigenous resources and reducing the environmental impacts resulting from transportation.

Requirements

Use building materials or products that have been extracted, harvested, or recovered, as well as manufactured within 500 miles of the project site for a minimum of 10 percent or 20 percent, based on cost, of the total materials value. If only a fraction of a product or material is extracted, harvested, or recovered and manufactured locally, then only that percentage (by weight) can contribute to the regional value. The minimum percentage regional materials for each point threshold is as follows:

Regional Materials	Points
10%	1
20%	2

Mechanical, electrical, and plumbing components and specialty items such as elevators and equipment must not be included in this calculation. Include only materials permanently installed in the project. Furniture may be included if it is included consistently in MR Credit 3: Materials Reuse, through MR Credit 7: Certified Wood.

Potential Technologies and Strategies

Establish a project goal for locally sourced materials, and identify materials and material suppliers that can achieve this goal. During construction, ensure that the specified local materials are installed, and quantify the total percentage of local materials installed. Consider a range of environmental, economic, and performance attributes when selecting products and materials.

Credits

CHAPTER 1

1. GBCI. *LEED AP Building Design + Construction Candidate Handbook,* October 2010 (2008), p. 7.

CHAPTER 2

1. Wikipedia website, http://en.wikipedia.org/wiki/Sustainability.
2. United Nations General Assembly, *Report of the World Commission on Environment and Development: Our Common Future* (1987). Transmitted to the General Assembly as an Annex to document A/42/427—Development and International Co-operation: Environment. Retrieved on February 1, 2009.
3. USGBC website, www.usgbc.org/DisplayPage.aspx?CMSPageID=1718.
4. GSA Public Buildings Service, "Assessing Green Building Performance: A Post Occupancy Evaluation of 12 GSA Buildings" (2008).
5. Environmental Protection Agency. *The Total Exposure Assessment Methodology (TEAM) Study* (1987).
6. See note 1.
7. Heschong Mahone Group, "Daylighting in Schools: An Investigation into the Relationship Between Daylighting and Human Performance" (1999).
8. USGBC website, www.usgbc.org/DisplayPage.aspx?CMSPageID=1718.
9. USGBC website, www.usgbc.org/DisplayPage.aspx?CMSPageID=124.
10. USGBC website, www.usgbc.org/DisplayPage.aspx?CMSPageID=124.
11. GBCI website, www.gbci.org/org-nav/about-gbci/about-gbci.aspx.
12. GBCI website. Disciplinary and Exam Appeals Policy, www.gbci.org/Files/Disc_ExamAppeals_Policy.pdf.

CHAPTER 3

1. USGBC website, www.usgbc.org/ShowFile.aspx?DocumentID=6715.

CHAPTER 4

1. EPA website, http://epa.gov/brownfields/about.htm.
2. USGBC, *Green Building and LEED Core Concepts Guide,* p. 31.
3. EPA website, http://epa.gov/brownfields/.
4. USGBC, *LEED Reference Guide for Green Building Design and Construction,* (2009), p. 40.
5. Ibid.
6. USGBC, *Green Building and LEED Core Concepts Guide,* p. 27.
7. Ibid.
8. Wikipedia website. http://en.wikipedia.org/wiki/Vehicle_Emissions.
9. USGBC. *Green Building and LEED Core Concepts Guide,* 1st edition (2009), p. 28.
10. "IPCC AR4 SYR Appendix Glossary" (PDF). Retrieved on April 20, 2010.

11. USGBC. *LEED Reference Guide for Green Building Design and Construction* (2008), p. 52.

12. USGBC, *LEED Reference Guide for Green Building Design and Construction* (2009), p. 10.

13. Ibid., p. 10.

14. Ibid., p. 116.

15. Ibid., p. 142.

16. Ibid., p. 143.

17. Ibid., p. 101.

CHAPTER 5

1. USGBC, *LEED Reference Guide for Green Building Design and Construction* (2009), p. 196.

2. Ibid., p. 627.

CHAPTER 6

1. USGBC website, www.usgbc.org/DisplayPage.aspx?CMSPageID=1718.

2. USGBC, *Green Building and LEED Core Concepts Guide*, p. 51.

CHAPTER 7

1. County of San Mateo, California. *San Mateo Countywide Guide to Sustainable Buildings* (2004), p. 3. www.recycleworks.org/pdf/GB-guide-2-23.pdf. Accessed December 2009.

2. Department of Natural Resources, Northeast Region. "Building Green at DNR—Northeast Region Headquarters Construction Waste & Recycling."

3. USGBC, *LEED Reference Guide for Green Building Design and Construction* (2009), p. 624.

4. Ibid., p. 638.

5. USGBC, *LEED Reference Guide for Green Building Design and Construction* (2009), Introduction, pp. xi and 335.

6. USGBC, *Green Building and LEED Core Concepts Guide*, p. 55.

CHAPTER 8

1. Environmental Protection Agency. The Total Exposure Assessment Methodology (TEAM) Study (1987).

2. USGBC, *Green Building and LEED Core Concepts Guide*, p. 59.

3. USGBC, *LEED Reference Guide for Green Building Design and Construction* (2009), p. 414.

4. USGBC, *Green Building and LEED Core Concepts Guide*, p. 60.

5. USGBC, *LEED Reference Guide for Green Building Design and Construction* (2009), p. 495.

6. USGBC, *Green Building and LEED Core Concepts Guide*, p. 60.

7. Heschong Mahone Group, "Daylighting in Schools: An Investigation into the Relationship between Daylighting and Human Performance" (1999).

8. USGBC, *LEED Reference Guide for Green Building Design and Construction* (2009), p. 433.

APPENDICES F, G, AND H

1. USGBC website. www.usgbc.org/DisplayPage.aspx?CMSPageID=220.

Index

The letter t following a page number indicates a table.

Sample Flashcards

1

Q. What is sustainable design?

2

Q. What savings have green buildings achieved?

3

Q. What are the eight strategies to improve IAQ during construction?

4

Q. What are the three strategies to improve IAQ by prevention and segregation methods?

5

Q. What are the four ways to earn Innovation in Design Credits?

6

Q. What are the benefits of an integrated project delivery (IPD)?

2

A. Up to 50 percent energy use reduction
40 percent water use reduction
70 percent solid waste reduction
13 percent reduction in maintenance costs

1

A. According to the Brundtland Commission of the United Nations' website: development that meets the needs of the present without compromising the ability of future generations to meet their own needs.

4

A. EQ Prerequisite 1: Environmental Tobacco Smoke (ETS) Control
EQ Credit 5: Indoor Chemical and Pollutant Source Control
EQ Credit 10: Mold Prevention (for Schools)

3

A. EQ Credit 3 .1: Construction IAQ Management—During Construction / EQ Credit 3: Construction IAQ Management (for CS)

EQ Credit 3.2: Construction IAQ Management—Before Occupancy (for NC and Schools)

EQ Credit 4.1: Low-Emitting Materials—Adhesives and Sealants

EQ Credit 4.2: Low-Emitting Materials—Paints and Coatings

EQ Credit 4.3: Low-Emitting Materials—Flooring Systems

EQ Credit 4.4: Low-Emitting Materials—Composite Wood and Agrifiber Products

EQ Credit 4.5: Low-Emitting Materials—Furniture and Furnishings (for Schools)

EQ Credit 4.6: Low-Emitting Materials—Ceiling and Wall Systems (for Schools)

6

A. Holistic approach versus linear approach with conventional projects
Brings all of the project team members together early to work collectively.
Begins as early as possible in the design process.
Team members share the risk and the rewards.
Helps to lower first costs and operating costs.
BIM.
Multilateral agreements.

5

A. Exemplary Performance
Innovation in Design
LEED Accredited Professional
The School as a Teaching Tool

7

Q. What is USGBC's mission statement?

8

Q. What four components are required for a team to submit for an Innovation in Design credit?

9

Q. What is GBCI's mission statement?

10

Q. Describe GBCI.

11

Q. What is a TAG?

12

Q. What are the two primary roles of USGBC?

13

Q. What are the two primary roles of GBCI?

14

Q. What are the four required strategies of EQ Credit 5: Indoor Chemical & Pollutant Source Control?

8

A. Intent of strategy

Suggested requirements for compliance

Suggested documentation proving compliance with requirements

A narrative describing the strategy implemented

7

A. To transform the way buildings and communities are designed, built, and operated, enabling an environmentally and socially responsible, healthy, and prosperous environment that improves the quality of life.

10

A. Provides third-party project certification and professional credentials recognizing excellence in green building performance and practice.

9

A. To support a high level of competence in building methods for environmental efficiency through the development and administration of a formal program of certification and recertification.

12

A. Develop LEED rating systems.

Provide education and research programs.

11

A. Technical advisory group within USGBC to help the LEED rating systems to evolve.

14

A. – 10' entryway system

– Separate exhaust areas of hazardous gases

– Use MERV 13 filters

– Dispose of chemicals properly by containment

13

A. Administering the project certification process with the help of certification bodies.

Administering the professional accreditation process.

15

Q. What is RT?

16

Q. What are the two differences between prerequisites and credits?

17

Q. What two components are credit weightings based on?

18

Q. What are the certification levels and coordinating point ranges for LEED?

19

Q. According to the minimum program requirements (MPRs), how many occupants must occupy any New Construction, Core & Shell, and Schools projects?

20

Q. Describe the MPR for whole-building energy and water use data.

21

Q. What is building density?

22

Q. What are the MPRs for reasonable site boundaries for LEED for New Construction, Core & Shell, and Schools?

16

A. Prerequisites are mandatory, as they address minimum performance achievements, and credits are optional.

Prerequisites are not worth any points, while credits are.

15

A. A measure of the amount of reverberation in a space and equal to the time required for the level of a study sound to decay by 60 dB after the sound has stopped. The decay rate depends on the amount of sound absorption in a room, the room geometry, and the frequency of the sound. RT is expressed in seconds.

18

A. Certified: 40–49 points
Silver: 50–59 points
Gold: 60–79 points
Platinum: 80 and higher

17

A. Environmental impacts and human benefits

20

A. All certified projects must commit to sharing with USGBC and/or GBCI all available actual whole-project energy and water usage data for a period of at least five years starting from the date that the LEED project begins typical physical occupancy if certifying under New Construction, Core & Shell, or Schools.

19

A. The LEED project must serve one or more full-time equivalent (FTE) occupant(s), calculated as an annual average in order to use LEED in its entirety.

22

A. 1. Boundary must include all contiguous land that is associated with and supports normal building operations.
2. Land in boundary must be owned by the same party that owns the LEED project.
3. For campus projects, 100 percent of the gross land area on the campus would be included within a LEED boundary if all buildings eventually get certified.
4. A property may be attributed to only a single LEED building.
5. Boundary may not unreasonably exclude land to achieve prerequisites or credits (i.e., gerrymandering).

21

A. Evaluates a building's total floor area as compared to the total area of the site and is measured in square feet per acre.

23

Q. Name the MPR for permanent buildings or spaces, applicable for all BD+C rating systems.

24

Q. What is considered a previously developed site?

25

Q. According to the MPRs, how many occupants must occupy any New Construction, Core & Shell, and Schools projects?

26

Q. What are the distances and associated grade levels for pedestrian access for school projects seeking SS Credit 4.1: Public Transportation Access?

27

Q. What must be achieved in order for a project to be eligible for certification?

28

Q. The distance boundary from an existing feature or natural body that a development is required to abide by is referred to as _____.

29

Q. What is a zero lot line?

30

Q. In a construction project, what is the site area?

24

A. Properties with existing buildings and hardscape but also those that were graded or somehow altered by human activity

23

A. All LEED projects must be designed for, constructed on, and operated on a permanent location on already existing land. No building or space that is designed to move at any point in its lifetime may pursue LEED certification.

26

A. For school projects to comply with Option 3: Pedestrian Access, the maximum walking radius must be less than three-quarters of a mile for grades K–8 and less than a mile and a half for grades 9 and higher for 80 percent of the total student population.

25

A. The LEED project must serve one or more FTE occupant(s), calculated as an annual average in order to use LEED in its entirety.

28

A. Setback. Common setbacks include minimum distance from the street and sidewalk, or minimum distance from a wetland or water body.

27

A. Complying with all minimum program requirements, achieving all prerequisites, and earning a minimum of 40 points

30

A. The total area within the project boundary of the applicant building including all area of the property, both constructed and nonconstructed areas

29

A. A development in which the building footprint is the same as the lot boundary. This is common in urban areas.

31

Q. What is the minimum building area-to-site area ratio required for a LEED project?

32

Q. What is an LPE?

33

Q. What are the six characteristics of credit interpretation requests?

34

Q. What are the three factors certification fees are based on?

35

Q. What are the four factors to address within the SS category?

36

Q. What is floor-to-area ratio?

37

Q. What are the strategies of Site Selection?

38

Q. What is community connectivity?

32

A. Licensed-professional exemption—the path decided on a submittal template to reduce documentation requirements

31

A. The gross floor area of the LEED project building must be no less than 2 percent of the gross land area within the LEED project boundary.

34

A. Rating system, membership, and square footage

33

A. Issued after a project is registered

Issued for a fee

Credit interpretation ruling issued in response

Submitted for clarification referencing *one* credit or prerequisite

Ruling not final

Submitted via LEED-Online

36

A. The proportion of the total floor area of a building to the total land area the building can occupy

35

A. Site Selection

Transportation

Site Design & Management

Stormwater Management

38

A. Proximity of project site to local businesses and community services such as parks, grocery stores, banks, cleaners, pharmacies, and restaurants. The LEED rating systems require a connection to at least 10 basic services.

37

A. SS Prerequisite 2: Environmental Site Assessment (Schools)

SS Credit 1: Site Selection

SS Credit 2: Development Density and Community Connectivity

SS Credit 3: Brownfield Redevelopment

39

Q. What is development density?

40

Q. What is a brownfield?

41

Q. What is site disturbance?

42

Q. What is prime farmland?

43

Q. What is a floodplain?

44

Q. What are the six types of sensitive sites to avoid for LEED projects?

45

Q. What is the referenced standard for brownfield sites?

46

Q. What are the four impacts of transportation?

40

A. Real property, the expansion, redevelopment, or reuse of which may be complicated by the presence or potential presence of a hazardous substance, pollutant, or contaminant. Cleaning up and reinvesting in these properties protects the environment, reduces blight, and takes development pressures off green spaces and working lands.

39

A. The total square footage of all buildings within a particular area, measured in square feet per acre or units per acre

42

A. Greenfield sites with soil appropriate for cultivation and agricultural growth and production

41

A. The amount of property affected by construction activity

44

A. 1. Prime farmland (defined by the U.S. Department of Agriculture): greenfield sites with soil appropriate for cultivation and agricultural growth and production
2. Floodplains/flood prone areas (land less than five feet above the 100-year floodplain level as defined by FEMA): land prone to flooding as a result of a storm
3. Habitat for any endangered or critical species
4. Within 100 feet of wetlands (defined by the Code of Federal Regulations [CFR])
5. Within 50 feet of a body of water (Clean Water Act)
6. Public parkland

43

A. Land prone to flooding as a result of a storm

46

A. Location
Vehicle technology
Fuel
Human behavior

45

A. ASTM E1903-97

47

Q. What is an alternative-fuel vehicle?

48

Q. What are the four SS credits to reduce the transportation impacts associated with the built environment?

49

Q. What is a stormwater prevention plan?

50

Q. What are the two credits that address stormwater management?

51

Q. What are native and adaptive plantings?

52

Q. What is potable water?

53

Q. What is imperviousness?

54

Q. What is perviousness?

48

A. SS Credit 4.1: Public Transportation Access

SS Credit 4.2: Bicycle Storage and Changing Rooms

SS Credit 4.3: Low-Emitting and Fuel-Efficient Vehicles

SS Credit 4.4: Parking Capacity

47

A. A vehicle that operates without the use of petroleum fuels, including gas-electric vehicle types. A minimum ACEEE Green score of 40 is required for compliance with LEED.

50

A. SS Credit 6.1: Quantity Control

SS Credit 6.2: Quality Control

49

A. A plan that describes all measures to prevent stormwater contamination, control sedimentation and erosion during construction, and comply with the requirements of the Clean Water Act

---

52

A. Drinking water supplied by municipalities or wells

51

A. Native vegetation occurs naturally, while adaptive plantings are not natural; they can adapt to their new surroundings. Both can survive with little to no human interaction or resources.

54

A. Surfaces that allow at least 50 percent of water to percolate or penetrate through them

---

53

A. Surfaces that do not allow 50 percent or less of water to pass through them

55

Q. What is stormwater runoff?

56

Q. What is a footcandle?

57

Q. What is the heat island effect?

58

Q. What is emissivity?

59

Q. What is solar reflective index (SRI) and the associated scale?

60

Q. What is albedo and the associated scale?

61

Q. What is a building footprint?

62

Q. What are the three credits that address salvaged materials and materials reuse?

56

A. A measurement of light measured in lumens per square foot

55

A. Rainwater that leaves a project site flowing along parking lots and roadways, traveling to sewer systems and water bodies

58

A. The ratio of the radiation emitted by a surface to the radiation emitted by a black body at the same temperature

57

A. Heat absorption by low-SRI, hardscape materials that contribute to an overall increase in temperature by radiating heat

60

A. The ability to reflect sunlight based on visible, infrared, and ultraviolet wavelengths on a scale from 0 to 1

59

A. A material's ability to reflect or reject solar heat gain measured on a scale from 0 (dark, most absorptive) to 100 (light, most reflective).

62

A. MR Credit 1.1: Building Reuse, Maintain Existing Walls, Floors, and Roof (for NC and Schools)/MR Credit 1 (for CS)

MR Credit 1.2 Building Reuse, Maintain 50 Percent of Interior Nonstructural Elements (for NC and Schools)

MR Credit 3: Materials Reuse

61

A. The amount of land the building structure occupies, not including landscape and hardscape surfaces such as parking lots, driveways, and walkways

63

Q. What are the three strategies to manage stormwater?

64

Q. What are the three types of water uses described in the WE category?

65

Q. What is the referenced standard used for indoor water use?

66

Q. What is baseline versus design case?

67

Q. What are examples of flow fixtures?

68

Q. How are flow fixtures measured?

69

Q. What are examples of flush fixtures?

70

Q. How are flow fixtures measured?

64

A. Indoor water
Outdoor water
Process water

63

A. Minimize impervious areas
Control stormwater
Harvest rainwater

66

A. The amount of water a conventional project would use as compared to the design case

65

A. EPAct 1992

68

A. Gallons per minute (gpm)

67

A. Sink faucets, showerheads, and aerators

70

A. Gallons per flush (gpf)

69

A. Toilets and urinals

71

Q. What is graywater?

72

Q. What are the LEED strategies to address reducing indoor water consumption?

73

Q. What are the strategies to reduce outdoor water consumption?

74

Q. How can nonpotable water use reduce water consumption?

75

Q. What are the uses for process water?

76

Q. What are the six strategies that address site design and management within the SS category?

77

Q. What are the benefits of utilizing a CxA?

78

Q. What is the baseline standard for energy performance?

72

A. WE Prerequisite 1: Water Use Reduction
WE Credit 2: Innovative Wastewater Technologies
WE Credit 3: Water Use Reduction

71

A. Wastewater from showers, bathtubs, lavatories, and washing machines. This water has not come into contact with toilet waste according to the International Plumbing Code (IPC).

74

A. Indoor: toilet and urinal flushing
Outdoor: irrigation
Process: building systems

73

A. Implement native and adapted plants.
Use xeriscaping.
Specify high-efficiency irrigation systems.
Use nonpotable water for irrigation.

76

A. SS Prerequisite 1: Construction Activity Pollution Prevention
SS Credit 5: Site Development
SS Credit 7: Heat Island Effect
SS Credit 8: Light Pollution Reduction
SS Credit 9: Site Master Plan (Schools)
SS Credit 10: Joint Use of Facilities (Schools)

75

A. Industrial uses, such as chillers, cooling towers, and boilers
Business operations, such as washing machines, ice machines, and dishwashers

78

A. ASHRAE 90.1 - 2007, Appendix G

77

A. Minimize or eliminate design flaws.
Avoid construction defects.
Avoid equipment malfunctions.
Ensure that preventative maintenance is implemented during operations.

79

Q. What are the uses for regulated energy?

80

Q. What are the uses for process energy?

81

Q. What two components should be evaluated when determining which refrigerants to use?

82

Q. What is ODP?

83

Q. What is GWP?

84

Q. What is the current percentage rate for recycling according to the EPA?

85

Q. What are the four components of the Energy & Atmosphere category?

86

Q. What are the two strategies to manage refrigerants within the EA category?

80

A. Computers, office equipment, kitchen refrigeration and cooking, washing and drying machines, and elevators and escalators. Miscellaneous items, such as waterfall pumps, and lighting that is exempt from lighting power allowance calculations such as lighting integrated into equipment, are also categorized as process energy uses.

79

A. Lighting: interior and exterior applications (parking garages, facades, site lighting)

HVAC: space heating, cooling, fans, pumps, toilet exhaust, ventilation for parking garages

Domestic and space heating for service water

82

A. Ozone-depleting potential

81

A. Refrigerants should be evaluated based on ODP and GWP impacts.

84

A. 32 percent

83

A. Global warming potential

86

A. EA Prerequisite 3: Fundamental Refrigerant Management

EA Credit 3: Enhanced Refrigerant Management

85

A. Energy efficiency

Tracking energy consumption

Managing refrigerants

Renewable energy

87

Q. How are electricity, natural gas, and liquid fuel each measured?

88

Q. What are the four strategies that address the tracking of energy consumption?

89

Q. What are the six types of eligible renewable energy sources for LEED projects?

90

Q. What are the two ways to incorporate renewable energy into a green building project seeking LEED certification?

91

Q. What is an REC?

92

Q. What are the two opportunities to address energy performance for a LEED project?

93

Q. What are the three components to address within the Materials & Resources category?

94

Q. What is a rapidly renewable material?

88

A. EA Prerequisite 1: Fundamental Commissioning

EA Credit 3: Enhanced Commissioning

EA Credit 5: Measurement and Verification/
EA Credit 5.1: Measurement and Verification, Base Building (for LEED CS)

EA Credit 5.2: Measurement and Verification, Tenant Submetering (for LEED CS)

87

A. Electricity is measured in kilowatts per hour, natural gas in therms, and liquid fuel in gallons.

90

A. Generate on-site renewable energy (EA Credit 2: On-Site Renewable Energy) and/or purchase green power, or RECs (EA Credit 6: Green Power).

89

A. Solar, wind, wave, biomass, geothermal power, and low-impact hydropower

92

A. EA Prerequisite 2: Minimum Energy Performance

EA Credit 1: Optimize Energy Performance

91

A. Renewable energy credit

94

A. Fiber or animal materials that must be grown or raised in 10 years or less

93

A. Salvaged materials and material reuse

Building material selection

Waste management

95

Q. Define recycled content.

96

Q. What referenced standard declares a material having postconsumer/preconsumer recycled content?

97

Q. Waste material that was generated from a manufacturing process and reintroduced to another manufacturing process, is referred to as _____.

98

Q. Material that was generated by household, commercial, industrial, or institutional end users, which can no longer be used for its intended purpose is referred to as _____.

99

Q. What are considered regional materials according to LEED?

100

Q. What type of documentation is required to prove compliance for FSC wood?

101

Q. Which elements are excluded from the calculations for recycled content, regional materials, and rapidly renewable materials?

102

Q. What are the four credits that address strategies to reduce the impacts of building material selection?

96

A. ISO 14021-1999—Environmental Label and Declarations

95

A. The percentage of materials in a product that are recycled from the manufacturing waste stream (preconsumer waste) or the consumer waste stream (postconsumer waste) and used to make new materials. Recycled content is typically expressed as a percentage of the total material volume or weight.

98

A. Postconsumer. Examples include construction and demolition debris, materials collected through recycling programs, and landscaping waste (ISO 14021).

97

A. Preconsumer. Examples include planer shavings, sawdust, bagasse, walnut shells, culls, trimmed materials, overissue publications, and obsolete inventories. Not included are rework, regrind, or scrap materials capable of being reclaimed within the same process that generated them.

100

A. FSC wood requires chain-of-custody documentation.

99

A. The amount of a building's materials that are extracted, processed, and manufactured close to a project site, expressed as a percentage of the total material cost. LEED considers regional materials as those that originate within 500 miles of the project site.

102

A. MR Credit 4: Recycled Content

MR Credit 5: Regional Materials
MR Credit 6: Rapidly Renewable Materials (for NC and Schools)
MR Credit 7: Certified Wood / MR Credit 6 (for CS)

101

A. Mechanical, electrical, and plumbing equipment and hazardous waste materials

103

Q. What are the minimum types of items to be recycled during operations to meet the requirements of the MR prerequisite?

104

Q. What are the 3Rs of waste management?

105

Q. What are the two strategies to reduce waste?

106

Q. What are the four components discussed in the EQ category?

107

Q. What are the types of VOCs?

108

Q. What are the different referenced standards for products that emit VOCs for NC and CS projects?

109

Q. How are VOCs measured?

110

Q. To comply with EQ Credit 4.4: Low-Emitting Materials—Composite Wood and Agrifiber Products, these products are not allowed to contain what type of resin? What type of resin is acceptable?

104

A. Reduce, reuse, and recycle

103

A. Paper, corrugated cardboard, glass, plastics, and metals

106

A. Indoor air quality (IAQ)
Thermal comfort
Lighting
Acoustics

105

A. MR Prerequisite 1: Storage & Collection of Recyclables
MR Credit 2: Construction Waste Management

108

A. Paints —Green Seal 11, Green Seal 3
Coatings—SMACNA 1113
Adhesives—Green Seal 36
Sealants—SCAQMD 1168
Carpet—Carpet and Rug Institute (CRI) Green Label Plus Program
Other Flooring—FloorScore

107

A. Volatile organic compounds include carbon dioxide, tobacco smoke, and particulates emitted from carpet, paints, adhesives, glues, sealants, coatings, furniture, and composite wood products.

110

A. Urea-formaldehyde resin is not allowed, although phenol-formaldehyde resin is.

109

A. Grams per liter (g/L)

111

Q. What is MERV? What is the range?

112

Q. What are the three ventilation strategies to address IAQ?

113

Q. What are the four environmental factors of thermal comfort defined by ASHRAE 55?

114

Q. What are the three credits that address thermal comfort?

115

Q. What are the EQ credit strategies that address lighting within a LEED building?

116

Q. What are the two strategies presented in the EQ category that address acoustic strategies to improve occupant comfort in schools?

117

Q. Of the six available Regional Priority credits, how many can count toward a project's LEED certification?

118

Q. A project's available Regional Priority points are determined by what project-specific element?

112

A. EQ Prerequisite 1: Minimum Indoor Air Quality Performance

EQ Credit 1: Outdoor Air Delivery Monitoring

EQ Credit 2: Increased Ventilation

111

A. Minimum Efficiency Reporting Value (MERV) filters range from 1 (low) to 16 (highest).

114

A. EQ Credit 6.2: Controllability of Systems, Thermal Comfort / EQ Credit 6 (for CS)

EQ Credit 7.1: Thermal Comfort, Design / EQ Credit 7 (for CS)

EQ Credit 7.2: Thermal Comfort, Verification (for NC and Schools)

113

A. Humidity, air speed, air temperature, and radiant temperature

116

A. EQ Prerequisite 3: Minimum Acoustical Performance

EQ Credit 9: Enhanced Acoustical Performance

115

A. EQ Credit 6.1: Controllability of Systems, Lighting (for NC and Schools)

EQ Credit 8.1: Daylight and Views, Daylight

EQ Credit 8.2: Daylight and Views, Views

118

A. Zip code

117

A. Four

119

Q. In order to find out the Regional Priority points for a LEED project, what must be done first?

120

Q. How many Innovation in Design points can a LEED Green Associate earn for a project seeking LEED certification?

121

Q. A project team diverts 97 percent of the nonhazardous construction waste away from a landfill. They earn all the points that are within the credit and an additional point that will be included in which category?

122

Q. What are the two components of a zoning requirement?

123

Q. What are some examples of uses that are defined in zoning ordinances?

124

Q. Within the SS category, LEED encourages a project team not to exceed the minimum number of _____, but encourages the team to exceed the minimum amount of _____, both as required by zoning.

125

Q. What best describes a regulation that restricts the height of a building?

126

Q. What are the five SMACNA guidelines?

127

Q. What must low-emitting products comply with for LEED for School projects?

128

Q. What must classroom furniture comply with for LEED for School projects?

120

A. Zero, only LEED APs are eligible.

119

A. Refer to the USGBC website and find your project's region.

122

A. The map of the zones and a text description of the requirements

121

A. Innovation in Design

124

A. Parking spaces and open space

123

A. Single-family residential, multifamily residential, commercial, and industrial

126

A. HVAC protection, source control, pathway interruption, housekeeping, and scheduling

125

A. Zoning ordinance

128

A. GREENGUARD, ANSI/BIFMA x7.1, ETV Large Chamber Test Protocol

127

A. California Department of Health Services Standard Practice for the Testing of Volatile Organic Emissions from Various Sources Using Small-Scale Environmental Chambers standard